OWLS

A GUIDE TO THE OWLS
OF THE WORLD

CLAUS KÖNIG, FRIEDHELM WEICK,

AND

JAN-HENDRIK BECKING

YALE UNIVERSITY PRESS
NEW HAVEN AND LONDON

Published 1999 in the United Kingdom by Pica Press (an imprint of Helm Information Ltd)
and in the United States by Yale University Press.

ISBN 0-300-07920-6
Library of Congress Cataloging in Publication Number 99-60571
Printed in Hong Kong.

A catalogue record for this book is available from the British Library.
The paper in this book meets the guidelines for permanence and durability of the Committee
on Production Guidelines for Book Longevity of the Council on Library Resources.

10 9 8 7 6 5 4 3 2 1

Contents

INTRODUCTION

Owls are fascinating birds. Most species spend the day hidden in the dense foliage of trees, in holes or in the dusky attics of large buildings. Normally humans, as diurnal beings, are only conscious of their presence from their vocalisations. Because of their nocturnal habits, owls have been regarded by superstitious humans as birds of ill omen. They have been associated with death, although the Greeks considered them wise. The Little Owl *Athene noctua*, abundant in the Mediterranean, was given its generic name *Athene* because of its association with the Greek goddess of wisdom, Pallas Athene, the patron deity of Athens, the dominant city of classical Greece. In Central Europe, Little Owls are locally still considered to be birds of ill omen, portending sickness and the approaching death of ill persons. But now civilised opinion has changed and at the end of the 20th century interest in these nocturnal birds has increased. Many owl species are protected by law worldwide but, through the destruction of their habitats and the use of pesticides, many species are severely endangered.

An increasing number of ornithologists (amateur and professional) go out at dusk or before dawn in order to study owls in the wild. Groups of owl enthusiasts in many countries exchange the results of their investigations and international meetings of owl specialists are no longer rare. Through international cooperation and research our worldwide knowledge of owls has increased. Nevertheless there are still gaps in our understanding of owl biology and behaviour. Some species are known almost entirely by skins in museums. Several species are extinct and their biology will remain a mystery. Studies of endangered species are much needed and adequate measures for their conservation must be devised.

Every year many bird books are published, but in most of them owls are treated cursorily. Books devoted to the order are rare and none of them deals with all the species. This demonstrates a lack of information on owl taxonomy and stresses the fact that it is still very difficult to identify several species correctly. Many species show a great degree of variation in plumage and coloration. Taxonomic studies based on comparing museum specimens alone cannot solve the problem and species limits in some genera are still poorly defined. Studies on ecology, behaviour and vocalisations are of overwhelming importance. We have tried to address these problems in this book, which describes all known owl species with illustrations and distribution maps. An accompanying double-CD covering over 80% of the world's species will greatly assist in the identification of this difficult group.

It is only possible to create a book like this through teamwork. Friedhelm Weick painted all 64 colour plates and made the numerous line-drawings in the text. He also compiled the caption text facing the plates and contributed several species accounts. He and Claus König gathered the owl literature references for the bibliography. Jan-Hendrik Becking wrote the species accounts for eastern and southern Asia and the Australasian region; Claus König was responsible for the European, African, Mascarene, western Asian and American species accounts. He also drafted the distribution maps. Claus König wrote the introductory chapters except for the one on molecular evolution, which was written by Michael Wink and Petra Heidrich of Heidelberg University.

This book may be used both as an identification guide and as a source of information on owl ecology and biology, especially for some of the lesser known species. It also points out where gaps in information exist. We hope to stimulate ornithologists to research these poorly known taxa and provide material for future editions. The book is a companion for all who research owls in the field; at home or in the laboratory it is a reference book for comparing observations and recorded voices.

ACKNOWLEDGEMENTS

The authors are greatly indebted to many institutions and people for kind and very helpful cooperation. Without their assistance it would not have been possible to undertake the large amount of work involved. We thank the following museums and other scientific institutions: Administración de Parques Nacionales, Buenos Aires, Iguazú, Salta, and Santa Cruz, Argentina (M. Jannes); American Museum of Natural History, New York, USA (M. LeCroy); Asociación Ornitológica del Plata, Buenos Aires, Argentina (R. Guerra, T. Narosky); British Museum of Natural History (Natural History Museum, Bird Section), Tring, UK (P. R. Colston); British Library, National Sound Archive, London, UK (R. Ranft); Laboratory of Ornithology, Cornell University, NY, USA; Dept. Biology, York College, PA, USA (Prof. R. Clark); Deutsche Forschungsgemeinschaft (German Research Foundation), Bonn, Germany; Florida State Museum of Natural History, Gainesville, USA (Dr J. W. Hardy, Dr T. Webber); Forschungsinstitut und Naturmuseum Senckenberg, Frankfurt a.M., Germany (Dr J. Steinbacher, Prof. Dr D. Peters); Fundación Vida Silvestre Argentina, Buenos Aires, Argentina (A. Johnson); Gesellschaft zur Förderung des Naturkundemuseums, Stuttgart, Germany; Institut für Pharmazeutische Biologie der Universität Heidelberg, Germany (P. Heidrich, Prof. Dr M. Wink); Institut für Zoologie der Universität Heidelberg, Germany (Prof. Dr H. Moeller); Institute of Zoology, Taipeh, Taiwan (Dr L. Liu-Severinghaus); IRSNB-Section Evol. Birds, Bruxelles, Belgium (Dr R. Lafontaine); Instituto Miguel Lillo, Tucumán, Argentina (Lic. E. Alabarce); Instituto Nacional de Entomología INESALT, Rosario de Lerma, Argentina (Dr M. Fritz); Instituto de Zoologia, Universidade de Campinas, SP, Brazil (Prof. J. Vielliard); Kansas Museum of Natural History, Kansas, USA (Dr M. Robbins); Konnikligh Museum van Midden Afrika, Tervuren, Belgium (Dr M. Louette); Louisiana State Museum of Natural History, Baton Rouge, USA; Museo Argentino de Ciencias Naturales, Buenos Aires, Argentina (Dr J. Navas, R. Straneck); Museo de Historia Natural de la Universidad de San Marcos, Lima, Peru (Dr I. Franke); Museo Nacional, Rio de Janeiro, Brazil (the late Prof. Dr H. Sick, D. Teixeira), Museo de Ciencias Naturales, University of Salta, Argentina (G. Hoy, Prof. Dr L. Novara); Museo de La Plata, La Plata, Argentina (Dr N. Bó); Museum für Naturkunde, Berlin, Germany (the late Dr G. Mauersberger, Prof. Dr B. Stephan, Prof. Dr D. Wallschläger, Dr Wunderlich); Museum Heineanum, Halberstadt, Germany (Dr Nicolai); Muséum d'Histoire Naturelle, St. Denis, Réunion (Dr M. Le Corre); Musée Zoologique de l'Université de Strasbourg, France (M. Wandhammer); Nationaal Naturhistorisch Museeum, Leiden, The Netherlands (Dr R. Dekker), National Museum of Natural History, Washington, USA (Dr J. T. Marshall); Natural History Museum, Helsinki, Finland (Dr P. Saurola); Naturhistorisches Museum, Basel, Switzerland (Dr R. Winkler); Naturhistorisches Museum, Wien, Austria (Dr K. Bauer, Dr E. Bauernfeind, Dr H. Schifter); Pfalzmuseum für Naturkunde, Bad Dürkheim (Dr R. Flößer); Staatliches Museum für Naturkunde, Stuttgart, Germany (R. Buob, M. Grabert, Dr A. Schlüter); Staatliches Museum für Naturkunde, Karlsruhe, Germany (Prof. Dr S. Rietschel); Staatliches Museum für Naturkunde, Dresden, Germany (S. Eck); Tierpark Berlin, Berlin, Germany (Dr Frädrich, Dr Grummt, Prof. Dr H. Klös); Übersee-Museum, Bremen, Germany (Dr H. Hohmann); Vogelpark Walsrode, Walsrode, Germany (R. Brehm); Vogelwarte Radolfzell, Möggingen, Germany (R. Schlenker); Wildlife Conservation Society, New York, USA (J. A. Hast); Zoologisches Forschungsinstitut und Museum Alexander Koenig, Bonn, Germany (Dr R. van den Elzen, Prof. Dr C. Naumann); Zoologische Staatssammlung des Bayerischen Staates, München, Germany (Prof. Dr J. Reichholf); Zoologisches Museum, Hamburg, Germany (Dr S. Hoerschelmann, Prof. Dr H. Koepcke); Zoologisk Museum, Copenhagen, Denmark (Dr J. Fjeldså, N. Krabbe).

We are also indebted in the recording of owl voices to the following for their kind cooperation and advice on several items: Dr R. Behrstock, Houston, USA; K. D. Bishop, Australia; Dr T. Butynski, Zoo Atlanta, Nairobi, Kenya; Prof. R. Clark, York College, USA; G. Dutson, Cambridge, UK; G. Ehlers, Leipzig, Germany; Dr R. Ertel, Remseck, Germany; R. Foerster, Iguazú, Argentina; Dr J. Haffer, Essen, Germany; Dr J. W. Hardy, Gainesville, Florida, USA; Dr G. P. Hekstra, Leidschendam, The Netherlands; Dr J. C. Heij, Netherlands; Dr D. G. W. Hollands, Orbost, Australia; Dr D. A. Holmes, Indonesia; S. N. G. Howell, Stinson Beach, California, USA; the late G. Hoy, Salta, Argentina; W. Jörlitschka, Pforzheim, Germany; Juni Adi, Indonesia; H. Kaiser, Villingen, Germany; Dr M. Kessler, Münster, Germany; Dr N. Krabbe, Quito, Ecuador; R. Krahe, Smithers, Canada; J. & I. Kuehl, Salta, Argentina; O. Lakus, Hambrücken, Germany; Dr F. Lambert, Bogor, Indonesia; Dr J. T. Marshall, Washington, USA; J Mazar Barnett, Argentina; Dr B.-U. Meyburg, Berlin, Germany; P. Morris, UK; the late Dr T. A. Parker III, Baton Rouge, USA; Dr M. S. Prana, Indonesia; the late Dr C. C. Olrog, Tucumán, Argentina; R. Ranft, National Sound Archive, London, UK; Dr P. C. Rasmussen, Smithsonian Institution, USA; O. v. Rootselaar, Renkum, The Netherlands; R. J. Safford, Surrey, UK; R. Schaaf, Ludwigsburg, Germany; Dr W. Scherzinger, Waldhäuser, Germany; D. Schmidt, Stuttgart, Germany; S. Smith, UK; R. Steinberg, Radevormwald, Germany; Prof. F. G. Stiles,

Bogotá, Colombia; R. Straneck, Cordoba, Argentina; D. V. M. Sudharto, Indonesia; Dr W. Thiede, Köln, Germany; Prof. Dr K. H. Voous, Huizen, The Netherlands; W. Weise, Clausnitz, Germany; Dr D. R. Wells, England.

For technical help in digitalising recordings, we thank D. Hagmann of Stuttgart, Germany. Special thanks are due to Pamela Rasmussen for critically reviewing the Old World *Otus* species and several other Asian owls. Above all we wish to give our most cordial thanks to Mrs. Ingrid König, who was a patient and well-informed assistant in the field and in the laboratory.

Last but not least we thank our publishers Christopher Helm and Nigel Redman for their guidance and patience throughout this project, Julie Reynolds and Marc Dando for their expertise in the design and production of the book, Nigel Collar for editorial assistance, and especially David Christie for his considerable skills in the editing of the species accounts.

Style and Layout of the Book

The introductory chapters are fairly brief, but many line drawings are included to illustrate the points discussed. The plates and species accounts comprise the greater part of the book. There is a strong emphasis on identification and vocalisation in the species accounts but other aspects of biology and ecology are also covered where known.

INTRODUCTORY CHAPTERS

Owls: an overview

This chapter gives an overview of owl biology and behaviour and is subdivided into a number of sections covering the following subjects: Morphology and Anatomy; Topography; Food; Hunting; Behaviour; Breeding; Vocalisations; and Systematics and Taxonomy.

Molecular Evolution and Systematics of the Owls

An invited chapter by Michael Wink and Petra Heidrich gives an up-to-date assessment of owl systematics according to DNA evidence. It also highlights that further changes in owl taxonomy are likely as more material becomes available for analysis.

The introductory chapters conclude with some hints on studying owls and an overview of owl conservation.

PLATES

The 64 colour plates illustrate all known species of owls, showing their different colour morphs and often their juvenile plumages. Many of the more distinct subspecies are also illustrated. The plate captions give, for each species, a brief summary of world range and the most important diagnostic features of each form or plumage illustrated.

SPECIES ACCOUNTS

Each genus begins with an introduction summarising key features of the genus and dealing with general structural differences which will enable separation from sympatric owl genera. Each species account is subdivided into sections as follows:

Names

Alternative English or scientific names are given where appropriate. Where relevant, species names are also given in other languages, namely French, German, Spanish or Portuguese.

Identification

These sections detail key features for field identification and should be used in conjunction with the plates. **Similar species**: Confusable species are mentioned, with a summary of the principal criteria for separation. This section is largely concerned with sympatric species. In some cases, no other species of owl occurs sympatrically with the species concerned.

Vocalisations

Voice transcriptions are included where available, most of which have been transcribed by the authors from tape recordings. Transcriptions of vocalisations emphasise the rhythm. Sequences written *how how...* mean that the 'barks' are uttered at intervals of more than one second, while a hyphenated *how-how-...* denotes shorter intervals (about 0.5 seconds), and *howhowhow...* indicates that the notes follow each other without noticeable breaks. Some vocalisations have a stress, *huwuwúbubu*. In this example, *ú* is short, whereas hooting notes are transcribed as *oo*; tones lying between *oo* and *ee* are expressed as *ew*.

Distribution

These sections commence with a brief summary of world range followed by a more detailed treatment. They should be used in conjunction with the maps. For several regions information is very scanty. The distributions given relate to the range of the species as a whole. In the case of polytypic species, the ranges of individual subspecies are given in 'Geographical Variation'.

Movements

Most owls are resident and sedentary, but a few are migratory, and others undertake local movements. This section covers all movements, both local and long distance, including altitudinal movements and vagrancy.

Habitat

Most species are dependent on trees to some extent, although some species inhabit grasslands or other open areas. Habitat preferences are given, including favoured tree species if known. Altitudinal ranges are also noted if known.

Description

These sections contain detailed descriptions of plumage features and, for ease of use, the section is subdivided into **Adult**, **Juvenile** and **Bare Parts**. For most polytypic species the nominate, or in some cases the most widespread, race forms the subject of the description. Where a species exhibits two or more colour morphs, these are usually described separately.

Measurements and weight

Wherever possible, measurements from the largest samples have been used, and refer to the race described in full under 'Description'; measurements for other races are detailed in 'Geographical Variation'. Mensural data given includes total length, wing length, tail length, and weight. All species' measurements are in millimetres unless otherwise stated (body length is always given in centimetres); weights are in grams.

Measurements were taken in the following ways. (1) **Wing length** The wing is closed and laid onto a special ruler (without pressing it down), but pushed it against the zero point at the lower end. Then the distance from wrist to wing-tip is measured. The measurement achieved in this way is called a chord. (2) **Tail length** The distance from the point where the shaft of the central feather emerges from the skin to its tip is measured with dividers. (3) **Wing-tip** The wing is closed and the distance that the primaries extend beyond the tips of the secondaries is measured. (4) **Total length** The distance is measured from the front edge of the crown to the tip of the tail, when the bird is laid on its back. Some authors measure from the tip of bill, but in owls this is difficult, as these birds have the bill in the middle of the face. Therefore it seems to be more sensible to measure from the crown.

Geographical Variation

We have attempted to describe briefly all recognised races, concentrating on the differences between them. Future taxonomic revisions are likely to subdivide certain polytypic species (or even amalgamate other taxa), and some possible 'splits' and 'lumps' have been noted in these sections. The range of each subspecies is briefly given, with measurements if available. The authors of the type descriptions for every accepted taxon are given in this section. Subspecies not recognised by us are detailed as synonyms.

Habits

Typical behavioural traits are noted in this section, although little is known for many species. We hope that the lack of information for some species may inspire others to undertake research into some of the lesser known owls.

Food

Where recorded, prey items are listed for each species, although the diet of many species is still poorly known. Many of the smaller owls are exclusively insectivorous, but larger species take a range of vertebrate prey.

Breeding

The nesting habits of each species, where known, are included in this section. Information presented includes breeding season, courtship, nest sites (most species build only rudimentary nests or re-use the nests of other birds), eggs and clutch size, incubation, brooding, and fledging. As with 'Habits', the breeding biology of many species is virtually unknown.

Status and Conservation

Information on the status of each species is given where known, together with any conservation recommendations. For some better known species, it has been possible to give details of conservation measures implemented, but most species are not protected and many are under threat from habitat destruction.

Remarks

Taxonomic problems or differences of opinion regarding taxonomic treatment are detailed in this section. Aspects of a species' biology or behaviour requiring further research are also highlighted here.

References

References given in the text and at the end of the species accounts are listed in full in the Bibliography.

MAPS

A map is included for each species. Generally, three intensities of shading indicate resident (70%), breeding visitor (50%), and wintering (30%) ranges. A cross indicates a vagrant record or an area of irregular occurrence. A question mark indicates an area of uncertain status.

tiny 13-16cm	**very small** 17-20cm	**small** 21-25cm	**small to medium-sized** 26-34cm	**medium-sized** 35-45cm
Xenoglaux	*Glaucidium*	*Aegolius*	*Tyto*	*Tyto*
Micrathene	*Otus*	*Athene*	*Phodilus*	*Lophostrix*
Glaucidium		*Glaucidium*	*Otus*	*Jubula*
		Otus	*Mimizuku*	*Bubo*
		Ptilopsis	*Ninox*	*Pulsatrix*
			Uroglaux	*Strix*
			Asio	*Surnia*
			Strix	*Ninox*
				Asio
				Nesasio

very large 64-72cm	**large** 57-63cm	**fairly large** 46-56cm
Bubo	*Bubo*	*Tyto*
	Nyctea	*Bubo*
	Scotopelia	*Scotopelia*
	Strix	*Pulsatrix*
	Ninox	*Strix*
		Ninox
		Asio

A selection of owls to illustrate relative differences in size between various genera.

OWLS: AN OVERVIEW

Owls are a group of chiefly nocturnal birds which share many patterns in behaviour, morphology and anatomy. All have a rather large, rounded head with eyes directed forward as in humans. Their plumage is soft, often rather fluffy and mostly cryptically coloured. All have a curved bill with a pointed tip, similar to diurnal birds of prey, and generally powerful talons with curved and sharp claws, as an adaptation for carnivory. Owls are ecologically the nocturnal counterparts to diurnal birds of prey, without being related with them. This phenomenon in biology is called convergence and is caused by adaptation. It may be found in several groups of animals or plants. For example the Old World and New World flycatchers, although superficially similar, are unrelated; the same is true of New and Old World vultures. Anatomically and behaviourally there are large differences between such groups although they occupy similar ecological niches.

The closest relatives of owls are, according to recent studies of DNA evidence, the nightjars (Caprimulgiformes). Systematically the owls are actually best placed between the parrots (Psittaciformes) and the Caprimulgiformes. Owls have caeca but no crop, while the reverse is the case in diurnal birds of prey.

When perched, owls show in general a very upright appearance. Many of them have ear-tufts, consisting of elongated feathers on the sides of the forehead. These have nothing to do with hearing. They serve as adornments which play a role in behaviour. The real ears are openings behind the rim of the facial disc and are situated at the sides of the head.

We recognise two surviving owl families: the barn, grass and bay owls (Tytonidae) and the 'true owls' (Strigidae). Most species belong to the latter family. Both have distinctive morphological and anatomical features.

MORPHOLOGY AND ANATOMY

In owls the eyes are set frontally as in humans. They are placed in sclerotic tubes or rings (see Fig. 2a). The visual field of owls is similar to ours (Fig. 1a); but, unlike us, their eyeballs are fixed. They cannot roll their eyes or move them in any way. Therefore they swivel their heads in order to see behind them. They can turn their heads through an arc of about 270°, thereby seeing backwards with great ease (Fig. 1b).

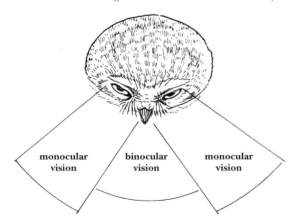

Figure 1a. Visual field of an owl.

Figure 1b. Short-eared Owl turning its head 180° (max. 270°).

The visual sense in owls is well developed. It would be wrong to think that owls see less well in daylight. At dusk or in the very subdued light at night, owls are able to distinguish more details than the human eye, but even in bright daylight they can see better than ourselves. Like us, they are blind in total darkness. The sclerotic sockets or tubes give their eyeballs a more oval shape (Fig. 2a). The retina is very large and densely equipped with rod cells, but with few or no uvular cells (Fig. 2b.). Therefore, although an owl's eye is designed to maximise shape outlines at the lowest light intensities, its ability to see colours is very much reduced or even lacking. More diurnal owls can to some extent distinguish colours, but their night sight is reduced.

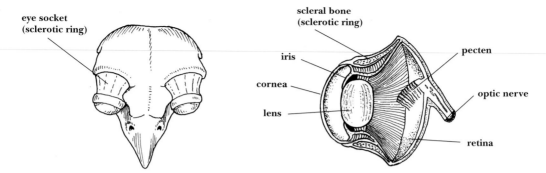

Figure 2a. Tubular eye.   **Figure 2b. Cross-section of an Eagle Owl's eye.**

Being active at dusk and night, owls need a highly developed acoustic sense. The ear openings are located in the auricular region at the side of the head which is often covered by the rim around the facial disc. The shape of the aperture varies according to species; it is often placed asymmetrically with a valve (operculum) covering the opening. The opening varies from a small, round aperture to a longitudinal slit with a large operculum. All members of the Tytonidae have rounded openings with large opercula, while in Strigidae the shape of the outer ear is more varied (Figs. 3a,b).

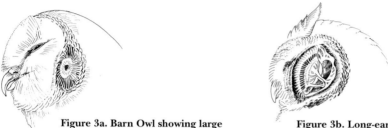

Figure 3a. Barn Owl showing large operculum and ear aperture.   **Figure 3b. Long-eared Owl showing ear aperture with complicated structure.**

Although an owl's frequency range is not much different from that of the human ear, its hearing is much more acute. This enables it to hear even the slightest rustle of an insect among dry leaves. The often asymmetrically-set ear openings give it an incredible ability to pinpoint the source of sounds. This is particularly true of the strictly nocturnal species such as the barn owls *Tyto* or Tengmalm's Owl *Aegolius funereus* (Fig. 5). These species also have a very pronounced facial disc, which is used to assist hearing. Its shape can be changed at will by special muscles and its function may be compared with the focusing apparatus of a searchlight. Owls may receive sound waves with a dilated or a more contracted facial disc, according to the distance of the detected sound. The more diurnal owls have in general a less well developed facial disc.

Figure 4a. Foot of Barn Owl (Tytonidae) and detail of serrated claw of the middle toe.

Figure 4b. Foot of Eagle Owl (Strigidae).

Owls have powerful talons with sharp, curved claws. The Tytonidae have inner and central toes of about equal length (Fig. 4a), while the Strigidae have an inner toe that is distinctly shorter than the central one (Fig. 4b).The claw of the central toe in the Tytonidae is serrated on its underside (see detailed sketch of a claw in Fig. 4a).

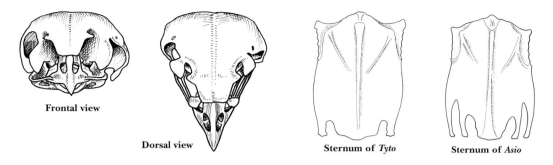

Frontal view

Dorsal view

Sternum of *Tyto*

Sternum of *Asio*

Figure 5. Skull of Tengmalm's Owl, showing the asymmetrical position of the ear-openings.

Figure 6. Different sterni in Tytonidae/Strigidae.

The skeleton of an owl is typically avian (Fig. 7). The skulls of species with asymmetrical ears are, however, different from others (Fig. 5). The Tytonidae and Strigidae may be separated by their breast-bones (Fig. 6): the former have a rather broad carina, becoming narrower towards the abdomen, and the lower edge of the breast-bone (sternum) has only a slight emargination on each side; in the Strigidae the carina is narrow at its upper part and becomes broader towards the belly, while the lower edge of the sternum has two deep emarginations on each side.

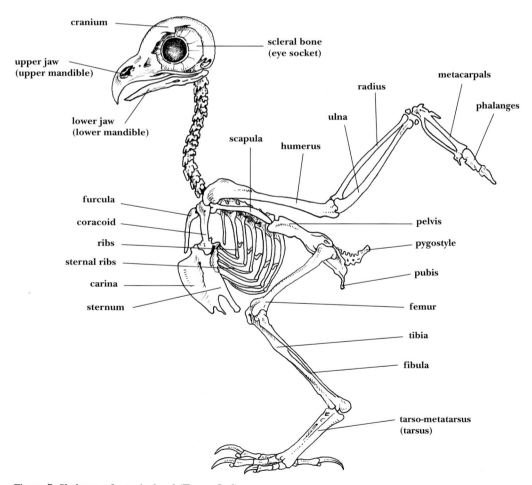

Figure 7. Skeleton of a typical owl (Tawny Owl).

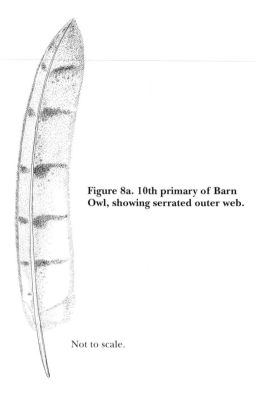

Figure 8a. 10th primary of Barn Owl, showing serrated outer web.

Not to scale.

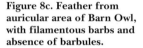

Figure 8b. Feather from the ruff of Barn Owl, with thick rachis and dense webbing.

Figure 8c. Feather from auricular area of Barn Owl, with filamentous barbs and absence of barbules.

Most owls fly noiselessly because of the structure of their feathers. The outermost (10th primary) flight feather has a 'combed' or serrated edge on its outerweb (Fig. 8a). This suppresses noise when cutting the air. The surface of the flight feathers is covered with a velvety structure absorbing sounds produced by moving the wings. The same applies to the loose, soft feathering of the body. More diurnal owls have a somewhat noisier flight than nocturnal ones.

The rim around the facial disc is like a ruff of rather stiff feathers (Fig. 8b), while around the auricular region the feathers have filamentous barbs in order to reflect sounds (Fig. 8c).

TOPOGRAPHY

Figure 9 shows sketches of typical owls:

(a) Whole body of a specimen of genus *Athene* (little owls). The foot consists of toes with claws and the tarsus or tarso-metatarsus. We use the expression 'foot' only when no part of it is specified. Mostly we use the terms 'tarsi' or 'toes'. Owls have four toes, three in front and one hind-toe. Of the front toes the outer one may be turned backwards.

(b) Head of a Long-eared Owl *Asio otus* with typical ear-tufts and showing on one eye the nictitating membrane, an opaque second eyelid, which may act as a protection to the eye in certain situations. This membrane keeps the eye clean and moist. Owls also have normal eyelids, which may be bare or finely feathered. The eye often has a brightly coloured iris and a dark or pink bare rim.

(c) Lateral view of an owl's head (type *Athene*) with the 'false eyes' or 'occipital face' on the nape. This pattern is characteristic of many *Glaucidium* and some *Athene* species and gives the impression of a face with dark eyes, whitish eyebrows and a whitish band below. It is a feature of many semi-diurnal species and it may have the purpose of deterring potential predators, as the owls are vulnerable when perched. The area surrounding the nostrils is called the cere and may be distinguished from the smooth horn of the bill by its rough surface.

(d) Wing and tail of an owl from above. The primaries are counted from the middle of the wing towards the tip and the secondaries from that point towards the body. When the wing length is measured, the wing has to be closed and the distance taken from the bend (wrist) to the longest primary feather. Tail length is the distance from the base of the central tail feather to the tip. Tail feathers are counted from the centre outwards. Each feather has a shaft and an outer and an inner web.

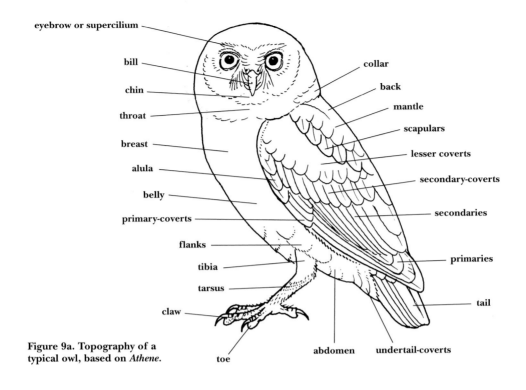

Figure 9a. Topography of a typical owl, based on *Athene*.

eyebrow or supercilium
bill
chin
throat
breast
alula
belly
primary-coverts
flanks
tibia
tarsus
claw
toe
abdomen
undertail-coverts
collar
back
mantle
scapulars
lesser coverts
secondary-coverts
secondaries
primaries
tail

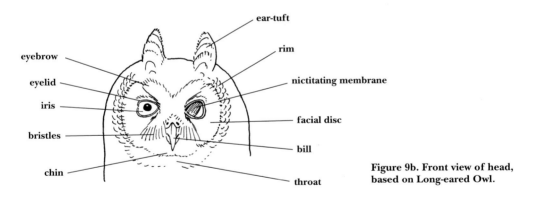

Figure 9b. Front view of head, based on Long-eared Owl.

ear-tuft
rim
nictitating membrane
facial disc
bill
throat
eyebrow
eyelid
iris
bristles
chin

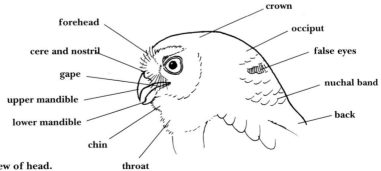

Figure 9c. Lateral view of head.

forehead
cere and nostril
gape
upper mandible
lower mandible
chin
throat
crown
occiput
false eyes
nuchal band
back

23

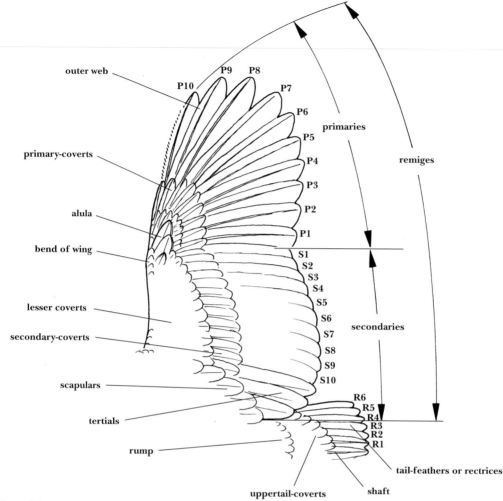

Figure 9d. Wing and tail of an owl (upperside).

FOOD

Owls are carnivorous. Their diet includes invertebrates such as insects, spiders, crabs, snails, earthworms and scorpions, and vertebrates from fish and amphibians to birds and mammals. Some species are specialised on certain prey. The food of Barn Owls consists mainly of mice, shrews and voles. If these are scarce, breeding success is low. Bay Owls *Phodilus badius* are less dependent on small mammals. Scops and screech owls *Otus* feed mainly on insects, while the food of the Eurasian Pygmy Owl *Glaucidium passerinum* consists of small rodents, shrews and birds. Little Owls have a varied diet which includes earthworms, insects and small mammals. Most eagle owls *Bubo* predate hares or young foxes and birds up to the size of ducks and gamebirds. Asian fish owls *Bubo*, subgenus *Ketupa*, are specialised on fish, as are the unrelated African fishing owls *Scotopelia*. Wood owls *Strix* and Asian and Australian hawk owls *Ninox* have a very varied diet. Long-eared and Tengmalm's Owls are very dependent in the breeding season on the supply of small mammals, especially voles. The Great Grey Owl *Strix nebulosa*, Snowy Owl *Nyctea scandiaca* and Northern Hawk Owl *Surnia ulula* similarly depend on an abundant supply of lemmings *Lemmus* or other northern voles for breeding success.

In Fig. 10 (a-g) some owls are shown carrying prey in their beaks. Prey is killed by crushing the skull and kneading the body with powerful talons. Many owls remain on the seized prey with half-spread wings, biting and kneading it at the same time, before flying to a perch to feed. Large prey is partly plucked on a perch. Pieces of it are torn off and swallowed. Smaller prey such as mice are often swallowed whole.

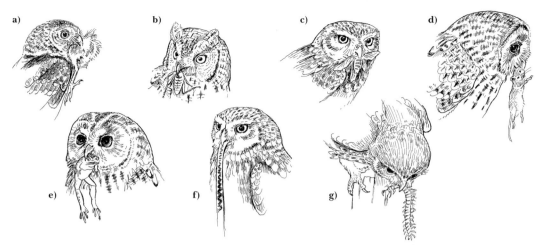

Figure 10. Owls and prey. a) *Glaucidium* **with remains of bird; b)** *Otus* **with bush cricket; c)** *Athene* **with moth; d)** *Strix* **with mouse; e)** *Strix* **with frog; f)** *Athene* **with viper; g)** *Ninox* **with centipede.**

When swallowing the eyes are closed. A Patagonian Pygmy Owl *Glaucidium nanum* has been observed gulping down whole an unfledged Austral Thrush *Turdus falcklandii*. Smaller owls pluck larger insects, tearing apart with their beaks the hard elytra or sturdy legs of beetles, while holding the prey in the talons of one foot and feeding on it in a parrot-like manner.

If prey is very abundant, owls will store the surplus food, which may be in the nest or in a nearby tree-hole or fork in a tree branch. Females incubate alone; their mates either bring food to the nest or deposit it nearby after calling her out. Towards the end of incubation or when the young have hatched, the female Eurasian Pygmy Owl often flies to the food deposit for herself.

HUNTING

Before catching prey, owls have to fly from their daytime roosts to their hunting areas, which may sometimes be quite far off. Their flight is light with rowing wingbeats alternating with gliding on more or less extended wings (Fig. 11a). Some larger owls (e.g. Eurasian Eagle Owl *Bubo bubo* and Short-eared Owl *Asio flammeus*) sometimes soar. When owls leave the perch, the legs dangle for a moment before they are pulled up against the tail (Fig. 12).

Figure 11a. Barn Owl flying (lateral view).

Figure 11b. Barn Owl swooping with talons streched forward.

Figure 12. Eurasian Eagle Owl after take-off with legs hanging.

Most species catch their prey from a perch (18), swooping down with opened wings and talons stretched forward (Fig. 11b, 15). Some (notably those using visual rather than aural search methods) employ a rather longer attack flight, e.g. eagle owls pursuing hares in open country, or pygmy owls dashing from cover to grasp its most avian prey. These latter and some others will take prey larger than themselves – Northern Hawk Owls may even take ptarmigans *Lagopus* spp. (Fig. 16) – while others take smaller prey such as bush-crickets plucked from leaves. Smaller insectivorous owls, notably *Otus* spp., may hawk insects in the air. Barn Owls hawk bats on the wing and, along with Short-eared Owls and Snowy Owls, they often

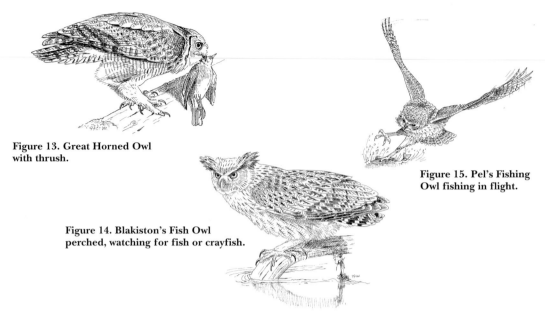

Figure 13. Great Horned Owl
with thrush.

Figure 15. Pel's Fishing
Owl fishing in flight.

Figure 14. Blakiston's Fish Owl
perched, watching for fish or crayfish.

quarter the ground in search of prey, dropping on small mammals in the grass, sometimes after a brief hover (see also Tengmalm's Owl in Fig. 20). Barn Owls, Long-eared Owls and Tawny Owls *Strix aluco* sometimes fly along hedgerows at dusk in order to flush out roosting birds. Fish and Fishing Owls are perch-and-pounce species, snatching prey as it rises near the water surface in the twilight (Figs. 14, 15), although some species also wade in the shallows after prey.

Figure 16. Northern Hawk
Owl hunting Red Grouse.

Figure 17. Eurasian Pygmy
Owl carrying prey in feet.

Figure 18. Little Owl starting
to pounce from fence.

Figure 19. Burrowing
Owl with beetle.

Smaller prey is carried away in the bill (Fig. 13) or eaten at once (Fig. 19). Larger prey is carried away in the talons (Fig. 17). All owls reject indigestible remains of food as pellets. These are dark, oval balls, containing hair, feathers, chitinous parts of insects and bones. They could be confused with fox droppings; but those are more elongated, never contain bones, and are of a more earthy quality. Foxes leave their droppings on stones, on mole hills or tree stumps; owl pellets are normally found below perches. Unlike raptor pellets, owl pellets contain even the smallest bones. Fresh Barn Owl pellets are always covered with a slightly glossy film of dried saliva. This film is lacking in pellets of the Strigidae.

Figure 20. Tengmalm's Owl hunting a mouse.

Figure 21. Short-eared Owl with vole.

Figure 22. Western Screech Owl swallowing prey whole.

BEHAVIOUR

A few owl species are partly active in the daytime; most are active at dusk or dawn; several are virtually inactive in the dead of night. In general activity begins around dusk. The owl, having spent most of the day motionless at its daytime roost, begins to stretch its wings and legs (Fig. 23) and to preen its plumage (Fig. 24) or to comb its head by scratching it with its claws (Fig. 25). Often the whole plumage is ruffled up and shaken or claws and toes are cleaned by nibbling with the bill. Then the owl silently leaves its roost, sometimes calling or singing, particularly during the reproductive cycle.

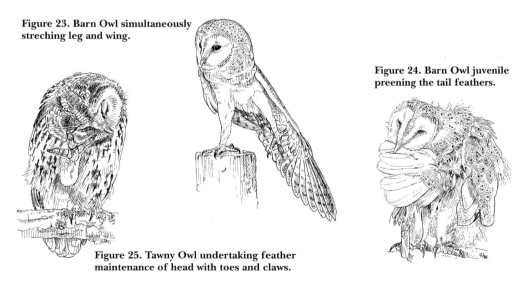

Figure 23. Barn Owl simultaneously streching leg and wing.

Figure 24. Barn Owl juvenile preening the tail feathers.

Figure 25. Tawny Owl undertaking feather maintenance of head with toes and claws.

Owls in general roost singly or in pairs. In the latter case allopreening may be observed at the daytime roost (Fig. 26). This behaviour is one of the inherited measures for fixing the pair-bond between mates. Although owls are territorial, some species may form flocks outside the breeding season especially during migration. Thus Short-eared Owls may be found roosting on the ground in meadows and on cultivated land such as potato-fields. In daytime during winter Long-eared Owls may congregate in dozens in trees for roosting even in urban parks, gardens and tree-lined avenues. On the ground below many pellets may be found giving an insight into their diet.

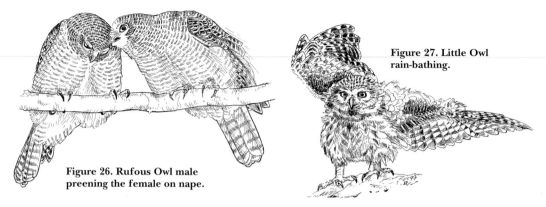

Figure 27. Little Owl
rain-bathing.

Figure 26. Rufous Owl male
preening the female on nape.

Owls love bathing. As with most birds they wade into shallow water and splash it around by pecking and shaking their heads, ruffling their body feathers and flapping their wings. They also like to bathe in rain (Fig. 27).

Figure 30. Northern Hawk
Owl: left, sleeked upright
posture; right, normal
posture on perch.

Figure 29. Common
Scops Owl screening.

Figure 28. Long-eared Owl: above, invisible
ear-tufts; below, erected ear-tufts.

Observation will disclose many expressive gestures. A relaxed owl carries its plumage rather loosely. Thus while the ear-tufts of Long-eared Owls are erected when the bird is on its guard, they are almost invisible when it is at its ease (Fig. 28). If frightened or in order to camouflage itself at its daytime roost, it becomes very slim, its feathers pressed closely to its body, making it very upright; it closes its eyes to a narrow slit and erects its ear-tufts straight up. Common Scops Owls *Otus scops* (Fig. 29) behave in the same way. Owls without ear-tufts also display similar behaviour (Fig. 30), freezing when frightened. Some other genera (e.g. *Aegolius* and *Glaucidium*) compress the feathers of the head so tightly to the head that the feathers around their facial discs suggest small ear-tufts. Many *Glaucidium* owls cock their tail when excited or alarmed and flick it from side to side (Fig. 31). Little Owls bob their body up and down when alert. Like many other owls they turn their heads from side to side in a curious way, probably to focus on an approaching object (Fig. 32). Similar behaviour may be observed in many species. If a potential enemy approaches its

Figure 31. Eurasian Pygmy Owl
tail-waving.

Figure 32. Little Owl
head-turning.

daytime roost, the owl either flies off immediately or assumes a threat posture before leaving. The body feathers are ruffled, the body bowed forward and the wings spread out, either hanging down or partly lifted above the body (Figs. 33, 34). Just before fledging or after it, young owls assume similar threatening postures (Fig. 34), accompanied by bill-snapping and hissing sounds. If touched, they defend themselves from a supine position by striking with their talons and biting with the bill. Owls may be very aggressive near the nest or fledged young. Tawny Owls and Ural Owls *Strix uralensis* are known to attack even humans fiercely, hitting them with their sharp claws in diving flights. Small owls can also be aggressive: the tiny female Eurasian Pygmy Owl will attack a human climbing a tree near the nest hole. The male dive-bombs a person imitating or playing back its song.

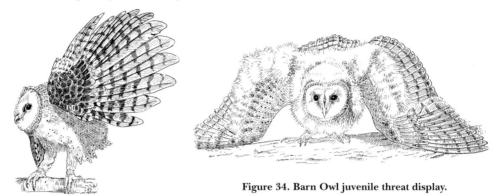

Figure 34. Barn Owl juvenile threat display.

Figure 33. Itombwe Owl stretching wing upwards.

In the wild, owls have been recorded typically reaching ages of 6-20 years, the larger species living longer. In captivity they may survive even longer.

Most owls are more or less resident. Some avoid the hard northern winters by moving southward, reaching areas where they are not normally found. In good reproductive years, in autumn northern owls invade the south. Northern Hawk Owls may be observed for instance in central or western Europe. Some resident owls near their northern limits of distribution suffer greatly in severe winters. Many die and local populations may go extinct from starvation. But after a severe winter, repopulation of the vacant territories quickly takes place.

BREEDING

When owls begin to sing and call the reproductive cycle has begun. The males claim their territories and potential nesting sites. In temperate climates this normally occurs in early spring; in the tropics at almost any time, but most often near the end of the dry season. Song is delivered from different perches in the territory, often but not always from near the future nesting site, sometimes even from outside the territory.

Females also sing; normally their song is higher in pitch and less clear. Often male and female may be heard duetting. After being paired, the female normally stops singing and uses other calls in its vocabulary to contact its mate and later its young. Unpaired owls (males as well as females) may sing persistently until they have found a mate. The song of both male and female has above all the purpose of claiming a territory and attracting a mate, the latter being more important for the female. After pairing the singing activity of males decreases considerably. After the female has accepted the future nesting site, male Tengmalm's Owls utter only a few phrases of song when bringing food to her inside the nesting hole. Later it only utters low notes. Voice is discussed more fully under 'Vocalisations' below, and special vocal features of individual species are treated in the species accounts. Unlike most songbirds, owls do not

Figure 35. Eurasian Eagle Owl singing.

open their bill visibly when singing. Instead, they inflate their throat into a small ball, which often shines as a white spot easily seen at dusk (Fig. 35). However, when giving other calls or cries, the bill is wide open (Fig. 36).

Figure 36. Little Owl calling.

Figure 37. Barn Owl copulation; male has handed over prey.

Some owls pair for life or at least for more than one breeding-season; others seek a new mate each year. Males are in general more faithful to their breeding territory; females tend to wander, sometimes occupying their own feeding territories, which may occasionally be united with the male's. The male will only occupy a territory if it meets his breeding demands and contains suitable nesting sites. He searches and inspects tree holes before embarking on courtship, scratching a shallow depression in the bottom of a selected hole and doing a little superficial housework. He advertises potential nesting sites to the female, guiding her around in his territory. He utters a song or some other vocalisation at the nest site, and may deposit prey as a courtship gift. The female then chooses one of the offered nest sites. After pairing, courtship display occurs near the nesting site. The birds often copulate on branches or nearby rocks; some *Tyto* and other species mate on the nest itself, the female carrying the male's gift in her bill (Fig. 37).

The nest sites of owls vary even within species. No owl constructs a real nest. Many scratch a shallow depression at the base of the nesting site; others mince pellets or remains of food with their bill in order to make a pad for the eggs. Grass owls *Tyto* trample a platform on the ground. Marsh *Asio capensis* and Short-eared Owls collect dry leaves, grass stems, etc., from around the nest to make an incomplete layer for the clutch. Sometimes tall grass or other vegetation at the nesting site is drawn together to make a shelter above the nest (Fig. 38). Barn Owls *Tyto alba* use corners in dusky attics of larger buildings (church towers, barns, etc.), holes in walls or rocks

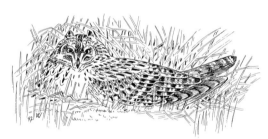

Figure 38. Short-eared Owl ground-nesting.

or hollow trees with large holes for nesting. They may accept artificial nestboxes placed behind the outside wall of the attics of larger buildings; optimal structures possess a quadrangular opening (20 x 15cm) about 15cm above the bottom of the box (Fig. 39). Many owls nest on cliff ledges, in holes or crevices of rocks or on bare ground (Fig. 40, 41). Eagle owls and some other larger species such as Ural Owls nest on ledges and in cavities in cliffs, abandoned nests of other birds or shallow cavities in tree stumps (Figs. 42, 43). The Great Grey Owl never uses hollow trees, always nesting in rather open sites. Owls living in deserts such as Hume's Owl *Strix butleri* mostly nests in rock cavities (Fig. 44). Most small to medium-sized owls nest in cavities. The tiny Elf Owl *Micrathene whitneyi* nests in holes made by woodpeckers in giant cacti or trees (Fig. 45). *Glaucidium* owls use similar holes. The Little Owl prefers holes in orchard trees, walls, cliffs, riverbanks or sand-pits; sometimes it nests under the eaves of buildings and in barns. Mounting special nestboxes in orchards can dramatically increase the Little Owl population (Fig. 46).

Figure 39. Barn Owl in nesting box.

Figure 40. Eurasian Eagle Owl rock-nesting.

Figure 41. Snowy Owl ground-nesting.

Figure 42. Great Grey Owl nesting on stump of broken tree.

Figure 43. Ural Owl in an old raptor's nest.

Figure 44. Hume's Owl nesting in rock cavity.

Figure 45. Elf Owl in hole of Gila Woodpecker in *Saquaro cachis* cactus.

Figure 46. Little Owl beside nesting box.

Figure 47. Burrowing Owl in nest burrow.

Figure 48. Tengmalm's Owl in nesting box.

Figure 49. Northern Hawk Owl in hole of dead tree.

The related Burrowing Owl nests in burrows in the ground (Fig. 47) which might have been dug by prairie dogs or rabbits, but are quite often excavated by the owls themselves. The tunnels may be several metres long, ending in a nest chamber. Tengmalm's and Northern Hawk Owls nest in tree-holes. The first usually uses the abandoned hole of a large woodpecker such as the Black Woodpecker *Dryocopus martius*, locally very frequently in artificial nestboxes (Fig. 48); the latter breeds in larger, rather open cavities in rotten tree stumps (Fig. 49).

All owls lay pure white eggs, oval in the Tytonidae, roughly spherical in the Strigidae. They are laid generally at intervals of a few days (normally two). Incubation often starts after the first egg is laid. Some species (e.g. *Glaucidium*) begin incubating only after the last or penultimate egg is laid. Only the female, fed by her mate, incubates. Prey is delivered either at the nest or near it, when the male summons the female to emerge. The male may cover the clutch in the brief absence of the female, but real incubation by males has not been proved. Males never have a brood-patch. When incubation starts from the first egg, the young hatch in laying sequence. When incubation starts after the clutch is almost complete, the young hatch within 1-2 days of each other. They are born with closed eyes and covered with a whitish natal down. This is gradually succeeded by a second coat, the so-called 'mesoptile', a fluffy, almost downy plumage. The mesoptile covers the body and head, while flight and tail-feathers resemble those of the adults. Many species of owl have no typical mesoptile, but resemble their parents, their body-feathering being only slightly fluffier and less distinctly marked. Sometimes they differ in coloration. The hatched chicks are normally first brooded and fed by the female alone; later on they are cared for by both parents. After fledging, the young move about calling for food. They are guided for some weeks, sometimes even months, by their parents. In some species at this time the residue of the mesoptile is still perceptible. Owls normally breed once per year. But when food is very abundant there are records of two and occasionally three clutches in species such as Barn Owl.

VOCALISATIONS

Owl vocalisations are poorly treated in bird books. Some calls are described; but the transcriptions are generally not very helpful as an aid to identification. Ornithologists belong to a diurnal species and tend therefore to look first for plumage patterns in order to separate one owl from another. However, the vocal patterns of nocturnal or crepuscular species are in general much more important than coloration or plumage as an aid to identification.

The owl has at its disposal a variably extended vocabulary depending on species. In all owls vocalisations are inherited and therefore of great taxonomic importance. Owls show little geographical dialect variation. There is also little variation in vocalisation between individuals; nor are vocal parameters different in the races of the same species. Where competition for food or nest sites is low, some species may develop individual variations. A typical example is Tengmalm's Owl, in which individual males may be recognised by their territorial songs, but despite this all show typical, specific patterns. If we compare the songs of the species from the Alps, Scandinavia and North America, we find some variation, but no essential differences between the three populations. In areas where species of the same size occur sympatrically, the individual variation is much less developed (e.g. American *Otus* or *Glaucidium*). Some books state that populations of the same species have different voices in different areas of their distribution. We have studied the evidence and found that either different phases of the vocabulary have been compared or that the birds belonged to separate species. Such studies have involved the Central American pygmy owls *Glaucidium* or South American screech owls *Otus*.

In order to build up a picture of the comparative vocalisations of different species, good recordings of their vocabularies are essential. First, we must know the territorial song. To establish this, studies in the field or on birds kept in aviaries will be necessary. Every vocalisation in an owl's vocabulary has a precise meaning. The song marks the territory and attracts the mate. Songs are uttered by all males and most females. Some taxa have two songs for different situations. In American screech owls *Otus*, both sexes utter a territorial song, the primary or A-song, and the secondary or B-song; the latter is used in courtship. The two sonograms (Figs. 50a, b) illustrate the A- and B-songs of the Tropical Screech Owl *Otus choliba*. The courtship song often has a more aggressive character than the territorial song. Courtship behaviour is expected to be more aggressive.

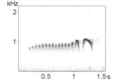

Figure 50a. Tropical Screech Owl: A-song of male.   **Figure 50b. Tropical Screech Owl: B-song of male.**

Old World *Otus*, like most owls, have only the A-song, which is used in aggressive situations as well as in courtship when duetting with the female. Common Scops Owls duet, the male's song being more pronounced and lower in pitch than the female's (Fig. 51a). Unpaired males may sing without noticeably stopping from dusk to dawn. Aggressive, single, piercing cries different from the song are uttered at irregular intervals (Fig. 51b). Unpaired females give a song similar to the male's, without the typical cadences but more drawn out. This type of song is seldom heard and may be a claim to a food territory. When a male approaches, this song changes into the higher-pitched, more lilting song uttered when duetting (Fig. 51c).

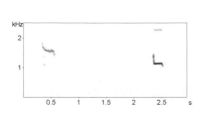

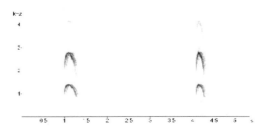

Figure 51a. Common Scops Owl: female and male duetting during courtship.   **Figure 51b. Common Scops Owl: aggressive call of male.**

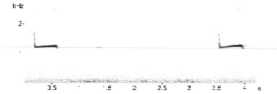

Figure 51c. Common Scops Owl: song of an unpaired female.

Typical vocalisations include territorial or courtship songs: aggressive calls, contact notes, begging-calls, cries of distress and alarm calls. Apart from vocal sounds, bill-snapping or wing-clapping sounds may be made. Studying the songs is usually sufficient to identify species, but allospecies may have similar songs, as normally they never meet. There may, however, be differences in vocabulary. As an example, the calls advertising potential nesting holes of two allopatric pygmy owls are shown here. In both cases the male flies to a potential hole in a tree (mostly made by a woodpecker), slips into it and utters advertising calls. Those of Ferruginous Pygmy Owl *Glaucidium brasilianum*, a resident of tropical and subtropical South America east of the Andes, are very different from those of the allopatric Austral Pygmy Owl *G. nanum*. The first gives high-pitched, rather piercing, cricket-like notes in irregular sequences, while the latter utters much lower, softly purring calls with a wavy character (Figs. 52a, b). The differences are easily discernible although the songs are similar, showing only slight differences in frequency of notes and tonal quality (Figs. 52c, d).

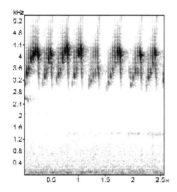

Figure 52a. Ferruginous Pygmy Owl: high chirping notes when advertising nest-hole.

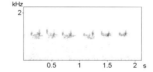

Figure 52b. Austral Pygmy Owl: cooing calls advertising potential nest-hole.

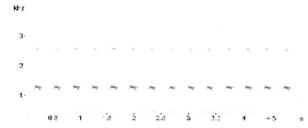

Figure 52c. Ferruginous Pygmy Owl: song of male.

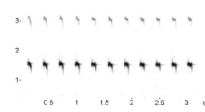

Figure 52d. Austral Pygmy Owl: song of male.

34

SYSTEMATICS AND TAXONOMY

Vocalisations are critical in owl taxonomy. However, there are also morphological differences between the two families and between the different species within them. Several species of owl have been lumped together as variants or races of the same species. The North American Eastern Screech Owl *Otus asio* and its Asian relatives in the *Otus bakkamoena* superspecies (consisting of at least four valid species) have been included by some authors in the single species *Otus asio*. Similarly, many South-East Asian *Otus* have been lumped as races of *O. scops*, even *O. insularis* from Mahé in the Seychelles. We now know that all these forms have different vocalisations, particularly songs, but we are also aware of strikingly different colour morphs in several owl species which do not represent separate species or races. These morphs often are wrongly described as phases; a phase is something temporary. In owls the colour morphs last a lifetime and reappear after each moult. A red-morph Tawny Owl will always be red.

Owl systematics have frequently been discussed and recent studies on DNA give clues to probable relationships. Two families may be accepted without argument: Tytonidae and Strigidae. The first may be separated into two genera, *Tyto* with 17 species and *Phodilus* with one species. We include the Itombwe Owl *Tyto prigoginei* in *Tyto*, as it shows typical barn owl patterns. All *Tyto* owls have well developed heart-shaped facial discs, rather small, dark eyes and relatively long legs with central and inner toes equal in length to the central toe. *Phodilus* has similar toe patterns and a serrated inner edge to the claw of the central toe; but the facial disc is very distinctly shaped and the legs are shorter with feathered tarsi.

The Strigidae comprises about 194 species in 24 genera. We include the genus *Ketupa* in *Bubo*, giving it the rank of subgenus. Asian fishing owls are obviously related to eagle owls and represent fishing *Bubo* species. On vocal patterns they appear to be more closely related to 'true' Asian *Bubo* than are *Bubo leucostictus* or *Bubo poensis* of Africa. The genus *Ciccaba* we include in *Strix*. We regard the Cuban Bare-legged Owl as a monotypic genus, *Gymnoglaux*, as this bird seems to be more related to *Athene* than to *Otus*. We also maintain the isolated Palau Owl *Pyrroglaux podarginus* in a genus of its own.

We treat the American screech owls *Otus* as members of subgenera *Megascops* and *Macabra*, as they differ from Old World scops owls in having two songs. However, on the basis of bioacoustical studies and DNA evidence, the American Flammulated Owl *Otus flammeolus* is related to the Old World scops owls and not screech owls. The Burrowing Owl we treat as a close relative of the Little Owl.

Following Ernst Mayr, we have applied the Biological Species Concept (BSC) to owls. So we regard as full species the members of a reproductive community which has evolved different patterns from members of another reproductive community. These patterns are often most easily perceptible vocally. Owls have not evolved distinct regional dialects and all vocalisations are inherited; therefore bioacoustics are the most important taxonomic criterion used to separate difficult species groups (e.g. *Glaucidium* and *Otus*). These studies have led to the recognition of several new species. Specific status can be substantiated by DNA-evidence and field studies. We know that in owl taxonomy the nucleotide substitutions in DNA-sequencing are variable at subspecific level between 0 and 1%. Greater gaps in nucleotide substitutions suggest species status. In Passeriformes, the nucleotide substitutions may be much greater and clinal vocal differences may be very striking.

The evidence may be summarised as follows. (1) Clearly distinguishable vocal patterns such as songs suggest different species, especially for sympatric taxa. (2) In allopatric, non-migratory species (allospecies) many vocal patterns may be similar or even identical; but this may not be taken as evidence of closer relationship and perhaps only indicates common ancestors. Allospecies are normally separated by large distances and are unlikely to come into contact with each other; thus, isolating mechanisms between them may not be necessary. This holds true for morphological as well as vocal patterns. Convergence may be the key. (3) In parapatric species (paraspecies) where the range may sometimes overlap, specific vocal parameters may be recognised in all studied cases. These may be barely distinguishable to the human ear, but are obviously different to the owls. Hybridisation may occasionally occur, but natural selection will not favour hybrids and populations of such birds will never be established.

Following these principles we have revised the owl taxa, especially those that present difficult problems. We recognise at least 212 species within the order Strigiformes, many of which have been recently described or have been separated from existing species through bioacoustical, ecological and molecular research.

Biometric criteria have also been applied such as the tail/wing index (length of tail : length of wing) or the hand/wing index (length of wing-tip rising above secondaries on closed wing x 100, divided by wing-length). Birds with long, pointed wings have a large index; birds with rounded wings have a small index.

In several species plumage may vary and colour morphs exist. Nevertheless some species may be separated by their plumage. For example, three species of *Athene* may be distinguished by the different markings on their heads: Little Owl *A. noctua* and Spotted Owlet *A. brama* have relatively well developed occipital faces which are absent or reduced to a narrow collar in Forest Owlet *A. blewitti*. The latter has a rather dark, virtually unspotted crown, while in Little Owl the crown is boldly streaked and in Spotted Owlet it is spotted with rounded dots (Fig. 53). Eye (iris) colour may also be diagnostic, but in the genus *Otus* several species may be found whose eye colour varies between brown, orange and yellow. Sometimes this may be caused by ageing. Coloration of the bill seems to be less variable.

Figure 53. a) Little Owl, white longitudinal spots above white nuchal band b) Spotted Owlet, white double-spots above white nuchal band c) Forest Owlet, only a few small white spots above the sparse white nuchal spots.

Most owls' feet are distinctive: they vary in size and shape and in the different feathering of the tarsus and toes, bare in some, sparsely bristled in others. Figure 54 demonstrates these differences. Most arise from adaptation for hunting or to climatic conditions.

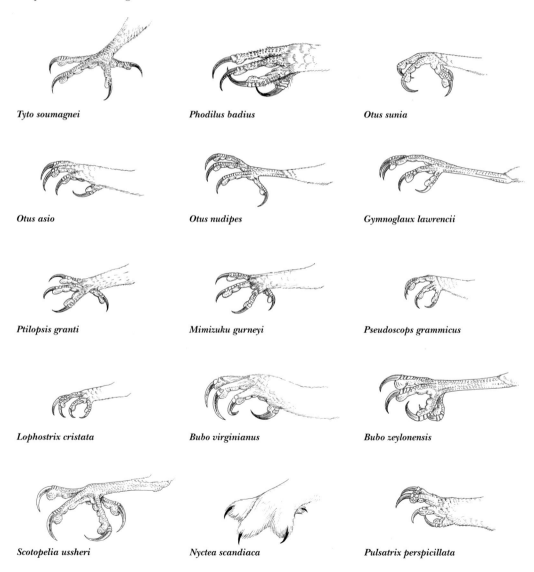

Tyto soumagnei

Phodilus badius

Otus sunia

Otus asio

Otus nudipes

Gymnoglaux lawrencii

Ptilopsis granti

Mimizuku gurneyi

Pseudoscops grammicus

Lophostrix cristata

Bubo virginianus

Bubo zeylonensis

Scotopelia ussheri

Nyctea scandiaca

Pulsatrix perspicillata

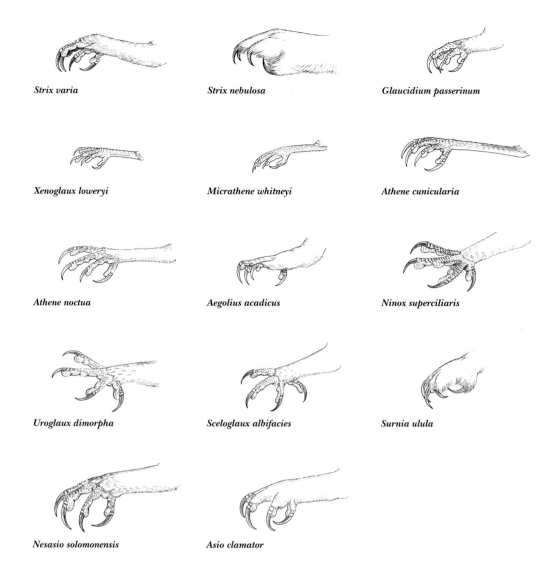

Strix varia

Strix nebulosa

Glaucidium passerinum

Xenoglaux loweryi

Micrathene whitneyi

Athene cunicularia

Athene noctua

Aegolius acadicus

Ninox superciliaris

Uroglaux dimorpha

Sceloglaux albifacies

Surnia ulula

Nesasio solomonensis

Asio clamator

Figure 54. Differences in the feet of a selection of owls (not to scale).

MOLECULAR EVOLUTION AND SYSTEMATICS OF THE OWLS (STRIGIFORMES)

by

Michael Wink and Petra Heidrich

INTRODUCTION

In 1857 Charles Darwin wrote to his friend T. H. Huxley:

> The time will come, I believe, though I shall not live to see it, when we shall have fairly true genealogical trees of each kingdom of nature...

Darwin was right in both his predictions, for it has taken over 130 years for his expectation to be realised: it is only in recent years that we can claim to have reached the stage when fairly true genealogical (today we use the term 'phylogenetic') trees can be established for nearly every group of organisms.

Phylogeny and systematics of birds and other organisms are traditionally based on morphological and anatomical characters; sometimes ecological, behavioural, acoustical or geographical data are included in the reconstruction of the underlying phylogenies. Since the main criterion is similarity, convergence due to adaptive traits can sometimes obscure the picture.

A real breakthrough for phylogenetic studies came with the advent of molecular and biochemical methods, such as protein electrophoresis, DNA-DNA-hybridisation, DNA restriction analyses (RFLP), or the amplification of marker genes by polymerase chain reaction (PCR) followed by DNA sequencing (overviews in Sibley and Ahlquist 1990, Avise 1994, Hillis and Moritz 1990, Hoelzel 1992, Mindell 1997). In particular, the analysis of nucleotide sequences by powerful computer programs, such as PAUP (Swofford 1993), PHYLIP (Felsenstein 1993) and MEGA (Kumar *et al.* 1993), has facilitated the reconstruction of phylogenies in all kingdoms of life. The molecular approach does not make the traditional analysis obsolete; on the contrary, it is complementary. Indeed, the right questions in molecular analysis can only be asked if we have a solid framework based on morphology, geography, behaviour and/or acoustics.

The analysis of mitochondrial genes is central today in most molecular studies on birds (Mindell 1997), since mtDNA evolves much faster than nuclear DNA. Among mitochondrial genes, many studies use the cytochrome b gene, which has the advantage that deletions, insertions or inversions are usually absent, so that the sequence alignment does not constitute a problem (as compared to ribosomal genes, which are also often used as markers). However, while cytochrome b is usually a good marker at the species and genus level, it loses resolution on divergence events which are more than 50 million years away. This is mainly due to multiple nucleotide substitutions at the same position, which can lead to homoplasy.

Cytochrome b sequences are available today for many groups of birds, such as the ratites, Pelicaniformes, Falconiformes, Ciconiidae, Procellariidae, Alcidae, Gruidae, Laridae, Stercorariidae, Psittacidae, Sylviidae, Paridae, Sittidae and Fringillidae (examples are: Kocher *et al.* 1989, Edwards *et al.* 1991, Birt *et al.* 1992, Cooper *et al.* 1992, Richman & Price 1992, Taberlet *et al.* 1992, Blechschmidt *et al.* 1993, Friesen *et al.* 1993, Helm-Bychowski & Cracraft 1993, Seibold *et al.* 1993, in press, Wink *et al.* 1993a,b, 1998, Avise *et al.* 1994, Hedges and Sibley 1994, Heidrich & Wink 1994, 1998, Wink 1994a,b, 1995, Heidrich *et al.* 1995a,b, 1996, 1998, Helbig *et al.* 1995, 1996, Wink & Seibold 1996, Wittmann *et al.* 1995, Gaucher *et al.* 1996, Griffiths 1997, Leisler *et al.* 1997 and Mindell 1997).

Trees which are based on sequence data are not necessarily unequivocal and correct. Problems can arise if the dataset is incomplete and does not contain all related taxa for a comparison ('undersampling'). The alignment can be critical for datasets containing gaps, insertion or deletions (as in rRNA genes). Nuclear copies of mitochondrial genes can bias a phylogeny (Quinn 1997). Also computer programs (i.e. character state, distance or maximum likely hood methods) and the evolutionary window to be analysed (i.e. problems of homoplasy) are of importance to obtain the correct tree. For mitochondrial genes it should be remembered that we can only trace maternal lineages ('gene trees') and that trees can be distorted by inbreeding and introgression. Some of these limitations have to be kept in mind when interpreting the phylogenetic trees presented in the following.

We have chosen the mitochondrial cytochrome b gene to study speciation and phylogeny of owls. Some results have already been published from our laboratory on tawny, screech and pygmy owls (Heidrich & Wink 1994, 1998, Heidrich *et al.* 1995). In this chapter we present results of our molecular investigation into the phylogenetic relationships in the genera *Tyto, Phodilus, Otus, Bubo, Ketupa, Nyctea, Strix, Pulsatrix, Glaucidium, Athene, Speotyto, Aegolius, Ninox, Asio* and *Surnia*. The missing genera mostly belong to monotypic genera, so that a general picture on the phylogeny of owls becomes possible with the present dataset. (We would be happy to receive blood, tissue or feather samples from species that are not included in our trees, since we hope eventually to arrive at a complete tree of the Strigiformes.)

MATERIAL AND METHODS

Detailed information on materials and methods use for DNA isolation, PCR, PCR primers, DNA sequencing and tree reconstruction has been produced (Wink 1994a, 1994b, 1995, Heidrich & Wink 1994, 1998, Heidrich *et al.* 1995, Leisler *et al.* 1997, Heidrich 1998). Sequences have been deposited with GeneBank. Details on methodology and sequence information can be obtained from the authors on request.

For most species we have determined cytochrome b sequences (1040 bp) for two or more individuals, so that the sequences used in this analysis are unequivocal and reliable (Heidrich 1998). For the molecular analysis (shown in Fig. 55) we have assembled a dataset consisting of a single cytochrome b sequence per taxon in those cases where significant haplotype differentiation was absent. We had samples of approximately 270 individuals of owls, and determined partial cytochrome b sequences (300 bp) for all of them. The partial sequences are helpful in identifying existing haplotypic differentiation (Fig. 56).

Distances (p-distance) are calculated as the proportion of nucleotide substitutions (in %) between pairs of taxa (Table 1). Distances correlate with divergence time: a 2% nucleotide substitution is estimated to be crudely equivalent to a million years of separation (Shields & Wilson 1987). This molecular clock provides a rough estimate for a temporal framework (Moore & DeFilippis 1997), but needs to be interpreted with caution, since the clock was not calibrated for owls.

Distances can be used to decide whether a taxon can be regarded as a distinct species: in owls a divergence of more than 1.5% is usually indicative of species level, and we advocate species recognition at this threshold when there is clear support from morphological and acoustic characters.

Bootstrap values provide an estimate of how well sequence data support a furcation. Although bootstrap values remain controversial, they can be helpful. On the basis of simulations under a wide range of conditons, Hillis & Bull (1993) concluded that nodes with calculated bootstrap values of 70% and higher actually occurred in 95% and more of simulated phylogenies. This means that a bootstrap value of 70% can be regarded as evidence for a well supported node (Moore & DeFilippis 1997).

PHYLOGENETIC RELATIONSHIPS WITHIN THE STRIGIFORMES

In occupying the niche of a nocturnal raptor, owls underwent several adaptations. Besides specialised hunting strategies, they developed a sophisticated acoustic communication system. Morphology varies relatively little in many owl species but the distinctive calls, which are inherited and not learned, are of considerable taxonomic value (Hekstra 1982, König 1991a,b, 1994a,b). If phylogenetic relationships are reconstructed on the basis of morphological characters alone, errors may result from the confusion caused by convergent traits that have nothing to do with underlying phylogeny.

The sequence dataset, involving one sequence per taxon, was analysed by Neighbour Joining (NJ) and Maximum Likelihood (ML). The resulting trees are congruent in most groupings (see Fig. 55a, b). Differences can be seen for *Ninox*, which is either placed as a sister group to the *Glaucidium/Athene* complex (ML) or at the base of the Strigidae (NJ). *Pulsatrix* either clusters as a sister group to New World *Otus* (NJ) or sits between *Strix* and *Bubo* (ML). Bootstrap values (NJ) indicate that the position of *Ninox* and *Pulsatrix* is not supported by significant values (Fig. 55b); we consider the ML groupings to be more likely, since ML has been considered as the best tree reconstruction method available at present.

As can be seen from Figs. 55-57, the distinction between the families Tytonidae and Strigidae is evident in all tree reconstructions and well supported by DNA data (Table 1).

Relationships within the family Tytonidae

Traditionally, two genera are distinguished within the Tytonidae: *Tyto* and *Phodilus*. This view is clearly supported by the sequence data (Figs. 55-57). The distance between the two genera is large (Table 1), i.e. their divergence from a common ancestor must have occurred more than nine million years ago.

Although several members of the *Tyto* complex have been recognised as distinct species (Sibley & Monroe 1990), several others are considered to be subspecies of *T. alba, T. novaehollandiae* or *T. capensis*. However, since morphological variation is pronounced, some of the subspecies may constitute sibling species. We have analysed the DNA of more than 20 individuals of *T. alba* and found a considerable degree of sequence variation between birds from different populations (up to 2%), indicating a strong degree of philopatry and reduced gene-flow between them. Fig. 56a shows their phylogeographic relationships: within Europe and Africa, birds originating from Germany, Ireland, Scotland, Austria or France have developed distinct haplotypes. *T. a. glaucops* from Hispaniola in the Caribbean has been separated as a distinct species since *T. glaucops* and *T. alba* are sympatric and do not interbreed (Sibley and Monroe 1990, Hume 1991). The sequence divergence of 8% (Table 1) definitely supports the treatment of *T. glaucops* as a distinct species. *T. a. pratincola*, which also lives in the West Indies, is clearly distinct from *T. alba* (8% sequence divergence) but less so from *T. glaucops* (1.7%), so might or might not merit species status, and if retained as a subspecies it presumably should be a subspecies of *T. glaucops*. Since barn owls have been introduced to many countries of the world by European settlers, the genetic make-up of local populations may be influenced by hybridisation between native and introduced birds.

Relationships within the family Strigidae

Glaucidium Pygmy owls of the genus *Glaucidium* occur in the Old and New World. Although their plumage is very similar in most instances (a factor which makes their taxonomy particularly difficult), they can be distinguished by a unique repertoire of vocalisations (König 1994b). We recently demonstrated that taxonomic classifications based on differing acoustic signals (König 1994b) could be corroborated by DNA sequence data (Heidrich *et al.* 1996). Figure 55 clearly shows that Old and New World species cluster in separate monophyletic clades which possess a common ancestry but diverged more than 7-8 million years ago (Table 1). We can certainly rule out the notion that *G. gnoma/ G. californicum* and *G. passerinum* are conspecific, as has been assumed by some authors based on their similar plumage patterns (Sibley & Monroe 1990). *Glaucidium perlatum* was considered a subspecies of *G. passerinum* by Eck & Busse (1973), but since genetic distances are higher than 6.5% (Fig. 56a) and vocal differences also exist, the taxa can be regarded as distinct species.

Within the *Glaucidium brasilianum* complex of South America, several distinct haplotypes have been recognised (Figs. 55, 57) in different regions of Argentina and Brazil. Because voices and sizes also differ, *G. tucumanum* has been considered a distinct species (Heidrich *et al.*, 1995) and *G. b. stranecki* a new subspecies (König & Wink 1995). *G. brasilianum* shares common ancestry with *G. peruanum*, *G. griseiceps* and *G. nanum* (Fig. 55), these species forming a monophyletic group. *G. bolivianum*, *G. jardinii* and *G. hardyi* also cluster in a common, apparently monophyletic group (Fig. 55). Birds of both complexes are clearly separated from *G. californicum* and *G. gnoma*, which have distinctive calls and distributions (*G. californicum* lives in North America, especially the Rocky Mountains, while *G. gnoma* ranges from Mexico to Central America). *G. minutissimum* from eastern Brazil clusters between the *bolivianum* and *californicum* group (Fig. 56a).

Athene/Speotyto Three species have been recognised in the genus *Athene*, i.e. *A. noctua*, *A. brama* and *A. blewitti*. As can be seen from Fig. 56a, *noctua* and *brama* are clearly separated also at the sequence level. Within *A. noctua*, we encountered a surprising phenomenon. Two genetic clusters are apparent, and are supported by high bootstrap values; genetic differences between both groups account for 6.4% nucleotide substitutions. A genetic distance of more than 1.5% is typical for species. Birds from cluster I derive from Israel and Turkey whereas those from cluster II are from Europe (Figs. 55, 56a). How can we explain these results? Both clusters might represent distinct species which have not been recognised by taxonomy so far. In this case, also morphological and acoustical differences should exist between both forms. Indeed, morphologically distinct subspecies have been described from Israel, which may explain the differences. In this case these birds would represent a separate species: *Athene lilith*.

We had no material of *blewitti* to work with. However, it should be noted that as yet unpublished morphological analysis suggests that it belongs in its own genus *Heteroglaux* (Rasmussen and Collar 1998).

Athene (*Speotyto*) *cunicularia* represents the genus *Athene* in the New World. Since DNA-DNA hybridisation suggested significant differences (Sibley and Monroe 1990), a separation into a monotypic genus appears justified. According to the sequence data, it is clear that *Speotyto* and *Athene* share common ancestry (divergence approximately six million years ago) and that they form a monophyletic group. Because of similarities in morphology, general appearance, vocal patterns, and in behaviour, however, we suggest merging *Speotyto* back in *Athene*.

Surnia The Northern Hawk Owl *Surnia ulula* of northern Eurasia and North America shares common ancestry and forms a monophyletic group with the *Glaucidium* complex of Old World origin (Figs. 1-3). Retention of a monotypic genus is thus open for debate, but might be justified because of morphological, behavioural and, last but not least, genetic differences.

Aegolius Owls of the genus *Aegolius* represent a third major monophyletic group (Figs. 55, 57) besides *Glaucidium/ Surnia* and *Athene*. Within *A. funereus*, some geographical differentiation is apparent (Fig. 56a) which requires further study. The North American *A. acadius* diverges with 12.9% nucleotide substitutions from *A. funereus*, implying divergence well over six million years ago (Table 1). Two geographically separated subspecies, *A. a. acadius* and *A. a. brooksii*, can be recognised (distance 0.7%). The South American *A. harrisii* is more closely related to the North American *A. acadius* than to *A. funereus* (Fig. 55), suggesting a common ancestor for the New World species. *Aegolius ridgwayi* from Central America could not be studied, as no tissue samples were available.

Ninox The genus *Ninox* comprises at least 20 species of mainly Australasian distribution. On general appearance they might be related to the *Glaucidium/Athene* complex. Indeed, in ML trees (and MP, not shown), *Ninox* clusters as a sister group to this complex (Fig. 55a). Also 12S mt rDNA support such an assumption (Mindell *et al.* 1997). We clearly need more taxa from the genus *Ninox* to resolve its phylogenetic position unambiguously.

Strix Tawny and wood owls (genus *Strix* with 21 species, including *Ciccaba*) always form a monophyletic clade in ML, MP, and NJ trees (Figs. 55-57) and cluster as a sister group to the *Bubo* complex.

DNA data show that *S. butleri* is a distinct species rather than a subspecies of *S. aluco*, and indeed closer to the African *S. woodfordii* than to *S. aluco* (Heidrich & Wink 1994). *Strix uralensis* appears as a sister group of *S. aluco*, as suggested from behaviour and general appearance; genetic distances (Table 1) imply that both taxa diverged from a common ancestor more than four million years ago.

The South American *S. rufipes* always clusters at the base of the *Strix* complex and could belong to a sister group to the Old World *Strix*, the two having diverged from a common ancestor 5-6 million years ago. Future studies of New World species will show whether this assumption is correct.

Within *S. aluco* from various parts of Europe and Israel we found no evidence of haplotypic differentiation, as observed for *Tyto alba* or *Asio otus* (Fig. 56b). Two distinct haplotypes can be seen in *S. uralensis*, probably reflecting phylogeographic differences between Scandinavian and birds from Eastern Europe (Fig. 56b).

Pulsatrix Four species are recognised in the Central and South American genus *Pulsatrix*, of which we were able to study *P. perspicillata* and *P. koeniswaldiana*. The phylogenetic position of *Pulsatrix* cannot, however, be resolved with certainty. In NJ trees (Fig. 55b) it clusters with the South American *Otus* complex, and in ML reconstructions between *Strix* (and *Ciccaba*) and *Bubo* (Fig. 55a); but clusters are not supported by high bootstrap values.

Otus, Mimizuku, Asio and Ptilopsis Morphologically, several owls with ears have been grouped in the genera *Bubo* (eagle owls), *Ketupa* (fish owls), *Otus* (scops and screech owls) and *Asio* ('eared owls'). According to our genetic analysis (Figs. 55-57), members of the genus *Otus* appear in at least three different monophyletic clades, indicating that the genus is polyphyletic; it therefore needs a systematic revision. The screech owls of the New World represent a distinct group which is separated from Old World *Otus* by genetic distances of between 12 and 16%, equivalent to 6-8 million years (Table 1). Within the screech owl complex, which has its centre of radiation in South and Central America, several species have been recognised on account of different acoustic repertoires (König 1994a). Sequence data corroborate these findings (Heidrich *et al.* 1995), thereby supporting the importance of vocalisations in owl taxonomy. *Otus atricapillus*, *O. usta* and *O. roboratus* are distinct species of common ancestry. *Otus sanctaecatarinae*, and probably *O. guatemalae* and *O. asio* (from North America), also belong to this assemblage. *Otus hoyi* and *O. petersoni* appear as sibling species, as do *O. albogularis* and *O. choliba* (Figs. 55, 56b).

Several Old World scops owls have been analysed (overview in Sibley & Monroe 1990). *Otus scops*, *O. lempiji*, *O. megalotis*, *O. longicornis*, *O. brucei* and *O. bakkamoena* have been included here as representatives of this group. As can be seen from Figs. 55 and 56b these birds fall into a common clade which is very distinct from the New World *Otus* complex. Using 12S mt rDNA sequences, Mindell *et al.* (1997) showed that *O. mirus*, *O. mindorensis* and *Mimizuku gurneyi* cluster together with *O. megalotis* and *O. longicornis*. Since we also studied the latter two species we can conclude that *O. mirus*, *O. mindorensis* and *Mimizuku gurneyi* are members of the Old World *Otus* group. Since *Mimizuku* clusters within this group it is doubtful whether this monotypic genus is valid (Miranda *et al.* 1997).

The African *O. leucotis* and *O. granti* differ both morphologically and genetically from the other Old World *Otus* species and have been placed in the genus *Ptilopsis*. In all reconstructions (Figs. 55-57) they figure as a sister group to *Asio* (to which they have some superficial resemblance). It is likely that '*P. leucotis*' represents two species: *P. leucotis* and *P. granti*, which are similar in size and plumage, but differ strikingly in voice and range; moreover, our DNA data (Fig. 56b) indicate a clear difference between them. *Asio otus* and *A. flammeus* always fall into the same clade (Fig. 56b) although they may have diverged more than five million years ago.

Altogether it seems obvious that other different monophyletic clades of *Otus* species should also be recognised taxonomically. Some haplotypic differentiation was discovered in *Otus atricapillus*, *O. usta*, *O. hoyi*, *O. petersoni*, *O. guatemalae*, *O. asio*, *Ptilopsis leucotis*, *Asio otus* and *A. flammeus* which deserves further study (Fig. 56b) to determine a possible phylogeographic pattern.

Bubo, Ketupa and Nyctea Eagle owls of the genus *Bubo* represent another prominent group of owls with ear-tufts. To date within this complex we have studied *B. bubo*, *B. ascalaphus*, *B. nipalensis*, *B. virginianus*, *B. magellanicus*, *B. africanus*, *B. bengalensis*, *B. sumatrana* and *B. lacteus*. According to phylogenetic relationships and distances (Figs. 55 & 56b; Table 1) these are all distinct species, although some have been treated as subspecies of *B. bubo* (Sibley and Monroe 1990).

The southernmost taxon of South American eagle owls differs in size, vocalisations and DNA (Figs. 55 & 56b) from *B. virginianus* and has been considered a distinct species, *B. magellanicus* (König *et al.* 1996).

Bubo ascalaphus, which occurs in North and West Africa, has been treated as a distinct species (Sibley and Monroe 1990). In our analysis nucleotide substitutions differ by 3.5% between *B. bubo* and *B. ascalaphus*. Moreover, *B. b. interpositus*, which is morphologically distinct from *B. bubo* and lives in the Israeli desert, is also genetically distinct (distance 2.8%) (Figs. 55 & 56; Table 1). Since a sequence divergence of more than 1.5% is indicative of species level, we regard it as justified to treat both taxa as distinct species particularly if supported by morphological and accoustic evidence.

We have analysed the sequences of some 20 individuals of *B. bubo* from Western and Central Europe. Many samples derived from birds found dead under powerlines or on roads, most of which were descendants of birds reintroduced to Germany and other countries during breeding programmes. A first analysis of the sequence data (Fig. 56b) shows a strong heterogeneity, indicating that birds from various origins and subspecies have been multiplied and released in the breeding programmes. Analysis before starting the breeding programme could have prevented this genetic mix.

The Snowy Owl *Nyctea scandiaca* shares its ancestry with *Bubo* (Figs. 55-57), especially with the New World *B. virginianus*, a finding which conforms with the arctic distribution of *Nyctea*. The separation from a common ancestor took place more than four million years ago. Since *Nyctea* represents a monotypic genus but unambiguously clusters within the *Bubo*-complex, the taxonomic consequence would be to lump *Nyctea* in *Bubo* and call the species *Bubo scandiaca*.

A similar situation obtains with *Ketupa*, of which four species have been described from South-East Asia. *Ketupa zeylonensis* and *K. ketupu* cluster as close relatives to Asian *Bubo* such as *B. nipalensis* and *B. sumatrana* (Figs. 55 & 56b). Moreover, the general appearance of *Ketupa* is similar to that of *Bubo*; because of genetic relationships (distance 9-10%) we agree with Amadon and Bull (1988) to merge *Ketupa* in *Bubo*.

PHYLOGENETIC POSITION OF OWLS AS COMPARED TO DIURNAL RAPTORS AND NIGHTJARS

Several hypotheses have been advanced concerning the evolution of owls. Linnaeus (1758) placed them with vultures, eagles and falcons in the order Accipitres. In 1827 they were separated from the diurnal raptors as a distict order by L'Herminier; soon afterwards Nitsch (1840) recognised the differences between Tytonidae and Strigidae. This view was supported by Fürbringer (1888) and Gadow (1892), who also stressed a closer relationship between Strigiformes and Caprimulgiformes, a view maintained by Wetmore (1930) and Mayr and Amadon (1951). Cracraft (1981), using a cladistic approach, went against this, concluding a closer relationship between owls and falcons, but Sibley and Ahlquist's (1990) study on DNA-DNA hybridisation reinstated the Caprimulgiformes as the nearest neighbour of the owls.

To test the owl/falcon and owl/nightjar hypotheses, we have assembled a dataset of cytochrome b sequences including the main genera of owls, members of the Galliformes and Casuariformes/Rheiformes as old and distinct outgroups, plus members of the Procellariiformes, Charadriiformes, Falconiformes (Falconidae, Sagittariidae, Pandionidae, Accipitridae, Cathartidae), Psittaciformes, Cuculiformes, Ciconiiformes and Gruiformes. The cytochrome b dataset was analysed by MP methods. The resulting bootstrap cladogram is shown in Figure 57.

Running parallel with our work, Mindell *et al.* (1997), using 12S mt rDNA, concluded that all diurnal raptors could be monophyletic. Our results, on the other hand, suggest that – although deeper (ordinal) branches are not well supported by bootstrap values – the Sagittariidae, Pandionidae and Accipitridae share an ancestry but appear separated from the falcons and Cathartidae. A similar conclusion had already been reached for the New World vultures (König 1982, Avise *et al.* 1994, Wink in press), which are no longer considered members of the Falconiformes (Sibley and Monroe 1990). Similar traits in morphology and behaviour of diurnal raptors are obviously based on convergence due to common life style and not due to common genealogy (Wink 1998, in press).

Figure 57 clearly shows that owls can be subdivided into two major lineages, representing the Tytonidae and Strigidae; together they form a monophyletic group. However, neither nightjars (Caprimulgidae) nor falcons (Falconidae) cluster as a closely related next neighbour to the Strigiformes. These groups usually cluster with unrelated orders (containing the Procellariiformes, Ciconiiformes, Charadiiformes, Pandionidae and Accipitridae). Using different methods for tree-building, such as NJ, MP or ML, we always obtained the same monophyletic groups, such as Strigidae, Tytonidae, Falconidae, Accipitridae,

Laridae, etc., all supported by high bootstrap values, but their positions in relation to each other differed and was not supported by significant bootstrap values. In some trees, we could see a monophyly of Falconidae, Accipitridae, Pandionidae and Sagittariidae; in others a relationship between Tytonidae and Falconidae. Because we could not obtain congruent trees, we conclude that it is difficult to reconstruct higher-order phylogeny of birds using cytochrome b and other mtDNA sequences.

Morphological and anatomical similarities between owls and falcons or nightjars, which were the base for the hypothesis of a closer relationships to owls, are probably based on convergence (as implied already by Bock and McEvey 1969, Mikkola 1983, Feduccia 1996), since they cannot be supported by our sequence data. Since cytochrome b is at its limits for such a comparison, covering probably 100 million years of evolution, a more conserved gene (preferably a nuclear gene) should be studied to confirm these findings.

CONCLUSION

As can be seen from Figs. 55 & 56, the phylogenetic trees inferred from cytochrome b gene sequences generally agree well with the classical taxonomy of owls (Sibley & Monroe 1990, Hume 1991, Burton 1992). Usually the genetic data agree with the attribution of species to a given genus. Exceptions are evident in *Otus*, where a paraphyletic origin is more likely than the present collection of species in a single genus.

The phylogenetic relationships between different genera could not be resolved with certainty in all instances. However, it is likely that the genera *Glaucidium, Athene, Aegolius* and *Surnia* derive from a common ancestor; the same applies to *Otus, Asio, Bubo* and *Strix*, and to *Tyto* and *Phodilus* (Fig. 55).

Cytochrome b sequence data are well suited to resolve phylogenetic relationships within genera and at the species level, but less so at the family and order level (Fig. 3). As mentioned before, several species of the *Glaucidium* and *Otus* complex have been recognised and described mainly by their vocal repertoires, in spite of their weak morphological differentiation. Cytochrome b sequence data have shown that these vocally distinct species are also genetically distinct (König 1994a,b, Heidrich *et al.* 1995, 1996).

In summary, sequence data of the mitochondrial cytochrome b gene provide another powerful tool (besides morphology, anatomy, behaviour and bioacoustics) to elucidate and reconstruct the evolutionary past and speciation in owls. Since the analysis of a single gene only provides a window for a particular evolutionary period, we need to include more progressive or more conservative genes (including both mtDNA and ncDNA) if we intend to solve other problems of microevolution or of higher-level classifications.

ACKNOWLEDGEMENTS

We thank W. Bednarek, G. Ehlers, O. Hatzofe, R. Krahe, D. Reynolds, A. Kemp, C. Fentzloff, W. Grummt, C. König, J. Yom-Tov, D. Ristow, E. Thaler, B. Etheridge and U. Schneppat for providing blood or tissues of owls. Our study of owl phylogenetics was undertaken in close collaboration with C. König (Stuttgart) whom we would like to thank for his help and encouragement.

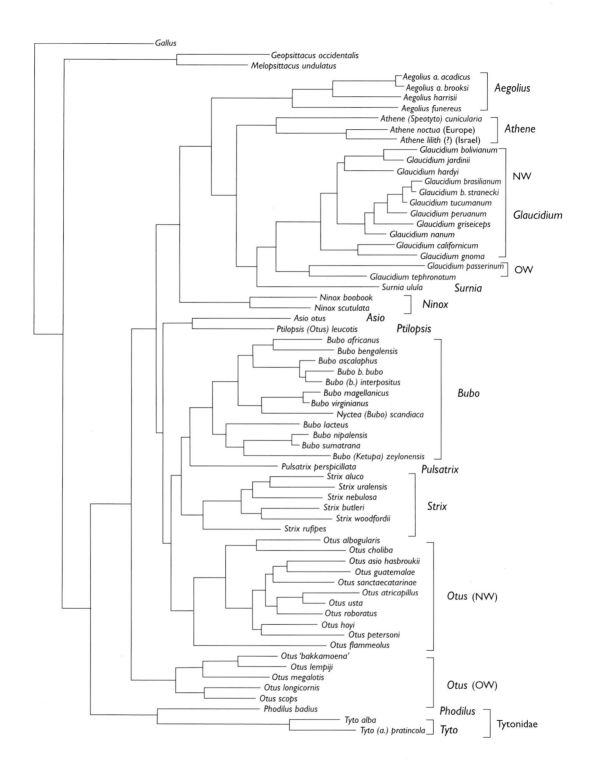

Figure 55a. Genetic relationships within the Tytonidae and Strigidae (based on 1040 nt of the cytochrome b gene): Maximum Likelihood tree. Branch lengths are proportional to genetic distances. (OW = Old World; NW = New World).

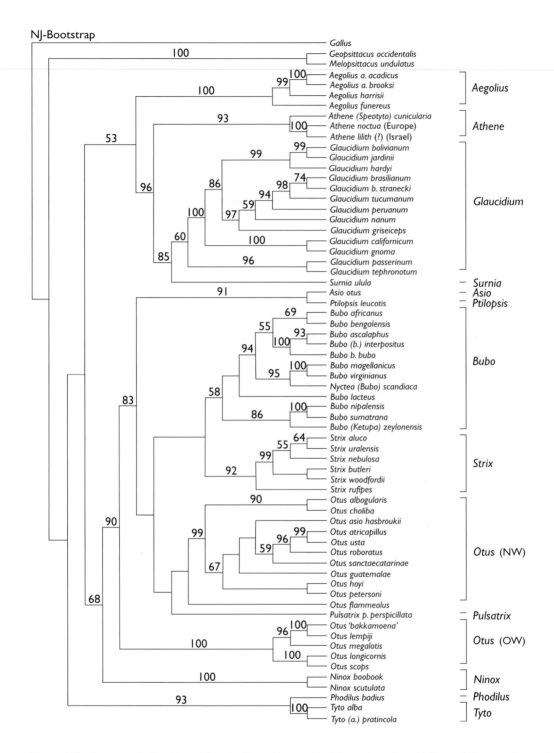

Figure 55b. Genetic relationships within the Tytonidae and Strigidae (based on 1040 nt of the cytochrome b gene): Bootstrap cladogram (100 replicates) reconstructed with the Neighbour Joining method using Jukes Cantor as a distance algorithm (other algorithms, such as Kimura 2, Tamura-Nei, do not change the tree topology). Bootstrap values (above 50%) are given in italics below the branch length values. (OW = Old World; NW = New World).

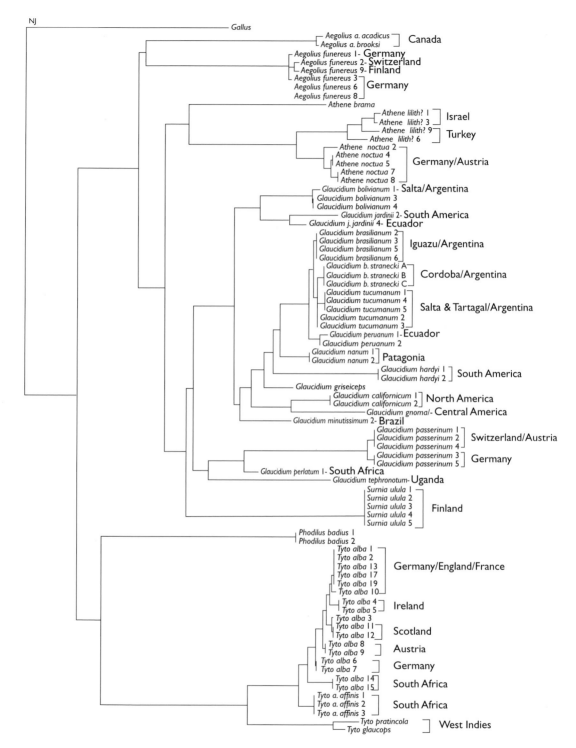

Figure 56a. Haplotypic differentiation in owls based on 300 bp of the cytochrome b gene. Analysis with NJ as in Fig. 55b; branch lengths are proportional to evolutionary distances. Phylogram of genetic relationships between several individuals per taxon of the Tytonidae and in the *Glaucidium/Athene* complex. Geographic origins are given after the species name when reliable data were available; in several instances samples came from zoo birds whose origin could not be established.

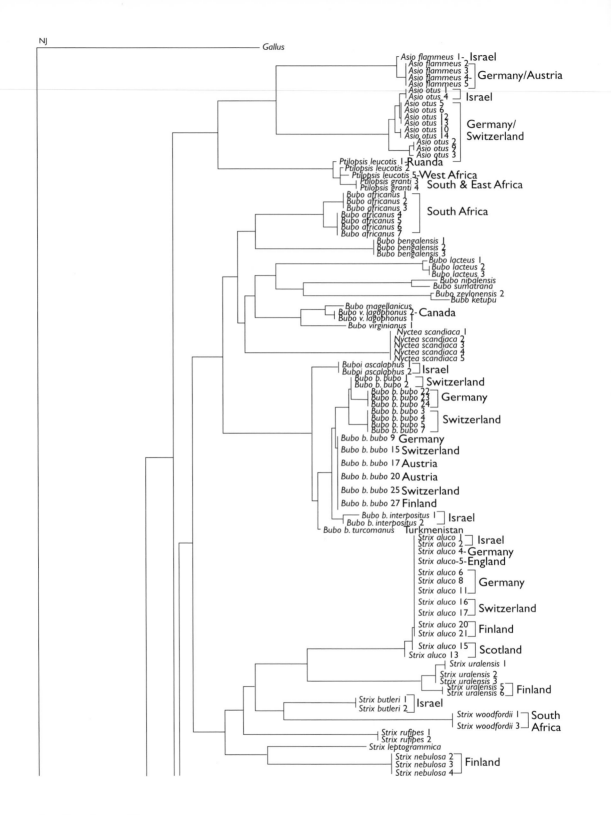

(continued on p.49)

(continued from p.48)

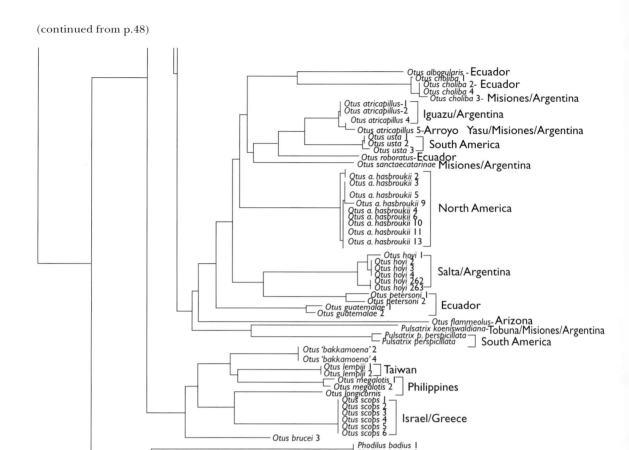

Figure 56b. Haplotypic differentiation in owls based on 300 bp of the cytochrome b gene. Analysis with NJ as in Fig. 55b; branch lengths are proportional to evolutionary distances. Phylogram of genetic relationships within the complex of 'eared owls' and *Strix*. Geographic origins are given after the species name when reliable data were available; in several instances samples came from zoo birds whose origin could not be established.

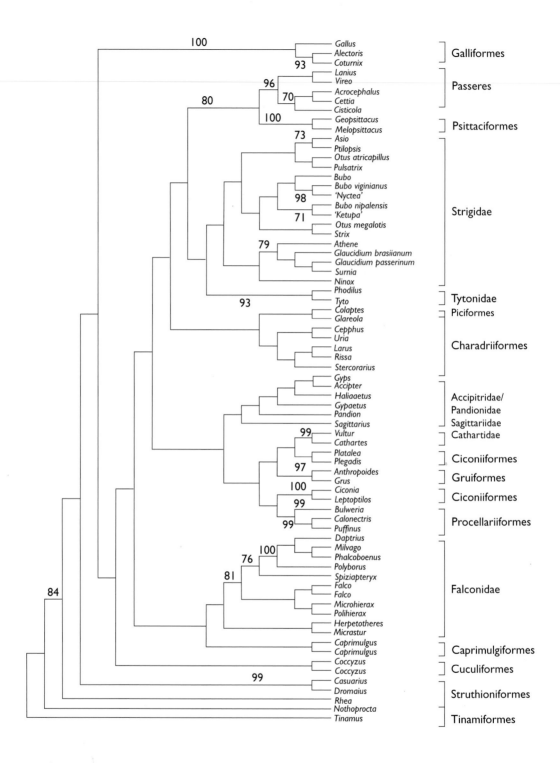

Figure 57. Genetic relationships between members of the Strigiformes and other orders of birds (based on 1040 nt of the cytochrome b gene): Bootstrap analysis (150 replicates) employing the Maximum Parsimony method with heuristic search (TBR branch swapping; tree length 5483 steps [sum of minimal possible lengths 1010, maximally 8114 steps]; consistency index CI= 0.184; retention index RI= 0.370). Sequence data from GeneBank or our own laboratory.

	77	78	80	84	86	88	89	93	95	97	98	100	113	114
77 Aegolius acadicus	-													
78 A. a. brooksi	0.00732	-												
80 A. funereus	0.12874	0.13210	-											
84 A. harrisii	0.08804	0.08910	0.12880	-										
86 Asio otus	0.17719	0.17640	0.17810	0.17874	-									
88 Athene cunicularia	0.17508	0.17047	0.18316	0.18366	0.18062	-								
89 A. noctua (Eur.)	0.18444	0.18270	0.18199	0.18741	0.19278	0.12950	-							
93 A. (n.) lilith (Isr.)	0.18792	0.18613	0.17396	0.17739	0.17662	0.13578	0.06467	-						
95 Bubo africanus	0.17861	0.17780	0.18184	0.19541	0.13901	0.15967	0.17956	0.17616	-					
97 B. ascalaphus	0.18634	0.18451	0.18399	0.18408	0.13853	0.16525	0.17322	0.18434	0.07866	-				
98 B. bengalensis	0.18433	0.18255	0.18054	0.17935	0.13215	0.16366	0.17793	0.17868	0.07455	0.03499	-			
100 B. b. bubo	0.18707	0.18623	0.18634	0.18933	0.13801	0.16827	0.18533	0.18529	0.08510	0.02345	0.09053	-		
113 B. (b.) interpositus	0.19160	0.19097	0.16364	0.16687	0.13801	0.16925	0.15879	0.18961	0.08091	0.09880	0.09278	0.02811	-	
114 B. lacteus	0.16164	0.16096	0.18328	0.18114	0.14300	0.16827	0.16284	0.17058	0.09440	0.09629	0.08674	0.09489	0.09999	-
115 B. magellanicus	0.18304	0.18353	0.18782	0.18022	0.14300	0.16925	0.16555	0.17856	0.08685	0.09727	0.09612	0.09904	0.09540	0.10531
116 B. nipalensis	0.17187	0.16992	0.18992	0.18382	0.13855	0.16531	0.16246	0.18230	0.09727	0.11576	0.11232	0.11889	0.11656	0.09157
117 B. sumatrana	0.17516	0.17220	0.17573	0.18057	0.13715	0.16261	0.18218	0.18427	0.09606	0.10902	0.11203	0.11441	0.11114	0.09152
122 B. virginianus	0.17934	0.17957	0.16117	0.15994	0.13585	0.16734	0.17147	0.18278	0.08274	0.09478	0.09022	0.09983	0.09580	0.10437
124 Glaucidium bolivia.	0.17420	0.17810	0.17628	0.15945	0.17545	0.14471	0.16971	0.17065	0.17736	0.17418	0.17737	0.17677	0.18338	0.16755
124 G. brasilianum	0.16297	0.16221	0.17815	0.15411	0.16480	0.13455	0.16594	0.16330	0.17986	0.17661	0.18182	0.17708	0.18071	0.15217
132 G. b. stranecki	0.16341	0.16263	0.16251	0.15000	0.16642	0.13841	0.16443	0.16524	0.18173	0.17845	0.18374	0.17899	0.18247	0.15374
136 G. tucumanum	0.16637	0.16669	0.17983	0.16170	0.17036	0.13457	0.16398	0.16704	0.18006	0.17903	0.18094	0.18067	0.18410	0.15564
140 G. californicum	0.17018	0.17171	0.18932	0.18114	0.17097	0.13781	0.15999	0.17572	0.17608	0.17833	0.17028	0.17380	0.17256	0.15471
141 G. gnoma	0.17088	0.17334	0.17226	0.18114	0.18770	0.13959	0.17004	0.16143	0.18445	0.18954	0.18507	0.18862	0.19115	0.15844
142 G. griseiceps	0.16001	0.15927	0.17031	0.16597	0.16267	0.12928	0.15867	0.16147	0.17668	0.17167	0.17208	0.17350	0.17801	0.15031
143 G. hardyi	0.16670	0.16702	0.17121	0.16535	0.16713	0.14377	0.16844	0.16844	0.17981	0.17140	0.17239	0.17822	0.17876	0.16372
145 G. jardinii	0.17706	0.17853	0.16392	0.15945	0.17118	0.13446	0.15049	0.16560	0.16774	0.15912	0.16648	0.16549	0.16299	0.14468
147 G. nanum	0.15306	0.15333	0.17595	0.15686	0.16209	0.13245	0.16581	0.16091	0.18144	0.18144	0.18708	0.18183	0.17776	0.15945
152 G. passerinum	0.17400	0.17329	0.16632	0.15975	0.19025	0.16237	0.16848	0.17246	0.17547	0.17338	0.18109	0.17498	0.17990	0.15783
153 G. peruanum	0.15879	0.16011	0.16326	0.15514	0.16686	0.13345	0.16034	0.16085	0.15047	0.15433	0.15859	0.15134	0.15561	0.13746
154 G. tephronotum	0.15428	0.15342	0.19503	0.18899	0.15975	0.14001	0.18972	0.16703	0.12072	0.16053	0.11587	0.11648	0.11648	0.10498
155 Bubo zeylonensis	0.18471	0.18389	0.19078	0.18245	0.15409	0.15736	0.16349	0.17276	0.12072	0.11685	0.11587	0.12200	0.11648	0.14756
156 Ninox boobook	0.19593	0.19406	0.19009	0.18608	0.16165	0.17104	0.15349	0.16761	0.16053	0.16698	0.16394	0.15357	0.16450	0.14357
157 N. scutulata	0.18630	0.18315	0.19009	0.18245	0.15559	0.15382	0.15349	0.16761	0.15301	0.15505	0.15471	0.14793	0.16007	0.14357
160 Nyctea scandiaca	0.18998	0.19029	0.18803	0.18608	0.15261	0.16166	0.17692	0.18428	0.10049	0.10844	0.10789	0.11479	0.10718	0.11467
161 Otus albogularis	0.17537	0.17320	0.17993	0.16247	0.15070	0.17389	0.18917	0.18563	0.13686	0.13940	0.13774	0.13637	0.14269	0.13193
166 O. asio	0.18202	0.18141	0.18783	0.17083	0.13693	0.15429	0.17700	0.18552	0.12821	0.13304	0.14108	0.12886	0.13099	0.12313
169 O. atricapillus	0.17474	0.17775	0.18141	0.17913	0.13916	0.15990	0.19211	0.19918	0.13854	0.14206	0.15134	0.13385	0.12464	0.12270
170 O. 'bakkamoena'	0.17840	0.17640	0.20082	0.16876	0.15304	0.16592	0.16211	0.17134	0.14412	0.14586	0.14103	0.13535	0.14343	0.12721
171 O. choliba	0.19294	0.19223	0.18185	0.17381	0.16388	0.17714	0.18325	0.18643	0.13530	0.15103	0.14491	0.14662	0.15170	0.13857
172 O. flammeolus	0.19632	0.19432	0.19346	0.17789	0.15794	0.17965	0.19192	0.19621	0.15284	0.15328	0.14750	0.14643	0.14892	0.14355
174 O. guatemalae	0.18669	0.18970	0.19213	0.17789	0.14478	0.17216	0.18488	0.18318	0.13600	0.15036	0.13710	0.13088	0.13308	0.12625
176 O. hoyi	0.17664	0.18477	0.20130	0.16733	0.13485	0.16633	0.16644	0.17646	0.13232	0.13912	0.13286	0.12630	0.13729	0.12124
179 O. lempiji	0.18979	0.18780	0.20825	0.17784	0.15880	0.18472	0.17672	0.18311	0.13215	0.14775	0.14982	0.13874	0.14367	0.13288
180 O. leucotis	0.17427	0.17114	0.19412	0.17091	0.11836	0.17102	0.17830	0.18157	0.14913	0.14432	0.13562	0.14043	0.14325	0.12970
182 O. longicornis	0.18754	0.18450	0.18567	0.16600	0.15066	0.16592	0.16890	0.17471	0.12400	0.13110	0.13196	0.12387	0.13029	0.12088
183 O. megalotis	0.18156	0.17851	0.19278	0.18914	0.15475	0.17714	0.17226	0.17421	0.13951	0.14606	0.14027	0.12303	0.12333	0.11447
184 O. petersoni	0.19149	0.18970	0.16600	0.18553	0.15873	0.17965	0.18459	0.18775	0.13992	0.13871	0.12422	0.11873	0.12333	0.12274
185 O. roboratus	0.18151	0.17961	0.18576	0.16804	0.13390	0.17111	0.18257	0.18410	0.14280	0.15036	0.14750	0.12794	0.12451	0.11012
187 O. sanctaecat.	0.18405	0.17640	0.19799	0.16504	0.13663	0.16824	0.16914	0.16899	0.13232	0.13912	0.14982	0.12855	0.12470	0.11810
189 O. scops	0.18146	0.18358	0.17346	0.17602	0.15859	0.18073	0.19042	0.17943	0.13625	0.12521	0.13411	0.13874	0.12376	0.10293
191 O. usta	0.17727	0.17906	0.17745	0.16705	0.14000	0.17755	0.18131	0.17943	0.13723	0.13013	0.13196	0.12922	0.12800	0.11340
194 Phodilus badius	0.18665	0.18358	0.17478	0.17627	0.13752	0.17855	0.18135	0.18390	0.13818	0.13818	0.13196	0.13038	0.12839	0.13114
206 Pulsatrix perspicill.	0.17989	0.18025	0.18294	0.18721	0.14367	0.16815	0.18459	0.18835	0.11919	0.18119	0.18112	0.18174	0.18733	0.13193
207 Strix aluco	0.17827	0.17845	0.18177	0.16705	0.13752	0.17324	0.18215	0.19181	0.18067	0.17876	0.17523	0.12303	0.17849	0.17460
209 S. butleri	0.17845	0.17515	0.18040	0.17627	0.15345	0.16994	0.18459	0.18446	0.11272	0.12167	0.12549	0.11873	0.12333	0.11447
211 S. nebulosa	0.17355	0.17378	0.18721	0.17828	0.15395	0.17706	0.18257	0.19473	0.13352	0.13654	0.12535	0.13241	0.13319	0.12274
213 S. ruffipes	0.17616	0.17845	0.19415	0.17742	0.13157	0.19086	0.18410	0.18274	0.12154	0.12065	0.12535	0.12795	0.12451	0.11012
216 S. urolensis	0.17367	0.17501	0.19304	0.17807	0.14569	0.16824	0.16914	0.16899	0.13755	0.13220	0.13925	0.11398	0.12470	0.11810
219 S. woodfordii	0.18405	0.18071	0.17346	0.18177	0.14065	0.18073	0.19042	0.18946	0.13723	0.13013	0.13411	0.12922	0.12800	0.11340
222 Surnia ulula	0.18146	0.17906	0.17745	0.18040	0.18782	0.15573	0.16910	0.16329	0.16329	0.13818	0.13196	0.13038	0.12839	0.13114
Tyto alba	0.18891	0.18822	0.18039	0.18040	0.18782	0.17755	0.18131	0.17943	0.17465	0.18119	0.18112	0.18174	0.18733	0.15733
T. (a.) pratincola	0.20761	0.20793	0.20051	0.20312	0.20754	0.20461	0.20300	0.20770	0.19566	0.19924	0.19768	0.19945	0.20157	0.18576
T. (a.) pratincola	0.21516	0.21699	0.20307	0.20985	0.20236	0.20618	0.21321	0.22102	0.20104	0.19939	0.19632	0.19171	0.19780	0.18759

	115	116	117	119	122	124	132	136	140	141	142	143	145	146
115 Bubo magellanicus	0.11502													
116 B. nipalensis	0.11178	–												
117 B. sumatrana	0.01735	0.01602	–											
119 B. virginianus	0.17017	0.10792	0.10462	–										
122 Glaucidium bolivi.	0.17252	0.18393	0.18114	0.16721	–									
124 G. brasilianum	0.17212	0.17080	0.16879	0.17158	0.07848	–								
132 G. b. stranecki	0.17276	0.17267	0.17052	0.17217	0.08369	0.00785	–							
136 G. tucumanum	0.16382	0.17656	0.17106	0.17158	0.08816	0.01782	0.01234	–						
140 G. californicum	0.18312	0.17885	0.17445	0.16122	0.07747	0.08717	0.09568	0.09289	–					
141 G. gnoma	0.17396	0.18282	0.18071	0.17500	0.10874	0.10241	0.10517	0.10603	0.06852	–				
142 G. griseiceps	0.16009	0.16163	0.16289	0.15982	0.08527	0.04557	0.04094	0.03840	0.08888	0.10981	–			
143 G. hardyi	0.16672	0.18061	0.17387	0.16200	0.08006	0.07704	0.07967	0.07608	0.09095	0.10064	0.08629	–		
145 G. jardinii	0.16798	0.16790	0.17561	0.16665	0.03672	0.08023	0.08199	0.07559	0.08683	0.11056	0.07977	0.06972	–	
146 G. nanum	0.18893	0.18184	0.15938	0.15807	0.07670	0.04224	0.03925	0.04031	0.08698	0.09296	0.04259	0.06808	0.07081	–
147 G. passerinum	0.17096	0.17824	0.17871	0.18368	0.14878	0.14916	0.14990	0.15036	0.15259	0.16083	0.14226	0.15420	0.13816	0.14770
152 G. perlatum	0.15352	0.16798	0.17368	0.16497	0.07434	0.03229	0.03138	0.02796	0.08965	0.10566	0.04369	0.06898	0.07060	0.04094
153 G. tephronotum	0.12251	0.16426	0.16144	0.15544	0.12434	0.11275	0.11552	0.11385	0.11561	0.12278	0.10954	0.11566	0.11826	0.10850
154 Bubo zeylonensis	0.15483	0.10201	0.09238	0.11591	0.18437	0.18583	0.18749	0.18922	0.18368	0.19680	0.18364	0.18761	0.18649	0.18369
155 Ninox boobook	0.15080	0.15253	0.15130	0.16155	0.17395	0.15993	0.16045	0.15897	0.16253	0.18004	0.14780	0.17390	0.16431	0.15925
156 N. scutulata	0.09007	0.15843	0.15730	0.15403	0.16046	0.16312	0.16380	0.16101	0.15387	0.17530	0.15442	0.16091	0.15531	0.16725
157 Nyctea scandiaca	0.14439	0.12601	0.12197	0.08124	0.16747	0.17201	0.17267	0.17211	0.18284	0.18552	0.16513	0.17278	0.16302	0.16541
160 Otus albogularis	0.13014	0.14932	0.14639	0.13802	0.17680	0.17467	0.17311	0.17351	0.18432	0.18001	0.16217	0.17678	0.18640	0.16637
161 O. asio	0.15025	0.13072	0.12598	0.12882	0.16974	0.16733	0.16325	0.16287	0.16753	0.17629	0.14296	0.17057	0.17243	0.15554
165 O. atricapillus	0.14096	0.15430	0.13860	0.13012	0.16660	0.16815	0.16179	0.18605	0.18006	0.18703	0.17623	0.18157	0.18171	0.17592
166 O. 'baikkamoena'	0.14946	0.14722	0.14562	0.14646	0.19056	0.18595	0.18455	0.17849	0.19460	0.19935	0.17658	0.19534	0.19269	0.17589
169 O. choliba	0.16460	0.15542	0.15449	0.14794	0.18024	0.17952	0.17554	0.18605	0.18895	0.18736	0.17066	0.18357	0.18171	0.17475
170 O. flammeolus	0.13340	0.14722	0.14247	0.15771	0.18195	0.18259	0.18629	0.18483	0.19355	0.20449	0.18772	0.19212	0.18728	0.18301
171 O. guatemalae	0.13770	0.12800	0.12678	0.13305	0.16748	0.17182	0.17009	0.17293	0.16416	0.17703	0.16328	0.17560	0.17743	0.16987
172 O. hoyi	0.15268	0.12373	0.12673	0.14041	0.17223	0.16666	0.16477	0.16432	0.16374	0.17348	0.16315	0.17033	0.17363	0.15922
174 O. lempiji	0.13046	0.14333	0.15546	0.15348	0.19618	0.19617	0.19808	0.19960	0.19669	0.19216	0.18600	0.19576	0.20101	0.18683
176 O. leucotis	0.15096	0.14765	0.12501	0.12726	0.16280	0.15627	0.15811	0.16074	0.16364	0.17418	0.15927	0.16859	0.16167	0.15541
179 O. longicornis	0.14080	0.14867	0.14051	0.14601	0.18337	0.18371	0.18449	0.18383	0.16368	0.18428	0.17271	0.18154	0.17368	0.17214
180 O. megalotis	0.15235	0.14498	0.14305	0.14152	0.18990	0.18217	0.18173	0.18109	0.18749	0.18584	0.16904	0.18398	0.18010	0.16976
182 O. petersoni	0.14072	0.14867	0.14247	0.15147	0.18510	0.17938	0.18009	0.18056	0.17488	0.18849	0.16913	0.17771	0.17656	0.17628
183 O. roboratus	0.14236	0.13914	0.13387	0.13877	0.17101	0.16498	0.15974	0.15811	0.17141	0.17081	0.14909	0.17013	0.17526	0.15966
184 O. sanctaecat.	0.14629	0.13962	0.13341	0.14138	0.17256	0.17259	0.16752	0.16818	0.16912	0.18212	0.15732	0.17972	0.18173	0.16492
185 O. scops	0.13387	0.14153	0.13764	0.14440	0.18515	0.18041	0.18120	0.17941	0.17414	0.18185	0.17740	0.18518	0.17427	0.17356
187 O. usta	0.17796	0.13324	0.12899	0.13099	0.17648	0.17059	0.16877	0.16735	0.17659	0.18138	0.16032	0.17266	0.18206	0.16579
189 Phodilus badius	0.13044	0.17611	0.17343	0.16886	0.17945	0.19262	0.19660	0.19552	0.17964	0.18382	0.17779	0.17891	0.17966	0.17996
191 Pulsatrix perspicill.	0.13235	0.10699	0.09912	0.12219	0.17769	0.17375	0.17335	0.17615	0.17072	0.17861	0.17061	0.17388	0.17627	0.16695
194 Strix aluco	0.11986	0.12581	0.12246	0.13127	0.17687	0.17591	0.17669	0.18050	0.17541	0.18845	0.16756	0.18769	0.17645	0.17216
206 S. butleri	0.13420	0.12848	0.13255	0.11524	0.16784	0.17429	0.17182	0.17798	0.15087	0.18496	0.16543	0.17497	0.17904	0.16946
207 S. nebulosa	0.13169	0.13689	0.13732	0.12842	0.18709	0.18923	0.19183	0.18957	0.17299	0.18938	0.17639	0.18310	0.18046	0.17755
209 S. ruffpes	0.13493	0.13083	0.12090	0.13142	0.16815	0.17035	0.16985	0.16722	0.17072	0.18280	0.16563	0.16350	0.16040	0.16700
211 S. uralensis	0.13387	0.13308	0.13329	0.13303	0.18411	0.17944	0.18019	0.18061	0.18242	0.18745	0.17284	0.18545	0.17697	0.17626
213 S. woodfordii	0.18962	0.11953	0.12069	0.13226	0.18448	0.18120	0.18606	0.18334	0.18286	0.18926	0.18523	0.18309	0.18068	0.17618
216 Surnia ulula	0.19838	0.18316	0.18106	0.18752	0.15990	0.15015	0.14735	0.14372	0.15053	0.15876	0.14302	0.13889	0.14419	0.14923
219 Tyto alba	0.19686	0.20933	0.21019	0.19117	0.20801	0.20909	0.20762	0.20678	0.20080	0.21285	0.19295	0.20804	0.20623	0.19172
222 T. (a.) pratincola	0.19903	0.20587	0.20750	0.19903	0.20523	0.21386	0.21356	0.21278	0.20080	0.22087	0.20393	0.20804	0.20079	0.19898

	147	152	153	154	155	156	157	160	161	165	166	169	170	171
147 *Glaucidium pass.*	–													
152 *G. peruanum*	0.14786	–												
153 *G. tephronotum*	0.10878	0.11095	–											
154 *Bubo zeylonensis*	0.18068	0.18663	0.17539	–										
155 *Ninox boobook*	0.17549	0.19963	0.15277	0.16738	–									
156 *N. scutulata*	0.18538	0.16308	0.15000	0.16952	0.08639	–								
157 *Nyctea scandiaca*	0.19285	0.16194	0.16564	0.13109	0.17328	0.16429	–							
160 *Otus albogularis*	0.18007	0.17556	0.16691	0.15008	0.15727	0.14727	0.14677	–						
161 *O. asio*	0.19418	0.17781	0.16022	0.13672	0.15082	0.15143	0.13189	0.10628	–					
165 *O. atricapillus*	0.18127	0.16498	0.15979	0.15819	0.17337	0.16797	0.16007	0.10025	0.08070	–				
166 *O. 'bakkamoena'*	0.19901	0.17859	0.16006	0.15894	0.15102	0.15015	0.15872	0.14512	0.15211	0.16160	–			
169 *O. choliba*	0.21247	0.18696	0.18218	0.16226	0.17256	0.15866	0.14092	0.09807	0.11078	0.11179	0.15820	–		
170 *O. flammeolus*	0.18965	0.18270	0.18808	0.14704	0.16473	0.16124	0.15535	0.13712	0.14786	0.14453	0.15479	0.15858	–	
171 *O. guatemalae*	0.17614	0.18745	0.16833	0.15031	0.16029	0.15866	0.16017	0.13489	0.13830	0.13129	0.14536	0.12006	0.13957	–
172 *O. hoyi*	0.17614	0.16746	0.15741	0.14215	0.15236	0.15112	0.14566	0.11105	0.08684	0.10141	0.14536	0.11833	0.14332	0.08589
174 *O. lempiji*	0.19018	0.19621	0.18138	0.16620	0.16175	0.16205	0.16296	0.14616	0.15316	0.16752	0.06099	0.16564	0.15942	0.15924
176 *O. leucotis*	0.17506	0.15597	0.15396	0.14196	0.15199	0.15252	0.13489	0.14668	0.13830	0.13129	0.14744	0.14855	0.14282	0.12624
179 *O. longicornis*	0.18071	0.18016	0.15620	0.16029	0.16064	0.14916	0.16017	0.14989	0.14315	0.16038	0.11497	0.15600	0.16579	0.13906
180 *O. megalotis*	0.18354	0.18063	0.16893	0.15593	0.15433	0.15995	0.15297	0.13827	0.14197	0.16814	0.09094	0.15865	0.16309	0.15193
182 *O. petersoni*	0.19155	0.17638	0.17055	0.15764	0.16294	0.15760	0.15583	0.12458	0.10930	0.10801	0.15143	0.11553	0.14647	0.10929
183 *O. roboratus*	0.19096	0.16787	0.15287	0.14737	0.15799	0.15178	0.14899	0.10538	0.08597	0.06500	0.14254	0.11222	0.15142	0.08104
184 *O. sanctaecat.*	0.19503	0.17310	0.16018	0.14689	0.15623	0.15034	0.15752	0.10150	0.08303	0.08004	0.16049	0.11208	0.14511	0.08320
185 *O. scops*	0.18299	0.17399	0.17144	0.16377	0.15859	0.15594	0.15811	0.14760	0.15004	0.16546	0.10311	0.15667	0.17579	0.13706
187 *O. usta*	0.19475	0.17009	0.16608	0.13774	0.15587	0.14760	0.14110	0.09683	0.07668	0.04360	0.14743	0.11378	0.14314	0.08534
189 *Phodilus badius*	0.19143	0.17490	0.17715	0.19770	0.18407	0.18651	0.17758	0.18945	0.16479	0.19166	0.18121	0.19893	0.20143	0.17066
191 *Pulsatrix perspicill.*	0.19076	0.18667	0.16879	0.16170	0.15765	0.15515	0.12902	0.12490	0.12789	0.12097	0.14451	0.13204	0.12960	0.12469
194 *Strix aluco*	0.19184	0.18070	0.16626	0.13584	0.16218	0.15488	0.13393	0.14517	0.14303	0.16013	0.14687	0.15274	0.15324	0.14318
206 *S. butleri*	0.18802	0.17332	0.16152	0.13735	0.17762	0.16142	0.12921	0.13161	0.12014	0.12503	0.13851	0.14039	0.16347	0.12263
207 *S. nebulosa*	0.19120	0.18416	0.16533	0.15160	0.16537	0.16143	0.14577	0.15342	0.14825	0.16208	0.15784	0.15677	0.16060	0.14231
209 *S. rufipes*	0.18883	0.17120	0.15702	0.12936	0.14821	0.13799	0.12867	0.13811	0.13026	0.14439	0.14447	0.13978	0.14354	0.12909
211 *S. uralensis*	0.19740	0.17823	0.16806	0.14309	0.16472	0.16268	0.14078	0.13886	0.14371	0.15411	0.16204	0.15984	0.15001	0.15074
213 *S. woodfordii*	0.20087	0.18151	0.16795	0.13780	0.16295	0.14937	0.14308	0.13974	0.13886	0.13417	0.14845	0.14922	0.14158	0.13891
216 *Surnia ulula*	0.15692	0.14325	0.13434	0.18469	0.17041	0.16429	0.18255	0.18221	0.13801	0.18479	0.17934	0.19760	0.20032	0.18834
219 *Tyto alba*	0.21426	0.20058	0.20548	0.21831	0.20918	0.21189	0.20016	0.19709	0.19569	0.19755	0.21203	0.21008	0.21311	0.20314
222 *T. (a.) pratincola*	0.22072	0.20957	0.20823	0.21323	0.20393	0.20846	0.19460	0.21590	0.18913	0.20039	0.21138	0.21174	0.21706	0.20848

Table 1. Pairwise nucleotide substitutions between owl taxa. Given are p-distances (in %) which correlate with divergence time (2% roughly equals one million years: Shields & Wilson 1987).

	172	174	176	179	180	182	183	184	185	187	189	191	194	206
172 Otus hoyi	-													
174 O. lempiji	0.14871	-												
176 O. leucotis	0.1241	0.15297	-											
179 O. longicorni	0.14169	0.11496	0.14394	-										
180 O. megalotis	0.13504	0.09299	0.13704	0.10679	-									
182 O. petersoni	0.09289	0.16341	0.14220	0.15459	0.15501	-								
183 O. roboratus	0.08025	0.15799	0.12858	0.14129	0.15022	0.08903	-							
184 O. sanctaecat.	0.08392	0.16760	0.12489	0.15296	0.16011	0.10351	0.07614	-						
185 O. scops	0.14031	0.11192	0.14293	0.07636	0.10759	0.15411	0.05704	0.15538	-					
187 O. usta	0.07771	0.15561	0.13141	0.14506	0.14708	0.09201		0.07459	0.14323	-				
189 Phodilus badius	0.17968	0.18044	0.17174	0.16863	0.17894	0.19049	0.17413	0.17422	0.17401	0.17530	-			
191 Pulsatrix perspicill.	0.11929	0.15385	0.12399	0.13703	0.14629	0.13116	0.12445	0.12804	0.13719	0.11595	0.17333	-		
194 Strix aluco	0.14982	0.14350	0.13207	0.14741	0.13748	0.15672	0.13972	0.15042	0.14747	0.13716	0.18847	0.12096	-	
206 S. butleri	0.12649	0.14849	0.12991	0.14872	0.15565	0.16434	0.12659	0.13041	0.16234	0.13233	0.18072	0.13440	0.08966	-
207 S. nebulosa	0.14817	0.15509	0.13632	0.15301	0.15581	0.14560	0.15053	0.14362	0.14905	0.13354	0.19066	0.12988	0.09139	0.08655
209 S. ruffpes	0.13179	0.15235	0.12222	0.14698	0.13779	0.14773	0.12433	0.13532	0.14511	0.12343	0.17778	0.11324	0.11627	0.10724
211 S. urolensis	0.13880	0.15940	0.13357	0.15097	0.15091	0.14973	0.13661	0.14442	0.15793	0.12992	0.18737	0.13249	0.08152	0.10368
213 S. woodfordii	0.13600	0.15901	0.13987	0.14816	0.15025		0.13476	0.14391	0.15481	0.13915	0.19016	0.12382	0.09167	0.08488
216 Surnia ulula	0.17314	0.19243	0.17122	0.19505	0.18489	0.17779	0.17389	0.18556	0.18961	0.17635	0.21015	0.18740	0.18265	0.17145
219 Tyto alba	0.19301	0.21986	0.20629	0.19511	0.21043	0.21107	0.19120	0.20284	0.20726	0.19837	0.17490	0.20549	0.23020	0.22080
222 T. (a.) pratincola	0.19943	0.21808	0.20319	0.19932	0.21712	0.21006	0.19230	0.20330	0.20846	0.21069	0.18725	0.19888	0.22749	0.22157

	207	209	211	213	216	219	222
207 S. nebulosa	-						
209 S. ruffpes	0.11222	-					
211 S. urolensis	0.09247	0.11715	-				
213 S. woodfordii	0.10795	0.11074	0.10480	-			
216 Surnia ulula	0.17887	0.16384	0.18700	0.18141	-		
219 Tyto alba	0.20379	0.20192	0.21127	0.21338	0.22988	-	
222 T. (a.) pratincola	0.20451	0.20569	0.20803	0.20525	0.22212	0.08080	-

LITERATURE

Amadon, D. & Bull, J. 1988. Hawks and owls of the world. *Proc. Western Found. Vertebr. Zool.* 3: 297-357.

Avise, J. C. 1994. *Molecular markers, natural history and evolution.* Chapman & Hall, New York.

Avise, J. C., Nelson, W. S. & Sibley, C. G. 1994. DNA sequences support for a close phylogenetic relationship between some storks and New World vultures. *Proc. Natn. Acad. Sci.* 91: 5173-5177.

Birt, T. P., Birt-Friesen, V. L., Green, J. M., Montevecchi, W. A. & Davidson, W. S. 1992. Cytochrome b sequence variation among parrots. *Hereditas* 117: 67-72.

Blechschmidt, K., Peter, H. U., de Korte, J., Wink, M., Seibold, I. & Helbig, A. 1993. Untersuchungen zur molekularen Systematik von Raubmöwen (Stercorariidae). *Zool. Jahrb. Syst.* 120: 379-387.

Bock, W. J. & McEvey, A. 1969. The radius and relationships of owls. *Wilson Bull.* 81: 55-68

Burton, J. A. 1992. *Owls of the world: their evolution, structure and ecology.* Peter Lowe, London.

Cooper, A., Mourer-Chauvire, C., Chambers, G. K., von Haeseler, A., Wilson, A. C. & Pääbo, S. 1992. Independent origins of New Zealand moas and kiwis. *Proc. Natn. Acad. Sci.* 89: 8741-8744.

Cracraft, J. 1981. Towards a phylogenetic classification of recent birds of the world (class Aves). *Auk* 98: 681-714.

Eck, S. & Busse, H. 1973. *Eulen.* Neue Brehm-Bucherei, Wittenberg-Lutherstadt.

Edwards, S. V., Arctander, P. & Wilson, A. C. 1991. Mitochondrial resolution of a deep branch in the genealogical tree for perching birds. *Proc. Royal Soc. London* B 243: 99-107.

Feduccia, A. 1995. Explosive evolution in tertiary birds and mammals. *Science* 267: 637-638.

Feduccia, A. 1996. *The origins and evolution of birds.* Yale Univ. Press, New Haven.

Felsenstein, J. 1985. Confidence estimates on phylogenies: an approach using the bootstrap. *Evolution* 39: 783-791.

Felsenstein, J. 1993. PHYLIP, version 3.5c, Department of Genetics, Univ. Washington, Seattle.

Friesen, V. L., Montevecchi, W. A. & Davidson, W. S. 1993. Cytochrome b nucleotide sequence variation among the Atlantic Alcidae. *Hereditas* 119: 245-252.

Fürbringer, M. 1888. *Untersuchungen zur Morphologie und Systematik der Vögel.* Amsterdam.

Gadow, H. 1892. On the classification of birds. *Proc. Zool. Soc. London:* 229-256.

Gaucher, P., Paillat, P., Chappuis, C., Saint Jalme, M., Lotfikhah, F. & Wink, M. 1996. Taxonomy of the houbara bustard, *Chlamydotis undulata* subspecies considered on the basis of sexual display and genetic divergence. *Ibis* 138: 273-282.

Griffiths, C. S. 1997. Correlation of functional domains and rates of nucleotide substitution in cytochrome b. *Mol. Phylogen. Evol.* 7: 352-365.

Hedges, S. B. & Sibley, C. G. 1994. Molecules vs. morphology in avian evolution: the case of the "pelecaniform" birds. *Proc. Natn. Acad. Sci.* 91: 9861-9865.

Heidrich, P. 1998. Untersuchungen zur molekularen Phylogenie ausgewählter Vogelgruppen anhand von DNA-Sequenzen des mitochondriellen Cytochrom b-Gens. Ph.D. thesis, Universität Heidelberg.

Heidrich, P. & Wink, M. 1994. Tawny owl (*Strix aluco*) and Hume's tawny owl (*Strix butleri*) are distinct species: evidence from nucleotide sequences of the cytochrome b gene. *Z. Naturforsch.* 49c: 230-234.

Heidrich, P., König, C. & Wink, M. 1995a. Molecular phylogeny of the South American screech owls of the *Otus atricapillus* complex (Aves, Strigidae) inferred from nucleotide sequences of the mitochondrial cytochrome b gene. *Z. Naturforsch.* 50c: 294-302.

Heidrich, P., König, C. & Wink, M. 1995b. Bioakustik, Taxonomie und molekulare Systematik amerikanischer Sperlingskäuze (Strigidae: *Glaucidium* spp.). *Stuttgarter Beitr. Naturk.* Ser. A, no. 534.

Heidrich, P., Ristow, D. & Wink, M. 1996. Molekulare Differenzierung von Gelb- und Schwarzschnabelsturmtauchern (*Calonectris diomedea, Puffinus puffinus, P. yelkouan*) und Großmöwen des Silbermöwenkomplexes (*Larus argentatus, L. fuscus, L. cachinnans*). *J. Orn.* 137: 281-294.

Heidrich, P., Amengual, J. & Wink, M. 1998. Phylogenetic relationships in Mediterranean and North Atlantic *Puffinus* shearwaters (Aves: Procellariidae) based on nucleotide sequences of mtDNA. *Biochem. Syst. and Ecol.* 26: 145-170.

Heidrich, P. & Wink, M. 1998. Phylogenetic relationships in holarctic owls (Order Strigiformes): evidence from nucleotide sequences of the mitochondrial cytochrome b gene. In R. D. Chancellor, F. Blanco & B.-U. Meyburg, eds. *Holarctic birds of prey*. Adenex & WWGBP.

Hekstra, G. P. 1982. Description of twenty-four new subspecies of American *Otus* (Aves, Strigidae). *Bull. Zool. Mus. Amsterdam* 9: 49-63.

Helbig, A. J., Seibold, I., Martens, J. & Wink, M. 1995. Genetic differentiation and phylogenetic relationships of Bonelli's Warbler *Phylloscopus bonellii* and Green Warbler *P. nitidus*. *J. Avian Biol.* 26: 139-153.

Helbig, A. J., Martens, J., Henning, F., Schottler, B., Seibold, I. & Wink, M. 1996. Phylogeny and species limits in the Palaearctic Chiffchaff (*Phylloscopus collybita*) complex: mitochondrial genetic differentiation and bioacoustic evidence. *Ibis* 138: 650-666.

Helm-Bychowski, K. & Cracraft, J. 1993. Recovering a phylogenetic signal from DNA sequences: relationships within the corvine assemblage (Class Aves) as inferred from complete sequence of the mitochondrial DNA cytochrome-b-Gene. *Molec. Biol. and Evol.* 10: 1196-1214.

Hillis, D. M. & Bull, J. J. 1993. An empirical test of bootstrapping as a method for assessing confidence in phylogenetic analysis. *Syst. Biol.* 42: 182-192.

Hillis, D. M. & Moritz, C. 1990. *Molecular systematics*. Sinauer Publishers, Sunderland.

Hoelzel, A. R. 1992. *Molecular genetic analysis of populations*. IRL-Press, Oxford.

Hume, R. 1991. *Owls of the world*. Dragons World, Limpfield.

Kocher, T. D., Thomas, W. K., Meyer, A., Edwards, S. V., Pääbo, S., Villablanca, F. X. & Wilson, A. C. 1989. Dynamics of mitochondrial DNA evolution in animals: amplification and sequencing with conserved primers. *Proc. Natn. Acad. Sci.* 86: 6196-6200.

König, C. 1982. Zur systematischen Stellung der Neuweltgeier (Cathartidae). *J. Orn.* 123: 209-214.

König, C. 1991a. Taxonomische und ökologische Untersuchungen an Kreischeulen (*Otus* spp.) des südlichen Südamerika. *J. Orn.* 132: 209-214.

König, C. 1991b. Zur Taxonomie und Ökologie der Sperlingskäuze (*Glaucidium* spp.) des Andenraumes. *Ökol. Vögel* 13: 15-76.

König, C. 1994a. Lautäußerungen als interspezifische Isolationsmechanismen bei Eulen der Gattung *Otus* (Aves: Strigidae) aus dem südlichen Südamerika. *Beitr. Naturkde.* Ser. A.

König, C. 1994b. Biological patterns in owl taxonomy, with emphasis on bioacoustical studies on neotropical pygmy (*Glaucidium*) and screech owls (*Otus*). Pp.1-19 in B.-U. Meyburg & R. D. Chancellor, eds. *Raptor conservation today*. Pica Press, Sussex, U.K.

König, C., Heidrich, P. & Wink, M. 1996. Zur Taxonomie der Uhus (Strigidae: *Bubo* spp.) im südlichen Südamerika. *Stuttgarter Beitr. Naturk.* Ser. A, no. 540.

König, C. & Wink, M. 1995. Eine neue Unterart des Brasilsperlingskauzes aus Zentralargentinien: *Glaucidium brasilianum stranecki* n. ssp. *J. Orn.* 136: 461-465.

Kumar, S., Tamura, K. & Nei, M. 1993. MEGA - Molecular Evolutionary Genetics Analysis. Version 1.0. Pennsylvania State University.

Leisler, B., Heidrich, P., Schulze-Hagen, K. & Wink, M. 1997. Taxonomy and phylogeny of reed warblers (genus *Acrocephalus*) based on mtDNA sequences and morphology. *J. Orn.* 138: 469-496.

Mayr, E. & Amadon, D. 1951. A classification of recent birds. *Amer. Mus. Novit.* 1496.

Mikkola, H. 1983. *Owls of Europe*. Poyser, Calton, U.K.

Mindell, D. P. 1997. *Avian molecular evolution and systematics*. Academic Press, San Diego.

Mindell, D. P., Sorenson, M. D., Huddleston, C. J., Miranda, H., Knight, A., Sawchuk, S. J. & Yuri, T. 1997. Phylogenetic relationships among and within select avian orders based on mitochondrial DNA. Pp.213-247 in D. P. Mindell, ed. *Avian molecular evolution and systematics*. Academic Press, San Diego.

Miranda, H. C., Kennedy, R. S. & Mindell, D. P. 1997. Phylogenetic placement of *Mimizuku gurneyi* (Aves: Strigidae) inferred from mitochondrial DNA. *Auk* 114: 315-323.

Moore, W. S. & DeFilippis, V. R. 1997. The window of taxonomic resolution for phylogenies based on mitochondrial cytochrome b. Pp.83-119 in D. P. Mindell, ed. *Avian molecular evolution and systematics*. Academic Press, San Diego.

Nitsch, C. L. 1840. *System der Pterylographie.* E. Anton, Halle.

Quinn, T.W. 1997. Molecular evolution of the mitochondrial genome. Pp.3-28 in D. P. Mindell, ed. *Avian molecular evolution and systematics.* Academic Press, San Diego.

Rasmussen, P. C. & Collar, N. J. 1998. Identification, distribution and status of the Forest Owlet *Heteroglaux* (*Athene*) *blewitti. Forktail* 14: 41-49.

Richman, A. D. & Price, T. 1992. Evolution of ecological differences in the Old World leaf warblers. *Nature* 355: 817-821.

Sambrook, J., Fritsch, E. F. & Maniatis, T. 1989. *Molecular cloning: a laboratory manual.* Second edition. CSHL, Cold Spring Harbour, New York.

Seibold, I., Helbig, A. J. & Wink, M. 1993. Molecular systematics of falcons (family Falconidae). *Naturwissenschaften* 80: 87-90.

Seibold, I., Helbig, A., Meyburg, B.-U., Negro, J. J. & Wink, M. in press. Genetic differentiation and molecular phylogeny of European *Aquila* eagles (Aves: Falconiformes) according to cytochrome b nucleotide sequences. In B.-U. Meyburg and R. D. Chancellor, eds. *Eagle studies.*

Shields, G. F. & Wilson, A. C. 1987. Calibration of mitochondrial DNA evolution in geese. *J. Molec. Evol.* 24: 212-217.

Sibley, C. G. 1994. On the phylogeny and classification of living birds. *J. Avian Biol.* 25: 87-92.

Sibley, C. G. & Ahlquist, J. E. 1990. *Phylogeny and classification of birds.* Yale Univ. Press, New Haven.

Sibley, C. G. & Monroe, B. L. 1990. *Distribution and taxonomy of birds of the world.* Yale University Press, New Haven.

Swatschek, I., Ristow, D., Scharlau, W., Wink, C. & Wink, M. 1993. Populationsgenetik und Vaterschaftsanalyse beim Eleonorenfalken (*Falco eleonorae*). *J. Orn.* 134: 137-143.

Swatschek, I., Ristow, D. & Wink, M. 1994. Mate fidelity and parentage in Cory's shearwater (*Calonectris diomedea*) Field studies and DNA-Fingerprinting. *Molec. Ecol.* 3: 259-262.

Swofford, D. L. 1993. PAUP: phylogenetic analysis using parsimony. Version 3.1.1. Illinois.

Taberlet, P., Meyer, A. & Bouvet, J. 1992. Unusual mitochondrial polymorphism in two local populations of blue tit *Parus caeruleus. Molec. Ecol.* 1: 27-36.

Wink, M. 1994a. PCR in der Evolutionsforschung. Pp.166-184 in M. Wink & H. Wehrle, eds. *PCR im medizinischen und biologischen Labor.* GIT-Verlag, Darmstadt.

Wink, M. 1994b. Molekulare Methoden in der Greifvogelforschung. *Greifvögel & Falknerei* 1993: 17-28.

Wink, M. 1998. Application of DNA-markers to study the ecology and evolution of raptors. In R. D. Chancellor, F. Blanco & B.-U. Meyburg, eds. *Holarctic birds of prey.* Adenex & WWGBP.

Wink, M. in press. Phylogeny of Old and New World vultures (Aves: Accipitridae and Cathartidae) inferred from nucleotide sequences of the mitochondrial cytochrome b gene. *Z. Naturforsch.*

Wink, M., Heidrich, P., Kahl, U., Witt, H.-H. & Ristow, D. 1993a. Inter- and intraspecific variation of the nucleotide sequence for cytochrome b in Cory's Shearwater (*Calonectris diomedea*), Manx Shearwater (*Puffinus puffinus*) and Fulmar (*Fulmarus glacialis*). *Z. Naturforsch.* 48c: 504-508.

Wink, M., Heidrich, P., & Ristow, D. 1993b. Genetic evidence for speciation of the Manx Shearwater (*Puffinus puffinus*) and the Mediterranean Shearwater (*P. yelkouan*). *Vogelwelt* 114: 226-232.

Wink, M., Heidrich, P. & Fentzloff, C. 1996. A mtDNA phylogeny of sea eagles (genus *Haliaeetus*) based on nucleotide sequences of the cytochrome b gene. *Biochem. Syst. and Ecol.* 24: 783-791.

Wink, M. & Seibold, I. 1996. Molecular phylogeny of Mediterranean raptors (families Accipitridae and Falconidae). Pp.335-344 in J. Muntaner & J. Mayol, eds. *Biology and conservation of Mediterranean raptors.* Monografia 4, SEO/BirdLife, Madrid.

Wink, M., Seibold, I., Lotfikhah, F. & Bednarek, W. 1998. Molecular systematics of holarctic raptors (Order Falconiformes). In R. D. Chancellor, F. Blanco & B.-U. Meyburg, eds. *Holarctic birds of prey.* Adenex & WWGBP.

Wittmann, U., Heidrich, P., Wink, M. & Gwinner, E. 1995. Speciation in the stonechat (*Saxicola torquata*) inferred from nucleotide sequences of the cytochrome b gene. *J. Zool. Syst. Evol. Research* 33: 116-122.

HOW TO STUDY OWLS

Although some owls are partly diurnal, most are rather difficult to find in daytime. If we want to study the life of owls, we must be prepared to be active at dusk or at night when our ears will be more important than our eyes. Owls like clear, moonlit nights without wind. The temperature is not so important. Windy or stormy nights are useless for owl studies. Wind affects the birds' soft, often fluffy plumage and the the noise of the wind rushing in the trees makes hearing more difficult, even for owls. Some owls are sensitive to falling atmospheric pressure. Unpaired Tengmalm's Owls are virtually silent if the atmospheric pressure falls during a calm, even clear night, giving way to rain next morning. Conversely, owls may call during nights with a slight drizzle if an increase in atmospheric pressure heralds a clear morning.

Owls are most vocally active at the beginning of the reproductive period, which in temperate zones is in springtime and in tropical areas falls towards the end of the dry season. Owl studies are therefore best timed to coincide with these periods. Males sing on different perches in their territory, sometimes close to the future nesting site, sometimes quite far away from it. The singing male must be followed from perch to perch in order to fix the boundaries of the territory. The presence of a female may often be deduced from the behaviour of the male. If one is nearby (or if the male meets an already paired couple), he will advertise nest sites to the potential mate. Numerous droppings, remains of prey and pellets under certain perches indicate the vicinity of an occupied nesting site. The male often roosts nearby in a sheltered place. During the daytime nothing much happens, but at dusk activity increases: some vocalisations may be heard, and often the female leaves the nest for a short while, or the male brings food to the nest. However, little will be heard from a distance; often vocalisations are so low that they may be perceived only at very close range.

Although many owls are confiding, they should not be disturbed. Observers need to move slowly or sit still out of sight, watching with good binoculars or recording calls on tape. All observations should be routinely recorded for later evaluation, noting date, time and weather conditions. The territories and nest sites should be mapped.

Several species of owl will breed in nestboxes, which makes it easier to inspect the nest and ring the young and their mother. Many studies of birds nesting in artificial nestboxes have been made of some northern species such as Tengmalm's, Pygmy, Ural and Tawny Owls, particularly in Scandinavia.

In the tropics, above all in rain- or cloudforests, owl studies are much more difficult than in temperate regions, although there are more species living in the same habitat. Our knowledge of the voices of tropical owls is incomplete. Walking around a tropical forest at night is not easy and the finding of nests is difficult. There are so many confusing night voices coming from different animals such as nightjars, frogs, crickets, cicadas and some mammals. Recordings should be thoroughly studied before making an expedition. In the forest the playback of recordings (or whistled imitations) may attract some owls. As already mentioned, some species become quite silent after courtship, but in general males react to the playback of their song, sometimes singing aggressively but often by flying unobtrusively to perch near the source of the 'intrusion'.

Dietary studies are very important. Collecting pellets below daytime-roosts or at nests will provide vital clues. Watching the nest may also reveal the prey species.

CONSERVATION

The greatest threat to owls, as to most other living creatures, is the increasing destruction of their natural habitats. The devastation of some tropical rainforests by logging is well documented, but illegal deforestation occurs in the developed world as well. The use of pesticides also endangers owls in common with all wildlife. In some regions owls are still persecuted as birds of ill omen. Trade in many species is prohibited under the Washington Convention (CITES); nevertheless a black market persists.

Some practical measures can be undertaken locally to aid owl conservation. The loss of nesting sites by tree felling may be partly compensated by constructing nestboxes and mounting them in trees. Nestboxes are available for many owl species, but in the case of Tawny Owls artificial nest sites are really not necessary. Tawny Owls will nest practically anywhere, even on the ground. Tengmalm's Owl on the other hand really does need help. Boxes should be hung in trees near forest clearings about 4-5m above ground (sometimes even higher). For Little Owls, nesting tubes are available which resemble hollow branches; the tube has to be mounted on a vertical tree branch in a suitable orchard. Barn Owls may be helped by mounting wooden boxes with an aperture of 15 x 20cm inside a barn or other large building such as a church tower. As owls do not build nests, the bottom of all nestboxes should be covered with a layer of vegetable mould or peat dust. Putting pellets in the nest box may sometimes make a Barn Owl feel at home.

Smaller tree-hole nesting owls suffer from mammalian predators such as martens *Martes* or racoons *Procyon*. Nests in abandoned woodpecker holes may be protected against predation by fixing cuffs of sheet iron around the tree trunk, about 1m below and 1m above the aperture, so that no mammal can maintain its grip. This technique has worked well for Tengmalm's Owls in south-west Germany. Nestboxes on tree trunks may be protected in the same way, but martens have learned to jump from above onto the roof of the box. To avoid this the box should be protected by a downhanging sheet, fixed to the trunk above the box, so that the marauder will slip off and fall down.

Some locally extinct species have been successfully reintroduced, given the right ecological circumstances. The Eurasian Eagle Owl has been reintroduced successfully in Central Europe. Eurasian Pygmy Owls have been reestablished in the Black Forest, where the species became extinct after the Second World War owing to deforestation and an increasing Tawny Owl population. After reafforestation, which helped reverse numbers of Tawny Owls, captive-bred Pygmy Owls were released in the late 1960s. A regular census has shown an increasing population (now around 200 pairs) throughout the Black Forest and birds are now emigrating to adjacent forested areas. However, a new threat to this population, and indeed to the health of the Black Forest as a whole, has arisen from the harmful effects of acid rain.

Hard winters with long-lasting snow cover are harmful to many owls, above all Barn and Long-eared Owls. Because they often congregate in daytime roosts in winter, Long-eared Owls can be helped by providing laboratory mice and one-day-old chicks from chicken farms. An open plastic vat is placed within sight of the roost, the bottom covered with straw or dry leaves. Before dusk several live laboratory (white) mice, together with some dead one-day-old chicks, are put in the vat. The mice crawling about in the straw produce a rustling noise which attracts owls as they disperse at dusk. When the owls' confidence has been won after catching a few mice, they also will take the dead chicks. After this, live mice are no longer necessary. In this way several populations of Long-eared Owl have been helped to survive severe winters. Similar methods may be used to feed Barn Owls at places where they have their daytime roosts.

Collar *et al.* (1994) listed 26 species of owls as globally threatened (Table 2) and a further 15 species as near-threatened (Table 3). In the light of taxonomic revisions since its publication, the description of several new species, and continuing habitat destruction in some parts of the world, it is likely that the number of threatened species is now even higher.

Madagascar Red Owl	*Tyto soumagnei* (EN)
New Britain Masked Owl	*Tyto aurantia* (VU)
Taliabu Masked Owl	*Tyto nigrobrunnea* (VU)
Manus Masked Owl	*Tyto manusi* (VU)
Itombwe Owl	*Tyto prigoginei* (VU)
White-fronted Scops Owl	*Otus sagittatus* (VU)
Sokoke Scops Owl	*Otus ireneae* (VU)
Javan Scops Owl	*Otus angelinae* (VU)
Mindanao Scops Owl	*Otus mirus* (VU)
Luzon Scops Owl	*Otus longicornis* (VU)
Mindoro Scops Owl	*Otus mindorensis* (VU)
Grand Comoro Scops Owl	*Otus pauliani* (CR)
Anjouan Scops Owl	*Otus capnodes* (CR)
Seychelles Scops Owl	*Otus insularis* (CR)
Palawan Scops Owl	*Otus fuliginosus* (VU)
Giant Scops Owl	*Mimizuku gurneyi* (EN)
Usambara Eagle Owl	*Bubo (poensis) vosseleri* (VU)
Philippine Eagle Owl	*Bubo philippensis* (EN)
Blakiston's Fish Owl	*Bubo blakistoni* (EN)
Rufous Fishing Owl	*Scotopelia ussheri* (EN)
Sichuan Wood Owl	*Strix davidi* (VU)
Albertine Owlet	*Glaucidium albertinum* (VU)
Forest Owlet	*Athene blewitti* (CR)
Powerful Owl	*Ninox strenua* (VU)
Sumba Boobook	*Ninox rudolfi* (VU)
Fearful Owl	*Nesasio solomonensis* (VU)

Table 2. List of Globally Threatened species of owls (Collar *et al.* 1994). Key: CR = Critical; EN = Endangered; VU = Vulnerable.

Lesser Sooty Owl	*Tyto multipunctata*
São Tomé Scops Owl	*Otus hartlaubi*
Andaman Scops Owl	*Otus balli*
Pemba Scops Owl	*Otus pembaensis*
Wallace's Scops Owl	*Otus silvicola*
Bearded Screech Owl	*Otus barbarus*
Colombian Screech Owl	*Otus colombianus*
Forest Eagle Owl	*Bubo nipalensis*
Tawny Fish Owl	*Bubo flavipes*
Spotted Owl	*Strix occidentalis*
Chestnut-backed Owlet	*Glaucidium castanonotum*
Long-whiskered Owlet	*Xenoglaux loweryi*
Unspotted Saw-whet Owl	*Aegolius ridgwayi*
Buff-fronted Owl	*Aegolius harrisii*
Andaman Hawk Owl	*Ninox affinis*

Table 3. List of Near-threatened species of owls (Collar *et al.* 1994).

PLATES
1-64

PLATE 1: BARN OWL

1   **Barn Owl** *Tyto alba*   **Text and map page 193**

Rather open habitats, including desert, grassland, moors, coastal plains, parkland, and otherwise widespread in lightly wooded and cultivated habitats, towns and cities. S Canada southward to tip of S America, Europe, NE Africa and sub-Saharan Africa (except rain-forest regions and Somalia), India and SE Asia, Indonesia, Australia; successfully introduced on several islands, including Hawaii, New Zealand and Seychelles. Eyes brownish-black; bill cream-white to whitish-pink.

1a   **Adult** (*ernesti*: Mediterranean region, merging with nominate *alba* in Spain) Very pale, with pure white, often unspotted underparts; above, pale yellowish-brown with indistinct grey veil and nearly white secondaries and tail feathers.

1b   **Adult** (nominate *alba*: British Isles and W Europe) Crown and upperparts yellowish-brown to orange-buff, partly covered by pale ashy-grey veil with scattered white and black spots; tail similar, with darker bars and often some grey pencil marks at tip; below, whitish or pure white with some dark spots.

1c   **Adult** (nominate *alba*) Individual from England (where sometimes separated as subspecies *hostilis*), in flight. Note that in genus *Tyto* none of the primaries is emarginated.

1d   **Adult** (*guttata*: C and E Europe) Dark morph, in flight.

1e   **Adult** (*guttata*) Dark morph, '*obscura*' type. Densely grey pencil marking above, with white and black spots on feather tips; orange-buff below with large and numerous dark and light spots.

1f   **Adult** (*guttata*) Buff-yellow morph, '*adspersa*' type. Light buff below with small spots.

1g   **Adult** (*guttata*) Typical morph. Light buff below with large spots.

1h   **Mesoptile** (nominate *alba*) Downy white chick and older young with fluffy, long downy plumage, but facial disc, rim and wing similar to adult.

1i   **Adult** (*hypermetra*: Madagascar and Comoro Islands) Similar to *guttata*, with stronger feet and longer tarsi. This subspecies is similar in plumage to the African race *affinis*, but somewhat larger in size.

1j   **Adult** (*stertens*: Pakistan, India and Sri Lanka east to Assam and Burma) Somewhat larger than nominate *alba*, with much greyer veil above, but similar in plumage to *javanica* (Burma to SW China, Thailand, Cambodia, Laos, S Vietnam, and Malay Peninsula to Borneo, Sumatra and Java).

1k   **Adult** (*thomensis*: São Tomé in Gulf of Guinea) Dark grey above on rufous-brown ground colour; yellow-ochre underparts; face very dark. Feet strong and powerful, with long tarsi.

1a   1b   1c   1d   1e   1f   1g   1h   1i   1j   1k

1995 Weick

1   Barn Owl *Tyto alba* **(cont.)**   **Text and map page 193**

1l   **Adult** (*delicatula*: Australia, Lesser Sundas and islands in Flores Sea, and Solomon Islands; introduced in New Zealand) Very short-tailed and pale. Very similarly coloured birds occur in SE New Guinea (*meeki*); Boang Island, Tanga and Bismarck Archipelago (*crassirostris*); Santa Cruz and Banks Islands and N New Hebrides (*interposita*); New Caledonia, S New Hebrides, Loyalty, Fiji, Tonga, Samoa and Society Islands (*lulu*).

1m   **Adult** (*pratincola*: North and Middle America to E Guatemala and E Nicaragua) Extremely variable in plumage, but normally with rather pale secondaries. Powerful feet and talons. Perhaps specifically distinct.

1n   **Adult** (*guatemalae*: W Guatemala, El Salvador, W Nicaragua to Panama, Canal Zone) In flight. Slightly larger in size and with somewhat darker plumage.

1o   **Adult** (*tuidara*: Brazil south of Amazon to Chile and Argentina, Tierra del Fuego) Dark morph, in flight. A highly variable subspecies with long tarsi.

1p   **Adult** (*tuidara*) Light morph. Typical of both morphs are the dark crown and occiput, contrasting with pale sides of head and neck. Also light-coloured secondaries, and long tarsi with powerful feet.

1q   **Adult** (*furcata*: Cuba, Isle of Pines, Grand Cayman and Cayman Brac Islands, Jamaica) Looks like a giant *ernesti*! Secondaries and tail feathers mostly uniform white; sometimes also with white primaries.

1r   **Adult** (*contempta*: temperate zone of Colombia and Ecuador to W Peru) Dark morph. A light morph also occurs. Highly variable in plumage above and below.

1s   **Adult** (*insularis*: Lesser Antilles) Dark plumage. Very similar to the subspecies from the Galápagos Islands (*punctatissima*).

2   Andaman Masked Owl *Tyto deroepstorffi*   **Text and map page 196**

Habitat similar to that of *T. alba*. South Andaman Islands.

2   **Adult** Small size but relatively strong feet and talons. Rufous-coloured face with orange-brown rim and chestnut streak before and behind the eyes. Dark brown above, freckled with buff and blackish, and white spots on occiput; back, scapulars, wing-coverts and uppertail-coverts dark brown, mottled with reddish-buff, and with greyish-white feather tips with a black-framed orange-buff spot; tail pale ferruginous-buff with 5 narrow bands and a pale tip. Below, bright golden-buff with tiny, triangular spots. Tibia and tarsus light ferruginous.

3   Ashy-faced Owl *Tyto glaucops*   **Text and map page 196**

Open country with scattered trees and bushes, often near human settlements; also open forest. Islands of Tortuga and Hispaniola (sympatric with *T. alba*).

3   **Adult** Ashy-grey facial disc, rufous rim. Dense dark vermiculations above; below, buffy-yellow with dark, arrow-like spots and zigzag flank bars. Eyes blackish-brown; bill pale horn-yellow.

4   Madagascar Red Owl *Tyto soumagnei*   **Text and map page 197**

Humid rain forest from 900 to 1,200m; primary forest with clearings, as well as secondary scrub. NE Madagascar.

4   **Adult** Small but relatively long-tailed barn owl with powerful feet and talons. Yellow-ochre; some are more rufous-ochre. Facial disc whitish with darker rim.

PLATE 3: MASKED OWLS AND GRASS OWLS

5 **New Britain Masked Owl** *Tyto aurantia* **Text and map page 198**

Tropical rain forest with clearings, also ravines with trees and shrubs. In lowlands and up to 1,830m in mountains. Endemic to island of New Britain in the Bismarck Archipelago.

> **5** **Adult** Relatively small and weak-footed barn owl with a golden-buff plumage and dark markings. Dark brown irides.

6 **Taliabu Masked Owl** *Tyto nigrobrunnea* **Text and map page 199**

Lowland forest. Known from a single specimen collected on Taliabu in the Sula Islands in the Moluccan Sea.

> **6** **Adult** Upperparts dark brown, with whitish speckles from crown to lower back and on tips of secondaries; primaries uniform dark brown without any pattern; tail with 3 darker bars. Dark tawny below, spotted whitish and dark brown. Legs feathered reddish-brown down to lower third of tarsus. Powerful feet and talons. Dark brown eyes.

7 **Eastern Grass Owl** *Tyto longimembris* **Text and map page 199**

Open grassland with tall, rank grass on dry ground, as well on wetlands. India to Vietnam and SE China, Taiwan, Philippines, Sulawesi, Flores, SE New Guinea and Australia; also New Caledonia and the Fijis.

> **7a** **Adult** (*chinensis*: SE China, Taiwan; Taiwan population sometimes separated as race *pithecops*) Much less uniform in plumage than other subspecies: dark-coloured head contrasting with tawny, dark-blotched back and lighter lower back, sides of neck and lesser wing-coverts; dark uppertail-coverts contrasting strongly with paler tail feathers. Dark brown eyes.
>
> **7b** **Adult male** (nominate *longimembris*: NE India to Assam, Burma, Vietnam, Malay Peninsula and Australia; birds from New Caledonia and Fiji Islands sometimes separated as race *oustaleti*) Dark and yellowish-ochre upperparts contrasting heavily with the whitish face and creamy undersurface.
>
> **7c** **Adult female** (nominate *longimembris*) Fawn-coloured wash on facial disc, rather more buff-yellow wash below.
>
> **7d** **Mesoptile** (nominate *longimembris*) Differs from young African Grass Owl in much lighter-coloured crown.
>
> **7e** **Adult** (*amauronota*: Philippines; probably includes '*papuensis*' of SE New Guinea and '*baliem*' of W Irian Jaya) Facial disc greyish-white; dark crown but rather dark upperparts; uniform greyish-white below.

8 **African Grass Owl** *Tyto capensis* **Text and map page 200**

Grassland and open savannas up to about 3,200m. From E Africa to the Cape, C Africa and Angola; isolated population in Cameroon.

> **8a** **Adult** Rather uniform, sooty-brown above, flecked and spotted, without buffy markings; below, whitish to cream-coloured with dark spots. Dark brown eyes.
>
> **8b** **Adult** In flight, showing the long wings and short tail with uniformly coloured central tail feathers.
>
> **8c** **Mesoptile** Showing the fluffy second coat, at age of about 18 days.

PLATE 4: MASKED OWLS

9   **Lesser Masked Owl** *Tyto sororcula*   **Text and map page 201**

Lowland forest and woodlands of Wallacea: islands of Tanimbar and Buru in Lesser Sundas.

     9   **Adult** Small size. Above, orange-buff ground colour with large grey-brown blotches and fine white spots; facial disc also orange-buff with a brown patch from eye to base of bill, and pale-spotted dark rim. Greater coverts and secondaries distinctly lighter grey-brown with darker bars; primaries darker grey-brown with dark bars and dense vermiculations. Underparts light creamy to buff with large spots. Tibia and tarsus creamy with light buffy spots. Dark brown eyes; yellowish-grey toes; creamy bill.

10   **Manus Masked Owl** *Tyto manusi*   **Text and map page 202**

Forest with clearings. Endemic on Manus Island in the Bismarck Archipelago.

     10   **Adult** Large size. Very similar in plumage to Australian Masked Owl, but with darker upperparts and pale ochraceous-buff underparts; flanks, thighs and tarsi light tawny with irregular brown spots. Facial disc whitish, with rufous-brown wash around the dark eyes.

11   **Australian Masked Owl** *Tyto novaehollandiae*   **Text and map page 202**

Forest and open woodland with adjacent cleared areas. Lowlands of south New Guinea, and Australia except the arid interior.

     11a   **Adult** (nominate *novaehollandiae*: New South Wales, Victoria and South Australia) Dark morph. Orange-buff ground colour above and below, with more V-shaped spots on breast and belly; facial disc with dirty buff wash. Dark eyes.

     11b   **Adult** (nominate *novaehollandiae*) Light morph. Lacks orange-buff ground colour. Has large white spots above, with sides of neck and underparts clear white and sparsely spotted; facial disc white, with small orange spot in front of eye.

     11c   **Adult** (*kimberli*: W Australia, Northern Territory and N Queensland) In flight. Somewhat paler in light morph than nominate.

     11d   **Mesoptile** (nominate *novaehollandiae*) White-faced; downy plumage white to creamy. Eyelids, cere and bare parts of feet pinkish.

     11e   **Adult** (*calabyi*: S New Guinea) Similar to the smaller Lesser Masked Owl, but with light facial disc, less contrasting secondaries, and somewhat paler below. Powerful feet.

12   **Sulawesi Masked Owl** *Tyto rosenbergii*   **Text and map page 203**

Rain forest, wooded areas and semi-open country near human settlements, from sea-level up to 1,100m. Sulawesi and adjacent islands.

     12   **Adult** Similar to dark-morph Australian Masked Owl, but with somewhat darker appearance owing to darker back and scapulars and more barring on secondaries; primary tips with black and white spots. Powerful feet. Dark eyes.

13   **Tasmanian Masked Owl** *Tyto castanops*   **Text and map page 204**

Forest and semi-open woodland. Tasmania.

     13a   **Adult female** Darker and larger than Australian Masked Owl, and with the most powerful feet of all *Tyto* species. Dark rufous facial disc, with brownish-black spots in front of dark brown eyes.

     13b   **Adult male** Somewhat smaller than female, often with much lighter-coloured face and underparts.

PLATE 5: MASKED, SOOTY AND BAY OWLS

14   Minahassa Masked Owl *Tyto inexspectata*   Text and map page 205

Tropical rain forest from about 250m up to 1,500m. Minahassa Peninsula in N Sulawesi.

14a   **Adult** Round-winged, small-sized barn owl with rufous appearance and relatively powerful feet. Pale rufous facial disc with dark-speckled rufous-brown rim; nuchal area and bend of wing darker than surrounding plumage. Dark brown eyes.

14b   **Adult** In flight, showing the numerous tail-bars.

15   Lesser Sooty Owl *Tyto multipunctata*   Text and map page 205

Rain forest and wet eucalypt forest with tall trees and hollow trunks. NE Australia in the Atherton region of NE Queensland.

15a   **Adult** Small, round-winged *Tyto*. Overall light sooty-grey, densely spotted and dotted whitish above and below. Light facial disc shaded sooty around the large blackish eyes, and having dark rim with tiny white speckles.

15b   **Adult** In flight, showing the light underwing-coverts.

16   Greater Sooty Owl *Tyto tenebricosa*   Text and map page 206

Rain and cloud forests, pockets of rain or wet eucalypt forests. New Guinea and SE Australia.

16a   **Adult** (*arfaki*: New Guinea and Jobi Island) Generally browner than nominate *tenebricosa*, with slightly larger white spots above and with distinctly barred tarsi. Blackish eyes; creamy bill; greyish-brown toes.

16b   **Adult** (nominate *tenebricosa*: SE Australia) Dark sooty-coloured plumage with somewhat lighter undersurface.

16c   **Adult** (nominate *tenebricosa*) In flight, showing the rounded and rather uniform wings.

16d   **Juvenile male** (nominate *tenebricosa*) Much darker head, facial disc and breast than adult.

17   Itombwe Owl *Tyto prigoginei*   Text and map page 207

Montane gallery forest and upper slopes with grass and light bush, from about 1,830m to 2,430m. C Africa, in Itombwe Mountains of E Zaire.

17   **Adult** Small rufous owl, superficially similar to Bay Owl, but with the typical heart-shaped facial disc of *Tyto* and several differences in plumage pattern. Bill more compressed and feet smaller.

18   Bay Owl *Phodilus badius*   Text and map page 208

Forest, from lowlands up to hill country and montane forest at about 2,300m, locally also secondary growth and plantations; hunts near water. NE India, Sri Lanka, southern SE Asia, Greater Sundas, Samar (Philippines) and some small Indonesian islands.

18a   **Adult** (*assimilis*: Sri Lanka) Head, back and bend of wing much darker than in all other races. Darker spots in front of and behind eyes.

18b   **Adult** (*assimilis*) In flight, showing the prominent ochre wing patch.

18c   **Adult** (*saturatus*: NE India, Nepal and Sikkim to N Thailand) Distinctly ochre-coloured scapulars, and pinkish tinge on face and underparts.

18d   **Adult** (nominate *badius*: Thailand and Malaysia to Greater Sundas and Samar, Philippines) Greyish frontal shield and pale tan underparts; paler than *assimilis* but darker than *parvus* or *saturatus*.

18e   **Adult** (*parvus*: Belitung Island, off SE Sumatra) Forehead, facial disc and underparts paler than in other subspecies. (Note that subspecies *arixuthus* from Bunguran in Natuna Islands has never been observed in the wild.)

14a

15a

14b

15b

16a

16c

16b

18b

16d

18e

17

18a

18c

18d

1995 WERK

PLATE 6: SCOPS OWLS

20   **Reddish Scops Owl** *Otus rufescens*   **Text and map page 212**

Humid forest, from lowlands up to about 1,300m. Peninsular Thailand, Malaysia, Sumatra, Java and Borneo; Sulu Archipelago (Philippines).

> **20a**   **Adult** (nominate *rufescens*: Sumatra, Java and Borneo). Light morph. Small reddish owl with conspicuous ear-tufts. Upperparts cinnamon-brown with white and black spots; scapulars with pale ochre outer webs and dark spots. Underparats cinnamon-buff with lighter shaft-streaks and black terminal spots. Eyes orange.

> **20b**   **Adult** (nominate *rufescens*) Dark morph. Much darker cinnamon-brown above and below, with similar pattern to light morph. (Subspecies *malayensis* is very similar in plumage.) Eyes orange to brown; bill yellow-horn; toes yellowish.

> **20c**   **Adult** (*burbidgei*: Sulu Archipelago) Darker on head and nape; also much darker facial disc, and more chestnut-brown on wings and tail.

21   **Cinnamon Scops Owl** *Otus icterorhynchus*   **Text and map page 213**

Humid lowland forest. Locally in equatorial belt of WC Africa, in NE Liberia (Mt Nimba), S Ghana, S Cameroon and NE Zaire.

> **21a**   **Adult** (nominate *icterorhynchus*: Liberia and Ghana) Light cinnamon-brown owl with buffy and white spots and conspicuous ear-tufts. Below, sandy-coloured with white longitudinal shaft marks, more spotted on belly. Feathered tarsi; eyes pale yellow.

> **21b**   **Adult** (nominate *icterorhynchus*) In flight, showing the sandy-coloured back, wings and tail contrasting with darker primary coverts and primaries.

> **21c**   **Adult** (*holerythrus*: Cameroon, E and C Zaire) Much darker cinnamon-coloured above and below, with similar pattern to nominate.

19   **White-fronted Scops Owl** *Otus sagittatus*   **Text and map page 211**

Humid forest, mostly in lowlands below 600m. SE Asia in Malay Peninsula and N Sumatra.

> **19**   **Adult** Large, long-tailed scops owl. Above, rufescent-brown with white, triangular, black-framed spots; scapulars whitish on outer webs. Forehead, supercilia and ear-tufts (partly) white; lacks neck-collar. Breast cinnamon, scalloped with blackish arrowheads; belly lighter, vermiculated rufous, with black arrowheads and shaft-streaks. Legs feathered to base of toes. Eyes brown.

22   **Sokoke Scops Owl** *Otus ireneae*   **Text and map page 214**

Brachystegia woodland. Lowlands of coastal E Kenya (Sokoke-Arabuku Forest); possibly wider distribution along E African coast (recently recorded in Tanzania).

> **22a**   **Adult** Light grey morph. Upperparts greyish with light and dark spots. Ear-tufts and supercilia white, spotted and mottled darker. Below, sandy-grey, vermiculated darker, and with white spots, black arrowheads and fine shaft-streaks. Eyes yellow.

> **22b**   **Adult** Rufous morph. Very similar pattern and vermiculations, but brighter rufous ground colour above and below.

> **22c**   **Adult** Dark brown morph. Similar pattern and barring, but dark brown ground colour, and spots more buffy than white. Facial disc with conspicuous concentric lines.

20a

21b

21a

20b

20c

21c

19

22a

22b

22c

PLATE 7: SCOPS OWLS

23 **Mountain Scops Owl** *Otus spilocephalus*   **Text and map page 214**

Humid forest and woodland in mountains from about 1,200m upwards. Pakistan, Nepal, N and E India and Burma, SE China, Taiwan, SE Asia (except Cambodia and S Vietnam), Sumatra, Java and Borneo.

23a **Adult** (nominate *spilocephalus*: Nepal and Sikkim east to Bangladesh and Burma). Small, pale rufous to ochraceous-buff owl with small ear-tufts, yellow eyes and cream bill. Face covered with strong bristles. Above, spotted whitish and black; scapulars white with black speckles. Below, white with rufescent barring and black arrowheads. (Subspecies *latouchi* of SE China to Laos is very similar in plumage.)

23b **Adult** (*hambroecki*: mountains of Taiwan) Shown perched and in flight. Slightly darker rufous above and below.

23c **Adult** (*huttoni*: Himachal Pradesh, Himalayas) Paler above and below than nominate.

23d **Adult** (*vulpes*: Malacca, Malay Peninsula) Light spots more buffy than white, less distinctly patterned and more rufous face than nominate.

23e **Adult** (*luciae*: Borneo) Extremely dark subspecies, lacking nuchal collar.

23f **Adult** (*vandewateri*: Sumatra) Dark, with distinct white scapulars and collar. (Sometimes considered conspecific with *O. angelinae*, but vocalisations suggest it to be a subspecies of *spilocephalus*.)

23g **Adult** ('*stresemanni*': Sumatra) Generally considered to be a pale morph of *vandewateri*, although plumage pattern somewhat different from typical individuals of that race: lacks dense vermiculations above, and spots below different in shape from those of other subspecies of *O. spilocephalus*.

24 **Javan Scops Owl** *Otus angelinae*   **Text and map page 216**

Montane virgin rain forest in interior of Java, between 900 and 3,000m above sea-level. Endemic to Java.

24a **Adult** Light morph. Lighter rufous than dark morph. Rather dark crown strongly contrasting with white supercilia and ear-tufts; buffy nuchal collar; light rufous facial disc. Pale underparts contrast strongly with upperparts.

24b **Adult** Dark morph (commoner). Shown perched and in flight. Much darker above and below than light morph, but still with distinct white supercilia and nuchal collar, also scapular spots. Yellow bill; bright orange-yellow irides. Inner webs of primaries unspotted.

48 **Nicobar Scops Owl** *Otus alius*   **Text and map page 241**

Wooded areas near sea-level. Endemic to Great Nicobar Island in the Bay of Bengal.

48 **Adult** Perched and in flight. Warm brown and finely barred above but lacking dark shaft-streaks on back and mantle. Underparts with heavy tricoloured barring, pale bars rather prominent on flanks, and dark shaft-streaks markedly reduced.

23a

23b

23b

23c

23d

23e

23f

23g

24a

24b

24b

48

48

97
Weick

PLATE 8: SCOPS OWLS

25 Mindanao Scops Owl *Otus mirus* **Text and map page 218**

Humid forest in the mountains of Mindanao, Philippines.

    25   **Adult** Small, dark owl with small ear-tufts and strong facial bristles. Very similar to Mountain and Javan Scops Owls (Plate 7), but with brown irides and different vocalisations.

26 Luzon Scops Owl *Otus longicornis* **Text and map page 219**

Humid forest of foothills and mountains, from 350m up to 2,200m. Endemic to Luzon, Philippines.

    26   **Adult** Small, buffy-brown owl with rather long ear-tufts, light supercilia, nuchal band and white throat. White scapular spots; back and rump rufous with black barring; wings and tail darker brown with dark bars. Breast rufous with dark spots; belly white with rufous and dark pattern. Yellow eyes.

27 Mindoro Scops Owl *Otus mindorensis* **Text and map page 219**

Montane, closed-canopy forest, above 870m. Endemic to Mindoro, Philippines.

    27   **Adult** Similar to Luzon Scops Owl in plumage, but much smaller and with shorter ear-tufts. More buffy-orange below, with different-shaped markings, and lacking white belly. Eyes yellow.

28 Flores Scops Owl *Otus alfredi* **Text and map page 220**

Humid forest in mountains above 1,000m. Endemic to Flores.

    27   **Adult** Relatively small, rufous-cinnamon scops owl with small ear-tufts. Back with some indistinct buffy-white cross-marks and with black-margined white scapulars; some black-tipped white spots on breast sides, and lower breast and belly with light grey-brown bars. Iris yellow.

29 São Tomé Scops Owl *Otus hartlaubi* **Text and map page 221**

Humid primary forest, also secondary forest and plantations, from sea-level up to 1,300m. Endemic to São Tomé Island in Gulf of Guinea.

    29a   **Adult** Brown morph. Small scops owl, this morph very similar to Luzon Scops, but with smaller ear-tufts, broad longitudinal shaft-streaks on back and finer barring below. Bare tarsi and toes yellow; eyes deep yellow.

    29b   **Adult** Rufous morph. Strongly rufous above and below, with wider shaft-streaks on undersurface and more buffy nuchal band and scapulars. Facial disc with distinctly rufous wash.

    29c   **Mesoptile** Fluffy rufous plumage with fine bars above an below.

30 Andaman Scops Owl *Otus balli* **Text and map page 222**

Semi-open areas with groups of trees, cultivated country and gardens with trees and bushes near buildings and settlements. Endemic to Andaman Islands.

    30a   **Adult** Brown morph. White eyebrows, lores and throat; large white blotches below. Bill and eyes yellow; feet dirty yellow.

    30b   **Adult** Rufous morph. Back less vermiculated than in brown morph, and with much smaller light spots on underparts; spots more buffy, less white than in brown morph.

    30c   **Adult** Rufous morph. In flight, showing contrast of rufous coverts and secondaries against browner primaries.

25

26

27

28

29a

29b

29c

30a

30b

30c

1997
WEICK

PLATE 9: SCOPS OWLS

31   Madagascar Scops Owl *Otus rutilus*   **Text and map page 223**

Forest and bushy country, from sea-level up to 1,800m. Madagascar, and Mayotte in Comoro Islands.

31a   Adult (nominate *rutilus*: Madagascar) Grey-brown morph. Rather larger than Common Scops Owl (Plate 10), with small ear-tufts, yellow eyes, and cryptic plumage with some rufous wash above and below. (From their vocalisations, birds from drier, western parts of Madagascar may represent a separate, undescribed species.)

31b   Adult (nominate *rutilus*) Rufous morph. Strongly rufous above and below, lacking the white spots on head and back of grey-brown morph, but still with light supercilia and scapulars.

31c   Adult (*mayottensis*: Mayotte) Very similar to grey-brown morph of nominate, but rather larger and darker, with more distinct nuchal band and a white throat. (Perhaps specifically distinct.)

32   Grand Comoro Scops Owl *Otus pauliani*   **Text and map page 224**

Mountain forest in primary or degraded state between 1,000m and 1,900m; also adjacent tree-heaths at upper forest edge. Endemic to Grand Comoro Island.

32   Adult Light morph. 'Earless' small scops owl, very similar in plumage to grey-brown morph of Madagascar Scops and light morph of Anjouan Scops, but distinctly smaller. (Also occurs as dark morph, similar to dark-morph Anjouan Scops.) Eyes yellow (sometimes brown?).

33   Anjouan Scops Owl *Otus capnodes*   **Text and map page 224**

Patches of primary forest on mountain slopes about 500m above sea-level. Endemic to Anjouan (Nzuani) in the Comoros Archipelago.

33a   Adult Rufous-brown morph. Hardly visible ear-tufts, indistinct scapular stripes, but ocellated with white spots on dark rusty and cryptic plumage. Eyes yellowish-green.

33b   Adult Dark morph. Varying from dark chocolate- to blackish-brown with numerous fine, buffy speckles.

33c   Adult Light morph, in flight. Similar in colour to light-morph Grand Comoro Scops, and with more and distinct white spots compared with rufous-brown morph.

34   Mohéli Scops Owl *Otus moheliensis*   **Text and map page 225**

Dense and humid forest. Endemic to Mohéli (Comoros Islands).

34a   Adult Brown morph. Hardly visible ear-tufts, relatively strong bill, bare lower third of tarsus and yellow-green irides. Scapulars with indistinct cinnamon outerwebs and one or two fine bars.

34b   Adult Rufous morph (head and chest). Finer streaking below and obsolete pattern above. Tail with indistinct barring.

35   Pemba Scops Owl *Otus pembaensis*   **Text and map page 226**

Semi-open country with groups of densely foliaged trees, also plantations. Endemic to Pemba Island, off E African coast.

35a   Adult Light morph. Plain, light tawny-rufous upperparts with fine pattern on head, back and mantle; scapulars distinctly white, margined dark, with buffy wash. Ear-tufts, face, lores, sides of neck and underparts creamy-white with few shaft-streaks and bars. Eyes yellow.

35b   Adult Rufous morph. Above, very similar to light morph, sometimes lacking bars on secondary coverts; buffy below, more densely vermiculated and barred on flanks and thighs.

31a

31b

31c

32

33a

33b

34b

33c

34a

35a

35b

1997 Weick

PLATE 10: SCOPS OWLS

36 **Flammulated Scops Owl** *Otus flammeolus* **Text and map page 227**

Open coniferous mountain forest, from 400 to 3,000m; common in forest with ponderosa and yellow pines, often mixed with oaks or aspen; favours forest with bushy undergrowth or mixed forest with Douglas firs. Western N America (British Columbia) along Rocky Mountains to Mexico, Guatemala; wintering south to El Salvador.

36a **Adult** (*idahoensis*: northern, long-winged migrant) Lighter in plumage, with finer pattern. Bill and toes greyish-brown; eyes dark brown. (A variant of this subspecies occurs, having more rufous tinge on facial disc, nape and scapulars.)

36b **Adult** (nominate *flammeolus*: S USA to Guatemala and El Salvador) Dark morph with coarse pattern. Somewhat darker than northern individuals, with coarser mottling and shaft-streaks, denser vermiculations. (Subspecies *rarus* from the highlands of Guatemala is darker and more brownish.)

36c **Adult** (nominate *flammeolus*) Rufous morph. Not so distinctly rufous as rufous morphs of other *Otus* species, having rufous to buffy-orange tinge on facial disc and scapulars, with similar pattern and vermiculations to the more greyish specimens.

36d **Mesoptile** (nominate *flammeolus*) Much lighter plumage than adult; fine bars above and below; rusty wash on facial disc and scapulars is typical of more rufous individuals.

37 **Common Scops Owl** *Otus scops* **Text and map page 228**

Semi-open and rather open country with scattered trees or small woods; cultivated areas with groups of trees; rocky landscapes, parks and Mediterranean scrub; in warm climates also in mountainous regions. S Europe (especially Mediterranean region), locally in C, E and W Europe; Africa north of Sahara, from Morocco to Tunisia; Asia Minor and east to C Asia.

37a **Adult** (*turanicus*: Turkmenistan to W Pakistan) Paler and more silvery-grey than nominate *scops*. Bill and toes grey; eyes yellow.

37b **Adult** (nominate *scops*: W and C Europe, Mediterranean region except Cyprus and SW Asia Minor, east to Crimea). Grey-brown morph. Greyish-brown above with streaks and vermiculations, cryptic pattern and less rufous tinge; somewhat paler below, with blackish shaft-streaks, barring and vermiculations and distinct white patches. Eyes yellow. (Subspecies *pulchellus*, distributed from Caucasus to the Yenisei, has a somewhat greyer appearance and more white above.)

37c **Adult** (nominate *scops*) Rufous-brown morph, also shown in flight. Distinctly browner above and below, with similar cryptic pattern, but lacking clear reddish tinge.

37d **Adult** (*cyprius*: Cyprus and SW Asia Minor) Much darker plumage (blackish pattern) and with clear white spots on hindneck and mantle.

37e **Mesoptile** (nominate *scops*) Less downy appearance than other young owls; lighter in colour than adult, with more indistinct barring and vermiculations.

37f **Juvenile** (nominate *scops*) Similar to adult, but with a more sandy-brown colour and less obvious barring and shaft-stripes.

36a

36b

36d

36c

37a

37b

37c

37c

37e

37d

37f

97
WEICK

PLATE 11: SCOPS OWLS

38 **Pallid Scops Owl** *Otus brucei*   **Text and map page 230**

Semi-open landscapes with trees and bushes, arid rocky gullies with scrub, from lowland up to 1,500m above sea-level. Middle East to W and C Asia, NW India, Afghanistan and Pakistan; occurrence on Socotra Island, off coast of Somalia, doubtful.

38a **Adult** (*obsoletus*: Syria, N Iraq, Turkmeniya, N Afghanistan and lowlands of Uzbekistan) Pale sandy-buff ground colour. Eyes yellow.

38b **Adult** (nominate *brucei*: E Aral Sea, Fergana basin and N Tadzhikistan and Kirgiziya). In flight. Somewhat darker sandy-grey and more distinctly patterned.

38c **Adult** (*exiguus*: Israel, C Iraq, S Iran, E Arabia, S Afghanistan and W Pakistan) Pale creamy-grey ground colour and less sharply defined pattern than *obsoletus* and *brucei*.

38d **Adult** (*socotranus*: Socotra, off coast of Somalia) Tiny, with a cream-grey ground colour, numerous speckles above and pale grey below. (Perhaps represents a separate species or is a race of African Scops Owl.)

39 **African Scops Owl** *Otus senegalensis*   **Text and map page 231**

Savanna with scattered trees and thorny scrub, also semi-open woodland and park-like areas, gardens, forest clearings, generally below 2,000m. Africa south of Sahara, except the southwest deserts of Namibia, also absent from the forested regions; Pagulu (Annobon) Island off coast of Gabon; recorded in southern Arabia. Eyes yellow.

39a **Adult** (*nivosus*: Tana river to Lalli Hills, SE Kenya) Very pale grey, with rather rufous tinge on back, wings and below (bars). (Adult of Arabian subspecies *pamelae* is similar to *nivosus*, but with a more sandy-grey ground colour.)

39b **Adult** (nominate *senegalensis*: sub-Saharan Africa except SE Kenya) Light morph of *latipennis* type. Greyer appearance and more rufous tinge, especially on ear-tufts and wing-coverts. Eyes yellow.

39c **Adult** (nominate *senegalensis*) Brown morph of *latipennis* type. Brown plumage, but similar pattern to light morph.

39d **Adult** (nominate *senegalensis*) Dark morph. Much darker-coloured, typical of Ugandan individuals (*ugandae* type).

39e **Adult** (*senegalensis*) Dark morph of *caecus* type. Rather darker than 39d, typical of specimens from Somalia and Ethiopia.

39f **Adult** (*feae*: Pagulu Island) Dark plumage, with the broadest dark stripes on undersurface.

38a

38b

38c

38d

38e

39a

39b

39c

39d

38e

39f

1992 林祥会

PLATE 12: SCOPS OWLS

40   Oriental Scops Owl *Otus sunia*   **Text and map page 232**

Open and semi-open woodland, parks, savannas with scattered trees and wooded riverside belts. India and Pakistan, Sri Lanka, Borneo, Andaman and Nicobar Islands, E Asia from Japan, E Siberia, Manchuria and E China to Malay Peninsula (Malacca), Taiwan; vagrant to Hong Kong and Aleutian Islands.

40a   **Adult** (*japonicus*: Hokkaido and Kyushu, Japan) Rufous morph. Specimens of this morph are very frequent. (Birds of the grey-brown morph are identical in plumage to race *stictonotus*.) Bill blackish-grey; eyes yellow.

40b   **Adult** (*stictonotus*: Manchuria, Amur and Ussuriland, south to China and Korea; migrant in SE China and Taiwan). Grey-brown morph. Rather larger than *japonicus*, but with similar light grey coloration. (Also occurs as a brown morph.)

40c   **Adult** (nominate *sunia*: Lower Himalayas from Kumaon to Bhutan, south to Punjab, Central Provinces, Bengal and Bangladesh). Grey-brown morph. With more rufous tinge and distinctly darker than *japonicus* or *stictonotus*.

40d   **Adult** (nominate *sunia*). Rufous morph. Lacks dark pattern above, more plain-coloured and much lighter (tawny-) rufous than *malayanus*.

40e   **Adult** (*rufipennis*: peninsular India from Bombay and Madras southward). Brown morph, in flight. In this morph very similar to brown *malayanus* and *modestus* (*modestus* perhaps synonym of *rufipennis*).

40f   **Adult** (*malayanus*: Malay Peninsula) Rufous morph. Much more chestnut-rufous plumage than in rufous morphs of other subspecies. Perhaps specifically distinct.

40g   **Adult** (*leggei*: Sri Lanka). Brown morph. Darkest plumage of all subspecies. Perhaps specifically distinct.

41   Elegant Scops Owl *Otus elegans*   **Text and map page 233**

Forested areas; originally mature forest with old trees, but has adapted to areas greatly altered by man. Ryukyu and Daito Islands, Lanyu Island off Taiwan; Calayan and Batan Islands (Philippines).

41a   **Adult** (nominate *elegans*: Ryukyus and Daito). Light rufous morph. Very similar plumage to Oriental Scops *sunia*, and with identical wing-formula, but larger and longer-winged.

41b   **Adult** (nominate *elegans*) Typical dark rufous morph. Specimens of both morphs similar in plumage to subspecies *botelensis* from Lanyu Island.

41c   **Adult** (nominate *elegans*) Dark morph. Showing the rounded wing with 4th primary longest. Bill dark horn; eyes deep yellow.

45   Seychelles Scops Owl *Otus insularis*   **Text and map page 238**

Forest and wooded areas, rather high in mountains. Endemic to Mahé Island, Seychelles; extinct on Praslin Island.

45a   **Adult** Typical plumage. Practically 'earless' scops owl. Densely spotted above and below: upper spots mostly washed ochre; white spots below on a buffy ground colour, with dark shaft-stripes and wavy bars. Lower third of tarsi unfeathered. Tarsi and toes greyish-yellow to greenish-white; eyes yellow.

45b   **Adult** In flight, showing P7 as longest primary on a rounded wing.

40a

40b

40c

40e

40d

40f

40g

41c

41a

45b

41b

45a

1997
WEICK

PLATE 13: SCOPS OWLS

42   **Mantanani Scops Owl** *Otus mantananensis*   **Text and map page 235**

Forest and wooded areas, also coconut groves. Mantanani Islands off N Borneo, and WC and SW Philippines. Small scops owl with short ear-tufts, distinctly rimmed facial disc, tarsi not feathered down to toes; eyes yellow; bill horn-coloured to grey; upperside with fine markings.

     42a   **Adult** (nominate *mantananensis*: Mantanani, Rasa and Ursula Islands off N Borneo) Rufous-brown morph, also in flight.

     42b   **Adult** (nominate *mantananensis*) Dark morph. Mottled dark brown, white and black, with pattern above very fine; strong black streaking on upper breast, belly much paler.

     42c   **Adult** (*sibutuensis* type: Sibutu Island, Sulu Archipelago) Smallest subspecies; more buffy on breast than rufous-brown *mantananensis*, with much paler wings. (Birds from Romblon, *romblonis*, and Cuyo, *cuyensis*, are very similar to this subspecies.)

43   **Moluccan Scops Owl** *Otus magicus*   **Text and map page 236**

Forest and wooded areas. Lesser Sunda Islands and Moluccas; population from Sula Mangoli (off Sulawesi) perhaps a separate species. Rufous-tinged facial disc in all morphs, lores white; scapulars of rufous morph with light buffy wash; indistinctly banded tail with dense vermiculations; eyes yellow.

     43a   **Adult** (nominate *magicus*: Moluccas, on Halmahera, Batjan, Seram, Ambon and Kep Obi) Grey-brown morph. Strong feet; tarsi mostly feathered down to toes, but more or less unfeathered on rear side.

     43b   **Adult** (nominate *magicus*) Deep rufous morph. Individual from Ambon, but occurs also on other Moluccan islands. Rufous wash on central tail feathers.

     43c   **Adult** (nominate *magicus*) Typical light buffy morph. Fine, distinct shaft-streaks and bars above and below.

     43d   **Adult** (*albiventris*: Lesser Sundas) Dark brown morph, with white belly. Tail very indistinctly banded and vermiculated. (Identical morphs occur on Buru Islands in Moluccas, often separated as subspecies *leucospilus* and *bouruensis*.) Birds from Wetar and Kep Barat Daja (subspecies *tempestatis*) are very similar to brown and rufous morphs of Sulawesi Scops Owl (Plate 14).

     43e   **Adult** (nominate *magicus*) Dark morph, in flight. Typical of individuals from Ambon, Halmahera and also Kep Obi.

     43f   **Mesoptile** (nominate *magicus*) Other mesoptiles with much paler buffy wash.

     43g   **Adult** (*sulaensis*: Sula Islands) Black mottling on crown coarse and rather broad. Tarsus unfeathered distally, rear of tarsus totally unfeathered. Probably specifically distinct.

44   **Biak Scops Owl** *Otus beccarii*   **Text and map page 237**

Forest and wooded areas. Biak Island in Geelvink Bay, off New Guinea.

     44   **Adult** Lacks shaft streaks above and below, but some streaks on forecrown. Underparts densely barred; indistinct collar. Tarsus feathered for 80% of its length, or down to toes. Eyes yellow.

42a 42a 42b 42c

43e 43a 43b 43c

43g

43f 43d 44

97 WEICK

PLATE 14: SCOPS OWLS

47   Sangihe Scops Owl *Otus collari*   Text and map page 240

Forests, secondary growth and agricultural land with trees, bushes or plantations, from sea-level up to 315m. Endemic to Sangihe Island, off N Sulawesi.

47   Adult Perched and in flight. Similar to Sulawesi Scops Owl but with longer and narrower wings and a rather long tail.

46   Sulawesi Scops Owl *Otus manadensis*   Text and map page 239

Humid forest, from lowland up to about 2,500m. Sulawesi, Peleng, Sangihe, Banggai Islands, and Kalidupa in the Tukangbesi Islands. Distinctly smaller than Moluccan Scops Owl (Plate 13), with smaller feet, tarsi feathered down to base of toes (or nearly), and less distinctly banded primaries on outer webs. In colour morphs, individual extension of scapular patches and supercilia similar to *O. magicus* group. Vocally different from *magicus*. (See also Sangihe Scops Owl, Plate 14.)

46a   Adult (nominate *manadensis*: range of species apart from Peleng and Siao) Grey-brown morph. Small but prominent ear-tufts. This and a yellowish-grey morph are the most common type of this species. Eyes yellow.

46b   Adult (nominate *manadensis*) Yellowish-grey morph. Pale ochraceous tinge, but similar pattern to grey-brown morph. (A rare rufous morph also occurs.)

46c   Adult (*mendeni*: Peleng Island) Rufous morph, type specimen. (A grey morph also occurs on Peleng, but only a few skins exist.)

46d   Adult (*siaoensis*: Siao Island). Type specimen. A tiny subspecies, known only from the type specimen. Distinct nuchal half-collars.

46e   Adult (nominate *manadensis*) Dark rufous morph, in flight. Rare morph, similar in pattern to other colour variants.

49   Simeulue Scops Owl *Otus umbra*   Text and map page 241

Broken forest, edges of forest on steep coast, also plantations. Endemic to Simeulue Island off NW Sumatra.

49   Adult Small, dark reddish-brown or olive-brown owl with distinct ear-tufts and greenish-yellow eyes. Lacks pale neck-collar of Enggano Scops Owl. Rufous below, with fine white and brown bars with black edges.

50   Enggano Scops Owl *Otus enganensis*   Text and map page 242

Forest and wooded areas. Endemic to Enggano Island, off SW Sumatra.

50   Adult Small, brown-mottled owl with prominent ear-tufts and yellow eyes. Dorsal coloration varies from chestnut to brownish-olive; greater coverts and secondaries distinctly paler, contrasting more with primary coverts and primaries than those of Simeulue Scops Owl. Below, varies from cinnamon to brownish-olive, more or less cross-barred and with double spots.

51   Rajah Scops Owl *Otus brookii*   Text and map page 243

Mountain forest, from about 1,200m up to 2,400m above sea-level. Highlands of Borneo and Sumatra.

51a   Adult (nominate *brookii*: NW Borneo) Rufous morph. Brownish to rufous-brown with conspicuous ear-tufts. Slightly larger than Collared Scops Owl (Plate 15) and with indication of occipital spot, a larger band on nape and a third on hindneck, forming a broad cervical collar. Eyes yellow; toes pale yellow.

51b   Adult (*solokensis*: Sumatra) Brown morph. Very similar to nominate *brookii* but browner dorsally, with three distinct collars on hindneck and nuchal area; broader blackish shaft-stripes below. Bill whitish; eyes brownish-yellow.

52 **Sunda Scops Owl** *Otus lempiji* **Text and map page 244**

Forest, second growth, woodland, open country and towns, from lowlands up to 2,400m. SE Asia to Sumatra (including Banka and Belitung), Borneo (including W Natuna Islands), Java and Bali (including Kangean Island).

52a **Adult** (nominate *lempiji*: Sumatra and Malay Peninsula east to Borneo and Natuna Islands) Grey-brown morph, dark-eyed. Long, prominent ear-tufts, blackish-marked head and uppracts; below, marked with arrowheads and rhomboid bars, more densely vermiculated than Indian Scops. Diagnostic pale nuchal band. Bill yellow; toes dirty yellow; eyes brown to bright orange-yellow.

52b **Adult** (nominate *lempiji*) Buffy morph, orange-eyed. Similar in pattern to grey-brown birds (and dark-eyed individuals are common). Feathered tarsi.

52c **Adult** (nominate *lempiji*) Grey-brown morph. In flight, showing rounded wings and dark dorsal colouring.

52d **Mesoptile** (nominate *lempiji*) Rufous morph. Ear-tufts inconspicuous; breast with dense dark rufous barring.

52e **Adult** (*hypnodes*: Pulau Padang, off Sumatra) Dark morph. (Also similar are subspecies *kangeana* from Kangean Island and *cnephaeus* from S Malay Peninsula, the latter perhaps specifically distinct.)

53 **Collared Scops Owl** *Otus lettia* **Text and map page 245**

Forest, second growth, woodland, open country and towns, from lowlands up to 2,400m above sea-level. E Himalayas from Nepal east to E Assam, south to E Bengal; Burma, Thailand, Hainan, Condor Island, S China and Taiwan. Eye colour varying from dark brown to brownish-orange.

53a **Adult** (nominate *lettia*: E Himalayas to E Bengal, Burma and Thailand) Buffy-grey morph. Distinctly lighter-coloured above and with shorter ear-tufts than Sunda Scops Owl. Eyes normally dark brown. (Subspecies *glabripes* from Taiwan is very similar in colour but with bare toes; *umbratilis* from Hainan is rather smaller, somewhat lighter above with darker marks.)

53b **Adult** (*erythrocampe*: S China) Rufous morph. Brown upperparts with buff markings, less greyish than nominate *lettia*; more golden-brown to chestnut-coloured eyes. With the white supercilia very similar to Japanese Scops Owl (Plate 16).

54 **Indian Scops Owl** *Otus bakkamoena* **Text and map page 246**

Forest, secondary woodland, open country and desert vegetation, and towns, from lowlands up to 2,200m. S Asia from SE Arabia to Pakistan, India and east to W Bengal, including Himalayas from Kashmir east to C Nepal, and Sri Lanka.

54a **Adult** (nominate *bakkamoena*: S India and Sri Lanka) Buffy morph. Dorsally somewhat lighter-coloured than Sunda Scops Owl. Conspicuous large ear-tufts, dark eyes. Distinct nuchal collar and also a second on hindneck. (Subspecies *marathae* similar in plumage, but rather larger.)

54b **Adult** (*gangeticus*: NW India) Grey morph. Larger and distinctly paler than nominate *bakkamoena*, smaller and paler than Collared Scops.

54c **Adult** (*deserticolor*: S Pakistan to SE Arabia) Typical pale individual. Dorsal and ventral surfaces without rufescent tinge, belly almost white.

54d **Adult** (*plumipes*: NW Himalayas) Grey morph. Densely feathered toes as Japanese Scops (nominate *semitorques* and *ussuriensis*), and very similar to that species, but differs in vocalisations and in brown (against red or yellow) eyes.

52a 52b 52e 53a

53b 52d 52c 54d

54a 54b 54c

97 Weick

55   **Japanese Scops Owl** *Otus semitorques*   **Text and map page 247**

Forest and woodland from lowland to mountains; woods near human habitation. E Asia in SE Siberia (Ussuriland and Sakhalin), Kuril Islands, Japan, Izu and Ryukyu Islands; winters in SE Asia.

55a   **Adult** (nominate *semitorques*: Kurile Islands, Hokkaido to Kyushu, and Quelpart Island) Large size, prominent ear-tufts. Fiery red-orange eyes; eyebrows, ear-tufts (partly) and throat whitish to clear white. Lacks rufous wash, colours more grey-brown and buff, with uniform appearance. Tarsi and toes densely feathered; strong bill. 7th primary longest on a more pointed wing.

55b   **Adult** (*ussuriensis*: Ussuriland and Sakhalin) In flight. Very similar to nominate, but with somewhat paler appearance and with yellow to orange-yellow eyes.

55c   **Adult** (*pryeri*: Izu and Ryukyu Islands) Differs from nominate *semitorques* in bare toes, yellow eyes, and strongly ferruginous wash above and below. Large bill, as nominate.

56   **Philippine Scops Owl** *Otus megalotis*   **Text and map page 248**

Tropical forest and secondary woodland. Philippines: Luzon, Marinduque, Catanduanes, Samar, Leyte, Dinagat, Bohol, Negros, Mindanao and Basilan. Eyes orange-brown.

56a   **Adult** (nominate *megalotis*: Luzon, Marinduque and Catanduanes) Rufous morph. Large scops owl with long ear-tufts and powerful feet. Tarsi feathered down to toes. Crown with dark mark in form of parallelogram; greater coverts more rufous than browner remaining wing-coverts and lighter secondaries; nuchal band contrasting with mantle. (A grey morph, similar in pattern, is frequent.)

56b   **Adult** (*nigrorum*: Negros) Rufous morph. Dorsal view, painted to smaller scale. Smaller than nominate *megalotis*, with distinct bright rufous crown, neck and face.

56c   **Adult** (*everetti*: Bohol, Samar, Leyte, Dinagat, Bohol, Mindanao and Basilan) Typical individual. Smaller and with browner plumage than nominate *megalotis*. Also dark parallelogram on head and nape. Tarsi not feathered down to toes. Ssp *boholensis* is synonym.

58   **Palawan Scops Owl** *Otus fuliginosus*   **Text and map page 250**

Tropical forest and secondary woodland. Lowlands of Palawan Island in W Philippines.

58   **Adult** Similar in size and colour to Philippine Scops Owl of race *everetti*, but differs in vocalizations. Broad nuchal collar, distinct pale scapulars and contrasting light greater coverts are significant. Eyes orange-brown.

57   **Mentawai Scops Owl** *Otus mentawi*   **Text and map page 249**

Lowland rain forest. Mentawai Islands off W Sumatra: Siberut, Sipura and Pagai.

57   **Adult** Dark rufous-brown scops owl with dark-mottled supercilia and ear-tufts. Powerful feet, bare toes. Lacks nuchal band but with small white dots on hindneck; dark rufous-brown below with herringbone markings and light spots. Some individuals are more blackish-brown, others more rufous. Eyes brown (sometimes yellow?).

59   **Wallace's Scops Owl** *Otus silvicola*   **Text and map page 251**

Forest and secondary woodland, from lowland up to 2,000m. Lesser Sundas (Flores and Sumbawa).

59a   **Adult** Female shown. Large scops owl with long ear-tufts. Above, pale grey with longitudinal black markings and deep brown vermiculations, scapulars with ochre-white markings; breast and flanks light buffish with black shaft-stripes and dark brown wavy cross-bars. Eyes dull orange.

59b   **Juvenile** Lighter, with more rufous wash, and inconspicuous pattern and ear-tufts.

55b

55a

56a

55c

58

56b

56c

57

59b

59a

1997
Weick

PLATE 17: SCREECH OWLS

60   Western Screech Owl *Otus kennicottii*   **Text and map page 251**

Natural woodland and cactus desert, mesquite and scrub, at up to 2,500m. Western N America and Mexico. More pointed wings, strong feet and bill, yellow eyes; facial disc greyish with distinct dark rim; tarsi and toes well feathered; bill black to grey.

60a   **Adult** (nominate *kennicottii*: Pacific coast of N America south to California) Cold-brown morph, male. Fuscous dorsal ground colour, coarsely and boldly patterned in blackish to buffy-fuscous. Bill black to grey. (Subspecies *bendirei* is somewhat larger and more plain brown above.)

60b   **Adult** (*aikeni*: SW USA to N Mexico) Pale grey morph. Pale grey dorsal ground colour with broad black streaks; below, with broad streaks and widely spaced conspicuous cross-bars. Bill black. (Subspecies *cineraceus* is smaller, with less coarse pattern.)

60c   **Adult** (*vinaceus*: Mexico) Typical individual. Small. Washed vinaceous above, with black streaks. Bill black. Toes bristled. (Subspecies *xanthusi* similar, but with less vinaceous wash.)

60d   **Adult** (*suttoni*: Rio Grande, Texas, to Mexican Plateau) Blackest subspecies. Blackish-grey above with bold pattern. Bill black. (Subspecies *cardonensis* is similar, but dorsally more blackish-brown and with dense cross-bars below.)

61   Eastern Screech Owl *Otus asio*   **Text and map page 253**

Open forest, orchards and villages, riparian woodland, deciduous forest and scrub. Eastern N America and NE Mexico. Compared with Western Screech Owl, ground colour rich and warmer brown, buff and ruddy (red morph common); eyes yellow; bill green to dull turquoise.

61a   **Adult** (nominate *asio*: SE Canada to SE USA, New England States, New York, Pennsylvania and S Michigan) Grey-brown morph. Rich brown above, varying to buffy, grey or ruddy, with coarse pattern; ventral markings coarse and sparse.

61b   **Adult** (nominate *asio*) Red morph. In flight, showing pointed wings and plain dorsal colouring.

61c   **Adult** (*mccalli*: S Texas, N and NE Mexico) Grey morph. Smaller than nominate *asio*. Large ear-tufts. Dorsal ground colour buffy-grey, finely textured but with broader shaft-streaks; coarse pattern below, with many buffy and white patches. Bill green to dull turquoise.

61d   **Adult** (*maxwelliae*: NW USA) Grey morph. Palest and least-marked subspecies, pale buffy-grey above and largely whitish below. (Also occurs in pale rufous morph.) Bill yellow to greyish-green. (Subspecies *hasbroucki*, from Oklahoma to Texas, has plain buffy-grey ground colour but a coarse texture with bold pattern, and has dense black streaks and bars below.)

61e   **Adult** (*floridanus*: Florida to Louisiana) Red morph. Buffy-rufous colour. (Extreme red morphs are similar to red morph of nominate *asio*, 57b.) Toes bristled; bill pale greenish-horn.

61f   **Neoptile** (nominate *asio*) White down, also on tarsi and toes.

61g   **Mesoptile** (nominate *asio*) Red morph. Iris pale yellow; plumage light ochre to buff, barred above and below.

61h   **Mesoptile** (nominate *asio*) Grey morph. Wings similar to adult; indistinct ear-tufts.

60a
60b
60c
60d
61a
61b
61c
61d
61e
61f
61g
61h

1997
Weick

PLATE 18: SCREECH OWLS

62 Oaxaca Screech Owl *Otus lambi*   **Text and map page 254**

Lowlands with coastal mangroves, deciduous woods with gullies, and dense woods at up to about 300m. Oaxaca, Mexico.

> **62**   **Adult** Similar to Eastern Screech Owl, but with vinaceous on brown ground colour above and below. Pattern coarser; facial rim less distinct; bill olive-green with yellow tip; toes less feathered, more bristled. Eyes yellow.

63 Pacific Screech Owl *Otus cooperi*   **Text and map page 255**

Upper tropical lowland mangroves, also foothills, deciduous woods with palms and giant cacti, at up to 330m. Pacific side of C America from Tehuantepec to Costa Rica.

> **63**   **Adult** Relatively large size with pale appearance (no red morph); powerful feet and bristled toes. Tawny-grey above, with fine pattern and narrow stripes; ventral cross-bars reduced to little freckled dots and broken vermiculations. Eyes yellow. (Form '*chiapensis*' slightly browner above.)

64 Whiskered Screech Owl *Otus trichopsis*   **Text and map page 256**

Pine-oak woodland between 1,600m and 2,600m. SW USA and C America (SE Arizona, Mexico, Nicaragua). Smaller feet and bill than Eastern Screech Owl, more distinct facial rim and longer, denser bristles around bill; cervical collar. Eyes yellow.

> **64a**   **Adult** (*aspersus*: Arizona, Sonora and Chihuahua) Grey morph. Light grey ground colour, broad black shaft marks, medium ventral cross-bars. (No red morph.)
>
> **64b**   **Adult** (nominate *trichopsis*: south end of Mexican Plateau) Grey morph. Darker grey-brown ground colour, broad blackish marks and coarse ventral cross-bars.
>
> **64c**   **Adult** (nominate *trichopsis*) Red morph. Dorsal cross-bars reduced or lacking; ventral cross-bars less coarse than in grey-brown morph. Some are brighter red.
>
> **64d**   **Adult** (*mesamericanus*: C El Salvador, Honduras, and Nicaragua) Red morph. Above, brown with rufous-edged feathers; below, fine pattern with cross-bars. (A dull red morph with same fine pattern is frequent.)

65 Bearded Screech Owl *Otus barbarus*   **Text and map page 257**

Humid subtropical mountain forest, from about 1,350m up to 1,850m. C Guatemala and adjacent Chiapas, Mexico. Small owl with short ear-tufts and spotted appearance, and with tarsi feathered down to toes; wings project beyond tail; toes pinkish, eyes yellow, bill horn-green.

> **65a**   **Adult** Grey morph. Grey-brown above, boldly blotched with small double spots; below, marked with ocellated cross-bars and arrowheads.
>
> **65b**   **Adult** Red morph. Pattern identical to grey morph, but suffused with rufous.

66 Balsas Screech Owl *Otus seductus*   **Text and map page 257**

Tropical foothills with open, deciduous woods and giant cacti, also closed woods without undergrowth at up to 540m. SW Mexico.

> **66**   **Adult** Somewhat larger than Pacific Screech Owl. Warm brown ground colour above overlaid with vinaceous-pink, shaft-streaks distinct and broad; densely and narrowly barred below, breast with bold black dots. Tarsi densely feathered. Eyes dark brown, rarely golden-brown. (No red morph known.)

67 Bare-shanked Screech Owl *Otus clarkii*   **Text and map page 258**

Humid forest edge, also thinner woodland, locally in mountains from 900m up to 2,350m. C and S America from Costa Rica and Panama to NW Colombia.

> **67**   **Adult** Rather large, attractively coloured owl. Tarsi bare for more than half length; ear-tufts hardly distinguishable from loose crown feathers. Beautiful ventral colouring in white, rufous and black, with more or less ocellated appearance. Eyes yellow.

PLATE 19: SCREECH OWLS

68 Tropical Screech Owl *Otus choliba* **Text and map page 259**

Open tropical woodland, forest edge, secondary forest, savanna, towns, bamboo stands. Costa Rica to N Argentina; Trinidad. Similar to Eastern Screech Owl, with shorter ear-tufts; eyebrows and throat whitish, tarsi feathered; eyes yellow.

68a Adult (nominate *choliba*: S Matto Grosso and São Paulo south through Paraguay to NE Argentina and Uruguay) Grey morph. Light-coloured owl with ochre and buffy wash dorsally; below, fine herringbone pattern and rather white blotches. Greyish face with distinct rim.

68b Adult (nominate *choliba*) Red morph. In flight, showing rounded wings and reduced pattern.

68c Adult (*luctisomus*: Pacific slope from Costa Rica to canal zone of W Panama, and Pearl Islands) Pale morph. Distinctly paler plumage than nominate *choliba*, with less ochre and buff wash.

68d Adult (*crucigerus*: E Colombia, NE Peru to NE Brazil and Trinidad) More rufescent above and below than nominate *choliba*; fluffy yellow-ochre spots ventrally, breast with dense cross-bars.

68e Mesoptile (*crucigerus*) Wings as adult, with fluffy, downy dorsal and ventral plumage and indistinct bars. Crown, lores and face whitish.

68f Adult (*decussatus*: C and S Brazil) Red morph. Above, warm brown ground colour and less black pattern; below, rufous wash, darker on breast, with fine herringbone pattern and fluffy buff-orange spots.

68g Adult ('*portoricensis*': Colombia and adjacent Ecuador) Red morph. Bright rufous-brown owl with more or less reduced bars and broad shaft-streaks. May be a dark rufous morph of *crucigerus*.

68h Adult (*duidae*: Mts Duida and Neblina in S Venezuela) Darkest subspecies. Very dark above, with coarse black patterning on ochraceous ground colour, and crown pure black; below, ochre ground colour with dense but fine pattern.

69 Maria Koepcke's Screech Owl *Otus koepckeae* **Text and map page 261**

Andes between 1,500m and 4,500m, subtropical and lower temperate dry woodland and cloud forest. N Peru.

69 Adult Similar to Peruvian Screech Owl and race *duidae* of Tropical Screech Owl, but with grey ground colour above and indistinct broad bars, lacking nuchal collar; below, with more white, bold black shaft-streaks and irregular wavy cross-bars. Eyes yellow; feet powerful, with ochraceous-feathered tarsi and bare greyish toes.

70 Peruvian Screech Owl *Otus roboratus* **Text and map page 262**

Arid woodland, mesquite and arid vegetation with large cacti, from near sea-level up to about 2,500m. N Peru and SW Ecuador.

70 Adult (nominate *roboratus*: between W and C Andes in N Peru) Black head, pale nuchal collar contrasting with dark mantle; strong patterning below, with rufous wash and white spots. Individual variation in width and intensity of dark shaft-streaks, density of cross-bars and vermiculations, also in dorsal and ventral ground colour. (A red morph also occurs.) Eyes yellow; toes blue-grey or grey-olive; tarsi feathered. (Subspecies *pacificus*, inhabiting coastal lowlands and foothills of NW Peru and one locality in Ecuador, is distinctly smaller, lighter in body mass and paler in plumage; may be specifically distinct, but voice is similar. See text illustration on p.262.)

68a

68c

68d

68b

68f

68g

68e

68h

69

70

1997 WEICK

PLATE 20: SCREECH OWLS

71 Montane Forest Screech Owl *Otus hoyi*   **Text and map page 263**

Dense montane forest. Argentina (Salta, Jujuy and Tucuman) and S Bolivia (Santa Cruz). Similar to Tropical Screech Owl in the grey morph, but with indistinct facial rim, darker face, and hindcrown edged by a white narrow line; eyebrows not clear white as on Tropical Screech; below, with wide shaft-streaks, broadly tipped, with few bars and ochraceous wash. Tarsi feathered down to toes; eyes yellow and bill green-yellow.

  71a Adult Red morph. With ochre-rufous wash above and below, especially on wing-coverts and breast.

  71b Adult Grey-brown morph. Darker-coloured dorsally, stronger shaft-stripes; below, identical in pattern to red morph.

  71c Adult Grey-brown morph. In flight, showing the typical light cervical band.

72 Rufescent Screech Owl *Otus ingens*   **Text and map page 265**

Cloud forest of W Andes, from 1,300m up to 2,100m. Venezuela to Bolivia. Reduced facial rim and ear-tufts, dusky appearance; eyes brown.

  72a Adult (nominate *ingens*: Ecuador) Distinct nuchal band contrasting with dark neck. Brown ground colour above more buffy and less vermiculated than in *minimus*.

  72b Adult ('*minimus*': C Bolivia to C Peru) Darker dorsal coloration, distinct nuchal band; below, more sandy wash and more densely vermiculated than nominate *ingens*. These differences are within individual variation, and we include *minimus* in the nominate form.

73 Cloud-forest Screech Owl *Otus marshalli*   **Text and map page 266**

Humid cloud and moss forest in Andes, from 1,900m up to 2,250m. E Peru: Pasco, Cuzco.

  73 Adult Above, with rich chestnut ground colour and blackish transverse markings, whitish spots on occiput and a buffy nuchal band; wings banded dusky and tawny, tail with eight rufous and black bands. Eyes dark brown; toes dirty whitish.

74 Colombian Screech Owl *Otus colombianus*   **Text and map page 267**

Cloud forest in mountains, from 1,200m up to 1,850m. Colombia and N Venezuela to N Ecuador. Smaller than Rufescent Screech Owl and with terminal half of tarsus bare; no white below; eyes dark.

  74a Adult Reddish morph. Similar to greyish morph, with same pattern and shaft-streaks, but with rufous wash over entire plumage.

  74b Adult Grey-brown morph. Light eyebrows, nuchal band and scapulars. Above, a little more grey-brown, especially on back and lesser wing-coverts; greater coverts and secondaries distinctly paler.

75 Cinnamon Screech Owl *Otus petersoni*   **Text and map page 268**

Cloud forest. N Peru.

  75 Adult Distinctly smaller than Colombian Screech Owl, with warm buffy-brown plumage; less vermiculated on breast and belly. Head rather darker than back, pale buffy collar. Tarsi feathered to within 5mm of toes. Bill pale green-grey; toes pale pink; eyes brown.

71a

71b

72a

73

72b

71c

74b

74a

75

1997
Weick

PLATE 21: SCREECH OWLS

76   **Northern Tawny-bellied Screech Owl** *Otus watsonii*   **Text and map page 269**

Humid lowland forest. E Colombia and W Venezuela to Surinam, south to E Ecuador, NE Peru and NW Amazonia.

> **76**   **Adult** Dull greyish owl with distinct ear-tufts, dirty orange to amber-coloured eyes and densely feathered tarsi; toes bare. Above, grey ground colour covered with small light freckles and spots, contrasting with dark shaft-streaks and vermiculations; densely vermiculated breast but distinctly lighter throat, and belly with herringbone pattern on rusty or sandy ground colour. (Some individuals darker above and more rufous below.)

77   **Southern Tawny-bellied Screech Owl** *Otus usta*   **Text and map page 270**

Lowland rain forest. Brazil and Peru south of Amazon to northern lowland Bolivia.

> **77a**   **Adult** Red-brown morph. Vocally different from Northern Tawny-bellied. Upper surface with more rufous wash, dark crown; breast with heavier shaft-streaks than Northern Tawny-bellied, belly dark rufous with dense vermiculations. Eyes warm brown.
>
> **77b**   **Adult** Dark morph. In flight, showing rounded wings with 6th primary the longest. Much darker above.

78   **Black-capped Screech Owl** *Otus atricapillus*   **Text and map page 271**

Tropical lowland forest. E Paraguay, adjacent S Brazil and extreme NE Argentina. Long ear-tufts, chestnut or brown (sometimes yellow) eyes; crown nearly uniform dusky blackish; rather distinct scapular stripe; irregular bars, streaks and vermiculations below; bill greenish, bare toes grey to greyish-brown.

> **78a**   **Adult** Red morph. Rufous-brown above, heavily streaked and barred; forehead, breast and belly more or less rufous-washed, with nearly white abdomen.
>
> **78b**   **Adult** Grey-brown morph. Sometimes with yellow irides. Distinct dark rim around facial disc; more strongly striped breast with dense cross-bars, belly with finer, irregular cross-bars and white blotches.
>
> **78c**   **Adult** Dark morph. Nearly black cap and hindneck, distinct nuchal band, back strongly striped and barred; breast with more pronounced pattern than belly.

79   **Long-tufted Screech Owl** *Otus sanctaecatarinae*   **Text and map page 272**

Subtropical woodland, often with conifers (*Araucaria*). SE Brazil, NE Argentina (Misiones) and Uruguay. Similar to a large version of Black-capped Screech Owl with more powerful talons; eyes yellow to brown; tarsi feathered.

> **79a**   **Adult** Grey morph. Lighter, more buffy and ochraceous in colour than Black-capped. Dark pattern on hindneck, distinct nuchal collar; below, similar in pattern to Black-capped.
>
> **79b**   **Adult** Brown morph. Typically with much coarser pattern below.
>
> **79c**   **Adult** Red morph, in flight. Much more rufous plumage than red morph of Black-capped.

PLATE 22: SCREECH OWLS

80   Vermiculated Screech Owl *Otus vermiculatus*   **Text and map page 274**

Upper tropical mountain forest, up to 1,200m. Costa Rica to Panama, NW Colombia and NW Venezuela. Light rufous face, indistinct facial rim, densely vermiculated; lower quarter of tarsi bare. Eyes yellow.

> **80a   Adult** Grey-brown morph. More densely vermiculated than Guatemalan Screech Owl; similar to Rio Napo Screech Owl, but less warm brown.
>
> **80b   Adult** Rufous morph. With bright rufous wash above and below; more indistinct pattern on head and back.
>
> **80c   Adult** Dark variant. In flight, showing rounded wings and extremely dark upper surface.

81   Roraima Screech Owl *Otus roraimae*   **Text and map page 275**

Endemic to Venezuelan rain forest: Mt Roraima and Mt Duida.

> **81   Adult** Darker than Guatemalan Screech Owl, and very different in coarser plumage pattern and cross-bars ventrally. Eyes yellow.

82   Guatemalan Screech Owl *Otus guatemalae*   **Text and map page 276**

Broadleaved woods and rain forest, tropical deciduous woods and thorn forest of the lowlands and foothills up into oak woodlands to 1,200m about sea-level. Mexico to Middle America. Distinct vermiculations, face more pale grey or brown; lower 1-4mm of tarsi bare. Eyes yellow.

> **82a   Adult** (nominate *guatemalae*: Isthmus of Tehuantepec, Mexico, to Honduras) Greyish morph. Less vermiculated than Vermiculated Screech Owl. Sandy-brown ground colour above; below, breast sandy-brown and densely patterned, belly more whitish and less mottled. (A red morph is frequent.)
>
> **82b   Adult** (*cassini*: Mexico, from Vera Cruz to Tamaulipas) Smaller and darker than nominate *guatemalae*. Plumage similar to Whiskered Screech Owl (Plate 18), but with ochre malar stripe, occipital and nuchal collars. Tarsi feathered down to joint of toes.
>
> **82c   Adult** (nominate *guatemalae*) In flight, showing upper surface (also typical of subspecies *hastatus* and *dacrysistactus* of W Mexico, E Honduras and N Nicaragua to N Costa Rica).
>
> **82d   Juvenile** (nominate *guatemalae*) Red morph. Wings as adult but with indistinct barring.

83   Rio Napo Screech Owl *Otus napensis*   **Text and map page 277**

Upper tropical mountain forest from 250m up to 1,500m. E Ecuador and E Colombia to N Bolivia. Dense vermiculations ending on lower breast and diminishing towards abdomen; tarsi feathered down to toes close to joint; eyes yellow, sometimes brown.

> **83a   Adult** (nominate *napensis*: E Ecuador and E Colombia). Dark cinnamon-brown morph. Brown-eyed individual, with typical white belly and abdomen.
>
> **83b   Adult** (*helleri*: E Peru) Light cinnamon-buff morph. With dense vermiculations on belly and abdomen. (Subspecies *bolivianus* less vermiculated, with distinct shaft-streaks and cross-bars on lower breast and belly.)

84   Puerto Rican Screech Owl *Otus nudipes*   **Text and map page 278**

Dense woodland, thickets and caves. Puerto Rico, Isla de Vieques, St Thomas, St John and St Croix. Lacks erectile ear-tufts; legs bare for more than half length; eyes brown; rounded wings as Guatemalan Screech Owl.

> **84a   Adult** (nominate *nudipes*: Puerto Rico) Rufescent morph. Underparts more heavily streaked and vermiculated than in *newtoni*. (Some have a more plain red colour dorsally; a brownish morph with more reduced pattern also occurs.)
>
> **84b   Adult** (*newtoni*: St Croix, Vieques, St Thomas and St John) Brownish-grey morph. Less densely vermiculated and streaked below.

80a

80b

83b

80c

81

82c

83a

82a

84a

84b

82d

82b

97
WEICK

PLATE 23: BARE-LEGGED, SCOPS AND SCREECH OWLS

87   **Cuban Bare-legged Owl** *Gymnoglaux lawrencii*   **Text and map page 281**

Limestone country with dense forest, thickets and caves. Cuba and Isle of Pines. Lacks erectile ear-tufts; eyes brown, sometimes yellow; long, bare tarsi; short-winged; relatively long tail with only 10 feathers.

87a   **Adult** More spotted above, and with banded tail, often distinct rufous tinge; below, with brown throat and drop-shaped shaft-streaks.

87b   **Probable subadult** Above, less spotted and with plain tail feathers; below, less distinct throat band and fewer shaft-stripes.

87c   **Adult** In flight, showing short, rounded wings and long tail and legs.

86   **Palau Scops Owl** *Pyrroglaux podarginus*   **Text and map page 280**

Mangrove, rain forest and villages. Lowlands of Palau (Micronesia). Rufous-coloured, small owl with hardly visible ear-tufts and bare tarsi.

86a   **Adult** Intermediate. (Much darker rufous and lighter-coloured morphs also occur, with greater or lesser amount of spots and bars.) Eyes orange-yellow; bill and toes whitish-cream.

86b   **Juvenile** Colour of eyes uncertain, may also be darker.

85   **White-throated Screech Owl** *Otus albogularis*   **Text and map page 279**

Humid forest and cloud forest, from 1,300m up to about 3,600m. Andes from Colombia and NW Venezuela, through Ecuador to Peru and C Bolivia. Large, dark owl with rounded head, no conspicuous ear-tufts but loose, fluffy crown feathers, lacking facial rim; lores brown, throat white; rounded wings and relatively long tail; eyes yellow to orange, bill yellow to olive-green; toes bare, yellow to pinkish flesh-coloured.

85a   **Adult** (nominate *albogularis*: Andes of Bogotá, Colombia, and Ecuador) Darker than *meridensis*, with more rufous-orange ventrally, less white on abdomen, and less freckled dorsally.

85b   **Adult** (*meridensis*: Andes of Mérida, Venezuela) Forehead and supercilia much whiter and crown and back more spotted than nominate *albogularis*; sides of head brown; dorsal spots larger and pale ochre; belly more buffy and with more white, especially on abdomen.

85c   **Adult** (*remotus*: E Andes from Peru to Bolivia) Darkest subspecies. Almost black above with cream-buff and white spots; secondaries and primaries with sandy-buff ground colour; belly and abdomen creamy-buff to white.

85d   **Adult** (*macabrum*: W Andes from Colombia and W Ecuador to W Peru) In flight. Similar to nominate, but with finer pattern below and reduced markings on inner webs of primaries.

PLATE 24: WHITE-FACED AND GIANT SCOPS OWLS

88 Northern White-faced Scops Owl *Ptilopsis leucotis*   **Text and map page 282**

Dry savanna and thornveld with scattered trees, arid open forest, woodland with closed canopy, edges and clearings. Sub-Saharan Africa, from Senegambia eastwards to Sudan, Somalia, N Uganda and N Kenya; in Uganda and Kenya, probably sympatric with Southern White-faced Scops Owl. Rather large scops owl with long ear-tufts, broadly dark-rimmed white face, heavily barred plumage, and yellow-orange to orange-red eyes; tarsi feathered down to middle of toes; toes bristled.

88a **Adult** Typical light morph. Above, pale greyish-brown, densely streaked and vermiculated; ear-tufts long, black-banded, more blackish on outer web; scapulars with white outer webs, edged black; tail and flight feathers with numerous light and dark bands. Below, somewhat lighter, with same pattern as dorsally.

88b **Adult** Light morph. In flight, showing rounded wings with 8th primary longest.

88c **Adult** Dark morph. Dark-crowned, with darker face and much darker ochraceous wash. (Formerly treated as subspecies '*nigrovertex*', but occurs with and interbreeds with light morph.)

88d **Mesoptile** Distinct facial rim, darker crown and back. Egg also shown.

88e **Adult** ('*margarethae*': frequent in Sudan) Probably only a pale, sandy-coloured morph.

89 Southern White-faced Scops Owl *Ptilopsis granti*   **Text and map page 283**

Dry savanna, thornveld. SW Kenya and Uganda, south to Cape Province and Natal, west to Namibia, Angola and Congo.

89 **Adult** Darker and more grey than Northern White-faced. Individual variation in both species, with light and dark birds, making separation difficult, but vocalisations different.

90 Giant Scops Owl *Mimizuku gurneyi*   **Text and map page 285**

Humid forest and secondary woodland in lowlands. SE Philippines: Dinagat, Siargao and Mindanao.

90a **Adult** Typical individual. A large and attractively coloured scops owl with long, slightly curved ear-tufts. Face unmarked rufous; crown dark rufous with dark brown stripes; upperparts and uppertail-coverts rufous with black spots, forming three long stripes; wings rufous with brown markings and bands; tail brown. Throat plain rufous; breast and flanks rufous with black shaft-streaks; belly lighter rufous to white, less streaked. Bill greyish-white; eyes warm brown; feet light grey, claws white, tipped dark grey.

90b **Adult** In flight, showing rounded wings with 7th or 6th primary longest.

88a

88b

90a

88c

88e

90

89

88d

1995 WEICK

PLATE 25: MANED, CRESTED AND JAMAICAN OWLS

91   Maned Owl *Jubula lettii*   **Text and map page 285**

Humid lowland forest. Cameroon east to Zaire, also Liberia and Ghana.

> **91a   Adult** Perched and in flight. Medium-sized (much as European Long-eared Owl). Varies somewhat in plumage, but always rufous. Crown and nape feathers elongated, long prominent ear-tufts. Facial disc rufous, finely barred and dark rimmed; throat white. Distinct scapular band; rufous lesser wing-coverts contrasting with remaining coverts and tertials; tail rufous with dusky bars. Upper breast finely vermiculated; lower breast and belly paler, streaked dusky brown. Legs plain rufous; bill and toes yellow, cere greenish; eyes deep yellow to orange.

> **91b   Juvenile** Densely covered with downy feathers, finely barred rufous; crown and face almost white. Wings and rectrices similar to adult.

92   Crested Owl *Lophostrix cristata*   **Text and map page 286**

Humid forest and second-growth woodland, also groves and thickets, from lowlands up to 1,500m. S Mexico to Panama, W and N Colombia, W Venezuela, the Guianas, E Ecuador, E Peru, N Bolivia and W Amazonian Brazil. Medium-sized owl with prominent white eyebrows continuing into long, erectile, partially white ear-tufts; highly variable in plumage (distinctive subspecies *stricklandi* perhaps a separate species).

> **92a   Adult** (nominate *cristata*: from upper Amazon southwards) Dark-faced chocolate-brown morph. Dark chocolate-brown upperside and breast, with uniform or light scapulars and paler-spotted and -banded wings, tail with fine bars; belly and legs tawny-buff, finely barred and vermiculated, but uniform abdomen and undertail-coverts. Eyes dark orange-brown to chestnut; tarsi feathered; cere and toes yellowish; bill horn-coloured with pale tip.

> **92b   Adult** (nominate *cristata*) Rufous-faced chocolate-brown morph. In flight, showing rounded wings with 7th primary longest. Similar to 91a, but with deep rufous face.

> **92c   Adult** (nominate *cristata*) Rufous-brown morph. Buffy-brown above, crown, neck and upper breast somewhat darker, but pale throat; paler buff below (or, frequently, whitish-grey). Dark brown lesser and median wing-coverts contrasting with paler greater coverts and remiges. Tail plain buffy.

> **92d   Adult** (*stricklandi*: S Mexico to W Panama and W Colombia) Typical individual. Tawny to chestnut face, dark-rimmed. Upperparts with much lighter scapulars, unspotted greater coverts and secondaries with fine vermiculations, outermost coverts sometimes with pale patches, primaries with few bars; densely barred below, bars wider on abdomen and undertail-coverts. Eyes yellow. (Darker-coloured individuals also occur.)

93   Jamaican Owl *Pseudoscops grammicus*   **Text and map page 288**

Forest edges, gardens near houses. Jamaica.

> **93   Adult** Perched and in flight. Small, tawny-brown owl with dark brown and black shaft-streaks, bars and flecks. Face amber to light cinnamon, bordered white, with rim speckled black and white; below, buffy-yellow to yellow-ochre, streaked dusky brown. Eyes hazel; legs and feet tawny; bill horn-yellow.

91a

91b

91a

92c

92b

92a

92d

93

93

1995 Weick

PLATE 26: GREAT HORNED OWLS

94   **Great Horned Owl** *Bubo virginianus*   **Text and map page 289**

Boreal forest and deciduous woodland, dry forested uplands, foothill ravines and river bottoms, aspen forest, isolated groves, grassland, and deserts with rocky canyons and steep gullies; from sea-level to 3,300m in Rocky Mountains and to 4,300m in Andes. Whole America, from Alaska to Argentina. Plumage darkest in warm and temperate climates, lightest in cold surroundings; females larger than males; eyes yellow, bill greyish; tarsi and toes densely feathered. (The number of recognised subspecies seems much too large, and many taxa require intensive study.)

94a   **Adult** (nominate *virginianus*: Canada to Florida) Typical female, perched and in flight. Neither darkly saturated nor strikingly pale; comparatively large amount of rusty-red. Black and white barring below in rather soft contrast; facial disc mostly clear rusty. Feathering of toes and tarsi varies from reddish-buff to cream. (Paler and darker grey individuals also occur.) (Subspecies *mesembrinus* from Costa Rica matches the more northerly nominate *virginianus* in plumage.)

94b   **Juvenile** (nominate *virginianus*) Downy plumage densely barred buff and grey; distinct rufous face and dark rim visible.

94c   **Adult** (*wapacuthu*: N and NE North America) Pale morph, female. Palest subspecies: much white, with little or no reddish visible below, and with pale shades of buff above. Mostly black and white, with white predominating. Face white or light ashy. Feet immaculate white to creamy or pale buff with some bars. (Whiter and darker individuals occur.) (Forms *subarcticus* and *occidentalis* are probably synonyms.)

94d   **Adult** (*saturatus*: NW North America from Alaska to California) Female. Very dark and saturated above, with black predominating. Face grey or reddish-grey to dark rusty. Feet grey to light buff, more or less barred. (A lighter-coloured morph occurs.) (This subspecies includes *heterocnemis* and *lagophonus* as synonyms.)

94e   **Adult** (*pallescens*: SE California, Arizona, New Mexico and C Texas south to Lower California and N Mexico) Female. Much smaller and much paler than nominate. (A darker morph, with darker colours predominating, is frequent.) (Subspecies *melanocercus* is here regarded as a synonym of *pallescens*.)

94f   **Adult** (*nigrescens*: NW Peru, Ecuador and Colombia) Female. Differs from all other subspecies in much blacker plumage and reduction of fulvous tints. Much darker than *saturatus*, with smaller size. (Subspecies *colombianus* is probably a synonym.)

94g   **Adult** (*nacurutu*: NW Venezuela, Guyana and Colombia southwards east of Andes to Bolivia, C Argentina and Uruguay) Typical individual. Similar to Magellan Great Horned, but rather larger, with longer and stronger bill, stronger talons, and ventral barring more widely spaced. Less fuscous than *nigrescens*. (Forms *scotinus* and *elutus* are probably synonyms.)

95   **Magellan Horned Owl** *Bubo magellanicus*   **Text and map page 290**

Rocky landscapes with pasture above timberline, semi-open *Nothofagus* forest rich in lichens and mosses, rocky semi-desert from sea-level to mountainous regions, locally near human settlements with parks. C Peru, Bolivia, Chile and Argentina south to Cape Horn.

95   **Adult** Light morph. Smaller than Great Horned Owl (*nacurutu*), with relatively smaller bill and feet and with denser barring below, and also very different vocally. Eyes yellow.

94a

94d

94a

94d

94b

94e

94d

94f

95

94g

1995 WEICK

96   Eurasian Eagle Owl *Bubo bubo*   **Text and map page 292**

Extremely variable habitat, from boreal coniferous and mixed deciduous forests to Mediterranean scrub, woody and grassy steppes, also rocky and sandy deserts; nests in Alps up to 2,100m (hunting to 2,800m), in Himalayas to 4,500m, in Tibetan highlands to 4,700m. Palearctic, from continental Europe and Scandinavia east across Russia to C Siberia, Sea of Okhotsk, Sakhalin and Japan, in south to Mediterranean region, Turkey, N Iraq, Iran, Afghanistan, Pakistan, India, Tibet, China and Korea. Plumage considerably darker in humid, oceanic regions than in arid continental areas; size increases from warm regions to cold northern areas or high-altidute surroundings.

96a   **Adult** (nominate *bubo*: Europe, south to France, Sicily, Greece, Romania and Ukraine, east to Moscow) Female, also in flight. Darkest race. Dorsal ground colour golden-brown to tawny-buff, crown, mantle, scapulars and upperwing-coverts with large black feather tips; hindneck and underparts broadly streaked black. (Scandinavian birds are darkest in colour.) Eyes bright golden-yellow to red-orange; bill greyish-black to black, cere olive-grey; claws black; tarsi and toes densely feathered. Intergrades with slightly smaller and greyer *hispanus* from Iberian Peninsula and (formerly) N Africa. (Subspecies *ruthenus*, east of nominate *bubo* to western Ural river and south to lower Volga basin, and *interpositus*, south of nominate in Bessarabia, Crimea, Caucasus, Asia Minor and Iran, are very similar in plumage, slightly greyer or darker, with less or more ochraceous wash.)

96b   **Mesoptile** (nominate *bubo*) Down long and soft, scapulars and greater upperwing-coverts rather feather-like; rusty-buff to dirty cream in colour. Eyes pale yellow to pale yellow-orange; cere bluish-grey.

96c   **Juvenile** (nominate *bubo*) Downy, long and soft, pale ochre and dirty cream mesoptile feathers. Eyebrows, area surrounding eyes, lores and throat white; scapulars, greater upperwing-coverts, secondaries and tail feathers similar to adult, but narrower, with more pointed tips; primaries hardly not visible or hardly so. Eyes yellow-orange.

96d   **Adult** (*sibiricus*: W Siberia and Bashkiria to middle Ob and W Altai, north to limits of forest) Female, also in flight. Pale ground colour mixed cream and white or clear white. Crown, hindneck and underparts only narrowly streaked black; limited spots on back, scapulars and upperwing-coverts, indistinctly vermiculated grey, cream or white; belly and flanks finely streaked and vermiculated. Tarsi and toes white. In flight, shows darker upperwing-coverts and dark tips to greater primary coverts. (Subspecies *yenisseensis* of C Siberia has slightly darker plumage, with light grey and ochre predominating.)

96e   **Adult** (*jakutensis*: NE Siberia) Male. Above, much darker and more brownish than *yenisseensis*; whitish belly more distinctly streaked and barred than *sibiricus*. (Subspecies *ussuriensis* of SE Siberia, N China and Kuriles rather darker above than *jakutensis*, with more ochre wash on belly.)

96f   **Adult** (*hemachalana*: Tien Shan and Fergana to Pamir Mountains, north to Kara Tau, south to Baluchistan and Himalayas; similar individuals known from Turkestan, Korea and S China) Male. A pale and distinctly brown race, similar to *swinhoei* of SE China and to the specifically distinct Rock Eagle Owl (Plate 28).

96a

96b

96c

96a

96d

96d

96f

96e

1995 WEICK

96   Eurasian Eagle Owl *Bubo bubo* (cont.)   **Text and map page 292**

96g   Adult (*omissus*: Turkmenia and adjacent Iran, Chinese Turkestan; intergrades with *turcomanus* and *hemachalana*) Male. Typical desert form. Pale ochre ground colour, less rusty than *nikolskii*; dark markings only slightly developed above and below. (Very similar to this subspecies is the rather smaller and greyer *turcomanus* from area between Volga and upper Ural east to Transbaikalia and W Mongolia.)

96h   Adult (*nikolskii*: Iran to Pakistan) Female, also in flight. Smaller than *omissus*, with more rusty wash, less dark dorsally, and with less dark and finer breast pattern and fine vermiculations on belly.

97   Pharaoh Eagle Owl *Bubo ascalaphus*   **Text and map page 294**

Open rocky woodland, desert. N Africa from Morocco to Egypt, Sinai Peninsula, Israel, Syria, W Iraq, Arabia, and across southern Sahara from Ethiopia and Sudan to Mauritania, Mali and Niger.

97a   Adult (nominate *ascalaphus*: N Africa east to Sinai and Israel/Palestine) Female, also in flight. Variable in colour. Short ear-tufts. Buff-orange ground colour with pinkish tinge. Dorsally rather blacker markings than Eurasian Eagle Owl, more triangular at feather tips; dark bands on flight feathers and tail sharp and rather narrow; also differently shaped spots on breast, belly with fine indistinct vermiculations. Eyes yellow to orange-red.

97b   Mesoptile (nominate *ascalaphus*) Buffy-coloured downy mesoptile feathers, paler on face, rim and tarsi; indistinct barring above.

97c   Adult (*desertorum*: W Iraq and Arabia, and southern Sahara) Female. Light sandy-pink to white ground colour, much-reduced pattern above and below. Eyes tawny-yellow to orange-yellow; also short ear-tufts. (Intergrades with nominate *ascalaphus* can be encountered in overlap areas.)

98   Rock Eagle Owl *Bubo bengalensis*   **Text and map page 295**

Forest, woodland and semi-desert, from lowlands up to mountains to about 2,400m. S Asia, from Pakistan and India to W Burma; overlaps with race *turcomanus* of Eurasian Eagle Owl in Kashmir.

98   Adult Typical richly coloured morph. Also in flight, showing pointed wings with 8th primary longest. Relatively small size, but with powerful feet; tarsi and toes fully feathered. Eyes orange-yellow to bright reddish-orange; bill horn-brown; claws horn-black. (A much darker morph also occurs, more dusky and densely patterned above and below.)

96g

96h

96h

97a

97a

98

98

97b

97c

1995 WEICK

PLATE 29: AFRICAN EAGLE OWLS

99 Cape Eagle Owl *Bubo capensis*   **Text and map page 297**

Grassland, evergreen forest, open rocky terrain, mostly in highlands above 2,000m. E Africa from
Ethiopia south to W Mozambique, E Zimbabwe, S Namibia and South Africa (where occurs at sea-
level). Large dark brown eagle owl with dark blotching on sides of breast; larger than Spotted Eagle
Owl (Plate 30), with more powerful feet; tarsi and toes densely feathered, soles yellow; eyes yellow to
yellow-orange; bill dusky horn.

99a **Adult** (nominate *capensis*: South Africa and S Namibia) Perched and in flight. Smallest
subspecies, with dark brown crown, long ear-tufts and off-white face. Dark-blotched breast
often with less rufous and buffy wash than in other subspecies.

99b **Mesoptile** (nominate *capensis*) About 20 days old. Completely covered with sparse off-white
down. Grey cere and yellow eyes.

99c **Juvenile** (nominate *capensis*) About 55 days old. Grey mesoptile feathers barred with dark
brown to rufous and with less distinct markings; head, throat and tarsi off-white to greyish-
white. Barely visible ear-tufts.

99d **Adult** (*dilloni*: Ethiopian highlands and S Eritrea) Rather smaller than nominate *capensis*, less
boldly marked above and below, no large white blotching on breast and belly, but distinctly
barred on white to rufous-washed belly and abdomen.

99e **Adult** (*mackinderi*: Kenyan highlands, reappearing at Iringa, Tanzania, and Mozambique, with
single record from Malawi) More ochre blotches above, and often with more rufous tinge
below, but noticeably large size is the only certain distinction from nominate *capensis*.

100 Akun Eagle Owl *Bubo leucostictus*   **Text and map page 298**

Mostly humid lowland forest. Uncommon resident in W Africa from Guinea, Liberia and Sierra Leone
east to Cameroon south to mouth of Congo River, east to Zaire and south to NW Angola.

100a **Adult** Above, rufous-brown with dusky wavy bars; head and ear-tufts dark brown with rufous
wash, facial disc with fine rufous barring; tail dusky brown with pale bars and white tip. White
below, marbled with dusky brown and with rufous bars. Considerable variation in density of
markings and of rufous wash. Feet small and weak, pale yellow; cere and bill pale greenish-
horn; eyes yellow.

100b **Adult** In flight, showing dark appearance and light-coloured nuchal area.

99a

99a

99d

99b

99c

99e

100b

100a

1975
WEICK

PLATE 30: AFRICAN EAGLE OWLS

101 Spotted Eagle Owl *Bubo africanus* Text and map page 299

Savanna, woodland except primary lowland forest, also semi-desert. Africa from Uganda, Kenya and southern limit of C African rainforest in Zaire and Gabon south to the Cape, and S Arabian Peninsula. Medium-sized eagle owl, notably smaller than Cape Eagle Owl (Plate 29) and with less contrasting markings and blotching, without dark patches on breast; finely barred underparts and weaker feet.

101a **Adult** (nominate *africanus*: Africa) Grey morph. Much individual variation in greyness and in markings. Undertail-coverts and thighs almost plain white or with rufous wash. Bill black; eyes yellow, rimmed black; toes dark horn-yellow. (An uncommon chestnut-coloured morph also occurs.)

101b **Adult** (nominate *africanus*) Brown morph. In flight, showing spotted appearance.

101c **Mesoptile** (nominate *africanus*) Completely covered with silky-white down. Cere pink; toes slate-blue.

101d **Juvenile** (nominate *africanus*) Whitish head, back and lesser wing-coverts sparsely barred brown; below, especially on breast, washed browner, less distinctly barred. Wings as adult.

101e **Adult** (*milesi*: Arabia, east to United Arabian Emirates and Oman) More tawny in colour. (Other described subspecies, such as *tanae* from Tana river, Kenya, and *trothae* from Namibia, seem to be paler local extremes without subspecific characters.)

102 Vermiculated Eagle Owl *Bubo cinerascens* Text and map page 301

Open wooded areas, savanna with acacia groves, rocky semi-desert, mountain slopes and bushland. Senegambia to Somalia, south to N Uganda and N Kenya; includes form *kollmannspergeri* from Chad.

102 **Adult** Above, more finely vermiculated, less spotted; below, fine bars and vermiculations. Overall, browner-washed than Spotted Eagle Owl. Eyes dark brown, rimmed pinkish-red (at all ages); cere and bill grey. Small size.

103 Fraser's Eagle Owl *Bubo poensis* Text and map page 302

Humid lowland forest. W and C Africa.

103a **Adult** (nominate *poensis*: Liberia east to Congo Basin, Zaire and SW Uganda, south to N Angola) Perched and in flight. Degree of rufous and density of barring varies considerably. Above, rufous and buff, barred with dusky brown; prominent long ear-tufts edged dusky brown; facial disc pale rufous, with distinct rim. Underparts pale rufous to white, barred dusky and rufous. Bill pale blue-grey; eyes brown, eyelids blue; feet pale blue-grey. (Juvenile plumage very similar to 103c.)

103b **Adult** (*vosseleri*, Usambara Eagle Owl: Bioko and N Tanzania) Known from only few specimens, but kept in captivity (zoos). Larger than nominate *poensis*. Breast more blotched, less regularly barred; more orange-rufous wash above and below; face orange-rufous. Belly with fine barring and shaft-streaks. (Considered a separate species by some authors.)

103c **Juvenile** (*vosseleri*) Known from only one specimen. Bill and feet pale bluish.

101a

101e

101b

103a

102

101c

101d

103b

103a

103c

1995 DIEICK

PLATE 31: AFRICAN EAGLE OWLS

104 Verreaux's Eagle Owl *Bubo lacteus*   **Text and map page 303**

Woodland, riparian forest, savanna and semi-deserts. Africa south of Sahara (absent from deserts in Namibia and tropical rain forests of W and C Africa).

104a **Adult** Perched and in flight. Pale, grey-brown, large eagle owl with fine white vermiculations and slightly greyish wash. Ear-tufts more dusky, off-white facial disc with broad dark rim; black bristles around bill. Scapulars, outer median and greater wing-coverts with whitish outer webs, remiges broadly banded with dark and light brown; all wing feathers densely vermiculated. Tail broadly barred dark and light brown, finely vermiculated. Below, grey-brown to buffy with fine vermiculations. Bill pale creamy-horn with dark grey base and cere; eyes dark brown, upper bare eyelid pink; feet horn; claws dark brown, tipped black.

104b **Mesoptile** Light grey down feathers with brown wash and faint darker bars; neoptile plumage completely creamy-white. Immatures similar to adult, often with browner wash.

105 Shelley's Eagle Owl *Bubo shelleyi*   **Text and map page 304**

Humid forest. Upper and Lower Guinea, Liberia, Ghana, Cameroon, Gabon and NE Zaire.

105a **Adult** Dark morph. Dusky brown above, with few white feathers on occiput between the large, dusky ear-tufts; facial disc darker brown than in the light morph; wings with darker ground colour and broader bars, especially on secondaries. Below, broadly barred dark brown with narrower white bars and terminal bands. Bill creamy-horn, base and cere blue; eyes dark brown; feet pale cream; claws pale grey and dark-tipped.

105b **Juvenile** Above and below, white with brown bars, and more or less rufous to buffy wash; head and neck much darker, with sooty wash. Remiges and rectrices similar to adult. Downy young undescribed.

105c **Adult** Typical light morph, also in flight. Much whiter above and below. Off-white face with darker bars; back and wings with more distinct light bars, less broad barring on secondaries; below, also less broad brown bars, showing more white ground colour with buffy wash.

104a

104a

104b

105b

105c

105c

105a

1995
WEICK

PLATE 32: SOUTH ASIAN EAGLE OWLS

106 Barred Eagle Owl *Bubo sumatranus*   **Text and map page 305**

Humid forest with pools and streams, from lowlands up to 1,600m above sea-level. S Burma, S Thailand, Malay Peninsula and Greater Sundas. Medium-sized eagle owl, blackish-brown above, finely barred with buff; long, outward-slanting ear-tufts; eyebrows white; eyes dark brown, bill and feet pale yellow.

  106a **Adult** (nominate *sumatranus*: S Burma to Malay Peninsula, Sumatra and Banka) Perched and in flight. Smaller than *strepitans*. Breast band with broad and dense bars on buff ground colour; more broken bars on belly, less widely spaced than in *strepitans*, on greyish-white ground colour.

  106b **Adult** (*tenuifasciatus*: Borneo) Size as nominate *sumatranus*, but breast band with finer bars, belly also finer-barred, and more dense unbroken bars on flanks.

  106c **Adult** (*strepitans*: Java and Bali) Larger size; cross-bars on buffy breast and greyish-white belly broad and well spaced.

  106d **Juvenile** (*strepitans*) Above and below, white mesoptile plumage with buffy-brown bars; face and throat unspotted white. Secondaries and tail feathers as adult.

107 Forest Eagle Owl *Bubo nipalensis*   **Text and map page 306**

Heavy forest, from evergreen and deciduous tropical lowland forest and forested hills to montane wet temperate forest up to 2,100m. Lower Himalayas from Kumaon eastwards to C Laos, south to Sri Lanka and S Thailand. Large eagle owl with heavy legs and toes, feathered tarsi; ear-tufts long, thick and conspicuous; similar in colour and habits to smaller Malaysian counterpart (106); eyes dark brown; bill and toes pale yellow.

  107a **Adult** (*blighi*: Sri Lanka) Distinctly smaller and lighter-coloured than nominate *nipalensis*. Lacks dark pectoral band; belly with somewhat honey-brown wash.

  107b **Adult** (nominate *nipalensis*: rest of range) Perched and in flight. Larger and darker above than *blighi*. Distinct honey-brown pectoral band, and larger bars on breast and belly. (Juvenile similar in plumage to young Barred Eagle Owl.)

106a

106a

106b

106d

106c

107b

107b

107a

1995 Weick

PLATE 33: SOUTH ASIAN EAGLE OWLS AND FISH OWLS

108 Dusky Eagle Owl *Bubo coromandus*   **Text and map page 307**

Riparian woodland, dense groves and stands of densely foliages trees, near water, in lowlands. Indian subcontinent south of Himalayas; also rare and of uncertain status in Burma, S Thailand and Malay Peninsula.

108a Adult (nominate *coromandus*: Indian subcontinent) Perched and in flight. Grey and sooty-washed large eagle owl, ear-tufts outward-slanting or erect and close to each other (like twin spires). Overall, including ear-tufts, greyish-brown, finely spotted and vermiculated with whitish, especially on underparts, with dark shaft-stripes. Scapulars buffy-white on outer webs. Wing and tail feathers dark brown with pale cross-bands and broad tips. Iris pale yellow; bill and cere leaden-bluish; toes plumbeous-grey, soles lighter grey. Tarsi feathered, toes bristled.

108b Adult (nominate *coromandus*) Showing ear-tufts erected.

109 Philippine Eagle Owl *Bubo philippensis*   **Text and map page 308**

Humid forest. Philippines. Small-sized and 'short-eared' eagle owl; tarsi feathered; irides yellow to golden-brown; bill tan with light tip; toes pale grey.

109a Adult (nominate *philippensis*: Luzon, Catanduanes) Perched and in flight. Above rufous ground colour with black shaft-stripes; tail dull rufous, barred with dark brown. Throat whitish. Below, pale buffy with fine dark shaft-streaks.

109b Adult (*mindanensis*: Samar, Leyte, Cebu, Mindanao) Similar to nominate *philippensis*, but distinctly darker rufous above; darker below, with broader and more numerous shaft-streaks.

110 Buffy Fish Owl *Bubo ketupu*   **Text and map page 309**

Tree-bordered waterways, riparian forest, rice paddies and mangroves, from lowlands up to 1,600m. S Burma and S Thailand to Malaya and Greater Sundas. Medium-sized, yellowish-brown fish owl with conspicuous ear-tufts; tarsi and toes bare; rich brown above, mottled with black and buffy edges, and rufous-buff below with black shaft-streaks.

110a Adult (nominate *ketupu*: entire range except Burma, Thailand, N Borneo and Nias Island) Rufous morph, female. Whole bird with deep rufous wash. Bare tarsi, feet greyish-yellow; eyes yellow; bill greyish-black.

110b Adult (nominate *ketupu*) Fulvous morph, also in flight. White lores and eyebrows. Crown, ear-tufts and underparts distinctly fulvous-tinged, also greater wing-coverts and flight and tail feathers.

111 Tawny Fish Owl *Bubo flavipes*   **Text and map page 310**

Riparian forest, at up to 1,500m in Nepal, 2,100m in Darjeeling. NW India and W China to SE China, Taiwan, south to NE Burma, N Laos and Vietnam. Similar to Brown (Plate 34) and Buffy Fish Owls, but more powerful, with distinct pale scapular band; tarsi feathered down to about half length, to about one third at rear; toes bare.

111a Adult Above, rich orange-rufous to tawny, with broad black shaft-stripes, strong buffy wash on greater wing-coverts and secondaries; wing and tail feathers banded dark brown and buff. Below, rich orange-rufous with dark brown shaft-streaks, broadest on chest. Eyebrows, lores and throat patch white. Eyes yellow; cere and bill greyish; feet pale greenish-yellow.

111b Adult In flight, showing the strong banding on wings and tail.

108a

108a

109a

108b

109a

109b

110b

110a

111b

110b

111a

Weick
95

PLATE 34: FISH OWLS

112 Blakiston's Fish Owl *Bubo blakistoni*   **Text and map page 311**

Riparian forest, beside rivers in undisturbed coniferous forest or dense mixed and broadleaved forest, thickets along streams, islands in fast-flowing waters, also dense forest bordering lakes, river mouths and sea coasts. E Asia, from N Sea of Okhotsk, Amur basin and Sakhalin south to Manchuria, N Korea, S Kuriles and N Japan. Very similar to large eagle owls, with tarsi completely feathered at front, but plumage less soft than in *Bubo*; toes naked, sparsely bristled and remarkably slender; facial ruff little developed; head flattened, ear-tufts dense and with a great number of feathers; long, heavy bill.

> **112a** **Adult** (*doerriesi*) Pale buffy head, back and underparts with fine shaft-stripes and rufous to brown barring and vermiculation; tail feathers with white ground colour and dark brown bands. Tarsi off-white to white.
>
> **112b** **Adult** (*doerriesi*) In flight. A pale subspecies, showing the white occipital spots. (Subspecies *piscivorus* from west of the Great Khingan Mountains, has rather paler plumage than *doerriesi*.)
>
> **112c** **Juvenile** (*doerriesi*: most of range except Sakhalin, Japan and W Manchuria) Showing the long, dense and downy plumage. Yellow eyes; bluish cere, bill and toes.
>
> **112d** **Adult** (nominate *blakistoni*: S Kuriles, Hokkaido, Japan, and Sakhalin) Smaller than *doerriesi*, with more fuscous plumage, much darker face, darker wing-coverts and more pale grey-brown (less pale buffy) ground colour. Lacks the white occipital spots, but has tail colours identical, not darker (*contra* Vaurie 1965).

113 Brown Fish Owl *Bubo zeylonensis*   **Text and map page 312**

Along streams or other waterways in forested lowlands and plains, especially overgrown ravines and steep river banks, often near human habitation. S Turkey east to SW Iran and NW Pakistan, India south to Sri Lanka and east to Indochina and SE China. Similar to smallest eagle owls, but with long bare tarsi, and feathers less soft than in other owls; toes bare, covered with granular scales, soles of feet with pointed scales; poorly developed facial disc, head flattened over eyebrows and with brown bushy ear-tufts; heavy bill.

> **113a** **Adult** (*leschenault*, India, Nepal, Bhutan, Assam, Burma, Thailand) Paler than nominate *zeylonensis*. Pale rufous ground colour, heavily streaked with black above; below, pale fulvous to whitish with fine wavy brown bars and bold blackish streaks. Prominent large white patch on throat and foreneck. Eyes pale yellow to bright golden-yellow; bill greyish-green; feet dusky yellow to pale greyish-yellow. Two other races, *semenowi* and *orientalis*, are probably only colour morphs (see text).
>
> **113b** **Adult** (*leschenault*) In flight, showing the rounded wings and long legs.
>
> **113c** **Adult** (nominate *zeylonensis*: Sri Lanka) Smaller size, darker plumage and shorter ear-tufts.

112c

113a

113c

112b

113b

112a

112d

1995
WEICK

PLATE 35: AFRICAN FISHING OWLS

114 Pel's Fishing Owl *Scotopelia peli*   **Text and map page 314**

Forested lowland rivers, lakes, swamps, riparian woodland, from sea-level to 1,700m. Africa, from Senegambia and Sierra Leone to S Cameroon and E Zaire, locally to Sudan and Somalia, south to Tanzania and patchily south to NW Angola and E South Africa. Large size; rufous plumage, barred above and streaked below; bare tarsi and toes.

> **114a** **Typical adult** Male, also in flight. Large individual variation in hues and markings, some with widely spaced narrow bars on breast, others with albinistic or melanistic feathers, a few heavily marked. Bill black, cere and base of bill grey; eyes dark brown; legs and feet pale yellow. (Forms *fisheri* and *salvagoragii* treated as synonyms.)
>
> **114b** **Juvenile** Downy body feathers white, with pale rufous wash on head, breast and mantle; light dusky spotting and barring above. Wings and tail pale rufous, barred as adult.
>
> **114c** **Immature** Similar to adult, but paler. Head, face, mantle, throat and underparts with pale rufous wash and faint dusky spotting; light barring on mantle and back. Wings and rectrices pale rufous, with dusky bars as adult.

115 Rufous Fishing Owl *Scotopelia ussheri*   **Text and map page 315**

Along river edges and lakes of lowland forest. Sierra Leone, Liberia, Ivory Coast and Ghana.

> **115** **Adult** Plain, rufous plumage, streaked below. Yellow eyes; pale yellow, bare tarsi and toes. (Immatures similar to adults, but paler. Downy young completely covered in white down, with pale rufous wash above, below clearly white.)

116 Vermiculated Fishing Owl *Scotopelia bouvieri*   **Text and map page 316**

Gallery and riparian forest along larger rivers. Congo Basin in S Cameroon, Gabon, Central African Republic, Congo, Zaire and N Angola.

> **116a** **Adult** Rufous above, densely vermiculated; white to sandy below, heavily streaked rufous-brown. Eyes dark brown; bill and cere yellow; bare tarsi and toes yellow to greyish-yellow.
>
> **116b** **Mesoptile** Downy head and back with slight cinnamon wash. Wings and tail similar to adult.

114c

114a

114a

114b

115

116a

116b

1995
WEICK

117 Snowy Owl *Nyctea scandiaca*   **Text and map page 317**

Tundra north of treeline; outside breeding season also other open country, fields and prairie. Circumpolar in Arctic: Greenland and Iceland, across N Eurasia to Sakhalin, Aleutians, Alaska and N Canada; winters south to USA, C Europe, C Russia, N China and Japan. Resembles eagle owls but plumage white, barred and spotted to varying extent with dark brown; relatively small rounded head, incomplete facial disc and small, seldom erected ear-tufts; dense and downy plumage; short bill and the legs largely concealed by long and dense feathers, on legs extending to claws. Sexually dimorphic in colour.

117a **Adult male** Perched and in flight. Nearly pure white. Eyes yellow; bill and claws black.

117b **Adult female** Perched and in flight. White plumage marked with dark-brown. Distinctly larger than male.

117c **Mesoptile** Nestling covered with white down, changing to sooty-grey above.

117d **Juvenile** Nestling with loose, downy feathers of greyish-brown; wings with visible remiges similar to adult.

117e **Juvenile** First incomplete plumage, moulting into first adult.

117f **Juvenile female** First-winter. (Young male resembles adult female, but smaller and less heavily barred, lacking strong bars on crown and neck.)

117c

117b

117a

117d

117e

117f

117b

117a

1995
WEICK

121 Band-bellied Owl *Pulsatrix melanota*   Text and map page 322

Dense humid forest at 700-1,600m. Colombia, E Ecuador E Peru and Bolivia.

121   **Adult** (nominate *melanota*: entire range except Bolivia) Perched and in flight. Relatively large, dark brown spectacled owl with white eyebrows, lores and throat. Narrow tawny-coloured border to brown breast band, the latter mottled with white and tawny, especially on centre of breast; belly white, barred rufous-brown and with pale orange to creamy wash. Eyes dark brown; tarsi feathered; toes bare; bill ivory. (Bolivian subspecies *philosica* is rather larger and slightly paler above.)

120 Tawny-browed Owl *Pulsatrix koeniswaldiana*   Text and map page 321

Tropical and subtropical forest and woodland in lowlands. E Brazil, C Paraguay and extreme NE Argentina.

120   **Adult** Perched and in flight. Smaller than other spectacled owls, with brown upperparts, distinctly tawny to fulvous eyebrows and cinnamon-yellow belly; broken brown chest band, white chin and darker, barred throat. Eyes brown; tarsi feathered; toes bristled.

118 Spectacled Owl *Pulsatrix perspicillata*   Text and map page 318

Tropical and subtropical forest, forest edge and clearings, also plantations and groves, from sea-level up to 1,500m. S Mexico through C America and south to Bolivia and N Argentina; Trinidad. Dark owl, strikingly blackish to dark brown above, with white crescents on black face; eyes yellow to orange-yellow.

118a   **Adult** (nominate *perspicillata*: Venezuela to Guianas, Mato Grosso, Brazil, and Ecuador) Perched and in flight. Crown blackish, hindneck dusky brown; pure white eyebrows, lores, edges of facial rim to sides of barred neck, also white foreneck; lower breast and belly whitish to pale yellow or ochraceous-buff. Tarsi feathered to near claws; toes with three scales. (Rare Trinidad subspecies *trinitatis* has less dark head and pale abdomen.)

118b   **Juvenile** (nominate *perspicillata*) Head, back and underside covered with white downy feathers; forehead, mask and chin patch distinctly blackish-brown. Wings and tail similar to adult, but with paler bars. In the final moulting stage, only the head is covered with white down.

118c   **Adult** (*saturata*: Oaxaca, Mexico, to Costa Rica and W Panama) Crown, lower hindneck and back sooty-blackish; lower breast, belly and abdomen deep buff, more or less barred sooty-black, sometimes only on flanks, sometimes extending down to tarsi. (Subspecies *chapmani*, from E Costa Rica to Ecuador, is similar to *saturata* but with deep buffy belly and abdomen unbarred.)

119 Short-browed Owl *Pulsatrix pulsatrix*   Text and map page 320

Semi-open forest, secondary growth and forest clearings in mountainous regions, also near human settlements. E Brazil, probably also extreme NE Argentina (E Misiones). Often regarded as subspecies of Spectacled Owl.

119   **Adult** Larger than Spectacled Owl, with remiges and rectrices not so distinctly banded. Eyes orange-brown to yellowish (?). More chocolate-brown in colour, with chest band extending farther down towards belly; much shorter eyebrows and less extensive throat band; lores, belly and abdomen with deep buffy colouring.

121

120

118a

121

120

118b

118a

118c

119

1995
LWEICK

122 Spotted Wood Owl *Strix seloputo*   Text and map page 323

Forest, plantations, villages, urban parks, also swamp forest and mangroves, from lowlands to 1,000m. SE Asia, Malay Peninsula, Java, possibly Sumatra, and Philippines (Palawan). Brown, white-spotted wood owl with relatively small, rounded head; eyes dark brown.

122a   Adult (nominate *seloputo*: S Burma, Thailand, Cambodia, S Vietnam and Malay Peninsula) Perched and in flight. Facial disc pale orange. Upperparts rufous-chocolate, marked with black-edged white spots; scapulars white with dark bars. Underparts white, washed rufous and barred dark brown; whitish chin. Eyes dark brown; bill grey to greenish-black; tarsi and toes feathered to distal end, bare soles yellow to grey. (Subspecies *baweana* from Java including Bawean Island is rather smaller and paler.)

122b   Adult (*wiebkeni*: SW Philippines, on Calamian Islands and Palawan) Above, scapulars and secondary bands more buffy washed; face dark buffy-orange; distinct brown throat band, and whole underparts, deeply washed yellow-buff to orange-buff.

123 Mottled Wood Owl *Strix ocellata*   Text and map page 324

Open country, lightly wooded plains, groves and farmland. Lowland India.

123a   Adult (nominate *ocellata*: S and C India, northeast to Bangladesh) Perched and in flight. A beautifully coloured wood owl with a rounded head. Above, mottled and vermiculated with reddish-brown, black, white and buff, black spotting on nuchal area predominating. Facial disc white with black concentric rings; rim white, black and chocolate-brown admixed. Below, chin and foreneck white, throat rufous-brown and black, stippled with white, rest of under parts white to orange-buff, narrowly barred blackish. Eyes dark brown, eyelids pink to red; bill horn-black; toes fleshy or dirty yellow.

123b   Adult (*grandis*: Kathiawar Peninsula, S Gujarat) Differs from nominate *ocellata* in larger size and in distinctly greyer, less black-spotted appearance above. (Subspecies *grisescens* from N India also larger and with paler, greyer, coloration above and paler rufous parts of plumage.)

124 Spotted Owl *Strix occidentalis*   Text and map page 325

Humid old growth and mature mixed coniferous forest, from near sea-level to montane and submontane zones. N America: British Columbia south to California and N Mexico. Dense plumage and thick-feathered tarsi resembling Barred Owl.

124a   Adult (nominate *occidentalis*: Nevada, C and S California). Perched and in flight. Rather smaller than Barred Owl (Plate 39). Large head with white spotting; dark appearance. Upperparts with white bars and spots, tail dark brown with 4-6 paler bars; underparts pale buff to whitish with coarse dark brown bars and scallops, and buffy hair-like feathers on breast and belly. Eyes dark brown; bill greenish-yellow; toes sparsely bristled and with yellow soles. (Subspecies *caurina* from British Columbia to N California is darker than nominate and perhaps only a dark morph.)

124b   Adult (*lucida*, Mountain Spotted Owl: SW USA to C Mexico) Paler appearance, with much yellowish-buff suffusion, markings larger and more distinct. (May be a separate species?)

124c   Juvenile (nominate *occidentalis*) Head, back and underparts covered with buffy to greyish downy feathers; face showing concentric rings. Wings and tail similar to adult.

122a

122b

123a

123a

123b

122a

124a

124a

124b

124c

1996
ZWEICK

125 Fulvous Owl *Strix fulvescens* Text and map page 326

Humid forest and pine-oak woodland. Mountains of Middle America from S Mexico to Honduras.

125 Adult Perched and in flight. Crown, nape and upperparts dark brown, head and nape coarsely scalloped tawny to ochraceous-buff. Facial disc pale grey-brown with dark brown rim; whitish eyebrows; forehead nearly uniform dark brown. Upperparts with sparse buffy bars, scapulars and wing-coverts boldly spotted, remiges with few pale buffy bars; tail dark brown with 3-4 pale cinnamon bars. Buffy to ochre ground colour below, upper chest coarsely barred dark brown, belly with heavy dark brown streaks, undertail-coverts nearly unmarked. Eyes dark brown; bill and toes yellow.

126 Barred Owl *Strix varia* Text and map page 327

Mainly dense woodland, swamps and riparian forest. N America, from Alaska to Mexico. Related to Ural Owl (Plate 40), but with relatively shorter tail and smaller claws; a chunky owl with dark barring on upper breast and dark streaking below, face with concentric rings and more or less distinct rim; dark eyes and yellow bill.

126a Adult (*helveola*: SC Texas and adjacent Mexico) Much lighter than nominate *varia*, cinnamon-buff to yellowish with pale wings and tail. Toes bare.

126b Adult (*georgica*: SE USA) Smaller and lighter-coloured than nominate *varia*, but distinctly darker than *helveola*, with darker wings and tail. Buffy-grey ground colour above; below, more ochraceous wash and darker rufous shaft-streaks.

126c Adult (nominate *varia*: Canada to E USA) Perched and in flight. More greyish-brown plumage with distinctly white spots above and below, and feathered toes. Visible bare parts yellow.

126d Adult (*sartorii*: C Mexico at 1,500-2,500m) Darkest race. Crown, nape and upperparts dark grey-brown with coarse but few white bars, scapulars boldly blotched whitish, tail with 4-5 whitish bars. Below, white ground colour, breast thickly barred dark grey-brown, belly heavily streaked, undertail-coverts nearly unmarked.

126e Mesoptile (nominate *varia*) Fluffy, whitish down, long and silky on back. Bare skin pinkish; bill pale yellow; cere blue-green. Flight feathers hardly visible; thighs covered with long down.

127 Sichuan Wood Owl *Strix davidi* Text and map page 328

Mountain forest up to 5,000m. C China in Sichuan and Tsinghai.

127 Adult Perched and in flight. A very dark owl, probably related to Ural Owl and with similar vocalisations, but face with concentric rings as on Great Grey Owl (Plate 40). Dark head and back with white streaking, distinctly light scapulars; wings dark grey-brown, banded and spotted pale; uppertail-coverts plain coloured, central tail feathers with fine scribbles. Below, greyish-white ground colour, darker on breast, and with longitudinal shaft-stripes with indication of cross-bars. Eyes dark brown; bill yellow; tarsi and toes feathered, soles yellow.

125

125

126a

126b

126c

127

126c

126d

127

126e

1996
Weick

128 Ural Owl *Strix uralensis*   **Text and map page 329**

Open coniferous forest, forest edge with alder and birch, in south mainly mature beech forest. Eurasia from Fennoscandia east to Siberia, south to Mongolia, Manchuria, Korea and Japan, also locally in mountains of E Europe (and reintroduced in Bavarian/Bohemian Forest); winters irregularly south to SE Europe. Relatively long-tailed, large owl with round facial disc, completely rimmed; eyes relatively small, dark brown.

128a Adult (nominate *uralensis*: E Russia to W Siberia, Yakutia and Sea of Okhotsk, south to Middle Volga, S Ural, Tyumen, Yalutrovsk and Kaink) Palest form. White ground colour with dark but narrow shaft-streaks, limited grey mottling and clouding on bases and tips of feathers; scapulars, most upperwing-coverts and underparts white, with narrow, contrasting streaks. Face white, small eyes dark brown, eyelids pink to red; bill horn-yellow to orange-yellow; soles greyish-yellow, claws dark brown to black.

128b Adult (*liturata*: N Europe from Lapland and Sweden south to Baltic regions, also E Alps, Carpathians and east to Volga; intergrades with nominate *uralensis*) In flight. Greyish to brownish-white, streaked dark brown, most clearly on underparts. Flight feathers and tail with broad, transverse dark brown bars on buffy or buff-white ground colour. Face greyish-white without any markings. (Subspecies *nikolskii* of Transbaikalia indistinguishable in plumage from adult *liturata*.)

128c Juvenile (*liturata*) Rather variable in colour, whitish-grey, hazel, dirty yellow or dull brown, feathers tipped white and with ill-defined broad and dark barring. Flight feathers similar to adult, tail hardly visible.

128d Adult (*macroura*: Carpathians, Transylvanian Alps to W Balkans) Slightly larger than nominate *uralensis*, with darker plumage, face with traces of concentric rings. Indication of cross-bars above and below. (Form *carpathica* treated as synonym.)

128e Immature (*macroura*) Melanistic morph. Colour entirely deep brown or chestnut, including face; paler spotting below and clearly banded tail and flight feathers. Mesoptile plumage also dark-coloured.

128f Adult (*fuscescens*: W and S Honshu and Kyushu, Japan) Smaller than European subspecies. More buffy-rufous above; ochraceous below with deep brown shaft-streaks, breast and belly distinctly white-blotched. Tarsi and toes feathered rufous. Face darker. (Subspecies *hondoensis* from N and C Honshu and Hokkaido more rusty-rufous in colour and less white on head and neck.)

129 Great Grey Owl *Strix nebulosa*   **Text and map page 331**

Mature lichen-covered coniferous forest, intermixed with larch and deciduous trees. N Eurasia and N North America. Large, long-tailed owl with large, rounded head; long, fluffy feathers; facial disc forms complete circle with concentric rings; eyes yellow, relatively small.

129a Adult (nominate *nebulosa*: North America from C Alaska south to British Columbia, Alberta, Manitoba and S Ontario, also mountains in W USA; irregular visitor to N USA and S Canada) Female. Rather larger and distinctly darker than *lapponica*, and barred below. Grey streaking above not so distinctly defined as in *lapponica*; less prominent white eyebrows and vertical dark throat band, bordered with more horizontal white bands, compared with larger white blotches and long black throat band in *lapponica*. Small, yellow eyes; bill wax-yellow.

129b Mesoptile (nominate *nebulosa*) Upperparts with feather-like, short and soft down; plumage white to off-white with dark olive-brown barring, below more indistinctly barred grey-brown. Growing wing feathers hardly visible. Eyes pale yellow; cere yellow or orange-tinged; bill with pink base and pale yellow tip.

129c Adult (*lapponica*: N Eurasia from Scandinavia to N Siberia, Anadyr and Koryakskland, south to S Siberia, Mongolia and Manchuria) Perched and in flight. Rather smaller and distinctly paler than nominate *nebulosa*. Individuals from E Eurasia slightly darker and more contrastingly marked than W Eurasian birds; birds from Sakhalin with rather darker and duller plumage.

128a

128d

128f

128e

129c

129a

129c

128b

128c

129b

LEVICK 96

130 Tawny Owl *Strix aluco*   **Text and map page 333**

Deciduous and mixed forest, open woodland, parks, gardens, coniferous forest, from lowlands up to 4,200m in Himalayas. Europe eastwards to W Siberia, E China and Taiwan, and locally NW Africa. Short-tailed and broad-winged owl with round head and circular facial disc; legs and toes strong and densely feathered; eyes dark brown, eyelids blue-grey, fleshy-bordered; bill yellow to greenish, pale-tipped, cere blue-grey to blackish; highly variable plumage with rufous, grey and intermediate brown morphs.

130a **Adult** (*mauretanica*: NW Africa) Dark morph. Medium-grey upperparts with dark grey bars and vermiculations, especially on crown and mantle. Facial disc with fine grey barring and distinct rim; throat white with rufous wash. Wings and tail more dark grey-brown than in nominate *aluco*. Below, white with dense dark-grey streaks and bars, especially on sides of breast and flanks.

130b **Adult** (nominate *aluco*: Europe from Scandinavia to Mediterranean and Black Sea, east to W Russia, intergrading with *siberiae*) Extreme rufous morph. Richly rufous-cinnamon plumage, including facial disc, with contrasting white eyebrows, lores and arcs above each eye. (Paler, less deep rufous birds, tawny-brown to tawny-buff, also occur.)

130c **Mesoptile** (nominate *aluco*) Long, feather-like down, colour variable as adult. Eyelids, cere and toes fleshy-pink; bill blue-grey; eyes with oily-bluish sheen.

130d **Adult** (nominate *aluco*) Intermediate, in flight. Usually termed grey morph in W Europe, but not so grey as birds from eastern or southeastern part of range or as *mauretanica*. Ground colour buff to pale cream with grey-brown to warm brown appearance. (W European subspecies *sylvatica* similar to nominate *aluco*, but smaller.)

130e **Adult** (*bidulphi*: NW India and Pakistan) Brown morph. Facial disc with distinct concentric rings. Closely barred on chin, throat and breast, belly with denser and stronger bars than nominate *aluco* (similar to Himalayan subspecies *nivicola*).

130f **Adult** (*siberiae*: W Ural to Irtysh) Pale grey morph. Larger and paler than nominate *aluco*, white predominating on head, back and underparts.

130g **Adult** (*sanctinicolai*: Iran and NE Iraq) Pale desert morph. Small. Pale grey and buff colours predominating (some individuals with more white on hindneck and below). Dark shaft-streaks on head and body narrow.

131 Hume's Owl *Strix butleri*   **Text and map page 335**

Rocky ravines and gorges in desert and semi-desert, palm groves in oases. Warm arid lower, middle and subtropical latitudes of SW Eurasia: Syria, Israel, NE and E Egypt (including Sinai), W and SE Arabia, possibly also Iranian shore of Persian Gulf (and coastal W Pakistan?).

131 **Adult** Perched and in flight. Small size, as smallest Tawny Owls, with fine, silky feather texture. Pale-faced, round-headed. Upperparts buff, mottled brown and grey, with pale collar; below, buffy-white, faintly marked. Tarsi feathered. Eyes orange-yellow to orange; bill horn-yellow; claws black.

130a

130b

130c

130d

130f

130e

131

130g

131

1995
Weick

132 Brown Wood Owl *Strix leptogrammica*   **Text and map page 336**

Deep tropical forest and dense jungle in lower hill tracts, also lowland primary forest in Sunda region. S India, Sri Lanka, S Burma, peninsular Thailand and Malay Peninsula, Borneo, Sumatra, Belitung and islands off W Sumatra, including Nias; absent Java and Bali. Highly variable in size and plumage; eyes dark brown to golden-brown; bill greenish-horn, cere bluish-grey; tarsi feathered, toes pale leaden, claws dusky grey.

132a **Adult** (*niasensis*: Nias Island, W Sumatran islands) Smallest subspecies. Warmer, rich coloration on whole plumage; deep rufous nuchal collar and face.

132b **Adult** (nominate *leptogrammica*: Sumatra, Banyak, Belitung, Sarawak and C and S Borneo) Perched and in flight. Head black, suffused with rufous, separated from mantle by cinnamon-buff to rufous band; wings and tail barred deep brown and light to dark cinnamon. Face rufous, rimmed black, with black around eyes; eyebrows and throat band whitish, Breast rufous with dark barring, belly creamy to buff with dark brown to blackish bars. (Forms *nyctiphasma*, *chaseni* and *myrtha* are treated here as synonyms.)

132c **Juvenile** (nominate *leptogrammica*) Downy feathers on head, back and underparts whitish with pale buff to tawny wash, with first indication of bars. Wings and tail similar to adult, but lighter in colour. Face buffy, with black rim.

132d **Adult** (*vaga*: N Borneo) Above, more fuscous to burnt umber than nominate *leptogrammica*. Darker than Indian *indranee*, and warmer-coloured than Himalayan Wood Owl. Buffy nuchal collar. Ventral: broad rich brown, black barred chest-band. White lower throat patch. Belly white to buff, barred with burnt umber. (Subspecies *maingayi* of S Burma to Malay Peninsula is similar in colour, but larger.)

132e **Adult** (*indranee*: C and S India, Sri Lanka) More variable in colour. Smaller and darker than Himalayan Wood Owl. Head darker than back; white, barred nuchal collar. Pale cinnamon below, heavily barred brown; cinnamon wash on sides of barred breast, but no distinct chest band.

134 Himalayan Wood Owl *Strix newarensis*   **Text and map page 338**

Dense evergreen forest, mostly in mountains. N Pakistan, India and Nepal east to N and C Burma, N Thailand, SE China, Hainan and Taiwan, south to S Laos. Largest species of this group, specifically distinct from Brown Wood Owl on grounds of very different voice and habitat.

134 **Adult** (nominate *newarensis*: Himalayas) Perched and in flight. Paler above, head somewhat darker; white nuchal collar, lighter face. Below, lacking distinct chest band of Brown Wood Owl; belly off-white to pale rufous with rufous to brown bars. Tarsi barred.

133 Bartels' Wood Owl *Strix bartelsi*   **Text and map page 337**

Undisturbed mountain forest. Mountains of W and WC Java.

133 **Adult** Similar in size to race *indranee* of Brown Wood Owl, but with different plumage and different voice. Broad ochraceous nuchal band. Secondaries and tail with more numerous bars, different from all subspecies of Brown Wood Owl and Mountain Wood Owl. Dark wings contrasting with paler scapulars.

132a

132b

132b

132d

132c

134

132e

133

134

96
Weick

PLATE 43: WOOD OWLS

135 African Wood Owl *Strix woodfordii* Text and map page 339

Forest and dense woodland. Senegambia to Ethiopia, through C Africa, including Bioko and Zanzibar, south to the Cape; single record from S Somalia. Medium-sized, round-headed owl with dark eyes surrounded by dark inner rings of facial disc; rufous plumage strongly barred with white.

135a **Adult** (nominate *woodfordii*: S Angola, S Zaire and SW Tanzania south to the Cape) Typical individual, also in flight. Head, neck and back dark rufous-brown with white bars and light nuchal band; scapulars with broad white spots. Throat and upper breast russet with white bars; belly distinctly barred white, russet and dark brown. Bill yellow; eyes dark brown, eyelids red; tarsi feathered, feet yellow-horn.

135b **Mesoptile** (nominate *woodfordii*) Downy rufous mesoptile feathers, barred white and brown. Remiges and rectrices hardly visible. Plumage hues and markings variable.

135c **Adult** (*nuchalis*: Senegambia to S Sudan and Uganda, south to N Angola and N and W Zaire) Darker above, but with heavy white bars; below, brighter chestnut-coloured, white bars more distinct and contrasting.

135d **Adult** (*nigricantior*: S Somalia, Kenya, Tanzania, Zanzibar and E Zaire) Dark grey-brown upperparts (sometimes blackish); distinct chest band, and more clearly barred below than nominate *woodfordi* or *nuchalis*. (Subspecies *umbrina* from Ethiopia and SE Sudan similar to *nigricantior*, but with browner upperside.)

136 Mottled Owl *Strix virgata* Text and map page 341

Dense forest and woodland, humid lowlands, also cloud forest up to 2,500m. Tropical America from Mexico to NE Argentina and S Brazil. Highly variable in plumage, also with light and dark morphs; eyes dark brown; bill horn to yellowish; toes grey to yellow.

136a **Adult** (nominate *virgata*: E Panama, Colombia, Ecuador, Venezuela and Trinidad) Dark morph. Almost blackish unspotted upperparts; dark face but distinct whitish lores, eyebrows and facial rim. Breast barred and streaked dark, belly white to buffy-orange with distinct shaft-stripes and cross-barred flanks.

136b **Adult** (*borelliana*: S Brazil, Paraguay and NE Argentina) Light morph. Predominantly brown above, spotted and barred white to pale buffy; outer scapulars tawny; wings dark, mottled and banded much paler. Below, white to buffy with heavy shaft-stripes. (Dark morph similar to nominate *virgata*. Subspecies *macconelli* of Guianas more rufous above and below, with densely barred breast and tendency towards barring on belly.)

136c **Adult** (*centralis*: S Mexico to W Panama) Paler above than *borelliana*, with more white visible; below, ochre ground colour and dense breast mottling.

136d **Adult** (*squamulata*: Mexico from Tamaulipas to Guerrero) Paler above than *centralis* and whiter below, with finer mottling on breast and finer streaking on belly.

137 Rufous-legged Owl *Strix rufipes* Text and map page 342

Dense lichen-rich forest and semi-open woodland. S South America. Medium-sized, round-headed owl, face with concentric rings, upperside and scapulars distinctly barred, underparts with three-coloured barring; feathered tarsi and toes, distal third bare; eyes brown, bill wax-yellow.

137a **Adult** (nominate *rufipes*: S Chile and S Argentina to Tierra del Fuego and Falkland Islands) Typical morph. Above, sepia-brown, spotted and barred white and orange; face and tarsi rufous-orange; wings and tail banded light brown to sepia and pale buff to white. Below, fine barring of sepia, brown and white.

137b **Adult** (nominate *rufipes*) Dark morph. Entire plumage much darker. Tawny ground colour, bars bold and merging. (Subspecies *sanborni* from Chiloé Island off Chile similar in colour to specimens from S Chile, perhaps a synonym.)

138 Chaco Owl *Strix chacoensis* Text and map page 343

Gran chaco from Paraguay to Argentina.

138 **Adult** Distinctly paler in plumage than Rufous-legged Owl. Face off-white with darker concentric rings; tarsi whitish with rufous bars. Formerly treated as conspecific with Rufous-legged Owl.

135a

135c

135a

135b

135d

136b

136a

136c

136d

138

137a

137b

1996 Weick

139 Rusty-barred Owl *Strix hylophila*   **Text and map page 344**

Forest and secondary growth. SE South America in Paraguay, SE Brazil and NE Argentina. Similar to Rufous-legged Owl, but with white scapulars; eyes brown; tarsi and base of toes feathered.

139a Adult Perched and in flight. Buffy-rufous above, barred dark. Face with buffy wash and dark concentric rings; distinct rim, with sides of neck paler. White below, breast with orange-buffy wash and dark bars; belly white to pale buffy, irregularly dark-barred.

139b Juvenile Covered with downy mesoptile feathers, white to pale buff and tawny; gradually acquires bars; facial disc lacking rings. Wings and tail similar to adult plumage.

140 Rufous-banded Owl *Strix albitarsus*   **Text and map page 345**

Dense, humid montane forest from 1,700m to 3,400m. W South America from Venezuela, Colombia and Ecuador to NW Peru and Bolivia.

140a Adult Perched and in flight. Small, round-headed and compact wood owl with rather short tail. Coarsely barred tawny and black. Below, especially on chest, marked with paler tawny, belly ocellated with white. Tawny face with black surrounding eyes, dark rim; white lores and eyebrows. Wings and tail barred blackish and buffy. Eyes orange-yellow; bill yellow; tarsi feathered down to yellow toes. (Form *tertia* from Ecuador, Peru and Bolivia is similar but lighter buffy above and with paler facial disc.)

140b Juvenile Different plumage and with dark eyes. Blackish mask, pale head and back with few dark bars. Below, lacking dense chest barring; belly more tawny-washed, streaked and barred dark and with white, ocellated spots. Wings as adult, but lacking vermiculations on lighter secondary bands.

141 Black-and-white Owl *Strix nigrolineata*   **Text and map page 346**

Humid forest, edge, deciduous woodland, dense swamps and mangroves, from lowlands up to 2,000m. Middle and NW South America, from S Mexico to NW Venezuela, W Ecuador and NW Peru. Medium-sized, round-headed wood owl.

141a Adult Perched and in flight. Crown, nape and upperparts blackish, tail with 4-5 narrow white bars. Face black, with rim and eyebrows speckled black and white. White below, narrowly barred blackish, this pattern extending around sides of neck in partial collar. Eyes dark; bill and feet orange-yellow.

141b Juvenile Whitish overall, narrowly barred blackish-brown above, and creamy below with narrow dark barring. Face, eyebrows and rim as adult. Wing-coverts as back; remiges and rectrices as adult. Eyes with oily-bluish sheen.

142 Black-banded Owl *Strix huhula*   **Text and map page 347**

Humid forest, from lowlands up to 1,400m. S America east of Andes, south to NE Argentina (Misiones) and SE Brazil. Rather smaller than Black-and-white Owl, and with yellow eyes.

142a Adult (nominate *huhula*: Colombia, the Guianas and N Brazil south to the Amazon and Bolivia) Perched and in flight. Entire plumage dark sooty with white bars, narrow above and fewer on head; chin black. Primaries distinctly blacker than rest of plumage; tail with four white bands and broad white tip. Tarsi feathered, barred black and white; eyes yellow (sometimes brownish?), eyelids reddish; bill and cere yellow; toes light yellow.

142b Adult (*albomarginata*: E Paraguay, NE Argentina, and E Brazil south to Santa Catarina) More blackish in plumage, with sooty secondaries and black-bordered white bars; white bars narrower, reduced on eyebrows and facial rim. Tarsi black with narrow fine bars.

142c Juvenile (nominate *huhula*) More fluffy and distinctly browner in colour than adult, with heavier white bars. Wings and tail as adult. Oily-bluish eyes; bill and toes yellow.

139a

139b

139a

140a

141b

141a

140a

140b

141a

142a

142a

142b

142c

1996
WEICK

143 Eurasian Pygmy Owl *Glaucidium passerinum* Text and map page 348

Semi-open coniferous and mixed forest, sometimes to the treeline, from 200m up to 2,150m. N and C Europe east through Siberia to Sakhalin and N China. Tiny owl with small, rather flat head and narrow tail; eyes yellow.

143a **Adult** (nominate *passerinum*: Europe to W Asia, east to Yenisei) Typical brown individual. Mainly dark dull brown, spotted buffy-white overall; lacks bold white scapular spots. Face lacks full disc; eyebrows and lores white. Nape with light area, and two dark spots, forming 'false eyes'. Flight feathers dark brown, narrowly barred buffy-white. Throat almost white, upper breast and sides of chest barred dark brown, but most of underparts white, sparsely spotted and streaked. Legs and base of toes feathered white; eyes, bill and toes yellow.

143b **Adult** (nominate *passerinum*) Dorsal view showing occipital face.

143c **Mesoptile** (nominate *passerinum*) At 12 days. Downy, feather-like plumage, softer than adult's, but not so downy as mesoptile stage of other owls such as *Strix* or *Asio*.

143d **Juvenile** (nominate *passerinum*) At 24 days. Plumage fully developed, but crown uniform and wings and tail not fully grown.

143e **Adult** (*orientale*: E Siberia, Sakhalin, Manchuria and N China) Perched and in flight. Identical to grey-morph nominate *passerinum*. Paler, greyer and less brown, with pure white spots.

144 Pearl-spotted Owlet *Glaucidium perlatum* Text and map page 351

Savanna, semi-open woodland, acacia country and dry bush. Sub-Saharan Africa from Senegambia east to Ethiopia and Somalia, south to Cape Province and west to Angola. Larger than Eurasian Pygmy Owl, with spotted rufous and cinnamon plumage and a white, streaked belly; false nuchal face obvious; eyes yellow, bill horn-yellow, cere brown, toes yellow-brown.

144a **Adult** (nominate *perlatum*: Senegambia east across Mali, Niger and Chad to W Sudan) Perched and in flight. Brighter and more contrastingly coloured than *licua*, with rufous neck and sandy back; below, larger white spots on flanks and heavy cross-barred stripes on belly.

144b **Adult** (nominate *perlatum*) Dorsal view showing occipital face.

144c **Juvenile** (nominate *perlatum*) Uniform crown and mantle, less rufous, and more prominent nuchal face.

144d **Adult** (*licua*: E Sudan, Ethiopia, Somalia, Uganda to N South Africa, Angola and Namibia) Paler than nominate *perlatum*. Head cinnamon-brown, nape ochre to buff, less rufous wing-coverts; belly white with fine dark shaft-stripes. (Forms *diurnum* and *kilimense* treated as synonyms.)

145 Red-chested Owlet *Glaucidium tephronotum* Text and map page 353

Forest, forest edge and clearings. Africa, from Liberia to Congo Basin, Uganda and W Kenya. Tiny, grey-headed owlet, lacking 'occipital face', but with whitish nuchal band; bill greenish-yellow, cere wax-yellow, eyes and feet yellow, claws yellow with black tips.

145a **Adult** (nominate *tephronotum*: Liberia, Ivory Coast and probably Ghana) Perched and in flight. Grey head and back, dusky mantle, chestnut wash on wing-coverts. Face, lores and eyebrows mostly white. Dusky tail with three incomplete white bars on inner webs. Breast white with brown spots; rufous-washed breast sides and flanks.

145b **Adult** (nominate *tephronotum*) Dorsal view showing neck collar.

145c **Adult** (*pycrafti*: Cameroon) Darker head, back and wings, dark chocolate-brown to brownish-grey; less rufous flanks black-spotted. (Subspecies *elgonense* from Uganda and Kenya is similar to *pycrafti*, but rather larger and with browner upperparts.)

143a

143e

143e

143b

144a

144a

143d

143c

144c

145a

144d

145a

145c

144b 145b

1995 Weick

146 **Northern Pygmy Owl** *Glaucidium californicum*   **Text and map page 354**

Coniferous and mixed forest. W North America, from Alaska south through Rocky Mountains to California and Arizona (and N Mexico?). Small, long-tailed owlet, similar to but not related to Eurasian Pygmy Owl (Plate 45); differs from Mountain Pygmy Owl in vocalisations, morphology and ecological requirements.

146a **Adult** (nominate *californicum*: SE Alaska and British Columbia south to NW California) Typical. Very similar to Eurasian Pygmy Owl, but with longer tail, bristled (not feathered) toes and swollen cere. Eyes and bill yellow.

146b **Adult** (nominate *californicum*) Red morph. In flight, showing more rounded wings compared with Mountain Pygmy Owl.

146c **Adult** (*pinicola*: W Montana and Idaho south to extreme E California, S Arizona and New Mexico, perhaps also N Mexico) Grey morph. (A red morph also occurs.)

146d **Adult** (*swarthi*: Vancouver Island) Darkest subspecies, typical of birds from this area. Reduced pale spots on head, back and wings.

147 **Cape Pygmy Owl** *Glaucidium hoskinsii*   **Text and map page 355**

Pine and pine-oak forest at about 1,500-2,100m; in winter probably also deciduous forest at lower altitudes. Mountains of S Baja California.

147a **Adult** female Smaller than Northern Pygmy Owl, with different vocalisations. Eyes and bill yellow; toes bristled. (Male has more sandy-grey upperside.)

147b **Adult** Dorsal view showing occipital face.

148 **Mountain Pygmy Owl** *Glaucidium gnoma*   **Text and map page 356**

Upland and highland forest, especially with pine. SW USA to Middle America (and extreme NW South America?). Smaller and shorter-tailed than Northern Pygmy Owl, with with more suffused shaft-streaks below.

148a **Adult** (nominate *gnoma*: S Arizona and New Mexico to C Honduras) Typical. With whiter throat and breast and browner face than Northern Pygmy Owl; sides of chest brown, finely spotted with buff. Eyes and bill yellow.

148b **Juvenile** (nominate *gnoma*) Uniform grey crown (some spots on forehead) and nape contrasting with brown upperparts; few pale spots on distal scapulars. No red morph known.

148c **Adult** (*cobanense*: Guatemalan highlands) Typical rufous morph. Bright rufous to chestnut above, with subdued paler spots on head; tail-bars pale buff to cinnamon. Sides of chest and flanks bright rufous with suffused stripes. (Possibly a separate species.)

148d **Adult** (*costaricanum*: Costa Rica to Panama and perhaps to extreme NW South America) Rufescent morph. Distinctly spotted on crown, back and wings; rufous wash on back and scapulars. Characteristic large white area on central breast and belly. Probably specifically distinct.

148e **Adult** (nominate *gnoma*) In flight, showing pointed wings and shorter tail than Northern Pygmy Owl.

149 **Cuban Pygmy Owl** *Glaucidium siju*   **Text and map page 358**

Semi-open woodland and forest edge, parks and bushy country. Cuba and Isle of Pines. Tiny, round-winged pygmy owl with different vocalisations from neighbouring species.

149a **Adult** (nominate *siju*: Cuba) Typical. Barely visible barring above; distinctly barred chest sides, with white central stripe in between. Yellow eyes and yellow, bristled toes. Obvious 'occipital face'.

149b **Adult** (nominate *siju*) Red morph (rare). Striped crown (also frequent in typical morph); breast with few rufous spots and bars. Bill yellow to yellowish-green.

149c **Adult** (*vittatum*: Isle of Pines) Dorsal view, showing the distinctly banded upperparts and 'false eyes'.

146a

146c

146b

148e

147a

147b

148b

148a

148c

148d

146d

149a

149b

149c

1996 WEICK

PLATE 47: CENTRAL AND SOUTH AMERICAN PYGMY OWLS

150 Tamaulipas Pygmy Owl *Glaucidium sanchezi*   **Text and map page 358**

Montane and cloud forest at 1,500-2,100m. NE Mexico in Tamaulipas and SE San Luis Potosi to Vera Cruz. Tiny and long-tailed owlet, sexes dimorphic; eyes, bill and feet yellow.

150a Adult female Crown, nape and upperparts washed cinnamon, distinctly redder than male; finely spotted forecrown. Tail with six pale, buffy-washed bars. Chest sides and streaks on underparts dark rufous-brown.

150b Adult male Grey-brown crown and nape, with some fine spots on forecrown; nape slightly contrasting with greyish-olive back. Chest sides and underpart streaks dark tawny to olivaceous-brown.

151 Colima Pygmy Owl *Glaucidium palmarum*   **Text and map page 359**

151 Adult Dry woodland, thorn forest, palm groves, semi-deciduous and locally deciduous forest, from sea-level up to 1,500m. W Mexico from Sonora to Oaxaca. Whole bird relatively greyish tawny-brown, palest on crown; tail with 6-7 pale bars. Eyes yellow.

152 Central American Pygmy Owl *Glaucidium griseiceps*   **Text and map page 360**

Rain forest and humid bushland and woodland, up to 1,300m. SE Mexico and large parts of Middle America to NW South America. Plumage redder overall than that of Amazonian or Subtropical Pygmy Owls.

152a Adult Crown and nape brownish-grey to grey-brown, contrasting with rich brown upperparts; forecrown, often extending to nape, finely spotted buff to white. Greater wing-coverts and secondaries more rufous-cinnamon than lesser coverts and primaries. Tail brown with 2-4 broken, whitish to buff bars. Below, whitish with rufous streaking; sides of chest rufous-brown, spotted buff.

152b Adult In flight, showing the contrasting secondaries.

152c Juvenile With unspotted grey crown and nape, contrasting with brown upperparts. Wing- and tail-bars are hardly visible.

153 Least Pygmy Owl *Glaucidium minutissimum*   **Text and map page 361**

Tropical and subtropical woodland with dense undergrowth, up to 1,000m above sea-level. SE Brazil and adjacent Paraguay (and NE Argentina?). Eyes yellow.

153a Adult Relatively short-tailed. Dark rufous-brown plumage overall. Tail with four visible whitish bars. Crown redder than on Central American or Amazonian Pygmy Owls.

153b Adult In flight, showing dark rufous-brown plumage.

153c Juvenile Similar to adult, but with nearly unspotted crown.

154 Amazonian Pygmy Owl *Glaucidium hardyi*   **Text and map page 362**

Tropical rain forest, from sea-level up to 350m. Amazonian South America, from Venezuela south to NE Bolivia.

154a Adult Relatively long-winged. Above, greyish rufous-brown, with a greyer head than Central American or Least Pygmy Owls; cinnamon upper mantle beneath the 'false eyes'. Sides of chest and underparts streaked rufous. Eyes, bill and toes yellow.

154b Adult In flight, showing the greyish head contrasting with mantle.

154c Adult Dorsal view showing occipital face.

155 Subtropical Pygmy Owl *Glaucidium parkeri*   **Text and map page 363**

Montane forest, between 1,450m and 1,975m. E Andes of Ecuador and Peru, locally to N Bolivia.

155 Adult Relatively long-winged and dark grey-brown, with distinct white spots on crown, nape, scapulars and wing-coverts; unspotted back. Tail with 4-5 visible white bands. Chest sides and underpart streaking more brown, less rufous. Eyes yellow.

150a

150b

152c

152a

151

152b

154c

153b

154b

153a

155

154a

153c

1996
WEICK

PLATE 48: SOUTH AMERICAN PYGMY OWLS

156 Andean Pygmy Owl *Glaucidium jardinii*   Text and map page 364

Montane forest up to *Polylepis* region. Andes of W Venezuela, NC Colombia and E Ecuador. Relatively long and pointed wings, large primary projection; eyes yellow.

156a **Adult** Typical. Grey-brown, densely spotted head, contrasting with rich rufous-brown back; blackish-edged white bars and spots on back and wings. Dark tail with 6-7 visible black-framed white spots and pale tip.

156b **Adult** Red morph. Crown more streaked than spotted; back indistinctly barred (not spotted) with pale rufous-buff; tail-bars washed pale rufous.

156c **Adult** Intermediate. Dorsal view, showing the wide nuchal half-collar.

156d **Adult** In flight, showing the pointed wings.

156e **Juvenile** Grey-brown morph.

157 Yungas Pygmy Owl *Glaucidium bolivianum*   Text and map page 365

Cloud forest (especially yungas) in E Andes. N Peru to Bolivia and N Argentina. Similar in size and plumage to Andean Pygmy Owl, but with different vocalisations and more rounded wings; eyes yellow.

157a **Adult** Typical grey morph. Longer tail than Andean Pygmy Owl, with 5-6 visible white bars, not extending to shafts. Flanks more striped than barred.

157b **Adult** In flight, showing more rounded wings and longer tail.

157c **Adult** Red morph. Tail with 6-7 rufous-washed spots, not extending to shafts.

157d **Adult** Dorsal view showing occipital face.

158 Peruvian Pygmy Owl *Glaucidium peruanum*   Text and map page 367

Dry bushland, thorn scrub with cacti and scattered trees, semi-open woodland, groves, riparian woodland, agricultural land with trees, even town parks (e.g. Lima), from sea-level to 3,500m. W Ecuador, W and SW Peru to northernmost Chile. Round-winged, tiny owlet similar to Yungas Pygmy Owl, with different vocalisations; eyes and toes yellow, bill greenish-yellow.

158a **Adult** Typical dark grey morph. With ochraceous zone on upper mantle beneath the 'occipital face'. Crown and nape with distinct fine white spots and streaks, back, scapulars and wing-coverts with large white spots, tail with 5-6 visible bars not extending to feather shafts.

158b **Adult** Red morph. Rufous-brown above, crown and nape with light shaft-streaks. Tail-bars with rufous wash, sometimes extending to shafts, light bands wider than in grey morph. Below, flanks more suffused with rufous, streaking more indistinct.

159 Austral Pygmy Owl *Glaucidium nanum*   Text and map page 368

Rather open forest, open country with shrubs, locally parks and farmland, in south also humid *Nothofagus* forest. S Andes from C Chile and Patagonia south to Tierra del Fuego. Relatively large and long-tailed owlet, less polymorphic (no foxy-red morph known); tail with 8-11 rufous or buffy bars; eyes yellow.

159a **Adult** Typical grey-brown morph. Relatively small eyes in comparison with Ferruginous Pygmy Owl. Crown, forehead and nape with light shaft-streaks. Below, streaked on a white ground colour, white areas on each side of breast extending down to flanks, also white central stripe from throat to abdomen.

159b **Adult** In flight, showing the densely barred tail.

159c **Adult** Dorsal view showing occipital face.

159d **Adult** Red morph. Identical in pattern to grey morph.

159e **Juvenile** Plain, unspotted crown, sparsely striped nape, indistinct 'occipital face'. Wings and tail not fully grown. Below, more uniform coloration, but light areas visible on flanks and centrally. Eyes more orange-yellow.

156a

156b

156e

156d

156c

157a

157c

157d

157b

158a

158b

159b

159c

159a

159e

159d

1996 Weick

160 Ferruginous Pygmy Owl *Glaucidium brasilianum*   Text and map page 370

Subtropical and tropical forest, edges, arid forest, thorn-scrub areas, parks and larger gardens. South America, from C and E Colombia and Venezuela south to Argentina and Uruguay. Highly polymorphic owlet with large variation in size; relatively large yellow eyes; bill yellow to yellowish-green; toes pale to dark yellow.

160a   **Adult** (*stranecki*: C and E Argentina and S Uruguay) Typical grey-brown morph. Large size. Plumage variable as in nominate *brasilianum*, but more distinctly striped below. Tail with 6-7 white to pale rufous bands. Smaller-scale dorsal view also shown. (Most specimens belong to a brown morph.)

160b   **Adult** (*stranecki*) Dorsal view showing occipital face.

160c   **Adult** (nominate *brasilianum*: NE Brazil south to E Paraguay, NE Argentina and N Uruguay) Typical brown male. Plain-coloured back, narrowly white-edged scapulars. Plain lesser wing-coverts and less distinct underpart stripes than in *stranecki*.

160d   **Adult** (nominate *brasilianum*) Red morph, in flight. Banded, rufous-washed tail.

160e   **Adult** (nominate *brasilianum*) Red morph. Dorsal view, showing plain rufous tail.

160f   **Adult** (*ucayalae*: Venezuela, Colombia and Amazonian Brazil south to E Ecuador, E Peru and Bolivia) Female, red morph. Bright rufous-brown crown concolorous with back, fine shaft-streaks not obvious. Tail uniform and brighter than back. Below, same dark markings as on back, heavily developed. (A brown morph with a light-barred tail is also frequent.)

160g   **Adult** (*duidae*: Mt Duida, Venezuela) Female. Darkest of all subspecies, darker and less rufous than *ucayalae*. Black-bordered nuchal band and black ear-coverts; crown and nape with fine white or ochraceous shaft-stripes. Tail black, with five white, incomplete bars.

161 Ridgway's Pygmy Owl *Glaucidium ridgwayi*   Text and map page 372

Arid forest, bushy country and giant cactus groves. S USA to Mexico, Panama and extreme NW South America. (Mostly regarded as subspecies of Ferruginous Pygmy Owl, but different vocalisations and DNA.)

161a   **Adult** (nominate *ridgwayi*: S Texas and E Mexico to Panama and extreme NW Colombia) Red morph. Rusty-brown. Lighter in colour but similar in pattern to Ferruginous Pygmy Owl. Tail always barred in this morph. Scapulars with roundish spots, greater wing-coverts more or less spotted. Bill and cere yellowish-green to greyish-yellow.

161b   **Adult** (nominate *ridgwayi*) In flight.

161c   **Adult** (nominate *ridgwayi*) Red morph. Dorsal view, showing uniform back and the rufous-washed tail-bands not extending to feather shafts.

161d   **Adult** (*cactorum*: S Arizona to Nayarit and Jalisco, W Mexico) Typical grey-brown morph. With buff to rufous bands on secondaries and tail (bands white in grey morph of nominate *ridgwayi*). Paler plumage in all morphs, also shorter wings and longer tail.

161e   **Adult** (*cactorum*) Dorsal view showing occipital face.

162 Chaco Pygmy Owl *Glaucidium tucumanum*   Text and map page 373

Dry forest and thorny scrub with cacti, arid bushy country, locally in or near settlements, up to 1,800m. SE Bolivia, NW and N Argentina and SW Paraguay. Small and dark owlet with distinct 'occipital face' and mostly plain mantle; eyes and bill yellow.

162a   **Adult** (nominate *tucumanum*: Argentina and Paraguay) Typical grey morph. Plumage without any tinge of brown. Wings and underpart stripes dark fuscous, wing-coverts without or with only few spots. Tail with 4-5 incomplete bars. (The taxon *pallens* of SE Bolivia has a whitish-spotted mantle.)

162b   **Adult** (nominate *tucumanum*) Grey morph. Dorsal view showing occipital face.

162c   **Adult** (nominate *tucumanum*) Red morph. Unspotted mantle, back, scapulars and wing-coverts, but tail with 6-7 visible rufous-washed bars extending to shafts.

160a

160b

160e

160d

160c

160f

160g

161a

161c

162a

162b

161b

162c

161d

161e

1997
KIECK

163 Collared Owlet *Glaucidium brodiei*   **Text and map page 375**

Montane and open hill forest between 800m and 3,200m. S Asia. A barred, grey-brown owlet with prominent white eyebrows and throat patch and buffy-rufous 'occipital face'; yellow underwing-coverts conspicuous in flight; eyes lemon-yellow.

163a Adult (nominate *brodiei*: Himalayas from Pakistan east to S China, south to Bangladesh, Malay Peninsula, Thailand, Sumatra, Borneo and Hainan) Grey morph, also in flight. Greyish head with numerous white and creamy spots; back barred sandy and dark; wings and tail whitish-spotted and barred. Grey, white-spotted breast band, sometimes interrupted centrally; middle breast and belly white; breast sides and flanks barred white, rufous and dark grey-brown. Lemon-yellow eyes; greenish-yellow bill and toes.

163b Adult (nominate *brodiei*) Rufous morph. Crown and back unspotted, nape with few spots. Distinct white scapular webs. Barring of wings, tail, breast and flanks suffused with rufous.

163c Adult (*tubiger*, synonymised with nominate: Thailand, Hainan and east to S China) Typical morph. Similar to nominate *brodiei*, but back, wings and flanks with more buffy to rufous wash.

163d Adult (*tubiger*) Rufous morph. With more banded appearance: barred back, wings and tail with wider-spaced rufous bands.

163e Adult (*pardalotum*: Taiwan) Paler above and below, with drop-shaped shaft-streaks on white belly.

164 Jungle Owlet *Glaucidium radiatum*   **Text and map page 376**

Deciduous forest and secondary jungle. Indian Peninsula and Sri Lanka. Distinctly larger than Collared Owlet, with similar barred plumage; fulvous to rufous underwing-coverts conspicuous in flight; eyes lemon-yellow, bill grey- to greenish-yellow, feet dirty greenish-yellow.

164a Adult (nominate *radiatum*: range of species apart from coastal SW India) Typical grey-brown morph, also in flight. Dark grey-brown above, barred pale buff to rufous. Eyebrows, chin, central breast and abdomen white; breast sides, sides of belly and flanks barred grey-brown, washed pale sandy to off-white.

164b Adult (*malabaricum*: coast of Malabar and Travancore) Rufous morph. Much darker, more rufous to chestnut on crown, nape, lower back, wings and sides of breast, but pale creamy tail-bands.

165 Chestnut-backed Owlet *Glaucidium castanonotum*   **Text and map page 377**

Dense forest of wet zone, from lowlands up to 1,950m. W Sri Lanka.

165 Adult Perched and in flight. Similar to Jungle Owlet, but bright chestnut back with few, narrow blackish cross-bars and more rufous on wings with few black bars and spots. Head and sides of breast as Jungle Owlet, but flanks, belly and abdomen with dark brown shaft-streaks instead of bars. Eyes yellow; bill yellow to greenish-horn, cere dusky greenish; feet yellowish-olive.

166 Sjöstedt's Owlet *Glaucidium sjostedti*   **Text and map page 378**

Humid lowland primary forest. Africa from Cameroon, Gabon and N Congo to NW and C Zaire.

166 Adult Perched and in flight. Extremely large *Glaucidium* owl with brightly coloured plumage. Plain cinnamon-rufous underwing-coverts conspicuous in flight. Head, neck and face barred dusky brown and white; back and scapulars deep chestnut, some feathers edged white; upperwing-coverts dark chestnut, few edged with white. Remiges and rectrices dusky brown, finely barred white; tail dusky, finely barred white. Throat plain white, breast cinnamon with fine brown barring, belly, tarsi and abdomen pale cinnamon-rufous with few brown bars. Eyes yellow.

163a

163a

163c

163e

163b

163d

164a

165

164a

164b

165

166

166

166

1996
WEICK

PLATE 51: AFRICAN OWLETS

167 African Barred Owlet *Glaucidium capense* **Text and map page 379**

Woodland, forest edge, secondary growth and riverine forest; primary forest in W Africa. From S Kenya south to E Cape Province, and southwest to Angola and Namibia; disjunct populations in Liberia, Ivory Coast, NW Zaire and SW Uganda. Larger than Pearl-Spotted Owlet (Plate 45), with relatively small feet; rounded head, no 'false eyes'; bill, cere and feet greenish-yellow, eyes yellow.

167a Adult (nominate *capense*: E Cape and Natal to S Mozambique) Larger and darker than *ngamiense*, with narrower tail-bands, and paler below with dark spots.

167b Adult (*ngamiense*: E Transvaal and N Botswana north to C Tanzania, including Mafia Island, and SE Zaire, west to Angola and Namibia) Perched and in flight. Mantle, back, wing-coverts and breast band more cinnamon than in nominate *capense*, with pale buff bars. Remiges and tail cinnamon-brown with buffy bars; scapulars white, edged brown (dark-edged in nominate). Belly whitish, with flanks washed pale buff and few rufous-cinnamon spots. Western birds tends to duller and greyer in plumage.

167c Juvenile (*ngamiense*) At 20 days, with white, downy head and moulting in mesoptile plumage.

167d Juvenile (*ngamiense*) At 35 days. Very similar to adult plumage, but barely visible primaries and rectrices.

167e Adult (*etchecopari*: forest of Liberia and Ivory Coast) Small and dark, with almost unmarked upperparts and narrow, barely visible tail-bands; less distinctly barred remiges. (Isolated distribution and vocalisations suggest that this may be a separate species.)

167f Adult (*scheffleri*: forest of NE Tanzania and S Kenya) Similar to *ngamiense*, but brighter chestnut-rufous breast and upperparts, and unbarred back beneath dark buffy-rufous nuchal band.

---

168 Chestnut Owlet *Glaucidium castaneum* **Text and map page 380**

Rainforest. NE Zaire and SW Uganda.

168 Adult Perched and in flight. Similar to race *scheffleri* of African Barred Owlet, but with brighter chestnut-coloured back; head ferruginous and spotted (not barred). Some show plain rufous upperwing-coverts. Eyes yellow.

---

169 Albertine Owlet *Glaucidium albertinum* **Text and map page 381**

Montane forest with dense undergrowth. Albertine Rift in NE Zaire and N Rwanda. Known only from five specimens.

169 Adult Perched and in flight. Size as African Barred Owlet. Warm maroon-brown head, spotted not barred; plain maroon-brown back, small creamy scapular spots, and almost unspotted lesser wing-coverts. Primaries 10 to 8 with uniform outer webs. Tail with seven visible narrow bars. Bare parts undescribed (painted as for related forms).

167b

167a

167c

167b

167d

167e

167f

169

168

169

168

1996 WEICK

PLATE 52: OWLETS AND ELF OWL

170 Asian Barred Owlet *Glaucidium cuculoides*   **Text and map page 381**

Open forest of pine, oak, rhododendron etc, also evergreen jungle, from lowlands up to 2,700m.
Himalayas from Pakistan east to NE India, SE Tibet and S China, south to SE Asia (not Malaya) and
Hainan. Larger than Jungle Owlet (Plate 50); iris lemon-yellow; bill greenish-yellow, cere horn-green;
feet grey to olive-yellow and claws horn-brown.

> **170a Adult** (nominate *cuculoides*: W Himalayas from Murree to Nepal) Dark brown to olive-brown,
> closely barred buffy to white, both above and below. White eyebrows, lores, chin, throat band,
> abdomen and undertail-coverts. White spots on outer webs of scapulars and greater coverts.
> Secondaries banded buff, tail banded whitish.

> **170b Juvenile** (nominate *cuculoides*) At 18 days, with mesoptile feathers just growing on head, back,
> breast and wings. Tail feathers not visible.

> **170c Adult** (*rufescens*: Sikkim, Bhutan, S Yunnan, south to Bengal and E Burma, Shan States and SE
> Tibet) In flight. (Includes *austerum* as synonym.)

> **170d Adult** (*persimile*: Hainan) More rufous than *rufescens*, especially on head, back, scapulars and
> upperwing-coverts.

> **170e Adult** (*bruegeli*: Tenasserim and Thailand east to S Laos, Cambodia and S Vietnam) Much
> paler than nominate *cuculoides*; also paler than *whitelyi* and rather smaller in size. Pale head
> and nape; pale and narrow barring. Primary coverts washed rufous. Belly and flanks with pale
> streaking. (Subspecies *deignani* treated as a synonym.)

> **170f Adult** (*whitelyi*: Sichuan, Yunnan, N Vietnam and SE China) Largest subspecies. Similar to
> nominate *cuculoides*, but with large white centre of breast, paler belly and wider flank-barring;
> few shaft-stripes on belly. Underwing-coverts off-white with fine shaft-streaks.

---

171 Javan Owlet *Glaucidium castanopterum*   **Text and map page 382**

Primary and secondary forest, gardens and villages. Lowlands and hills of Java and Bali.

> **171 Adult** Perched and in flight. Size similar to Asian Barred Owlet. Upperparts rufous-chestnut,
> scapulars white on outer webs. Head, nape, neck and sides of breast barred brown and ochre,
> centre of breast and belly whitish, with chestnut-striped flanks; bold white chin patch, brown
> and buff gorget. Eyes yellow; bill greenish, tipped yellow; feet greenish-yellow.

---

172 Long-whiskered Owlet *Xenoglaux loweryi*   **Text and map page 383**

Humid cloud forest. E Andes in N Peru (Rio Mayo).

> **172 Adult** Perched and in flight. Smallest owl. No ear-tufts but with whiskers extending out from
> sides of facial disc, and with bristles at base of bill projecting beyond bill and cere and
> extending upwards between eyes. Entire plumage finely barred, with white eyebrows, sides of
> neck and scapular spots; body plumage soft, long and dense. Iris amber-brownish; bill
> greenish-grey with yellow tip, cere pinkish-grey; tarsi and toes fleshy-pink.

---

173 Elf Owl *Micrathene whitneyi*   **Text and map page 384**

Cactus desert, dry woodland, thorn forest, locally also semi-open swampy bushland. SW USA to C
Mexico. Eyes yellow.

> **173a Adult** (nominate *whitneyi*: SW California to SW New Mexico and Sonora) Brown morph.
> Brown upperparts, and conspicuous cinnamon blotching below. (Grey morph has more
> brownish-grey plumage, but also with tiny buff or pale tawny spots and identical in pattern.)

> **173b Adult** (*idonea*: Lower Rio Grande Valley, south to EC Mexico). Above, paler grey-brown; tail-
> bands broader and paler. Below, with more white and a paler wash. (Subspecies *sanfordi* of S
> Baja California similar, but less whitish below.)

> **173c Adult** (*graysoni*: Socorro Island, W Mexico) In flight. Above, more olive-brown, with broad,
> deep cinnamon-buff tail-bands. Less white below, blotched cinnamon.

170c

170e

170f

170d

170a

170b

171

171

172

172

173a

173b

173c

WEICK 96

PLATE 53: LITTLE OWLS

174 Burrowing Owl *Athene cunicularia*   **Text and map page 386**

Open country, including grassland desert and farmland. W North America and Mexico to S South America. Long-legged owlet with bristled toes, yellow eyes, greenish-horn bill; face with brownish patch, white eyebrows and fore-collar; varies in depth and intensity of coloration, presence of dark bars and spots below, and size. Some southern subspecies overlap and intergrade (the number of races recently recognised is too high).

174a Adult (*hypugaea*: W North America south to Baja California and C Mexico, W Panama) Perched and in flight. Intermediate in size, and heavily marked ochraceous to warm sepia plumage. Broad chest band with pale buffy spots; white belly boldly barred and with pale sandy to creamy wash.

174b Adult (*floridana*: Florida and Bahamas) Darker warm brown than *hypugaea*, with narrow, less spotted breast band and much whiter belly.

174c Adult (*troglodytes*: Hispaniola, with Gonave and Beata Islands) Smaller and darker than *floridana*, with broad, white-spotted chest band and more barring below.

174d Juvenile (*hypugaea*) Remiges and rectrices as adult, but downy lesser wing-coverts. Crown, nape and back mostly light buff. Uppertail-coverts and underparts immaculate pale buff to white; sides of chest, sometimes whole upper chest, shaded and barred brown; uniform brown throat band.

174e Adult (*juninensis*: Andes of C Peru south to W Bolivia and NW Argentina) Pale pinkish-buff in colour, with large white blotches above. Few fawn-coloured ventral bars, and large whitish area on belly. (Form *punensis* from W Ecuador to W Peru similar in plumage and large size, probably a synonym.)

174f Adult (*grallaria*: N to SE Brazil) Darker above than *hypugaea*, with rufous wash and small scapular spots. Below, dark, distinctly spotted chest band, belly with few rusty bars and pale buffy wash.

174g Adult (nominate *cunicularia*: Chile, Bolivia, Paraguay, Uruguay, S Brazil and Argentina south to Tierra del Fuego) Large brown subspecies, densely spotted above and barred below. Distinctly paler in southern parts of its range.

174h Adult (*pichinchae*: Andes of W Ecuador) Dark grey-brown above, without rufous shades and with fine, dense spots, larger on nape and scapulars. Wings narrowly banded, tail with buffy-washed bars on outer feathers. Below, narrow dark barring, denser on chest; abdomen almost unspotted. (Subspecies *tolimae* from W Colombia similar in plumage, but with smaller size.)

175 Forest Owlet *Athene blewitti*   **Text and map page 387**

Forest of C India. Rediscovered in 1997 near Bombay, after absence of any records since 1884.

175 Adult Perched and in flight. Larger, shorter-winged and longer-tailed than Spotted Owlet (Plate 54). Eyes yellow; bill yellow; tarsi feathered, and feet more massive than those of Spotted. Crown sepia-brown, unspotted or faintly spotted; back plain, with much-reduced spotting. Tail broadly banded with white (bands wider than 5mm). Continuous collar and large white throat patch extending to centre of abdomen; sides of breast barred dark grey-brown. Tarsi white.

174a

174b

174c

174d

174a

174e

174f

174g

175

174h

175

1996
WEICK

PLATE 54: LITTLE OWLS

176 Little Owl *Athene noctua*   **Text and map page 389**

Open country with trees and bushes, e.g. farmland, rocky country, steppe and semi-desert, open woodland, and urban parks. Eurasia and N Africa, south to Mauretania, Sahara, Red Sea coast and Somalia, Himalayas and Korea; introduced in New Zealand. Rather small, 'earless', compact and tubby owl, less arboreal and more terrestrial, with spotted upperparts and streaked or spotted underparts and relatively long legs; plumage colour highly variable; feathered and bristled tarsi, more bare at rear; tarsi yellow to greyish-yellow, toes grey-brown to blackish; bill lemon to greenish-yellow, cere slate-grey to blackish; eyes lemon-yellow, eyelids dark slate-blue.

176a Adult (nominate *noctua*: C Europe, south to Italy and east to NW Russia) In flight. Dark russet-brown above; whitish below, with russet-brown streaks, these rather narrower than in *vidalii*. Reduced tail-bars.

176b Neoptile (nominate *noctua*) With short and dense first down, white with grey mottling.

176c Juvenile (nominate *noctua*) Rather like adult, but paler ground colour, less contrasting upperpart spots and face, pale creamy neck sides and indistinct white throat patch.

176d Adult (*vidalii*: W Europe, north to Britain and east to Belgium) Darkest subspecies. Rather cold, dark fuscous-brown with olive tinge; clearer white spots above than in nominate *noctua*. Streaked umber-brown below. (Subspecies *ludlowi* from Ladakh and Tibet very similar in colour, but distinctly larger.)

176e Adult (*indigena*: Balkan Peninsula, Aegean Islands, Asia Minor and Ukraine, east to Ural river and Caspian) Paler, russet to greyish olive-brown, more rufous than nominate *noctua*.

176f Adult (*bactriana*: Iraq and Iran east to Pakistan and northeast to Lake Balkhash) Grey morph. Large size, feathered toes. Pale greyish-brown, similar to grey morph of *glaux*.

176g Adult (*glaux*: N Africa east to Egypt) Rufous morph. Similar to rufous morph of *bactriana*, but smaller and varying from pale rufous to brownish-buff. Irregularly spotted tail. (Subspecies *saharae* similar in plumage to *glaux* or somewhat paler, treated as synonym.)

176h Adult (*lilith*: S Turkey through Levant to Arabian Peninsula, overlapping with *bactriana* in east of range) Palestine birds much whiter on crown, nape, back and wings as in all desert forms. Less streaked below. (Possibly a separate species according to voice and DNA evidence.)

176i Adult (*spilogastra*: Sudan to N Ethiopia) Small size, thinly bristled legs. Paler than *glaux*, with light, almost unspotted belly. (This and *somaliensis* may represent a separate species.)

176j Adult (*somaliensis*: SW Ethiopia to N Somalia) Dwarfish subspecies with thinly bristled legs. Darker than *spilogastra*, with fewer white markings on head.

177 Spotted Owlet *Athene brama*   **Text and map page 391**

Open and semi-open country, including farmland, open forest, edges, semi-desert and villages, from lowlands up to 1,400m. S Iran, east to India and Indochina; overlaps with Little Owl in Middle East. Differs from Little Owl in nape pattern and barred (not striped) underparts; eyes yellow; bill greenish-horn, cere dusky green; feet dirty yellowish-green.

177a Adult (nominate *brama*: S India, south of 20°N) In flight. Smallest subspecies; darker than *indica*. Above, brown with shades of grey and rufescent, and small spots; nape with larger spots forming collar. Forehead, eyebrows and lores white to pale buffy; wings spotted and banded white, tail with narrow white bars.

177b Adult (*pulchra*: Burma, S Yunnan, Thailand, Cambodia, Laos and S Vietnam) Small size. Rather darker than nominate *brama*, with slaty tinge, and larger white spots.

177c Adult (*ultra*: NE Assam) Darkest and largest race, with reduced white spotting.

177d Adult (*indica*: Afghan frontier east to Assam and Bangladesh and south in Indian Peninsula to 20°N) Paler and larger than *brama*. Less brown, more clay-coloured wings and tail, clearly marked with white. (Subspecies *albida* from Iran and Baluchistan is similar in colour to *indica*.)

176a

176g

176b

176f

176j

176d

176i

176e

176h

176c

177a

177c

177b

177d

1996 WEICK

178 Tengmalm's Owl *Aegolius funereus*   Text and map page 392

Natural coniferous forest, locally deciduous and mixed forest, from lowlands up to at least 3,000m. Eurasia and North America. Small, round-headed owl, dark brown and spotted above, white and blotched below, with dull white facial disc with black upper corners, distinct rim and white eyebrows; feathered tarsi and toes; eyes bright yellow; bill pale horn to bluish; soles greyish-yellow.

    178a   **Adult** (nominate *funereus*: N and C Europe to W Siberia) Perched and in flight. Above, more russet-brown tinge; below, paler with large white blotching.

    178b   **Mesoptile** (nominate *funereus*) Loose and soft mesoptile down all chocolate-brown, with darker face and indistinct whitish eyebrows, lores and base of bill.

    178c   **Juvenile** (nominate *funereus*) Growing wings and tail visible and similar to adult. Body chocolate-brown.

    178d   **Adult** (*magnus*: NE Siberia to Kamchatka) Pale grey-brown above, with large white spots on nape, scapulars, wing-coverts and chest; below, mostly white. (Subspecies *sibiricus* of C Siberia to Sakhalin and NE China similar in plumage; *pallens* from N Mongolia intermediate between nominate *funereus* and *magnus*.)

    178e   **Adult** (*richardsoni*: N North America, south locally to Oregon and New Mexico) Darker than nominate *funereus*, warmer brown above with smaller white spots; below, large throat patch, more distinct warm brown pattern and white spots.

181 Buff-fronted Owl *Aegolius harrisii*   Text and map page 398

Primarily montane forest, in Andes from 1,700 up to 3,100m. South America.

    181   **Adult** (nominate *harrisii*: Andes of Venezuela, Colombia and Ecuador to Bolivia) Round-headed owl, dark brown above. Creamy forehead, with white eyebrows and lores; facial disc creamy, with black upper corners above yellow eyes, and dark facial rim bordered creamy. Broad pale ochre nuchal band and scapulars; spotted wing-coverts and banded wings and tail. Black throat patch and plain creamy to pale ochre underparts. Tarsi feathered, toes bare. (Subspecies *dabbenei* of NW Argentina is similar to nominate *harrisii*; *iheringi* of E Brazil and immediately adjacent areas also similar, but lacks throat patch and has more buffy facial rim and blacker hindneck.)

179 Northern Saw-whet Owl *Aegolius acadicus*   Text and map page 395

Forest, especially coniferous, swampy woodland, locally drier and more open country. N America south to C Mexico. Smaller than Tengmalm's Owl; pointed wings; reddish-brown above, white below with reddish streaks; red face streaky-looking, no dark rim; pale scapulars; bill dark; eyes and toes yellow; tarsi and toes (partly) feathered; white underwing-coverts.

    179a   **Adult** (nominate *acadicus*: British Columbia east to Newfoundland, and south to California, Arizona and N Mexico) Perched and in flight. Head narrowly streaked with white, nape with large white spots. Secondaries and outer primaries spotted with white on outer webs. Tail with 2-3 broken narrow white bands and white tip.

    179b   **Juvenile** (nominate *acadicus*) White eyebrows and lores contrast with uniform chocolate-brown head, back and breast band. Wings and tail as adult. Chin dull white, often invisible; rest of underparts plain tawny- to cinnamon-buff.

    179c   **Adult** (*brooksi*: Queen Charlotte Islands) Dark grey to sepia above, ochre nuchal band extending to sides of neck; below, with pale to rich ochre and rusty wash densely blotched and streaked sepia-brown.

180 Unspotted Saw-whet Owl *Aegolius ridgwayi*   Text and map page 397

Edges of montane and cloud forest, open woodland, in highlands between 1,350m and 2,500m. S Mexico to Costa Rica and Guatemala.

    180a   **Adult** (nominate *ridgwayi*: Costa Rica, S Mexico and Guatemala) Similar to young Northern Saw-whet Owl, without white spots above. Wood-brown underwing-coverts. Bill black, eyes yellow. (We consider *rostratus* from Guatemala to be a synonym.)

    180b   **Adult** ('*tacanensis*': Chiapas, Mexico) Possibly a hybrid of *acadicus* x *ridgwayi*.

178a

178d

178a

178c

178b

178e

181

179a

180b

180a

179b

179a

179c

1994 Weick

PLATE 56: HAWK OWLS

182 Rufous Owl *Ninox rufa*   **Text and map page 399**

Tropical rain forest, wet forested gullies and wooded swamps, from lowlands up to 1,800m. New Guinea, Aru Islands and N Australia. Large, rufous-coloured and long-tailed owl, male larger than female, with forehead, crown, upperparts and wings dark rufous, finely barred light brown; tail similar, but with broader bars; face blackish-brown; throat and underparts rich rufous with fine, narrow cream bars; legs feathered; eyes yellow; bill pale horn with short, dark bristles; toes pale yellow.

> **182a Adult** (nominate *rufa*: N Western Australia and Northern Territory) Typical. Large, and rather light in colour above and below.
>
> **182b Adult** (*queenslandica*: E Queensland) Darker above, cheeks rather dark; below, much colder brown cross-bands.
>
> **182c Adult** (*humeralis*: New Guinea and Waigeo) In flight. Above, dark as *queenslandica*; below, rather browner, less cinnamon. (Subspecies *aruensis* from Aru Islands much smaller than all other forms of this species.)
>
> **182d Mesoptile** (nominate *rufa*) Head, back and underparts covered with whitish down; dark face, wings and tail similar to adult.
>
> **182e Juvenile** (nominate *rufa*) Darker than adult with broader barring below.

183 Powerful Owl *Ninox strenua*   **Text and map page 401**

Densely forested ravines, woodland and scrub. SE Australia. Largest Australian owl, huge and dark, long-tailed but relatively small-headed; large, yellow eyes, indistinct facial disc; feathered tarsi, feet powerful and yellow, talons brown; large bill bluish-horn.

> **183a Adult** Perched and in flight. Ground colour above varies from grey-brown to dark brown. Forehead creamy-white, crown and nape finely spotted; back and wings irregularly barred creamy. Tail with six paler bars. Prominent eyebrows.
>
> **183b Juvenile** White, downy feathers on head, back and underside; growing feathers on crown and face. Scapulars, wings and tail as adult.

184 Barking Owl *Ninox connivens*   **Text and map page 402**

Riparian forest, woodland and savanna, in lowlands. Moluccas, New Guinea and Australia. Medium-sized, long-tailed, brown-grey owl with white-spotted wings, strongly streaked breast and yellow eyes; bill dark horn or blackish; legs pale yellow.

> **184a Adult** (nominate *connivens*: S Queensland, New South Wales, Victoria and S Australia; absent from C Australia and Nullarbor Plain) Dark morph, in flight. Forehead, crown and face dark grey-brown, upperwings and back with large white spots, tail indistinctly barred; streaked dark brown below.
>
> **184b Adult** (nominate *connivens*) Light morph. Rather paler grey-brown in colour and less distinctly striped below. (Subspecies *assimilis* from E New Guinea, Vulcan and Dampier Islands much smaller in size, but similar in plumage.)
>
> **184c Adult** (*rufostrigata*: Moluccas in Morotai, Halmahera, Bacan and Obi) Clearly browner plumage, especially underpart streaking, than nominate *connivens*.
>
> **184d Juvenile** (nominate *connivens*) With mesoptile feathers on crown, face and chest. Wings as adult, short tail feathers invisible.

182a

182b

182c

182d

182e

183a

183a

184a

184b

183b

184c

184d

1995 Weick

PLATE 57: HAWK OWLS

185 Sumba Boobook *Ninox rudolfi*   **Text and map page 403**

Open forest and farmland, in lowlands up to 500m. Sumba in Lesser Sundas.

> **185** **Adult** Larger than Morepork or Southern Boobook. Dark brown with rufous wash above, spotted on crown, nape and back; secondary coverts with two rows of bars, flight feathers with more bars than on related species. Throat plain white; rest of underparts washed rufous, with rufous-brown barring. Brown eyes, feathered tarsi, pale yellow toes.

186 Morepork *Ninox novaeseelandiae*   **Text and map page 404**

Forest and farmland. New Zealand and surrounding islands.

> **186** **Adult** (nominate *novaeseelandiae*: range of species apart from Lord Howe and Norfolk Islands) Small, dark-coloured owl with cinnamon-buff streaking on head and neck, and ocellated spots on breast and belly; highly variable plumage. Feathered tarsi, toes bare to bristled and yellow to yellow-brown; eyes bright yellow; bill dark with pale tip. (Subspecies *albaria* from Lord Howe Island, apparently extinct, light brown above and ocellated light brown below, and the slightly darker *undulata* from Norfolk Island are very similar in plumage to Tasmanian race *leucopsis* of Southern Boobook, 187h.)

187 Southern Boobook *Ninox boobook*   **Text and map page 405**

Varied habitats, from forest and farmland to desert, including parks and urban areas. Indonesia and New Guinea region, Australia and Tasmania. Small and highly variable owl; eyes yellowish-green, bill and toes grey, tarsi feathered. Taxonomic position unclear, requiring further research and study on its relationship to Morepork; subspecies *lurida*, different in plumage and habitat, may represent separate species.

> **187a** **Adult** (*fusca*: Lesser Sundas on Timor, Roma and Leti) Dark, cold grey-brown colour, without any trace of brown or rufous. (Subspecies *pusilla* from New Guinea, with similar plumage, perhaps a synonym.)

> **187b** **Adult** (*cinnamomina*: Lesser Sundas on Babar Islands) Entirely deep cinnamon.

> **187c** **Adult** (*lurida*, Red Boobook: rainforest of NE Queensland) Smaller and much darker than all other Australian subspecies. (Perhaps specifically distinct.)

> **187d** **Adult** (*ocellata*: inland S and W Australia, Queensland and Northern Territory) Light morph. Highly variable in size and colour. Paler in this morph than any other subspecies.

> **187e** **Adult** (*ocellata*) Dark morph. Odd individuals sometimes dark. (Form *moae* from Moa Island very similar in colour to this.)

> **187f** **Adult** (nominate *boobook*: S Queensland, New South Wales, Victoria and South Australia to SW Australia) Perched and in flight. Large subspecies with varying plumage. Brown above, heavily spotted white to creamy on scapulars and upperwing-coverts; forehead, crown, nape and back sepia, indistinctly streaked fawn to buffy; barred tail often suffused rufous-brown. Creamy-white eyebrows, lores and throat, dark face. Breast and belly with heavy dusky streaking. (Subspecies *halmaterina* of Kangaroo Island and *rufigaster* from SW Australia are synonyms.)

> **187g** **Juvenile** (nominate *boobook*) Mesoptile feathers on crown, face and breast. Greater wing-coverts and remiges are visible; tail hardly obvious.

> **187h** **Adult** (*leucopsis*: Tasmania, possibly straggling to Victoria and New South Wales) Smallest subspecies. Similar in colour to nominate *boobook*, but with small white dots on upperparts, especially on head and neck; strongly ocellated rufous-orange underparts.

185

187f

186

187a

187b

187c

187g

187d

187f

187e

187h

1996
Weick

PLATE 58: HAWK OWLS

188 Brown Hawk Owl *Ninox scutulata*　　　　　　　**Text and map page 407**

Forest and other wooded areas, gardens, often near water, from lowlands up to 1,300m. E and SE Asia from India to E Siberia and Japan, south to Sri Lanka, Malay Peninsula and Indonesia. Slender, dark-coloured and long-tailed owl, small- and round-headed; wings of northern, migratory birds pointed, those of residents more rounded; heavily dark-streaked on white ground colour below; eyes yellow; bill bluish-black, cere dull green; tarsi feathered, toes bristled and yellow.

188a　**Adult** (*japonica*: Ussuriland, SE Manchuria, N Korea and Japan; winters in Philippines, possibly also Greater Sundas). Palest subspecies. Pale chocolate-brown above, grey-brown on head and neck. Light eyebrows, lores and throat. Below, cream to white, with greyish rufous-brown streaking. Tarsi cream and brown. (Forms *florensis* and *ussuriensis* are synonyms.)

188b　**Adult** (nominate *scutulata*: Sumatra, Riau, Lingga and Bangka) Perched and in flight. Above, more chocolate-brown, with rufous tinge on wings. Below, rich rufous-brown streaking; chin and abdomen creamy-white, rest with pale buffy wash.

188c　**Mesoptile** (nominate *scutulata*) Similar to adult, but wings and tail short, still growing. Fluffy dark upper chest, thick remnants of down on head, neck and back.

188d　**Adult** (*lugubris*: N and C India) Grey-brown above, with white-spotted shoulders and scapulars. Throat and foreneck fulvous, streaked brown; rest of underparts white, washed pale fulvous, with reddish-brown streaks and more broken bars on belly. Tail barred black and tipped white.

188e　**Adult** (*randi*: Philippines) Above, as nominate *scutulata*, but more rufous-washed; below, darker-streaked. Larger feet and bill.

188f　**Adult** (*obscura*: Andaman and Nicobar Islands) Dark chocolate-brown above, with head and primary coverts blackish-brown; below, dark brown to rufous-brown, with barely visible white on abdomen.

188g　**Adult** (*javensis*: W Java) Very dark above; densely streaked below, with broken heart-shaped spots on belly.

188h　**Adult** (*borneensis*: Borneo and Natuna Islands) Dark and small, as *javensis*. Below, darker and more densely streaked and barred than *javensis*.

---

189 Andaman Hawk Owl *Ninox affinis*　　　　　　　**Text and map page 408**

Lowland forest. Andaman and Nicobar Islands.

189　**Adult** (nominate *affinis*: Andamans) Perched and in flight. Smaller and much browner than Brown Hawk Owl, with bright rufous tinge on wings and tail; scapular spots and wing- and tail-bars buffy to pale rufous; unspotted wing-coverts. Below, buffy to pale ashy ground colour, streaked bright rufous. Eyes yellow. (Subspecies *isolata* from Nicobar Islands is distinctly larger and browner in colour than nominate *affinis*.)

---

190 Madagascar Hawk Owl *Ninox superciliaris*　　　　　　　**Text and map page 409**

Rain forest, gallery forest, dry deciduous forest, thorn scrub and villages. Lowlands of NE, S and W Madagascar. Sexes similar. Brown, white-spotted crown; face tan-grey; distinct white eyebrows and throat; chin light brown. Bill and toes white to pale yellow; eyes dark brown.

190a　**Adult** Light morph, perched and in flight. Uniform brown above, with white-spotted scapulars and wing-coverts; remiges brown, with some white spots on inner secondaries and distinctly white-spotted primaries. Below, widely spaced brown bars on fulvous-washed white ground colour.

190b　**Adult** Dark morph. Darker above; dense barring on breast, and darker buffy to fulvous wash on flanks and feathered tarsi.

188a

188b

188c

188b

188e

188d

188g

188f

188h

189

190a

189

190a

190b

1996 Weick

PLATE 59: HAWK OWLS

191 Philippine Hawk Owl *Ninox philippensis*　　　　**Text and map page 410**

Forest edge, scrub. Philippines. Small, round-headed owl, brown to buffy and highly variable; eyes yellow, bill greenish with yellow tip, yellow toes densely bristled.

> **191a**　**Adult** (nominate *philippensis*: Luzon, Marinduque, Polillo, Buad, Catanduanes, Samar, Leyte) Typical individual, also in flight. Above, pale cinnamon-brown, washed rufous, with white spots on scapulars and wings; tail dark brown with paler bars. Below, white with tawny wash, stripes ill-defined.

> **191b**　**Juvenile** (nominate *philippensis*) Above, plain cinnamon-brown, with smaller scapular spots and fewer wing-spots; less distinctly barred remiges and dark-banded tail. Below, suffused tawny-rufous; lower part of tarsi bare. (Subspecies *proxima* from Masbate and *ticaoensis* from Ticao similar to juvenile, but with larger size and shorter tail; *centralis* from Panay to Siquijor and Bohol also similar to juvenile birds, but larger, longer-tailed and without rufous tint.)

> **191c**　**Adult** (*spilocephala*: Mindanao, Basilan, Dinagat, Siargao) Head and neck spotted or barred. Striped below or with tendency towards bars; breast with bright tawny wash, belly paler. (Subspecies *reyi* from the Sulu Archipelago is similar to *spilocephala*, but with prominent rufous barring on head and back.)

> **191d**　**Adult** (*spilonota*: Cebu, Sibuyan, Tablas, Camiguin Sur) Larger than *mindorensis*. Differs from all other subspecies in white, coarsely spotted and barred underparts.

192 Mindoro Hawk Owl *Ninox mindorensis*　　　　**Text and map page 411**

Forest. Mindoro, Philippines. Formerly treated as conspecific with Philippine Hawk Owl (see text).

> **192**　**Adult** Head, neck and back spotted or barred, scapulars with few large spots. Below, entirely vermiculated and barred, with dark-tinged chest and bright orange-rufous wash to belly and abdomen.

193 Ochre-bellied Hawk Owl *Ninox ochracea*　　　　**Text and map page 412**

Dense humid forest, up to 800m. Sulawesi and Buton. Sometimes referred to as *Ninox perversa*, but *N. ochracea* has priority.

> **193**　**Adult** Perched and in flight. Dark chestnut above, tinged brown, with dusky crown; large white scapular spots, white-spotted wing-coverts, buffy-barred remiges. Below, white throat, cinnamon-tawny breast and tawny-ochre belly. Yellow eyes.

194 Solomon Hawk Owl *Ninox jacquinoti*　　　　**Text and map page 412**

Forest. Solomon Islands. Medium-sized owl with two differently coloured subspecies groups.

> **194a**　**Adult** (nominate *jacquinoti*: Santa Isabel and New Georgia) Perched and in flight. Rufous-brown to blackish above, with numerous spots and bars; central tail feathers barred or unbarred. White eyebrows, throat, foreneck and belly; Brown-barred breast, at sides suffused with pale brown, belly with fine buffy-washed shaft-lines. Eyes and feet yellow; bill pale olive. (Subspecies *floridae* from Florida Island differs only in size; *eichhorni* from Bougainville, Choiseul and Treasure Islands differs in smaller size and coarser barring above; *mono* from Mono Islands has reduced white spotting on wings.)

> **194b**　**Adult** (*granti*: Guadalcanal) Lacks spotting and barring on head, back and scapulars; reduced spots and bars on wings and tail. White below, with heavy rufous-brown bars, more densely barred on breast sides. Eyes brown, sometimes yellow? (Subspecies *roseoaxillaris* from San Cristóbal is more rufous-cinnamon above, with some ochre nape spots, has white throat patch, darker breast, cinnamon belly with creamy bars and spots, pale abdomen, undertail-coverts and thighs, and pale pink axillaries.)

191a

191a

191d

192

191c

191b

194b

193

193

194a

194a

96
WEICK

195 Jungle Hawk Owl *Ninox theomacha* Text and map page 413

Humid forest, from lowlands up to 2,000m. New Guinea region. Very variable in size and plumage; eyes yellow to golden-yellow; bill black with white tip, cere greenish-black; tarsi feathered, legs dull brown to yellow.

195a **Adult** (nominate *theomacha*: New Guinea) Perched and in flight. Uniform deep chocolate-brown above, except for some light secondary spots. Below, throat and upper breast nearly plain dark brown, with some paler streaks on throat; lower breast, belly and tarsi bright rufous chestnut, more buffy on abdomen and undertail-coverts.

195b **Adult** (*hoedtii*: Waigeo and Misool) Similar to nominate *theomacha*, but duller above; sides of head brown rather than sooty. Lighter-coloured and distinctly striped on throat and foreneck.

195c **Adult** (*goldii*: D'Entrecasteaux Archipelago) Larger size. Above, similar in colour to nominate *theomacha*, but duller and with some tiny wing spots; much paler below, tawny to whitish, with distinct chestnut-brown streaking.

195d **Adult** (*rosseliana*: Louisiade Archipelago) In flight. Plumage as *goldii*, but with much whiter markings below.

196 Speckled Hawk Owl *Ninox punctulata* Text and map page 414

Farmland and cultivations, open woodland, often near habitations, from sea-level up to 800m (once 2,300m). Sulawesi. Dull reddish-brown above, with small white dots, including on wing-coverts and secondaries, with blackish-brown facial mask, white eyebrows, throat and neck sides; very variable below; eyes brown.

196a **Adult** Typical individual, perched and in flight. Below, white patch on breast, white belly, abdomen and tarsi, flanks with broad bars and buffy-rufous wash.

196b **Adult** Variant. Nearly uniform brown breast band, broadly barred rufous flanks, and white zone from lower breast down to abdomen, slightly buffy-washed. Tibia buffy, tarsi whitish.

197 Russet Hawk Owl *Ninox odiosa* Text and map page 415

Lowland and hill forest. New Britain.

197 **Adult** Perched and in flight. Similar to Speckled Hawk Owl, but longer-tailed and brighter. Bright rufous-brown upperparts with white spots and bars, larger white scapular spots. Below, bright rufous-brown chest band, barred white; belly white, heavily barred on flanks and with sharp shaft-streaks. Eyes orange-yellow. Tarsi feathered; toes bristled and yellowish-brown.

195a

195a

195b

195c

196a

195d

197

196a

197

196b

1996
WEICK

PLATE 61: HAWK OWLS

198 Moluccan Hawk Owl *Ninox squamipila* **Text and map page 416**

Thickets and forest, up to 1,750m. Moluccas and Tanimbar Islands. Eyes yellow (but nominate *squamipila* with brown irides), cere yellow, bill pale grey; feet bristled, bare parts yellow.

> **198a** **Adult** (nominate *squamipila*: Seram) Typical individual, also in flight. Dark reddish-brown above, darker on head; white-barred scapulars, rusty-barred wings and tail. Breast rufous with narrow dusky bars; belly and abdomen white, barred rusty to blackish.
>
> **198b** **Adult** (*hypogramma*: Halmahera, Ternate and Bacan) Light morph. Above, rusty-brown with cold, dusky crown; scapulars and greater coverts with white bars. Upper breast reddish-brown with dark barring; lower breast down to abdomen white, barred darker and with rufous wash.
>
> **198c** **Adult** (*hypogramma*) Dark morph. Scapulars and wing-coverts with few or no bars; white below, rufous-washed and densely barred, undertail-coverts barred white and rusty.
>
> **198d** **Adult** (*hantu*: Buru) Individual with wing spots. Dark rufous above, bright rufous to ochraceous below. Forehead, lores and chin whitish; below, barred dark to light rufous and white, undertail-coverts barred rufous and white or plain pale rufous.
>
> **198e** **Adult** (*hantu*) Lacking wing spots. Similar to 198d, but less rufous bars on nape, few pale rufous scapular spots. (Christmas Island Hawk Owl *Ninox natalis*, a separate allopatric species restricted to Christmas Island, is not illustrated: very similar in colour to *N. s. hantu*, but differs in vocalisations.)
>
> **198f** **Adult** (*forbesi*: Tanimbar Islands) Crown, back and chest much lighter-coloured than in all other forms. Mantle, scapulars and wing-coverts barred ochre-rufous and white, primary coverts plain and darker, wings and tail barred white; belly white with pale ochre-rufous bars. Feathered tarsi pale rufous.

199 Christmas Island Hawk Owl *Ninox natalis* **Text and map page 418**

Thickets and forest. Christmas Island.

> **199** **Adult** Similar to Moluccan Hawk Owl, but much smaller, with lighter, tawny-brown head. Tibia and tarsus feathered rufous-ochre with rufous-brown mottling up to the end of the metacarpus. Toes sparsely covered with pale horn-coloured bristles.

200 Manus Hawk Owl *Ninox meeki* **Text and map page 418**

Forest. Manus, in Admiralty Islands, Bismarck Archipelago.

> **200** **Adult** Perched and in flight. Rufous-brown, distinctly ochraceous-tinged hawk owl. Crown of male uniform rufous-brown, of female with barring; distinctly barred nape, scapulars, wing-coverts, rump and tail. Ear-coverts dark brown. Throat pale, breast tawny, rest of underparts white with rufous-brown streaking. Tarsi partly feathered and bristled, toes bristled and pale yellow; eyes pale yellow; bill slaty-blue, tip pale horn.

201 Bismarck Hawk Owl *Ninox variegata* **Text and map page 416**

Forest. E Bismarck Archipelago. Dark rufous-brown owl, more or less spotted above, light below with distinct barring; brown or yellow eyes, yellow bill and feet.

> **201a** **Adult** (nominate *variegata*: New Britain and New Ireland) Typical individual, also in flight. Dark sepia-brown above, with barred scapulars and spotted or barred wings and tail. Dark brown face. Throat pale, upper breast dark-coloured and barred, rest of underparts whitish with rufous-brown bars.
>
> **201b** **Adult** (*superior*: New Hanover) Light morph. Paler above, forehead slightly spotted; distinctly spotted and barred on mantle, back and wings. Pale face. Below, large and pale throat patch, light and barred breast band and fine brown barring on rest of underparts.

198a

198a

198b

198c

198d

198e

199

200

198f

199

200

201a

201b

201a

1996 Weick

PLATE 62: HAWK OWLS

203 Laughing Owl *Sceloglaux albifacies* **Text and map page 420**

Open country. New Zealand: now extinct. A relatively large owl with yellowish-brown plumage streaked dark brown, scapulars white-edged, head, hindneck and back edged whitish to pale yellowish, wings and tail brown with pale bars; tarsi feathered, yellowish to rufous-buff; toes bristled, fleshy to pale yellow, claws dark brown; bill horn-coloured, basally black; eyes dark orange to rufous.

203a Adult (nominate *albifacies*: South Island and Stewart Island) Perched and in flight. Above and below, rather lighter-coloured than *rufifacies*; whitish face, eyebrows and lores. Secondary coverts with distinctly whiter bars.

203b Adult (*rufifacies*: North Island) Perhaps only a rufous morph. More rufous-washed face, and rather darker rufous above and below.

204 Northern Hawk Owl *Surnia ulula* **Text and map page 421**

Rather open coniferous forest, forest edge and moorland. N Eurasia and N North America; partly migratory. Slim and medium-sized owl with Peregrine-like flight, pointed wings, long, graduated tail, bright yellow eyes, and pale yellow to greenish-yellow bill; dark brown above with heavy white spotting and streaking on head, back and wings, white-barred tail; white face with heavy black rim; white below, closely barred with slaty-black; white feathered tarsi and toes.

204a Adult (nominate *ulula*: N Eurasia from Scandinavia east to Siberia, Kamchatka and Sakhalin; in winters occasionally south south to C Europe) Perched and in flight. Smaller and lighter than *caparoch*, and much whiter on head, back and scapulars. Below, finer barring on white ground colour. (Subspecies *tianschanica* from Tien Shan intermediate in size and colour between nominate *ulula* and *caparoch*.

204b Mesoptile (nominate *ulula*) Unfledged, at 3 weeks, with distinct dark facial disc.

204c Juvenile (nominate *ulula*) Lacks dark mask; wings and tail growing larger.

204d Adult (*caparoch*: N North America from Alaska and Canada south to N Michigan; winters south to S Canada and N USA) Perched and in flight. Somewhat larger and with darker plumage than nominate *ulula*, less white-spotted above, and more narrowly barred tail. Large blackish bars on sides of foreneck. More heavily barred below, and with distinct brown wash on flanks and abdomen.

202 Papuan Hawk Owl *Uroglaux dimorpha* **Text and map page 419**

Forest, forest edge and gallery forest, from lowlands up to 1,500m. New Guinea, including Yapen Island.

202 Adult Perched and in flight. Slim, medium-sized hawk owl, small-headed, round-winged and long-tailed. Barred blackish-brown on back, wings and tail, on a rufous ground colour. Face, head and underparts streaked on whitish to pale rufous ground colour, darkest on chest. Forehead, eyebrows, throat and foreneck white with fine dark streaking. Base of bill white with fine, long and black bristles; tarsi feathered down to joint of pale toes; eyes yellow.

203a

203b

203a

204a

204d

204b

204c

202

204d

204a

202

1996 Weick

PLATE 63: EARED OWLS AND ALLIES

205 **Fearful Owl** *Nesasio solomonensis*   **Text and map page 422**

Lowland and hill forest. Bougainville, and Solomon Islands (Choiseul and Santa Isabel).

> **205** **Adult** Similar to Short-eared Owl, but without ear-tufts and with powerful bill and feet. Face rufous, dark around eyes, with white eyebrows, lores, chin and throat; white foreneck and upper breast, spotted and streaked blackish. Back and lesser wing-coverts streaked and barred; larger coverts, remiges and tail barred pale to rufous-brown. Tawny below, with dark streaking and hint of rufous bars. Feathered tarsi tawny, toes bristled; eyes yellow, bill black.

206 **Stygian Owl** *Asio stygius*   **Text and map page 423**

Forest, dense woodland and semi-open country, in hills and mountains up to 3,000m and above. Middle America, including Caribbean, and N South America. Medium-sized, slender owl with long ear-tufts; sooty-black above with whitish mottling, fuscous face; eyes orange-yellow; bill black, cere grey; toes fleshy and bristled, tarsi feathered.

> **206a** **Adult** (nominate *stygius*: Colombia, Venezuela and Ecuador, patchily south to SE Brazil and N Argentina) Darkest subspecies. Scapulars slightly spotted and barred; fine bars on outer webs of wing-coverts and secondaries; tail indistinctly barred. Below, heavily marked on throat and breast, belly with deep buffy wash. (Subspecies *siguapa* from Cuba, Isle of Pines, Gonave and Hispaniola is similar, but rather paler above and whiter below; *noctipetens* treated as a synonym.)
>
> **206b** **Adult** (*robustus*: Mexico to Nicaragua and Belize) Perched and in flight. Greyer above, with more distinct spotting on back, scapulars and secondaries; tail more distinctly banded. Below, with finer pattern and more whitish colour. (Form *lambi* treated as synonym.)

207 **Long-eared Owl** *Asio otus*   **Text and map page 424**

Coniferous, mixed and deciduous forest, edges and clearings, second growth, sometimes even in urban areas. Palearctic and N America. Rich buffy-brown, dark-streaked, long-eared owl with distinct facial disc and rim; eyes yellow to orange; bill and claws black, cere grey; tarsi and feet feathered.

> **207a** **Adult** (nominate *otus*: Azores, NW Africa, Iberia and British Isles east across Europe and C Asia, east to Japan, Manchuria and Ussuriland; winters south to Egypt, NW India and S China) Perched and in flight. Warm buff face, orange eyes. Below, heavily streaked and blotched on chest, more finely streaked but less barred on belly. (Subspecies *canariensis* smaller, with rather darker plumage, and paler, more mottled and vermiculated below.)
>
> **207b** **Neoptile** (nominate *otus*) Short, soft white down. Bare skin pink, bill bluish, cere pink-grey.
>
> **207c** **Mesoptile** (nominate *otus*) Long and soft, creamy to pale buff second down. Barred dusky grey to grey-brown. Flight feathers and tail similar to adult, not fully grown.
>
> **207d** **Adult** (*wilsonianus*: N America from Canada south to S USA; winters south to Florida and C Mexico) Eyes yellow, face golden-rufous. Above, more mottled and vermiculated; large white spots on crown, nape and scapulars. Below, rufous-white ground colour, more distinctly barred than nominate *otus*.

208 **Abyssinian Long-eared Owl** *Asio abyssinicus*   **Text and map page 426**

Forested areas. Highlands of NE Africa. Larger than Long-eared Owl, with more orange-rufous colour; more spotted than streaked below, with distinct barring and blotching, dividing incomplete white bars into blocks, giving chequered effect; eyes orange; feet powerful.

> **208a** **Adult** (nominate *abyssinicus*: Ethiopian highlands). Typical 'golden' specimen.
>
> **208b** **Adult** (*graueri*: Mt Kenya, Ruwenzori Mts south to E Zaire). Rather smaller, and distinctly darker and greyer than nominate *abyssinicus*.

209 **Madagascar Long-eared Owl** *Asio madagascariensis*   **Text and map page 427**

Rain and gallery forest, and dry deciduous forest. Madagascar.

> **209** **Adult** Sexes dimorphic in size. Blackish-brown above, mixed with golden-tawny. Face tan, with dark around eyes, pale eyebrows and lores, and distinct rim. Long, graduated ear-tufts. Below, dark-blotched chest, heavily streaked and barred belly and flanks. Powerful bill and feet, much stronger than on Abyssinian Long-eared. Eyes orange-yellow.

205

206b

206b

206a

207c

207a

207d

207a

207b

209

208a

208b

210 Striped Owl *Asio clamator*   **Text and map page 428**

Open and semi-open grassland, marshland, scrub, humid forest edge and woodland, from lowlands up to 1,600m. Middle and S America. Long-eared, robust, pale-faced owl; tarsi and toes feathered; eyes brown.

210a Adult (nominate *clamator*: Colombia, Venezuela, Peru and N and C Brazil) Perched and in flight. Darkest, heavily streaked subspecies. Ochraceous-buff above and below. Heavy streaking on head and nape, streaked and mottled blackish on back and wings, with light-spotted scapulars and wing-coverts. White eyebrows and lores, buffy face. White chin and throat, dark-blotched chest, belly with fine dark streaks. Tarsi plain buff. (Subspecies *forbesi* from S Mexico to Panama smaller and paler.)

210b Adult (*midas*: Bolivia and N Argentina to SE Brazil and Uruguay). Largest and palest subspecies. (Subspecies *oberi* from Tobago is known only from the type.)

210c Juvenile (nominate *clamator*) Dark eyes, distinct facial rim, but growing wings and tail are hardly visible.

---

211 Short-eared Owl *Asio flammeus*   **Text and map page 429**

Open country, tundra, marsh, moorland, grassland etc, also forest edge. N America, Greater Antilles, S America, Hawaiian Islands, Eurasia and NW Africa; northern and southernmost birds migratory. Long-winged, small-headed owl with heavily streaked, pale yellow-brown to ochre-white plumage, short ear-tufts usually invisible; dark wingtips and dark, broadly streaked chest obvious; pale face, with black surrounding yellow eyes.

211a Adult (nominate *flammeus*: N America, Eurasia and NW Africa) Typical individual, also in flight. Variable in ground colour, density and colour of streaking, and pattern. Bleaching and wear have marked influence, buff, tawny and cinnamon changing to white. N American specimens have stronger bill and feet.

211b Neoptile (nominate *flammeus*) Dense pinky-buff down. Bare parts pink to greyish.

211c Juvenile (nominate *flammeus*) Soft and long, indistinctly barred mesoptile feathers. Obvious dark face. Growing wings similar to those of adult.

211d Adult (*suinda*: S Peru, C Chile, Bolivia and Brazil south to Tierra del Fuego) Similar to nominate *flammeus*; more or less darker rufous in colour and rather smaller or larger in size, with stronger bill and feet.

211e Adult (*galapagoensis*: Galápagos Islands) Darkest, most buffy-rufous subspecies. Blackish face; more heavily marked and banded above and below. Smaller size.

---

212 Marsh Owl *Asio capensis*   **Text and map page 431**

Grassland, marsh and moorland, from lowlands up to 3,000m. Locally in NW and sub-Saharan Africa and Madagascar. Medium-sized, long-winged and dark-eyed owl, dark brown above, with dark brown and white face, dark brown chest and more or less lighter-coloured underparts; tarsi feathered, toes bristled; bill black, eyes brown.

212a Adult (nominate *capensis*: very patchily from Senegambia to Ethiopia and south to the Cape) Perched and in flight. Below, with dense barring, wider-spaced on belly and with distinct shaft-streaks. Noticeably smaller than *hova*. (Subspecies *tingitanus* from NW Africa is smaller, darker above and with whiter spots below.)

212b Juvenile (nominate *capensis*) Downy mesoptile feathers on head, back and underside. Growing wings and tail clearly visible.

212c Adult (*hova*: Madagascar) Much larger and stronger, with powerful bill and feet. Narrowly barred secondaries, more broadly barred primaries and tail. More barred and spotted below.

210a

210b

210a

210c

211a

211c

211a

212a

212a

211b

212b

211d

211e

212c

1996Weick

ORDER: OWLS (STRIGIFORMES)
FAMILY TYTONIDAE: BARN, GRASS AND BAY OWLS

Inner toe equal in length to middle toe: this is one of the most striking differences between members of this family and the true owls (Strigidae). Additional differences exist in skeleton (e.g. hind margin of sternum entire, furcula joined to keel of sternum) and plumage. 18 species.

Barn and Grass Owls, Genus *Tyto* Billberg, 1828

Rather long-legged owls with long wings and relatively short tail. Facial disc more or less heart-shaped; rim of feathers around disc whose inner (central) edges run to the base of the bill, forming a narrow vertical ridge of two parallel lines. Claw of central toe finely serrated on its inner edge. Cosmopolitan. We include the Itombwe Owl in this genus, and not in *Phodilus*, as photos of a recently caught bird show great similarities with barn owls and not with the Bay Owl *Phodilus badius* (e.g. the facial disc is that of a typical *Tyto*). Many *Tyto* owls require intensive study to clear up their taxonomic status, but this important work can be done only by a revision of the whole genus, including bioacoustical and molecular-biological (DNA) investigations. In addition, the biology, vocalisations and ecology of many taxa are poorly known or totally unknown. 17 species.

1 BARN OWL
Tyto alba   Plates 1 & 2

French: Chouette effraie
German: Schleiereule
Spanish: Lechuza de Campanarios
Portuguese: Suindara

IDENTIFICATION A medium-sized owl with heart-shaped facial disc, relatively long legs and no ear-tufts. Eyes relatively small, blackish. Upperparts yellowish-brown, with darker bars on flight feathers and tail; back with an ashy-grey tinge, suggesting a fine grey veil, with small black-bordered white spots. Underparts vary from white to clay-brownish, with or without fine dark spots. **Similar species** Other species of the genus *Tyto*. In Europe, this species is the only representative.

VOCALISATIONS A long, harsh screech is uttered both in flight and when perched: *chrrrrreeh*. This seems to have the function of a song, indicating the territory, and is given chiefly by the male, repeated at irregular intervals. The female utters a similar song, especially during courtship. A shrill purring is uttered against an intruder of the same species. Female and young birds beg with snoring sounds, which may be heard during the night for hours on end from a nest with chicks. When feeding their offspring, adults give series of metallic clicking sounds. Long-drawn, rushing sounds are aggressive vocalisations against enemies near the nest. Nestlings utter chirping notes when uneasy.

DISTRIBUTION Worldwide more than 30 subspecies have been described, all in temperate or warm climates. Absent from cold climates. See Geographical Variation and distribution map.

MOVEMENTS Adults are mostly resident. When food becomes scarce, however, many birds may emigrate. Directions in which they move vary, but in Europe very often towards the southwest; longest recorded distance from breeding place nearly 500km. In severe winters, entire populations of sedentary adults may sometimes even starve. Once independent, young disperse in autumn in various directions: longest known distance of a ringed bird 1,625km. Later, they tend to settle to breed in the region of their birth.

HABITAT Rather open countryside, such as pastureland, grassland, hilly landscapes with scattered trees, etc., cultivations, mostly near human settlements. Often in villages or even towns surrounded by open or semi-open country. In Europe, avoids higher altitudes and regions with more than 40 days of permanent snow cover. May roost in trees and taller bushes during daytime, but most frequently uses barns, attics of large buildings or church towers as day haunt. Outside Europe, inhabits open country, open forest with hollow trees, rocky canyons or ravines with steep walls, and also human settlements, but usually avoids dense forest and barren deserts; it is never found in the tundra region, and because of its low tolerance to cold avoids such areas as Siberia, N Russia, northern North America, N Scandinavia, and high altitudes in Asia (Himalayas).

DESCRIPTION *T. a. alba* **Adult** Crown and upperparts yellowish-brown to orange-buff, covered partly by a pale ashy-grey veil marked with scattered white spots surrounded by black. Tail similar with few darker bars and with white dots towards tips of feathers. Underparts whitish or pure white with a few small, dark drop-shaped spots (females often with more spots on underparts than males). Facial disc white, with brownish wash between lower edge of eye and base of bill; rim brown. Legs feathered white nearly to base of toes, the latter bare and hardly bristled. **Juvenile** Downy chicks white. Mesoptile plumage of young is similar to that of adult plumage, but more 'fluffy' because of their long, whitish underdown. **Bare parts** Eyes brownish-black. Bill whitish-pink. Toes pale greyish-brown, on underside dirty yellowish. Claws brownish-black.

MEASUREMENTS AND WEIGHT No evident difference in size between males and females. Total length about 34cm; wingspan 90-98cm. Wing (from wrist to tip) 260-309mm. Weight of males 250-357g, of females 320-480g.

GEOGRAPHICAL VARIATION Of the 35 or so described subspecies, we recognise 30; 18 are listed in full here (13 of them shown on plates 1 and 2), followed by 12 considered probably acceptable.

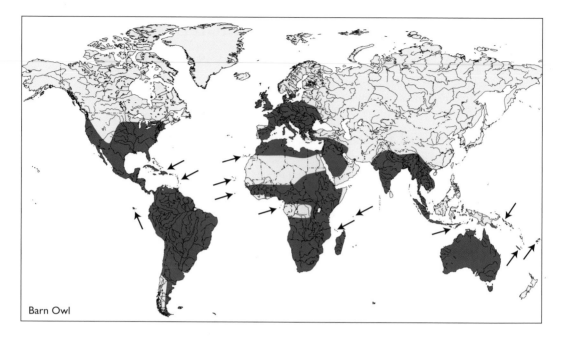

Barn Owl

T. a. alba (Scopoli, 1769). British Isles and W Europe; from E France eastwards merges with C European subspecies *guttata*, and in W Germany hybrids of the two may be found, showing a wide variety of colorations. See Description. Wing 278-302mm; tail 110-115mm.

T. a. guttata (C. L. Brehm, 1831). C and E Europe. Darker than nominate. Upperparts more orange-brown, with more pronounced grey veil; facial disc whitish, becoming brownish towards base of bill; underparts brownish-yellow with blackish spots; legs feathered pale brownish-yellow. Wing 270-300mm; tail 122-137mm; weight 241-380g.

T. a. ernesti (Kleinschmidt, 1901). Mediterranean region, merging with nominate *alba* in Spain. A very pale subspecies with pure white, often unspotted underparts; in flight, appears nearly white. Upperparts pale yellowish-brown with indistinct grey veil, and nearly white secondaries; facial disc white, with brownish wash between lower edge of eye and base of bill, rim less prominent than in other subspecies. Wing 281-309mm; tail 110-126mm.

T. a. affinis (Blyth, 1862). Africa south of Sahara. Similar to *guttata*, but with stronger feet and longer, sparsely feathered tarsi. Wing 270-312mm; tail 110-140mm.

T. a. hypermetra Grote, 1928. Madagascar and Comoro Islands. A rather large subspecies, similar in plumage to *affinis*, but with more distinct, brownish rim around disc and more boldly spotted underparts. Wing-coverts with a very pale area. Wing 300-320mm; tail 120-140mm.

T. a. stertens Hartert, 1929. Pakistan, India and Sri Lanka, east to Assam and Burma. Similar to nominate *alba*, but upperparts with prominent bluish-grey veil and little or no yellowish on back and head. Underparts white, very finely spotted dark. Wing 262-322mm; tail 119-129mm.

T. a. thomensis (Hartlaub, 1852). São Tomé. A very dark race, with dark grey upperparts finely spotted white. Facial disc and underparts yellowish-brown, the latter with dark, arrow-like dots. Wing 241-264mm; tail 97-114mm; weight of 1 male 380g.

T. a. delicatula (Gould, 1837). Australia, Tasmania, Timor, Solomon Islands; introduced New Zealand. Very short-tailed, like a grass owl [7, 8]. Upperparts with light grey veil, no yellowish-brown on back; facial disc and whole underparts white, with few dark spots on sides of breast, very few on wings; rim around disc rather indistinct. Wing 247-294mm; tail about 119mm; weight 230-470g.

T. a. pratincola (Bonaparte, 1838). N and C America from British Columbia to Florida and to E Guatemala and E Nicaragua, also locally in Caribbean (e.g. Hispaniola). A large subspecies, with relatively large feet. In plumage similar to nominate race, but breast more distinctly spotted dark; wings very often with rather large, pale area on secondaries. Wing 337-370mm; tail 125-157mm. (The races *furcata* and *guatemalae* may in reality represent only varieties of *T. a. pratincola*, as the latter shows a wide polymorphy, and the differences in size, especially in wing length, are not significant.)

T. a. guatemalae (Ridgway, 1873). Nicaragua and W Guatemala to Panama. Very similar to *pratincola*. Wings mainly without pale area on secondaries. Wing 312-385mm; tail 134-145mm.

T. a. tuidara (J. E. Gray, 1829). South America east of Andes and south of the Amazon from Brazil to Argentina and Tierra del Fuego. Similar in coloration to *pratincola*, but smaller and paler. Back with more prominent greyish veil; underparts white with fine, dark spots. A light and a dark morph exist. Wing 290-334; tail 113-143mm.

T. a. furcata (Temminck, 1827). Cuba, Isle of Pines (Isla de la Juventud), Grand Cayman, Cayman Brac

194

and Jamaica. Very similar to *pratincola*, but back more yellowish-brown with fine, dark spots. Edge of wings orange-brown; secondaries mainly whitish, forming light patch on wings. Wing 337-354mm; tail 134-152mm.

T. a. contempta (Hartert, 1898). Temperate Ecuador and Colombia to W Peru. Smaller than *furcata*. Very variable in coloration. Edge of wings whitish; back with greyish veil, becoming more prominent on wings; underparts pale yellowish-brown with dark spots; facial disc white with a fine dark and a whitish rim. Wing 293-300mm.

T. a. insularis (Pelzeln, 1872). Lesser Antilles in Caribbean: St Lucia, St Vincent, Bequia, Union, Carriacou, Grenada. Similar in size to nominate race, but with dark greyish veil on upperparts and on wings; facial disc brownish-white with black-spotted brownish rim; underparts brownish with dark, arrow-shaped spots; bill yellowish. Plumage rather identical to *punctatissima* from Galápagos (the two forms may possibly belong to a separate species, *Tyto punctatissima*). Wing 226-243mm; tail 100-108mm.

T. a. schmitzi (Hartert, 1900). Madeira. This subspecies has only 4-5 wing-bars. Wing 268-286mm; tail 107-116mm.

T. a. gracilirostris (Hartert, 1905). Canary Islands: Fuerteventura and Lanzarote. Bill more slender than in other races. Wing 235-270mm; tail 94-105mm.

T. a. detorta Hartert, 1913. Cape Verde Islands: Santiago and St Vincent. Similar to a very dark *guttata*, but with larger spots above and more prominent bars on primaries. Wing 272-297mm; tail 116-124mm.

T. a. javanica (Gmelin, 1788). Burma, SW China, Thailand, Cambodia, Laos, S Vietnam, Malay Peninsula, S Borneo, Sumatra, Java, including Kangean Island. Feet powerful. Whitish to yellow and rufous below. Wing 265-323mm; tail 119-127mm.

Of additional subspecies described, we list here those 12 which we think to be valid, even if they are difficult to distinguish from others:

T. a. erlangeri W.L. Sclater, 1921. Middle East, Iraq, Iran, Arabia.

T. a. meeki (Rothschild & Hartert, 1907). SE New Guinea, Vulcan and Dampier Islands.

T. a. crassirostris Mayr, 1935. Boang Island, Tanga Group, Bismarck Archipelago.

T. a. interposita Mayr, 1935. Santa Cruz Islands, Banks Islands and N Vanuatu (New Hebrides).

T. a. lulu (Peale, 1848). New Caledonia, S New Hebrides, Loyalty, Fiji, Tonga, Samoa and Society Islands.

T. a. lucayana Riley, 1913. Bahamas.

T. a. nigrescens (Lawrence, 1878). Lesser Antilles: Dominica.

T. a. bargei (Hartert, 1892). Lesser Antilles: Curaçao.

T. a. subandeana L. Kelso, 1938. Tropical zones of Colombia and Ecuador.

T. a. hellmayri Griscom & Greenway, 1937. Guianas to Amazon, west to Surinam.

T. a. punctatissima (G. R. Gray, 1838). Galápagos Archipelago.

T. a. hauchecorni Kleinschmidt, 1940. Chile.

HABITS In general lives singly or in pairs. By day, roosts in holes of walls, in attics of large buildings, in barns or in similar sites, and sometimes in trees with dense foliage.

Although often strictly nocturnal, it is not uncommon for this species to emerge at dusk or to be active at dawn, and it is occasionally seen in flight during full daylight. Flight noiseless, with soft wingbeats interrupted by gliding.

FOOD Mainly small mammals, such as mice, rats, voles and shrews, but also catches birds. Some Barn Owls specialise in hunting bats. Small reptiles, frogs or larger insects sometimes serve as prey, too. Preferred prey weight is between 5g and 30g, but the bird is able to carry off animals weighing up to 200g. Hunts from a perch, such as a pole on farmland, but frequently also on the wing; in latter case, the owl usually quarters field margins, edges of ditches or other places with rough grass, often hovering before dropping on to prey. It locates prey primarily by its delicate sense of hearing and swoops down to seize a small rodent with its powerful talons. Aerial prey (e.g. bats) may also be captured. The victim is normally is killed by a bite to the hindneck, after which it is carried away in the bill. Mice or small birds are swallowed whole; larger birds are held tight with the claws and plucked with the bill. The body of the prey is eaten piece by piece. Bones, feathers and hair are regurgitated as blackish pellets, these having a silky gloss caused by a film of saliva (typical of barn owls).

BREEDING Barn Owls normally pair for life. At the beginning of the reproductive period the male flies in circles around the breeding site, and utters his screeching song both perched and on the wing. Male and female reinforce the pair-bond by indulging in mutual aerial pursuits, and at the nest site both utter purring sounds before copulating. A dark place inside a larger building (e.g. barn, church tower, etc), a nestbox, a deep hole in a wall, and similar places are commonly used sites; outside C Europe, hollow trees and cavities between rocks quite often serve as breeding places.

The clutch is normally 4-7 eggs, laid at intervals of 2 days, but in years of rodent plagues ('vole-years') up to 15 eggs may be laid in a single clutch. The pure white eggs are somewhat more elongated than those of other owls. No nest is built, the eggs being laid on a layer of decayed pellets. The female incubates alone, during which she is fed by the male, who quite often deposits a fair amount of food at the nest site. Incubation begins with the first egg and lasts 30-35 days. The young hatch at intervals of 2 days and are therefore different in size, which can be very striking in cases of large clutches. The male brings in all the food and passes it to the female, who offers small morsels to the chicks by touching their bill and uttering clicking sounds. At 8-11 days the eyes of the nestlings begin to open, and by about 3 weeks young take pieces of food from the nest floor. At 5-6 weeks they walk towards their food-bearing parents and swallow the offered prey whole. Normally the later-hatched nestlings grow a bit faster than their older siblings, so that all are more or less the same size on fledging. When food is scarce, smaller nestlings starve or are killed, and are then eaten by their siblings. During cold weather the owlets form a pyramid at the nest site, the larger ones warming the smaller. At about 44 days of age the young walk about near the nest, which they finally leave when about 60 days old. They continue to be fed by their parents, who deliver prey to them. Gradually they become independent, and at an age of about 3 months they are chased out of the breeding area, primarily by the female, following which they begin to disperse. Sexual maturity is reached towards the end of the first year.

Barn Owls normally breed once a year, but in years

when food is abundant they may breed twice or even three times. In times of food shortage, no eggs are laid or breeding attempts may fail. This species may reach an age of about 21 years.

STATUS AND CONSERVATION In Europe this species is rather common, but the population may fluctuate according to food supply. In temperate climates it is greatly dependent on the winter weather conditions: if these are severe, with long-lasting snow cover, entire populations may starve (as Barn Owls show no tendencies for storing body fat), butut such populations may be restored by birds immigrating from warmer climates. In C Europe this owl is threatened chiefly by the lack of adequate nesting sites, a result of modern construction of buildings and mechanisation in agriculture; it may be assisted rather easily, however, by putting up nestboxes at suitable sites in barn lofts or church towers which offer permanent open access to the owls. Like other owls, the Barn Owl suffers in areas where pesticides are used. Moreover, its habit of hunting near roads, above all in winter, means that many are killed by traffic.

REMARKS The taxonomy of *Tyto alba* is not yet fully clarified. Some forms described as subspecies may be no more than morphs or variations, while others could be separate species.

REFERENCES Bezzel (1985), Boyer & Hume (1991), Brandt & Seebass (1994), Buehler (1981, 1988), Buehler & Epple (1980), Bunn *et al.* (1982), Dunning (1993), Eck & Busse (1973), Epple (1985), Glutz von Blotzheim & Bauer (1980), Hollands (1991), König (1961), Mikkola (1983), Sick (1985), Voous (1988), Witt (1984).

---

2   ANDAMAN MASKED OWL
Tyto deroepstorffi   Plate   2

French: Effraie des Andamanes
German: Andamanen-Schleiereule

IDENTIFICATION Similar in shape and size to Barn Owl [1], but brighter in colour. Upperparts greyish-brown with chocolate-brown patches and orange-buff (not white) spots, lacking Common's typical greyish veil; rim around facial disc orange-brown. Feet with more powerful talons. **Similar species** All races of Barn Owl have a greyish veil with white spots and no prominent orange-brown rim around facial disc. Other species of the genus *Tyto* may be similar.

VOCALISATIONS As this owl has usually been treated as a race of Barn Owl, there are no reports on its voice.

DISTRIBUTION Known only from the S Andamans.

MOVEMENTS Nothing known; probably sedentary.

HABITAT Probably similar to that of Barn Owl.

DESCRIPTION Adult Entire upperparts, including wing-coverts, greyish-brown with chocolate-brown patches and fine rufous spots. Primaries, secondaries and tail with few darker bars. Facial disc fulvous-brown with a prominent, orange-brown rim. Breast light brownish-yellow with dark brown spots, becoming lighter towards belly; abdomen whitish. Legs feathered whitish-ochre to base of toes.

Juvenile Probably similar to young Barn Owl. **Bare parts** Eyes blackish-brown. Bill cream-coloured. Toes dark pinkish-grey. Claws purple-grey.

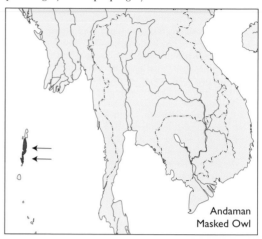

Andaman
Masked Owl

MEASUREMENTS AND WEIGHT Wing 250-264mm; tail 113mm. Weight unknown.

GEOGRAPHICAL VARIATION Monotypic: *Tyto deroepstorffi* (Hume, 1875). Only two skins are known, one with much lighter coloration below.

HABITS Unknown. Surely a nocturnal bird.

FOOD Probably similar to that of Barn Owl.

BREEDING Probably similar to that of Barn Owl.

STATUS AND CONSERVATION Uncertain. Further investigation required.

REMARKS We recognise *Tyto deroepstorffi* as distinct from *T. alba* because it lacks the greyish veil with white-and-black spots which is a typical and obvious feature of all races of the latter; in addition, the feet are much more powerful than those of Barn Owl. It is likely that *T. deroepstorffi* may replace *T. alba* ecologically on the S Andamans, where it seems to be an endemic species. Further investigation of the vocalisations, ecology and biology of this taxon are needed in order to confirm its taxonomic status.

REFERENCES Brandt & Seebass (1994), Eck & Busse (1973), Hume (1875), Voous (1988).

---

3   ASHY-FACED OWL
Tyto glaucops   Plate   2

French: Effraie d'Haiti
German: Hispaniola-Schleiereule

IDENTIFICATION A medium-sized, handsome, 'earless' owl, similar to Barn Owl [1], but with an ashy-grey facial disc and an orange-brown rim. Body yellowish-brown, finely vermiculated with black above, and with dark arrow-like spots below. **Similar species** Other species of the genus *Tyto*. This species is significantly smaller than the Caribbean races of Barn Owl, one of which lives alongside it on Hispaniola.

VOCALISATIONS Little known. Several rapid trills of clicking sounds are followed by a rasping wheeze of about 2-3 seconds' duration, which may represent the song. According to recordings, the vocalisations of Ashy-faced Owl differ from those of Barn Owl.

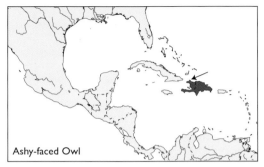

Ashy-faced Owl

DISTRIBUTION Endemic to the islands of Hispaniola and Tortuga in the Caribbean.

MOVEMENTS Apparently a sedentary bird.

HABITAT Open country with scattered trees and bushes, often near human settlements; also in open forest.

DESCRIPTION Adult Upperparts yellowish-brown with blackish vermiculations. Edge of wings near wrist orange-brown. Wings yellowish-brown, finely mottled dark; primaries, secondaries and tail with few dark bars. Facial disk ashy-grey, with faint brownish wash at lower edge of eyes; rim prominent orange-brown. Whole underparts yellowish-brown with dark arrow-shaped spots. Legs rather long, feathered yellowish-brown. Toes bare greyish-brown, sparsely bristled. **Juvenile** Similar to young Barn Owl. **Bare parts** Eyes blackish-brown. Bill yellowish-horn. Claws blackish-brown.

MEASUREMENTS AND WEIGHT Total length about 33cm. Wing around 255mm; tail 127mm. Weight: no data.

GEOGRAPHICAL VARIATION Monotypic: *Tyto glaucops* (Kaup, 1852). No details are known of any variation between populations on Hispaniola and Tortuga.

HABITS Probably similar to those of Barn Owl.

FOOD Small mammals (mice, rats, etc) and small birds, as well as reptiles, frogs and insects.

BREEDING Apparently similar to that of Barn Owl.

STATUS AND CONSERVATION As an endemic species of just two Caribbean islands, this owl may be considered endangered by human civilisation. Since the taxon has hitherto been considered conspecific with Barn Owl, relatively little is known of its true status.

REMARKS Although *Tyto glaucops* lives side by side with the larger *T. alba pratincola*, and in more or less the same habitat, interbreeding has never been observed. The taxon must therefore be considered a full species, as the different vocalisations suggest. Studies on this endemic species are urgently needed, above all for its conservation.

REFERENCES Boyer & Hume (1991), Brandt & Seebass (1994), Burton (1992), Eck & Busse (1973), Hardy *et al.* (1990), Voous (1988).

4   MADAGASCAR RED OWL
Tyto soumagnei   Plate   2

Other name: Madagascar Grass Owl

French: Effraie de Madagascar
German: Malegasseneule

IDENTIFICATION A relatively small barn owl, ochre-yellow to reddish-ochre above with many fine, blackish spots; facial disc heart-shaped, whitish, with darker wash between lower edge of eyes and base of bill, and dark rim. Underparts ochre with scattered fine, blackish dots. Talons powerful. **Similar species** Combination of coloration and size distinctive. Could be confused with sympatric Barn Owl [1], but that species is larger and differs in colour, especially in much paler underparts.

VOCALISATIONS Poorly known. The song is a loud hissing screech of about 1.5 seconds' duration, similar to the song of Barn Owl, but more vigorous and downward-inflected, dropping in pitch halfway through the call: *cheeerrrooorrr*. In addition, calls such as *wok-wok-wok* are considered to have an alarm function.

DISTRIBUTION Endemic to Madagascar.

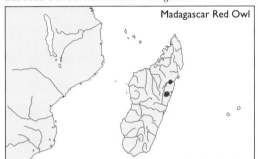

Madagascar Red Owl

MOVEMENTS Nothing known.

HABITAT Humid rainforest in NE Madagascar between 900m and 1,200m. Has been found in primary forest with clearings, as well as in secondary scrub, or in semi-open, forested habitats (created by deforestation). Recent studies discovered the owl at sea-level on Masoala Peninsula, where it inhabited forest edge and plantations or other secondary habitats modified by man. A radio-tagged bird was observed within a range of 210ha from October to December 1994: 50% of the identified locations were along forest edge and newly created tavies (shifting agricultural plots), 36% in rice fields and 14% in cultivated tavies.

DESCRIPTION Adult Overall ochre-reddish to yellow-ochre. Upperparts with fine blackish spots, these becoming larger towards tail and on wings. Tail relatively long. Facial disc white, with brownish wash between lower edge of eyes and base of bill; rim brown. Underparts as upperparts, but with only scattered, very fine dark dots. **Juvenile** Not described. **Bare parts** Eyes dark sooty-blackish. Bill light grey. Toes smoky-grey, scarcely bristled. Claws greyish-brown.

MEASUREMENTS AND WEIGHT Total length about 27.5cm. Wing 212-215mm; tail 100-120mm. Weight of a captured individual was 323g; one female weighed 435g.

GEOGRAPHICAL VARIATION Monotypic: *Tyto soumagnei* (Milne-Edwards, 1878).

HABITS A strictly nocturnal bird, which has been observed hunting in clearings of dense rainforest. Nine day roosts were found in ravines with secondary growth and bananas, where dense canopies were used, about 3.7m above ground.

FOOD Shrew-like tenrecs *Microgale* and small rodents up to the size of black rat *Rattus rattus* have been found as prey, but probably also takes other small vertebrates and insects.

BREEDING Virtually nothing published on breeding. Apparently uses natural tree cavities for nesting. Breeding biology may be similar to that of locally sympatric Barn Owl.

STATUS AND CONSERVATION A very rare and endangered species. Few observations exist, but this owl may perhaps have been overlooked owing to confusion with the larger Barn Owl. Since 1934, there have been only about six records: one in 1973, one in 1993, and at least four in 1994. The status and distribution, as well as ecology and behaviour, need intensive study to develop protective measures. Listed as Endangered by BirdLife International.

REMARKS Apart from recent studies of a radio-tagged bird, very little is known about this endangered species. Comparative studies on *T. soumagnei* and *T. alba* are very important to understanding the biology of the Madagascar Red Owl. The Peregrine Fund has begun with studies on endemic bird species in Madagascar, including *T. soumagnei*.

REFERENCES Aurivillius (1995), Boyer & Hume (1991), Brandt & Seebass (1994), Burton (1992), Collar *et al.* (1994), Eck & Busse (1973), Langrand (1990), Thorstrom *et al.* (1997).

---

5 NEW BRITAIN MASKED OWL
Tyto aurantia   Plate   3

Other names: New Britain Barn Owl

French: Effraie de Nouvelle Bretagne
German: Goldeule

IDENTIFICATION A relatively small barn owl, generally pale golden-rufous with dark markings, the facial disc pale yellowish-brown with rufous-brown rim. Upperparts are covered with dark V-shaped markings, these becoming smaller towards head, and underparts spotted with brown dots. Tail and flight feathers with few dark bars. **Similar species** Other species of the genus *Tyto*, but none of those has golden-rufous plumage with V-shaped markings on back and wing-coverts.

VOCALISATIONS Little information. According to reports from local inhabitants, this owl is known as 'a kakaula', from its call. Hissing or screeching notes are also reported, but no tape recordings have been available to us.

DISTRIBUTION Endemic to New Britain in the Bismarck Archipelago.

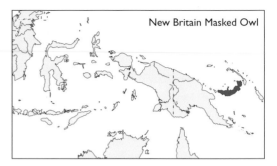
New Britain Masked Owl

MOVEMENTS Apparently sedentary. Nothing is known about movements.

HABITAT Tropical rainforest with clearings, as well as ravines with trees and shrubs, are reported as typical habitats. The owl has been found from lowlands up to about 1,830m in the mountains.

DESCRIPTION Adult Plumage overall pale golden-rufous, somewhat darker on back. Upperparts with dark brown V-shaped markings, these rather large on wing-coverts and back, becoming smaller on hindneck and crown; inside the V-markings is a light patch with a dark spot, rather prominent on wing-coverts and back. Facial disc pale yellowish-brown, with finely dark-speckled reddish-brown rim. Primaries, secondaries and tail feathers with few dark brown bars, primaries with a dark spot near tip. Underparts slightly paler than upperparts, with dark brown, indistinctly heart-shaped spots. Legs rather long, feathered pale orange-brown down to base of bare toes. Bill rather powerful in relation to body size, but feet and claws relatively weak. **Juvenile** Probably similar to other species of genus. **Bare parts** Eyes blackish-brown. Bill ashy-white. Toes yellowish-grey to brownish-grey. Claws brown, becoming darker towards tip.

MEASUREMENTS AND WEIGHT Total length 27-33cm. Wing 220-230mm. Weight: no data.

GEOGRAPHICAL VARIATION Monotypic: *Tyto aurantia* (Salvadori, 1881).

HABITS Nocturnal, like other barn owls. Nothing is known about its behaviour.

FOOD This owl is said to feed on small rodents, but will probably also prey on other small vertebrates, as well as on insects.

BREEDING Nothing known.

STATUS AND CONSERVATION Endemic to New Britain, where it is uncommon to rare. Being confined to a single island, the species would appear rather vulnerable to man-induced changes to its habitat. Listed as Vulnerable by BirdLife International.

REMARKS The biology and ecology of this species are poorly known and require study.

REFERENCES Boyer & Hume (1991), Brandt & Seebass (1994), Burton (1992), Collar *et al.* (1994), Eck & Busse (1973).

---

6 TALIABU MASKED OWL
Tyto nigrobrunnea   Plate 3

French: Effraie de Taliabu
German: Taliabu-Schleiereule

IDENTIFICATION In general appearance similar to other barn owls, but brown with uniform dark brown wings, secondaries with whitish tips. Tail brown with three dark bars. Facial disc pale reddish-brown. Upperparts with white speckles; deep golden-brown below with many dark spots. **Similar species** The only barn owl with uniform brown wings lacking any markings on primaries.

VOCALISATIONS Unknown.

DISTRIBUTION This bird is known only from a single female specimen collected on the island of Taliabu in the Sula Archipelago, in the Moluccan Sea, and a recent sight record near Tubang in NE Taliabu.

Taliabu Masked Owl

MOVEMENTS Unknown.

HABITAT The only specimen known was reported to have been found in a lowland forest.

DESCRIPTION Adult Only one specimen known (skin stored at Staatliches Museum für Tierkunde in Dresden, Germany). Upperparts dark brown, with whitish speckles from crown to lower back and on wing-coverts. Primaries uniform dark brown and unmarked; secondaries mainly uniform brown, but tips whitish. Tail brown with three darker bars. Facial disc pale reddish-brown, becoming darker towards eyes; rim nearly the same colour. Underparts deep golden-brown with dark spots, some of latter with pale areas. Legs feathered reddish-brown to lower third of tarsus. Talons powerful. **Juvenile** Unknown. **Bare parts** Eyes blackish-brown. Bill blackish-grey. Bare part of tarsus and toes grey. Claws blackish.

MEASUREMENTS AND WEIGHT Total length 31cm. Wing 283mm; tail 125mm. Weight unknown.

GEOGRAPHICAL VARIATION Monotypic: *Tyto nigrobrunnea* (Neumann, 1939).

HABITS Unknown.

FOOD Unknown, but probably similar to that of its congeners.

BREEDING Unknown.

STATUS AND CONSERVATION Formerly only known from a single specimen collected 60 years ago. Since 1939 no reliable observations of this bird had been made. A recent sight-record in October 1991 proves that the taxon still survives on Taliabu, but must be extremely rare. Listed as Vulnerable by BirdLife International.

REMARKS Studies on the ecology and biology of this species are essential for this almost unknown owl.

REFERENCES Boyer & Hume (1991), Brandt & Seebass (1994), Burton (1992), Collar *et al.* (1994), Eck & Busse (1973), Neumann (1939), Stones *et al.* (1997), White & Bruce (1986).

7 EASTERN GRASS OWL
Tyto longimembris   Plate 3

French: Effraie de prairie
German: Östliche Graseule

IDENTIFICATION A medium-sized, long-legged barn owl with lower half of tarsi unfeathered. Plumage very variable, but upperparts more or less dark brown with yellowish-ochre flecks and small whitish spots; underparts vary from pale ochre to white, more or less spotted black. Facial disc pale brownish-yellow to white, with rim not very pronounced. Tail relatively short, with 3-4 dark bars. Eyes relatively small compared with Barn Owl [1]. **Similar species** The very similar African Grass Owl [8] has sooty-blackish upperparts without any yellowish flecks.

VOCALISATIONS Generally said to be rather silent, but vocalisations little studied. Thin, high screeching sounds are described and probably represent a song. At the nest, female utters hissing sounds. A high cricket-like chirruping, audible only at very close range, is uttered by the male in flight, when returning with food. A high sibilant *pseeo00* given in flight near nest possibly serves as alarm-call. Nestlings utter high-pitched wheezing and snoring calls.

DISTRIBUTION From India to Vietnam and SE China, Taiwan, Philippines, Sulawesi, Flores, SE New Guinea and Australia; also New Caledonia and Fiji.

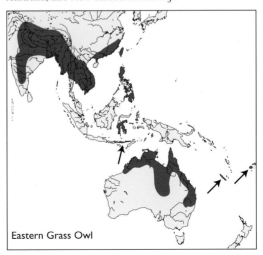

Eastern Grass Owl

MOVEMENTS More or less nomadic, and in years with plagues of small rodents many show a tendency to follow the migrations of their favoured prey, or to disperse to locate other centres of food abundance. Some populations are sedentary.

HABITAT Typical habitat is open grassland with tall, rank grass, both on dry ground and in wetland areas.

DESCRIPTION *T. l. longimembris* **Adult** Upperparts dark brown with yellowish-ochre flecks and small whitish spots. Facial disc white (males) or with fawn-coloured wash (most females). Wings very long, with three dark bars on primaries; wing-coverts similar to back. Tail relatively short, with 3-4 dark bars. Underparts white to whitish-cream with scattered small dark spots. Legs feathered whitish to about two-thirds down tarsus; lower third and toes bare. **Juvenile** Downy chicks pale ochre. **Bare parts** Eyes blackish-brown. Bill whitish-cream. Lower third of tarsus and toes yellowish-grey. Claws blackish-brown.

MEASUREMENTS AND WEIGHT Total length 38-42cm; wingspan 103-116cm. Wing of males 273-322mm, of females 321-348mm; tail 114-139mm. Weight 265-450g.

GEOGRAPHICAL VARIATION Six or more subspecies have been named. We treat here only four of them.

   T. l. longimembris (Jerdon, 1839). NE India to Assam, Burma, Vietnam, Malay Peninsula, Sulawesi, Flores and Australia, New Caledonia and Fiji. See Description. (Birds from New Caledonia and Fiji sometimes separated as *oustaleti*.)

   T. l. chinensis Hartert, 1929. SE China and Taiwan. Facial disc pale yellowish-brown to ochre; head dark brown with tiny whitish spots; centre of back yellowish-brown with irregular dark brown patches, so that upperparts appear much less uniform than in other races; underparts cream-coloured to ochre with small dark spots. Wing about 340mm. (Taiwan population sometimes separated as *pithecops*.)

   T. l. amauronota (Cabanis, 1872). Philippines. Facial disc greyish-white, crown dark brown with small white spots; upperparts less dark than in other races; underparts white with few tiny dark spots. Wing of type 330mm.

   T. l. papuensis (New Guinea). Differs from nominate by plain facial disc, and paler upperparts and underparts. (Includes *baliem* of W Irian Jaya).

HABITS Normally lives singly or in pairs; when food is abundant (rodent plagues), may breed semi-colonially or groups up to several dozens may hunt in same area. Nocturnal, but sometimes flies during daytime. This species is adapted for a life on the ground. Normally hides under shelter of high grass; when disturbed, flies a short distance before taking cover again in dense grass. Flight noiseless with soft wingbeats, as with others of genus.

FOOD Small rodents such as mice and rats are the favoured prey. When these are scarce, may also take other small vertebrates and larger insects. Generally hunts on the wing, swooping down on their victim and seizing it with their powerful talons.

BREEDING Nests on ground. Nest a shallow depression under a dense tussock of grass; by walking to and from nest, the owls very often create a tunnel in the dense grass, which is used as 'runway' by both adults. Normally 3-8 eggs, dull white and equal in size to those of Barn Owl: 36.1-

44.0 x 28.2-36.0mm (eggs of similar African Grass Owl about 24% bigger). Only the female incubates, and is fed by the male during this period. Incubation, starting from first egg, lasts 42 days. Breeding biology is similar to that of Barn Owl. Nestlings fledge at 2 months; some time before this they walk around and hide near the nest, returning to it when their parents return with food.

STATUS AND CONSERVATION Apparently common locally, but use of agricultural pesticides represents a threat.

REMARKS This species is considered by some authors as conspecific with the *T. capensis*, being similar in coloration. This may, however, be due to convergence, as both owls occupy similar habitats in their different continents. The difference in egg size may indicate separate evolution.

REFERENCES Ali & Ripley (1969), Bezzel (1985), Boyer & Hume (1991), Brandt & Seebass (1994), Burton (1992), Higgins (1999), Hollands (1991), Voous (1988).

8 AFRICAN GRASS OWL
Tyto capensis   Plate 3

French: Effraie du Cap
German: Afrika-Graseule

IDENTIFICATION A long-legged owl with rather uniform sooty-brown upperparts, finely flecked or spotted whitish. Back without yellowish markings. Wings very long and tail relatively short, latter with uniform brown central feathers. Underparts whitish-cream with small dark spots. **Similar species** Eastern Grass Owl [7] of Asia has the dark brown coloration of the back broken by yellowish markings. The two grass owls are the only *Tyto* species with blackish-brown back and light underparts.

VOCALISATIONS Similar to those of Barn Owl [1], but less strident. Hunting birds often utter clicking sounds in flight. A high-pitched sibilant tremolo of 1-2 seconds' duration seems to be the song of the male. Young and female at the nest utter hissing sounds.

DISTRIBUTION E Africa from Ethiopian highlands south to the Cape, and across S Zaïre to N Angola; an isolated population occurs in Cameroon.

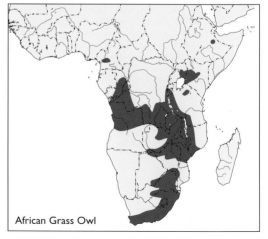

African Grass Owl

MOVEMENTS Apparently sedentary.

HABITAT A typical bird of moist grassland and open savanna at up to 3,200m. Although it prefers moister habitats than Marsh Owl [210], it may also be found on dry grassland. Also occupies higher altitudes, e.g. moors in the Aberdares and on Mt Kenya in E Africa. The habitat is normally characterised by long and dense grass.

DESCRIPTION Adult Entire upperparts from crown to lower back and wing-coverts rather uniform sooty blackish-brown, with scattered small white spots and greyish flecks. Facial disc whitish-cream, with thin yellowish-buff rim densely spotted dark. Primaries and secondaries light brownish-grey with darker bars and yellowish bases. Tail short, central feathers uniform brown, outer ones becoming lighter (almost white) towards edge, and showing about four dark bars. Underparts whitish to creamy-brownish with dark spots. Underwings whitish to pale golden-brown. Legs feathered whitish to lower third of tarsi; latter as well as toes bare, slightly bristled. **Juvenile** Downy chicks initially have a whitish coat, replaced at about 18 days by a dense and very fluffy second coat, pale brownish-buff in colour (mesoptile). Facial disc brownish, paler towards rim. Immatures unspotted dark above and deep golden-brown below, often still showing fluffy down of mesoptile. **Bare parts** Eyes brownish-black. Bill whitish to pale pink. Lower third of tarsi and toes pale yellowish-grey. Claws dark greyish-brown to blackish.

MEASUREMENTS AND WEIGHT Total length 38-42cm. Wing 283-345mm; tail 115-125mm. Weight 355-520g.

GEOGRAPHICAL VARIATION Plumage is rather variable individually. Although four races have been described (*capensis*, *cameroonensis*, *liberatus* and *damarensis*), these are hardly distinguishable in appearance and we doubt that they really represent subspecies. We therefore treat this species as monotypic: *Tyto capensis* (A. Smith, 1834).

HABITS A nocturnal bird, only rarely seen flying during daytime. These owls always roost on the ground in tall, often tangled grass, where they create a domed platform by trampling down surrounding grass. In the same way they also produce tunnels (used also as 'runways') which may be several metres long and connect with other tunnels; a domed platform at the end of such a tunnel serves as nest or daytime roost. Often roosts in pairs, and sometimes small parties may have roosts quite close to one another. Such places are used over fairly long periods, and many droppings and pellets can be found there. Becomes active after sunset and hunts at night; when food is scarce or when hungry nestlings are to be fed, may be seen on the wing also in early morning or late afternoon.

FOOD Preferred prey consists of small rodents and other small mammals, taken from the ground. May also capture bats, larger insects and small birds in the air, as well as on ground. Normally flies with soft wingbeats in wavering flight low over ground, listening and watching for prey, but will also hunt from a perch.

BREEDING Breeds from December to August, mainly February-April. Monogamous. Size of occupied territory seems to vary according to population density and food supply. Two nests were found about 300m apart. A shallow hollow lined with grass at the end of a 'grass tunnel serves as nest. The female lays 2-4 pure white eggs, which are bigger than those of Eastern Grass Owl: 37.4-45.0 x 30.0-36.0mm (av. 41.1 x 32.7mm). Laying interval normally 2 days. The female incubates alone, and is fed by the male. Incubation starts with the first egg and lasts between 32 and 42 days. The young are fed for about 10 days by the brooding female, with food delivered by the male; thereafter both parents feed the chicks. When nestlings are about 4 weeks old, the female no longer roosts at the nest. At 5 weeks the young begin to wander around the nest, and at 7 weeks they make their first attempts at flying. After leaving the nest, the young remain with the parents for about 3 weeks, then become independent.

STATUS AND CONSERVATION A locally rather common bird which is legally protected.

REMARKS Some authors suggest that Eastern and African Grass Owls are races of the same species. We give both specific rank, as their similarity seems to be due to convergence.

REFERENCES Boyer & Hume (1991), Burton (1992), Dunning (1993), Eck & Busse (1973), Fry *et al.* (1988), Voous (1988).

---

9   LESSER MASKED OWL
Tyto sororcula   Plate   4

French: Effraie masquée mineure
German: Tanimbar-Schleiereule

IDENTIFICATION A typical *Tyto* owl, very similar in plumage to but smaller than Australian Masked Owl [11]. **Similar species** Other species of the genus *Tyto*. Best distinguished from Australian Masked Owl by its smaller size.

VOCALISATIONS Three rapidly screeched whistles over a period of 2 secs, sometimes preceded by 3-4 slower, more drawn-out, higher pitched screeches are attributed to this species (Bishop & Brickle 1999).

DISTRIBUTION The islands of Tanimbar and Buru in the Lesser Sundas. Known only from three records of collected specimens: two from Tanimbar, one from Buru.

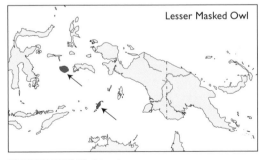

MOVEMENTS Nothing known.

HABITAT Presumed to live in lowland forest. Sometimes hides in limestone caves during daytime.

DESCRIPTION Adult Upperparts from crown to rump and to wing-coverts greyish-brown with orange patches, coarsely spotted with black-bordered white dots (yellowish basal parts of the greyish-brown feathers shine through the dark surface, giving an irregularly mottled appearance). Facial disc pale rufous-brown, with brownish rim finely speckled ochre-yellow; brownish wash around eyes, extending to base of bill. Flight and tail feathers greyish to rufous-brown with darker bars. Entire underparts whitish with coarse brown dots. Feet feathered whitish to base of toes, the latter bare. **Juvenile** Not known. **Bare parts** Eyes blackish-brown. Bill yellowish-cream. Toes yellowish-grey. Claws blackish-brown.

MEASUREMENTS AND WEIGHT Total length about 31cm. Wing of Tanimbar specimens 227mm (male), 235mm (female); of Buru specimen 251mm (female). Weight: no data.

GEOGRAPHICAL VARIATION The single bird collected on Buru may represent a geographical race, *T. s. cayelii* (Hartert, 1900); as only three specimens of this species exist, however, no conclusions can be drawn on any possible variations. We therefore regard this species as monotypic: *Tyto sororcula* (T. L. Sclater, 1783).

HABITS There are no observations on this species in the wild.

FOOD Unknown, but probably similar to that of its congeners.

BREEDING Nothing known. Perhaps nests in hollow trees?

STATUS AND CONSERVATION This handsome owl is probably rare and endangered. The conservation of lowland forest on the islands of the Lesser Sundas is surely the best way to preserve this virtually unknown taxon.

REMARKS Studies on taxonomy, distribution, ecology and biology of this owl are urgently needed, above all for its conservation.

REFERENCES Bishop & Brickle (1999), Boyer & Hume (1991), Brandt & Seebass (1994), Burton (1992), Coates & Bishop (1997), White & Bruce (1986).

10 MANUS MASKED OWL
Tyto manusi   Plate 4

French: Effraie de Manus
German: Manus-Schleiereule

IDENTIFICATION A rather large barn owl (about 49cm) with greyish-brown upperparts spotted white and black, with ochre patches. Whitish below, becoming pale ochraceous-buff towards belly and feet, coarsely spotted brown from breast to thighs. **Similar species** Australian Masked Owl [11] is very similar, but less dark above (the two have frequently been thought conspecific).

VOCALISATIONS Not known.

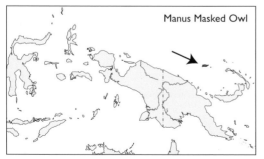

Manus Masked Owl

DISTRIBUTION Known only from Manus Island in the Bismarck Archipelago.

MOVEMENTS Apparently resident.

HABITAT Forest with clearings.

DESCRIPTION Adult Upperparts from crown to rump and wing-coverts relatively dark greyish-brown with white spots and blackish flecks, with some of the ochraceous-buffy bases of feathers visible and giving appearance of irregular yellowish patches. Facial disc whitish, with rufous-brown wash around eyes and towards base of bill; rim speckled dark. Wings and tail light yellowish-brown with indistinct darker bars. Underparts whitish-cream, becoming pale ochraceous-buff towards belly and thighs, and irregularly spotted brown from neck to lower breast and thighs; underwing-coverts white. Tarsi feathered pale ochraceous-buff; toes bare, slightly bristled. **Juvenile** Downy chicks in first and second coats probably similar to Australian Masked Owl. **Bare parts** Eyes blackish-brown. Bill cream to pinkish-white. Toes yellowish-grey to greyish-brown. Claws dark greyish-brown, shading to black at tips.

MEASUREMENTS AND WEIGHT Total length 49cm. Wing 275-301mm; tail 122-133mm. Females in general somewhat larger than males. Weight: no data.

GEOGRAPHICAL VARIATION Monotypic: *Tyto manusi* Rothschild & Hartert, 1914.

HABITS Probably similar to those of Australian Masked Owl.

FOOD Small rodents and other small vertebrates. Probably also larger insects.

BREEDING Probably nests in hollow trees.

STATUS AND CONSERVATION Probably rare and possibly endangered; no records since 1934. Very little is known about this owl, as it has usually been treated as no more than a race of Australian Masked Owl. Listed as Vulnerable by BirdLife International.

REMARKS The taxonomy of *T. manusi* and *T. novaehollandiae* needs more detailed study, including comparison of bioacoustics and molecular biology. The ecology and biology of both species should also be compared.

REFERENCES Boyer & Hume (1991), Burton (1992), Collar *et al.* (1994), Eck & Busse (1973), Rothschild & Hartert (1914).

11 AUSTRALIAN MASKED OWL
Tyto novaehollandiae   Plate 4

French: Effraie masquée d'Australie
German: Neuhollandeule

IDENTIFICATION A relatively large barn owl (37-47 cm) with powerful feet, and with greyish-brown back spotted white and black, sometimes with yellowish or orange-buffy patches, and facial disc whitish to pale rufous-brown. Feet feathered to base of toes. White to pale orange-buff below with dark, often arrow-shaped spots. Pale and dark morphs may be distinguished. **Similar species** Similar to the smaller

Barn Owl [1] and to other *Tyto* species except the grass owls [7, 8], which are more or less uniform dark brown above with fine whitish spots, and the sooty owls [15, 16], which are wholly sooty-grey with fine white spots. Feet more powerful than on Barn Owl.

VOCALISATIONS Similar to those of Barn Owl, but much louder and more rasping. A strange, wild cackling is described, rising and falling in volume. After perching with food, the male utters cackling notes, but ending with a high rattling shriek. The male calls to his mate near the nest with soft, rather musical, cooing notes, audible only at close range. The female beckons the male to the nest with rasping calls. During copulation, the female utters a single high-pitched squeal. Nestlings utter hissing sounds like those of Barn Owl.

DISTRIBUTION Lowland of S New Guinea (including Daru Islands) and Australia (except the arid interior).

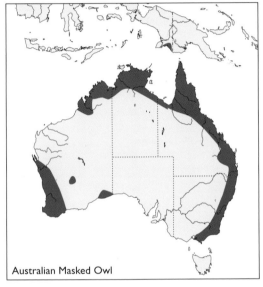

Australian Masked Owl

MOVEMENTS Apparently sedentary.

HABITAT Forest and open woodland with adjacent clearings. Locally, uses underground caves as daytime haunt.

DESCRIPTION *T. n. novaehollandiae* Adult *Light morph*: Upperparts, including wing-coverts, greyish-brown, peppered with white and black spots. Facial disc white, with chestnut shading around the eyes; distinct rim speckled lighter and darker brown. Wings and tail brownish-grey with few darker bars. Underparts white with rather coarse dark markings, often arrow-shaped. Feet fully feathered to base of toes, varying in colour from whitish to orange-buff. *Dark morph*: Ground colour of upperparts and underparts orange-buff; facial disc buff to pale rufous-brown. **Juvenile** Downy plumage of first and second coats whitish. Immatures similar to adult, but with more fluffy appearance. **Bare parts** Eyes dark brown to blackish. Bill whitish. Toes yellowish-grey to pale pinkish-grey, slightly bristled. Claws dark greyish-brown, darker towards tip.

MEASUREMENTS AND WEIGHT Total length 37-47cm. Wing of males 290-318mm, of females 299-358mm; tail 119-150mm. Weight 545-673g.

GEOGRAPHICAL VARIATION Of the described subspecies we treat three here.

T. n. novaehollandiae (Stephens, 1826). New South Wales, Victoria and South Australia. See Description.
T. n. kimberli Mathews, 1912. Western Australia, Northern Territory and N Queensland (except York Peninsula). Very variable in coloration, but always white below. Upperparts rather pale. Wing 293-332mm; tail 123-144mm.
T. n. calabyi Mason, 1983. S New Guinea between Merauke and the Fly River delta. Back generally darker than in nominate *novaehollandiae*, with more yellowish patches; white spots larger and surrounded black. Whitish below, sparsely spotted brown. Wing 305mm; tail 130mm.

HABITS A nocturnal, relatively shy and secretive bird. By day it roosts in dense foliage of tall trees or in hollow tree trunks; sometimes uses underground caves and holes between rocks. Male utters its screeching song normally from a perch in a tall tree. Generally quiet and difficult to find.

FOOD Small mammals up to the size of rabbits are the most important prey. In addition, also preys on small birds and lizards. Hunts on the wing or from a perch.

BREEDING No nest is constructed. Normally uses hollow trunks of tall eucalyptus trees, where the 2-4 dull white eggs (43 x 49mm) are laid on decayed debris and discarded prey remains; locally, eggs laid on bare rock or sand in underground caves. The female incubates alone, during which she is fed by the male. Breeding biology probably similar to that of Barn Owl, but nestlings fledge at 10-12 weeks.

STATUS AND CONSERVATION The status of this owl is uncertain, as its secretive habits make it difficult to locate. Reported to have declined regionally in Australia.

REMARKS The ecology, behaviour and taxonomy of *T. novaehollandiae* require more research.

REFERENCES Boyer & Hume (1991), Burton (1992), Dunning (1993), Eck & Busse (1973), Hollands (1991), Mason (1983), Mees (1964), Pizzey & Doyle (1980).

---

12   SULAWESI MASKED OWL
Tyto rosenbergii   Plate   4

Other names: Sulawesi or Celebes Barn Owl

French: Effraie de Rosenberg
German: Celebes-Schleiereule

IDENTIFICATION Similar in size to Australian Masked Owl [11], but with more numerous bars on flight feathers and with more prominent, reddish-brown rim around whitish facial disc. Brownish-grey above with scattered spots, these with lower half white and upper black. Pale fulvous below with brown spots, and some brownish edges to breast feathers. Feet very powerful. **Similar species** The only other *Tyto* owl in Sulawesi is Minahassa Masked Owl [14], which is much smaller (27-33cm) than its larger relative (41-51cm).

VOCALISATIONS Calls typical for the genus. The song

203

of the male is an eerie, dry, creaky, rasping screech, lasting for about 1 second and somewhat wavering; with a downward inflection: *chreeochreoh* or *chreeeeho*. When begging for food, juvenile gives a loud screaming hiss of about 1 second, repeated every few seconds (P. Morris *in litt.*). Short, hoarse *chreap* calls also recorded near a nest with young.

DISTRIBUTION Sulawesi and adjacent islands.

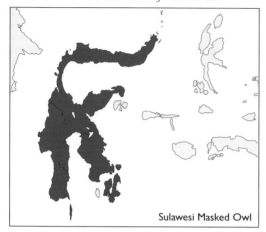

Sulawesi Masked Owl

HABITAT Rainforest, wooded areas and semi-open landscape near human settlements, from sea-level up to about 1,100m.

DESCRIPTION Adult Upperparts greyish-brown with obvious black-and-white spots. Wing feathers with 5-8 darker bars, tail feathers with 4-5 darker bars on paler brownish-grey ground; tips of tail feathers densely mottled darker and lighter brownish-grey, with a white spot near central fringe. Facial disc whitish, becoming somewhat darker towards eyes; rim rufous-brown with darker speckles. Underparts pale ochre, with faint brown edges to feathers on foreneck and upper breast and some darker spots, the latter becoming more prominent on lower breast and flanks. Tarsi feathered pale ochre almost to base of toes; latter bare and sparsely bristled. Talons very powerful. **Juvenile** Probably similar to others of genus. **Bare parts** Eyes blackish-brown. Bill whitish-cream. Toes greyish-brown. Claws dark brown to blackish.

MEASUREMENTS AND WEIGHT Total length 41-51cm. Wing 331-360mm; tail 139-165mm. Weight: no data.

GEOGRAPHICAL VARIATION A race described from Peleng (Banggai Archipelago, off Sulawesi) is known only from the type specimen: *T. r. pelingensis* Neumann, 1939. It is smaller with more scaly black spots on chest. Wing 296mm. In the absence of further material we consider this species to be monotypic: *Tyto rosenbergii* (Schlegel, 1866).

HABITS A nocturnal bird. Regularly found near villages. Hunts over clearings and cultivation, as well as forest edges.

FOOD Probably small vertebrates. Rats and shrews recorded from pellets.

BREEDING Not recorded.

STATUS AND CONSERVATION Poorly known. A rather widely distributed owl on Sulawesi, and one which does not seem to be affected by deforestation as it also occurs in rather open habitats near human settlements.

REMARKS This species needs intensive study, as nearly all of its life is unknown.

REFERENCES Bishop (1989), Boyer & Hume (1991), Burton (1992), Coates & Bishop (1997), Eck & Busse (1973), Holmes & Phillips (1986), P. Morris (pers. comm. 1999), White & Bruce (1986).

13　TASMANIAN MASKED OWL
Tyto castanops　　　　　　Plate　4

French: Effraie de Tasmanie
German: Tasmanien-Schleiereule

IDENTIFICATION Largest of all *Tyto* and with the most powerful talons. Mainly greyish-brown above, with white and black spots. Facial disc pale chestnut-brown to brownish-buff, with darker, sometimes blackish zone around eyes and extending towards base of bill. Underparts boldly marked with relatively large dark spots. **Similar species** Australian Masked Owl [11] is similar, but somewhat smaller and distinctly lighter, with generally lighter facial disc; underparts less boldly spotted.

VOCALISATIONS Similar to those of Australian Masked Owl.

DISTRIBUTION Tasmania.

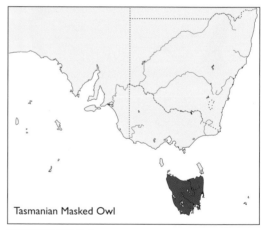

Tasmanian Masked Owl

MOVEMENTS Unknown.

HABITAT Forest and semi-open wooded areas.

DESCRIPTION Adult Females are darker and larger than males. *Female:* Upperparts rather dark greyish-brown, peppered with white and black spots; wing-coverts similar. Flight feathers greyish-brown with some darker bars and fulvous-brown markings. Tail feathers greyish-brown with four darker bars. Facial disc pale chestnut to brownish-buff, with darker, often nearly black zone around eyes which extends towards base of bill; rim very prominently brown, speckled darker. Underparts fulvous with rather large dark spots. Tarsi feathered fulvous-brown to base of toes. *Male:* Generally lighter in colour; facial disc brownish-white, and underparts whitish or pale fulvous with smaller dark brown spots. **Juvenile** Similar to Australian Masked

Owl. **Bare parts** Eyes blackish-brown. Bill whitish-cream. Toes greyish-brown to yellowish-grey. Claws blackish-brown.

MEASUREMENTS AND WEIGHT Total length 47-51cm. Wing of males 310-347, of females 344-387mm; tail of males 140-163mm, of females 150-178mm. Weight up to 1260g.

GEOGRAPHICAL VARIATION Monotypic: *Tyto castanops* (Gould, 1837).

HABITS Similar to those of Australian Masked Owl, which it replaces ecologically in Tasmania.

FOOD Mainly smaller mammals up to the size of rabbits, but also takes smaller birds and lizards.

BREEDING Similar to that of Australian Masked Owl. Normally nests in hollow trees. The 2-4 white eggs are incubated by the female alone.

STATUS AND CONSERVATION Apparently not rare in Tasmania, whereas Australian Masked Owl is said to have declined regionally in Australia.

REMARKS This species is considered by some authorities a geographical race of *T. novaehollandiae*. We treat it as a separate species because of the obvious differences in size and coloration between males and females, not exhibited so conspicuously by *T. novaehollandiae*.

REFERENCES Boyer & Hume (1991), Burton (1992), Hollands (1991), Mees (1964).

---

14   MINAHASSA MASKED OWL
Tyto inexspectata   Plate   5

Other names: Minahassa Barn Owl

French: Effraie de Minahassa
German: Minahassa-Schleiereule

IDENTIFICATION A relatively small barn owl (27-31cm) with relatively short and rounded wings, carpal area dark greyish-brown with white and orange-brown spots. Upperparts greyish-brown with orange-yellow to rusty-red patches and relatively large white spots, these bordered black on upper edge. Fulvous-white to pale ochre below, with fine blackish spots. Facial disc srikingly small compared with body-size. **Similar species** Distinctly smaller than the sympatric Sulawesi Masked Owl [12] (41-51cm) which has a relatively much larger facial disc.

VOCALISATIONS Apparently recently tape-recorded, but details not yet available.

DISTRIBUTION Minahassa Peninsula in N Sulawesi, where it occurs alongside the larger Sulawesi Masked Owl.

MOVEMENTS Unknown.

HABITAT Rich tropical rainforest with lianas, ferns, palms and epiphytic plants, as wellas drier, degraded forests, from about 250m up to 1,500m.

DESCRIPTION Adult Crown to upper back greyish-brown, speckled white and black; half-collar on hindneck darker than surrounding plumage; rest of upperparts more golden-brownish, somewhat mottled greyish, with relatively large white spots bordered black on their upper

half. Wings and tail ochre with several dark bars; narrow zone at edge of wing from carpal to base of primaries dark greyish-brown with white and orange-brownish spots. Facial disc small, pale cream, tinged reddish, with brownish shading around eyes and towards base of bill; rim rufous-brown with some darker speckles. Underparts fulvous-white to pale ochre with fine blackish spots. Legs feathered uniform ochre to base of toes, the latter bare. **Juvenile** Unknown. **Bare parts** Eyes blackish-brown. Bill whitish-cream. Toes reddish-grey to greyish-brown. Claws blackish-brown.

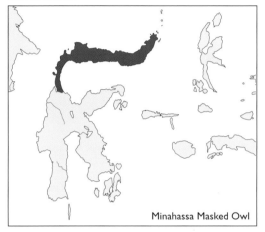
Minahassa Masked Owl

MEASUREMENTS AND WEIGHT Total length 27-31cm. Wing 239-272mm; tail 102-122mm; males smaller than females. Weight: no data.

GEOGRAPHICAL VARIATION Monotypic: *Tyto inexspectata* (Schlegel, 1879).

HABITS Nocturnal. Ecology and behaviour unknown.

FOOD Probably as for other species of *Tyto*, with small mammals predominant.

BREEDING Unknown. Probably nests in hollow trees in early April.

STATUS AND CONSERVATION No information.

REMARKS The biology and some other aspects of the Minahassa Masked Owl remain totally unknown.

REFERENCES Bishop (1989), Boyer & Hume (1991), Burton (1992), Coates & Bishop (1997), Eck & Busse (1973), Fletcher (1998), van Marle (1940), White & Bruce (1986).

---

15   LESSER SOOTY OWL
Tyto multipunctata   Plate   5

French: Effraie suie mineure
German: Flecken-Ruâeule

IDENTIFICATION A sooty-grey barn owl, somewhat paler below, and densely spotted and dotted whitish above and below. Eyes relatively large for a barn owl. Facial disc greyish-white, becoming sooty towards and around eyes. Flight feathers grey with some distinct darker bars. **Similar species** Greater Sooty Owl [16] is larger and darker, with

205

relatively smaller eyes, upperparts less spotted (and spots smaller), and flight feathers uniform sooty with only indistinct darker bars.

VOCALISATIONS A rather high-pitched, strident descending whistle seems to be the song; it is sometimes likened to the sound of a falling bomb or the whistling of a boiling kettle. Trilling sounds uttered by both sexes have been reported. When approaching the nest with food, the male gives a high, piercing trill, all notes on the same pitch.

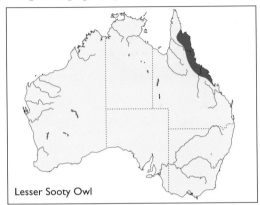

Lesser Sooty Owl

DISTRIBUTION NE Australia in the Atherton region of NE Queensland.

MOVEMENTS Unknown.

HABITAT Rainforest and wet eucalypt forest with tall trees and hollow trunks.

DESCRIPTION Adult Upperparts from crown to lower back and to wing-coverts sooty-grey, densely spotted and dotted white, spots becoming rather large on back and wing-coverts. Wings and tail grey with several darker bars. Facial disc contrastingly whitish, shading into sooty-blackish towards and around eyes; rim dark sooty with few tiny white flecks. Underparts lighter than upperparts, boldly speckled and mottled pale grey and blackish; underwings light greyish. Legs feathered greyish to base of toes, the latter bare. **Juvenile** Downy chicks sooty-grey. Mesoptile plumage appears more or less indistinguishable from adult. **Bare parts** Eyes black. Bill pale greyish-brown. Toes greyish-brown. Claws as toes, but somewhat darker.

MEASUREMENTS AND WEIGHT Total length 32-38cm; wingspan 86cm. Wing 237-263mm. Weight 450g (1 male), 540g (1 female).

GEOGRAPHICAL VARIATION Monotypic: *Tyto multipunctata* (Mathews, 1912).

HABITS Strictly nocturnal. Hides during daytime in dense foliage, between tangles of aerial roots, in crevices of all kinds, and beneath overhanging banks. Hunts in clearings and near roads, but also inside forest.

FOOD Chiefly small mammals, taken from the ground or from trees. Has a remarkable ability to hunt in almost total darkness and during rain. Prey is normally sighted and caught from a perch.

BREEDING Territory said to be about 50-60ha in size. Aged hollow trees (often eucalyptus) are used for nesting; nest holes may be very high above the ground (up to 30m!). The female lays 1-2 oval white eggs (41-42 x 36-39mm) on a mat of debris inside the hole. She incubates alone for 40-42 days. Breeding biology poorly known. Normally only one chick hatches, and is fed by both parents; it fledges at 3 months.

STATUS AND CONSERVATION Probably threatened or even endangered by deforestation.

REMARKS Long supposed to be a race of Greater Sooty Owl, this taxon is nowadays accepted as a separate species, being different in size and coloration from the Australian and New Guinean subspecies of *T. tenebricosa*. Further investigations are needed on both species.

REFERENCES Boyer & Hume (1991), Burton (1992), Eck & Busse (1973), Hollands (1991).

16   GREATER SOOTY OWL
Tyto tenebricosa   Plate   5

French: Effraie suie
German: Ruâ-Schleiereule

IDENTIFICATION Larger and darker than Lesser Sooty Owl [15], with relatively smaller eyes. Entirely sooty brownish-black, underparts somewhat lighter, and both upperparts and underparts with small whitish spots. Facial disc pale greyish-brown, darker around eyes. Flight feathers and tail greyish-brown, with rather indistinct darker bars on wing, somewhat more prominent on tail. **Similar species** Lesser Sooty Owl is smaller and paler, with boldly white-spotted plumage and relatively larger eyes, and facial disc more whitish and contrasting noticeably with surrounding dark plumage.

VOCALISATIONS Most vocalisations are similar to those of Lesser Sooty Owl, but generally lower in pitch. The characteristic call (song ?) is a piercing downslurred shriek, lasting about 2 seconds, having some similarity with the sound of a falling bomb. When male approaches the nest with food, he gives a high, piercing trill. During courtship both sexes utter soft chirruping trills, and during copulation one bird (female ?) utters a single squeal. Incubating female solicits food by snoring calls. Nestlings beg with wheezing trills.

DISTRIBUTION New Guinea and SE Australia.

MOVEMENTS Unknown.

HABITAT Confined to rain and cloud forest in New Guinea and to pockets of rainforest or wet eucalypt forest in SE Australia. From sea-level to about 2,000m in New Guinea.

DESCRIPTION *T. t. tenebricosa* **Adult** Upperparts from crown to lower back dark sooty blackish-brown, with fine white spots on crown becoming larger towards back and wing-coverts. Flight feathers rather uniform dark greyish-brown with some indistinct darker bars; tail similar, with more distinct bars. Facial disc greyish-brown, lighter towards lower rim and darker towards eyes and base of bill; rim dark greyish-brown. Underparts greyish-brown, lighter towards belly, with small whitish spots and mottling. Feet densely feathered light greyish-brown to base of bare toes. **Juvenile** Downy chicks whitish to greyish-white.

Immatures similar to adult, but with darker facial disc. **Bare parts** Eyes blackish. Bill whitish-cream. Toes pale greyish-brown. Claws dark brown.

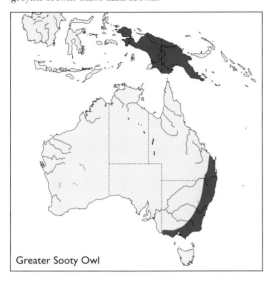

Greater Sooty Owl

MEASUREMENTS AND WEIGHT Total length 35-50cm; wingspan 103cm. Wing 243-343mm; tail 116-145mm. Weight 500-700g (males), 750-1000g (females).

GEOGRAPHICAL VARIATION Two races are described.
T. t. tenebricosa (Gould, 1845). SE Australia: SE Queensland to E Victoria. See Description. Wing 285-343mm; tail 145mm.
T. t. arfaki (Schlegel, 1879). New Guinea and adjacent Jobi Island. Generally browner than nominate race, and tarsi mottled darker and lighter greyish-brown. White spots slightly larger than in nominate. Wing 243-300mm; tail 116-132mm.

HABITS Strictly nocturnal. During daytime it hides in crevices and hollow tree trunks, as well as in dense foliage of tall trees; sometimes in caves.

FOOD Predominantly small mammals, but also small birds.

BREEDING Mostly from January to June. Territories much larger than those of Lesser Sooty Owl, comprising about 200-800ha. A cavity in an old tree is normally used as nest, sometimes a rock cave. Normally 1-2 white oval eggs (44-52 x 36-41mm), laid on a mat of debris. Incubation about 42 days; often only one chick hatches. Both parents feed the young, which fledge at 3 months and are fed and cared for by both parents for some months thereafter.

STATUS AND CONSERVATION Unknown because of its elusive behaviour, but probably rare and endangered.

REMARKS Both species of sooty owl are in need of more detailed studies.

REFERENCES Boyer & Hume (1991), Burton (1992), Eck & Busse (1973), Hollands (1991).

17   ITOMBWE OWL
Tyto prigoginei   Plate 5

Other names: African Bay Owl

French: Chouette du Congo
German: Prigogine-Eule

IDENTIFICATION Superficially similar to Bay Owl [18] and equal in size, but with facial disc very similar to the heart-shaped disc of typical barn owls. Feet and bill smaller. Underparts russet-cream with many black-fringed white spots. Scapulars and wing-coverts with a dark greyish veil. **Similar species** Bay Owl is characterised by its peculiarly shaped facial disc, in addition to which it lacks the greyish veil on wing-coverts and is less spotted on generally lighter underparts.

VOCALISATIONS Unknown.

DISTRIBUTION Known only from a single collected specimen, two sight records and one trapped individual, all in EC Africa (near Lake Tanganyika). The type locality is in the Itombwe Mountains of E Zaïre.

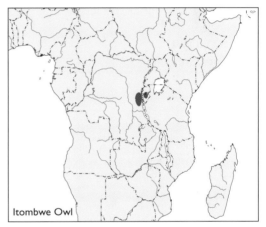

Itombwe Owl

MOVEMENTS Unknown.

HABITAT Montane gallery forest and upper slopes with grass and light bush, from about 1,830m to 2,430m. In 1951, a single specimen was collected in the Itombwe Mountains at 2,430m in montane forest. Two presumed sightings, each of a single individual (1970 and 1989), were in a tea estate in Burundi and in a montane forest of this region. On 1st May 1996, an individual (probably female) was netted at 1,830m above sea-level within dense, slightly degraded forest of southern Itombwe; it was ringed and released.

DESCRIPTION Adult Crown and nape chestnut-brown with many black-and-white spots; hindneck and sides of neck paler and more yellowish; mantle chestnut-brown with black-fringed white spots. Scapulars and fore wing-coverts blackish, finely vermiculated grey and russet, suggesting a faint dark veil. Primaries chestnut with about six blackish bars; tail similar in colour, with seven narrow black bars. Facial disc russet-cream with brown rim. Underparts russet-cream with many longish black-fringed white spots. Feet feathered creamy to base of toes. **Juvenile** Unknown. **Bare parts** Eyes very dark brown. Bill laterally compressed, yellowish-horn. Toes yellowish-grey. Claws greyish-brown with darker tip.

MEASUREMENTS AND WEIGHT Single live individual (probably female): total length about 24cm; wingspan 63cm. Single skin (female): wing 192mm; tail 93mm. Weight 195g.

GEOGRAPHICAL VARIATION Monotypic: *Tyto prigoginei* (Schouteden, 1932).

HABITS Apparently strictly nocturnal.

FOOD Unknown.

BREEDING Unknown. Probably nests in holes of trees.

STATUS AND CONSERVATION Apparently rare and endangered. Listed as Vulnerable by BirdLife International.

REMARKS The Itombwe Owl has been described as belonging to the genus *Phodilus*, but we have some doubts about this classification. The superficial similarity with *Phodilus badius* is perhaps only due to convergence. A photograph of the recently netted bird shows what is to us a typical *Tyto* owl with heart-shaped facial disc, very different from the disc of Bay Owl. Nothing is known about the vocalisations and DNA of Itombwe Owl, and research in these fields is urgently requested. The results may show that this owl should indeed be placed in the genus *Tyto*, as we suggest here, or in a separate genus within Tytonidae.

REFERENCES Boyer & Hume (1991), Burton (1992), Butynski *et al.* (1997), Collar *et al.* (1994), Fry *et al.* (1988), Prigogine (1973), Schouteden (1952).

Bay Owls, Genus *Phodilus* Geoffroy Saint-Hilaire, 1830

Relatively small owls with a 'mask-like' facial disc, suggesting ear-tufts, and with an obvious, more or less V-shaped frontal shield of short feathers extending to base of bill. Rim of stiff feathers around disc, muscle movements of which allow variable facial aspect. Wings rounded. Tarsi relatively short. (For anatomical details, see Marshall 1966.) Eyes dark brownish-black. Central claw finely serrated as in *Tyto*. Pellets with silky coating as in *Tyto*. 1 species (we include the African taxon *prigoginei* in the genus *Tyto*).

18   BAY OWL
Phodilus badius   Plate   5

French: Chouette baie
German: Maskeneule

IDENTIFICATION A relatively small owl (23-33cm) with short rounded wings, somewhat resembling a small, short-legged barn owl, but with different (not heart-shaped), rather vertically elongated facial disc in which upper edges rise over crown at both sides, suggesting ear-tufts. Disc vinous-pink, with dark chestnut-brown around eye. Chestnut-brown above, spotted with black and yellow. Paler below, vivid light chestnut-brown with rosy tinge, speckled with black and with narrow buff shaft-streaks. Feet powerful, tarsi fully feathered to toe joint. **Similar species** Barn Owl [1] is much larger, has more rounded, heart-shaped silky-white facial disc, and has white (sometimes buff-tinged) underparts usually very sparsely spotted with dark brown (in Asia).

VOCALISATIONS A rising series of four whining whistles, *woo-woo-wee-wee*, often repeated many times; sometimes in descending sequence. These whistles are given from a stationary position, and sometimes alternate with a series of different and shorter whistles, *kleet-kleet-kleet'* or *kleek-kleek-kleek*, as the bird flies about. Pairs often duet together. Usually starts calling at about 18:30-19:00 hours. Very noisy during breeding season, particularly after midnight (12:00-03:00 hours), and sometimes calls suddenly during night when nervous or disturbed by intruders.

DISTRIBUTION SW India (Kerala, only one specimen: see Geographical Variation), Sri Lanka (lowland wet zone and hill zone to about 1,200m), Nepal, Sikkim, Assam (Brahmaputra river), Nagaland, Manipur, Burma and Thailand, east to S China (Tonkin), south through Malay Peninsula to Greater Sundas; recorded also in Philippines (Samar).

MOVEMENTS Resident.

HABITAT Dense evergreen primary and secondary forest in lowlands (but as yet not close to sea coast), particularly foothills, submontane forest and montane forest up to 1,700-1,800m in India and continental SE Asia. In Java, preferred habitat is foothills (200-1,000m) and submontane forest (1,000-1,500m), but forest destruction has caused it to move from hill and middle zones to montane forest (e.g. Mt Slamet, C Java, 1,740m; Mt Raung, E Java, 1,800m); also occurs in densely foliaged groves between farmland and rice fields in cultivated areas or in fruit-tree plantations near forest edge (pers. obs.). Hunts near water. Lowlands to about 2,300m.

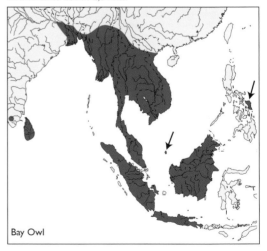
Bay Owl

DESCRIPTION *P. b. badius* Adult Elongated facial disc whitish-vinaceous, with broad frontal tract and striking chestnut-brown feathers around each eye; feathers of rim tipped blackish and chestnut-brown; forehead chestnut. Crown and nape chestnut, speckled with black and buff shaft-spots. Mantle and back to uppertail-coverts somewhat lighter chestnut, spotted with black and buff shaft-streaks, with bases bright buff (each mantle feather has 2-3 black spots on shaft). Tail chestnut with small black bars. Wing with outer two primaries (10th and 9th) with white on outer webs and banded with black or chestnut edges, 8th and 7th also with white on outer web near tip. Throat creamy-vinous. Underparts vivid light chestnut-brown with rosy tinge, speckled with blackish-brown and buff. Feet powerful, tarsi fully covered to toe joint or nearly so with pinkish-vinacous feathers, becoming lighter near toe joint. Middle toe serrated as *Tyto*, with scale-like notches. **Juvenile** Plumage with whitish down. **Bare parts** Eyes dark brown or brownish-black. Bill creamy-yellow or pinkish-horn. Toes yellowish-brown or pinkish-buff. Claws paler.

MEASUREMENTS AND WEIGHT Female slightly larger than male. Total length 22.5-29cm. Wing 168-239mm; tail 75-97mm. Weight: 150-220g.

GEOGRAPHICAL VARIATION Six subspecies are recognised. The species becomes smaller and darker from north to south.

P. b. badius (Horsfield, 1821). E and C Burma, south through Tenasserim to Malay Peninsula, S Thailand, Sumatra, Nias, Java, Bali, Borneo; also Samar in Philippines (one record; see Remarks). See Description. Wing 180-207mm; tail 75-90mm.

P. b. saturatus Robinson, 1927. Nepal, Sikkim, Bhutan (?), Assam north and south of Brahmaputra river, Nagaland, Manipur, N Burma, N Thailand, Cambodia, Vietnam and Tonkin. A large race. Upperparts chestnut, sparsely speckled; inner webs of primaries chestnut, barred black. Wing 214-239mm; tail 92-97mm.

P. b. assimilis Hume, 1877. Sri Lanka. Smaller than *saturatus*. Upperparts dark brown, speckled; inner webs of primaries brown, barred black. Wing 197-203mm; tail 81-89mm.

P. b. ripley Hussain & Khan, 1978. Kerala, SW India; known only from one specimen, collected at Periasolai in southern section of Nelliampathy Hills, south of the Palghat Gap. A rather small, darker and extremely vermiculated and speckled form. Upperparts chocolate-brown, finely stippled; inner webs of primaries vinous, barred dark brown. Wing 208mm; tail 81mm.

P. b. parvus Chasen, 1937. Belitung Island, off SE Sumatra; rather rare, known only from a eight museum specimens. A small race compared with Javan topotypes. Wing 172-180mm. Also somewhat smaller feet and shorter bill.

P. b. arixuthus Oberholser, 1932. North Natunas, off NW Borneo: Bunguran; known only from the holotype. Similar to nominate *badius* from Java. Upperparts, underparts, face and legs lighter; white spots on tertials, back and scapulars much larger. Total length in flesh 261mm; wing 185mm; tail 71mm.

HABITS Strictly nocturnal. Rather elusive. Reported to be very ill at ease in daylight, spending the daytime in holes and hollows in tree trunks. Nevertheless, these owls were regularly observed by day perched on a branch in the forest, preferentially sheltered above by palm leaves or beneath a thick horizontal bend of a rattan, usually no more than about 1.5-2m above the forest floor, and generally so fast asleep (with closely contracted eyes and

typical vertically elongated and folded disc) that they could be grabbed by their feet (this is curious, as *Phodilus*, when awake or hunting, orientates particularly by sounds and not by sight). This behaviour is quite different from that experienced with some other owl species (e.g. *Ninox*), which are always fully awake and alert before the observer has located them. When disturbed by day, the Bay Owl may fly very rapidly through dense stands of young trees, skilfully avoiding these obstacles, and can even fly through a maze of lianas. An individual kept in an aviary was observed to perch sideways on sapling stems, its huge feet grasping the vertical stalk in the manner of a tit clinging to an upright twig. Moreover, the bilateral extensions of the facial ruff can be turned in the direction of a sound source and seem therefore to assist in focusing sound waves upon the ear openings. When agitated or cornered, it may rock the body from side to side, then suddenly bow its head deeply so that it is facing more or less backwards between its own feet; in this position it shakes its head slowly from side to side before suddenly flinging it up, exposing the pale facial disc with enormous wide-staring black eyes and open bill. This bluff-and-escape behaviour is known also for Barn Owl, as well as for some *Otus* species.

FOOD Small rodents (rats and mice) and bats, birds, lizards, frogs, and beetles and other large insects such as grasshoppers. A bird kept in captivity was not choosy with food: it ate fish (!), rats, and the flesh from carcases of shot birds. Captives became very tame and could be observed at close distance; at dusk they responded to a whistle, and accepted food offered by hand. The stomach of the Samar (Philippines) specimen contained remains of a small snake. Pellets as those of *Tyto*, with a silky tar-like coating. Hunts from a perch, sharpening its gaze by rocking the head rhythmically from side to side (almost hypnotic to the observer), and flies through dense stands of young trees beneath the forest canopy to make a capture. Its relatively short and rounded wings make it well adapted for this method of hunting.

BREEDING Breeding season March-May in Nepal, Sikkim, etc; in Sri Lanka, three young of different sizes in November; in Java, eggs March-July (Bartels collection). Nests in tree holes (unlined), rotten tree trunks or stumps, in cavities or in leaf layers of *Arenga pinnata* palms (Java). Clutch 3-5 eggs (Nepal, Sikkim), 3 (Sri Lanka), usually 2 (Java): 34.5 x 30.0 mm (n = 30; India); 39.0 x 30.7 mm (range 38.0-40.6 x 30.2-31.1 mm, n = 4; Java, Bartels collection). Eggs laid at about 2-day intervals and, as incubation starts with first egg, they hatch asynchronously at the same intervals; chicks in same nest always show disparity in size. Only the female incubates, and is fed by the male at the nest. Incubation and fledging periods unknown.

STATUS AND CONSERVATION Rather rare and occurring at low population density. Particular threats include forest destruction and other habitat changes. Can easily been kept in captivity.

REMARKS The taxonomic position of *Phodilus badius* within the Tytonidae is often discussed. Its loud, musical and complicated vocalisation is remarkable and completely unlike the rasping snores or hissing sounds of *Tyto* species (with the exception of *T. tenebricosa*). The head-bowing behaviour is not exclusive to Tytonidae, but is also found among some *Otus* species. Its osteology, especially the skull, is different from that of *Tyto* (immense skull and big eyes set far apart). The curved humerus, stout forearm and short, broad manus suggest quick wingbeats and versatility of a forest-dwelling raptor. With regard to bird lice (Mallophaga), *Phodilus* harbours a species of *Strigiphilus* (*S. marshalli*) similar to species of that genus found in Strigidae owls, and showing only superficial resemblance to *S. rostratus* that infests Barn Owl. Some authors therefore prefer to place Bay Owl in an intermediate position in its own family, Phodilidae. Note that the Philippine specimen of *Phodilus badius* was lost in the destruction of the Bureau of Science, Manila, during the Second World War in 1945; it was described as *Phodilus riverae* by McGregor in 1927, but without comparison with any of the races of *P. badius*, and was therefore consigned to synonymy by Peters (1940).

REFERENCES Ali & Ripley (1969), Boyer & Hume (1991), Burton (1992), Dickinson *et al.* (1991), Eck & Busse (1973), Henry (1978), Hussain & Kahn (1978), King *et al.* (1995), Kuroda (1936), Marshall (1966), McGregor (1927), MacKinnon & Phillipps (1993), Rand & Rabor (1960), Voous (1988), Wells (1986).

FAMILY STRIGIDAE: TRUE OWLS

Inner toe remarkably shorter than central toe. Claw of inner toe not serrated. Facial disc round, oval or square (not heart-shaped). Plumage very variable in coloration, many species with different colour morphs, often called phases. The individual colour morphs or polymorphy of plumage patterns existing in several species are retained for life. More or less prominent 'ear-tufts' present in several taxa. We currently recognise 194 species.

Scops and Screech Owls, Genus *Otus* Pennant, 1769

In general relatively small owls (total length between 16mm and 28cm), most with erectile ear-tufts and short, rounded wings.

The taxonomic status of some taxa is uncertain and needs more research, including on bioacoustics and molecular biology (DNA). We currently recognise 67 species of *Otus*. The American screech owls (except *Otus flammeolus*) represent a subgenus, *Megascops*, though our studies suggest that this should be raised to a full genus. All members of this subgenus have two different songs: a primary (territorial) song and a secondary (courtship or aggressive) song. We term these, respectively, the A-song and the B-song. The A-song is mostly a long trill or sequence of single notes in more or less rapid succession, while the B-song is relatively short, often with a characteristic rhythm; B-songs in particular are uttered by males and females when duetting in courtship. The Old World scops owls and the American *O. flammeolus* (the only American taxon belonging to this group) utter only one type of song, which is never a long trill. Because it has only one song type, we separate the Cuban taxon *lawrencii* generically from *Otus*, placing it in its own monotypic genus *Gymnoglaux*. The Palau Scops Owl we treat in the monotypic genus *Pyrroglaux*, and the two white-faced scops owls we place in *Ptilopsis*.

19 WHITE-FRONTED SCOPS OWL
Otus sagittatus   Plate   6

French: Hibou à front blanc
German: Weiâstirn-Zwergohreule

IDENTIFICATION Although a small owl (25-28cm), relatively large for a scops owl, with relatively long tail (more than 100mm). Wings rounded. Plumage overall chestnut-rufous with prominent white forehead, extending laterally into large ear-tufts. Rather small indistinct spots on upperside, and pale rufous underside, a little more greyish-brown on throat and breast, with small rounded black spots, the largest on centre of belly. Tarsus feathered, toes naked; eyes brown. **Similar species** Largest of all SE Asian *Otus* owls and the only one with such long tail and prominent white forehead. Javan Scops Owl [24] also has white forehead, but is much smaller and does not overlap in range. Most other scops owls are distinctly smaller, with shorter tail.

VOCALISATIONS The song of the male is a hollow whistle, *hoooo*, beginning and ending abruptly; it is repeated at long intervals. A trapped individual uttered a low, soft moan.

DISTRIBUTION Peninsular Burma, locally (from 12°N), peninsular Thailand and Malay Peninsula; one doubtful record in N Sumatra (Aceh).

MOVEMENTS Unknown, probably resident. The only Sumatran specimen (BMNH: Aceh, undated) may have involved a vagrant, unless the species is an overlooked resident.

HABITAT Evergreen forest, and rather degraded swampy forest. Suspected (but not proved) to be a lowland specialist. Found in rainforest or tall secondary forest in lowlands and hills of Malay Peninsula, where occurs to about 600-700m (three individuals netted in the understorey at Pasoh Forest Reserve, Negri Sembilan).

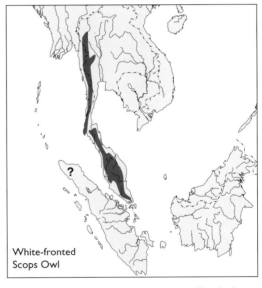

White-fronted
Scops Owl

DESCRIPTION Adult Forehead to beyond level of eyes, together with superciliary stripe extending to ear-tufts, white with pinkish tinge, obscurely vermiculated with fuscous. Facial disc pale rufous, with broad ring of deep rufous-chestnut feathers around eyes, and the whole bordered by black-tipped feathers; loral bristles whitish with black tips. Upperparts rufous-chestnut, mantle and back with small, triangular, buffy-white spots with black lower margin, inner scapulars with similar but larger spots; outer scapulars yellowish-white to rufous on outer webs, with 3-4 moderately sized black spots on shafts. Wings rounded, with ground colour similar to back, with some darker and lighter brown bars. Tail chestnut-rufous with about 10 tranverse blackish bars, more distinct on outer feathers and towards base. Chin, behind and above jaw, a patch of close-set feathers forming a partial ruff, pinkish-white with black tips. Underparts pale rufous, finely vermiculated with brown on breast and throat, each feather with pale or whitish centre broken by roundish black shaft-spot, the largest on centre of belly. Tarsus feathered, rufous. **Juvenile** Undescribed. **Bare parts** Eyes deep brown to dark honey-brown. Bill bluish-white. Cere pale bluish-green. Toes flesh-pink and claws bluish-white.

MEASUREMENTS AND WEIGHT Total length 25-28cm. Wing 175-192mm; tail 108-125mm. Weight about 109-139g.

GEOGRAPHICAL VARIATION Monotypic: *Otus sagittatus* (Cassin, 1848).

HABITS Little known. A very elusive bird.

FOOD Insects, chiefly moths (stomach contents).

BREEDING Season in Thailand (Samkok) and Malay Peninsula (Perak) February and March. Birds trapped in July/August (Malay Peninsula) in heavy moult of flight feathers (primary 7). Nests in tree holes. Clutch 3-4 eggs, white and roundish: 34.2 x 28.5mm (Baker).

STATUS AND CONSERVATION Said to be rare, but in suitable habitats (e.g. Negri Sembilan, Malaya) it was observed to be no less common than more widespread species such as Reddish and Sunda Scops Owls [20, 52]. Threatened by the extensive deforestation of lowlands taking place within its small range. Listed as Vulnerable by BirdLife International.

REMARKS This owl's biology and vocalisations are very poorly known. Its life history and ecology, need to be studied before it becomes very rare, or even extinct.

REFERENCES Baker (1927), Boyer & Hume (1991), Burton (1992), Chasen (1939), Collar *et al.* (1994), Dunning (1993), Eck & Busse (1973), King *et al.* (1995), Lekagul & Round (1991), MacKinnon & Phillipps (1993), Medway & Wells (1970, 1976), Wells (1999).

20 REDDISH SCOPS OWL
Otus rufescens Plate 6

French: Hibou rouge
German: Rötliche Zwergohreule

IDENTIFICATION A small (15-18cm), rather uniform rufous-brown scops owl with ear-tufts, slightly spotted (never vermiculated) with black on body. Upperparts with triangular pale fulvous spots, largest on mantle and wing-coverts and becoming shaft-stripes on back and rump. Underparts orange-brown with sparse small black spots, absent on flanks. Bright chestnut-brown or orange-brown eyes. **Similar species** Mountain Scops Owl [23] is much less distinctly spotted overall, and in the region of overlap has shorter ear-tufts. Sunda Scops Owl [52] is never strongly rufous or distinctly spotted, and has a prominent collar and dark brown eyes. White-fronted Scops Owl [19] is much larger, with white forehead and long tail.

VOCALISATIONS Little studied. The song consists of prolonged, hollow whistles, *heeooh*, repeated at regular intervals of about 7-10 seconds, each note first rising and then dropping in pitch. The birds call particularly on moonlit nights.

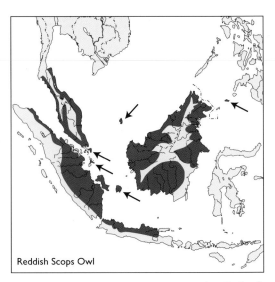

Reddish Scops Owl

DISTRIBUTION Extreme south of peninsular Thailand, Malay Peninsula, Sumatra, Java, Borneo, and (?) Sulu Islands (Philippines).

MOVEMENTS Resident.

HABITAT Lowland evergreen, foothill and submontane rainforest, up to 1,000m (e.g. Mt Pangrango, Java); also logged primary and secondary forest (Sumatra). Mostly lowlands, but recorded up to 1,300m.

DESCRIPTION *O. r. rufescens* Adult *Light morph*: Upperparts including crown tawny rufous-brown, with elongated or triangular pale fulvous spots bordered on one or both sides with black, spots becoming larger on mantle and wing-coverts and more or less shaft-stripes on back and rump; scapulars with pale ochre (not white) outer webs and dark spots. Prominent ear-tufts flecked with white, blackish and rufescent-brown. Facial disc cinnamon-buff, becoming lighter towards edge, bordered by dark brown rim. Primaries ochre with very prominent blackish bars; secondaries ochraceous-brown with darker brown bars. Tail rufous-brown, similar to secondaries, mottled with black and with indistinct pale bars (clearest on central rectrices). Underparts cinnamon-buff, with sparse spots similar to those on upperparts. Relatively large feet feathered nearly to base of toes, feathering pale buff. *Dark morph*: Similar in pattern to light morph, but much darker cinnamon-brown above and below. **Juvenile** Downy chicks have rufous-brown underside, more dark rufous-brown down on crown and mantle, lighter on rump; undeveloped flight feathers unmarked dark rufous-brown. Juveniles like adult, but far less speckled. **Bare parts** Iris chestnut-brown or amber-brown, eyelids reddish-brown. Bill horn-white. Feet pale flesh.

MEASUREMENTS AND WEIGHT Total length 15-18cm. Wing 127-132mm; tail 58-68mm; tail index (tail/wing) 47-52%; long toes, index (central toe/tarsus) 70-85%. Weight about 77g.

GEOGRAPHICAL VARIATION Three subspecies.
   O. r. rufescens (Horsfield, 1821). Sumatra, Java and Borneo. See Description.
   O. r. malayensis Hachisuka, 1934. Malay Peninsula and

S peninsular Thailand. Slightly more rufous than nominate race. Wing (unsexed) 132mm.

O. r. burbidgei Hachisuka, 1934. Sulu Islands in S Philippines. Similar to nominate race, but head and nape darker, facial disc and rim also much darker, and more chestnut-brown on wings and tail; throat finely vermiculated dark. (The validity of this subspecies is doubtful, as the differences in plumage may fall within the range of individual variation or polymorphy. This taxon is based on a single specimen, the provenance of which has been doubted.)

HABITS Little known. Very elusive. Nocturnal. Frequents dense lower parts and middle storey of primary and tall secondary forest, and is generally encountered at rather lower levels in the forest than most other *Otus* species.

FOOD Stomach contents reveal mainly grasshoppers, crickets and other insects. Two stomachs of Javan individuals also contained remains of crabs.

BREEDING Little known. In Java, eggs found March-April and a downy nestling in mid July. Breeds in tree holes, also in old barbet or woodpecker holes. Eggs white and rounded.

STATUS AND CONSERVATION Rather rare, and certainly locally threatened or even endangered by deforestation and forest fires.

REMARKS As many tropical SE Asian owls, this species requires extensive study of its biology and ecology.

REFERENCES Boyer & Hume (1991), Chasen (1939), Dickinson *et al.* (1991), Dunning (1993), Eck & Busse (1973), King *et al.* (1995), Lekagul & Round (1991), Marshall (1978), MacKinnon & Phillipps (1993), Medway & Wells (1976).

---

21   CINNAMON SCOPS OWL
Otus icterorhynchus   Plate 6

Other names: Sandy Scops Owl

French: Petit-duc à bec jaune
German: Gelbschnabel-Zwergohreule

IDENTIFICATION A relatively small scops owl (18-20cm), buffy to sandy in colour with blackish-edged whitish spots. Eyes pale yellow; bill and cere cream-yellow. **Similar species** Common Scops Owl [37] is about equal in size, but greyer, with greyish-brown bill, and a different voice.

VOCALISATIONS Poorly studied. A whistled *kweeah* with downward inflection, and a *kewhurew* or *kewhurr*, each lasting about 2.5 seconds and dropping slightly in pitch and volume. This note is uttered at intervals of several seconds.

DISTRIBUTION Liberia, Ivory Coast, Ghana, Cameroon, Gabon and C and E Zaïre.

MOVEMENTS Resident.

HABITAT Humid lowland forest.

DESCRIPTION *O. i. icterorhynchus* **Adult** Upperparts light cinnamon-brown with buffy and white spots, the latter with

blackish tips or edges. Scapulars with whitish webs edged dark, forming band on folded wing. Outer webs of primaries spotted white; inner webs and secondaries cinnamon, barred dark brown. Tail cinnamon with dark-edged rufous bars. Facial disc cinnamon-brown with some darker concentric lines. Ear-tufts speckled and mottled rufous, white and blackish. Underparts paler than upperparts, with whitish spots becoming larger and more prominent on abdomen; underwing-coverts plain pale buff. Feet feathered pale buffy to base of toes. (A wide variety of individual variation in coloration exists in this species, with lighter and darker morphs also known.) **Juvenile** Mesoptile similar to adult, but barred on back and plain below. Downy coat unknown. **Bare parts** Eyes pale yellow. Bill and cere cream-yellow. Toes pinkish-cream, tinged yellowish. Claws dull whitish with grey tips.

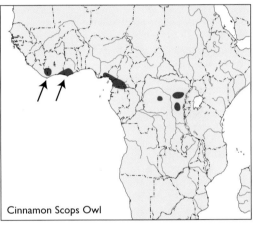

Cinnamon Scops Owl

MEASUREMENTS AND WEIGHT Total length 18-20cm. Wing 117-147mm; tail 70-79mm. Weight 61-80g, mean 73.3g.

GEOGRAPHICAL VARIATION Two races are described.
  O. i. icterorhynchus (Shelley, 1873). Liberia, Ivory Coast and Ghana. See Description.
  O. i. holerythrus (Sharpe, 1901). Cameroon, Gabon and E and C Zaïre. More deep cinnamon-brown than nominate race, and no white spots on outer webs of greater upperwing-coverts. Wing 140-144mm; tail 67-78mm.

HABITS Poorly known. Apparently a nocturnal bird, and is difficult to locate. Roosts in tree holes.

FOOD Insects.

BREEDING Virtually unknown. A nestling was found in May in Zaïre, and juveniles in April in Cameroon; laying period probably February-March. The white eggs are laid in holes in trees.

STATUS AND CONSERVATION Probably rare and possibly endangered by deforestation.

REMARKS A poorly studied species.

REFERENCES Bannerman (1953), Boyer & Hume (1971), British Sound Archive (1998), Dunning (1993), Fry *et al.* (1988).

22 SOKOKE SCOPS OWL
Otus ireneae   Plate 6

French: Petit-duc de Sokoke
German: Sokoke-Zwergohreule

IDENTIFICATION A small scops owl (16-18cm) with grey, rufous and dark morphs. Yellowish bill; spotted underparts, lacking dark streaks; facial disc often with concentric lines. Eyes pale yellow. **Similar species** Superficially similar Common Scops Owl [37] always has a dark (not yellow) bill, and has blackish shaft-streaks on underparts, as well as differences in voice.

VOCALISATIONS A series of 5-9, sometimes more, rather high whistled notes, *goohk-goohk-...*, at rate of about three notes every 2 seconds. Such series are repeated at intervals and are the song of the male. Nothing else known of the vocabulary.

DISTRIBUTION Not discovered until 1966, and thereafter considered an endemic species in Sokoke-Arabuko Forest near the southeastern coast of Kenya; recent discoveries of this owl in the foothill forest of the Usambara Mountains in NE Tanzania, however, suggest that it may have a wider distribution on the E African coast.

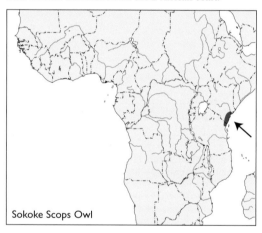

Sokoke Scops Owl

MOVEMENTS Resident.

HABITAT *Cynometra-Manilkara* forest, extending rarely into adjacent *Brachystegia* woodland. Lives in woodland with trees taller than 3-4m. Between 50m and 170m above sea-level; in Tanzania between 200m and 400m.

DESCRIPTION Adult *Grey and dark brown morphs*: Upperparts greyish or dark brown, crown streaked blackish. Erectile ear-tufts mottled and spotted light and dark. Nape spotted light and dark. Mantle similar to crown, mottled and spotted light and dark. Facial disc light greyish-brown or pale rufous-buff, with faint, slightly darker concentric lines. Tail barred dark on slightly lighter ground colour. Primaries barred white and dark brown, inner primaries and secondaries paler. Scapulars with whitish spots on outer webs, forming white scapular stripe on folded wing. Underparts greyish-brown with black-tipped white spots and dark vermiculations. *Rufous morph*: Similar, but ground colour above and below bright rufous. **Juvenile** Not described. **Bare parts** Eyes pale yellow. Bill and cere pale

yellow with pinkish wash. Toes pale greyish-brown. Claws dark brown with blackish tip.

MEASUREMENTS AND WEIGHT Total length 16-18cm. Wing 113-115mm; tail 60-66mm. Weight of 2 males 46g and 50g; mean unsexed 50.3g.

GEOGRAPHICAL VARIATION Monotypic: *Otus ireneae* Ripley, 1966.

HABITS Nocturnal. Daytime roosts generally in lower canopy of trees. Habits otherwise unknown.

FOOD Apparently small insects.

BREEDING Unknown. Probably nests in holes in trees.

STATUS AND CONSERVATION Rare, with a world population of about 1,000 pairs, but apparently common locally. Restricted range, however, could expose it to various threats, in particular deforestation. This owl's habitat is now designated a protection zone and the species itself is protected by law in Kenya. With sponsorship from the Peregrine Fund, its ecology and measures needed for its conservation are currently being studied in order to ensure the future survival of this delightful owl. Listed as Vulnerable by BirdLife International.

REMARKS Ecology and biology of this little owl are poorly known.

REFERENCES Boyer & Hume (1991), Collar *et al.* (1994), Dunning (1993), Fry *et al.* (1988), Ripley (1966), Virani (1995), Zimmerman *et al.* (1996).

23 MOUNTAIN SCOPS OWL
Otus spilocephalus   Plate 7

Other names: Spotted Scops Owl

French: Petit-duc de Montagne
German: Gefleckte Zwergohreule, Fuchseule

IDENTIFICATION A small scops owl (about 18cm) with short, blunt wings (especially SE Asian populations) and short and ill-defined ear-tufts (except Taiwan). Overall plumage rich tawny-rufous or ochraceous-buff or dull grey-brown, densely vermiculated, freckled and spotted with blackish or dark brown. Many races (some polymorphic) and considerable individual variation; general coloration ranging from rufous, tawny or foxy-brown to buffy greyish-brown; no prominent blackish shaft-streaks either above or below; upperparts, including crown, spotted whitish and black; underparts barred whitish, rufescent or buff, with small, often triangular, paired black and white spots. Tail at least 65mm, generally longer. Eyes pale yellow to more golden-yellow. **Similar species** Reddish Scops Owl [20] has chestnut- or amber-brown eyes, and slightly shorter wings and tail. White-fronted Scops Owl [19] is much larger, with relatively long tail (over 100mm), white forehead, no nuchal collar, and brown eyes. Collared Scops Owl [53] is much larger, is mottled and striped dark brown on a light buffy-grey or buffy-rufous ground, has only indistinct barring below, and has dark brown or orange eyes. Indian Scops Owl [54] and Sunda Scops Owl [52] have longer ear-tufts, no barring below, and normally brown eyes. Oriental Scops Owl [40] is very boldly streaked below. Common Scops Owl [37] has a 'bark-like' plumage pattern above and streaks below. Javan Scops Owl [24], endemic to that island, has prominent white-frosted eyebrows, usually a buffy-white nuchal collar, and a number of sparse black stripes or blotches below (confined mainly to sides of breast and flanks); also clear golden-orange eyes. Rajah Scops Owl [51] of Sumatra and Borneo, is much larger, very dark brown (and far less rufous) above, with prominent double collar around hindneck and long ear-tufts, is unbarred, but with blackish stripes and irregular spots with vermiculations on underparts, and has orange-yellow eyes.

VOCALISATIONS The male's song is a plaintive, relatively high-pitched double whistle (like sound of a hammer on an anvil), *whew-whew* or *plew-plew*, with very slight interval (0.5-1.0 seconds) between the two notes, which are pure and silvery in quality. It is uttered with great persistance at intervals of about 6-12 seconds. The female's call, very seldom heard, is a single soft note in antiphony to that of male, their songs finally becoming a couplet.

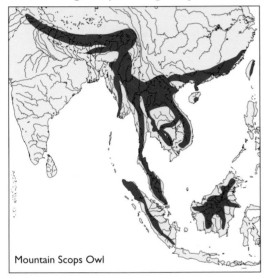

Mountain Scops Owl

DISTRIBUTION Pakistan, Nepal, and Himalayas in N and E India to Sikkim and Burma, SE China, Taiwan, south to SE Asia (except Cambodia and S Vietnam?), Malay Peninsula, Sumatra and Borneo.

MOVEMENTS Usually resident. The northern subspecies locally descend from higher to lower elevations in winter.

HABITAT Confined to humid forest. In the north frequents temperate hill evergreen forest of oak, pine and chestnut, and in the south montane tropical rainforest (also partly containing chestnut and oak). Lives and forages in lower parts of very dense vegetation of trees and scrubs, preferentially within tall primary forest or its fringes. Usually occurs between 600m and 2,600m, mostly above 1,200m.

DESCRIPTION *O. s. spilocephalus* **Adult** Upperparts dark tawny-brown or rufous-brown, vermiculated with blackish. Facial disc rufous-brown, the bristly feathers pale at base and tipped blackish, ear-coverts and cheeks barred blackish, ruff whitish or rufous-buff with obsolete bars of blackish and dark brown or blackish tips. Forehead and sides of crown, including short ear-tufts, sometimes paler and buffish; crown with numerous pale rufescent spots

edged with black, these often broadening on hindneck and back into bars, most numerous and forming more or less ill-defined collar on hindneck. Inner scapulars form prominent row of feathers with clear white outer webs and bold black tips. Median wing-coverts usually boldly marked with buff and black. Primaries barred rufous-brown and dark brown. Tail rufous-brown, with blackish bars mottled and broken by chestnut bands. Underparts whitish, barred rufescent, with small, triangular, paired black and white spots. Tarsus densely feathered up to and often right over base of toes. **Juvenile** Overall more dull rufous and more fluffy than adults; head and crown barred with narrow blackish-brown lines, back with broader ones, while underside also barred but very faintly. **Bare parts** Iris golden-yellow or greenish-yellow. Bill horn-coloured, whitish or wax-yellow. Feet whitish, pale flesh or fleshy-brown.

MEASUREMENTS AND WEIGHT Total length about 18-20cm. Wing 133-155mm. Tail 65-92mm. Toe-index (central toe/tarsus) usually 58-70%. Weight averages 60-77g (all races). *O. s. vandewateri* (Mt Kerinci, Sumatra) 85g; *O. s. hambroecki* (Taiwan) 53-112g.

GEOGRAPHICAL VARIATION Very variable species, also individually variable within populations. Wide colour variation makes peripheral races appear like different species. Many subspecies described, but racial boundaries can often be drawn only arbitrarily: general trend is that tawny populations, like the nominate race, become slightly darker and more boldly marked from north to south; extent of feathering of distal end of tarsus tends to decrease from north to south (varies between races, but can sometimes also vary within populations). Bare-part colours vary also to some degree: iris yellow (pale yellow, lemon-yellow, golden-yellow); bill whitish-flesh, pale flesh, pinkish-horn, horny, wax-yellow, cinnamon); feet pale flesh (whitish, pale pinky-white, fleshy-brown). Some taxa described as races may be good species, or perhaps only aberrant morphs.

O. s. spilocephalus (Blyth, 1846). E Himalayas from C Nepal eastward through Sikkim, Bhutan and Arunachal Pradesh to Assam hills and areas north of Brahmaputra river. See Description. Occurs in rufous and more greyish-buff morphs, with intermediate forms; dichromatism limited mainly to this race and *latouchi*, (extreme grey morphs of nominate very difficult to separate from *huttoni*). Fully feathered tarsus. Wing 137-151mm; tail 77-90mm. *O. s. rupchandi* Koelz, 1952 from hill areas south of Brahmaputra river (Nagaland, Manipur and Bangladesh) is regarded as a synonym.

O. s. huttoni (Hume, 1870). W Himalayas from about Murree in Pakistan eastward through Himachal Pradesh, Garhwal and Kumaon to C Nepal, where intergrades with nominate race. Differs from nominate in being generally much paler and greyish-brown, lacking rich rufous tinge; above, speckled greyish-brown, conspicuously marked on crown and nape with paired spots of black and white; below, speckled brown and white, with indistinct fine pale stippling on breast and abdomen. Tarsus densely feathered up to and often right over base of toes. Wing 135-144mm; tail 71-76mm.

O. s. latouchi (Rickett, 1900). SE China to Laos. Like nominate race, but more rufous, varying from rufous to buffy-brown. Distal 2-5 mm of tarsus bare. Wing 140-151mm; tail 77mm.

O. s. hambroecki (Swinhoe, 1870). Mountains of Taiwan. A rather robust race. Upperside fuscous or chestnut-brown with bold, coarse pattern, and distinct whitish hindneck-collar of heavily black-tipped feathers; underside often somewhat rusty and 'bark-like', with a few dark spots connected by many fine vermiculations, bars or pencil-lines and with small dark speckles; unlike other races, ear-tufts rather long. Distal 4-6mm of tarsus bare. Wing 145-151mm. In this race females tend to be longer-winged and heavier than males. So far as reported, song is typical of the species, though intervals between songs are 1 second longer than those in Thailand.

O. s. siamensis Robinson & Kloss, 1922. Mountains of Thailand and southern Annam. Darker than nominate. Distal end of tarsus sparsely feathered or bare. Wing 138-142mm; tail 65mm.

O. s. vulpes (Ogilvie-Grant, 1906). Malay Peninsula. Very similar to *luciae* in darkness, but general colour above and below foxy-red and more uniform in tone; black markings much reduced, especially on top of head and rather coarse, especially in W Malaysian birds. Distal 3-4mm of tarsus bare. Total length 17.7cm (in flesh); wing 137mm; tail 68.5mm.

O. s. luciae (Sharpe, 1888). Mountains of Borneo. On average more buffy-brown, freckled with black, and with coarse pattern of black markings. Tarsus has the distal 3-8mm bare. Wing 134mm; tail 70mm.

O. s. vandewateri (Robinson & Kloss, 1916). Mountains of Sumatra. Somewhat like *luciae* in coloration, but with more pronounced hindcollar of black-tipped white feathers. Tarsi usually bare for 5-6mm to half their length distally. Total length 19cm (in flesh); wing 138mm; tail 70mm. (Sometimes considered conspecific with Javan Scops Owl, but its vocalisations indicate that it is a subspecies of Mountain Scops. We include *Otus stresemanni* (Robinson, 1927) from Mt Kerinci, Sumatra (915m), as an exceptionally pale morph of *O. s. vandewateri*.)

HABITS A nocturnal species, starting its activity during and after dusk; far less diurnal in its habits than *Glaucidium* species. Frequents deep and shady gullies and ravines, foraging in the lower parts of the densest forest trees. For its songpost it selects a horizontal bare branch beneath a concealing umbrella of foliage or large-leaved plants, such as palm, wild banana leaves, etc. Males call from stationary positions within territories small enough for 3-4 other males to be heard from one spot. It is usually impossible not to hear this owl within a few minutes of entering a suitable habitat in dense, cool mountain forest at night, at almost any time of the year. The owl readily answers imitated whistles but never approaches closer.

FOOD Stomachs examined revealed remains of Coleoptera, small moths and other insects. Although never observed hunting, it probably hawks insects in the air.

BREEDING Known only for northern races *huttoni* and nominate *spilocephalus*. Season March/April-June. Nests invariably in holes 1.5-7.5m from the ground in dead trees; usually a large, natural hole, but sometimes uses abandoned nest hole of woodpecker or barbet. Nest unlined. Eggs usually 3-4 (less often 2 or 5), pure white, roundish, with smooth texture: 31.9 x 27.6mm. The female incubates alone and is fed by the male.

STATUS AND CONSERVATION Although sometimes locally frequent, and in places even common, the species is threatened in some areas by forest destruction.

REMARKS The taxonomy and the biology of this complex species need to be studied and require revision. Its relationships to other taxa are unclear, although some consider Flores Scops Owl [28] closely related (Widodo *et al.* 1999). In particular, the taxonomic status (and habitat preference) of the pale morph of race *vandewateri*, the so-called *Otus stresemanni*, needs to be verified, since it is sometimes given species rank, and also in view of the fact that *vandewateri* is listed as a full species by Peters (1940).

REFERENCES Ali & Ripley (1981), Baker (1927), Boyer & Hume (1991), Eck & Busse (1973), King *et al.* (1995), MacKinnon & Phillipps (1993), Marshall (1978), Marshall & King (1988), Peters (1940), Roberts & King (1986), Robinson (1928), Voous (1988), Widodo *et al.* (1999).

24 JAVAN SCOPS OWL
Otus angelinae   Plate 7

French: Petit-duc de Java
German: Angelina-Zwergohreule

IDENTIFICATION A relatively small owl (16-18cm) with almost unmarked rusty-brown or pale rufous facial disc, and conspicuous whitish-frosted eyebrows leading into prominent ear-tufts. Breast and belly pale rufous, with somewhat darker fine vermiculations, and with herring-bone-like shaft-stripes on breast sides and flanks; often a prominent whitish or pale buff, distinctly black-tipped, nuchal collar. Eyes golden-yellow or orange-yellow; bill and feet pale fleshy. **Similar species** Mountain Scops Owl [23] is similar in size or marginally larger, but has smaller ear-tufts (except on Taiwan and Sumatra), characteristic triangular bicoloured twinned spots on breast and belly, and yellow eyes; in addition, it does not occur in Java. The last applies also to Rajah Scops Owl [51], the presumed occurrence of which in Java is based on a misidentification; this owl is much larger, darker above and more densely freckled and blotched below, and has two collars, one on hindneck and a buffy band on nape or hindcrown. Sunda Scops Owl [52] is about equal in size to Javan Scops, but is more squat and sturdier-looking, and is heavily mottled and vermiculated with sharply contrasting dark brown and black markings on a light sandy or grey-brown ground colour.

VOCALISATIONS No territorial or advertising song is known, and this owl is habitually non-vocal. Only in conditions of extreme stress and agitation (as when intruder approaches fledged young) does it produce a very hard, explosive disyllabic hoot, *poo-poo*, with an interval of 0.6 seconds between the two notes, the first note lasting 0.3 seconds, and the second (always lower in pitch than the first) 0.2 seconds. The notes are repeated a number of times at intervals of several seconds, and then abruptly stop. This vocalisaton is given by both sexes, the female's slightly higher in pitch; it is possibly related to territorial song and evoked by displacement behaviour, as known for a number of birds (including some owl species, e.g. Eurasian Eagle Owl [96]), a supposition strengthened by the fact that in the closely related Rajah Scops Owl the same type of call acts as territorial song. In addition, a male Javan Scops Owl, after feeding fledged young, often uttered a low trisyllabic and soft *wook-wook-wook*; this may be a 'subsong', used as a comfort-call. Both sexes emit cat-like hissing sounds, *tch-tsischschsch*, of surprisingly constant duration (0.3 seconds), less scratchy than similar notes (food- or begging-calls) of the young, and evidently used as contact-calls. During feeding, active bill-snapping of the young can usually be heard, more intensive if they are more hungrier; before and during feeding, young also produce a rapid metallic twittering or chittering *gickickick*, rather similar to twittering sounds of young Barn Owls [1] when being fed.

DISTRIBUTION Mountains of Java, at altitudes of 900-2,500m. Definite records from Mt Halimun, Mt Salak, Mt Gede/Pangrango, Mt Tangkubanprahu, Mt Papandayan and Mt Ceremay in W Java, and Ijen Highlands in E Java. No record exists from C Java, but it is likely that this owl occurs along the whole central mountain chain of the island (from Halimun in the west to Ijen Highlands in the east), its detection hampered by its being rare, elusive and non-vocal. Endemic.

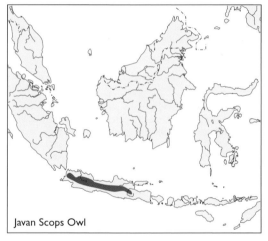

Javan Scops Owl

MOVEMENTS Resident.

HABITAT Montane primary rainforest and its fringes. A family with two fledglings observed on Mt Gede/Pangrango at 1,500-1,600m, where the forest had luxuriant undergrowth beneath an upper canopy of old trees of *Altingia exelsa* and oak, about 40-55m high and with base diameter of up to 2.5 m; the owls kept mainly to the middle and lower storeys of the forest.

DESCRIPTION *O. a. angelinae* **Adult** (Some individual variation, from lighter to darker individuals, latter more common.) Facial disc uniform rufous, sometimes nearly light chestnut-brown; bristly feathers around bill white, tipped black. Prominent white eyebrows, extending along forehead to ear-tufts. Ear-tufts rather long (33-35mm) with clear white inner webs, and dark brown to black outer webs decorated with some lighter spots; white tuft feathers often edged with black and some transverse, dark rufous bars. Crown dark brown or dark rufous-brown with dark feather centres. Nuchal collar often prominent, a row of whitish or pale buff feathers with bold black tips. Upperparts dark rufous-brown, sprinkled with light vermiculations and light and dark rufous spots and freckles;

distinct row of upper scapular feathers with clear white outer webs and black at tip and edges. Wings dark brown and with about five buffy, rather broad cross-bars. Tail dark rufous-brown with indistinct bars and mottling. Underparts light rufous with somewhat darker rufous fine vermiculations; breast sides and flanks with conspicuous black herringbone-like markings. Tarsus fully feathered up to and sometimes extending well over toe joint. Relatively long toes. **Juvenile** Overall dark rufous-brown, crown with fine dark cross-bars, which become broader on mantle, back and rump; underside darker rufous-brown than adult, with tendency towards faint dark rufous bars and with a few elongated, rather broad dark brown shaft-stripes (indicating the later characteristic herringbone pattern of stripes of adult plumage). **Bare parts** Iris golden-yellow or orange-yellow, eyelids reddish-brown. Bill dark straw-yellow or pale greyish-yellow, more brownish near cutting edges. Feet fleshy or pinkish-flesh, soles a little darker. Claws dark fleshy, browner near tip.

MEASUREMENTS AND WEIGHT Total length 16-18cm. Wing 135-149mm; tail 65-67mm. Weight of one male 75g (Cibodas, Mt Gede/Pangrango); four others (unsexed), trapped at same locality, 81.1-90.6g.

GEOGRAPHICAL VARIATION Two subspecies.
    O. a. angelinae (Finsch, 1912). W Java. See Description.
    O. angelinae subsp. nov. E Java: Sodong Jerok, Ijen Highland, at 1,170m. Known only from a single specimen (formerly misidentified as *O. brookii*). Similar to nominate race, but larger. Wing 163mm.

HABITS Completely nocturnal; activity starts only after dusk (18:00 hours). Frequents the lower and middle storeys of tall virgin montane rainforest. During daytime often roosts at low level or hides in low tangled vegetation, often on a bare branch in rather exposed position, relying on its very effective camouflage colours; when detected, adopts concealing attitude, the 'sleeked-upright' posture (common to most scops owls), the body stretched upward with feathers sleeked and eyes half-closed. Also roosts or conceals itself on small epiphytic bird's-nest ferns *Asplenium nidus*, an owl having been flushed from such a site on two occasions (see also Breeding).

FOOD Larger insects (beetles, grasshoppers, crickets, moths etc); occasionally also takes small lizards and snakes. In one case, praying mantids (Mantidae) comprised 38% of the food delivered to young; these insects are most active at night, as are the species of grasshopper (Tettigoniidae, Gryllidae and Phasmidae) regularly brought to young. Potential prey are located by their movements, but probably also by sound (e.g. stridulations of Tettigoniidae). The few observations of hunting technique indicate that prey is seized with the claws from a branch, stem or leaf, or even from the ground; no indication that insects are caught in flight (when beetles, moths or other apparently suitable insects flew close to the owls, they were ignored). Prey items were often more sluggish insects. Adults generally dismember large prey items such as beetles (removing the elytra) and the larger winged insects (mantids) by transferring the prey from bill to feet, holding it in the claws, and pulling it apart, before presenting pieces to the young.

BREEDING No definite nest sites have ever been found, but probably breeds in tree holes, as do most scops owls; possibly also on epiphytic bird's-nest ferns, from which this owl species has twice been flushed. Three observations of a family with two fledged young, suggesting that the full clutch is 2 eggs; size differences between young suggest asynchronous egg-laying and hatching, the interval estimated at 3-4 days. Fledged young are fed by both parents, which accompany them for a further 3-4 weeks.

STATUS AND CONSERVATION An elusive bird, rather difficult to locate. Its status is therefore uncertain, but it doubtless may be considered rare. As an endemic species of the montane forest of Java, it is endangered by the destruction of virgin forest. Listed as Vulnerable by BirdLife International.

REMARKS Javan Scops Owl is related to Rajah Scops Owl of Sumatra and Borneo and has sometimes been considered conspecific with it, but we treat it as a full species; a proposed relationship with Mountain Scops Owl, as suggested by some authors, is very improbable, as the vocalisations are very different from this species. While there are some morphological differences between the taxa *O. brookii* and *O. angelinae*, our main argument for recognising *angelinae* as a full species is based on its behaviour: Javan Scops Owl differs in its habitual silence, this feature being apparently innate (many attemps to elicit response with playback experiments of its recorded vocalisations failed, at all seasons, including at sites where it certainly does occur and had been seen shortly beforehand, whereas Rajah Scops Owl can be readily attracted by playback or imitations of its song); and, when a pair of Rajah Scops Owls with young is disturbed, it reacts very aggressively, with an extensive vocabulary of gruff and growling notes, quite unlike Javan Scops Owl under similar circumstances.

REFERENCES Andrew & Milton (1988), Becking (1994 and in prep.), Collar *et al.* (1994), Marshall & King (1988), Voous (1988). Durwyn Liley (pers. comm. 1995).

---

25 MINDANAO SCOPS OWL
Otus mirus Plate 8

French: Petit-duc de Mindanao
German: Mindanao-Zwergohreule

IDENTIFICATION A small, dark scops owl (about 19cm) with short ear-tufts. Facial disc with indistinct light and dark brown concentric lines, and some longer whiskers protruding from rim. Very dark and contrastingly marked; heavily spotted and blotched above with blackish, some rufescence near feather bases; pale below, especially on belly, with bold, sharply defined black streaks and crossbars. **Similar species** The only scops owl on Mindanao. The only other Philippine scops owl resembling it is Luzon Scops Owl [26] but that is more finely marked, more rufescent, with longer ear-tufts, and confined to Luzon.

VOCALISATIONS According to tape recordings made by N. Bostock, the song of the male is a disyllabic, melancholic whistle, the second note slightly more forced than the first. These couplets are uttered in long series at intervals of about 10-15 seconds: *pli-piooh, pli-piooh*. They are very different from the high mellow whistles of Sulawesi Scops Owl [46] and the guttural, three or four notes of Oriental Scops [40].

Mindanao Scops Owl

DISTRIBUTION Mindanao, Philippines. Recorded from Mt Hilong, Angusan Province, in N Mindanao (type locality), and from Mt Apo in S Mindanao; also found recently on Mt Katanglad. Endemic.

MOVEMENTS Resident.

HABITAT Montane rainforest; restricted to forest above 650m (?).

DESCRIPTION Adult Wings short and rounded. Facial disc pale greyish-brown with concentric rings of blackish spots, and some dark bristles reaching beyond rim of disc. Eyebrows whitish, continuing towards tips of ear-tufts, which are small. Upperparts greyish-brown, spotted brownish and black; scapulars with rather large whitish areas on outer webs, but no distinct whitish row across shoulder. Flight and tail feathers barred light and dark. Underparts buffy-whitish to whitish-cream with blackish spots and herringbone-like pattern. Distal third of tarsus and toes bare. **Juvenile** Unknown. **Bare parts** Iris yellow in Mt Katanglad birds. Bill dark greenish-grey. Cere greenish-yellow to greyish. Toes light greyish to whitish-yellow.

MEASUREMENTS AND WEIGHT Total length 19cm. Wing 127-131mm; tail 58mm. Weight: 64.5g.

GEOGRAPHICAL VARIATION Monotypic: *Otus mirus* Ripley & Rabor, 1968.

HABITS A nocturnal bird, but details of habits unknown.

FOOD Probably mainly insects and other arthropods.

BREEDING Unknown.

STATUS AND CONSERVATION Apparently rare within its small range, where continuing destruction of forest habitat represents a major threat. Listed as Vulnerable by BirdLife International.

REMARKS A poorly known species. Studies on its ecology and biology, as well as its vocalisations, are urgently needed.

REFERENCES Dickinson *et al.* (1991), Collar *et al.* (1994), Marshall & King (1988), P. Morris (pers. comm. 1999), Ripley & Rabor (1968).

26 LUZON SCOPS OWL
Otus longicornis   Plate 8

French: Petit-duc de Luzon
German: Luzon-Zwergohreule

IDENTIFICATION A small scops owl (19-21cm), above pale rufous with dark brown and black mottling, speckles and freckles, and long ear-tufts (31mm), whitish eyebrows, a white collar, and white and rufous underparts heavily marked with black, breast more rufous and belly whiter. Eyes yellow. **Similar species** In Philippines, Mindoro Scops Owl [27] is smaller, with shorter ear-tufts, is buffier below, and is endemic to Mindoro; Mindanao Scops Owl [25] darker and less rufous, with heavier markings overall and shorter ear-tufts, and is found only on Mindanao; the race of Philippine Scops Owl [56] on Luzon is much larger, with powerful talons, well feathered legs and toes, orange-brown eyes, and nuchal collar contrasts with back.

VOCALISATIONS According to tape recordings made by P. Morris, the song of the male is a melancholic, somewhat drawn-out whistle with a downward inflection: *wheehuw wheehuw wheehuw...* uttered at intervals of about 3-5 seconds. In addition, a similar but rather bisyllabic whistle, dropping slightly in pitch with the first note running into the second, is uttered in series, perhaps expressing excitement (e.g. after playback). These double notes are repeated at intervals of about 5-10 seconds: *whewhíuh whewhíuh whewhíuh...* .

DISTRIBUTION Luzon in Philippines, where confined to forest above 350m. Recent observations in Quezon National Park in S Luzon (14°N, 121°50'E), and on Mts Cetaceo and Dipalayag in Sierra Madre (northwest of Manila); in S Luzon, also found in provinces of Bulacan (15°N, 121°05'E) and Camarines Sur (13°40'N, 123°20'E) between 360 and 1,800m. Endemic.

Luzon Scops Owl

MOVEMENTS Resident.

HABITAT Forest in foothills and mountains. Frequents closed-canopy forest. Found in pine forest from 1,800m in Camarines Sur Province to as low as 360m in Bulacan Province. In type locality at La Trinidad (now a suburb of Baguio, with scattered remnants of pine forest), now absent. 350-2,200m.

DESCRIPTION Adult Forehead pale, eyebrows white, and a complete white collar, the feathers blackish at tips; collar usually more narrow but distinct on hindneck. Rictal bristles with white bars and black tips, the longest bristles about 28mm. Ear-tufts coloured like head, the longest feathers 31mm. Ear-coverts barred with white, blackish-brown and rufous. Upperparts bright ochraceous-buff, the feathers with streaks and irregular bars of blackish-brown, mostly near tips. Wing blackish, mottled and speckled with black and rusty-brown. Tail and tertials narrowly but inconspicuously barred. Chin whitish; throat white with some black-tipped rufous feathers; breast rich rufous, boldly mottled with black and less so with white; abdomen and flanks largely white, feathers mottled with black and rusty-brown. Slender bill laterally compressed. Tarsi thin, bare for 10-11mm above toe joint, i.e. feathered for slightly more than half of length; long slender claws. **Juvenile** Natal down pure light grey; soon replaced by a soft grey plumage barred with brown, darker on head and upperparts. **Bare parts** Iris bright yellow. Bill dingy dull green, tip and cutting edges dark brown. Cere dirty flesh at base, but dull yellowish-green over nostrils. Feet whitish-flesh. Claws grey.

MEASUREMENTS AND WEIGHT Total length 19-21cm. Females perhaps a little larger than males. Wing 142-153mm; tail 72-74mm. Weight: no data.

GEOGRAPHICAL VARIATION Monotypic: *Otus longicornis* (Ogilivie-Grant, 1894).

HABITS A nocturnal bird. No detailed knowledge of habits.

FOOD As with most scops owls, insects are the main prey.

BREEDING Nest with three downy young found in May at Benguet. Nests in holes of aged trees. Eggs 2-3, white and roundish.

STATUS AND CONSERVATION Although this owl is currently not uncommon locally, it has become rare in places as a result of habitat loss. Continuing deforestation remains a clear threat. Listed as Vulnerable by BirdLife International.

REMARKS This species' ecology, biology and vocalisations need study.

REFERENCES Collar *et al.* (1994), Dickinson *et al.* (1991), DuPont (1971), McGregor (1909).

27 MINDORO SCOPS OWL
Otus mindorensis   Plate 8

French: Petit-duc de Mindoro
German: Mindoro-Zwergohreule

IDENTIFICATION A small, buffy-brown scops owl, vaguely streaked above and finely streaked and barred below, with medium-length ear-tufts and yellow eyes. **Similar species** Reports of an undescribed *otus* on Mindoro are due to unfamiliarity with the song of Mindoro Hawk Owl [192]. Compared with allopatric Luzon Scops Owl [26], smaller, buffier and more vaguely marked overall, with shorter ear-tufts.

VOCALISATIONS The territorial song of the male is a series of single, whistled notes, uttered at variable intervals of at least 5 seconds: *whoow, whoow, ...* The single hoots are similar in tone to the song of Tawny Owl [130], but somewhat higher in pitch and easily imitated by whistling; they have a single frequency of 0.9kHz and a duration of about 0.4 seconds.

DISTRIBUTION Endemic to Mindoro in the Philippines. Reported from Mt Halcon, Mt Ilong and Mt Baco, as well as C Mindoro.

Mindoro Scops Owl

MOVEMENTS Resident.

HABITAT Montane, closed-canopy forest with homogenous extension, above 870m.

DESCRIPTION Adult Mantle, back and rump brown with black shaft-streaks, these having short lateral 'branches' forming irregular bars. Forehead and area above eye uniform pale buff or whitish. Crown rufous with black shaft markings and spots. Nuchal collar buffy, but narrow and almost obsolete. Underparts mostly buffy, with only narrow white bars (in contrast to Luzon Scops Owl). Tarsus feathered for half its length; long toes. **Juvenile** Undescribed. **Bare parts** Iris bright yellow. Bill dull greenish-yellow, cutting edges dark brown. Cere dirty flesh. Legs whitish-flesh. Claws grey.

MEASUREMENTS AND WEIGHT Total length 18.5cm. Wing 135mm; tail 63mm. Weight: no data.

GEOGRAPHICAL VARIATION Monotypic: *Otus mindorensis* (Whitehead, 1899).

HABITS A nocturnal bird which hides during daytime in dense foliage or natural holes. After dark, the birds start singing to claim their territories.

FOOD Apparently insects constitute the majority of the prey, as with most scops owls.

BREEDING Unknown. The holotype had well-developed eggs when collected in January 1896. Probably nests in holes in aged trees.

STATUS AND CONSERVATION Up to nine individuals have been heard singing along a 1.5km length of track,

suggesting that the species was rather common in that area (a plateau where the track bisected homegenous montane forest at 1,300-1,450m above sea-level). Although locally common, the species is threatened by increasing forest destruction. Listed as Vulnerable by BirdLife International.

REMARKS The biology of the Mindoro Scops Owl needs study.

REFERENCES Collar *et al.* (1994), Dickinson *et al.* (1991), du Pont (1971), Evans *et al.* (1993), Marshall & King (1988).

28 FLORES SCOPS OWL
Otus alfredi   Plate 8

French: Petit-duc de Flores
German: Flores-Zwergohreule

IDENTIFICATION A relatively small (about 20cm), dark rufous-brown scops owl with small ear-tufts. Almost plain dark rufous-brown above, outer webs of scapulars forming white band across shoulder; forehead and crown finely mottled and vermiculated light. Finely barred cinnamon and whitish below, without dark shaft-streaks. Eyes yellowish. **Similar species** Moluccan Scops Owl [43] is not cinnamon-brown above and is more barred and streaked below. Wallace's Scops Owl [59] is rather dull, pale greyish-brown, with brownish barring and blackish shaft-streaks below.

VOCALISATIONS Unknown; repeated attempts by various observers to locate this owl by voice have failed, so it must either vocalise infrequently, only seasonally, have an unusual song, or be rare.

A relatively high *goohk* given at intervals of several seconds has been recorded in lowland forest on Sumba, where the birds sang from branches above the canopy. This may possibly be the song of Flores Scops Owl (indicating a new locality in its distribution). Also on Sumba, a slightly higher 'song' (female?) was recorded, in duet with the 'deeper-singing' bird (male?). The songs may also, of course, be of an undescribed species.

DISTRIBUTION Western Flores in the Ruteng and Todo mountains, Lesser Sundas. An owl seen and recorded on nearby Sumba might be this species.

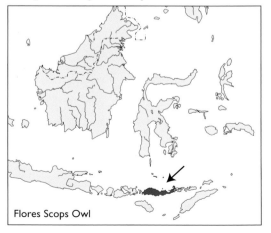

Flores Scops Owl

MOVEMENTS Resident.

HABITAT Probably humid forest in the mountains, above 1,000m. After a century with no recorded sightings, rediscovered in 1994 at 1,400m above sea-level in humid montane forest on SW Flores. If the recorded songs from Sumba are of this species, then it would also occur at lower altitudes on this island.

DESCRIPTION Adult Crown cinnamon-brown with very fine light vermiculations. Eyebrows buffy-whitish. Ear-tufts small, of same coloration as forehead and crown. Facial disc cinnamon-brown, not contrasting with surrounding plumage; rim of facial disc mostly obscured by lengthened auriculars; thin rim indistinctly darker outer webs of auriculars partly white. Upperparts nearly uniform foxy cinnamon-brown; outer webs of scapulars white, forming white band across shoulder. Flight feathers barred whitish-buff and cinnamon-brown. Tail banding obsolete. Underparts dirty white, densely marked with indistinct cinnamon-brown bars and fine vermiculations; no dark shaft-streaks; sides of upper breast and neck sparsely flecked black. Distal quarter of tarsus bare. **Juvenile** Nearly uniform pale rufous with only vague barring, and more distinct tail bands than adult. **Bare parts** Eyes yellow; rims pinkish. Bill and cere orange-yellow. Toes dull yellowish. Claws yellowish-horn without dark tips.

MEASUREMENTS AND WEIGHT Total length 19.2-20.7cm. Wing 146-160mm; tail about 78mm. Weight: no data.

GEOGRAPHICAL VARIATION Monotypic: *Otus alfredi* (Hartert, 1897).

HABITS Unknown.

FOOD Unknown.

BREEDING Unknown. Probably nests in cavities of trees.

STATUS AND CONSERVATION Known only from three specimens, collected in 1896, until rediscovered in 1994. A juvenile specimen was collected in May 1994, and another individual was netted in March of the same year but not recognised as this species until 1998; in addition a recent sight record was made in September 1997. The conservation status of this species was not evaluated due to taxonomic confusion, but as a restricted range species it must be threatened by continuing loss of habitat.

REMARKS Ecology and biology of this species are unknown. Some authors consider it clearly related to Mountain Scops Owl. It was briefly erroneously considered to be the red morph of Moluccan Scops Owl, but it differs from all members of this group in many ways, being much closer to Mountain Scops Owl. Nevertheless, this treatment resulted in its temporary exclusion from world lists and conservation plans.

REFERENCES Boyer & Hume (1991), Coates & Bishop (1997), Hartert (1897), Linsley *et al.* (1999), Marshall & King (1988), Mayr (1944), Monk *et al.* (1997), Rasmussen (1998), Sibley & Monroe (1991), White & Bruce (1986), Widodo *et al.* (1999).

29   SÃO TOMÉ SCOPS OWL
Otus hartlaubi   Plate   8

French: Petit-duc de São Tomé
German: Hartlaub-Zwergohreule

IDENTIFICATION A small scops owl (18cm) with very small ear-tufts, yellow eyes, bold markings but lacking vermiculations, and wings and tail essentially unbanded. Tarsi largely unfeathered. Greyish-brown and rufous morphs exist. The song is characteristic. **Similar species** African Scops Owl [39], occurring on Pagalu (Annobon) Island less than 200km to the southwest, has feathered tarsi and is very heavily streaked below, with prominently banded wings and tail.

VOCALISATIONS The song is a low, rather raucous *kwow* uttered at intervals of about 15-20 seconds. It is totally different from the trilled song of African Scops Owl and the flute-like note of Common Scops Owl [37].

DISTRIBUTION Found only on São Tomé Island in the Gulf of Guinea. An unconfirmed report exists from nearby Principe.

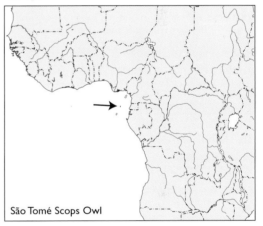

São Tomé Scops Owl

MOVEMENTS Resident.

HABITAT Humid primary forest, but also secondary forest and plantations. Sea-level up to 1,300m.

DESCRIPTION Adult *Grey-brown morph*: Upperparts nearly solid dark brown with indistinct rufous and dark markings. Feathers of crown, nape and back with blackish shaft-streaks, nape with some dark-edged white spots. Facial disc pale brown, darker near eyes; rim rufous. Ear-tufts very small. Scapulars with very large whitish areas forming scapular stripe. Primaries essentially unbarred brownish, mottled with buffy-brown and whitish; secondaries brown with fine vermiculations. Tail nearly unbanded, with vague narrow buffy bars and pale rufous vermiculations. Underparts whitish with fine brown and rufous barring, and blackish shaft-streaks along which the bars converge. Distal quarter or so of top of tarsus unfeathered but sides and rear bare. *Rufous morph*: Similar to grey-brown morph, but ground colour dark reddish-brown and black markings more prominent. **Juvenile** Downy coat undescribed. Mesoptile of both morphs paler than adult, with fine barring above and below. **Bare parts** Eyes deep yellow (sometimes brown?). Bill and cere yellow, tip of bill washed greyish. Tarsi and toes yellowish-ochre. Claws brown.

MEASUREMENTS AND WEIGHT Total length around 18cm. Wing 123-141mm; tail 66-72mm. Females somewhat larger than males. Weight about 79g.

GEOGRAPHICAL VARIATION Monotypic: *Otus hartlaubi* (Giebel, 1849).

HABITS A nocturnal bird. By day roosts in dense foliage or close to tree trunks, where well camouflaged; sometimes uses holes in trees as daytime roost.

FOOD Mainly insects, such as grasshoppers, beetles and moths. Also preys on small lizards. Frequents dense foliage at lower levels of forest for hunting, sometimes also descending to ground.

BREEDING Virtually unknown. Probably nests in natural cavities in trees; two nestlings unable to fly were found on the ground, which may suggest that this owl is perhaps occasionally a ground nester. Clutch probably consists of 2 white eggs.

STATUS AND CONSERVATION Probably rare. As it is restricted to one small island it may be endangered, but little is known about this small owl.

REMARKS Further research is required on this species' biology. Unlikely on morphological and geographical grounds to belong to the *manadensis* superspecies as suggested by Marshall (1978).

REFERENCES Chappuis (1978), Collar & Stuart (1985), Dowsett & Dowsett-Lemaire (1993), Fry *et al.* (1988), de Naurois (1975).

30 ANDAMAN SCOPS OWL
Otus balli Plate 8

French: Petit-duc des Andamanes
German: Andamanen-Zwergohreule

IDENTIFICATION A small (18cm) brown or rufescent scops owl with short ear-tufts. Crown flecked blackish and buffy-white; underparts finely vermiculated light and dark, with whitish spots which have black, often arrow-shaped lower tips (these much larger in brown morph than in rufous one). Eyes, bill and bare toes yellow. **Similar species** Oriental Scops Owl [40], which occurs in Andamans as winter visitor (and probable breeding resident), has a blackish-streaked crown and is much more boldly streaked below, without larger white spots; it also differs vocally.

VOCALISATIONS The territorial song consists of strong purring notes somewaht similar to African Scops Owl [39], *curroo curro curro...*, with the 'r' typically rolled. The interval between notes is about 2 seconds. The single notes are often preceded by 1-3 faint *tek* notes, only heard at close range. These verses are repeated at intervals of several seconds. The female has a similar, but higher-pitched song. Single subdued, hoarse calls are also uttered.

DISTRIBUTION Endemic to the Andaman Islands in the Bay of Bengal.

MOVEMENTS Unknown.

HABITAT Semi-open areas with groups of trees, cultivated

countryside with trees, near buildings and settlements, also gardens with bushes and trees.

DESCRIPTION Adult Occurs in brown and rufous morphs, the latter less boldly patterned than the brown morph. Ear-tufts small. Facial disc pale brown with some concentric lines, edge of disc faintly rimmed dark. Upperparts brown with more or less rufous tinge; crown spotted whitish-buff and black, nape similar and with fine vermiculations; mantle with buffy-whitish spots, tipped black; scapulars with dark-edged whitish to pale buff outer webs. Flight feathers and tail barred dark and light. Throat whitish; rest of underparts brown, finely vermiculated darker, with relatively large whitish spots with black lower tips (blackish tips often arrowhead-shaped). Tarsi not totally feathered to base of toes; distal third is bare. **Juvenile** Not described. **Bare parts** Eyes yellow. Bill yellowish-horn. Cere yellowish. Toes dirty yellow. Claws horn with darker tips.

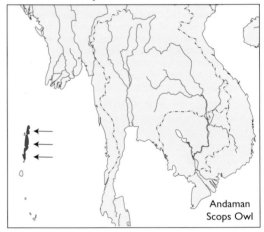

Andaman
Scops Owl

MEASUREMENTS AND WEIGHT Total length 18-19cm. Wing 138-143mm; tail 75-81mm. Weight: no data.

GEOGRAPHICAL VARIATION Monotypic: *Otus balli* (Hume, 1873). Apart from individual variation in both brown and rufous morphs, nothing known.

HABITS A strictly nocturnal owl, which appears rather confiding towards man. By day it roosts in trees or bushes, sometimes inside buildings, becoming active at dusk. In settlements, roofs of houses are often used as perches.

FOOD Primarily insects and their larvae. Shows a preference for caterpillars, which it catches by sidling in parrot-like manner along boughs of small trees and bushes.

BREEDING Season mid February to mid April. Nests in cavities in trees, normally old holes of woodpeckers or barbets. The 2-3 pure white eggs (mean 30.5 x 27.1mm) are laid directly on to the floor of hole, and incubated by the female alone. Even though the species is not rare, its biology is poorly known.

STATUS AND CONSERVATION Rather frequently observed and not uncommon. It lives in relatively close association with man and agriculture, and is therefore less threatened than many other tropical owls.

REMARKS This species' relationship with other scops owls is still unclear. It has been thought a relative of *Otus spilocephalus*, but is probably not very closely related. It may be to some extent related to *O. sunia*, which lives in similar habitats in the Indian subcontinent and locally in the Andaman and Nicobar Islands.

REFERENCES Boyer & Hume (1991), Marshall & King (1988), Rasmussen (1998).

31   MADAGASCAR SCOPS OWL
Otus rutilus   Plate 9

French: Petit-duc malgache
German: Madagascar-Zwergohreule

IDENTIFICATION Small, but larger (19-23cm) than Common Scops Owl [37] and with greyish bill and yellow eyes, and rather small ear-tufts. Grey, rufous and brown morphs are known. Cryptically coloured like all scops owls, it is difficult to spot in the field. Best identified by its voice. **Similar species** The Madagascar Scops Owl is almost certainly polytypic, with western birds averaging greyer, but best identified in the field on voice (see Vocalisations).

VOCALISATIONS The song is a series of 5-9 short, hollow and clear *oot* notes, uttered rather rapidly (about 3 per second), with a break of several seconds before the next series begins. In the drier areas of the west, a different song has been recorded which apparently belongs to another taxon: *gurrok-gurrok-gurrok* (generally 3-5 notes per phrase). The song of birds from Mayotte Island is similar in tone to that of nominate *rutilus*, but the single notes are longer and the sequence slower; this allopatric form, isolated by a large distance, may be specifically distinct: '*Otus mayottensis*'.

DISTRIBUTION Madagascar and Mayotte (Comoro Islands). The drier areas of W Madagascar are inhabited by vocally distinct populations, but its range limits are yet to be defined.

Madagascar Scops Owl

MOVEMENTS Apparently resident.

HABITAT Forest and rather humid bushy country. Drier areas with shrubs, brush and scattered trees in the west are inhabited by populations which average greyer and differ vocally. Sea-level up to 1,800m.

DESCRIPTION *O. r. rutilus* **Adult** *Brown morph*: Facial disc whitish-brown, rim dark brown. Ear-tufts small. Upperparts and crown pale brown, mottled with ochre and whitish markings, and with black shaft-streaks sometimes showing

herringbone-like pattern. Scapulars with white areas, edged blackish, showing as scapular stripe across closed wing. Primaries greyish-brown with lighter and darker barring, less conspicuous on secondaries. Tail with lighter and darker bars. Underparts ochraceous to pale greyish-brown with rusty-brown vermiculations, and blackish shaft-streaks showing somewhat herringbone-like pattern. Tarsi feathered pale greyish-brown to base of toes. *Rufous morph*: Similar, but ground colour rusty-brown and dark markings often obsolete. *Grey morph*: Similar, but ground colour more greyish. Western birds show a predominance of grey morphs, while eastern birds are frequently of the rufous morph. **Juvenile** Not known. **Bare parts** Eyes yellow. Bill and cere pale greyish-brown. Toes greyish-brown. Claws blackish-brown.

MEASUREMENTS AND WEIGHT Total length 19-23cm. Wing 145-175mm; tail 55-80mm. Males slightly smaller than females. Weight of males 85-107g, of females 112-116g.

GEOGRAPHICAL VARIATION Two subspecies recognised, but these may be separate species. In addition, population of drier regions of W Madagascar probably represents a third taxon.

   O. r. rutilus (Pucheran, 1849). Madagascar. See Description.
   O. (r.) mayottensis Benson, 1960. Mayotte in Comoro Islands. Similar to brown morph of nominate *rutilus*, but a little larger, with larger ear-tufts and white throat. Wing 166-175mm. See Vocalisations for differences in song. (Perhaps specifically distinct from *O. rutilus*.)

HABITS Nocturnal. During daytime it conceals itself in dense foliage, between branches or by perching tight against a trunk.

FOOD Insects, especially moths and beetles. Perhaps also small vertebrates. Flies from tree to tree to hunt insects; quite often takes prey, e.g. moths, on the wing, but also comes to the ground to capture food.

BREEDING Eggs have been found on ground under dead branches, but the owl doubtless prefers natural holes in trees or on the ground. Clutch 3-4 white eggs, incubated by female. Breeding biology is very poorly known.

STATUS AND CONSERVATION Locally rather common. Nothing is known about its population dynamics.

REMARKS The Mayotte race is sometimes thought to be specifically distinct, as the sequence of phrases of its song is shorter, the single notes are longer, and the intervals between single notes are longer, although the quality of its song is rather similar to that of nominate. Further research is required to determine its taxonomy, and in particular bioacoustical, ecological and molecular-biological studies should be undertaken. Studies are in progress to clarify the taxonomic status of the population from drier areas in W Madagascar.

REFERENCES Benson *et al.* (1976), Boyer & Hume (1991), Goodman *et al.* (1997), Langrand (1990), Lewis (1997), Louette (1988), Marshall (1978), Morris & Hawkins (1998), Rasmussen *et al.* (in prep.), Safford (1993, 1996).

32 GRAND COMORO SCOPS OWL
Otus pauliani   Plate 9

French: Petit-duc du Karthala
German: Comoren-Zwergohreule

IDENTIFICATION An 'earless' scops owl with finely barred crown and vermiculated underparts with scarcely any dark shaft-streaks. Facial disc shows several concentric lines. Eyes vary from yellow to dark brown. **Similar species** The only other owl on Grand Comoro is the much larger and very different Barn Owl [1]. No other scops owl on the Comoros has such finely barred and vermiculated plumage.

VOCALISATIONS The song consists of a long series of short, somewhat 'bent' notes, e.g. *gluk-gluk-gluk-gluk-...*, about 2 per second. It begins with few more drawn-out notes, e.g. *choo*; the following sounds become shorter and are downward-inflected, and are repeated in series for ten or more minutes (once, more than 1,200 notes counted in one sequence). Female apparently utters a call like *choeiet* about every 3 seconds, duetting with male.

DISTRIBUTION Endemic to Njazidja (Grand Comoro Island), where confined to Mt Karthala.

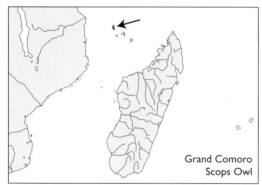

Grand Comoro
Scops Owl

MOVEMENTS Apparently resident.

HABITAT Mountain forest in primary or degraded state, also adjacent tree-heath at upper forest edge. Between 460m and 1,900m above sea-level.

DESCRIPTION Adult *Light morph*: Facial disc grey-brown, with some darker concentric lines around eyes. Ear-tufts not visible. Remarkably uniform in coloration above, dark greyish-brown, finely barred or vermiculated darker and with some lighter spots; scapulars buff with indistinct dark bars. Underparts ochraceous-buff with very few dark shaft-streaks and dense pattern of darker vermiculations; undertail- and underwing-coverts whitish. Distal part of tarsus unfeathered. Talons rather weak. *Dark morph*: Apparently similar to dark morph of Anjouan Scops Owl [33] (but no dark morph specimen exists). **Juvenile** Unknown. **Bare parts** Eyes yellow or brown; in the holotype described as yellow, and also by Safford (1993), and this supported by a colour photo by A. Lewis (1997), but four recently observed individuals (three males, one female) had dark brown eyes, suggesting that iris colour is variable. Bill and cere greyish-brown. Tarsi and toes yellowish-grey to pale greyish-brown. Claws blackish-brown.

MEASUREMENTS AND WEIGHT Total length 20cm. Wing 141-144mm; tail 73mm. Weight of a single specimen 69.5g.

GEOGRAPHICAL VARIATION Monotypic: *Otus pauliani* Benson, 1960.

HABITS A little known nocturnal bird which becomes active at dusk. Reported to be highly territorial, approaching very closely when its call is imitated. It is said to fly slowly with undeliberate, shallow wing-flutterings. When perched, it holds its wings rather loosely drooped along the body, giving a long-winged, short-tailed impression (Herremans *et al.* 1991).

FOOD Insects. The weak talons suggest that it normally preys on invertebrates.

BREEDING Unknown. Probably nests in holes in trees.

STATUS AND CONSERVATION Total population is estimated to be more than 1,000 pairs. Although the species is doubtless endangered by habitat fragmentation, it seems to be holding its own even in degraded forest. The situation may worsen, however, with increasing deforestation, and the introduced Common Myna *Acridotheres tristis* poses an additional, and serious threat. Prompt action is therefore needed to protect this owl from extinction. Listed as Critical by BirdLife International.

REMARKS Although *O. pauliani* has been thought to be a race of *O. rutilus*, bioacoustical and morphological studies have clearly shown it to be a full species. Although known from sight records, only a single specimen exists of this species.

REFERENCES Benson (1960), Boyer & Hume (1991), Collar *et al.* (1994), Herremans *et al.* (1991), Louette (1988), Safford (1993).

33 ANJOUAN SCOPS OWL
Otus capnodes   Plate 9

French: Petit-duc d'Anjouan
German: Anjouan-Zwergohreule

IDENTIFICATION A small scops owl (20cm) with very rudimentary, almost non-existent ear-tufts. Three colour morphs known. **Similar species** This is the only owl on Anjouan; it is larger and heavier than Grand Comoro Scops Owl [32], with much more powerful talons. Mohéli Scops Owl [34] is generally more rufescent.

VOCALISATIONS The song consists of a series of prolonged whistles, similar to call of Grey Plover *Pluvialis squatarola*: *peeooee* and *peeoo*, repeated 3-5 times at varying intervals of 0.5-1.0 seconds. Each series is separated from the next by an interval of at least 10 seconds. Also utters single notes. Apart from the song, a harsh screech call is known, *chrreeoeeh*, lasting about 1.5 seconds.

DISTRIBUTION Endemic to Anjouan (Ndzuani) in the Comoro Islands.

MOVEMENTS Not known.

HABITAT Patches of primary forest on mountain slopes upwards of 550m above sea-level.

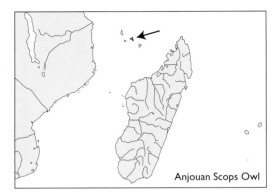

Anjouan Scops Owl

DESCRIPTION Adult *Light morph*: Facial disc whitish-cream, with narrow dark concentric lines around eyes; rim of disc dark. No visible ear-tufts. Upperparts greyish-brown, feathers with dark centres and greyish-buff edges, giving somewhat mottled appearance; scapulars buffy and barred, not forming a conspicuous stripe. Flight and tail feathers with several darker and lighter bars. Underparts similar to back, with fine barring and dark shaft-streaks, latter sometimes with herringbone-like pattern. Tarsi heavily feathered front and back, feathering ending abruptly at distal third. *Rufous-brown morph*: Similar to light morph, but less speckled whitish and generally with rufous-brown coloration. *Dark morph*: Overall dark chocolate-brown to earth-brown, rather uniform, with fine buffy speckles. **Juvenile** Unknown. **Bare parts** Eyes yellowish-green. Bill and cere horn-coloured. Toes and bare parts of tarsus dull yellowish-grey with greenish tint. Claws blackish-brown.

MEASUREMENTS AND WEIGHT Total length about 20cm. Wing 158-173mm; tail 80mm. Weight (one bird) 119g.

GEOGRAPHICAL VARIATION Monotypic: *Otus capnodes* (Gurney, 1889).

HABITS During daytime the owl roosts in natural holes in aged trees, leaving at dusk to hunt. Little is known about its biology and habits.

FOOD Probably insects.

BREEDING Nests in holes in thick trunks of mature trees.

STATUS AND CONSERVATION Rediscovered in June 1992, having not been seen by ornithologists since 1886. The population is estimated at about 100-200 pairs (or even fewer). Deforestation and hunting by man seem to be the most serious threats to its survival. Listed as Critical by BirdLife International.

REMARKS The Anjouan Scops Owl needs intensive study of its biology and ecology. It is doubtless a full species, and not a race of *O. rutilus*.

REFERENCES Collar *et al.* (1994), Lewis (1996), Louette (1988), Safford (1993 and *in litt.*).

34   MOHÉLI SCOPS OWL
Otus moheliensis   Plate   9

French: Petit-duc de Mohéli
German: Mohéli-Zwergohreule

IDENTIFICATION A rufescent-brown, medium-sized scops owl with reduced ear-tufts and ill-defined facial disc. Back barred and mottled with blackish; outer webs of scapulars cinnamon, with one or two fine dark bars. Lower third or so of tarsus bare; bill dark, relatively large. Eyes greenish-yellow. A red morph exists. **Similar species** Grand Comoro Scops Owl [32] is smaller and paler and has a much weaker bill, while Anjouan Scops Owl [33] is less rufescent. Both have feathered tarsi to the base of the toes but are best distinguished by their different vocalisations.

VOCALISATIONS Little studied. The song of the male is described as an aspirated hissing whistle in series of 1-5 notes. A screech, similar to that of Anjouan Scops, is also described.

DISTRIBUTION Endemic to Mohéli (Mwali), in Comoro Islands.

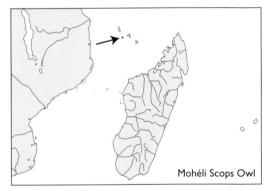

Mohéli Scops Owl

MOVEMENTS Probably resident.

HABITAT Dense, humid forest, rich in epiphytes, between 450m and 790m on the slopes and on the summit of Mohéli Island.

DESCRIPTION Adult Facial disc silky pale brown; rim inconspicuous, outlined with thin dusky edge. Ear-tufts short and rather inconspicuous. Upperparts rufescent-brown with irregular blackish barring and mottling; nape densely mottled with blackish, forming a dusky 'collar'; outer webs of scapulars light cinnamon with 1-2 fine dark bars. Outer webs of flight feathers regularly barred with buffy dots near the base and rufescent-brown towards tips; inner webs uniform brown. Tail feathers brown, mottled with rufescent-brown or indistinctly barred. Throat whitish with buffy suffusion; rest of underparts buffy-cinnamon with blackish shaft-streaks, abdomen finely barred chamois or cinnamon-buff; thighs and feathered parts of tarsi with scaly brown spots. Lower third of tarsi unfeathered. (An individual of a rufous morph has also been described.) **Juvenile** Unknown. **Bare parts** Eyes greenish-yellow. Bill dusky horn. Unfeathered parts of tarsus and toes grey, undersurface of toes yellowish-flesh.

MEASUREMENTS AND WEIGHT Total length about 22cm. Wing (chord) of males 155-164 mm, of female

161mm; tail (1 female) 71mm. Weight of 1 male 95g, of 1 female 116g.

GEOGRAPHICAL VARIATION Monotypic: *Otus moheliensis* Lafontaine & Moulaert, 1998.

HABITS Strictly nocturnal, becoming active after sunset. At this time and later at night, the male may be heard singing; vocalisations were recorded in September.

FOOD Probably mainly insects and spiders.

BREEDING Unknown.

STATUS AND CONSERVATION The total population is estimated at about 400 individuals. At present, this species appears to be still rather numerous in the forest of the summits and mountain slopes, but these are subject to continuing destruction. This species must therefore be classified as endangered. The density recorded in untouched forest was one individual per 5ha or so, while in degraded forest the figure was one individual in 10ha.

REMARKS This species was only described in 1998. Its recent discovery means that the suggestion of translocating Anjouan Scops Owls to Mohéli is out of the question. The biology of this owl requires research, as also do its vocalisations and its relationship with other species of scops owls.

REFERENCES Lafontaine & Moulaert (1998).

---

35   PEMBA SCOPS OWL
Otus pembaensis   Plate   9

French: Petit-duc de Pemba
German: Pemba-Zwergohreule

IDENTIFICATION A rather uniform rufous or grey, rufous-tinged scops owl with short ear-tufts and more or less prominent whitish eyebrows. Central tail feathers plain rufous, outer ones barred dark brown on outer webs. Eyes yellow. **Similar species** The only owl on Pemba Island apart from the much bigger and very different Barn Owl [1]. Flores Scops Owl [28] from Indonesia is also rather plain rufous above but its tail is fully barred.

VOCALISATIONS The song consists of a long sequence of hollow, monosyllabic notes, uttered at irregular intervals, sometimes in succession with intervals of 0.5-1 second: *hoo hoo hoo...* . Voice of male lower than that of female. Pairs duet: *hoo ho hoo hoo ho hoo...* . The shorter note is higher pitched and represents the song of the female duetting with the longer and much hollower *hoo* of the male. Like most owls the birds bill-click in defence behaviour.

DISTRIBUTION Endemic to Pemba Island, off N Tanzanian coast of E Africa.

MOVEMENTS Resident.

HABITAT Semi-open landscape with groups of densely foliaged trees, and plantations, especially of cloves.

DESCRIPTION Adult *Light morph*: Facial disc pale buff, with darker but not very distinct rim. Ear-tufts short. Upperparts rather unmarked plain rufous, with several darker streaks on crown, sometimes also on nape. Fore-

head, eyebrows and mantle with fine dusky bars and vermiculations. Outer webs of scapulars whitish-buff with dark tips, forming dark-barred pale line across shoulder. Flight feathers barred darker and lighter. Central tail feathers plain, outer ones barred dark on outer webs. Underparts pale grey tinged rufous, finely vermiculated light rufous, grey and white, with a few narrow streaks on breast and flanks. Tarsi profusely feathered to base of toes front and rear; claws large. *Rufous morph*: More uniformly rufous, flanks sometimes with vague broad barring. **Juvenile** Downy young undescribed. Juvenile with vaguely cinnamon-barred whitish down, unstreaked crown barred with white, tail somewhat banded. **Bare parts** Eyes yellow. Bill dull greenish to yellow with dark tip. Toes grey with yellow soles. Claws dark greyish-brown with blackish tips.

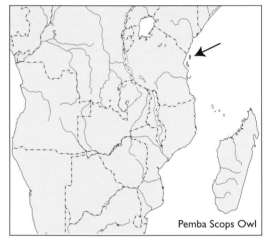

Pemba Scops Owl

MEASUREMENTS AND WEIGHT Total length about 20cm. Wing 148-155mm; tail 73-79mm. Weight: no data.

GEOGRAPHICAL VARIATION Monotypic: *Otus pembaensis* Pakenham, 1937.

HABITS During daytime the bird roosts in dense foliage of trees or in dense undergrowth low above ground. It becomes active at sunset and starts singing; less vocally active after dark. Calls from different perches, as well as in flight. When leaving a tree, it dives down and flies rather low above the ground before swooping up into another.

FOOD Insects. These are either caught from a perch, by dropping on to them, or are hawked in flight.

BREEDING Probably breeds from August to October in tree holes. Breeding biology unknown.

STATUS AND CONSERVATION Fairly common, but restricted range renders it vulnerable.

REMARKS Formerly considered a subspecies of *O. rutilus*. Studies are required on its biology and ecology.

REFERENCES Pakenham (1937, 1979), Fry *et al.* (1988), Safford (1993), Zimmerman *et al.* (1996).

36 FLAMMULATED SCOPS OWL
Otus flammeolus   Plate 10

French: Petit-duc d'Amérique
German: Ponderosa-Zwergohreule
Spanish: Tecolote Flameado

IDENTIFICATION A small scops owl (16-17 cm) with cryptic plumage. Facial disc and scapulars have rusty or cinnamon-buff areas. Eyes dark brown. **Similar species** Western and Eastern Screech Owls [60, 61] are larger, have yellow eyes, and lack rusty areas on scapulars, as well as having totally different, trilling songs.

VOCALISATIONS The song is a relatively deep *woop* with ventriloquial effect, repeated at regular intervals of about 2-3 seconds. Double notes of the same quality may be uttered when the bird is excited. Somewhat resembles voice of Common Scops Owl [37], which has a similarly spaced song of single but much higher-pitched notes.

DISTRIBUTION From W North America (British Columbia) south along Rocky Mountains to Mexico, Guatemala and El Salvador.

Flammulated Scops Owl

MOVEMENTS In the northern parts of its range only a summer visitor, migrating southwards in autumn to winter in warmer climates, e.g. in Mexico.

HABITAT Open coniferous mountain forest, especially forest with ponderosa and yellow pines, quite often mixed with oak or aspen; in most cases, habitats characterised by bushy undergrowth. Also occupies mixed forest with Douglas fir. From 400m up to about 3,000m.

DESCRIPTION *O. f. flammeolus* **Adult** Rufous and greyish morphs exist. Facial disc greyish-brown, washed with pale chestnut or rusty-brown; rim dark chestnut to blackish-brown. Erectile ear-tufts small. Entire upperparts cryptic greyish-brown with fine blackish mottles and shaft-streaks; scapulars with large rusty-tinged areas forming orange-buffy scapular stripe. Flight feathers with contrasting lighter and darker bars, less prominent on secondaries; tail similar in coloration. Underparts greyish-brown, mottled lighter and darker, with rusty spots and blackish shaft-streaks. Legs feathered greyish-brown to base of toes.

Juvenile Downy chicks whitish. Mesoptile similar to adult plumage, but with dark barring on underparts, crown, nape and back; facial disc tinged rusty. **Bare parts** Eyes dark brown. Bill relatively weak, greyish-brown. Cere similar in colour. Toes greyish-brown. Claws blackish-brown.

MEASUREMENTS AND WEIGHT Total length 16-17cm. Wing 133-149mm; tail 66-69mm. Weight 45-63g.

GEOGRAPHICAL VARIATION Weak and clinal; differences obscured by individual variation. Six subspecies have been described, but we only recognise three here.

    O. f. flammeolus (Kaup, 1853). Mountains of SW USA south to Mexico, Guatemala and El Salvador. See Description. (We include *meridionalis* in the nominate.)
    O. f. idahoensis Merriam, 1891. Northern part of species' range in W North America. Highly migratory. Longer-winged than nominate. (We include *frontalis* and *borealis* in *idahoensis*.)
    O. f. rarus Griscom, 1937. Highlands of Guatemala. Darker and more brownish than nominate *flammeolus*. Wing 127-144mm; tail 65-70mm.

HABITS Lives in pairs. A nocturnal bird, activity beginning after sunset or at dawn. By day roosts close to tree trunks, where well camouflaged by its plumage pattern, resembling a piece of broken branch; when nervous, becomes very slim, sleeking the plumage tightly and stretching the body upwards, with small ear-tufts erected ('ears' rather inconspicuous when plumage carried loose). This owl is difficult to detect; best way is to listen for the typical song, or to provoke response of territorial birds by playback of recordings.

FOOD Mainly nocturnal insects and spiders, especially moths. Flies from tree to tree in search of favoured food or chases moths above the canopy of trees, seizing prey with the bill. Larger prey are held in the talons and eaten piece by piece.

BREEDING Sometimes several pairs may nest quite close to one another, so that borders of territories must overlap. At beginning of breeding season in spring, males sing from their territories in order to attract females. A hole (mostly produced by a woodpecker) in a branch or in a tree trunk is used as nest; also accepts nestboxes for owls or American Kestrels *Falco sparverius* for breeding. The 3-4 pure white, rounded eggs are laid directly on to dry material on bottom of cavity. The female incubates alone and is fed by the male, who brings food to the nest. Incubation, lasting 3-4 weeks, begins after the first egg has been laid. Young are fed by both parents. After 3-4 weeks they leave the nest, and are cared for by both parents for about 4-5 weeks.

STATUS AND CONSERVATION Generally uncommon or local, but may be rather frequent in some areas.

REMARKS We consider this owl to be more closely related to the Old World *Otus* than to the American screech owls, both morphologically and vocally. The latter have more or less trilling songs or rather rapid sequences of generally higher-pitched notes, whereas that of *O. flammeolus* is similar to the songs of scops owls of the Old World.

REFERENCES Boyer & Hume (1991), Dunning (1993), Eck & Busse (1973), Pyle (1997), Scott *et al.* (1987), Voous (1988).

French: Hibou Petit-duc
German: Zwergohreule
Spanish: Autillo

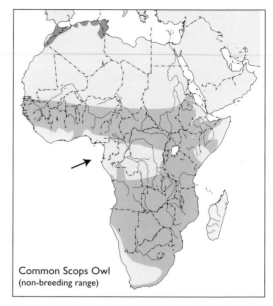

Common Scops Owl
(non-breeding range)

IDENTIFICATION A rather small scops owl (size somewhat larger than a thrush) with cryptic plumage pattern very like the bark of an old tree. Wings relatively long, tail short; erectile ear-tufts small. Eyes yellow. **Similar species** This is the only species of the genus *Otus* in Europe. Elsewhere, it overlaps with several other *Otus* owls which are similar in size and plumage pattern. From the Middle East to Pakistan may occur sympatrically with Pallid Scops Owl [38], the latter being generally paler and having a less bark-like colour pattern with more prominent ventral streaks. Indian Scops Owl [54] has dark brown eyes. Oriental Scops Owl [40] is more heavily streaked below, has longer ear-tufts, more rounded wings and has a frequent rufous morph. All are best distinguished by vocal patterns.

VOCALISATIONS The song of the male consists of single, monosyllabic flute-like notes with downward inflection: *kyoot*, lasting 0.2-0.3 seconds. These notes are repeated at intervals of about 2-3 seconds in long sequences. The unpaired female utters a similar but longer drawn-out song; when in contact with a male, she emits higher-pitched and slightly hoarse notes. During courtship male and female duet, so that the listener may get the impression of a two-syllable song of higher- and lower-pitched notes. Soft *phew* notes serve as contact-calls. In alarm, both sexes utter a loud, piercing *kweeoh*, similar to a call of Little Owl [176]. During copulation a high twittering is uttered. Larger nestlings and fledged young beg with faint single *chew* notes. In their first autumn, young males utter a song similar to that of adults, but somewhat hoarse in quality.

DISTRIBUTION S Europe (especially Mediterranean region), locally in C, E and W Europe, and Africa north of the Sahara from Morocco to Tunisia, Asia Minor and eastwards to C Asia.

MOVEMENTS In general migratory, but locally with resident populations (e.g. on Mallorca). European birds normally winter in the savannas of W and E Africa, north of the rainforest. In autumn the owls leave their breeding areas between August and November, returning between late March and late April (depending on breeding area).

HABITAT Semi-open or rather open country with scattered trees or small woods, cultivated areas with groups of trees, rocky landscapes, parks, avenues of trees along roads, gardens with mature trees, Mediterranean scrub and garrigue; in warm climates also in mountainous regions. Does not occur in dense forest. Winters chiefly in savannas with trees.

DESCRIPTION *O. s. scops* Adult Facial disc greyish-brown, finely mottled; rim around disc not very prominent. Erectile ear-tufts difficult to see or virtually invisible when plumage held loose (head then appears rounded and 'earless'). Above, greyish-brown with blackish streaks, pattern resembling the bark of old tree. Crown similar, with blackish shaft-streaks. Scapulars white on outer webs,

with blackish central streak and black tip. Flight feathers barred dark and light, as is the short tail. Underparts greyish-brown, somewhat lighter than back, with blackish shaft-streaks, and some thin cross-bars and dark vermiculations; several shaft-streaks much broader than others and with heavier horizontal vermiculations. Tarsi feathered to base of toes. (Reddish morph very rare.) **Juvenile** Downy chick whitish. Mesoptile and juvenile plumage similar to adult, but texture of plumage more 'woolly', with more prominent vermiculations on breast, crown and upper back. **Bare parts** Eyes yellow. Bill grey. Toes grey. Claws greyish-brown with darker tips.

MEASUREMENTS AND WEIGHT Total length 16-21cm. Wing 143-168mm; tail 67-75mm. Weight 60-135g, females heavier than males.

GEOGRAPHICAL VARIATION We distinguish five subspecies, *cycladum* being included within nominate race.
> *O. s. scops* (Linnaeus, 1758). W, S and SE Europe, North Africa, locally in E and C Europe. See Description.
> *O. s. mallorcae* von Jordans, 1924. Balearic Islands, where normally resident. Similar to nominate, but in general paler.
> *O. s. cyprius* (Madarász, 1901). Cyprus and Asia Minor. Similar to nominate race but darker, with distinct white spots, and slightly larger. Wing 150-167mm.
> *O. s. turanicus* (Loudon, 1905). Turkmenistan to W Pakistan. Paler and more silvery-grey than nominate race. Wing 149-165mm.
> *O. s. pulchellus* (Pallas, 1801). Caucasus to the Yenisei; winters south to Sind and adjacent parts of India. Greyer than nominate race. Wing 145-167mm.

HABITS A strictly nocturnal bird, most active from after sunset to midnight. Normally not very shy. By day it roosts in trees (mostly close to the trunk or in dense foliage), cavities in old trees or rocks, holes in walls, etc; with its cryptic plumage pattern, and with eyes closed to a narrow slit, it is rather indistinguishable from the surrounding bark or rock. Evening activity normally begins with a brief

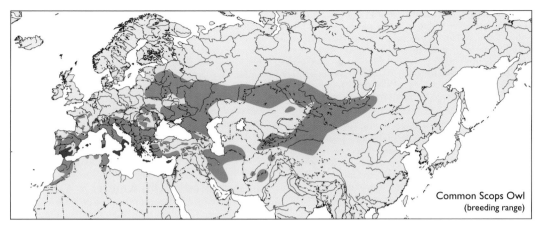

Common Scops Owl
(breeding range)

verse of song, either at the roosting place or from a perch nearby; occasionally some notes may be heard from the roost during daytime. At the start of the breeding season vocal activity is very frequent, and males may be heard singing nearly all night, with a peak before midnight and between 02:00 hours and dawn; duetting of male and female is usually heard before copulation. After pair formation song activity decreases, and notes of song are heard only occasionally, while unpaired males sing intensively virtually all night; some birds may be heard singing in autumn. This owl is territorial and males, especially in spring, may be provoked to sing by playback (or imitation) of their song; in such situations, males and sometimes pairs may be attracted very close to the imitator.

FOOD Mostly insects, such as grasshoppers, beetles, moths and cicadas; spiders and earthworms are also taken, as well as small vertebrates such as small mammals, small birds, reptiles (geckos) and frogs. Often approaches lamps in order to catch insects settled on them or on nearby walls, and then captures in particular moths and even craneflies by swooping on them. Larger prey are normally caught by swooping on them from a perch. Small prey are taken with the bill; larger animals (e.g. mice, larger locusts or beetles) are seized with the talons, and held between the toes of one raised foot for consumption (in the same manner as parrots, eating 'from the hand').

BREEDING On its return from winter quarters, the male begins to sing on calm nights; residents (e.g. on Balearic Islands and locally in S Spain) start singing in February. The female answers, and the birds start duetting; copulations are frequent after such duets. The male then flies to a potential cavity, enters and sings from the opening; once the female has accepted the cavity, having inspected it, the pair may be watched every evening near the nesting site. Natural cavities in trees, rocks or walls, woodpecker holes in tree trunks or thick branches, or holes in steep banks of ditches or sand-pits, even under roofs, are used; also accepts nestboxes.

Laying begins in late April or in May to first half of June, occasionally in July. The female lays usually 3-4 (sometimes only 2 or even up to 6) white, rather spherical eggs directly on to the bottom of the cavity, at 2-day intervals: mean egg size 31 x 27mm. Incubation begins with the second egg and is by the female alone, fed by the male, who brings food to the nest. The eggs hatch after 20-31 days (in general after about 25 days), according to

climatic conditions. The female broods and feeds the young up to about 18 days, and a few days later leaves the nest to help her mate bring in food. The chicks' eyes begin to open at 6-8 days, and are are fully open at 11-13 days. About 6-9 days after hatching, the young regurgitate pellets. At an age of 3-4 weeks they leave the nest, landing on the ground and climbing up into trees or bushes by using their bill and claws, and fluttering with their wings. When about 33 days old they are fully capable of flight. They are cared for and fed by both parents for 4-5 weeks, thereafter becoming independent. Sexual maturity is reached at an age of about 10 months.

Normally one brood per year.

STATUS AND CONSERVATION In C Europe this owl is rare, whereas in the Mediterranean it may be quite abundant locally (e.g. on Mallorca). In S France local populations have decreased during recent years, probably owing to modern agricultural methods and the use of pesticides, coincident with loss of adequate habitats. Increasing populations of potential predators (e.g. Tawny Owl [130]) may also lead to decreases in numbers of Common Scops Owls (e.g. in the Camargue). In some cases, nestboxes may help boost the breeding population.

REMARKS We separate this owl specifically from its African (south of Sahara) and E Asian relatives because of ecological and bioacoustical patterns, further reinforced by DNA evidence.

REFERENCES Bezzel (1985), Dunning (1993), Eck & Busse (1973), Kalby *et al.* (1983), König (1970), Koenig (1973).

38   PALLID SCOPS OWL
Otus brucei   Plate 11

Other names: Striated Scops Owl, Bruce's Scops Owl

French: Petit-duc de Bruce
German: Streifen-Zwergohreule

IDENTIFICATION Size much as Common Scops Owl [37], and very similar to that species in appearance, but distinctly streaked on back and wing-coverts, and with plumage less 'bark-like' in pattern, lacking rufous patches and more uniformly coloured. Base of toes slightly feathered; eyes yellow. **Similar species** Common Scops Owl is generally darker, with a bark-like pattern on back and wing-coverts, and totally bare toes; best distinguished from Pallid Scops by its different, much higher-pitched song. Oriental Scops Owl [40] is about equal in size, but is less streaked on back and wing-coverts, and occurs in a rather frequent red morph (lacking in Pallid Scops). Indian Scops Owl [54] and Collared Scops Owl [53] are much darker, less streaked, and have dark, orange or reddish-brown eyes.

VOCALISATIONS The male's song consists of well-spaced hollow, dove-like notes (similar to those of Stock Pigeon *Columba oenas*) uttered in long sequences: *whookh-whookh-whookh-whookh-*.... Intervals between the single notes vary between 0.6 and nearly 1 second; the single notes are longer than in Common Scops Owl and often end with a slightly rising bleating sound, *whookhwww*. Single, generally lower hoots are uttered by both sexes as contact between mates. A single barking call and rattling sounds are given in alarm. (The song of the taxon on Socotra Island off Somalia, said to be a race of Pallid Scops Owl, is unknown; if it consists of purring notes, this owl may be a race of African Scops Owl [39].)

DISTRIBUTION From the Middle East (SC Turkey, N Syria, Iraq, Iran, E Arabia) to W and C Asia, south to Afghanistan, Pakistan and NW India; has bred Israel. The form on Socotra Island, off the coast of Somalia, is considered by various authors a subspecies of Pallid, African or Oriental Scops Owls; we believe that it may belong with one of the first two, if it is not an endemic species.

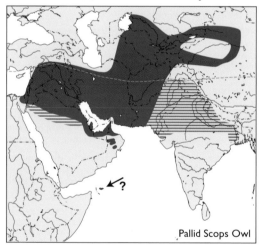

Pallid Scops Owl

MOVEMENTS Present all year in SE Arabia and in Iran (and on Socotra). Other populations are mostly migratory, wintering in Levant, NE Egypt and Arabia and in India south to Bombay.

HABITAT Semi-open country with trees and bushes, riverine habitats, deserts with rocky hills, human settlements with gardens and trees. In Jerusalem, has been observed near ancient walls of the historic part of the city. In Pakistan, found in arid hills up to about 1,500m, where it inhabits rocky gorges with few trees.

DESCRIPTION *O. b. brucei* **Adult** Facial disc much paler than on Common Scops Owl, with faint dark rim. Small erectile ear-tufts, rather invisible when plumage of head held loose. Crown with fine blackish shaft-streaks. Upper-

parts typically paler than on Common Scops, often more yellowish-ochre, with thin though fairly obvious blackish shaft-streaks; back without bark-like colour pattern; scapulars with indistinct row of whitish feathers, edged blackish at rear end. Flight and tail feathers barred darker and lighter. Underparts pale greyish or pale ochre-yellow with dark shaft-streaks, latter quite faint in light morphs. Tarsi feathered, the feathering extending slightly on to basal portion of toes. **Juvenile** Downy chicks white. Mesoptile similar to adult, but with a more 'woolly' texture, and almost without ear-tufts; crown, nape, upper back and underparts finely barred dark. **Bare parts** Eyes light yellow; yellowish-grey in juvenile. Bill dark greyish-horn. Toes greyish-brown. Claws blackish-brown.

MEASUREMENTS AND WEIGHT Females mostly somewhat larger and heavier than males. Total length 18-21cm. Wing 147-170mm (Socotran population only 125-135mm); tail 66-84mm. Weight 100-110g.

GEOGRAPHICAL VARIATION Four subspecies, although one of these may possibly belong to African Scops Owl.
O. b. brucei (Hume, 1873). C Asia east of Aral Sea, Fergana basin, and N Tadzhikistan and Kirgiziya. See Description.
O. b. obsoletus (Cabanis, 1875) SC Turkey, N Syria and N Iraq east to N Afghanistan and lowlands of Uzbekistan. Very similar to nominate race and probably better included within it.
O. b. exiguus Mukherjee, 1958. C Iraq, E Arabia and S Iran to S Afghanistan and W Pakistan. General coloration pale sandy. Wing 150-163mm.
O. (b.?) socotranus (Grant & Forbes, 1899). Socotra Island. Very pale, and heavily speckled above. Smallest race. Wing 125-135mm. (Its isolated distribution and very small size suggest that this taxon may be specifically distinct from *O. brucei*, perhaps representing an endemic species or a race of *O. senegalensis*.)

HABITS This owl is not strictly nocturnal, but resembles Little Owl [175] in being partly diurnal. May be seen hunting in early morning or late afternoon, though most activity is at night. Holes in walls or river banks, hollow trees or dense foliage serve as daytime haunts.

FOOD Insects (beetles, grasshoppers, moths, etc) and spiders are the preferred food, but also preys on small mammals (mice, shrews), lizards and small birds. Hunts mostly from a perch, swooping down to catch its prey on the ground or from a branch. Sometimes captures prey (e.g. flying insects, bats) on the wing.

BREEDING Returns to its breeding areas earlier than Common Scops Owl and begins breeding somewhat earlier (this is evident in places where the two species live side by side). In early spring, the male sings at dusk near potential nesting sites. No nest is built, the eggs being laid directly on the floor of a cavity, mostly a woodpecker hole in a tree trunk or branch, or a hole in a wall, river bank or between rocks, sometimes in an old nest of Black-billed Magpie *Pica pica*. Reproductive biology similar to that of Common Scops. The 4-6 white eggs (about 29 x 26mm to 31.7 x 28.1mm) are incubated by the female, which is fed by the male.

STATUS AND CONSERVATION Locally rather frequent, but the use of pesticides may be regarded as a potential danger in some areas.

REMARKS *Otus brucei* has often been considered a race of *O. scops*, but it is doubtless a separate species, living sympatrically with latter in some regions without interbreeding; studies of vocal patterns and DNA evidence have proved the specific status of Pallid Scops Owl. The owls on Socotra Island require research into their bioacoustics and DNA to determine whether they are a race of *O. brucei* (which we doubt) or of *O. senegalensis*, or represent another, perhaps endemic species.

REFERENCES Boyer & Hume (1991), Cramp (1985), Dementiev & Gladkov (1951), Etchécopar & Hüe (1964), Fry *et al.* (1988), Gallagher & Roger (1980), Meinertzhagen (1948).

---

39   AFRICAN SCOPS OWL
Otus senegalensis   Plate 11

French: Petit-duc africain
German: Afrika-Zwergohreule
Spanish: Autillo africano

IDENTIFICATION Very small, similar in size and coloration to Common Scops Owl [37], but with dark markings much heavier and more obvious and plumage pattern less bark-like. Feathers of back and scapulars often edged rusty. Ear-tufts small and blade-shaped when erected. Song different from that of Common Scops. **Similar species** Common Scops Owl winters in Africa north of the tropical rainforest, where it may occur alongside resident African Scops; the two are best separated by voice, but in general the plumage of African Scops has much heavier dark markings, the feathers of back and scapulars often edged reddish-brown (rusty), and different wing-formula. Northern White-faced and Southern White-faced Scops Owls [88, 89] are much larger, with a white face, a broad blackish rim around facial disc, long ear-tufts, and yellowish-orange to red eyes; both may occur in the same habitat as African Scops. São Tomé Scops Owl [29] is more uniform in coloration, with nearly invisible ear-tufts, and lower half of tarsi unfeathered; it is confined to the São

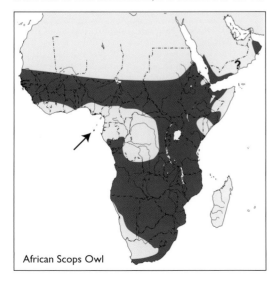

African Scops Owl

Tomé Archipelago. Pallid Scops Owl [38], rather pale, with fine dark streaks and almost unbarred, and a totally different song, does not occur in Africa, but a taxon on Socotra is recognised by some authors as a race of Pallid Scops.

VOCALISATIONS The song of the male is a short purring trill, about 0.4-1 seconds in duration, delivered in long sequences at intervals of 5-8 seconds: *kjurrrr*. (The flute-like notes of Common Scops are uttered at intervals of 2-3 seconds.) The female has a similar but slightly higher-pitched song, given during courtship when duetting with the male. In alarm, both sexes utter a shrill cry. Soft growling notes, hissing sounds, short soft trills, and bill-clicking are also given.

DISTRIBUTION Africa south of the Sahara, including Pagalu (Annobon) Island off the coast of Gabon; absent from forested regions of Mali, Equatorial Guinea, Gabon and Congo, and from the southwest deserts of Namibia. We include the form inhabiting S and SW Arabia as a race of this species.

MOVEMENTS Resident.

HABITAT Savanna with scattered trees and thorny shrubs, semi-open woodland, park-like areas (e.g. mopane woodland in S Africa), gardens with some mature trees, and forest clearings. Generally below 2,000m.

DESCRIPTION *O. s. senegalensis* **Adult** Grey and brown morphs exist; all colour patterns may vary individually. Facial disc with fine vermiculations and dark rim. Crown and forehead with relatively broad shaft-streaks. Ear-tufts small, but well developed. Upperparts grey or brownish with darker streaks and fine vermiculations; feathers of mantle and upperwing-coverts often edged rufous; scapulars with whitish areas forming white band across shoulder. Flight and tail feathers barred dark and light, outer webs of primaries with large white spots. Tip of wing more rounded than on Common Scops Owl: P9 with no emargination and much shorter than P8, and PP8, 7 and 6 of equal length (on Common Scops, P9 and P8 equal, with P7 shorter and P6 much shorter than P8, and outer web of P9 emarginated in outer half). Underparts similar in colour to upperparts but often somewhat lighter, with dark streaks and fine vermiculations. Tarsi feathered to base of toes. **Juvenile** Downy young whitish. Immatures (mesoptile) similar to adult, but less distinctly marked and with a more 'woolly' texture to plumage. **Bare parts** Eyes yellow. Bill blackish-horn. Toes dusky greyish-brown. Claws blackish-brown.

MEASUREMENTS AND WEIGHT Total length 16-19cm. Wing 117-138mm; tail 50-70mm. Weight 46-62g; 1 female *pamelae* 71g.

GEOGRAPHICAL VARIATION Four subspecies.

O. s. senegalensis (Swainson, 1837). Sub-Saharan Africa, except western forest belt, central rainforest (Congo Basin), W Namibia and western S Africa). See Description. (We include *latipennis*, *ugandae* and *caecus* as colour morphs of nominate.)

O. s. nivosus Keith & Twomey, 1968. SE Kenya from lower Tana river to Lali Hills. A very pale subspecies, pale grey above and below; belly and undertail-coverts whitish. Wing 117-119mm; tail 54mm.

O. s. feae (Salvadori, 1903). Pagalu (Annobon) Island. Darker and more broadly streaked. Wing 120-125mm.

O. s. pamelae Bates, 1937. SW and SE Arabia. A rather

pale subspecies. Wing 134-148mm. (This form has been considered by some authors a race of Pallid Scops Owl or Oriental Scops Owl [40]; we recognise it as a subspecies of African Scops Owl, which has a more or less identical song.)

HABITS A nocturnal bird. During daytime it roosts in dense foliage, against a branch or tree trunk, or in a hole; when approached, it becomes very slim by adopting an upright position, erecting the ear-tufts and closing the eyes to a thin slit, thus well camouflaged; if approached too closely, it flies to another roost. Pair-members sometimes roost together. In general more social than Common Scops Owl, pairs nesting relatively close to one another (even in a loose colony). At dusk, just before or after leaving the day roost, the male begins to sing; during the courtship period, song may be heard almost throughout the night. Often several males may be heard from one place. Can be stimulated to sing, or even attracted close, by playback or imitation of its song.

FOOD Mostly insects, such as grasshoppers, beetles, moths, crickets, etc, but occasionally takes spiders, scorpions and small vertebrates (e.g. rodents, frogs, geckos, small passerine birds). Generally hunts from a perch, swooping to the ground to seize prey, but many insects are hawked in flight.

BREEDING Monogamous. Normally nests solitarily; locally, several pairs may nest quite close to one another, but each claiming its own territory, which may be relatively small. During courtship male and female may be heard duetting. Male advertises potential nesting sites to female by singing from entrance of a tree hole, often one made by a woodpecker; if the female accepts the site, she roosts in it during daytime. The 2-3 white eggs are laid directly on to the floor of the nest hole. The female incubates alone and is fed by the male, which normally roosts near the nest, singing briefly after sunset before leaving its daytime roost; the female quite often answers from the hole. Incubation, usually lasting 24 days, starts with the second egg. The chicks' eyes open 3 days after hatching. They are fed by the female, with food brought by the male, until they are 18 days old, after which both parents feed them. At about 3-4 weeks the young leave the nest; they soon begin to catch prey, but are fed by both parents until they are 60 days old. Moult of the mesoptile feathers takes place at an age of 40-80 days. Sexual maturity is reached at 8 months.

STATUS AND CONSERVATION Rather common throughout its range in Africa. As it lives primarily on insects, it may be threatened locally by the use of pesticides.

REMARKS Since the African Scops Owl varies individually in plumage pattern, we treat only four subspecies as valid taxa, including Arabian *pamelae* in this species because of its vocal patterns.

REFERENCES Boyer & Hume (1991), Cramp (1985), Dunning (1993), Fry *et al.* (1988), Gallagher & Roger (1980), Voous (1988), Zimmerman *et al.* (1996).

40   ORIENTAL SCOPS OWL
Otus sunia   Plate 12

French: Petit-duc oriental
German: Orient-Zwergohreule

IDENTIFICATION Similar to Common Scops Owl [37] in size (16-19cm), but underparts more boldly streaked, plumage coloration with less bark-like pattern, and ear-tufts somewhat larger. In the hand, Oriental Scops has more rounded wings, usually showing four or five primaries beyond the longest tertial (Common Scops shows six or seven). A red morph is common. Eyes yellow. **Similar species** Common Scops Owl has a bark-like pattern to its plumage and smaller ear-tufts, but best separated by voice. Collared Scops Owl [53], Indian Scops Owl [54], Japanese Scops Owl [55] and Sunda Scops Owl [52] have a well-developed collar around hindneck and orange or brown eyes, Indian Scops also being darker with dark brown eyes. Mountain Scops Owl [23] is unstreaked below (except on Taiwan) and finely vermiculated. Elegant Scops Owl [41] is larger and longer-winged, and less boldly streaked. All are best distinguished by vocal patterns, which are specifically distinct.

VOCALISATIONS The song consists of a sequence of trisyllabic phrases of resonant, throaty notes, similar in pitch to those of Common Scops Owl, but whistles less clear, more rasping, and with different rhythm: *kroik ku kjooh, kroik ku kjooh,...*, audible over distance of several hundred metres. The regularity of this evenly spaced rhythm during long sequences is diagnostic of this owl. In S China, the second and third notes are more drawn together, giving the song a slightly different rhythm: it is not known whether this is due to individual or to geographical variation, but in every case each phrase consists of three notes as with typical birds, *króik-kukjóohk*. Recordings from Thailand sound different in rhythm and involve a four-note phrase, *kroik-kuk-kújooh*: this difference, very obvious in sonagrams, suggests that the Thailand population may perhaps be specifically distinct from others. Similar are the songs of Sri Lankan birds, which are distinctly smaller than all other subspecies. Young birds utter a high trill when begging for food.

DISTRIBUTION N Pakistan (Punjab), India and Nepal east to Bangladesh and Assam, Sri Lanka, E Asia from Japan (Hokkaido and Kyushu), E Siberia, Manchuria, Taiwan and E China to Malay Peninsula (Malacca); also resident in Andaman and Nicobar Islands, where perhaps also winter visitor. Vagrant to Hong Kong and the Aleutian Islands.

MOVEMENTS Southern populations are resident. Birds from E Siberia and Japan migrate to winter in India and China.

HABITAT Open and semi-open woodland, parks, savannas with scattered trees, wooded riverside belts. Hunts mostly near forest edges or in open country; in Sri Lanka, also near street lights in urban areas. In areas where Oriental and Common Scops Owls overlap in range, Oriental prefers riversides with trees, with Common found in wooded areas higher up.

DESCRIPTION *O. s. sunia* **Adult** Grey-brown, reddish-grey and rufous morphs exist. *Rufous morph*: Facial disc light rufous, whitish around bill and with white eyebrows; narrow dark rim. Upperparts rather plain rufous, with dark streaking on forehead and crown; scapulars have whitish-buffy spots with blackish edges. Wings and tail banded dark and light, as in most scops owls. Underparts somewhat lighter than back, becoming buffy-whitish towards belly; feathers of neck and breast have dark shaft-streaks with fine horizontal vermiculations, suggesting faint herringbone pattern. Tarsi feathered to base of toes. *Other morphs:* Much more spotted and streaked above; pattern of underparts similar to rufous morph, but with greyish-brown or reddish-grey ground colour. **Juvenile** Downy chicks whitish. Mesoptile similar to adult plumage, but markings less prominent and feathers of a more 'woolly' texture, with much faint barring on underparts and on back. **Bare parts** Eyes yellow. Bill blackish-grey. Toes greyish-brown. Claws blackish-brown.

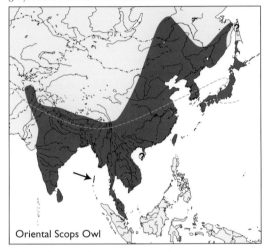

Oriental Scops Owl

MEASUREMENTS AND WEIGHT Total length 16-20cm. Wing 119-158mm; tail 49-75mm. Weight 75-95g.

GEOGRAPHICAL VARIATION Eight subspecies recognised. Some taxa may be specifically distinct from *O. sunia*.

O. s. sunia (Hodgson, 1836). Pakistan (Punjab) and Nepal to Bhutan, Bangladesh ans Assam. See Description. Wing 135-154mm; tail 60-70mm.

O. s. stictonotus (Sharpe, 1875). Manchuria, Amur and Ussuriland south to N China and Korea; winters in SE China and Taiwan. Largest and palest subspecies. Wing 138-158mm; tail 68-72mm.

O. s. japonicus Temminck & Schlegel, 1850. Japan. Rufous morph very frequent. Grey morph similar to *stictonotus*. Wing 143-153mm; tail 65-75mm.

O. s. modestus (Walden, 1874). Andaman Islands. Differs from other races in wing shape (P1=P6, or P6/7 or P7/8). Wing 137-143mm; tail 62mm.

O. s. nicobaricus (Hume, 1876) Nicobar Islands. A rufous subspecies differing from *rufipennis* in having dark vermiculations on upperparts.

O. (s.) malayanus (Hay, 1847). S China (from W Yunnan to Guangdong) South to Malay Peninsula. Tarsus less feathered than in nominate race. Dark brown and rufous morphs, latter with much chestnut-rufous in plumage. Wing 145-150mm; tail 61-66mm. (We include *distans* from Thailand in this taxon.)

O. (s.) rufipennis (Sharpe, 1875). Peninsular India from Bombay and Madras southward. Dark subspecies, similar in plumage to *malayanus*. Wing 122-135mm; tail 52-68mm.

O. (s.) leggei Ticehurst, 1878. Sri Lanka. Smallest and darkest subspecies. A cinnamon-bay morph exists. Wing 119-127mm; tail 49-54mm.

HABITS A nocturnal bird, activity beginning at dusk. During daytime roosts in dense foliage, against a tree trunk or in holes; if detected, stretches vertically, with plumage sleeked, ear-tufts erected and eyes almost closed, when almost invisible against surroundings. After sunset males begin to sing. Behaviour is otherwise little known.

FOOD Insects and spiders are the favourite prey; in addition, takes small vertebrates. Hunts both from a perch and in flight. Prey is often caught on the ground, where the owl swoops down on it. Insects or spiders are sometimes taken from bushes or branches, quite often in the canopy of a tree.

BREEDING Season February-May in Indian subcontinent. At the start of the breeding period the male sings near potential nesting sites, mostly holes in trees or walls, locally nestboxes. It advertises such holes to the female by entering and singing from the entrance. Male and female duet during courtship. The 3-4 white eggs are laid directly on to the floor of the nest. The female incubates alone and is fed by the male, who brings food to the nest. Breeding biology poorly known.

STATUS AND CONSERVATION This owl is probably rather common in many parts of its range, but is scarce in some (e.g. Pakistan, Sri Lanka). Numbers may be boosted locally by provision of nestboxes.

REMARKS The taxonomy of the Oriental Scops Owl is not yet clear. Perhaps 1-2 more species may be involved. The non-migratory, southern populations may possibly represent separate species. The taxa on the Andamans and Nicobars require further investigation. The different songs of Thailand and Sri Lankan birds support such a speculation. Studies on bioacoustics and molecur biology are needed. A pair of scops owls which bred on Pulo Perak (off NE Sumatra) in 1976 were photographed (but no specimens exist). They have been listed as *O. magicus*, but are probably *O. s. nicobaricus* (Rasmussen 1998).

REFERENCES Ali & Ripley (1969), Boyer & Hume (1991), Eck & Busse (1973), Grimmett *et al.* (1998), King *et al.* (1975), Rasmussen (1998), Roberts & King (1986), Voous (1988), Wells (1999).

41 ELEGANT SCOPS OWL
Otus elegans   Plate 12

Other names: Ryukyu Scops Owl

French: Petit-duc élégant
German: Schmuck-Zwergohreule

IDENTIFICATION A long-winged, medium-sized scops owl, with long ear-tufts, finely mottled and vermiculated plumage overall with reduced streaking, a grizzled facial disc with rufous around rim, and yellow eyes. Race *calayensis* is ochraceous overall with shorter wings. **Similar**

species Oriental Scops Owl [40] is smaller, with much shorter wings and ear-tufts, and generally appears less slim and more 'podgy'. Indian Scops Owl [54] has dark brown eyes and a buff nuchal collar. Japanese Scops Owl [55] is much paler, and has very long ear-tufts, a nuchal collar and deep orange-red eyes. Mountain Scops Owl [23] is much smaller, and finely barred below and spotted above. All are easily distinguished by voice. No other scops owl occurs within the limited range of race *calayensis*.

VOCALISATIONS The song of the male is a characteristic hoarse *kew-guruk*, repeated at regular intervals (15-30 times per minute depending on season and island). The notes are less guttural than in Oriental Scops, but most typical is the different rhythm. The call of the female is suspected to be different.

DISTRIBUTION Ryukyu (Nansei-shoto) and Daito Islands south of Japan, Lanyu (Lan Yü) Island off SE Taiwan), and also Batan, Calayan and perhaps other small islands north of Luzon in the Philippines.

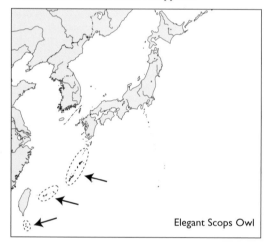

Elegant Scops Owl

MOVEMENTS Northern populations are probably partly migratory, southern ones sedentary.

HABITAT Forested areas. Originally inhabited mature forest with old trees, but has adapted locally to areas greatly altered by man. On Lanyu, this owl occurs from sea-level up to the highest elevation (548m).

DESCRIPTION *O. e. elegans* **Adult** *Buffy-greyish morph*: Facial disc pale greyish-brown with narrow dark rim. Ear-tufts relatively long, with blackish outer webs and rufous inner webs. Crown and forehead with dark streaks; eyebrows whitish. Upperparts buffy greyish-brown with dark shaft-streaks and fine vermiculations, mantle with some whitish spots; scapulars buffy-whitish with dark lower edges, forming whitish line across shoulder. Flight and tail feathers barred light and dark. Underparts somewhat lighter than upperparts, becoming nearly whitish towards abdomen; feathers with dark shaft-streaks and fine dark horizontal vermiculations, suggesting a more or less herringbone pattern. Tarsi heavily feathered almost to base of toes; feet and claws relatively large. *Rufous morph*: General coloration darker rufous-brown but pattern not obscured. **Juvenile** Downy chicks probably whitish. Mesoptile similar to adult. **Bare parts** Eyes yellow. Bill dark horn. Toes greyish-brown. Claws blackish-brown.

MEASUREMENTS AND WEIGHT Total length about 20cm. Wing 163-178mm; tail 85-101mm. Weight: 100-107g.

GEOGRAPHICAL VARIATION Three subspecies are recognised here.

O. e. elegans (Cassin, 1852). Ryukyu (Nansei-shoto) and Daito Islands. See Description. (The population on Daito is considered a distinct subspecies by some authors: *O. e. interpositus.*)

O. e. botelensis Kuroda, 1928. Lanyu Island off Taiwan. Longer-winged than nominate, with even more finely marked, less streaked, generally paler plumage. It also has a somewhat different call.

O. e. calayensis McGregor, 1904. Batan, Calayan and perhaps other small islands north of Luzon, Philippines. General coloration ochraceous (yellow- to rufous-ochre), with solid ochre facial disc partly edged black, a crisply black-streaked crown, medium-length black-streaked ear-tufts, white eyebrows nearly lacking, fine dark streaking on lower throat, upperparts warm brown finely freckled and barred darker, nearly unstreaked, scapular spots large but ochraceous and inconspicuous; abundant fine white barring and black streaking on underparts, wing and tail banding prominent dark brown and buff; wing shorter and more rounded than nominate. Wing 169mm; tail 85mm. (We consider *batanensis* to be a synonym of *calayensis*.)

HABITS Nocturnal. Habits virtually unknown, but probably similar to those of other scops owls.

FOOD Insects, such as beetles, grasshoppers, crickets, moths; also spiders and small vertebrates.

BREEDING Breeding season: April-July. Nests in holes, often those of woodpeckers, in old trees, occasionally in the axils of coconut palms. Clutch size usually 3-4 eggs (mean size 32.4 x 29.0mm). Up to five nestlings have been found at one nest on Lanyu; on same island, observed to make second breeding attempt when the first failed. Duration of incubation unknown. Young fledge after 32 days.

STATUS AND CONSERVATION Common on Nansei-shoto wherever suitable habitat remains. It is most widespread on Amami, northern Okinawa and Iriomote. Total population on Lanyu estimated by Severinghaus as about 150-230 individuals. Lack of potential nest sites is locally a severe threat, since many trees with holes are lost through deforestation; provision of nestboxes could assist in countering this problem. On Lanyu, these owls are also under pressure from hunting and should be regarded as at best vulnerable, and possibly even endangered.

REMARKS Since this owl has long been regarded as a subspecies of *Otus sunia* or even of *O. scops*, its biology is little studied. According to the latest research, however, *Otus elegans* has to be considered specifically distinct from those two taxa. On morphological grounds, *calayensis* may not be correctly placed in this species.

REFERENCES Brazil (1991), Dickinson *et al.* (1991), Eck & Busse (1973), King (1981), Marshall (1978), (Rasmussen *in litt.*), Severinghaus (1986, 1989 and *in litt.*).

42 MANTANANI SCOPS OWL
Otus mantananensis   Plate 13

French: Petit-duc de Mantanani
German: Philippinen-Zwergohreule

IDENTIFICATION A medium-sized scops owl with large feet and claws, prominent irregularly marked ear-tufts, a conspicuous dark-rimmed facial disc, a dark patch over eye, streaked throat and underparts, brown to rufescent and white barring on underparts. A rufous-brown morph is also known. Eyes yellow; bill grey. **Similar species** In C Philippines, Luzon Scops Owl [26] and Mindoro Scops Owl [27] inhabit humid forest of those respective islands, while Mindanao Scops Owl [25] lives in the mountains of Mindanao in S Philippines; all are smaller, with much smaller, less extensively feathered legs and have yellow eyes. Palawan Scops Owl [58] and Philippine Scops Owl [56] do not occur on the small islands inhabited by the present species, and are darker above with conspicuous hindcollars and long ear-tufts.

VOCALISATIONS The territorial song is a series of deep, nasal, grunting notes (somewhat goose-like), uttered at intervals of several (normally about 5-6) seconds: *kwoank, kwoank,....* Often these notes are followed by a slightly deeper and more gruff *kro-kro-kro-kro-kro*, which we believe to be probably the female singing in duet with her mate.

DISTRIBUTION Mantanani Island off N Borneo; also islands of WC Philippines (Calamian, Cuyo, Romblon etc.) and SW Philippines (Tumindao and Sibutu in Sulu Archipelago).

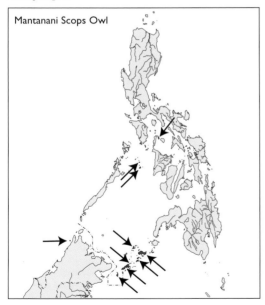

Mantanani Scops Owl

MOVEMENTS Resident.

HABITAT Forest and wooded areas, also coconut groves and casuarina. Hunts along forest edges and in clearings.

DESCRIPTION *O. m. mantananensis* **Adult** Rufous-brown and grey-brown morphs occur. Facial disc rather distinctly rimmed dark. Upperparts greyish-brown (greyish-brown morph) or reddish-brown (rufous-brown morph) with black pattern of mottling and freckles; scapulars with whitish outer webs, forming row across shoulder. Flight and tail feathers barred light and dark. Underparts lighter in colour than upperparts, peppered black, with belly paler than breast. Tarsi heavily feathered but with a narrow zone bare at base of toes. **Juvenile** Unknown. **Bare parts** Eyes yellow. Bill greyish-horn. Toes and bare part of tarsi pale greyish-brown. Claws dark horn.

MEASUREMENTS AND WEIGHT Total length 18cm. Wing 136-175mm. Tail 74-76mm. Weight about 106g.

GEOGRAPHICAL VARIATION Four subspecies recognised. Populations differ in the amount of rufous, which decreases from north to south.

    O. m. mantananensis (Sharpe, 1892). Mantanani (off Borneo) and Rasa and Ursula (both off S Palawan). See Description.

    O. m. romblonis McGregor, 1905. Banton, Romblon, Tablas, Sibuyan, Tres Reyes, Semirara (WC Philippines). Pale rufous overall, with a rufous eye-patch and pale grey border, finely black-striped upperparts, very heavily streaked underparts with prominent rufous-and-white barring, tertials and uppertail surface nearly unbanded, rufescent white tarsal feathering. Wing 158mm.

    O. m. cuyensis McGregor, 1904. Cuyo Is., and Dicabaito and Linapacan (Calamian Islands) in WC Philippines. Brown overall heavily marked with black, especially edges of facial disc, streaks overall, heavy dark-feathered tarsi, prominent brown, cinnamon and white barring below, and dark brown eye-patch. Wing 175mm.

    O. m. sibutuensis (Sharpe, 1893). Sibutu and Tumindao in Sulu Archipelago. Dull brown overall with indistinct, irregular, vague markings, buffy, heavily marked scapular spots, dark tarsal feathering. Wing 136mm. (We regard *steerei* as a synonym.)

HABITS A nocturnal bird which hides during daytime in dense foliage, in coconut groves, or against trunks of trees, as well as in holes. Behaviour unknown.

FOOD Mostly insects and other arthropods, probably also small vertebrates.

BREEDING A female collected in May contained an egg ready to be laid. Nests in holes of old trees, perhaps also in other cavities. Nothing else known.

STATUS AND CONSERVATION Locally common, perhaps threatened by forest destruction.

REMARKS This little-known species is in need of studies on its ecology, behaviour and reproduction, as well as on its taxonomy and vocalisations.

REFERENCES Dickinson *et al.* (1991), Dunning (1993), Eck & Busse (1973), Marshall (1978), MacKinnon & Phillipps (1993), P. Rasmussen (*in litt.*).

43 MOLUCCAN SCOPS OWL
Otus magicus   **Plate 13**

French: Petit-duc des Molukkes
German: Molukken-Zwergohreule

IDENTIFICATION A small to medium-sized scops owl (20-23cm) with bold dark mottling above and blackish shaft-streaks with some horizontal vermiculations below. Belly lighter than breast. Ear-tufts moderate-sized, long in race *albiventris*; dark rim around brownish facial disc not very prominent. Buffy, reddish and brown morphs are known. Eyes yellow; tarsal feathering very variable. **Similar species** Sulawesi Scops Owl [46] is smaller than the Moluccan races and less stocky, with weaker bill and feet, and different voice. Sangihe Scops Owl [47] is also smaller, with shorter ear-tufts and a different voice. Simeulue Scops Owl [49] and Enggano Scops Owl [50] from those two respective islands off Sumatra also have yellow eyes but are much darker, nearly all rufous, and their vocalisations are different. Seychelles Scops Owl [45] has indistinct ear-tufts and has lower parts of tarsi bare. Mantanani Scops Owl [42] has a more distinctly rimmed facial disc and it also differs vocally.

VOCALISATIONS The territorial song is a deep, rough croak, uttered at intervals of several seconds. The single note may be described as *kwoark*, somewhat resembling the sound of a single cut produced by sawing a hollow trunk with a large-toothed saw. When the bird is excited, intervals between notes may be shorter. Pairs duet during courtship, the song of the female being very similar but slightly higher in pitch. Both sexes utter single calls, deep and croaking in the male (similar to song) and somewhat higher but also rough and rasping in the female, *kwoirkh*.

DISTRIBUTION Lesser Sundas (Lombok, Sumbawa, Flores, Lomblen, Wetar), Moluccas (Morotai, Halmahera, Ternate, Bacan, Obi, Buru, Ambon, Seram) and possibly the Aru Islands.

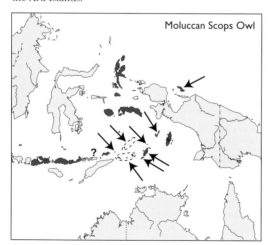

Moluccan Scops Owl

MOVEMENTS Resident.

HABITAT Lowlands and near coast. Forest, secondary growth, swamp forest (mangroves), coastal coralline-limestone forest, heavily wooded limestone cliffs, fruit trees or large trees in villages, *Cocos* palm plantations near

habitations, and farming areas interspersed with large trees. Foothills to 1,500m on Flores; also common to 900m on Buru.

DESCRIPTION *O. m. magicus* **Adult** Very variable in ground colour; more or less brown, yellowish-brown (buffy), reddish-brown (fulvous), greyish-brown and sepia-brown morphs are known, and barring may vary from weak (rather indistinct) to very pronounced. (Compared with Sulawesi Scops Owl, Moluccan Scops is larger, with plumage usually not finely patterned, but any pattern is coarse or somewhat indistinct, and inner webs of primaries are clearly barred.) Facial disc tinged rufous, not very prominently rimmed dark; loral feathers whitish. Ear-tufts short, but well visible. Upperparts with bold dark mottling, but variable; outer webs of scapulars with some larger areas of buffy-whitish, forming indistinct row across shoulder (sometimes difficult to see). Flight feathers barred light and dark. Tail indistinctly barred, with dense vermiculations. Underparts with blackish shaft-streaks and some horizontal vermiculations; belly paler than breast. Bill and feet strong. Tarsi unfeathered distally to 6-9 mm before toe joint. **Juvenile** Like adult, but spots and freckles more faint or indistinct and feathers more fluffy; also, feathers of head, crown and neck have narrow dark brown cross-bars. **Bare parts** Iris yellow. Bill and cere pale yellowish-grey. Toes greyish-brown. Claws dark horn.

MEASUREMENTS AND WEIGHT Total length 20-23cm. Wing 150-197mm; tail 70-101mm. Weight 114-165g.

GEOGRAPHICAL VARIATION Eight subspecies recognised, although one of these is sometimes treated as full species. There is considerable variation in size, with the Moluccan forms being much larger than the Lesser Sundas forms; the only character that seems to unite them all is the heavily banded tertials and tail in adults.

O. m. magicus (S. Müller, 1841). S Moluccas: Seram, Ambon. See Description. Wing 172-186 mm (Seram), 178-197mm (Ambon).

O. m. bouruensis (Sharpe, 1875). S Moluccas: Buru. Tarsi more heavily feathered and for more of tarsus; pattern much less spotted and more striped, especially below, usually pale grey, sometimes warm brown, never ochraceous. Wing 172-192mm; tail 101mm.

O. m. morotensis (Sharpe, 1875). N Moluccas: Morotai, Ternate. Very like *leucospilus* but much darker overall than most individuals of that race. Wing 168-188mm; tail 96mm.

O. m. leucospilus (G. R. Gray, 1860). N Moluccas: Halmahera, Bacan. Much less spotted above than nominate wit a distinct pale face. Wing 163-174mm (Halmahera), 170-175mm (Bacan).

O. m. obira Jany, 1955. N Moluccas: Obi. Wing 168-172mm (Obi).

O. m. tempestatis (Hartert, 1904). Lesser Sundas: Wetar, Kep Barat Daya. Small, with weak feet and claws. Polymorphic, with grey and orange-rufous morphs, the former finely patterned overall (pale spots and dark streaks above), the latter very different-looking, with bold orange bars below; always has strong streaks at least on crown, streaks elsewhere may be reduced in rufous morph; tarsi entirely covered with short feathers; ear-tufts short and rounded. Vocalisations unknown. Wing 150-171mm; tail 70-75mm.

O. m. albiventris (Sharpe, 1875). Lesser Sundas: Lombok, Sumbawa, Flores, Lomblen. Small, with weak feet and claws. Markings below typically bolder than for grey *tempestatis*, and contrast between basically brown breast and largely white belly; ear-tufts exceptionally long, dark-spotted and with some rufous, tarsus entirely feathered. No true rufous morph; some variability in warmth of coloration. Wing 159-161mm; tail 76-84mm.

O. (*m.*) *sulaensis* (Hartert, 1898). Sula Islands off Sulawesi. Known only from two adult specimens and a juvenile. Dark and richly coloured, with coarse markings; tarsi only about half feathered in front, and completely bare in the rear; primaries with solid dark inner webs and pale flecks only on outer webs; scapulars spots with large irregular dark patches. Vocalisations apparently very different. Wing 170mm. (Sometimes considered to be a full species, Sula Scops Owl.)

HABITS A nocturnal bird which hides away during daytime. At dusk and at night, both sexes may be heard duetting. The behaviour of this species is little studied; may approach, singing loudly, during tape playback of its songs (e.g. on Buru).

FOOD Apparently chiefly insects and other arthropods; small vertebrates may occasionally be taken.

BREEDING Nestlings found in November/December on Ambon. Probably breeds in cavities in trees. The eggs are pure white.

STATUS AND CONSERVATION Locally common in many areas, but status not known on others (e.g. Wetar); at least some forms occur in heavily degraded habitats.

REMARKS The taxonomic status of several forms of this owl is not yet clear. Some subspecies may be only morphs, while at least one may prove to be a separate species. There is still insufficient material (especially molecular-biological and bioacoustical data) available for secure conclusions, and we therefore include *sulaensis*, as a subspecies of *O. magicus* until further information is available. The different vocalisations of *sulaensis*, however, have led some to think there was an undescribed owl on the Sula Isalnds.

In the past, *O. alfredi* has been incorrectly synonymised with *O. m. albiventris*, and also *O. alius* has been attributed to *O. magicus*.

REFERENCES Boyer & Hume (1991), Clark & Smith (in prep.), Davidson *et al. (1994),* Dunning (1993), Eck & Busse (1973), Finsch (1899), Lambert & Rasmussen (1998), Marshall (1978), Rasmussen (1998, *in litt.*), Sibley (1996), White & Bruce (1986), Widodo *et al.* (1999).

---

44   BIAK SCOPS OWL
Otus beccarii   Plate 13

Other names: Beccari Scops Owl

French: Petit-duc de Beccari
German: Beccari-Zwergohreule

IDENTIFICATION A small owl (about 25cm) with moderate-length ear-tufts, lacking any trace of dark shaft-streaks above and below, but few fine streaks on forecrown. Barred overall (except on mantle) with light and dark; hindneck may have indistinct collar of blackish and light bars; occurs in rufous-brown and 'black' phases. Eyes yellow. **Similar species** Moluccan Scops Owl [43] is distinctly streaked dark below and above. Mantanani Scops Owl [42] has more distinctly rimmed facial disc, has underparts marked with shaft-streaks, and also differs vocally. Nicobar Scops Owl [48] is much drabber, with more barred crown and mantle, and well-banded tertials and tail.

VOCALISATIONS The male's song is a sequence of hoarse croaking notes, similar to that of Moluccan Scops Owl.

DISTRIBUTION Endemic to Biak Island off NW New Guinea.

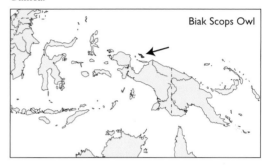
Biak Scops Owl

MOVEMENTS Resident.

HABITAT Heavy forest and wooded areas; locally near human settlements.

DESCRIPTION Adult 'Black' morph has blackish barring overall alternating with white; rufous-brown morph predominatly cinnamon-rufous with white barring below, cinnamon-brown above and finely vermiculated. Facial disc pale brownish, indistinctly rimmed by a blackish edge and whitish spots. Ear-tufts moderate-length and finely barred dusky. Crown finely barred blackish, with few fine streaks on forecrown; nape barred blackish and white or pale buffy, forming indistinct collar. Upperparts brown, rather densely barred and mottled with blackish and whitish. Outer webs of scapulars mainly white, with subterminal bar first, then black, and terminating with a black fringe, forming whitish row of spots across shoulder. Flight and tail feathers barred dusky and light. Throat white, finely vermiculated blackish; rest of underparts lighter brown, densely barred blackish and pale buff; no distinct shaft-streaks. Tarsi feathered almost to base of toes, latter bare. **Juvenile** Unknown. **Bare parts** Eyes yellow. Bill dusky, streaked yellowish. Cere pale horn. Toes dusky yellow. Claws dusky.

MEASUREMENTS AND WEIGHT Total length around 25cm. Wing of a male and a female 171mm, and tail 79mm and 83mm respectively. Weight: no data.

GEOGRAPHICAL VARIATION Monotypic: *Otus beccarii* (Salvadori, 1876).

HABITS Strictly nocturnal.

FOOD Chiefly insects and spiders, but probably also small invertebrates.

BREEDING Nests in holes in trees. The pure white eggs are laid directly on the floor of the nesting hole.

STATUS AND CONSERVATION This species is only known from three specimens and a few sight records. Much of the forest on Biak has been destroyed or degraded, posing a serious threat to the long-term survival of this little-known species.

REMARKS Despite the similarity of its song to that of Moluccan Scops Owl, we consider *beccarii* a full species because of its strikingly different plumage and its allopatric and isolated distribution.

REFERENCES Marshall (1978), Mayr & Meyer de Schauensee (1939), Rand & Gilliard (1967), Rasmussen (1998), White & Bruce (1986).

45   SEYCHELLES SCOPS OWL
Otus insularis   Plate 12

French: Petit-duc scieur
German: Seychellen-Zwergohreule

IDENTIFICATION A buffy, practically 'earless' scops owl (around 20cm) with bare tarsi and relatively long toes. Crown rather densely spotted and streaked black; underparts indistinctly barred whitish and rather broadly streaked black. Eyes yellow. **Similar species** This is the only small owl in the Seychelles. Moluccan Scops Owl [43], sometimes considered conspecific with the present species because of its similar song, has well-developed ear-tufts (as do most other scops owls) and has tarsi feathered nearly to base of toes.

VOCALISATIONS The song is similar to the croaking of Moluccan Scops Owl, but more drawn out and less grunting with shorter intervals between notes (differences between the two species are best seen in sonagrams). The female has a similar, slightly higher-pitched song, often given in duet with male; such duets sound like a hand-saw operating on a thick, dry branch, *kroahk - kraa, kroahk - kraa,....*, often interspersed with guttural knocking notes such as *tok tok.*

DISTRIBUTION Probably endemic to Mahé Island in the Seychelles. Formerly occurred also on other islands of this archipelago, but now extinct on these. A few pairs may still exist on Praslin.

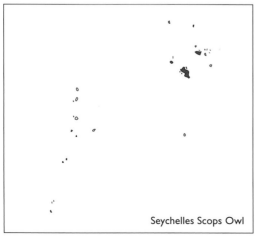

Seychelles Scops Owl

MOVEMENTS Resident.

HABITAT Upland forest and wooded areas with nearby water, between 250m and 600m; may occasionally be observed at lower altitudes. Before the arrival of man, this owl probably inhabited all wooded areas from the lowlands to the mountains, but destruction of forest caused it to retreat into the hills, where adequate habitat still exist. Its ecology is practically unknown.

DESCRIPTION Adult General coloration buff-brown. Facial disc light buffy-brown with darker mottling; rim prominent, blackish. Crown buffy-brown with black streaks, spotted white. Upperparts mottled light and dark; outer webs of scapulars whitish, edged dark, forming white band across shoulder; wing-coverts buffy-brown with dark shaft-streaks and some vermiculations. Wings and tail barred dark and light. Underparts lighter than upperparts, with relatively broad blackish streaks and faint darker as well as whitish barring. Relatively long-legged; most of tarsi and rather long toes bare. **Juvenile** Said to be similar to adult. **Bare parts** Eyes yellow. Bill greyish-yellow with darker tip. Bare tarsi and toes pale greyish-yellow to greenish-white or pinkish-grey. Claws dark horn.

MEASUREMENTS AND WEIGHT Total length around 20cm. Wing of one male 163 mm, of one female 173mm. Weight: no data.

GEOGRAPHICAL VARIATION Monotypic: *Otus insularis* (Tristram, 1880).

HABITS A totally nocturnal bird which is best located by its 'sawing' vocalisations. It may be attracted by playback of its song, to which it quite readily responds. During daytime it roosts in trees or bushes. Recent observations indicate that it exhibits extreme site-fidelity.

FOOD Apparently mainly geckos, but also tree frogs and insects.

BREEDING No nest has ever been found, but probably breeds in holes of old trees or in clefts in rocks.

STATUS AND CONSERVATION From 1909 this owl was presumed extinct, but in 1959 it was rediscovered on Mahé. Although there have been several sightings in recent years (1990s), the species is extremely rare and in danger of extinction; the total population was estimated at about 80 pairs (possibly more) in 1992-93, but it may have declined since then. The owl may survive if the remaining areas of upland forest can be protected against exploitation and encroachment by developers. Listed as Critical by BirdLife International.

REMARKS This owl has been thought by some authors to be a subspecies of Moluccan Scops Owl [43], but has been isolated from that species for a very long time. It is therefore best to treat Seychelles Scops Owl as a full species, because of its allopatric distribution and different appearance. Both species are non-migratory.

REFERENCES Boyer & Hume (1991), Burton (1992), Collar *et al.* (1994), Ertel (pers. comm. 1997), Marshall (1978), Penny (1974), Safford (1993).

46 SULAWESI SCOPS OWL
Otus manadensis   Plate 14

Other names: Celebes Scops Owl

French: Petit-duc de Manado
German: Manado-Zwergohreule

IDENTIFICATION A small (about 20cm), extremely variable scops owl with moderate-length ear-tufts, yellow eyes, prominent white eyebrows that curve around bill, dark brown cheeks surrounded by paler areas, and typically indistinctly banded uppertail and tertials; tarsi normally fully feathered; feet and claws weak. **Similar species** Moluccan Scops Owl [43] is much larger in the Moluccas; small Lesser Sundas races have more prominently banded uppertail and tertials. Sangihe Scops Owl [47] is drabber, more finely marked, with paler cheeks but darker patches between eyes and bill, and longer, narrower wings. Both species differ vocally.

VOCALISATIONS The song of the male consists of rather clear, upward-inflected notes, repeated at intervals of about 6 seconds. The single note may be described as a plaintive, somewhat syncopated *ooeehk* of about 0.4 seconds in duration and ranging between 1 and 1.5kHz. The song of the female is similar, but slightly higher in pitch, less clear and with less upward inflection. This is very different from the deep, croaking vocalisations of Moluccan Scops Owl. In addition, rapid giggling notes of increasing amplitude but with steady frequency have also been described.

DISTRIBUTION Sulawesi, Siau and Peleng (Banggai).

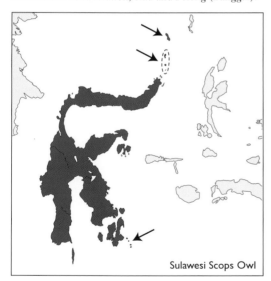

Sulawesi Scops Owl

MOVEMENTS Resident.

HABITAT Humid forest, from the lowlands up to about 2,500m (on Sulawesi).

DESCRIPTION *O. m. manadensis* **Adult** Facial disc brownish or sepia-coloured, bordered by black-tipped feathers; a usually incomplete whitish supercilium ending above eyes; whitish or pale lores and chin. Ear-tufts short (20-30mm), but prominent. Upperparts sepia and fuscous-grey, densely but irregularly freckled and mottled with dark brown or sepia-brown, feathers with dark shaft marks; interscapular feathers show pattern of bands and dark shaft-streaks and, beside shaft-streaks, paired buffy 'windows' (ocelli). Flight feathers with broad buff and dark brown bands, inner webs of primaries plain or with poorly defined light barring. Chest similar in colour to back, or more rufous; lower part of underside boldly but sparsely streaked on white background, with freckled remnants of cross-bars condensed on those feathers possessing streaks. Tarsus feathered to toes on front and back; feet and claws weak. (There is also a rufous morph, although very scarce, and a yellowish-grey morph; apparently no intergrades.) **Juvenile** Similar to adult, but feathers of, especially, crown and hindneck show pattern of fine dark brown bars. **Bare parts** Iris orange-yellow to yellow. Bill dirty yellowish-horn. Toes yellowish-grey. Claws horn.

MEASUREMENTS AND WEIGHT Total length 19-20cm. Wing 142-162mm; tail 63-86mm. Weight about 88g.

GEOGRAPHICAL VARIATION Four subspecies, one of which may be a full species.
   O. m. manadensis (Quoi & Gaimard, 1830). Sulawesi. See Description.
   O. (m.) siaoensis (Schlegel, 1873). Siau Island. Known only from one specimen (holotype). Much smaller, with very small ear-tufts; despite very short wing and tail (which are very narrowly banded), head and feet relatively large. Wing 127mm; tail 55mm. (Perhaps specifically distinct.)
   O. m. mendeni Neumann, 1939. Peleng (Banggai). Known from three adult and one juvenile specimens; two adults grey phase, very finely speckled above, finely vermiculated below with black and rufous streaks; tarsus largely bare. Wing 142-151 mm. (Status uncertain.)
   O. m. kalidupae (Hartert, 1903). Tukangbesi Islands off Sulawesi (= Kalidupa). Tarsi feathered down to toes. Distinct dark rim around facial disc. Crown with narrow dark streaking. Outer webs of scapulars with large white spots and dusky barring. Tail indistinctly barred. Eyes ochre to orange-yellow. Bill blackish at tip, base of mandible horn. Toes dirty white. Wing about 168mm.

HABITS A nocturnal bird, becoming active at dusk. Roosts by day in trees.

FOOD Probably insects and other arthropods, as well as small vertebrates.

BREEDING Probably breeds in holes in trees. Biology unknown.

STATUS AND CONSERVATION Locally relatively common (e.g. on Sulawesi), but threatened by forest destruction.

REMARKS The relationship of *Otus manadensis* with other Indonesian scops owls is not yet clear. The Siau subspecies *siaoensis* is distinctly smaller, with tiny ear-tufts; it may represent a separate species. Recently, a new species has been described from Sangihe Island (see 47): it is very similar in plumage to *O. manadensis*, but has longer and narrower wings and its song differs, but more material is desirable to clarify the position of this new taxon.

REFERENCES Boyer & Hume (1991), Coates & Bishop

(1997), Clark & Smith (in prep.), Coomans de Ruiter & Maurenbrecher (1948), Dunning (1993), Eck & Busse (1973), Finsch (1898, 1899), Holmes & Phillips (1996), Lambert & Rasmussen (1998), White & Bruce (1986).

47 SANGIHE SCOPS OWL
Otus collari Plate 14

French: Petit-duc de Sangihe
German: Sangihe-Zwergohreule

IDENTIFICATION A rather small scops owl (19-20cm) with small, moderate-sized ear-tufts and yellow eyes; overall has a drab, indistinctly marked appearance. **Similar species** Very similar in appearance and coloration to Sulawesi Scops Owl [46], but with longer, narrower wings, and a rather long tail; typically more finely patterned below, with paler auriculars and a dark patch between eye and bill; supercilia less pronounced and smaller. Song considerably different from Sulawesi Scops Owl. The Moluccan Scops Owl [43] is larger in the Moluccas, and in the Lesser Sundas, *O. m. albiventris* has longer ear-tufts, more distinct markings on the underparts and a whiter abdomen; *O. m. tempestatis* has broader streaks below, and more prominently banded tertials and tail.

VOCALISATIONS From the several existing recordings, the song is clearly and consistently different from Sulawesi Scops Owl. While the territorial song of male Sulawesi Scops consists of somewhat syncopated, breathily whistled notes with a marked upward inflection, with the single notes lasting about 0.4 seconds, the songs of Sangihe Scops Owl are more modulated, slurred, clearer, and somewhat higher (between 1.65 and 1.85kHz). The single notes are slightly longer (about 0.7 seconds), more drawn out with a clear downward inflection and rising again at the end: *peeyuuwit*, downslurred for most of its duration and ending with an upslurred, short *wit*; the intervals between the single notes may vary between 0.3 and 11 seconds.

DISTRIBUTION Endemic to Sangihe Island, N of Sulawesi.

MOVEMENTS Unknown.

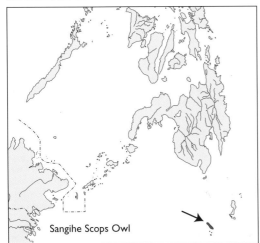

Sangihe Scops Owl

HABITAT Forest, secondary growth and agricultural land with trees, bushes or plantations, in lowlands and on mountain slopes. Recorded from sea-level to at least 315 m on the lower slopes of hills.

DESCRIPTION Adult Very similar in coloration and plumage patterns to some individuals of the polymorphic Sulawesi Scops Owl, especially to immatures. Facial disc paler than surrounding plumage, becoming darker between eye and bill; rim around disc rather pronounced, with light and dark tips of feathers; eyebrows whitish, not very obvious and ending above bill. Ear-tufts of medium length, with buff spots, black streaks and elliptical tips. Upperparts drab brownish with dark shaft-streaks, rather prominent vermiculations and prominent buffy spotting; scapulars with pale buff outer webs with triangular darker tips, forming a pale row across shoulder. Flight feathers banded dark brown and buff; tertials not prominently banded. Tail with narrow irregular buff bars and wider dark brown bands. Throat markedly lighter than surrounding plumage; underparts slightly lighter than upperparts, with fine 'sketchy' background pattern, most shaft-streaks relatively long and narrow with reduced cross-barring. Tarsi feathered to base of the toes, the latter bare; toes and talons relatively weak. **Juvenile** Unknown. **Bare parts** Eyes pale yellow with dark rim to eyelids. Cere and bill brownish-horn. Toes pale brownish-grey. Claws with base pale brown, shading towards dark tips.

MEASUREMENTS AND WEIGHT Total length about 20cm. Wing (flattened and straightened) 158-166 mm; tail 70.1-79mm. Weight (1 male specimen) 76g.

GEOGRAPHICAL VARIATION Monotypic: *Otus collari* Lambert & Rasmussen, 1998.

HABITS Unknown. Nocturnal.

FOOD Probably mainly insects.

BREEDING Unknown. Probably nests in holes in trees.

STATUS AND CONSERVATION Apparently rather common and widespread on Sangihe Island, occurring in plantations, so unlikely to be endangered.

REMARKS The narrower and longer wings of Sangihe Scops Owl, as well as vocalisations, support its recognition as a separate species; but DNA studies and comparative studies of the complete vocabularies of these two owls are needed in order to clarify the situation.

After publication of the description, a fifth (previously unreported) Sangihe specimen was located in the MNHN (Paris) collection; this specimen upholds the mensural and plumage characters based on the type series. In addition, two more individuals photographed subsequently are similar in appearance. The supposedly identical songs of this species with *O. manadensis* were not based on comparisons of tape-recorded songs, when the striking differences become evident.

REFERENCES Coomans de Ruiter & Maurenbrecher (1948), Lambert & Rasmussen (1998), Marshall (1978), Riley (1997), Wardill (in press), White & Bruce (1986).

48 NICOBAR SCOPS OWL
Otus alius   Plate 7

French: Petit-duc de Grand Nicobar
German: Nicobaren-Zwergohreule

IDENTIFICATION A typical scops owl, smaller than most forms of Moluccan Scops Owl, predominantly warm brown and finely barred above, but lacking dark shaft-streaks on back and mantle. Ear-tufts evenly and finely barred, rounded and of medium length, facial disc slightly paler than rest of plumage and with not very prominent dark rim. Outer webs of scapulars with rounded white spots forming row across shoulder. Underparts with heavy tricoloured barring, pale bars rather prominent on flanks, and dark shaft-streaks markedly reduced. Tarsi feathered, but most of distal portion and rear bare. Colour of eyes unknown, but assumed to be yellow. **Similar species** Andaman, Oriental and Moluccan Scops Owls [30, 40, 43], as well as all other SE Asian scops owls except Biak Scops [44], have dark shaft-streaks on upperparts. Simeulue Scops Owl [49] much more rufous and uniform but with dark streaks below; smaller and with dark streaks on forecrown.

VOCALISATIONS Song unknown. The only known female vocalisation, according to one observation, is a rising, long-drawn, melancholic moaning note lasting 2-2.5 seconds, *oün*, repeated after 3-5 seconds, the bird 'pouring out its steady moaning note continuously for more than 30 minutes or so'. If this were the female's song, the male's might be similar but lower in pitch.

DISTRIBUTION Apparently endemic to Great Nicobar Island in the Bay of Bengal.

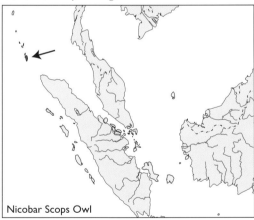

Nicobar Scops Owl

MOVEMENTS Unknown, but probably resident.

HABITAT Little known. Wooded areas near sea-level.

DESCRIPTION Adult Known only from two specimens collected on Great Nicobar. Upperparts warm brown, rather densely barred dusky; mantle to lower back with dark bars about 2mm wide and light bars about 1.7mm wide. Crown and nape similar, but with finer bars; no nuchal collar. Eyebrows paler than surrounding plumage, finely mottled dark. Ear-tufts medium-sized with rounded tips, similar in coloration to eyebrows. Facial disc slightly paler than surrounding plumage and with some darker vermiculations, indistinctly and thinly rimmed darker

brown. Outer webs of scapulars with large rounded white spots, surrounded by blackish, forming distinct row across shoulder. Flight and tail feathers barred lighter and darker brown. Throat pale cinnamon; upper breast cinnamon-brown with fuscous bars and few dark shaft-streaks; lower breast, flanks and belly with rather heavy whitish, cinnamon and dusky brown bars and markedly reduced shaft-streaks. Tarsi sparsely feathered, rear edge and lower part bare. Bare toes and claws relatively large. **Juvenile** Unknown. **Bare parts** No data for fresh or live birds. Eye colour unknown, but assumed to be yellow; narrow bare blackish orbital ring. Bill yellowish-brown with darker tip and cutting edges. Cere (dried study skins) dull yellowish-brown. Toes dark yellowish-brown. Claws dusky horn.

MEASUREMENTS AND WEIGHT Total length unknown. Holotype: wing (flattened) 161mm; tail 74.4mm; tarsus 28.6mm; ear-tufts 20.4mm. Weight unknown.

GEOGRAPHICAL VARIATION Monotypic: *Otus alius* Rasmussen, 1998.

HABITS Probably nocturnal.

FOOD One individual was said to have eaten a spider and a beetle, the other a gecko.

BREEDING Unknown.

STATUS AND CONSERVATION Unknown. This owl may perhaps occur also on Little Nicobar, on the basis of geographic proximity of this island to Great Nicobar. The species may be rare and/or endangered.

REMARKS As this taxon has been described from just two skins, its relationships with other SE Asian *Otus* species needs study, as do its biology, vocalisations and ecology. Its wing formula suggests relationship with the geographically nearest taxa *umbra* and *enganensis*.

REFERENCES Abdulali (1967, 1972, 1978), King (1997), Marshall (1978), Rasmussen (1998).

49 SIMEULUE SCOPS OWL
Otus umbra   Plate 14

Other names: Mentaur Scops Owl

French: Petit-duc de Mentaur
German: Simeulue-Zwergohreule

IDENTIFICATION A very small (16-18cm), all-rufous scops owl with some dark streaking on crown and underparts, and white barring on underparts. **Similar species** The only scops owl on Simeulue Island off NW Sumatra. Enggano Scops Owl [50], endemic to Enggano Island (more than 1,000km away off SW Sumatra), is very similar, but much larger, and with larger ear-tufts.

VOCALISATIONS The song of the male is a clear *took took tutook*, repeated at short intervals, sometimes with incomplete verses consisting of only 2-3 notes in a stuttering rhythm. The single notes may rise gradually in pitch from verse to verse or even within the same verse, this very obvious when duetting with female. The female's song in duet is similar, but higher in pitch. Often it utters only a single, whining 'mewing' note, repeated at short but often irregular intervals: *kweeuk*.

Simeulue Scops Owl

50 ENGGANO SCOPS OWL
Otus enganensis   Plate 14

French: Petit-duc d'Enggano
German: Enggano-Zwergohreule

IDENTIFICATION A small, brown scops owl (18-20.5cm) with prominent ear-tufts. Dorsal coloration varies from chestnut to olive-brown, with indistinct nuchal collar dividing nape from mantle. Eyes yellow. **Similar species** Simeulue Scops Owl [49] is very similar, but has no trace of nuchal collar, less contrasting pattern on greater wing-coverts and flight feathers, and greenish-yellow eyes. Mentawai Scops Owl [57] is a dark owl, blotched and mottled dark brown, has no nuchal collar and has yellow or brown eyes.

VOCALISATIONS The vocalisations are said to differ from those of Simeulue Scops Owl (Ben King *in litt.*).

DISTRIBUTION Endemic to Enggano Island off the southwest coast of Sumatra.

Enggano Scops Owl

MOVEMENTS Resident.

HABITAT Forest and wooded areas.

DESCRIPTION Adult Very similar to Simeulue Scops Owl, but with more contrasting fine dark or blackish vermiculations. Facial disc light rufous-brown, with circularly orientated white-shafted feathers. Forehead with a few small black-tipped white feathers; ear-tufts more prominent and longer than Simeulue Scops Owl, fulvous-brown and with some sparse whitish, dark-shafted and black-rimmed feathers. Lores and chin whitish. Upperparts dark rufous-brown to brownish-olive, darker on crown and in irregular patches on back, with indistinct nuchal collar; shoulder with row of outer-scapular feathers having white 'windows', framed in lighter rufous and rimmed by dark rufous borders. Flight feathers plain dark rufous with indistinct fine, blackish vermiculations; greater coverts and secondaries clearly paler (contrast more with primaries and their coverts than on Simeulue Scops Owl). Underparts lighter than back, varying from cinnamon to brownish-olive, more or less cross-barred and with double spots: breast somewhat more rufous, with black shaft-streaks and a few black bars and vermiculations, upper breast with a few dark-barred and dark-shafted white feathers; belly feathers broadly rimmed dark rufous, those near flanks and lower abdomen becoming darker; under-tail-coverts white with broad (3-4mm) rufous borders. Tarsi

---

DISTRIBUTION Endemic to Simeulue Island off the NW Sumatran coast.

MOVEMENTS Apparently sedentary.

HABITAT Broken forest and forest edges on steep coast, but also clove plantations.

DESCRIPTION Adult Facial disc rufous with indistinct rim. Ear-tufts short, but rather prominent. Upperparts dark rufous, with vague dark vermiculations; scapulars with buffy and whitish outer webs, edged black, forming short whitish stripe across shoulder. Flight and tail feathers barred dark brown on rufous. Underparts slightly lighter than upperparts, with some white barring and thin dark shaft streaks on underparts. Tarsi feathered nearly to base of toes. **Juvenile** Not described. **Bare parts** Eyes greenish-yellow. Bill grey. Toes grey. Claws horn with dark tips.

MEASUREMENTS AND WEIGHT Total length 16-18cm. Wing 143mm. Tail 61mm. Weight about 95g.

GEOGRAPHICAL VARIATION Monotypic: *Otus umbra* (Richmond, 1903).

HABITS A nocturnal bird which performs a syncopated duet of male and female, not only from a perch but also on the wing. General biology and behaviour otherwise practically unknown.

FOOD Apparently mainly insects and other arthropods.

BREEDING Probably nests in holes in trees. Reproduction unknown.

STATUS AND CONSERVATION Rather frequent but, as an endemic species confined to a single island, it is probably threatened by the destruction of suitable habitat.

REMARKS The relationship of *Otus umbra* with other scops owls of the region is unknown. It has been considered a subspecies of *O. scops* or of *O. sunia*; it has also been proposed that *O. umbra* and *O. enganensis* be treated as races of the same species. We consider all these suggestions dubious, because of vocal patterns. According to our present knowledge, Simeulue Scops Owl is a species in its own right.

REFERENCES Boyer & Hume (1991), Dunning (1993), MacKinnon & Phillips (1993), Marshall (1978), Marshall & King (1988), Rasmussen (1998).

fully feathered to toe joint, mottled rufous and white. **Juvenile** Not described. **Bare parts** Eyes yellow. Bill bluish-horn. Feet bluish-grey. Claws darker horn.

MEASUREMENTS AND WEIGHT Total length 18-20.5cm. Wing 142-167mm; tail 64-83mm Weight: 100-110g

GEOGRAPHICAL VARIATION Monotypic: *Otus enganensis* Riley, 1927.

HABITS Nocturnal bird. Habits not described.

FOOD Apparently mainly insects, spiders and other arthropods.

BREEDING Probably nests in holes in trees. Reproduction unknown.

STATUS AND CONSERVATION Uncertain. Probably rather common. May be under threat from loss of habitat.

REMARKS A more or less unknown bird which requires study. Its relationship with other scops owls of the region is unclear. We treat it as a valid species.

REFERENCES Boyer & Hume (1991), MacKinnon & Phillips (1993), Marshall (1978), Marshall & King (1988).

51 RAJAH SCOPS OWL
Otus brookii   Plate 14

French: Petit-duc de Brooke
German: Radscha-Zwergohreule

IDENTIFICATION A medium-sized (21.5-25cm) dark brownish scops owl with long ear-tufts. Rufous to brownish above, coarsely mottled, freckled and speckled with black and dark brown, with broad collar on hindneck and smaller one on nape. Light whitish-rufous below, coarsely freckled with rufous vermiculations and irregular dark brown shaft markings. Fully feathered tarsus, bare toes. Eyes orange-yellow or chrome-yellow. **Similar species** Reddish Scops Owl [20] and Mountain Scops Owl [23] are smaller and more reddish, with small spots and speckles. Sunda Scops Owl [52] is about the same size, but uniformly dark brown on back, with less pronounced pale nuchal collar, and whitish-buff below with dark black streaks and numerous tiny wavy bars.

VOCALISATIONS *O. b. brookii* The song of nominate race is poorly known. Hose (1929), who collected the only two specimens, stated: 'Its note is clear, and at first almost startling, but is repeated monotonously with no change of inflection', adding that 'The Kayans have a bird-call, made of a short length of bamboo, which when blown is so exactly like the note of the real bird, that it will always answer back, and so to say join in the conversation'. *O. b. solokensis* Territorial song a double hoot, uttered rather explosively, and somewhat reminiscent of the song of Javan Scops Owl [24] but somewhat lower in pitch, as expected from a larger bird. The two notes are on the same pitch, the second rarely a little higher, and about equal in duration at 0.2 seconds, with the interval between them 0.7 seconds. The song is repeated at variable intervals, mostly 7-10 seconds by actively calling birds. Males readily respond to playback of recordings or to imitations, and approach closer. If disturbed or alarmed in the presence of young, it produces a wide vocabulary of short gruff and growling notes.

DISTRIBUTION Montane regions of Sumatra and Borneo.

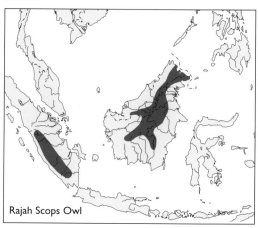

Rajah Scops Owl

MOVEMENTS Resident.

HABITAT Tropical montane rainforest to cloud forest, apparently frequenting middle storey of dense forest. Between about 900m and 2,500m, mostly 1,200-2,400m.

DESCRIPTION Adult Broad white band on side of crown extending to ear-tufts, and with hint of pale occipital patch. Ear-tufts long (up to 48.5mm), with prominent white inner webs. Upperparts deep fuscous or rufous, densely freckled, mottled and speckled with blackish shaft markings and dark brown wavy bars interspersed with more sparse lighter spots. Double collar of white or whitish-buff feathers with distinct large black markings at tips, the lower collar (on hindneck) broader than upper (on nape) and extending to form cervical collar. Underparts light rufous, variably mottled and blotched with dark rufous and black; sometimes only a few irregular shaft-streaks with many dark rufous wavy lines or vermiculations (*O. b. solokensis*), or nearly white ground colour heavily blotched with dark rufous and blackish-brown markings, leaving pattern of large white ocelli (*O. b. brookii*). Feet powerful. Tarsus heavily feathered up to and sometimes beyond proximal (or first) toe joint; toes bare. **Juvenile** Only juvenile *solokensis* known: crown, mantle and back dark rufous-brown with fine dark brown cross-barring; underside whitish-rufous, freckled with darker rufous and shaft-streaks, ocelli pattern hardly developed. **Bare parts** Iris chrome-yellow, orange-yellow or dark orange. Bill pale yellow; or upper mandible greyish-yellow, more grey or blackish near tip and cutting edges, with lower mandible grey. Toes yellowish-flesh or pale grey. Claws yellow, becoming dark grey or black at tip.

MEASUREMENTS AND WEIGHT Females tend to be a little larger. *O. b. brookii*: Total length 24 cm (in flesh). Wing 167-171mm; tail 81 mm (holotype); ear-tufts 35.5mm. *O. b. solokensis*: Total length 21.5-25cm. Wing 163-181 mm, av. about 172mm; tail 70-83.5mm; ear-tufts 28-48.5mm. Weight: no data.

GEOGRAPHICAL VARIATION Two subspecies.
   O. b. brookii (Sharpe, 1892). Mountains of NW Borneo, from where only two specimens known, both

collected by Charles Hose in Sarawak: one (holotype, BM 1892.8.25.3), taken on Mt Dulit at 1,525m in May 1892, is in perfect condition; the other (AMNH No. 629912), from Mt Mulu at 915m in October 1893, was very damaged by shot (wing 162+mm, tail 78+mm). Plumage with more rufous tinge.

O. b. solokensis (Hartert, 1893). Mountains of Sumatra, where seen or collected at localities along entire central mountain chain (Bukit Barisan) from north to south: Mt Leuser, Blangkejeren, Gayo Highlands, 1,500-2,000m (Aceh); Mt Sibayak, 1,400-1,800m, Berastagi, Karo-Batak Highlands (Sumatra Utara); Solok Mountains, c. 1,400-1,600m, 35km NE of Padang, Padang Highlands, and Mt Kerinci, 1,400-2,225m (Sumatra Barat); Rejang, 1,200m, Barisan Range (Bengkulu). Plumage browner above and with more yellowish tinge. Bill paler.

HABITS Unknown.

FOOD Stomach contents contained remains of insects, mainly Coleoptera, Orthoptera (grasshoppers, Tettigoniidae and Gryllidae) and moths, and once a frog.

BREEDING Families contained two fledged young, these fed and accompanied by both parents in July. No other details known.

STATUS AND CONSERVATION Uncertain, but almost surely endangered. Deforestation in mountain regions is a serious threat. In N Borneo, clear-felling and forest fires are a most severe threat to the virtually unknown nominate race, apparently not observed by ornithologists for a century or more and perhaps already extinct.

REMARKS Examination of the two specimens of the nominate race and about ten of *solokensis* revealed that the nominate has exceptionally soft and fluffy plumage, very boldly blotched on belly and flanks with broad (open) ocellar markings narrowly framed with black and dark rufous lines, whereas *solokensis* had more normal stiff feathers, not fluffy, and small ocellar markings always contiguous with the dark shaft-streaks; further, the bill of nominate (dried skin) was dark grey, compared with whitish-yellow in dried skins of *solokensis*. It may be that the Bornean form is a separate species, but this is difficult to determine with only two specimens available of a possibly extinct population.

REFERENCES Boyer & Hume (1991), Hose (1927, 1929), MacKinnon & Phillipps (1993), Marle & Voous (1988), Marshall (1978), Robinson & Kloss (1924), Smythies (1968).

---

52   SUNDA SCOPS OWL
Otus lempiji   Plate 15

French: Petit-duc de Sunda
German: Sunda-Zwergohreule

IDENTIFICATION A medium-sized (20-23cm) sandy-brown owl, spotted and mottled dark brown and black, with rounded wings, large ear-tufts and ill-defined hindneck-collar. Light buffish-brown above, mottled, spotted and freckled with black and buff, and light grey-buff (grey-brown morph) or more rufous-buff (rufous morph) below with small arrowhead-like streaks crossed by fine wavy bars and vermiculations. Fully feathered tarsi. Eyes usually deep brown, sometimes orange or bright yellow. **Similar species** No other owl with similar black and buff spotting normally occurs in same range and habitat. Mountain Scops Owl [23] is usually found at higher elevations and is distinctly smaller, more reddish and with bolder markings. Common Scops Owl [37] is distinguished by its large white scapular patches and lack of collar. Collared Scops Owl [53] is similar to Sunda Scops in coloration, but has a different, downward-inflected song.

VOCALISATIONS A musical, 'querying' *woouk woouk ......* with upward inflection and uttered at relatively long intervals of 10-15 seconds is the song of the male. It is repeated for long periods, normally from dusk onwards, but sometimes from as early as late afternoon on cloudy days. The female has a similar but higher-pitched song, also with 'interrogative' tone, *woik woik ....* Often the song is a long monologue, but in the breeding season pairs tend to duet, with pauses between calls becoming relatively shorter and one bird answering exactly when the other pauses. Song of males of S Malay Peninsula population (*cnephaeus*) is a resonant *kwook* without inflection, uttered at longer intervals.

DISTRIBUTION SE Asian mainland and neighbouring islands to Malay Peninsula, Sumatra (including Bangka and Belitung), Borneo (including W Natuna Islands), Java and Bali (including Kangean Island).

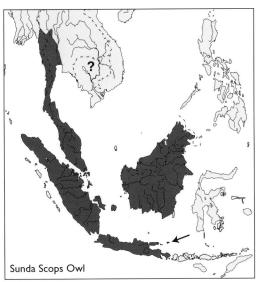

Sunda Scops Owl

MOVEMENTS Resident.

HABITAT Frequents middle and lower storeys of forest and secondary growth, plantations, wooded gardens and partly cleared country, including villages and suburban and urban areas with trees. Attracted by human activities and habitations, even occurring in large towns provided they contain enough trees for cover, roosting and breeding. Avoids undisturbed primary rainforest. Occurs from sea-level to about 2,000m, occasionally to 2,400m.

DESCRIPTION *O. l. lempiji* Adult Plumage very variable and probably also varying individually within populations; grey-brown, grey-buff and rufous morphs, colour patterns

of which may also intergrade. Facial disc rufous-buff, broadly margined with black. Forehead and eyebrows pinkish-buff, more variegated with black posteriorly. Crown blackish; ear-tufts buffy, broadly edged black on outer webs. Upperparts sandy-brown, mottled and freckled with black and buff, and blotched with black; somewhat ill-defined collar on hindneck, usually of sandy-buff colour, the feathers tipped with black and with traces of bars. Wings dark brown with sandy vermiculated barring, outer webs of quills with buffy bars interspaced with dark ones. Underparts grey-buff or rufous-buff (different morphs) with arrowhead- or chevron-like black shaft markings interconnected with fine cross-bars or vermiculations, interspaces often densely peppered with minute black spots. Tarsus fully feathered to toe joint, sometimes well over toe joint. **Juvenile** Downy plumage pure white (Malay Peninsula), dark grey or rufous-grey (Java), or bright rufous. Immatures have generally irregular and indistinct markings on brownish-buff ground colour, with strong tendency to cross-barring, especially on head. **Bare parts** Iris usually dark brown, occasionally bright or orange-yellow; eyelids pale pinky-brown. Bill horny-white. Cere yellowish-horn, sometimes with greenish tinge. Toes horny-white. Claws somewhat darker or more brownish.

MEASUREMENTS AND WEIGHT Total length 20-23cm. Wing 143-162mm; tail 70-78mm. Weight 90-140g (average 107.5 for 10 specimens).

GEOGRAPHICAL VARIATION We recognise four subspecies, one of them possibly specifically distinct.
   O. l. lempiji (Horsfield, 1821). Malay Peninsula, Sumatra, Bangka, Belitung, Java, Borneo, Natuna Islands. See Description. Wing 136-156mm; tail 70-78mm. (We include *lemurum* as a synonym.)
   O. (l.) cnephaeus Deignan, 1950. S Malay Peninsula. Smaller than nominate. (Probably occurs locally alongside nominate *lempiji*, and likely to be a separate species according to male's song: see Vocalisations.)
   O. l. hypnodes Deignan, 1950. Pulau Padang, off E Sumatra. Overall darker and more rufous in the dark morph. Wing 142-159mm.
   O. l. kangeana Mayr, 1938. Kangean Island. Smaller than nominate, with paler plumage. Wing 144-147mm.

Sunda Scops Owl
Otus (lempiji) cnephaeus

HABITS Nocturnal. Seldom seen in daytime, when it hides up in thickly foliaged trees, palms or bamboo groves. Calls from a perch but, unlike many other owls, not from exposed branch but always from centre of a usually densely foliaged tree. Males shift songposts at regular intervals, but on their rounds usually visit the same trees; after a short break calling is resumed from a different tree, suggesting that the bird may be hunting for food in the interval. The call is heard throughout the year.

FOOD Mainly insects, such as large Coleoptera species, Orthoptera (grasshoppers, crickets), mantids and moths; sometimes small birds are taken, such as nestlings of munias *lonchura*. Food is usually sought near the ground around houses and huts of native villages or streets and houses in towns. In villages, it habitually hunts nocturnal insects attracted by cow dung or poultry droppings around houses. Some stomachs examined were crammed with cockroaches (Blattidae) and a particular type of black dung beetle (Scarabacoidea, *Lamellicornis*). The Sumatran (Minangklabau) name for this owl is 'kuas cirit ayam', which means 'fowl's-excrement owl'.

BREEDING Main breeding season February-April, sometimes also June or July. Breeds in natural holes or hollow trees or palms, also between the erect, dead leaf sheets of sugar/oil/coconut palms *Arenga/Elaeis/Cocos*. In contrast to most owls, which lay in an unlined hole, sometimes builds an actual nest of vegetable fibres (most often those of *Arenga saccharifera*, but also plant-fibre material from other sources), an untidy heap of material forming the base on which usually 2 eggs, rarely 3, are laid. Eggs like those of all owl species, pure white, roundish, often with some gloss: about 33.5 x 28.8mm.

STATUS AND CONSERVATION Very common, occurring even in densely populated areas when enough trees are present.

REMARKS Research is required on the birds of the S Malay Peninsula, where a vocally distinct population (*cnephaeus*) occurs. The relationship of the taxa *alboniger* and *manipurensis* with *O. lempiji* is not clear and requires further study. We here consider them to belong to *O. lettia*. See remarks under Collared Scops Owl.

REFERENCES Becking (unpublished), Deignan (1950), King *et al.* (1995), Robinson (1927).

---

53   COLLARED SCOPS OWL
Otus lettia   Plate 15

French: Petit-duc à collier
German: Halsband-Zwergohreule

IDENTIFICATION A medium-sized (23-25cm) sandy-brown owl, spotted and mottled dark brown and black, with relatively pointed wings and rather small ear-tufts. Eyes dark brown to orange. Song always contains downward-inflected notes. **Similar species** Sunda Scops Owl [52], Indian Scops Owl [54] and Japanese Scops Owl [55] are similar in size and coloration, but are easily distinguished by their different songs: Sunda Scops, which is darker above and has longer ear-tufts, utters a melodious 'questioning', upward-inflected *woouk* (male) or higher-pitched *woik* (female); Indian Scops gives more yelping, unmelodious notes with upward inflection, such as *wuatt* or *what?*; and Japanese Scops utters deep notes with no inflection.

VOCALISATIONS The song is a single hoot, repeated at somewhat longer intervals (15-20 seconds) than the quite different calls of Sunda and Indian Scops Owl. Males utter a downward-inflected *kwúo* and females a slightly higher-pitched and more mewing *kwiau*, duetting during courtship. When disturbed, both sexes utter series of

chattering notes: *wakwakwakwakwakwak...* or *uattuattuatt-uattuatt....*

DISTRIBUTION E Himalayas from E Nepal east to Assam, south to E Bengal, Burma, Thailand, Hainan, S China and Taiwan.

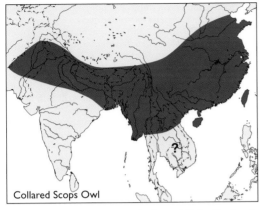

Collared Scops Owl

MOVEMENTS Migrates to S India and Malay Peninsula in winter.

HABITAT Forest, including sal, oak, pine, deodar forest around hill stations, second growth, also groves of trees and bamboo stands around habitations, open country and towns. From plains and submontane tracts to about 2400m.

DESCRIPTION *O. l. lettia* **Adult** Resembles Sunda Scops Owl, but distinctly lighter-coloured above and with shorter ear-tufts. Light buffish-brown above, mottled, spotted and freckled with black and buff, and light grey-buff (grey-brown morph) or more rufous-buff (rufous morph) below with small arrowhead-like shaft-streaks. Tarsus fully feathered to the base of the toes. **Juvenile** Indistinguishable from Sunda Scops Owl. **Bare parts** Iris dark brown to orange, or yellowish-brown. Bill greenish-horn, paler at base, blacker at tip; lower mandible pale dusky yellow. Feet and claws fleshy-grey to dusky olive; pads yellowish-white.

MEASUREMENTS AND WEIGHT Total length 23-25cm, females usually larger. Wing 158-168mm; tail 75-91mm. Weight 108-170g.

GEOGRAPHICAL VARIATION We recognise four subspecies.

    O. l. lettia (Hodgson, 1836). E Himalayas to E Assam, E Bengal, Burma and Thailand. See Description. (We include *alboniger* and *manipurensis* as synonyms.)
    O. l. erythrocampe (Swinhoe, 1874). S China. Upperparts brown with buff markings, less greyish than nominate race, with white supercilia, very similar to Japanese Scops Owl. Eyes more golden-brown to chestnut. Wing 173-180mm; tail 91mm.
    O. l. glabripes (Swinhoe, 1870). Taiwan. Similar in plumage to Japanese Scops Owl, but has totally bare toes. Wing 178-188mm.
    O. l. umbratilis (Swinhoe, 1870). Hainan. Compared with *glabripes*, somewhat lighter above and with darker markings. Smaller in size. Wing 161-183mm; tail 83mm.

HABITS Nocturnal, and seldom seen by day. Spends daytime lurking in some dark corner on a densely foliaged branch, perched upright and motionless, effectively disguised as a snag. Its presence in a locality is detected only by its distinctive voice at night; singing continues intermittently throughout the night, in runs of 10-15 minutes' duration or longer.

FOOD Beetles, grasshoppers and other insects, but in general has a more varied diet than Sunda and Indian Scops Owls, including lizards, mice and small birds. An individual of nominate race, shot at 02:30 hours (when calling), had its stomach packed with a freshly ingested field mouse.

BREEDING Season February-May. Nests in a natural hollow or woodpecker hole in a tree trunk or dead stump, mostly at moderate height (about 2-5m up). Eggs 3 or 4, rarely 5, similar in shape and colour to those of related species: 32.3 x 28.1mm. Incubation period and other details of breeding biology unrecorded.

STATUS AND CONSERVATION Widespread, but local. Generally not uncommon in those localities where it occurs.

REMARKS *O. lettia*, *O. lempiji*, *O. semitorques* and *O. bakkamoena* have in the past been lumped together as a single species: *O. bakkamoena*. Although they are all very similar in plumage, they are vocally and genetically distinct. The entire group urgently needs a revision to determine which species the various taxa described as subspecies should be attributed.

REFERENCES Ali & Ripley (1981), Dementiev & Gladkov (1951), Voous (1988).

---

54 INDIAN SCOPS OWL
Otus bakkamoena   **Plate 15**

French: Petit-duc des Indes
German: Hindu-Halsbandeule

IDENTIFICATION A medium-sized (19-23cm) sandy-brown owl, spotted and mottled dark brown and black, with rounded wings and large conspicuous ear-tufts. Upperparts light buffish-brown, mottled, spotted and freckled with black and buff, and underparts light grey-buff (grey-brown morph) or more rufous-buff (rufous morph) with small arrowhead-like shaft-streaks interconnected by fine wavy transverse bars and vermiculations. A distinct nuchal collar and also a second collar on nape. Eyes dark brown. **Similar species** Sunda Scops Owl [52] is darker above, while Collared and Japanese Scops Owls [53, 55] are similar in size and coloration; all three have less prominent ear-tufts, and also differ vocally (see Collared Scops Owl).

VOCALISATIONS The male's song is a regularly spaced, interrogative *what?......what?* or *wuatt*; series are interrupted by pauses. An occasional series of slowly repeated bubbling or chattering *ackackackack...* on ascending scale, strung out for 5 seconds or so, usually interposed with normal notes but sometimes heard independently.

DISTRIBUTION SE Arabia to S Pakistan, NW Himalayas, India east to W Bengal, including Himalayas from Kashmir east to C Nepal, and south to Sri Lanka.

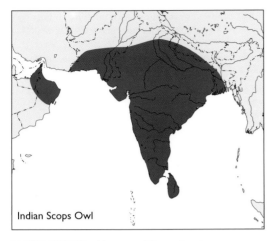

Indian Scops Owl

MOVEMENTS Resident, possibly partly migratory.

HABITAT Forest and secondary woodland, desert vegetation, and groups of densely foliaged trees in gardens, mango orchards and other fruit trees around villages and cultivation. From lowlands to 2,200m.

DESCRIPTION *O. b. bakkamoena* **Adult** Facial disc pale greyish-brown, rather distinctly rimmed by blackish spots. Forehead and eyebrows paler than surrounding plumage. Ear-tufts rather long and prominent. Upperparts slightly paler than on Sunda Scops Owl, greyish-brown with darker and lighter markings; outer webs of scapulars dirty cream or whitish-buff, not very prominent and not forming distinct shoulder stripe. Flight and tail feathers inconspicuously barred lighter and darker. Underparts ochraceous-buff, becoming paler towards belly, with relatively few dark shaft-streaks and wavy cross-bars, especially on upper breast and flanks. **Juvenile** Pale grey or pale to warm fulvous, narrowly barred all over with dusky brown, these bars covering even face and chin. **Bare parts** Eyes hazel or brown. Bill greenish horn-brown, paler on lower mandible, darker at tip. Cere dusky green. Mouth pink. Toes brownish-flesh to greenish-yellow. Claws pale horn-brown.

MEASUREMENTS AND WEIGHT Total length 19-23cm. Wing 135-185mm; tail 64-94mm. Weight 125-152g.

GEOGRAPHICAL VARIATION Numerous subspecies have been described, but only some seem to be valid, and several others belong to different species. We recognise five subspecies here.

O. b. bakkamoena Pennant, 1769. S India and Sri Lanka. See Description. Wing 135-152mm; tail 64-67mm.

O. b. marathae Ticehurst, 1922. Central provinces of India to Sambalpur and Manbhum in SW Bengal. Similar in plumage to nominate *bakkamoena*, but in general less rufous and much more grey in overall tone, and larger. Wing 152-162mm.

O. b. gangeticus Ticehurst, 1922. NW India. Somewhat larger and distinctly paler than nominate; smaller and paler than Collared Scops Owl. Wing 153-167mm.

O. b. plumipes (Hume, 1870). NW Himalayas from Murree to Naini. Toes densely feathered as in Japanese Scops Owl, and rather similar in plumage to that species. Differs, however, in vocalisations and in dark

eyes (red or yellow in Japanese). Wing 173-185mm; tail 89-94mm.

O. b. deserticolor Ticehurst, 1922. SE Arabia to S Pakistan. Desert race. Very pale; lacks rufous tinge above and below, and belly almost white. Wing 165-175mm.

HABITS Seldom seen in daytime, when it hides up in thickly foliaged trees.

FOOD Mainly insects (beetles, grasshoppers and others), but occasionally vertebrates (lizards, mice and small birds).

BREEDING Nests in tree hollows, usually at moderate height. Eggs 3-4, white and roundish: about 33 x 27mm.

STATUS AND CONSERVATION Widespread, and locally common.

REMARKS The ecology and biology, as well as the taxonomy, of this species and related taxa need study. See remarks under Collared Scops Owl.

REFERENCES Ali & Ripley (1981), Baker (1927), Boyer & Hume (1991), Dementiev & Gladkov (1951), Roberts & King (1986), Voous (1988).

55 JAPANESE SCOPS OWL
Otus semitorques   Plate 16

French: Petit-duc du Japon
German: Japan-Halsbandeule

IDENTIFICATION A small (21-25.5cm) sandy greyish-brown owl, spotted and mottled dark brown and black, with more pointed wings and long, prominent ear-tufts. Upperparts light greyish-brown, lacking rufous wash, and mottled, spotted and freckled with black and buff. Eyebrows, ear-tufts (partly) and throat whitish to clear white. Underparts greyish-buff with small arrowhead-like shaft-streaks interconnected by fine wavy transverse bars and vermiculations. Grey double collar, one on hindneck and one on nape. Strong bill. Tarsi and toes fully feathered in two subspecies, toes bare in one. Eyes bright red or orange-yellow. **Similar species** Collared Scops Owl [53], Indian Scops Owl [54] and Sunda Scops Owl [52] are similar in size and coloration to Japanese Scops, but Japanese never has brown eyes. All are best separated by voice.

VOCALISATIONS A rather deep, mournful *whoop* uttered at long intervals is the song of the male. A weak, cat-like mew has also been described.

DISTRIBUTION SE Siberia (Ussuriland and Sakhalin); S Kuril Islands (Kunashiri, Shikotan, and north to Uruppu); Japan from Hokkaido to Kyushu, and Sado, Shikoku, Tsushima, Quelpart, Goto and Yaku-shima, Izu Islands (Hachijo) and Ryukyu Islands (Okinawa and Yagachi-shima).

MOVEMENTS Resident and migratory. Nominate *semitorques* is largely resident, but moves locally and occurs in the Seven Islands of Izu in winter. *O. s. ussuriensis* winters in C and S Korea (reported to also to be a common passage migrant and uncommon summer visitor in Korea) and also in N China (Shandong, where perhaps also partly resident).

247

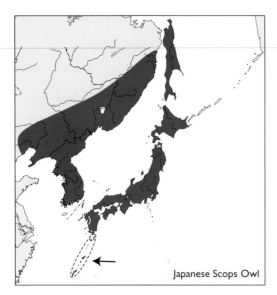

Japanese Scops Owl

HABITAT Woods and forest, wooded gardens, lowland areas with trees; often in or around villages and suburbs, particularly in winter. Lowlands to mountains.

DESCRIPTION *O. s. semitorques* **Adult** Facial disc pale greyish-brown with minute dark flecks; rim narrow, but rather prominent. Forehead lighter than crown. Eyebrows whitish, extending nearly to tips of prominent ear-tufts. Upperparts sandy greyish-brown with blackish and buffy-whitish markings; hindneck and nape each with a light collar. Outer webs of scapulars with small lighter areas, but no distinct scapular stripe. Flight and tail feathers barred light and dark; wings pointed, with 7th primary longest. Underparts pale greyish-buff with dark herring-bone-like patterns. Tarsi and toes feathered. **Juvenile** Downy chicks whitish. Mesoptile greyish-buff, diffusely barred on head, mantle, back and underparts. **Bare parts** Eyes fiery to dark red; more yellowish in juveniles. Bill and cere greyish-horn. Claws horn.

MEASUREMENTS AND WEIGHT Total length 21-25.5cm. Wing 151-191mm; tail 86-98mm. Weight about 130g.

GEOGRAPHICAL VARIATION We recognise three subspecies.

O. s. semitorques Temminck & Schlegel, 1850. S Kuril Islands and Japan (Hokkaido to Yaku-shima); Izu and Ryukyu Islands in winter. See Description. Wing 166-191mm; tail 86-98mm.

O. s. ussuriensis (Buturlin, 1910). Ussuriland and Sakhalin; winters (breeds?) in C and S Korea and N China. Very similar to nominate *semitorques*, but somewhat paler in appearance and with yellow to orange-yellow eyes. Wing 159-176mm.

O. s. pryeri (Gurney, 1889). Izu (Hachijo) and Ryukyu Islands (Okinawa and Yagachi-shima). Differs from nominate in bare toes, dark yellow eyes, and strong ferruginous wash above and below (less greyish). Bill large, as in nominate. Wing 151-173mm.

HABITS Strictly nocturnal. Roosts by day among dense foliage or in tree holes.

FOOD Larger insects, spiders, frogs, small mammals and birds.

BREEDING Nests in natural tree holes or hollow trees, or in old raptor nests or in buildings. Clutch usually (?) 4 eggs, white and roundish: 36.6 x 30.7mm.

STATUS AND CONSERVATION Widespread, and locally not uncommon.

REMARKS As with the three closely related preceding species, the Japanese Scops Owl requires more study. See remarks under Collared Scops Owl.

REFERENCES Brazil (1991), Dementiev & Gladkov (1951), Gore & Won (1971), Higuchi & Momose (1980), Marshall (1988), Schönwetter (1967), Vaurie (1965), Voous (1988).

56   PHILIPPINE SCOPS OWL
Otus megalotis   Plate 16

French: Petit-duc des Philippines
German: Philippinen-Halsbandeule

IDENTIFICATION A small owl (about 20-28cm), but relatively large for a scops owl, with long ear-tufts and powerful feet. Grey morph has blackish crown, whitish eyebrows extending to ear-tufts, and upperparts greyish dark brown or heavily mottled and vermiculated blackish, with some white and rufous, and with narrow whitish-buff nuchal collar; throat shows broad whitish-buff ruff of dark-tipped feathers, and underparts are grey with dark arrowhead-like shaft-streaks with some cross-markings. Rufous morph the same, but more rufous (instead of greyish) above and below. Eyes orange-brown. **Similar species** No other owl of this size and pattern occurs in the Philippines. Reddish Scops Owl [20], found in Sulu Islands, is smaller and much more rufous. Giant Scops Owl [90] is much larger, and has breast and belly light rufous with well-demarcated dark brown streaks and drop-like markings.

VOCALISATIONS Song an explosive series of 3-6 descending notes, each with rising inflection, but longer than the similar notes of Sunda Scops Owl [52]. J. Marshall reports: 'A second bird, presumably its mate, uttered only the first one or two notes of the song. The frequency of its calls varied from one song at dawn or dusk on some nights to one or more bouts with an interval of 5-30 minutes between songs on other nights'. A most peculiar and powerful cry, uttered shortly after nightfall, is best described as *oik-oik-oik oohk*, with an interval between each *oik* and the *oohk*, a well-drawn-out sound.

DISTRIBUTION Philippine Islands, excluding Palawan. See Geographical Variation.

MOVEMENTS Resident.

HABITAT Tropical forest and secondary woodland, usually dense forest from 300m to 1,200m.

DESCRIPTION *O. m. megalotis* **Adult** *Rufous morph*: Light rufous-fawn all over, with discrete vermiculations and mottling of dull blackish, a little coarse on ear-tufts and wing-coverts, almost obsolete on underparts. Greater and primary wing-coverts rufous-fawn, very coarsely and thickly vermiculated with blackish, forming 5-6 indistinct bars. Flight feathers blackish with 6-7 fawn-coloured bars, these very distinct on outer primaries, gradually becoming more obscure with blackish frecklings, until obsolete on secondaries. Tail with 6-7 similarly coloured bars, more or less obscured by blackish freckling. Underwing ashy-brown with fulvous bands. Tarsus feathered to toe joint; fulvous, slightly mottled with rufous. *Grey morph:* Similar, but general coloration greyish-brown. **Juvenile** Top of head and neck rufous-buff, finely barred with black; upperside of face rufous, the feathers of facial disc with faint white shaft-streaks; throat rufous-buff, faintly barred with black; remaining underparts rufous-buff, becoming whitish-buff with fine dusky bars on lower abdomen and thighs; tarsi whitish with obscure dusky bars. **Bare parts** Iris warm orange-brown. Bill pale horn or flesh, more yellowish on lower mandible. Cere pinkish. Toes pale flesh, yellowish-brown or whitish-grey. Claws flesh-coloured, faintly tinged with olive or dark grey.

Philippine Scops Owl

MEASUREMENTS AND WEIGHT Total length 20-28cm. Wing 146-203mm; tail 70-108mm; ear-tufts 37mm. Weight 180-310g.

GEOGRAPHICAL VARIATION Three subspecies.

O. m. megalotis Walden, 1875. Luzon, Marinduque and Catanduanes. See Description. Wing 185-203mm; tail 89-108mm; ear-tufts 37mm. (Form *whiteheadi* is a synonym of *megalotis*.)

O. m. everetti (Tweeddale, 1897). Samar, Leyte, Dinagat, Bohol, Mindanao and Basilan. Differs from nominate in being smaller (wing 158-171 mm, tail 71-92mm) and in tarsus feathering not reaching toes. (Form *boholensis* is a synonym.)

O. m. nigrorum Rand, 1950. Negros. Differs from *everetti* in being smaller (wing 146-148 mm, tail 70mm) and in having head and neck bright rufous.

HABITS Nocturnal. A family group of two parents with one young was found roosting in a partly uprooted, dead and decaying tree on the top of a ridge, the exposed part of the root system providing a very safe and convenient roost for the owls. The amount of excrement found at the site indicated that the birds must have remained there for quite a long time. Seems to frequent deserted forest roads for hunting; reported often to start to fly only a metre or so before reached by walkers, usually flying less than 3m before landing again.

FOOD Insects (stomach contents).

BREEDING A very young owlet was collected in Lepato (Luzon) in February; immatures observed in Negros in May, estimated from their ages to have been hatched in January-February. Probably breeds in tree holes or in root sytems of upturned decaying trees (see Habits). In two cases, a family with one young observed.

STATUS AND CONSERVATION Presumed to be locally not rare.

REMARKS These Philippine forms of scops owl were previously treated as races of *O. bakkamoena*; on the basis of their calls, however, all but the Palawan form *fuliginosus* [58] are combined in the species *O. megalotis*.

REFERENCES Boyer & Hume (1991), Dickinson *et al.* (1991), DuPont (1971), Marshall (1978), McGregor (1909), Ogilvie-Grant (1895c), Rabor (1979), Whitehead (1899).

57   MENTAWAI SCOPS OWL
Otus mentawi   Plate 16

French: Petit-duc de Mentawai

German: Mentawai-Zwergohreule

IDENTIFICATION A small owl (22cm), dark blackish-brown above, with whitish eyebrows and ear-tufts mottled with dark brown, and paler below, peppered with black and small distinct dark shaft-streaks. Rufous-brown morph has ground colour of underside rich chestnut or chestnut-tawny. No collar. Tarsus fully feathered to base of toes. Eyes yellow or brown. **Similar species** No other scops owl occurs on Mentawai Islands.

VOCALISATIONS The song of the male is a series of 3-4 rough barking notes, *how-how-how*, repeated at intervals of several seconds. Female gives single or series of somewhat hoarse and slightly vibrating *huwéw* notes, higher in pitch than male's song, sometimes duetting with mate. Duet by pair-members includes added notes, becomes gruffer, and fades towards end; female follows the male's phrases and repeats them in synchrony. Another principal call is a bold cry with rising inflection, mono- or disyllabic, *po-po*; the owl's native name is taken from this call.

DISTRIBUTION Mentawai Islands, off W Sumatra: reported from Siberut, Sipura, and N and S Pagai.

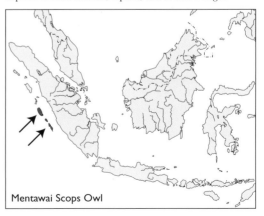

Mentawai Scops Owl

MOVEMENTS Resident.

HABITAT Inhabits lowland rainforest; also occurs in human settlements (villages).

DESCRIPTION Adult *Rufous-brown morph*: Facial disc rufous, bordered with black-tipped feathers. Eyebrows pale buff with dark mottling, leading to similarly coloured ear-tufts, the latter not very prominent. Upperparts dark rufous-brown, darker on crown and nape, with dark shaft-streaks on back; no nuchal collar, but some feathers with small white dots. Outer scapular feathers blotched whitish and black, forming distinct row. Wing-coverts mottled and freckled with dark brown. Underparts rufous-brown or chestnut, with herringbone-like shaft markings enclosed by single or paired white ocelli; ground colour becoming paler towards lower abdomen and undertail-coverts. Tarsus fully feathered to and sometimes beyond toe joint. Toes bare. Relatively powerful talons. *Blackish-brown morph*: Basic colour more blackish-brown and less rufous (see Identification). **Juvenile** Not described. **Bare parts** Iris brown, sometimes yellow. Bill greyish-horn. Toes grey. Claws dark horn.

MEASUREMENTS AND WEIGHT Total length 22cm. Wing 157-166mm; tail: 84mm. Weight: no data.

GEOGRAPHICAL VARIATION Monotypic: *Otus mentawi* Chasen & Kloss, 1926.

HABITS Nocturnal. Individuals of forest-dwelling populations are usually more shy and keep well hidden, whereas those inhabiting villages are bolder and therefore more conspicuous, often perching on bare limbs, banana leaves or coconut fronds. The species responds to and is attracted by playback of its calls.

FOOD Insects.

BREEDING Unknown.

STATUS AND CONSERVATION Locally common.

REMARKS This owl is sometimes treated as a race of the Sundan *O. lempiji*, but is better treated as a separate species on account of its very different vocalisations. It is remarkable that no *Otus* owl is known from the nearby Batu Islands and Nias, to the north of the main Mentawai group.

REFERENCES Chasen & Kloss (1926), König & Weick (unpublished), Marshall (1978).

---

58   PALAWAN SCOPS OWL
Otus fuliginosus   Plate 16

French: Petit-duc de Palawan
German: Palawan-Halsbandeule

IDENTIFICATION Resembles race *everetti* of Philippine Scops Owl [56], but is smaller (about 19cm), is more rufous above and has a reduced but prominent collar on hindneck. Face and chin rufous-brown, not white, and underparts rufous-brown with heavy dark brown streaks. Eyes orange-brown. **Similar species** No other scops owl occurs on Palawan.

VOCALISATIONS The male's song is a rasping, disyllabic,

deep croak, resembling a dry branch being cut with a handsaw: *krarr-kroarrr* ..., repeated at intervals of several seconds.

DISTRIBUTION Philippines: Palawan Island.

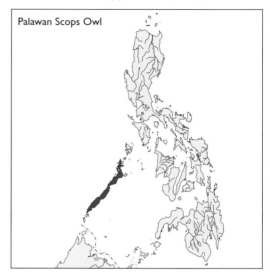

Palawan Scops Owl

MOVEMENTS Resident.

HABITAT Tropical forest and secondary woodland in lowlands.

DESCRIPTION Adult Overall rich brown, vermiculated and spotted as in typical *Otus* species. Facial disc rufescent-brownish with numerous dark flecks; rim around disc not prominent. Forehead and eyebrows whitish, finely flecked dark. Ear-tufts short, but more prominent than on Mentawai Scops Owl [57]. Crown darker brown. A pale collar on nape is prominent. Outer webs of scapulars with rather large whitish areas, forming whitish row across shoulder. Primaries with very pale bars, contrasting with dark rest of feathers. Underparts rufescent-brown with dark vermiculations and several arrow-shaped blackish markings. Tarsi feathered to base of toes. **Juvenile** Undescribed. **Bare parts** Eyes light orange-brown. Bill and cere pale brownish-horn. Toes yellowish-grey. Claws dark horn.

MEASUREMENTS AND WEIGHT Total length 19-20cm. Wing 139mm. Weight: no data.

GEOGRAPHICAL VARIATION Monotypic: *Otus fuliginosus* (Sharpe, 1888).

HABITS Unrecorded.

FOOD Insects.

BREEDING Probably nests in tree holes.

STATUS AND CONSERVATION Rare and endangered. Listed as Vulnerable by BirdLife International.

REMARKS This little-known species requires study.

REFERENCES Collar *et al.* (1994), duPont (1971), Marshall (1978), Marshall & King (1988), McGregor (1909).

59 WALLACE'S SCOPS OWL
Otus silvicola   Plate 16

French: Petit-duc de Wallace
German: Wallace-Zwergohreule

IDENTIFICATION A small dark owl, relatively large (23-27cm) for a scops owl, with long ear-tufts. Pale greyish-brown above, with black herringbone-like shaft-streaks and more reddish-brown vermiculations, scapulars with dark shaft marks and ochre-white markings and flight feathers barred dark brown and buff. No pale collar. Breast and flanks light buff with black shaft-stripes and dark brown wavy cross-bars. Tarsus fully feathered; talons powerful. Eyes dull orange-yellow. **Similar species** Moluccan Scops Owl [43] is smaller (20cm), with relatively small ear-tufts, brighter yellow eyes and usually more whitish lores, and is more rufous in the rufous morph, while the brown morph is extremely variable in markings (obscure or miniaturised spotting, or clear dark shaft-stripes and ocelli); in addition, substantial vocal differences exist between the two species. Flores Scops Owl [28] is much smaller (19cm), cinnamon-coloured and with small ear-tufts.

VOCALISATIONS Territorial song is a long series of gruff notes on the same pitch, uttered at intervals of about 1 second: *rrow*. A deep *hwomph*, repeated 9-18 times, is also reported.

DISTRIBUTION Sumbawa and Flores, in Lesser Sunda Islands.

Wallace's Scops Owl

MOVEMENTS Resident.

HABITAT Tropical lowland forest to submontane forest, also secondary woodland, around farms and in the town of Ruteng (Flores). The song (along with that of Moluccan Scops Owl) was heard in wooded ravines in lowland farming areas near Maumere (Flores), as well as throughout the virgin montane rainforest south of Ruteng (at least to 1,600m). Lowlands to 2,000m.

DESCRIPTION Adult Light-coloured face with whitish eyebrows (but white not extending to ear-tufts). Ear-tufts rather long, mottled dark brown and buff, without white on inner border. Upperparts pale grey-brown, with black herringbone-like shaft-streaks on a reddish or buffy-brown background with some darker vermiculations; no pale collar; scapulars with ochre-white markings. Remiges with dark brown and buff bars. Tail brown with rather in-

conspicuous and narrow buff bars. Underparts whitish-buff or light buff with sparse, bold blackish herringbone-like streaks and well-defined dark brown wavy cross-bars. Tarsus and proximal phalanx usually densely feathered, as also is part or all (laterally) of second phalanges. Rest of toes bare. **Juvenile** Overall lighter in colour and more fluffy; ground colour usually more rufous-washed, and feather patterns rather inconspicuous both on upperside and underside, and also on ear-tufts. **Bare parts** Iris dull orange-yellow. Bill and cere greyish-horn. Toes pale greyish-brown. Claws horn.

MEASUREMENTS AND WEIGHT Total length 23cm. Wing 202-251mm; tail 101-141mm. Weight: no data.

GEOGRAPHICAL VARIATION Monotypic: *Otus silvicola* (Wallace, 1864).

HABITS A strictly nocturnal bird which hides away during daytime. Invariably perches high up in a tree or in concealment and therefore difficult to observe; tends also to call from such a position. Peak of vocal activity is said to be between 22:00 and 23:00 hours.

FOOD Mainly insectivorous.

BREEDING Unrecorded. A male in December had enlarged testes.

STATUS AND CONSERVATION Locally not rare, but probably under some threat from forest destruction.

REMARKS Like many scops owls of Indonesia, this species is in need of study. The first description, by Wallace, was based on a juvenile; Hartert described an adult and the differences between it and the holotype.

REFERENCES Boyer & Hume (1991), Butchart *et al.* (1996), Coates & Bishop (1997), Hartert (1897), Marshall (1978).

60 WESTERN SCREECH OWL
Otus kennicottii   Plate 17

Syn: *Megascops kennicottii*

French: Scops d'Elliot
German: West-Kreischeule
Spanish: Tecolote Occidental

IDENTIFICATION A typical screech owl, medium-sized (about 23cm) and with short ear-tufts and yellow eyes. Most birds belong to a greyish morph, while the red one is much rarer. It has a blackish bill. **Similar species** Eastern Screech Owl [61] is very similar but has a greenish bill, and a red morph is rather frequent. Whiskered Screech Owl [64] is much smaller (16.5-19cm), with relatively small feet and a greyish bill, and occurs in a red and a grey morph. Both are more coarsely streaked below than Western Screech Owl. Flammulated Scops Owl [36] is small (15-17cm), has dark brown eyes and has rufescent markings in the plumage; it is a bird of mountain forest. Balsas Screech Owl [66] is larger (24-26.5cm), and has dark brown eyes; it is endemic to SW Mexico. All are best separated by voice.

VOCALISATIONS The A-song of the male is a short trill followed immediately by a longer one, rising slightly in pitch and dropping again near the end: *urrr - uhrrrrrrrrr*.

The female utters a similar, but higher-pitched A-song. The B-song (similar in both sexes, the female's higher in pitch) is a short sequence of 5-10 accelerated notes in 'bouncing-ball' rhythm, ending with a trill (the notes running together): *bu bu-bubububurrrr*.

DISTRIBUTION West of the Rocky Mountains from northern Canada to central Mexico; eastern limits of distribution uncertain. Probably overlaps locally with Eastern Screech Owl and occasional interbreeding is known, especially near the USA/Mexican border.

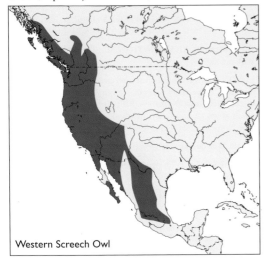

Western Screech Owl

MOVEMENTS Partly migratory in the northern part of its range, migrating southward in winter, but most of the population is apparently resident. Those living at higher altitudes may move to lower ones in winter.

HABITAT Arid to semi-humid open woodland, especially pine/oak forest. Also semi-open areas with scattered trees or groups of trees and shrubs, riparian forest, semi-desert with large cacti, and suburban areas with gardens and parks.

DESCRIPTION *O. k. kennicottii* **Adult** Two colour morphs exist: a grey morph and a rare red one, the latter found more in the northern part of range. *Grey morph*: Facial disc light brownish-grey, finely mottled and vermiculated darker; rim dark, edged by light speckles, not very prominent. Eyebrows slightly lighter than surrounding plumage, but generally not very prominent. Ear-tufts short and pointed, prominent when erected. Bristles at base of bill blackish. Crown and upperparts brownish-grey with blackish shaft-streaks and fine vermiculations; scapulars with whitish outer webs, edged black, forming a line of white spots across shoulder. Flight feathers boldly barred light and dark. Tail less distinctly barred. Underparts lighter than upperparts, with blackish shaft-streaks and irregular lateral branches; upper breast with some very broad shaft-streaks resembling black spots. Tarsi feathered to base of toes, the latter bristled and partly feathered. Talons relatively powerful. *Red morph*: Similar in pattern, but with a more rufescent-brown general coloration, though never as foxy-red as in Eastern Screech Owl. **Juvenile** Downy chicks are whitish. Mesoptile densely barred on head, mantle and underparts. **Bare parts** Eyes bright yellow, edges of eyelids black. Bill and cere blackish. Toes greyish-brown. Claws blackish-horn.

MEASUREMENTS AND WEIGHT Total length 21.5-24cm. Wing 136-193mm (females larger than males); tail 72-104mm. Weight of males 88-178g, of females 92-215g.

GEOGRAPHICAL VARIATION Several races have been described, but some of these may represent only individual variation, as the species is rather polymorphic (as most *Otus*). We recognise eight subspecies, even if the taxonomic status of some may be doubtful.

O. k. kennicottii (Elliot, 1867). S Alaska and NW Canada to coastal N California. See Description. Wing averages around 174mm.

O. k. bendirei (Brewster, 1882). Idaho, Montana, Washington and Oregon. Wing of males about 184mm, of females 189-193mm; tail 76-90mm.

O. k. aikeni (Brewster, 1891). SW USA to N Mexico. The palest grey subspecies. Wing 144-165mm; tail 73-85mm.

O. k. yumanensis Miller & Miller, 1951. S USA, Baja California, and C Mexico. Pale pinkish-grey. Wing 149mm.

O. k. cardonensis Huey, 1926. S California and Pacific slope of Baja California. General coloration rather dark, with a 'salt-and-pepper' pattern above; vermiculations and bars denser than in other subspecies. Wing 145-152mm; tail 72-80mm.

O. k. xanthusi (Brewster, 1902). S Baja California. A small and pale race. Wing 144-149mm.

O. k. vinaceus (Brewster, 1888). Mexico. Grey plumage with vinaceous wash (red-wine colour); fine ventral bars in form of wavy rows of wine-coloured dots. Wing 136-154mm.

O. k. suttoni Moore, 1944. Texas to Mexican Plateau. Darkest subspecies. Wing 152-168mm.

HABITS A nocturnal bird, normally not shy. Activity generally begins 20-30 minutes after sunset, at which time both types of song may be heard. The male leaves its daytime roost close to a trunk or in dense foliage and flies around in the territory, perching at several stations to sing or from which to hunt. Flight is noiseless, with soft wing-beats and gliding. When disturbed at the roost, it becomes motionless, as if mesmerised, and may sometimes be caught by hand. When alarmed, the owl assumes a concealment posture, upright and with the feathers held very tight, the ear-tufts erected and the eyes closed to thin slits; the usual outline is thereby distorted, perhaps in order to avoid being mobbed by diurnal birds. On the other hand, the birds are very aggressive when the nest site is approached, and may even attack humans by swooping over their head, sometimes scratching it with their claws. Utters bill-snapping or aggressive calls in such situations.

FOOD Mainly insects and other arthropods, but also small vertebrates such as small mammals, birds, frogs and reptiles. The prey may sometimes be larger than the owl itself. During the cold months of the year, prey consists of small mammals and birds; these are stored at several different cavities in which the owls roost by day, or where they shelter during poor weather on winter nights. The owls accumulate much fat in autumn, to provide energy reserves for winter. Food is caught by swooping from a perch, gripping it with the powerful talons or with the bill. Bats or flying squirrels are often caught on the wing.

BREEDING In late February, even earlier in the very south, the male begins to sing at dusk, moving around its territory and singing from different perches; during this period it may be easily attracted by playback of the song. At about the same time the female appears in the male's territory. She also sings, and finally the pair duet near the future nest site. The male courts the female by running up and down a branch, crouching and uttering rasping calls; normally, copulation follows such displays. Some weeks later, the female selects one of the winter roosting cavities, which the male has previously advertised. A natural hole in an aged tree, an abandoned woodpecker hole or a nestbox may serve as nest site.

The 3-7 pure white eggs, measuring 38 x 32mm, are laid directly on to the bottom of the cavity, normally at intervals of 2 days. The female incubates alone, beginning with the first egg, and is fed my her mate, who brings food to the nest. Incubation lasts 26 days. The young hatch asynchronously, according to sequence of laying, and are brooded and fed by the female. When brooding is no longer necessary, both parents feed the young, which leave the nest at an age of 4 weeks. They are cared for and fed by the parents for a further 5-6 weeks, before they become independent.

STATUS AND CONSERVATION This species is locally rather common, or at least frequent, throughout its range. Like the Eastern Screech Owl, it accepts nestboxes, and may therefore be encouraged to breed in areas with few natural holes. As an insect-eater, or preying on rodents, it is adversely affected by the use of pesticides.

REMARKS The Western Screech Owl is in need of a taxonomic revision with respect to the large number of described subspecies. We suspect that most of these are merely morphs or even individual variations, being described from only few specimens. This is one of the cases discussed critically in the chapter on taxonomy in the introductory section of this book.

REFERENCES Boyer & Hume (1991), Burton (1992), Dunning (1993), Hardy *et al.* (1989), Hekstra (1982), Howell & Webb (1995), Marshall (1967), Marshall & King (1988), Voous (1988).

---

61   EASTERN SCREECH OWL
Otus asio   Plate 17

Syn: *Megascops asio*

French: Scops d'Amérique
German: Ost-Kreischeule
Spanish: Tecolote Oriental

IDENTIFICATION Very similar to Western Screech Owl [60], but with a greenish-olive bill. A foxy-red morph is very frequent. Facial disc more prominently rimmed dark, especially on the lower half of both sides. Eyes yellow; talons relatively large, with bristled and partly feathered toes. **Similar species** Western Screech Owl has a blackish bill, and its red morph is rare and never as foxy-coloured as in Eastern Screech Owl. Flammulated Scops Owl [36] is much smaller, with dark brown eyes, has rufous markings in the greyish-brown plumage, and lives at higher altitudes. Balsas Screech Owl [66] is larger and has brown eyes. Oaxaca Screech Owl [62] is similar to Eastern Screech Owl, but has bare (not bristled) toes and is endemic to Oaxaca in Mexico. Whiskered Screech Owl [64] is smaller, with coarsely streaked underparts and much smaller talons. All are best distinguished by voice.

VOCALISATIONS The A-song of the male is a quavering, toad-like trill of 3-5 seconds' duration, repeated after some seconds. It is a rapid sequence of staccato notes, slightly accelerating and ending abruptly: *gurrrrrrrrrrrrt*. The female has a similar but higher pitched A-song. The B-song is a horse-like 'whinny', uttered also by the female in duet with the male during courtship. When playing back this species' songs in its territory, mostly the B-song is uttered by the male in order to chase off the apparent intruder. Both A- and B-songs may be given in duets. Young emit hissing or scratching sounds when begging for food.

DISTRIBUTION E North America from E Montana and the Great Lakes to the Gulf of Mexico south to Tamaulipas in NE Mexico, and from S Ontario to Florida. Overlaps in distribution with Western Screech Owl near the USA/Mexico border at the 'Big Bend' of Rio Grande.

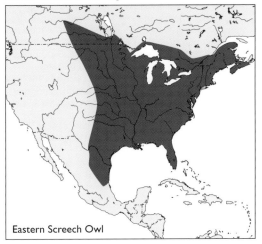

Eastern Screech Owl

MOVEMENTS Most populations are sedentary. Some northernmost birds may move a little southward in severe winters.

HABITAT Open deciduous and riparian woodland, sub-urban gardens and parks.

DESCRIPTION *O. a. asio* Adult A greyish-brown, a grey and a red morph may be distinguished, and intermediates also occur; red morph is most common in the south, while the two other morphs predominate in the northern parts of the range. *Greyish-brown morph:* Facial disc pale greyish-brown, finely mottled or vermiculated darker; rim around disc blackish, most prominent on basal half of both sides. Eyebrows paler than surrounding plumage. Ear-tufts short, prominent when erected. Whiskers at base of bill light greyish-brown. Upperparts greyish-brown, with blackish shaft-streaks and fine transverse bars or vermiculations. Crown like back, with blackish shaft-streaks and fine, dark vermiculations. Scapulars with blackish-edged whitish outer webs, forming line of white spots across shoulder. Flight feathers barred light and dark, but less prominently than on Western Screech Owl. Tail greyish-brown, mottled and vermiculated dark, with several thin light bars. Underparts less coarsely marked than on Western Screech Owl. Tarsi feathered to base of toes, the latter partly feathered and bristled. *Grey and red morphs:* Similar in

253

pattern, but general coloration grey or foxy-red respectively. **Juvenile** Downy chick whitish. Mesoptile similar to adult in coloration, but indistinctly barred light and dark on head, mantle and underparts. **Bare parts** Eyes bright yellow, edges of eyelids blackish-brown. Bill and cere greenish-olive. Toes greyish-brown. Claws dark horn.

MEASUREMENTS AND WEIGHT Total length 20-23cm. Wing 145-177mm; tail 72.5-91mm. Weight of males 100-210g, of females 150-235g.

GEOGRAPHICAL VARIATION As with Western Screech Owl, many subspecies have been described, many of them probably representing only intermediates between the three morphs or individual variation. We therefore treat only six subspecies.

O. a. asio (Linnaeus, 1758). S Carolina, Georgia, Virginia, Oklahoma. See Description. Wing 162-172mm.

O. a. maxwelliae (Ridgway, 1877). N USA, west of the Great Lakes. Bill greenish-yellow. Above, pale grey or buffy-grey; below, general coloration whitish. Red morph very pale. Wing 168-174mm; tail 76-100mm.

O. a. naevius (Gmelin, 1788). SE Canada to NE USA. Largest subspecies, with much white below, especially on abdomen. Wing 154-177mm; tail 68-83mm.

O. a. floridanus (Ridgway, 1873). Florida and Gulf coast to Louisiana. Red morph predominant. Underparts more rufescent than whitish; upperparts dark rusty-brown. Wing 145-156mm.

O. a. hasbroucki Ridgway, 1914. Oklahoma to Texas. Underparts with broad lateral markings. One specimen: wing 165mm; tail 80mm.

O. a. mccalli (Cassin, 1854). S Texas to NE Mexico. Grey morph much more mottled dark above than other races. Red morph paler than in nominate race. Wing 146-160mm; tail 72-80mm.

HABITS A nocturnal bird which roosts during daytime in holes in trees, in nestboxes, close to tree trunks or in dense foliage. Activity begins after sunset. Habits similar to those of Western Screech Owl.

FOOD Insects and other arthropods, small mammals (including bats and flying squirrels), birds, and other small vertebrates. Hunting behaviour similar to that of Western Screech Owl.

BREEDING Natural holes in trees, and nestboxes, are used as nesting sites. Like its western counterpart, it shows a tendency to breed in contact with neighbours; 'groups' of several pairs may be found, with the nests rather close to one another, while adjacent areas are not occupied, even if the habitats are practically identical. The 3-7 pure white eggs, averaging 35.5 x 30mm, are laid directly on to the bottom of the cavity and incubated by the female alone; during incubation, about 26 days, she is fed by the male. Breeding biology similar to that of Western Screech Owl. Young fledge at about 4 weeks of age.

STATUS AND CONSERVATION Widespread and locally common, although many are killed by cars when hunting near roads. Adversely affected by the use of pesticides. As some other owls, this species may be helped by the provision of nestboxes.

REMARKS Eastern and the Western Screech Owls were long considered conspecific. Although indeed rather closely related, they are without doubt separate species;

interbreeding may occur where their distributions overlap, but there are no areas of hybrid populations. (Occasional hybridisation may occur in many bird species, and is no sign of conspecificity.) In general, subspecies of birds intergrade gradually from one to the other at the borders of their distribution. As vocalisations are the most important interspecific isolating mechanisms in owls, the different vocal patterns of the two taxa are a clear reason for regarding them as distinct species, this being fully supported by DNA evidence. Nevertheless, comparative studies on ecology, behaviour and biology should be undertaken in order to detect differences between these two related species; since they have long been treated as a single species in the literature, and observations have not differentiated between them, we cannot specify any biological differences between Eastern and Western Screech Owls.

REFERENCES Boyer & Hume (1991), Burton (1992), Dunning (1993), Eck & Busse (1973), Howell & Webb (1995), Marshall (1967), Marshall & King (1988), Voous (1988).

---

62 OAXACA SCREECH OWL
Otus lambi   Plate 18

Syn: *Megascops lambi*

French: Scops d'Oaxaca
German: Oaxaca-Kreischeule
Spanish: Tecolote de Oaxaca

IDENTIFICATION Similar to Eastern Screech Owl [61] in size and coloration, but above and below more intensively vinaceous, upperparts much darker, and toes softly bristled instead of partly feathered. Wings relatively rounded owing to reduced outer six primaries. Bill olive-green to brown, with yellowish tip; eyes yellow. **Similar species** Eastern Screech Owl is distributed south to NE Mexico (Tamaulipas), and is not found on the Pacific side of SW Mexico (Oaxaca); its toes are more feathered than bristled. Western Screech Owl [60] has a blackish bill, and is distributed much farther north. Flammulated Scops Owl [36] has brown eyes and is much smaller; it is a bird of higher elevations. Balsas Screech Owl [66] is much larger, with brown eyes, and occurs only in the Río Balsas Valley of SW Mexico. Whiskered Screech Owl [64] is smaller and more coarsely streaked below. Guatemalan Screech Owl [82] has bare toes. All are best distinguished by voice.

VOCALISATIONS A gruff, somewhat guttural, grunting trill followed by a staccato, *croarrr-gogogogogogok*, represents probably the A-song, while the B-song seems to be a 'whinny' similar to that of Eastern Screech Owl. The female's songs are similar, but higher in pitch. Vocal patterns little studied.

DISTRIBUTION Endemic to the Pacific slope of Oaxaca in SW Mexico.

MOVEMENTS Unknown; probably resident, as the rounded wings suggest.

HABITAT Thorn wood with candelabra cacti and palms, often surrounding coastal swamps with mangroves. Found from sea-level up to about 1,000m.

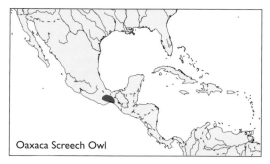

Oaxaca Screech Owl

DESCRIPTION Adult Facial disc greyish, with rather conspicuous dark rim. Upperparts similar in pattern to Balsas Screech Owl, but more intensively vinaceous than latter. Crown dark, contrasting with frosty areas around face and hindneck. Underparts with strong vinaceous wash and herringbone-like patterns on single feathers, mixed with suffused vermiculations. Tarsi feathered to base of toes, the latter softly bristled (not feathered). **Juvenile** Not described. **Bare parts** Eyes yellow. Bill and cere olive-green to brownish-olive, bill with yellowish tip. Toes pale greyish-brown. Claws dark horn with blackish tips.

MEASUREMENTS AND WEIGHT Total length about 20cm. Wing 148-166mm; tail about half wing length. Weight around 125g.

GEOGRAPHICAL VARIATION Monotypic: *Otus lambi* Moore & Marshall, 1959.

HABITS Nocturnal and crepuscular. Habits similar to those of other screech owls.

FOOD As that of most screech owls.

BREEDING Unknown. Probably nests in holes in trees.

STATUS AND CONSERVATION Uncertain.

REMARKS Has been described as a race of Eastern Screech Owl. The latter is distributed east of the Rocky Mountains and reaches its southernmost point in SE Mexico, while Oaxaca Screech Owl occurs on the Pacific slope (where it lives more than 1600 km south of the southernmost race of Western Screech Owl), and between the two another species is found, the much larger and heavier Balsas Screech Owl, which has brown eyes. On the basis of distribution, and also because of its plumage pattern, we suggest that *Otus lambi* be treated as a distinct species, which perhaps became separated from Eastern Screech Owl in the Pleistocene. Although their similar vocalisations indicate that in former times the two may have been conspecific, they should now be regarded as allospecies, as they no longer have any contact with each other; in such circumstances (two species with allopatric distribution) there is no need for voice patterns to change, and therefore similarity in voice does not point to conspecificity (there are several similar examples where taxonomic status has been demonstrated by DNA evidence, and not only among owls). Despite this, a taxonomic revision of this group of screech owls will require extensive research to clarify the exact status of this taxon.

REFERENCES Hardy *et al.* (1989), Hekstra (1982), Moore & Marshall (1959).

63 PACIFIC SCREECH OWL
Otus cooperi   Plate 18

Syn: *Megascops cooperi*

French: Scops de Cooper
German: Mangroven-Kreischeule
Spanish: Tecolote de Cooper

IDENTIFICATION A medium-sized to relatively large screech owl (about 24cm) with crown and prominent ear-tufts barred blackish and facial disc distinctly rimmed dark. Talons relatively powerful; toes covered with stiff bristles; eyes yellow. **Similar species** Eastern and Western Screech Owls [61, 60] have partly feathered toes and no barring on crown and ear-tufts. Balsas Screech Owl [66] is more heavily built and has brown eyes. Oaxaca Screech Owl [62] is smaller and has a dark (not barred) crown. Flammulated Scops Owl [36] is a much smaller highland bird with brown eyes. Whiskered Screech Owl [64] is much smaller, with weak talons and a dark-streaked crown, and is a bird of mountain forest.

VOCALISATIONS A series of relatively deep hoots beginning in a rapid, trilled sequence, becoming more accentuated and slower towards the middle of the strophe and maintaining an evenly spaced staccato to the end. These series are repeated at intervals of several seconds and are probably the B-song, which is uttered in a similar but higher-pitched manner by the female, particularly when duetting: *gurrrgogogogogo*. The A-song has not been described. A single low, gruff *woof*, uttered by both sexes, may be a contact-call.

DISTRIBUTION Southern Pacific slope of Mexico (SW Oaxaca and Chiapas) to Costa Rica.

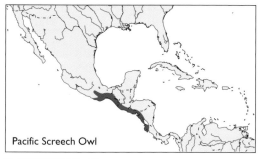

Pacific Screech Owl

MOVEMENTS Resident.

HABITAT Arid to semi-arid woodland, semi-open landscapes with scattered trees, giant cacti, palms and shrubs, also swampy forest and mangroves. Lowlands up to 330m.

DESCRIPTION Adult No red morph is known. Facial disc pale greyish with fine darker vermiculations; rim around disc blackish. Small ear-tufts barred blackish. Upperparts relatively pale greyish-brown with dark mottling and streaks, feathers of crown with fine dark shaft-streaks and rather coarse dark barring. Scapulars with blackish-edged whitish outer webs, forming a white band across shoulder. Wing-coverts edged whitish, producing second light band across closed wing. Primaries prominently barred light and dark; secondaries and tail feathers less distinctly barred. Underparts slightly lighter than upperparts, with thin blackish shaft-streaks and dark vermiculations. Tarsi feathered to base of toes, the latter covered with stiff bristles. Talons relatively powerful. **Juvenile** Probably similar to other screech owls. **Bare parts** Eyes yellow. Cere and bill greenish. Toes brownish-flesh. Claws dark horn with darker tips.

MEASUREMENTS AND WEIGHT Total length 23-25.5cm. Wing 162-178mm; tail 74-84mm. Weight 145-153g.

GEOGRAPHICAL VARIATION Monotypic: *Otus cooperi* (Ridgway, 1878). We distinguish no geographical subspecies, but treat the form '*chiapensis*' as a slightly browner variant.

HABITS A little-known bird. Habits are probably similar to those of other screech owls.

FOOD Apparently mostly insects and other arthropods, but the powerful talons suggest that small vertebrates are also taken as prey.

BREEDING Similar to that of other screech owls. The pure white eggs are laid in holes in trees.

STATUS AND CONSERVATION Uncertain. Studies are needed.

REMARKS The taxonomic status requires clarification. This owl appears to be a valid species, and not a subspecies of Western Screech Owl. The vocalisations are quite different, and some other factors support its status as a separate species. Modern molecular-biological studies should help to clarify the relationships of this little-known owl.

REFERENCES Boyer & Hume (1991), Dunning (1993), Hardy *et al.* (1989), Howell & Webb (1995), Marshall & King (1988).

---

64 WHISKERED SCREECH OWL
Otus trichopsis   Plate 18

Syn: *Megascops trichopsis*

French: Scops tacheté
German: Flecken-Kreischeule
Spanish: Tecolote bigotudo

IDENTIFICATION A small screech owl (about 18cm) occurring in a grey and a red morph, with very small, often invisible ear-tufts and yellow eyes. Bill dark grey, with rather prominent long whiskers around the base; feet relatively small, with bristled toes. A bird of upland forest. **Similar species** Flammulated Scops Owl [36] is about the same size, but has brown eyes and has 'flammulated' pattern in plumage. Bearded Screech Owl [65] is also a bird of mountains, but has bare pinkish toes and coarsely scalloped underparts. Other screech owls occurring within the region are larger. In addition, all differ in voice.

VOCALISATIONS The A-song is a series of hoots, similar to the song of Tengmalm's Owl [178]: an equally spaced *bububúbububub*, mostly with emphasis on third note, slightly falling in pitch at the end. The B-song is a hollow hooting, often uttered in duet with the female: *buru-bububup, buru-bububup,...* (like morse-code signal). The female's voice is slightly higher in pitch.

DISTRIBUTION From SE Arizona through Mexico to Nicaragua.

Whiskered Screech Owl

MOVEMENTS Resident.

HABITAT Mountain forest (pine-oak woodland) from about 750m to 2,500m, mostly above 1,600m. Locally, it may be found together with Flammulated Scops Owl and Western Screech Owl in the same habitat.

DESCRIPTION *O. t. trichopsis* **Adult** A grey and a red morph may be distinguished, the latter more in the south. *Grey morph*: Facial disc light greyish, with indistinct darker concentric lines around eyes; rim prominent blackish. Ear-tufts short, prominent only when erected. Long, markedly wispy whiskers at base of bill. Upperparts greyish to brownish-grey with blackish shaft-streaks and dark horizontal branches, also with fine vermiculations. Crown like back, with broad blackish shaft-streaks and dark vermiculations. Scapulars with blackish-edged white outer webs, forming a white line across shoulder. Wings and tail feathers barred light and dark. Underparts lighter than upperparts, rather densely vermiculated and with broad blackish shaft-streaks, especially on upper breast. Tarsi feathered to base of toes, the latter bristled. Talons relatively weak. *Red morph*: Similarly but less prominently patterned, but with general coloration rufous. **Juvenile** Similar to other screech owls. **Bare parts** Eyes relatively large, yellow. Cere and bill darker grey. Toes greyish-brown. Claws greyish-horn with darker tips.

MEASUREMENTS AND WEIGHT Total length 16.5-19cm. Wing 139-160mm; tail 71-91mm. Weight of males 70-104g. of females 79-121g.

GEOGRAPHICAL VARIATION We recognise three subspecies.
    O. t. trichopsis (Wagler, 1832). Highlands of C Mexico. See Description. Wing 145-160mm.
    O. t. aspersus (Brewster, 1888). Arizona to N Mexico. No red morph. Wing mean 144mm; tail mean 70mm.
    O. t. mesamericanus van Rossem, 1932. S Mexico to Honduras and Nicaragua. Wing 139-154mm.

HABITS A nocturnal bird which hides during daytime close to a tree trunk or in dense foliage. At dusk it becomes active, and the male starts singing. At the beginning of the breeding season, male and female may be heard duetting near the potential nesting site. Territory is defended throughout the year, and male may be very aggressive towards intruders. Playback of songs may stimulate males or females to sing, and to approach close to the imaginary rival.

FOOD Mainly insects and other arthropods, such as grasshoppers, locusts, praying mantises, crickets, beetles, moths, spiders, as well as caterpillars (even hairy ones). In addition, occasionally takes small vertebrates. Hunts insects by foraging between branches, less frequently from a perch.

BREEDING A natural cavity is used for breeding, mostly an abandoned woodpecker hole in a tree. Lays 3-4 white eggs, average 33 x 27.6mm. Female alone incubates, during which she is fed by her mate. When the young hatch, the male also brings food to the nest, while the female shares in catching prey for the nestlings. The breeding biology is little studied.

STATUS AND CONSERVATION Locally frequent, but further studies are needed.

REMARKS As with many owls, the biology of the Whiskered Screech Owl is only poorly known.

REFERENCES Boyer & Hume (1991), Dunning (1993), Hardy *et al.* (1989), Howell & Webb (1995), Marshall (1967), Marshall & King (1988), Voous (1988).

65　BEARDED SCREECH OWL
Otus barbarus　　　　　　　Plate 18

Syn: *Megascops barbarus*

Other names: Santa Barbara or Bridled Screech Owl

French: Scops à moustache
German: Tropfen-Kreischeule
Spanish: Tecolote barbudo

IDENTIFICATION A small (about 18cm), relatively dark screech owl with yellow eyes, very short (often nearly invisible) ear-tufts and a striking, scalloped pattern on the underparts. Eyebrows whitish and bill greenish. Toes naked and bright pinkish. The wings project beyond the short tail. **Similar species** Whiskered Screech Owl [64] has bristled, greyish-brown toes and a grey bill, lacks the scalloped pattern below, and its wingtips do not project beyond the tail. Other screech owls occurring in the same region are larger. All are best separated by voice.

VOCALISATIONS The A-song of the male is a rapid, somewhat cricket-like, strident trill, increasing in volume and breaking off rather abruptly: *teerrrrrrrrrrrt*. The duration of each phrase is 3-5 seconds, and these are repeated at intervals of several seconds. The female has a similar but slightly higher-pitched song. The B-song is unknown. A series of single, soft *dewd* calls is often uttered by the female, when the male announces his arrival with song.

DISTRIBUTION Highlands south of the Mexican isthmus, from Chiapas (Mexico) to C Guatemala.

MOVEMENTS Resident.

HABITAT Humid pine-oak forest in the highlands, mostly between 1,800m and 2,500m.

DESCRIPTION Adult Grey and red morphs occur. *Grey morph:* Facial disc pale greyish-brown, with darker concentric lines around eyes; rim of disc dark brown or blackish brown. Eyebrows whitish, speckled greyish-brown. Ear-tufts very small, often not visible. Upperparts dark greyish-brown with whitish and buffy spots, as well as darker markings. Crown dark greyish-brown with rounded whitish

and buffy dots. Scapulars with blackish-edged whitish outer webs, forming a whitish line across shoulder. Wings barred light and dark, relatively long, protruding far beyond tip of relatively short tail, which is barred light on a dark ground. Underparts pale greyish-brown to dirty whitish, individual feathers with dark shaft-streaks and irregular lateral branches; on upper breast, the basal parts of individual feathers have a rounded white spot on each side of the central streak, giving 'ocellated' appearance. Tarsi feathered to base of toes, latter naked. *Red morph:* Less clearly marked, with patterns more suffused on a reddish general coloration. **Juvenile** Not described. **Bare parts** Eyes yellow. Bill and cere greenish. Toes bright pinkish. Claws horn with darker tips.

Bearded Screech Owl

MEASUREMENTS AND WEIGHT Total length 16.5-19cm. Wing 126-144mm; tail 63.5-76mm. Weight about 69g.

GEOGRAPHICAL VARIATION Monotypic: *Otus barbarus* (Sclater & Salvin, 1868).

HABITS Nocturnal. Habits probably similar to those of other screech owls. Elusive.

FOOD Probably mainly insects and other arthropods.

BREEDING Probably nests in cavities in trees (woodpecker holes, etc). Nest and eggs apparently undescribed.

STATUS AND CONSERVATION Uncertain, but probably rare and likely to be endangered.

REMARKS The Bearded Screech Owl is a little-known species. Its biology and ecology require extensive study.

REFERENCES Boyer & Hume (1991), Dunning (1993), Hardy *et al.* (1989), Howell & Webb (1995), Marshall & King (1988).

66　BALSAS SCREECH OWL
Otus seductus　　　　　　　Plate 18

Syn: *Megascops seductus*

French: Scops du Balsas
German: Balsas-Kreischeule
Spanish: Tecolote del Balsas

IDENTIFICATION A relatively large (about 25cm), greyish-brown screech owl with short ear-tufts, brown eyes, and powerful talons with large, bristled toes. Bill greenish. No red morph is known. **Similar species** Western Screech Owl [60] and Oaxaca Screech Owl [62] are smaller and have yellow eyes, as also have Guatemalan and Whiskered Screech Owls [82, 64]. Flammulated Scops Owl [36] and

Bearded Screech Owl [65] are much smaller, and are highland birds. All are best distinguished by voice.

VOCALISATIONS A rather loud series of gruff notes accelerating to a trill ('bouncing-ball' rhythm), *bookh-bookh-bokbokbobobobrrrrr*, we judge to be the A-song of the male. This series is repeated after some seconds. The female has a similar song, but slightly higher in pitch. Both sexes utter another song (B-song?), which consists of a series of gruff, screaming 'whinnying' sounds.

DISTRIBUTION SW Mexico, from the lowlands of S Jalisco and Colima to Río Balsas drainage of Michoacán and C Guerrero.

Balsas Screech Owl

MOVEMENTS Resident.

HABITAT Arid semi-open to open areas with scattered trees and shrubs, and thorn woodland, from about 600m to 1,500m.

DESCRIPTION Adult No red morph known. Facial disc greyish-brown, mottled and vermiculated brownish; rim around disc blackish-brown, edged pale. Eyebrows not very prominent, and ear-tufts short. Crown greyish-brown with blackish-brown shaft-streaks, some whitish spots and brown vermiculations. Above, greyish-brown overlaid with vinaceous-pink, with dark streaks and vermiculations; scapulars with whitish outer webs, forming a whitish band across shoulder; wing-coverts tipped whitish, creating light second band on closed wing. Flight and tail feathers barred light and dark. Underparts lighter than upperparts, with rather thin dark shaft-streaks and faint vermiculations; upper breast with several broad dark brown or deep chestnut shaft-streaks, giving neck and upper breast an irregularly spotted appearance. Tarsi feathered to base of toes, the latter strongly bristled. **Juvenile** Not described, but probably similar to other screech owls. **Bare parts** Eyes tobacco-brown to (rarely) golden-brown. Bill and cere greenish. Toes large, greyish-brown. Claws horn with darker tips.

MEASUREMENTS AND WEIGHT Total length 24-26.5cm. Wing 169.5-182mm; tail 89.5-95.5mm. Weight 158-165g.

GEOGRAPHICAL VARIATION Monotypic: *Otus seductus* Moore, 1941.

HABITS Probably as those of other screech owls.

FOOD Insects and other arthropods, but also small vertebrates.

BREEDING Probably breeds in holes in trees (e.g. woodpecker holes). The eggs are white.

STATUS AND CONSERVATION Uncertain.

REMARKS The Balsas Screech Owl is often considered a race of Western Screech Owl, but it is much larger (in

particular, much heavier) than its northern counterpart and has brown eyes. In addition, the voice is different. We treat it as full species, as suggested by vocal patterns. This owl is poorly known, and there is very little information on its ecology, biology, habits and bioacoustics. Studies are therefore needed in order to make comparisons with other related taxa in Mexico and Central America.

REFERENCES Dunning (1993), Hardy *et al.* (1989), Hekstra (1982), Howell & Webb (1995), Marshall & King (1988).

67 BARE-SHANKED SCREECH OWL
Otus clarkii   Plate 18

Syn: *Megascops clarkii*

French: Scops de Clark
German: Nacktbein-Kreischeule
Spanish: Tecolote de Clark, Lechucita Serranera

IDENTIFICATION A relatively large screech owl (about 24cm) with an obviously large head, small ear-tufts, and bare distal third of tarsi. Underparts with broken dark streaks and bars and whitish, rather square dots on each side of the shaft-streaks, giving a scalloped or rather 'ocellated' appearance. Toes naked; eyes pale yellow. **Similar species** All other *Otus* species occurring within the same range have the tarsi feathered to the base of the toes. Vocalisations are also specific.

VOCALISATIONS The A-song of the male is a relatively deep, trisyllabic *woohg-woohg-woohg*, repeated at intervals of several seconds. The B-song is a rhythmical *bubu booh-booh-booh*, with emphasis on the third and fourth notes, the latter sometimes slightly higher in pitch; this verse is repeated at intervals of several seconds, often in duet with the partner. The female's songs are slightly higher in pitch. Fast toots in groups of three, given in flight, seem to have an aggressive quality. The vocalisations are little studied.

DISTRIBUTION Locally from Costa Rica to Panama and extreme NW Colombia.

Bare-shanked Screech Owl

MOVEMENTS Resident.

HABITAT Montane cloud forest from about 900m to 2,350m, where it prefers dense forest and forest edge, but may also be found in thinned woodland.

DESCRIPTION Adult Facial disc cinnamon to tawny-brown, indistinctly rimmed dark. Ear-tufts short. (Head appears rather large compared with body.) Upperparts rich brown to dull rufous, heavily spotted, vermiculated and mottled with black; hindneck buffy; scapulars with blackish-edged white outer webs, forming a white band across shoulder. Flight feathers barred with cinnamon-buff; tail barred light and dark. Underparts pale brown with buffy or cinnamon tinge, mixed with white on chest; shaft-streaks blackish, with dusky and rufous horizontal bars or vermiculations; from lower breast to belly, large squarish-shaped white dots at each side of the central streak on most feathers, giving 'ocellated' appearance (similar to the much smaller Bearded Screech Owl); thighs mostly buff. Lower third of tarsi bare, as are toes. **Juvenile** Downy chick whitish. Young at fledging cinnamon-buff above, speckled with white and barred with dusky; buffy below, barred with dull cinnamon; no ear-tufts visible. **Bare parts** Eyes pale yellow. Bill greenish- or bluish-grey. Cere horn. Bare parts of tarsi and toes horn to flesh-coloured. Claws dark horn with darker tips.

MEASUREMENTS AND WEIGHT Total length 23-25cm. Wing 176-190mm; tail 86-99mm. Weight 123-186g.

GEOGRAPHICAL VARIATION Monotypic: *Otus clarkii* Kelso & Kelso, 1935.

HABITS Little known. A nocturnal bird, roosting by day in trees with dense foliage or a thick cover of epiphytes. It hunts at dusk and during the night at forest edges, in clearings and occasionally in canopy. Song is normally delivered from high in trees; like most owls, it may be stimulated to sing or even to approach by playback of its song. This owl shows a tendency to be social: quite often groups of 'family size' are found fairly close together, even during breeding season.

FOOD Prey includes large insects, such as beetles and orthopterans, as well as spiders, shrews, small rodents and probably other small terrestrial vertebrates. These are normally taken from the ground or from branches by seizing them with the talons.

BREEDING Probably breeds in natural cavities in trees (knotholes) or in holes made by woodpeckers. Egg-laying occurs from February to May. Fledged young have been seen from May to August. The reproductive biology requires study.

STATUS AND CONSERVATION Uncertain; in general apparently rare, but locally frequent. Threatened by the destruction of dense cloud forest.

REMARKS A little-known owl with a rather restricted distribution. Studies are required on its ecology and biology, in particular with respect to identifying protective measures.

REFERENCES Boyer & Hume (1991), Dunning (1993), Hardy *et al.* (1989), Hekstra (1982), Hilty & Brown (1986), Marshall & King (1988), Stiles & Skutch (1989).

---

68 TROPICAL SCREECH OWL
Otus choliba   Plate 19

Syn: *Megascops choliba*

French: Scops de Choliba
German: Choliba-Kreischeule
Spanish: Alicuco común
Portuguese: Corujinha-do-mato

IDENTIFICATION A relatively small screech owl (about 22cm) with short ear-tufts and yellow eyes. When relaxed, with plumage held loose, the small ear-tufts are often invisible. Combination of dark herringbone-like pattern below (each feather with narrow shaft-streak with 4-5 thin lateral branches on whitish grey-brown or pale rufescent ground) and lack of whitish fringe on hindneck is highly characteristic of the species. Polymrphic: occurs in grey, brown and red morphs, with intermediates. **Similar species** Both Black-capped and Long-tufted Screech Owls [78, 79] may occur sympatrically with Tropical Screech Owl: former is slightly larger, and has a dark, nearly uniform crown, longer ear-tufts, a whitish fringe surrounding hindneck, and less herringbone-like pattern below; Long-tufted is much larger and heavier, with longer ear-tufts. Montane Forest Screech Owl [71] inhabits montane cloud forest on eastern slopes of C Andes, where it may overlap locally with Tropical Screech Owl at lower and warmer elevations: it has short ear-tufts, a whitish fringe around hindneck, and a much coarser pattern below with many shaft-streaks spade-like in shape, and the eyes are yellow. All are best separated, however, by vocal patterns. Northern and Southern Tawny-bellied Screech Owls [76, 77] are darker, with amber-yellow or brown eyes, long ear-tufts and different songs. Cloud-forest and Cinnamon Screech Owls [73, 75] are rufescent-brown, with different plumage patterns and brown eyes, and normally live at higher altitudes. Guatemalan, Vermiculated and Rio Napo Screech Owls [82, 80, 83], as well as other similar species, lack Tropical Screech's very typical herringbone-like pattern on the underparts. Bare-shanked Screech Owl [67] has the lower part of the tarsi unfeathered. Note also that Tropical Screech Owl is the only Neotropical screech owl with such a characteristic song.

VOCALISATIONS The A-song is a short, purring trill, followed by two accentuated clear notes: *gurrrrku-kúk*. When excited (e.g. after playback), the final notes may be more numerous and uttered in 'stuttering' rhythm, *gurrrrku-kúk-gukúk-gugukoohk*. The female utters a similar song to the normal A-song of the male, but slightly higher-pitched, and sings less frequently. The B-song (given also by both sexes) is a bubbling *bububúbubu*, similar to the song of Tengmalm's Owl [178], and is often heard during courtship or when the birds begin to sing at dusk; it is frequently uttered as a prelude to the A-song, and is often given also in response to playback in an occupied territory. When alarmed, emits a hollow laughing *hahahaha hahaha hahaha...* on a descending scale. A soft *woog* seems to function as contact.

DISTRIBUTION From Costa Rica through Central America and large parts of South America east of the Andes, south to N Argentina and Uruguay, the southernmost limit of distribution being in the Argentine province of Buenos Aires. Also on Trinidad. Absent from W Ecuador, W Peru and Chile.

MOVEMENTS Not known.

HABITAT Open forest, savanna with scattered trees or small woods, farmland with woods and groups of trees, forest edges, clearings in rainforest, dry forest, open or semi-open country with thorny shrubs, urban parks, pastureland with scattered trees, riverine forest, and plantations. Avoids heavy and dense primary forest, as well as temperate cloud or mist forest. Prefers warm climates, and normally found below 1,500m; occurs locally at higher altitudes when the climate is adequate, and may then overlap in range with Montane Forest Screech Owl and some other species in areas of transistion between dry and montane forest ('bosques de transición').

Tropical Screech Owl

DESCRIPTION *O. c. choliba* **Adult** Markedly polymorphic: greyish-brown, brown and red morphs may be distinguished, the first of these in general the most common. *Greyish-brown morph*: Facial disc pale grey-brown, somewhat mottled; rim around disc very prominent, blackish. Eyebrows whitish, continuing towards ear-tufts, latter small and pointed. Upperparts greyish-brown with dark streaks and mottling. Crown as back and mantle, with blackish shaft-streaks; hindneck without whitish fringe. Scapulars with dark-edged whitish or pale ochre outer webs, forming a row of whitish or yellowish spots across shoulder. Primaries and secondaries barred light and dark. Tail feathers mottled, indistinctly barred. Underparts whitish-grey, individual feathers with herringbone-like pattern of dark, mostly relatively thin shaft-streak with 4-5 lateral branches. Tarsi feathered to base of toes. *Red and brown morphs*: In the red morph, the general coloration is rusty or cinnamon-buffish; in the brown morph, brownish colours predominate. **Juvenile** Downy chick whitish. Mesoptile feathering of half-grown young distinctly barred. **Bare parts** Eyes light yellow to golden-yellow. Bill and cere light greenish-grey. Toes grey. Claws dark horn with blackish tips.

MEASUREMENTS AND WEIGHT Total length 20.4-23cm; some females may be larger. Wing 148-180mm; tail 86-104mm; span of talons about 33mm. Weight 97-152g.

GEOGRAPHICAL VARIATION Since the species is polymorphic, many of the described subspecies may represent only morphs or individual variation; some previously described races are in fact separate species, and not at all closely related to *O. choliba* (e.g. the two following species). Of the many described taxa of Tropical Screech Owl, we recognise nine subspecies.

 O. c. choliba (Vieillot, 1817). S Mato Grosso, São Paulo (Brazil), south to E Paraguay. See Description. Wing 148-165mm; tail 86-104mm.
 O. c. luctisomus Bangs & Penard, 1921. Pacific slope of Costa Rica to canal zone of Panama, and Pearl Islands off NW Colombia. Wing 172-180mm; tail 88-95mm.
 O. c. margaritae Cory, 1915. N Colombia, N Venezuela and Margarita Island. Wing 161-168mm.
 O. c. crucigerus (Spix, 1824). E Colombia and E Peru

to NE Brazil, and Trinidad. Body-feathers with fluffy yellowish spots. Wing 165-174mm. (Form described as *O. c. portoricensis* is perhaps as synonym of rufous morph of *O. c. crucigerus*.)
 O. c. duidae Chapman, 1927. Mt Duida and Mt Neblina in S Venezuela. A very dark subspecies with rather uniform crown and a broken, whitish collar on hindneck (latter absent in other races). Perhaps specifically distinct endemic of Mt Duida, but comparative studies on vocalisations are lacking. Wing 155-167mm; tail (1 specimen) 82mm.
 O. c. decussatus (Lichtenstein, 1823). C and S Brazil. Smaller and lighter than *crucigerus*, with whitish spots on mantle. Wing 162-165mm.
 O. c. uruguaiensis Hekstra, 1982. SE Brazil (Santa Catarina, Rio Grande do Sul), NE Argentina and Uruguay. Shaft-streaks on underparts rather prominent; body-feathers with fluffy buffy-rufous marks. Wing 165-180mm.
 O. c. surutus L. Kelso, 1941. Bolivia. Wing 160-178mm.
 O. c. wetmorei Brodkorb, 1937. Chaco of Paraguay and Argentina, NW Argentina, south to Mendoza and N Buenos Aires. Wing 157-169mm. (*O. c. alilicuco* is a synonym of *wetmorei*).

HABITS A nocturnal bird which becomes active at dusk. By day it roosts in dense foliage of a tree or bush, often within a thorny shrub or in dense epiphytes on a trunk. Very often the male starts to sing from its daytime roost, uttering a few verses of the B-song, before flying to song perches, where it delivers the A-song. During courtship, males and females duet, and often roost together. Not normally shy, and can be observed at rather close range, but becomes relatively shy where persecuted by man. At night, it may be found perched in rows of trees or bushes along roads, or on telephone wires. As with other screech owls, the flight is noiseless, with rather soft wingbeats and gliding.

FOOD Primarily insects, such as moths, cicadas, grasshoppers, crickets, mantids and beetles, but also spiders and occasionally small vertebrates. Forages at lower levels of trees, as well as in bushes or on the ground. Hunts also from roadside trees or telephone wires, taking prey either on the ground or from branches.

BREEDING South of the equator, males normally begin to sing in August or early September; courtship is mostly in September; one male from Rio Grande do Sul had enlarged testes in early September, indicating sexual activity. Both sexes are vocally active during courtship. The male advertises potential nesting sites to the female by flying to them and singing from the entrance. Natural holes in trees, as well as holes made by woodpeckers, are used as nest site. The 1-3 white eggs, averaging 34.3 x 29.3mm, are laid directly on to the bottom of the cavity. On 24 October, a nest with eggs about to hatch was found in Misiones (Argentina), about 3m above ground in a dead trunk without canopy: the female alone incubated; the male carried food to the nest in his bill, delivering prey at the entrance or inside the hole, and when approaching the nest gave some low verses of A-song. Even though this owl is a rather common bird, little is known about its biology.

STATUS AND CONSERVATION A widespread and locally quite common owl, which is absent only in deserts, treeless regions, heavy montane forest and dense rainforest (except at forest edges and near clearings). As an insect-eater, it may be affected locally by the use of pesticides.

Because of its habit of frequently hunting along roadsides, many are killed annually by traffic.

REMARKS This owl apparently has no very close relatives in South America. The taxonomy of many forms described as subspecies needs clarification, and studies on the species' ecology, behaviour and biology are also required.

REFERENCES Belton (1985), Dunning (1993), Heidrich *et al.* (1994), Hekstra (1982), Hilty & Brown (1986), König (1994 and unpublished), Sick (1985), Stiles & Skutch (1991), Voous (1988).

69 MARIA KOEPCKE'S SCREECH OWL
Otus koepckeae Plate 19

Syn: *Megascops koepckeae*

French: Scops de Maria Koepcke
German: Koepcke-Kreischeule
Spanish: Urcututú de Koepcke

IDENTIFICATION A rather dark grey screech owl (about 24 cm) with prominent ear-tufts, a dark crown and virtually no whitish fringe around hindneck. Broadly streaked underparts without vermiculations. Eyes yellow. A bird of high-altitude wooded areas in W Andes of Peru. **Similar species** Peruvian Screech Owl [70] also has yellow eyes, but is smaller (about 20cm) and less coarsely patterned below, has a whitish fringe around the blackish crown and prominently whitish eyebrows, and is more a lowland bird; very similar but much smaller (about 17.5cm) is the form *pacificus* of Peruvian (Tumbes Screech Owl) of arid lowland areas of NW Peru. White-throated Screech Owl [85] lives at high altitudes, but is larger and generally darker, lacks ear-tufts, and has orange eyes and a white throat. Peruvian Pygmy Owl [158] is much smaller, with a relatively longer tail, a rounded head without ear-tufts, and yellow eyes.

VOCALISATIONS According to Maria Koepcke (*in litt.*), the song is a sequence of 8-10 low *uk* notes, slightly rising in pitch and with the last note falling. No other descriptions.

DISTRIBUTION High Andean slopes of N and NW Peru (e.g. Cordillera Blanca in Ancash, upper Marañón), south to the department of Lima (e.g. Bosque de Linday), perhaps farther south.

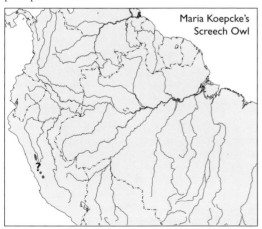

Maria Koepcke's Screech Owl

MOVEMENTS Unknown.

HABITAT Temperate or oligothermic woodland or patches of wood on Andean slopes above 2,500m and up to about 4,500m (*Polylepis* woodland).

DESCRIPTION Adult Facial disc whitish, speckled or mottled dark, becoming lighter towards outer edge; rim prominent, blackish. Eyebrows whitish, not very prominent. Ear-tufts relatively short, with dark shaft-streaks. Forehead and bristles around bill white. Crown blackish-brown with fine light brown speckling, becoming ochre-whitish towards forehead; hindcrown with only trace of a pale fringe, often hard to detect. Upperparts dark greyish-brown or brown with dark, relatively broad, laterally ill-defined shaft-streaks and dark transverse branches, and ochre to whitish spots; only little tendency towards vermiculation. Scapulars with blackish-edged whitish outer webs, forming line of whitish spots across shoulder. Flight feathers not very distinctly barred dark and light, primaries with uniform dark tips. Tail feathers dark brown with thin ochre bars and small speckles. Underparts greyish-white with broad blackish-brown shaft-streaks and few irregular lateral branches; sides of neck and upper breast washed with pale brownish-ochre. Tarsi feathered ochre with brown speckles to base of toes. **Juvenile** Not described. **Bare parts** Eyes yellow, with dark eyelids. Cere and bill bluish-horn, bill with lighter tip. Toes greyish-brown. Claws dark horn with darker tips.

MEASUREMENTS AND WEIGHT Total length around 24cm. Wing 172-177mm; tail 95-104mm. Weight 113-121g.

GEOGRAPHICAL VARIATION Monotypic: *Otus koepckeae* Hekstra, 1982. No different colour morphs are described, but individual variation is frequent.

HABITS A nocturnal bird, roosting during daytime in trees or bushes with dense twigs and foliage. Not shy. When disturbed during day, flies to a nearby roost offering more or less equivalent shelter. General behaviour and biology, however, practically unknown.

FOOD Probably mainly insects, as suggested by its small feet.

BREEDING Nothing known, but probably breeds in holes in trees or in other cavities, such as beneath fallen branches etc on the ground.

STATUS AND CONSERVATION Unknown, but probably not uncommon locally.

REMARKS Maria Koepcke, when first discovering this owl in the Cordillera Blanca, thought it to be a new, high-altitude race of Peruvian Screech Owl. After her death, the bird was described, quite erroneously, as a race of Tropical Screech Owl [68]. It has since been given specific rank. Its ecology, biology, behaviour and bioacoustics require extensive study, although this is difficult in the region of Peru in which it occurs.

REFERENCES Hekstra (1982), Koepcke (1964, manuscript and *in litt.*), Koepcke & Koepcke (1958), Marshall & King (1988).

70 PERUVIAN SCREECH OWL
Otus roboratus   Plate 19

O. (r.) roboratus
O. (r.) pacificus

Syn: *Megascops roboratus*

Other names: Tumbes Screech Owl (*O. (r.) pacificus*)

French: Scops du Pérou/Scops de Tumbes
German: Peru-Kreischeule/Tumbes-Kreischeule
Spanish: Urcututú occidental/Urcututú de Tumbes

IDENTIFICATION A medium-sized screech owl (about 20cm) occurring in both a grey and a red morph. Crown dark, surrounded by a whitish fringe from eyebrows to hindneck; underparts with rather thin shaft-streaks and irregular lateral branches. Eyes yellow. The lowland form *pacificus*, Tumbes Screech Owl, is much smaller (about 17.5cm) and shorter-tailed than the mountain form from the Bagua area of N Peru, and is probably specifically distinct. **Similar species** Maria Koepcke's Screech Owl [69] is larger, without (or with barely marked) whitish surround to dark crown, and with underparts much more coarsely patterned with relatively broad shaft-streaks; it lives at 2,500-4,600m in the W Peruvian Andes south to about Bosque de Linday in department of Lima, perhaps extending farther south. White-throated Screech Owl [85] is larger, without ear-tufts, and has orange eyes and a prominent white throat patch. Peruvian Pygmy Owl [158] is smaller, with no ear-tufts, and partly diurnal; it may occur locally together with Peruvian (including lowland Tumbes), Maria Koepcke's or White-throated Screech Owl, but is easily distinguished by its longer, distinctly barred tail.

VOCALISATIONS Little studied, and the vocalisations of the two taxa have in most cases been merged. The A-song is a purring trill of about 1.5-2 seconds in duration and with a slight downward inflection towards the end, and consists of a very rapid sequence of *u* notes, beginning softly and increasing in volume to a peak, then gently fading away: *kwurrrrrrr*. These trills are characteristic of the taxon *pacificus* and are repeated at intervals of several seconds; the mountain form utters longer trills with equally spaced notes and an 'undulating' quality in pitch. The B-songs likewise seem to differ. Explosive 'yelping' calls are uttered in aggressive situations: *pacificus* gives a *kew, kew,...* with downward inflection, and *roboratus* utters *kyui, kyui,...* with marked upward inflection.

DISTRIBUTION Coastal plains and Andean foothills of W Ecuador and NW Peru, south to the department of Lambayeque (*pacificus*). A separate population lives in the drainage of the rivers Chinchipe and Marañón between the W and C Andes in N Peru; north of the Marañón depression, the distribution reaches to the adjacent mountains of S Ecuador (*roboratus*).

MOVEMENTS Unknown; probably resident.

HABITAT Tumbes Screech Owl (*pacificus*) inhabits the Arid Tropical Zone: open countryside with cacti, bushes and scattered groups of trees in coastal lowlands and on lower Andean slopes (mostly below 500m) with dry deciduous forest; preferred habitats are mesquite woodland and acacia scrub in plains or on arid hillsides. Peruvian Screech Owl (*roboratus*) inhabits slopes and hilly country between about 500m and 1,200m; the typical habitat is dry deciduous woodland with bushes.

DESCRIPTION *O. (r.) roboratus* **Adult** A greyish-brown and a red morph may be distinguished. *Greyish-brown morph*: Facial disc light greyish-brown, speckled and finely vermiculated darker; rim around disc dark blackish-brown. Ear-tufts short. Crown blackish-brown, bordered by whitish line from eyebrows to hindneck. Upperparts dark greyish-brown with blackish shaft-streaks and some dark transverse vermiculations; scapulars with blackish-edged whitish outer webs, forming line of whitish spots across shoulder. Flight feathers distinctly barred light and dark. Tail mottled and indistinctly barred light and dark. Underparts pale greyish-brown with relatively fine shaft-streaks and irregular transverse branches, as well as fine vermiculations; some feathers on sides of upper breast may have blackish shaft-streaks becoming broader, nearly spade-shaped towards tip. Tarsi feathered to base of toes. *Red morph*: General coloration light rufous, with dark markings dark brown rather than blackish. **Juvenile** Downy chick whitish. Young in mesoptile plumage densely barred below; crown not prominently marked. Juvenile plumage similar to adult, but more 'fluffy' and less clearly marked; eyes pale yellow-olive. **Bare parts** Eyes golden-yellow to pale yellow, with pinkish-olive eyelids. Bill and cere greyish-olive, bill with yellowish tip. Toes greyish-olive to brownish. Claws dark horn with darker tips.

Left, *O. (r.) roboratus*; right, *O. (r.) pacificus*.

MEASUREMENTS AND WEIGHT Total length 17.5cm (*pacificus*) to 20cm (*roboratus*). See Geographical Variation.

GEOGRAPHICAL VARIATION Two subspecies may be distinguished, separated by the western range of the Andes; the western taxon of the lowlands probably represents a separate species (see line-drawings).

O. (r.) roboratus Bangs & Noble, 1918. Drainage of rivers Chinchipe and Marañón, between W and C Andes. See Description. Wing of males about 167mm, of females about 170mm; tail of both sexes about 92mm; weight about 144-162g.

O. (r.) pacificus Hekstra, 1982. Tumbes Screech Owl. W Ecuador, coastal Peru and foothills of W Andes from Tumbes to Lambayeque. Much smaller than nominate race, and rim around facial disc less prominent. Also occurs in two colour morphs (grey and rufous), but general coloration is paler and dark markings below much less bold. Rufous morph much more frequent than in *roboratus*. Bill greenish olive-grey with pale greenish tip. Wing about 140mm; tail about 77mm; weight of 1 female (from Piura, W Peru) 87.7g, 1 unsexed 70g.

HABITS A nocturnal bird, roosting during daytime in dense foliage or dense bushes. Apparently not very shy. It may be attracted and stimulated to sing by playback of the A-song.

FOOD Probably mainly or almost exclusively insects. Caterpillars, orthopterans, grasshoppers, beetles and their larvae, and crickets have been found as prey.

BREEDING Breeds in holes in trees, perhaps also in abandoned mud nests of Pale-legged Hornero *Furnarius leucopus*. Breeding biology unknown.

STATUS AND CONSERVATION Locally uncommon to rather common. The destruction of habitat by grazing goats, and the felling of trees and cutting of shrubs for firewood, represent threats for this owl, which is dependent on trees with holes for breeding. Loss of suitable sites may be compensated for by the provision of nestboxes, as well as by the use of mud nests of horneros as nesting sites (a habit adopted by Peruvian Pygmy Owls).

REMARKS Apparently two species. Being little known, they need further investigation, especially with regard to their ecology, behaviour, vocalisations, breeding and general biology. Both taxa are specifically distinct from Tropical and Guatemalan Screech Owls [82], as well as from Maria Koepcke's. Vocal patterns and DNA evidence have proven the specific rank of *roboratus* from the Marañón-Chinchipe drainage in N Peru. Coastal *pacificus* requires specific confirmation by additional studies, especially on bioacoustics and molecular biology; it is very likely that it will be shown to be a full species.

REFERENCES Dunning (1993), Hardy *et al.* (1989), Johnson & Jones (1990), Koepcke (1964, manuscript and *in litt.*), Marshall & King (1988), Williams & Tobias (1997).

71 MONTANE FOREST SCREECH OWL
Otus hoyi
Plate 20

Syn: *Megascops hoyi*

French: Scops de Hoy
German: Bergwald-Kreischeule
Spanish: Alicuco yungueño

IDENTIFICATION A medium-sized screech owl with small ear-tufts, yellow eyes, and facial disc well defined laterally by a relatively broad, blackish rim. Eyebrows lighter than surrounding plumage, pale colour continuing to ear-tufts, but mostly with obvious notch just above eyes breaking line between base of bill and ear-tufts. Crown streaked and mottled dark, but never suggesting a black 'cap'; hindneck with pale collar-like line. Underparts boldly streaked blackish (shaft-streaks with 2-3 horizontal branches), each side of upper breast with two rows of dark shaft-streaks widening spade-like towards tip. **Similar species** Tropical Screech Owl [68] is smaller, with shorter ear-tufts and weaker talons, pale band between bill base and ear-tufts unbroken, and underparts less coarsely streaked (shaft-streaks normally not spade-like towards tip, but feathers of breast and belly with herringbone-like pattern of rather thin lines); normally found at lower altitudes, and only locally sympatric with Montane Forest Screech Owl in ecotone between dry, thorny woodland and montane forest; song also totally different. Rio Napo Screech Owl [83] is of similar size to present species, but has underparts densely vermiculated and barred, with inconspicuous thin shaft-streaks, and eye colour varying between brown and yellow; distributed east of Andes from E Ecuador to Bolivia, where it may overlap in range with Montane Forest but occupies different habitat (lives in tropical rainforest at about 300m above sea-level in Cochabamba, Bolivia, while present species probably found in the montane forest of Cordillera de Cochabamba); its song is similar to Montane Forest's, but with faster sequence of notes at slightly higher pitch (more like that of Guatemalan Screech Owl [82]).

VOCALISATIONS The A-song of the male is a long trill of clear staccato notes, uttered at a frequency of almost exactly 11 notes per second. These verses are repeated at intervals of several seconds; they begin very softly and faintly, increase gradually in volume to a peak (this maintained for some seconds), and end rather abruptly after a slight decrease in volume: bubububu.....bububop. The female's A-song is similar, but higher in pitch and less clear in tone (often more tinny). The A-song is obviously the territorial song, which is uttered at the beginning of the breeding season and brings male and female together; both sexes may be heared duetting at that time. Playback of the A-song may stimulate territorial males to respond and to approach close to the supposed rival. Once the pair-bond is formed, the A-song is only occasionally uttered, e.g. when the male announces his arrival with food near the nest.

When an unpaired male enters an occupied territory and sings, male and female (the latter leaving the nest) mostly answer with the B-song, which probably has an aggressive character. The latter is also given when the birds are disturbed by playback of their songs, as well as during courtship display just before copulation. The B-song is a short staccato sequence of equally spaced *ou* notes beginning softly and increasing in volume to a peak, then ending abruptly. The male's notes are clear; in females they are higher-pitched and more guttural, often beginning with scratchy notes. During copulation twittering sounds are uttered.

A slightly hoarse *chuío* is uttered by both sexes and probably has a contact function. In aggressive situations, both sexes utter loud, drawn-out notes rising slightly in pitch in a short sequence of about 4-5 notes, each lasting about 0.8 seconds: *ooh ooh ooh-ooh-ooh*, the sequence accelerating somewhat towards the end.

DISTRIBUTION From Cochabamba in Bolivia to Salta, Jujuy, Tucumán and perhaps Catamarca in Argentina.

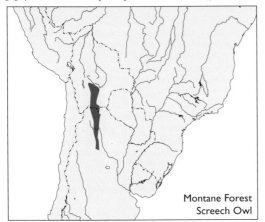

Montane Forest
Screech Owl

MOVEMENTS Not known. Birds of higher elevations locally probably move to lower areas in winter.

HABITAT Montane forest on E Andean slopes and pre-Andean mountains (e.g. Sierra de Santa Bárbara and Cerro Calilegua in Jujuy, El Rey National Park in Salta, Valle de Tafí in Tucumán), from about 1,000m up to 2,800m. Normally found in the Southern Yungas or 'Tucumán-Bolivian Forest', where epiphytes are common and survive the dry season on the moisture of mist and clouds ('Selva de Neblina'). Most trees here are deciduous, but even in the dry season (southern winter) the forest appears somewhat green owing to the richness of epiphytic plants, such as *Tillandsia*, orchids, mosses and climbing cactus; dense undergrowth of shrubs, climbing bamboo *Chusquea* and many creepers make access difficult. In the southern summer, the forest is dense and often totally shrouded in clouds and mist, producing a very slight drizzle. The soil is always covered with dead leaves. Montane Forest Screech Owls may be found from the lower parts, where Myrtaceae predominate, up to the 'Aliso zone', where alders *Alnus* are the dominant trees. Many aged trees have natural holes, or cavities produced by woodpeckers.

DESCRIPTION Adult Occurs in three morphs: a grey, a brown and a red one, brown morph being the most common. *Brown morph*: Facial disc greyish-brown, finely vermiculated dark; rim at both sides of disc very prominent, blackish. Ear-tufts short. Eyebrows lighter than surrounding plumage, pale colour extending towards ear-tufts but mostly notched above eyes, so that pale line appears broken. Crown and upperparts greyish-brown with dark shaft-streaks and vermiculations; crown sometimes with some rather broad shaft-streaks, making crown centre darker (but never creating blackish 'cap' as on Black-capped Screech Owl [78]); hindneck bordered by whitish feathers, forming narrow line. Scapulars with dark-edged whitish outer webs, forming whitish band across shoulder. Flight and tail feathers barred dark and light. Underparts slightly lighter than upperparts, feathers with dark shaft-streaks with 2-3 horizontal branches; on each side of upper breast, two obvious blackish rows of dark shaft-streaks widening sharply towards tip in spade-like pattern, creating suggestion of somewhat 'cravat'-like appearance (note that similar pattern may be found on many other species, too, but not on Tropical and Rio Napo Screech Owls). Tarsi feathered to base of toes. *Grey and red morphs*: Plumage patterns similar, but ground colour grey or rusty-brown. **Juvenile** Not described. **Bare parts** Eyes bright yellow (holotype had dull yellowish-orange eyes, but this was due to discoloration caused by head wound). Bill and cere greenish-yellow. Toes greyish-brown to yellowish-grey or brownish-flesh. Claws dark horn with blackish tips.

MEASUREMENTS AND WEIGHT Total length 23-24cm. Wing 170-177mm; tail 88-98mm; span between tips of middle and hind toes (without nail) about 38mm. Weight 115-145g. Females slightly larger and heavier than males.

GEOGRAPHICAL VARIATION Monotypic: *Otus hoyi* König & Straneck, 1989.

HABITS A nocturnal bird. Activity begins after sunset, at beginning of dusk, when male flies to a song perch (if not already roosting there), which is normally in the centre of the crown of an old tree with dense foliage or a dense cover of epiphytes on the branches. Using playback of both song types, males and females may be attracted and stimulated to sing; up to five or six birds (both sexes) may approach quite closely, indicating a rather high population density in some places (up to five singing males have been heard from the same spot at two localities in Salta, N Argentina). Territories seem to be rather small, and the owls show some tendency to form loose colonies; thus, several males may be heard at one place, while in very similar habitats only a few kilometres away in the same forest the species is apparently absent. Attracted birds utter both song types, mainly the B-song, and may be watched at close range, as the owls are not at all shy. The flight is noiseless, with soft wingbeats.

FOOD Principally insects and spiders. Several individuals have been observed catching locusts (Tettigoniidae) and moths from twigs or leaves of bushes at the forest edge; prey was taken with the talons, then grasped with one of them and eaten from the raised 'fist' (like a parrot, or many falcons and owls). Also hunts in the upper storeys of old trees, as well as among undergrowth. Some prey is taken from the ground.

BREEDING Normally begins to sing in August and September; copulation observed in mid September in Salta (Argentina); egg-laying may occur in late September or early October, depending on annual climatic conditions, in Argentina. A natural cavity or, particularly, one produced by a larger woodpecker (e.g. Black-bodied Woodpecker *Dryocopus schulzi*) is used as nest site. The eggs, laid on to the bottom of the cavity, are probably incubated by the female alone; she is fed by the male at the hole entrance. Clutch size and incubation period unknown, but presumably 2-3 eggs are laid. Breeding biology unknown.

STATUS AND CONSERVATION Locally rather common, but ever-increasing loss of habitat (deforestation, overgrazing by cattle) represents a threat. Locally, the species is found in rather small patches of forest on steep slopes, where the nature of the terrain makes extensive tree-felling difficult.

REMARKS This species and Black-capped and Long-tufted Screech Owls [78, 79] of SE Brazil and NE Argentina (Misiones) all have allopatric distributions, while Montane Forest Screech Owl is parapatric with Rio Napo Screech Owl (E Ecuador to Cochabamba in Bolivia). All probably belong to the same species group, but bioacoustics and molecular biology have shown each one to be a full species.

REFERENCES Burton (1991), Heidrich *et al.* (1993, 1994), König (1991, 1994 and unpublished), König & Straneck (1989), Marshall (1991).

---

72   RUFESCENT SCREECH OWL
Otus ingens   Plate 20

Syn: *Megascops ingens*

French: Scops de Salvin
German: Salvin-Kreischeule
Spanish: Urcututú de Salvin

IDENTIFICATION A large screech owl (25-28cm) with small ear-tufts and honey-brown eyes. Sandy-brown above, vermiculated dark; facial disc sandy-brown, without distinct rim; hindcrown with buffy-whitish border. Tarsi feathered to base of toes. **Similar species** Colombian Screech Owl [74] is about the same in size, but has lower portion of tarsi bare; it is distributed on the western slopes of the Andes (Rufescent is found only on eastern slopes). Cinnamon Screech Owl [75] is very similar, but about 15% smaller; Cloud-forest Screech Owl [73] is much more boldly patterned below, with nearly square-shaped whitish dots; White-throated [85] has practically no ear-tufts and has orange eyes; Rio Napo [83] has eyes sometimes brown and sometimes yellow, and is much smaller; Southern Tawny-bellied [77] is a bird of lowland rainforest. The other *Otus* species possibly occurring within the range of Rufescent Screech Owl have yellow eyes. All are best distinguished by voice.

VOCALISATIONS The A-song is described as a long phrase (about 10 seconds' duration) of about 50 equally spaced *ut* notes in rather rapid succession. A series of evenly pitched notes, accelerating suddenly after about the fourth one (similar to sound of a bouncing ball), but with a slightly longer space before the final note, seems to be the B-song, uttered by both sexes: *bu bu bu bu búbubububu-bu.*

DISTRIBUTION Eastern slopes of Andes locally from Venezuela to Peru and N Bolivia.

MOVEMENTS Resident.

HABITAT Humid forest rich in epiphytes on mountain slopes, from about 1,200m to 2,500m above sea-level.

DESCRIPTION *O. i. ingens* **Adult** Facial disc buffy-brown, slightly marked with darker concentric lines around eyes; rim not distinctly outlined. Ear-tufts short. Crown indistinctly scalloped buffy and dark. Upperparts sandy to olive-tawny or grey-brown, with fine dark vermiculations and some fine whitish spots; scapulars with whitish-buffy edges, forming faint light band across shoulder (underdown buffy, not whitish). Flight feathers barred cinnamon and dusky. Tail with cinnamon and darker brown bars. Underparts lighter than upperparts, with few thin shaft-streaks and fine dark and buffy-whitish vermiculations. Tarsi densely feathered to base of toes. Talons relatively powerful. **Juvenile** Downy chick whitish-buff, becoming densely mottled dusky when older. **Bare parts** Eyes honey-brown. Cere and bill olive-yellow. Toes yellowish-grey. Claws pale horn with darker tips.

Rufescent Screech Owl

MEASUREMENTS AND WEIGHT Total length 25-28cm. Wing of males 183.5-200mm (av. 192.0mm), of females 188-208mm (av. 196.0mm); tail of males 94-106mm (av. 101.2mm), of females 102-112mm (av. 106.1mm). Weight of males 134-180g (av. 154g), of females 140-223g (av. 182g).

GEOGRAPHICAL VARIATION Shows some individual variation, and some of the described subspecies appear to be only morphs. We recognise two races, considering forms *minimus* and *aequatorialis* as merely variations of the nominate. In addition, an undescribed taxon living in the isolated coastal mountains north of Maracay, Venezuela, may represent a third subspecies: three specimens were collected at Pico Guacamayo at about 1700 m, but, as they were said to differ vocally from *O. i. venezuelanus*, this taxon may be specifically distinct from Rufescent Screech Owl.

    O. i. ingens (Salvin, 1897). E Ecuador to N Bolivia. See Description.

    O. i. venezuelanus Phelps, 1954. Venezuela to E Colombia. Paler and slightly smaller than nominate race.

HABITS A strictly nocturnal bird, which becomes active at dusk. During daytime it roosts among epiphytes on thick branches, often close to the trunk. A single bird was found on two consecutive days at the same roost, about 7m above ground in a pocket of moss against a trunk. Biology and habits poorly known.

FOOD Larger insects and spiders, as well as small vertebrates.

BREEDING Probably breeds in natural holes in trees, where the pure white eggs are laid directly on to the bottom of the cavity. Reproductive biology requires study.

STATUS AND CONSERVATION Uncertain, but probably rare (perhaps sometimes overlooked) and locally endangered by forest destruction.

REMARKS This is a little-known bird. Its relationship with other screech owls is not yet clear, but it is probably related to some degree to Colombian Screech Owl, Cinnamon Screech Owl (with which it occurs sympatrically) and Cloud-forest Screech Owl. All can apparently be regarded as full species. The undescribed taxon of Pico Guacamayo, Venezuela (see Geographical Variation), requires study to clarify its taxonomic status.

REFERENCES Boyer & Hume (1991), Hardy *et al.* (1989), Hekstra (1982), Hilty & Brown (1986), Fitzpatrick & O'Neill (1986), Fjeldså & Krabbe (1990).

---

73 CLOUD-FOREST SCREECH OWL
Otus marshalli   Plate 20

Syn: *Megascops marshalli*

French: Scops de Marshall
German: Nebelwald-Kreischeule
Spanish: Urcututú de Marshall

IDENTIFICATION A medium-sized (19-23cm), rufescent-coloured screech owl with facial disc broadly rimmed black, very short ear-tufts and brown eyes. Belly pattern consists of transverse white spots separated by blackish shaft-streaks and rufous bars; upperparts chestnut with blackish transverse markings (neither streaked nor spotted), and whitish band across shoulder. Tarsi feathered to base of toes. **Similar species** The only screech owl of E Andean cloud forest with such a conspicuous pattern on the underside. Rufescent Screech Owl [72] is much larger, Cinnamon Screech Owl [75] is rather uniform cinnamon without bold pattern below and lacks whitish shoulder band, and Southern Tawny-bellied Screech Owl [77] is a bird of lowland rainforest. All are best distinguished by vocal patterns.

VOCALISATIONS Poorly studied. The A-song seems to be a monotonous series of single notes between *ee* and *u* in tone (like the German 'ü') in a rather rapid, staccato sequence; it somewhat resembles the A-song of Northern Tawny-bellied [76], but is much shorter in duration and higher-pitched. (We have studied a tape recording made by J. Weske at Cordillera de Vilcabamba, which may well be of this species.) The B-song is unknown.

DISTRIBUTION E Peru in departments of Cuzco (Cordillera de Vilcabamba) and Pasco (Cordillera Yanachaga).

MOVEMENTS Resident.

HABITAT Cloud forest rich in epiphytes and mosses, at about 1,920-2,240m above sea-level. The tallest trees in these forests reach 40m in height, forming a broken and irregular canopy, with undergrowth dense and rather impenetrable, with climbing bamboo *Chusquea* and tree ferns; emergent trees are festooned with mosses, ferns, orchids and other epiphytes. Rain and mist occur very frequently. The species normally lives at higher elevations than Rufescent Screech Owl. In places occurs together with Yungas Pygmy Owl [157].

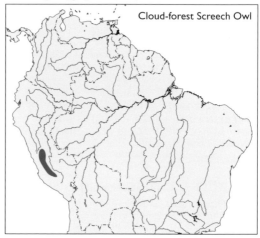

Cloud-forest Screech Owl

DESCRIPTION Adult Facial disc rufous, broadly rimmed black. Superciliary and loral feathers whitish basally, tipped rufous. Ear-tufts short. Crown as back, but feathers more extensively marked black centrally, with rufescent and black barring; hindcrown with whitish border, tipped rufescent and dusky. Upperparts rich chestnut-brown, irregularly barred and mottled with blackish, typical feathers of central back having four wavy blackish cross-bars on a chestnut background; outer webs of scapulars whitish or pale buffy, with a blackish area near tip of each web. Flight feathers barred dusky and tawny. Tail with eight rufous and blackish bars. Feathers of throat and upper breast rufous with relatively broad dusky shaft-streaks and some dark barring; lower breast rufescent-whitish with scattering of blotchy black spots; belly whitish with dusky shaft-streaks and few cross-bars, giving irregularly white-spotted or even ocellated appearance (each feather has a dusky shaft-streak and two dark cross-bars bordered with rufous, leaving three pairs of white spots). Tarsi feathered to base of toes, the latter bare. **Juvenile** Downy chick undescribed. Young similar to adult, but tail feathers with ten (instead of eight) bars. **Bare parts** Eyes dark brown. Cere and bill greyish-yellow. Toes flesh-coloured. Claws pale horn with darker tips.

MEASUREMENTS AND WEIGHT Total length 19-23cm. Wing 151.5-164mm; tail 84.6-91.5mm. Females slightly larger than males. Weight averages 115g.

GEOGRAPHICAL VARIATION Monotypic: *Otus marshalli* Weske & Terborgh, 1981.

HABITS Nocturnal. Habits probably similar to those of other screech owls. Requires study.

FOOD Probably mainly insects and other arthropods.

BREEDING Virtually unknown. According to gonadal condition, breeding seems to be in progress from late June to mid August, sometimes even earlier in the year. Probably breeds in natural holes in trees.

STATUS AND CONSERVATION Uncertain. Locally rather abundant, as in the Cordillera de Vilcabamba at 2130-2190m above sea-level. It may be threatened by forest destruction.

REMARKS This owl is probably related to Cinnamon Screech Owl, and to Southern Tawny-bellied of lowland rainforest. We do not accept the view of some other authors that it related to Bare-shanked or Bearded Screech Owls [67, 65], as we do not consider similarities in plumage patterns to be an indication of relationship.

REFERENCES Boyer & Hume (1991), Fjeldså & Krabbe (1990), Marshall & King (1988), Weske & Terborgh (1981).

74 COLOMBIAN SCREECH OWL
Otus colombianus   Plate 20

Syn: *Megascops colombianus*

French: Scops de Colombie
German: Kolumbien-Kreischeule
Spanish: Urcututú de Colombia

IDENTIFICATION An almost uniform rufescent-brown or greyish-brown screech owl (two morphs) with short ear-tufts, relatively long legs and brown eyes. Scapulars without any white on outer webs; lower half of tarsi bare. Talons rather powerful. **Similar species** Similarly sized Rufescent Screech Owl [72] has shorter legs, with tarsi densely feathered to base of toes, and has allopatric distribution (occurs only on eastern slopes of Andes). Cinnamon Screech Owl [75] is very similar to Colombian in plumage, but about 15% smaller, with weaker talons, and tarsi feathered nearly to base of toes; it is locally sympatric with Colombian on eastern slopes of Andes. Unlike other species mentioned here, which birds of mountain forest, Southern Tawny-bellied Screech Owl [77] lives only in lowland rainforest, to about 600m; it is much darker, brown-eyed, and has longer ear-tufts, and tarsi feathered to base of toes. Rio Napo Screech Owl [83] is smaller, mostly rufescent-brown with dense dusky barring on breast and belly, has has yellow (sometimes brown) eyes. White-throated Screech Owl [85] has no ear-tufts, has orange eyes, and is generally dusky brown with a white throat; it generally lives higher in the mountains, even in elfin forest around 3,600m. All are well separated by voice.

VOCALISATIONS The A-song of the male is a series of equally spaced flute-like notes on the same pitch, preceded by 1-2 weak introductory notes: *bu-bu bubububububububububu*. Such verses are repeated at intervals of several seconds. At a distance, only the louder sequences are audible.

DISTRIBUTION Western slope of the Andes in Colombia and N Ecuador.

MOVEMENTS Resident.

HABITAT Cloud forest with dense undergrowth and rich in epiphytic plants, from about 1,300m up to about 2,300m.

DESCRIPTION Adult Two colour morphs occur, a cinnamon-reddish and a greyish-brown one. *Grey-brown morph*: Facial disc greyish-brown with no distinct rim. Eyebrows somewhat lighter than facial disc and crown. Ear-tufts short. Crown with dusky shaft-streaks and dark mottling; border of hindcrown with pale buffy rim, broken

by dark spots. Upperparts greyish-brown, finely mottled and vermiculated dusky; scapulars with buffy-brownish outer webs, thus generally lacking obvious pale stripe across shoulder. Flight and tail feathers barred lighter and darker. Underparts rather uniform greyish-brown with fine dusky vermiculations and mottling, as well as some blackish shaft-streaks and cross-bars. Tarsi sparsely feathered on upper part, the lower parts (more than lower half) totally bare. Talons rather powerful, feet relatively long. *Reddish morph*: Generally cinnamon-reddish, and less distinctly patterned than grey-brown morph. **Juvenile** Downy chick buffy-whitish. Mesoptile similar to adult, but more fluffy and finely barred below and on head and mantle. **Bare parts** Eyes brown, darker in red morph; rims of eyelids yellowish. Cere and bill yellowish-grey. Toes pale brownish-flesh. Claws pale horn with darker tips.

Colombian Screech Owl

MEASUREMENTS AND WEIGHT Total length 26-28cm. Wing of males 175-186mm (av. 181.5mm), of females 176.5-185mm (av. 181.2mm); tail of males 90-96mm (av. 93.5mm), of females 95-103mm (av. 98.5mm); tarsus of males 34-37mm (av. 35.8mm), of females 33-36mm (av. 34.2mm) (though slightly smaller than *O. ingens*, tarsi are longer, averaging 34.2- 35.8mm as against 32.2-33.1mm in *ingens*). Weight of males 150-156g, of females about 210g.

GEOGRAPHICAL VARIATION Monotypic: *Otus colombianus* Traylor, 1952.

HABITS A nocturnal bird. Its habits are poorly known.

FOOD Larger insects and other arthropods, also small vertebrates.

BREEDING Probably breeds in natural holes in trees. Biology needs study.

STATUS AND CONSERVATION Uncertain, probably rare. Threatened by forest destruction.

REMARKS Although we treat Colombian Screech Owl as a full species, its taxonomic status requires further research, as do its biology and ecology.

REFERENCES Boyer & Hume (1991), Hardy *et al.* (1989), Fjeldså & Krabbe (1990), Fitzpatrick & O'Neill (1986), Marshall & King (1988).

75   CINNAMON SCREECH OWL
Otus petersoni   **Plate 20**

Syn: *Megascops petersoni*

French: Scops de Peterson
German: Zimt-Kreischeule
Spanish: Urcututú acanelado

IDENTIFICATION A relatively small screech owl (about 21cm) characterised by warm buffy-brown plumage, short to medium-long ear-tufts, a narrow buffy nuchal collar, and tarsi feathered nearly to base of toes. Eyes dark brown. No white scapular spots. **Similar species** Colombian Screech Owl [74] is about 15% larger (wing 176.5-192mm versus 153-165.5mm), and more vermiculated on breast and belly, with tarsi distally unfeathered. Rufescent Screech Owl [72] is greyer and larger (about same size as Colombian), with whitish outer edges and spots on scapulars. Southern Tawny-bellied Screech Owl [77] is similar in size, but more dusky; it lives in lowland rainforest, and never penetrates into the mountain forest inhabited by Cinnamon. Rio Napo Screech Owl [83] lives at lower altitudes, and in its red morph is densely vermiculated dusky below; it has yellow (sometimes brown) eyes.

VOCALISATIONS The A-song is a series of equally spaced *u* notes in rather rapid succession (faster than Colombian's), slightly rising at first, then dropping in pitch: *bubububububububu...*, about 5-7 notes per second. Each phrase begins at slightly lower volume, reaches full peak after a few notes, and breaks off abruptly at the end (not fading away), such phrases being repeated after a pause of several seconds. The female has a similar but higher-pitched song. The B-song is unknown. Single *whew* calls, uttered at intervals of 1-2 seconds, may represent contact-calls.

DISTRIBUTION Forested eastern foothills of Andes from S Ecuador (Cordillera de Cutucú) south to N Peru on the E Andean slopes. Possibly also in the Andes of Colombia.

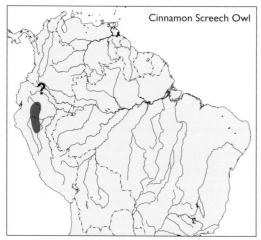

Cinnamon Screech Owl

MOVEMENTS Resident.

HABITAT Moist cloud forest with dense undergrowth and rich in mosses and epiphytic plants, between 1,690m and 2,450m. Locally sympatric with Rufescent Screech Owl.

DESCRIPTION Adult Facial disc warm cinnamon-brown (like back), most feathers finely vermiculated or barred blackish (4-5 bars on each feather), gradually shading to darker brown towards rim; rim blackish, but not very obvious. Eyebrows paler than surrounding areas. Ear-tufts of moderate length (longest feather about 29mm), mottled blackish towards tip. Crown slightly darker than back (no buffy underdown). Upperparts cinnamon-brown, finely vermiculated with double wavy bars, alternately darker and paler (on most feathers of mantle, darker vermiculations break up distally into mottling); underdown feathers of back buffy; scapulars pale cinnamon, generally indistinctly marked dusky (no whitish outer webs); wing-coverts as back and mantle. Flight feathers barred light buff and dark cinnamon. Tail banded brown and blackish (about eight bars of each). Underparts warm cinnamon-buff, throat feathers and breast finely mottled with dark wavy bars or vermiculations; lower breast and belly nearly uniform cinnamon. Tarsi feathered to within 5mm of toes, distal feathering becoming sparse. **Juvenile** Not described. **Bare parts** Eyes dark brown. Cere and bill pale grey-green. Toes pale pinkish-flesh. Claws pale horn with darker tips.

MEASUREMENTS AND WEIGHT Total length about 21cm. Wing of males 153-165.5mm (av. 157mm), of females 155-161.5mm (av. 157.3mm); tail of males 81-90mm (av. 85.6mm), of females 85-90.5mm (av. 86.8mm); tarsus 25-29mm (av. 27.3mm). Weight of males 88-119 g (av. 97g), of females 92-105g (av. 98g).

GEOGRAPHICAL VARIATION Monotypic: *Otus petersoni* Fitzpatrick & O'Neill, 1986. Some individual variation occurs, with general coloration ranging from more reddish to darker cinnamon.

HABITS A nocturnal bird. Where sympatric with Rufescent Screech Owl, it prefers higher elevations (as does Cloud-forest Screech Owl [73] when occurring together with Rufescent), but in a few places both Cinnamon and Rufescent Screech Owls may be found living alongside each other at the same elevation.

FOOD Apparently mainly insects, but small vertebrates may also be taken occasionally.

BREEDING According to gonad size and the stage of moult, it may be assumed that the breeding season is prior to the dry months of July and August. Probably breeds in natural cavities in trees, though no nest has yet been found. Breeding biology unknown, but probably similar to that of other screech owls.

STATUS AND CONSERVATION Uncertain. Like all forest owls, it must be under threat from forest destruction.

REMARKS Thought by some authors to be a subspecies of Rufescent or of Colombian Screech Owl. With the first it occurs sympatrically; and compared with the allopatric Colombian it is about 15 % smaller, and has much shorter tarsi which are feathered nearly to the base of the toes. All three differ vocally. A closer relationship might exist between Cinnamon and Cloud-forest Screech Owls, or with the two lowland tawny-bellied [76, 77]; Northern Tawny-bellied has a similar A-song, but the notes are run together faster and the phrases are much longer. In any case, all these taxa are in need of study in a number of aspects.

REFERENCES Boyer & Hume (1991), Fitzpatrick & O'Neill (1986), Hardy *et al.* (1989), Marshall & King (1988), Weske & Terborgh (1981).

76 NORTHERN TAWNY-BELLIED SCREECH OWL
Otus watsonii   Plate 21

Syn: *Megascops watsonii*

French: Scops de Watson
German: Watson-Kreischeule
Spanish: Urcututú de Watson

IDENTIFICATION A relatively dark, medium-sized screech owl (19-23cm) having dark greyish-brown upperparts with small light freckles and spots, so that the bird appears covered with a thin layer of dust. Ear-tufts relatively long, mostly dusky. Upper breast dusky brown with darker and lighter mottling; rest of underparts rusty or sandy-brown with relatively thin dark shaft-streaks and cross-bars, as well as fine vermiculations. Tarsi feathered to base of toes; eyes amber-yellow to brownish-orange. **Similar species** The extremely similar (until recently mostly treated as conspecific) Southern Tawny-bellied Screech Owl [77] is slightly larger, with a more rufous wash above, and with darker crown and much heavier (broader) shaft-streaks below, the belly mostly dark rufous with dense vermiculations; it is distributed south of the Amazon, but overlaps locally in distribution with its northern counterpart. The two have totally different songs and may be regarded as parapatric taxa. Tropical Screech Owl [68] may also be sympatric locally; it has yellow eyes and a typical herringbone-like pattern on breast and belly. Cinnamon Screech Owl [75] is overall warm cinnamon-brown and inhabits cloud forest.

VOCALISATIONS The A-song of the male is a long (up to about 20 seconds) regular series of *u* notes uttered in rapid succession, beginning softly, increasing in volume and finally fading out: *bubububububububu....* It is similar to the A-song of Cinnamon Screech Owl, but with a slightly faster succession of notes (in addition to which, Cinnamon has much shorter phrases, which end abruptly instead of softly fading away). The B-song seems to be a short sequence of *u* notes in a morse-code-like rhythm. The female has a similar but mostly higher-pitched song.

DISTRIBUTION Lowlands from E Colombia to W and S Venezuela, Surinam, NE Ecuador, NE Peru and Amazonian Brazil (north of the Amazon). In Amazonia, it seems to overlap locally with its southern counterpart, and occasional hybridisation may be possible in these areas. (Some authors mention the occurrence of Northern Tawny-bellied at elevations of up to 2,100m in Perijá Mountains in extreme NE Colombia/NW Venezuela and also northeast of the Orinoco; we suspect that this may be due to confusion with another, perhaps undescribed species, as we regard the present species as a typical lowland form.)

MOVEMENTS Resident.

HABITAT Lowland rainforest, to about 600m above sea-level. It is reported to occur up to 2,100m in the Perijá

Mountains (extreme NE Colombia/NW Venezuela) and north-east of the Orinoco. Although it may occur locally with Tropical Screech Owl (e.g. at forest edges and clearings), it is more a bird of the interior of primary forest.

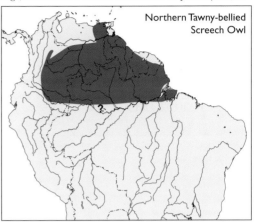

DESCRIPTION Adult Facial disc greyish-brown, with indistinct darker rim. Upperparts, including mantle, wing-coverts and crown, dark greyish-brown, peppered with small light and dark freckles, vermiculations and spots, giving appearance of being covered with a fine layer of dust; scapulars normally without whitish outer webs. Flight and tail feathers barred light and dark; outer webs of secondaries peppered light and dark, giving dusty appearance. Upper breast relatively dark earth-brown, vermiculated and flecked light, throat paler; rest of underparts tawny or pale rusty-brown with relatively thin shaft-streaks and cross-bars, as well as lighter and darker vermiculations. Tarsi densely feathered to base of toes. Talons relatively weak (similar to Cinnamon Screech Owl). **Juvenile** Not described. **Bare parts** Eyes amber-yellow to light brownish-orange. Cere and bill greenish-grey. Toes pale ochre-brown. Claws horn with darker tips.

MEASUREMENTS AND WEIGHT Total length 19-23cm. Wing 158-175mm; tail 86-99mm. Weight 114-130g.

GEOGRAPHICAL VARIATION Monotypic: *Otus watsonii* (Cassin, 1848).

HABITS A nocturnal bird, which may start singing just before dusk. It lives at medium height in primary forest, but also descends to undergrowth. Little other information.

FOOD Mainly insects, but probably also occasional small vertebrates.

BREEDING Probably similar to that of other screech owls. Studies are needed.

STATUS AND CONSERVATION Uncertain, but probably threatened by forest destruction.

REMARKS We separate the Northern Tawny-bellied Screech Owl specifically from its southern counterpart because of vocal differences. Where the two overlap in range, hybrids may occasionally occur, as suggested by recordings of apparent 'intermediate' songs. Occasional hybridisation does not, however, indicate conspecificity, as many examples show; so long as there is no zone of regular intergrading, the specific character of both taxa is not in question.

The occurrence of this species at higher elevations in montane forest requires confirmation. If proven, this taxon would exhibit an unusually wide altitudinal span, ranging from humid, tropical lowland forest to moist, subtropical cloud forests.

REFERENCES Boyer & Hume (1991), Fitzpatrick & O'Neill (1986), Hardy *et al.* (1989), Hilty & Brown (1986), König (1994), Marshall & King (1988).

77 SOUTHERN TAWNY-BELLIED SCREECH OWL
Otus usta   Plate 21

Syn: *Megascops usta*

French: Scops d'Usta
German: Usta-Kreischeule
Spanish: Urcututú de Usta
Portuguese: Corujinha-orelhuda

IDENTIFICATION Very similar to Northern Tawny-bellied [76], but slightly larger (23-24cm), with a rufous wash above, a darker crown, and more broadly-streaked underparts. A dark and a light morph exist: the first is rather blackish-brown above, and has a tawny-buff ground colour on lower breast and belly; rare light morph has a pale ochraceous-buff ground colour on lower breast, becoming nearly whitish-buff towards belly The medium-sized ear-tufts are more blackish, and the eyes warm brown. **Similar species** Northern Tawny-bellied Screech Owl is very similar in size and plumage pattern (see above), but has a totally different song. Tropical Screech Owl [68] lives in more open parts of the forest, at edges or near clearings, and has yellow eyes, short ear-tufts and a different song. Rio Napo Screech Owl [83] has yellow (sometimes brown) eyes and densely vermiculated underparts, and the ear-tufts are very short; its A-song is a long trill. Cinnamon Screech Owl [75] is a bird of mountain forest.

VOCALISATIONS The A-song of the male is a long series (up to 20 seconds and more) of equally spaced hollow hoots, beginning softly, increasing gradually in volume and dying away at the end of the phrase: *whoo-whoo-whoo-whoo-whoo...*, at about 2 notes per second. The B-song is probably a series of bouncing *u* notes beginning rapidly and becoming gradually slower towards the end: *bububu-bu-bu--bu–bu–bu bu bub.*

DISTRIBUTION Amazonian Colombia, Peru and Brazil, south to lowland forest of N Bolivia and Mato Grosso (Brazil). May perhaps overlap with its northern counterpart in SE Ecuador or in Amazonian Peru.

MOVEMENTS Resident.

HABITAT Tropical primary lowland forest, locally near clearings or forest edges. Generally a bird of the forest interior, living in the lower storey of primary forest or second growth.

DESCRIPTION Adult A dark, a rufous and a light morph exist, as well as much individual variation (see below). Facial disc brown with a thin blackish rim. Ear-tufts medium-sized, rather prominent, blackish. Crown slightly darker than back. Upperparts dark earth-brown with a

slight rufous wash, finely freckled and spotted light, giving dusty appearance; scapulars brownish, without whitish outer webs. Flight and tail feathers barred light and dark. Underparts ochraceous-tawny, becoming lighter towards belly, with blackish shaft-streaks and cross-bars, as well as lighter and darker vermiculations. Tarsi thickly feathered to base of toes. *Morphs*: Differ in basic coloration: dark morph is dark greyish-brown, rufous morph is dark red-brown, and light morph is relatively light brownish-grey (with light facial disc). **Juvenile** Similar to other young screech owls, with barred underparts, head and mantle. **Bare parts** Eyes warm brown. Cere and bill greyish-brown with greenish suffusion. Toes greyish-yellow to brownish. Claws horn with darker tips.

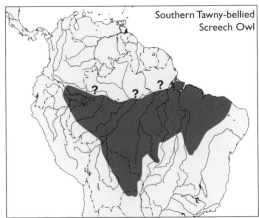

Southern Tawny-bellied Screech Owl

MEASUREMENTS AND WEIGHT Total length 23-24cm. Wing 164-173mm; tail 86-99mm. Weight about 115-141g.

GEOGRAPHICAL VARIATION Monotypic: *Otus usta* (Sclater, 1859). Wide individual variation, as well as the existence of three colour morphs (see Description), makes any geographical distinctions difficult to assess.

HABITS A nocturnal bird which sometimes begins to sing early at dusk. The behaviour is similar to that of other screech owls, but it prefers the interior of forest, rarely ascending more than 10m above ground in the lower storey.

FOOD Mainly insects and other arthropods, but apparently sometimes also small terrestrial vertebrates.

BREEDING Natural holes in trees are used as nesting sites. Breeding biology poorly known.

STATUS AND CONSERVATION Uncertain. Locally not rare, but no doubt vulnerable to forest destruction.

REMARKS The specific epithet *usta* is an eponym; the spelling '*ustus*' used by some authors (matching the gender with that of '*Otus*') is therefore incorrect. Although this species is superficially very similar in size and plumage patterns to Northern Tawny-bellied Screech Owl, we treat it as a separate species and not as a southern subspecies of Northern; the two occur locally together in the same forest and they exhibit too many vocal differences to be regarded as conspecific. DNA evidence indicates some relationship between Southern Tawny-bellied and Black-capped Screech Owl [78], the two perhaps belonging to the same superspecies.

REFERENCES Boyer & Hume (1991), Burton (1992), Dunning (1993), Fitzpatrick & O'Neill (1986), Hardy *et al.* (1989), Marshall & King (1988), Sick (1985).

---

78 BLACK-CAPPED SCREECH OWL
Otus atricapillus   Plate 21

Black-capped Screech Owl

Syn: *Megascops atricapillus*

Other names: Variable Screech Owl

French: Scops variable
German: Schwarzkappen-Kreischeule
Spanish: Alicuco tropical
Portuguese: Corujinha-sapo

IDENTIFICATION A medium-sized screech owl (about 23cm) with a blackish crown, rather prominent ear-tufts, and mostly brown (sometimes golden or amber-yellow) eyes. General coloration and colour patterns very variable; grey, dark and red morphs may be found at the same locality. **Similar species** Long-tufted Screech Owl [79] is larger, with longer ear-tufts and more powerful talons, and the crown darker only in the central area; it is an endemic of SE Brazil, Uruguay and NE Argentina (Misiones). Tropical Screech Owl [68] is smaller, with short ear-tufts and yellow eyes; it is widely distributed in tropical and subtropical South America. Both are easily distinguished by voice.

VOCALISATIONS The A-song of the male is a long trill, normally of about 8-10 seconds but sometimes up to 15-20 seconds, beginning very quietly and increasing gradually in volume, then breaking off rather abruptly; normally a rather constant 14 notes per second. The pitch is slightly higher than in Montane Forest Screech Owl [71], with a more rapid sequence of notes. It is very similar to the songs of the allopatric Rio Napo and Guatemalan Screech Owls [83, 82]. The verses are repeated after a pause of some seconds. The female's A-song is higher in pitch, with a tinny quality, and normally less long. The B-song of the male is a short sequence of staccato notes (about 2.5-3 seconds' duration) in 'bouncing-ball rhythm' (table-tennis ball dropping on a hard surface), the individual notes clear. The female's B-song is similar, but slightly higher-pitched, often with a tinny quality.

When startled, both sexes utter explosive calls, singly or in a short sequence. These are totally different from calls of Montane Forest Screech Owl in similar situations. Single soft *yewoh* calls (audible only at close range) are given by male and female as contact between each other.

DISTRIBUTION E Brazil from about S Bahia and Rio de Janeiro south to Paraná and Santa Catarina, east to E Paraguay (Amambay plateau) and NE Argentina (northernmost Misiones); in Argentina, the southermost limit seems to be north of the river Urugua-i (not to be confused with the river Uruguay!). It is generally found in regions with more than 350 frost-free days, as in Argentina in the vicinity of Iguazú, where the owl is rather abundant in extensive forest (Iguazú National Park, forest of the 'Peninsula', etc); in Paraguay, it is abundant in the reserve of Cerro Corá on the Amambay plateau.

MOVEMENTS Unknown, but probably resident.

HABITAT Extensive rainforest (primary and secondary forest) with often very dense undergrowth. The habitat is mostly 'jungle-like', with climbing bamboos *Chusquea*, *Philodendron*, and *Tillandsia* epiphytes; the presence of old trees with holes is very important. May also occur near forest edges, sometimes quite close to roads with heavy traffic, or near human settlements. Being a bird of warm climates, it can be found at up to about 600m in the northern part of its range, while in the south (Misiones) it inhabits lowland forest at up to 250m.

DESCRIPTION Adult Highly variable in coloration and plumage patterns, and in general three colour morphs (dark, red and grey) may be distinguished, dark being commonest. *Dark morph*: Facial disc dirty brown, finely vermiculated dark; rim of disc prominent, dark brown or blackish at both sides. Eyebrows somewhat lighter than facial disc, vermiculated with brown, pale colour extending in unbroken line from base of bill to the rather prominent ear-tufts. Crown nearly uniform dark brown to blackish; hindneck with narrow whitish or pale yellowish-ochre margin. Upperparts dark earth-brown, mottled and vermiculated with light brown or buff; outer webs of scapulars pale yellowish-ochre or yellowish-white with dark edges, forming pale line across shoulder. Primaries and secondaries barred dark and light. Tail feathers mottled light and dark, but only indistinctly barred. Underparts lighter than upperparts, more warm brown; feathers with dark shaft-streaks, often widening spade-like at tip, especially at both sides of upper breast (2-3 dark, often slightly curved branches extend from central shaft-streak to the edges); in addition, entire underside is finely vermiculated dark. Tarsi feathered to base of toes. *Red morph*: General coloration rufous, with darker upperparts and a dark cap. *Grey morph*: Lacks brown or rufous in the greyish plumage, and the dark patterns are very prominent. **Juvenile** Not described. **Bare parts** Eyes normally dark brown or chestnut, especially in dark morph; individuals of grey and red morphs occasionally have golden or amber-yellow. Bill and cere greenish-yellow. Toes brownish-grey to pale flesh-brown. Claws dark horn with blackish tips.

MEASUREMENTS AND WEIGHT Total length around

23cm. Wing 170-184mm (av. 175mm); tail 98-110mm; span of talons (tip of middle toe to hind toe, without claws) about 40mm. Weight (5 males) 115-138g.

GEOGRAPHICAL VARIATION Monotypic: *Otus atricap-illus* (Temminck, 1822). The species varies individually on a large scale. (Note that all three morphs may be found in the same forest; we have observed individuals of each morph within an area of about 2km².)

HABITS A nocturnal bird, roosting by day in dense foliage of trees or in cavities. At dusk, the male leaves its roost and flies to a song perch in a tree or tall bush with dense foliage; it sometimes sings a few verses at the roost. This species shows a tendency to settle in loose contact with other pairs, and quite often several males may be heard singing from the same place. In playback experiments (A- or B-song), several males, and sometimes also females, may be attracted quite close to the observer; on one such occasion, two different males were observed singing from the same tree, only 2m or so from each other. The birds are not at all shy and can be observed at close range. When undisturbed, the owls normally sing and move about in the middle canopy of medium-sized trees, but playback may attract them into rather low undergrowth. The flight is noiseless, with soft wingbeats and gliding. When relaxed, they hold the plumage rather loose, but in most cases the pointed ear-tufts can still be seen, even against the starlit sky.

FOOD Mainly insects, especially locusts (Tettigoniidae), cicadas, moths and beetles, but also spiders and probably occasionally small vertebrates. Usually hunts from a perch, taking prey from branches, leaves or tree trunks, or from the ground. Hunting birds often frequent low undergrowth.

BREEDING Nests in holes in trees, either natural cavities or abandoned nest holes of woodpeckers. The male sings near potential nesting sites and 'demonstrates' them to the female. Clutch probably 2-3 white eggs, laid directly on to the bottom of the nest hole. The female alone incubates, during which period she is fed by her mate, who brings food to the nest in its bill; the male announces his approach with short verses of song or soft contact-calls. Breeding biology otherwise unknown, but probably similar to that of other screech owls.

STATUS AND CONSERVATION Despite being still rather common locally, the species is under threat from increasing forest destruction. It requires extensive rainforest where the birds can settle in loose groups; these 'colonies' seem to be important in maintaining a stable population, and can be developed only in larger unbroken tracts of forest.

REMARKS Some authorities have lumped this species with other screech owls, such as Guatemalan, Rio Napo, Montane Forest and Long-tufted. Our own studies on ecology, zoogeography, bioacoustics and molecular biology do not, however, support this view. Nevertheless, the biology and distribution of Black-capped Screech Owl are poorly known and require study.

REFERENCES Heidrich *et al.* (1994), König (1991, 1994 and unpublished), Marshall *et al.* (1991).

79 LONG-TUFTED SCREECH OWL
Otus sanctaecatarinae   Plate 21

Syn: *Megascops sanctaecatarinae*

French: Scops de Salvin
German: Santa Catarina-Kreischeule
Spanish: Alicuco grande
Portuguese: Corujinha-sapo grande

IDENTIFICATION Similar to Black-capped Screech Owl [78], but larger (26-27cm) and heavier (average weight 170-190g), with much more heavily built body, longer ear-tufts and much more powerful talons. Rather coarsely marked dark above, crown darker only in centre; dark shaft-streaks below, widening gradually towards tips of feathers, and with few lateral branches, underparts with little or no dark vermiculation. Eyes normally yellow, sometimes light brown. **Similar species** Black-capped Screech Owl is smaller, distinctly lighter in weight and slimmer, with weaker talons; has crown nearly plain blackish, dark markings less coarse, and underparts normally densely and finely vermiculated; eyes generally dark brown or chestnut, occasionally bright yellow. Tropical Screech Owl [68] is much smaller, with short ear-tufts, relatively weak talons, and typical herringbone-like pattern on underpart feathers; hindneck without whitish fringe, and eyes yellow. Both are best distinguished by vocal patterns. Pygmy owls of this region are much smaller, with longer tail, and without ear-tufts. Buff-fronted Owl [181], which may occur sympatrically with all above-mentioned species, has yellow eyes, a large, rounded head without ear-tufts, and plain pale cinnamon or ochraceous-buff underparts; its song is a high-pitched, wavering trill.

VOCALISATIONS The A-song of the male is a guttural, rapid trill of normally about 6-8 seconds' duration, but when excited (e.g. attracted by playback) it may utter longer verses. The song starts as very faint grunting and increases gradually in volume and slightly in pitch, before ending abruptly. It is similar to the A-song of Black-capped Screech Owl, but less clear, with a ventriloquial character, giving the impression of two birds singing simultaneously (this is well evident on sonagrams, where the very prominent harmonics give impression of a second voice above the 'ground notes'). The verses are repeated at intervals of several seconds. The female's A-song is similar, but higher in pitch, shorter in duration, and with a tinny, somewhat hoarse character.

The B-song of the male is a 'reverse bouncing-ball' verse, uttered mostly in duet with the female. Normally the female begins and her mate joins in, finishing his song after hers. Such duets may be heard at the beginning of the breeding season. The male's B-song begins rather rapidly with short notes, these becoming longer with increasing intervals between them: *burrbububu-bu-bu-bu-bu-bu bu*. One verse lasts about 4-5 seconds, the single notes equally high in pitch but initially weak and increasing gradually in volume. The female's B-song is a sequence of hoarse, scratching, heron-like notes, totally unlike vocalisations of other screech owls: *kra-kra-kra-kra-...*, the verse lasting about 3-4 seconds and repeated at intervals of several seconds. In duet with the male, the female begins and the male joins in at about the middle of her verse, so that, at the end of the duet, only the remainder of the male's verse is heard. The two verses are so well interwoven that the listener could gain the impression of a single bird singing two different phrases. Very excited females (especially after playback) may utter prolonged verses of about 5-7 seconds' duration, consisting of disyllabic, hoarse notes: *karre-karre-karre-....*

An upward-inflected *vieweed* seems to have a contact function. We heard it given by a female while the male sang nearby.

DISTRIBUTION SE Brazil (Santa Catarina and Rio Grande do Sul, perhaps also São Paulo). Has also been found in Uruguay and NE Argentina (Sierra de Misiones).

Long-tufted
Screech Owl

MOVEMENTS Apparently sedentary.

HABITAT Semi-open forest, open pastureland with scattered wooded areas, upland moors with *Araucaria* woodland; also edges of forest with adjacent farmland, when also near and even in human settlements with scattered trees and groups of trees. Normally above 300m and up to about 1000m. Seems to avoid extensive, dense rainforest, preferring semi-open habitats. In the Sierra de Misiones, we found this owl at 350m in subtropical semi-open forest of the Urugua-i Province Park, and at 680m in secondary-growth woodland within farmland in a valley at Cerro Tigre (between Bernardo de Irigoyen and Tobuna): at both localities, Ferruginous Pygmy Owl [160], Tropical Screech Owl and Rusty-barred Owl [139] were present; at the Cerro Tigre site, we heard Buff-fronted Owl and Short-browed Owl [119] singing from an adjacent dense secondary forest.

DESCRIPTION Adult Three colour morphs may be distinguished, brown being the most common. *Brown morph*: General coloration yellowish-brown to ochraceous-buff. Facial disc ochre-brown, almost unmarked; rim around disc laterally quite prominently defined dark. Ear-tufts rather bushy, with relatively long tips. Crown similar to back, but with dark central zone; whitish fringe around hindneck. Upperparts brown with slight ochre tinge; feathers of mantle and back with rather broad dark shaft-streaks, each of these widening into 2-3 triangular spots on each side (the dense, fine vermiculations of Black-capped Screech Owl are more or less absent); scapulars with dark-margined whitish outer webs, forming row of light spots across shoulder. Primaries and secondaries barred dark and light. Tail feathers more distinctly barred than on Black-capped Screech Owl. Underparts similar

to Black-capped, but pattern much coarser and virtually lacking dense, fine vermiculations. Tarsi feathered to base of toes. *Grey morph*: Similar, but with general grey coloration. *Red morph*: Mostly dusky rufous-brown, with dark markings less prominent. **Juvenile** Not described. **Bare parts** Eyes normally light yellow to orange-yellow, but individuals with light brown eyes occur, especially in brown morph. Bill and cere greenish-grey. Toes light greyish-brown. Claws dark horn with blackish tips.

MEASUREMENTS AND WEIGHT Total length 22.5-28.1cm, median 26.3cm. Wing 182-210mm (av. about 190mm); tail 100-110mm; span of talons (from tip of central toe to tip of hind toe, without claws) about 45mm. Weight of 7 males 155-194 g (median 170 g), of 8 females 174-211 g (median 189.5 g).

GEOGRAPHICAL VARIATION Monotypic: *Otus santae-catarinae* (Salvin, 1897). Some taxa described as subspecies of Long-tufted or Black-capped Screech Owl (which have in most cases not been treated as different species) are clearly only morphs.

HABITS A nocturnal bird which becomes active at or, occasionally, just before dusk. During daytime it roosts singly in dense foliage of trees; one was reported to spend the day in a eucalyptus. In our experience, this species seems to be shyer than Black-capped Screech Owl and is more difficult to approach. A singing male may be attracted by playback, but it normally approaches less close to the observer than the smaller species; females also react to playback of their typical hoarse scratching B-song. Near the nest site they may be quite aggressive, and make diving flights over the head of the observer playing back the song, but normally they will not perch very close; there may be exceptions, however, where the birds are accustomed to human activities. The flight is silent, with soft wingbeats.

FOOD Mainly insects, above all grasshoppers, mantids, beetles, moths and cicadas; also spiders and small vertebrates. Prey is normally caught by swooping down from a perch, and is taken from branches or leaves or from the ground.

BREEDING The male begins singing at dusk at the start of the reproductive cycle, normally in late August or early September. Males examined in October and November had enlarged testes; one female in November had only a small ovary with slightly enlarged follicles and had probably laid earlier. These data suggest that breeding in general occurs between late August and late November, but there may be exceptions: we heard a pair duetting in early November, obviously in nuptial display; at the same place (Cerro Tigre, Misiones) we found a pair duetting (B-songs) in the second half of August, although no singing was heard at the site in November of the following year, nor in October or November of the previous one, even though the birds were present.

A natural hole (or one produced by a larger wood-pecker) is used for nesting. In a small wood at Cerro Tigre, we found a nest hole in a thick, almost vertical branch of a black laurel *Laurus*, about 5m from the ground; the cavity, a natural knothole with a rather rounded entrance, had doubtless been used by the owls for several years, as we watched them at the same place on a number of occasions between 1991 and 1995. Breeding behaviour probably similar to that of other screech owls. The eggs are pure white. The female apparently incubates alone, being fed by her mate.

STATUS AND CONSERVATION Although locally rather common (e.g. in Rio Grande do Sul and Santa Catarina), this owl is threatened by the destruction of its habitat by overgrazing with cattle, felling and burning. Mainly for these reasons, it is probably rather rare in the Argentine Sierra de Misiones, where it seems to reach the westernmost limit of its range.

REMARKS Like many owls, the Long-tufted Screech Owl needs study, especially with regard to its requirements for survival. Bioacoustics, morphology, ecology and molecular biology (DNA evidence) appear to have clarified its taxonomy: it seems to be a full species, parapatric with Black-capped and allopatric with Montane Forest Screech Owl [71]. (Note also that Long-tufted is much more heavily built than Black-capped, this being obvious in osteological comparisons: humerus, femur and tarsus are distinctly larger and thicker; the talons are much larger and much more powerful.)

REFERENCES Belton (1984), Hardy *et al.* (1989), Heidrich *et al.* (1994), Hekstra (1982), König (1991, 1994 and unpublished), Sick (1985).

---

80   VERMICULATED SCREECH OWL
Otus vermiculatus   Plate 22

Syn: *Megascops vermiculatus*

French: Scops vermiculé
German: Kritzel-Kreischeule
Spanish: Telocote vermiculado

IDENTIFICATION A relatively small screech owl (20-23cm) with short ear-tufts, bright yellow eyes and bare brownish-pink toes. Greyish-brown and rufous morphs occur. Whitish scapular stripe rather prominent; underparts with fine dark shaft-streaks, densely vermiculated dark and light. Light rufous-brown facial disc, indistinctly rimmed; lighter eyebrows indistinct or even absent. Bill greyish-olive with greenish tint. **Similar species** Guatemalan Screech Owl [82], often thought conspecific with Vermiculated, differs vocally; the two are very similar in plumage, but Guatemalan is less densely vermiculated and more coarsely streaked, and has prominent whitish eyebrows. Peruvian Screech Owl [70] has a dark crown and lives in dry habitats; Bearded [65] is smaller, with wingtips reaching far beyond tail, and has an 'ocellated' pattern on lower breast and belly; Tropical [68] has a typical herringbone-like pattern below; Pacific [63] is larger, with bristled toes; Bare-shanked [67] is larger, with lower portion of tarsi bare; and Whiskered [64] has relatively small and bristled toes. All are best distinguished by voice.

VOCALISATIONS The A-song seems to be a very rapid purring trill of about 5-8 seconds' duration, beginning softly, gradually increasing a little in pitch and volume, and dropping slightly in pitch on the last 5 notes and becoming fainter before breaking off. The individual *u* notes are given in very rapid succession, with 17 notes per second, faster than in Guatemalan Screech Owl (14 per second). Females have a similar, slightly higher-pitched and shorter song. The B-song is probably a very short, purring trill (1-1.5 seconds), falling strongly in pitch and having a 'melancholy' character: *rreeoorr*. It has some similarity with that of Peruvian Screech Owl, but is much

shorter and more downward-bent. Females have a similar but slightly higher B-song, sometimes duetting with males.

In addition, a scratchy, sibilant *ghoor* is uttered by both sexes and may have a contact function. A sharp *prrrowr* with rising inflection seems to be an aggressive call. (See also Remarks.)

DISTRIBUTION Costa Rica, Panama, and extreme (mostly coastal) NW South America in NW Colombia and N Venezuela.

Vermiculated Screech Owl

MOVEMENTS Resident.

HABITAT Humid tropical forest with many epiphytes, up to about 1,200m.

DESCRIPTION Adult Rufous and greyish-brown morphs are known. *Grey-brown morph:* Facial disc rufous-brownish, finely vermiculated dark; rim very indistinct. No prominent pale eyebrows. Ear-tufts short, mottled and vermiculated dark and light. Crown with blackish shaft-streaks and dark mottling or indistinct barring; hindcrown with indistinct pale collar. Upperparts greyish-brown with warmer brown tinge; mantle and back warm greyish-brown with whitish or pale buffy spots, dark shaft-streaks and cross-bars, as well as indistinct vermiculations (dark markings not very obvious); scapulars with whitish outer webs, spotted or mottled with dark, forming whitish, sometimes partly broken stripe across shoulder. Flight and tail feathers barred light and dark (tips of wings project beyond tail). Underparts pale greyish-brown, feathers with thin dark shaft-streaks, cross-bars and dense, fine vermiculations (latter the most prominent pattern on undersurface). Tarsi feathered nearly to base of toes, the latter bare. *Rufous morph:* Similar in plumage pattern, but general colour rufous-brown, and dark patterning less prominent. **Juvenile** Similar to other screech owls. **Bare parts** Irides bright yellow, with slight orange wash towards pupil. Cere and bill greyish-olive with greenish tinge. Toes pinkish-brown. Claws pale horn with darker tips.

MEASUREMENTS AND WEIGHT Total length 20-23cm. Wing 150-170mm; tail about 80mm (shorter than on Guatemalan). Weight about 107g.

GEOGRAPHICAL VARIATION Monotypic: *Otus vermiculatus* Ridgway, 1887. Individual variation is frequent.

HABITS Similar to those of other screech owls. A nocturnal bird, which may (as most screech owls) be stimulated to sing by playback of its song.

FOOD Apparently mainly insects; perhaps also small vertebrates.

BREEDING Breeds in cavities in trees (woodpecker holes, knotholes, etc). Breeding biology poorly known.

STATUS AND CONSERVATION Uncertain. Probably threatened by forest destruction.

REMARKS We treat this taxon as a full species, as it has A- and B-songs which differ from those of Guatemalan Screech Owl; interbreeding or hybrids between the two are not known. Vermiculated Screech Owl seems to replace Guatemalan from Costa Rica southward to NW Colombia and N Venezuela. Because Vermiculated has until now been thought, incorrectly, to be a race of Guatemalan Screech Owl, the vocalisations of the two have not been distinguished. Bioacoustic studies are needed for the whole '*guatemalae-vermiculatus* group'.

REFERENCES Boyer & Hume (1991), Dunning (1993), Hardy *et al.* (1989), Howell & Webb (1995), Marshall (1967), Marshall & King (1988), Marshall *et al.* (1991), Stiles & Skutch (1989).

---

81   RORAIMA SCREECH OWL
Otus roraimae   Plate 22

Syn: *Megascops roraimae*

French: Scops de Roraima
German: Roraima-Kreischeule
Spanish: Curucucú de Roraima

IDENTIFICATION Similar in size to Guatemalan and Vermiculated Screech Owls [82, 80], but much darker and more coarsely patterned, especially below, where the dark, relatively broad shaft-streaks have broad cross-bars and no vermiculations. Scapulars have very prominent dark-edged whitish outer webs; back appears barred, as feathers often have pale elongated spots at each side of the dark shaft-streak. Ear-tufts small; eyes yellow. **Similar species** Within its range (mountains of Roraima and Duida in Venezuela), there is only one other screech owl, subspecies *duidae* of Tropical Screech Owl [68] (which may possibly represent a separate species, too): that has a typical herringbone-like pattern on underparts, a well-pronounced rim around facial disc and a different song. Northern Tawny-bellied Screech Owl [76] is a bird of lowland primary forest, with a different song.

VOCALISATIONS The A-song of the male is a rather high-pitched trill (higher than Guatemalan's) of about 5-8 seconds' duration, with about 50 *u* notes in one phrase. This begins softly, increases in volume but on a descending scale, and towards the end the notes become fainter before breaking off. The speed is similar to that of Guatemalan Screech Owl (about 14 notes per second), but that species has much longer phrases and at lower pitch. The female has a similar but slightly higher-pitched song. The B-song and other vocalisations are unknown.

DISTRIBUTION Probably endemic to the mountainous regions of Roraima, Duida and Neblina in Venezuela/Brazil.

MOVEMENTS Resident.

HABITAT Rainforest on the slopes of the tepuis and other steep mountains between 1,000m and 1,800m above sea-level, perhaps locally at lower elevations.

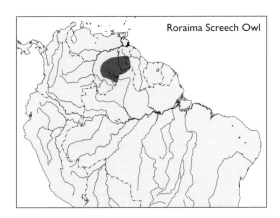

Roraima Screech Owl

DESCRIPTION Adult Facial disc brownish with rufous suffusion and dark mottling; rim of disc more prominent than on Vermiculated Screech Owl, but much less than on Tropical. Eyebrows paler than surrounding plumage. Ear-tufts very short and pointed, mostly dark, contrasting with light eyebrows. Hindcrown without distinct nuchal collar. Upperparts in general relatively dark rufous-brown, feathers with darker shaft-streaks and pale buffy to nearly whitish oval spots on each side of central streak (pattern less conspicuous on crown), these pale spots often having a dark dot near centre; scapulars with distinct buffy-whitish outer webs, edged dark, forming light row across shoulder. Flight and tail feathers barred light and dark. Underparts pale ochraceous-buff, with broad, dark shaft-streaks on sides of upper breast and thinner ones on rest of underside, the feathers with dark brown and rufous cross-bars on each side of the central streak, giving underparts a coarsely patterned appearance. Tarsi feathered almost to base of toes, the latter bare. **Juvenile** Not described. **Bare parts** Eyes bright yellow. Cere and bill dull olive. Toes pale brownish with pinkish tinge. Claws horn with darker tips.

MEASUREMENTS AND WEIGHT Total length 20-23cm. Wing 150-170mm. Weight: no data.

GEOGRAPHICAL VARIATION Monotypic: *Otus roraimae* (Salvin, 1897).

HABITS Probably similar to those of other screech owls.

FOOD Apparently mainly insects and other arthropods; probably also small vertebrates at times.

BREEDING Not described. Probably nests in cavities of trees (e.g. woodpecker holes, knotholes).

STATUS AND CONSERVATION Uncertain.

REMARKS We consider *roraimae* a full species, separating it from Guatemalan and Vermiculated Screech Owls on vocal and zoogeographical grounds. It is probably an endemic of the Guayana Mountains, reaching from Mt Duida to Mt Roraima and Cerro Neblina.

REFERENCES Marshall *et al.* (1991), König (unpublished), Meyer de Schauensee & Phelps (1978).

82 GUATEMALAN SCREECH OWL
Otus guatemalae **Plate 22**

Syn: *Megascops guatemalae*

French: Scops de Guatémala
German: Guatemala-Kreischeule
Spanish: Telocote variable

IDENTIFICATION Similar in size and coloration to Vermiculated Screech Owl [80], but tarsi feathered to base of toes, the latter longer and slimmer and dusky flesh in coloration. Tail relatively longer (tips of wings do not project past tail); underparts more distinctly streaked (with cross-bars) and less densely vermiculated. Crown more or less barred dark on greyish-brown ground; eyebrows whitish; ear-tufts small. Bill greenish-olive; eyes yellow. Grey and red morphs occur. **Similar species** Vermiculated Screech Owl has a relatively shorter tail and is more finely vermiculated below; crown with darker spots or shaft-streaks, instead of broad barring; B-song strikingly different. Bearded Screech Owl [65] is smaller, with 'ocellated' underside and a very short tail. Western, Eastern, Oaxaca and Pacific Screech Owls [60-63] have feathered or bristled toes. Bare-shanked Screech Owl [67] is much larger, with lower half of tarsi bare, while Balsas Screech Owl [66] is also much larger and heavier and has brown eyes. Whiskered Screech Owl [64] is smaller, more coarsely streaked, and has bristled toes. All are best separated by vocal patterns.

VOCALISATIONS The A-song of the male is a long trill of *u* notes (14 per second), sometimes lasting up to about 20 seconds; after a pause of several seconds, this is repeated. The song starts softly, increases gradually in volume and slightly in pitch, and finally breaks off abruptly. It is higher in pitch than the A-song of Vermiculated Screech Owl, and much longer in duration (and Vermiculated utters the individual notes in more rapid succession, 17 per second). The female has a similar but slightly higher-pitched song, with a tinny character, mostly of shorter duration than the male's A-song. The B-song is a short sequence of accelerating staccato notes with rhythm of a table-tennis ball bouncing on a hard surface: *bup bup bup-bup-bupbubububurrt*. A similar, slightly higher-pitched song is given by the female in courtship duets with her mate.

DISTRIBUTION Mexico, on the Pacific slope from about S Sonora to Oaxaca, and on the Atlantic side from Tamaulipas south to Yucatán and E Chiapas. Also Belize, Guatemala, Honduras, Nicaragua and N Costa Rica.

MOVEMENTS Resident.

Guatemalan Screech Owl

HABITAT Humid to semi-arid forest (evergreen or semi-deciduous), as well as dense scrubby woodland. From sea-level up to about 1,500m.

DESCRIPTION *O. g. guatemalae* **Adult** Greyish and red morphs are known. *Grey morph*: Facial disc greyish-brown with fine vermiculations; rim around disc consisting of a fine row of blackish spots (somewhat more distinct than on Vermiculated). Eyebrows whitish, contrasting with darker surrounding plumage. Ear-tufts short and pointed, relatively dark and contrasting with whitish eyebrows. Crown similar to back, but blackish markings rather broad and prominent on upper edges of feathers, giving lightly barred appearance; hindneck with pale, not very prominent collar. Upperparts rather dark greyish-brown with blackish shaft-streaks, cross-bars, flecks and vermiculations; scapulars with blackish-edged whitish outer webs, forming a whitish row across shoulder. Flight and tail feathers barred dark. General colour of underparts paler than upperparts, with blackish shaft-streaks and cross-bars (more prominent than on Vermiculated); brownish vermiculations on upper breast, fewer or none on lower areas; throat whitish. Tarsi feathered to base of toes, the latter bare and relatively long. *Red morph*: Generally rufous, with dark patterns less prominent. **Juvenile** Downy chick whitish. Mesoptile similar to adult, but with indistinct barring on head, nape and mantle, as well as on underparts. **Bare parts** Eyes yellow. Bill and cere greenish. Toes dusky flesh. Claws horn with darker tips.

MEASUREMENTS AND WEIGHT Total length 20-23cm. Wing 140-178.5mm, normally around 150mm; tail 89-94mm. Weight 91-123g.

GEOGRAPHICAL VARIATION Of the many described subspecies, we treat here only four; the others either represent apparently individual variations or are separate species.

O. g. guatemalae (Sharpe, 1875). Mexico (from S Vera Cruz) to Guatemala and Honduras. See Description. Wing 152-178.5mm.

O. g. hastatus (Ridgway, 1887). W Mexico from Sonora to Sinaloa. Back with 'hastate' pattern: on light tawny-brown ground colour, pagoda-shaped marks, with distinct black streaks crossed by rows of small black dots. Wing 153-165mm.

O. g. cassini (Ridgway, 1878). Mexico from Vera Cruz to Tamaulipas. Smallest and darkest race. More coarsely patterned than other subspecies, with ochre malar stripe and lighter occipital and nuchal collar. Wing 150-152mm; tail 68-78mm.

O. g. dacrysistactus Moore & Peters, 1939. N Nicaragua and E Honduras to N Costa Rica. Similar to nominate *guatemalae*, but paler above and more vermiculated below. Wing 164-171mm.

HABITS A nocturnal bird which hides away during day in dense foliage or natural cavities in trees. Very difficult to see, even when singing, as it rarely chooses an open song perch. May be stimulated to sing and to come closer by playback or imitation of its songs. General behaviour is similar to that of other screech owls.

FOOD Chiefly insects and larger arthropods, the rather long, slender toes being well adapted to catch insects such as mantids, phasmids, etc; small rodents and other small terrestrial vertebrates are occasionally reported as prey. Hunts rather frequently at forest edge or in clearings, where it may be seen hunting insects in flight. Prey is caught by swooping on it from a perch, or in flight. Insects are taken from branches, from the ground, or on the wing.

BREEDING Natural tree cavities (especially woodpecker holes and knotholes) are use as nesting site, with normally 2-3 white eggs laid on the bottom debris already present in the hole. Breeding biology similar to that of other screech owls, but requires study.

STATUS AND CONSERVATION Uncertain, but locally not yet rare. Forest destruction represents a threat.

REMARKS We separate *Otus guatemalae* specifically from the taxa *vermiculatus*, *roraimae* and *napensis* on vocal and zoogeographical grounds. Guatemalan Screech Owl is to us a Mexican bird which extends south to Nicaragua, Honduras and N Costa Rica. From Costa Rica to NW South America Vermiculated Screech Owl is found, which has different vocalisations. In mountains of E Venezuela lives an isolated (perhaps endemic) taxon, which may also occur in surrounding forest at lower elevations: Roraima Screech Owl [81] is characterised by plumage pattern and voice. The E Andean Rio Napo Screech Owl [83] and Guatemalan are allopatric, their ranges being separated by the range occupied by Vermiculated; though superficially similar to Vermiculated, Rio Napo has different vocalisations, above all the B-songs. Doubtless all are related and probably belong to the same superspecies (*Otus guatemalae*), having specific rank as allospecies or paraspecies.

REFERENCES Dunning (1993), Hardy *et al.* (1989), Hekstra (1982), Howell & Webb (1995), König (1994 and unpublished), Marshall (1967), Marshall *et al.* (1991), Stiles & Skutch (1989), Voous (1988).

---

83   RIO NAPO SCREECH OWL
Otus napensis   Plate 22

Syn: *Megascops napensis*

French: Scops du Rio Napo
German: Rio Napo Kreischeule
Spanish : Telocote del Rio Napo

IDENTIFICATION Very similar to Vermiculated Screech Owl [80], but with prominent whitish eyebrows. In general, a relatively small (about 21cm), greyish-brown or rufescent screech owl with fine (not prominent) darker and lighter markings. Ear-tufts short, distinctly darker than pale eyebrows; hindcrown without distinct pale collar; rim of facial disc very indistinct or even absent. Eyes yellow, sometimes brown. **Similar species** Vermiculated has relatively longer wings, projecting slightly beyond tips of tail feathers, lacks prominent whitish eyebrows, and its the toes are longer; no brown-eyed individuals have yet been found. Northern and Southern Tawny-bellied Screech Owls [76, 77] are much darker, with longer ear-tufts, and both live at lower altitudes in dense primary forest. Rufescent and Colombian Screech Owls [72, 74] are much larger and heavier. Cloud-forest Screech Owl [73] has a dark-rimmed facial disc and more coarsely patterned underparts. Cinnamon Screech Owl [75] is nearly uniform cinnamon-brown, and has no row of whitish spots across shoulder. White-throated Screech Owl [85] lives at much

higher elevations, is larger and has no ear-tufts; its throat is very distinctly white. Tropical Screech Owl [68] is of about the same size, but normally avoids dense forest; it has a rather prominent herringbone-like pattern on its underside and no pale-edged hindcrown. All are best separated by vocal patterns.

VOCALISATIONS The A-song is very similar to that of the allopatric Guatemalan Screech Owl [82], but shorter in duration. It starts quietly, increases gradually in volume and pitch, then drops slightly in pitch without altering volume; towards the end the volume is slightly reduced, before the phrase breaks off. As with Guatemalan, 14 notes are uttered per second. A single phrase lasts about 7-10 seconds. The female has a similar A-song, but normally shorter and slightly higher-pitched (often with a tinny quality). The B-song is totally different from those of Guatemalan and Vermiculated, being a slightly accelerating sequence of downward-inflected notes, introduced by a short trill: *gurreeo gyo-gyo-gyo-gyo-gyo*. It is uttered by both sexes, in situations similar to those in which other screech owls give B-song. A single, somewhat drawn-out mewing *kaweeoh* obviously has an aggressive character, as it is often uttered in alternation with phrases of the B-song by male and female when disturbed near the nest site by playback.

DISTRIBUTION From E Ecuador and E Colombia along the E Andean slope to Peru and N Bolivia.

Rio Napo Screech Owl

MOVEMENTS Resident.

HABITAT Dense rainforest, from about 250m up to 1,500m.

DESCRIPTION *O. n. napensis* Adult A dark cinnamon-brown and a light cinnamon-buff morph are known. *Dark morph*: Facial disc brownish-cinnamon, finely vermiculated darker, not contrasting with the surrounding plumage; rim around disc mostly indistinguishable from surrounding plumage. Eyebrows very pale, almost whitish, contrasting with dark, short ear-tufts. Crown dark cinnamon-brown, densely vermiculated, spotted and streaked blackish; hindcrown without pale collar; Upperparts dark cinnamon-brown with blackish speckles, vermiculations and streaks; scapulars with white outer webs, edged blackish, forming distinct row of white spots across shoulder. Flight and tail feathers barred light and dark (wing-tips do not reach tip of tail). Underparts pale buffy-brown, darker on upper breast, with thin dark shaft-streaks, some cross-bars, and rather densely vermiculated on upper breast. Tarsi feathered to base of toes, the latter bare and shorter than on Guatemalan. **Juvenile** Similar to Guatemalan Screech Owl. **Bare parts** Eyes yellow, sometimes brown. Bill and cere pale leaden-bluish. Toes pale greyish-brown to flesh. Claws horn with darker tips.

MEASUREMENTS AND WEIGHT Total length 20-22.7cm. Wing 157-175mm. Weight: no data.

GEOGRAPHICAL VARIATION Three subspecies.
    O. n. napensis Chapman, 1928. E Ecuador and E Colombia. See Description. Wing 157-174mm.
    O. n. helleri Kelso, 1940. Peru. Paler than nominate race. Light morph brighter cinnamon-rufous than nominate form. Below, densely vermiculated to belly, shaft-streaks very thin, inconspicuous. Wing 162-175mm.
    O. n. bolivianus Bond & de Schauensee, 1941. N Bolivia in Cochabamba (type specimen with yellow eyes was collected at mouth of Rio Chaparé, at about 300 m). Similar to *napensis*, but upper breast almost lacking vermiculations, lower breast and belly marked with several shaft-streaks and cross-bars.

HABITS Similar to those of other screech owls.

FOOD Chiefly insects and other arthropods; locusts (Tettigoniidae) are a favourite prey. Perhaps also takes small vertebrates.

BREEDING Similar to that of other screech owls. Lays in natural holes in trees.

STATUS AND CONSERVATION Uncertain. Locally not rare; at Cerros del Sira (Peru), 14 individuals were netted near an expedition camp 900m above sea-level in dense mountain forest. Apparently threatened by forest destruction.

REMARKS We treat this owl as separate species on the grounds of morphology (ratio of wings to tail, size of talons, colour of bill), vocal evidence and zoogeographical aspects: see under Guatemalan Screech Owl.

REFERENCES Bond & Meyer de Schauensee (1941), Chapman (1928), Hardy *et al.* (1989), Hilty & Brown (1986), Kelso (1940), König (1994 and unpublished), Marshall *et al.* (1991).

---

84   PUERTO RICAN SCREECH OWL
Otus nudipes   Plate 22

Syn: *Megascops nudipes*

French: Scops de Puerto Rico
German: Puerto Rico-Kreischeule
Spanish: Telocote de Puerto Rico or Múcaro

IDENTIFICATION A greyish-brown or rufescent screech owl (20-22cm) with more than half of tarsi bare, a rounded head without ear-tufts, and brownish eyes. No distinct rim around facial disc; underparts with dark shaft-streaks,

cross-bars and vermiculations. **Similar species** Cuban Bare-legged Owl [87] has very long, totally bare tarsi, a whitish to pale buffy facial disc, and prominent whitish eyebrows; it is brown above with some whitish and darker spots, and brownish-white below with dark shaft-streaks, and has a relatively long tail. All other species of screech owl in the Caribbean have ear-tufts. Note that there are only two species of true owl on Puerto Rico, the present species and Short-eared Owl [211], which is much larger and has yellow eyes and short ear-tufts.

VOCALISATIONS The A-song of the male is a short, relatively deep, somewhat guttural, toad-like quavering trill of about 3-5 seconds' duration, *rrurrrrrr*. The B-song is a shorter trill (about 2 seconds), which begins rather softly, rises gradually in pitch and volume to a peak, then drops and fades away rather rapidly: *rruorrr*. The songs of the female are similar, but higher-pitched. When duetting (B-song), male and female are so well synchronised that one could believe that a single bird were singing with two voices. A soft cackling *gu-gu* may have a contact function. A loud *coo-coo* is quite often uttered, too, this giving the bird its Virgin Islands name of 'Cuckoo Bird'. A hoarse croaking may sometimes be heard.

DISTRIBUTION Puerto Rico, Isla de Vieques, Isla de Culebra and adjacent Virgin Islands (e.g. St Thomas, St Croix, St John, Tortola).

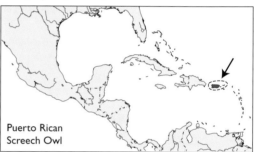

Puerto Rican
Screech Owl

MOVEMENTS Resident.

HABITAT Dense woodland; also thickets and caves.

DESCRIPTION *O. n. nudipes* **Adult** A brownish-grey and a less common rufescent morph are known. *Brownish-grey morph*: Facial disc greyish-brown, with darker vermiculations arranged more or less in concentric rows; no distinct rim. Eyebrows only indistinctly lighter than surrounding plumage. Ear-tufts lacking. Upperparts greyish-brown, spotted, slightly barred and streaked darker, and flecked lighter; crown as mantle, but dark markings more or less in longitudinal rows; scapulars with whitish portions, these forming indistinct pale row across shoulder. Flight and tail feathers barred dark and light; whitish bars on tail much thinner than darker ones. Underparts similar in general colour to upperparts, but lighter, and becoming gradually whitish towards belly, individual feathers with dark shaft-streaks and cross-bars; upper breast with many brown vermiculations, lower parts with few, and abdomen nearly all whitish. Only uppermost part of tarsi feathered, the rest bare. Toes also bare. *Rufescent morph*: Similar in pattern, but general coloration pale rufescent-brown or rather foxy ochraceous-buff. **Juvenile** Downy chick whitish. Mesoptile similar to adult, but less clearly patterned, and more barred light and dark on underparts, crown and mantle. **Bare parts** Eyes brown. Cere and bill greenish-yellow. Tarsi and toes greyish-yellow. Claws dark horn with blackish tips.

MEASUREMENTS AND WEIGHT Total length 20-22cm. Wing 145-173mm; tail about 86mm. Weight 103-154g.

GEOGRAPHICAL VARIATION Two races treated, but validity of this subdivision unclear. Racial separation perhaps due more to polymorphy.

O. n. nudipes (Daudin, 1800). Puerto Rico. See Description. Wing 154-173mm.

O. n. newtoni (Lawrence, 1860). Virgin Islands. Less densely vermiculated and streaked below. Wing 145-163mm.

HABITS A nocturnal bird, hiding away during day in dense foliage of trees or in thickets; also uses caves in cliffs as daytime haunt. Calls in early morning and in evening, and birds can be attracted by making thin mouse-like squeaks. Little is known of its behaviour.

FOOD Mostly insects and other arthropods; occasionally also small vertebrates.

BREEDING Little studied. Breeding season apparently April-June. Crevices in limestone cliffs, caves, and holes in trees (woodpecker holes, knotholes) are used as nesting sites; even cavities under eaves of houses serve for breeding. The female lays 2-3 white eggs, which she incubates alone, being fed by her mate.

STATUS AND CONSERVATION Although this owl appears to be still common on Puerto Rico, it is rare in the Virgin Islands. Recent reports suggest that the species is extinct on Vieques; and in the Virgin Islands habitat loss, as well as egg predation by Pearly-eyed Thrashers *Margarops fuscatus*, have reduced its numbers to the point where it is now considered critically endangered.

REMARKS The Puerto Rican Screech Owl is doubtless related to other screech owls, but specifically distinct from Guatemalan, even though the two have somewhat similar A-songs. It is endemic to Puerto Rico and adjacent islands in the Caribbean.

REFERENCES Bond (1974), Dunning (1993), Hardy *et al.* (1989), Hekstra (1982), Raffaele *et al.* (1998), van der Weyden (1973, 1975).

85 WHITE-THROATED SCREECH OWL
Otus albogularis   Plate 23

Syn: *Macabra albugularis*

French: Scops à gorge blanche
German: Weiâkehl-Kreischeule
Spanish: Curucucú gargantiblanco

IDENTIFICATION A relatively large (about 28cm), dark screech owl with practically no ear-tufts, but with a fluffy-feathered head. Shoulders without whitish row of feathers; chin and throat with large, very prominent, white zone on each side of bill, contrasting greatly with surrounding dark plumage; rim around facial disc very inconspicuous or lacking. Eyes orange-yellow. **Similar species** No other

screech owl of higher regions of the Andes has such a prominent white throat. Comination of general dark coloration, relatively large size, white throat, total lack of white scapular stripe and the fluffy-feathered head make this species very characteristic. Vocal patterns are also very important distinction from other species, e.g. Maria Koepcke's, Montane Forest, Rufescent, Cloud-forest, Colombian and Rio Napo Screech Owls [69, 71, 72, 73, 74, 83].

VOCALISATIONS One song of the male is a sequence of equally spaced and gradually descending hollow, rather mellow hoots in relatively rapid succession (about 4-5 notes per second). Such phrases are repeated at intervals of about 5-10 seconds. Male and female may sometimes be heard duetting, the voice of the female being slightly higher in pitch: *wububúbubububu.* Another song consists of 7-30 gruff but hollow notes in rhythmic series: *chuchurrochurro-churrochurro-churrochurro-gugugugugug.* Both sexes may utter this song in duet, too. It is not certain which one is the A-song and which is the B-song, but in other screech owls the A-song (primary or territorial) is normally a longer series, while the B-song (secondary or nuptial song, mostly duetting with female, but also in aggressive situations) is generally short; accordingly, the A-song would be the long rhythmic series, while the short sequence of descending hoots would represent the B-song, but this remains unproven and further studies of the species' vocal behaviour are needed. Single hoots probably serve to maintain contact between mates or with fledged young.

White-throated Screech Owl

DISTRIBUTION Andean forest from Colombia and NW Venezuela south through Ecuador and Peru to C Bolivia (Cochabamba).

MOVEMENTS Apparently resident.

HABITAT Montane forest (rain and cloud forests) from about 1,300m up to 3,600m above sea-level, mainly between 2,000m and 3,000m; habitat is mostly characterised by dense forest rich in epiphytes and with bamboo thickets. In higher regions, found also in semi-open areas with patches of woodland. Extends from the subtropical to the upper temperate zone.

DESCRIPTION *O. a. albogularis* **Adult** Facial disc dark, without distinct rim. Eyebrows whitish, but not very prominent. Crown as mantle, but with fluffy feathers carried rather loose and giving head a tousled appearance. Upperparts dark fuscous-brown with blackish mottles, and some tiny rufous or buffy and whitish spots (but no row of whitish spots across shoulder). Wings and relatively long tail barred light and dark, the light bars on tail feathers very thin. Underparts tawny-buff, darker on upper breast, becoming paler and more buffy towards abdomen, feathers with dusky shaft-streaks and cross-bars; throat with large oval area of white on each side of bill (this pattern more prominent than on any other *Otus* species). Tarsi feathered buffy to base of toes, the latter bare. **Juvenile** Downy chick dirty whitish. Mesoptile pale buffy-grey with orbital discs and long bristles above bill; underparts, mantle and crown evenly barred dusky. On fledging, similar to adult but less distinctly marked. **Bare parts** Eyes orange-yellow. Cere and bill greenish-yellow to greenish-grey. Toes yellowish-grey to brownish-flesh. Claws pale horn with darker tips.

MEASUREMENTS AND WEIGHT Total length 25-28cm. Wing 190-218mm; tail about 127mm. Weight about 185g.

GEOGRAPHICAL VARIATION We recognise four subspecies. Other named races may involve polymorphy only.

O. a. albogularis (Cassin, 1848). Andes of Colombia amd Ecuador. See Description.

O. a. meridensis (Chapman, 1923). Andes of Mérida, Venezuela. Forehead and eyebrows whitish, crown more spotted than in nominate race; belly paler, with whitish abdomen. Wing 196-207mm.

O. a. remotus Bond & Meyer de Schauensee, 1941. E

Andes from Peru to Bolivia. Darkest subspecies. Almost black above, with cream-buff and whitish spots; general colour of belly and abdomen creamy-buff to whitish. Wing 203-218mm. (We include *obscurus* in *remotus*.)

O. a. macabrum (Bonaparte, 1850). W Andes from Colombia and Ecuador to W Peru. Similar to nominate race, but underparts more finely patterned; markings on inner webs of primaries reduced. Wing 190-213mm.

HABITS Strictly nocturnal. Behaviour little studied.

FOOD Mainly insects and other arthropods, but evidently also small vertebrates.

BREEDING Requires study. One female with enlarged ovary was found in July (C Peru); pulli found in October (Ecuador); juveniles observed in January (Ecuador), March (C Peru), and September (Venezuela). Said to nest either on the ground among grass or ferns, or in open nests of other birds in bushes or trees; one incubated egg was found in a deserted cup nest above ground; probably also uses holes in trees if these are available.

STATUS AND CONSERVATION Uncertain.

REMARKS This owl is sometimes placed into a monotypic genus *Macabra*, but according to DNA evidence it is quite closely related to owls of the subgenus *Megascops*. It shares with the latter the two different songs (A- and B-songs). We therefore leave it within *Otus*, where it may be placed in the subgenus *Macabra*.

REFERENCES Fjeldså & Krabbe (1990), Hardy *et al.* (1989), Hilty & Brown (1986), Marshall & King (1988), Meyer de Schauensee & Phelps (1978).

Palau Scops Owl, Genus *Pyrroglaux* Yamashina, 1938

Small, long-legged owls without visible ear-tufts. Legs rather long; tarsi and toes bare. One species on Palau Islands. We place the Palau Scops Owl in the genus *Pyrroglaux* because it seems to us less closely related to scops owls of the genus *Otus*, but further studies will be necessary to clarify its taxonomy.

86   PALAU SCOPS OWL
Pyrroglaux podarginus   Plate 23

Syn: *Otus podarginus*

French: Petit-duc de Palau
German: Palau-Zwergohreule

IDENTIFICATION A small (22cm), dark rufous owl with hardly visible ear-tufts and bare tarsi. Forehead and superciliary area whitish, tinged with rufous-buff, and narrowly barred blackish-brown; facial disc with narrow concentric dark rufous-brown rings; breast and abdomen narrowly barred with white and black. Darker and lighter colour morphs exist. Bill and feet whitish; eyes brown or orange-yellow. **Similar species** None. The only other owl on Palau Islands is the Short-eared Owl [211], which is very much larger and quite different in appearance.

VOCALISATIONS The song of the male is a series of clear single notes (similar to the alarm call of a Blackbird *Turdus merula*) uttered at intervals of almost 1 second: *kwuk kwuk...*

When excited, the intervals become shorter and finally disyllabic, usually returning to single notes which fade away: *kwuk-kwuk... kwuk-kwuk... kwugook kwugook... kwuk kwuk.* The single notes may vary in length and quality, sometimes softer, sometimes harder. (Description of vocalisation from a recording by D. W. Steadman in January 1997.) The voice of the female is similar, but higher in pitch. Male and female duet during courtship.

DISTRIBUTION Palau Islands (Micronesia): reported from the islands of Koror, Babelthuap, Peleliu, Urukthabel and Angaur.

MOVEMENTS Resident.

HABITAT Mangrove, rainforest and villages in lowlands. At night, very common around villages (Koror); specimens have been obtained at night with the use of a flashlight (Coultas).

DESCRIPTION Sexes claimed not to be exactly alike. **Male** Facial disc pale rufous-buff with narrow darker rufous-brown concentric rings. Forehead and superciliary area whitish, tinged with rufous-buff, and narrowly barred

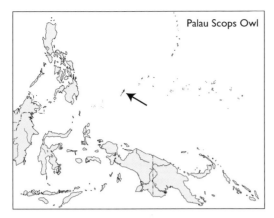
Palau Scops Owl

with white shaft-streaks and white spots; underparts more heavily barred. **Bare parts** Iris brown or orange-yellow. Bill, tarsi and toes whitish.

MEASUREMENTS AND WEIGHT Total length 22cm; females presumably average a little larger. Wing 155-163mm (av. 159)mm; tail 82-90mm (av. 84)mm. Weight: no data.

GEOGRAPHICAL VARIATION Monotypic: *Pyrroglaux podarginus* (Hartlaub & Finsch, 1872).

HABITS Nocturnal, keeping in mangrove thickets during daylight hours. Moves around considerably during the night in search of food, particularly in villages. Calls, however, in stationary position on a perch, where it remains for only about 3 minutes or so before moving again.

blackish-brown; feathers a base of upper mandible with long, blackish shafts. Crown and upperparts rufous-brown, some neck feathers narrowly barred with brown and white. Wings sandy-rufous with pale rufous-buff bars. Tail rufous, indistinctly barred dark brown. Throat more whitish-rufous; breast pale rufous, feathers barred with white and black; abdomen paler rufous. Tarsus bare. (Much darker and lighter rufous morphs exist.) **Female** Resembles adult male, but darker brown above with fine blackish vermiculations; underparts may be pale or dark rufous with slight or heavy white and brown bars and spots. **Juvenile** Down plumage pale rufous, lighter on abdomen and belly, darker on breast and back. Immature resembles adult male, but upperparts darker brown, with forehead, crown and back barred ochraceous and black; scapulars

FOOD Insects and other arthropods; also earthworms.

BREEDING Breeding season February-March. Nests in hollow trees or tree holes. Clutch 3-4, egg size 34.3 x 31.7mm.

STATUS AND CONSERVATION Surveys made in 1945 on Koror and Peleliu: 33 pairs were found on Koror (approximately half of the total population), with four pairs on Peleliu. Another expedition in 1945 did not find the owl in the southern Palaus. Highly endangered.

REMARKS Yamashina introduced the generic name *Pyrroglaux* for this species in 1938, as it appeared rather different from *Otus*, in which it had previously been placed.

REFERENCES Baker (1951), Boyer & Hume (1991), Marshall (1949), Mayr (1944), Yamashina (1938).

Bare-legged Owl, Genus *Gymnoglaux* Cabanis, 1855

Similar to screech owls, but without ear-tufts, and with long, bare tarsi and a relatively long tail with only 10 feathers. Vocalisations differ considerably from those of screech owls. Only one species, in Cuba and Isle of Pines (Isla de la Juventud).

87 CUBAN BARE-LEGGED OWL
Gymnoglaux lawrencii   Plate 23

Syn: *Otus lawrencii*

Other names: Cuban Screech Owl

French: Scops de Cuba
German: Kuba-Kreischeule
Spanish: Cotunto

IDENTIFICATION A round-headed, relatively small owl with long, bare legs. Very similar to Burrowing Owl [174], but much smaller. No ear-tufts; eyebrows very prominent, whitish. Generally brown above, dark-streaked brownish-white below. Tail relatively long, wing-tips at most reaching middle of tail. Eyes brown (and yellowish?). **Similar species** Burrowing Owl is larger, with feathered or bristled tarsi and toes, yellow eyes, and barred (not streaked) underside; in Cuba, it breeds more or less only in the west. Cuban Pygmy [149] is smaller, with shorter legs, feathered tarsi and relatively small yellow eyes.

VOCALISATIONS The song is a soft, accelerating *coo-coo-*

coo-guguguk, becoming slightly higher-pitched towards end. The female sometimes answers with a high-pitched, downward-inflected *yiu-yiu-yiu*.... This species has no distinguishable A- and B-songs.

DISTRIBUTION Cuba and Isle of Pines (Isla de la Juventud).

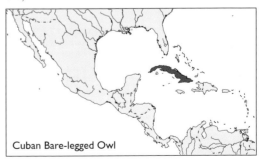
Cuban Bare-legged Owl

MOVEMENTS Resident.

HABITAT Forest, thickets, and semi-open limestone country with caves and crevices.

DESCRIPTION Adult Facial disc whitish-buff with very indistinct rim. Prominent whitish eyebrows. No ear-tufts. Upperparts brown (occasionally rufescent), with blackish spots on crown and hindneck; feathers of mantle and wing-coverts with whitish tips and darker areas in centre; some scapulars with small whitish areas, so that row of whitish spots across shoulder very indistinct or sometimes practically absent. Outer webs of primaries with whitish spots, inner webs uniform brownish; secondaries with thin whitish bars. Only 10 tail feathers: outer ones with thin whitish bars, central feathers uniform (sometimes all tail feathers plain). Underparts cream-whitish with buffy suffusion; neck and throat more or less washed with buffy-brown, finely spotted black; entire underparts with distinct, drop-shaped dark shaft-streaks. Long tarsi and toes totally bare. **Juvenile** Downy chick whitish. Mesoptile similar to adult, but less spotted above. In first-year plumage, tail feathers normally plain brown (but this may also occur in adults). **Bare parts** Eyes brown (sometimes yellowish?); possible that younger birds have brown eyes, older ones yellowish. Cere and bill greyish-yellow. Tarsi and toes yellowish-brown. Claws horn with darker tips.

MEASUREMENTS AND WEIGHT Total length 20-23cm. Wing 137-154mm; tail 71-88mm. Weight: no data.

GEOGRAPHICAL VARIATION Monotypic: *Gymnoglaux lawrencii* (Sclater & Salvin, 1868).

HABITS A nocturnal bird. During daytime it roosts in densely foliaged trees, thickets, crevices in rocks, or in caves. Like Burrowing Owl, this species is often found on the ground, where it searches for prey. With its relatively short, rounded wings and relatively long tail, this owl is able to fly elegantly in densely forested areas, as well as among rocks.

FOOD Chiefly insects and other arthropods; also takes frogs and, rarely, small birds. Frequently hunts on the ground; also hunts from a perch, swooping down on its victim.

BREEDING Reported to breed during first 6 months of the year. A hole or crevice in cliffs, a tree cavity or a cave in limestone country is used as nesting site. Normally 2 white eggs are laid, incubated by the female alone.

STATUS AND CONSERVATION Uncertain. Reported as rather common in most of its range.

REMARKS Cuban Bare-legged Owl differs in many aspects from all screech owls of the subgenus *Megascops*, e.g. it has no known B-song. We therefore follow most recent authors in placing it in its own monotypic genus, *Gymnoglaux*. It may be more closely related to the genus *Athene*: the latter (*A. cunicularia*) breeds in Cuba but is more or less confined to the western part of the island, and it may be that Cuban Bare-legged Owl replaces Burrowing Owl generally on Cuba. DNA analysis is needed to clarify the true relationship of Cuban Bare-legged Owl.

REFERENCES Bond (1974), Boyer & Hume (1991), Eck & Busse (1973), Hardy *et al.* (1989), Hekstra (1982), Raffaele *et al.* (1998).

White-faced Scops Owls, Genus *Ptilopsis* Kaup, 1848

Relatively large scops owls with large orange to red eyes, long ear-tufts and dark-streaked light greyish plumage. Toes feathered at the base, often to halfway along. According to DNA evidence, the white-faced scops owls are very different from typical scops owls of the genus *Otus*; we therefore place them in a separate genus, *Ptilopsis*, which has much larger eyes and has ear-openings twice as large as those of any *Otus*. We recognise two species, which are similar in plumage but have totally different songs.

88 NORTHERN WHITE-FACED SCOPS OWL
Ptilopsis leucotis   Plate 24

French: Petit-duc à face blanche de Temminck
German: Temminck-Weißgesichteule

IDENTIFICATION A rather large scops owl (19-24cm) with long ear-tufts and a black-rimmed white facial disc. Plumage very pale greyish-brown with dark streaks and fine vermiculations. Eyes amber-yellow to orange; feet feathered to about middle of toes. **Similar species** The long ear-tufts, together with the very pale, dark-streaked plumage and the white, broadly rimmed facial disc, distinguish both species of white-faced scops owl from all other scops owls. Southern White-faced Scops Owl [89] is very similar to Northern, but in general greyer and darker above, with eye colour varying from orange-red to ruby-red. The two are best separated by their totally different songs.

VOCALISATIONS The song of the male is a disyllabic, mellow fluting *po-prooh*, repeated several times at intervals of 4-8 seconds. The first note is very short. It is followed after a very short break of about 0.6s by a prolonged *prooh*. The female's song is similar, but weaker and higher in pitch. A low *to-whit-to-wheet* is probably a contact-call, uttered by both sexes. In defensive situations, emits squeaky growls. Young birds beg with hissing sounds.

DISTRIBUTION Africa south of the Sahara, from Senegambia eastwards to Sudan, Somalia, N Uganda and N Kenya. In Kenya and Uganda, probably overlaps in distribution with Southern White-faced Scops Owl.

MOVEMENTS Resident.

HABITAT Savanna with scattered trees, dry open forest, woodland with closed canopy, forest edges and clearings. Preferred habitats are dry savannas with thorn trees. Absent in deserts and dense tropical rainforest.

DESCRIPTION Adult Two colour morphs may be distinguished. *Light morph*: Facial disc whitish, with broad blackish rim. Ear-tufts long, often with blackish tips. Upperparts rather pale greyish-brown with many dark shaft-streaks and faint vermiculations; scapulars with white outer webs, edged dark. Flight and tail feathers barred light and dark greyish-brown. Underparts somewhat lighter than upperparts, with dark shaft-streaks and fine vermiculations. Basal half of toes feathered. *Dark morph*: Similar, but general coloration much darker and with an ochraceous tinge; facial disc brownish-white, crown blackish, ear-tufts with blackish centres. **Juvenile** Downy chick whitish. Mesoptile greyish-white with greyish-brown tips, especially on crown, nape and back; rim of facial disc dark grey-brown. **Bare parts** Eyes vary from deep amber-yellow to orange; juveniles have yellow eyes. Bill yellowish-horn. Toes dusky brown. Claws blackish.

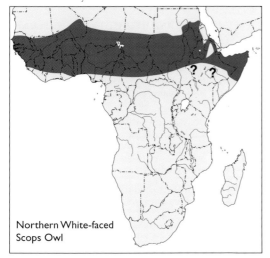

Northern White-faced
Scops Owl

MEASUREMENTS Total length 19-24cm. Wing 171-206mm; tail 79-101mm. Females larger than males.

GEOGRAPHICAL VARIATION Monotypic: *Ptilopsis leucotis* (Temminck, 1820).

Blackish-crowned birds were originally regarded as a subspecies, *P. l. nigrovertex*, but are now known to be merely a dark morph; this occurs alongside the light morph and interbreeds with it, and both morphs may be found in the same nest.

Similarly, a particularly pale morph, rather frequent in Sudan, is often treated as race *P. l. margarethae* (von Jordans & Neubaur, 1932); we consider it likely to be no more than a pale morph.

HABITS A nocturnal bird, roosting by day against a tree trunk, in dense foliage, in thorny shrubs, etc. At its daytime roost, perches upright with feathers held rather tight to the body, appearing very slim, and with ear-tufts erected and eyes closed to fine horizontal slits; well camouflaged as well by this posture, as well by coloration. Often male and female roost quite close to one another at the same site; outside breeding season, several individuals may be found at the same daytime roost. When roosting birds are approached, they threaten by growling and jerk the body back and forth; in greater aggression they bend forward, raise the back feathers, extend the wings, snap with the bill and hiss. At dusk, the owls leave the roost for a prominent lookout, where they often start singing. Song may be heard at any time of the night, but most frequently at dusk or just before dawn.

FOOD Invertebrates and small vertebrates, such as moths, crickets, beetles, scorpions, spiders, and small reptiles; birds and mammals (especially rodents and shrews); takes proportionately more vertebrates than do owls of the genus *Otus*. Prey is generally swallowed whole, even small

birds being swallowed without being plucked. Pellets are generally regurgitated at the roost, beneath which a number may be found if the site is used for a longish period. Hunts from a perch, swooping down on its prey on the ground.

BREEDING The occupied territory is defended by both sexes. Can be very aggressive near the nest, making aerial attacks on intruders. When food is abundant, several pairs may nest quite close together: at least four pairs have been found in 10km², with distance between two nests only about 200m, though territories still defended by each pair. Territory size, however, unknown. At the start of the reproductive cycle the male is vocally very active, singing from different perches in its territory or at potential nesting sites. During courtship male and female often duet. Approaching the female, the male bobs head up and down, continuing to sing, and his mate answers with song or a chirruping call, which probably has a begging function. Potential nest sites are advertised by the male. Natural holes or hollows and crevices in old trees, or quite often old stick nests of larger birds in bushes or trees, are used for breeding; chosen site is normally 2-8m above ground, and nest site may be used for several years by the same pair.

Laying has been recorded from January to September. Normally one clutch per year. Usually lays 2-3 (1-4) white shiny eggs, measuring 36.6-37.3 x 30.3-31.3mm, at intervals of about 2 days. Incubation, starting with the first egg, is by the female alone (the male sometimes covers the clutch for a short time when she leaves the nest), her mate bringing food to her in the bill; the female turns the eggs at least 8 times in one night. Incubation period is about 30 days. The chicks are brooded and fed by the female, with prey delivered to the nest by the male. At 7 days they are able to sit up, and by day 16 the white neoptile down is gradually replaced by the more greyish-brown mesoptile. At 27 days of age young appear fully feathered, and may leave the nest to climb around nearby branches. By 30-32 days they are able to fly well. They are cared for and fed by both parents for at least 2 weeks after leaving the nest.

STATUS AND CONSERVATION Uncommon to locally rather common and widespread in suitable habitats; abundance may vary locally. Rare in Somalia. As most owls, it may be vulnerable owing to the use of pesticides and the destruction of habitat.

REMARKS We give specific rank to the southern counterpart of this owl because of significant differences in their vocalisations and molecularbiological evidence.

REFERENCES Boyer & Hume (1991), Eck & Busse (1973), Fry *et al.* (1985), van der Weyden (1975).

89 SOUTHERN WHITE-FACED SCOPS OWL
Ptilopsis granti   Plate 24

French: Petit-duc à face blanche de Grant
German: Grant-Weiâgesichteule

IDENTIFICATION Very similar to the northern taxon [88], but more pure grey in general coloration. Crown and upperparts deeper grey with black shaft-streaks. Facial disc nearly pure white, with greatly contrasting broad black rim. Adults have mostly red eyes. **Similar species** Northern White-faced Scops Owl is light greyish-brown with an ochraceous tinge, has weaker talons, and contrast between the whitish (slightly ochraceous-tinged) facial disc and the black rim is less marked; best separated by vocal patterns. African Scops Owl [39] is much smaller and has yellow eyes. Common Scops Owl [37], a winter visitor to Africa, is greyish-brown with bark-like plumage pattern; like African Scops, it has yellow eyes and small ear-tufts.

VOCALISATIONS The song begins with a rapid, stuttering staccato trill, followed by a rather clear, somewhat drawn-out note: *whhhhhhhu-hóoh*, the *hóoh* often slightly rising in pitch. This verse is repeated at intervals of several seconds. It somewhat resembles the song of Tropical Screech Owl [68] of South America, but with staccato (rather than trilled) introduction. Other vocalisations are probably similar to those of Northern White-faced; as the two species have until recently been considered conspecific, however, studies on their vocal patterns are urgently needed.

DISTRIBUTION Africa from S Uganda and S Kenya south to the Congo, Angola, Namibia and to the northern Cape Province and Natal.

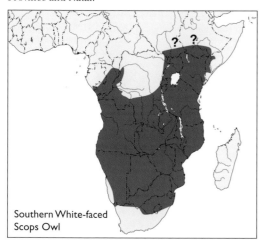

Southern White-faced Scops Owl

MOVEMENTS In general resident. Occasional movements to regions with a temporarily rich supply of prey (rodent plagues) may be observed.

HABITAT Savanna with scattered groups of trees and thorny shrubs, dry open woods (e.g. mopane woodlands), wooded areas along rivers, forest edges and clearings. Avoids dense rainforest and treeless deserts.

DESCRIPTION Adult General coloration nearly pure grey with clear and well-pronounced blackish markings. Facial disc nearly pure white, contrasting greatly with broad black rim. Ear-tufts long, of same coloration as crown and without black tips or centres, but streaked and vermiculated blackish. Upperparts relatively dark grey without any tinge of brown or ochraceous, feathers of crown, nape and mantle with well-pronounced black shaft-streaks and many fine vermiculations; outer webs of scapulars white, edged black, forming white line across shoulder; upperwing-coverts with black streaks and fine mottling. Flight and tail feathers barred light and dark. Underparts lighter grey, with fine blackish shaft-streaks and fine dark

vermiculations (latter less prominent than on Northern White-faced). Tarsi feathered pale grey to basal half of toes. Talons more powerful than on northern counterpart. **Juvenile** Downy chick white. Mesoptile similar in coloration to adult, but less distinctly marked. At fledging, similar to parents but with shorter ear-tufts and less pronounced plumage patterns. **Bare parts** Eyes orange-red to red in adult; young have yellowish-grey eyes, which become yellow before fledging. Bill pale creamy-horn. Bare parts of toes dusky greyish-brown. Claws blackish-horn.

MEASUREMENTS AND WEIGHT Total length 20-24cm. Wing 191-206mm; tail about 90mm. Weight of males about 190g, of females 240-275g.

GEOGRAPHICAL VARIATION Monotypic: *Ptilopsis granti* (Kollibay, 1910). Some individual variation between lighter and darker individuals, but this has no taxonomic significance.

HABITS Strictly nocturnal. Comparative studies are needed of the behaviour of the two white-faced scops owls, which have until now been considered conspecific; any differences in habits between the two taxa have not therefore been elaborated.

FOOD Larger insects, spiders, scorpions, small birds, reptiles and small mammals; largest recorded prey were bush-squirrel *Paraxerus* and doves *Streptopelia*, which are very large for the owl's size. Prey are held with the powerful talons and torn apart with the bill. Prey is normally taken from the ground or from branches. Hunt from perches, dropping down and gliding low over the ground, before swooping up to a new perch.

BREEDING Natural holes in tree trunks or thick branches are used for breeding, but nest platforms of larger birds may also serve as nest site. At the start of the reproductive cycle the male sings intensively, especially at dusk, but the birds may be heard throughout the night. During courtship, male and female duet; later, the female answers her mate with a faint shriek. The clutch is generally of 2-3 pure white eggs, measuring 38.1-42.4 x 31.3-34.5mm (slightly larger than those of Northern White-faced), normally laid between May and November, locally with a peak in July and August (dry season). Incubation, from the first egg, is by female alone and lasts 30 days; during this period the female is fed by the male, who brings food to the nest. The young fledge at 4 weeks of age, and a few days later are able to fly quite well. They are cared for by both parents for at least 2 weeks more.

STATUS AND CONSERVATION Locally rather common. Since the species feeds mainly on insects and small mammals, it is endangered in regions where pesticides are used.

REMARKS Even though the two white-faced scops owls are very similar in plumage and size (which has led to the erroneous assumption that they are conspecific), their nuptial songs are totally different. Comparative studies on their ecology, biology, behaviour and vocalisations will help to shed light on the specific differences between these two closely related species, which perhaps overlap locally in distribution.

REFERENCES Boyer & Hume (1991), Eck & Busse (1973), Fry *et al.* (1988), König (1991), van der Weyden (1975).

Giant Scops Owl, Genus *Mimizuku* Hachisuka, 1934

A monotypic genus. This relatively large owl was formerly often placed in the genus *Otus*, but it is so different from *Otus* owls, and so much larger, that it is better placed in a genus of its own. According to DNA studies, it is, however, more closely related to *Otus* than to *Bubo*.

90 GIANT SCOPS OWL
Mimizuku gurneyi   Plate 24

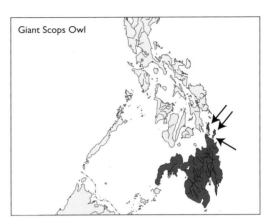

Giant Scops Owl

Other names: Lesser Eagle Owl, Mindanao Owl

French: Hibou de Gurney
German: Mindanao-Ohreule

IDENTIFICATION A relatively large (30-35cm), brown owl, spotted and streaked blackish, with long ear-tufts. Buffy-whitish below, with large oval or drop-shaped black spots on breast, and belly and abdomen white. Facial disc pale rufous-buff with blackish rim; eyebrows frosty whitish. Eyes honey-yellow to warm brown; talons powerful. **Similar species** This owl's characteristic breast pattern, together with its size and general appearance, makes it quite unmistakable. All *Otus* owl are much smaller, while eagle owls are larger and heavier.

VOCALISATIONS According to tape-recordings by P. Morris, the song of the male consists of a growling, melancholic call, with a somewhat hoarse quality. This note is repeated at intervals of 10-20 seconds, often in series of 5-10 notes. The single calls always fall slightly in pitch: *wuaah, wuaah... .*

DISTRIBUTION S Philippines: recorded on Mindanao, Siargo and Dinagat. Absent from Marinduque.

MOVEMENTS Resident.

HABITAT Lowland rainforest and second growth, from sea-level up to about 1,200m. One record of a female at 2,938m seems doubtful to us (and perhaps due to confusion of feet with metres!).

DESCRIPTION Adult Facial disc light rufous-brown; rim thin, consisting of black spots. Eyebrows frosty white, fading into buffy, black-spotted long ear-tufts. Forehead and crown streaked black. Upperpartse dark rufous-brown with blackish shaft-streaks; outer webs of scapulars whitish-buff, edged blackish; wing-coverts dark brown with black shaft-streaks. Flight and tail feathers banded dark and light. Underparts whitish-buff, becoming creamy-white on belly and abdomen; breast with large drop-shaped or oval black spots. Tarsi feathered to base of toes. Talons

powerful. **Juvenile** Unknown. **Bare parts** Eyes brown. Bill greenish-yellow to greyish-white. Toes pale greyish-brown. Claws pale horn with dark tips.

MEASUREMENTS AND WEIGHT Total length 30-35cm. Wing 223-274mm; tail 109-139mm. Weight: No data.

GEOGRAPHICAL VARIATION Monotypic: *Mimizuku gurneyi* (Tweeddale, 1879).

HABITS Strictly nocturnal. Biology and behaviour unknown.

FOOD Probably small vertebrates (e.g. mammals, birds) and larger insects.

BREEDING Unknown.

STATUS AND CONSERVATION Rare, occurring at natural low density. As with all forest birds in the Philippines, it is threatened by the destruction of forest. Listed as Endangered by BirdLife International.

REMARKS This very poorly known owl urgently requires studies on its ecology and biology.

REFERENCES Boyer & Hume (1991), Clark & Mikkola (1989), Collar *et al.* (1994), Delacour & Mayr (1946), Dickinson *et al.* (1991), DuPont & Rabor (1973), Eck & Busse (1973), Hachisuka (1935), Marshall & King (1988), Miranda *et al.* (1997), Ripley & Rabor (1961).

Maned Owl, Genus *Jubula* Bates, 1929

Medium-sized owls with long, bushy ear-tufts extending towards the nape. Only one species, endemic to tropical W and C Africa.

91 MANED OWL
Jubula lettii   Plate 25

French: Hibou à crinière
German: Mähneneule

IDENTIFICATION A medium-sized owl (30-44cm) with

bushy, rather long ear-tufts extending to nape, giving a maned appearance. Crown reddish-brown, scaled white, forehead and eyebrows whitish; underparts ochraceous-buff with prominent blackish shaft-streaks. Eyes deep yellow. **Similar species** The maned head is characteristic of this owl, and no similar species is found in Africa. Scops owls of genus *Otus* are much smaller, with small ear-tufts; eagle owls are heavier, with much more powerful talons, and have differently shaped ear-tufts; fishing owls have fluffy head feathers but no ear-tufts, and their eyes are dark brown.

VOCALISATIONS The song is described as a mellow hooting *who*, followed after an interval of about 10 seconds by another, slightly higher-pitched *who*, the two notes repeated in the same succession for some time. Some doubt exists, however, over whether these recorded vocalisations really are of this species; some authors suspect that the notes may be uttered by Vermiculated Fishing Owl [116], living in similar habitats, and confusion is possible. Until clear evidence becomes available, the described vocalisations of Maned Owl must remain open to doubt.

DISTRIBUTION Africa from Ghana and Liberia to Cameroon, and east to Zaïre.

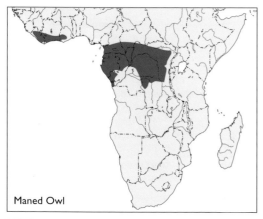

Maned Owl

MOVEMENTS Resident and sedentary.

HABITAT Primary lowland forest and gallery forest with abundant creepers, preferring the vicinity of rivers or lakes. Has never been found outside forested areas.

DESCRIPTION Adult Facial disc light rufous, finely vermiculated dusky brown; rim blackish-brown. Forehead and eyebrows white; crown feathers rufous with white borders, giving scaly appearance. Ear-tufts long and bushy and, together with elongated feathers of sides of head and nape, giving maned appearance. Upperparts rufous or chestnut-brown with dark and light markings; mantle and back chestnut with some barring; scapulars pale buffy with dark-edged whitish outer webs, forming a light band across shoulder; wing-coverts chestnut-brown with dark vermic-

ulations and shaft-streaks. Flight feathers light chestnut with four dark bars. Tail barred rufous and dark. Throat white; rest of underparts rufous, becoming buffer and lighter towards belly; upper breast with many fine white vermiculations, feathers from upper to lower breast with very prominent dark shaft-streaks. Feathering of tarsi buffy. Toes unfeathered. **Juvenile** Downy chick undescribed. Mesoptile rufous-brown, with faint barring on pale rufous underparts and with less developed 'mane'; flight and tail feathers similar to adult. **Bare parts** Eyes deep yellow to orange-yellow. Bill yellow. Cere yellowish-green. Toes yellow, with some grey patches on upperside. Claws brownish-horn with dark tips.

MEASUREMENTS AND WEIGHT Total length 30-44cm. Wing 241-285mm; tail 147-179mm. Weight of 1 female 183g.

GEOGRAPHICAL VARIATION Monotypic: *Jubula lettii* (Büttikofer, 1889).

HABITS Rather unknown. A nocturnal bird which often roosts among creepers in tangled primary forest. Emerges from its day haunt at dusk and flies to open perches, where it may be seen against the dusky sky.

FOOD Chiefly larger insects such as grasshoppers, crickets and beetles; in addition, takes small vertebrates.

BREEDING Practically unknown. A pair with full-grown young was observed in February in Liberia; one fledgling in late December in Cameroon; laying in Zaïre estimated in March/April. Probably nests in natural holes in old trees or in abandoned nests of larger birds. According to available data, clutch is of 3-4 white eggs; incubation period reported to be about 28 days. Young leave the nest at 33 days of age.

STATUS AND CONSERVATION The estimated density is about 1 pair in 1-1.5km² of forest. Although this suggests that the owl is not too rare, its distribution is insufficiently known and its true status therefore remains doubtful. In any case, the increasing destruction of tropical rainforest must be a threat.

REMARKS Some authors suggest lumping the genus *Jubula* with the South American *Lophostrix*. We do not agree, however, as we believe the superficial similarity between the two to be due to convergence. We regard *Lophostrix* and *Jubula* as not closely related.

REFERENCES Chappuis (1978), Clark & Mikkola (1989), Dowsett-Lemaire (1992, 1996), Eck & Busse (1973), Fry *et al.* (1988), Kemp (1989).

Crested Owl, Genus *Lophostrix* Lesson, 1836

Medium-sized dark owl with long erectile ear-tufts. The latter somewhat resemble the 'mane' of African *Jubula*, but they are less interwoven into the 'mane' than in the African counterpart. We consider this an example of convergence, rather than an indication of close relationship.

92   CRESTED OWL
Lophostrix cristata   Plate 25

French: Hibou à casque
German: Haubeneule

Spanish: Lechuza copetona
Portuguese: Coruja-de-carapuca

IDENTIFICATION A medium-sized (about 40cm), rather uniform brown or grey-brown owl with large, white ear-tufts and white eyebrows. Rather plain below, except for very fine, dense vermiculations; scapulars and wing-coverts with white spots. Eyes brown (yellow in the grey morph, which is also considered a different subspecies). Grey, dark, and light brown to rufous-brown morphs exist. **Similar species** The only Central and South American owl of lowland rainforest with unstreaked underparts and long, white ear-tufts and eyebrows.

VOCALISATIONS The song is a rather frog-like croak, which can also be confused with the similar but disyllabic call of Bare-throated Tiger Heron *Tigrisoma mexicanum*. It begins with a stuttering rattle, which accelerates to a purring, guttural and rough croak: *k-k-kk-kk-krrrrrroa*. At a distance, the introductory, lower notes are inaudible, so that the song sounds like *grrrrroa*. This song is uttered at intervals of several seconds.

DISTRIBUTION Locally from S Mexico through Central America to Venezuela, Surinam, the Guianas, Amazonian Colombia, Ecuador, Peru, Brazil and Bolivia.

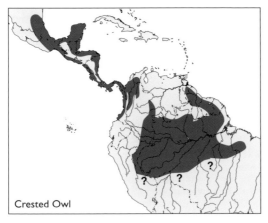

Crested Owl

MOVEMENTS Resident.

HABITAT Lowland rainforest with undergrowth, mainly primary forest but also second growth, up to about 1,500m. Prefers the vicinity of water.

DESCRIPTION *L. c. cristata* **Adult** At least two colour morphs may be distinguished, a dark chocolate-brown and a lighter rufous-brown (a third, greyish, morph is regarded as a different subspecies: *stricklandi*). *Chocolate-brown morph*: Crown, facial disc and upper breast uniform deep chocolate-brown, with dark rim around disc almost invisible. (In this morph, some individuals have rufous facial disc.) Forehead, eyebrows and most of ear-tufts white. Rather plain dark chocolate-brown above, wing-coverts and outer webs of primaries with whitish dots. All flight feathers barred light and dark. Tail feathers rather uniform chocolate-brown with very fine darker mottling. Underparts below upper breast pale brownish with numerous faint brown vermiculations. Tarsi feathered to base of toes. *Rufous-brown morph*: General colour light rufous-brown instead of dark chocolate. (For grey morph, see Geographical Variation.) **Juvenile** Head and body plumage whitish; facial disc and flight and tail feathers as adult. **Bare parts** Eyes normally dark brown; individuals with orange-yellow or deep yellow eyes have been recorded, especially in greyish morph (or subspecies *stricklandi*). Bill yellowish-horn to dark horn. Toes light greyish-brown. Claws dark horn with blackish tips.

MEASUREMENTS AND WEIGHT Total length 38-43cm. Wing 309-340mm; tail about 215mm. Weight 425-620g.

GEOGRAPHICAL VARIATION As the individual variability of the three colour morphs is large, it is difficult to judge whether all four described subspecies are valid taxa. We treat here three subspecies, and include *amazonica* in the nominate race.

L. c. cristata (Daudin, 1800). South America east of Andes, from Venezuela, Surinam and the Guianas to Colombia and the Amazon region south to N Bolivia. See Description.

L. c. wedeli Griscom, 1932. E Panama. Wing (1 specimen) 280mm.

L. (c.) stricklandi Sclater & Salvin, 1859. S Mexico to W Panama and W Colombia. In general light greyish-brown; outer webs of scapulars whitish with dark edges, forming pale band across shoulder; facial disc blackish, fading into rufous around eyes. Eyes yellow. Wing 298-325mm; tail 171-203mm. Song shorter, *kworrr*, repeated at irregular intervals. (Perhaps specifically distinct from *Lophostrix cristata*.)

HABITS Strictly nocturnal. During daytime it roosts in dense vegetation, especially in thickets along rivers, pair-members quite often roosting together. When disturbed at its day roost, the bird becomes very slim and erects the ear-tufts high. At dusk, song is delivered from perches in middle canopy of the forest. Singing birds may be heard throughout the night.

FOOD Chiefly larger insects, but probably also small vertebrates. The hunting behaviour has not yet been studied.

BREEDING Normally breeds in dry or early wet season, apparently nesting in natural holes in old trees. Biology poorly known.

STATUS AND CONSERVATION In undisturbed primary forest still rather common, but endangered where forests are destroyed. As with many nocturnal birds, its true status is unknown.

REMARKS The taxon *stricklandi* differs from other members of this species mainly in having yellow (instead of brown) eyes. This phenomenon is known to exist in some other species, such as Black-capped Screech Owl [78], where dark brown, reddish-brown and deep yellow eyes may be found in birds inhabiting the same area. As the eyes of *stricklandi* seem always to be yellow, however, this may be a sign of specific differentiation (at least in the case of a subspecies), and there may also be some difference in vocalisations. To clarify the situation, intensive studies on behaviour, bioacoustics and molecular biology are required.

REFERENCES Dunning (1993), Eck & Busse (1973), Hilty & Brown (1986), Sick (1985), Stiles & Skutch (1989).

Jamaican Owl, Genus *Pseudoscops* Kaup, 1848

Medium sized owls with prominent ear-tufts, similar to *Asio* (Long-eared Owl [205]), but with hazel-brown eyes. One species, endemic to the Island of Jamaica.

93 JAMAICAN OWL
Pseudoscops grammicus   Plate 25

French: Hibou de Jamaique
German: Jamaica-Ohreule
Spanish: Lechuza de Jamaica

IDENTIFICATION A medium-sized (31cm), generally warm brown owl with streaked underparts, rather long ear-tufts and hazel-brown eyes. Facial disc warm brown, fading into whitish in a narrow zone near dark rim, so that the face appears double-rimmed. No white on scapulars. **Similar species** Short-eared Owl [211] is more boldly streaked, is yellowish to whitish-ochre below and dark greyish-brown above, and has very short ear-tufts (situated above centre of forehead) and yellow eyes; it is a straggler and irregular breeder (though recently commoner) in the Caribbean.

VOCALISATIONS A rough frog-like croak, *k-kwoarrr*, repeated at intervals of several seconds, is quite often heard. A repetition at intervals of *to-whoo* notes is probably the song. An upslurred, wailing *kwe-eeh* seems to be a contact-call.

DISTRIBUTION Jamaica.

MOVEMENTS Resident.

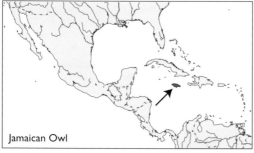

Jamaican Owl

HABITAT Woodland and semi-open country with scattered groups of trees, from the lowlands up into mountainous regions; also gardens with trees. The occurrence of this little-known owl is dependent on the existence of wooded areas or at least small wooded patches in rather open countryside.

DESCRIPTION Adult Facial disc warm rufous-brown, fading to whitish towards the dark rim (forming apparent second rim just before outer edge of disc). Forehead and crown with dark mottling, ear-tufts also mottled brown and blackish. Upperparts rather uniform warm brown, mantle, scapulars and wing-coverts with blackish arrow-shaped markings and fine vermiculations; no white spots on scapulars. Flight and tail feathers barred light and dark. Underparts slightly lighter than upperparts, with long dark shaft-streaks and fine brown vermiculations. Tarsi feathered rufescent-brown to base of toes. **Juvenile** Downy chick white. **Bare parts** Eyes hazel-brown. Bill pale grey to horn-yellow. Toes greyish-brown. Claws dark horn with blackish tips.

MEASUREMENTS AND WEIGHT Total length 31-33cm. Wing 197-229mm; tail 96-130mm. Weight: no data.

GEOGRAPHICAL VARIATION Monotypic: *Pseudoscops grammicus* (Gosse, 1847).

HABITS A strictly nocturnal bird. Regularly uses same daytime roost. Habits otherwise virtually unknown.

FOOD Larger insects and spiders, small vertebrates (e.g. lizards, rodents, tree frogs, possibly small birds).

BREEDING Nesting has been recorded from March to October, but recently reported as probably December-June. Lays 2 white eggs in a natural hole in the trunk of an old tree, sometimes in well-concealed fork between the broad bases of two branches. No nest is built. Incubation is by the female, who is fed by the male during this period. Breeding biology unknown.

STATUS AND CONSERVATION Common and widespread but probably at some risk, chiefly through destruction of forest amd woodland.

REMARKS The relationships of this owl are not clear. We believe that it may be related to owls of the genus *Asio*, which have rather similar contact-calls, but this may be due to convergence. Molecular-biological studies are needed to shed light on this.

REFERENCES Boyer & Hume (1991), Downer & Sutton (1990), Eck & Busse (1973), Hardy *et al.* (1989), Raffaele *et al.* (1998).

Horned Owls, Eagle Owls and Fish Owls, Genus *Bubo* Duméril, 1806

In general large, heavy owls with prominent ear-tufts and powerful talons. Tarsi and toes feathered or bare. Eyes yellow, orange or brown. Distributed in Eurasia, Indonesia, Africa and America; absent from Australia, New Guinea and islands of that region. We treat the Asian fish owls as members of the genus *Bubo*, retaining the name *Ketupa* only as a subgenus; doubtless all are rather closely related to eagle owls, differing only in being specialised on fish. According to DNA evidence, the genera *Nyctea* and *Scotopelia* are so closely related to *Bubo* that they might also be included in this genus. We treat them traditionally as separate genera and recognise 20 species in *Bubo*.

French: Grand-duc américain
German: Virginia-Uhu
Spanish: Buho americano or ñacurutú
Portuguese: Jacurutú

IDENTIFICATION A very large, powerful owl with prominent ear-tufts (largest 'eared' owl in whole America), large yellow eyes and very powerful, fully feathered talons. Female larger than male. General coloration varies from pale greyish to buffy-brown; underparts coarsely barred light and dark, with several dark patches on upper breast. Pure white throat very prominent when inflated during calling. **Similar species** Magellan Horned Owl [95] is smaller and lighter, with weaker talons and smaller bill, and underparts more narrowly and more finely barred dark and light; vocalisations very different. Stygian Owl [206] is much smaller and darker, without barring below. Striped Owl [210] is also smaller, has brown eyes and is streaked below. Short-eared Owl [211] has very small ear-tufts near centre of upper rim of facial disc; its underparts are streaked and its eyes yellow. All are well characterised by their vocal patterns.

VOCALISATIONS The song of the male is a deep, resonant *bu-bubú booh booh*, repeated at intervals of several seconds; sometimes not completed. The female has a similar song, but with a different rhythm: *bu-bububú booh*. During courtship, male and female may be heard duetting. Both sexes also utter strident screams. When advertising a potential nesting site or when offering food to the female, the male utters guttural clucking sounds. Young beg for food with hoarse discordant screams.

DISTRIBUTION America, from Alaska to Central and South America south to Brazil and C Argentina. Absent from the Pacific slope and central parts of the Andes from Peru to Chile, also from Patagonia and Tierra del Fuego.

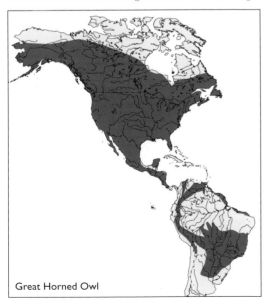

Great Horned Owl

MOVEMENTS In general resident. When food becomes scarce, or in hard winters, some northern birds may move southward for winter.

HABITAT Semi-open landscape with trees, groves, open woodland and shrubs; also rocky areas with woods and bushes, and even near human settlements or in larger parks; locally rocky semi-deserts with large cacti and shrubs. Locally up to about 4,000m, sometimes higher. Absent from heavy or primary rainforest (e.g. Amazon region) or dense cloud forest.

DESCRIPTION *B. v. virginianus* **Adult** Females generally larger than males, but with no differences in plumage. General coloration varies individually. Facial disc rusty-brown to ochraceous-buff, lighter around eyes; blackish rim very prominent on each side. Eyebrows whitish, rather prominent. Ear-tufts long and somewhat tousled. Upperparts warm brownish-buff, mottled and vermiculated with greyish-brown, black and whitish. Crown similar in coloration to mantle, but rather finely barred dark and light. Outer webs of scapulars with rather large whitish areas, irregularly marked with few dark transverse bars; row of whitish spots across shoulder not very obvious. Flight and tail feathers distinctly barred dark and light; outer webs of primaries brownish-buff, inner webs much paler. Underparts brownish-buff, becoming paler towards belly; throat whitish (very prominent when inflated during calling); upper breast with blackish blotches and some cross-bars; rest of underparts coarsely barred light and dark. Tarsi and toes densely feathered, leaving very small zone at upper base of claws bare. Talons very powerful. **Juvenile** Downy chick whitish. Mesoptile pale brownish-buff with indistinct dark barring on underparts, back and mantle; feathers fluffy. **Bare parts** Eyes yellow, eyelids with blackish edge, giving face a 'fierce' expression. Bill and cere greyish. Partly bare tips of toes greyish-brown. Claws dark horn with blackish tips.

MEASUREMENTS AND WEIGHT Total length 43-56cm. Wing 313-395mm; tail 190-250mm; bill (culmen) 43-52mm. Weight about 1,000g, females heavier than males.

GEOGRAPHICAL VARIATION The number of named subspecies seems too large, and some may be based only on individual variation and should therefore be treated as synonyms; requires taxonomic study. We recognise only 10 subspecies, even some of these being of doubtful validity.

   B. v. virginianus (Gmelin, 1788). Canada to Florida and Costa Rica. See Description. Wing 320-380mm. (The virtually identical *mesembrinus* of Costa Rica is probably a synonym of *virginianus*.)
   B. v. saturatus Ridgway, 1877. North America from Alaska to California. Mostly very dark and saturated above; facial disc varying from reddish-grey to dark rusty; feathering of feet more or less barred dark. Wing 356-383mm. (We include *heterocnemis* and *lagophonus* as synonyms of this subspecies.)
   B. v. wapacuthu (Gmelin, 1788). Northernmost and NE North America. Palest subspecies, white predominating in plumage; little or no reddish suffusion below; above, very pale buff with dark markings; facial disc whitish to pale ashy-grey. Wing 337-395mm. (The forms *subarcticus* and *occidentalis* are probably synonyms.)
   B. v. pacificus Cassin, 1854. SW USA, east to Nevada,

south to Baja California. Similar to the following subspecies. Wing 313-370mm.

B. v. pallescens Stone, 1897. SE California, Arizona, New Mexico and Texas, south to N Mexico. Smaller and paler than nominate form. Wing 330-375mm. (We consider the form *melanocercus* a synonym.)

B. v. elachistus Brewster, 1902. S Baja California, south from about 30°N. Smallest subspecies in North America. Similar in coloration to *saturatus*. Wing 305-330mm; tail 175-211mm.

B. v. mayensis Nelson, 1901. Mexico to W Panama. Similar to nominate race. Wing 320-355m.

B. v. nigrescens Berlepsch, 1884. Ecuador and Colombia. Darkest subspecies, with coarsely barred and mottled upper breast blackish; back and mantle with large black blotches. Wing of males 345-365mm, of females 351-381mm. (The form *colombianus* is probably a synonym.)

B. v. deserti Reiser, 1905. Bahia, Brazil. Similar to *nacurutu*, of which probably a synonym.

B. v. nacurutu (Vieillot, 1817). South America east of Andes in NW Venezuela, Guyana, Peru through Bolivia (absent from Amazon area) and Paraguay to C Argentina (Buenos Aires province) and Uruguay. Wing of males 330-354mm, of females 340-376mm; bill (culmen) 43-52mm. (The forms *scotinus* and *elutus* are probably synonyms.)

HABITS Activity generally begins at dusk, but in some regions the owl may be seen alert in late afternoon or early morning. Roosts among dense foliage of trees or bushes, in crevices or holes in cliffs, between rocks or in a crotch of thick branches in an old tree; here the bird spends the day in an upright position, with ear-tufts erected and eyes closed to a thin slit. At dusk it often utters a few calls from its roost, before flying to an open songpost, often rocks, exposed bare branches etc, to deliver the song. Normally several perches are used for marking the occupied territory, or in order to attract a female. When singing, the male bows forward, so that the whole body is horizontal with tail slightly cocked and wings hanging down; in this posture, the throat is inflated like a white ball beneath the bill (at dusk, this 'white ball' is very prominent, indicating the site of the singing male). The female normally does not display such a posture when uttering her song. Both sexes may be very aggressive towards intruders (even man) during the breeding season, especially when they have young.

FOOD Smaller mammals up to the size of rabbits, hares or oppossums are the most common food; also takes birds to the size of ducks, geese, herons and medium-sized birds of prey (even other species of owl), reptiles, frogs, spiders and larger insects. Hunts mostly in open or semi-open areas, at the edges of forest or in clearings, generally from a perch, from which it swoops down on prey; sometimes detects prey from the air and drops down to seize it. Kills prey by using the powerful talons and by biting head with the bill. The victim is then carried to a suitable site for eating or is taken to the nest. Surplus food is quite often stored at special depots in the territory.

BREEDING The breeding cycle starts in winter, when nights are long. After having marked the territory and defined the boundaries in relation to those of neighbours, the male normally makes contact with a female, often the same one as in previous years. Both may be heard duetting during courtship. The male offers potential nesting sites to its mate by trampling and walking around, uttering guttural sounds combined with song phrases. Often the chosen site is the same as in previous years. Frequently used sites are an abandoned nest of a large bird (e.g. hawk), a large hollow in a tree where a thick branch has broken away, a sheltered depression on a cliff ledge, a cave entrance, a trough-shaped site on the ground at the base of a trunk or between rocks, etc; sometimes breeds in heron's nest within a heronry. When advertising the breeding site, the male scratches the bottom in order to deepen the depression.

The female normally lays 2 (sometimes, when food is abundant, up to 6) white eggs of tennis-ball shape, 50-60 x 43-50mm. She incubates alone for 28-35 days, beginning with the first egg, and being fed by her mate, who brings food to the nest; when food is plentiful, it is stored at the nest, where it may become rotten in times of surplus. The young hatch with a whitish coat of down. They stay at the nest site for about 7 weeks, but are not able to fly well before 10-12 weeks; some therefore fall from the nest before fledging. The young are very noisy when begging for food. They are cared for by both parents into summer or even to the beginning of autumn, after which they disperse. Sexual maturity is reached in the following year.

STATUS AND CONSERVATION Although widespread and locally frequent, the Great Horned Owl has to be considered endangered in some regions by transformation of its habitat (especially by agriculture), human persecution and the use of pesticides.

REMARKS Our studies indicate that the horned owl occurring in the Andes from Peru to Tierra del Fuego and Cape Horn is specifically distinct from Great Horned Owl; it is much smaller, with totally different vocalisations. Even though both species are large and vocally active, however, the limits of their distribution require study. Since the two have to now been regarded as conspecific, the taxonomy of the whole *virginianus/magellanicus* complex should be investigated thoroughly, with emphasis on vocalisations.

REFERENCES Amadon & Bull (1988), Boyer & Hume (1991), Fjeldså & Krabbe (1990), Hardy *et al.* (1989), Hilty & Brown (1986), Howell & Webb (1995), König *et al.* (1996), Narosky & Yzurieta (1987), Sick (1985), Stiles & Skutch (1989), Traylor (1958), Voous (1988).

95   MAGELLAN HORNED OWL
Bubo magellanicus   Plate 26

French: Grand-duc de Magellan
German: Magellan-Uhu
Spanish: Tucúquere

IDENTIFICATION Smaller (about 45cm) than Great Horned Owl [94], with weaker talons, relatively small bill (culmen less than 43mm), and smaller, rather narrow and pointed ear-tufts. Underparts with fine dark barring, much denser and more regular than on its larger counterpart; upper chest sparsely marked with some dark dots. Rim around facial disc more pronounced than on Great Horned. Eyes yellow. **Similar species** Great Horned Owl is larger and heavier, with totally different vocalisations.

All other owls occurring in the range of Magellan Great Horned are smaller: Striped Owl [210] has brown eyes and is streaked below; Short-eared Owl [211] is also streaked below and has tiny ear-tufts near centre of forehead; Rufous-legged Owl [137] has no ear-tufts and brown eyes; Rufous-banded Owl [140] also lacks ear-tufts, has yellow eyes and lives in montane forest of tropical South America.

VOCALISATIONS The song of the male consists of two deep hoots with emphasis on the second, followed by a low guttural purring: *bu-hóohworrrr*. This may be the source of the local name 'tucúquere'. At a distance only the two hoots are easily heard, as the purr is rather low in volume. Female utters a similar song, but with a longer purr. The single phrases are repeated at intervals of several seconds. Male and female may be heard duetting during courtship.

DISTRIBUTION Andes of C Peru, Bolivia and Argentina, nearly all Chile, Patagonia and Tierra del Fuego to Cape Horn.

Magellan Horned Owl

MOVEMENTS In general resident; young birds may wander, especially in autumn. Some movement of southernmost populations towards warmer areas have been observed in winter.

HABITAT Rocky landscapes with pasture in mountains above timberline, semi-open Patagonian and Fuegian *Nothofagus* forest rich in lichens and mosses, and rocky semi-desert from sea-level to mountainous regions. Locally near or even in human settlements with parks, e.g. in Patagonia, where this species is abundant.

DESCRIPTION Adult Sexes alike in plumage, but females larger and heavier than males. Light and dark morphs are known; intermediates also occur. *Light morph*: Facial disc light greyish-brown to ashy-grey, becoming whitish towards bill and chin; rim around disc prominent blackish, separating chin from throat by a thin, dark line. Eyebrows lighter than crown, but not very prominent. Ear-tufts dark brown to blackish, relatively thin and pointed, not tousled. Crown greyish-brown with lighter and darker shaft-streaks

and fine mottling. Upperparts greyish-brown with blackish shaft-streaks, and brownish mottling, dots and dark cross-bars; scapulars without prominent whitish outer webs, the latter more or less mottled with greyish-brown, white and black. Flight and tail feathers barred blackish and greyish-brown. Throat white, bordered ventrally by a row of dark dots; rest of underparts pale brownish-grey to whitish with fine, regular dark brown to dark grey barring (light bands between dark bars much narrower than on Great Horned Owl); upper chest with some dark blotches on a barred ground; abdomen nearly plain whitish. Talons and toes feathered dirty white (feathering on toes less dense than on Great Horned, so toes appear thinner). Talons much weaker than on Great Horned. *Dark morph*: Generally darker and browner, with less white on underparts. **Juvenile** Similar to Great Horned Owl. **Bare parts** Eyes bright yellow, eyelids with thin blackish edge. Bill and cere greyish. Claws dark horn with blackish tips.

MEASUREMENTS AND WEIGHT Total length about 45cm. Wing of males 306-339mm (median 329.0mm), of females 330-358mm (median 342.9mm). Birds from Peru and Bolivia are somewhat larger. Bill (culmen) 37-42mm (median 38-39mm) (note that bill of parapatric race *nacurutu* of Great Horned Owl measures 43-52mm). Weight of one male from Calafate (Santa Cruz), Argentina: 830g.

GEOGRAPHICAL VARIATION Monotypic: *Bubo magellanicus* Lesson, 1828. The form *andicolus* may be a valid, slightly larger subspecies of higher elevations in the Andes.

HABITS A mostly nocturnal bird which becomes active at dusk; in the south, it may occasionally be observed before sunset. During daytime the owl roosts alone on a branch close to the trunk, often well concealed by lichens or foliage; also uses crevices in cliffs, ledges or cave entrances on rocky slopes as roosting sites. Behaviour little studied, but seems to be similar to that of Great Horned Owl. Beyond that, we have never seen the singing male adopt the horizontal posture typical of its northern counterpart. Both parents may be very aggressive in the vicinity of the nest.

FOOD Primarily small mammals up to the size of hares, but also birds and reptiles. Probably takes larger insects and spiders, too.

BREEDING Reproductive biology little studied, since observations on this and the previous species united in the literature. As most owls, is strictly territorial. Male sings from different perches in its territory; during courtship, male and female duet. When population is dense, as locally in Patagonia, the stationary observer can hear pairs in adjacent territories singing. A sheltered spot by an overhanging rock, a wider crevice or hole in a steep cliff or between rocks is normally used as nesting site. In *Nothofagus* forest the owls may nest in a shallow depression on the ground, often at the base of a trunk or under broken branches and trees. The male scratches at the nest site in order to deepen the depression. If tree nests of larger birds are available, these are also used for breeding.

Normally 2-3 white eggs (median 50.5 x 42.1mm) are laid from late winter, directly on to the base of the depression. Incubation, starting from the first egg, is by the female alone, being fed by her mate, who brings food to the nest. The young are fed by both parents. They leave the nest before they are able to fly, and walk around the nesting site.

STATUS AND CONSERVATION In Patagonia and Tierra del Fuego locally rather frequent. We discovered several occupied territories near Lago Argentino (Argentine province of Santa Cruz), where we also found birds killed by road traffic. Doubtless many owls become road casualties, but this is not yet a serious influence on the population, as there are still many areas without roads in this region. Human persecution, which exists locally, may cause more severe damage to populations, especially in tourist areas.

REMARKS According to voice and DNA evidence, Magellan Horned Owl is specifically distinct from Great Horned Owl. The two may be regarded as paraspecies, overlapping in range locally, as for instance in NW Argentina, where the lowlands (e.g. Argentine Chaco in Salta province) and foothills of the E Andes are occupied by *B. v. nacurutu* while in the rocky 'Quebradas' and above the timberline (at about 3,000-4,000m) *B. magellanicus* is found. Both species require further study, above all to clarify the boundaries of their distribution. Beyond that, the ecology and behaviour of Magellan Great Horned Owl are poorly known and require thorough investigation.

REFERENCES Araya & Millie (1986), Fjeldså & Krabbe (1990), Johnson & Goodall (1967), König *et al.* (1996), Narosky & Yzurieta (1987), Traylor (1958).

96 EURASIAN EAGLE OWL
Bubo bubo   Plates 27 & 28

French: Hibou grand-duc
German: Uhu
Spanish: Buho

IDENTIFICATION A very large and heavy owl (58-71cm) with prominent ear-tufts, powerful, fully feathered talons and bright orange eyes. Mainly rusty-brown with black markings above and below; underparts lighter, with irregular blackish spots and prominent broad streaks on upper breast, lower parts with dark shaft-streaks and fine cross-bars, giving lower breast and belly a somewhat barred appearance. Facial disc indistinctly rimmed. **Similar species** This is the largest 'eared' owl with fully feathered toes. Long-eared Owl [207] is much smaller (crow-sized) and has a very prominent blackish rim around facial disc. Short-eared Owl [211] has yellow eyes and very short ear-tufts, and is streaked below. Pharaoh Eagle Owl [97] of North Africa and the Middle East is smaller and more sandy-coloured, with black spots on upper breast and a pale face, ear-tufts speckled dark and light, and eyes yellow to orange; it differs vocally from Eurasian Eagle Owl, with which it occurs (or formerly occurred?) sympatrically in the Atlas Mountains of Morocco and Algeria. The fish owls of the subgenus *Ketupa* [110-113] are also relatively large, but have very tousled ear-tufts, and bare tarsi or at least bare toes. Snowy Owl [117] is largely white, with no ear-tufts. Great Grey Owl [129] lacks ear-tufts, and has a large rounded head, small, yellow eyes, and grey plumage with dark markings.

VOCALISATIONS The song of the male is a deep, resonant hoot, stressed at the beginning and dropping at the end: *búoh*, the two syllables very much drawn together and suggesting almost a single, downward-inflected note (the scientific name *bubo* clearly derives from the male's

song). These hoots are uttered at intervals of about 8-10 seconds. The female has a similar but higher-pitched song which is clearly disyllabic and with emphasis on the second syllable, *huhóoh*, with both syllables on the same pitch. Male and female duet during courtship. A rapid staccato series of *u* notes is uttered by the male during nuptial display and when advertising the nesting site to the female. The latter gives a hoarse, nasal scream when demanding food from its mate or for contact with the latter. When disturbed or in aggression, a heron-like 'crack' and bill-snapping are given by both sexes. Just before copulation, male and female emit clucking and clicking notes. Young beg with hoarse screams similar to the female's food-call.

DISTRIBUTION Widespread but locally very rare or absent in continental Eurasia (absent Britain, Ireland and Iceland) and North Africa, from the Iberian Peninsula and (only in former times?) Atlas Mountains of Algeria and Morocco to N Scandinavia and Siberia, N India, Himalayas, east to Sakhalin, and from E Siberia (Okhotsk) south to S China. Accidentally and locally on islands of northernmost Japan.

MOVEMENTS In general resident, but some (mainly younger?) individuals of northern and eastern populations show a tendency to move to warmer regions in harsh winters. Once independent, immatures wander.

HABITAT Primarily rocky landscapes, often with scattered trees, small groves or bushes, from sea-level to above timberline. Also open forest with clearings, cultivated open or semi-open areas with quarries, steep slopes with rocks and bushes, rocky cliffs in river valleys, taiga forest with clearings. Locally near human settlements. Avoids dense, extensive forest.

DESCRIPTION *B. b. bubo* Adult Facial disc greyish-brown with buffy suffusion; rim around disc slightly darker, thin and not very prominent. Eyebrows and feathering around bill whitish. Long, prominent ear-tufts pointed, mainly blackish. Crown buffy-brown with dark brown or blackish bars and vermiculations, appearing relatively dark. Upperparts buffy-brown with blackish streaks and cross-bars, mantle with much black, neck with buffy-brown underplumage predominating over blackish markings (therefore much lighter than crown and mantle); scapulars with no white on outer webs. Flight and tail feathers buffy-brown with blackish or dark brown bars. Alula nearly uniform blackish-brown. Throat white, very prominent when calling; rest of underparts buffy orange-brown, with blackish streaks from below throat to upper breast; lower underparts with dark shaft-streaks and fine cross-bars (herringbone-like pattern). Tarsi and toes densely feathered. Talons very powerful. **Juvenile** Downy chick whitish. Mesoptile pale buffy-brown, with many indistinct darker bars on underparts, head, mantle and back; ear-tufts indicated by fluffy feathers; flight and tail feathers similar to adult. On fledging, much mesoptile down still present on head. **Bare parts** Eyes golden-yellow to bright orange; juvenile has yellow-orange irides with 'milky' suffusion, which disappears when about half-grown. Cere greyish-olive. Bill blackish. Relatively long and powerful claws blackish-brown with black tips.

MEASUREMENTS AND WEIGHT Total length 58-71cm. Wing 378-518mm; tail 240-310mm. Weight of males 1,570-2,800g, of females 1,750-4,200g. Size increases from south to north and from lowlands to high altitudes.

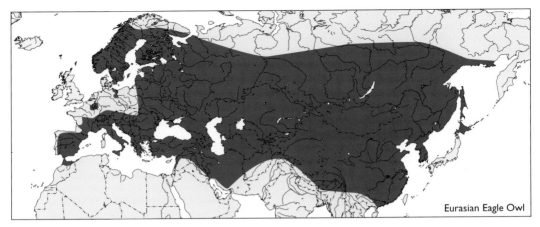

Eurasian Eagle Owl

GEOGRAPHICAL VARIATION Many subspecies have been described, some reflecting only individual variation, while others are in reality separate species. We recognise 14 subspecies, one of which is probably best regarded as a separate species.

    B. b. bubo (Linnaeus, 1758). Europe from Pyrenees and Mediterranean east to the Bosporus and Ukraine, north to Scandinavia, Moscow and NW Russia. See Description. Wing of males 435-480mm, of females 455-500mm; bill of males 45-51mm, of females 50-56mm.

    B. b. hispanus Rothschild & Hartert, 1910. Iberian Peninsula and (only formerly?) wooded areas of Atlas Mountains in Algeria and Morocco. Similar to nominate, but lighter, greyer and slightly smaller. Wing 420-495mm.

    B. b. ruthenus Buturlin & Zhitkov, 1906. East of a line from Moscow to Pechora, to Ural river and south to mouth of Volga river. Lighter and greyer than nominate, and less buffy. Wing 440-515mm.

    B. (b.) interpositus Rothschild & Hartert, 1910. Bessarabia, Crimea, Caucasus, Asia Minor, Palestine, Syria and Iran. Darker and more rusty than *ruthenus*. Wing 425-502mm. DNA evidence suggests that this form is specifically distinct form *B. bubo*.

    B. b. sibiricus (Gloger, 1833). W Siberia and Bashkiria to middle Ob river and W Altai Mountains, north to limits of the taiga. Very pale: general coloration creamy-white with dark markings, crown, hindneck and underparts streaked blackish, lower breast and belly indistinctly barred; primary coverts dark, contrasting with rest of wing. Wing 435-515mm. (The form *baschkiricus* we regard as a synonym.)

    B. b. yenisseensis Buturlin, 1912. C Siberia between Ob river, Lake Baikal, Altai Mountains and N Mongolia. Darker, greyer, with more yellowish ground colour than *sibiricus.* Wing 443-518mm. (The form *zaissanensis* we regard as a synonym.)

    B. b. jakutensis Buturlin, 1908. NE Siberia. Much darker and browner above than *yenisseensis*, more distinctly streaked and barred below than *sibiricus.* Wing 455-503mm.

    B. b. ussuriensis Polyakov, 1915. SE Siberia to N China, Sakhalin and Kuriles. Darker above than *jakutensis*, with more ochre wash on underparts. Wing 430-502mm. (We regard *dauricus* and *borissowi* as synonyms.)

    B. b. turcomanus (Eversmann, 1835). Between Volga and upper Ural, Caspian coast and Aral Sea, east to Transbaikalia and Tarim basin to W Mongolia. Greyer, but similar to *hemalachanus*. Wing 418-512mm. (We regard *tarimensis* as a synonym.)

    B. b. omissus Dementiev, 1932. Turkmenia and adjacent Iran, Chinese Turkestan. A typical desert form: general coloration pale ochre; dark markings not very prominent on underparts. Wing 404-460mm. (We regard *gladkovi* as a synonym.)

    B. b. nikolskii Zarudny, 1905. Iran to Pakistan. Smaller than *omissus*, with more rusty wash; less dark above. Wing 378-465mm.

    B. b. hemachalana Hume, 1873. From Tien Shan to Pamir Mountains, north to Kara Tau, south to Baluchistan and the Himalayas. General coloration light brown, mantle not darker than back; ear-tufts more brownish instead of blackish. Wing 450-505mm. (We regard *auspicabilis* and *tibetanus* as synonyms.)

    B. b. kiautschensis Reichenow, 1903. Korea, and China south to Sichuan and Yunnan. Smaller and darker than *ussuriensis*, with thinner shaft-streaks. Wing 410-485mm. (We regard as synonyms the following: *setschuanus, inexpectatus, tenuipes, jarlandi.*)

    B. b. swinhoei Hartert, 1913. SE China. Relatively small, rufescent form, somewhat similar to *kiautschensis*. Wing 410-465mm.

HABITS Active mainly at dusk or at night to dawn. Roosts by day singly or in pairs in trees or in rock crevices, mostly well hidden. At the beginning of the breeding season, males may be heard singing as early as 1 hour before sunset. Lowest activity around midnight. The flight is nearly noiseless, with soft wingbeats, interrupted by gliding when flying over long distance; sometimes soars.

FOOD Mammals, ranging in size from small rodents and shrews to hares; in C Europe hedgehogs are a favourite prey, as well as rats taken at refuse dumps. Birds to the size of herons and buzzards are taken, as well as reptiles, frogs, sometimes fish, larger insects and even earthworms. Occasionally eats carrion, when live prey is scarce. Preferred prey between 200g and 1,900g in weight. Generally hunts from a perch, but may also hunt in searching-flight. Kills prey with the powerful talons and by biting its head with the bill, after which the owl carries its victim to a perch (often top of a rock) and tears it into pieces for swallowing; small prey are swallowed whole. Larger birds are plucked before eating.

293

BREEDING Territorial, but territories of neighbouring pairs may partly overlap. Male and female duet during courtship. Very often pairs for life. The male advertises potential breeding sites to its mate, scratching a shallow depression at the future site and uttering staccato notes and clucking sounds. Cliff ledges sheltered by overhanging rocks, larger crevices between rocks, and entrances to caves in cliffs are most favoured nesting sites, but abandoned nests of larger birds may be used, too. If no such sites are available, may nest on the ground between rocks, under fallen trunks, under a bush, or even rather exposed at the base of a tree trunk: in such cases sites on steep slopes preferred, but not essential, and may thus nest on the ground in semi-open taiga, or on ledges of river banks. Often several potential depressions are offered to the female, who selects one; this quite often used again in subsequent years. No nesting material is added.

Laying begins in late winter, sometimes even at the end of January. Lays 1-4 white eggs (56.0-73.0 x 44.2-53.0mm; weight when fresh 75-80 g), normally at intervals of 3 days. 1 clutch per year. The female incubates alone, starting from the first egg, for 31-36 days, fed on the nest by her mate. Young hatch at shorter intervals than would be expected from the laying schedule. Their eyes open on day 4, and they are brooded for about 2 weeks; the female stays with them at the nest for 4-5 weeks. For the first 2-3 weeks the male brings food to the nest or deposits it nearby, and the female feeds small pieces to the young. After 3 weeks the chicks start to feed themselves and now begin to swallow smaller items whole, although accidents occasionally happen when the prey is too large and gets stuck in the nestling's throat; we found a dead nestling with a whole Common Moorhen *Gallinula chloropus* in its gape. At 5 weeks the young walk around the nesting area, and at 52 days of age are able to fly a few metres. They leave ground nests at 22-25 days old, while elevated nests (on cliff ledges or in old tree nests of other birds) are left at an age of 5-7 weeks. Fledged young are cared for by both parents for about 20-24 weeks. They become independent between September and November (C Europe) and leave the parents' territory or are driven out by them. At this time the male begins to sing again on calm evenings and to inspect future potential nesting sites. Young reach maturity in the following year, but normally breed in the wild when 2-3 years old.

Eurasian Eagle Owls may live to more than 60 years in captivity; in the wild, about 20 years might be the maximum (oldest known ringed bird reached 19 years).

STATUS AND CONSERVATION This owl is endangered in many parts of Europe, where local extinctons have been caused by human persecution. Recently, successful reintroductions have been made at many suitable locations in C Europe by releasing captive-bred individuals, though many of these were killed on roads, on railway tracks and through collisions with power lines. In addition, the species is very sensitive to disturbance at the nest site, and nests should not therefore be approached; mountaineers should also avoid cliffs occupied by these owls. In some parts of its range, this handsome, powerful owl is endangered by habitat destruction and the use of pesticides. Although protected by law in most countries, human persecution still persists locally.

REMARKS The taxonomy of *Bubo bubo* requires study, including of its distribution and geographical variation. Two taxa formerly treated as subspecies have already proved to be separate species: Pharaoh and Rock Eagle Owls [97, 98] differ vocally and according to DNA evidence. DNA studies suggest that *interpositus* might also be given specific rank.

REFERENCES Boyer & Hume (1991), Bezzel (1985), Dementiev & Gladkov (1951), Eck & Busse (1973), Glutz von Blotzheim *et al.* (1980), Hölzinger (1987), König (1979), Voous (1988), Wink & Heidrich (*in litt.* 1999).

97 PHARAOH EAGLE OWL
Bubo ascalaphus Plate 28

French: Grand-duc nordafricain
German: Wüstenuhu
Spanish: Buho del Sáhara

IDENTIFICATION A pale sandy-ochre eagle owl with a creamy-whitish or pale ochre facial disc, thinly rimmed dark. Distinctly smaller than Eurasian Eagle Owl [96], with decidedly shorter ear-tufts speckled light and dark (not blackish); throat white, and upper breast spotted with dark, more or less drop-shaped dots. Bill blackish; eyes yellow to deep orange. Tarsi and toes feathered, somewhat sparsely near base of claws. Talons less powerful than those of the larger and darker race *hispanus* of Eurasian, with which it occurs (or formerly occurred) sympatrically on southern slope of Atlas Mountains in Algeria. **Similar species** Eurasian Eagle Owl is larger, much darker and heavier, and differs vocally, in proportions and in DNA. Hume's Owl [131] of Middle East is smaller and round-headed and lacks ear-tufts. Long-eared Owl [207] is slimmer, smaller and boldly striped below.

VOCALISATIONS The song of the male is normally higher in pitch than Eurasian Eagle Owl's: a short, downward-inflected *búo*, higher-pitched than song of male Long-eared Owl. The female has a similar but higher-pitched song. During courtship, a trisyllabic call is uttered with emphasis on the first syllable, and slightly higher-pitched second and third: *hú-huhooh*, this phrase sometimes being uttered incompletely. (Male Eurasian utters only two syllables, the second more drawn out.) The female gives a higher-pitched, again mainly trisyllabic phrase of hoots. Such phrases are repeated at intervals of about 8 seconds. During courtship the sexes duet. Young beg with hoarse screams: *cheht* and *chewcht*. This owl's vocalisations are little studied; since most authors have treated it as conspecific with Eurasian Eagle Owl, the literature does not differentiate between the voices of the two species.

DISTRIBUTION N and NW Africa from the southern slopes of the Rif and Atlas Mountains to most of the Sahara (south to Chad), Mauritania, Mali, Niger, N Egypt, Sudan and NW Ethiopia, Arabia, Syria, Israel and Palestine to W Iraq. Locally sympatric with race *interpositus* of Eurasian Eagle Owl.

MOVEMENTS Resident.

HABITAT Rocky deserts and semi-deserts, mountains with gorges and cliffs, dry, rocky mountain slopes with scattered trees or shrubs, outcrops of oases, occasionally in dry savannas.

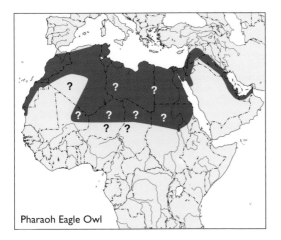

Pharaoh Eagle Owl

DESCRIPTION *B. a. ascalaphus* **Adult** Facial disc plain pale tawny, rimmed by a row of fine blackish spots; face more rounded, less horizontally oval than Eurasian Eagle Owl's, giving it a different expression. Ear-tufts relatively short and pointed, pale tawny with dark speckles and tawny-brown edges. Crown pale tawny with numerous blackish spots. Upperparts tawny-rufous, marked dark and light (shoulders slightly darker than back), individual feathers with dark shaft-streak, a broad blackish tip and whitish spots on each side of shaft-streak, giving blotched effect; scapulars as back and mantle. Flight and tail feathers barred light and dark. Throat white; rest of underparts pale tawny-brown to sandy-coloured, upper breast with dark drop-shaped shaft-streaks and few cross-bars; lower underparts finely marked dark, individual feathers having thin shaft-streak and thin horizontal bar (barring less prominent than on Eurasian, which has a herringbone-like pattern with many cross-bars). Tarsi and toes feathered pale tawny; feathering more sparse towards base of claws. **Juvenile** Downy chick whitish, with buffy suffusion on forehead, wings and rump. Mesoptile resembles adult, but more fluffy and barred on upperparts and (very slightly) on upper breast; ear-tufts not yet developed. **Bare parts** Eyes yellow to deep orange. Cere greyish. Bill black. Tips of toes sooty-brown. Claws blackish-brown with darker tips.

MEASUREMENTS AND WEIGHT Total length 46-50cm. Wing of males 325-411mm, of females 348-416mm (for comparison, Atlas race *hispanus* of Eurasian Eagle Owl has wing of males 420-470mm, of females 450-495mm); tail of males 177-224mm (median 196mm), of females 188-233mm (median 217mm). Weight: no data.

GEOGRAPHICAL VARIATION We recognise two subspecies. Intermediates occur where these overlap.
  B. a. ascalaphus Savigny, 1809. N Africa from Morocco to Egypt, Sinai Peninsula, Israel/Palestine. See Description. Wing 328-416mm.
  B. a. desertorum Erlanger, 1897. W Iraq, Arabia, across S Sahara from Ethiopia and Sudan to Mauritania, Mali and Niger. Smaller and much paler than nominate. Wing 325-390mm.

HABITS Becomes active after sunset. Roosts by day between rocks, either on the ground or high above it in steep precipice, in cliff crevices or in cave entrance; may also roost in trees, if these are present. When disturbed at its daytime roost, may fly rather far away to land in open

country. Behaviour little studied, but may be similar to that of Eurasian Eagle Owl.

FOOD Mostly small vertebrates, such as mammals, birds and reptiles, but also larger insects and scorpions. Rodents make up the main diet, especially *Gerbillus* and *Ctenodactylus*, as well as hares, bats, desert foxes, hedgehogs. Normally hunts from a perch.

BREEDING Male and female generally pair for life, maintaining same territory for years. The male announces his presence at dusk. Courtship display similar to that of Eurasian Eagle Owl. A shallow scrape among rocks, in a crevice or down a well serves as nesting site, which is mostly in darkness; on newly desertified fringes of sub-Sahara, tree holes or old nests of larger birds are used. Lays 2-4 (mostly 2) white eggs (55-62 x 45-50mm) directly on to the bottom of the nest; laying interval 2-4 days. The female incubates alone, from the first egg, and is fed on the nest by the male. Breeding biology probably similar to that of other eagle owls. Reaches maturity in the year following birth, but in the wild does not normally breed before 2 years of age.

STATUS AND CONSERVATION Uncertain. May be locally endangered by human persecution.

REMARKS This owl is doubtless closely related to its Eurasian counterpart, but vocalisations and DNA evidence indicate that it is specifically separated from it. The sympatry of race *hispanus* of Eurasian Eagle Owl with Pharaoh Eagle Owl in the Algerian Atlas also argues in favour of their being different species; whether *hispanus* is yet extinct there is not known, but some time ago the two species could be encountered alongside each other on the southern slope of the Atlas. The biology and behaviour of Pharaoh Eagle Owl demands study, as observations have been merged with those of Eurasian in the literature.

REFERENCES Cramp (1985), Dementiev & Gladkov (1951), Dowsett & Dowsett-Lemaire (1993), Fry *et al.* (1988), Glutz von Blotzheim *et al.* (1980), Voous (1988).

98   ROCK EAGLE OWL
Bubo bengalensis   Plate 28

Other name: Indian Eagle Owl

French: Grand-duc des Indes
German: Bengaluhu

IDENTIFICATION In general smaller (50-56cm) than Eurasian Eagle Owl [96], with which it is considered conspecific by some authors. Similar in coloration to latter, but with more pointed wings (8th primary longest; on Eurasian 8th and 7th of equal length) and tips of toes unfeathered. Talons very powerful in relation to size. Crown darker than forehead; facial disc oval-shaped, tawny-buffish, rather prominently rimmed blackish. Eyes orange to deep orange-red. **Similar species** Eurasian Eagle Owl, which overlaps in distribution with Rock in Kashmir (where the two may live side by side), is larger and heavier, with underparts more prominently streaked; toes totally feathered and wings more rounded. The locally sympatric Brown Fish Owl [113] has yellow eyes, bare tarsi and toes, and tousled ear-tufts. Long-eared Owl [207] is much smaller and slimmer, with boldly streaked underparts. All differ further in vocalisations.

VOCALISATIONS The male's song is a rather deep (but higher than Eurasian's), resonant, double-noted hoot on one pitch, with emphasis on the more prolonged second syllable: *bu-whúoh*. These hoots are repeated at intervals of several seconds. The song of the female is similar, but slightly higher-pitched. At nest, a sequence of clucking notes may be heard, as well as a series of *huwúo-huwúo-huwúo-...*, uttered by both sexes, the female higher in pitch. In aggression both sexes hiss menacingly, fluffing their plumage and spreading their wings, a posture displayed by many owls in such situations.

DISTRIBUTION W Himalayas, Pakistan to India (south to region south of Madras), Kashmir, Nepal, Assam and Burma. Absent from Sri Lanka.

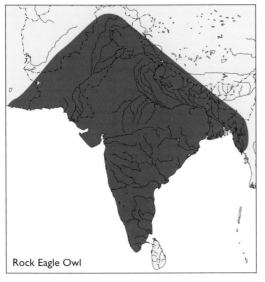

Rock Eagle Owl

MOVEMENTS Resident.

HABITAT Rocky hills with bushes, steep earth banks, wooded country with ravines, old mango orchards in the neighbourhood of human settlements, semi-deserts with rocks and thorny brush. Lowlands up to about 2,400m.

DESCRIPTION Adult Darker and lighter morphs occur, differing only in intensity of ground colour. Facial disc fulvous-brown to buffy, with thin but prominent blackish rim. Eyebrows whitish to above centre of eyes, then continuing at upward angle as a blackish line leading to mainly dark ear-tufts. Forehead buffy-brown with some small blackish flecks, becoming more numerous towards crown, which is densely spotted black (crown appears dark). Upperparts tawny-brown, mottled and streaked with blackish-brown; outer webs of scapulars often partly whitish, sometimes suggesting indistinct whitish row across shoulder. Flight and tail feathers tawny-buff, barred blackish-brown. Wing-tips rather pointed: P8 primary (counted from inner wing; = P3 counted from outermost) longest. Chin and throat white. Underparts fulvous, becoming whitish towards centre; upper breast with relatively small dark streaks, rest of underparts with fine

shaft-streaks and faint cross-bars, the shaft-streaks disappearing more and more towards abdomen, so that latter appears faintly barred. Tarsi and toes feathered fulvous, outer toe joints bare. **Juvenile** Downy chick whitish with buffy suffusion. Mesoptile with indistinct, narrow fulvous-brown bars on underparts, head and mantle; ear-tufts not developed; dark barring on primaries less blackish than on adult. **Bare parts** Eyes orange-yellow to deep orange-red. Cere greyish. Bill greenish-horn to slaty-black. Tips of toes greenish-slate. Claws dusky black.

MEASUREMENTS AND WEIGHT Total length 50-56cm. Wing of males 364-390mm, of females 375-425mm; tail 185-227mm. Weight of 1 male 1,100g.

GEOGRAPHICAL VARIATION Monotypic: *Bubo bengalensis* (Franklin, 1831).

HABITS In general nocturnal, but may be seen perched on top of an exposed rock well before sunset and after sunrise. During daytime roosts on a bough in thick foliage, in crevice between rocks or on sheltered ledge of a clay cliff flanking a ravine, or even in ruined or abandoned buildings. Flies with slow, deliberate wingbeats, interspersed with long bouts of gliding on outstretched wings; usually flies quite close to ground. When intruders approach a nest with chicks, the parents frequently resort to diversionary tactics, feigning wing injury.

FOOD Primarily field rats and mice, but birds up to the size of peafowl, reptiles, frogs, crabs and large insects are also taken. The large pellets (up to 150 x 40mm) may be found below nest site or under daytime roost; they normally contain predominantly fur and bones of rodents. Hunts mostly from a perch, sometimes in a low foraging flight.

BREEDING Breeds chiefly February-April, but considerable local variation between October/November and May. Territorial. The nest is a shallow saucer-like scrape on bare soil, this being scratched out by both sexes, especially by male. It may be on a sheltered rock ledge, in a recess in a clay cliff flanking a ravine or river bank, sometimes even on the ground under a bush or between rocks on a slope. The 2-4 white eggs (53.6 x 43.8mm), laid directly on to the soil, are incubated by the female alone, starting from the first egg; incubation period 35 days. Reproductive biology probably similar to that of Eurasian Eagle Owl.

STATUS AND CONSERVATION Uncertain. Not uncommon in suitable habitats.

REMARKS This owl has been considered by many authors a subspecies of Eurasian Eagle Owl, and observations of both species have therefore been merged. Intensive study of its ecology, behaviour, distribution and taxonomy is required, in order also to gain more detailed knowledge for its conservation. According to vocal patterns and DNA evidence, Rock Eagle Owl is specifically distinct from the very similar but larger Eurasian Eagle Owl, with subspecies *turcomanus* of which it overlaps in range and lives sympatrically in Kashmir.

REFERENCES Ali & Ripley (1969), Baker (1927), Dementiev & Gladkov (1951), Eck & Busse (1973), King & Dickinson (1995).

99 CAPE EAGLE OWL
Bubo capensis   **Plate 29**

French: Grand-duc du Cap
German: Kapuhu

IDENTIFICATION A relatively large eagle owl (46-61cm), dark brown above, with prominent ear-tufts and yellow to orange-yellow eyes. Dark-marked below, sides of upper breast densely blotched blackish. Tarsi and toes densely feathered. Talons powerful. **Similar species** Spotted Eagle Owl [101] is smaller, spotted and barred below, without dense blackish blotching on sides of upper breast; eyes yellow. Vermiculated Eagle Owl [102], also smaller and more greyish, is finely barred and vermiculated below; eyes dark brown with pink or reddish edges of eyelids. Verreaux's Eagle Owl [104] is much larger, and pale brownish-grey with fine and dense vermiculations; eyes brown, eyelids fleshy pink, ear-tufts rather fluffy.

VOCALISATIONS The song of the male is a powerful, rather explosive, deep hoot, followed by a faint (very weak in volume), short note: *bóowh-hu*. This phrase is repeated at intervals of several seconds and uttered mostly from rather exposed perches. The female normally gives a slightly higher-pitched song, sometimes duetting with the male (but not so frequently as Spotted Eagle Owl). When approaching the female during courtship, the male utters a trisyllabic *cu-cóo-cu*, bowing to its mate. The latter gives a drawn-out, nasal, wheezing *chrrreeh* when demanding food. Similar food-calls are uttered by young. When alarmed, both sexes give barking *wack wack wack...* or *werp werp...* notes. The female utters clucking notes when offering food to the nestlings.

DISTRIBUTION E and S Africa, from Eritrea and Ethiopia south to Kenya, Tanzania, Zimbabwe, Mozambique and Cape Province to S Namibia. Distribution irregular and local, depending on habitat conditions.

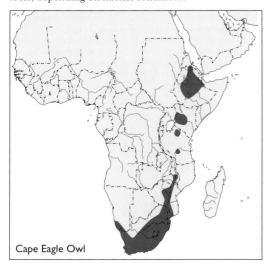

Cape Eagle Owl

MOVEMENTS Generally resident, but sometimes straggles around territory outside breeding season. Young birds wander after having reached independence.

HABITAT Predominantly mountainous regions and hilly country with rocky areas, rocky gorges excavated by rivers and adjacent wooded gulleys, but not dependent on mountains and lives in e.g. the flat Karroo in Cape Province. Hunts also in open savanna. Locally, visits human settlements and even towns to roost and to feed on feral pigeons.

DESCRIPTION *B. c. capensis* **Adult** Facial disc pale fulvous-brownish, distinctly rimmed black or dark brown, rim becoming broader towards neck. Ear-tufts prominent, mostly dark brown, with inner edge pale brownish. Crown fulvous-tawny to greyish-brown with blackish spots and mottling. Upperparts dark brown with whitish, black and fulvous-tawny spots or mottling; outer webs of scapulars with large white areas and dark dots (row across shoulder rather indistinct); wing-coverts with large white spots forming whitish bar on closed wing. Flight and tail feathers barred light and dark. Throat white. Underparts light fulvous-brown, shading into whitish towards middle of breast and belly; sides of upper breast densely blotched black, rest of underparts with some blackish spots and coarse, 'hastate' bars. Tarsi and toes densely feathered. **Juvenile** Downy chick whitish, becoming spotted dark in early mesoptile plumage. Mesoptile dull brownish-white, with dark barring on head, mantle, back and underparts. **Bare parts** Eyes orange-yellow to orange; yellow in juveniles. Cere greyish. Bill dusky horn. Toes (on sparsely feathered outermost tips) brownish, with yellowish bare underside. Claws dark horn with blackish tips.

MEASUREMENTS AND WEIGHT Total length 46-61cm. Wing 343-418mm; tail 155-256mm. Weight of males 905-1387g, of females 1240-1800g.

GEOGRAPHICAL VARIATION We distinguish three subspecies.
B. c. capensis A. Smith, 1834. South Africa and S Namibia. See Description. Wing 355-393mm; tail 145-240mm; weight 905-1400 g.
B. c. dillonii des Murs & Prevost, 1846. Ethiopian highlands and Eritrea. Less coarsely marked below, with distinct barring on lower breast and belly; in general browner. Wing 341-413mm.
B. c. mackinderi Sharpe, 1899. Kenya, Tanzania to Zimbabwe, Malawi and Mozambique. Largest subspecies. Similar to nominate in coloration, but with more fulvous-tawny in plumage. Wing 378-428mm; tail 184-256mm; weight 1220-1800g.

HABITS Largely nocturnal, but may be seen occasionally after sunrise or before sunset. During daytime it roosts between rocks, in crevices or holes in cliffs, in the shade of sheltered rock ledges, sometimes in trees with dense foliage, or even on the ground under a bush; locally, may roost on buildings, even in towns, if suitable sites exist (e.g. in Johannesburg and Pretoria). Often male and female roost close together, especially before breeding season. Before leaving its roost, the male normally utters some phrases of song.

FOOD Mammals, from small rodents and shrews up to the size of hares, birds to the size of francolins and Hamerkop *Scopus umbretta*, reptiles, frogs, scorpions, crabs and larger insects. Majority of prey are medium-sized mammals and birds. Pellets large (68-140 x 25-35mm, av. 90 x 30mm) and often contain larger bones; they can be found at the nest site or below day roosts. A pair with two half-grown chicks is estimated to require about 650-750g per day (= 1-3 mole rats per night). Hunts from prominent perches from which provide a good view over the terrain.

On spotting prey, the owl descends in gliding flight, killing its victim with its powerful talons and by biting its head.

BREEDING Territorial, with relatively large territories. Where the population is dense (e.g. on Mau Plateau, Kenya), a territory may measure only 2.5km²; in Zimbabwe, 8-10 pairs were recorded in 620km². The male advertises the occupied territory by singing. Duets with the female are rare. During courtship, the male bows up and down in front of its upright, silent female and utters rhythmic hoots (see Vocalisations) in rapid sequence. A shallow scrape on a sheltered rock ledge, in a cave entrance, between rocks, or even on the ground under a bush is used as nest; sometimes stick nests of larger birds in trees or tall bushes are used. Normally one clutch per year; sometimes breeds only in alternate years.

The normally 2 (1-3) white eggs (52-57 x 43-48mm, fresh weight 62 g) are laid directly on to the soil, at intervals of at least 2 days. Incubation, by the female alone, lasts 34-38 days, during which time the female is fed by the male. Young hatch at intervals of up to 4 days, and weigh 42-51g at hatching; at 20 days they weigh 500g, and at 40 days 1,000g. Their eyes open at 6-8 days. The female broods the chicks, feeding them with small pieces of prey brought to the nest by the male; in one night usually one food item is delivered, which may be a whole prey or parts of a larger, dismembered one. When the chicks are 11-13 days old, buff down emerges from mesoptile plumage. By 17 days, the female leaves the young for some of the time, but roosts with them; she leaves the chicks completely when they are 3-4 weeks old, but always remains near the nest, as also does the male during daytime. At 3 weeks the mesoptile plumage is well developed, with buff and dark barring, and the eye colour begins to turn from yellow to yellow-orange; at 4-5 weeks the facial disc is clearly developed, and flight and tail feathers apparent. If the nesting site permits, the young wander away from the nest at about 45 days of age. At about 70-77 days they can fly well. They are cared for up to an age of about 6 months (ear-tufts now well developed), and then hoot regularly. Sexual maturity is reached during the following year.

STATUS AND CONSERVATION Although widespread, this species is locally rare or absent, but in some areas rather frequent to common (e.g. Mau Plateau in Kenya). Breeding success averages between 50% and 60%. Predation of nests, especially those on ground, roadkills and casualties caused by power lines and barbed wire are reported. In addition, the use of pesticides to control rodents may be a threat.

REMARKS A rather well-studied species, but vocalisations and taxonomy require further investigation.

REFERENCES Benson & Irvin (1967), Boyer & Hume (1991), Fry *et al.* (1985), Newman (1985, 1987), Steyn (1982), Zimmerman *et al.* (1996).

---

100   AKUN EAGLE OWL
Bubo leucostictus   Plate 29

French: Grand-duc tacheté
German: Akun-Uhu, Gelbfuâ-Uhu

IDENTIFICATION A relatively small (40-45cm), dark

eagle owl, finely vermiculated above, with prominent ear-tufts and yellow eyes. Facial disc with fine rufous concentric lines; underparts pale brown with a rufous wash, mottled and barred dark and light and with some large blackish-brown spots. Bill greenish-olive; tarsi feathered, but toes bare and yellowish; talons relatively small and weak. **Similar species** This is the only W African eagle owl with yellow eyes. Vermiculated Eagle Owl [102] is finely vermiculated below, and has dark brown eyes rimmed fleshy-red; toes are feathered. Fraser's Eagle Owl [103] has shorter and more fluffy ear-tufts, dark brown eyes and greyish bare toes, and is coarsely barred below. Shelley's Eagle Owl [105] is much larger, with heavy barring above and below; eyes brown, toes feathered. Verreaux's Eagle Owl [104] is much larger, with fleshy-pink eyelids, dark brown eyes, and finely vermiculated grey-brown plumage.

VOCALISATIONS An accelerating series of short, knocking notes has been heard from birds responding to each other: *kok kok-kok-kokokokok*. It is not yet clear if this is the territorial song, but it could be. A high-pitched wailing *heuuuw*, rising in pitch, is given by the female when begging for food. A similar call is uttered by begging young, which are said also to emit chirruping notes. When alarmed, both sexes give quacking notes.

DISTRIBUTION W Africa from Guinea, Sierra Leone, Liberia, Ivory Coast, Ghana and Nigeria to Cameroon, south to mouth of Congo river, eastwards to Zaïre and south to NW Angola.

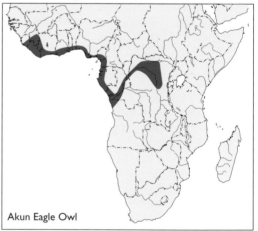

Akun Eagle Owl

MOVEMENTS Resident.

HABITAT Lowland rainforest, primary and old secondary forest with clearings, forest edges, forested islands in large rivers. Probably found only in lowlands.

DESCRIPTION Adult Facial disc light rufous with fine, darker concentric lines; rim thin and blackish. Ear-tufts prominent, with dusky outer edge. Crown dark brown with fine white spots, especially around base of ear-tufts. Upperparts brown to rufescent-brown, with dense dusky vermiculations and wavy bars; scapulars with large areas of white on outer webs, showing as an indistinct whitish row across shoulder. Flight and tail feathers barred light and dark; feathers of tail tipped white. Throat white, edged with dusky barring towards neck. Underparts pale brownish on upper chest, becoming whitish on middle breast and belly; densely vermiculated and barred dark from below throat to upper breast, rest of underparts less densely barred but with relatively large white and blackish-brown dots; abdomen white with small dusky spots. Tarsi feathered and dark (owing to dense dark barring) to base of toes, the latter bare. **Juvenile** Downy chick white. Mesoptile nearly all white with widely spaced rufous-brown bars. Remnants of whitish mesoptile plumage still present up to about 1 year, by when similar to adult. **Bare parts** Eyes pale yellow. Bill and cere pale greenish-yellow. Toes pale yellow. Talons weak and relatively small, blackish.

MEASUREMENTS AND WEIGHT Total length 40-45cm. Wing of males 292-338mm, of females 310-332mm; tail 190-219mm. Weight of males 486-536g, of females 524-607g.

GEOGRAPHICAL VARIATION Monotypic: *Bubo leucostictus* Hartlaub, 1855.

HABITS Nocturnal. Often active on moonlit nights. During daytime normally roosts singly on large branches within foliage of large forest trees, mostly high above ground; pair-members sometimes roost together. When disturbed at its roost, the owl snaps with the bill, puffs out feathers and droops wings.

FOOD The major part of the diet apparently consists of larger insects such as beetles, cicadas, cockroaches and locusts; possible also takes small vertebrates, but this remains unproven. Has been watched hawking flying cockroaches at dusk. When feeding at a perch, holds the prey with one foot and nips off small pieces with the bill.

BREEDING Poorly known. According to ovaries of collected specimens, laying seems to occur in November-December (Sierra Leone), April, September and December (Liberia), November-January (Gabon) and March and August-September (Zaïre). Apparently often nests in a shallow scrape on the ground, young nestlings having been found at such sites on three occasions.

STATUS AND CONSERVATION Uncertain. An uncommon bird of tropical W Africa. Probably endangered by forest destruction.

REMARKS In particular, this owl's biology, ecology, vocalisations and habits require study.

REFERENCES Boyer & Hume (1991), Brosset & Erard (1986), Eck & Busse (1973), Fry *et al.* (1985), Jellicoe (1954).

---

101 SPOTTED EAGLE OWL
Bubo africanus　　　　　　　　Plate 30

French: Grand-duc africain
German: Fleckenuhu

IDENTIFICATION A relatively small eagle owl (45cm) with prominent ear-tufts, and yellow eyes rimmed by black edges of eyelids. Similar to the South American Magellan Horned Owl [95]. Upperparts dusky brown with whitish spots; pale greyish-brown to creamy-white below, distinctly barred dark, upper breast with dark blotches, especially at sides. Tarsi feathered, toes feathered nearly to tip; talons not very powerful. **Similar species** Vermiculated Eagle Owl [102] is slightly smaller, browner, and is finely vermiculated (less spotted) above and densely barred and

vermiculated below; eyes dark brown, with fleshy-reddish edges of eyelids. Cape Eagle Owl [99] is much larger and heavier, more coarsely marked below, with blackish blotches at sides of upper breast; eyes orange-yellow. Akun Eagle Owl [100] is smaller, with bare, yellow toes and pale yellow eyes. All other eagle owls of Africa have dark brown eyes.

VOCALISATIONS The full song of the male consists of three intergrading notes followed after a short break of about 0.2-0.3s by a drawn-out, somewhat deeper hoot: *wúhuhu-whooh*; this is often introduced by several double-noted hoots, *buo-hooh buo-hooh*. The female's song is similar, but higher in pitch. When duetting, the female's song follows the male's hooting so closely as to give impression of a single bird singing. Both sexes also utter single hoots at different volumes, usually when alarmed; in such situations they also give a wailing *keeow*. Probably connected with courtship is a fast *hokok-hokokokok* by the male. The female utters a humming call and clucking notes during courtship. When scraping out the nest depression, and also when attending chicks, clucking notes are given. Chicks initially beg with a faint *cheep*, when older with a loud ventriloquial wheezing *scheee*. Adults and young give bill-snapping, hissing and chittering in different situations.

DISTRIBUTION Sub-Saharan Africa from Kenya and Uganda south to the Cape, and from there north to the southern borders of the C African rainforest of Zaïre and S Gabon. Locally in S Arabia.

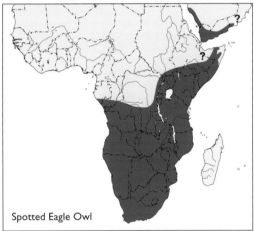
Spotted Eagle Owl

MOVEMENTS Resident.

HABITAT Open or semi-open woodland with shrubs and bushes, mostly with sparse ground cover, savanna with thorny shrubs and scattered trees, and rocky hillsides with groups of trees and bushes. Also semi-deserts, as in the Kalahari. Avoids dense rainforest. From sea-level up to 2,100m.

DESCRIPTION *B. a. africanus* **Adult** Facial disc whitish to pale ochre with fine dark barring; rim blackish. Ear-tufts prominent, often erected. Upperparts dusky brown with whitish or pale buff spots, giving spotted effect (especially on mantle); outer webs of scapulars with larger white areas, but not forming conspicuous row across shoulder. Flight and tail feathers barred light and dark. Chin white. Underparts whitish, finely barred dark; upper breast with several dark greyish-brown blotches; abdomen nearly plain white, suffused with pale buff. Tarsi feathered dirty whitish with some faint brown bars. Toes feathered almost to tips. (A rare buff morph occurs, with paler ground colour to plumage.) **Juvenile** Downy chick white. Mesoptile finely barred whitish and brown. **Bare parts** Eyes yellow to orange-yellow, with blackish edges of eyelids; juveniles have greyish-yellow eyes, becoming yellow before fledging. Cere grey. Bill black. Bare tips of toes dark horn. Claws dark brown to blackish.

MEASUREMENTS AND WEIGHT Total length about 45cm. Wing 290-370mm; tail 184-262mm. Weight 487-850g; males normally lighter than females, mostly 550-620g, females 640-730g.

GEOGRAPHICAL VARIATION We recognise two subspecies. Others have been described, but are possibly no more than variants.

 B. a. africanus (Temminck, 1821). From Uganda, Kenya and the southern limit of C African rainforest in Zaïre and Gabon south to the Cape. See Description. Wing 290-370mm. (The described forms *tanae* from SE Kenya and *trothae* from Namibia may be extreme pale variations rather than true subspecies.)
 B. a. milesi Sharpe, 1886. S Arabia to United Arab Emirates and Oman. More tawny in colour than nominate, and smaller. Wing 302-330mm. (Vocalisations are said to differ somewhat from those of African nominate, suggesting that *milesi* may be specifically distinct; it is allopatric. More study needed.)

HABITS Mostly nocturnal, but sometimes active before sunset. During daytime it roosts in trees, in rock crevices and cave entrances, at sheltered sites on cliff ledges, on the ground between rocks, under a bush or high grass, sometimes in burrows of larger mammals. In trees it sits mostly close to the trunk, with feathers compressed and ear-tufts erected; eyes are normally closed to a small slit, especially when the bird is approached. When flushed, it may perch rather openly, and is then often mobbed by diurnal birds. Male and female sometimes roost together, billing and allopreening. Generally leaves its roost at dusk and flies to a perch, from where it sings or watches for prey.

FOOD Larger insects (e.g. beetles) and other arthropods (including spiders and scorpions), small mammals (shrews, rodents, ground squirrels, hedgehogs, young hares, etc), birds (up to the size of terns and falcons) and reptiles are the favourite prey. In South Africa, 67% of food was invertebrates, 17% mammals and 14.5% birds, the remainder consisting of reptiles and frogs. Small rodents, when abundant, may constitute the major part of the diet. This owl is said also to eat carrion. Normally hunts from a perch, gliding down on to prey; sometimes dashes at roosting birds or hawks flying insects, bats and possibly nightjars. When water is available, it drinks regularly.

BREEDING Probably pairs for life. The occupied territory is claimed by regularly singing (white throat then conspicuous). Territories may be relatively small; in Zimbabwe, three pairs were found in 5.8 km². Male and female may be heard duetting, primarily during breeding season. Courtship poorly known, but perhaps similar to that of other eagle owls. Nest is a shallow scrape on the ground, between rocks, in a sheltered site on a cliff ledge,

in a hollow tree or on the platform of an abandoned tree nest of a larger bird; even the large colonies of Sociable Weavers *Philetarius socius* may be used as nest platforms, and sometimes holes in walls of buildings are used. Ground nests may be among grass, under a bush, on a steep slope or on an earth bank. The same site is sometimes used for several years.

Lays mostly 2-4 white eggs, at intervals of 1-4 days; eggs average 49.1 x 41.1mm. In South Africa, a peak in laying is noted between July and October (dry season); in other parts of Africa, laying varies throughout the year, but drier weather conditions seem to be preferred. The female incubates alone, being fed on the nest by her mate; she sits very tight, but leaves the nest up to three times per night for periods of 6-28 minutes each. Incubation, starting from the first egg, takes 30-32 days. Eyes of young begin to open at 7 days; eye colour grey, becoming gradually yellow when about 2 weeks old, at which age mesoptile down begins to replace the first white, downy plumage. When about 4 weeks old the nestlings begin to walk or clamber around the nest, displaying threat posture typical of many owls: raised plumage, half-open wings, hissing and bill-snapping. At about 6 weeks the plumage is well developed, only underparts and mantle showing remnants of barred mesoptile; the facial disc is now well developed and the eyes bright yellow. The female broods the chicks closely for the first 10 days, feeding them with morsels of food (mainly mammals and birds) brought by the male; prey normally delivered decapitated and consists often of larger animals. The normal diet is rodents (mice, rats, etc) and birds, which are caught predominantly outside the breeding season. After 12 days, the female spends less time with the nestlings, which are now able to gulp down prey whole. Like the male, she will defend the nest and attack intruders, or perform injury-feigning distraction displays. If sites are suitable (e.g. on ground), young leave the nest when 30-38 days old, not yet able to fly well; in elevated positions, they leave at 40-42 days, flying well by 48 days. Thereafter, they remain unobtrusive for a few days, then become more mobile, begging loudly and following the parents. For about 5 weeks after fledging the young are fed by both parents, and by 7 weeks are able to kill their own prey. The exact age of full independence is unknown. Sexual maturity is reached in the following year.

Spotted Eagle Owls may reach an age of more than 10 years (precise data lacking).

STATUS AND CONSERVATION Widespread over its range and locally frequent. Endangered locally by the use of pesticides, nest predation by larger carnivores, human persecution, bush fires, road traffic, and collisions with barbed-wire fences.

REMARKS The Spotted Eagle Owl needs intensive taxonomic research, including study of its vocalisations, behaviour, ecology and molecular biology. This should help to clarify whether the allopatric Arabian population *milesi* is conspecific (representing a subspecies) or whether it may be specifically distinct. The species' northern distributional limits in Africa are much farther south than the southernmost coast of Arabia. More contact could exist with the specifically distinct Vermiculated Eagle Owl, which reaches the African coast of the Red Sea; this, however, has dark brown eyes and is densely vermiculated, whereas *milesi* has yellow eyes and more resembles Spotted Eagle Owl (though is more tawny). One Arabian record of a bird with brown eyes may have involved a Vermiculated

Eagle Owl, living on the opposite side of the Red Sea. Apart from these problems, comparative studies of the parapatric taxa *africanus* and *cinerascens* are needed, above all on their vocalisations, behaviour, ecology and molecular biology.

REFERENCES Aurelian (1957), Boyer & Hume (1991), Fry *et al.* (1988), König & Ertel (1979), Newman (1985, 1987), Steyn (1982), Voous (1988), Zimmerman *et al.* (1996).

102 VERMICULATED EAGLE OWL
Bubo cinerascens   Plate 30

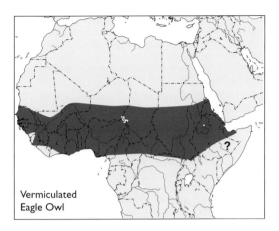

Vermiculated
Eagle Owl

French: Grand-duc vermiculé
German: Wellen-Uhu

IDENTIFICATION A relatively small (about 43cm), greyish-brown eagle owl with less prominent ear-tufts than Spotted Eagle Owl [101]. Finely vermiculated and less spotted above, densely vermiculated and barred below, upper breast with several dark dots. Eyes dark brown, rimmed by fleshy-reddish edges of eyelids. **Similar species** Spotted Eagle Owl is slightly larger, with longer ear-tufts, more coarsely barred underparts, and yellow eyes with black edges of eyelids. Akun Eagle Owl [100] is darker, with yellow eyes and bare, pale yellow toes. Cape Eagle Owl [99] is much larger and more heavily built, coarsely marked below, with black blotches on each side of upper breast, and with eyes orange-yellow. Shelley's Eagle Owl [105], also much larger, has very prominent barring below and a pale creamy-horn bill; eyes dark brown, ear-tufts short and fluffy. Fraser's Eagle Owl [103] has dark brown eyes, fluffy ear-tufts, and coarse barring below; general coloration tawny-buff, with plain tawny, prominently dark-rimmed facial disc; toes totally bare and pale blue-grey. Verreaux's Eagle Owl [104] is very large and heavy, with short, fluffy ear-tufts and dark brown eyes, and eyelids bare and fleshy-pink; general coloration 'milky' brown with faint but dense vermiculations above and below, with white outer webs of scapulars forming prominent white band across shoulder.

VOCALISATIONS As this owl has hitherto been considered a race of Spotted Eagle Owl, observations on its vocalisations have not been differentiated but have been merged with those of the latter. Comparative studies on the vocabulary of the two taxa are urgently needed. The song of male Vermiculated recorded in Mali and Ivory Coast consists of a clearly disyllabic *kuo-wooh*, the first syllable rather explosive, with the second (after a break of about 1.4s) slightly downward-inflected, deeper and somewhat drawn out. These double notes are uttered at intervals of several seconds. It is therefore very different from that of Spotted Eagle Owl.

DISTRIBUTION Sub-Saharan Africa from Senegambia and Cameroon eastwards north of the rainforest to Ethiopia, Somalia, S Sudan, N Kenya and N Uganda.

MOVEMENTS Resident. Locally, moves to higher altitudes in hot summers.

HABITAT Rocky semi-desert (e.g. fringes of Sahara), open and semi-open savanna with thorn bushes and scattered trees, rocky mountain slopes and open hilly landscapes; the habitat is normally rather dry. Avoids dense forest and rainforest.

DESCRIPTION Adult Facial disc pale greyish-brown, finely vermiculated darker in form of more or less concentric lines; blackish rim around disc broader and more prominent than on Spotted Eagle Owl. Eyebrows whitish, ear-tufts shorter and blunter than on Spotted. Upperparts greyish-brown with many dark vermiculations and a few lighter and darker spots; crown slightly darker than mantle and back, the mantle rather densely vermiculated; outer webs of scapulars with much white, sometimes showing as indistinct white row across shoulder. Flight feathers barred light and dark. Tail feathers pale greyish-brown, dark bars fewer and more widely spaced than on Spotted. Throat white. Underparts pale greyish-brown, finely and densely vermiculated dark brown, upper chest with several dark dots (concentrated at sides); abdomen whitish, densely vermiculated dark. Tarsi feathered, toes partly bare. **Juvenile** Similar to Spotted Eagle Owl, but eyes always dark. **Bare parts** Eyes dark brown, rimmed by fleshy-reddish edges of eyelids. Cere brownish-grey. Bill lead-grey (not blackish-horn as on Spotted). Bare parts of toes greyish-brown. (Coloration of bare parts apparently specifically important, as it is invariably the same from Senegambia to Somalia and N Kenya.)

MEASUREMENTS AND WEIGHT Total length about 43cm. Wing of males 284-333mm (median of 30 males 309mm), of females 298-338mm (median of 27 females 324mm); tail 170-200mm. Weight about 500g, females heavier than males.

GEOGRAPHICAL VARIATION Monotypic: *Bubo cinerascens* Guérin-Méneville, 1843. The form *kollmannspergeri* from Chad is perhaps only a pale variant; we do not, therefore, treat this form as a subspecies, but more study is needed to clarify the situation.

HABITS A nocturnal bird, normally leaving its daytime roost at dusk. The roost may be in a crevice of a cliff, between rocks, in a tree, in a hole in a wall or earth bank, under a bush or among rocks on the ground. Behaviour requires study, especially for comparison with Spotted Eagle Owl.

FOOD Larger insects and other arthropods, small mammals and birds, reptiles and frogs are taken. Normally hunts from a perch, but probably also hawks flying insects and bats.

BREEDING Laying said to be mostly from November to April almost throughout the species' range; in July in

Somalia, in August in Nigeria. In general, lays 2-3 white eggs (49-50 x 39-40mm) in a shallow scrape on the ground or among rocks, or in a sheltered site on a cliff ledge; sometimes uses nest platform of larger bird in tree. Breeding biology probably similar to that of Spotted Eagle Owl; requires study.

STATUS AND CONSERVATION Uncertain, as limits of distribution not fully clarified, but seems to be locally not rare.

REMARKS We separate Vermiculated Eagle Owl from Spotted Eagle Owl because of its plumage pattern and bare-part coloration, which are constant from Senegambia to Somalia; retention of patterns (e.g. always dark eyes) over such distances, without intergrading at any locality, argues against subspecific treatment. Unfortunately, we have no detailed evidence on vocal patterns. Interbreeding of the two taxa has not yet been observed; although their distributions seem to overlap in N Kenya and Uganda, no indications of hybrid populations or intergrading have been observed. Comparative studies on the vocabulary of Vermiculated and Spotted Eagle Owls are urgently required in order to shed light on their taxonomy.

REFERENCES Boyer & Hume (1991), Burton (1992), Fry *et al.* (1988), Voous (1988), Zimmerman *et al.* (1996).

103 FRASER'S EAGLE OWL
Bubo poensis Plate 30

Other names: Usambara or Nduk Eagle Owl (*vosseleri*)

French: Grand-duc à aigrettes
German: Guinea-Uhu

IDENTIFICATION A relatively small eagle owl (39-42cm) with 'tousled' ear-tufts, prominently dark-rimmed facial disc and bare, greyish-blue toes. Bill pale bluish-grey; eyes dark brown with bluish edges of eyelids. General coloration rufous and buff with variable dark markings; underparts coarsely barred dark on pale rufous or ochre-whitish ground, upper breast with dark blotches, especially at sides. **Similar species** The allopatric form *vosseleri*, which is probably a separate species (Usambara Eagle Owl: see Geographical Variation, below), has darker brown barring and in general more orange-rufous wash, is more coarsely and irregularly barred dark below, with fine shaft-streaks and many blackish blotches on upper breast, and is slightly larger. Akun Eagle Owl [100] is darker, with pale yellow eyes and bare yellow toes. Vermiculated Eagle Owl [102] is paler and greyer, with dense vermiculations below, and dark eyes rimmed by fleshy-reddish edges of eyelids. Shelley's Eagle Owl [105] is much larger, more dark brown (not buffy or rufescent) and with coarse barring above and below; eyes brown, toes feathered, ear-tufts relatively short and fluffy. Verreaux's Eagle Owl [104] is very large and heavy, rather uniform 'milky' brownish, densely and finely vermiculated above and below, with bare and prominently pink eyelids with pale orange edges rimming dark brown eyes.

VOCALISATIONS The song of the male is a very long, deep trill of rapid staccato notes, somewhat guttural: *korororororor....* It resembles the noise of a generator in operation. A double hoot, *twowooht*, with second note higher in pitch and more whistled, is also uttered; these

hoots are repeated at intervals of 3-4 seconds and are similar in pitch to the song of male Tawny Owl [130]. Single soft mewing notes, *wooh*, are given by both sexes. Also reported are moaning sounds, probably a begging-call. As with all owls, bill-snapping forms part of the vocabulary. The form *vosseleri* (see Geographical Variation) has a very similar 'mechanical' trilled song, and also gives a double hoot; possible differences between the two taxa require study.

DISTRIBUTION From tropical forested W Africa eastwards to Zaïre and SW Uganda, south to extreme NW Angola (primary rainforest of the Congo Basin). The allopatric form *vosseleri* is reported to occur in the Usambara Mountains of NE Tanzania.

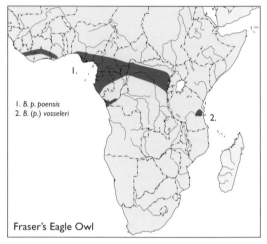

1. *B. p. poensis*
2. *B. (p.) vosseleri*

Fraser's Eagle Owl

MOVEMENTS Resident.

HABITAT Chiefly lowland primary evergreen rainforest, forest edges and clearings within forest, secondary forest and cardamom plantations. In Cameroon from sea-level up to about 1,600m; in the Usambara Mountains of Tanzania (*vosseleri*), between 900m and 1,500m.

DESCRIPTION *B. p. poensis* **Adult** Sexes alike, but females somewhat larger; degree of rufous coloration and density of barring vary individually. Facial disc pale rufous, with relatively broad dusky rim. Eyebrows lighter than surrounding plumage. Ear-tufts 'tousled', rather prominent. Upperparts rufous and buffy-brown, barred with dusky brown; scapulars with pale buffy to creamy-whitish, dark-edged outer webs, suggesting a row of pale dots across shoulder. Flight and tail feathers rather narrowly barred light and dark. Chin whitish, but prominent only when calling. Underparts pale rufous, shading to whitish on abdomen and undertail-coverts, with rufous-edged dark bars; broad dusky tips of feathers on upper breast give dark-blotched effect. Tarsi feathered to base of toes, rather faintly and densely barred. **Juvenile** Downy chick whitish. Mesoptile very pale rufous, almost white, marked all over with narrow dark brown bars; facial disc prominently rimmed dusky; indistinct ear-tufts fluffy and darker than surrounding plumage; facial bristles dark, contrasting with pallid facial disc; alula and flight and tail feathers similar to adult, contrasting with whitish mesoptile. Mesoptile feathers of underparts replaced by true contour feathers when about 1 year old. **Bare parts** Eyes dark brown, rimmed by pale bluish edges of bare eyelids. Bill and cere pale blue-grey. Toes bluish-grey. Claws dark greyish-horn.

MEASUREMENTS AND WEIGHT Total length 39-42cm. Wing of males 281-318mm (av. of 10 birds 301mm), of females 296-333mm (av. of 10 birds 320mm); tail of males 153-174mm (median 163mm), of females 157-179mm (median 170mm). Weight of 1 male 575g, of 4 females 685-815g (median 746g); 2 unsexed fledglings weighed 641g and 653g.

GEOGRAPHICAL VARIATION Varies considerably in coloration and plumage pattern throughout its range, making any true geographical variation difficult to determine. The taxon *vosseleri* probably represents an allopatric species.

> **B. p. poensis** Fraser, 1853. From Liberia to Congo Basin of Cameroon, Zaïre and SW Uganda, south to northernmost W Angola. See Description.
> **B. (p.) vosseleri** Reichenow, 1908. Usambara or Nduk Eagle Owl. Endemic to Usambara Mountains of NE Tanzania. Slightly larger (wing 342-350mm), with orange-rufous facial disc broadly rimmed blackish (rim more prominent than in nominate *poensis*); upper breast more densely blotched blackish, rest of underparts more irregularly barred and faintly streaked. (Allopatric distribution, and differences in size, plumage pattern and perhaps voice may indicate specific separation, but available data seem to us at present insufficient for any definitive decision to be made.)

HABITS Little studied. Nocturnal, becoming active at dusk. Roosts by day within foliage of trees, up to about 40m above ground; at this time, it is mobbed by diurnal birds when located by them. Normally leaves its roost at dusk to hunt, mostly from a perch. Singing is recorded mostly at dusk and early in the night, as well as before dawn.

FOOD Small mammals (such as mice, squirrels, bats, and galago), birds, frogs and reptiles, as well as insects and other arthropods, form the bulk of its diet. This owl is said to eat fruit occasionally.

BREEDING Poorly known. Most vocally active in Gabon June-September. Laying estimated in February and May in Liberia, in November in Ghana, in July-December in Cameroon, in August and December in Zaïre and in March in Uganda; in October, December, January and February in Tanzania (*vosseleri*). Captive birds in Nigeria laid in October. Nestlings have been found on the ground, and one was observed peering out of a large cavity in a tree; this suggests that it may nest on the ground as well as in tree holes. Eggs pure white. Post-fledging dependence seems to be long, as young do not acquire full plumage until about 1 year of age.

STATUS AND CONSERVATION Uncertain, but doubtless threatened by forest destruction and probably (at least locally) by human persecution. Usambara population (*vosseleri*) listed as Vulnerable by BirdLife International.

REMARKS Very little is known about the ecology, behaviour, vocalisations, distribution, taxonomy and reproductive biology of this handsome, probably endangered owl. The possible specific status of *vosseleri* requires confirmation through studies of such aspects.

REFERENCES Boyer & Hume (1991), Brosset & Erard (1986), Collar & Stuart (1985), Collar *et al.* (1994), Fry *et al.* (1988), Moreau (1964), Olney (1984), Zimmerman *et al.* (1996).

104   VERREAUX'S EAGLE OWL
Bubo lacteus   Plate 31

French: Grand-duc de Verreaux
German: Blaâuhu

IDENTIFICATION A very large eagle owl (60-65cm), the largest and heaviest owl of Africa. Rather uniform greyish-brown, with light vermiculations above and a row of whitish spots across shoulder, and with dense fine vermiculations below; ear-tufts 'tousled' and somewhat fluffy. Talons very powerful, with feathered toes. Eyes dark brown, eyelids bare and pink (very conspicuous); rims around eyes dark, with ochre lashes on upper eyelid. **Similar species** Shelley's Eagle Owl [105] is nearly as large, but is coarsely barred below, with general coloration much darker, and lacks pink eyelids. All other eagle owls of Africa are much smaller, or have yellow to orange eyes.

VOCALISATIONS The male's song is an irregularly spaced sequence of very deep grunting, nasal notes: *gwonk gwok-gwok gwonk-gwokwokwok gwonkwogwonk gwonk....* This phrase is repeated after several seconds. The female utters a similar song. Females and large chicks give loud, drawn-out, high piercing whistles when begging for food. A sonorous *whok* uttered by both sexes seems to have an alarm function. Male gives soft bubbling calls when calling female to the nest. In addition, grunting notes and rasping screams are uttered by both sexes. Young chicks chitter, hiss and snap with the bill.

DISTRIBUTION Africa south of Sahara, south to the Cape; absent from desert in Namibia and tropical rainforest of W and C Africa (Congo Basin).

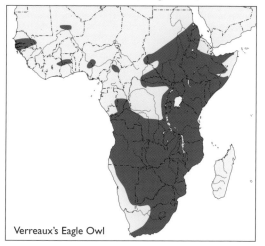
Verreaux's Eagle Owl

MOVEMENTS Resident.

HABITAT Dry savanna with scattered trees and thorny shrubs, riverine forest with adjacent savanna, groups of trees and small, semi-open woods in open countryside.

Most common in open savanna and semi-deserts, un-common in well-developed woodland, and absent from heavy forest. A rather typical bird of the thorny savannas in E Africa. From sea-level up to about 3,000m.

DESCRIPTION Adult Sexes alike, but females larger and heavier than males. Facial disc off-white, with broad blackish rim. Bristles around bill blackish. Upperparts pale grey-brown (suffused 'milky') with fine whitish vermic-ulations, the latter darker on 'tousled', somewhat fluffy ear-tufts and on mantle; scapulars with large areas of white, forming whitish row across shoulder. Flight and tail feathers barred light and dark. Throat white, prominent when calling. Underparts lighter greyish-brown with fine light and dark vermiculations, darkest on upper breast and lightest on flanks and feathered tarsi. Toes feathered. **Juvenile** Downy chick completely covered with creamy-white down. Mesoptile pale greyish with fine vermic-ulations and some dark barring; rim around facial disc less prominent. **Bare parts** Eyes dark brown, rimmed by brown edges of eyelids; upper eyelids naked and pink-coloured, with ochre eyelashes. Cere blue-grey. Bill pale creamy-horn with dark grey base. Bare parts of toes horn. Claws dark brown with black tips.

MEASUREMENTS AND WEIGHT Total length 60-65cm. Wing of males 420-477mm (median of 18 birds 448mm), of females 447-490mm (median of 22 birds 465mm); tail of males 220-275mm (median 244mm), of females 230-273mm (median 254mm). Weight of 4 males 1615-1960g (median 1704g), of 6 females 2475-3115 g (median 2625g).

GEOGRAPHICAL VARIATION Monotypic: *Bubo lacteus* (Temminck, 1820).

HABITS Normally nocturnal, but will swoop on potential prey at any hour of the day. By day it roosts on large, often horizontal branches, mostly well shaded and sheltered, with sites often used over fairly long periods; pair and fledged young may sometimes roost quite close together; pair-members often seen allopreening at their roost. At dusk, leaves its day roost and flies to different perches, used as lookouts for prey; also sings from such perches. Hunts mainly in the early part of the night. This species regularly bathes in rain or in shallow water; when very hot, it flutters white throat for cooling.

FOOD Mostly medium-sized mammals and some larger birds; also eats carrion. Locally, hedgehogs are a favourite prey, their spiny skins being characteristically peeled off and discarded (a technique used also by Eurasian Eagle Owls [95]). Mammals preyed on include young monkeys, warthog piglets, springhares, hares, genets, hyraxes, ground squirrels, fruit bats, rats and mice. Birds taken range in size from waxbills and weavers up to herons, Secretary-birds *Sagittarius serpentarius*, ducks, nestlings of vultures, francolins and young cranes. In addition, reptiles, frogs, toads, fish and arthropods (including insects, millipedes, spiders and scorpions) are caught. The owl is able to carry away in flight prey of 1.8kg (mongoose) or a young, half-grown vervet monkey. Requires about 5% of body weight in food per day. Catches prey by gliding down quickly on to it from a perch. Also hawks flying insects, grasping them with the talons, and dashes into foliage to catch roosting birds or galagos. Sometimes runs about on the ground after insects, or wades into shallow water after fish. Occasionally, flies low over bushes to surprise potential prey.

BREEDING Monogamous; lives in pairs. The pair defends its territory with deep grunting calls or phrases of song, sometimes in duet; song carries up to 5km. In courtship the birds perch near each other, producing fast stuttering hoots, bob up and down, and flick open the wings slightly. Allopreening is frequent. Normally uses abandoned stick nest of a larger bird, such as a vulture, Secretary-bird, Hamerkop *Scopus umbretta*, crow, etc; sometimes large hollows in old trees are used. Breeds annually, mainly in the dry season; sometimes only every 2-3 years, perhaps according to food supply.

Generally lays 2 white eggs (mean 62.6 x 51.4mm) at an interval of about 1 week; fresh weight of first egg 101.6g, of second 93.1g. The female alone incubates and is fed by her mate, who often roosts near the nest. Incubation lasts 38-39 days. Young hatch within 7 days of one another, and on hatching weigh 60-70g. Pink eyelids are already evident at 1 week old. The second chick usually disappears within the first 2 weeks (cannibalism, starvation?); only occasionally do both chicks fledge. The female broods the chick up to about 20 days. Later the parents roost near nest, grunting in alarm if approached; rarely, intruders are attacked. Young leave the nest 62-63 days after hatching and before able to fly, but fly well 2 weeks after fledging. They mostly remain hidden in trees or bushes and are rather inactive until about 3 months old; at 5 months they are able to catch prey. A ringed 9-month-old bird had moved 24km from its nest area. Sometimes young remain with their parents for up to 2 years, before breeding on their own. Sexual maturity is reached at 3-4 years.

One bird survived 15 years in captivity.

STATUS AND CONSERVATION Widespread, but locally rare and endangered by the use of pesticides and human persecution.

REMARKS Although a very large and widespread bird, much of its life cycle requires further study.

REFERENCES Avery *et al.* (1985), Boyer & Hume (1991), Brown (1965), Burton (1992), Fry *et al.* (1988), König & Ertel (1979), Newman (1985, 1987), Steyn (1982), Wilson & Wilson (1982).

105 SHELLEY'S EAGLE OWL
Bubo shelleyi   Plate 31

French: Grand-duc bandé
German: Bindenuhu, Sperberuhu

IDENTIFICATION A large eagle owl (53-61cm), dark above with light barring, and with whitish underparts heavily barred dark. Facial disc off-white with brown concentric lines; ear-tufts 'tousled'. Eyes dark brown; tarsi and toes feathered; bill pale creamy-horn. **Similar species** The only large, heavily built and, below, heavily barred eagle owl of W African lowland forest. All other sympatric species are distinctly smaller. Akun Eagle Owl [100] has pale yellow eyes and bare, yellowish toes. Fraser's Eagle Owl [103] is much smaller, more warm tawny and with bare bluish-grey toes, and is less heavily barred below.

VOCALISATIONS The song is a loud wailing *kooouw*, uttered at irregular intervals of several seconds. When stressed, captive individuals gave a continuous soft peeping.

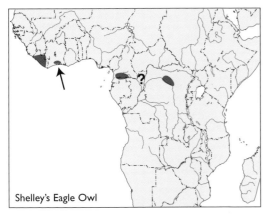

Shelley's Eagle Owl

STATUS AND CONSERVATION Apparently very rare and endangered, with forest destruction a principal threat.

REMARKS Ecology, behaviour and the entire biology of Shelley's Eagle Owl are unknown. Studies are needed, in particular to determine more about this powerful owl's requirements for its survival.

REFERENCES Boyer & Hume (1991), Chapin (1960), Colston & Curry-Lindahl (1986), Fry *et al.* (1988), Good (1952), de Roo (1966), Schouteden (1966).

106 BARRED EAGLE OWL
Bubo sumatranus   Plate 32

Other name: Malay Eagle Owl

French: Grand-duc de Malaisie
German: Malayen-Uhu

IDENTIFICATION A large owl (40-46cm) for this region, with barred underparts and long, outward-slanting, finely barred ear-tufts, and with breast always much darker than belly. Tarsus entirely feathered to toe joint. **Similar species** In Indonesia, can be confused with Brown Wood Owl [132] or Bartels' Wood Owl [133], but *Strix* species have no ear-tufts; moreover, the toes of Barred Eagle Owl are naked, while on Brown Wood Owl feathering extends over toe joint and only the two last digits are naked, and on Bartels' Wood Owl feathering reaches over all toes almost to claws. Some similarity exists also with Forest Eagle Owl [107], which is, however, somewhat more boldly spotted below, but the two species apparently do not overlap in distribution (note that Forest and Barred Eagle Owls evidently belong to the same superspecies). Differs from fish owls [109-112] in having fully feathered tarsi.

VOCALISATIONS A deep hoot, *hoo* or *hoo-hoo*, slightly dropping in pitch towards the end of the hoot with an interval of 1.9-2.0 sec between the hoots of the double-hoot. Also a noisy 'cackling' of various syllables, fearful shrieks and strangulated noises in the early evening.

DISTRIBUTION S Burma (S Tenasserim), S Thailand, Malay Peninsula, Sumatra, Bangka, Borneo, Java and Bali.

MOVEMENTS Resident.

HABITAT Evergreen forest with pools and streams, gardens with large, densely foliaged trees (Botanical Gardens, Bogor, Java), groves in cultivated country, sometimes not far from habitations. Usually from sea-level to 1,000m, seldom higher, to about 1,600m (Cibodas Nature Reserve, Mt Gede, W Java).

DESCRIPTION *B. s. strepitans* **Adult** Face and lores dirty greyish-white, with distinct white eyebrow which is continuous with ear-tufts. Ear-tufts long and outward-slanting or slightly upward-angled, blackish-brown and with inner webs delicately barred with white or rufous. Upperparts brown, crossed and mottled with numerous zigzag bars of tawny-rufous, rather broad on back. Uppertail dark brown with about six whitish or tawny bars and white at tip. Chest rufous-brown (varying individually in degree of darkness); rest of underparts white with scattered irregularly shaped spots and distinctly cross-

DISTRIBUTION Widely scattered in Upper and Lower Guinea, Liberia, Ghana, Cameroon, Gabon and NE Zaïre. At present, fewer than 20 specimens known.

MOVEMENTS Resident.

HABITAT Primary lowland forest of tropical W and C Africa.

DESCRIPTION Adult Lighter and darker morphs occur. *Light morph*: Facial disc off-white to pale tawny with fine, dark concentric lines; rim around disc prominent, blackish-brown. Ear-tufts mainly dark brown, partly barred lighter. Bristles around base of bill brown. Crown and mantle dusky brown, sometimes with a few whitish feathers in centre of crown or towards nape; rest of upperparts dark brown with buffy-whitish bars. Flight and tail feathers barred dark and light. Throat white, but normally concealed under barred plumage (prominent only when calling). Underparts off-white, heavily barred dark brown from upper breast to belly. Tarsi feathered dirty white with several dusky bars or spots. Toes nearly all feathered, leaving extreme tips bare. *Dark morph*: Facial disc browner. Generally more dark brown above, only sparsely barred light. Underparts darker with broader dusky bars, more 'scaly' on upper breast. **Juvenile** Downy chick not described, but probably has whitish down. Mesoptile overall barred off-white and brown; flight and tail feathers as adult. **Bare parts** Eyes dark brown. Cere bluish-grey. Bill pale creamy-horn with bluish wash near base. Bare parts of toes pale cream. Claws pale greyish-horn with darker tips.

MEASUREMENTS AND WEIGHT Total length 53-61cm. Wing 420-477mm; tail 240-266mm. Weight of 1 male 1257g; females presumably heavier.

GEOGRAPHICAL VARIATION Monotypic: *Bubo shelleyi* (Sharpe & Ussher, 1872).

HABITS A nocturnal bird which roosts during daytime among foliage, sometimes quite low above ground.

FOOD Powerful talons suggest that medium-sized mammals and birds are the major part of the diet. A large flying squirrel was once found as prey. A captive individual required about 110g of meat daily.

BREEDING Unknown. In Zaïre, a large nestling was found in September and one recently fledged young in early April, while another in mesoptile plumage was recorded in early November. In Liberia, persistently singing birds were observed in March.

barred with fulvous or dark brown. Tarsus feathered to and sometimes a little over toe joint. **Juvenile** Natal down pure white. Juvenile has head, breast, belly and back conspicuously white, banded with dark brown; ear-tufts white, also with fine brown bars. The brown-fulvous adult colour appears first in flight feathers and rectrices, then on rump. **Bare parts** Iris dark brown or dark hazel; in some (a minority) said to be yellow (cf. Robinson & Kloss 1918, 1924). Bill and cere pale yellow, cere sometimes with greenish cast. Claws greenish-lead or blackish-brown.

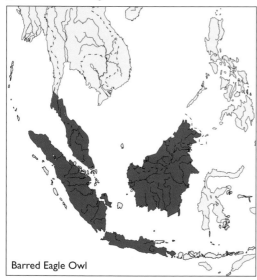

Barred Eagle Owl

MEASUREMENTS AND WEIGHT Total length 40-46cm. Females sometimes slightly larger than males. Weight: 1,427-1,606g (av. 1,525g).

GEOGRAPHICAL VARIATION Three races are recognised.
B. s. sumatranus (Raffles, 1822). Sumatra, Bangka and Malay Peninsula. Small; bands on belly not quite so pronounced as and more widely spaced than on Javan birds. Wing 323-358mm; tail 183-190mm.
B. s. strepitans (Temminck, 1821). Java and Bali. Considerably larger; cross-bars on lower underparts broad and far apart. Wing 370-417mm; tail 186-200mm.
B. s. tenuifasciatus Mees, 1946. Borneo. Similar in size to nominate, but bands on belly finer and closer together.

HABITS Roosts by day singly or in pairs, hidden in a lofty tree with dense foliage, often near the trunk. When the female is at the nest, the male usually remains in the neighbourhood in a dark part of a shady tree.

FOOD Large insects (grasshoppers, Coleoptera), birds, small mammals (mainly rodents: rats and mice), and reptiles (snakes). In captivity it was not choosy, but accepted small fish and all kinds of fresh meat of birds and mammals; one was so fierce that it killed and ate a Changeable Hawk Eagle *Spizaetus cirrhatus* kept in the same aviary.

BREEDING Probably pairs for life. This owl is very attached to particular nesting sites, and when not disturbed will return year after year; when one partner dies or is killed, the surviving mate will continue to occupy

the same site with another partner. Nests in large tree holes, but in Java and Sumatra also very commonly on the top of large bird's-nest ferns *Asplenium nidus*. Clutch always 1 egg: white, broad roundish oval with almost identical poles, 59.8 x 47.9mm (Bartels). In Java, eggs found in February-April and nest with young in May-June; in Sumatra, nestlings or dependent young observed in March-May; in Borneo, young in February-March.

STATUS AND CONSERVATION Not uncommon, but in Java and Sumatra less common than Buffy Fish Owl [110]. Populations at rather low density (large territories).

REMARKS As with many owls, the details of this species' life are not well known and require much study.

REFERENCES Boyer & Hume (1991), Eck & Busse (1973), Kuroda (1936), MacKinnon & Phillipps (1993), Mees (1946), Robinson & Kloss (1918, 1924).

107 FOREST EAGLE OWL
Bubo nipalensis   Plate 32

Other name: Spot-bellied Eagle Owl

French: Grand-duc du Népal
German: Nepaluhu

IDENTIFICATION A large, powerful owl (about 63cm), brown overall, with black-and-white horizontal or sideward-slanting ear-tufts, fully feathered legs and dark brown eyes. **Similar species** Eurasian Eagle Owl [96] is immediately distinguished by its orange-yellow eyes; Forest Eagle Owl differs also from that species in its characteristic juvenile plumage, which is similar to Barred Eagle Owl [106] and quite distinct from that of the adult.

VOCALISATIONS A low, deep and far-sounding double hoot with 2-second interval between the *hoo* notes. Also utters a mournful scream, first rising and then falling in tone.

DISTRIBUTION Lower Himalayas from Kumaon eastwards to N and C Burma and to C Laos and C Vietnam, south to Sri Lanka and S Thailand.

MOVEMENTS Resident.

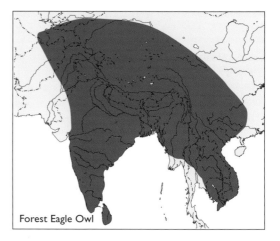

Forest Eagle Owl

HABITAT Dense evergreen and moist deciduous forest such as tropical valleys, terai (alluvial hilly country interspersed with tracts of dense forest) and duars (Himalayan foothills) in the north, and sholas (montane evergreen wet temperate forest) in the southern hills in India and Himalayas; tropical rainforest in Burma, Thailand, Laos and Vietnam. From lowlands and foothills to about 1,500m; in Himalayas, mostly about 900-1,200m but sometimes higher (to 2,100m or above); to about 1,800m in Sri Lanka.

DESCRIPTION *B. n. nipalensis* Adult Ear-tufts dark brown, inner (rarely also outer) webs barred with fulvous-white. Bristly feathers of lores and cheeks brownish-white with black shafts. Upperparts dark brown with black bar-like markings and edged with pale buff, and with feather bases barred fulvous (mostly concealed); scapulars broadly buff with dark brown bars; wing-coverts dark brown, lessers with narrow buffy white-edges, median and greater coverts with broad buff edges mottled with brown. Primaries dark brown with lighter brown bars; secondaries more broadly barred with buffy-brown. Tail dark brown with fulvous bars. Throat and underparts fulvous or fulvous-white, barred with dark brown, the bars becoming broad spots on abdomen, vent and undertail-coverts. **Juvenile** Pale buff or whitish-buff, paler on head, with upperparts barred dark brown; underparts white, washed with buff and barred (though less conspicuously) with dark brown. Adult colour pattern appears first in primaries and secondaries. **Bare parts** Iris dark brown. Bill wax-yellow or yellow. Toes dusky yellow. Claws pale horn, darker at tip.

MEASUREMENTS AND WEIGHT Total length about 63cm. Weight: c. 1,300-1,500g.

GEOGRAPHICAL VARIATION Two subspecies are recognised.

B. n. nipalensis Hodgson, 1836. Lower Himalayas from Kumaon (Pakistan) eastward through Nepal, Sikkim, Bhutan, Arunachal Pradesh and Assam hills north and south of the Brahmaputra river to Nagaland, Manipur and Bangladesh, and also N and C Burma, parts of Thailand, Laos and C Vietnam; peninsular India in Western Ghats and associated hills from Belgaum (c. 16°N) south through W Mysore and Kerala, and Shevaroy Hills (S Eastern Ghats). See Description. Wing 425-470mm; tail 229-250mm.
B. n. blighi Legg, 1878. Sri Lanka. Smaller than nominate race, slightly darker above, and with narrower and fewer bars on underparts. This population, however, doubtfully distinct from birds of S India. Wing 370-412mm; tail 184-215mm.

HABITS Largely nocturnal, spending the day dozing on a densely foliaged bough in the forest, but sometimes on the move and even hunting during daytime.

FOOD Chiefly game birds, including pheasants. A bold and powerful owl, capable of overpowering such large birds as peafowl and junglefowl, and reported to kill jackals, hares, and fawns of barking deer *Muntiacus muntjac*, also takes lizards, snakes and fish. Pounces on large birds asleep at their night roosts in trees or bamboo clumps

BREEDING In the Himalayas breeds in February-March, in Kerala in December-January; an egg collected in N Cachar in June. Nest is a hollow in an old tree, or may use a deserted stick nest of an eagle or other bird of prey; sometimes lays on bare soil in a cave or horizontal fissure in a rock scarp. Clutch 1 egg, white, roundish oval with a smooth surface; 10 eggs averaged 61.2 x 49.9mm. Both sexes are said to share in incubation, but this is doubtful: males simply cover the clutch, without incubating, when the female leaves for a short period. Reported to be very fierce and aggressive in defence of its egg or young.

STATUS AND CONSERVATION Uncommon. Lives at low densities, in large territories.

REMARKS In colour pattern, behaviour and biology this owl is very similar to Barred Eagle Owl. As the two are fully allopatric, they evidently must belong to the same superspecies.

REFERENCES Ali & Ripley (1969), Boyer & Hume (1991), Burton (1992), Lekagul & Round (1991), Voous (1988).

108 DUSKY EAGLE OWL
Bubo coromandus   Plate 33

French: Grand-duc sombre
German: Koromandeluhu

IDENTIFICATION A large owl (48-50cm) with grey or sooty-washed plumage and pale yellow eyes, and with distinct ear-tufts which, on perched bird, stand erect and quite close together (like double spires). **Similar species** Rock Eagle Owl [98] is generally more tawny and has orange (not yellow) eyes.

VOCALISATIONS A deep, resonant, accelerating, croaking *kro-kro-krokrohohohoho* is uttered both day and night; towards the end, the single notes are given in very rapid staccato sequence, resembling a tremolo. The croaking song is reminiscent of the sound made by a large ball dropped from a height and bouncing to a halt, becoming fainter and quicker with each successive bounce. Male and female may be heard duetting during courtship. Like many *Bubo* species, also gives loud snapping *tuck-tuck* of the mandibles when disturbed at nest or irritated.

DISTRIBUTION Indian subcontinent south of the Himalayas, from Sind, Punjab and Uttar Pradesh east through the terai and duars of Nepal to Assam south of Brahmaputra river, Manipur and Bangladesh, south over the northern half of the Indian peninsula at least to Mysore and the Nilgiris; also occurs rarely (status uncertain) in Burma eastwards to Arakan and south to Tenasserim, and in S Thailand and Malay Peninsula.

MOVEMENTS Resident.

HABITAT Widely distributed in well-wooded and well-watered country, not in arid or desert regions. Found in old mango plantations, dense groves, roadside avenues of ancient tamarind *Tamarindus indica* and other densely foliaged trees, in proximity of water and habitations, normally in the (alluvial) plains.

DESCRIPTION *B. c. coromandus* Adult Facial disc whitish with dark shafts; ear-tufts darker and to a large extent unmottled brown. Whole plumage very pale grey with dark brown shaft-lines, broad and indistinct above, more narrow and sharply defined below, and vermiculated light brown to whitish all over (tiny broken wavy bars); on underparts, brown is less extensive and white shows up much more. Primaries dark brown with indistinct paler bars of mottled brown and fulvous. Tail with broad bars of mottled brown and fulvous and with white tip. Tarsus feathered to or beyond toe joint. **Juvenile** Natal down short, pure white. Fledged juvenile rufous overall, with head and neck dirty grey; whole plumage has a rather mealy appearance owing to longer down tips. **Bare parts** Iris bright yellow. Bill bluish-ivory. Cere bluish-lead (or greyish-white or pale lavender), tip pale yellowish-horn. Toes (unfeathered tips) plumbeous or pale brown, soles lighter. Claws darker to blackish-brown.

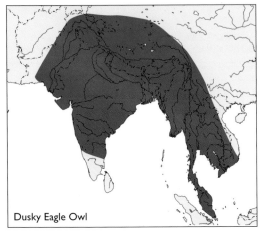

Dusky Eagle Owl

MEASUREMENTS AND WEIGHT Females larger and heavier than males. Total length 43-50cm. Wing 380-435mm; tail 187-224mm. Weight: no data.

GEOGRAPHICAL VARIATION Two subspecies.

B. c. coromandus (Latham, 1790) Indian subcontinent south of Himalayas, east to Assam south of the Brahmaputra, Manipur and Bangladesh, south to Mysore and the Nilgiris. See Description.

B. c. klossi Robinson, 1911. Burma (Arakan, Tenasserim), S Thailand and Malay Peninsula. Plumage similar to nominate, but much darker. Wing 390mm; tail 190mm.

HABITS Although by no means entirely nocturnal, this owl usually spends the daytime in the seclusion of a shady bough or foliage, becoming active an hour or so before sunset. Not really deterred by daylight, having been seen on the move or even hunting by day, particularly in cloudy, drizzling weather (though not during brightest and hottest hours). Usually in pairs. Very faithful to localities when unmolested, pairs often inhabiting the same grove year after year. May frequently be heard calling at all hours of the day. Most vocal during the rainy and cold seasons.

FOOD Small mammals, birds, reptiles, frogs, fish and large insects. Items identified in stomachs and remains of food brought to nestlings include rats, hares, squirrels, coots, pond herons, Red-wattled Lapwings *Vanellus indicus*, once a Shikra *Accipiter badius*, rollers, pigeons, parakeets, and, in particular, House Crows *Corvus splendens* and Jungle Crows *C. (macrorhynchos) levaillantii* (Baker). Insects are mainly water beetles *Dytiscus*. Two dead porcupines were once found in the nest of a pair of these owls. Large prey are evidently decapitated at the site of capture, as their skulls are never found in pellets.

BREEDING Breeding season overall spans November to April: principally December-January in N India, somewhat later in the south. Abandoned stick nests of larger birds in the fork of large tree such as *Ficus, Stephegyne, Dalbergia* or similar, preferably standing in or near water, and not infrequently close to habitation, are used for nesting; also old nests of kites, vultures and eagles, which it sometimes lines with a few green leaves. Lays normally 2 (sometimes only 1) typical owl eggs, white and a roundish oval in shape; 40 eggs averaged 59.3 x 48.2mm. They are laid at an interval of several days, resulting in great disparity in size between the chicks; usually, only the larger and stronger one survives. Both sexes are said to share in incubation. Incubation and fledging periods unknown.

STATUS AND CONSERVATION Not uncommon in India and Bangladesh in suitable habitats, such as well-wooded country and near water. Very rare in easternmost parts of range, and in Malaya known only from three museum specimens, all from N Perak (G. Semanggol, Krian district and Dindings district).

REMARKS Reproductive biology and behaviour require study, in particular the supposed role of the male in incubation (generally, only females incubate).

REFERENCES Ali & Ripley (1969), Baker (1927, 1934), Robinson (1911), Voous (1988).

109 PHILIPPINE EAGLE OWL
Bubo philippensis   Plate 33

French: Grand-duc des Philippines
German: Streifenuhu

IDENTIFICATION A medium-sized owl (40-43cm) with medium-long (about 33mm), conspicuous, outward-slanting ear-tufts. Tawny-rufous to dark brown above with blackish streaks, tail dull rufous-brown with dark brown barring; chin light rufous, throat whitish, rest of underparts pale rufous-brown with dark brown streaks. Tarsus feathered to toe joint, toes naked. Eyes yellow. **Similar species** In the Philippines confusable only with Mindanao Owl [90], though that species is far more rufous, with breast and flanks marked with broad drop-shaped streaks (not narrow streaks), and has brown (not yellow) irides. Confusion with Short-eared Owl [211] perhaps conceivable owing to the streaked appearance of its underparts, but very unlikely because Short-eared lives in very different habitats (open country), has inconspicuous ear-tufts, and has both legs and toes fully feathered.

VOCALISATIONS According to a tape-recording by P. Morris, the song of the male consists of long series of deep staccato notes, given at intervals of about 4 seconds: *bububububu..., bubububu..., bubububu...*, fading away at the end. A high-pitched screaming call appears to be a vocalisation of the female begging for food.

DISTRIBUTION Philippines: recorded from the islands of Luzon, Catanduanes, Mindanao, Samar and Leyte.

MOVEMENTS Resident.

HABITAT Forest, often near rivers and lakes, at lower elevations.

Philippine Eagle Owl

DESCRIPTION *B. p. philippensis* **Adult** Facial disc tawny, with brown central streaks and fulvous bases to feathers. Crown, forehead and ear-tufts as upperparts, but somewhat more narrowly streaked. Tawny-rufous above, each feather with a broad brown central line, giving a closely striped appearance. Tail dull rufous-brown with dark brown bars. Chin pale rufous, throat whitish. Underparts buffy-white, streaked with dark brown (centres to feathers), each streak with narrow edging of rufous at each side, decreasing in width towards abdomen; lower abdomen almost unmarked. Tarsi fully feathered to toe joint. Toes naked. **Juvenile** Not described. **Bare parts** Iris yellow. Bill horn-blue at base, yellow at tip. Cere similar horn-blue but darker. Toes pale dingy blue, light grey or fleshy-brown. Claws light horn-coloured to blackish.

MEASUREMENTS AND WEIGHT Total length 40-43cm. Wing 341-356mm; tail 162-178mm. Weight: no data.

GEOGRAPHICAL VARIATION Two subspecies recognised.

    B. p. philippensis Kaup, 1851. Luzon, Catanduanes. See Description. Wing 341-350mm.
    B. p. mindanensis (Ogilvie-Grant, 1906). Samar, Leyte, Mindanao. Differs from nominate race in having upperparts darker and underparts with darker and more numerous streaks; may also be larger, but this doubtful. Wing 341-355mm.

HABITS Unknown.

FOOD Unknown, but the structure of its legs and feet indicates that it feeds on small mammals and birds.

BREEDING Unknown.

STATUS AND CONSERVATION A Philippine endemic, uncommon or rare throughout its restricted range. Listed as Endangered by BirdLife International. Main causes are extensive habitat destruction and possibly also persecution, and this species is in need of protection. Recent records more or less confined to Luzon.

REMARKS The biology and ecology of this species are poorly known, and studies will no doubt assist with its conservation.

REFERENCES Boyer & Hume (1991), Collar *et al.* (1994), Delacour & Mayr (1945, 1946), Dickinson *et al.* (1991), Eck & Busse (1973), McGregor (1909).

110 BUFFY FISH OWL
Bubo ketupu   Plate 33

Syn: *Ketupa ketupu*

Other name: Malay Fish Owl

French: Hibou pêcheur malais
German: Sunda Fischuhu

IDENTIFICATION A rather large owl (38-48cm), overall yellowish-brown, much variegated with pale buff, feathers edged tawny, and with distinct sideward-directed ear-tufts. Facial disc ill-defined; tail and wings broadly barred yellowish and dark brown, wings very rounded in flight; underparts yellowish-brown, rich buff or fulvous (depending on morph) with broad black shaft-stripes. Relatively long, unfeathered tarsi. **Similar species** In some areas sympatric with Brown Fish Owl [113], but that species has some barring below, as well as streaks. Also with Tawny Fish Owl [111], on which, however, rufous of underparts is much richer, almost orange-rufous, tail more narrowly barred, face more whitish (buff or rufous on other fish owl species), and tarsi feathered to more than halfway down at front.

VOCALISATIONS Hissing sounds and a rattling *kutook, kutook, kutook, kutook, kutook, kutook,...*, as well as a ringing *pof-pof-pof-...* and high *hie-ee-ee-eek-keek* notes. Particularly noisy before breeding, and pairs indulge in bouts of duetting which continue for many minutes.

DISTRIBUTION S Burma, south and east to peninsular Thailand and Annam, Malay Peninsula, Riau Archipelago, Sumatra with neighbouring islands on west side (Nias, etc), Bangka, Belitung, Java, Bali and Borneo.

MOVEMENTS Resident. Exceptionally, vagrants recorded (one specimen recovered at Cocos Keeling Is., Indian Ocean, 1,050km outside main range).

HABITAT Common in woody areas near water, such as wooded banks of rivers, lakes and fish ponds, rice paddies, often close to villages and human habitation; but also in mangrove forest and other less inhabited or uninhabited coastal areas. Lowlands from sea-level to 1,600m.

DESCRIPTION *B. k. ketupu* **Adult** Ear-tufts long. Upperparts blackish-brown, feathers broadly margined with rufous and with pale rufous or whitish spots near tips. Head and neck as upperparts, except that tips of feathers lack pale spots; outer scapulars fulvous on outer webs; wing-coverts as back, but with much larger pale spots. Primaries and secondaries dark brown, banded with whitish or fulvous. Rectrices dark brown with whitish tips and 3-4 whitish bands. Underparts rufous-buff or fulvous with narrow dark brown shaft-stripes, these becoming narrower and fewer in number on abdomen and undertail-coverts; flanks and thighs unstreaked. Tarsi relatively long, bare. **Juvenile** Upperparts more rufous than adult, narrowly streaked with blackish-brown and less spotted with white (or lacking white altogether); rectrices with 5-6 irregular narrow whitish bands; underparts very narrowly

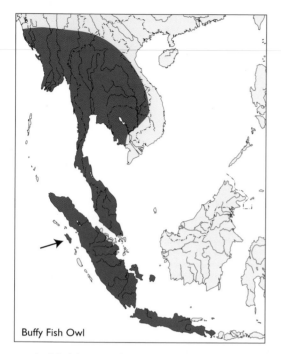

Buffy Fish Owl

the ground below the roost. Food remains have never been found beneath a nest site, but only in the nest. Fishes from a perch at the water's edge or from a tree on a wooded bank, swooping down to snatch prey from the surface or in the water, in much the same manner as a fish eagle. Also walks in shallow streams and brooks, snatching at crabs, frogs, fish and aquatic insects.

BREEDING Eggs found mainly February-April, but also breeds less commonly in May-July (W Java) or in April and September-January (Malay Peninsula). Frequently nests on top of bird's-nest ferns *Asplenium nidus*, but also in fork of a thick bough covered by ferns, moss and orchids, or in tree holes or, more rarely, in caves in rocky sites (e.g. waterfalls). Nest simply a small depression scratched out in centre of a bird's-nest fern or in humus-rich debris of decayed leaves, with no special structure or lining; sometimes uses old nest of raptor (e.g. Brahminy Kite *Haliaster indus*). Lays 1 egg, broadly oval, nearly round, and dull white or with moderate gloss: 48 x 52mm, 48.3-59.1 x 42.7-48.6mm (av. 57.4 x 47.0mm, n = 8; W Java); 48.5 x 42.9mm and 54.9 x 44.5mm (Malay Peninsula).

STATUS AND CONSERVATION Locally rather common. In regions with fish ponds, this owl is sometimes persecuted because of its fish-catching habits.

REMARKS The smallest and most southerly representative of the subgenus *Ketupa*.

REFERENCES Boyer & Hume (1991), Burton (1992), Chasen (1939), Eck & Busse (1973), Gibson-Hill (1949, 1950), Kuroda (1931), MacKinnon & Phillipps (1993), Voous (1988).

streaked dark brown and faintly barred whitish. **Bare parts** Iris yellow, rimmed black. Bill black or greyish-black. Tarsi and toes yellowish-grey or brownish-yellow.

MEASUREMENTS AND WEIGHT Females always larger than males. Total length 38-48cm. Wing 329-390mm; tail 160-181mm. Weight: 1,028-2,100g (av. 1,293g).

GEOGRAPHICAL VARIATION Four subspecies recognised.

    B. k. ketupu (Horsfield, 1821). Malay Peninsula, Riau Archipelago, Sumatra, Bangka, Belitung, Java, Bali, and Borneo (except portion occupied by *pageli*). See Description.

    B. k. aagaardi (Neumann, 1935). S Burma, south and east to peninsular Thailand and Annam. Similar to nominate *ketupu* from Java, but much paler, especially below. Wing 315-345mm.

    B. k. pageli (Neumann, 1936). Eastern coast of Sarawak, N Borneo. Similar to nominate *ketupu* from Java, but far more reddish or brick-red. Wing 310-330mm.

    B. k. minor Büttikofer, 1896. Confined to island of Nias, off west coast of Sumatra. A smaller race. Wing 295-300mm. (Also named *Bubo ketupu buettikoferi* Chasen, 1935.)

HABITS During the daytime, this owl shelters, often singly, in rather dark places such as densely foliaged trees near its nesting site. Easily disturbed, it is often already wide-awake before being located by the observer.

FOOD A large proportion of the diet consists of fish, along with reptiles, frogs, toads and insects; rats, mice and large insects (beetles) are also commonly eaten. Sometimes takes bats, and also feeds on carrion or carcases (reported feeding on a dead crocodile and remains of a badger *Mydaus javanensis* in Java). This species does not produce firm pellets or pellets of any real consistency; bones and frog and insect remains are ejected in pieces and fall to

111 TAWNY FISH OWL
Bubo flavipes   **Plate 33**

Syn: *Ketupa flavipes*

French: Hibou pêcheur roux
German: Himalaja Fischuhu

IDENTIFICATION A rather large owl (48-58cm), rich orange-rufous or tawny with broad dark shaft-stripes, much buff on scapulars and wing-coverts, and dark brown wings and tail with buff bars and tips. Usually shows a white throat patch. Tarsi partly feathered (nearly two-thirds at front); eyes yellow. **Similar species** Buffy Fish Owl [110] is far less orange-rufous, and has unfeathered tarsi. Brown Fish Owl [113] differs in its much browner colour, as well as its striped underparts with pinkish-white barring and brown vermiculations on each side of the stripes, and its bare tarsi.

VOCALISATIONS A deep *whoo-hoo*, like that of Brown Fish Owl, and a curious, very cat-like mewing call.

DISTRIBUTION Himalayas and from W China south to N Burma, N Laos and Vietnam, and C and SE China and Taiwan.

MOVEMENTS Resident.

HABITAT A forest owl frequenting the banks of hill and submontane streams. To 1,500m in Nepal and to 2,100m in Darjeeling.

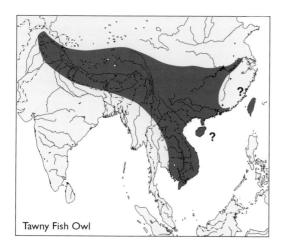

Tawny Fish Owl

DESCRIPTION Adult In general appearance very like Buffy Fish Owl, but larger, and with upperparts much richer in colour, almost orange-rufous, the central dark markings on feathers broader and the spots concolorous with the rufous edges. Underparts very deep and rich rufous, with dark red-brown streaks broader and more numerous; white patch on throat generally much better developed. Tarsi feathered to about two-thirds their length at front and sides and for about one-third at rear. **Juvenile** Like Buffy Fish Owl, but more richly coloured and much bigger. Compared with adult, juvenile has distinct spots and narrower and broader streaks on upperside; underpart plumage downy, chin white, and streaks finer and paler; tarsi covered with down to about 2.5cm above base of middle toe. **Bare parts** Iris yellow. Bill horn-black, sometimes a little yellowish at extreme tip. Legs yellowish-grey, dingy greenish or slaty-green. Claws horn-black.

MEASUREMENTS AND WEIGHT Females larger. Total length 48-58cm. Wing 410-477mm; tail 215-227mm. Weight: no data.

GEOGRAPHICAL VARIATION Monotypic: *Bubo flavipes* (Hodgson, 1836).

HABITS This is the most powerful and fierce of all species of fish owl. Diurnal, even hunting by day, it is sluggish until late afternoon; when disturbed, it prefers to sit still and allow itself to be watched rather than take to the wing.

FOOD As this owl hunts particularly along streams, its main diet consists of fish, crabs, lizards and large Coleoptera. Remains of bamboo-rats *Rhizomys* are regularly found around the nest, and once remains of a small porcupine *Hystrix brachyura*. Its powerful strength, however, enables it frequently to kill junglefowl, pheasants and wood-partridges.

BREEDING Season November-February in India, December-February in Assam. Little known. Sometimes lays on bare earth in a hollow in a ravine or river bank, with no lining added; in Cachar, India, said often to use old nests of fish eagles quite high in trees, these not repaired and no lining added. Normally 2 eggs, sometimes 1, roundish oval and white, very similar to those of Brown Fish Owl: 56.0-58.8 x 45.3-48.3mm (av. 57.1 x 46.9mm, n = 10).

STATUS AND CONSERVATION Locally not uncommon.

REMARKS Biology, behaviour and vocalisations are poorly known and require study.

REFERENCES Ali & Ripley (1969), Baker (1927, 1934), Boyer & Hume (1991), Burton (1992), Eck & Busse (1973), Voous (1988).

112 BLAKISTON'S FISH OWL
Bubo blakistoni   Plate 34

Syn: *Ketupa blakistoni*

French: Hibou pêcheur de Blakiston
German: Riesenfischuhu

IDENTIFICATION A very large owl (60-71cm, wingspan about 2m) with long and broad, almost horizontally slanting ear-tufts. Plumage spotted greyish-brown, marked below with fine dark brown wavy bars and bold streaks; dark brown to chestnut facial disc, dark bill and yellow eyes. Tarsi feathered, toes bare. **Similar species** Eurasian Eagle Owl [96] is darker overall, with broader streaks on breast, and has orange (not yellow) eyes.

VOCALISATIONS A short, deep song, *boo-boo uoo* or *foo-foroo*, like that of an eagle owl. Elaborate duet songs are also described. Food-call of young is a long-drawn-out and slurred trill, *pirriririrr....*

DISTRIBUTION E Siberia from the basins of the Amur and Ussuri and their tributaries the Bolschaja, Ussurka, Bikin and Khor to Okhotsk coast, south to Sakhalin (south of Tyme river), Lake Khanka and regions south of Vladivostok, possibly adjacent parts of Korea, and in a restricted area west of the Great Khingan Mountain range in NW and W Manchuria, and Heilongjiang in China; also Hokkaido (Japan) and southernmost Kuriles (Kunashiri, Shikotan, Etorofu).

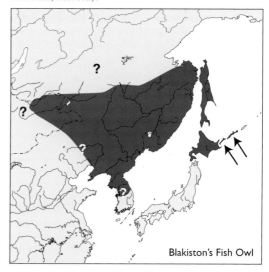

Blakiston's Fish Owl

MOVEMENTS Resident. Although many are thought to leave the Bikin river valley, Ussuriland, in winter, there is no indication of their destination.

HABITAT Riverine forest, undisturbed coniferous forest,

chiefly along fast-flowing rivers and streams which remain at least partly ice-free in winter (e.g. in Great Khingan); dense coniferous, mixed and broadleaved forest in wide river plains with islands in fast-flowing waters and permanent wells that do not freeze over (Ussuriland); in the Kuriles, inhabits dense fir and spruce forest with some deciduous trees bordering lakes, river mouths and sea coasts. Fishes also on rocky sea coasts in the far north.

DESCRIPTION B. b. blakistoni Adult Lores of facial disc tawny-brown with narrow black shaft-stripes; above eyes, around bill base and on forehead a row of small, stiff, almost completely white feathers; chin largely white. Rest of head and upperparts brown with blackish-brown shaft-stripes and buff feather tips, hindneck with traces of barring; back darker (dark brown colour more dominant), mantle somewhat lighter and more rufous and with blackish-brown bars as well as dark brown shaft-streaks. Wings deep brown with numerous buffy-yellowish bars. Tail dark brown with 7-8 cream-yellow bars. Underparts light buff-brown with blackish-brown shaft-streaks and narrow light brown wavy cross-bars (these feathers pale ashy at base); undertail-coverts cream-coloured with few dark markings. Tarsi feathered, mostly unmarked creamy-coloured. Toes bare. **Juvenile** Natal down white. Later the quills emerge, and the wing-coverts have a large dark brown spot in centre, a narrow almost black shaft-stripe and white margins (more variegated compared with adult). **Bare parts** Iris yellow. Bill bluish-grey with yellowish-white mandible tips. Toes lead-grey. Claws dark horn-black.

MEASUREMENTS AND WEIGHT Females larger than males. Total length 60-71cm. Wing 501-560mm; tail 285-290mm. Weight: no data.

GEOGRAPHICAL VARIATION Four subspecies recognised.

B. b. blakistoni (Seebohm, 1884). Hokkaido, N Japan, and Kuriles. See Description. Wing 510-527mm; tail (1 specimen) 281mm.

B. b. doerriesi (Seebohm, 1895). E Siberia south to Vladivostok region and Korean border area. Larger, with large white patch on top of head; tail less regularly marked and bars incomplete. Wing 510-560mm; tail 285-290mm.

B. b. karafutonis (Kuroda, 1931). Sakhalin. Smaller than nominate race (wing about 501mm) and darker, especially on back and ear-coverts; tail with narrower dark brown bars and the light bars more numerous (8-9, as against 7-8 in nominate).

B. b. piscivorus (Meise, 1933). W Manchuria. Paler overall than *doerriesi*, ground colour of underparts greyish-white (not buff-brown); tail-bars not fully creamy-yellow, central rectrices having white inner webs almost to base; chin pure white; as *doerriesi*, a large white occipital spot. Wing 547mm.

HABITS Hunts at onset of dark (Manchuria); also reported to be equally active at dusk, during the day and at night (at Bikin river and other tributaries of the Ussuri), but this was during the brood-rearing season, when northern summer nights are relatively short. In contrast to other owls, it spends much time on the ground, even trampling out conspicuous trails along river banks; in winter, footprints have been found in the snow around air holes in river ice. There are reports of winter concentrations of 5-6 owls near rapids and non-freezing springs.

FOOD Chiefly fish (sometimes of considerable size: Amur pike, catfish, burbot, trout, salmon) and the crayfish *Astacus schrenckii*, and grass frogs (sometimes fed in large quantities to young); in winter, also mammals up to the size of hares, martens, cats and small dogs. Captures prey (fish, etc) by entering water and wading through shallows, or by lying in wait at water's edge and pouncing on prey.

BREEDING Does not breed every year, probably as a result of food supply and conditions. Laying begins as early as mid March, when ground and trees still covered with snow; on Kunashiri (Kuriles), a nestling was found in April. In dense riparian forest of the Bikin and other tributaries of the Ussuri, nests have been reported in hollow trees, often poplar *Populus* and Manchurian ash *Fraxinus* up to 12-18m high, as well as on fallen tree trunks and on the forest floor. Nest holes usually very wide and spacious. Clutch size 1-3, usually 2. Eggs similar in shape and colour to those of other *Bubo* owls: 62.2 x 49.0mm and 62.4 x 48.5mm. The male provides food for the incubating female and later also for the young. Incubation period about 35 days. Young leave the nest within 35-40 days, but still require parental care and may need to be fed for some months.

STATUS AND CONSERVATION Rare and endangered throughout its range. Listed as Endangered by Birdlife International. Total population estimated at not more than a few hundred pairs in Siberia (including Sakhalin and Kuriles) and probably fewer than 100 individuals in Japan. Some 30 nesting pairs were found along a 350km stretch of the Bikin river valley. In Siberia it concentrates around air holes in river ice in winter, making it vulnerable to hunters, fur-trappers and fishermen. Protection programmes have been initiated, including the provision of nestboxes, and the population has recently shown signs of an increase.

REMARKS Some authors regard this owl as no more than a northern race of Brown Fish Owl [113]. The skull of Blakiston's Fish Owl seems not to differ from that of Eurasian Eagle Owl, nor do other skeletal details differ from those of *Bubo* species.

REFERENCES Boyer & Hume (1991), Brazil (1991), Brazil & Yamamoto (1983), Burton (1992), Collar *et al.* (1994), Dementiev & Gladkov (1951), Ford (1967), Hartert (1913), Knystautas & Sygnev (1987), Kuroda (1931), Meise (1933, 1992), Pukinski (1975), Sayers (1976), Voous (1988).

113 BROWN FISH OWL
Bubo zeylonensis   Plate 34

Syn: *Ketupa zeylonensis*

French: Hibou pêcheur brun
German: Fischuhu

IDENTIFICATION A rather large owl (48-56cm) with long and pointed, outward-facing ear-tufts, white at base and black towards tip. Facial disc rather ill-defined, tawny with black shaft-streaks. Overall rufous-brown, heavily streaked above with black or blackish-brown; underparts pale fulvous-whitish with fine wavy brown bars and bold blackish streaks; prominent white patch on throat and foreneck. Eyes bright golden-yellow; tarsus and toes bare. **Similar**

species Buffy Fish Owl [110] is smaller, its facial disc lacks black shaft-streaks and its underparts are unbarred. Tawny Fish Owl [111] has a pale face, no bars below, and tarsi about two-thirds feathered at front. Blakiston's Fish Owl [112], unlikely to occur sympatrically, is considerably larger and has somewhat darker tawny-brown to chestnut-coloured facial disc.

VOCALISATIONS The male's song is a deep, trisyllabic *tu-whoo-hu*; sometimes also a doleful, almost human-sounding moan, *oomp-ooo-oo*, answered by his mate with an 'assenting' *oo*. Also recorded is a deep, hollow-sounding *boom-boom* or *boom-o-boom* with peculiar reverberating, ventriloquistic quality, repeated at intervals; this call, when suddenly 'exploding' in the stillness of the forest, has a distinctly eerie effect.

DISTRIBUTION Locally distributed from SW Asia Minor, Iraq and adjacent parts of Iran to Sind and NW Pakistan, all of India south of the Himalayas, Sri Lanka, Assam, Burma, Thailand, Vietnam, and SE China (SE Yunnan, Guangxi, Guangdong, Hainan).

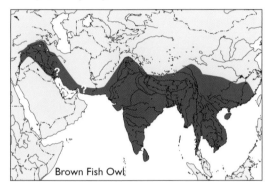

Brown Fish Owl

MOVEMENTS Resident.

HABITAT Generally found in fairly thick lowland forest and open but well-wooded country, but always in neighbourhood of water. Old mango groves or plantations, occasionally even roadside and canalside avenues and densely foliaged trees along streams and tanks; overgrown eroded ravines and steep river banks are favourite haunts. In west of range more arid habitats, though still with access to water. Commonly found near human habitations. Lowlands to about 1,400m, locally to 2,000m.

DESCRIPTION *B. z. leschenault* **Adult** Facial disc tawny with black shaft-streaks. Upperparts light chestnut-brown with broad, black shaft-stripes; lower back, rump and uppertail-coverts a little paler and with narrow shaft stripes; scapulars, tertials and wing-coverts considerably mottled with whitish, the outer webs of outer scapulars white. Remiges and rectrices dark brown, barred and tipped dusky buff. Throat white with dark shaft-stripes. Underparts with fine, wavy pale brown to rufous cross-bars and bold black shaft-streaks. **Juvenile** More rufescent, with narrower and browner shaft-streaks; paler and duller below, with shaft-streaks narrower, and mere trace of white throat patch. Birds in their 2nd year are duller and paler than 3rd-years. **Bare parts** Iris golden-yellow. Bill pale greenish-grey, dusky on culmen and tip. Legs and feet dusky yellow. Claws horn-brown.

MEASUREMENTS AND WEIGHT Total length 48-56cm,

females often larger. Wing 365-457mm; tail 186-214mm. Weight 1105g (1, unsexed).

GEOGRAPHICAL VARIATION Four subspecies have been described, although Voous (1988) considers that *B. z. semenowi* and *B. z. orientalis* are only colour morphs; he includes them in *leschenault*.

B. z. leschenault (Temminck, 1820). All of India south of Himalayas, to Assam, Burma (except northeastern part) and Thailand. See Description. Wing 371-417mm.
B. z. zeylonensis (Gmelin, 1788). Sri Lanka. Smaller and darker than *leschenault*. Wing 365-383mm.
B. z. semenowi Zarudny, 1905. SW Asia Minor, Israel (extinct), Iraq and adjacent parts of Iran to Sind and Pakistan; in more arid or desert areas. Very pale and buff race. Upperside bright loamy-coloured with greyish-isabelline tinge; underside much paler, especially lower breast and abdomen, and with darker brown bars of same tone as upperparts. Above, shaft-streaks much narrower than in nominate race. Wing of 1 male 378mm, of 1 female 381mm.
B. z. orientalis Delacour, 1926. NE Burma, Vietnam and SE China. Darker above, with larger and blacker markings; ground colour of underparts more buff, not so yellow. Wing 365-457mm (2 males 395mm and 400mm).

HABITS Roosts in large trees during daytime, leaving its diurnal retreat well before sunset. Semi-diurnal and is frequently seen abroad, and even hunting, in daylight, especially in cloudy weather. Fond of bathing and will waddle into the shallows, ruffling its feathers, before drying and carefully preening the plumage.

FOOD Mainly fish, frogs and crabs; also rodents, birds, reptiles (once a monitor *Varanus* of about 28cm), and large beetles. Has been observed feeding on the putrefying carcase of a crocodile. Watches for prey from a perch, such as a stump overlooking a pool, or a rock in middle or on edge of a stream, often flying up and down, at times almost skimming the water. Fish are scooped up from near the surface.

BREEDING Season November-March (chiefly January-February) in N India, December-March in the peninsula; about April in Sri Lanka. Breeds in abandoned stick nests of larger birds on a rock ledge near water or in cleft of a rocky bank, or in ruins of old buildings; nest sometimes also a cradle in the fork of an old tree such as mango or fig, occasionally in old nest of a fish eagle. Vicinity of nest always littered with regurgitated pellets and various food remains. Lays 1 or 2 white eggs, roundish with smooth surface: 10 eggs averaged 58.4 x 48.9mm; eggs of northern populations may be slightly larger.

STATUS AND CONSERVATION Generally common through the lowlands, less so in hills and submontane or montane forest to about 2,000m. Locally not rare along watercourses and forest streams with rocky pools up to 1,400m, e.g. in India in the Nilgiri, Palni and other hills. In Sri Lanka, this is the commonest owl.

REMARKS This species' biology and behaviour, as well as its vocalisations, require further study.

REFERENCES Ali & Ripley (1969), Baker (1927, 1934), Boyer & Hume (1991), Burton (1992), Dementiev & Gladkov (1951), Eck & Busse (1973), Voous (1988).

African Fishing Owls, Genus *Scotopelia* Bonaparte, 1850

Medium-sized to large owls without ear-tufts. All three species are adapted for fishing. Talons powerful, with long, curved claws; tarsi and toes bare, soles with spicules. Flight feathers rather stiff, without recurved barbs on leading edge of outer primaries. Feathers of head and nape long and loose. Confined to Africa south of the Sahara, inhabiting rivers and lakes with adjacent forest or wooded areas in tropical lowlands. According to recent molecular biological studies, the genus *Scotopelia* is closely related to *Bubo*. Further taxonomic investigation may lead to the inclusion of *Scotopelia* in *Bubo*, reducing *Scotopelia* to the rank of subgenus.

114 PEL'S FISHING OWL
Scotopelia peli   Plate 35

French: Chouette-pecheuse de Pel
German: Pel-Fischeule

IDENTIFICATION A large (51-61cm), rufous owl, with fine dusky barring and spotting above. Head with long rufous feathers, mostly carried loose, sometimes giving impression of a tousled crown; underparts pale rufous-buff with dusky shaft-streaks ending in a rounded spot at tips. Tarsi and toes bare, talons powerful with long, curved claws; eyes blackish-brown; bill black, cere grey. **Similar species** Rufous Fishing Owl [115] is much smaller and brighter rufous, with honey-brown eyes, and with shaft-streaks on underparts not ending in rounded spots. Vermiculated Fishing Owl [116] is similar in size to preceding species, but has dark brown eyes, densely vermiculated upperparts, whitish underparts rather heavily streaked dark, and yellow bill and cere.

VOCALISATIONS The song of the male is a deep, sonorous, horn-like boom, first a single note and then a higher-pitched *huhuhu*. Also utters a rather ringing hoot, usually followed by a deeper and softer grunt. The pitch of the first hoot is much higher than the notes of most eagle owls: *whoommmm-wot*. When singing, throat and upper breast are greatly inflated. The female's song is similar, but slightly higher in pitch and ending with a double note. The song phrases are repeated at intervals of about 10 seconds. Both sexes utter penetrating trills when feigning injury. Female and large young beg with wailing cries, *wheeoouu*. Small chicks emit cheeping notes.

DISTRIBUTION Patchily distributed in Nigeria, Senegambia, Guinea and Sierra Leone; C Africa from the coast eastwards to E Zaire and discontinuously to Sudan, Somalia, Kenya and Tanzania, from Zaire patchily southward to Zimbabwe, Botswana and E South Africa.

MOVEMENTS In general resident, but moves to other hunting areas when food conditions change, e.g. through drying-out of rivers.

HABITAT Forest along rivers and lakes, from swamps and estuaries at sea-level up to about 1,700m. Riverine forest with large trees is favourite habitat, as well as islands in large rivers, swamps or lakes with groups of old trees, so long as the islands are not too far from the bank.

DESCRIPTION Adult Sexes alike, but female often less rufous. Facial disc not very prominent, rufous-brown with indistinct rim. Head and nape with long feathers, mostly carried loose and giving head a tousled appearance. Upperparts rufous-brown with fine dusky barring, dark spots and some streaks. Flight and tail feathers barred light and dark. Throat white, prominently inflated when sing-ing. Underparts pale rufous-buff with dusky shaft-streaks, these ending in a more or less rounded spot at tips of individual feathers; thighs and underwing-coverts plain light rufous. Tarsi and toes bare, pale straw-colured; soles with spicules instead of scales. **Juvenile** Downy chick white. Mesoptile on head, hindneck and underparts whitish with buffy wash, unmarked; mantle initially as head, later, along with wings and tail, similar to adult but paler, less rufous, at which stage young leave the nest. First full plumage paler than adult; by 15 months, similar to adult. **Bare parts** Eyes dark brown, almost blackish-brown. Cere grey. Bill black, grey at base. Tarsi and toes pale straw-coloured. Claws grey-horn with darker tips.

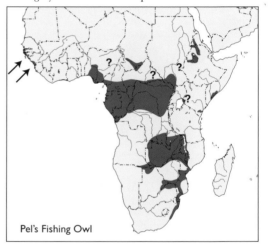

Pel's Fishing Owl

MEASUREMENTS AND WEIGHT Total length 51-61cm. Wingspan 153cm. Wing of 7 males 423-447mm (median 431mm), of 6 females 407-445mm (median 426mm); tail 207-243mm. Weight of 4 females 2055-2325g (median 2188g).

GEOGRAPHICAL VARIATION Monotypic: *Scotopelia peli* Bonaparte, 1850. Because of the rather large individual variation in coloration, we do not recognise any subspecies. The forms *fisheri* and *salvagoragii* are probably synonyms.

HABITS In general nocturnal and vocally most active on moonlit nights, especially towards dawn. Sometimes seen by day when food becomes scarce. During daytime normally roosts on large branches of trees, often male and female quite close together; the same site is quite often used for some time. At dusk, leaves the roost and perches on stumps, branches, etc over the water.

FOOD Fish up to the weight of 2kg, but normally between 100g and 200g; sometimes takes frogs, crabs or mussels. The pellets are yellowish and crumble when dry; measure 40 x 20mm. Prefers branches overhanging water as hunting perches. Detects fish by the ripples they cause on the surface, then glides down to seize the prey with its powerful talons and swoops up to a perch, only rarely immersing the body; the owl generally does not therefore get wet when hunting fish. Sometimes forages by wading into shallow water near sandbanks.

BREEDING Breeds mostly during dry season, when the water is low and clear and fish more easily detected. Monogamous and territorial, residing along a stretch of river or lakeshore. All activities take place in the vicinity of water. Territory is claimed by intensive hooting, especially at beginning of breeding season. Territories may be rather small when population density high: in Botswana, 23 territories found along 60km of river, with 1 pair/km in some parts, and shortest distance between nests 250-300m; in Kruger National Park (Transvaal), 5-8 pairs encountered in 18km of Levubu river. Courting birds utter duets of grunting and hooting notes from a branch. The nest is a natural hollow or cavity in an old shady tree close to water, quite often a hollow formed where thick branches emerge from the trunk; no material is added.

Normally lays 1-2 white eggs directly on to the bottom of the nest: eggs average 62.5 x 52.1mm and weigh (fresh) 85g. The female lays when water levels at peak or falling, so that brood-feeding timed to coincide with period when water low and prey concentrated. Female incubates alone, fed by her mate. Incubation about 32 days, starting probably with first egg. Young may hatch up to 5 days apart, which suggests similar laying intervals. At hatching, chick weighs 60-70g; eyes open at 7 days, and at 20 days already weighs 500g; on fledging, at 68-70 days, weighs 1400-1700g. The second-hatched chick often disappears (probably starves). Young remain in parental territory at least 6-9 months after fledging, assuming first true feathers by 10 months of age.

When disturbed at the nest, the female performs distraction displays, uttering high trills with bill wide open and feigning injury. May attack African Fish Eagles *Haliaeetus vocifer* which come too close to the nest.

STATUS AND CONSERVATION Locally rather common, in many areas only scattered. Depends on large waters with abundant fish and nearby trees or forest. Water pollution may be a threat to populations locally.

REMARKS Behaviour, vocalisations and taxonomy require further study, especially for comparison with the two other species in this genus.

REFERENCES Atkinson *et al.* (1994), Boyer & Hume (1991), Brown (1976), Campbell (1977), Claffey (1997), Dowsett-Lemaire (1996), Fry *et al.* (1988), Liversedge (1980), Zimmerman *et al.* (1996).

---

115 RUFOUS FISHING OWL
Scotopelia ussheri   Plate 35

French: Chouette-pecheuse à dos roux
German: Rotrücken-Fischeule

IDENTIFICATION Rather large (46-51cm), with no ear-tufts and with facial disc indistinct. Mantle and back plain tawny-rufous, scapulars with whitish outer webs forming white row across shoulder. Eyes honey-coloured to warm, dark brown; tarsi and toes bare, pale yellowish; bill blackish-grey. **Similar species** Pel's Fishing Owl [114] is

larger, and spotted and barred above. Vermiculated Fishing Owl [116] is about the same size as Rufous, but is densely vermiculated above and prominently streaked below, with bill and cere yellowish-horn.

VOCALISATIONS The song is described as a low, deep moaning *whoo*.

DISTRIBUTION W Africa: Sierra Leone, Liberia, Ivory Coast and Ghana. Locally sympatric with the larger Pel's Fishing Owl.

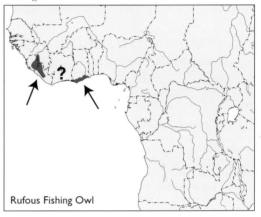

Rufous Fishing Owl

MOVEMENTS Resident.

HABITAT Forest, especially primary forest, along large rivers and lakes.

DESCRIPTION Adult Facial disc light cinnamon, very indistinct and only faintly rimmed tawny-rufous. Upperparts plain tawny-rufous, forecrown with some indistinct lighter mottling; scapulars with whitish outer webs, forming white row across shoulder. Flight and tail feathers barred light and dark. Underparts pale cinnamon, slightly darker on upper breast, with narrow dusky rufous shaft-streaks; thighs and underwing-coverts plain buff. Tarsi and toes bare. **Juvenile** Downy chick completely white. Mesoptile not described, but probably similar to Pel's Fishing Owl. Immature paler than adult. **Bare parts** Eyes warm dark brown. Cere lead-grey. Bill blackish-grey, at base lighter and more similar in colour to cere. Tarsi and toes pale yellow. Claws pale horn with darker tips.

MEASUREMENTS AND WEIGHT Total length 46-51cm. Wing 330-345mm; tail 166-205mm. Weight of 1 male 743g.

GEOGRAPHICAL VARIATION Monotypic: *Scotopelia ussheri* Sharpe, 1871.

HABITS Poorly known, but probably similar to those of Pel's Fishing Owl.

FOOD Probably mainly fish. Catfish found in one stomach. Hunts mainly from branches overhanging water.

BREEDING Poorly known, but may be similar to that of Pel's Fishing Owl. In Sierra Leone, eggs laid in September and October; in Liberia, juveniles moulting into adult plumage (about 6 months after fledging) were found in July. Probably only one young is raised.

STATUS AND CONSERVATION Apparently rare. Main threats are habitat destruction and persecution by man. Listed as Endangered by BirdLife International.

REMARKS A rather unknown bird, as it is apparently rare and therefore little studied. The eye colour has been described as yellow, but recent observations and photographic documentation prove that it is dark brown, as in the two other species of the genus. This probably highly endangered species requires study.

REFERENCES Atkinson *et al.* (1996), Boyer & Hume (1991), Burton (1992), Collar & Stuart (1985), Collar *et al.* (1994), Colston & Curry-Lindahl (1986), Fry *et al.* (1988).

---

116 VERMICULATED FISHING OWL
Scotopelia bouvieri Plate 35

French: Chouette-pecheuse de Bouvier
German: Marmor-Fischeule

IDENTIFICATION A rather large (46-51cm), 'earless' owl with dark brown eyes and a yellowish bill. Upperparts brown, densely vermiculated dark, with much white on outer webs of scapulars; whitish to sandy below, heavily streaked dark brown. **Similar species** Rufous Fishing Owl [115] is similar in size, but plain rufous-tawny above and less heavily streaked below, with bill blackish-grey. Pel's Fishing Owl [114] is larger, barred and spotted above, without white on outer webs of scapulars, and below has narrow streaks ending in drop-shaped spots; bill dark grey to blackish.

VOCALISATIONS The song, often uttered in duet with the female, consists of a low croaking hoot followed by a sequence of about 4-8 short notes, often disyllabic. It is said to be similar to the song of Maned Owl [91], which also duets with its mate. A low wailing call is also described and recorded, apparently uttered by immatures at the stage of becoming independent, probably in order to claim a territory.

DISTRIBUTION C African forest from near the Atlantic coast (S Cameroon, Gabon) to NE Zaire and NW Angola.

Vermiculated Fishing Owl

MOVEMENTS Resident.

HABITAT Forested areas near rivers or lakes, but also in flooded areas of normally dry forest, and even some distance from any water. Its presence is not dependent on water or the availability of fish.

DESCRIPTION Adult Facial disc not very prominent, light rufous, with indistinct dark brown rim. Upperparts cinnamon-brown, finely vermiculated with dark brown, crown more streaked; scapulars with larger areas of white on outer webs. Flight and tail feathers barred dark and light. Underparts dirty whitish to very pale rufous (general coloration varies individually), heavily streaked with dark brown; thighs, undertail-coverts and underwing-coverts plain off-white. Tarsi and toes bare. **Juvenile** Downy chick white. Mesoptile mainly white, often with faint cinnamon wash on head, nape, face and underparts. **Bare parts** Eyes dark brown. Cere bright yellow. Bill yellowish-horn with darker tip. Tarsi and toes chrome-yellow. Claws blackish.

MEASUREMENTS AND WEIGHT Total length 46-51cm. Wing 302-330mm; tail 167-203mm. Weight: do data.

GEOGRAPHICAL VARIATION Monotypic: *Scotopelia bouvieri* Sharpe, 1875.

HABITS A nocturnal bird. May be heard calling all year around.

FOOD Fish, crabs, frogs, small birds and mammals.

BREEDING Peak of vocal activity seems to be in May-October; nestlings collected in Zaire suggest laying between November and December. Populations may be rather dense locally, and several singing pairs may be heard from the same place. Male and female duet during courtship; unpaired younger birds utter a low wailing call, probably in order to claim a territory among occupied ones. Found to nest in old nests of larger birds. Breeding biology unknown, but probably similar to that of Pel's Fishing Owl. Young matures slowly; 3 months after fledging, the whitish mesoptile still covers the body. Usually raises only one chick per year.

STATUS AND CONSERVATION Uncertain. According to recent studies, this owl is apparently not so rare as has been supposed. Locally, it may even be rather abundant, as, contrary to previous belief, it is not dependent on water or the occurrence of fish.

REMARKS This species requires further study, in particular comparative studies on its ecology, behaviour and biology.

REFERENCES Atkinson *et al.* (1994), Boyer & Hume (1991), Brosset & Erard (1986), Dowsett-Lemaire (1996), Fry *et al.* (1988), Sharpe (1875).

Snowy Owl, Genus *Nyctea* Stephens, 1826

A large owl without visible ear-tufts. Plumage of adult nearly all white; facial disc very indistinct. Eyes relatively small, bright yellow. Tarsi and toes thickly feathered white. Mesoptile dark greyish-brown, moulting gradually into mostly white, dusky-spotted and -barred subadult plumage. Circumpolar distribution; one recent species. According to recent molecular biological studies, the genus *Nyctea* is closely related to *Bubo* and may be included in this genus in the future.

117 SNOWY OWL
Nyctea scandiaca Plate 36

French: Harfang des neiges
German: Schnee-Eule

IDENTIFICATION A large (52.5-66cm), mostly white owl, normally without visible ear-tufts (very short tufts may be erected in some situations), and with bright yellow eyes. Head relatively small. Females larger and more dusky-patterned than nearly all-white males. Toes thickly feathered white; bill and claws blackish. **Similar species** This is the only all-white owl in the Holarctic. Eurasian Eagle Owl [96] is slightly bigger, with prominent ear-tufts and larger orange eyes, and even the palest races are much darker, especially on upperside. Great Horned Owl [94] is similar in size, but always has a dark back, very prominent ear-tufts and yellow eyes, and, as with Eurasian Eagle Owl, even the palest individuals are much darker than Snowy.

VOCALISATIONS The song of the male is a monotonous sequence of normally 2-6 (sometimes more) rough notes, similar in rhythm to the barking of a dog: *krooh krooh krooh krooh....* It is uttered mostly from a perch, but sometimes also in flight. The female has a similar, higher-pitched and more guttural song with the same rhythm, but single notes often disyllabic, *khuso*. Females also utter chirping and high screaming notes, similar to calls of nestlings. Both sexes give clucking series when excited.

DISTRIBUTION Circumpolar, from Greenland and Iceland across N Eurasia to Sakhalin, Alaska and N Canada, with southernmost limit between 60° and 55°N; range includes Spitsbergen, W and N Scandinavia, N Russia and N Siberia, Anadyr and Koryakland, Commander and Hall Islands, Aleutians, Alaska and Labrador. Winters south to USA, C Europe, C Russia, N China and Japan.

MOVEMENTS Most leave the dark arctic winter for regions farther south. Southern limit of winter distribution normally from Ireland and Scotland across C Eurasia (S Scandinavia, E Baltic area, C Russia and SW Siberia) to Sakhalin, S Kamchatka, the Aleutians and S Canada. In some years invasions occur, and the species may be observed farther south than usual. Stragglers have been recorded as far south as the Azores and Bermuda.

HABITAT Open arctic tundra with mosses, lichens and some rocks, often preferring areas with slight elevations such as hummocks. In the very north, often breeds near the coast. Outside breeding season in open landscapes, especially near seashores.

DESCRIPTION Sexes differ in the degree of dusky patterning on white plumage; female also larger and heavier than male. **Adult male** Facial disc white and ill-defined, base of bill thickly feathered. Upperparts plain white, with few dusky spots on miniature ear-tufts (tufts normally invisible), on alula and at tips of some primaries and secondaries. Tail feathers nearly all white, sometimes with indistinct terminal bars. Underparts all white. Tarsi and toes thickly feathered white. **Adult female** Spotted and slightly barred brown on crown and upperparts. Flight and tail feathers faintly barred brown. Underparts white, with brown spotting and barring on flanks and upper breast. **Juvenile** Downy chick greyish-white. Mesoptile dark greyish-brown, this gradually replaced by plumage showing dark barring on white. On fledging, young bird has an irregularly mottled or blotched appearance: head mostly still dark, with contrasting white eyebrows and other white areas of face. **Bare parts** Eyes bright yellow, rimmed by blackish edges of eyelids. Cere dark grey, normally concealed by dense feathering. Bill blackish. Claws blackish.

MEASUREMENTS AND WEIGHT Total length of males 52.5-64cm, of females 59-66cm. Wing of males 384-429mm, of females 428-462mm; tail of males 206-222mm, of females 217-241. Weight of males 710-2500g (median 1730g), of females 780-2950g (median 2120g).

GEOGRAPHICAL VARIATION Monotypic: *Nyctea scandiaca* (Linnaeus, 1758).

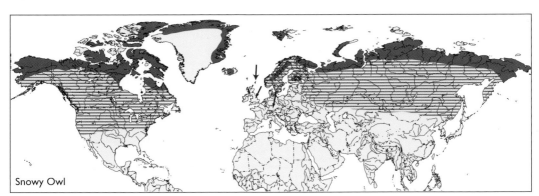

Snowy Owl

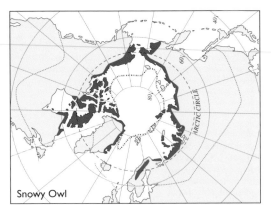

Snowy Owl

HABITS Active during daytime from dawn to dusk. Often on the ground, perched mostly on a slight elevation or on a rock. Walks and runs quickly. Flies with rowing wingbeats, interrupted by gliding on stretched wings. Male claims territory by singing from elevated points or during display flights over it. When displaying, he flies on an undulating course with series of wingbeats and gliding with wings held in a V, finally dropping rather vertically to the ground. In the nesting area the birds are rather aggressive, especially the male, which attacks intruders by diving at them; female more often feigns injury in order to distract a potential enemy.

FOOD Primarily small mammals, especially lemmings and other voles; also birds up to the size of ptarmigans *Lagopus* and ducks, beetles, crustaceans, and occasionally fish. Outside breeding season, mostly smaller mammals and birds, as well as carrion. Prey are eaten on the ground, small items (e.g. voles) being swallowed whole, larger prey torn into suitably sized pieces; birds are often partially plucked before eating. Hunts from a perch, gliding on to prey, sometimes over a fairly long distance.

BREEDING Often pairs for life. Breeds once per year, but in years when food is scarce many pairs will not breed. Territory size normally about 3km², but may vary according to abundance of food and density of population. Male marks territory by display flights and singing; female answers her mate with song during courtship. Male advertises potential nest sites by scratching the ground and spreading his wings over it. The nest is a shallow depression on an eminence in open tundra with a view over the surrounding landscape; any taller plants obstructing view are plucked away.

Laying normally begins during early May to the first ten days of June. The 3-11 (generally 7-9) pure white eggs, laid directly on to the ground, average 56.4 x 44.7mm and weigh (fresh) 47.5-68.0g (median 60.3g); laying interval normally 2 days. Incubation, beginning with the first egg, is by the female alone, fed by her mate, who brings food to the nest; surplus prey is stored near the nest. Incubation period 32-33 days, young hatching at intervals of several days and brooded by the female. When the first chick is about 3 weeks old, the female shares in hunting for prey and both parents feed the offspring. When about 2 weeks old, the young may walk around the nest site, which they leave at 18-28 days, when still unable to fly. First attempts to fly begin at 35 days, and by 50-60 days the young fly well. They are cared for and fed by their parents for about 2-3 months. Sexual maturity is reached in the following year, but first breeding normally occurs at the end of the second year of life.

May reach an age of about 10 years in the wild; in captivity, ages of 25 and even 28 years have been recorded.

STATUS AND CONSERVATION This species' presence and apparent numbers are largely dependent on the amount of food available. In 'lemming years' Snowy Owls may be locally very abundant, while in years with only few voles they can be rare or even absent from the same localities; in the latter circumstances, they often move to areas where food is more plentiful, but may not breed. These beautiful owls may be locally threatened by the use of pesticides.

REMARKS Although the biology of the Snowy Owl is reasonably well known, further studies would be useful. The genus *Nyctea* is probably quite closely related to *Bubo*.

REFERENCES Bezzel (1985), Boyer & Hume (1991), Eck & Busse (1973), Glutz & Bauer (1980), Josephson (1980), König (1967), Portenko (1972), Saurola (1997), Voous (1988), Wiklund & Stigh (1983).

Spectacled Owls, Genus *Pulsatrix* Kaup, 1848

Medium-sized to rather large owls with rounded heads without ear-tufts. Light pattern of face suggests spectacles. Eyes large, orange-yellow or brown. Talons rather powerful. Throat and foreneck separated from rest of underparts by a dark breast-band. Songs mostly series of guttural knocking notes without any hooting sounds. Four species, confined to forested areas of tropical and subtropical America from Mexico to Argentina.

118 SPECTACLED OWL
Pulsatrix perspicillata   Plate 37

French: Chouette à lunettes
German: Brillenkauz
Portuguese: Murucututu
Spanish: Urucureá Grande or Buho de Anteojos

IDENTIFICATION A large (41-48cm), broad-winged owl without ear-tufts, and with dark facial disc contrasting with white 'spectacles' (long eyebrows, malar, and loral streaks), yellowish-green bill and bright orange-yellow eyes. Chin black, throat white. Dark brown above; pale yellowish-buff below, with broad dark brown band across chest. Powerful talons with almost totally feathered toes. **Similar species** In SE Brazil and NE Argentina (Misiones), may co-occur locally with similar-sized Short-browed Owl [119]; latter has plain brown crown and mantle; eyebrows pale creamy-buff, rather short (reaching just behind eyes), lower part of facial disc not broadly rimmed white but faintly marked pale creamy-buff; breast band brown, indistinctly broken at centre; toes only sparsely feathered at base; eyes yellowish-brown to warm brown. Tawny-browed Owl [120] is very similar, but smaller, with ochraceous-tawny eyebrows and belly, dark chestnut eyes, and different song. Band-bellied Owl [121] is about the same size as Spectacled Owl, but has dark eyes and white eyebrows, brown chest band broken by buffy-whitish barring, rest of underparts whitish with reddish-brown barring, and different voice; it lives in montane forest of N Andes between 700m and 1,600m.

VOCALISATIONS Rather poorly known. The territorial song of the male is an accelerating sequence of guttural knocking notes, becoming weaker and lower in pitch towards end: *pokpokbogbogbogbobobo*. The female's song is similar, but somewhat higher in pitch. Male and female duet near breeding site. A disyllabic screaming call similar to a steam-whistle is uttered mostly by the female: *kewheeer*, with emphasis on the drawn-out, second syllable. Young beg with harsh, high-pitched *keeew* calls.

DISTRIBUTION From S Mexico through Central America, Venezuela, the Guianas, Colombia, Ecuador, E Peru, Amazonian Brazil south to Bolivia and N Argentina. Also present on the Caribbean island of Trinidad.

Spectacled Owl

MOVEMENTS Apparently resident.

HABITAT Rather dense tropical and subtropical forest with aged trees; occurs in interior of dense rain forest, as well as near clearings or at forest edge. Also plantations and groves. Can be found also at higher altitudes, to about 1,500m, in subtropical montane forest, e.g. in Costa Rica.

DESCRIPTION *P. p. perspicillata* **Adult** Face dark brown, bordered by long white eyebrows, white lores and white malar streaks, forming 'spectacles'. Throat white, forming semi-collar; chin black. Rest of head and neck uniform blackish-brown, much darker than back. Upperparts uniform dark brown, merging into more blackish coloration of hindneck. Remiges and rectrices barred with lighter grey-brown. Broad chest band brown; breast and belly uniform pale yellowish-buff. Feet and toes almost fully feathered creamy-buff. **Juvenile** Recently hatched chick covered with whitish down. In juvenile plumage, body mainly feathered white, with grey-brown barring on wing-coverts; face blackish, more or less heart-shaped, and contrasting strongly with fluffy white body; wings and tail

brown with lighter barring. (Since this species takes up to five years to reach full adult plumage, breeding birds in immature plumage may be found.) **Bare parts** Iris bright orange-yellow. Bill and cere yellowish-horn with greenish tint towards tip. Unfeathered parts of toes whitish or pale grey. Claws dark.

MEASUREMENTS AND WEIGHT Total length of males about 41-48cm, females larger and heavier. Wing of males 314-338mm, of females up to 345mm; tail 173-191mm. Weight of males 591-761g, of females 765-980g.

GEOGRAPHICAL VARIATION Five subspecies described, three of which are poorly marked.
    P. p. perspicillata (Latham, 1790). NW South America to E Peru and Mato Grosso, Brazil. See Description.
    P. p. saturata Ridgway, 1914. S Mexico to N Costa Rica and W Panama. Differs from nominate race mainly in uniform sooty-black head and back and in often having fine dark barring at sides of belly, sometimes also on breast. Wing 329-335mm; tail 182-204mm.

The following forms show less distinct patterns, and are simply listed here:
    P. p. chapmani: E Costa Rica to NW Ecuador, except Pacific slope of W Panama. Wing 326-346mm; tail 183-192mm.
    P. p. trinitatis: Trinidad.
    P. p. boliviana: Bolivia to N Argentina.

HABITS Unsociable. More or less strictly nocturnal. Activity normally begins after dusk and lasts to dawn. By day roosts singly in trees with dense foliage, after dusk flying with soft wingbeats from perch to perch, watching the ground. Vocal activity is most frequent on calm, moonlit nights.

FOOD In general smaller mammals, sometimes up to the size of an opossum *Didelphys*, but also takes smaller birds up to the size of a pigeon. In addition, preys on larger insects and caterpillars, which it snatches from the ground or from foliage; locally, may take crabs and large spiders. Hunts from a perch, swooping down to seize prey with its strong claws.

BREEDING Breeding behaviour little. Male claims territory by singing from an elevated perch, often in the upper third of a tall tree. Female answers by singing, and duets may be heard especially on moonlit nights. A large natural cavity in a thick branch or in a tree trunk serves as nest site. Lays 2 white eggs (average 45.5 x 38mm) directly on the bottom of the cavity, incubated by the female for about 5 weeks. Chicks fed mainly by the female, while the male brings food to the nest. Young (often only one) leave the nest at about 5-6 weeks of age, still unable to fly well; cared for by parents for several months (sometimes nearly a year). Spectacled 0wls may breed in immature plumage, as it may take up to 5 years for full adult plumage to be attained.

STATUS AND CONSERVATION Generally uncommon, but may be rather common locally, e.g. in Costa Rica, Colombia and the Amazon. As with most owls, detailed population studies are lacking. The species may be endangered in areas suffering extensive deforestation. It is most important that the natural habitat of this amazing owl be maintained, to secure its conservation.

REMARKS It is clear that the original *Pulsatrix perspicillata* involves more than one species of spectacled owl, but comparative studies on ecology and vocalisations, as well as DNA analyses, are still lacking. We separate the SE Brazilian form specifically from *P. perspicillata*, as *Pulsatrix pulsatrix*, because of its morphology and vocal patterns, as well as the fact that the two overlap locally without hybridisation.

REFERENCES Belton (1984), Eck & Busse (1973), Hilty & Brown (1986), Hume & Boyer (1991), Narosky & Yzurieta (1987), Sick (1985), Stiles & Skutch (1989).

119 SHORT-BROWED OWL
Pulsatrix pulsatrix   Plate 37

Other name: Brown Spectacled Owl

French: Chouette à lunettes de surcils courts
German: Kurzbrauen-Brillenkauz
Spanish: Urucureá de cejas cortas
Portuguese: Murucututu de sobrecelhas cortas

IDENTIFICATION Similar in size to Spectacled Owl [118] but often heavier, and with crown and nape brown, not contrasting with back and mantle. Eyebrows pale creamy-buff and rather short, reaching only just behind eyes, and lower part of facial disc bordered by rather narrow creamy-buff area from throat to lores. Breast band brown, indistinctly broken in centre. Eyes brownish to pale orange-brown; toes only sparsely feathered, rest bare, whitish. **Similar species** Spectacled Owl has white 'spectacles', with crown and nape distinctly darker (more blackish) than back and mantle, breast band dark brown to blackish and not broken in centre, eyes bright orange-yellow, and toes almost fully feathered. Tawny-browed Owl [120] is much smaller, with long pale tawny eyebrows, a broadly broken breast band and dark chestnut eyes; toes almost totally bare, whitish with greenish tint. Band-bellied Owl [121] has long, white eyebrows, a thin buffy collar below throat, and a brown, buffy-mottled breast band, with rest of underparts whitish with broad rusty-brown feather edges, giving banded appearance. All differ vocally. Rusty-barred Owl [139] is much smaller, rusty-brown and densely barred, with facial disc more developed, being rusty-brown with dark concentric lines; eyes dark brown. Black-banded Owl [142] is densely barred black and light grey above and below, and has orange-yellow eyes.

VOCALISATIONS Little studied, as species has hitherto been merged with Spectacled Owl. The song is a resonant, slowly bubbling *bup bup bup bup...* at constant pitch, and not accelerating as that of Spectacled. Male and female often duet during courtship, the two sexes differing in pitch.

DISTRIBUTION E Brazil from about Bahia south to Rio Grande do Sul (Aparados da Serra National Park), probably also in adjacent NE Argentina (one observation of a singing male at Cerro Tigre, near Bernardo de Irigoyen in E Misiones, in 1991). In northern parts of its range overlaps with Spectacled Owl; locally sympatric with Tawny-browed Owl.

MOVEMENTS Resident.

HABITAT Semi-open forest (primary or secondary

growth) or forest with clearings and aged trees, especially *Araucaria*, in mountainous regions. Also near human settlements. The male at Cerro Tigre sang on a bare branch of a high tree a few metres off the road from Bernardo de Irigoyen to Tobuna: surroundings were secondary growth with dense undergrowth of climbing bamboo *Chusquea* and several clearings with settlements; also found in the vicinity were Tropical and Long-tufted Screech Owls [68, 79], Rusty-barred Owl, Ferruginous Pygmy Owl [160] and Buff-fronted Owl [181].

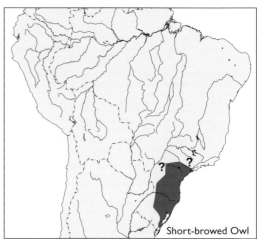
Short-browed Owl

DESCRIPTION Adult Facial disc warm earth-brown, indistinctly rimmed lighter; lower part bordered by thin pale buffy collar from throat to lores, feathering around bill of similar coloration. Eyebrows short, creamy-buff, reaching just behind eyes. Crown and nape concolorous with upperparts, rather plain earth-brown. Flight and tail feathers barred light and dark (barring on tail rather dense, similar to Spectacled Owl, not so widely spaced as on Tawny-browed). Throat pale buffy. Brown breast band indistinctly broken in centre of upper breast; rest of underparts clear yellowish-brown. Tarsi feathered pale yellowish brown. Toes sparsely feathered at base, with rather bare outer portions. **Juvenile** Unknown, but probably similar to Spectacled Owl. **Bare parts** Eyes brownish orange-yellow to rich yellow. Bill and cere light green. Bare parts of toes dirty white, tinged greyish-green. Claws greyish-horn with dark tips.

MEASUREMENTS AND WEIGHT Total length of 1 male 510mm, of 1 female 523mm. Wing 363-364mm; tail 211mm. Weight of 1 male 1075g, of 1 female 1250g.

GEOGRAPHICAL VARIATION Monotypic: *Pulsatrix pulsatrix* (Wied, 1820).

HABITS A nocturnal bird. The observed male sang after dusk; it was rather shy, and flew away when approached at distance of about 60m. In SE Brazil, is said to perch high on bare branches of *Araucaria*.

FOOD Probably similar to that of Spectacled Owl, consisting mainly of smaller mammals, birds and other vertebrates.

BREEDING Both sexes were found in breeding condition in early July (Rio Grande do Sul). Breeding biology unknown. Probably nests in large holes in trees.

STATUS AND CONSERVATION Apparently rare. Threatened by human persecution and destruction of natural habitats.

REMARKS The ecology, behaviour, vocalisations and biology of this owl are poorly studied. We separate it as a distinct species from the Spectacled Owl because of its different vocalisations and very different plumage patterns, but a final decision will be possible only when our hypothesis has been tested by molecular-biological studies.

REFERENCES Belton (1984), Boyer & Hume (1991), Eck & Busse (1973), König (unpublished).

120 TAWNY-BROWED OWL
Pulsatrix koeniswaldiana   Plate 37

Other name: White-chinned Owl

French: Chouette de Koeniswald
German: Kleiner Brillenkauz or Koeniswald-Kauz
Spanish: Urucureá Chico
Portuguese: Murucututu-de-barriga-amarela

IDENTIFICATION Very similar to Spectacled Owl [118], but smaller (about 40cm). Eyebrows yellowish-tawny, eyes chestnut. Large white spot on chin (hence alternative name of White-chinned Owl), brown chest band brown somewhat broken in centre, rest of underparts yellowish-cinnamon. Feet feathered, but toes bare. Bars on flight and tail feathers white. **Similar species** Spectacled Owl and Short-browed Owl [119] are both larger (up to about 52.5cm): the first has feathered toes, white eyebrows and orange-yellow eyes, and flight and tail feathers banded light greyish-brown (not white); the second has very short buffy eyebrows and brownish-orange to yellow eyes. Band-bellied Owl [121] is somewhat larger, and has a whitish belly heavily barred with rufous-brown, and white eyebrows. Buff-fronted Owl [181] is much smaller (about 20cm), lacks broad chest band, and has yellow or orange-red eyes. Rusty-barred Owl [139] has dark brown eyes and is densely barred rusty-brown and whitish below, without broad chest band.

VOCALISATIONS Poorly known. Territorial song of the male is a guttural, muffled sequence of short, grunting notes, with emphasis on the second, the following notes becoming weaker and accelerating somewhat towards the end: *bobórrboborborbrr*. The female has a similar, slightly higher-pitched song. Male and female duet near breeding site. Single notes of similar sound quality are also uttered: *croorrr*.

DISTRIBUTION E Brazil from Espírito Santo, Rio de Janeiro and Minas Gerais to Pará and Santa Catarina; also E Paraguay and NE Argentina (Misiones).

MOVEMENTS Apparently resident.

HABITAT Tropical and subtropical forest with old trees, often mixed with conifers (*Araucaria angustifolia*), in mountainous regions. In this habitat, it may be found locally together with Tropical and Long-tufted Screech Owls [68, 79], Rusty-barred Owl, Ferruginous Pygmy Owl [160] and Buff-fronted Owl.

Tawny-browed Owl

DESCRIPTION Adult Facial disc dark brown. Eyebrows and loral streaks yellowish-tawny, forming incomplete 'spectacles'. Large white patch on chin. Crown and upperparts uniform dark brown. Wings dark brown. Tail brown with about 4-5 narrow white bars and white terminal band. Large brown patch on each side of upper chest, forming broad, rather broken chest band; rest of underparts yellowish-cinnamon, feathers of belly sometimes narrowly edged slightly darker, this becoming more prominent on older, bleached skins. (This latter fact may have inspired artists, e.g. in Eck & Busse, Narosky & Yzurieta, and Sick, to paint the species with a barred belly, a feature we have never seen on live birds or on museum specimens protected from bleaching effect of light. The structure of the feather edges suggests a narrow, slightly darker zone, which is not prominent on unbleached skins; light causes the rest of such a feather to bleach more rapidly than the edge, and all illustrations showing barred belly depict the ground colour of the underside as very pale, lacking yellowish-cinnamon tone, and also show rather white eyebrows, which suggests that these patterns may be due to bleaching.) **Juvenile** Juvenile plumage similar to that of Spectacled Owl, but face browner and eyes dark, not yellow. **Bare parts** Iris chestnut. Bill and cere yellowish-horn, sometimes with greenish tint. Toes whitish-grey, often with greenish tint. Claws yellowish-grey with darker tips.

MEASUREMENTS AND WEIGHT Total length about 40cm, females somewhat larger than males. Wing about 300-440mm; tail about 170mm. Weight of 1 female from Misiones (Argentina) 481g.

GEOGRAPHICAL VARIATION Monotypic: *Pulsatrix koeniswaldiana* (Bertoni & Bertoni, 1901). Individual differences exist in the tint of the belly and the sometimes slightly darkened edges of the feathers of the underside.

HABITS Unsociable. Normally strictly nocturnal. During daytime roosts singly in trees. After dusk flies around with soft wingbeats, perching very often on thick branches, often covered with epiphytes. May be attracted by playback of its song and by imitation of voices of other owl species.

Males sing particularly on calm, moonlit nights, and pair-members may be heard duetting near breeding site.

FOOD Small mammals and birds, as well as other small vertebrates and larger insects. Hunting behaviour similar to that of Spectacled Owl.

BREEDING Very little is known about breeding. Nests in a natural hole in an old tree. Normally lays 2 white eggs, incubated by the female alone, the male delivering food to his mate; incubation, from first egg, lasts about 5 weeks. Hatchlings are brooded and fed by the female. At about 5-6 weeks the young leave the nest, but are not yet able to fly well; they are accompanied and fed by both parents for several months.

STATUS AND CONSERVATION Not much is known about the status of this handsome owl. Our own experience suggests that it is uncommon to rare and loxcally endangered. It is dependent on more or less intact mountain forest in its rather restricted area of distribution.

REMARKS Tawny-browed Owl is doubtless a separate species, and not a race of Band-bellied Owl as some authors suggest. Studies on its biology and ecology are required.

REFERENCES Burton (1992), Eck & Busse (1973), Hume & Boyer (1991), König (unpublished), Narosky & Yzurieta (1987), Sick (1985).

121 BAND-BELLIED OWL
Pulsatrix melanota   Plate 37

French: Chouette à lunettes striée
German: Bänder-Brillenkauz
Spanish: Lechuzón Barrado

IDENTIFICATION A large owl (about 48cm) without ear-tufts, dark brown above with some paler mottling, and whitish below with prominent rusty-brown barring and a broad brown chest band mottled with whitish-buff. Facial disc dark brown with white 'spectacles'. Throat with whitish half-collar. Eyes dark reddish-brown; feet feathered, toes bare. **Similar species** Spectacled Owl [118] has yellow eyes and no rusty barring on belly. Tawny-browed Owl [120] has yellowish-tawny eyebrows and no rufous barring below. Rusty-barred Owl [139] is smaller (about 35cm), lacks broad dark chest band, and is geographically separated from Band-bellied. Rufous-banded Owl [140], also smaller (35cm) and without broad chest band, lives in humid montane forest at higher altitudes. All have different voices.

VOCALISATIONS Very poorly known. The territorial song is a very rapid sequence of popping notes, introduced by a short purring call, the popping notes with emphasis on the third: *hoorr-gogogógog*. In addition, single muffled hoots are attributed to this species.

DISTRIBUTION Only patchily known. Colombia, E Ecuador, Peru east of the Andes, and Bolivia.

MOVEMENTS Probably sedentary.

HABITAT Humid and dense montane forest between 700m and 1,600m, locally lower or in some cases higher.

DESCRIPTION *P. m. melanota* **Adult** Facial disc dark brown. Eyebrows and loral streaks white, forming incomplete 'spectacles'. White patch on throat bordered by dark area, below which a white half-collar. Upperparts dark brown with some paler mottling. Dark wings banded narrowly with white. Tail dark brown with about six narrow white bars and white terminal band. Underparts buffy-whitish with prominent rufous-brown bars; upper chest with broad brown band, mottled with whitish and buffy tones. Feet feathered whitish-buff, toes bare. **Juvenile** Plumage unknown, but probably similar to other *Pulsatrix*. **Bare parts** Iris dark reddish-brown. Bill and cere pale horn. Toes pale greyish-brown. Claws horn-coloured with darker tips.

Band-bellied Owl

MEASUREMENTS AND WEIGHT Total length 44-48cm. Wing 284-287mm; tail about 170mm. Weight: no data. Female somewhat larger and heavier than males.

GEOGRAPHICAL VARIATION Because of the paucity of available museum material, it is difficult to judge whether any distinct races exist. Besides the nominate form *P. m. melanota* (Tschudi, 1844) from Colombia, E Ecuador and E Peru, the subspecies *P. m. philosica* has been described by Todd (1947) from the Yungas of Cochabamba in Bolivia: wing of 1 specimen 305mm.

HABITS Unsociable and apparently nocturnal. Virtually nothing else is known of its behaviour.

FOOD Probably as that of Spectacled and Tawny-browed Owls.

BREEDING Unknown. Probably nests in natural cavities in trees.

STATUS AND CONSERVATION Status unknown. Probably rare, and may be endangered by deforestation.

REMARKS This species may have a wider distribution in the montane forest of the E Andes, but hitherto there are only few, very local records.

REFERENCES Eck & Busse (1973), Hilty & Brown (1986), Hume & Boyer (1991), Todd (1947).

Wood Owls, Genus *Strix* Linnaeus, 1758

Medium-sized to large owls with large, rounded head without ear-tufts. Eyes relatively large, dark brown, yellow or orange. Plumage mostly cryptic, several species with different colour morphs. We merge the genus *Ciccaba* with *Strix*, as we cannot find any clear generic difference between the two; moreover, DNA evidence suggests that all taxa concerned should belong to the same genus. We recognise 20 species. Distribution nearly worldwide, except Madagascar, Australia, New Guinea and islands of South Pacific, where the genus is replaced by *Ninox*.

122 SPOTTED WOOD OWL
Strix seloputo   Plate 38

French: Chouette obscure
German: Pagodenkauz

IDENTIFICATION A medium-sized owl (44-47cm) without ear-tufts. Upperparts rich brown, profusely marked with large white spots; underparts white, distinctly barred with black. Facial disc rufous, eyes dark brown. Tail dark brown below, with 5-6 visible yellowish-buff or tawny bars. Tarsus and toes feathered. **Similar species** Brown Wood Owl [132] has more yellowish-buff (not white) underparts more narrowly barred, facial disc dark rufous with black rim and prominent black eye-rings, and whitish-rufous supercilium; also forehead, crown and nape unspotted dark brown, breast dark rufous, and tail with far more (about eight) visible bars, the brown bars being less broad.

VOCALISATIONS The song is different from that of any other species of wood owl: it begins with a rolling staccato *hoo-hoo-hoo* and ends with a prolonged and deep drawn *hoo*. Also utters a loud, quivering, eerie *chuhua-aa* regularly on emerging from daytime retreat, and again before retiring at dawn, as well as from time to time (but not frequently) during the night. On other occasions mostly a mellow, metallic hoot; also, an occasional harsh screech very similar to Barn Owl's [1]. Particularly active and vocal in breeding season.

DISTRIBUTION S Burma, Thailand, Cambodia, S Vietnam and Malay Peninsula, discontinuously to Java, Bawean Island and Palawan, Philippines. Absent from Sumatra and Borneo, although two unconfirmed sight records for Sumatra, where it may be an overlooked species.

MOVEMENTS Sedentary.

HABITAT Frequents plantations, partially cleared forest, evergreen secondary forest, forest edges, and parks in both towns and villages; forages freely in open and semi-open country, orchards and parks, as well as between houses in areas with much parkland. Also inhabits unpopulated, rather remote regions such as swamp forest and mangroves near the coast. From sea-level to about 1,000m.

DESCRIPTION *S. s. seloputo* Adult Facial disc reddish-buff or rufous. Head blackish-brown, feathers with large white spots and golden-buff bases, spots becoming bar-shaped on nape. Upperparts overall rich brown, profusely spotted with white; mantle, back and uppertail-coverts rather paler, chocolate-brown, with black-margined white bars and spots; outer scapulars with white bars bordered with black, bars broadening towards innermost. Primaries brownish, outer ones with narrow incomplete bars on outer webs. Chin buff, a large white patch on throat; rest of undersurface buff, barred black and white, the white bands

broader; thighs and feathered tarsi white, washed with buff and barred with black; feathering of toes unbarred. **Juvenile** Natal down whitish. Juvenile with upper plumage mostly banded white and dark brown; subadult with upperwing-coverts broadly tipped white, and rather more white in scapulars. **Bare parts** Iris dark brown. Bill black. Cere greenish-black. Visible parts of toes dark olive. Claws horn-coloured.

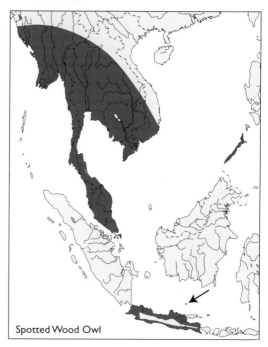

Spotted Wood Owl

MEASUREMENTS AND WEIGHT Total length 44-47cm, females larger than males. Wing 338-363mm; tail 190-229mm. Weight: 650-900g (av. 779.5g).

GEOGRAPHICAL VARIATION Three subspecies recognised.

S. s. seloputo Horsfield, 1809. S Burma southward over Malay Peninsula, Thailand, Cambodia, Vietnam, Java. See Description.

S. s. baweana Oberholser, 1917. Bawean Island. Resembles nominate *seloputo*, but much smaller and paler; white spots on upper surface much reduced, more roundish, and less inclined to form bars; dark brown bars on underparts much narrower. Wing 297mm.

S. s. wiepkeni Blasius, 1888. Palawan and Calamian Islands, Philippines. Distinguished from nominate by more rufescent undersurface lacking white bars; upperside chocolate-brown with white spots; underside tawny-rufous, narrowly barred blackish-brown;

face more orange-rufous. Wing 330mm. (Synonym: *Syrnium whiteheadi* Sharpe.)

HABITS Strictly nocturnal, becoming active at dusk. Roosts by day, often in pairs, close to the trunk, and always in densely foliaged tall trees or groves of trees. Birds can be particularly vocal, sometimes duetting, when they emerge soon after dusk and again when they retire at dawn.

FOOD Mainly rats and mice, small birds and large insects, especially large Coleoptera. Loose, ellipsoidal pellets (about 3-4 x 2cm) collected from beneath roosts often found to contain remains of Tree Sparrows *Passer montanus*.

BREEDING Breeds in tree holes or in open branches, sometimes also on the top of a bird's-nest fern *Asplenium nidus*, often high up in a tall tree. Eggs usually 2, sometimes 3, very rounded oval with both ends alike, pure white, with satiny surface and fair amount of gloss (2 Malay Peninsula av. 49 x 42mm; 2 Java av. 50 x 43mm); laid on the wood or leaf debris (bird's-nest fern) with no nesting material added.

STATUS AND CONSERVATION Not uncommon, but rather sparsely distributed (low density). Its rather cryptic appearance means that it is easily overlooked, since it rests by day in large, thickly foliaged trees, although often not far from human habitation.

REMARKS This species' biology and behaviour are in need of study.

REFERENCES Boyer & Hume (1991), Eck & Busse (1973), MacKinnon & Phillipps (1995), Voous (1988).

---

123 MOTTLED WOOD OWL
Strix ocellata   Plate 38

French: Chouette indienne
German: Mangokauz

IDENTIFICATION A medium-sized (about 46cm), yellowish-red owl, beautifully mottled and vermiculated above with reddish-brown, black and white. Facial disc white, with prominent black concentric rings; below, throat chestnut and black, breast and belly white and golden-buff to orange-buff, narrowly barred with blackish. Eyes dark brown; tarsus and toes feathered, reddish-buff. **Similar species** Brown Wood Owl [132] has underparts more yellowish-buff (not reddish), and facial disc tawny (not white) with black rim and prominent, nearly blackish rings around eyes.

VOCALISATIONS In the breeding season, especially, a loud, quivering, eerie *chuhua-aa* uttered regularly on emerging from the daytime retreat, and again before retiring at dawn; also from time to time during the night, but not frequently. This may have the function of a territorial song. At other times gives mostly a single mellow, metallic hoot; occasionally a harsh screech similar to that of Barn Owl [1]. Particularly active and vocal during breeding season.

DISTRIBUTION India, from the Himalayas eastward to lower Bengal and south to S Nilgiris and Pondicherry. Does not occur in Sri Lanka.

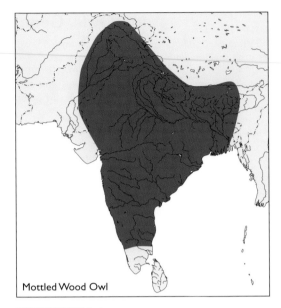
Mottled Wood Owl

MOVEMENTS Sedentary.

HABITAT Lightly wooded plains: open woodland and groves of old trees (e.g. mango *Mangifera*, ancient tamarind *Tamarindus*, banyan *Ficus*, and similar densely foliaged trees) on outskirts of villages and cultivated land.

DESCRIPTION *S. o. ocellata* **Adult** Facial disc white, finely barred concentrically with black. Nape white and black with chocolate colour admixed. Upperparts beautifully mottled and vermiculated with reddish-brown, black, white and buff. Large amount of yellowish-buff on wings (very conspicuous in flight). Throat chestnut and black, stippled with white; prominent white half-collar on side of neck; rest of underparts white with golden-buff to orange-buff, narrowly barred blackish. **Juvenile** Nothing recorded. **Bare parts** Iris dark brown, eyelids dusky pink or dull coral-red. Bill horny-black, paler at tip; mouth pale yellowish-pink. Feet brownish-flesh or dirty yellowish-brown, soles yellow. Claws horny-black.

MEASUREMENTS AND WEIGHT Total length 38-46cm, females presumably larger than males. Wing 320-372mm; tail 174-216mm. Weight: no data.

GEOGRAPHICAL VARIATION Three subspecies are recognised.
    S. o. ocellata (Lesson, 1839). Southern race: widely distributed throughout peninsular India from S Kerala and Tamil Nadu northward through Mysore, Andhra Pradesh, Maharashtra, Gujarat, Madhya Pradesh, Orissa to Bangladesh; zone of intergrading with northern population (*S. o. grisescens*) undetermined. See Description. Wing 320-353mm; tail 174-200mm.
    S. o. grandis Koelz, 1950. Kathiawar Peninsula, in S Gujarat. Differs from nominate *ocellata* in being much larger and in averaging greyer above; size of black areas on back and nape reduced. Wing 360-372mm; tail 200-215mm.
    S. o. grisescens Koelz, 1950. Northern part of Indian subcontinent, from base of the Himalayas south to an undetermined boundary; apparently absent Assam

and possibly Bangladesh. Differs from nominate race in slightly larger size and lighter coloration of upperparts: black bars on scapulars and on wing and tail feathers narrower; black and white spots in rufous area of neck mostly white, (largely black in nominate); rufous parts of plumage often paler. Wing 338-346mm; tail 190mm.

HABITS Largely nocturnal. Pair-members spend the day perched together and dozing on a branch hidden among foliage; when disturbed, they will fly long distances in bright sunlight without apparent discomfort, eventually sweeping up to settle well within seclusion of the foliage canopy (unlike *Bubo*, which prefers to alight on peripheral branches).

FOOD Rats, mice and other rodents, and birds up to the size of domestic pigeon; also lizards, crabs, beetles and large insects. A large scorpion complete with sting was found in one stomach.

BREEDING Season November-April for nominate *ocellata*, February and March for race *grisescens*. Nests in natural hollows, practically unlined. Eggs normally 2, occasionally 3, creamy-white and roundish; 18 averaged 51.1 x 42.6mm. Incubation period and other details unknown.

STATUS AND CONSERVATION Rather common, and widely distributed throughout peninsular India to lower Himalayas.

REMARKS As with many tropical owls, more studies on its biology are required.

REFERENCES Ali & Ripley (1969), Baker (1927, 1934), Boyer & Hume (1991), Burton (1992), Eck & Busse (1973), Voous (1988).

---

124 SPOTTED OWL
Strix occidentalis   Plate 38

French: Chouette tachetée
German: Fleckenkauz
Spanish: Buho manchado

IDENTIFICATION A medium-sized owl (40.5-48cm) with a large, rounded head without ear-tufts. General coloration dark rufous-brown, boldly spotted white on above and below, with abdomen heavily barred brown and white. Eyes relatively large, blackish-brown; tarsi and toes feathered. **Similar species** Barred Owl [126] is larger, lighter, distinctly barred on upper breast and boldly streaked on rest of underparts (abdomen streaked, not barred), with eyes blackish-brown. Fulvous Owl [125] has a pale face and streaked, fulvous underparts. Great Horned Owl [94] is larger, with prominent ear-tufts and yellow eyes. Great Grey Owl [129], also larger, is generally grey and has rather small, yellow eyes. Long-eared Owl [207] is smaller, with long ear-tufts and orange eyes.

VOCALISATIONS The song of the male is a series of four explosive hoots in a typical rhythm: *whoop wu-hu hoo*. Female has a similar but higher-pitched and somewhat hoarser song. A high, upward-inflected *ooeeht* is uttered mainly by the female during breeding season, having probably a contact function. Single low hoots are uttered by both sexes.

DISTRIBUTION W North America from British Columbia to California; also Arizona, New Mexico and SW Texas to C Mexico, although this population (*lucida*) may represent a separate species, Mountain Spotted Owl (see Geographical Variation).

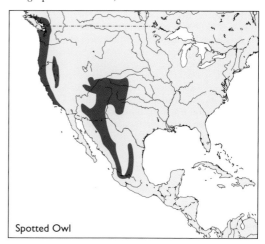

Spotted Owl

MOVEMENTS Resident. Some birds (especially immatures) may wander outside breeding season.

HABITAT Dark or well-shaded coniferous and mixed forest from sea-level to about 2,700m in the interior; in mountainous regions, inhabits forested slopes as well as deep gorges with aged forest or wooded areas on their flanks. Cool, moist ambient climate and the vicinity of water seem to be important.

DESCRIPTION *S. o. occidentalis* **Adult** Facial disc pale buffy-brown with some darker concentric lines; rim around disc dark brown, not very prominent. Crown dark rufous-brown with whitish flecks and small spots. Upperparts dark rufous-brown with many transverse or spear-shaped white spots; scapulars with relatively large areas of white on outer webs. Flight feathers barred light and dark; tail feathers dark brown with several narrow whitish bars and whitish terminal band. Throat whitish; upper breast barred whitish and dark brown, lower breast and belly boldly marked dark brown and white, individual feathers being dusky at base, along shaft and bordering tip, with a large white rounded spot at each side of central streak (pattern generally gives a white-spotted appearance to underparts, becoming more barred on lower belly); abdomen boldly barred dark brown and white. Tarsi and toes feathered. **Juvenile** Downy chick whitish. Mesoptile indistinctly barred above and below. **Bare parts** Eyes blackish-brown. Cere yellowish-horn. Bill pale greenish-yellow. Claws dusky horn.

MEASUREMENTS AND WEIGHT Total length 40.5-48cm. Wing 325-331mm; tail about 225mm. Weight of males 518-694g, of females 548-760g.

GEOGRAPHICAL VARIATION

S. o. occidentalis (Xantus, 1859). Nevada, C and S California. See Description. Wing 300-331mm; tail 191-213mm.

S. o. caurina (Merriam, 1898). British Columbia to N California. Darker than nominate race and perhaps only a dark morph. Wing 315-325mm.

S. (o.) lucida (Nelson, 1903). Arizona, New Mexico

and SW Texas to C Mexico. Lighter than nominate form, and more profusely spotted white. May well be a different species, Mountain Forest Owl, but further details are required to clarify its taxonomy.

HABITS A nocturnal, rather 'tame' bird. By day, it normally roosts in deep shade on a high branch of an old tree, in a large knothole or in a cliff cavity; in summer perches lower down, where temperatures are not so high, and may then be approached quite closely. Being not very fond of high temperatures, the owl moves to cooler, shaded places in hot weather, and then prefers to roost on north-facing slopes with dense, moist coniferous forest. When disturbed during daytime, it flies to another shaded perch. Leaves roost towards dusk. Song is delivered from various different perches.

FOOD Mostly small mammals and birds, but also lizards, frogs and insects; locally, flying squirrels, pocket-gophers, bats, deer mice and wood rats are favoured prey. Birds up to the size of pigeon are taken. It may be supposed that this owl, being sedentary, feeds throughout the year on all suitable prey that it can catch. Recorded prey species (e.g. flying squirrels and wood rats, as well as crossbills *Loxia*) suggest that it prefers to hunt through the middle stratum of the forest; ground-dwelling species such as deer mice, brush rabbits, shrews and moles have been found to be less frequent than arboreal ones. Hunts from a perch, swooping on to prey in noiseless flight; while most prey are taken from the ground or branches, bats are mostly captured on the wing.

BREEDING Nests mostly in holes in tree trunks, potholes and other cavities in cliffs, or in cave entrances on steep slopes of narrow canyons; also uses abandoned stick nests of Common Ravens *Corvus corax*, Golden Eagles *Aquila chrysaetos* or other birds of prey in cliffs or on trees, always well shaded from sunlight. Normally lays 2 white eggs (sometimes up to 4); the female incubates alone, fed by her mate. Breeding biology poorly known, but probably similar to that of Barred, Ural and Tawny Owls [128, 130].

STATUS AND CONSERVATION Uncertain. Locally threatened by forest destruction, as this owl needs dense, cool forest to survive. Intensive logging has also allowed the larger and more powerful Barred Owl to extend its range westwards, where in places it may be a threat to its smaller counterpart through predation. The problem of hybridisation also arises, as the genetic barriers between the two species appear to be very weak; hybrids are already known in the wild, and increasing hybridisation would constitute an additional hazard.

REMARKS The biology of this handsome, rather 'tame' owl needs study, primarily in order to determine the requirements for its conservation.

REFERENCES Barrows (1981), Boyer & Hume (1991), Burton (1992), Gould (1977), Hardy *et al.* (1989), Marcot & Gardetto (1980), Snyder & Wiley (1976), Voous (1988).

125 FULVOUS OWL
Strix fulvescens   **Plate 39**

French: Chouette fauve
German: Gilbkauz
Spanish: Buho fulvo

IDENTIFICATION A rather large (40.5-45cm), round-headed owl without ear-tufts, and with pale ochraceous facial disc rimmed dark brown. Upperparts rusty-brown with whitish spots; pale fulvous-brown below, with barred upper breast and rather broadly streaked rest of underparts. Bill yellow; eyes blackish-brown; toes partly feathered. **Similar species** Barred Owl [126] is very similar in plumage pattern, but larger, lighter and greyer, and mostly with densely feathered toes. Spotted Owl [124] is boldly spotted below, not streaked. Mottled Owl [136] is much smaller, generally dark brown with brown facial disc and brown eyes, and rather prominent whitish eyebrows. Black-and-white Owl [141] has a blackish head with dark facial disc, dusky upperparts, greyish-white underparts finely barred blackish, bill and bare toes yellow and eyes dark brown. Great Horned Owl [94] is larger and heavier, with yellow eyes and prominent ear-tufts. Stygian Owl [206] is about the same size as Fulvous Owl, but with dusky plumage, dark face, yellow eyes and prominent ear-tufts, and is boldly marked below with herringbone pattern and spots. Striped Owl [210] is boldly streaked below, and has a pale, dark-rimmed face, brown eyes and very prominent ear-tufts.

VOCALISATIONS The song of the male is more like that of Spotted Owl than that of Barred (though latter has been thought to be conspecific with Fulvous), a rhythmic sequence of rather low, short and accentuated hoots: *who-wuhú-woot-woot*, the number of single hoots varying according to excitement, as do intervals between phrases. Somewhat similar to the song of Great Horned Owl, but higher in pitch and with much shorter intervals between single (never drawn-out) notes. The female has a similar but higher-pitched song, often uttered in duet with male. Also gives parrot-like, nasal *gwao* calls, singly or in series, as well as single hoots.

DISTRIBUTION Mexico south of the Isthmus (Chiapas) to Guatemala, El Salvador and Honduras. Separated from Barred Owl by a stretch of only 50-100km between the mountains of Chiapas and the mountainous regions of Oaxaca.

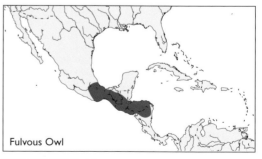

Fulvous Owl

MOVEMENTS Resident.

HABITAT Montane pine-oak forest and humid forest at 1,200-3,000m.

DESCRIPTION Adult Facial disc pale ochraceous, darkening around eyes; narrow rim of disc dark brown. Eyebrows whitish. Upperparts dark rufous-brown with whitish and pale buffy flecks and scalloped with short ochraceous bars. Flight feathers barred dark and light; tail feathers with few (3-5), rather broad light and dark bars. Underparts ochraceous-fulvous, with brown barring on neck, sides of head and upper breast; rest of underparts rather broadly streaked rufescent-brown. Tarsi feathered ochraceous-fulvous; toes feathered only near base, rest bare. **Juvenile** Downy chick whitish. Mesoptile similar to Barred Owl, but more cinnamon-brown, barred with pale yellowish-orange and white. **Bare parts** Eyes blackish-brown. Cere yellowish. Bill corn-yellow. Bare parts of toes yellowish-grey. Claws dusky horn with darker tips.

MEASUREMENTS Total length 40.5-45cm. Wing 300-333mm; tail 185-203mm. Generally about 20% smaller than Mexican populations of Barred Owl.

GEOGRAPHICAL VARIATION Monotypic: *Strix fulvescens* (Sclater & Salvin, 1848).

HABITS A nocturnal bird, roosting during daytime at well-shaded sites in trees or in natural holes. Habits similar to those of Tawny Owl [130] and Spotted Owl.

FOOD Small mammals and birds, frogs, lizards, insects and other arthropods. Prey are normally caught from a perch.

BREEDING Generally uses natural holes in tree trunks as nesting sites. Lays 2-5 (mostly 2-3) white eggs directly on to the bottom of the cavity; female incubates alone, for 28-30 days, starting with the first egg. Breeding biology little known, but probably similar to that of other members of the genus.

STATUS AND CONSERVATION Uncertain. Forest destruction probably represents a threat.

REMARKS We separate this owl specifically from the Barred Owl because of its significantly smaller size in comparison with Mexican populations of the latter living less than 100km to the north, and on the grounds of its different vocalisations. The species obviously requires further research, particularly comparative studies in relation to Barred and Spotted Owls, and with regard to measures needed for its conservation.

REFERENCES Boyer & Hume (1991), Burton (1992), Hardy *et al.* (1989), Howell & Webb (1995), Monroe (1968), Voous (1988).

---

126 BARRED OWL
Strix varia   Plate 39

French: Chouette barrée
German: Streifenkauz
Spanish: Buho barrado

IDENTIFICATION A rather large (50-60cm), greyish-brown or brown owl with barred upper chest, rest of underparts being boldly streaked dusky or rufescent-brown. Head large and rounded, without ear-tufts. Facial disc pale greyish-brown with several darker concentric lines. Bill pale straw-yellow; eyes blackish-brown; tarsi and toes feathered, in southern races more bristled. **Similar species** Fulvous Owl [125] is smaller, with fulvous tones in plumage, and has a pale, plain facial disc without darker concentric lines. Spotted Owl [124] is similar in size, but boldly spotted below and darker above. Great Grey Owl [129] is generally grey, with a very large, rounded head and relatively small yellow eyes. Great Horned Owl [94] is larger, with prominent ear-tufts and yellow eyes. Long-eared Owl [207] is smaller and slimmer, with prominent ear-tufts and orange eyes.

VOCALISATIONS Two different songs of the male are known: one is a deep barking sequence of guttural notes, increasing in volume and ending with an explosive, disyllabic hoot with accent on the second syllable, *ok-ok-ok-ok-ok-ok-ok-buhooh*; the other is a rhythmic *who-hú-buhooh who-hú-buhooh*. Both are repeated at intervals of several seconds. We believe that these song differences, rather than representing geographical variation, give expression to the 'mood' of the bird. The situation may be similar to that found with the screech owls of the genus *Otus* (all of which have two different types of song, A- and B-songs), the first song perhaps expressing aggression. Ural Owl [128] utters hoarse, barking calls in aggression, which may correspond to the barking sequence of Barred Owl, to which Ural is apparently rather closely related; Tawny Owl [130] also has two different songs, one of which is the territorial song and the other (a rolling trill) is uttered during courtship, with a more or less yelping *kwatt-kwatt...* being given in aggression (see Tawny Owl). Considering all possibilities, however, the most plausible explanation seems to be that the barking song type has an aggressive function, in which case the rhythmic song would be the territorial one. Females and juveniles beg with high scratching *skreechch* notes.

DISTRIBUTION Widely distributed in North America east of the Rocky Mountains, south to Florida and S Mexico (Oaxaca); also extends from about the Great Lakes in a narrow belt across the Rockies to British Columbia, south to Washington, Oregon and N California. As a result of logging operations, it is expanding its range on the Atlantic side of North America, where it now overlaps with that of the Spotted Owl.

MOVEMENTS In general resident, but some wandering movements when food is scarce.

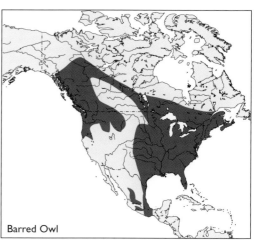

Barred Owl

HABITAT Old coniferous and mixed forest, often in riverine bottomlands or on swampy ground, but also similar habitats in mountainous regions. Not confined to extended forest, but found also in semi-open wooded areas, locally in large parks with mature trees, and in natural forest cleared by logging (thus enabling its westward expansion).

DESCRIPTION *S. v. varia* **Adult** Facial disc pale greyish-brown with darker concentric lines; rim around disc not very prominent. Sides of head and neck barred light and dark. Upperparts brown to greyish-brown (lighter than Spotted Owl), scalloped with whitish bars on crown, back and mantle; wing-coverts spotted whitish. Flight feathers barred whitish-buff and brown; tail brown or greyish-brown with 4-5 whitish bars. Underparts pale greyish-brown to dirty whitish; upper breast and foreneck densely barred light and dark (like sides of head and neck), rest of underparts boldly streaked dark to rufescent-brown. Tarsi feathered; toes nearly totally feathered (note that toes more bristled in southern subspecies). **Juvenile** Downy chick whitish. Mesoptile fluffy brownish-white, with indistinct darker barring on back, head and mantle, as well as on underparts. **Bare parts** Eyes dark brown to blackish-brown. Cere pale horn. Bill pale yellowish with slight greenish tint. Bare parts of toes yellowish-grey. Claws dark horn with blackish tips. Juvenile has a pinkish skin and a pale-blue-green cere.

MEASUREMENTS AND WEIGHT Total length 50-61cm. Wing 312-376mm; tail about 229mm. Weight of males median 630g, of females median 800g (maximum to about 1050g). Females normally larger and heavier than males.

GEOGRAPHICAL VARIATION Four subspecies.
 S. v. varia Barton, 1799. British Columbia to N California and southeast to E USA. See Description. Wing of males 312-325mm, of females 320-351mm.
 S. v. georgica Latham, 1801. SE USA, south of N Carolina to Georgia and Florida. About 3% smaller than nominate race, with feathering of toes reduced.
 S. v. helveola (Bangs, 1899). Texas and adjacent lowlands of Mexico. Pale cinnamon ground coloration; toes rather bare or slightly bristled. Wing 330-355mm.
 S. v. sartorii (Ridgway, 1873). Montane regions in C and S Mexico (Oaxaca)), from 1500m up to 2500m. Darkest race. Toes rather bare. Wing 340-380mm; tail 220-257mm.

HABITS Nocturnal. By day it roosts well hidden in dense foliage of a tree, usually rather high above ground, sometimes on a branch close to a broad trunk or in a natural tree hole; mobbed by small birds when discovered by them during daytime, and in such situations may be attacked by diurnal birds of prey. At the nest can be very aggressive towards intruders, and will also attack humans if they approach the nest or fledged young.

FOOD Principally small mammals, but birds, other vertebrates and arthropods also form part of its diet. Of 2,234 prey items, 76% were mammals, 6% birds, 2.5% other vertebrates (including frogs, lizards and fish), and 16% insects and other arthropods. Mammalian prey includes voles, mice, rats, cotton rats, shrews, moles, chipmunks, squirrels, cottontails, young hares, opossums, weasels, minks and bats. About 30 species of bird have been recorded as prey, from warblers to swallows, flickers *Colaptes*, crows and smaller owls, occasionally poultry. Snails and slugs have also been noted as prey. Like Tawny Owl, it usually hunts from a perch, but will also will flush and capture night-roosting birds; bats may be caught on the wing, too. Again like Tawny, it is able to catch fish by wading in shallow water.

BREEDING The territory is claimed by singing from different perches. Territory size has been studied by radio telemetry: in Minnesota, one pair occupied about 226 ha in mixed hardwood-conifer habitats. Usually nests in natural holes in trees in deep, dark woods, but nests have frequently been found in hollow live oaks, and stick nests of diurnal raptors (e.g. hawks) and other large birds are also used and squirrel dreys are accepted; in the south, nests have been found between fronds of palmetto palm leaves, in holes of broken palm stems and rotten snags; may even nest on the ground in a hollowed-out depression; locally, nestboxes are accepted. Suitable nesting holes in trees are often used for several years, even up to about 25 years, but in such cases it is not certain whether the same adults were always involved (Barred Owls normally do not reach such an age in the wild) or whether, more probably, a male offspring had brought its mate to a site familiar to him.

Normally lays 2-3 white eggs (up to 5 possible) directly on to the base of the nest, no material being added. Incubation starts with the first egg and is by the female alone, fed by her mate; incubation lasts about 28 days. Chicks brooded by the female for 3 weeks; at 6 weeks they leave the nest, and are cared for and fed by their parents for several weeks more.

STATUS AND CONSERVATION Uncertain. Logging actually favours the expansion of this species in the W USA, but with increasing forest destruction it eventually loses its habitat. Forest and woods with old trees (with natural holes) are necessary for its occurrence, and their replacement by plantations of younger trees with thin trunks is inadequate. Locally, experiments with nestboxes (with side entrance not smaller than 18cm) placed high in trees have proved successful; while this may help the owls in some regions, it will not solve the problem of conservation on a wider scale.

REMARKS Comparative studies of Barred, Spotted and Fulvous Owls would be of great interest, above all to clarify their ecological and biological differentiation, as well as their relationships with other *Strix* owls.

REFERENCES Bent (1938), Bosakowski *et al.* (1987), Boyer & Hume (1991), Burton (1992), Earhart & Johnson (1970), Eck & Busse (1973), Fuller *et al.* (1973), Hardy *et al.* (1989), Johnson (1987), Monroe (1968), Scott *et al.* (1987), Siddle (1984), Snyder & Wiley (1976), Voous (1988).

---

127 SICHUAN WOOD OWL
Strix davidi   Plate 39

French: Chouette de David
German: Davidskauz

IDENTIFICATION A rather large (about 58cm), dark owl with pale facial disc with darker concentric lines. Head and back dark with whitish streaking, uppertail-coverts plain, and central tail feathers with fine scribbles; greyish-white below, boldly streaked dark and with indication of cross-bars. Eyes dark brown; bill yellow; tarsi and toes feathered. **Similar species** Very similar to Ural Owl [128], of which often considered to be a race, but dark patterning of plumage darker, more blackisk-brown, less rufous-brown than nearest race of Ural (*fuscescens*, Japan), and does not occur sympatrically with that species. Can be confused with Tawny Owl [130] (if it occurs in Sichuan), but that species is much smaller (36-46cm) and not so greyish-white or brownish-white below.

VOCALISATIONS Calls (song?) are described as a long, quivering hoot and barking *kbau kbau*, as well as a harsh *kee-wick*.

DISTRIBUTION Recorded only from the mountains of W China, from C and W Sichuan west to the region of Paohing (Moupin) and Batang in C Sikiang, also in SE Qinghai near Pan Ma (Sai-lai-tang), about 100°E, 32°50'N.

Sichuan Wood Owl

MOVEMENTS Resident.

HABITAT Old coniferous mixed forest; also tall and dense forest stands of spruce, fir and pine alternating with alpine meadows and rather open areas with low vegetation. About 2,700-4,200m, at times perhaps to 5,000m.

DESCRIPTION Adult Very similar to Ural Owl, but markings much darker. Facial disc white, with some indication of concentric dark lines (unlike Ural), and clearly marked rim. Pale spots on head whiter than on Japanese race *fuscescens* of Ural, and moreover spots are paler and larger on nape and mantle, and ground colour of underparts also paler, but dark patterning of plumage is darker, blackish-brown (more rufous-brown in *fuscescens*). Tail rather long, tipped with white; outer feathers blacker, with pale bars less conspicuous. Underparts streaked (not spotted as in some *fuscescens*). **Juvenile** Not yet described. **Bare parts** Probably little different from Ural Owl; eyes dark brown.

MEASUREMENTS AND WEIGHT Total length 58-59cm. Wing 371-372mm; tail 266 (290)mm. Weight: no data. Females always much larger and heavier than males.

GEOGRAPHICAL VARIATION Monotypic: *Strix davidi* (Sharpe, 1875).

HABITS Probably not different from those of Ural Owl.

FOOD Unknown, but probably much as for Ural Owl (see latter).

BREEDING Unknown.

STATUS AND CONSERVATION Probably endangered. Listed as Vulnerable by BirdLife International. Appears to be rare within its known range, where extensive deforestation is taking place.

REMARKS This little-known owl is sometimes considered an isolated subspecies of Ural Owl. Studies of all aspects of its life are urgently needed.

REFERENCES Boyer & Hume (1991), Burton (1992), Collar *et al.* (1994), Eck & Busse (1973), Etchécopar & Hüe (1978), Sharpe (1875), Voous (1988).

---

128 URAL OWL
Strix uralensis   Plate 40

French: Chouette d'Oural
German: Habichtskauz

IDENTIFICATION A rather large (58-61cm), round-headed owl without ear-tufts, and with relatively long tail with wedge-shaped tip. Round facial disc plain pale greyish-brown to whitish, with relatively small, dark brown eyes. Greyish-brown to brown above, with whitish markings; underparts pale greyish-brown, boldly streaked dark brown, without cross-bars. Wings boldly barred light and dark. Bill yellowish; tarsi and toes feathered. **Similar species** Sichuan Wood Owl [127] is darker and its facial disc has darker concentric lines; eyes dark brown. Tawny Owl [130] is much smaller, with short tail and relatively large head, and occurs in grey, brown and red morphs; underparts with dark shaft-streaks and cross-bars, not heavily streaked; eyes dark brown, larger than Ural Owl's. Great Grey Owl [129] is larger, with huge, rounded head and small, yellow eyes, and its facial disc has numerous concentric lines. Eurasian Eagle Owl [96] is much larger, with prominent ear-tufts and orange eyes. Long-eared Owl [205] is smaller and slimmer, with prominent ear-tufts and orange eyes.

VOCALISATIONS The song of the male is a deep rhythmic sequence of notes, with a short pause after the first double note: *wúhu huw-hohuwo*. This phrase is repeated at intervals of several seconds. The female has a similar but hoarse and slightly higher-pitched song, giving it a more 'barking' character. Both partners may duet during courtship. In addition, a heron-like *kraoh* is uttered by both sexes. Rough barking series of nasal notes are given by male and female in aggression. A hoarse *kuwat* is probably used as contact-call. Young beg with hoarse *chrreeh* calls, lower-pitched than those of Tawny Owl.

DISTRIBUTION N Europe, from Norway, Sweden, Finland and the Baltic Repubics, through N Russia and Siberia to Korea, coast of the Okhotsk Sea, Sakhalin and Japan; also locally in Poland, Czech Republic, Slovakia, Slovenia, Croatia and Balkan countries; very locally in the Bohemian Forest and in the 'Bavarian Forest' National Park in Germany (where it has been reintroduced). Single stragglers have been recorded in N Germany (e.g. Harz Mountains, Lüneburger Heide).

MOVEMENTS Adults are in general sedentary, while immatures may wander distances of up to about 150km;

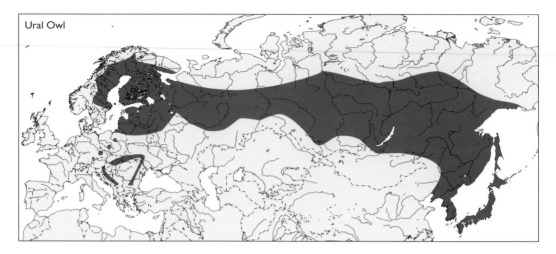

Ural Owl

occasional individuals may straggle even farther and remain there for some time. Winters irregularly south to SE Europe. Siberian populations show some tendency to move southwards in severe winters.

HABITAT Mature, not too dense, deciduous and mixed forest with clearings. In north, breeding habitat is similar to that of Northern Goshawk *Accipiter gentilis*: rather open coniferous or mixed forest with tall trees and some clearings, often near bogs, and often mixed with alder and birch. In southern parts of range, e.g. Transylvania, occurs mainly in old beech forest.

DESCRIPTION *S. u. uralensis* **Adult** Light and dark morphs occur, the former being more numerous. *Light morph*: Facial disc rather round and prominent, uniform dirty whitish to pale ochraceous-grey; rim around disc consisting of rows of small dark spots. Upperparts pale greyish-brown, mottled, spotted and streaked with whitish and dusky; scapulars with rather large areas of white. Flight feathers conspicuously barred light and dark; tail rather long, wedge-shaped, with dark and pale greyish-white bars. Throat whitish; remaining underparts very pale greyish-brown to dirty white, heavily streaked brown. Tarsi and toes rather thickly feathered pale greyish-brown to dirty whitish-cream. **Juvenile** Downy chick white. Mesoptile pale dirty whitish, barred with greyish-brown on head, nape, mantle and underparts. **Bare parts** Eyes relatively small, very dark brown. Cere dirty yellow. Bill pale yellow-horn. Claws yellowish-brown with darker tips.

MEASUREMENTS AND WEIGHT Total length 58-61cm. Wing 295-415mm; tail 253-326mm. Weight of males 503-950g, of females 569-1307g.

GEOGRAPHICAL VARIATION We recognise seven subspecies.

S. u. uralensis Pallas, 1771. E Russia, Siberia, to Yakutia and Okhotsk coast, south to Middle Volga, S Ural, Tyumen, Yalutrovsk and Kaink. See Description. Wing 340-380mm. (We include the form *buturlini* in nominate.)
S. u. liturata Tengmalm, 1793. N Europe from Lapland and Sweden to Baltic region, E Alps, Carpathians, east to Volga; intergrades with nominate *uralensis*. Darker than nominate. Wing 342-382mm.
S. u. macroura Wolf, 1810. NW Carpathians, Tran-

sylvanian Alps to W Balkans. Larger and darker than *liturata*. A coffee-brown morph exists. Wing 354-415mm. (We include the form *carpathica* as a synonym of macroura.)
S. u. yenisseensis Buturlin, 1915. C Siberian plateau to Transbaikalia. Wing 328-370mm.
S. u. nikolskii Buturlin, 1907. Transbaikalia north to Vitim, Sakhalin, south to Korea. Similar to *liturata*, but head and shoulders more brownish, light areas whiter. Wing 310-355mm. (We include *daurica*, *tatibanai* and *coreensis* as synonyms of *nikolskii*.)
S. u. fuscescens Temminck & Schlegel, 1847. W and S Honshu to Kyushu, Japan. Upperparts marked with yellowish rufescent-brown; underparts yellowish-rusty with dark brown streaks and often with rounded white spots; feathering of tarsi and toes brownish. Wing 310-332mm.
S. u. hondoensis (Clark, 1907). Hokkaido and N and C Honshu, Japan. More rusty-brown; white on head and back reduced. Wing 295-347mm. (We include the form *japonica* within *hondoensis*.)

HABITS Active chiefly at night, with peaks at dusk and just before dawn; during brood-rearing period also during daytime, especially in northern parts of range. Roosts on a branch close to a trunk or in dense foliage; normally not shy and may be approached quite closely. Very aggressive near the nest, when male and female will attack human intruders in diving flight, scratching them with the powerful claws.

FOOD A large variety of mammals, birds, frogs and insects. Voles, shrews, mice and rats, and other mammals up to the size of smaller hares are the main prey, voles constituting about 60-70%. Birds up to the size of Black Grouse *Tetrao tetrix* have been reported, but at a much lower rate. Surplus food is stored at the nest or at nearby depots. Hunts mainly from perches.

BREEDING The male claims its territory by singing from different perches; during courtship, may be heard duetting with its mate. Generally pairs for life and maintains same territory for many years. Territories are on average about three times larger than those of Tawny Owls; in Sweden, about 3,000 pairs of Ural Owls were found in 150,000km². Potential nesting sites include large natural holes in trees, cavities left by large broken-off branches, hollow trunks where canopy has been broken ('chimney stacks'), fissures and holes in cliffs or between rocks, and holes in buildings; may also use old stick nests of larger birds such as Northern Goshawk *Accipiter gentilis*, buzzards *Buteo* etc, as well as squirrel dreys; in Fennoscandia, makes large-scale use of nestboxes locally.

The 3-4 (1-6) white eggs measure 46.5-52.3 x 39.0-44.0mm and weigh (fresh) about 46-48g; laid directly on to the bottom of nest, at intervals of about 2 days. Female incubates alone, beginning with the first egg, and is fed by her mate; incubation lasts 28-35 days. Young hatch at about same intervals as eggs are laid, the female staying with them almost until fledging. Nestlings leave the nest site when about 35 days old, and can fly fairly well at about 45 days; they are cared for and fed by both parents for about 2 months after leaving the nest.

Young reach sexual maturity during their first year of life.

STATUS AND CONSERVATION Locally not uncommon, especially where making use of nestboxes. Decreasing numbers are reported from areas where hollow and broken trees are removed from forest. The erection of nestboxes with an opening of about 16cm in diameter has proved a very successful conservation measure in Finland.

REMARKS Although this species' biology is rather well known, further taxonomic research is required on the various described races. The ecological hierarchy of Ural and Tawny Owls in Fennoscandia should be investigated in more detail; the larger and more powerful Ural Owl apparently influences the distribution of its smaller counterpart.

REFERENCES Bezzel (1985), Boyer & Hume (1991), Burton (1992), Dementiev & Gladkov (1951), Holmberg (1974), König (1969), Lahti 1972), Lindblad (1967), Linkola & Myllymäki (1969), Mikkola (1972, 1983), Saurola (1987, 1997), Scherzinger (1980), Voous (1988).

129 GREAT GREY OWL
Strix nebulosa   Plate 40

French: Chouette lapone
German: Bartkauz

IDENTIFICATION A large (61-69cm), grey to greyish-brown owl, mottled and streaked dark, with a rather huge, rounded head without ear-tufts and small, piercing yellow eyes. Feathers long and fluffy, suggesting a very large bird, which in reality has only a relatively small body. Facial disc round, with many dark concentric lines; blackish area beneath bill, resembling a black beard (hence German name Bartkauz, meaning 'bearded owl'). Tail relatively long. Tarsi and toes densely feathered. **Similar species** Ural Owl [128] is smaller, boldly streaked below, has dark brown eyes, and facial disc is pale and lacks dark concentric markings. Sichuan Wood Owl [127], confined to mountains of Sichuan in C China, is similar, but is darker than Ural Owl and has dark concentric lines on facial disc. Barred Owl [126] is also smaller, and has a greyish-brown, whitish-barred back and a pale facial disc with darker concentric lines (much less marked than on Great Grey), with eyes blackish-brown. Spotted Owl [124] is smaller, brown, spotted with white above and below, and has dark

brown eyes. Tawny Owl [130] is much smaller, with relatively large, brown eyes; plumage variable (grey, brown and rufous morphs frequent), with row of whitish scapular spots. Eurasian Eagle Owl [96] is larger and more powerful, with prominent ear-tufts and orange eyes. Great Horned Owl [94] is somewhat smaller, with prominent ear-tufts and rather large, yellow eyes.

VOCALISATIONS The male's song is a sequence of deep mellow hoots, slightly accelerating towards end and falling in pitch: *húwo-húwo-húwo-húwo-húw-huhuhuhuw*, not particularly loud, but audible at rather long distances on calm nights. The female's song is similar, but rather hoarse and mostly higher in pitch, uttered by unpaired females and sometimes during courtship. A high-pitched *ooeeh* is given by the female when soliciting food. Young emit a similar call. Adults also give cackling and guttural notes.

DISTRIBUTION Boreal zones in the Holarctic forest belt from Fennoscandia through Siberia to Sakhalin and Anadyr Plateau north of Kamchatka, across the Bering Sea to Alaska and N Canada, east to Hudson Bay and south in the Rocky Mountains to N California, Idaho and Wyoming.

Great Grey Owl

MOVEMENTS A nomadic bird which breeds in areas where food (especially voles) is plentiful; may be fairly abundant in areas when there are peaks of vole populations, while in other years it may be absent from these same regions. True irruptions into areas with good food supply have been observed, and in such cases stragglers can occur, and may even breed, far south of their normal limits of distribution. In Europe vagrants may reach Ukraine and NE Germany, and in America the region of New York.

HABITAT Mature and normally extensive boreal, mostly lichen-covered forest of spruce and pine, sometimes mixed with birch, larch and poplar, often near swampy clearings or other open areas. In mountains ascends to subalpine regions, e.g. to 2,400m in the Sierra Nevada of California and to 3,200m above sea-level in Utah. Outside breeding season, may also be seen in other types of landscape, occasionally near and in human settlements.

DESCRIPTION *S. n. nebulosa* Adult Facial disc circular, grey, with many dark concentric rings. Short eyebrows and lores whitish, forming white X in centre of face. Blackish patch beneath bill, suggesting a black 'beard'. Upperparts dark grey with brownish tint, densely vermiculated and mottled darker, with indistinct dusky streaks. Flight feathers barred darker and lighter grey to greyish-brown.

Great Grey Owl

Tail relatively long, barred and mottled grey and dusky. Tarsi and toes densely feathered grey, with dusky mottling. Talons somewhat less powerful than Ural Owl's. Underparts lighter greyish with dark vermiculations, mottling and suffused longitudinal dark streaks; abdomen barred dusky. **Juvenile** Downy chick whitish-grey. Mesoptile pale greyish, with dusky bars and whitish mottling above and below, giving cryptic coloration; face dusky. **Bare parts** Eyes relatively small (diameter about 12-14mm) compared with Ural (15-16mm) and Tawny Owls (16-17mm), bright yellow, surrounded by blackish edge of eyelids. Cere greyish-yellow. Bill yellowish-horn. Claws dark brown with blackish tips. Young birds have pale yellowish-grey eyes and greyish-yellow cere and bill.

MEASUREMENTS AND WEIGHT Total length 61-69cm. Wing of males 405-477mm, of females 438-490mm; tail 295-330mm. Weight of males 660-1110g (median 884g), of females 977-1900 (median 1186g).

GEOGRAPHICAL VARIATION We recognise two taxa as valid subspecies.

S. n. nebulosa J.R. Forster, 1772. North America from Alaska to California and an area between Hudson Bay and the Great Lakes. See Description. Streaks on underparts more suffused than in Eurasian *lapponica*, somewhat barred below, and generally darker and more grey. Wing of males 405-477mm, of females 438-483mm.

S. n. lapponica Thunberg, 1798. N Eurasia, from Fennoscandia through Siberia to Sakhalin and north of Kamchatka (absent from peninsula), south to Lake Baikal, Kazakhstan, Mongolia and Manchuria. Often lighter, less grey than nominate race; streaking on underparts more prominent, without barring. Wing of males 430-450mm, of females 460-490mm.

HABITS Active at night, but also at dusk and just before dawn; sometimes active by day during breeding season. Roosts on branches, often close to the trunk or in canopy. Mostly seen singly or in pairs; outside breeding season often wanders around and roosts in groups. Can be very aggressive near the nest, and will even attack and injure human intruders. May be attracted and stimulated to sing by playback of its song. Flies with soft, slow wingbeats.

FOOD Chiefly small mammals, especially voles; latter about 90% of food during breeding season, and this owl may breed in fair numbers when these are abundant. Also takes shrews (especially in winter), squirrels, smaller hares, and birds up to the size of grouse; in addition, frogs and large beetles are caught. Normally hunts from a perch.

BREEDING Monogamous. Song may be heard in autumn, but primarily between March and May. Territory may vary in size according to food abundance, topography, etc: 10-25km² in some cases, and in others only about 2.6km² or occasionally as little as 0.47km² (three nests in distance of about 400m). Uses abandoned stick nests of larger birds (buzzards *Buteo*, Osprey *Pandion haliaetus*, Northern Goshawk *Accipiter gentilis*, etc), sometimes driving away the original owners; sometimes nests on top of broken or rotten snags, as well as on rocks or similar localities, and even in shallow depressions on the ground at base of a tree.

Lays 3-6 (2-9) pure white eggs (average 53.2 x 42.4mm in Europe, 54.2 x 43.4mm in North America); as with most owls, clutch size depends on abundance of food, and if this is very scarce the birds will not breed at all or may even emigrate. Eggs are laid at intervals of about 2 days, directly on to the bottom of the nest, with no material added. The female incubates alone, being fed by her mate, who delivers food to her bill to bill or stores surplus prey on the rim of the nest; incubation starts with the first egg and lasts 28-30 days, the eggs hatching at similar intervals to laying. Young leave the nest at an age of 20-30 days, when not yet able to fly; at 5-6 weeks they fly well. Sexual maturity is reached in the following year.

Great Grey Owls may live to about 7 years in the wild, perhaps longer at times. In captivity, they have reached an age of 27 years.

STATUS AND CONSERVATION So long as the boreal forest is preserved from clear-felling, acid rain and the use of pesticides, the Great Grey Owl's future remains assured. Its populations seem to be rather stable, annual fluctuations being natural and due to relative abundance of food. Locally, the species may be helped by the provision of artificial nesting platforms of sticks mounted in trees at suitable sites, a method which has proved successful in Sweden and Canada. In Sweden, the acceptance of a nestbox (type not stated) has been recorded. Hunting and the trade in wild birds may be a threat locally, although this owl is protected by law throughout its range.

REMARKS Although rather well studied, several questions concerning the biology of the Great Grey Owl and its relationship to other members of the genus *Strix* remain unanswered. This species seems to us to be somewhat removed from its congeners.

REFERENCES Bent (1938), Bezzel (1985), Boyer & Hume (1991), Bull *et al.* (1987), Burton (1992), Craighead & Craighead (1956), Cramp (1985), Dementiev & Gladkov (1951), Eck & Busse (1973), Glutz & Bauer (1980), König (1970), Mikkola (1981, 1983), Nero (1980), Saurola (1997), Voous (1988), Wahlstedt (1974), Winter (1982).

130 TAWNY OWL
Strix aluco   **Plate 41**

French: Chouette hulotte
German: Waldkauz
Spanish: Cárabo común

IDENTIFICATION Commonest owl in C Europe. A medium-sized (36-46cm), chunky owl with large, round head without ear-tufts, prominent facial disc rimmed dusky, and blackish-brown eyes rimmed by pale fleshy edges of blue-grey eyelids. Plumage coloration very variable: grey, brown and red morphs occur, sometimes intergrading. Above and below, streaked dusky with several cross-bars (herringbone pattern). Tail rather short, wings broad. Tarsi and toes densely feathered; talons rather powerful. **Similar species** Ural and Great Grey Owls [128, 129] are both much larger, the former with smaller, dark brown eyes, underparts boldly streaked dusky and without cross-bars, and long, distinctly barred tail, and Great Grey with huge, round head, rather circular facial disc with many dusky concentric lines, and small yellow eyes. Hume's Owl [131] is smaller, more sandy-coloured, and has orange-yellow to pale ochraceous-orange eyes. Brown Wood Owl [132] is larger, with prominent orange-buff facial disc and large, dark brown eyes, is finely barred off-white and brown below, and has warm brown upperparts more or less barred whitish. Mottled Wood Owl [123] has a prominent white throat, is finely barred off-white and brown from crown to mantle and below, and has brown eyes. Spotted Wood Owl [122] is heavily barred pale buffy and dusky below, and has plain creamy-white facial disc contrasting with surrounding plumage and dark brown eyes. Marsh Owl [212] has small ear-tufts and is rather uniform earth-brown above, with pale facial disc. Short-eared Owl [211] has short ear-tufts, yellow eyes and streaked underparts, while Long-eared Owl [207] has prominent ear-tufts and orange eyes. All eagle owls and fish owls [94-113] are much larger, with prominent ear-tufts.

VOCALISATIONS The male utters a characteristic song, well known in Europe: a clear, fluted, long-drawn hoot with wailing quality, consisting of about three notes drawn together into one, often with upward inflection and emphasis in the middle, followed after a brief pause by a very short *uk* and continuing after a further short interval with a long tremolo of staccato notes, often rising or falling slightly in pitch and drawn out at end. This phrase, repeated at intervals of several seconds, may be transcribed as *whoóoh uk whoooooooooh*. The female's song is similar but hoarser, less clear, and somewhat higher in pitch. During courtship, both sexes also utter long, rolling trills in duet, the female's voice higher in pitch. Male and female give rather soft *kuit* calls, probably having a contact function, and piercing *coo-wik* or *cu-weeht* cries, apparently expressing aggression. When disturbed at the nest, utters series of yelping *uett-uett-uett-...* notes. Young beg with drawn-out *cheeh* or *cheheeh*.

DISTRIBUTION Britain and continental Eurasia, from Iberian Peninsula in the south and Scandinavia in the north to W Siberia, and from Greece, Asia Minor and the Middle East to the Caspian Sea and Turkestan to E China and Taiwan; present in Sardinia and Sicily, rare in Mallorca, and absent from Ireland, Corsica, Crete, Rhodes and Cyprus. Occurs locally in N Africa (Morocco to Tunisia, Mauritania).

MOVEMENTS Resident. Immatures may wander up to about 100km, occasionally farther; Scandinavian birds recorded moving up to 745km.

HABITAT Semi-open deciduous and mixed forest with clearings, riverine forest, parks, larger gardens with old trees, open landscapes with wooded patches, and avenues of trees in open farmland; occupied pure coniferous forest only near edges, or when clearings and rides exist. Also

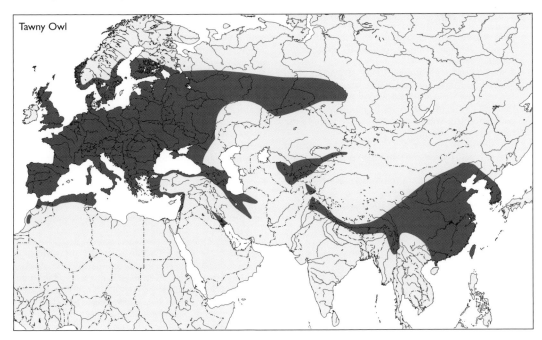

Tawny Owl

inhabits rocky country with scattered trees and bushes. Locally near or in human settlements, and even towns and cities where timbered gardens or tree-lined pavements are present. Found from lowlands, up to 4,200m in Himalayas.

DESCRIPTION *S. a. aluco* **Adult** Markedly polymorphic, with grey, brown and rufous morphs, as well as intermediates between these. *Brown morph:* Facial disc pale brownish with some indistinct dusky concentric lines; rim around disc dark brown. Bristles around base of bill and eyebrows off-white. Upperparts generally brown, feathers with dusky streaks and some cross-bars, forehead and forecrown darker than rest of upperparts; scapulars with whitish outer webs, forming whitish row across shoulder. Flight feathers barred lighter and darker brown; tail feathers brownish above with darker mottling, outer ones with some indistinct bars. Underparts pale ochraceous to brownish-white with dark brown streaks and suffused cross-bars. Tarsi feathered brownish-white, also most of toes, leaving only very tips bare. Claws powerful and curved. *Other morphs:* Rufous or grey coloration replaces the brown. **Juvenile** Downy chick white. Mesoptile pale brownish- or greyish-white, densely barred with diffuse brown, grey or reddish. **Bare parts** Eyes blackish-brown, rimmed by pale flesh-coloured edges of bluish-grey eyelids. Cere yellowish-horn. Bill pale yellowish to ivory-coloured. Toes grey. Claws light horn with dark greyish-brown tips. Juvenile has prominently pink-rimmed eyes with opaque pupil, and cere, eyelids and toes pale flesh-coloured.

MEASUREMENTS AND WEIGHT Total length 36-46cm. Wing 255-343mm; tail 148-210mm. Weight of males 385-475g (median 440g), of females 480-660g (median 553g). Females normally larger and heavier than males.

GEOGRAPHICAL VARIATION Because of considerable polymorphy, the geographical subspecies are difficult to tell apart; taxonomic status of several forms is uncertain. Here we treat 11 subspecies, some of which may be specifically distinct.

S. a. aluco Linnaeus, 1758. N and C Europe from Scandinavia to the Mediterranean and Black Sea, east to W Russia. See Description. Wing of males 268-286mm (median 275mm), of females 268-298mm (median 286mm).

S. a. mauretanica (Witherby, 1905). NW Africa from Morocco to Tunisia and Mauritania. Wing 273-296mm.

S. a. sylvatica Shaw, 1809. Britain, W Europe south to Iberian Peninsula. More boldly patterned than nominate race. Wing 248-278mm. (We include the form clanceyi in this race.)

S. a. siberiae Dementiev, 1933. C Russia, from west of Ural to Irtysh. Larger and paler than nominate. Wing 280-311mm.

S. a. sanctinicolai (Zarudny, 1905). Iran, NE Iraq. Pale desert form. Wing 255-285mm.

S. a. wilkonskii (Menzbier, 1896). Asia Minor and Palestine to N Iran and Caucasus. Has a coffee-brown morph. Wing 255-285mm. (We include the form obscurata in this race).

S. a. harmsi (Zarudny, 1911). Turkestan. Wing 300-332mm.

S. (a.) bidulphi (Scully, 1881). NW India, Pakistan. Grey morph predominates. Wing 285-343mm.

S. (a.) nivicola (Blyth, 1845). Himalayas from Nepal to Assam, and from N Burma to Thailand and SE China. A mountain form. Underparts more barred

than streaked. Wing 282-322mm. (We include the form obrieni in this race).

S. (a.) yamadae Yamashina, 1836. Taiwan. Wing 280mm.

S. (a.) ma (Clark, 1907). Korea and NE China. Wing 272-299mm.

HABITS Generally nocturnal, but sometimes active during daylight when young have to be fed. Flies agilely among trees with relatively quick wingbeats, but also glides on extended wings over open spaces, or hovers. Roosts by day among dense foliage, on a branch close to the trunk, in a natural hole in a tree or rock, in hole or crevice of wall, in attic of larger building, in barn or shed, inside church tower, sometimes in chimney of house. Vocally very active; song heard particularly in autumn, winter and early spring on clear (often moonlit) calm nights, when male claims territory; like other owls, shows little tendency to sing in windy weather. Can be very aggressive near nest, or when young have fledged; even human intruders are attacked in diving flight and may be injured, especially by the female. May be stimulated to sing or to approach by playback of its song, sometimes attacking apparent potential rival!

FOOD Takes a wide variety of mammals, birds, frogs, reptiles and even fish; larger insects, earthworms, snails etc also form part of its diet. Largest mammal prey are rats, squirrels and hamsters; largest birds pigeons, smaller owls, coots *Fulica* and crows. Much more of a generalist than Great Grey and Ural Owls, former being a specialist on small rodents (especially voles), while Ural is less specialised on rodents and also preys on much larger animals (e.g. hares, Black Grouse *Tetrao tetrix*). Small prey (e.g. mice) are swallowed whole, others torn into pieces; birds are plucked before being consumed. Indigestible items, such as hair, feathers, bones and chitin, are regurgitated in large pellets (about 25.3 x 21.0mm to 45 x 21mm). Normally hunts from a perch, but also flushes roosting birds in the dark and snatches them on the wing; catches larger insects and bats in flight.

BREEDING Monogamous, and territorial all year round. Young birds select territories and look for partners in autumn, and can be very vocal on calm nights; males normally begin to sing in late winter. Natural holes in trees, Black Woodpecker *Dryocopus martius* holes, nestboxes, holes in steep river banks, crevices and caves in cliffs, holes in walls of buildings, etc are used as nesting sites, as well as attics, church towers, barns and outhouses, stick nests of larger birds (e.g. crows, buzzards *Buteo*), burrows of larger mammals (e.g. fox or badger), and shallow depressions on the ground at base of a tree or under a bush. The male advertises various potential sites to his mate by singing from the entrance, slipping inside, and so on, the female finally choosing one. Once selected, a nesting site is often used for many years. Female scratches out a shallow hollow at the base of the nest, and sometimes tears pellets into pieces as a cushion for the eggs.

Laying normally begins in March, sometimes as early as February. One clutch per year. Lays 3-5 (2-9) pure white eggs (average 47.6 x 39.2mm, weight about 40g) at intervals of 2-3 days. The female incubates alone, starting with the first egg, for 28-29 days; she is fed by her mate, who brings food to the nest. Eggs hatch at about the same intervals as laying. The female broods the chicks and feeds them morsels of prey until about 2 weeks, at which time they swallow mice whole; she continues to give food to the young until they fledge, after which the male also feeds them. Young leave the nest at an age of 29-35 days; they often land on the forest floor, from where they flutter and climb into bushes, trying to reach higher parts of trees (if found on the ground, they should not be removed: they are not abandoned and will soon reach a secure spot to await their food-bearing parents). At about 7 weeks they fly well and accompany their parents. When about 3 months old, young become independent and begin to disperse. Sexual maturity is reached within 1 year.

Tawny Owls may live to 18-19 years in the wild, and in captivity up to 27 years or perhaps more.

STATUS AND CONSERVATION In C Europe a rather common species. Nestboxes, although accepted frequently, are not necessary from the point of view of conservation. On the contrary, Tawny Owls are powerful predators on smaller species of owl, and it would be unwise to increase their population artificially. Locally, smaller species, including Common Scops, Eurasian Pygmy, Little and Tengmalm's Owls [37, 143, 176, 178], have suffered severe predation by Tawny Owls, especially when populations of the latter have been high. Indeed, Tawny Owl was one of the most important factors (besides logging) in the extinction after the Second World War of the Eurasian Pygmy Owl in the Black Forest, where this species had been successfully reintroduced in the late 1960s following a reduction in the Tawny population caused by natural factors (including forest regeneration). Nevertheless, Tawny Owl may be threatened locally by pesticides, traffic and electrocution from power lines.

REMARKS A well-known species, but some questions relating to its life are still awaiting solution.

REFERENCES Baker (1934), Beven (1982), Bezzel (1985), Boyer & Hume (1991), Burton (1992), Conrad (1977), Cramp (1985), Dementiev & Gladkov (1951), Eck & Busse (1973), Glutz & Bauer (1980), Hölzinger (1987), Hosking & Newberry (1945), Klaas (1981), König (1967, 1969), König et al. (1994), Meeus (1981), Mikkola (1983), Rockenbauch (1978), Saurola (1997), Steinbach (1980), Stresemann (1940), Vaurie (1965), Voous (1988), Wendland (1972, 1980).

---

131 HUME'S OWL
Strix butleri   Plate 41

French: Chouette de Butler
German: Fahlkauz

IDENTIFICATION A rather small to medium-sized owl (30-33cm) with rounded head without ear-tufts and orange-yellow eyes. Underparts creamy-white with pale ochraceous-buffy spots and bars. Tarsi feathered, toes bare. Perches more at an angle than upright. **Similar species** Tawny Owl [130] is larger and much darker, always has dark brown to blackish eyes and partly feathered toes, and typically perches upright. The Middle East race *lilith* of Little Owl [176] is also very pale, but much smaller, and has lemon-yellow to sulphur-yellow eyes and a 'flat' facial disc, white-spotted upperparts and streaked underparts, and toes bristled. Pharaoh Eagle Owl [97] is much larger, with prominent ear-tufts.

VOCALISATIONS The song of the male is a clear, rhythmic hooting, higher-pitched than Tawny's, consisting of a drawn-out hoot followed after a short pause by two staccato disyllabic notes with a very short pause between them: *whooh wúhu-wúhu*. This phrase is repeated at intervals of several seconds. The rest of the vocabulary needs study. A sequence (about 2-3 seconds' duration) of booming *bu* notes, increasing in volume and somewhat accelerating towards the end, has been described as agitated response to playback or to a rival singing nearby.

DISTRIBUTION Middle East from S Israel, Lebanon, Syria and Jordan to Arabian Peninsula and NE Egypt; possibly also S Iran and coastal areas of Baluchistan (Pakistan).

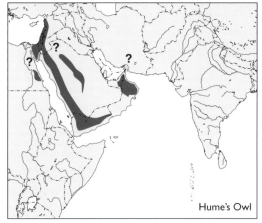

Hume's Owl

MOVEMENTS Resident.

HABITAT Gorges and ravines in rocky deserts and semi-deserts, arid, rocky mountains with springs or slow-draining rain pools, and palm groves in oases.

DESCRIPTION Adult Feathers of a fine silky texture. Facial disc nearly circular, pale buffy-grey with thin dusky rim. Crown and nape spotted brown and dusky, sometimes with pale longitudinal lines crossing forehead and crown. Upperparts greyish-ochraceous or sand-coloured, with dusky streaks and fine vermiculations on mantle and back; scapulars with dusky shaft-streaks and whitish outer webs, forming whitish row across shoulder. Flight and tail feathers barred lighter and darker (wings narrower and relatively longer and tail shorter than on Tawny Owl). Underparts creamy-white to pale ochraceous, shading gradually into white on belly and abdomen; breast and flanks barred and spotted with orange-buff, shaft-streaks being inconspicuously darker. Tarsi feathered whitish-cream to base of toes; latter bare, or only sparsely feathered at base, but with fine silky-feathered covering on underside (adaptation to perching on hot desert substrate?). Talons much weaker than Tawny's. **Juvenile** Downy chick white. Mesoptile similar to very pale Tawny Owl, but with yellowish eyes. **Bare parts** Eyes yellowish-orange to sandy-yellow, rimmed by dusky edge of eyelids. Cere pale ochraceous. Bill yellowish-horn, sometimes with pale greenish tint. Toes yellowish-grey. Claws light horn, shading into dark brown towards tips.

MEASUREMENTS AND WEIGHT Total length 30-33cm. Wing 243-256mm; tail of males 134-140mm, of females about 150mm. Weight 214-220g. Females larger and heavier than males.

GEOGRAPHICAL VARIATION Monotypic: *Strix butleri* (Hume, 1878).

HABITS A nocturnal bird, becoming active at dusk. During daytime it roosts in holes or caves in rocky landscapes. Habits poorly studied.

FOOD Small mammals (e.g. rock gerbils), small birds, reptiles (e.g. lizards and geckos), grasshoppers and other insects, scorpions and other arthropods. Hunts mainly from a perch, but sometimes hawks insects in the air. Often hunts small animals crossing roads at night, and may then sometimes be killed by cars.

BREEDING Singing most often heard in February and March. Cavities, crevices, holes and caves in steep slopes of rocky ravines or gorges in arid mountains are favourite breeding sites. No nest is built; lays up to 5 white eggs directly on to base of nest site. Normally the female alone incubates, but in one case the male clearly shared this duty; incubation period about 35 days. Young leave the nesting site on fledging, when about 37 days old.

STATUS AND CONSERVATION Uncertain, but locally (e.g. in S Israel) less rare than supposed according to number found killed on roads. In its desert habitat has to compete for food with at least four other species of owl, the larger of which also prey to it: Barn Owl [1], Pharaoh Eagle Owl and Little Owl, and in northern areas of its range Tawny Owl. Among threat factors, accidents on roads seem to be rather important. Nothing is known of the effects of pesticides used in oases.

REMARKS This owl is in need of further study of its ecology (e.g. competition for food with other owls and diurnal raptors), biology and behaviour. In addition, its relationship with other owls of genus *Strix* is not yet fully clarified.

REFERENCES Aronson (1980), Boyer & Hume (1991), Burton (1992), Cramp (1985), Fry *et al.* (1985), Gallagher & Rogers (1980), Goodman & Sabry (1984), Hüe & Etchécopar (1970), Jennings (1977, 1983), Leshem (1979, 1981), Mendelssohn *et al.* (1975), Mikkola (1983), Shirihai (1996), Silsby (1980), Voous (1988).

---

132 BROWN WOOD OWL
Strix leptogrammica   Plate 42

French: Chouette leptogramme
German: Malaienkauz

IDENTIFICATION A medium-sized to rather large owl (34-45cm) without ear-tufts and with much rufous in plumage. Facial disc very rufous or maroon, with black around eyes and at base of bill, eyebrows rufous or fulvous, throat and chest immaculate rufous or chestnut-red. Crown mainly dark brown, nape and collar uniform rufous, mantle and back vivid chestnut-red with broad blackish-brown bars; wings and tail barred reddish-brown and buff; underparts reddish-buff with browner bars. Tarsus feathered, toes feathered at base; eyes dark brown. Lowland species. **Similar species** Bartels' Wood Owl [133] has facial disc more ochraceous-tawny, lacks prominent rufous on throat and chest, lacks chestnut or maroon

collar, has upperparts uniform sepia-brown or yellowish-brown and unbarred, and has toes fully feathered; is also a submontane and montane species, never occurring at sea-level or in lowland forest, and has a fundamentally different voice. Himalayan Wood Owl [134] is larger, and differs vocally.

VOCALISATIONS A series of three or four rather short hoots, *hoo-ho-hooh*, the final hoot longer and somewhat stressed, or *oot-oot-tu-whoo*, is probably the song of the male. The opening notes are normally very faint and audible only at close range. A mellow, musical, hollow-sounding *tok....tu-hoo* is also recorded, the initial *tok* (sometimes doubled) a low undertone and audible only at close range. Also emits a variety of weird, eerie shrieks and chuckles, as well as bill-snapping. In addition, utters various other notes when agitated or excited, especially when its young are approached (e.g. by a troop of macaques), flapping its wings violently against foliage and threatening with bill-snapping, growls, hoarse hoots, *huh huh huh*, and a short barking *wow wow wow*. Begging-call of young a hoarse, wheeze, quivering at end, *eeeerrrr*.

DISTRIBUTION S India, Sri Lanka, S Burma, peninsular Thailand, Malay Peninsula, Sumatra, Belitung and islands off W Sumatra (Nias, etc), and Borneo. Absent Java and Bali.

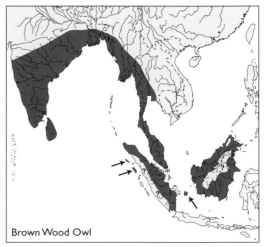

Brown Wood Owl

MOVEMENTS Sedentary.

HABITAT Strictly a forest species, frequenting heavy tropical forest along the sea-coast, in lowlands and in lower hills; lowland primary forest in Sunda region. Occurs from sea-level to about 500m.

DESCRIPTION *S. l. leptogrammica* **Adult** Facial disc dark fulvous, chestnut or maroon-brown, with black feathers around eyes and distinct rufous or fulvous (not whitish) eyebrows; short, black, bristle-like pre-ocular feathers. Crown dark chocolate-brown; pronounced maroon-coloured collar; mantle and back chestnut-red, broadly barred with dark brown to blackish. Primaries barred chestnut and black; secondaries and wing-coverts fulvous, barred with tawny-ochre and rufous; tail similarly barred and tipped with white. Throat and chest immaculate rufous or chestnut-red; rest of underparts reddish-buff with browner bars. Tarsi feathered; toes feathered at base, the distal two (or sometimes more) phalanges bare. **Juvenile**

Natal down pale rufous-buff, gradually assuming barring of juvenile plumage. Juvenile has facial disc buff, bordered with small dark brown or black line, feather around eyes black, pre-ocular bristles short and black; crown to mantle very pale rufous or ochraceous-buff, faintly barred with russet (markings on forehead, crown and nape rather inconspicuous); wings reddish-buff with dark rufous bands; tail cream-coloured, banded with dark rufous and tipped white; underparts very pale ochraceous-buff with faint rufous bars. **Bare parts** Iris dark brown. Cere plumbeous. Bill greenish-horn, bluish near base. Toes pale leaden. Claws dusky plumbeous.

MEASUREMENTS AND WEIGHT Total length 34-45cm, females larger than males. Wing 291-400mm; tail 151-229mm. Weight: c. 800-1,100g.

GEOGRAPHICAL VARIATION Five subspecies recognised.

S. l. leptogrammica Temminck, 1831. Sumatra, Banyak, Belitung, Sarawak, and S and C Borneo. See Description. (We include the taxa *chaseni*, *myrtha* and *nyctiphasma* as synonyms.)

S. l. vaga Mayr, 1938. N Borneo: Benkoker and Sandakan. Averages larger than nominate. Entire coloration duller, more greyish-brown, less rufous; light bars on upperparts less well defined, narrower, pale brown (not tawny). Wing 297-339mm. (The form *rileyi* is a synonym.)

S. l. niasensis (Salvadori, 1887). Nias Island, off W Sumatra. A small race. Throat and upper chest vivid chestnut/maroon-coloured. Wing 270-285mm; tail 151-157mm.

S. l. maingayi (Hume, 1878). S Burma, peninsular Thailand and Malay Peninsula. Deeper- and richer-coloured: facial disc rich rufous; collar almost black; upperparts very rich and dark, crown and nape darker than back; underparts dark fulvous, white throat patch conspicuous, breast much suffused with chocolate-brown (sometimes appearing almost wholly chocolate-brown). Wing 328-373mm.

S. l. indranee (Sykes, 1832). C and S India in Western and Eastern Ghats (Malabar, Nilgiris), and Sri Lanka. Wing 291-400mm; tail 170-229mm. (Doubtfully distinct from *maingayi*. The form *ochrogenys* is treated as a synonym of *indranee*.)

HABITS Strictly nocturnal. Spends the day perched in a dark, densely foliaged, often rather lofty tree. If intruded upon, seeks to elude observation by compressing itself into shape resembling a stub of wood, while watching the intruder through half-closed eyes; if this ruse fails, it flies off silently, threading its way skilfully between trunks. Particularly vocal on moonlit nights, and rather noisy during the breeding season.

FOOD Small mammals, such as rats, mice and shrews, and small birds and reptiles.

BREEDING Season in S India January-March; on Nias, a half-grown young collected in first half of January; on Belitung, a nestling with downy feathers, but quills half grown, on 15 June. Nest a few feathers placed in a tree hole or the hollow of a forked trunk; reports of nesting very rarely on shelf of cliff face require confirmation. Normally 2 eggs, 49.9 x 44.1 (India).

STATUS AND CONSERVATION Rather rare, but locally not uncommon at times (e.g. Sri Lanka); rather elusive.

REMARKS The 'original' *Strix leptogrammica*, extending from W Himalayas east to SE China and Taiwan, and south to Greater Sundas, including Java (thus incorporating both *bartelsi* and *newarensis*), is considered to be a species complex rather than a single species. See present treatment.

REFERENCES Ali & Ripley (1969), Baker (1927, 1934), Boyer & Hume (1991), Burton (1992), Eck & Busse (1973), MacKinnon & Phillipps (1995), Voous (1988).

133 BARTELS' WOOD OWL
Strix bartelsi   Plate 42

French: Chouette de Barthels
German: Bartelskauz

IDENTIFICATION A medium-sized owl (39-43cm) without ear-tufts, and with fulvous-tawny (not rufous or maroon) facial disc bordered with black. Prominent black feathers around eyes, whitish to fulvous eyebrows (sometimes extending above the eyes as superciliary streak?). Crown and nape dark sepia-brown; collar, if present, yellowish-buff (not pronounced). Upperparts dark sepia-brown, sometimes with rather unobtrusive light yellowish-buff markings; below, throat buff, chest fawn-coloured or rufous with darker bars, breast and belly rufous with fine dark rufous bars. Tarsus feathered, toes almost fully feathered; eyes dark brown. **Similar species** Similar-sized Brown Wood Owl [132] is far more rufous and chestnut-brown and with dark rufous or maroon facial disc; moreover, has very distinct maroon-coloured throat and collar (lacking on Bartels'), vivid rufous-brown or chestnut mantle and back very clearly and broadly barred dark brown or blackish-brown (Bartels' is uniform sepia-brown above), and at least the two distal phalanges of toes bare (toes feathered nearly to tip on Bartels').

VOCALISATIONS An single drawn-out *hoo*, far-carrying and audible to at least several hundred metres, perhaps farther, is uttered at long intervals, never as a 'flurry' of calls. The call is extremely explosive and sudden, at close range having a very eerie and almost terrifying effect. It is also so powerful that it fades away gradually (this also obvious from sonograms); in narrow mountain valleys or glens, it produces an echo effect. In the Sundalands of W Java, the sound is associated with the mysterious 'ahul', a supposed bird-apeman.

DISTRIBUTION W Java, where it occurs in some well-known localities such as Mt Halimun, Mt Pangrango/Gede, Mt Salak, and Mt Ciremai on the border of W and C Java. No records from C and E Java. Also apparently known from Sumatra, and possibly Borneo (see Remarks).

MOVEMENTS Resident.

HABITAT Undisturbed mountain forest and edges, from 1,000m to 2,000m.

DESCRIPTION Adult Facial disc tawny-rufous or ferruginous, above eyes (eyebrows) more whitish-fulvous; around eyes a rather broad blackish ring of feathers, which extends upward to side of crown; bristle-like pre-ocular feathers relatively long, black with white tips. Crown very dark sepia-brown, nearly black; collar, if present, yellowish-buff. Mantle and back sepia-brown, virtually unmarked and lighter in colour than crown; scapulars lighter than remiges, more yellowish-buff with dark bands. Primaries and secondaries barred rufous-buff and dark brown, usually with buff edges and tips; uppertail rufous with about seven broad dark brown bars, bars less conspicuous on undertail. Chin and throat buff (yellowish-brown); chest and upper breast fawn-coloured (tawny-russet) suffused with rufous, and barred with dark rufous; lower breast and belly light rufous, with fine dark rufous bars (plumage of abdomen very soft). Tarsus and toes (nearly to tips) feathered rufous-hazel with fine dark rufous barring; toe feathering terminates in two horny scales at distal end of last phalanx before claw. **Juvenile** Not described, but a sight record suggests rufous down with fine dark rufous barring. **Bare parts** Iris dark brown. Bill bright bluish-plumbeous, becoming lighter towards tip, tip horn-white or yellowish. Non-feathered parts of toes bright plumbeous; soles whitish-flesh or dark grey. Claws horn-brown or dusty blackish-grey.

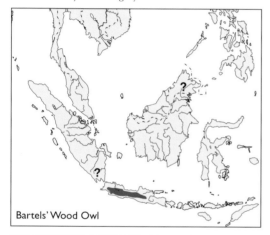

Bartels' Wood Owl

MEASUREMENTS AND WEIGHT Total length 39-43cm, females larger than males. Wing 335-380mm; tail 191-215mm; middle toe 35-37mm. Weight 1,000-1,300g.

GEOGRAPHICAL VARIATION Monotypic: *Strix bartelsi* (Finsch, 1906).

HABITS Very little known. Often found in pairs. Usually keeps to dense, undisturbed montane forest, and more rarely forest edges. Its presence is often betrayed by the mobbing behaviour of Ashy Drongos *Dicrurus leucophaeus*.

FOOD Mainly large insects such as large Coleoptera, but also small mammals such as rodents; a fruit-eating bat *Cynopterus* has been recorded among stomach contents.

BREEDING Nothing known, but probably nests in hollow trees. Probably pairs for life.

STATUS AND CONSERVATION Rare, and even then heard more often than seen. Occurs only in a rather restricted area in W Java, where severely threatened by clearance of mountain forest in its main localities. Studies of its ecology and biology are urgently needed.

REMARKS Among the three syntypes of *Strix leptogrammica myrtha* described by Bonaparte (1850), one of the series (all labelled 'Sumatra') is from another locality as it is from another collector (!); this specimen is considerably

larger and has other features (e.g. uniform mantle without barring, feathered toes) consistent with *Strix bartelsi*. Mayr (1938) described under *Strix leptogrammica vaga* (White-head coll., AMNH), among material from N Borneo, immature specimens which appeared considerably larger than the adults and with somewhat different plumage pattern; it may be possible that these are referable to *Strix bartelsi*.

The taxonomic status of the northern forms of the '*Strix leptogrammica*' complex was rather unsatisfactory and needed revision. These constitute a rather coherent and evidently a mutually closely related group of large owls, considerably larger then *S. leptogrammica* and *S. bartelsi*. They have more or less the same plumage pattern as the latter species, although their overall coloration is duller, more greyish-brown and less rufous; they lack cross-barring on the upperside and have more whitish underparts, their abdomen being less suffused with ochraceous or rufous, and they have nearly completely feathered toes. Moreover, like *S. bartelsi*, they are all mountain species. Their voices, however (so far as known and described; tapes not available) are different from those of both *S. bartelsi* and *S. leptogrammica*. It is likely that they represent a separate group, somewhat similar to *S. bartelsi* in plumage (unbarred upperparts, nearly fully feathered toes), but differing vocally and in some other aspects such as breeding biology. For this reason they are treated here as a separate species, *S. newarensis*.

REFERENCES Boyer & Hume (1991), Bonaparte (1850), Eck & Busse (1973), Mayr (1938), MacKinnon & Phillipps (1995), Ripley (1977), Voous (1988).

134 HIMALAYAN WOOD OWL
Strix newarensis   Plate 42

French: Chouette des Himalayas
German: Himalaya-Waldkauz

IDENTIFICATION A rather large owl (46-53cm) without ear-tufts, and with whitish or very pale ochraceous facial disc framed with dark brown. Very prominent white supercilium extending well over eyes; black around eyes not so prominent. Rather whitish underparts closely barred with very dark brown. Eyes dark brown; tarsus feathered; toes feathered except for two last horny scales of distal phalanx. **Similar species** Both Brown and Bartels' Wood Owls [132, 133] have a more southerly distribution and are smaller. Confusion with a *Bubo* species is unlikely, as those have ear-tufts and are much darker brown in plumage.

VOCALISATIONS A low double hoot, *tu-whoo*, is the song of the male. A sound somewhat like that of a male domestic pigeon, and loud bill-snapping when annoyed. Series of several deep and eerie hoots, repeated periodically, are recorded from Taiwan.

DISTRIBUTION Throughout the Himalayas from Pakistan (Punjab) to Nepal, Sikkim, N and C Burma (Shan States), N Thailand, Laos, N Vietnam (Annam, Tonkin), SE China in provinces of Anhui, Jiangxi, Zhejiang and Fujian and N Guangxi Zhuang, and islands of Hainan and Taiwan. Occurs between about 1,000m and 2,500m, sometimes as high as 4,000m.

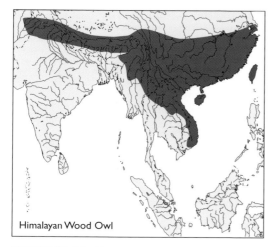

Himalayan Wood Owl

MOVEMENTS Resident.

HABITAT Dense evergreen forest; prefers undisturbed mountain forest. Probably forages in more open areas of forest.

DESCRIPTION *S. n. newarensis* **Adult** Facial disc whitish, very pale ochraceous or very pale fulvous-brown, sometimes with narrow (obsolescent) darker brown bars, and bordered by small row of blackish-brown feathers; central parea of disc, around eyes and near base of bill, black. Shafts of long, bristle-like, pre-ocular feathers black, but lateral parts of these, especially near base, greyish. Broad pure white superciliary band extends from bill base over the eye to as far as its posterior angle, and sometimes even beyond (outside black central ring). Crown to mantle dark sepia-brown without any barring; scapulars, wings and uppertail-coverts much barred with white, giving a rather light-coloured or whitish appearance. Bands on tail feathers contain more white compared with Brown and Bartels' Wood Owls (see above). Chin somewhat mixed with sepia-brown, pure white patch on throat; rest of underparts very pale fulvous or buffy-white, suffused with brown on breast, and closely barred with very dark brown. Tarsus and toes feathered, whitish, finely barred with sepia or fulvous-brown. **Juvenile** Not described. **Bare parts** Iris dark brown. Cere plumbeous. Bill greenish-horn, bluish near base. Toes pale leaden. Claws dusky plumbeous, paler at bases.

MEASUREMENTS AND WEIGHT Total length 46-53cm, females larger than males. Wing 367-442mm; tail 223-262mm. Weight of 1 male 970g.

GEOGRAPHICAL VARIATION Four subspecies recognised.

    S. n. newarensis (Hodgson, 1836). Throughout Himalayas, from Pakistan (Punjab) to Nepal and Sikkim and probably farther east, at 1,000-2,500m, sometimes to 4,000m. See Description. Wing 382-412mm.
    S. n. laotiana Delacour, 1926. S Laos and N Vietnam (Annam). Darker upperside, especially head; more buff below. Wing 377mm.
    S. n. ticehursti Delacour, 1930 (new name for *S. n. orientalis* Delacour & Jabouille, 1930, syn. *S. n. shanensis* Baker, 1935). N Burma (Shan States), N Laos, N Vietnam (Tonkin), SE China (N Guangxi Zhuang,

Jiangxi, Fujian, Zhejiang and Anhui); 1,200-2,000m. Somewhat smaller than nominate. Wing 355-395mm.
    S. n. caligata (Swinhoe, 1863). Hainan and Taiwan. Slightly larger than nominate. Wing 388-401mm. (Possibly a synonym of nominate.)

HABITS Strictly nocturnal; calls more often at dusk than later the night. During day keeps in pairs within heavy forest, this perhaps more to escape mobbing by diurnal birds than to avoid any disabling effects of sunlight. When detected, often mobbed by drongos *Dicrurus*, the loud, raucous noise of which often attracts other bird species. Very shy; easily disturbed at its daytime retreat by the faintest footstep, flying swiftly and noiselessly away from the intruder, threading its way with ease through the maze of tree trunks and branches, and moving ever farther off if followed.

FOOD Small mammals (rats and mice) and large squirrels; birds, not only small ones but species as large as pheasants, junglefowl and, particularly, bamboo-partridges *Bambusicola* and hill-partridges *Arborophila*; also reptiles such as small monitor lizards, etc. Rats, doves and remains of a Jungle Myna *Aethiopsar fuscus* have been identified among stomach contents. Probably hunts more often in open spaces of the forest and streamside openings than in closed forest.

BREEDING Season February-April in Himalayas. Probably pairs for life. More reliable records indicate that its breeding biology differs somewhat from that of Brown and Bartels' Wood Owls. In Himalayas, it was found nesting in caves or cavities of cliffs, and similar regular association with caves or dark caverns for breeding noted also in Taiwan. The nest is a simple hollow scratched out at the foot of a cliff or, less often, in a hollow at the base of a cliff-growing tree. The eggs appear always to be laid on the bare ground, with no pretence at a nest. Eggs normally 2, sometimes only 1, white, very broad subspheroidal: 16 averaged 56.2 x 45.9mm. Incubation 30 days in one case.

STATUS AND CONSERVATION Rare, and rarely seen or encountered. Threatened by deforestation of habitat.

REMARKS We consider *Strix newarensis* a separate species on the basis that its vocalisations are different from those of *S. leptogrammica* and it is a bird of montane habitats. Its biology requires more detailed study, as do its distribution and taxonomy.

REFERENCES Ali & Ripley (1969), Baker (1927, 1934), Eck & Busse (1973), Ripley (1977), Severinghaus & Blackshaw (1980), Voous (1988).

135 AFRICAN WOOD OWL
Strix woodfordii   Plate 43

French: Chouette africaine
German: Afrika-Waldkauz

IDENTIFICATION A medium-sized (about 35cm), round-headed owl without ear-tufts. General coloration warm brown, above with white spots, below barred dusky and rufous on brownish-white. Scapulars with white outer webs. Face brown, eyebrows and lores whitish. Eyes dark brown; bill and bare toes yellowish. **Similar species** Marsh Owl

[212] has tiny ear-tufts and is rather plain brown above, without white spotting, lacks white on scapulars, and has dusky bill and blackish-rimmed dark brown eyes. Eagle owls [e.g. 99-104] are much larger, with prominent ear-tufts. Maned Owl [91] has yellow eyes and mane-like feathers on head. Owlets [e.g. 144, 145, 166-169] are much smaller and have yellow eyes.

VOCALISATIONS The song of the male is a loud, rather explosive, rhythmic sequence of clear hoots, *whúbu-wúbubu-wubú*, this phrase repeated at intervals of several seconds. The female often duets with its mate at a higher pitch, and with the first double note not staccato but somewhat drawn-out and followed by a slightly longer pause: *whuhóoh wúbubu-wubú*. Female also utters a high *wheeow*, often answered by the male with a single or a series of low hoots. Near the nest, both sexes give soft single hoots. Young beg with wheezing *schree* calls; deep snoring sounds are also recorded. As with other owls, adult and young utter bill-snapping in aggressive situations.

DISTRIBUTION Africa south of Sahel Zone from Senegambia to Ethiopia, south to Angola, Botswana, Zimbabwe, Mozambique and South Africa (Transvaal and along the eastern coast to the Cape).

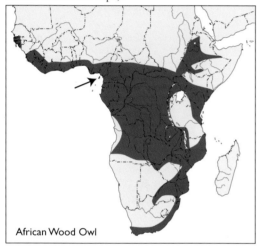
African Wood Owl

MOVEMENTS Resident.

HABITAT Forest, from edge of primary forest to dense woodland; also riverine forest and plantations. From sea-level up to 3,700m.

DESCRIPTION *S. w. woodfordii* **Adult** Some individual variation in general coloration. Facial disc pale buffy-brown with darker concentric lines, shading into a dusky ring around eyes. Rest of head and neck dark brown, spotted white. Mantle, back and uppertail-coverts dusky rufous, individual feathers with narrow white subterminal bars, white shaft-streaks and buff vermiculations; scapulars with white outer webs, forming white row across shoulder. Flight and tail feathers barred light and dark. Underparts russet, densely barred whitish and brown. Tarsi feathered light buff with pale brown bars; toes bare. **Juvenile** Downy chick white with a pink skin; weight at hatching 73g. Mesoptile pale rufous, tipped white above and barred white and brown below. **Bare parts** Eyes dark brown, eyelids and edges around eyes fleshy red. Bill and cere yellowish. Toes yellow-horn. Claws greyish-brown.

MEASUREMENTS AND WEIGHT Total length 30.5-35cm, females larger than males. Wing 223-299mm; tail 112-176mm. Weight of males 242-270g (median 250g), of females 285-350g (median 300g).

GEOGRAPHICAL VARIATION We distinguish four subspecies.

S. w. woodfordii (A. Smith, 1834). S Angola, S Zaire and SW Tanzania to the Cape. See Description. Wing of males 223-269mm, of females 235-264mm; weight of females up to 350g.

S. w. umbrina (Heuglin, 1863). Ethiopia and SE Sudan. Browner than nominate, more clearly barred with white below. Wing 246mm.

S. w. nigricantior (Sharpe, 1897). S Somalia, Kenya, Tanzania, Zanzibar, E Zaire. Generally more blackish than nominate. Wing 234-258mm; weight of 2 males 220g and 240g.

S. w. nuchalis (Sharpe, 1870). Senegambia to S Sudan and Uganda, south to N Angola and N and W Zaire. General colours brighter rufous and chestnut, white markings on upperparts broader; underparts with fine vermiculations and breast clearly barred. Wing 231-273mm; weight of 6 males 253-281g, of 3 females 285-305g.

HABITS Strictly nocturnal, but may fly by day when flushed. During daytime roosts singly or in pairs in dense cover, mostly high in trees; before leaving roost, it stretches frequently. Vocal activity begins at nightfall; often sings from exposed perches, e.g. from top of canopy. Responds to playback and may be stimulated and even attracted by playback of its song; sometimes more than one bird may approach the source of the sound. When the nest or fledged young are approached by humans, the adults feign injury.

FOOD Mostly insects, such as grasshoppers, crickets, cicadas, mantises, moths, caterpillars, beetles, etc, but also takes frogs, reptiles, small birds, small rodents and shrews. Small items are swallowed whole. Most prey is caught from a perch, the owl normally watching its victim intently before swooping down on it; also hawks flying insects in the air and snatches small animals from vegetation in flight.

BREEDING Pair occupies territory throughout the year, and is particularly vocal before start of breeding season. A natural hole in a tree, often where a large branch has broken off, is the normal nesting site; occasionally uses stick nests of larger birds in a tree, or nests on the ground at base of a trunk or beneath a fallen log. Usually lays 2 (1-3) white, rounded eggs (about 42.9 x 37.7mm), at intervals of 2-4 days. Female incubates alone, starting with the first egg, while fed by her mate; incubation period 31 days (per egg). Young hatch at similar intervals to eggs being laid; by 10 days their eyes open, at which stage mesoptile plumage begins to grow through down. Female broods the chicks until they are about 3 weeks old, then leaves them unattended at night in order to help the male bring food to the nest, the pair usually staying close to the nest site. At 23-37 days young leave nest, still unable to fly, and remain in cover nearby, where they are fed by both parents; by 46 days they fly well and accompany their parents. The family remains together until about 4 months after fledging.

STATUS AND CONSERVATION In suitable habitats a rather common bird, although may be endangered locally by forest destruction.

REMARKS This owl was formerly placed in a different genus, *Ciccaba*, along with several other species all distributed in Neotropical America. Since these owls are also doubtless closely related to *Strix*, however, we treat them here under the same genus.

REFERENCES Boyer & Hume (1991), Brosset & Erard (1986), Burton (1992), Fry *et al.* (1988), Harvey (1977), Marchant (1948), Scott (1980), Steyn (1982), Steyn & Scott (1973), Zimmerman *et al.* (1996).

136 MOTTLED OWL
Strix virgata　　　　　　　Plate 43

French: Chouette striée
German: Sprenkelkauz
Spanish: Lechuza (or Buho) café, Lechuza estriada
Portuguese: Coruja-do-mato

IDENTIFICATION A medium-sized (30.5-35.5cm), round-headed owl without ear-tufts. Light and dark morphs exist. Facial disc brown, with white eyebrows and whiskers. Dark brown above, flecked and sparsely barred whitish to pale buff, with whitish row of spots across shoulder; tail with 3-4 narrow whitish bars. Underparts whitish or pale buff, streaked dark brown. Dark morph is generally darker, with buff to ochraceous-buff, coarsely streaked underparts. Eyes dark brown; tarsi feathered, toes bare and grey; bill pale bluish-grey. **Similar species** Spotted, Fulvous and Barred Owls [124-126] are much larger, while Spectacled owls [118-121] are larger and have characteristic plumage pattern. Rusty-barred Owl [139] is rufescent-brown and barred below. Black-and-white Owl [141] has blackish head and mantle separated by a broad dark-barred light collar, and underparts distinctly barred blackish and whitish; bill and toes yellow. Black-banded Owl [142] is overall barred blackish and whitish, the bill is yellow and the eyes are orange-yellow. Crested Owl [92] has long, whitish ear-tufts. Stygian Owl [206] is much larger, with prominent ear-tufts and yellow eyes, and Striped Owl [210] has dark brown eyes in a pale facial disc and prominent ear-tufts.

VOCALISATIONS Rather large repertoire. The territorial song of the male is a series of rather equally spaced, short guttural hoots with explosive character and somewhat frog-like: *gwow gwow gwow gwow gwow gwot*. Such sequences are repeated at intervals of several seconds. In some situations, said to utter rather deep and guttural series of staccato notes accelerating gradually towards end, like sound produced by a table-tennis ball bouncing on a hard surface (similar but higher-pitched notes are given by some screech owls [e.g. 60, 66, 72, 78, 79, 82]). (These series very much resemble in pitch and rhythm the song of Spectacled Owl [118]; as we have never heard a 'bouncing-ball song' from Mottled Owls, we have a suspicion that the recorded vocalisation on which this description is based may have been confused with the song of Spectacled, which is locally sympatric with Mottled.) The female often answers its singing mate with a high whinny, somewhat similar to the B-song of Eastern Screech Owl [61], *wheeahrr*. Series of resonant, fairly soft hoots are also given by both sexes in duet.

DISTRIBUTION From Mexico (Sonora and Nuevo León) south to Central America and forested South America, from Venezuela and Ecuador to NE Argentina (Misiones) and SE Brazil (Rio Grande do Sul). Absent from the Pacific slope of the Andes south of Ecuador. In Misiones, we found it living rather sympatrically with Tropical and Black-capped Screech Owls [68, 78], Rusty-barred and Black-banded Owls and Ferruginous Pygmy Owl [160].

Mottled Owl

MOVEMENTS Resident.

HABITAT Primary and secondary humid forest, drier wooded areas, plantations and even thorny forest, from sea-level to about 2,500m. Most common in humid lowland forest.

DESCRIPTION *S. v. virgata* **Adult** Light and dark morphs occur. *Light morph*: Facial disc brown, with white eyebrows and whiskers. Upperparts dark brown, flecked and sparsely barred whitish to pale buff; outer webs of scapulars white, forming whitish row across shoulder. Flight feathers dark brown, barred whitish or pale grey; tail feathers dark brown above, with 3-4 narrow whitish bars. Underparts whitish to pale buff, mottled dusky at sides of breast; rest of underparts streaked brown. Tarsi feathered, toes bare. *Dark morph*: In general darker, with underparts darker yellowish- or ochraceous-buff and breast sides heavily mottled dark brown; eyebrows and whiskers less prominent. **Juvenile** Downy chick whitish. Mesoptile pale buff to ochraceous-buff, indistinctly barred above; facial disc whitish, bill pale pink. **Bare parts** Eyes pale dark brown. Cere pale bluish-grey. Bill pale bluish-grey to yellowish-grey with slight greenish tinge. Toes grey to yellowish- or brownish-grey. Claws pale horn with darker tips.

MEASUREMENTS AND WEIGHT Total length 30.5-35.5cm. Wing 228-274mm; tail 145-170mm. Weight 176-305g, females heavier than males.

GEOGRAPHICAL VARIATION As with many owls, individual variation is rather large. Of the described races, we accept the six which are treated here.

　　S. v. virgata (Cassin, 1848). Panama east of Canal Zone, Colombia, Ecuador, Venezuela and Trinidad. See Description. Wing 242-249mm.
　　S. v. squamulata (Bonaparte, 1850). Mexico from

341

Sonora and Tamaulipas to Guerrero. Smaller than nominate. Wing about 228-265mm.

S. v. centralis (Griscom, 1929). S Mexico to W Panama. More distinctly barred light above than nominate. Wing 225-243mm.

S. v. macconnellii Chubb, 1916. Guianas. Underparts show tendency towards barring. Wing about 238mm.

S. v. superciliaris (Pelzeln, 1863). Lower Amazon, Brazil. Slightly larger than nominate and more reddish-brown. Wing about 274mm.

S. v. borelliana (Bertoni, 1901). SE Brazil, Paraguay, NE Argentina. Relatively dark; white markings of nominate replaced by pale ochraceous-buff. Wing about 256mm.

HABITS A strictly nocturnal bird which becomes active, and begins to call, at dusk. During daytime it roosts among dense foliage of trees and thickets, within creepers rising up tree trunks, or in natural holes. Little is known of this owl's behaviour. Is easily attracted by playback during courtship period.

FOOD Small mammals (especially mice), reptiles (even snakes), amphibians, and insects and other arthropods; probably also takes small birds, as these mob the owl when detecting it by day. Normally hunts from a perch, but may also hawk insects in the air.

BREEDING Territorial. Male claims territory by singing. Lays February-April in Costa Rica, February-May in Colombia and September-November in NE Argentina (Misiones). A natural hole in a tree normally serves as nesting site, but sometimes uses old nests of larger birds. Generally lays 2 white eggs, incubated by female alone. Breeding biology rather unknown, but probably similar to that of congeners.

STATUS AND CONSERVATION Uncertain, but locally fairly common. May be threatened by forest destruction.

REMARKS This species' ecology, behaviour, vocalisations and breeding biology require study.

REFERENCES Belton (1984), Boyer & Hume (1991), Burton (1992), Eck & Busse (1973), Hardy *et al.* (1989), Haverschmidt (1968), Hilty & Brown (1986), Howell & Webb (1995), König (unpublished), Meyer de Schauensee & Phelps (1978), Narosky & Yzurieta (1987), Sick (1985), Stiles & Skutch (1989), Voous (1988).

---

137 RUFOUS-LEGGED OWL
Strix rufipes   Plate 43

French: Chouette à pieds rouge
German: Rostfußkauz
Spanish: Lechuza bataraz, Concón

IDENTIFICATION A medium-sized (33-38cm), round-headed owl without ear-tufts. Facial disc pale orange-brown to pale ochraceous, mostly with indistinct concentric lines; throat white. Sepia above, distinctly barred light, especially on head, nape and hindneck, back spotted white and buff; underparts heavily marked with neat bars of white, buff and blackish. Eyes dark brown; tarsi and toes feathered orange-brown to cinnamon-buff. **Similar species** Chaco

Owl [138] is much paler, with facial disc off-white with darker, more pronounced rings, no distinct white eyebrows, and tarsi and toes feathered dirty cream-white to pale orange-buff with some dark bars; also differs vocally. Great Horned and Magellan Horned Owls [94, 95] are larger, with yellow eyes and prominent ear-tufts. Striped Owl [210] has a pale face, brown eyes and prominent ear-tufts, and is streaked below. Short-eared Owl [211] has short ear-tufts, is streaked below, and has yellow eyes surrounded by blackish facial area.

VOCALISATIONS The song of the male is a rather guttural, fast series starting with 3-4 grunting notes in rapid succession, followed by a loud sequence of guttural notes with relatively clear quality: *kokoko-kwowkwowkwówkwow kwowkwowkwok*. The female utters a similar but slightly higher-pitched song. Both may be heard duetting during courtship. When excited, may (especially the female) begin the loud guttural sequence with 2-3 explosive yelping notes before continuing with the *kwow* notes: *kokoko-kwaihkwaihkwowkwówkwowkwowkwowk*. Females beg with a high-pitched scream.

DISTRIBUTION C Chile and S Argentina (Patagonia) to Tierra del Fuego, occasionally the Falkland Islands.

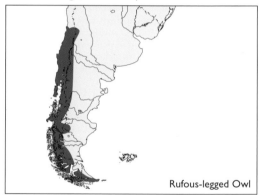

Rufous-legged Owl

MOVEMENTS In general resident, but young birds may wander outside breeding season.

HABITAT Inhabits rather dense and moist lichen- and moss-laden *Nothofagus* forest on mountain slopes or in lowlands, semi-open forest and woodland, sometimes with *Araucaria* stands.

DESCRIPTION *S. r. rufipes* **Adult** General coloration varies individually. Facial disc pale ochraceous to light orange-brown, mostly with indistinct darker concentric lines. Eyebrows and lores prominently whitish-buff. Upperparts sepia-brown, with dense, fine whitish barring on head, crown and hindneck; rest of upperparts more or less barred and spotted whitish and buff; scapulars with spots of white and pale buff, not very prominent. Flight and tail feathers barred light buff and dusky. Throat whitish, often finely barred dusky in upper region; underparts otherwise bright cinnamon-buff, rather densely barred with white and blackish ('tricoloured barring'); underwing-coverts light cinnamon-buff, sparsely barred and blotched dusky. Tarsi and toes feathered cinnamon-buff, mostly plain, sometimes with few dark bars. **Juvenile** Downy chick whitish. Mesoptile warm buff, diffusely barred dusky, with whitish flecks on head and a tawny facial disc. **Bare parts**

Eyes dark brown. Cere and bill pale yellowish-horn. Claws brownish-horn with blackish tips.

MEASUREMENTS AND WEIGHT Total length 33-38cm. Wing 241-290mm; tail 139-182mm. Weight about 350g. Females mostly larger and heavier than males.

GEOGRAPHICAL VARIATION We recognise two subspecies, one perhaps representing only a dark morph.
>*S. r. rufipes* King, 1828. S Argentina and C Chile south to Tierra del Fuego and Falklands. See Description. Wing 250-275mm; tail 150-160mm.
>*S. r. sanborni* Wheeler, 1938. Chiloe Island off C Chile. Smaller then nominate, and eyebrows less prominent. Wing 241-245mm; tail about 140mm. (Perhaps a synonym of the nominate.)

HABITS Poorly known. A nocturnal bird, becoming active at dusk. Roosts by day on a branch, mostly close to a lichen-covered trunk, in dense foliage or in natural hole. Rather elusive and difficult to observe in places where it is not common.

FOOD Diet consists of small rodents and birds, reptiles, and insects and other arthropods. Hunts chiefly from a perch.

BREEDING Little known. One large pullus found in May (Chile). Apparently territorial all year round. A natural cavity in the trunk of a tree is normally used as nesting site; in Chile, eggs found once in old raptor nest in a high tree in rather open country; exceptionally, may possibly nest on the ground (beneath fallen trunk, under bush, etc). Lays 2-3 pure white eggs directly on to the bottom of the nest; 3 Chilean eggs average 42.4 x 31.8mm. Breeding biology unknown, but probably similar to that of other *Strix* owls.

STATUS AND CONSERVATION Uncertain. May be locally less rare than generally supposed, as the bird is rather elusive. May be threatened locally by, above all, forest destruction and the use of pesticides.

REMARKS Although known since 1828, this owl's ecology, behaviour, vocalisations and reproductive biology have been very little studied. It is highly probable, therefore, that the Chaco population, formerly treated as a race of Rufous-legged Owl, really is specifically distinct, as suggested by recent comparative studies of vocalisations, and it is treated as such here. The two taxa (which are not migratory) do not overlap in distribution, but are separated by the SC Andes and the woodless Pampas south of Buenos Aires, so they are allospecies belonging to the same superspecies or species-group.

REFERENCES Araya & Millie (1986), Boyer & Hume (1991), Burton (1992), Eck & Busse (1973), Fjeldså & Krabbe (1990), Hardy *et al.* (1989), Johnson & Goodall (1967), König (unpublished), Mazar Barnett (pers. comm. 1999), Narosky & Yzurieta (1987), Straneck & Vidoz (1995).

138 CHACO OWL
Strix chacoensis   **Plate 43**

French: Chouette du Chaco
German: Chaco-Waldkauz
Spanish: Lechuza chaqueña

IDENTIFICATION A medium-sized owl (about 35cm)

without ear-tufts and with toes feathered on basal half. Much paler than Rufous-legged Owl [137], and buffy coloration reduced or lacking. Facial disc off-white, rather densely marked with dark concentric lines, and without distinct whitish eyebrows; underparts off-white, barred dark brown. Tarsi and toes feathered creamy-white or pale orange-buff, sparsely barred darker. Eyes dark blackish-brown. **Similar species** Rufous-legged Owl [137], found only in Patagonian Argentina, Chile and Tierra del Fuego, always has rufous feathering on tarsi and toes, is shorter-tailed, and also differs vocally. Magellan Horned Owl [95] is larger, and has ear-tufts and yellow eyes. Short-eared Owl [211] is striped below, and has small ear-tufts, a dusky face and yellow eyes. Striped Owl [210] has prominent ear-tufts and brown eyes, and is distinctly marked below with broad shaft-streaks.

VOCALISATIONS The song of the male is a croaking or deep grunting, rather frog-like *crococro craorr-craorr craorr-craorr*, with emphasis on the first *craorr*. The trisyllabic introductory note is very low, while the following two double notes are very loud. When the bird is excited, it may utter additional double notes in sequence after the low introduction. Sometimes only double notes are given at longer intervals. The female has a very similar but slightly higher-pitched song. Both may be heard duetting during courtship or when defending territory. Single *craorr* calls and a harsh, drawn-out shriek may also be given.

DISTRIBUTION Chaco of Argentina and Paraguay, south to Córdoba and Buenos Aires province.

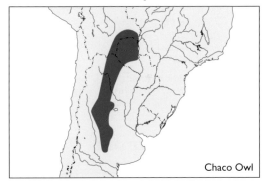
Chaco Owl

MOVEMENTS Resident.

HABITAT Semi-open, rather dry landscapes with thorny shrubs in hilly country, often with giant cacti and small groups of trees. We encountered this owl on a mountain slope covered with thorny shrubs, with giant cacti and some scattered trees (e.g. *Chorisia insignis*), near the town of Salta, Argentina, at about 1,300m above sea-level.

DESCRIPTION Adult Facial disc pale greyish-white with narrow darker concentric lines; rim of disc inconspicuous. Upperparts dark greyish-brown, barred and mottled with whitish and buff, crown and nape rather finely barred light and dark with some pale orange-buffy bars; wing-coverts coarsely blotched with white and pale orange-buff on dark greyish-brown. Flight feathers boldly barred dark greyish-brown and orange-buff; tail dark greyish-brown with few narrow pale buffy bars. Throat white. Foreneck and upper breast rather finely barred dark greyish-brown and greyish-white, bars becoming more bold with wider intervening spaces towards abdomen; lower breast and abdomen suffused with very pale orange-buff. Tarsi and upper half of toes feathered very pale orange-buff or cream-coloured with few darker bars or spots. **Juvenile** Downy chick whitish. Mesoptile very fluffy, pale greyish-brown, often with buffy suffusion; facial disc pale greyish. **Bare parts** Eyes blackish-brown. Bill horn, becoming yellowish at tip. Bare parts of toes greyish-brown. Claws reddish-horn with darker tips.

MEASUREMENTS AND WEIGHT Total length about 35cm. Wing 250-290mm; tail 160-182mm. Weight about 330g.

GEOGRAPHICAL VARIATION Monotypic: *Strix chacoensis* Cherry & Reichensberger, 1925.

HABITS Nocturnal, activity beginning at dusk. During daytime normally roosts in dense bushes or trees, sometimes on the ground, in general well camouflaged.

FOOD Small mammals, birds and other small vertebrates, and insects and other arthropods.

BREEDING Holes in trees are often used for breeding; may sometimes nest on the ground under a bush or a fallen trunk. Lays 2-3 pure white eggs directly on to the bottom of the hole; only the female incubates. Breeding biology similar to that of other *Strix* owls.

STATUS AND CONSERVATION Little known. Locally appears to be not uncommon.

REMARKS The Chaco Owl has been regarded as a subspecies of Rufous-legged Owl, but recent studies have shown the two to be separate species. Their distributions are allopatric, and both are non-migratory; in addition, their territorial songs are very different. We therefore follow Straneck & Vidoz (1995) in treating them as two valid species. Moreover, it would appear that Chaco Owl is more closely related to Rusty-barred Owl that it is to Rufous-legged Owl.

REFERENCES Boyer & Hume (1991), Hardy *et al.* (1989), König (unpublished), Mazar Barnett (pers. comm. 1999), Narosky & Yzurieta (1987), Straneck & Vidoz (1995).

---

139 RUSTY-BARRED OWL
Strix hylophila   Plate 44

Other name: Brazilian Owl

French: Chouette du Brésil
German: Brasilkauz, Rostkauz
Spanish: Lechuza listada
Portuguese: Coruja listrada

IDENTIFICATION A rusty-brown, medium-sized owl (about 35.5cm) with a rounded head without ear-tufts. Facial disc rufescent-brown with rather prominent dusky concentric lines; upperparts rusty-brown, barred pale buff; below, coarsely barred buffy and brown. Eyes dark brown; bill yellowish; tarsi feathered, toes bare and yellowish. **Similar species** Chaco Owl [138] is similarly patterned, but never has rusty-coloured upperparts, its toes are feathered, and it may overlap in range only locally in the eastern Chaco. Mottled Owl [136] is streaked below, while Black-banded Owl [142] is blackish and finely barred whitish all over, with yellowish-orange eyes. Stygian Owl [206] has yellow eyes and prominent ear-tufts, and Striped Owl [210] has brown eyes in a pale face and prominent

ear-tufts. Buff-fronted Owl [181] is smaller, with plain yellowish-cinnamon underparts and yellow eyes. Short-browed Owl [119] is larger, with dark breast band and plain, pale orange-brown underparts. Tawny-browed Owl [120] has a brown breast band broken in the centre, rest of underparts plain pale yellowish-cinnamon, and chestnut eyes.

VOCALISATIONS The song of male and female is similar in its frog-like, deep grunting quality to that of Chaco Owl, but with different rhythm: *crocróh-crocróhcrocro* or *crocrocrocróh-crocróhcrocro*. The first example is slightly higher in pitch than the second; both may often be heard when the birds duet, especially when stimulated by playback, but we are not yet certain which phrase of the song belongs to the male and which to the female. The higher-pitched one is heard more frequently, but normally females have a higher voice than males, in which case females would be more vocal when defending the territory; the other possibility is that females have a lower voice than males, which would be in contrast to all other owls. More study is clearly required. This species also responds to playback of other owl songs. A deep *craorr* is uttered singly. The female gives a guttural, upward-inflected *ooeehrr*, with scratching quality at end. During courtship, low clucking and screeching sounds may also be heard.

DISTRIBUTION E Brazil from Rio de Janeiro and Minas Gerais south to Rio Grande do Sul, E and S Paraguay and northernmost NE Argentina (Misiones).

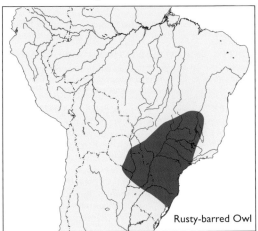
Rusty-barred Owl

MOVEMENTS Resident.

HABITAT Primary and secondary forest, often with dense undergrowth of climbing bamboo, etc, such habitats frequently containing many creepers as well as epiphytic plants; also wooded areas with secondary growth near human settlements. From lowlands up to about 1,000m.

In NE Argentina (Misiones), we observed pairs at about 150m above sea-level near Iguazú, in dense, tangled secondary forest with clearings; at 350m at Parque Provincial Urugua-i, at the edge of remnant primary forest and secondary growth with many creepers and epiphytes; and at 760m on the slope of Cerro Tigre in the Sierra de Misiones, close to the Brazilian border, in a large patch of dense secondary forest with rather impenetrable undergrowth, surrounded by clearings and farmland with several 'ranchos' (nearby secondary forest continued along the slopes, but many clearings created by logging and, especially, by burning were visible). At Iguazú, Tropical and Black-capped Screech Owls [68, 78], Mottled and Black-banded Owls and Ferruginous Pygmy Owl [160] occurred sympatrically with Rusty-barred; at the second locality, we also observed Tropical Screech, Long-tufted Screech [79] and Ferruginous Pygmy; and around the same locality in the Sierra de Misiones, we observed Tropical and Long-tufted Screech, Short-browed Spectacled, Ferruginous Pygmy, Buff-fronted and Stygian Owls.

DESCRIPTION Adult Facial disc rather rounded, rusty-brown with dusky brown concentric lines; rim around disc brown, but not very prominent. Upperparts dark to warm brown, densely barred with rusty-orange; scapulars with buffy and whitish areas on outer webs. Flight and tail feathers barred buff or rusty and brown. Underparts orange-buff, becoming lighter towards belly, coarsely barred brown. Tarsi feathered, toes bare. **Juvenile** Downy chick white. Mesoptile similar to Rufous-legged Owl, but more buffy. **Bare parts** Eyes dark brown. Cere and bill yellowish-horn. Toes yellowish. Claws horn with darker tips.

MEASUREMENTS AND WEIGHT Total length 35.5-36.7cm. Wing about 280mm; tail 173mm. Weight of males 315-340g, of females 345-365g. Females larger and heavier than males.

GEOGRAPHICAL VARIATION Monotypic: *Strix hylophila* Temminck, 1825.

HABITS A nocturnal bird, roosting during day in dense cover of foliage, between creepers, in natural holes in trees or close to the trunk on a branch. Male and female defend the territory and sing in duet to drive away intruders; they respond well to playback not only of their own song, but also of songs of other owl species.

In late October 1991, in Parque Provincial Uruguai, we attracted a pair by playback of the song of a male Long-tufted Screech Owl in a territory of the latter known to us for years. One Rusty-barred approached, at first silently, perched on a branch near us, looked around and finally began to sing; some moments later, another bird with a similar but slightly lower-pitched voice sang nearby; we stopped playback. The first bird then flew to its mate and both duetted from the same branch, facing us; using a torchlight, we could identify the birds easily enough, but it was impossible to tell which was the male and which the female. When we continued playback of the screech owl, both Rusty-barred approached silently in undulating flight and passed close to the loudspeaker, then perched on a nearby branch and started duetting again; we stopped playback, and after some minutes both disappeared. We supposed that these birds were feeding chicks, and so were eager to catch a potential prey. Neither in this nor in following years could we find Long-tufted Screech Owls in this territory, which had been occupied since 1991 by Rusty-barred Owls; apparently, these powerful predators either had driven out the former owners or, and we think more probably, had killed and eaten them.

FOOD Small mammals and birds, reptiles and probably also amphibians, as well as insects and other arthropods, make up the varied diet.

BREEDING In the Sierra de Misiones, we observed a pair during courtship on 28th August 1992; from their behaviour, we estimated that laying might occur between late August and early September in Misiones. Both sexes are vocally very active during breeding season. In general, a natural hole in a tree serves as nesting site; one was about 12m above ground. Lays 2-3 white eggs at intervals of about 2 days, these incubated by the female alone, fed by her mate, for 28-29 days. Young hatch at similar intervals to laying, leaving nest at age of 35 days; at 4 months they are independent. They reach sexual maturity during the next year, when at least 12 months old.

STATUS AND CONSERVATION Uncertain. Locally in suitable habitats not rare, but in general an endangered species, which depends on larger forested areas. In Misiones, it may be considered rare. Logging and burning of forest seem to be the major threats for this fascinating species.

REMARKS As the vocalisations of both Rusty-barred and Chaco Owls are totally different from those of other members of the genus *Strix*, it is possible that the two are not so closely related to the latter as their external appearance would suggest. This owl's ecology, biology and habits need study, in particular in order to develop measures for its conservation.

REFERENCES Boyer & Hume (1991), Burton (1992), Eck & Busse (1973), Hardy *et al.* (1989), König (1994 & unpublished), Narosky & Yzurieta (1987), Sick (1985).

140 RUFOUS-BANDED OWL
Strix albitarsus   Plate 44

French: Chouette striée rouge
German: Rötelkauz
Spanish: Lechuza patiblanca

IDENTIFICATION A medium-sized (30-35cm), round-headed owl without ear-tufts. Facial disc tawny, shading into blackish around eyes, with pale buffy concentric lines and dusky rim. Dark brown above, barred and spotted orange-buff; wings and rather short tail barred blackish and buffy. Upper breast coarsely barred tawny and blackish; rest of underparts buff-tinged off-white, individual feathers with dark shaft-streak and one cross-bar, giving lower breast and belly somewhat chequered appearance. In coloration similar to Rusty-barred Owl [139], but with orange-yellow eyes, whitish toes, and no large white areas on scapulars. **Similar species** White-throated Screech Owl [85] is smaller and much darker (more blackish), with very prominent white throat, and lacks coarse barring below. Black-banded Owl [142] is overall blackish, finely barred white, has orange-yellow eyes, and lives in lowland forest. Mottled Owl [136] has dark brown eyes, and is streaked without cross-bars on lower breast and belly. Band-bellied Owl [121] is larger, dusky above, barred chestnut on whitish below, and has dark brown eyes contrasting with white eyebrows and lores ('spectacles'). Stygian and Striped Owls [206, 210] and the much larger Great Horned Owl [94] have prominent ear-tufts.

VOCALISATIONS The song of the male consists of a rapid sequence of 4-5 short, deep and guttural notes followed after a short pause by an explosive, decidedly higher-pitched, very loud and somewhat drawn-out hoot: *gwogwo-gwogwo gwóoh*. Also utters single gruff hoots.

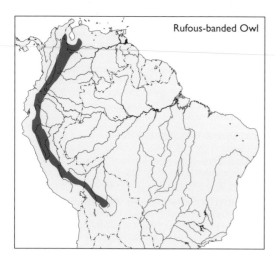

Rufous-banded Owl

DISTRIBUTION Patchily distributed from Venezuela, Colombia and Ecuador to northernmost NW Peru, and from northern Peru on the E Andean slopes south to Bolivia.

MOVEMENTS Resident.

HABITAT Dense montane and cloud forest with thick undergrowth, epiphytes and mosses, from about 1,700m up to about 3,400m above sea-level. Also semi-open areas with scattered groups of trees near the páramo zone.

DESCRIPTION Adult Facial disc tawny, shading into blackish around eyes, with pale buffy concentric lines; rim around disc dusky. Eyebrows and lores buffy-white. Upperparts dark brown, heavily barred and spotted orange-buff. Flight and tail feathers barred blackish and buffy. Breast buffy-white to pale ochraceous, dark brown mottling and indistinct barring on upper breast suggesting indefinite band; rest of underparts whitish, individual feathers divided by dark central streak and one terminal cross-bar, giving chequered or 'ocellated' appearance, as lower breast and belly are covered with large, squarish, silvery-white spots. Tarsi feathered off-white, toes bare. **Juvenile** Downy chick whitish. Mesoptile uniformly buff, with blackish mask and brown eyes. **Bare parts** Eyes orange-yellow; brown in young birds. Cere and bill yellowish-horn. Toes dirty white to creamy-white. Claws pale horn with darker brown tips.

MEASUREMENTS AND WEIGHT Total length 30-35cm. Wing about 274mm. Weight: no data.

GEOGRAPHICAL VARIATION Monotypic: *Strix albitarsus* (Bonaparte, 1850). Because of the relatively large individual variation and the few museum specimens available for comparison, we do not separate the forms *opaca* and *tertia* subspecifically. The latter, from Ecuador, Peru and Bolivia, is generally paler and more buffish above, with paler facial disc.

HABITS Virtually unknown. A strictly nocturnal bird which roosts during daytime in dense cover among branches, epiphytes and dense foliage.

FOOD Rather unknown. Apparently takes small mammals and insects, perhaps also other vertebrates and arthropods. Like many owls, it hunts chiefly from perches.

BREEDING A recently fledged bird was found on 22nd June in Colombia. Probably nests mainly in holes in trees.

STATUS AND CONSERVATION Uncertain. Probably rather rare. Threatened by forest destruction.

REMARKS The biology, ecology, behaviour and taxonomy of this species are very little known and require study; as the owl lives mostly in areas with unstable political situations, however, the necessary research is difficult to carry out.

REFERENCES Boyer & Hume (1991), Burton (1992), Eck & Busse (1973), Fjeldså & Krabbe (1990), Hardy *et al.* (1989), Hilty & Brown (1985), Meyer de Schauensee & Phelps (1978), Ridgely & Gaulin (1980).

141 BLACK-AND-WHITE OWL
Strix nigrolineata   Plate 44

French: Chouette noire et blanche
German: Bindenhalskauz
Spanish: Lechuza blanquinegra

IDENTIFICATION A medium-sized (35-40cm), round-headed owl without ear-tufts. Blackish-brown above, with a prominent hindneck-collar barred whitish and dusky; off-white below, with blackish-brown barring, throat with blackish bib. Bill and bare toes yellow; eyes dark brown. **Similar species** Black-banded Owl [142] is blackish-brown, overall barred whitish, with bill yellow, bare toes pale ochraceous and eyes orange-yellow. Rusty-barred Owl [139] is barred rusty and brown above and below, Rufous-banded Owl [140] being similar to Rusty-barred but with chequered or 'ocellated' lower breast and belly, and both have dark brown eyes. Stygian Owl [206] has prominent ear-tufts and yellow eyes.

VOCALISATIONS The song is a phrase consisting of a rather rapid sequence of low, deep, somewhat guttural notes, gradually increasing in volume, followed after a very short pause by a loud, explosive and higher-pitched *wow* with wailing quality, this sometimes followed by a faint, short *ho*: *wúo-wúo-wúo-wúo-wúo-... -wow* or *wúo-wúo-wúo-wúo-... -wow ho.* These phrases are repeated at intervals of several seconds. The female has a similar but slightly higher-pitched song. A protracted, high-pitched *who-ah* is also described. Young utter an rising, breathy shriek.

DISTRIBUTION From S Mexico through Central America to NW Colombia, NW Venezuela and W Ecuador.

MOVEMENTS Resident.

HABITAT Rain forest with clearings, forest edges, and semi-open, swampy or flooded woodland; also gallery forest and mangrove thickets. Sometimes near human settlements. From sea-level up to about 2,000m.

DESCRIPTION Adult Facial disc blackish; rim and eyebrows densely speckled whitish. Rest of head, crown and nape sooty blackish-brown; prominent collar around hindneck, barred dusky and whitish. Rest of upperparts dark sooty-brown. Primaries darker than secondaries, all barred lighter grey; tail sooty-blackish with 4-6 narrow whitish bars and white terminal band. Throat with blackish bib; rest of underparts whitish, rather densely barred blackish. Tarsi feathered, barred dusky and whitish; toes bare. **Juvenile** Downy chick whitish. Mesoptile overall whitish, above narrowly barred blackish-brown, below creamy-white with dusky barring. **Bare parts** Eyes dark brown; juvenile has dusky oily-bluish eyes. Cere yellowish. Bill orange-yellow. Toes orange-yellow. Claws yellowish-horn.

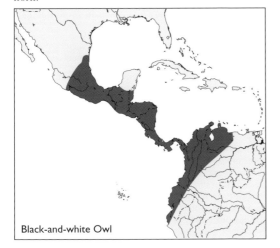

Black-and-white Owl

MEASUREMENTS AND WEIGHT Total length 35-40cm. Wing 225-293mm; tail 165-175mm. Weight 350g.

GEOGRAPHICAL VARIATION Monotypic: *Strix nigrolineata* Sclater, 1859.

HABITS Strictly nocturnal. Solitary or in pairs. During daytime well hidden in dense foliage, among creepers or on a branch close to the trunk, normally considerably high above ground; male and female may be found roosting together. Perches on branches at middle or upper level.

FOOD Primarily insects, especially beetles and orthopterans, but also small mammals (including bats) and other small vertebrates (birds, frogs?). Prey normally caught from a perch, but sometimes hawked in the air or taken on the wing from branches or leaves. Often hunts along forest edge; sometimes attracted to bright lights with swarming insects.

BREEDING Poorly known. Generally lays 2 white eggs in a natural hole in a rotten stump or tree trunk; the female incubates alone, while the male tends to her needs.

STATUS AND CONSERVATION Uncertain. Doubtless threatened by forest destruction and the use of pesticides.

REMARKS Some authors believe this species to be conspecific with Black-banded Owl. The two differ, however, not only in size and plumage pattern, but also in voice, and we therefore treat them as different species.

REFERENCES Boyer & Hume (1991), Burton (1992), Hardy *et al.* (1989), Hilty & Brown (1985), Howell & Webb (1995), Meyer de Schauensee & Phelps (1978), Stiles & Skutch (1989).

142 BLACK-BANDED OWL
Strix huhula   Plate 44

French: Chouette obscure
German: Zebrakauz
Spanish: Lechuza negra
Portuguese: Coruja-preta

IDENTIFICATION A medium-sized (30.5-36cm), sooty-brown to blackish owl densely marked all over with whitish wavy bars. Head rounded, without ear-tufts, facial disc blackish with concentric white lines; blackish bristles around bill. Eyes orange-yellow; bill and bare toes yellowish-horn. **Similar species** Black-and-white Owl [141] is slightly larger, and has dark brown eyes, unbarred blackish crown and back, and a prominent hindneck-collar barred whitish and dusky. Mottled Owl [136] is dark brown above and streaked below, with brown eyes. Rusty-barred Owl [139] is barred rusty and brown above and coarsely barred brown, buffy and creamy below, with dark brown eyes. Stygian Owl [206] has prominent ear-tufts and yellow eyes.

VOCALISATIONS Poorly studied. The song of the male is a phrase of various hoots in typical rhythm, a rather rapid series of 3-4 deep guttural notes, increasing gradually in volume, followed after a pause by a louder, somewhat bouncing, short downslurred hoot, sometimes with a second hoot after a break: *whohohoho whuo* or *whohoho whuo whó*. This is repeated after a while. The female utters a similar but higher-pitched, more wailing song. Also recorded are higher-pitched hoots in a sequence of 2-3 notes: *how-how* or *how-how-how* (female?). Vocalisations of this species from Iquitos, Peru and N Argentina are virtually identical.

DISTRIBUTION South America east of the Andes, from Colombia, Venezuela and Ecuador to the Amazon, south to Bolivia, Paraguay, N Argentina (Misiones and Jujuy) and SE Brazil (Santa Catarina).

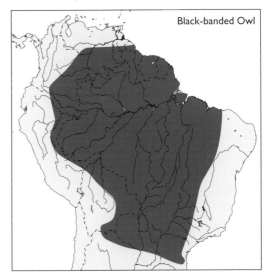

Black-banded Owl

MOVEMENTS Resident.

HABITAT Tropical and subtropical rainforest, forest clearings, and coffee and banana plantations in forested

347

areas. Generally in lowlands, to about 500m, but locally also higher in cloud forests on Andean slopes. Recorded at 1,100m in Calilegua, N Argentina.

DESCRIPTION *S. h. huhula* **Adult** Facial disc blackish, densely marked with whitish concentric lines; rim of disc and eyebrows finely speckled whitish. Bristles around bill blackish. Upperparts sooty-brown to blackish, forehead and crown to lower back with dense, narrow whitish wavy bars; no scapular stripe. Flight feathers sooty-brown with some lighter bars; tail feathers sooty blackish-brown with 4-5 whitish bars and a white terminal band. Chin with blackish spot; rest of underparts distinctly barred blackish and white, the white bars somewhat broader than on upperparts. **Juvenile** Downy chick whitish. Mesoptile browner than adult plumage, heavily barred with whitish. **Bare parts** Eyes orange-yellow; subadult may have brown eyes; young birds have dark eyes with an 'oily' appearance. Cere and bill yellowish-horn to pale orange-yellow. Toes yellowish. Claws light horn with darker tips.

MEASUREMENTS AND WEIGHT Total length 30.5-36cm. Wing 250-261mm; tail about 165mm. Weight of 1 unsexed specimen 397g.

GEOGRAPHICAL VARIATION Like many owls, this species exhibits considerable individual variation. Taking this into account, we recognise only two subspecies.
   S. h. huhula Daudin, 1800. Colombia, the Guianas and N Brazil to the Amazon and Bolivia. See Description. Wing 243-270mm; tail 147-165mm.
   S. h. albomarginata Spix, 1824. E Paraguay, NE Argentina in Misiones, and E Brazil south to Santa Catarina. Generally more blackish than nominate, with clearer white bars. Wing 265-280mm; tail 165-171mm.

HABITS Poorly known. Strictly nocturnal. During daytime roosts in well-concealed site in tree, becoming active at dusk. Just before nightfall on 26th August 1992, we heard a pair duetting near a clearing in dense secondary rain forest near Iguazú (Misiones, Argentina): the songs were delivered from the upper areas of high trees, the male being much more vocal.

FOOD Probably chiefly insects, especially locusts, mantises and beetles; also small mammals and other small vertebrates.

BREEDING Unknown. Probably breeds in natural holes in trees or rotten stumps.

STATUS AND CONSERVATION Uncertain, but probably often overlooked. Threatened by forest destruction, as we witnessed personally in NE Argentina.

REMARKS Black-banded and Black-and-white Owls are sometimes considered conspecific. We do not agree with this arrangement, as the two have different vocalisations and overlap in range in N South America. The different descriptions of vocalisations of Black-banded do not represent geographical 'dialects', but are different calls within this species' relatively large vocabulary. Studies on ecology, behaviour, vocalisations and breeding biology are needed.

REFERENCES Boyer & Hume (1991), Burton (1992), Eck & Busse (1973), Hardy *et al.* (1989), Hilty & Brown (1985), Mazar Barnett (pers. comm. 1999), Meyer de Schauensee & Phelps (1978), Narosky & Yzurieta (1987), Partridge (1956), Sick (1985).

Pygmy Owls, Genus *Glaucidium* Boie, 1826

Very small to tiny owls with rounded head without ear-tufts and with yellow eyes. Talons relatively powerful in some species. When alarmed, adopt upright posture with plumage held close to the body, the feathers of facial rim then suggesting small tufts at sides of forecrown. Facial disc not very distinct, often marked with concentric lines; eyebrows often prominently whitish. Nape of most with large pale-bordered dark patch on each side, suggesting false eyes ('occipital face'). Often partly diurnal and sing from exposed perches; normally not very shy. Many species cock tail and flick it from side to side. 30 species.

Most Asian and some African species lack the 'occipital face' but have barred head and nape, and do not cock and flick tail. These should probably be removed from this genus, as they seem to be more closely related to the genus *Athene*; we consider them to be members of a subgenus, *Taenioglaux*. According to DNA evidence, the American pygmy owls are not closely related to those of the Old World.

143 EURASIAN PYGMY OWL
Glaucidium passerinum   Plate 45

French: Chouette chevechette
German: Sperlingskauz
Spanish: Mochuelo chico

IDENTIFICATION A very small (15-19cm), round-headed owl without ear-tufts. General coloration dark rufescent- to greyish-brown, above spotted whitish, below streaked brown on off-white; breast sides mottled brown. Facial disc indistinct, pale greyish-brown and with fine dusky spots arranged in concentric rings; eyebrows and lores whitish. Nape with two large, blackish spots surrounded by whitish; crown finely spotted whitish. Tail brown to grey-brown with five narrow whitish bars. Tarsi and toes feathered; eyes relatively small, yellow. Often cocks tail and flicks it from side to side. **Similar species** Collared Owlet [163] is similar in size, but barred orange-buff above, more barred than streaked below, with large whitish areas on throat and foreneck, as well as on belly; nape with occipital face; toes bare. Little Owl [176] is larger, more boldly spotted white above, rather densely spotted, mottled and streaked dark on off-white below, with facial disc very narrow and laterally ill-defined, and has occipital face and lemon-yellow eyes; lives in different habitats. Tengmalm's Owl [178] is larger and has a well-defined, rounded to square facial disc, yellow eyes, the tarsi and toes thickly feathered, and nape with occipital face. Common Scops Owl [37] has 'bark-patterned' plumage, small ear-tufts and yellow eyes. Oriental and Japanese Scops Owls [40, 55] have well-developed ear-tufts and are larger. Brown Hawk Owl [188] is much larger, brown above and boldly streaked dark below, with relatively large yellow eyes and bare yellow toes.

VOCALISATIONS The song of the male is a rather long sequence of well-spaced (about 2-second intervals), monotonous, clear fluted notes: *gewh, gewh, gewh,....* When excited, the single notes are followed by a rapid succession of about 3-6 staccato notes, sometimes with trilling character: *gewh-gogogog, gewh-gogogogog,....* The female also has a monotonous, but higher-pitched and 'thinner' song; when excited, it resembles the male's, but with less clear quality and a 'cackling' character. Both sexes also utter a sequence of about 5-7 drawn-out notes, rising gradually on the scale, with a 'false' or broken tone at the end. Particularly before and after breeding season, such 'scale songs' are given singly at dusk or dawn as introduction to normal (monotonous) song; in autumn, only scales are uttered by immatures wandering in search of an unoccupied territory.

Soft, feeble *gew* calls are given by both sexes (females somewhat higher-pitched) as contact. Male often gives single, soft *sewh* notes (instead of song) when bringing food to female; latter emits a very high-pitched, rather piercing *seeht* when begging. Both sexes give short series of accelerating *giu* notes, increasing gradually in volume and pitch when uneasy: *giu, giu giu-giu-giugiugiuk; giu* calls are also given singly.

Male advertises nesting hole by singing from the entrance and uttering a rapid succession of staccato notes, *gygygygygygyg*, alternating between shorter and longer phrases, sometimes with a stuttering character; he also gives such staccato sequences when flying to the perched female for copulation, during which shrill twittering calls are uttered.

Young give very high-pitched calls, often double-noted, with vocal quality of kinglets *Regulus*: *seeh, see-seeht*; when nervous, they utter chirping sounds.

DISTRIBUTION C and N Europe (Norway, Sweden, Finland) eastward to E Siberia, the mouth of the Amur river, and Sakhalin, Manchuria and N China; in C Europe, occurs in mountainous regions such as the Alps, Jura, Black Forest, C and N Germany (locally at lower altitudes), Vosges, Harz Mountains, Bohemian Forest, Tatra, Carpathians, etc, also in N Greece, and perhaps very locally in the Pyrenees.

MOVEMENTS Adults in general resident; in severe winters, some (mainly females) may move to lower altitudes for a short time. Immatures show a rather marked tendency to move about in autumn and winter, occasionally straggling perhaps as far as Britain. On the Baltic Sea coast several individuals have been ringed on migration in spring and autumn, indicating that probably Siberian birds show a greater tendency (in some years irruptive) to move about than those of C Europe, where most adults are territorial all year round. Largest recorded distance from breeding grounds of ringed birds about 300km.

HABITAT Primarily coniferous forest of the boreal zone (taiga) and corresponding montane coniferous and mixed forest in higher mountains, from about 700m in the Black Forest (locally lower) and 900m in the Alps up to the timberline. In mountains of C Germany generally above 200-400m, in northern regions also in lowland taiga with spruce, larch, pine, alder and birch. Prefers semi-open mature forest with some clearings and with more or less natural character. The forest structure seems to be the most important factor for this species' occupation: richly structured habitat with aged trees, clearings, dense groups of young spruce, etc. Nesting sites are often surrounded by moist or swampy terrain with small ponds or creeks with open water and groups of younger spruces nearby.

DESCRIPTION *G. p. passerinum* **Adult** Facial disc indistinctly defined laterally, pale greyish-brown with some darker concentric lines formed by minute dark spots. Eyebrows whitish. Upperparts dusky chocolate- or greyish-brown, crown finely spotted creamy-whitish, back and mantle with small whitish dots near lower edge of individual feathers; nape with two large blackish spots surrounded by whitish, suggesting eyes (occipital face). Flight feathers barred dusky and light; tail feathers brown with about five narrow whitish bars. Throat whitish; rest of underparts off-white, with brown mottling on sides of breast and flanks and brown streaks from throat to belly. Tarsi and toes feathered whitish to brownish-white. **Juvenile** Downy chick white. Mesoptile similar to adult plumage, not so fluffy as most other young owls; crown plain, unspotted, eyebrows and white chin spot very prominent; facial disc rather dark. **Bare parts** Eyes relatively small, yellow, rimmed by blackish edge of eyelids. Cere grey. Bill yellowish-horn. Small unfeathered parts of toes yellowish. Claws dark horn with blackish tips.

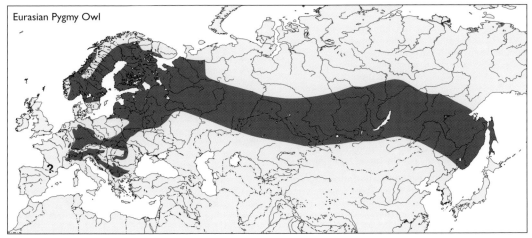

Eurasian Pygmy Owl

MEASUREMENTS AND WEIGHT Total length of males 15.2-17cm, of females 174-190mm. Wing of males 92-102mm, of females 100-112mm; tail 60-69mm. Weight of males 50-65g (average 58g), of females 67-77g (median 73g).

GEOGRAPHICAL VARIATION Rather little variation, except that general coloration may grade from dusky rufescent-brown to more greyish-brown. We distinguish two subspecies.

> **G. p. passerinum** (Linnaeus, 1758). C and N Europe east to Yenisei in Siberia. See Description.
> **G. p. orientale** Taczanowski, 1891. E Siberia, Manchuria, Sakhalin and N China. Greyer generally, and spots clearer white. Wing 94-108mm.

HABITS Most active, including vocally, at dusk and dawn, but also during daytime; normally no activity at night, but unpaired birds may sing frequently on calm, clear or, particularly, moonlit nights as they move around their territories. Roosts singly on branches, mostly well sheltered.

When claiming its territory, male sings from tops of trees, using different perches; unpaired females may also sing from treetops. Males defend territory vigorously; when attracted by playback or imitation, some will even attack humans with diving flights. (Playback should not be used for fun or for 'twitching' purposes, as the owls can become very excited and suffer from stress; moreover, in defending their territory they become less alert to danger, and more exposed to larger predators.) As the owls often sing during daytime, small passerines 'learn' that the treetop song is that of an enemy, so they approach it in fair numbers, mobbing the potential predator. This typical reaction of tits, kinglets, finches and others may be provoked by imitating the male's song, and the passerines' reaction to this, since it is learned and not inherited, may give clues to the owls' presence in certain areas of forest; because the males do not sing frequently all year round, however, passerines 'forget' their enemy's song (within 3-4 weeks) and cease to react. Daytime singing decreases rather abruptly when the female starts laying, and increases again in autumn. Reacting passerines may therefore often be recorded only near the nesting site during the breeding season. Use of this method should therefore be restricted to the period before and after breeding, and for scientific purposes only, not to 'tease' the birds.

Displays a large number of expressive postures. When excited, cocks tail, flicking it from side to side. In anger, raises the feathers of body and head, the latter then appearing relatively large in comparison with the small eyes. When frightened, becomes very slim, displaying an upright posture with feathers held very tight to the body; as the head feathers are rather long, small tufts appear at both sides of the forecrown in this posture.

Moves with woodpecker-like undulating flight over large distances. When aggressive, glides on outstretched wings from perch to perch or attacks with diving flights. In the nesting area it moves at medium height among trees, using mostly dry branches for perching. In hot weather, the birds open the bill and flutter the throat. Fond of bathing, especially the female during breeding season.

FOOD Small mammals, especially voles, mice and shrews, up to the size of semi-adult Water Voles *Arvicola terrestris* and Forest Dormice *Eliomys quercinus*; small birds up to size of Hawfinch *Coccothraustes coccothraustes*, young thrushes *Turdus* and Common Crossbill *Loxia curvirostra*

can form high percentage (locally more than 60%) of diet; reptiles (lizards, small snakes) are taken rarely, as well as some insects. Surplus food is stored at deposits (e.g. holes in trees, on branches, in nestboxes, etc), which are often essential for winter survival; defrosts frozen prey by perching on a branch with prey in one of the talons and held under the body. In winter, single owls will visit feeding stations locally during daytime to catch small birds there. During breeding, food is stored near the nest.

Hunting behaviour similar to that of a Northern Sparrowhawk *Accipiter nisus* or a shrike *Lanius*. Catches ground prey from a perch; watches intently for some time, bowed forward, flicking wings and cocked tail, before swooping on to the potential prey. Small birds often caught in dashing flight from ambush.

BREEDING Monogamous. Male and female sometimes pair for more than one breeding season. In all cases the male is very territorial, and may occupy the same territory for up to about 7 years; subsequently, another male (one of its offspring?) may take over the territory. Pair formation begins in autumn, and following a break in midwinter is resumed towards end of winter and in early spring. Females are less territorial; may leave breeding grounds after having raised young. Territory size varies between about 1 and 2km², depending on topography, food supply and population density, averaging about 1.5km²; in a study area in the Black Forest (SW Germany), the highest density was 4 pairs in 10km². Neighbouring males in territories they have occupied for several years often show little aggression towards each other; they are less vocally active than those with newly occupied territories or in areas of much lower population density.

On calm evenings in late winter or spring (between February and May, depending on climatic conditions), male sings at different places in territory; if already paired, the female soon joins male. Unpaired birds often duet. Once paired, female increasingly replaces singing by *seeht* calls. Male guides female around territory, copulating at different places, often far from future nesting site. The male advertises various sites to its mate, or the previous year's hole is only one visited; eventually, both approach closer to the future nesting site, which male demonstrates by entering, singing from entrance and uttering staccato trills from the entrance or from inside. This is normally a cavity produced by Great Spotted *Picoides major* or Three-toed Woodpecker *P. tridactylus*, sometimes a nestbox; nest holes are most often in coniferous trees, but also in birch and beech, mainly in live trees but also in dead and rotting trunks. The female inspects the hole, and decides whether to accept it; she stays near the chosen hole or visits it at dusk, and is fed in the vicinity by the male, who delivers prey to her bill to bill. Copulation takes place several times every evening and early morning.

Lays mostly 3-7 (sometimes more) white eggs (27.0-31.0 x 21.7-24.0mm, fresh weight 8-9g) directly on to the bottom of the hole, at normally 2-day intervals. Incubation, starting when last egg being laid, is by female alone, leaving briefly every evening or morning to be fed by the male, who calls her when bringing food; incubation lasts 28-29 days. Female often enlarges the cavity, using bill to tear small wood chips from inner wall. Young hatch almost synchronously and are brooded by female until about 9-10 days old, at which age their eyes open. Male brings food, calling female off nest; she takes it back into the hole and feeds the young; later, male more often deposits food near nest, where female collects it. When nestlings are about 3 weeks old, they begin to peer out of the hole; female then roosts near the nest, entering only to feed young or remove waste etc.

The female throws heaps of feathers, hair, eggshells and pieces of wood, excrement, prey remains etc out of the hole, all of which accumulate at base of nest tree; often some feathers or hair are stuck around the hole entrance; when not in nest hole, she prefers roosts near the nest tree, beneath which many droppings and pellets accumulate (a clue that an occupied nest is nearby).

Young leave nest at 30-34 days, whole brood normally over 3-4 days, and are able to fly some distance; once fledged, they do not return to nest, but normally roost quite close to one another, often in body contact and allopreening. They remain near nest for about 3-4 days, and are then led by their parents to other parts of the territory, being located by their high-pitched calls. For about one week female alone feeds fledglings, then male shares duty and finally feeds alone, while the female departs to moult. The male cares for the young for about 4-6 weeks, after which they are independent and begin to disperse. They reach sexual maturity when about 1 year old, and may breed in the following spring at an age of 9-10 months.

In the wild Eurasian Pygmy Owls may live to an age of about 6-7 years, sometimes longer in captivity.

STATUS AND CONSERVATION Locally not rare. In Germany, seems currently to be expanding its range. Locally common in Finland, using artificial nestboxes.

Reintroduced in the Black Forest after the Second World War, but logging operations, coupled with increasing population of Tawny Owls [130] following habitat changes, led to its extinction in 1965-67. Reforestation of clearings, consequently reducing food supply for the larger predator in winters with much snow, led in turn to a decline in Tawny Owls. The opportunity was taken to release captive-bred ringed Eurasian Pygmy Owls in the S Black Forest in 1968-71: as early as 1970 one pair bred successfully, the male having been released in 1968, and other ringed males had occupied territories in the N Black Forest, some breeding successfully. Recent censuses put the Black Forest population at about 200 pairs in 1997. In autumn, single birds (young?) appeared in areas up to about 100km outside the Black Forest; new records and increasing numbers are reported from other mountains in Germany. This is probably a temporary situation due to acid-rain damage, which enables increases in several insect populations which are a basic food for small passerines, which in turn enlarge the diet of these owls; and woodpeckers produce more holes in the damaged trees, providing new nesting sites. This tiny owl therefore actually profits from an ecologically dangerous situation. But damaged trees are less resistant to storms, which are beginning to harm larger areas, and this, in conjunction with increasing forest disease, will doubtless eventually lead to a critical situation for the owls, as changing habitats will again encourage more Tawny Owls to breed, as has already happened locally. The fear is that the situation may return to that which obtained after the war, when the Eurasian Pygmy Owl became extinct in the Black Forest through such factors. Experience shows how important it is to preserve adequate habitats for the conservation of this fascinating little owl, and that the current situation is obviously just a peak before a deep

trough! We hope that measures to prevent this event can be found in time.

REMARKS A rather well-studied owl in C and N Europe, but the species merits intensive study in the eastern parts of its range, too, above all on the ecological hierarchy between this and other birds.

REFERENCES Bezzel (1985), Glutz & Bauer (1980), Hölzinger (1987), Klaus et al. (1982), König (1968, 1969, 1970, 1981), König & Kaiser (1985), König et al. (1995), Mikkola (1983), Möckel (1980), Rudat & Wiesner (1981), Saurola (1997), Scherzinger (1970, 1976, 1981), Voous (1988).

---

144 PEARL-SPOTTED OWLET
Glaucidium perlatum   Plate 45

French: Chevêchette perlée
German: Perl-Sperlingskauz

IDENTIFICATION A very small owl (17-20cm) with rounded head without ear-tufts. Slightly larger and heavier than Eurasian Pygmy Owl [143], and with remarkably powerful talons. General coloration of upperparts brown in different shades, with many rounded whitish spots rimmed by narrow dusky edge, giving 'pearled' appearance; nape with occipital face; outer webs of scapulars whitish, outlined with black, forming whitish row across shoulder. Tail dark brown with several rows of whitish, dusky-edged spots. Underparts off-white, streaked brown, with some brown mottling on sides of upper breast and flanks. Tarsi feathered, but toes only sparsely bristled; eyes pale yellow. **Similar species** African Barred Owlet [167] has no 'pearl-like' spots on upperparts and no occipital face on nape, is barred on crown, forehead and upper breast, and rest of underparts spotted dusky. Red-chested Owlet [145] has sides of chest and flanks strongly suffused with orange-buff, rest of underparts whitish with dusky spots, upperparts dark without white on scapulars, tail blackish with large, rounded white spots; nape with occipital face. African Scops Owl [39] has distinct ear-tufts and well-defined facial disc, yellow eyes, lacks occipital face.

VOCALISATIONS As with most *Glaucidium*, vocabulary rather large. Song of male is a series of somewhat drawn-out, clearly fluted whistles rising gradually in volume and in pitch: *few-few-few-few-few-...*; after a short pause several explosive glissando notes with downward inflection are uttered, *péeooh péeooh....* The female gives a very similar, slightly higher-pitched song and also the glissando notes. Male and female may often be heard duetting. At dusk or dawn, singing of both sexes is mostly initiated by a series of clear, drawn-out notes on a rising scale, similar to Eurasian Pygmy Owl, but with single notes much more protracted and without a 'false' final note: *whooh-wewh-weeh-weeh-weeht.* A short *keeowít* by both sexes apparently has a contact function.

When advertising a nesting site to the female, the male sings from the entrance of the cavity and then withdraws inside, giving a series of 'wailing' notes.

Very high, explosive, somewhat drawn-out, piercing *wheet* whistles probably have an alarm function; we heard them from both sexes when young had fledged and a hawk flew past nearby. The fledglings stopped begging, became motionless, with feathers held close to the body, and adopted a very upright posture.

When soliciting food, female and young utter metallic, high ringing chitter, *chrigigirr*.

DISTRIBUTION Africa south of the Sahara: from Senegambia to Ethiopia and W Somalia and south to N Cape Province and, in the west, north through Namibia to NW Angola; absent from deserts and dense rain forest in W and C Africa.

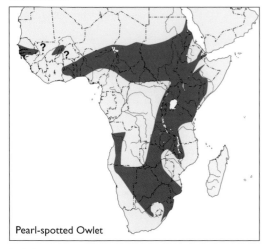
Pearl-spotted Owlet

MOVEMENTS Resident.

HABITAT Open savanna with short grass or little ground cover, scattered trees and thorny shrubs (acacias); avoids landscapes covered with long grass. Also dry, semi-open woodland (e.g. mopane woodland), and semi-open riverine forest with adjacent savanna. Absent from heavy tropical rain forest and montane forest, as well as from treeless deserts.

DESCRIPTION *G. p. perlatum* **Adult** Sexes alike; female in general (but not always) larger and heavier than male. No ear-tufts, but in alarmed posture, when plumage sleeked, small tufts at sides of head may be visible. Facial disc ill-defined, pale greyish-brown with some diffuse concentric lines; eyebrows whitish, rather prominent. Upperparts chestnut-brown, somewhat paler (sometimes nearly sand-coloured) on mantle and back, finely spotted whitish on forehead and crown; nape with two large sooty-brown spots, diffusely bordered whitish (occipital face); mantle with white spots, bordered blackish (suggesting pearls); scapulars with whitish outer webs and narrow dusky edges, forming prominent white row across shoulder. Flight feathers barred light and dark; tail feathers brown, with black-rimmed whitish spots in about 6 rows. Throat whitish; rest of underparts off-white, upper breast and flanks with brownish or rufous wash, sides of upper breast and flanks mottled brown and, as breast and belly, streaked dusky brown. Tarsi feathered off-white with brown spots, toes sparsely bristled. **Juvenile** Downy chick completely covered with white down; skin pinkish. Mesoptile similar to adult (as with all *Glaucidium*, less fluffy than most other owls), but streaking on underparts less clear, crown and mantle unspotted. **Bare parts** Eyes pale yellow; deep yellow in immatures. Cere brown. Bill yellowish-horn. Toes brownish-yellow. Claws horn with darker tips.

MEASUREMENTS AND WEIGHT Total length 17-20cm. Wing of males 100-113mm, of females 107-118mm; tail 77-81mm. Weight of males 68-85g, of females 77-100g (occasionally heavier, according to body condition).

GEOGRAPHICAL VARIATION We distinguish two subspecies, regarding the taxa *diurnum* and *kilimense* as synonyms of *licua*.

> *G. p. perlatum* (Vieillot, 1818). From Senegambia through Mali, Niger and Chad to W Sudan. See Description.
> *G. p. licua* (Lichtenstein, 1842). E Sudan, Ethiopia, Somalia, Uganda, Kenya, Tanzania, south to N South Africa, westwards to Namibia and W Angola. Paler than nominate, with cinnamon-brown head and crown; wing-coverts with less rufous, more sandy-brown; underparts whiter, with thinner dusky streaks. Wing 100-108mm.

HABITS Active mainly at dusk and dawn, but also during daytime and occasionally on moonlit nights. Prefers to sing from exposed perches, often from tops of bushes or trees. When excited, cocks tail and flicks it from side to side in similar fashion to Eurasian Pygmy Owl, but in a more shrike-like manner, with longer jerks. Habits similar to those of other pygmy owls, but more nocturnal than Eurasian, its much larger eyes enabling it to hunt at night, (rather difficult for Eurasian Pygmy Owl, whose sight in dim light is about the same as a human's). Flies longer distances in undulating flight, with rapid wingbeats alternating with gliding, and swoops up to perch.

FOOD Large, powerful talons enable this owl to catch rather big prey and to seize flying insects or bats in the air. Highest percentage of food seems to be arthropods, such as orthopterans, beetles, spiders, millipedes, etc; also takes birds up to the size of larger weavers, and small mammals and reptiles, as well as snails. Recorded diet in Namibia was 65% arthropods, 19% snails, 10% reptiles, 5% small rodents, and 1% other invertebrates. Apparently the most easily caught prey seems to form the highest percentage of food, probably with a certain preference for arthropods; the Namibian findings should not, therefore, be taken as general. According to our own observations in South Africa, many small birds were taken by a pair living in mopane woodland, where such prey were very abundant. Most hunting done from perches.

BREEDING Monogamous. Male and female claim territory by singing in duet, but normally defend only immediate surroundings of the nest site, where they sing regularly (strikingly different from Eurasian Pygmy Owl, which may sing at great distance from the future nesting place). Several singing birds may therefore be heard from the same observation point, and distance between occupied nests may be only 200-500m. Holes made by woodpeckers or barbets in tree trunks and thick branches are used for nesting; these range from 1.20m to about 10m above ground. Male advertises potential site by singing near it and from the hole entrance; when female approaches, he withdraws inside the hole, changing his song to series of wailing notes. Female inspects potential sites and selects one, often occupying the entrance or roosts close to the hole, calling for her mate to feed her. After feeding, copulations are frequent. Courtship may continue for 3-4 weeks before laying. Single-brooded.

Lays 2-4 white eggs (median 31.0 x 25.8mm) directly on to bottom of nest hole, at intervals of 2 days. Incubation, starting before last egg laid, is by female alone, fed by her mate inside the nest hole (not outside as is case with Eurasian Pygmy Owl); when female leaves the nest for brief time, male often slips into the hole to cover eggs; incubation lasts 29 days. Young hatch with closed eyes, these opening at about 13 days, and are fed by both parents by night and day. No nest-cleaning is known to take place (unlike Eurasian Pygmy). Nestlings leave nest permanently when 31 days old, at which age they are able to fly short distances; normally they hide near the nest, where they are fed by both parents. After some days they are led away by parents, and become independent a few weeks later. Young reach sexual maturity in less than 1 year.

STATUS AND CONSERVATION Uncertain. Locally rather common. May be endangered in some areas by bush fires and the use of pesticides.

REMARKS This species has been considered closely related to Eurasian Pygmy Owl, with suggestion that the two form a superspecies. Our studies on vocalisations and behaviour do not suport this; in addition, DNA evidence has shown that the two species are rather well separated.

REFERENCES Boyer & Hume (1991), Eck & Busse (1973), Fry *et al.* (1985), König (unpublished), Scherzinger (1978), Steyn (1979, 1982), Zimmerman *et al.* (1996).

---

145 RED-CHESTED OWLET
Glaucidium tephronotum   Plate 45

French: Chevêchette à pieds jaunes
German: Rotbrust-Sperlingskauz

IDENTIFICATION A very small (17-18cm), round-headed pygmy owl. Above, dark brown or greyish with unspotted forehead and crown, nape with indistinct occipital face, scapulars without white outer webs. Primaries plain dusky greyish-brown, secondaries with some spotting or barring; tail feathers dusky, with 3-4 large, white rounded spots. Underparts off-white, sides of breast and flanks strongly washed with rusty-orange, spotted blackish from neck sides to belly. Eyes yellow; tarsi feathered; toes sparsely bristled, and yellow. **Similar species** African Barred Owlet [167] is barred on upper chest, has barred crown and white scapular line, and lacks occipital face. Pearl-spotted Owlet [144] has crown spotted with white, whitish scapular line, is streaked below, and tail is relatively long with rows of dusky-edged whitish spots. Albertine Owlet [169] has spotted head, barred mantle and unmarked back and uppertail-coverts, with underparts spotted maroon; lacks occipital face. Sjöstedt's Owlet [166] is larger, with rufescent-chestnut back and barred crown and mantle, no occipital face, relatively long tail, and underparts buffy with darker barring. Chestnut-backed Owlet [165] has plain rufous mantle and upperwing-coverts, and often white scapular row. Scops owls of genus *Otus* have distinct ear-tufts and a more cryptic plumage.

VOCALISATIONS Poorly studied. Male utters 2-20 high whistling notes at 2-second intervals, with break of 2-5 seconds between series. Female gives a similar but higher-pitched song in a more rapid sequence (intervals between single notes about 1 second).

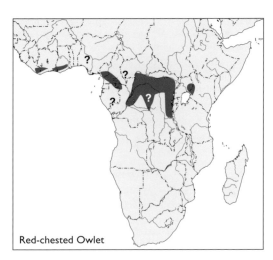

Red-chested Owlet

DISTRIBUTION W Africa from Liberia, Ivory Coast, Ghana, S Cameroon and Congo Basin to Uganda and W Kenya (Mt Elgon, Kakamega, Nandi and Mau Forests).

MOVEMENTS Resident.

HABITAT Primary rain forest and forest-scrub mosaic at up to 2,150m; also forest edges and clearings.

DESCRIPTION *G. t. tephronotum* Adult Facial disc and forehead light grey, flecked white. Upperparts dark grey, with broad white bars on neck and lower nape, grading into dusky brown of mantle, back and rump; nape with indistinct occipital face. Primaries plain dusky brown, secondaries with indistinct barring; tail feathers dusky brown, with 3 incomplete white bars forming rounded spots on inner webs. Throat white; breast whitish with large dark brown spots, sides of breast washed with rufous, shading into extensive rufous on flanks; rest of underparts pale rufous-buff. Tarsi feathered pale plain rufous-buffy; toes sparsely bristled. **Juvenile** Not described. **Bare parts** Eyes yellow. Cere waxy yellow. Bill greenish-yellow. Toes yellow. Claws yellowish with dark tips.

MEASUREMENTS AND WEIGHT Total length 17-18cm. Wing of males 99-113mm, of females 103-127mm; tail 67-87mm. Weight of males 71-95g, of females 75-103g. Females mostly larger and heavier than males.

GEOGRAPHICAL VARIATION Apart from individual variation, the species seems to vary geographically. We recognise four subspecies, one of these perhaps a synonym.
   G. t. tephronotum Sharpe, 1875. Liberia, Ivory Coast, probably Ghana. See Description. Wing 99-109mm.
   G. t. pycrafti Bates, 1911. Cameroon. Dark chocolate-brown above; underparts less rufous than nominate, with black spots. Wing 104-109mm.
   G. t. medje Chapin, 1932. Congo Basin, Zaire, SW Uganda and W Kenya. Slaty above, with less chestnut than nominate; larger. Wing 113-127mm.
   G. t. elgonense Granvik, 1934. Uganda and Kenya at Mt Elgon, Kakamega, Nandi and Mau Forests. Darker and browner above than *pycrafti*, and larger. Wing about 127mm; weight of 9 males 80-95g (median 90g), of 1 female 103g. (Perhaps a synonym of *medje*.)

HABITS Active at dusk and night, but partly diurnal. Roosts during daytime in holes in trees. Sometimes hunts on overcast afternoons. Behaviour practically unknown.

FOOD Insects, above all beetles, mantises, grasshoppers, moths, cockroaches, etc. Also small mammals up to the size of smaller rats and small birds.

BREEDING Unknown. Probably nests in old tree holes of woodpeckers or barbets. A female collected in Ghana in February had just completed laying.

STATUS AND CONSERVATION Uncertain, but apparently rare. Probably threatened by forest destruction.

REMARKS This is one of the owl species whose biology, behaviour, vocalisations, taxonomy and ecology are rather unknown. Studies are urgently needed, as the habitats of this handsome owl are severely threatened.

REFERENCES Boyer & Hume (1991), Eck & Busse (1973), Fry *et al.* (1985), Zimmerman (1972), Zimmerman *et al.* (1996).

---

146 NORTHERN PYGMY OWL
Glaucidium californicum   Plate 46

French: Chevêchette de l'Amérique du Nord
German: Rocky Mountains-Sperlingskauz
Spanish: Mochuelo norteamericano

IDENTIFICATION A very small pygmy owl (17-19cm) with rounded head, relatively long tail and rounded wing-tips. Prominent occipital face. Very similar to Eurasian Pygmy Owl [143], but toes bristled, not feathered; also, cere around nostrils very much swollen, forming rather prominent, broad-coniform 'buckles' (characteristic of the American pygmy owls, being absent or at least less developed in Old World Eurasian Pygmy). Tips of wings rounded. Coloration very variable: grey, brown and red morphs occur. **Similar species** Mountain Pygmy Owl [148] is smaller, with pointed wing-tips, shorter tail (less than 64mm); coloration and markings similar to Northern, and also polymorphic, but underparts less clearly streaked, white on throat, neck and upper breast more extensive; best distinguished by voice. Cape Pygmy Owl [147] is smaller, but more or less indistinguishable from Northern by plumage pattern; tail averages shorter (about 64mm, against 70mm), wing-tips rounded; vocally distinct. Ridgway's Pygmy Owl [161] has forehead and crown streaked, not spotted, tail more densely barred (6-7 light bars) barred light and dark (mostly rufous and brown); previously considered a subspecies of Ferruginous Pygmy Owl [160], which is strictly South American. Tamaulipas and Colima Pygmy Owls [150, 151] are smaller, with much shorter tail, and both have spotted crown. All above-mentioned species have an occipital face, and are best distinguished by vocal patterns. Elf Owl [173] is tiny, with a very short tail, and is finely vermiculated and blotched cinnamon below, lacks occipital face, and has tarsi and toes bristled. Northern Saw-whet Owl [179] is larger, with rounded facial disc and relatively large, yellowish-orange eyes. Screech owls of genus *Otus* have ear-tufts.

VOCALISATIONS The song of the male is a series of equally spaced hoots (intervals about 2 seconds), similar to that of Eurasian Pygmy Owl but lower in pitch and somewhat dropping, with ventriloquial qualty: *gwoo gwoo gwoo gwoo....* The female utters a similar but higher-pitched and less clear song. As with its Eurasian and African counterparts [143, 144], both sexes also utter a sequence of notes on rising scale. Male bringing food to the nest announces his arrival with high whinnying sounds. Female and young beg with chittering calls. The vocabulary needs more study.

DISTRIBUTION W North America, from British Columbia and southernmost Alaska south through the Rocky Mountains to California and Arizona, perhaps also to mountains in northernmost Mexico.

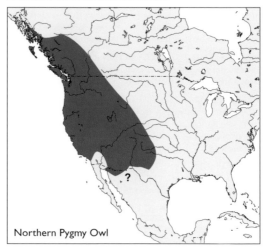

Northern Pygmy Owl

MOVEMENTS Resident. In winter, northern populations may move from higher to lower elevations. Immatures wander.

HABITAT Coniferous and mixed forest with old trees in mountainous regions, but also at lower elevations.

DESCRIPTION *G. c. californicum* **Adult** Sexes alike, but females in general larger and heavier than males. Grey, red and brown morphs, as well as intermediates, are known. *Brown morph*: Facial disc rather 'flat', pale greyish-brown with some darker concentric rings, indistinctly rimmed; eyebrows whitish. Upperparts brown, crown with rather dense, small whitish spots; nape with two large blackish dots surrounded by diffuse whitish zone (occipital face); rest of upperparts with some whitish or pale buffy spots, scapulars with partly whitish outer webs. Flight feathers barred light and dark; tail feathers brown, with about 6 incomplete whitish bars on both webs, hardly reaching central shaft. Throat and foreneck whitish; sides of chest and upper flanks brown with several small white spots, rest of underparts whitish with prominent dark brown streaks. Tarsi feathered off-white, toes sparsely bristled. *Grey morph*: Generally grey, with whitish patterns more pure white. *Red morph*: Rusty-brown; markings as in brown morph. **Juvenile** Downy chick whitish. Mesoptile as in other *Glaucidium*, less fluffy than most owls; crown unspotted. **Bare parts** Eyes bright yellow. Cere greenish-yellow; around nostrils distinctly swollen, shaped like coniform buckles. Bill yellowish-horn. Toes greyish-yellow. Claws greyish-horn with darker tips.

MEASUREMENTS AND WEIGHT Total length 17-19cm. Wing 86-105mm; tail 66-72.5mm. Weight of 1 male from California 52g, normally about 70g; females heavier than males.

GEOGRAPHICAL VARIATION Highly polymorphic, with

three morphs and intermediates, and geographical sub-species therefore very difficult to distinguish. Bearing this in mind, we recognise three subspecies.

G. c. californicum Sclater, 1857. S Alaska to British Columbia, south to California. See Description. (We include the taxon *grinnelli* as a synonym.)

G. c. swarthi Grinnell, 1913. Vancouver Island. Very dark. Wing 86-96.5mm; tail of 1 specimen 66mm.

G. c. pinicola Nelson, 1910. W Montana, Idaho, Utah to E California, Arizona and New Mexico; perhaps also in conifer forest of mountains of northernmost Mexico. Occurs in grey and red morphs. Mantle more spotted than in nominate. Wing 94-105mm; tail 70-78.7mm.

HABITS Little studied. At least partly diurnal. When seen by day, mostly mobbed by small passerines. Imitation or playback of song may also provoke this mobbing reaction, and can clue to the presence of this owl (see Eurasian Pygmy Owl).

FOOD Similar to that of Eurasian Pygmy Owl, but with higher percentage of insects, frogs and reptiles. Birds up to the size of California Quail *Callipepla californica* and mammals to chipmunk size are caught, being about twice as large as the owl itself.

BREEDING Although this species has been bred success-fully in captivity, little is known about its reproductive biology. Probably similar to that of Eurasian Pygmy Owl, but no nest sanitation has been reported. Holes made by woodpeckers are normally used for nesting; no material is added. Lays 3-7 white eggs (median 26.6 x 24.3mm, somewhat more elongated than Eurasian Pygmy Owl's) directly on to bottom of hole. Female alone incubates, male feeding her near nesting site or inside the hole.

STATUS AND CONSERVATION Uncertain. Locally not rare. May be endangered, at least locally, by logging and the use of pesticides (see also Eurasian Pygmy Owl). Has not yet been reported to accept nestboxes.

REMARKS Hitherto, at least three species (146-148) have been lumped as one under the name *Glaucidium gnoma*. These three taxa, however, formerly treated as races, differ primarily in vocalisations, but also ecologically and accord-ing to DNA evidence; biometric and morphological differences exist, too. We may therefore state with some confidence that they are not different races with differing 'dialects', but in fact separate species: they are treated as such here. Since all have previously been lumped, detailed studies on the ecology, behaviour, taxonomy and biology of the different taxa are urgently needed.

REFERENCES Balgooyen (1969), Bent (1938), Boyer & Hume (1991), Burton (1992), Earhart & Johnson (1970), Eck & Busse (1973), Hardy *et al.* (1989), Heidrich *et al.* (1995), Howell & Webb (1995), König (1994), Miller (1955), Monroe (1968), Norton & Holt (1982), Ridgway (1914), Robbins & Howell (1995), Snyder & Wiley (1976), Voous (1988).

147 CAPE PYGMY OWL
Glaucidium hoskinsii   Plate 46

French: Chevêchette de Basse Californie
German: Hoskins-Sperlingskauz
Spanish: Tecolotito del Cabo

IDENTIFICATION A very small (about 16cm), round-headed pygmy owl. Very similar to Northern Pygmy Owl [146], but smaller and with shorter tail (about 64mm, against 70mm). Wing-tips rounded. Plumage pattern similar to northern counterpart, but underparts more finely and more densely streaked; general coloration above sandy-rufous to sandy-grey, with prominent occipital face. No red or grey morphs known. **Similar species** This is the only pygmy owl of S Baja California, where it is endemic. For comparison with other pygmy owls, see Northern Pygmy Owl. Elf Owl [173] is smaller, with a shorter tail, unstreaked underparts, and lacks occipital face.

VOCALISATIONS The male's song is a rather slow sequence of double notes, about five in 30-40 seconds, with some single notes thrown in: *whew-whew, whew-whew, whew, whew-whew,...*; intervals between double or single hoots are about 5-15 seconds, and one double note lasts about 2 seconds. Song is often preceded by a quavering *huhuhu...*; sometimes begins with several single notes before series of double notes given. Vocalisations require further study.

DISTRIBUTION Endemic to mountains of S Baja California, down to the cape.

Cape Pygmy Owl

MOVEMENTS Resident, but sometimes moves to lower elevations in winter.

HABITAT Pine and pine-oak forest, about 1,500-2,100m above sea-level. In winter, probably also deciduous forest at lower altitudes (about 500m above sea-level).

DESCRIPTION Adult Sexes alike, but females often more reddish. No grey or red morphs known. Facial disc as in other pygmy owls, eyebrows whitish. Upperparts sandy grey-brown with reddish tint, latter more pronounced on females; crown finely spotted with whitish; nape with two large blackish or dark brown spots, edged above by whitish, below by pale buff; mantle and back irregularly spotted light; scapulars with pale buff spots. Flight feathers barred light and dark; tail feathers dark brown with normally six incomplete narrow whitish bars, not reaching central shaft of feather. Underparts off-white, with prominent white spot on throat and central foreneck, surrounded by greyish-brown mottling and streaking; sides of upper breast and partly flanks mottled greyish-brown, rest of underparts rather densely streaked dusky. Tarsi feathered, toes bristled. **Juvenile** Undescribed, but probably similar to Northern Pygmy Owl (with unspotted crown). **Bare parts** Eyes yellow, rimmed by blackish edge of eyelids. Cere swollen around nostrils in coniform 'buckling', pale greenish-grey. Bill greenish-yellow. Toes yellowish-grey. Claws horn with darker tips.

MEASUREMENTS AND WEIGHT Total length 15-16.5cm. Wing 88-91mm; tail about 64mm. Weight about 50-65g; females heavier than males.

GEOGRAPHICAL VARIATION Monotypic: *Glaucidium hoskinsii* Brewster, 1888.

HABITS Little studied. Partly diurnal. Probably similar to those of most pygmy owls.

FOOD Insects and other arthropods, small mammals, reptiles and birds.

BREEDING Unknown. Probably nests in old woodpecker holes.

STATUS AND CONSERVATION Rare. As an endemic species with a very restricted range, it is doubtless threatened, principally by habitat destruction.

REMARKS This owl has been considered a race of Mountain Pygmy Owl [148], but it has rounded (not pointed) wings similar to the decidedly larger Northern Pygmy Owl, which also has a totally different voice. We treat it as an allospecies to *Glaucidium gnoma*, which lives in the mountains of the Mexican mainland.

REFERENCES Heidrich *et al.* (1995), Howell & Robbins (1996), Howell & Webb (1995).

148 MOUNTAIN PYGMY OWL
Glaucidium gnoma　　　　　Plate 46

French: Chevêchette des montagnes
German: Gnomen-Sperlingskauz
Spanish: Mochuelo serrano, Tecolotito serrano

IDENTIFICATION A very small pygmy owl (15-16.5cm). General coloration varies from dark brown to foxy-rufous; crown finely spotted whitish or pale buff, nape with occipital face. Similar to Northern Pygmy Owl [146], but smaller and with shorter tail (no overlap between species), wing-tips rather pointed, not rounded as in two preceding species; underparts more diffusely streaked, with large, long whitish area from throat to centre of breast. Eyes yellow. **Similar species** Northern Pygmy Owl is larger, with longer tail and rounded wing-tips (see above). Cape Pygmy Owl [147] is about equal in size to Mountain Pygmy, but has rounded wing-tips, underparts clearly (not diffusely) streaked, and whitish throat and centre of foreneck forming rounded white area bordered on lower edge (on breast) by streaking. Ridgway's Pygmy Owl [161] has streaked (not spotted) crown. Tamaulipas, Colima and Central American Pygmy Owls [150-152] are smaller, with spotted crown and much shorter tail. All are best distinguished by vocal patterns. Elf Owl [173] is smaller and shorter-tailed, lacks occipital face and is unstreaked below.

VOCALISATIONS The song of the male consists of a mostly prolonged series of short staccato notes, given in double hoots with some single notes thrown in, producing an irregular character: *gew-gew gew-gew gew-gew gew gew gew-gew gew....* A song described from mountains of Costa Rica and Panama differs from this type in being series of constant double notes (couplets) given at intervals of about 1 second, lacking irregularity; more study is needed to determine whether these differences are specific or merely individual variations. The former, typical, song often starts hesitantly with a slightly ringing, rapid sequence of notes, *huhuhuhuhu....* Young beg with a chipping twitter.

DISTRIBUTION Highlands of N and C Mexico, from Chihuahua, Coahuila, Nuevo León and Tamaulipas south to Central America and perhaps extreme NW South America; northernmost limit probably extends to mountains of southernmost Arizona and New Mexico. May overlap locally with Northern Pygmy Owl, from which it is easily distinguished by voice.

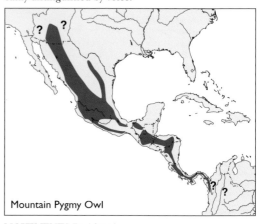
Mountain Pygmy Owl

MOVEMENTS Resident.

HABITAT Particularly pine-oak, pine and humid pine-evergreen forest in mountainous regions, from about 1,500m to 3,500m.

DESCRIPTION *G. g. gnoma* **Adult** Females generally larger and heavier than males. Facial disc pale brownish or rufous, speckled lighter and darker; eyebrows rather narrow, whitish. Crown finely speckled with whitish or pale buffy; nape with two large blackish or dark brownish spots, edged buffy-whitish above and pale cinnamon-buff below. Upperparts with greyish-brown, dark brown or rufous general coloration (according to one of the three known morphs, but intermediates exist, too), mantle and back with whitish and buffy spots; outer webs of scapulars partly spotted whitish or pale cinnamon-buff. Flight feathers barred light and dark; tail brown to rufescent with 5-6 narrow whitish (grey or brown morphs) or pale buffy (rufous morph) bars. Underparts off-white to whitish-buff, with rather plain area from throat to lower breast; sides of upper breast and partly flanks mottled brown or rufescent and whitish, rest of underparts streaked dusky or rufescent (according to morph). Tarsi feathered, toes bristled. **Juvenile** Downy chick whitish. Mesoptile resembles adult, but crown always unspotted greyish, differing very much in coloration from mantle and back. **Bare parts** Iris yellow. Cere yellowish-grey, typically swollen around nostrils; cere more greyish on immature. Bill horn-yellow. Toes yellowish-grey. Claws brownish-horn with darker tips.

MEASUREMENTS AND WEIGHT Total length 15-16.5 cm. Wing 82-92 mm; tail 57-64 mm. Weight 55-64 g, females heavier than males.

GEOGRAPHICAL VARIATION We distinguish three subspecies, two of which probably represent separate full species.

G. g. gnoma Wagler, 1832. Southernmost Arizona and New Mexico to S Mexico and C Honduras. See Description.

G. (g.) cobanense Sharpe, 1875. Guatemala, perhaps to Costa Rica (see below). Slightly smaller. Bright rufous morph predominant; light bars on tail narrowly edged dusky, underparts very diffusely streaked; wingtips less pointed than in nominate race. Wing of 1 specimen 87.5mm. (Perhaps a full species, Guatemalan Pygmy Owl, but vocalisations apparently undescribed. See also next subspecies.)

G. (g.) costaricanum Kelso, 1937. Costa Rica to Panama. Very dark, underparts more mottled than streaked; smaller than nominate, with wing-tips more pointed. Wing of 1 male from volcano Turrialba in Costa Rica 96 mm, tail 54mm; primary index 20.8. Another bird from Irazú volcano in Costa Rica, however, has wing 99.3mm, tail 58mm, and primary index only 7.5; tail has light bars narrowly edged dusky (as in cobanense), upperparts slightly mottled and spotted buffy or rusty, and underparts streaked rather than mottled. We believe that this latter individual may be distinct from the other Costa Rican specimen: if so, then the Turrialba bird would be costaricanum, and the Irazú specimen a dark morph of cobanense. (From the different wing-tip shape and the pattern of the underparts, the Irazú bird may be a valid species, distinct from G. gnoma: Guatemalan Pygmy Owl Glaucidium cobanense. The Turrialba owl may perhaps also be distinct from G. gnoma, as it has much more pointed wings and a very differently patterned undersurface. The song of the Costa Rican taxon costaricanum is a series of mostly equally spaced double notes, very similar to the song of typical G. gnoma, these vocal patterns showing the former to be a member of the gnoma group and not, as sometimes believed, a subspecies of G. jardinii of the Andes of N South America, which has a totally different song. Most recent studies suggest treating costaricanum as a full species: Costa Rican Pygmy Owl Glaucidium costaricanum.) Wing of 8 males median 91.5mm, of 1 female 99.1mm; tail of 8 males median 53.1mm, of 1 female 57.5mm; weight of 3 males median 66g.

HABITS Partly diurnal, but active mostly at dusk and dawn. Also heard singing on moonlit nights. May be attracted by playback or imitation of its song. When active by day, it is often mobbed by small birds.

FOOD Mainly insects, especially orthopterans and beetles, but also small mammals, birds and reptiles.

BREEDING Poorly known, but probably similar to that of other American pygmy owls. Holes in trees (especially woodpecker holes) are used for nesting. Lays 2-4 white eggs directly on to the bottom of the hole. Female alone incubates, fed by the male. No nest sanitation has been observed; such behaviour seems to be restricted to Eurasian Pygmy Owl [143].

STATUS AND CONSERVATION Uncertain, but seems to be locally not rare. Forest destruction is apparently the most endangering factor.

REMARKS Since different taxa have hitherto been merged into a single species (Glaucidium gnoma), observations of what are in reality different species have been attributed to one, giving rise to much confusion. Although the taxonomy of the whole group is still not properly clarified, G. californicum and G. gnoma are certainly separate species and the same appears to hold for G. hoskinsii; the taxa costaricanum and cobanense, however, require intensive study, but it is quite clear that the former is not a subspecies of the South American G. jardinii.

Pygmy owls observed and collected near San Antonio in the W Cordillera of Colombia and near Mindo and Gualea on the Pacific Andean slope of W Ecuador belong to a different, newly named taxon distributed in cloud forest of the slopes of the NW Andes. Since the description of this new species has only very recently been published, and after the manuscript of the present book had already been typeset, only a brief description of it is given below.

REFERENCES Hardy *et al.* (1989), Heidrich *et al.* (1995), Howell & Webb (1995), König (1991, 1994), Miller (1955, 1963), Ridgway (1914), Robbins & Stiles (1999), Voous (1988), Wolf (1976).

148X CLOUD-FOREST PYGMY OWL
Glaucidium nubicola   Not illustrated

IDENTIFICATION This newly discovered species is similar in plumage to other Neotropical pygmy owls of higher altitudes, but is slightly larger and heavier, and has less barring or spotting on sides of chest and flanks than the taxa costaricanum, jardinii and bolivianum. The black marks on the hindneck ('false eyes') are always bordered white, not rufous as in costaricanum. Crown and auricular area brown with sepia-bordered white spots; mantle, back, scapulars, upperwing-coverts and rump dark brown, washed dark rufous-brown, with bold white (often rufous-tinged) spots on scapulars and wing-coverts; tail blackish with five incomplete whitish bars (appearing as irregularly shaped spots); throat and centre of chest white, sides of chest brown with inconspicuous whitish spots. Eyes, bill and unfeathered (but bristled) toes yellow.

MEASUREMENTS AND WEIGHT Wing of 5 males average 92.2mm, of 1 female 95.8mm; tail of 5 males median 47.2mm, of 1 female 49.8mm. Weight of 3 males median 76.1g, of 1 female 79g.

VOCALISATIONS The song suggests a relationship with the gnoma-costaricanum group, being long sequences of 'couplets'. The latter consist of longer notes than those of G. gnoma and G. costaricanum.

DISTRIBUTION This new species is distributed in cloud forest on the Pacific slope of the W Andes from Colombia to W Ecuador, and perhaps south to northernmost Peru.

REMARKS Probably a member of the gnoma species-group, as suggested by vocalisations and DNA evidence. Much more study is needed on this group of related species.

REFERENCES Robbins & Stiles (1999).

149 CUBAN PYGMY OWL
Glaucidium siju   Plate 46

French: Chevêchette de Cuba
German: Cuba-Sperlingskauz
Spanish: Sijú

IDENTIFICATION A very small pygmy owl (about 17cm) with rounded head, wing-tips relatively rounded. Cere around nostrils less swollen than in other American pygmy owls. Nape with occipital face, crown spotted light; mantle and back more or less distinctly barred; upper breast densely barred laterally, leaving plain whitish zone from throat to belly, with flanks and lower breast spotted brown or buffy. Tail with 5-6 narrow light bars. Eyes yellow. Grey-brown and reddish (rare) morphs occur. **Similar species** The only pygmy owl in Cuba and Isle of Pines. Cuban Bare-legged Owl [87] has long, bare tarsi and often brown eyes. Burrowing Owl [174] is much larger and lives in open country.

VOCALISATIONS The song of the male is a series of equally spaced single notes with intervals of about 4 seconds between each, the tonal quality similar to that of Mountain Pygmy Owl [148] but the rhythm more like that of Northern Pygmy Owl [146] (single, well-spaced hoots): *tew, tew, tew,...*. A rapid series of accelerating, twittering notes, increasing gradually in pitch, is quite often heard from both sexes: *wewewhitititititirrr*.

DISTRIBUTION Endemic to Cuba and the Isle of Pines (Isla de la Juventud).

Cuban Pygmy Owl

MOVEMENTS Resident.

HABITAT Semi-open woodland, plantations, larger parks with old trees, and bushy country.

DESCRIPTION *G. s. siju* **Adult** A greyish-brown and a reddish morph occur. *Grey-brown morph*: Facial disc pale greyish-brown, indistinctly speckled dusky; eyebrows narrow, whitish. Crown spotted whitish; nape with occipital face, the blackish spots narrowly bordered whitish above, ochraceous-buff below. Upperparts greyish-brown, irregularly spotted whitish and buff; mantle indistinctly barred, scapulars not prominently marked lighter. Flight feathers barred light and dark; tail brownish-grey with 5-6 narrow whitish bars, often edged dusky. Underparts off-white, densely barred brownish-ochraceous on sides of upper breast, leaving unmarked longitudinal area in centre from throat to lower breast; rest of underparts spotted and streaked brown. Tarsi feathered, toes bristled. *Red morph*: General coloration rufescent-brown. **Juvenile** Downy chick white. Mesoptile similar to adult, but crown unspotted. **Bare parts** Eyes yellow, rimmed by dusky edge of eyelid. Cere yellowish-grey. Bill yellow-horn. Toes yellowish. Claws dusky horn with darker tips.

MEASUREMENTS AND WEIGHT Total length about 17cm. Wing about 90mm; tail 61mm. Weight 55-92g, females heavier than males.

GEOGRAPHICAL VARIATION Two subspecies.
    G. s. siju (D'Orbigny, 1839). Cuba. Wing 87-104mm; tail 54-67mm; weight of males 55-57g, of females 66.5-73.5g.
    G. s. vittatum Ridgway, 1914. Isle of Pines. More distinctly barred above; larger. Wing 84-109mm; tail 69-73mm; weight of males 65-68g, of females 84-92g.

HABITS Partly diurnal; often mobbed by small birds. Behaviour similar to that of other pygmy owls.

FOOD Mostly insects and small reptiles, but also small mammals and birds. Hunts mainly from a perch.

BREEDING Little known. In general uses abandoned holes of woodpeckers for breeding. Female lays 3-4 white eggs and incubates alone. Breeding biology probably similar to that of other pygmy owls; no nest sanitation has been observed.

STATUS AND CONSERVATION Uncertain. Locally rather common.

REMARKS Relationship with other American *Glaucidium* is unclear. This is the only American pygmy owl in which the cere is not prominently swollen buckle-like around nostrils. DNA studies could be one means of solving the taxonomic problem. On the other hand, it is striking that birds on Isle of Pines, only a few miles off Cuba, are so much larger and heavier. Studies on the whole ecology and biology of this fascinating little owl are needed.

REFERENCES Boyer & Hume (1991), Dunning (1993), Eck & Busse (1973), Hardy *et al.* (1989), Heidrich *et al.* (1995), König (1994), Wallschläger (unpublished).

150 TAMAULIPAS PYGMY OWL
Glaucidium sanchezi   Plate 47

French: Chevêchette de Tamaulipas
German: Tamaulipas-Sperlingskauz
Spanish: Telocotito tamaulipeco

IDENTIFICATION A tiny pygmy owl (12-15cm). Tail relatively long, with 5-6 pale bars (often 1-2 concealed). Overall cinnamon-brown, female redder than male; forecrown with few whitish flecks, hindcrown rather unspotted, mantle and unspotted. Eyes yellow. **Similar species** Mountain Pygmy Owl [148] is larger, with relatively shorter tail and spotted mantle. Ridgway's Pygmy Owl [161] has a streaked crown. Colima Pygmy Owl [151] is much paler, and has an allopatric distribution.

VOCALISATIONS The song consists of 2-3 rather high-pitched hollow and somewhat drawn-out notes, always 2 per second, given at regular intervals and repeated after a while: *phew-phew, phew-phew-phew, phew-phew-phew*. A trembling roll may precede the song.

DISTRIBUTION Mountains of NE Mexico, from Tamaulipas and SE San Luis Potosí to Vera Cruz.

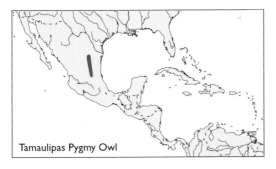

Tamaulipas Pygmy Owl

MOVEMENTS Resident.

HABITAT Humid evergreen and pine-evergreen montane and cloud forest at 1,500-2,100m above sea-level.

DESCRIPTION Sexes differ. **Adult male** Facial disc brownish, flecked white to pale buff; short eyebrows whitish. Crown, nape and upperparts rich olive-brown, with greyer crown. Forecrown finely spotted light cinnamon to whitish, spots extending along sides of crown to nape; nape with occipital face. Wing-coverts spotted light, scapulars with indistinct lighter areas on outer webs. Flight feathers barred dark and light; tail brown with 5-6 broken whitish bars. Underparts whitish, with rufous-brown streaking and rufescent-brown mottling on sides of upper breast, spotted buff. Tarsi feathered, toes bristled. **Adult female** Differs in having crown, nape and upperparts rufous-brown. **Juvenile** Downy chick white. Mesoptile similar to adult, but crown greyer and unspotted. **Bare parts** Eyes yellow. Cere yellowish-grey; in immature more greyish. Bill horn-yellow. Toes yellowish-grey. Claws horn with darker tips.

MEASUREMENTS AND WEIGHT Total length 12-15cm. Wing 86-93.5mm; tail 50-57mm. Weight of males 51-55g, females heavier.

GEOGRAPHICAL VARIATION Monotypic: *Glaucidium sanchezi* Lowery & Newman, 1949.

HABITS Partly diurnal. Habits poorly studied.

FOOD Probably mainly insects and small vertebrates.

BREEDING Little studied. Breeds mainly in abandoned holes of woodpeckers. Breeding habits probably similar to those of other pygmy owls; no cleaning of nest has been observed. When young leave the nest, they are able to fly short distances.

STATUS AND CONSERVATION Uncertain. Probably endangered by habitat destruction (logging).

REMARKS Like most owls, this tiny bird needs study on its ecology, taxonomy, behaviour and reproductive biology, in particular to identify measures for its conservation.

REFERENCES Heidrich *et al.* (1995), Howell & Robbins (1995), Howell & Webb (1995), König (1991, 1994).

---

151 COLIMA PYGMY OWL
Glaucidium palmarum   Plate 47

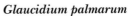

French: Chevêchette de Colima
German: Colima-Sperlingskauz
Spanish: Tecolotito colimense

IDENTIFICATION A very small pygmy owl (14-15cm). Sandy grey-brown to olive-brown above, crown fully spotted whitish to pale buff, nape with occipital face and a narrow cinnamon band below it across base of nape. Tail brown with 3-4 visible, slightly broken pale bars. Underparts whitish, with buffy to cinnamon streaking and brown mottling on sides of upper breast. Eyes yellow. **Similar species** Tamaulipas Pygmy Owl [150] is darker, has only forecrown and sides of crown spotted, and is allopatric. Mountain Pygmy Owl [148] is larger, with more visible light bars on tail and a spotted mantle. Ridgway's Pygmy Owl [161] is larger, with longer tail and streaked (not spotted) crown. Central American Pygmy Owl [152] has a greyer, less spotted crown, contrasting with more rufous upperparts; it inhabits tropical rain forest, not montane areas or thorny shrub. Elf Owl [173] has no occipital face, and is finely vermiculated, not streaked, below.

VOCALISATIONS The song of the male consists of series of hollow, short notes, often increasing in number (up to about 24 or more in one phrase), about three notes per second: *whew-whew-whew, whew-whew-whew-whew-whew, whew-whew-whew-whew-whew-....* Intervals between phrases are relatively long. It is somewhat similar to that of Ridgway's Pygmy Owl, but the phrases are normally much shorter and the tempo is slower. The series are often preceded by shivering rolls.

DISTRIBUTION W Mexico along the Pacific coast from C Sonora to the Isthmus of Tehuantepec (Oaxaca).

Colima Pygmy Owl

MOVEMENTS Resident.

HABITAT Dry, tropical woodland from sea-level up to about 1,500m, including thorny woods in foothills, palm groves, semi-deciduous forest up into dry oak woodland; sometimes in dry pine-oak woods, where it may be found sympatrically with Mountain Pygmy Owl. Locally, occurs in ravines ('barrancas') at the upper edge of tropical deciduous forest; has also been recorded from forest with swampy substrate.

DESCRIPTION Adult Facial disc pale ochraceous with indistinct darker concentric lines; eyebrows short, whitish. Upperparts greyish tawny-brown, mantle slightly more greyish than crown, forehead to nape rather densely spotted whitish or pale buff; nape with occipital face, below which a cinnamon band across hindneck; scapulars with indistinct pale buffy spots; wing-coverts slightly spotted pale buff. Flight feathers barred light and dark; tail greyish-brown with 6-7 buffy-whitish bars, of which normally 3-4 visible (two concealed by uppertail-coverts). Underparts off-white, sides of upper breast and streaking on rest of underparts cinnamon-brown. Tarsi feathered, toes bristled. **Juvenile** Downy chick whitish. Mesoptile similar to adult, but crown unspotted grey, contrasting with brown upperparts, forehead sometimes with few lighter flecks; nape with occipital face, but cinnamon band below it lacking or very indistinct. **Bare parts** Eyes yellow. Cere and bill yellowish-horn. Toes pale yellowish. Claws horn with darker tips.

MEASUREMENTS AND WEIGHT Total length 14-15cm. Wing of males 81-85mm, of females 84-88mm; tail of males 51-54mm, of females 53.3-55.7mm. Weight of males about 50g, females heavier.

GEOGRAPHICAL VARIATION Montypic: *Glaucidium palmarum* Nelson, 1901.

HABITS Partly diurnal. Behaviour little studied, but probably similar to that of other pygmy owls. May be attracted by playback or imitation of its song. Is mobbed by small birds when seen by day.

FOOD Probably mostly insects, but also small vertebrates.

BREEDING Not described. Probably nests in abandoned holes of woodpeckers.

STATUS AND CONSERVATION Uncertain. Locally rather common.

REMARKS As the taxa *sanchezi*, *palmarum* and *griseiceps* have traditionally been considered races of Least Pygmy Owl [153], detailed observations on the different species are lacking. All three are doubtless valid species and specifically distinct from Least, which occurs only in E Brazil, and all are best distinguished by different vocalisations. The three Mexican/Central American 'Least' Pygmy Owls are rather closely related to each other, but are clearly distinct from Amazonian Pygmy Owl [154], which is superficially very similar (but this similarity seems to be due to convergence and not to true relationship). According to DNA evidence, Amazonian Pygmy Owl, which also has an unspotted back, is related to Yungas Pygmy Owl [157] from the montane forest of Peru to NW Argentina, which has a spotted mantle; both utter trills, which the other three species do not, although Andean Pygmy Owl [156] of the N Andes does have a 'stuttering' trill-like song. (The six different species of 'Least' Pygmy Owl are shown together on Plate 47 in order to facilitate their comparison, not because they may be closely related.)

REFERENCES Burton (1992), Heidrich *et al.* (1995), Howell & Robbins (1995), Howell & Webb (1995), Ridgway (1914), Robbins & Howell (1995).

152 CENTRAL AMERICAN PYGMY OWL
Glaucidium griseiceps   Plate 47

French: Chevêchette à tete grise
German: Yucatán-Sperlingskauz
Spanish: Mochuelo centroamericano

IDENTIFICATION A very small pygmy owl (14-15cm). Crown and nape brownish-grey, contrasting with rich brown rest of upperparts, and with minute whitish spots, these less dense towards nape, which has occipital face. Tail with 2-3 visible, broken whitish bars. Off-white below, mottled rufous-brown on chest sides and streaked rufous-brown on flanks and lower breast, leaving longitudinal plain whitish zone from throat to centre of breast. Ground colour of primaries greyish-brown, of secondaries rufescent-brown. Eyes yellow. **Similar species** Tamaulipas and Colima Pygmy Owls [150, 151] are allopatric: both have more light bars on tail, former has crown spotted only near forehead and at sides, latter is much paler and has sandy-brown crown rather densely spotted. Mountain Pygmy Owl [148] is larger and has spotted back. Ridgway's Pygmy Owl [161] has streaked, not spotted, crown, a longer tail, and is generally larger.

VOCALISATIONS The male's song consists of series, varying in length, of equally spaced (3 per second), rather accentuated, hollow, ringing notes, starting mostly with sequence of 2-4 notes, followed by run of up to about 18 notes, these phrases being repeated after intervals of variable length: *pew-pew-pew-pew, pew-pew-pew-pew-pew-pew-pew, pew-pew-....* Also quavering trills. As with related species, vocabulary needs study.

DISTRIBUTION SE Mexico and Central America to NW South America (NW Colombia, NW Ecuador).

Central American Pygmy Owl

MOVEMENTS Resident.

HABITAT Humid tropical evergreen forest and humid bushland, from sea-level up to about 1,300m.

DESCRIPTION Adult Facial disc pale grey-brown, flecked whitish, with indistinct concentric lines; short eyebrows whitish. Crown and nape brownish-grey, forecrown with minute whitish spots, spotting sometimes extending to hindcrown; nape with prominent occipital face. Mantle and back plain rich brown. Primaries greyish-brown with rows of light spots; secondaries rufous-brown with pale buffy bars. Tail brown with 2-3 visible, broken whitish bars (4-5 bars, but two normally concealed by uppertail-coverts). Underparts off-white, with large whitish zone from throat to central breast; sides of upper breast mottled rufescent-brown, flanks and rest of underparts boldly streaked rufous-brown. Tarsi feathered to base of toes, latter bristled. **Juvenile** Downy chick whitish. Mesoptile similar in structure and coloration to adult, but crown unspotted grey (sometimes with whitish flecks on forehead), contrasting with rich brown upperparts; barring of tail may vary from whitish to pale cinnamon. **Bare parts** Eyes yellow. Cere and bill yellowish-horn with slightly greenish tint. Toes pale yellowish. Claws horn with dark tips.

MEASUREMENTS AND WEIGHT Total length 14-15cm. Wing 84.5-90mm; tail 46-52mm. Weight of males 49.5-51.7g, females heavier.

GEOGRAPHICAL VARIATION Monotypic: *Glaucidium griseiceps* Sharpe, 1875.

HABITS Partly diurnal. May be attracted by playback or imitation of its song. Behaviour little studied.

FOOD Insects, probably also spiders, and small mammals, birds and other vertebrates.

BREEDING Poorly known. Apparently nests in abandoned holes of woodpeckers and perhaps also in opened old nests of termites on trees.

STATUS AND CONSERVATION Uncertain. Locally not rare, but may be threatened by habitat destruction (logging).

REMARKS Has traditionally been considered a race of Least Pygmy Owl [153], which in reality is confined to E Brazil. Like most pygmy owls, it is in need of study.

REFERENCES Heidrich *et al.* (1995), Howell & Robbins (1995), Howell & Webb (1995), König (1991, 1994), Robbins & Howell (1995).

---

153 LEAST PYGMY OWL
Glaucidium minutissimum　　Plate 47

French: Chevêchette naine
German: Zwerg-Sperlingskauz
Spanish: Caburé enano
Portuguese: Caburé miudinho

IDENTIFICATION A very small pygmy owl (about 15cm). Wing-tips rather rounded, although some specimens show more pointed wing-tips (see Geographical Variation). Crown to back rather uniform warm brown, crown finely spotted whitish or pale buff, nape with occipital face, mantle plain. Off-white below, streaked rufescent, especially on flanks and lower breast; white patch around throat, bordered laterally by rufous-brown mottling and below by rufous-brown streaks. Tail with 3-4 visible whitish, laterally elongated spots. Eyes yellow. **Similar species** Amazonian Pygmy Owl [154] has a more greyish-brown crown, contrasting with unspotted brown mantle; allopatric. Ferruginous Pygmy Owl [160] is larger, with longer tail, crown more streaked than spotted, scapulars often with whitish spots on outer webs, tail with more bars or plain rufous.

VOCALISATIONS The song of the male is a rather high, hollow double note, somewhat drawn out, repeated at intervals of several seconds; the first note of the couplet lasts about 0.25 seconds, the second about 0.2 seconds, with the pause between them about 0.35 seconds: *hew-hew, hew-hew, hew-hew,....* This song is very similar to that of Tamaulipas Pygmy Owl [150], but lower-pitched and with the second note always shorter than the first (in Tamaulipas Pygmy, both notes are of equal length and the pause between the two slightly longer).

DISTRIBUTION E Brazil from N Bahia south to Santa Catarina, east to Goiás, Paraná and adjacent Paraguay. Perhaps also very locally in E Misiones (NE Argentina), bordering Santa Catarina.

Least Pygmy Owl

MOVEMENTS Resident.

HABITAT Evergreen rainforest and forest edge, in tropical and subtropical climates. Seems to avoid secondary growth. Occurs from sea-level up to about 1,000m; in SE Brazil, relatively common in foothills at altitudes of 500-800m.

DESCRIPTION Adult Facial disc pale greyish-brown with some rufescent concentric lines; eyebrows whitish. Crown and upperparts dusky cinnamon-brown to rufous-brown, crown with tiny whitish flecks, nape with prominent occipital face; mantle and back plain warm brown, wing-coverts with few light speckles. Flight feathers indistinctly barred light and dark; tail cinnamon-brown with 3-4 visible broken whitish bars (more rounded than on Mexican or Central American 'Least' Pygmy Owls). Rounded whitish area around throat, bordered above by narrow rufous band, laterally by dense, rufescent-brown mottling forming patches with few light spots; rest of underparts off-white with prominent rufous streaking. Tarsi feathered, toes bristled. **Juvenile** Downy chick whitish. Mesoptile similar to adult in coloration and structure, but crown unspotted rufescent-brown, not greyish, forehead sometimes with few pale flecks. **Bare parts** Eyes yellow. Cere yellowish-grey. Bill yellowish-horn with slight greenish tint. Toes yellowish. Claws horn with darker tips.

MEASUREMENTS AND WEIGHT Total length about 15cm. Wing 82.5-91mm; tail 57-59mm; tail/wing ratio 0.62-0.65. Weight about 50g, females heavier than males.

GEOGRAPHICAL VARIATION Monotypic: *Glaucidium minutissimum* (Wied, 1821).

Examination of museum specimens revealed some birds with rather rounded wing-tips, all of which originated from SE Brazil (Paraná, São Paulo, Santa Catarina); other skins labelled 'Brazil' had pointed wing-tips, and were more or less identical in coloration and plumage pattern to the rounded-winged owls. We doubt that these difference are due to geographical variation, and it seems to us more probable that another, specifically distinct taxon is involved. We have neither voice recordings nor DNA data for these birds, however, so we assume that the owls with rounded wing-tips are true *Glaucidium minutissimum*, while those with pointed wings might perhaps be '*Glaucidium pumilum*' (regarded as a synonym of *minutissimum*) or an undescribed taxon. The problem can be solved only by intensive studies of vocalisations and by DNA evidence.

HABITS Partly diurnal, but active mostly at dusk and dawn. Behaviour little studied, but probably similar to that of other American pygmy owls. Relatively tame towards man. When seen by day, mobbed by small birds.

FOOD Mostly insects, but also small vertebrates.

BREEDING Virtually unknown. Probably breeds in abandoned holes of woodpeckers in trunks or larger branches.

STATUS AND CONSERVATION Uncertain. Found to be locally not rare in region between Rio de Janeiro and Santa Catarina. As the species seems to avoid secondary growth, it is doubtless threatened by logging activities in primary forest.

REMARKS Since the 'Least Pygmy Owl' has traditionally been thought to be distributed from Mexico to the Amazon and E Brazil, detailed studies on the ecology and habits as well as on the whole biology of the several species involved are lacking. A further problem has recently been presented by the Brazilian specimens with different wing shapes, which might be two distinct species. Bioacoustical studies on 'Least Pygmy Owls' in Brazil are as important as that on their counterparts in Mexico and Middle America.

REFERENCES Burton (1992), Hardy *et al.* (1989), Heidrich *et al.* (1995), Howell & Robbins (1995), König (1991, 1994), Robbins & Howell (1995), Sick (1985), Vielliard (1989).

---

154 AMAZONIAN PYGMY OWL
Glaucidium hardyi   Plate 47

French: Chevêchette d'Amazonie
German: Amazonas-Sperlingskauz
Spanish: Mochuelo amazónico
Portuguese: Caburé amazônico

IDENTIFICATION A very small pygmy owl (14-15cm) with relatively short tail; wings relatively long, but with rather rounded tips. Crown and nape notably greyer than plain brown mantle and back, upperwing-coverts slightly spotted light. Crown with rather dense small off-white dots and some larger scaly markings; nape with occipital face and ochraceous-buffy nuchal band. Tail brown with normally three visible broken whitish bars. Off-white below with rufescent-brown streaks, breast sides mottled rufescent. Eyes and toes bright yellow to golden-yellow. **Similar species** Ferruginous Pygmy Owl [160] is larger with longer tail, latter either with more bars varying from buffy-white to pale reddish-brown, or plain chestnut; eyes yellow, crown with shaft-streaks. Screech owls (genus *Otus*) are larger, and have small ear-tufts. Subtropical Pygmy Owl [155] has outer webs of scapulars and upperwing-coverts spotted whitish, and lives at higher altitudes. All are best distinguished by voice.

VOCALISATIONS The male's song is a melodious trill, falling slightly in pitch towards the end, normally consisting of series of about 10-30 short, fluted notes in a rapid sequence (about 11 notes per second), phrase lasting about 2.5-3 seconds and repeated at variable intervals: *bewbewbewbewbewbewbewbew....* Vocabulary is under study.

DISTRIBUTION Amazonian South America, from Venezuela (Orinoco) to E Ecuador, E Peru, C and NE Brazil and NE Bolivia.

Amazonian Pygmy Owl

MOVEMENTS Resident.

HABITAT Primary tropical rain forest of the Amazon, up to about 350m above sea-level in lower foothills of the Andes. Lives mostly in canopy of forest, where branches are heavily laden with epiphytic plants. Often occurs together with Ferruginous Pygmy Owl and Northern Tawny-bellied Screech Owl [76] and, south of the Amazon, with Southern Tawny-bellied Screech Owl [77].

DESCRIPTION Adult Facial disc pale greyish-brown with fine brownish flecks; short eyebrows whitish. Crown greyish-brown, marked with small off-white dots and some larger scaly markings; nape with occipital face (two large blackish spots surrounded by light area) and, below this, an ochraceous-buff narrow nuchal band. Mantle unspotted, slightly rufescent earth-brown, rest of upperparts similar, contrasting with greyish head; wing-coverts with few, not very prominent light spots. Flight feathers barred light and dark; tail dark brown with normally three visible broken whitish bars. Underparts off-white, with large, unmarked patch from throat to central breast; sides of upper breast densely mottled rufous-brown with few whitish spots, flanks and rest of underparts boldly streaked reddish-brown. Tarsi feathered, toes bristled. **Juvenile** Not described. **Bare parts** Eyes bright yellow to golden-yellow. Cere dirty greenish-yellow. Bill yellowish-horn with olive or greenish tint. Toes golden-yellow. Claws horn with darker tips.

MEASUREMENTS AND WEIGHT Total length 14-15cm. Wing 90.5-94mm (1 bird from E Peru had wing 96mm); tail 45-52mm; tail/wing ratio varies between 0.48 and 0.55. Weight of 2 males from E Peru 56.5g and 63g.

GEOGRAPHICAL VARIATION Monotypic: *Glaucidium hardyi* Vielliard, 1989.

HABITS Partly diurnal. Normally lives in the upper storey of primary forest, probably descending to ground only occasionally, and is therefore difficult to observe. (The lower to medium storey is often inhabited by Ferruginous Pygmy and Southern Tawny-bellied Screech Owls, while Amazonian Pygmy Owl lives high above them.) When seen by day, the owl is mobbed by small birds. May be attracted by playback or imitation of its song.

FOOD Mainly insects, but probably also small tree-dwelling mammals, birds and reptiles.

BREEDING Not studied, but probably as for other pygmy owls. Apparently uses abandoned holes of woodpeckers as nest; these may be very high up in trees.

STATUS AND CONSERVATION Uncertain, as difficult to observe and limits of distribution only roughly known. This tiny owl is doubtless threatened by deforestation of its habitat, together with changes in the whole ecosystem.

REMARKS Recent studies (bioacoustics, DNA) have clearly shown that the Amazonian Pygmy Owl is a distinct species. Its entire ecology and biology, as well as taxonomy, require further study. According to vocalisations and DNA evidence, it seems to be more closely related to Andean and Yungas Pygmy Owls [156, 157] than to the 'Least Pygmy Owl complex'.

REFERENCES Hardy *et al.* (1989), Heidrich *et al.* (1995), Howell & Robbins (1995), Howell & Webb (1995), König (1991, 1994 and unpublished), Robbins & Howell (1995), Sick (1985), Vielliard (1989).

---

155 SUBTROPICAL PYGMY OWL
Glaucidium parkeri Plate 47

French: Chevêchette subtropicale
German: Zamora-Sperlingskauz
Spanish: Mochuelo de Zamora-Chinchipe

IDENTIFICATION A very small pygmy owl (about 15cm). Facial disc finely speckled whitish and brown. Brown above, crown and sides of head with distinct greyish tone, rather boldly spotted with white dots narrowly bordered blackish, prominent occipital face with narrow (often concealed) whitish nuchal collar below; scapulars with rather prominent whitish spots. Tail dusky brown with normally four visible whitish bars. White below, throat and centre of upper breast plain, sides of upper breast dark rufescent-brown with some white speckles, rest of underparts clearly streaked dark chestnut. Eyes yellow.
Similar species Ferruginous Pygmy Owl [160] is larger, with longer tail either unbarred rufous or with 6-7 rufous to whitish bars; crown mostly streaked. Peruvian Pygmy Owl [158] is larger, with much longer tail, and rufous morph rather frequent; inhabits semi-arid bushland and open, rather dry forest from sea-level up to 3,500m in W Andes. Central American Pygmy Owl [152] lives at lower altitudes, and has grey crown contrasting with more rufescent-brown back. Andean Pygmy Owl [156] normally lives at higher altitudes, and has longer wings with pointed tips, mantle not plain but flecked light, and underparts more mottled than streaked. Yungas Pygmy Owl [157] lives in montane forest and might occur sympatrically with Subtropical Pygmy in Peru or N Bolivia; has distinctly longer tail, is less clearly streaked below, and mantle and back are irregularly spotted light with more or less 'hastate' pattern. Amazonian Pygmy Owl [154] inhabits tropical rainforest below 350m; spotting on crown and sides of head without dark edging, streaking on underparts less clear, normally only three white bars visible on tail. All are best distinguished by voice.

VOCALISATIONS The song of the male consists of short phrases (normally 2-4, sometimes up to 6 notes) given at intervals of several seconds. One phrase of four rather high-pitched notes lasts about 2 seconds, but the notes are not equally spaced: it begins normally with two notes in a couplet (interval between notes about 0.1 seconds), followed after interval of about 0.25 seconds by another note and finally after about 0.3-0.35 seconds by the final one. The song thus has a hesitant character: *hew-hew–hew––hew*.

DISTRIBUTION Poorly known: Andes from SE Ecuador (Cordillera del Cóndor, Cordillera de Cutucú) to Peru (e.g. Cerros del Sira) and N Bolivia.

MOVEMENTS Resident.

HABITAT Humid subtropical montane and cloud forest, rich in epiphytes and creepers, between 1,450m and 1,975m above sea-level.

DESCRIPTION Adult Facial disc pale greyish-brown, finely speckled white and brown. Upperparts dark brown, slightly greyer on crown, latter and sides of head densely spotted with whitish dots narrowly edged dusky; prominent occipital face with (often concealed) whitish collar below; mantle plain dark brown, with slight dull olivaceous wash towards wing-coverts; outer webs of scapulars and upper-wing-coverts with rather bold whitish spots, basally edged dusky. Flight feathers with white irregularly shaped spots (not buffy as in other pygmy owls); tail blackish-brown with five incomplete white bars of irregularly shaped spots. Underparts white, with large plain patch between throat and centre of upper breast; sides of neck and upper breast rufescent-brown with small whitish flecks, flanks and underparts from lower breast downwards clearly streaked olive-washed chestnut. Tarsi feathered, toes bristled.
Juvenile Not described. **Bare parts** Eyes yellow. Cere and bill greenish-yellow. Toes yellow. Claws dark horn.

MEASUREMENTS AND WEIGHT Total length about 15cm. Wing of 3 males 89.1-97.1mm, of male holotype

91,8mm; tail 46.6-53.4mm, of holotype 48.5mm. Weight of 3 males 59.1-63.1g, of holotype 62g.

GEOGRAPHICAL VARIATION Monotypic: *Glaucidium parkeri* Robbins & Howell, 1995.

HABITS Partly diurnal. Frequents upper storeys of forest and forest edges. Has been observed in canopy about 30m above ground.

FOOD Probably mainly insects.

BREEDING Unknown. Probably breeds in abandoned holes of woodpeckers at considerable height above ground.

STATUS AND CONSERVATION Uncertain. As with other birds inhabiting primary forest, it is endangered by forest destruction.

REMARKS This recently described new species requires study, including of its relationship with other Neotropical pygmy owls.

REFERENCES Heidrich *et al.* (1965), Howell & Robbins (1995), Robbins & Howell (1995).

156 ANDEAN PYGMY OWL
Glaucidium jardinii　　　　Plate 48

French: Chevêchette des Andes
German: Anden-Sperlingskauz
Spanish: Mochuelo andino

IDENTIFICATION A very small (15-16cm) dark brown or buffy orange-brown pygmy owl, with wings relatively long with rather pointed tips. Head and crown finely spotted whitish to pale buff, sometimes with indistinct pale shaft-streaks, eyebrows rather prominent whitish. Warm chocolate-brown above, irregularly spotted light buff or orangey-brown with lighter mottling, spotting and barring. Rather large, white or whitish-buff (red morph) throat patch; sides of chest and flanks densely mottled dusky brown or orange-buff, lower breast indistinctly mottled and streaked dark. Tail with 6-7 broken whitish bars, or dark brown with 6-7 pale orange-buff bars, not reaching central shaft. Eyes yellow. **Similar species** Subtropical Pygmy Owl [155] is smaller and clearly streaked rufescent-brown below. Yungas Pygmy Owl [157] has throat to lower breast plain whitish, flanks and lower parts of underside distinctly streaked dusky, occipital face bordered below by narrow ochraceous nuchal collar, mantle and back marked with often 'hastate' pale spots, tail blackish or dark brown with 5-6 broken whitish or pale orange-buff bars, and wings with rounded tips. The recently described Cloud-forest Pygmy Owl [148X] is slightly larger and heavier, and lives in cloud forests on the W slope of the Andes. Amazonian Pygmy Owl [154] has unspotted mantle, is smaller, with shorter tail, and lives below 350m. Ferruginous Pygmy Owl [160] is absent from montane forest, living at lower altitudes; has longer tail which either has 6-7 rather narrow bars or is plain rufous, and crown often with light shaft-streaks (not spots). All are best distinguished by voice.

VOCALISATIONS The song of the male consists of two different phrases. It begins normally with 4-5 short,

stuttering trills, uttered at regular intervals of about 0.35 seconds, followed after a similar interval by about 5-10 staccato notes in rapid succession (4 per second, with interval of about 0.15 seconds between each); after several seconds a new phrase begins. The short trills consist of a rather explosive note, increasing in volume and slightly in pitch, of about 0.3 seconds' duration, followed by a very rapid (rather stuttering) series of 2-3 very short staccato notes, one trill lasting about 0.6 seconds: *puéehtututu—puéehtututu—puéehtututu—puéehtututu—tew-tew-tew-tew-tew-tew*. Long sequences of *tew* notes at regular intervals (about 3-4 notes per second) are frequent.

DISTRIBUTION Andes of Venezuela (Cordillera de Mérida), NC Colombia and C and E Ecuador, south to Morona-Santiago and the Marañón depression. Absent from W cordillera of Colombia, and from whole W slope of the Andes, as well as south of the Marañón depression. Type locality is Quito in Ecuador.

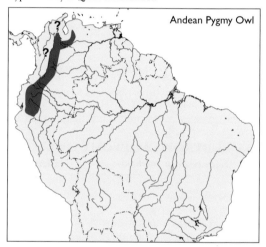

Andean Pygmy Owl

MOVEMENTS Resident.

HABITAT Semi-open montane and cloud forest, patches of *Polylepis* woodland, and elfin forest near the Páramos. From about 2,000m above sea-level up to timberline (to 3,500m, locally even higher).

DESCRIPTION Adult Red and dark brown morphs are known, as well as intermediates. *Brown morph*: Facial disc pale greyish-brown with darker concentric lines; eyebrows rather prominent, whitish. Upperparts dark, warm earth-brown; crown with minute, sometimes slightly drop-shaped, whitish or pale buffy spots and occasionally very thin shaft-streaks; nape with occipital face; mantle and back with slightly more rufous wash than crown, with irregular light spots. Flight feathers barred light and dark; tail blackish, with 5-6 irregular whitish spot-bars not reaching shafts of rectrices. Throat white, separated from large white patch on foreneck and upper breast by a narrow brown band; sides of upper breast dark brown, mottled light and dark, flanks with dusky mottling and some indistinct streaking; centre of belly whitish. Tarsi feathered brown and white, toes bristled. *Red morph*: Overall brown with orange-rufous tinge, or orange-buff; crown dotted light buffy, or marked with some narrow shaft-streaks together with spots; mantle and back mottled, spotted and barred rufous and brown. Tail dark brown with 6-7 irregular oval, buffy spots in rows, suggesting bars. Underparts mottled and indistinctly streaked orange-buff and buffy-whitish; pale throat patch much smaller than in brown morph. **Juvenile** Downy chick whitish. Mesoptile similar to adult in coloration and structure, but crown unspotted, and less clearly marked below. **Bare parts** Eyes yellow. Cere and bill yellowish-horn. Toes yellow. Claws dark horn with blackish tips.

MEASUREMENTS AND WEIGHT Total length 15-16cm. Wing 97-106mm; tail 59-69mm; tail/wing ratio 0.57-0.69 (median 0.62); primary index about 15.0. Weight about 60g, females heavier than males.

GEOGRAPHICAL VARIATION Monotypic: *Glaucidium jardinii* (Bonaparte, 1855).

Central American birds, described as *Glaucidium jardinii costaricanum* are specifically distinct from Andean Pygmy Owl, whose distribution is confined to the Andes of NW South America, south to the Marañón depression. Pygmy owls of the taxon *costaricanum* from the mountains of Costa Rica to Panama, and perhaps to extreme NW South America (W Colombia), are probably related to Mountain Pygmy Owl [148] and might therefore be treated as a subspecies of that (according to vocal and DNA evidence), although very recent and ongoing studies suggest that they may perhaps prove to represent a separate species. For further details, see Mountain Pygmy Owl.

HABITS Probably similar to those of other pygmy owls. Partly diurnal and relatively often seen by day, when it is mobbed by small birds. Over larger distances has undulating flight with rapid wingbeats and gliding; on alighting, tail is often cocked and twisted from side to side.

FOOD Small birds, insects and other arthropods, small mammals, and other vertebrates. The prey is normally caught from a perch.

BREEDING Poorly known. Abandoned woodpecker holes in tree trunks, thick branches or even in dead stumps are used for nesting. Clutch size in general 3 white eggs. Breeding behaviour probably similar to that of other American pygmy owls.

STATUS AND CONSERVATION Uncertain. Locally rather frequent.

REMARKS Studies on the taxonomy, biology and ecology and, above all, on the bioacoustics and behaviour of the pygmy owls inhabiting montane forest in the Neotropics are needed in order to understand the specific limits between the taxa involved. According to our current knowledge, *Glaucidium jardinii* is endemic to the NW Andes, and specifically distinct from all other taxa which have traditionally been merged with it.

REFERENCES Fjeldså & Krabbe (1990), Hardy *et al.* (1989), Heidrich *et al.* (1995), Howell & Robbins (1995), König (1991, 1994), Miller (1963), Robbins & Stiles (1999), Wolf (1976).

157 YUNGAS PYGMY OWL
Glaucidium bolivianum   Plate 48

French: Chevêchette des Yungas
German: Yungas-Sperlingskauz
Spanish: Mochuelo yungueño, Caburé yungueño

IDENTIFICATION A very small pygmy owl (about 16cm), similar to Andean Pygmy Owl [156], but with rounded wing-tips and longer tail. Grey, brown and rufous morphs occur. Occipital face prominent, with narrow pale ochraceous-buff nuchal collar below it; crown rather densely marked with rounded or rhomboid whitish to pale buffy spots and some larger scaly dots, sometimes with pale shaft-streaks (elongated drop-shaped). Back irregularly spotted with light dots, often hastate-shaped. Off-white to pale buff below, with dark mottling on sides of upper chest, white throat separated from plain whitish central underparts by narrow dusky band (often slightly triangular), flanks and breast sides distinctly streaked dark. Tail blackish to dark brown with 4-5 visible broken pale bars. Eyes yellow. **Similar species** Andean Pygmy Owl has pointed wing-tips and a shorter tail, crown less densely marked with smaller spots, underparts more mottled and barred than streaked; no grey morph known. Subtropical Pygmy Owl [155] is smaller, with much shorter tail, unspotted mantle, and clear dark rufous-brown streaking on white underparts. Ferruginous Pygmy Owl [160] is mostly larger, very variable in coloration, and has crown normally marked with light shaft-streaks, tail with either more light bars or plain rufous; inhabits semi-open evergreen forest and tropical rain forest with clearings and edges. Peruvian Pygmy Owl [158] is very similar to Yungas, but more heavily streaked dark below, and with larger whitish spots (more rounded than hastate) on back and scapulars, and coloration very variable; distributed on Pacific side of W Ecuador and Peru, in semi-arid country and rather dry woodland on Andean slopes. Chaco Pygmy Owl [162] normally has an unspotted mantle (in both grey and rufescent morphs), crown and sides of head spotted whitish (pale buff in rufescent morph), with some very thin shaft-streaks on forehead and, sometimes, also on crown; distributed in arid, thorny shrubland and dry 'monte chaqueño', not entering humid montane forest.

VOCALISATIONS As Andean Pygmy Owl, Yungas has two different phrases in its song, which normally starts with 2-3 melodious (thrush-like) fluted whistles, ending with a tremolo, followed by a series of slightly drawn-out hollow notes, equally spaced and at relatively slow tempo (about 1.5-2 notes per second): *wuéeurrrr wuéeurrrr wuéeurrrr whew-whew-whew-whew-....* The second part is the commonest vocalisation, often uttered for minutes without break, while the 2-3 'introductory' whistles are relatively seldom heard. The whistle begins softly, rising gradually in volume and pitch, and ends with a downward-inflected tremolo, the whole lasting about 0.75-1.5 seconds, and is uttered normally 2-3 times at intervals of about 1 second. Then, after a break of about 0.7 seconds, the series of equally spaced notes (1.5-2 notes per second) begins: these may be given in shorter (6-10 notes) or longer sequences (50 or even more), with intervals of several seconds between each.

Females have a similar but slightly higher-pitched song, sometimes given in duet with the male, and normally of lesser intensity than the male's.

Short sequences of metallic twittering notes are uttered by female and fledglings when begging.

A male, which we had attracted by playback and which approached rather closely, stopped singing after a while, perched on a low branch a few metres away and began preening; some minutes later, it turned its head several times and we heard single, soft, very faint and somewhat plaintive *ooéeo* calls at varying intervals. We suppose that these notes may have a contact function. Similar calls were uttered by both sexes in a nesting area, without being provoked by playback.

DISTRIBUTION Slopes of the E Andes, from N Peru to Bolivia and N Argentina (Jujuy, Salta, Tucumán), including outlying higher mountains (e.g. Cerro Calilegua, Sierra de Santa Bárbara in Jujuy, El Rey National Park in Salta).

Yungas Pygmy Owl

MOVEMENTS Resident.

HABITAT Humid or temporarily humid montane and cloud forest, rich in epiphytes and creepers, from about 1,000m above sea-level to near timberline at 3,000m (locally even higher). Most common in 'yungas' (dense cloud forest with tangled undergrowth at 1,000-2,500m), reaching from 'Nogal' zone (predominant tree species *Juglans australis*) to 'Aliso' zone (dominated by *Alnus jorullensis*). This habitat of 'Southern Yungas' (partly deciduous Tucumán-Bolivian Forest) is shared in N Argentina with Montane Forest Screech Owl [71] and Buff-fronted Owl [181]. Often these forests are on steep slopes with humid and very densely tangled undergrowth, including climbing bamboo, in ravines; the tallest trees generally reach 20-25m, towering singly or in groups over the closed forest 'roof' about 10-15m up.

DESCRIPTION Adult Grey, brown and red morphs exist, brown being commonest; as the holotype belongs to the grey morph, however, description is based on that. *Grey morph*: Facial disc rather flat and poorly developed (as in all pygmy owls), pale greyish-brown with dusky flecks; eyebrows white. Upperparts dusky grey-brown with numerous whitish spots. Crown rather densely marked with more or less rounded, whitish dots and larger, scaly pale ochraceous markings, giving irregular scaly appearance

(single bird from Aconquija in Tucumán has many shaft-streaks, shaped like elongated spots, while another from same locality has spotted crown). Nape with prominent occipital face of two large black spots, edged whitish above and pale ochraceous below, forming narrow ochraceous nuchal collar. Mantle and back dark greyish-brown, with irregular whitish and pale ochraceous, often hastate-shaped spots; outer webs of scapulars partly whitish, but not very prominent. Flight feathers barred light and dark; tail blackish with six broken whitish bars (more or less oval spots, not reaching shaft of rectrix). Underparts off-white, with dusky greyish-brown mottled areas at sides of upper breast; throat white, bordered basally by narrow, dusky band, and below it to centre of breast a large rather rounded area of plain whitish, continuing in narrow zone to belly and abdomen; flanks and rest of underparts distinctly streaked dusky. Tarsi feathered, mottled dusky and whitish; toes bristled. *Brown morph*: Similar in pattern to grey morph, but general coloration warm, dark brown; whitish bars on blackish tail, normally only five. *Red morph*: General coloration rusty orange-brown; light markings on upper surface similar to other morphs. Tail dark brown with seven rows of oval, pale orange-brown spots, hardly reaching rectrix of each feather. Underparts similar in pattern to other morphs, but general coloration orange-brown; throat patch and area along centre of underside whitish (white areas larger than in red-morph Andean Pygmy Owl). **Juvenile** Downy chick probably whitish. Mesoptile similar to adult, but underparts less distinctly streaked and crown unspotted, slightly greyer than rest of upperparts. **Bare parts** Eyes golden-yellow. Cere and bill greenish-yellow. Toes dirty yellow. Claws dark horn with blackish tips.

MEASUREMENTS AND WEIGHT Total length about 16cm. Wing 94-105mm; tail 64-72.5mm. Females larger than males. Holotype (male) from Salta, Argentina: total length 161mm, wing 94mm, tail 67mm. Median tail/wing ratio about 0.70 (in Andean Pygmy Owl about 0.62); median primary index about 6.8 (in Andean about 15). Weight of 20 males averaged 59.6g, of 13 females 66.5g.

GEOGRAPHICAL VARIATION Monotypic: *Glaucidium bolivianum* König, 1992.

The grey morph seems to be restricted in range to the Southern Yungas between Tucumán and S Bolivia (to bend of Andes in Santa Cruz); here we saw only grey and red morphs. North of the big bend of the Andes the brown morph is predominant, while the red morph occurs throughout range. Northern birds may belong to an undescribed subspecies. Individual variation in plumage pattern is rather large: two birds from Aconquija (Tucumán), collected at 3,000m above sea-level (in Buenos Aires Natural History Museum), have a different crown pattern: one has more or less rhomboid whitish spots, the other has spots and many distinct shaft-streaks shaped like elongated drops.

HABITS Less diurnal than congeners. Activity normally begins at dusk; also vocally active on calm, moonlit nights and around dawn. In an area in N Argentina, where we found several pairs, we observed single individuals only twice (during over 150 visits in different years!) for a short while between sunset and dusk; all other observations were at dusk or on moonlit nights. No doubt there is some vocal activity during daytime, especially before dusk and around dawn, as small birds give mobbing response to imitation of the owl's song: we observed this reaction by small passerines and hummingbirds in different territories occupied by pairs of this owl, which we heard regularly at dusk and on some clear nights, when it was easily stimulated to sing or sang spontaneously; apart from the two cases mentioned above, all efforts to attract this species or to stimulate it to sing failed during daytime.

At the start of the breeding season (in Argentina, normally August/September) males begin singing at dusk, giving 2-3 fluted phrases and continuing with series of hollow, rather high 'toots'. The male moves around its territory while singing at intervals, mostly in the canopy region but sometimes from exposed perches. The peak of vocal activity is before eggs are laid. Singing then decreases and the birds lose interest in responding to imitations or playback, and during incubation vocal activity is low; in the nesting area, males may answer only with the soft, plaintive call.

FOOD Insects, other arthropods and small birds seem to be the major diet, but probably also takes other small vertebrates. We observed males several times carrying a small bird in the talons, but the gloomy light made it impossible to determine the species. This species forages primarily in the canopy and in dense foliage below it, for which its relatively long tail and rounded wings make it well adapted.

BREEDING Territories in N Argentina varied between 0.5 and 1km² on forested slopes; from one point on a slope, we could hear up to five males singing on several evenings. Abandoned woodpecker holes, normally rather high above ground, are used for breeding. Breeding biology almost unknown, but probably similar to that of other pygmy owls. The female incubates alone, while the male brings food, which may be delivered in the nest hole or outside if the female has come out to be fed.

STATUS AND CONSERVATION Uncertain. In N Argentina obviously endangered, and declining locally because of forest destruction; this may also be the case elsewhere. In an area well known to us since 1987 (the type locality), we formerly counted up to five singing males from one point, but between 1991 and 1995, at the same place, only one pair was found; in this area, the forest has been seriously damaged by logging, burning, and cattle grazing.

REMARKS This owl is apparently much less active by day than other *Glaucidium* species, especially the northern Andean Pygmy Owl; comparative studies would be of great interest. Its ecology, taxonomy, vocalisations and behaviour are under study by ourselves in Argentina, in cooperation with Argentine colleagues.

REFERENCES Fjeldså & Krabbe (1990), Heidrich *et al.* (1995), König (1991, 1994 and unpublished), König & Straneck (1989), Robbins & Stiles (1999), Straneck *et al.* (1987).

---

158 PERUVIAN PYGMY OWL
Glaucidium peruanum   Plate 48

French: Chevêchette du Pérou
German: Peru-Sperlingskauz
Spanish: Mochuelo peruano, Paca paca

IDENTIFICATION A very small pygmy owl (15-17cm) with tips of wings rather rounded, similar to Yungas and Ferruginous Pygmy Owls [157, 160], from which it differs vocally. Grey, brown and red morphs are known. Grey morph of higher altitudes normally has crown with larger and smaller rounded whitish dots, while birds living at lower altitudes often have crown with whitish or pale buff shaft-streaks and drop-shaped spots; white spots on back and scapulars larger and more rounded than on Yungas Pygmy Owl; occipital face bordered below by narrow ochraceous collar; underparts prominently streaked; tail dusky, with 5-6 visible broken whitish bars. Brown morph is similar in pattern, but general coloration dark brown instead of dusky greyish-brown. Red morph normally has streaked crown; tail brown with more or less distinct, rufescent barring, or rusty-brown with indistinct, often rather narrow and sometimes irregularly spaced brown bars, the light bars (6-7) often much wider than dark ones. **Similar species** Ferruginous Pygmy Owl is similarly highly polymorphic, but always lacks ochraceous nuchal collar below occipital face; it lives east of the Andes, not on the Pacific slope. Yungas Pygmy Owl has wing-tips rather rounded, has smaller, often hastate, light spots on back and mantle, and is less clearly streaked below, the red morph with crown more spotted than streaked; inhabits montane forest of E Andes. Both are best distinguished by voice.

VOCALISATIONS The song of the male is a rapid sequence of short, distinctly upslurred staccato notes, about 6-7 per second: *toitoitoitoitoitoitoitoitoit...* (Ferruginous Pygmy Owl utters about three notes per second). The phrase varies in length, and is normally repeated at short intervals. Female has a similar but slightly higher-pitched song. The very rapid sequence and the upslurred, short staccato notes are typical for this species. When excited, gives rather high-pitched, short *chirrp* notes, either singly or in series of normally 5-10 separated by intervals of about 0.35 seconds; the notes are higher in pitch, clearer and more metallic than those of Ferruginous Pygmy.

DISTRIBUTION From W Ecuador to SW Ecuador (Loja), W and SW Peru (Pacific slope) and northernmost Chile. From sea-level up the Andean slopes to Ancash, Apurímac and Arequipa.

Peruvian Pygmy Owl

MOVEMENTS Resident.

HABITAT Semi-arid bushland, thorny scrub with cacti and scattered trees, semi-open, dry or semi-arid woods, rather open landscape with groves or scattered groups of trees, eucalyptus plantations, riparian woodland, agricultural land with trees, and urban parks (e.g. in Lima). From sea-level up to 3,000m, locally even higher (Arequipa). Type locality is thorny scrub with some trees near Ninabamba in Apurímac (Peru), at 2,100m.

DESCRIPTION Adult Grey, brown and red morphs are known. Holotype is of the grey morph, which is therefore used as basis for description. *Grey morph*: Very similar to grey-morph Ferruginous Pygmy Owl. Upperparts dark greyish-brown, mantle and back with whitish spots of variable size and shape, often more or less rounded (not hastate); outer webs of scapulars with larger areas of whitish. Forehead with very small and narrow pale shaft-streaks, crown to nape and sides of head with smaller and larger whitish spots and some fine speckles (birds from lower elevations, e.g. Lima, often have some spots and many prominent elongated drop-shaped shaft-streaks on crown); nape with occipital face edged whitish above, and with narrow ochraceous nuchal collar below. Flight feathers barred light and dark; tail dark greyish-brown with 6-7 broken whitish bars (normally 4-5 visible), not reaching shafts of rectrices. Underparts whitish, with relatively large whitish throat patch; sides of upper breast densely mottled dark greyish-brown with few whitish speckles, rest of underparts boldly streaked dark greyish-brown. Tarsi feathered greyish-brown, mottled with off-white; toes bristled. *Brown morph*: Similar in pattern to grey morph; crown more finely spotted light and general coloration dark earth-brown. *Red morph*: Upperparts rusty-brown with pale buffy or whitish flecks and dots; crown normally with light buffy shaft-streaks. Tail normally rufescent-brown with about seven lighter rusty-brown or orange-buff bars, which may reach shafts (light bars quite often rather diffuse and wider than dark ones). Underparts off-white to pale buffy with orange-brown markings, less distinctly patterned than in grey and brown morphs. **Juvenile** Downy chick whitish. Mesoptile similar to adult, but crown plain, unspotted. **Bare parts** Eyes yellow. Cere and bill greenish-yellow. Toes yellow. Claws dark horn with blackish tips.

MEASUREMENTS AND WEIGHT Total length 15-17cm. Wing of male (holotype) 98mm, of 4 females 101-109mm; tail of male (holotype) 67.5mm, of 4 females 69-75mm; tail/wing ratio 0.68-0.73 (wing-tips rounded, primaries at most only slightly exceeding secondaries on folded wing). Weight of 3 males 58-62g, of 1 female 64.5g.

GEOGRAPHICAL VARIATION Monotypic: *Glaucidium peruanum* König, 1991. Highly polymorphic, but populations of higher and lower altitudes may perhaps belong to different subspecies. More study needed.

HABITS Partly diurnal. May be seen in bright daylight, even perched in exposed position. We observed a red-morph individual near Guayaquil (W Ecuador) perched on a telephone wire, close to the mud nest of Pale-legged Hornero *Furnarius leucopus* on a wooden mast: when we approached, it adopted a slim posture, facing us, and then suddenly turned around, jumped to the nest and slipped inside it; we supposed that this bird was a female with eggs or chicks, because it entered the nest instead of flying away (similar behaviour can be observed with Little Owls [176]).

Vocal activity is frequent at dusk, sometimes also on clear nights; by day, singing may be provoked by playback or imitation of song. Small birds give mobbing response to playback in areas where the owl is present.

FOOD Insects and small birds seem to be the major food, but locally small mammals and other small vertebrates may account for a considerable percentage of the diet. Prey is normally caught from a perch.

BREEDING Little studied. Males are very territorial and defend their territories, even making diving attacks against intruders (and in response to playback). Old woodpecker holes in trees (and large cacti?) seem to be the most common nesting site; occasionally, mud nests of horneros on branches, telephone masts etc, and possibly even holes in walls or river banks, may be used. The female incubates alone. Breeding biology not described, but probably similar to that of other American pygmy owls.

STATUS AND CONSERVATION Uncertain. Locally apparently not rare. Often living in agricultural areas, it may be threatened by the use of pesticides.

REMARKS Until 1991, this species was considered conspecific with Ferruginous Pygmy Owl, being merged with nominate race of latter. The very different vocalisations, some morphological patterns, ecological and zoogeographical aspects and DNA evidence have shown, however, that Peruvian Pygmy Owl is a distinct species. Since it has previously been merged with Ferruginous Pygmy, next to nothing is known of its biology. Research on the whole biology, including behaviour and vocalisations, as well as on taxonomy (geographical variation) and distribution, will be of great import.

REFERENCES Araya & Millie (1986), Fjeldså & Krabbe (1990), Hardy *et al.* (1989), Heidrich *et al.* (1995), Johnson & Goodall (1967), Koepcke (1964), Koepcke & Koepcke (1958), König (1991, 1994 and unpublished), Krabbe (pers. comm. and recordings), T. A. Parker (pers. comm.), Parker *et al.* (1982).

159 AUSTRAL PYGMY OWL
Glaucidium nanum   Plate 48

French: Chevêchette de Patagonie
German: Patagonien-Sperlingskauz
Spanish: Caburé patagónico (Argentina), Chuncho (Chile)

IDENTIFICATION A very small to small pygmy owl (17-21cm) with prominent occipital face. Forehead and crown with distinct whitish or pale buffy shaft-streaks, eyebrows and lores whitish; dark greyish-brown or rufous above with whitish spots, outer webs of scapulars with large areas of white. Dark brown or rufescent-brown tail with 8-11 pale buff to rusty-orange narrow bars, light bars normally narrower than dark ones, bars reaching shafts of rectrices. Off-white to whitish-buff below with rather fine but dense dusky shaft-streaks, and rather plain whitish on flanks and in centre of underparts. Eyes yellow. **Similar species** Southernmost subspecies of Ferruginous Pygmy Owl [160] is about equal in size, but is more boldly streaked below and tail is less densely barred; eyes relatively larger. Peruvian Pygmy Owl [158] is smaller, with wing-tips more rounded, and has ochraceous nuchal collar, crown more spotted than streaked and tail less densely barred; in red morph, light bars on tail are wider than dark ones. Both differ voally. Burrowing Owl [174] is larger and longer-legged, with underparts more barred.

VOCALISATIONS The song of the male is a rapid sequence of rather hard, staccato, very short, equally spaced notes, about 3.5-5 per second: *kü-kü-kü-kü-kü-kü....* A sequence may consist of 20-30 notes, sometimes more, repeated at intervals of several seconds. The female has a similar but higher-pitched and less 'full' song. In excitement, both sexes utter a rather metallic chirping *chrickchrickchrickchrick*, often introduced by metallic ticking, *tick-tick-ticktick-chrickchrick...*; four *chrick* notes per second. Female and young beg with metallic chirps, *trigigigirrr* or *trigigick*. Male advertising potential nesting sites sings from the entrance and, from inside, utters a soft cooing sequence, undulating in volume, together with some single clicking notes. Both sexes emit low *duid* calls and a drawn *diuh*. During copulation, high twittering series may be heard.

DISTRIBUTION Argentine Patagonia from Rio Negro to Tierra del Fuego; Chile from south of the Atacama Desert to Tierra del Fuego.

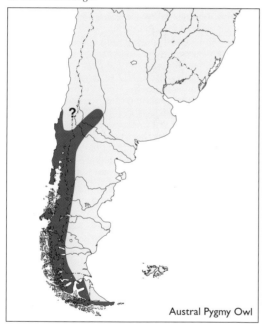

Austral Pygmy Owl

MOVEMENTS In general resident. In harsh winters, some individuals (primarily immatures) from southernmost populations may migrate northwards up to C Argentina. Migration to NW Argentina requires confirmation.

HABITAT Open landscape with shrubs and groups of trees, rather open forest on Andean slopes, and humid *Nothofagus* forest in S Patagonia and Tierra del Fuego; locally in parks and on farmland with scattered trees or small groves. Also in arid areas with shrubs and ravines, where it may nest in burrows of other birds in banks.

DESCRIPTION Adult Red and grey-brown morphs are known, but in general much less polymorphic than

Ferruginous or Peruvian Pygmy Owls. *Grey-brown morph*: Facial disc pale greyish-brown with fine dark flecks and streaks; eyebrows and lores whitish. Upperparts dark greyish-brown, spotted whitish (dots variable in size and shape). Forehead finely streaked whitish, crown with distinct, dense whitish to pale buff shaft-streaks; occipital face prominent, bordered above and below by whitish (no ochraceous nuchal collar). Mantle and back irregularly spotted light, outer webs of scapulars with large areas of white. Flight feathers barred light and dark; tail dark greyish-brown, with about 8-11 very narrow buffy bars that reach shafts of rectrices, light bars in general narrower than dark ones. Underparts off-white, with dark greyish-brown, whitish-speckled patches at sides of upper breast; white throat patch relatively small, continuing into narrow zone in middle of underside, with further narrow white flank panel from about breast to thighs, area between central and flank panels densely marked with narrow and relatively short shaft-streaks. Tarsi feathered whitish, mottled with greyish-brown; toes bristled. *Red morph*: Similar in pattern to grey-brown morph, but dark greyish-brown replaced by rufous-brown (never as foxy-reddish as Peruvian or Ferruginous Pygmy Owls). Intermediates between the two morphs also occur. **Juvenile** Downy chick whitish. Mesoptile similar to adult, but patterns less distinct, crown unspotted. **Bare parts** Eyes light yellow; in immatures deep yellow, often with orange tint. Cere and bill greenish-yellow. Toes yellow. Claws dark horn with blackish tips.

MEASUREMENTS AND WEIGHT Total length 17-21cm. Wing of males 93-104mm, of females 97-108mm; tail of males 65-73mm, of females 68-76mm. Weight of males 55.4-74g, of females 69.6-100g.

GEOGRAPHICAL VARIATION Monotypic: *Glaucidium nanum* (King, 1828). Birds from C Chile often have light tail-bars wider than dark ones; they have been described as *G. n. vafrum* but we regard this as probably a synonym.

HABITS Partly diurnal, but also active at night. Exposed perches are often used for singing. In general not shy; may be seen perched rather openly in bright daylight, but normally keeps among foliage. Can be very aggressive in response to playback. Flight over larger distances undulating, with rapid wingbeats and gliding; flies low over ground and swoops up to a perch. When seen by day, mobbed by many small birds, which also give mobbing response to imitation of its song and approach closely: this is a clue to this owl's presence in an area, as the small birds 'learn' that the vocalisations are those of a predator on them (in Patagonia, e.g. Thorn-tailed Rayadito *Aphrastura spinicauda*, White-crested Elaenia *Elaenia albiceps*, Patagonian Sierra-finch *Phrygilus patagonicus*, House Wren *Troglodytes aedon*, Rufous-collared Sparrow *Zonotrichia capensis* and other small birds may gather around the source of the call).

FOOD Insects (up to about 50%), small mammals (about 32%) and birds (about 14%) are the major prey, with about 2% reptiles; dragonflies are also captured. Prey may be rather large, e.g. up to size of Chilean Tinamou *Nothoprocta perdicaria* weighing about 160g, Eared Dove *Zenaida auriculata* (137g) and Falkland Thrush *Turdus falklandii* (94.3g); among mammals, Bennett's chinchilla rat *Abrocoma bennetti* weighing 80g and other rodents between 24g and 80g have been reported as prey. Scorpions and spiders are taken occasionally. Near Lago

Argentino (Santa Cruz), we observed a male plundering a House Wren nest containing chicks just about to fledge: the owl returned at intervals of about 15 minutes, taking one chick after another and carrying it to its own nest with young; the adult wrens, together with other small birds, scolded and mobbed the owl, which appeared unbothered by their attentions.

BREEDING Male starts singing normally in August or September, and reproductive activity generally begins in October. The territory is about 1km² in size; locally smaller when population is larger, e.g. in Los Glaciares National Park in Santa Cruz, Argentine, where from one spot we heard four males singing. Nesting by two pairs in the same tree has been reported, but this seems doubtful to us. The male advertises potential nesting site by singing near it, slipping into the hole and singing from the entrance; when a female approaches, he withdraws inside and emits an undulating cooing interspersed with clicking sounds. The female often inspects the hole and the male leaves, watching the entrance; if she leaves, he flies with cooing notes to the hole and tries to attract her again. Male often deposits food inside the cavity; female normally accepts this 'gift' and pair-bond begins to be firmly established. Copulation takes place near the nest site.

Nest is normally a hole in a trunk, mostly made by Chilean Flicker *Colaptes pitius*, often rather low down (1-2m above ground); we found nests in trunks of *Nothofagus antarctica* and *N. pumilio*. Burrows made by mammals or birds (e.g. Dark-bellied Cinclodes *Cinclodes patagonicus*) in river or road banks are also used, as well as holes in walls of buildings. The same nesting holes are often used in successive years.

Lays 3-5 white eggs directly on to the floor of the hole, at intervals of about 2 days. Incubation, by female alone, starts when the last egg is being laid and lasts about 26-28 days. In contrast to Eurasian Pygmy Owl [143], no cleaning of the nest was observed, and no food remains or pellets were found beneath occupied nests. The young leave the nest when about 4-5 weeks old, and are able to fly short distances; they are cared for by both parents for at least 3-4 weeks more. In the following year they reach sexual maturity. We found recently fledged young in early and mid December, as well as in early January in S Patagonia.

In the wild, this species may reach an age of 6-7 years, possibly more in captivity.

STATUS AND CONSERVATION Locally not rare. Where population density is high, occupied nests may be only about 200m (or even less?) apart. In agricultural areas, may be threatened by use of pesticides.

REMARKS This owl has been often regarded as a sub-species of Ferruginous Pygmy Owl because of similarities in plumage and song. Apart from song, however, the remaining vocabulary is very different from that of Ferruginous, and this, along with DNA evidence, shows clearly that the two are different species, being generally allopatric and locally perhaps parapatric. Biology and behaviour of both need more study.

REFERENCES Araya & Millie (1986), Barros (1950), Fjeldså & Krabbe (1990), Heidrich *et al.* (1995), Housse (1945), Humphrey *et al.* (1970), Jiménez & Jaksic (1989), Johnson & Goodall (1967), König (1987, 1991, 1994 and unpublished), Narosky & Yzurieta (1987), Olrog (1948, 1979), Vuilleumier (1985).

160   FERRUGINOUS PYGMY OWL
Glaucidium brasilianum   Plate 49

French: Chevêchette du Brésil
German: Brasil-Sperlingskauz
Spanish: Caburé común
Portuguese: Caburé do sol

IDENTIFICATION A very small to small pygmy owl (17-20cm) with very variable coloration and plumage pattern, as well as body size. Grey, brown and red morphs, as well as intermediates, are known, making it therefore very difficult to distinguish from other species of pygmy owl. Forehead and crown normally with light shaft-streaks; occipital face prominent, edged whitish to pale ochre but without ochraceous nuchal collar; mantle and back either plain or irregularly spotted whitish or buff, scapulars with much whitish or pale buff. Off-white to pale buff below, distinctly streaked. Tail dark brown, grey-brown or rufous, with 6-7 broken whitish or orange-buffy bars, or plain rufous, but variable (see Description and Geographical Variation). **Similar species** Least, Amazonian and Sub-tropical Pygmy Owls [153-155] are smaller, with shorter tail, and crown spotted (not streaked). Chaco Pygmy Owl [162] is smaller, with crown spotted and only slightly streaked, mantle and back unspotted and scapulars generally without whitish on outer webs, and lives in dry habitats. Andean and Yungas Pygmy Owls [156, 157] have crown more spotted than streaked, and live in montane forest at higher altitudes. Austral Pygmy Owl [159] has tail rather densely barred (8-11 rufescent or buffy, never white, bars) and is less polymorphic; it has an allopatric distribution in Patagonia and Chile south of the Atacama Desert. Also allopatric is Peruvian Pygmy Owl [158] (Pacific slope from W Ecuador to N Chile), which has a narrow ochraceous nuchal collar and often a spotted crown. Ridgway's Pygmy Owl [161] has tail more densely barred (most often rufescent, less frequently whitish, similar to Austral Pygmy) and crown boldly streaked. All are best separated by voice.

VOCALISATIONS The song of the male consists of long series of equally spaced notes, three per second, with a somewhat bell-like ringing character: *poip-poip-poip-poip-poip-*.... Each phrase may contain 20-30 notes or even more when excited, with phrases repeated after an interval of several seconds. The female has a similar but higher-pitched and less 'clear' song. During courtship, male and female may be heard duetting, but female very soon utters just a high-pitched twitter, *trigigigick*, in response to male. When excited (e.g. attracted by playback), both sexes utter several rather metallic *chirrp* notes at regular intervals of two per second, sometimes irregularly at longer intervals; females especially introduce such notes with accelerated sequence of ticks, *tjick–tjick-tjicktjicktjick - chirrrp – chirrrp –* .... When advertising a potential nesting site, the male utters short sequence of very high-pitched, cricket-like trills, *tsreep-tsreep-tsreep-tsreep-tsreep*; before copulation, male gives stuttering *ducky-duck-ducky-ducky-duck-ducky* in flight; during copulation a high twitter is given. A soft *dew* given by both sexes seems to have a contact function. Young beg with faint squeezing sounds, *cheep, cheep-cheep,*..., and emit short, metallic twittering sounds.

DISTRIBUTION From N South America east of the Andes (E Colombia, Venezuela, E Ecuador, the Guianas and N

Brazil), south through the Amazon to E Bolivia, E Paraguay, Uruguay and C Argentina to La Pampa and Buenos Aires province.

MOVEMENTS Resident. Young birds may wander about.

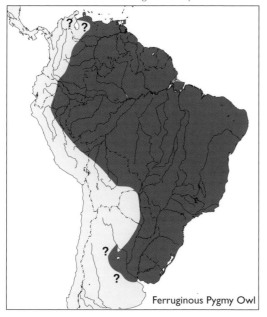

Ferruginous Pygmy Owl

HABITAT Tropical and subtropical (mostly humid) primary or secondary forest with clearings, forest edges, riverine forest, pastureland with groups of trees and bushy areas, parks and large gardens with old trees and thick bushes. Normally below 1,500m; does not enter montane or cloud forest. Prefers evergreen or semi-deciduous forest with undergrowth in lowlands; rather common in subtropical and tropical rain forest of E Brazil, E Paraguay and NE Argentina (Misiones), where inhabits forest with dense undergrowth. Absent from arid landscapes with giant cacti and thorny scrub.

DESCRIPTION *G. b. brasilianum* **Adult** Highly polymorphic, occurring in grey, brown and red morphs, with intermediates; in nominate race, brown morph most common, red rather common, grey rather rare. *Brown morph*: Facial disc pale ochraceous-brown with darker flecks; eyebrows whitish. Upperparts warm earth-brown, crown with narrow pale buffy shaft-streaks, nape with occipital face of black 'eye-spots' bordered whitish above and pale ochraceous below (but not forming narrow nuchal collar); mantle and back either plain or irregularly spotted pale buff to whitish, uppertail-coverts with rufous tint; scapulars with pale buffy edges of outer webs, wing-coverts spotted whitish or whitish-buff. Flight feathers barred light and dark; tail dark brown with 6-7 broken whitish bars (not reaching shafts of rectrices). Underparts off-white, sides of upper chest densely mottled brown with some lighter flecks, rest of underparts streaked brown. Tarsi feathered brown and pale buff, toes bristled. *Grey morph*: Similar to brown morph in plumage pattern, but general coloration greyish-brown and light markings whitish. *Red morph*: Upperparts rusty-brown, more or less spotted buff, crown with pale buffy shaft-streaks. Tail rusty-brown with narrow dark brown bars, the dusky bars

narrower than rusty spaces between; sometimes plain rusty-brown without markings. Underparts pale buffy with rusty-brown streaks. **Juvenile** Downy chick whitish. Mesoptile similar to adult, but markings less clear and crown plain. **Bare parts** Eyes yellow. Cere and bill greenish-yellow. Toes pale yellow. Claws dark horn with blackish tips.

MEASUREMENTS AND WEIGHT Total length 17-20cm. Wing 93-108mm; tail 55-76mm. Weight of males 46-74g (median 61.4g), of females 62-95g (median 75.1g); 1 female of largest race (*stranecki*) weighed 107g.

GEOGRAPHICAL VARIATION Because of considerable individual polymorphy, it is difficult to distinguish different subspecies. We recognise six races, one of which may be specifically distinct.

G. b. brasilianum (Gmelin, 1788). From Maranho and Ceará in NE Brazil south to Mato Grosso, São Paulo, Paraná, Rio Grande do Sul, E Paraguay, NE Argentina and N Uruguay. See Description. Wing 93-106mm; tail about 68mm.

G. b. medianum Todd, 1916. N Colombia, N Venezuela, N Surinam, N Guianas. Relatively small, grey-brown morph with broken whitish tail-bars frequent; red morph or birds with rufescent tail-bars less common than grey-brown morph. Wing 95-99mm; tail 58-65mm.

G. b. phaloenoides (Daudin, 1800). Islands of Trinidad and Margarita, perhaps intergrading somewhere in N Venezuela with *medianum*. Similar to *medianum*. Wing 99-104mm.

G. b. duidae Chapman, 1929. Probably endemic to Mt Duida in Venezuela, but perhaps also in other mountains of this region. Very dark, with unspotted mantle, crown with fine whitish or ochraceous shaft-streaks; tail blackish with incomplete whitish bars; wnderparts with white throat patch and rather dense, dark brown streaking. Wing 95-101mm; tail 55-62mm.

G. (b.) ucayalae Chapman, 1929. S Venezuela, Amazonian Colombia and Amazonian Brazil south to E Ecuador, E Peru and Bolivia. Red morph rufescent-brown above, crown indistinctly streaked, tail uniform chestnut or very indistinctly barred darker; brown morph similar to red, but general coloration less rufescent; underparts of both rather densely streaked, throat patch white. Wing 98-106mm; tail 58-65mm. (This form may be specifically distinct from *G. brasilianum*, as its song has a more hollow quality with more staccato notes. DNA evidence also suggests separation.)

G. b. stranecki König & Wink, 1995. S Uruguay, and C and E Argentina from Entre Rios and Córdoba to La Pampa and Buenos Aires; in more open habitats with shrubs and small woods, locally in parks and large gardens near or even in human settlements. Crown distinctly streaked pale ochraceous or buff; brown and red morphs with tail barred buffy and brown; less frequent grey morph with broken whitish bars on dusky brown tail. Largest subspecies: wing 102-108mm, tail 70-76mm; weight of males about 70-76g, of females 85-93g (1 female from La Pampa 107g).

HABITS Partly diurnal; may be seen in bright daylight on exposed perches. May also sing by day, and often rather easily stimulated to sing by playback or whistled imitation of its song, when it will sometimes attack the imitator with diving flights. Principal activity at dusk or around dawn; sometimes vocally active on clear, calm nights. During daytime normally roosts within shelter of foliage in trees or bushes, but always alert. When excited cocks tail and flicks it from one side to the other. When seen by day, it is often mobbed by small birds, which also give mobbing response to imitations of its song. The flight is undulating, with rapid wingbeats and gliding.

FOOD Insects, small birds and other small vertebrates make up the main food. Birds up to the size of a thrush (Creamy-bellied Thrush *Turdus amaurochalinus*) and Eared Dove *Zenaida auriculata* have been recorded as prey; we found decapitated individuals of these species in food depots of the race *stranecki* in shrubby pastureland with small woods in Calamuchita (Córdoba province, Argentina). In NE Argentina (Misiones), imitations of Ferruginous Pygmy Owl elicited fierce mobbing responses by Pale-breasted Thrush *T. leucomelas*; it would seem likely that this thrush, smaller than *T. amaurochalinus*, is also preyed on by the smaller nominate race. The powerful talons suggest that this pygmy owl is able to catch prey larger than itself. In forest it forages and moves about at medium height and near the ground. Normally hunts from a perch, but may catch a bird or insect among foliage in sudden dashing flight.

BREEDING Territorial for most of year. Peaks of vocal activity are in late winter and autumn in subtropical areas, nearly all year in the tropics. Male advertises potential nesting sites by singing from a nearby perch or by flying with series of cricket-like chirps to the hole, entering and singing, or chirping from the entrance, or from inside the cavity. For copulation, on a branch near the nest, the male utters series of 'stuttering' notes as it glides towards the female, perched in a rather horizontal position with tail slightly raised; copulation is accompanied by a high twitter, then the male flies off with stuttering notes and loud chirps. The female normally stays all day near the nest, entering occasionally or remaining some time inside, before going to roosting at nearby perch.

Abandoned woodpecker holes in trees, mud nests of Rufous Horneros *Furnarius rufus*, burrows in banks, or even holes in walls and opened nests of termites in trees may be used for breeding; no material is added. The nest site is normally rather high up, but may also be at lower heights; we found one in Córdoba (Argentina) a little more than 2m above ground in an abandoned hole of Golden-breasted Woodpecker *Colaptes melanochloros melanolaimus*, and another in Misiones (NE Argentina) was in a hole of Green-barred Woodpecker *C. m. melanochloros* about 5-6m up in a dead stump.

Lays 3-5 white eggs (about 29 x 23mm) directly on to the bottom of the nest-hole, where the sexes together scratch a shallow depression; the male may be more active in scratching inside the cavity during courtship; sometimes chips of wood are torn from the wall of the cavity. A nest in Córdoba contained 5 recently laid eggs in mid October; in Misiones, a hole was advertised by the male several times on 9th September, by which date no eggs were present; our observations in Misiones suggest that laying occurs in October. Eggs are laid at 2-day intervals, incubation starting with the final egg and lasting 24-27 days. The female incubates alone and is fed by her mate, who brings food into the nest or drops prey at certain deposits, from where the female collects it when leaving the nest for a short break. Newly hatched chicks weigh about 4 g; they are initially fed only by the female, later by both parents,

and remain in the nest about 4 weeks. When young leave, they are already able to fly a short distance; they remain a few days near the nest, hidden among foliage, keeping contact with their parents by metallic chirping calls, and are cared for by both parents for at least 2-3 weeks. Sexual maturity is reached in the following spring.

STATUS AND CONSERVATION At least locally common, e.g. in subtropical, semi-open secondary forest with dense undergrowth and in remnants of primary forest with clearings in SE Brazil and NE Argentina. Forest destruction is an endangering factor. In some areas, 'Caburés' (pygmy owls) are taken by man because of the superstitious belief that feathers or parts of these birds bring fortune and success in love to the person possessing them; for similar reasons these owls are kept in cages as pets, although this is prohibited in most countries. Other small owls may also suffer from this superstitious tradition.

REMARKS Although this species is widespread and rather common, little is known of its taxonomy and biology. Many data given here are based on our own experience. The taxonomy of many described forms, however, remains to be clarified, and distributional limits therefore are in many cases uncertain (e.g. *G. ridgwayi*, *G. peruanum*, *G. tucumanum*), while specific or subspecific patterns require more study. Vocal and molecular-biological evidence is still lacking for some taxa, and it is not clear whether *medianum*, *duidae* and *phaloenoides* really are subspecies of *G. brasilianum*. A problem also exists in E Brazil (Espirito Santo), where rather large individuals (almost the size of *stranecki*) of a grey and a red morph occur among 'normal-sized' nominate Ferruginous Pygmy Owls; whether these differences in body size are due to individual polymophy or are an indication of an undescribed species has yet to be determined. The whole '*brasilianum* complex' is in need of taxonomic revision.

REFERENCES Boyer & Hume (1991), Burton (1992), Chapman (1922, 1929), Diesener (1971), Dunning (1985), Hardy *et al.* (1989), Heidrich *et al.* (1995), Kemp (1989), König (1991, 1994 and unpublished), König & Wink (1995), Voous (1988).

---

161 RIDGWAY'S PYGMY OWL
Glaucidium ridgwayi   Plate 49

French: Chevêchette de Ridgway
German: Ridgway-Sperlingskauz
Spanish: Tecolotito de Ridgway

IDENTIFICATION A highly polymorphic species, very similar in size and plumage to Ferruginous Pygmy Owl [160] and hitherto usually considered conspecific with it. Crown more densely streaked and tail with 6-8 bars, latter mostly rufous or pale buffy (even in grey-brown morph), birds with whitish tail-bars being relatively rare. Occipital face prominent, nape without ochraceous nuchal collar; mantle irregularly spotted light, scapulars with much whitish on outer webs. Below, boldly streaked on off-white. Eyes yellow. **Similar species** All other pygmy owls in this species' range have tail less densely barred and crown spotted rather than streaked. Elf Owl [173] is much smaller, with shorter tail and without occipital face.

VOCALISATIONS The song of the male is similar to that of Ferruginous Pygmy Owl, but sequence of notes slower (about 2.5-3 notes per second), and hollower in character. In addition, gives a faster and more insistent *whi-whi-whi-...*, breaking into bursts of high, yelping twitters; these vocalisations are very different from those of Ferruginous Pygmy, and might have the same function as the latter's cricket-like chirps. Also gives irregular, short series, similar to those of Colima Pygmy Owl [151].

DISTRIBUTION SW USA (S Arizona and Texas) to Mexico, from Sonora and Tamaulípas, and south to Panama and extreme NW South America (NW Colombia).

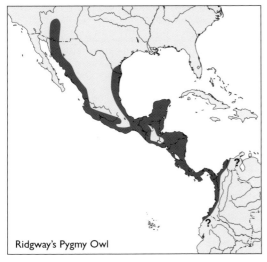

Ridgway's Pygmy Owl

MOVEMENTS Resident.

HABITAT Semi-open areas with thorny scrub and giant cacti, scattered patches of woodland in open landscapes, plantations, open, mostly dry woods, and evergreen secondary growth. From sea-level up to about 1,500m, locally slightly higher; in general in lowlands, not in montane forest.

DESCRIPTION *G. r. ridgwayi* **Adult** Very polymorphic, with grey-brown and red morphs, as well as intermediates. *Greyish-brown morph*: Facial disc light brown, flecked whitish; eyebrows whitish. Upperparts greyish-brown, forehead and crown rather densely streaked pale buff to whitish, nape with occipital face edged pale buff; mantle slightly darker than crown, irregularly spotted whitish-buff; wing-coverts barred light and dark, outer webs of scapulars with large whitish areas forming distinct row of spots across shoulder. Flight feathers barred light and dark; tail dark brown with 6-8 rufescent, ochraceous or whitish bars. Throat patch off-white, sides of upper breast greyish-brown with buffy streaks and spots; rest of underparts boldly streaked brown or greyish-brown. Tarsi feathered, toes bristled. *Red morph*: Similar in pattern to greyish-brown morph, but general coloration rufous to orange-brown; tail always barred rufous. **Juvenile** Downy chick white. Mesoptile similar to adult, but patterns less clear; crown often greyer than back, plain, with fine light shaft-streaks on forehead. **Bare parts** Eyes pale yellow. Cere and bill greenish-yellow. Toes yellowish. Claws dusky horn with blackish tips.

MEASUREMENTS AND WEIGHT Total length 16.5-18.5cm. Wing 85-100mm; tail of males 56-64mm, of females 57-70mm. Weight about 60-70g, females larger and heavier than males.

GEOGRAPHICAL VARIATION We recognise two subspecies.

G. r. ridgway Sharpe, 1875. Lower Rio Grande Valley in Texas to E Mexico and south to C America, Panama and extreme NW Colombia. See Description. Wing 89-100mm; tail 56-64mm.

G. r. cactorum Van Rossem, 1937. S Arizona to Nayarit and Jalisco in W Mexico. General coloration greyer; light bars of tail never white, always rufescent or buff. Wings shorter and tail longer than in nominate: wing 85-95mm; tail 59-70mm.

HABITS Partly diurnal, but most activity at dusk and dawn; sometimes active by night. During daytime mostly hidden among foliage, but sometimes on exposed perch in bright sunshine; often mobbed by small birds, including in response to imitation of its song. May be stimulated to sing and approach by playback or imitation of song. In semi-deserts often perches on tops of giant cacti. Flight over larger distances is rather straight, with rapid wingbeats alternating with gliding.

FOOD Mostly insects, small birds, reptiles and small mammals. Forages at medium height in wooded areas, or in bushes near ground. The prey is normally caught from a perch, or in dashing flight into thickets or dense foliage.

BREEDING Similar to that of Ferruginous Pygmy Owl. Nests in woodpecker holes in trees or giant cacti; sometimes opened nests of termites in trees may be accepted. The female lays 3-5 white eggs and incubates alone. Breeding biology little studied, but probably similar to that of other pygmy owls.

STATUS AND CONSERVATION Uncertain. Locally common.

REMARKS Hitherto considered a race of Ferruginous Pygmy Owl. We separate the two taxa as allopatric species on the basis of DNA evidence and vocalisations; moreover, they seem to show some differences in ecology and behaviour. Further studies are needed, however, conclusively to resolve this question, revising the whole '*brasilianum* complex'. *Glaucidium brasilianum* probably represents a superspecies, with various related allospecies and paraspecies which have already reached species level.

REFERENCES Boyer & Hume (1991), Burton (1992), Heidrich *et al.* (1995), Howell & Webb (1995), König (1991), Stiles & Skutch (1989), Van Rossem (1937), Voous (1988).

---

162 CHACO PYGMY OWL
Glaucidium tucumanum   Plate 49

French: Chevêchette du Chaco
German: Chaco-Sperlingskauz
Spanish: Caburé chaqueño
Portuguese: Caburé do Chaco

IDENTIFICATION A very small pygmy owl (16.5-17.5cm) similar to Ferruginous Pygmy Owl [160], but with less individual variation, though occurs in grey, brown and red morphs. Commonest is grey morph, with rather dark grey-brown or slaty-grey upperparts and unspotted mantle, scapulars without (or with only indication of) lighter spots, forehead with fine whitish shaft-streaks, crown with some fine streaks grading into rounded spots on hindcrown and sides of head; tail blackish-brown with 5-6 broken whitish bars; off-white below, with large dusky areas on chest sides, rest of underparts heavily streaked dusky. Eyes bright yellow. Red morph pale rufescent-brown, with brown and rufescent bars on tail, crown indistinctly streaked and spotted. Brown morph similar in pattern to grey morph, but warm brown, scapulars sometimes with whitish areas; back and mantle may show some light spotting. **Similar species** Ferruginous Pygmy Owl normally somewhat larger, and much more polymorphic individually; crown more streaked than spotted; habitat different and vocalisations distinct. Yungas Pygmy Owl [157] very similar, but has rounded or drop-shaped spots on crown and an ochraceous nuchal collar; inhabits montane and cloud forest, which Chaco Pygmy Owl does not penetrate, and has different vocalisations.

VOCALISATIONS The song of the male is a series of equally spaced, distinctly upward-inflected staccato notes in relatively slow succession (about two notes per second): *toik-toik-toik-toik-....* These series, of about 10-30 notes (sometimes many more!), are repeated at intervals of several seconds. Song normally starts rather softly with notes on even pitch, increasing gradually in volume and finally reaching the yelping, upward-inflected quality, this being typical for this species. The female has a similar but higher-pitched and less 'clear' song. Duet occur during courtship. Both sexes utter, when excited, single *uik* notes, sometimes accelerating into short sequence and followed by mellow *chirrp* notes, lower and more melodic than those of Ferruginous Pygmy, *chewrr, chewrr,....* Female gives a short twitter when begging.

DISTRIBUTION Bolivian, Paraguayan and Argentine Chaco, south to Tucumán, N Córdoba and Santiago del Estero.

MOVEMENTS Probably resident.

Chaco Pygmy Owl

HABITAT Semi-open dry forest ('monte chaqueño'), thorny scrub with scattered trees and giant cacti, and semi-arid and arid bushy country with scattered trees or small groves, from about 500m up to about 1,800m above sea-level if habitat is suitable. Avoids montane forest. Locally, near or in human settlements with gardens or parks. Near the Argentine town of Salta, it occurs principally in hilly country with thorny scrub, scattered trees (e.g. *Chorisia insignis, Prosopis nigra, Aspidosperma quebracho-blanco*) and giant cacti (*Trichocereus terschecki*), at 1,100-1,500m; also in dry, semi-open and thorny forest near Tartagal (N Argentina, close to Bolivian border), between about 500m and 700m. Everywhere, we found it sympatric with Tropical Screech Owl [68], locally also with race *chacoensis* of Rufous-legged Owl [137].

DESCRIPTION *G. t. tucumanum* Adult Grey, brown and red morphs are known, grey the commonest. *Grey morph*: Facial disc dusky, finely flecked whitish or pale buff; eyebrows whitish. Upperparts dark greyish-brown with slight olive tint or rather dark slaty-grey; forehead with very narrow whitish shaft-streaks; forecrown with some narrow, short shaft-streaks, grading into more or less rounded whitish spots on centre and hindcrown, as well as on sides of head; nape with prominent occipital face, rimmed whitish (no ochraceous nuchal collar); mantle and back unspotted, scapulars without whitish on outer webs. Flight feather barred whitish and dusky; tail very dark grey-brown with 5-6 incomplete whitish bars. Underparts off-white, sides of upper chest dark greyish-brown with some whitish flecks; rest of underparts heavily but slightly diffusely streaked dark greyish-brown, sometimes with slight violet tint. Tarsi feathered, toes bare. *Brown morph*: Similar in pattern to grey morph, but general coloration more earth-brown. *Red morph*: General coloration reddish-sandy to pale rufescent-brown, mantle plain, scapulars edged paler; tail brown with 6-7 orange-rufous or cinnamon-buffy bars. **Juvenile** Downy chick whitish. Mesoptile similar to adult, but crown unmarked. **Bare parts** Eyes light to bright yellow; yellowish-grey in younger nestlings. Cere and bill greenish-yellow. Toes yellowish-green above, yellow below; pale greyish-blue to greyish-yellow in juveniles. Claws blackish.

MEASUREMENTS AND WEIGHT Total length 16.5-17.5cm. Wing of males 90-95.5mm, of females 94-99.5mm; tail of males 60.5-68mm, of females 63-68.5mm. Weight 52-56g, females normally not distinctly heavier than males.

GEOGRAPHICAL VARIATION Apart from different colour morphs, individual variability of plumage patterns is not very large. We distinguish two subspecies.

    G. t. tucumanum Chapman, 1922. Argentine and Paraguayan Chaco south to N Córdoba, Tucumán and Santiago del Estero (near southern limit may overlap with race *stranecki* of Ferruginous Pygmy Owl; infertile hybrids between the two are known). See Description. Grey morph predominant.
    G. t. pallens Brodkorb, 1938. Bolivian Chaco, Sierra de Chiquitos. Brown and red morphs known. Brown morph light brown to warm earth-brown, with irregularly light-spotted back and mantle; crown with many rounded pale buffy dots, forehead with tiny shaft-streaks; tail brown with 5-6 incomplete whitish bars. Red morph has pale shaft-streaks on crown, distinct whitish areas on scapulars, tail barred brown and orange-rufous or cinnamon-buff.

HABITS Partly diurnal, but general activity at dusk and dawn. Solitary males may be heard singing for hours on calm, moonlit nights. Giant cacti or trees and taller bushes are used as perches for singing; otherwise perches mostly among branches, so difficult to spot. May be stimulated and attracted by imitation of its song or by playback. Small birds give mobbing response to imitation of its song, and mob the owl if they locate it by day. Flight over larger distances is rather straight, sometimes slightly undulating, with rapid wingbeats alternating with glides on extended wings.

FOOD In the dry season, small birds seem to be its main prey; also takes small mammals, reptiles and insects. The percentage of insects increases during brood-rearing (after the dry season, when insects become much more numerous). Forages and moves around in shrubs or trees at lower height, often near ground. Hunts mostly from perches, swooping on to prey on the ground, but also takes small birds among foliage in dashing flight.

BREEDING Territorial. Male defends territories of about 1km² or more. Intensive singing normally starts in the second half of September or in October, with eggs normally laid in the second half of October or in early November; young fledge in December. One clutch per year. Woodpecker holes in trees or giant cacti are the most common nesting sites, but natural holes in trunks may also be used; we believe that burrows of small mammals or birds in banks may sometimes be accepted for breeding. Often uses the same holes for several years. Female lays 3-5 white eggs and incubates alone, while fed in the nest by her mate. Breeding biology poorly known, but probably similar to that of Ferruginous Pygmy Owl.

STATUS AND CONSERVATION Uncertain. Locally not rare. We found it rather abundant near Tartagal, between Salta (N Argentina) and the Bolivian border. Threatened by destruction of its habitat (particularly by burning) and by superstitious traditional customs (feathers, parts of the owl and live birds trapped and kept in cages for fortune in love, etc).

REMARKS Although *Glaucidium tucumanum* and the taxon *pallens* have been described as subspecies of Ferruginous Pygmy Owl, we regard the taxon *tucumanum* as specifically distinct from *brasilianum* because of vocal and DNA evidence, as well as differences in ecology. The illustration in Boyer & Hume (1991) appears to depict a specimen of *G. tucumanum* (perhaps slightly too brown) in its typical habitat. From its small size, more spotted than streaked head and distribution, the taxon *pallens* is probably a race of *Glaucidium tucumanum*. In northernmost Argentina and southernmost Bolivia (Tarija) both taxa seem to intergrade, inhabiting temporary dry, semi-open forest and farmland with shrubs and patches of wood.

It seems to us that *G. tucumanum* is distributed over the whole dry Gran Chaco, being replaced in adjacent humid areas of the north and east, as well as in cooler regions with higher precipitation in the south, by *G. brasilianum*. Our studies (in the field and the laboratory) indicate clearly that very often several species are involved when references to '*Glaucidium brasilianum*' are made. Further studies, especially in the field, are needed, however, to resolve the very difficult problem of the entire '*brasilianum* complex'.

REFERENCES Boyer & Hume (1991), Burton (1992), Chapman (1922), Heidrich *et al.* (1995), Howell & Robbins (1995), Howell & Webb (1995), König (1991, 1994 and unpublished), Narosky & Yzurieta (1987), Olrog (1979), Voous (1988), Wink & Heidrich (unpublished).

---

163 COLLARED OWLET
Glaucidium brodiei   Plate 50

Other name: Collared Pygmy Owlet

French: Chevêchette à collier
German: Wachtel-Sperlingskauz

IDENTIFICATION A very small owl (about 15cm), being a miniature version of Asian Barred Owlet [170]. Overall, barred grey-brown with a prominent white supercilium, rufous half-collar on mantle, and white patch on throat; from behind, the collar together with a black spot on each side of the nape look deceptively like a staring owl face (occipital face). Also occurs in a rufous or chestnut morph. **Similar species** Asian Barred Owlet is larger (about 20cm).

VOCALISATIONS A pleasant four-note bell-like whistle, *tew - tewtew - tewt*, uttered in 3-4 runs, repeated at intervals. There is a distinct interval between the first and second notes and the third and fourth, but none between the second and the third. The call is often incomplete, ending with *tewtew*. The bird bobs its head from side to side, producing a marked ventriloquial effect, making it hard to locate. The call commences very softly, sounding as if the bird is miles away, and then becomes louder, until one finds the bird sitting overhead.

DISTRIBUTION Himalayas east to China and Taiwan, south to Sumatra and Borneo.

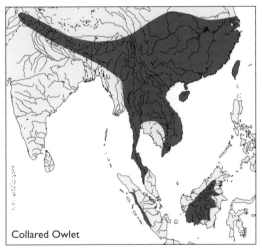

Collared Owlet

MOVEMENTS Resident.

HABITAT Usually submontane to dense montane forest with open spaces or clearings, at up to about 3,200m. Sometimes also in open hill forest.

DESCRIPTION *G. b. brodiei* **Adult** Light brown face with well-defined white supercilium, chin sometimes white, moustachial streak prominently white. Crown, nape, ear-coverts and sides of neck dull grey-brown or reddish-brown, marked with broken bars and spots of whitish-fulvous or rufous of various shades; broad fulvous or rufous half-collar on hindneck, feathers edged with dark brown and with black bases showing through and forming black patch on each side of neck (occipital face). Remainder of upperparts brown, barred whitish-fulvous to rufous; scapulars with white outer webs, forming bold streak on each side of back. Primaries blackish-brown, first two unmarked, the rest increasingly notched with shades of rufous on outer web and barred with white on base of inner web. Throat with white patch; underparts white, fulvous-white or rufous-white, with broad dark brown bars on breast and flanks, which become fewer and more drop-like on abdomen. (On the whole the colour is very variable: of 100 skins in BMNH, six colour groups could be identified irrespective of provenance.) **Juvenile** Fully barred on back as adult, but head more streaked. **Bare parts** Iris bright lemon-yellow or more straw- to golden-yellow. Cere and gape greenish or bluish. Bill greenish-yellow, darker at base. Legs and feet pale greenish-yellow to olive-grey, soles paler and more yellow. Claws dark horn.

MEASUREMENTS AND WEIGHT Total length 14-15cm. Wing 81-101mm; tail 56-69mm. Weight of 2 males 52g and 53g, of 1 female 63g; females usually larger and heavier.

GEOGRAPHICAL VARIATION Two subspecies are recognised.

> **G. b. brodiei** (Burton, 1835). Himalayas from Pakistan eastward through Nepal, Assam and S China (north to Anhwei), south to Malay Peninsula and N Vietnam, Hainan, Sumatra and Borneo. See Description. (Described forms *sylvaticum* from Sumatra, *borneense* from Borneo and *tubiger* from Thailand east to S China regarded as synonyms; *Glaucidium peritum* described from Sumatra also a synonym.)
>
> **G. b. pardalotum** (Swinhoe, 1863). Taiwan. Head olive-brown, spotted and marked with ochreous; broad buff collar from one shoulder to other, with black spot on each side near scapulars; reddish tinge of upperparts of nominate deepens into deep olive-brown; belly, vent and lower flanks white, flanks with dark spots.

HABITS Diurnal. Usually seen perched on thinly foliaged branch in a tall forest tree; flies about freely in open sunshine, even hunting and calling persistently at midday. Also crepuscular, but less nocturnal than other owls; does not call in middle of night. Suffers ceaseless mobbing from small birds during day; it has been suggested that the occipital face may be of value in discouraging attacks from the rear. Flight a series of rapid wingbeats punctuated by glides.

FOOD Small birds, mice, lizards, and cicadas, grasshoppers, beetles and other large insects. Extremely bold and fierce for its size, sometimes pouncing on birds almost as large as itself, and carrying these to a perch in its talons. The victim is pinned under the foot, torn up and devoured with vicious upward pulls of the bill.

BREEDING Season in the Himalayas March to June, mainly April-May. Nest is an unlined natural hollow, sometimes very large, or an old barbet or woodpecker hole, 2-10m up in a tree trunk (often very rotten) standing in fairly open places in the forest or at clearings. Normally lays 4 white roundish eggs, sometimes 3 or 5: about 29 x 24mm.

STATUS AND CONSERVATION Locally not rare.

REMARKS Although this widespread species is not un-common, more information on its biology, behaviour and ecology is needed.

REFERENCES Ali & Ripley (1981), Baker (1927), Mees (1967), Voous (1988).

164 JUNGLE OWLET
Glaucidium radiatum   Plate 50

Syn: *Taenioglaux radiatum*

French: Chevêchette de la jungle
German: Dschungel-Sperlingskauz

IDENTIFICATION A small (about 20cm), round-headed owlet. Dark brown above, conspicuously barred with pale rufous; chin, supercilium and moustachial streak, middle of breast, and abdomen white; rest of underparts dark, barred dark olive-brown and white or rufous-white. **Similar species** Collared Owlet [163] is smaller, and has a rufous half-collar and an occipital face. Asian Barred Owlet [170] is larger, much more closely barred with whitish above and below, and abdomen has dark striations.

VOCALISATIONS Starts with a loud and slow *kao* repeated 2-3 times, followed by series of *kao-kuk* (or *koo-kuk*), of about 5 seconds' duration, quickening in tempo and fading at the end. Nuptial song (?) a soft, musical, rather ventriloquistic *cur-cur-cur-cur-er*, fading towards end, uttered on moonlit nights monotonously for about 15 minutes, with short pauses. Sometimes an occasional pleasant bubbling *woioioioioioioi....keek*, the final note in a much higher key (confusion with nightjar *Caprimulgus* possible?).

DISTRIBUTION Pakistan, Nepal to Bhutan, and peninsular India.

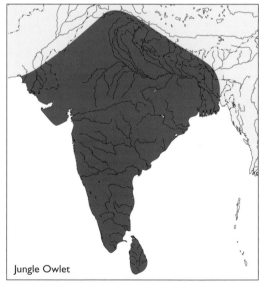

Jungle Owlet

MOVEMENTS Resident.

HABITAT Submontane moist deciduous forest (Himalayas) and secondary jungle; especially partial to teak-bamboo areas in foothills; occurs locally up to about 2,000m.

DESCRIPTION *G. r. radiatum* **Adult** Chin, short supercilium, moustachial streak and patch on breast pure white. Upperparts dark brown with narrow bars of pale ochraceous or rufous; bars on back, rump and uppertail-coverts often almost pure white. Underparts white, more or less tinged rufous to lower breast and paling to pure white on vent and abdomen, barred grey-brown on breast sides, belly sides and flanks. Tarsi feathered, toes finely bristled. (Some birds are much greyer than others, more particularly on lower back and tail; this is unconnected with provenance, but in the nature of individual variation, i.e. grey morph.) **Juvenile** Undescribed. **Bare parts** Iris bright lemon-yellow. Cere and gape bluish. Bill greenish-yellow. Toes greenish-yellow or brown to olive-grey, soles yellowish. Claws dark horn-brown.

MEASUREMENTS AND WEIGHT Total length about 20cm, females sometimes a little larger. Wing 124-134mm; tail 63-84mm. Weight 88-114g, 2 males each 114g.

GEOGRAPHICAL VARIATION Two subspecies.

    G. r. radiatum (Tickell, 1833) W Himalayas of Pakistan eastwards through Nepal and Sikkim to Bhutan, south through peninsular India in appropriate biotopes (locally to about 2,000m in Nilgiris) and south of a line from Almora to Baroda, with western extension to Mt Abu area. See Description.

    G. r. malabaricum (Blyth, 1846). Malabar coastal strip from S Konkan (about 16°N), south through Goa, W Mysore and Kerala; chiefly in lowland open forest and foothills, locally to about 1,500m. Much darker and more rufous than nominate, some individuals practically bright chestnut, especially on upperparts, wings, breast and flanks.

HABITS Frequents the tops of tall trees, usually on steep hillsides, and usually singly or in pairs. Largely crepuscular, and most active an hour or so before dusk and likewise before sunrise, but also on move during the night. Fond of sunbathing in early morning or late afternoon, and also flies about freely, and even hunts, in daytime, especially in cloudy, drizzling weather; normally, however, retires during the day to some leafy branch or a tree hollow, particularly to escape the mobbing of small diurnal birds. When perched upright and motionless (after disturbance), with its head screwed round to stare at the intruder, it looks deceptively like a snag of a dead branch. When calling, the head is slightly lowered, giving the bird a hunchback profile, and the tail is wagged from side to side.

FOOD Feeds mostly on locusts, grasshoppers, cicadas and other large insects; also takes molluscs, lizards, small birds and mice.

BREEDING Nests in a natural hollow or abandoned woodpecker or barbet hole in the trunk or branch of a tree standing in open forest, 3-8m from the ground. Season March-April. Lays 3 or 4 white roundish eggs: 28 eggs average 31.5 x 26.8mm.

STATUS AND CONSERVATION Locally not rare.

REMARKS Ali & Ripley (1981) and Marshall & King (1988) regard *Glaucidium castanonotum* as a subspecies of Jungle Owlet. We disagree, and give *castanonotum* specific rank, as Chestnut-backed Owlet [165].

REFERENCES Ali & Ripley (1981), Baker (1927), Boyer & Hume (1991), Burton (1992), Eck & Busse (1973), Marshall & King (1988), Scherzinger (1968), Voous (1988).

165 CHESTNUT-BACKED OWLET
Glaucidium castanonotum   Plate 50

Syn: *Taenioglaux castanonotum*

French: Chevêchette de Sri Lanka
German: Sri Lanka-Sperlingskauz

IDENTIFICATION A small owl (about 19cm) with bright chestnut upperparts, crown, nape and hindneck narrowly barred blackish, and white underparts streaked (rather than barred) with olive-brown or blackish-brown. **Similar species** Jungle Owlet [164] is very similar in shape, size and general appearance, but has mantle barred dark brown and white instead of plain chestnut, and lacks blackish shaft-streaks on underparts. Differs from scops owls (*Otus*) in absence of ear-tufts; moreover, scops owls are usually dark brown or grey, heavily marbled, mottled and streaked with black, although they do also occur in more rufous or chestnut morphs (but are never barred on mantle, crown and nape).

VOCALISATIONS The song of the male is a long series of somewhat purring *krew* or *kru* notes in rapid succession: *krewkrewkrewkrew*. The phrases begin softly, gradually increasing in volume and finally breaking off. Sequences are normally repeated at intervals of several seconds.

DISTRIBUTION Confined to Sri Lanka.

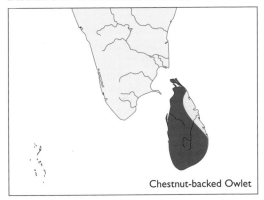

Chestnut-backed Owlet

MOVEMENTS Resident.

HABITAT Widely distributed in small numbers throughout the dense forest of the humid zone of Sri Lanka and the western slopes of hills, to about 1,950m. More a forest bird than Asian Barred Owlet [170], but it occurs in the vicinity of Colombo, where in the past it was not rare.

DESCRIPTION Adult Very similar to Jungle Owlet: differs in chestnut back, scapulars and wing-coverts; white underparts marked with blackish shaft-streaks, and bars on flanks. Pale bars on head are narrow and rufous-ochre. (Some individuals have white spots on outer webs of scapulars.) Tarsi feathered, toes sparsely bristled. **Juvenile** Undescribed. **Bare parts** Iris bright yellow. Cere dusky greenish. Bill yellowish or greenish-horn. Toes greenish-olive or yellow, soles paler and more yellow.

MEASUREMENTS AND WEIGHT Total length 19-20cm. Wing 122-140mm; tail 56-68.5mm. Weight around 100g, females probably somewhat larger and heavier.

GEOGRAPHICAL VARIATION Monotypic: *Glaucidium castanonotum* (Blyth, 1852).

HABITS Very diurnal in its habits, often hunting and calling in broad daylight, but very shy and wary, and seldom seen. It frequents the tops of high trees, usually on steep hillsides.

FOOD Mainly insects such as beetles, but also mice, small birds, small reptiles, etc; occasionally larger vertebrate prey, but only when young are being fed.

BREEDING Nests in holes in trees or coconut palms. Season March-May. Lays 2 oval eggs: av. 35 x 28mm.

STATUS AND CONSERVATION In the 19th century this species was far more common. Its habitat is dwindling and its range therefore contracting owing to the clearance of forest for plantations, etc. Nevertheless, it sometimes occurs also in thickly planted native gardens.

REMARKS This owl's biology, habits and vocalisations are poorly known and require study.

REFERENCES Ali & Ripley (1981), Baker (1927, 1934), Boyer & Hume (1991), Eck & Busse (1973), Henry (1955), Voous (1988), Wait (1925).

166 SJÖSTEDT'S OWLET
Glaucidium sjostedti   Plate 50

Syn: *Taenioglaux sjostedti*

French: Chevêchette à queue barrée
German: Pracht-Sperlingskauz

IDENTIFICATION A small owl (about 25cm), but relatively large for a pygmy owl. Head and neck dusky brown, densely barred whitish, without occipital face; dark chestnut-rufous above, barred lighter on upper back; wings blackish, barred whitish. Below, densely barred brown on pale cinnamon-buff; throat white. Underwing-coverts plain cinnamon-rufous, very conspicuous in flight. Tail rather long with narrow whitish bars. Eyes yellow. **Similar species** African Barred Owlet [167] is smaller, with whitish underparts barred dark only on upper breast, rest of underparts spotted. Chestnut-backed Owlet [165] has a spotted rather than barred crown, plain rufous-chestnut back, and spotted whitish lower breast, with tail densely barred brown and buff. Red-chested Owlet [145] has plain crown and is spotted below. Scops owls (*Otus*) have small ear-tufts.

VOCALISATIONS Poorly known. The male's song consists of 2-4 notes in about 2 seconds, *kroo-kroo-kroo*, the series repeated at intervals of about 1 second. Male and female also give (sometimes in duet) more liquid notes, accelerating, then dropping in volume and pitch at the end of the series: *kroo kroo-krookrookrookroo*.

DISTRIBUTION Cameroon, Gabon, N Congo, and Zaire (very locally, primarily in NW).

MOVEMENTS Resident.

HABITAT Lowland primary forest, but also at higher altitudes on Mt Cameroon. Avoids forest edges, keeping to the interior parts.

DESCRIPTION Adult Facial disc indistinct, dusky brown, finely barred whitish; eyebrows white. Forehead, crown

and nape dusky brown, finely barred whitish; mantle and back deep chestnut, with light barring on upper back; greater upperwing-coverts dusky brown, washed with chestnut and tipped whitish; outer webs of scapulars finely barred pale cinnamon. Flight feathers dusky brown, finely barred whitish; tail dusky brown with narrow whitish bars. Throat plain white; underparts cinnamon, finely barred dark brown, abdomen and undertail-coverts pale cinnamon-rufous; underwing-coverts plain pale cinnamon-rufous. Tarsi feathered cinnamon-rufous to base of toes, latter sparsely bristled. **Juvenile** Downy chick undescribed. Mesoptile similar to adult but paler, barring on upper breast and flanks darker. Half-grown chicks have pale buff down on underparts. **Bare parts** Eyes yellow. Cere and bill pale yellow. Toes pale yellow. Claws yellowish-horn.

MEASUREMENTS AND WEIGHT Total length about 25cm. Wing of males 154-165mm, of females 167-168mm; tail (unsexed) 83-110mm (median 94mm). Weight about 140g.

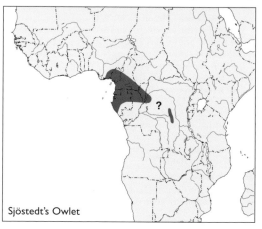

Sjöstedt's Owlet

GEOGRAPHICAL VARIATION Monotypic: *Glaucidium sjostedti* Reichenow, 1893.

HABITS Little known. Active mostly at dusk and dawn, but also by night and sometimes during daytime. Singing is recorded mostly at dusk and down, rarely during daytime. By day normally roosts in dense foliage, where it is mobbed by small birds when detected. Unlike 'typical' *Glaucidium*, does not cock tail and flick it from side to side.

FOOD Insects, especially grasshoppers and dung beetles, small rodents, reptiles, birds (especially nestlings or young fledglings), crabs and spiders. Hunts mostly at night, in understorey of forest within about 2m of the ground. The prey is normally caught from a low perch; open nests of small birds are plundered when they contain young.

BREEDING Breeding habits not well known. Territorial. The territory size is probably 10-12ha; in Gabon, two males have been heard singing about 400m apart. Peak of vocal activity in Gabon from September to October. Laying was recorded in Gabon in July, and chicks have been found in Cameroon in February, May, August, November and December. Natural holes in trees are used for nesting; one was found only 1.5m above the ground. Lays at least 2 white eggs (about 34 x 28mm) directly on to the bottom of the nest hole; female incubates alone, for about 28 days. The nestlings fledge at an age of about 31 days and are cared for and fed by their parents for a few weeks more.

STATUS AND CONSERVATION Uncertain. Generally uncommon, but rather frequent in Gabon. Forest destruction represents threat.

REMARKS The biology, behaviour, ecology, distribution and vocalisations of Sjöstedt's Owlet are poorly known and need study, the more so because the species may be declining rapidly in numbers as a result of habitat destruction.

REFERENCES Boyer & Hume (1991), Brosset & Erard (1986), Dunning (1993), Eck & Busse (1973), Fry *et al.* (1988), Kemp (1989).

---

167 AFRICAN BARRED OWLET
Glaucidium capense   Plate 51

Syn: *Taenioglaux capense*

French: Chevêchette à poitrine barrée
German: Kap-Sperlingskauz

IDENTIFICATION A small owlet (21-22cm) without occipital face. Crown and nape barred whitish on dark greyish-brown; mantle and back cinnamon-brown, narrowly barred with buff. Upper breast barred dusky brown on pale buff or whitish; rest of underparts off-white with relatively large, dusky spots. Tail rather densely barred pale buff and cinnamon-brown. Eyes yellow. Does not cock tail and flick it from one side to the other. **Similar species** Pearl-spotted Owlet [144] is smaller, streaked below and spotted on crown and back. Sjöstedt's Owlet [166] is larger, with longer tail, and densely barred on whole underparts, with chestnut mantle with light barring; tail with narrow whitish bars. Chestnut Owlet [168] has spotted (not barred) crown and plain chestnut back. Scops owls (*Otus*) have a cryptic plumage below, longer wings and small ear-tufts.

VOCALISATIONS The song of the male is a series of often slightly downward-inflected, equally spaced notes, about two per second: *kweeo-kweeo-kweeo-...kew-kew-kew*. The female gives a similar but slightly higher-pitched song. Both sexes utter, when excited, series of short purring and vibrating trills, alternating in pitch, *pjurr—prorr—pjurr—prorr—pjurr—...*, the interval between trills about 1 second; these notes sometimes accelerate and run together. Croaking notes are uttered if disturbed at the roost. At the nest, male and female give soft *twoo* calls. Chicks beg with rapid sequences of *chip* notes.

DISTRIBUTION From S Kenya to the eastern Cape, through C African woodland to Angola and Namibia; also Mafia Island. Disjunct, allopatric populations are found in Liberia and Ivory Coast (possibly representing a separate species).

MOVEMENTS Resident.

HABITAT Open areas with riverine forest, woods with large trees, forest edge and secondary growth. The birds of Ivory Coast and Liberia (*etchecopari*) inhabit primary forest.

DESCRIPTION *G. c. capense* Adult Facial disc brownish with white concentric lines; eyebrows whitish, not very prominent. Head and nape greyish-brown to dark earth-brown with fine whitish bars. Mantle, back and uppertail-coverts dark cinnamon-brown, barred narrowly buff; scapulars cinnamon-brown with whitish outer webs and dark brown tips. Flight feathers barred cinnamon-brown and rufous-brown; tail cinnamon-brown, densely barred with pale buff. Throat and upper breast buffy-whitish, densely barred cinnamon-brown; rest of underparts off-white with light buffy wash, with large brown dots at tips of several feathers; underwing-coverts whitish-buff with some brown spots. Tarsi feathered whitish with rufous wash; toes bristled. **Juvenile** Downy chick white. Mesoptile similar to adult, but browner and less barred on back and less spotted below. **Bare parts** Eyes yellow. Cere and bill pale greenish-grey with yellowish tint. Toes brownish-yellow to yellowish-olive. Claws horn with darker tips. Juveniles have tongue and gape blackish, not pink as in Pearl-spotted Owlet.

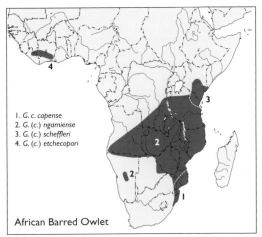

1. *G. c. capense*
2. *G. (c.) ngamiense*
3. *G. (c.) scheffleri*
4. *G. (c.) etchecopari*

African Barred Owlet

MEASUREMENTS AND WEIGHT Total length 21-22cm. Wing of males 123-143mm, of females 131-150mm; tail of males 82-93mm, of females 77-93mm. Weight of males 103-132g (median 117g), of females 100-139g (median 122g).

GEOGRAPHICAL VARIATION We recognise four subspecies, all of which may prove to be full species. (The form *castaneum* we separate specifically, as Chestnut Owlet.)

G. c. capense (A. Smith, 1834). E Cape to eastern coast of Natal and S Mozambique. See Description. Wing 136-150mm.

G. (c.) ngamiense (Roberts, 1932). E Transvaal and N Botswana north to C Tanzania, including Mafia Island, and SE Zaire, west to Angola and Namibia. Greyer and slightly smaller than nominate. Wing 131-147mm. (Sometimes considered specifically distinct. The forms *robertsi* and *clanceyi* are synonyms and intergrades.)

G. (c.) scheffleri Neumann, 1911. NE Tanzania and E Kenya (e.g. in Tsavo region). Smaller than nominate. Wing 132-140mm. Similar to *ngamiense*, but back sometimes unbarred. (Sometimes considered specifically distinct.)

G. (c.) etchecopari Erard & Roux, 1983. Liberia and Ivory Coast. Lives in primary forest. Upperparts very dark, almost unmarked; few pale narrow bars on tail. Much smaller than all other races. Differs vocally. Wing 123-132mm; weight of males about 83g, of females 93-119g. (May be specifically distinct.)

HABITS Partly diurnal. Main vocal activity at dusk and

379

dawn, but also active on calm, clear nights. Often seen on exposed perches looking for prey, even during daytime. Normally roosts within cover, sometimes in a natural hole in a tree. When detected during daytime, often mobbed by small passerines. Flight low with whirring wingbeats, swooping up to perch. Seems to be fond of bathing.

FOOD Small mammals and birds, reptiles, frogs, insects and other arthropods, including scorpions and caterpillars. The prey is normally caught from a perch.

BREEDING Male and female sing together when claiming territory; singing is most frequent prior to breeding. Laying normally takes place in September and October to November in E and S Africa. A natural cavity in a tree is used as nest; this may be about 3-6m above ground, and is normally about 15-30cm deep. Lays 2-3 white eggs (average 32.1 x 27.1mm) at 2-day intervals directly on to the floor of the hole. Incubation begins with the second egg; incubation period unknown. The young are fed by both parents after dusk, with no food deliveries during daytime. At 30-33 days the nestlings leave the nest, being cared for for some time by both parents; by 7 months they may sing like adults, and reach sexual maturity by the next breeding season.

STATUS AND CONSERVATION Uncertain. May be threatened by habitat destruction and the use of pesticides.

REMARKS The biology, ecology and behaviour, as well as taxonomy, of the African Barred Owlet needs study. In particular, the vocalisations of the races mentioned above should be investigated. It is possible that the four subspecies described actually represent four separate species, the allopatric and non-migratory *etchecopari* being a particularly strong candidate.

REFERENCES Brooke (1983), Carlyon (1985), Dowsett & Dowsett-Lemaire (1993), Dunning (1993), Erard & Roux (1985), Fry *et al.* (1988), Kemp (1989), König & Ertel (1979), Steyn (1979, 1982).

---

168 CHESTNUT OWLET
Glaucidium castaneum   Plate 51

Syn: *Taenioglaux castaneum*

French: Chevêchette marronne
German: Kastanien-Sperlingskauz

IDENTIFICATION A small owlet (20-21.5cm) without occipital face. Similar to African Barred Owlet [167], but somewhat smaller; crown spotted, not barred whitish, and mantle and back plain chestnut. Eyes yellow, bill greenish-yellow. Does not cock and flirt tail. **Similar species** African Barred Owlet is larger and has crown mainly barred light, while spotting (if present) is reduced to forehead; mantle and back barred buff. Pearl-spotted Owlet [144] is distinctly streaked below and has prominent occipital face. Albertine Owlet [169] has cream-spotted forehead and crown, leading into cream bars on nape and upper mantle, with rest of upperparts plain maroon-brown; tail brown with seven narrow whitish bars. Red-chested Owlet [145] has a dark grey head contrasting with dark brown back, upperparts plain, tail with large white spots.

VOCALISATIONS The song of the male is a melancholic

sequence of whistled, somewhat rolling notes accelerating towards the end: *kyurr-kyurr-kyurr-...kyurrkyurrrkyurr*.

DISTRIBUTION NE Zaire (Semliki Valley) and SW Uganda (Bwamba Forest).

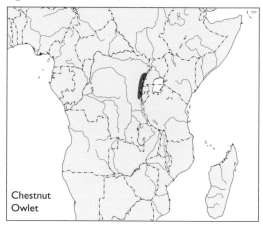

Chestnut Owlet

MOVEMENTS Resident.

HABITAT Primary forest and other extensive rain forest.

DESCRIPTION Adult Facial disc brownish with lighter bars and flecks; eyebrows whitish. Upperparts chestnut to rufous-brown, crown spotted whitish, mantle and back plain chestnut, outer webs of scapulars whitish; upperwing-coverts often unbarred. Flight feathers barred brown and buff; tail brown, barred buff (less narrowly than on African Barred Owlet). Upper breast densely barred brown and buff, rest of underparts off-white, heavily spotted brown. Tarsi feathered, toes bristled. **Juvenile** Not described, but probably similar to African Barred Owlet. **Bare parts** Eyes yellow. Cere and bill greenish-yellow. Toes dirty yellow to greenish-yellow. Claws horn with darker tips.

MEASUREMENTS AND WEIGHT Total length 20-21.5cm. Wing 128-139mm. Weight median about 100g, females mostly larger and heavier than males.

GEOGRAPHICAL VARIATION Monotypic: *Glaucidium castaneum* Neumann, 1893.

HABITS Poorly known. Partly diurnal. Inhabits mostly lower storeys in dense forest. Is mobbed by small birds when seen by day. Does not cock and flirt tail when excited.

FOOD Small mammals, birds and other vertebrates, as well as insects and other arthropods. The prey is normally caught from a perch or by foraging in undergrowth.

BREEDING Not described. Probably similar to that of African Barred Owlet.

STATUS AND CONSERVATION Uncertain. Probably threatened by forest destruction.

REMARKS As this species has previously been considered a race of African Barred Owlet, specific observations are lacking. Studies on ecology, biology and behaviour (including vocalisations) are needed for comparison with other taxa of the '*Glaucidium capense* complex', in order to resolve taxonomic questions. These may perhaps reveal that more species are involved, and justify raising *etchecopari*, *ngamiense* and *scheffleri* to species level.

REFERENCES Boyer & Hume (1991), Brooke *et al.* (1983), Burton (1992), Erard & Roux (1983), Fry *et al.* (1988), König & Ertel (1979), Prigogine (1985), Zimmerman *et al.* (1996).

169 ALBERTINE OWLET
Glaucidium albertinum   Plate 51

Syn: *Taenioglaux albertinum*

French: Chevêchette du Graben
German: Albert-Sperlingskauz

IDENTIFICATION A small owlet (about 20cm) without occipital face. Warm maroon-brown above, crown spotted with cream-coloured flecks, mantle and back plain; hindneck and outer webs of scapulars with cream-coloured spots, horizontally elongated on hindneck (slightly bar-like). Tail dark brown with seven narrow creamy-white bars. **Similar species** African Barred Owlet [167] is slightly larger, crown barred light and tail rather densely barred brown and buff, with mantle and back barred. Pearl-spotted Owlet [144] has prominent occipital face and is streaked (not barred or spotted) below. Red-chested Owlet [145] has a dark grey head with unspotted crown and plain dark brown back and mantle; tail with large, rounded white spots.

VOCALISATIONS Undescribed.

DISTRIBUTION Albertine Rift in NE Zaire and N Rwanda. Known from only five specimens.

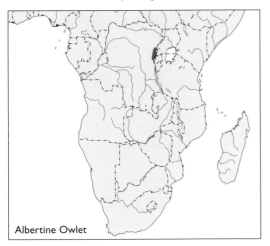

Albertine Owlet

MOVEMENTS Resident.

HABITAT Montane forest with dense undergrowth, from about 1,100m to 1,700m above sea-level.

DESCRIPTION Adult Facial disc brownish with some lighter flecks; eyebrows whitish. Upperparts warm maroon-brown, forehead, crown and nape with cream-coloured spots of different size; hindneck spotted creamy-white, several spots being horizontally elongated; mantle and back plain, scapulars with creamy-white outer webs. Outermost 3 primaries plain brown, rest of flight feathers barred lighter and darker brown and spotted with creamy-

white; tail dark brown with seven narrow whitish or cream bars. Chin white, throat maroon; upper breast maroon with broad cream bars, rest of underparts whitish with maroon-brown spots, especially on flanks. Tarsi feathered, toes bristled. **Juvenile** Undescribed. **Bare parts** Undescribed, but probably similar to African Barred Owlet.

MEASUREMENTS AND WEIGHT Total length about 20cm. Wing 126-138mm; tail 61-70mm. Weight of 1 female 73g.

GEOGRAPHICAL VARIATION Monotypic: *Glaucidium albertinum* Prigogine, 1983.

HABITS Partly diurnal. Type specimen was collected in dense undergrowth of primary montane forest.

FOOD Insects have been recorded as food, but probably also feeds on small vertebrates.

BREEDING Not described. Probably nests in natural holes in trees.

STATUS AND CONSERVATION Uncertain. As endemic resident of the Albertine Rift, this owlet may be endangered by forest destruction. Listed as Vulnerable by BirdLife International.

REMARKS A rather unknown owl. Its ecology, behaviour, vocalisations and entire biology need study. Its relationship to other owlets of the '*Glaucidium capense* complex' is unknown.

REFERENCES Boyer & Hume (1991), Collar *et al.* (1994), Fry *et al.* (1988), Prigogine (1983, 1985).

170 ASIAN BARRED OWLET
Glaucidium cuculoides   Plate 52

Syn: *Taenioglaux cuculoides*

French: Chevêchette barrée
German: Kuckuck-Sperlingskauz

IDENTIFICATION A small (23cm), round-headed owlet without occipital face. Resembles Jungle Owlet [164], but larger. Dark brown (or olive-brown), closely barred whitish above and below, with prominent white throat patch; abdomen whitish with dark brown streaks. **Similar species** Collared Owlet [163] has an occipital face and a spotted, not barred, crown and is much smaller. Jungle Owlet is somewhat smaller, usually with barred (not streaked) abdomen.

VOCALISATIONS Normal call a crescendo of harsh squawks. In the breeding season, a continuous bubbling musical whistle of about 4-7 seconds, *wowowowowowow-owowowwo...*, very reminiscent of the opening notes of the song of a barbet, is probably the male's song. Occasionally gives a variant of this, *woiwoiwoiwoiwoi.....keek*, as Jungle Owlet.

DISTRIBUTION W Himalayas of Pakistan east to Nepal, Bhutan and Burma, and across S and SE China, south to Hainan and SE Asia.

MOVEMENTS Resident. Possibly moves locally to lower elevations outside the breeding season.

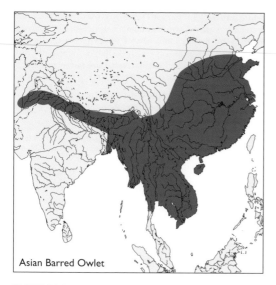

Asian Barred Owlet

averages decidedly smaller. Wing 131-161mm. (We treat *deignani* as a synonym.)

G. c. whitelyi (Blyth, 1867). Sichuan, Yunnan and SE China south of Yangtse river. Wing 154-168mm; tail 93-114mm. (We regard *delacouri* as a synonym.)

G. c. persimile Hartert, 1910. Hainan. More rufous than *rufescens*, especially on head, back, scapulars and upperwing-coverts.

HABITS Largely diurnal; often found sitting out on bare branches or dead tree stumps in full sunlight, and hunting freely at any time of day. Vocal at all hours of the day, but most noisy at dawn and for a couple of hours after sunrise. Subjected to relentless mobbing by small birds as soon as its presence is detected; sits statue-like during mobbing attacks, betraying its agitation only by swinging its tail from side to side for minutes on end. Flight undulating as other owlets, series of rapid flaps followed by a pause with wings closed.

FOOD Beetles, grasshoppers, cicadas and other large insects; also takes lizards, mice and small birds. Has been observed to catch a Common Quail *Coturnix coturnix* flying past, seizing it in the air like a hawk.

BREEDING Nest an unlined natural hole in a tree trunk or a suitable disused barbet or woodpecker hole. Normally 4 eggs, white and rounded: average size (30) 35.8 x 30.4mm.

STATUS AND CONSERVATION Rather common.

REMARKS Peters (1940) regarded *Glaucidium castanonotum* and *G. castanopterum* as races of *G. cuculoides*, but we give both of those specific rank according to the 'biological species concept' (see introductory chapters). This species' biology, behaviour and vocalisations are in need of further study, as also is the taxonomy of the whole '*Glaucidium radiatum/cuculoides* complex'.

REFERENCES Ali & Ripley (1981), Baker (1927, 1934), Boyer & Hume (1991), Burton (1992), Dunning (1993), Eck & Busse (1973), King *et al.* (1995), Marshall & King (1988), Voous (1988).

HABITAT Open submontane (or montane) forest of pine, oak, rhododendron, etc; also subtropical and tropical evergreen jungle at lower elevations in the foothills. In the foothills normally extends to submontane tract around 2,100m, but locally to montane levels at about 2,700m.

DESCRIPTION *G. c. cuculoides* **Adult** White supercilium as far back as eye; white moustachial streak. Whole upperside, sides of head and neck and wing-coverts dull brown or olive-brown, or faintly tinged rufous, closely barred fulvous-white or dull rufous-white. Tail dark brown with about six whitish or pure white bars. Distinct white patch on throat; breast barred dark brown and dull fulvous-white; upper abdomen with paler brown and pure white bars, lower part more streaked than barred. Tarsi feathered; toes bare, sparsely bristled. **Juvenile** Chick covered with short white down all over. Juvenile (immature) barred only on wings and tail, in general more rufous, with head and nape spotted paler rufous, and underparts streaked. **Bare parts** Iris lemon-yellow. Cere greenish-horn. Bill yellowish-green. Toes greyish olive-yellow or dull horn-green, pads chrome-yellow. Claws horn-brown.

MEASUREMENTS AND WEIGHT Total length 23-25cm, females usually (not always) a little larger than males. Wing 131-168mm; tail 75-114mm. Weight 150-176g.

GEOGRAPHICAL VARIATION We recognise five subspecies; two other subspecies mentioned in Peters (1940) are now given species rank.

G. c. cuculoides (Vigors, 1831). Lower ranges of W Himalayas from Murree and Mussorie (Pakistan) to E Nepal and W Sikkim). See Description. Wing 143-162mm; tail 75-96mm.

G. c. rufescens Baker, 1926. Sikkim, Bhutan, SE Tibet, Assam hills south of Brahmaputra river, and N Burma (Shan States), south to Bangladesh, N Laos and N Vietnam. Much richer rufous-brown; particularly rich rufous on underparts, breast more streaked, less barred. Wing 141-162mm; tail 78-90mm. (We regard *austerum* as a synonym.)

G. c. bruegeli (Parrot, 1908). Tenasserim, Thailand, S Laos, Cambodia and S Vietnam. Like preceding race, but less dark brown above, less rufous below, and

171 JAVAN OWLET
Glaucidium castanopterum   Plate 52

Syn: *Taenioglaux castanopterum*
French: Chevêchette de Java
German: Java-Sperlingskauz

IDENTIFICATION A largish owlet (23-27cm) with uniform rufous-chestnut back. Outer webs of scapulars white, forming broad band on each side of mantle; tail dark brown, closely barred with ochraceous. Head and neck barred dark brown and ochraceous. Upper breast brown, barred ochraceous, rest of underside white and streaked with bright rufous-chestnut. **Similar species** In Java and Bali no other owlet of this size and plumage pattern. Javan Scops Owl [24] has ear-tufts (when erected), and abdomen feathers with black central streak and fine, wavy rufous cross-bars.

VOCALISATIONS A staccato *sempok.....sempok....sempok*, with regular time intervals, is the male's song. Another version, beginning with slow *sempok* notes, gradually accelerating and rising in pitch, and finally ending in a loud laughter-like trill, is probably the fully developed song; often it seems as if the bird is trying to raise the pitch to a great height, but it then ends suddenly and quite unexpectedly. After a pause, the series starts again. The nestlings' food-call is a high-pitched *tjeet...tjeet...tjeet...*, uttered constantly even during daytime.

DISTRIBUTION Java and Bali.

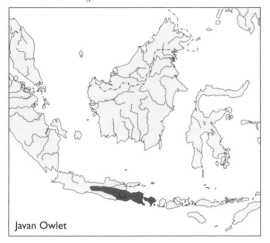

Javan Owlet

MOVEMENTS Resident.

HABITAT Forest and woodland in lower regions, particularly dense primary lowland rain forest, occasionally also submontane or montane forest; also thick bamboo jungle interspersed with broadleaved trees. At Mt Pangrango, W Java, it occurs rather rarely at 1,000-1,500m (Lake Situ Gunung), and on Mt Papandajan in primary forest up to 2,000m. Breeding has also been observed in coastal forest close to the sand beach at Pelabuanratu, W Java. Optimal habitat is hill country at about 500m, where it is locally rather common. Also enters gardens and villages.

DESCRIPTION Adult Head, nape and sides of breast brown, barred with ochraceous. Cheek feathers white, narrowly tipped brown. Upperparts rufous-chestnut; outer

webs of scapulars white. Tail dark brown with seven rather narrow ochraceous bands, including terminal one. Chin whitish, throat feathers banded dark brown and ochraceous (as sides of neck and head); rest of undersurface white, streaked bright rufous-chestnut; feathers of lower breast rufous, broadly margined with white on both webs; flank feathers chestnut on outer web, white on inner. Tarsi feathered, toes sparsely bristled. **Juvenile** Downy chick whitish. Fledglings same colour as adult, but much duller. **Bare parts** Iris bright sulphur-yellow. Cere olive-green. Bill light greenish-yellow, more yellow at tip and on cutting edges. Toes light olive-green, soles greenish-yellow or yellow.

MEASUREMENTS AND WEIGHT Total length 23-27cm. Wing 144-150mm; tail 76-97mm. Weight: No data.

GEOGRAPHICAL VARIATION Monotypic: *Glaucidium castanopterum* (Horsfield, 1821).

HABITS Frequents tops of high trees, usually on steep hillsides. Rather crepuscular, and most active an hour or so before dusk and likewise after sunrise; rather silent during the night. Also diurnal, however, calling at midday, and flies freely and even seen to hunt (capturing a snake) and feed nestlings during day.

FOOD Mainly large insects such as beetles, grasshoppers, crickets, stick insects, cockroaches and mantids. Also takes spiders, scorpions, myriopods, centipedes (*Scolopendra*), lizards and small snakes, and occasionally small birds and mice.

BREEDING Breeding season February-April. Breeds in natural tree holes, sometimes with the entrance rather large for the size of the bird; also in deserted woodpecker or barbet holes. Nest unlined. Normally 2 eggs, roundish: average size (8) 33.5 x 29.5mm.

STATUS AND CONSERVATION Rare, but locally more common in undisturbed lowland or hill forest. Main threat is loss of rainforest habitat.

REMARKS The biology and behaviour of this species are in need of further study.

REFERENCES Amadon & Bull (1988), Bartels (unpublished), Becking (unpublished), Boyer & Hume (1991), King *et al.* (1995), MacKinnon & Phillipps (1995).

Long-whiskered Owlet, Genus *Xenoglaux*
O'Neill & Graves, 1977

Tiny owls with long, fan-like whiskers around bill, reaching beyond facial disc. Eyebrows prominent whitish. Overall brownish, finely mottled darker, with throat whitish; flight feathers dusky. Tail very short, 12 feathers. Eyes light orange-brown. Toes and tarsi bare, flesh-coloured. One species.

172 LONG-WHISKERED OWLET
Xenoglaux loweryi   Plate 52

French: Chouette de Lowery
German: Lowery-Zwergkauz
Spanish: Mochuelito de Lowery

IDENTIFICATION A tiny (13-14cm), very short-tailed

owlet without occipital face. Long, fan-like whiskers around base of bill and on sides of facial disc, reaching beyond edge of disc. General coloration warm brown, finely vermiculated darker; eyebrows prominent, yellowish-white. Tarsi and toes bare, latter flesh-coloured; eyes pale orange-brown. **Similar species** No other owl in the world is similar to Long-whiskered Owlet. Within its range, pygmy owls (*Glaucidium*) are larger, with longer tail, have distinct occipital face, and are streaked below, not finely vermiculated.

VOCALISATIONS Unknown. Short, mellow whistles repeated at intervals of about 10 seconds might be contact-calls of this tiny owl; these have been heard at dusk in the area where this owl is found. In addition, a two-part vocalisation, consisting of 3-5 similar whistles followed by a series of faster, slightly higher-pitched notes, could be the song of the male.

DISTRIBUTION Known only from Deptamento San Martín in the E Andes of N Peru (valley of Rio Mayo, northwest of Rioja).

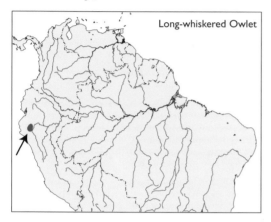

Long-whiskered Owlet

MOVEMENTS Resident.

HABITAT Upper subtropical zone. Humid cloud forest with very dense undergrowth (often climbing bamboo), laden with mosses, orchids, ferns and other epiphytes, between 1,890m and 2,100m above sea-level. The forest canopy is 6-9m in sheltered valleys, about 4m in exposed sites.

DESCRIPTION Adult Facial disc brown, not prominent; around base of bill fan-like whiskers, and similar but even longer whiskers at sides of disc projecting clearly beyond edge. Upperparts from crown to uppertail-coverts warm brown, densely vermiculated dark brown to blackish, lower nape with collar of large whitish spots; scapulars each with distinct whitish subterminal spot on outer web. Primaries dull black, with small light spots on edge of outer webs and irregular whitish area at base of inner web. Tail dull brown, mottled lighter and darker. Underparts similar to upperparts, but with many whitish vermiculations, increasing in number towards belly. Tarsi and toes bare. **Juvenile** Unknown. **Bare parts** Eyes pale orange-brown to amber-orange; eyelids dark blackish-brown. Cere pinkish-grey. Bill greenish-grey with yellowish tip. Tarsi and toes flesh-pink. Claws pale horn with darker tips.

MEASUREMENTS AND WEIGHT Total length 13-14cm. 1 male (holotype) wing 105.2mm, tail 50.3mm; wing of 2 females 100mm and 104.6mm, tail 51.7mm and 55.4mm. Weight of male 47g, of 2 females 46g and 51g.

GEOGRAPHICAL VARIATION Monotypic: *Xenoglaux loweryi* O'Neill & Graves, 1977.

HABITS Active at dusk. Not shy; may be attracted by imitation of the short, mellow whistles or of its presumed song. Moves more by hopping and fluttering among dense vegetation and undergrowth. The three known specimens were caught in mist-nets during the night.

FOOD Probably mainly insects.

BREEDING Unknown.

STATUS AND CONSERVATION Uncertain. Although it seems to be frequent in the small area of its distribution, it is doubtless one of the rarest owls of the world. It may be endangered in particular by forest destruction. Listed as Near-threatened by BirdLife International.

REMARKS Known only from three collected specimens, but observations of calling birds and one sight record have been made at other localities in the same area. This species' biology, ecology, behaviour, vocalisations, etc are unknown, as is its systematic status and relationship to other owls. A proposed close relationship to *Glaucidium* owls seems to us unlikely.

REFERENCES Burton (1992), Collar *et al.* (1994), O'Neill & Graves (1977).

Elf Owl, Genus *Micrathene* Coues, 1866

Tiny owlets without ear-tufts or occipital face. General plumage greyish-brown with fine darker and lighter vermiculations; narrow whitish eyebrows; scapulars with large whitish areas on outer webs. Tail relatively short, only 10 feathers. Tarsi and toes bristled. One species.

173 ELF OWL
Micrathene whitneyi   Plate 52

French: Chouette elfe
German: Elfenkauz
Spanish: Tecolotito enano

IDENTIFICATION A tiny, short-tailed owlet (13-14cm), greyish-brown and densely vermiculated lighter and darker. Forehead with some ochre spots; outer webs of scapulars whitish, forming prominent row across shoulder. Wings relatively long, tail with 3-4 narrow pale bars. Tarsi and toes bristled; eyes pale yellow. Nocturnal. **Similar species** Pygmy owls (*Glaucidium*) have distinct occipital face and are streaked below; tarsi feathered, tail longer. Screech owls (*Otus*) are larger and have more or less distinct ear-tufts. Burrowing Owl [174] is long-legged, much larger, and boldly spotted brown and whitish.

VOCALISATIONS The song of the male is a rapid sequence of slightly accelerating, short, whistled, rather yelping notes, rising slightly in pitch: *guwewíwiwiwiwirk*. This phrase, which may consist of up to about 20 notes, is repeated at intervals of several seconds. A similar but slightly higher-pitched song is uttered by the female. Both sexes also give single, piercing, downward-inflected calls at variable intervals, *kweeo! kweeo!...*, as well as hoarse, scratchy notes and a plaintive, drawn-out *hee-ew* with ventriloqual quality.

DISTRIBUTION From SW USA (S Arizona, New Mexico, S Texas) to C Mexico, Baja California and Socorro Island.

MOVEMENTS Mostly migratory. Northern populations winter in C Mexico and on the Pacific slope north to Sinaloa. Resident in Baja California and on Socorro Island.

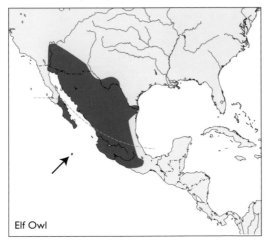

Elf Owl

HABITAT Open semi-deserts with shrubs and giant cacti, dry, wooded areas, semi-arid wooded canyons, and thorny forest; occurs locally in semi-open bushland with scattered trees on swampy substrate. From sea-level up to about 2,000m.

DESCRIPTION *M. w. whitneyi* **Adult** General coloration varies between more greyish and more brown. Facial disc brownish, diffusely vermiculated; eyebrows whitish, narrow. Upperparts greyish-brown, densely vermiculated lighter and darker; forehead with some ochre spots, nape with narrow whitish nuchal collar, wing-coverts with whitish spots; outer webs of scapulars whitish, forming prominent white row across shoulder. Flight feathers barred whitish and ochraceous-buff. Tail with 3-4 narrow pale bars (only 10 tail feathers). Underparts whitish, densely mottled and vermiculated greyish-brown and cinnamon (appearing rather plain grey-brown from distance). Tarsi and toes bristled. **Juvenile** Downy chick whitish. Mesoptile similar to adult, but forehead and crown unspotted greyish, pale spots on upperparts indistinct, underparts mottled grey and whitish. **Bare parts** Eyes pale yellow, edges of eyelids blackish. Cere pale greyish-brown. Bill pale greyish-horn

with yellowish-horn tip. Tarsi and toes pale greyish-brown. Claws dark horn.

MEASUREMENTS AND WEIGHT Total length 13-14.5cm. Wing 101.5-112mm; tail 48-58mm. Weight 35.9-44.1g.

GEOGRAPHICAL VARIATION We distinguish four subspecies.

    M. w. whitneyi (Cooper, 1861). SW USA to N Mexico. See Description.

    M. w. idonea (Ridgway, 1914). SE California to SW New Mexico and Sonora. Greyer above than nominate, tail-bars broader and paler; paler below.

    M. w. sanfordi (Ridgway, 1914). S Baja California. Darker below than *idonea*.

    M. w. graysoni Ridgway, 1886. Socorro Island off W Mexico. More olive-brown above, tail with broad cinnamon-buff bars.

HABITS Nocturnal. Activity begins at dusk; often sings throughout night. During daytime, roosts in holes made by woodpeckers in giant saguaro cacti or trees; also hides among foliage. Does not cock and flirt tail.

FOOD Mostly insects and other arthropods. Swoops on prey from a perch. May be attracted to camp fires, to catch insects coming to the light.

BREEDING Territorial; northern populations leave territory in autumn to winter in C Mexico. Song is delivered from exposed perches claim territory or to attract a female. Holes made by woodpeckers (e.g. Gila Woodpecker *Melanerpes uropygialis*, Northern Flicker *Colaptes auratus*) in a saguaro cactus or in a tree are used for breeding. In April or May, lays 2-5 (normally 3) white eggs (about 25.9 x 22.9mm) directly on to the bottom of the nest hole; the laying intervals is 1-2 days. Incubation lasts about 2 weeks; the male is said to share in incubation. Both parents feed young, and care for them for some time after fledging.

STATUS AND CONSERVATION Uncertain. Locally not rare. May be threatened by the use of pesticides.

REMARKS This owl's ecology and biology need further study. Above all, the role of the male in incubation should be clarified; among owls, normally only the female incubates and the male occasionally covers the clutch when female has left for a short while. The species' relationship with other owls is not clear; we doubt that it is closely related to pygmy owls.

REFERENCES Boyer & Hume (1991), Burton (1992), Eck & Busse (1973), Hardy *et al.* (1989), Howell & Webb (1995), Ridgway (1914), Sprunt (1965), Voous (1988).

Little Owls, Genus *Athene* Boie, 1822

Small owls without ear-tufts. Wings often rather rounded, tail relatively short (12 tail feathers). Plumage generally boldly spotted whitish above on dusky grey or sandy-brown ground; crown mostly streaked or spotted whitish, nape with indistinct occipital face (two blackish areas surrounded by pale). Underparts off-white, spotted, barred or streaked dark. Tarsi relatively long; toes bristled. Eyes yellow to sulphur-yellow. We include the genus *Speotyto* in *Athene* on the grounds of similarities in morphology, behaviour and vocalisations and on DNA evidence. Four species (one in America, three in the Old World).

    The recently rediscovered *Athene blewitti*, previously considered extinct, seems to be rather separated from the three other species of *Athene*, as it inhabits primary forest and shows morphological differences. Further investigations may perhaps indicate removing it from *Athene*; we currently place it in the subgenus *Heteroglaux*.

174 BURROWING OWL
Athene cunicularia   **Plate 53**

French: Chouette des terriers
German: Kaninchen-Eule
Spanish: Buho llanero, Lechuza vizcachera
Portuguese: Coruja-de-campo

IDENTIFICATION A small (18-26cm), rather long-legged owl without ear-tufts, with head and facial disc rather flat. Boldly spotted whitish and brown above, eyebrows prominently whitish; below, spotted and barred light and dark. Tarsi relatively long, sparsely feathered; toes bristled. Tail relatively short. Eyes bright yellow. Partly diurnal, in open landscapes, not in forest. **Similar species** Pygmy owls (*Glaucidium*) are smaller, with relatively longer tail and prominent occipital face. Cuban Bare-legged Owl [87] is much smaller, and has totally bare tarsi and toes. Screech owls (*Otus*) are slimmer, nocturnal, and have small ear-tufts. Elf Owl [173] is tiny, with fine vermiculations on greyish-brown plumage.

VOCALISATIONS Vocally very active, with a rich vocabulary. The song of the male is a hollow, plaintive *cu-cuhooh*, repeated at intervals of several seconds. It varies somewhat individually and according to excitement of the bird. The female utters a similar but slightly higher-pitched song. Both sexes give a chattering *kwekwekwekweeh* when alarmed, increasing in volume to a loud, harsh *jaket-jakjaket... gowaeh-keket-gowaeh* and a wooden rattle; a screeching *chreeh-ket-ket-ket* is uttered in similar situations. A clucking *chee-gugugugugug* seems to have a contact function. Young utter dry rattling sounds (like a rattlesnake!), and hiss when disturbed at the nest.

DISTRIBUTION From the plains of W North America south to Central America and patchily southeast to the Atlantic coast; also Hispaniola, very locally in W Cuba and some other islands of the Caribbean. Locally in NW South America and the Andean region, primarily on eastern (not forested) and western slopes; rather widely distributed in E South America from Pará in Brazil south to Patagonia and Tierra del Fuego, where it recently almost became extinct.

MOVEMENTS Northern populations are mostly migratory, and many winter south to Honduras. Vagrants have been observed outside normal range of distribution. Central and South American populations are mainly resident.

HABITAT Open country with bushes or scattered trees, semi-deserts and deserts, mountain slopes with ravines and scattered bushes, open arid areas in the Andes, open grassland with patches of short vegetation, rather open pastureland with bushes and some trees, agricultural land, and Patagonian plains with ravines. From sea-level up to about 4,500m locally.

DESCRIPTION *A. c. cunicularia* Adult Facial disc pale brownish, contrasting with prominent white eyebrows; below disc a distinct whitish throat band. Upperparts brown, forehead and crown with whitish streaks and dots, the rest irregularly dotted whitish to pale ochraceous with relatively large, rather rounded spots. Flight feathers barred light and dark; tail brown with 3-4 pale bars. Underparts whitish to pale buff, rather densely barred

dusky brown. Tarsi rather long, sparsely feathered; toes bristled. **Juvenile** Downy chick pale grey-brown to whitish. Mesoptile similar to adult, but crown unspotted, underparts more diffusely marked, facial disc whitish with dusky zones on outer edge of eyes. **Bare parts** Eyes bright yellow. Cere greyish-brown. Bill greyish-olive. Toes olive-grey. Claws dark horn with blackish tips.

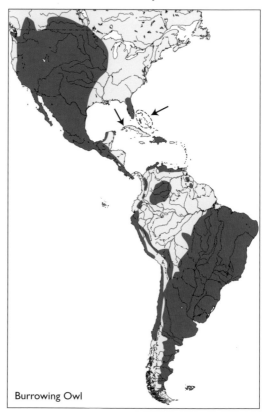

Burrowing Owl

MEASUREMENTS AND WEIGHT Total length 18-26cm. Wing 142.5-200mm; tail 63.5-114mm. Weight of males 129-185g (median 151g), of females 120-228g (median 159g); 1 unsexed 250g.

GEOGRAPHICAL VARIATION The total of about 21 different subspecies described appears to us as too high. Two races (*guadeloupensis, amaura*) are extinct. The species shows a rather wide individual variability in size and weight. We therefore recognise only 13, treating the others as synonyms.

A. c. cunicularia (Molina, 1782). N Chile from Taracapá to Cautín, Argentina (from Tucumán) to Paraguay, Rio Grande do Sul in S Brazil, Uruguay, and south to Tierra del Fuego. See Description. Wing 179-200mm; tail 78-114mm; 1 unsexed bird 250g. (We include *partridgei* as a synonym.)

A. c. grallaria (Temminck, 1822). Dry interior of Brazil from Maranho and Piauhy south through Goiás and Bahia to SE Mato Grosso and Paraná. Above, relatively dark with rufous wash and small scapular spots; dark below, distinctly spotted chest band, lower breast and belly with few rusty bars and buffy wash. Wing 168-198mm.

A. c. hypugaea (Bonaparte, 1825). From British Columbia east to C Manitoba, south to Mexico and W Panama. Broad chest band with pale buffy spots; whitish lower breast and belly boldly barred and with sandy or creamy wash. Wing 164.5-178mm.

A. c. floridana (Ridgway, 1874). Patchily in E USA, widely distributed in Florida. Narrow, sparsely spotted chest band, coloration of underparts rather white. Wing 154.5-170mm.

A. c. troglodytes (Wetmore & Swales, 1886). Hispaniola, Beata and Gonave in Caribbean. Smaller and darker than *floridana*; broad, spotted chest band. Wing 153-161.5mm; tail 64.5-76.5mm.

A. c. rostrata (Townsend, 1890). Clarion Island off west coast of Mexico. Wing 160-169mm.

A. c. nanodes (Berlepsch & Stolzmann, 1892). Pacific coast of Peru to northernmost Chile. A relatively small desert form. (Form *intermedia* probably a synonym.)

A. c. brachyptera (Richmond, 1896). Margarita Island and N and C Venezuela. Very short-winged. Wing 142-152mm. (The taxon *apurensis* may be a synonym.)

A. c. tolimae (Stone, 1899). W Colombia. Similar to *pichinchae* but smaller. (The taxon *carrikeri* may be a synonym.)

A. c. juninensis (Berlepsch & Stolzmann, 1902). Andes of Peru, south to Andean regions of W Bolivia and NW Argentina. Upperparts pale buff with large whitish blotches; barring on underparts fawn-coloured and rather open. Wing 193-213mm. (The taxon *punensis* is probably a synonym.)

A. c. boliviana (Kelso, 1939). Arid habitats in Bolivia and N Argentina; intergrades with nominate race in Tucumán.

A. c. minor (Cory, 1918). Savanna of upper Rio Branco in Brazil and adjacent parts of Guyana and Surinam. Wing of 1 specimen 142.5mm.

A. c. pichinchae (v. Boetticher, 1929). Andes of W Ecuador, probably intergrading with *juninensis*. Dark grey-brown above, finely spotted whitish; dusky barring below rather dense. Wing about 175mm.

HABITS Largely diurnal, but most active at dusk, sometimes at night. Highly terrestrial; often seen perched on a rock, a mound of earth or telegraph or fence posts, bobbing up and down when excited. Frequently roosts on one foot. Flight over longer distances is undulating, with rapid wingbeats and a swooping glide.

FOOD Beetles and other insects, spiders, scorpions, small mammals, reptiles and occasionally other small vertebrates. The prey is normally caught from a perch, sometimes by hovering above the ground.

BREEDING Although territorial, often nests in loose colonies of several pairs; in such cases, only a small area around the nest is defended. Several males may be heard calling quite close to one another. A burrow of a small mammal (e.g. prairie-dog or vizcacha) in the ground or a bank is used for nesting, but quite often the owls excavate a burrow themselves; the opening is normally surrounded by very short vegetation or may even be in bare ground; areas with tall grass are avoided. The nest chamber can be about 1m below ground, with the often meandering tunnel up to 3m long. The owls collect cattle dung which they place around the entrance, sometimes also lining the chamber; this striking behaviour seems likely to be a means of camouflaging the nest against mammalian predators,

which are often distracted by the odour of the dung (experiments have shown that the owls replace dung if it is removed). Apart from Short-eared Owl [211], this is the only owl species known to bring material to the nest.

The female lays 2-11 (normally 5-6) white eggs (31 x 26mm) and incubates for about 4 weeks; the male is said to share in incubation, but this requires confirmation (males of some owl species occasionally cover the eggs without incubating when the female takes a brief break from her duties). The young are fed and cared for by both parents, including for a while after leaving the nest.

STATUS AND CONSERVATION Uncertain. Locally rather frequent, otherwise rare. The species is adversely affected by pesticide use and the transformation of prairie landscapes into agricultural land. Grazing livestock (especially sheep) often destroy burrows by trampling, which may have been the main reason for a rapid decline of this owl noted in Tierra del Fuego. Campaigns in the USA in the early 20th century aimed at eradicating prairie dogs led to a remarkable decline in Burrowing Owl populations. Large clearings in wooded areas have aided colonisation by this owl, but poisoning of small rodents in such areas has reversed the trend again.

REMARKS Although rather well known, this amazing owl requires further study, e.g. on the role of the male in incubation, reproductive biology, behaviour and geographical variation.

REFERENCES Boetticher (1929), Boyer & Hume (1991), Burton (1992), Clark (1997), Clark *et al.* (1978), Eck & Busse (1973), Fjeldså & Krabbe (1990), Haug *et al.* (1993), Howell & Webb (1995), Humphrey *et al.* (1970), Johnson (1967), Koepcke (1970), Peters (1940), Scherzinger (1988), Voous (1988).

175 FOREST OWLET
Athene blewitti   Plate 53

Syn: *Heteroglaux blewitti*

Other names: Forest Spotted Owlet, Blewitt's Owl

French: Chouette des forêts
German: Blewitt-Kauz

IDENTIFICATION A small owl (23cm) similar in appearance to Spotted Owlet [177], but heavier and with different markings. Crown unspotted or with faint miniature whitish dots; back nearly plain, with spotting much reduced; tail with broad white bands more than 5mm in width and a white terminal band (except in worn plumage). Upper chest with uniform broad dark area; throat, as well as most of central breast and belly, white; flanks broadly barred. **Similar species** Little Owl [176] differs in having streaked abdomen. Spotted Owlet is much more spotted, particularly on crown (except in juvenile), with curved eyebrows and white behind auriculars, lacks plain band across breast, centre of lower breast and belly are heavily barred and spotted, and back has scattered subterminal spots; although larger in body size than Spotted, Forest Owlet has relatively shorter wings.

VOCALISATIONS Primary song consists of short, melodious, querulous *uwww* or *uh-wuwwww* notes in series, with intervals of 4-15 seconds; typically given in full daylight. An infrequent call is described as long series of *kweek... kweek* notes. A low, flat, buzzing hiss lasting 2-3 seconds and rising slightly near the end is given by resting birds.

DISTRIBUTION Only known from four sites (all below 500m), two in West Khandesh (N Maharashtra), and one each in E Madhya Pradesh and W Orissa. No acceptable records for 113 years until its rediscovery (two birds) in November 1997 in N Maharashtra, near Shahada. Since then only definitely reported from the immediate area.

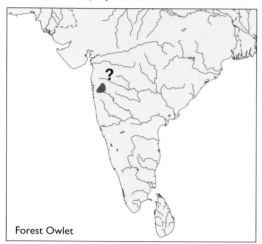

Forest Owlet

MOVEMENTS Resident.

HABITAT Dry and humid deciduous forest, from 200-500m elevation.

DESCRIPTION Adult Facial disc whitish-brown with a few darker vermiculations; eyebrows prominently whitish and straight. Crown plain brown with few miniature whitish speckles, ear-coverts pale brown lacking white rear border; sides of head and neck, as well as mantle, unspotted greyish-brown; indistinct occipital face with nape collar reduced; scapulars and wing-coverts with few whitish spots. Flight feathers (P1 equal to P7 or shorter than P6) barred white and blackish; short tail brown with rather broad (more than 5mm) whitish bars and whitish terminal band (except in worn plumage). Underparts white, with broad dark throat band (hidden in normal posture) and nearly uniform grey-brown breast (sometimes partially broken in middle), contrasting with large whitish throat patch and plain whitish centre of lower breast and belly; flanks and breast sides with broad dark brown banding. Tarsus feathered pure white; upper surface of long thick toes with soft whitish feathering. Claws relatively very heavy. **Juvenile** Not described. **Bare parts** Iris pale yellow, eyelids black. Cere dirty yellow. Bill yellowish. Toes dirty yellowish. Claws blackish.

MEASUREMENTS AND WEIGHT Total length about 23cm. 3 males wing 145-154mm, tail 68-72.5mm; 2 females wing 147.5-148mm, tail 63-70mm. Weight of 1 male 241g.

GEOGRAPHICAL VARIATION Monotypic: *Athene blewitti* (Hume, 1873).

HABITS Largely diurnal, it routinely hunts, sings, flies and perches in broad daylight. Does not often sing at night. During the cool season often sits in full sun on bare

topmost branches, rhythmically flicking its tail. During the hot season often rests much of the day in the shady mid-strata. Not much persecuted, or avoided by small birds. Performs a bobbing display in which head is lowered to cover feet, then owlet stands tall to show very conspicuous white belly and leg feathering. Flight direct, agile, strong and not undulating.

Forest Owlet.

FOOD Probably typically larger prey than Spotted Owlet, given that skull and talons are much more massive. In November 1997, one was seen with bill smeared with blood, suggesting that it had been feeding on vertebrate prey. In June 1998, one was seen mid-morning feeding on a medium-sized lizard; also seen foraging on the wet ground after heavy rains, apparently feeding on invertebrates.

BREEDING Unknown. The observers of the November 1997 individuals report that the two birds were in different stages of moult: one had rather worn plumage, while the other had recently moulted. These differences suggest that the worn individual was an adult, and the other probably a bird of the year in its first full plumage.

STATUS AND CONSERVATION Since its discovery in 1872, Forest Owlet had been known from only seven museum specimens, indicating that it must have been rare and local even in the 19th century. A bird alleged by Meinertzhagen to have been collected in October 1914 at Mandvi on the Tapti river (21°16'N, 73°22'E), about 220km north of Bombay, would have been the latest specimen, but the claim has recently been shown to have been fraudulent; recent examination proved that it was a restuffed specimen relabelled with false data from a series collected in the late 19th century (Rasmussen & Collar 1999). The 1997 sighting demonstrates that the species is not yet extinct; it is, however, obviously extremely rare, and highly threatened by severe destruction of its lowland deciduous forest habitat. Listed as Critical by BirdLife International.

REMARKS This species clearly requires intensive study of its ecology, biology, behaviour, vocalisations and systematics before it becomes extinct. The tail-flicking behaviour (see Habits) argues against a close relationship with other *Athene* owls and suggests closer affinity with pygmy owls (*Glaucidium*); we therefore suggest placing this species in the subgenus *Heteroglaux*. It differs from other *Athene* species (including *Speotyto*) in osteology of the skull and tarsometatarsus, as well as in primary song (Rasmussen & Collar in prep.).

REFERENCES Ali & Ripley (1969, 1987), Baker (1927), Boyer & Hume (1991), Burton (1992), Collar *et al.* (1994), Eck & Busse (1973), Gallagher (1998), Ishtiaq (1998), King & Rasmussen (1999), Rasmussen (1998), Rasmussen & Collar (1998, 1999), Rasmussen & Ishtiaq (in press 1999), Voous (1988).

---

176 LITTLE OWL
Athene noctua   Plate 54

French: Chouette chevêche
German: Steinkauz
Spanish: Mochuelo común

IDENTIFICATION A small (19-25cm), relatively long-legged, 'chunky' owl with short tail, and rather flat head with indistinct facial disc. Dark greyish-brown to sandy-coloured above, rather densely spotted whitish to pale ochre; below, boldly spotted and streaked brown or ochraceous. Eyes lemon-yellow. Tarsi feathered (lower parts sometimes bristled), toes bristled. Often perches in exposed sites (e.g. fence posts, telephone poles, earth mounds, heaps of stones), bobbing body up and down when excited. Flight undulating. **Similar species** Eurasian Pygmy Owl [143] is smaller, with relatively longer tail, and lives in coniferous and mixed forest (where Little Owl is absent). Common and Pallid Scops Owl [37, 38] are slimmer, with small ear-tufts and a more bark-like, cryptic plumage pattern. Spotted Owlet [177] is diffusely barred below and has bright yellow eyes. Tengmalm's Owl [178] has a much more rounded head and thickly feathered toes, and is a forest bird.

VOCALISATIONS The song of the male is a rising *goohk* with 'interrogative' character, repeated at intervals of several seconds. With excitement, it grades into a cat-like, rather explosive *kwéeo*, repeated several times. The female sometimes utters a similar but higher-pitched song. Both give piercing series of shrill yelping notes when disturbed: *kwiff-kwiff-kwiff-kwiff-....* A cackling *kekekek* and a short *kyu* probably have a warning function. Both sexes give soft *uhk* notes in contact. Larger nestlings beg with scratchy, somewhat hissing notes, *shreeh*.

DISTRIBUTION Britain (except in north; introduced), and Eurasia from Iberia north to Denmark, S Sweden and Latvia, east to Asia Minor, Levant, Arabia, C and E Asia to China and Manchuria, south to N Africa and Red Sea coast to Somalia and Eritrea. Introduced in New Zealand.

MOVEMENTS Resident. Young birds wander about and may settle up to 200-600km from the locality of their birth; normally, they are found at an average range of about 50km from the natal site.

HABITAT Open country with groups of trees and bushes, rocky country (e.g. valleys with cliffs), deserts and semi-deserts with rocks or ruins, oases, pastureland with scattered trees, orchards with old fruit trees, along rivers and creeks with pollarded willows and other trees, parkland, and edges of semi-open woodland; locally around farmhouses or barns, even in human settlements with surrounding cultivated land with trees. From sea-level up into open montane regions (to about 3,000-4,600m in the Himalayas), avoiding forest; in C Europe normally below 700m.

DESCRIPTION *A. n. noctua* Adult Facial disc ill-defined, greyish-brown with light mottling; whitish eyebrows

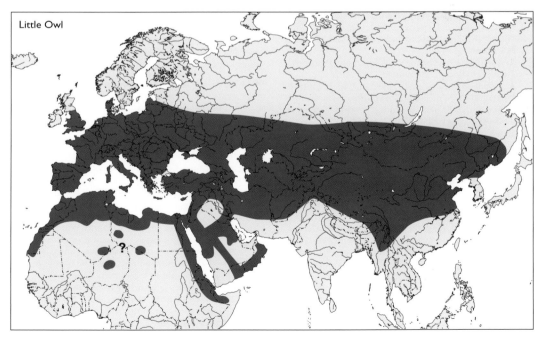

Little Owl

prominent. Upperparts dark brown, heavily spotted with whitish dots; forehead and crown streaked and spotted whitish, nape with indistinct occipital face. Flight feathers barred whitish and dark brown; tail dark brown with few whitish or pale ochre bars. Throat plain whitish, separated from diffusely light- and dark-spotted neck and upper breast by narrow brown collar; rest of underparts whitish, boldly streaked dark brown, belly rather plain whitish. Tarsi relatively long, feathered whitish; toes bristled. **Juvenile** Downy chick white, slightly mottled with pale grey on upperside. Mesoptile similar to adult, but markings more suffused, spotting less distinct and structure of body plumage more fluffy. **Bare parts** Eyes sulphur-yellow to pale yellow; half-grown chicks have yellowish-grey eyes. Cere olive-grey. Bill greyish-green to yellowish-grey. Toes pale grey-brown. Claws dark horn with blackish tips.

MEASUREMENTS AND WEIGHT Total length 19-25cm. Wing 129-187mm; tail 69-96mm. Weight 108-210g, females normally heavier than males.

GEOGRAPHICAL VARIATION Many subspecies are described, mostly based on individual variation of few specimens. More rufous and more greyish morphs occur. We therefore treat several taxa as synonyms and recognise a total of 11 geographical races, some of which may be specifically distinct.

A. n. noctua (Scopoli, 1769). C Europe, north to Denmark, south to Italy, east to NW Russia and N Albania. See Description. Wing 151-177mm; tail 75-85mm; weight 120-265g. (We include the form *sarda* of Sardinia and other W Mediterranean islands in this race).

A. n. vidalii Brehm, 1857. W Europe from Spain and Portugal to Belgium; introduced in England, from where spread to Wales and S Scotland. Darker than nominate, dark fuscous-brown with olive tinge above, with spots clearer white; streaked dark umber-brown below. Wing 151-170mm.

A. n. glaux (Savigny, 1809). N Africa from Morocco southwest to Mauritania, south to the Sahara and east to Egypt. More cinnamon-brown, streaked and spotted white; tail unevenly spotted buff; toes greenish-yellow. Wing 150-163mm. (We include *saharae* and *solitudinis* as synonyms.).

A. n. orientalis Severetzov, 1873. Turkestan, Dzungaria, Tien Shan. Wing 152-169mm.

A. n. ludlowi Baker, 1924. (Tibetan Owlet) Ladakh, Tibet, eastwards through Tibetan plateau facies of N Sikkim and N Bhutan, reaching 3,000-4,600m above sea-level. Larger than nominate. Chocolate-brown above, spotted white; dirty white below with grey-brown wash on breast. Bill bright yellow, toes grey with yellow soles. Wing 169-187mm.

A. n. plumipes Swinhoe, 1870. Altai and south of Lake Baikal to Mongolia, NE China and Korea. Toes more densely covered with plumes rather than bristles. Wing 156-170mm.

A. n. indigena Brehm, 1855. S Albania, Greece, Romania, Bulgaria and Ukraine, east to Caspian Sea, south to Asia Minor, Aegean islands and Crete. Paler than nominate. Wing 158-172mm.

A. n. bactriana Blyth, 1847. (Hutton's Owlet) Transcaspia eastwards to Lake Balkhash, south to Iraq, Iran and Afghanistan, east to Ladakh. Overlaps with *ludlowi* in Ladakh. Sandy-brown above, spotted with white; wings and tail broadly barred whitish. White below, heavily sreaked chocolate-brown. Wing 153-175mm.

A. (n.) lilith Hartert, 1913. S Turkey, Syria, Israel, and Arabian Peninsula, overlapping with *bactriana* in Iraq and W Iran. Very pale sandy-brown; occipital face rather distinct; less streaked below. Wing 154-168mm. (According to DNA evidence from birds in S Turkey, *lilith* may be specifically distinct from *Athene noctua*; song also differs in lacking latter's typical upward-inflected 'interrogative' character; *lilith* gives somewhat drawn and slightly hoarse *gwiah* at intervals.).

A. (n.) spilogastra (Heuglin, 1863). Red Sea coast of from Sudan to N Ethiopia. A very small, rather pale form. Wing 146-147mm.

A. (n.) somaliensis Reichenow, 1905. SW Ethiopia to N Somalia. Smallest race. Crown less spotted than in *spilogastra*. Wing 129-144mm. (The two smallest taxa, may perhaps represent a separate species: '*Athene spilogastra*'.)

HABITS Most active at dusk, but also partly by day and at night. Often roosts by day in dense foliage, in openings of holes, sometimes on open perches such as telephone wires, fence posts, bare branches, rocks, etc; when disturbed at its roost, it first adopts a slim, upright position, then bobs body up and down and finally flies away or withdraws into a nearby hole. Vocally active nearly all year, especially around courtship period; may be stimulated and attracted by playback of its song. Male normally begins to sing at dusk, and is sometimes vocal by day; during courtship singing may be heard also at night, especially on clear, calm nights; in windy weather vocal activity is much reduced or even ceases. When leaving perch, it drops down and flies low over the ground, before sweeping up to another perch. Flight is undulating, with rapid wingbeats alternating with glides. Both sexes may be aggressive near nest.

FOOD Insects, primarily beetles and grasshoppers, other arthropods, small reptiles and frogs, small mammals and birds, as well as earthworms. Does not pluck bird prey, but discards the wings and tail. Pellets are about 30-40 x 10-19mm in size. Surplus food is stored in deposits, mostly in holes. The prey is normally caught from a perch, by swooping down on it; often hops and moves about on the ground in search of food.

BREEDING Territorial, defending its territory by singing or by aggressive behaviour against intruders. The male sings at different perches in its territory, particularly near the future nesting site; often duets with female during courtship. Territory size is in general about 0.5km², so locally several singing males may be heard from one point. Male advertises potential nesting site by singing near it or from the entrance. Copulation normally occurs near the nest on a bare branch or a rock, wall, etc. Natural holes in trees or pollarded willows are used for nesting, favourite sites being hollow branches of old fruit trees; artificial nestboxes are often accepted (see Status and Conservation); also uses holes or cavities in walls, under eaves, in earth or clay banks of rivers or ravines, in cliffs and in walls of sand-pits, and abandoned mammal burrows in the ground, holes in termite mounds, etc. The nest hole may thus be at ground level or 0.2-10m above ground.

In C Europe, laying normally occurs in April to mid May. Lays usually 3-6 white eggs (av. 34.4 x 29.6mm), at 2-day intervals, directly on to the bottom of the cavity in a shallow depression created 1-2 weeks earlier. Incubation, starting before the final egg is laid, is by the female alone, fed by her mate, and lasts 22-28 days; young of a captive pair hatched after only 19 days, but this is exceptional. Chicks hatch blind, their eyes opening at an age of 8-10 days; the female broods them for about 1 week, and feeds them alone, with food brought into the nest by the male. Young leave the nest a about 35 days and are then fed by both parents; at about 38-46 days they are able to fly some distance, and when 2-3 months old they are independent and leave the territory. Reach sexual maturity before 1 year old. Normally one brood per year; occasionally double-brooded when food is abundant.

Little Owls may reach an age of about 15-16 years, but normally less.

STATUS AND CONSERVATION Although locally rather abundant within its range, populations of C Europe are under some threat from pesticide use and the destruction of habitat by modern agriculture; particularly serious is the loss of old fruit trees with holes or of pollarded willows along creeks. Artificial nesting-tubes about 1m in length and 16cm wide, with an opening 6-8cm in diameter at one side, mounted on vertical branches in extensively used orchards, has proved a good means of increasing Little Owl populations. Many individuals become victims of road traffic when hunting at night, while severe winters with much snow may lead to huge losses among populations.

REMARKS Bioacoustical and molecular-biological studies of the 'dwarfish' forms of NE Africa and the pale Middle East taxa are needed in order to determine whether these are separate species or merely very distinct subspecies. DNA studies of birds from S Turkey (*lilith*) suggest specific difference, as do vocal patterns.

REFERENCES Ali & Ripley (1969), Bezzel (1985), Burton (1992), Cramp (1985), Dementiev & Gladkov (1951), Dunning (1993), Eck & Busse (1973), Exo (1981, 1983), Exo & Hennes (1980), Fry *et al.* (1988), Furrington (1979), Glutz & Bauer (1980), Hölzinger (1987), König (1967, 1969), Pfister (1999), Scherzinger (1988), Schönn *et al.* (1991), Ullrich (1980), Voous (1988).

---

177 SPOTTED OWLET
Athene brama   Plate 54

French: Chouette brame
German: Brahma-Kauz

IDENTIFICATION A small (21cm), squat, white-spotted owl with round head and yellow eyes. Tail relatively short with narrow white bars and very little pale at tip. **Similar species** Forest Owlet [175] is heavier-bodied, with more uniform upperparts and more contrasting underparts, a different face pattern, and short stout heavily white-feathered legs and feet. Little Owl [176], also a little bigger, differs in its longitudinally streaked abdomen and crown.

VOCALISATIONS The song is probably a harsh screeching *chirurrr-chirurrr-chirurrr-...* followed by, or alternating with, *cheevak, cheevak, cheevak*, and a variety of equally discordant screeches and chuckles. Particularly noisy in the breeding season.

DISTRIBUTION Southern Asia, from Iran to Vietnam; present throughout most of Indian subcontinent (except Sri Lanka) and SE Asia (except peninsular Thailand and Malaysia).

MOVEMENTS Resident.

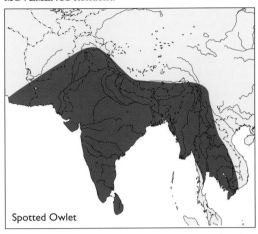
Spotted Owlet

HABITAT Open or semi-open country, including semi-deserts, also within and on outskirts of villages and cultivation, groves with old trees, and ruins; avoids heavy forest. From sea-level locally to about 1,400m.

DESCRIPTION *A. b. indica* **Adult** Forehead and lores white to pale buffy. Curved white supercilia; auriculars dark, contrasting with white rear edge. Crown, sides of head and upperparts earth-brown, sometimes more grey, sometimes rather rufescent, marked with small white spots; nape with very large white spots forming collar, back with large white spots, scapulars with broad white edges. Wings spotted and banded white, tail with narrow white bars. Chin, throat, and front and sides of neck white; a band (usually narrow and broken) below this dark brown; remainder of underparts whitish, spotted and mottled with brown, sometimes with broken bars; lacks large pure white areas on underparts. Tarsi feathered, toes bristled, claws small. **Juvenile** Chick with pure white down; short, very soft prepennae over whole body, except for apteria of lateral neck, anterior body sides and sides of spinal tract. Juvenile much like adult, but with softer plumage, usually less white on crown and mantle, these sometimes virtually unspotted; vague dark streaks below breast. **Bare parts** Iris pale to deep golden-yellow. Cere dusky green or greenish-brown. Bill greenish-horn, sometimes darker, sometimes more yellow on culmen. Toes dirty yellowish. Claws dark horny, soles yellowish.

MEASUREMENTS AND WEIGHT Total length 19-21cm, females usually somewhat larger than males. Wing 143-171mm; tail 65-93mm. Weight 110-114g.

GEOGRAPHICAL VARIATION There is much variation in colour within all races, but southern birds tend to be much darker and less spotted than pale northern birds. We recognise five subspecies.

A. b. indica (Franklin, 1831). From Afghan frontier (Kohat and Peshawar) eastwards through Punjab and Jammu (in plains and along Himalayan submontane tract, locally to about 1,400m), and through Nepal, Sikkim and Bhutan to Assam north and south of Brahmaputra river, south to Bangladesh and peninsular India (south to about 20°N, where intergrades with nominate race). See Description. Wing 149-171mm.

A. b. brama (Temminck, 1821). Peninsular India south of about 20°N; absent Sri Lanka, though occurring on Rameswaram Island about 30km from its northern tip. Differs from *indica* in being considerably darker and smaller. Wing 153-163mm.

A. b. albida Koelz, 1950. Iran, Baluchistan. Tends to average slightly paler than *indica*. Wing 154-167mm.

A. b. ultra Ripley, 1948. NE Assam north and south of Brahmaputra and Luhit rivers. Somewhat larger and darker than *indica*, with white spotting considerably reduced. Wing 164-168mm.

A. b. pulchra Hume, 1873. C Burma, Shan States and S Yunnan, south to S Burma, Thailand, Cambodia and SW Vietnam. A small dark race, much darker than *indica* and slightly darker than nominate *brama*; differs further from latter in having larger white spots, and less brown, more slaty, tinge in general coloration. Wing 143-158mm. (We regard *mayri* as a synonym.)

HABITS Largely crepuscular and nocturnal, but sometimes seen by day. Normally emerges around dusk and retires by sunrise to its roost in a tree hole or branch, where pairs and small (family?) groups huddle together. At dusk, perches on fence posts, telegraph wires or other vantage points to look for prey; often near street lights. Its flight is deeply undulating, like that of other small owls, consisting of a few rapid flaps followed by a glide with wings pressed to body.

FOOD Chiefly beetles, moths and other insects; also earthworms, lizards, mice and small birds. Hunts from a perch, pouncing on an unwary insect, and occasionally launching aerial sallies to seize winged termites in flight; commonly uses street lamps as hunting bases, hawking beetles and moths attracted to the light. Dismembers insects in its claws and then raises one foot to its bill, in similar fashion to a parakeet consuming a nut.

BREEDING Season February-April in the north; southern races breed November-March. Nests in natural tree hollows, holes in dilapidated wall, or in cavities in eaves of both deserted and occupied human dwellings; in semi-desert areas where suitable trees are scarce, occupies cavities in the sides of ravines and earth cliffs (as Little Owl). The nest is sometimes lined with a little grass and feathers. The 3 or 4, occasionally 5, white, roundish oval eggs (50 average 32.2 x 27.1mm) hatch asynchronously, as incubation starts with the first egg; this results in considerable disparity in the size of nestlings within same brood.

STATUS AND CONSERVATION Generally rather common. In some localities, every banyan, tamarind or mango tree hold a resident pair of this species. Often found in the neighbourhood of human habitations.

REMARKS This owl's biology and vocalisations need more study.

REFERENCES Ali and Ripley (1969, 1987), Baker (1927, 1934), Boyer & Hume (1991), Burton (1992), Eck & Busse (1973), Rasmussen & Collar (1998), Scherzinger (1988), Suresh Kumar (1985), Voous (1988).

Forest Owls, Genus *Aegolius* Kaup, 1829

Small owls with a large, round head without ear-tufts. Wings relatively long. Facial disc well developed, rather rounded or square. Eyes yellow or orange-yellow; edges of eyelids blackish. Tarsi feathered, toes feathered or bare. Openings of ears large and asymmetrical. All four species live in extensive forest (one in the Holarctic, three in America).

178 TENGMALM'S OWL
Aegolius funereus   Plate 55

Other names: Boreal Owl (North America)

French: Chouette de Tengmalm
German: Rauhfusskauz
Spanish: Lechuza de Tengmalm

IDENTIFICATION A small (20-23cm), whitish-spotted greyish-brown owl (body size about that of a small domestic pigeon) with relatively large, yellow eyes, large rounded head without ear-tufts, very prominent, rather square facial disc, short tail, relatively long wings, and densely feathered tarsi and toes. **Similar species** Eurasian Pygmy Owl [143] is much smaller, with flatter facial disc and relatively small yellow eyes. Little Owl [176] has a rather flat facial disc and is spotted and blotched light and dark, with toes bristled, not thickly feathered. Tawny Owl [130] is much larger and has large, dark brown eyes.

VOCALISATIONS The best known of all vocalisations is the territorial song of the male; this varies rather widely among individuals in all populations, whether in Europe, Asia or North America, with no different regional dialects. It consists of a series of poop notes, followed by a break before the next 'verse' starts, and may be uttered in a rather regular pattern of verse and break during a protracted period of the night. The individual notes normally begin rather faint and mellow, then increase to full power and finally break off abruptly, a verse generally consisting of 6-8 poop notes, often with emphasis on the third: *bubububu-bububu* (*u*-sound in all cases a short staccato *oo*), the sound always '*ocarina*-like'. The length of the break between verses depends on degree of excitement; with leisurely singing birds, it is normally about 3-4 seconds. On calm, often moonlit nights, songs may carry about 1km or more.

This song varies individually both in the pitch of the '*u*' and in the rate at which notes are given, with individual variation also in the number of poop notes and their character: some birds utter only series of about three notes in very slow succession, while others produce a dozen or more notes in very rapid succession; some sound very mellow and musical, and others have a more 'yelping' character. These patterns make it possible to distinguish between all the males in an area; the differences do not reflect different meanings, but are simply variations of the territorial song of the male.

When a female approaches a singing male, the song verses become stuttering, with irregularly spaced sequences of notes: *bububu-bu-bubu-bubububu-....* This 'stutter song' normally leads into a long, mellow trill, which may consist of up to about 350 (normally fewer!) notes in rapid succession: *wuwuwuwuwu....* It is delivered from potential nest holes in order to indicate their existence to the female. A short trill is uttered in flight when pursuing the female, or just before and after copulation.

To contact a breeding female, the male emits a low *wood*, or *wood-woohd*. In aggressive situations, he delivers a whipcrack-like *zjuck*, similar to a call of the European Red Squirrel *Sciurus vulgaris*.

The female has a song similar to the male's, but fainter, slightly higher-pitched and less clear, *guiguigui...*; it is delivered very infrequently.

Aggressive females utter a sharp *jack*, as well as a hoarse *oohwack* (somewhat similar to a Tawny Owl call) and croaking (heron-like) sounds, *kraihk, kwahk*; the male also makes similar sounds. When the male announces his arrival with either a short trill or *wood* calls, the female answers from inside the hole with a high-pitched *seeh*, sometimes with a verse of suppressed song. The female's contact-call is a mewing, somewhat hoarse *zuihd*.

Fledged birds beg with short, hissing *cheet* calls. Nestlings utter similar calls in the nest hole, as well as series of clicking sounds when uneasy.

DISTRIBUTION In the north, this owl's distribution is similar to that of the coniferous belt of the Holarctic. South of this, it occurs locally in Europe (e.g. Lüneburger Heide and other lowland forest in the plains of N Germany) and is generally confined to mountainous regions, e.g. Harz, Solling, Eifel, Venn, Odenwald, Thuringian and Saxon mountains, Carpathians, the Balkans, Bohemian and Black Forests, Vosges and Alps, as well as some mountains in Greece and very locally in the Pyrenees. In Europe the general distribution is rather coincident with that of the Norway Spruce *Picea abies*. Isolated populations exist e.g. in the Caucasus, Tien Shan and Himalayas.

In North America, the distribution is largely confined to forest areas of the Rocky Mountains and the northern coniferous belt. To the east of the Rockies it occurs south as far as New Mexico, and to the west in forest from Alaska to Oregon.

MOVEMENTS Partly migratory, especially northern populations. During migration may occur in habitats and at sites (even in towns) where it has never been recorded breeding. Northern birds may migrate up to about 1,000km. Adult males are rather sedentary everywhere and remain in the breeding area, while females and young birds may disperse quite far (up to 200-500km in Europe). Migrants from N Europe sometimes cross the Baltic and North Sea.

HABITAT Mostly fairly natural coniferous forest with old trees, and with some scattered or grouped deciduous trees, in mountainous regions; in the north also in lowlands. In N Europe and in Siberia found in vast forest of spruce and even birch *Betula* in the lowlands; in North America lives in similar habitats and especially in coniferous forest of Rocky Mountains. A very important element is the presence of suitable nest holes, mostly woodpecker holes; in Europe normally shares habitat with Black Woodpecker *Dryocopus martius*, in North America with Pileated *D. pileatus*. If nestboxes are provided, may also colonise uniform, artificial spruce forest; locally, occurs in deciduous forest with beech *Fagus sylvatica*, birch and oak *Quercus*, so long as these contain old woodpecker holes.

Typical habitat normally characterised by rather extensive forest (mostly coniferous) of aged trees, with clearings and groups of young conifers (e.g. tree nurseries), the floor often humid and partially covered with mosses. Sometimes found in younger forest when some remaining old trees with woodpecker holes, especially beech or pine, tower high above surrounding wood. In parts of the Jura Mountains in SW Germany, inhabits beech forest with nearby groups of spruces and clearings; such woods, with little or low undergrowth and with freestanding tall, slim and aged beeches with their dense canopy of leaves, give a 'dome-like' impression. Mature coniferous forest with Norway spruce, silver fir *Abies alba* and Scots pine *Pinus silvestris* quite often gives similar impression (e.g. in the Black Forest).

Ranges from plains up to slopes or summits of mountains; locally in forested valleys. Where Tawny Owl population is high, Tengmalm's Owl has little chance to survive; its altitudinal range towards lower regions is therefore very often limited by the Tawny Owl, which is less resistant to cold and snow. Occurs from plains up to 1,200m in C and S Germany, to 2,000m in the Alps and in Asia, and to about 3,000m in Rockies.

DESCRIPTION *A. f. funereus* **Adult** Sexes alike, but female heavier and a bit larger; in many cases coloration of facial disc may give hint to sex, appearing more uniform ochraceous-whitish on female, tinged greyish towards rim on male. Facial disc round or rather square, whitish, surrounded by dark rim with tiny white spots; small dark zone between eyes and base of bill. Above, greyish-brown to dark earth-brown, forehead and crown with small white dots, back and wing-coverts with larger white dots; hindneck spotted and mottled with dark and whitish markings. Primaries and secondaries with rounded whitish spots; tail dark brown with 4-5 bars of whitish dots. Underparts whitish, spotted and streaked greyish-brown. Tarsi and toes densely feathered. (Body plumage is normally carried rather loose, so that the owl appears larger than it really is; when frightened, becomes very slim

Tengmalm's Owl

by pressing plumage very tight to body, facial disc then appearing elongated, with pointed 'corners' at upper edge which may suggest small ear-tufts, but this due only to compressing of facial disc laterally and not analogous with 'real' ear-tufts of other owl species.) **Juvenile** First downy plumage after hatching (neoptile) white, not very dense, so reddish skin shows through. Downy plumage begins to be replaced after 1 week by rather uniform dark chocolate-brown juvenile plumage (mesoptile): only eyebrows and a streak on both sides of chin are whitish, contrasting with dark facial disc; flight and tail feathers dark brown, already showing similar pattern to adult, but with fewer and smaller white spots; eyes initially pale yellowish-grey, becoming yellow before fledging. A few weeks after fledging, uniform brown body plumage has been moulted and young very much resembles adult, but somewhat darker. **Bare parts** Eye colour varying from pale to bright yellow; eyes rimmed by blackish edges of eyelids. Cere and bill yellowish-horn. Claws dark horn to blackish-brown with extremely sharp blackish tips.

MEASUREMENTS AND WEIGHT Total length 20-23cm. Wing of males 158-178mm (most around 169mm), of females 164-185mm (most about 176mm); tail 91-106mm (median 99.7mm). Weight of males during breeding season 90-113g (av. 101.4g), of females 126-194g (av. 166.8g); chicks just after hatching 8g.

GEOGRAPHICAL VARIATION Becomes paler and greyer from west to east. Seven subspecies.

A. f. funereus (Linnaeus, 1758). Europe, locally from Scandinavia to Pyrenees, the Alps, eastwards to Greece, and from Baltic Republics to Russia north of Caspian Sea. See Description. Wing 162-182mm.

A. f. magnus (Buturlin, 1907). NE Siberia and Kamchatka. Lighter above, more ashy grey-brown, with heavy white spotting; dark markings on underparts rather faint. Larger than nominate. Wing 172-191.5mm; weight of 1 specimen 109g.

A. f. sibiricus (Buturlin, 1910). From C Siberia to Sakhalin and NE China. Paler and more spotted than nominate. Wing 166-182mm.

A. f. pallens (Schalow, 1908). Siberia east of Caspian Sea to N Mongolia. Very much like *sibiricus*. Wing 162-181mm.

A. f. beickianus Stresemann, 1928. N Kansu in C China. Very dark, similar to North American *richardsoni*. Wing 166-182mm.

A. f. caucasicus (Buturlin, 1907). Caucasus and Crimea. Smaller and darker than nominate. Wing 151-159mm.

A. f. richardsoni (Bonaparte, 1838). N North America. Larger, darker and more boldly patterned than nominate. Wing 174-185mm.

HABITS Almost strictly nocturnal, activity beginning at dusk and ending before sunrise. Unsociable. Roosts by day quite well concealed on a branch close to the trunk, mostly of a conifer. Adult males are territorial, but territories may be quite small, so that neighbouring males sometimes sing only a few hundred metres or less from each other without any aggressive reactions; where the population is large, several males may be heard from the same place, and individual differences in songs clearly noticeable (see Vocalisations). Song perches are quite often near potential nest holes (or nestboxes). Normally three peaks of singing during night: one just before dark, another some time later lasting to just before midnight,

and a third during a few hours before sunrise; unmated males may sing during these three periods nearly without a break, and some very ardent males may also sing around midnight. Vocally active only on calm, mostly clear nights: windy weather or an approaching depression suppresses singing, although drizzle, light snowfall or mist normally do not if a high-pressure zone is imminent; virtually no singing heard on windy or stormy nights (even if bright moonlight) or when heavy rain.

Tengmalm's is one of the owl species in which males sing intensively only so long as they are unmated; once he has acquired a female, the male will utter only a short song or a trill (very often just the wood calls) when announcing his arrival with food. For censusing, it is therefore important to begin listening early in the year (about mid February) in order not to miss any singing males. Males start singing normally when the snow begins to disappear and the first free patches of soil appear, so the start of the song period may vary from year to year, although never later than March even if there is still deep snow cover. Male may sing for only a very short period (sometimes only one or a few days) if successful in finding a mate very early in the year; intensively singing males are always unpaired.

Flight is noiseless, unhurried, with soft wingbeats, and straight.

FOOD Primarily small rodents, especially voles, but also shrews and sometimes moles *Talpa*; insects have not been recorded. Birds are taken only occasionally, especially in years with few rodents; in such years breeding success is very low, many birds do not breed, and there is little vocal activity, so enormous fluctuations of populations noted over the course of several years, due to food supply; rather cool and very wet springs are in general 'bad' years for most owl species. Cannibalism among nestlings very frequent in years when food is scarce.

Often perches on branches or tree trunks, investigating the ground. In such a situation it turns its head rather slowly from one side to the other, listening towards the ground; has an enormous ability for acoustical localisation of a rustling mouse on the forest floor. If a potential prey is located, it swoops on it from its perch. Birds are caught at dusk or dawn, in similar manner. Small rodents or shrews are quite often swallowed whole. Pellets (about 22 x 12mm) may be found mostly around the day roost.

BREEDING Polyandry and polygyny are not infrequent; if a clutch is destroyed by a predator early in the year, the female often settles and breeds with another male. Pair-bond is seasonal; the male retains the nesting area (often even the same nest hole) for several years, while females leave their mate after breeding. Territories can be quite small (often much less than 1km²). Nests mostly in holes produced by large woodpeckers (e.g. *Dryocopus*) in the trunks of tall trees, but sometimes natural holes in trees are used; special nestboxes are widely accepted locally. The height above ground is not important: holes produced by Black Woodpeckers are normally 7-14m above the forest floor, sometimes lower or even higher; nestboxes may be placed only 2.5m up on trunks, and even holes between 1m and 2m above ground have been used successfully.

The male begins to inspect potential holes (or boxes) in late winter, often sites used as deposits for food during the past weeks. It slips repeatedly into the cavity, and scratches on the floor until a shallow depression is produced, which the female later enlarges; no nest is built.

Quite often a fresh prey item is deposited in the cavity. On a calm evening the male begins to sing from a perch (mostly high up in a tree) near potential holes; if the site is in a narrow valley or hollow, he may sing from the upper edge of the slope so as to be heard as far as possible.

When a female approaches with *jack* or *zuid* calls, the male swoops to the cavity, slips inside and begins the 'stutter song' or utters a long trill, occasionally singing from the entrance; if interested, the female flies to the hole and slips in, while the male leaves; usually she finds a prey item inside. If the hole is to her liking, she will inspect it several times and eventually accept it; if not, she will leave and look for another male with a more acceptable nesting place, and the male will then start singing again. If the male is successful, he will stop singing, and visit only every evening to copulate with the female; hole-advertising, accompanied by trills and 'stutter songs', continues for a few evenings until the female occupies the hole and stays inside during daytime. Each night she leaves for a short time and copulations take place; when in the hole, she is fed by the male, who delivers prey at the entrance, sometimes inside the cavity. The female reacts to scratching at the tree trunk; she quickly appears at the entrance and looks out.

A few days after occupying the hole, the female lays normally 3-6 white eggs (32.6 x 26.6mm), at 1-day intervals; occasional larger clutches (up to about 11 eggs) may indicate the presence of a second female. She incubates alone for 28-29 days, starting with the first egg, and is fed during this period and also after hatching by the male, either inside the hole or at the entrance. Chicks hatch at roughly the same intervals as the eggs are laid, and thus differ in size; their eyes open after about 10 days, and they are fed by the female with food brought by the male. No nest sanitation, so the young are reared on a stinking layer of pellets, rotting food remains and excrement. At about 30-32 days they leave and disperse around the nesting area; not yet able to fly well, they quite often land on the forest floor, in which case they hide in the vegetation or try to climb up bushes or trees by using claws and bill, fluttering their still rather short wings, uttering contact-calls to the parents in the evening (see Vocalisations). They are accompanied and fed for about 4-6 weeks. Sexual maturity is reached at about 9 months.

Tengmalm's Owl may live for at least 7-8 years.

STATUS AND CONSERVATION Generally uncommon to rare, with some populations endangered particularly by deforestation; mature forest with groups of younger trees and clearings, where rodents are abundant, is essential for natural occurrence. Locally, may be rather common, especially where conservation measures (provision of nestboxes, protection of trees with nest holes, etc) are undertaken.

This species' most serious predators are larger owls (in Europe, mainly Tawny Owl) and martens *Martes*. In some years, the latter destroy a very high percentage of broods and kill many females on the nest (in most cases, eggshells and feathers found near nest tree): during the early stages of breeding, the female leaves the hole when a marten approaches; at later stages (e.g. around hatching), she very often withdraws inside and is then taken by the predator. In Europe, pine *M. martes* and stone martens *M. foina* are the most dangerous predators. A proven method of protecting cavities is by fixing a strip of sheet-metal or plastic, about 50cm wide, around the trunk below

the hole, and another above it, to prevent access by martens; nestboxes can be similarly protected, or special 'anti-marten' boxes can be used. It is important that there are no trees or stronger branches closer than 4-5m to the nest (a pine marten can leap over a distance of 3-4m). Nestboxes should have an aperture of about 8cm (best 7cm wide and 9cm high), i.e. too small for a Tawny Owl to enter. Deforestation at higher altitudes provides more habitat for rodents and thus encourages more Tawny Owls; creation of clearings and roads through extensive forest is therefore disadvantageous to Tengmalm's.

In Germany, the Nuthatch *Sitta europaea* has proved a problem locally through its habit of reducing the size of hole entrances with plastered mud; this behaviour extends to Black Woodpecker holes and large nestboxes, with the result that the owl can no longer enter and the potential breeding site is lost. Moreover, there are several recorded instances of Nuthatches even walling in brooding female Tengmalm's Owls: the male owl continued to feed its mate for a while through the small hole, and the female and young, unable to emerge through the opening, had to be rescued by breaking the mud wall; on several occasions, however, nest inspection was too late and female and young had starved.

Like all owls, Tengmalm's is highly vulnerable to pesticides, which can have an enormous negative effect on populations when used against voles or sprayed on clearings.

REMARKS This widespread species is one of the better known owls of the northern hemisphere.

REFERENCES Bezzel (1985), Dementiev & Gladkov (1951), Frochot (1963), Glutz & Bauer (1980), Hölzinger (1987), König (1964, 1965, 1967, 1968, 1969, 1979, and unpublished), Korpimäki (1981), Kuhk (1949, 1950, 1952, 1953), Möckel (1983), Schelper (1979), Voous (1988).

179 NORTHERN SAW-WHET OWL
Aegolius acadicus   Plate 55

French: Chouette-Scie
German: Sägekauz
Spanish: Tecolotito Cabezón

IDENTIFICATION A small owl (17-19mm) with relatively large, round head. Brown above, whitish with warm rufous-buff streaks below; crown with numerous white shaft-streaks; rim of facial disc rather unmarked. Bill blackish; eyes orange-yellow. **Similar species** Unspotted Saw-whet Owl [180] is more uniform above and below, and Tengmalm's Owl [178] is bigger.

VOCALISATIONS Common name is derived from the shrill, rasping call, sounding like a saw being sharpened: *screerrave*. This is uttered by both sexes and seems to have an aggressive character, and is perhaps ethologically comparable with the hoarse calls of Tengmalm's Owl.

Territorial song is long sequences of high and mellow 'toots' uttered regularly in a rather even rhythm at medium speed (about two notes per second): *tew-tew-tew-....* The single notes sound like water dripping into a half-filled bucket. This song, repeated after a short break, is uttered by males on calm nights in early spring. A metallic note, resembling the sound of a hammer striking an anvil, is given when the birds are excited (compare *zjuck* call of Tengmalm's). Calls of young probably similar to those of young Tengmalm's.

DISTRIBUTION Wide range in North America, but with more southerly distribution than Tengmalm's Owl, with which it overlaps in north and west. Occurs south of a line from Newfoundland and the mouth of the St Lawrence in the east to Queen Charlotte Islands, north of Vancouver, in the west. In the east extends to North Carolina, and in the west to S Arizona and in higher mountains as far as C Mexico (Oaxaca).

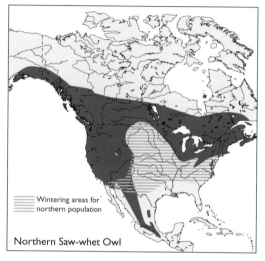

Wintering areas for northern population

Northern Saw-whet Owl

MOVEMENTS Partially migratory, especially northern populations. Short-distance migrant, appearing outside breeding season in regions or habitats where never previously recorded, and in winter may therefore be found in Louisiana, Georgia and Florida. In certain years, especially in autumn (September), many may be observed on passage, probably blown off course by strong winds.

HABITAT Dense woodland, often with moist or swampy ground; breeds mostly in the coniferous belt of N North America, with spruce *Picea* and fir *Abies* forest. Locally, especially in the Mexican mountains, it is found in more open and drier country with pine *Pinus*, other conifers and oak *Quercus* woodland. In autumn, moves into deciduous woods, e.g. in the E USA, and can then be found particularly in moist and riverine groves with alders *Alnus*, aspens *Populus* and willows *Salix*.

DESCRIPTION *A. a. acadicus* **Adult** Facial disc brownish, with whitish zone around eyes, forming radial white streaks towards edge of disc, and with blackish spot between base of bill and eyes; disk without dark rim. Rest of head warm brown or grey-brown, rather densely covered with white shaft-streaks, especially on forehead. Mantle and rest of upperparts brown with white spots. Flight feathers spotted white; relatively short tail with normally three rows of white spots on both webs of rectrices. Below, whitish with soft reddish-buff streaks. Toes slightly feathered. **Juvenile** Chick has whitish downy plumage. Mesoptile chocolate-brown, resembles young Tengmalm's Owl. At fledging, juvenile plumage is similar: facial disc brown, faintly rimmed white, with eyebrows and forehead white; above, plain chocolate-brown; breast like back, forming indistinct breast band,

rest of underparts pale brownish or ochraceous-buff. **Bare parts** Eyes orange-yellow, surrounded by blackish edge of eyelids; juvenile with iris yellowish, eyes with pinkish rim of skin. Bill and cere blackish. Claws dark horn with blackish tips.

MEASUREMENTS AND WEIGHT Total length 17-19cm. Wing 132-144mm; tail about 72mm. Weight of adults about 80-90g, females heavier than males.

GEOGRAPHICAL VARIATION We distinguish three geographical subspecies.

A. a. acadicus (Gmelin, 1788). From British Columbia east to the Gulf of St Lawrence and south to California, Arizona and N Mexico. See Description.

A. a. brooksi (Fleming, 1916). Queen Charlotte Islands, British Columbia. Known as 'Queen Charlotte Owl'. Very dark above; underparts with pale to rich ochraceous-buff wash, densely blotched and streaked dusky. Wing of 1 male 140mm; mean weight of males 84.8g, of females 99.6g.

A. a. brodkorbi Briggs, 1954. Sierra Madre de Oaxaca, SW Mexico. Paler than nominate, and with less whitish spotting on primaries and tail feathers. (Overlaps in range with *A. ridgwayi* and occasional hybrids may occur, as suggested by an 'intermediate' specimen: '*A. ridgwayi tacanensis*'.)

HABITS Strictly nocturnal and normally unsociable; larger numbers occasionally observed during migration. During daytime roosts singly in dense foliage of trees, mostly close to the trunk, normally not very high above the ground, and is perfectly camouflaged as it closes its eyes and fluffs out its feathers; if approached too closely, the bird becomes very slim, turning one wing in front of the body like a shield. Activity begins at late dusk. Males begin to sing in late winter or early spring near potential nest holes (or nestboxes). Little is known about the mating display, but it may be somewhat similar to that of Tengmalm's Owl: as with latter, the main purpose of the male's song is to attract a female, and as soon as he is mated he stops singing rather abruptly; thus, parallels may be drawn between the two species in terms of vocal activity (see Tengmalm's Owl). Behaviour apparently also similar to that of Tengmalm's. One individual, radio-tracked over a protracted period, hunted from 20 minutes after sunset to 20 minutes before sunrise, over an area of 114ha; most of time was spent on different perches on lookout for prey, and the owl hunted mainly in wooded areas; when the first snow fell, it moved into more open country. The flight is noiseless and soft.

FOOD Mostly small rodents and shrews, and occasionally preys on small birds, frogs and insects. Hunting behaviour similar to that of Tengmalm's Owl.

BREEDING As with Tengmalm's Owl, there seems to be no pair-bond beyond breeding season. The male advertises by singing and entering potential holes (woodpecker holes, natural cavities in tree trunks, nestboxes, etc) to females; no nest is constructed. The female lays 3-7 white eggs (av. 29.9 x 25mm), at 2-day intervals, directly on to the floor of the nest hole. She incubates alone for 21-28 days, from the first egg, so the young hatch at intervals. In periods of prey scarcity, the smaller chicks starve and are eaten by their siblings; pellets, excrement and food remnants are not removed from the nest. Scratching of the tree trunk causes the female immediately to appear at the hole entrance, an inherited behaviour in response to the predatory activity of martens *Martes*. At about 4 weeks the young leave the nest in their chocolate-brown juvenile plumage, and are accompanied and fed by their parents (particularly the male) for some weeks; they then begin to moult the body plumage, after which they very much resemble their parents. Sexual maturity is reached at 9-10 months.

STATUS AND CONSERVATION Because of its secretive behaviour this owl's status is uncertain, but it may be locally frequent. It does not in fact appear to be in any way endangered, but likely events in the near future are not known. Essential for its conservation is that large forest areas are retained intact and that its food supply remains uncontaminated. The species may be assisted by the provision of nestboxes in areas where it is known to be present, and by measures similar to those used for Tengmalm's Owl in order to protect breeding sites from potential predators.

REMARKS The taxonomic status of the form '*tacanensis*' requires study to establish whether it is a hybrid, an aberrant morph or a good subspecies. We consider that a hybrid *acadicus* x *ridgwayi* is the most likely explanantion.

REFERENCES Bent (1938), Boyer & Hume (1991), Burleigh (1958, 1972), Burton (1992), Dunning (1993), Eck & Busse (1973), National Geographic Society (1989), Peterson (1980), Steinberg (1997), Voous (1988).

---

180 UNSPOTTED SAW-WHET OWL
Aegolius ridgwayi   Plate 55

French: Chouette de Ridgway
German: Ridgwaykauz
Spanish: Lechucita parda

IDENTIFICATION A compact, small (18cm) owl with large round head and rather broad, rounded wings. Whitish eyebrows; upperparts uniform brown, underparts buffy with indistinct cinnamon-brown band across chest; short tail plain brown. Toes unfeathered or sparsely bristled. Bill dusky; eyes yellow. **Similar species** Northern Saw-whet Owl [179] has head and crown streaked whitish and is streaked below, with blackish bill. Tengmalm's Owl [178] is larger, has thickly feathered toes, and has rounded white spots on crown. Pygmy owls (*Glaucidium*) are much smaller, with boldly marked underparts, and screech owls (*Otus*) have small ear-tufts.

VOCALISATIONS Very little known. The territorial song of the male consists of a verse repeated several times at short intervals. This is of 4-10 mellow, somewhat melancholic 'toots', on an even pitch and more or less equally spaced, very like the song of Northern Saw-whet Owl but mellower and lower in pitch; a tree frog of the genus *Anotheca* has a very similar song, which may lead to confusion in the field, but this frog lives at lower altitudes than the owl. A high-pitched trill is described from excited birds.

DISTRIBUTION S Mexico and Central America, south to Panama.

MOVEMENTS Apparently sedentary.

Unspotted Saw-whet Owl

HABITAT Montane and cloud forest with oaks *Quercus*, from at least 2,000m up to the timberline. Frequents canopy and forest edge, as well as pastures with groups of tall trees.

DESCRIPTION Adult Facial disc brownish with indistinct darker rim; eyebrows, chin and lores whitish, contrasting with dark face. Rest of head and entire upperparts earth-brown, head and mantle sometimes a little darker than the rest, crown sometimes with fine whitish shaft-streaks. Wings brown, with narrow white edges to alulae and primaries; inner secondaries with white spots. Tail uniform brown, inner (normally not visible) webs of rectrices with few white spots. Breast dull cinnamon-brown, forming indistinct broad band; belly plain yellowish to pale ochraceous-buff. **Juvenile** Downy plumage unknown. Juvenile similar to adult, but with softer (more 'downy') plumage, breast sometimes with faint pale streaking. **Bare parts** Eyes yellow to brownish-yellow. Cere and bill yellowish-horn. Toes flesh-coloured with some buffy bristles. Claws dark brownish-horn.

MEASUREMENTS AND WEIGHT Total length 17-19cm. Wing 133-146mm; tail about 64mm. Weight about 80g.

GEOGRAPHICAL VARIATION The lack of sufficient material for comparative studies makes subspecific splitting very difficult, as nothing is known about individual variability. Two doubtful subspecies have been described: *A. r. tacanensis* from S Mexico, and *A. r. rostratus* from Guatemala. A bird found in S Mexico shows a pattern intermediate between this species and Northern Saw-whet Owl: whitish underparts with buffy-reddish streaking, indistinct band across chest, also whitish radial streaks from around eyes towards rim of facial disc, and plain back and crown, with tail uniform brown. The question arises as to whether an individual with such a pattern may be a hybrid between the two species or whether it represents a distinct morph. It has also been argued that this coloration might be the true adult plumage of *Aegolius ridgwayi*, with younger birds reaching sexual maturity when still in a plumage similar to the juvenile one. More investigations in the field are required to clarify this problem.
　　We consider this species to be monotypic: *Aegolius ridgwayi* (Alfaro, 1905).

HABITS A strictly nocturnal bird, and unsociable. Flight with rapid wingbeats, fluttery in character. Virtually nothing is known about its behaviour.

FOOD Probably mainly small rodents and shrews, as well as small birds and bats. No information is available on the possibility of insects being included as part of the diet.

BREEDING Probably nests in cavities, e.g. woodpecker holes in trees. Eggs presumably white, as in all owls.

STATUS AND CONSERVATION Status uncertain, as records are very scattered. Listed as Near-threatened by BirdLife International. Probably often overlooked, it may be less rare than generally thought. Like other forest owls, it is threatened above all by deforestation. Studies on status and ecology will be of great interest, especially with respect to the conservation of this almost unknown owl.

REMARKS Some authors treat Unspotted Saw-whet Owl as a subspecies of Northern Saw-whet. We do not agree with this hypothesis. The taxonomic status of the S Mexican and the Guatemalan birds is uncertain; the forms *tacanensis* and *rostratus* may well be hybrids of *A. ridgwayi* x *A. acadicus*.

REFERENCES Boyer & Hume (1991), Collar *et al.* (1994), Dunning (1993), Eck & Busse (1973), Ridgely (1976), Stiles & Skutch (1989), Voous (1988).

---

181 BUFF-FRONTED OWL
Aegolius harrisii   Plate 55

French: Choutte d'Harris
German: Gelbstirnkauz
Spanish: Lechucita acanelada
Portuguese: Caburé-acanelado

IDENTIFICATION An unmistakable, rather colourful, small (about 20cm), somewhat 'podgy' owl without ear-tufts, with short tail and large, round head. Upperside dark brown to blackish-brown, somewhat spotted white and buff; underparts mainly yellowish-buff. Forehead with a triangular yellowish-buffy area pointing towards base of bill. **Similar species** Spectacled, Short-browed and Tawny-browed Owls [118-120] are much larger and have a broad, dark breast band. No other owl is as colourful as Buff-fronted as to be confused with it.

VOCALISATIONS Little known. The male's territorial song consists of very rapid trills with a 'quivering' character, rather high-pitched (between 0.8 and 1.25kHz) and uttered in very rapid staccato (15-16 notes per second), similar to some South American screech owls (*Otus*) but higher in pitch: *gyrrrrryrrrrrryrrrr...* (*y* is between '*u*' and '*ee*' in sound), lasting about 7-10 seconds. The general character is somewhat irregular, as the verse increases and drops in volume. Soft, single, rather high-pitched *u* calls probably serve as contact. A short series of accelerating staccato notes falling in pitch seems to have an alarm function, and is often introduced by single, upward-inflected hoots with a wailing character; we heard this from the male near nest. Female gives a thin, very high-pitched *tseet* when calling to its mate to be fed. Fledged young beg with a hissing, somewhat rasping *cheet*.

DISTRIBUTION Andes from Venezuela to Ecuador and southward on the eastern slope to N Argentina (Tucumán); some records from the E Paraguayan Chaco. A rather isolated population lives in E Brazil (from Goiás south to Rio Grande do Sul and Uruguay) and adjacent regions of Paraguay and Argentina (Misiones). Distribution seems to be very scattered and local, and the species' total range is apparently only superficially and poorly known; may have been overlooked in some areas.

Buff-fronted Owl

MOVEMENTS Nothing known, but seems to be largely sedentary.

HABITAT Primarily montane and cloud forest alternating with clearings and pastures, up to near timberline: wooded areas, especially with 'nogal' (*Juglans*) and 'aliso' (*Alnus*) trees, and even in 'queñoa' (*Polylepis*) groves up to locally 3,000m and more. Also occurs at lower altitudes in rather dense forest with tall trees and dense undergrowth. In NW Argentina (Salta) has been recorded in the 'Tucumanian-Bolivian Forest' (Southern Yungas) between 1,200m and 1,800m, where it occupies the same habitat as Yungas Pygmy Owl [157] and Montane Forest Screech Owl [71]. In Misiones, has been found in semi-open subtropical rain forest with scattered *Araucaria angustifolia*, alternating with clearings and pastures, at 600-700m in Sierra de Misiones, where it shares the habitat with Long-tufted Screech Owl [79]; recorded in Goiás (Brazil) in similar type of habitat at 1,000m. In the Paraguayan Chaco, a few records from temporary dry forest.

DESCRIPTION *A. h. harrisii* **Adult** Facial disc round with narrow blackish rim, bordered buffy; blackish-brown area from eye to edge of disc, bordering yellowish-buffy forehead (can appear to have small ear-tufts, especially when alarmed bird 'folds' disc); chin with dark brown or blackish bib, nearly merging into thin blackish rim. Above, dark chocolate-brown with few rounded white spots and some buffy ones; narrow yellowish-buff collar around neck, contrasting with dark back; scapulars, wings and tail with white rounded spots. Breast and belly plain yellowish to ochraceous-buff. Tarsi feathered to base of toes, toes bare. **Juvenile** Downy plumage unknown. Young fledglings resemble adult, but have unspotted back and the colours are fainter. **Bare parts** Eyes yellow. Cere yellowish-grey. Bill yellowish to pale bluish-green. Toes pale yellow. Claws dark brown.

MEASUREMENTS AND WEIGHT Total length about 19-20cm. Wing 142-164mm; tail about 80mm. Weight 104-155g; 1 female from Salta (NW Argentina) 152g.

GEOGRAPHICAL VARIATION Three subspecies.

A. h. harrisii (Cassin, 1849). Andes of Venezuela and Colombia to Bolivia. See Description. Wing 142-164mm.

A. h. dabbenei Olrog, 1979. Tucumán and Salta in NW Argentina. Darker purple-brown on upperparts, pale cinnamon-ochre below; eyes light yellow. Wing of type 146mm, tail 82mm.

A. h. iheringi (Sharpe, 1899). E Brazil and adjacent areas of Argentina and Paraguay. Rim around facial disc blackish; no dark bib on chin; above, more blackish than nominate, and buffy spots on mantle form V; eyes normally orange; toes sometimes sparsely bristled buffy.

HABITS An unsociable bird, strictly nocturnal. Almost nothing is known about its behaviour. The male sings in its territory, normally among dense foliage in treetops. During the song period, it may be stimulated to sing or to approach by imitating or playback; during incubation and post-fledging periods, males rarely sing, nor do they normally respond with song to playback.

FOOD Probably small vertebrates and perhaps larger insects.

BREEDING The breeding season seems to vary according to climatic conditions. In Salta (Argentina), males in full song have been recorded in November in some years and during the first days of October in others; in another year, at the same locality in late September, three recently fledged young were found but no singing was recorded then, and no adult reacted to playback of song, although the juveniles could be attracted (watched first in rather high and thick bushes below tall trees, later fairly high up in dense foliage of latter). In 1995, egg-laying was recorded in early November. Nests in cavities, especially in woodpecker holes, at variable heights above ground; a nest on a mountain slope at about 1,500m in Salta was a natural cavity, with entrance about 8cm in diameter, about 5m above the forest floor in a *Juglans australis* tree. Clutch size and duration of incubation unknown.

STATUS AND CONSERVATION Listed as Near-threatened by BirdLife International. Probably rare and locally absent, but may be overlooked because of its secretive habits. The infrequently heard song may be confused with the trills of Montane Forest, Black-capped and Guatemalan Screech Owls [71, 78, 82], all of which are, however, lower in pitch and never have a 'quivering' character. Buff-fronted Owl seems to be uncommon in the Sierra de Misiones (Argentina), where it is obviously declining as a result of deforestation. The species is probably endangered by forest destruction, a familiar situation in South America. The preservation of extensive montane forest will doubtless help the survival of this handsome, little-known owl.

REMARKS The biology of Buff-fronted Owl is poorly known. Its taxonomy and behaviour (including vocalisations) also need study; the allopatric form *iheringi* from SE Brazil may perhaps be specifically distinct.

REFERENCES Boyer & Hume (1991), Collar *et al.* (1994), Dunning (1993), Fjeldså & Krabbe (1990), Hilty & Brown (1986), Kessler (pers. comm.), König (1994, 1999), Olrog (1979), Sick (1985).

Hawk Owls, Genus *Ninox* Hodgson, 1837

Small to large owls with a rounded head without ear-tufts. Tail relatively long, wings long with pointed tips. Facial disc very indistinct. Nostrils located on front of swollen cere (not at sides). Distributed from E Siberia to Japan, Philippines, New Guinea, Australia, New Zealand, Sri Lanka, Malaysia, and Sunda Islands and other islands of the Indo-Pacific region. One species inhabits Madagascar. At least 20 species; some taxa currently considered subspecies may prove to be full species.

182 RUFOUS OWL
Ninox rufa   Plate 56

French: Chouette rouge
German: Roter Buschkauz, Rostkauz

IDENTIFICATION A rather large hawk owl (40-50cm) with pale-barred dark brown upperparts, and buff underparts with fine transverse brown bars. Forehead and throat pale, sides of face dark, with dusky area around eyes. Eyes bright yellow. **Similar species** Powerful Owl [183] is larger (60-65cm), with dark brown upperparts barred with white and pale brown, and underparts streaked; partly allopatric with Rufous Owl, but confined to S Australia from Portland, Victoria, southwards. Southern Boobook [187] is smaller (30-35cm), with upperparts pale to dark brown with white spots on wing and back, and underparts with cream to buff streaks and mottling, and has orange eyes. Barking Owl [184], somewhat similar in size (38-43cm), differs in being smoky-brown above with large white spots on wings, and whitish below with dark grey to rusty streaks.

VOCALISATIONS The male's song recalls that of Powerful Owl: a slow, rather mournful, deep double hoot that sounds like *wooh-hoo* (duration 1 second), second note shorter and often slightly higher than first, repeated many times at intervals of 2-6 seconds. Although sounding somewhat similar, the call is not so loud and powerful as that of Powerful Owl. During courtship, male gives six or seven single hoots at intervals of about 1 second; also occasionally a short, less far-carrying, sharp single note. The female has a similar but higher-pitched song and also utters a sheep-like bleating call; on the nest, utters murmuring sounds for contact with chicks. Young beg with repeated wheezing trills.

DISTRIBUTION New Guinea, Aru Islands, Waigeo, and tropical N Australia (where three distinct, separated populations).

MOVEMENTS Resident.

HABITAT Tropical rain forest, monsoon forest, and wet forested gullies and adjoining thick woodland; also swamp woodland. In New Guinea, occurs in lowlands and lower mountains, locally up to about 1,850m.

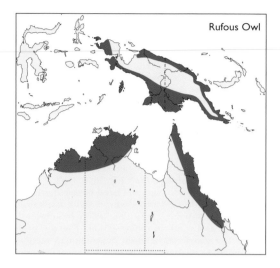

Rufous Owl

DESCRIPTION *N. r. humeralis* **Adult** Forehead whitish to base of bill, contrasting with dusky, nearly blackish-brown facial disc (ill-defined). Upperparts dark brown, crown and nape densely barred pale buff, feathers of back and mantle edged narrowly pale. Flight feathers barred light and dark. Tail relatively long, dark brown with about eight narrow pale bars. Underparts white or orange-buff, finely barred with rufous-brown. Tarsi feathered; toes bare, sparsely bristled. **Juvenile** Downy young have head and underparts pure white, except for distinct dark facial disc. Immature similar to adult. **Bare parts** Eyes bright yellow. Cere and bill leaden greyish-horn. Toes yellowish. Claws black.

MEASUREMENTS AND WEIGHT Total length 40-50cm, males larger than females. Wing 260-383mm; tail 180-228mm. (Size varies with subspecies.) Weight of males 1,150-1,300g, of females 700-1,050g.

GEOGRAPHICAL VARIATION We recognise six subspecies.

N. r. humeralis (Bonaparte, 1850). New Guinea and Waigeo Island. See Description. Wing 306-337mm; tail 228mm.

N. r. aruensis (Schlegel, 1866). Aru Islands: known only from Wokam Island. Like *humeralis*, but smaller. Wing 260-270mm; tail 185mm.

N. r. rufa (Gould, 1846). Tropical N Australia, i.e. Western Australia (N Kimberleys) and Northern Territory (Arnhem Land). Large race, fairly light in colour above and below. Wing of males 374-383mm, of females 347-357mm.

N. r. marginata Mees, 1964. Queensland: known only from east coast (from Claude River to Cairns). Slightly darker on back than nominate race, but conspicuously smaller. Wing 313-352mm. (This taxon may be a synonym of *queenslandica*).

N. r. queenslandica Mathews, 1911. E Queensland in region of Mackay: rare (for long known only from the holotype); roosts and nests in fragments of rain forest, particularly gallery rain forest, forages in surrounding woodland, rarely occurs in extensive stands of forest and appears to require a mosaic of habitat. A large, dark subspecies. Darker above, much colder brown bars on undersurface (compared with *marginata*); cheeks rather dark. Wing length similar

to *marginata*. (Taxonomic status doubtful, as taxon based on single skin only.)

N. r. meesi Mason & Schodde, 1980. E Cape York Peninsula, south to at least Cooktown (?). Very few records of this small, pale subspecies, as its habitat on Cape York Peninsula is so remote and not yet surveyed. (Status doubtful; perhaps only a light morph of *marginata*.)

HABITS Seldom seen, and little known. Roosts by day, singly or in pairs, in thickly foliaged trees with commanding view of its surroundings; each pair appears to have a number of roosts. Presence mostly revealed by calls at night and by scolding of other birds, especially butcherbirds *Cracticus* and drongos *Dicrurus*, at daytime roosts. A very shy bird, which usually slips away from its roost when an intruder approaches, but during the breeding season both pair-members defend the nest very aggressively against intruders, including humans.

FOOD Small arboreal mammals, such as gliding possums (e.g. sugar glider *Petaurus breviceps*), large fruit bats (flying foxes *Pteropus*) and certain kinds of rats. Also takes some birds and large insects.

BREEDING Breeding season from June in Northern Territory to September in NE Queensland. At the beginning of breeding season male and female roost together (often on the same branch), and at dusk or somewhat later male begins to sing. Female approaches male, uttering bleating sounds, and before copulating male often preens her nape while she picks at his toes with her bill; copulation generally follows immediately after this, and female then flies directly to the nest. A large hollow up to about 30m above ground in the trunk or a thick branch of a big tree serves as nesting site. The normally 2 (occasionally 1-3) white, rather spherical eggs (about 49-54 x 44-48mm) are laid on decayed debris at the bottom of the cavity, at intervals of about 3 days. The female incubates alone for 37 days. The young leave the nest by about 50 days, when able to fly a little but still with some down plumage; they are accompanied and fed by their parents for several months, even to the following breeding season.

STATUS AND CONSERVATION Rare to very uncommon. In the past, much suitable habitat, both rain forest and woodland, has been cleared, and clearance for agriculture still continues in most parts of the species' range. Hollow trees required for nesting are particularly vulnerable to fire. In the western parts of its Australian range, gallery rain forest is being invaded by exotic weeds such as rubber vine *Cryptostegia grandis*, with unknown effects on nest-site and prey availability. In E Australia, nest trees in suitable habitat of the subspecies *queenslandica* occur 3-4km apart, with foraging ranges estimated at 400-800ha; based on the distribution of nest sites, the total population has been estimated at about 1,000 pairs.

REMARKS See excellent photos (also of other Australian nightbirds) in Hollands (1991). A revision of the different races would be sensible, as would studies on biology and ecology of this obviously endangered species.

REFERENCES Beehler (1986), Coates (1985), Hollands (1991), Mason & Schodde (1980), Pizzey (1980), Rand & Gilliard (1967), Reader's Digest (1976), Schodde & Mason (1980), Simpson & Day (1984), Slater (1970).

183 POWERFUL OWL
Ninox strenua   **Plate 56**

French: Chouette géante
German: Riesenkauz

IDENTIFICATION Largest owl in Australia (55-63cm), lacking ear-tufts and with golden-yellow eyes. Tail relatively long and head relatively small (not typically owl-like). Upperparts dark grey-brown, mottled and barred with whitish; underparts white with bold grey-brown V-shaped barring. Talons very powerful. **Similar species** No other *Ninox* species of this size; moreover, chevron-shaped barring of underparts characteristic, absent in all other *Ninox*. Barking Owl [184] is much smaller (38-43cm), smoky-brown above with large white spots on wings, and whitish below with dark grey to rusty streaks and yellow eyes. Rufous Owl [182] is smaller, dark brown above, with pale buffy edges to feathers of mantle and back, a blackish face, and with dense pale buff and rufous-brown barring on underparts.

VOCALISATIONS The male's song is an impressive low, rather mournful, far-carrying double hoot, *whoo hooo*, each note lasting more than half a second, with a short pause between the two, second note often slightly higher in pitch. The female utters a similar but higher-pitched song. During courtship, male and female duet; when laying, females stop singing. Unpaired males are much more vocally active than paired ones. Near the nest, both sexes utter sheep-like bleating, somewhat tremulous sounds. Young beg with thin chirruping trills.

DISTRIBUTION SE Australia, from Dawson River in SE Queensland to Portland in W Victoria.

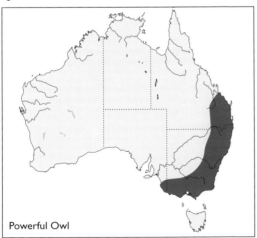

Powerful Owl

MOVEMENTS Resident.

HABITAT Usually tall humid forest. Dense mountain gullies; forested ravines; wetter, heavily timbered subcoastal ranges; coastal forest and woodland; coastal scrub; pine plantations. Prefers wetter, heavily timbered areas; found mostly in wet sclerophyll forest.

DESCRIPTION Adult Facial disc indistinct, dark brown; prominent white eyebrows. Upperparts dark brown or grey-brown, mottled and barred with white and pale brown; underparts whitish, barred with dark brown V-shaped markings. Tail rather long, with about six narrow whitish bars. Tarsi feathered to base of toes; toes bare, sparsely bristled. Powerful talons. **Juvenile** Immature has back and wings paler, more heavily barred white; face white, with dark eye patches; whitish below with sparse fine dark streaks, faint barring on flanks. **Bare parts** Iris bright yellow. Bill bluish-horn. Toes dull yellow. Claws dusky.

MEASUREMENTS AND WEIGHT Total length 55-63cm, males larger than females. Wing of males 397-437mm, of females 381-410mm; tail about 280mm. Weight of males 1,130-1,700g, of females 1,050-1,600g.

GEOGRAPHICAL VARIATION Monotypic: *Ninox strenua* (Gould, 1838).

HABITS Lives permanently in pairs. By day roosts singly, in pairs or in family groups of 3-4, in foliage or on a fairly open tree in forest or woodland, often clutching part-eaten remains of prey. Several roosting sites are used, and may be occupied intermittently for many years. Easily approached by day; shy and difficult to observe at night. Slow, deliberate flight on huge wings. May be very aggressive near nest (especially males). When disturbed during incubation, female often deserts.

FOOD Feeds on birds and mammals. In S Australia, its diet consists mainly of small to medium-sized tree-living mammals, especially great glider possum *Schoinobates volans* and ringtail possum *Pseudocheirus peregrinus*; also eats sugar gliders *Petaurus breviceps* and, less often, young brush possums *Trichosurus vulpecula*, rats and young rabbits. Preys on birds such as kookaburras *Dacelo* and magpies *Gymnorhina*. Tears prey apart and consumes it piecemeal. Will sometimes take part of a prey item to its roost, carefully place it on the branch and hold it all day in its talons, then eat it before leaving the roost in the evening. Clutching of part-eaten prey remains near roost is also reported.

BREEDING Breeds in winter (May to June). Behaviour probably similar to that of Rufous Owl. A large hollow at least 10-15m above ground, often much higher, in the trunk of a tall tree serves as nest; nesting trees are often located at the head of a gully. Usually lays 2 white eggs (about 55 x 46mm), at interval of about 4 days, on rotten wood on to the floor of nesting cavity. Female alone incubates, for about 38 days, and is fed by her mate outside the nest; during incubation, the male may be fiercely aggressive towards intruders in the nesting area (but not always), and even attack humans. Young fledge by 7-8 weeks, still wearing patches of down, and are accompanied and fed by both parents for some months, sometimes until the following breeding season, when they sometimes inhibit the adults from breeding.

STATUS AND CONSERVATION Uncommon. Listed as Vulnerable by BirdLife International. The main threat is the loss of old-growth forest (nesting sites), and intensive forestry which reduces prey density. Information on population size is based largely on the spacing of calling birds: home-range estimates 400-1,450ha (av. 600-800ha); Victoria population 500 pairs; in New South Wales 1,000-10,000 individuals. In both New South Wales and Queensland, this species is considered uncommon rather than rare.

REMARKS In Australia, this owl is sometimes known as 'Eagle Owl' or 'Great Scrub Owl'. Its biology, and especially its population dynamics, require more study.

REFERENCES Boyer & Hume (1991), Burton (1992), Collar *et al.* (1994), Davey (1989), Fley (1968), Garnett (1992), Hollands (1991), Mees (1964), Morris *et al.* (1981).

---

184 BARKING OWL
Ninox connivens   Plate 56

Other name: Winking Owl

French: Chouette aboyeuse
German: Kläfferkauz

IDENTIFICATION A medium-sized (38-43cm), very robust owl without ear-tufts, but with piercing yellow eyes. Tail relatively long. Upperparts smoky-brown, with large white spots on wings; underparts whitish with dark grey to rusty streaks. Tarsi feathered; toes sparsely bristled. Talons powerful. Eyes relatively large. **Similar species** Powerful Owl [183] is much larger (about 60cm), with relatively smaller head, and has bold chevrons on underparts. Southern Boobook [187], somewhat smaller (30-35cm), has large whitish eyebrows and a dark area around each eye, is reddish-brown below with thick brown and white streaks or heavy white mottling, and has pale yellowish-grey eyes. Rufous Owl [182] is larger, and densely barred below.

VOCALISATIONS A fast, remarkably dog-like bark, *wuk-wuk* or *wuf-wuf*, preceded by a short low groan (audible only at close range), is the male's song. The female utters a similar but somewhat higher-pitched double-noted bark. These songs are repeated softly at first, becoming explosive and far-carrying. The rapid barking notes are repeated many times at intervals of a few seconds. Pairs commonly perform antiphonal duetting, with the female immediately following the male. These vocalisations are given during the night and at dawn, but sometimes also during daytime. Usually very vocal, and choruses of barking may be interspersed with 'growling' sounds. Occasionally, a terrifying loud, high-pitched, tremulous (drawn-out and strangled) scream is produced, usually during the winter (breeding season); this call has earned the owl the name of 'screaming-woman bird', though it seems to be uttered very seldom. In addition, a low groaning hoot of almost cow-like quality is given by the female when calling to its young. Both sexes utter dog-like snarls in aggression. Young beg with thin chirrups.

DISTRIBUTION Northern Moluccas, New Guinea, and more humid parts of Australia. In Australia occurs on mainland and some coastal islands in the north, being widespread in some regions (Queensland, New South Wales) and rare in others; apparently absent or very rare in arid regions or those without large trees.

MOVEMENTS Resident.

HABITAT Inhabits both temperate as subtropical forest. Mainly open country with groups of larger trees, woodland, dense scrub, and savanna. Occurs in foothills and timber along watercourses, often those penetrating otherwise open country; also swamp and riverine woodland. Sometimes roosts in rain forest, but needs more open

country for hunting and hollow trees for breeding. In mainly New Guinea recorded only in the lowlands, but on Karkar Island up to 1,040m.

Barking Owl

DESCRIPTION *N. c. connivens* **Adult** Forehead, crown and facial disc brown, the latter indistinctly rimmed; eyebrows whitish, very narrow, sometimes invisible. Upperparts smoky-brown, dark grey or grey-brown (depending on locality and individual variation), with large white spots or blotches on wings and lower back, and a few conspicuous whitish spots on scapulars and wing-coverts, but considerable variation in degree of spotting. Tail feathers grey-brown with pale brown bars and tip. Throat pale buff. Underparts creamy-buff to whitish with bold brown to chestnut streaks, but considerable variation in pattern among specimens even from same locality (streaks vary from narrow to broad and from dark to lighter, and are sharply defined on a nearly pure white background, or underparts are heavily tinged tawny). Tarsi feathered; toes bare, sparsely bristled. **Juvenile** Immature similar to adult. **Bare parts** Iris yellow. Cere and bill greenish yellow-grey. Toes dull yellow or yellowish-brown. Claws horn, becoming dusky towards blackish tips.

MEASUREMENTS AND WEIGHT Total length 35-45cm. Wing 244-325mm; tail 143-198. Weight 425-510g. Sexual differences in size and weight less obvious than in the two preceding species.

GEOGRAPHICAL VARIATION We recognise five subspecies.

N. c. connivens (Latham, 1801). Western Australia, South Australia, Victoria, New South Wales and Queensland. See Description. The largest and darkest race. Greyish-brown above; dark greyish-brown striations below. Wing 282-325mm. (We regard the form *addenda* as a synonym.)

N. c. rufostrigata (G. R. Gray, 1860). Moluccas: Morotai, Halmahera, Bacan, Obi. Clearly browner, less grey-brown on underparts, especially the streaks on underparts; not so small as *assimilis*. Wing 258-300mm.

N. c. assimilis Salvadori & D'Albertis, 1875. E New Guinea, on north coast west to Ramu River, including Karkar Island, on south coast as far west as Merauke; also Vulcan and Dampier Islands. Very small, smaller than other races, and overall browner, less grey-brown. Wing 244-277mm; weight of 1 male 380g, of 1 female 430g.

N. c. occidentalis Ramsay, 1886. Western Australia, Northern Territory and NW Queensland. Differs from nominate in being much browner, less greyish, above, and having streaks on underparts much browner. Wing 272-310mm.

N. c. peninsularis Salvadori, 1875 (1876). Cape York Peninsula, Queensland; also Thursday Island and Banks (Moa) Island in Torres Strait. Similar to nominate race, but smaller. Upperparts slightly darker; stripes below slightly browner, less grey. Wing 257-288mm. (Taxonomic status uncertain.)

HABITS Usually found in pairs that occupy territories all year around. Each pair has a number of daytime roost sites, usually in a leafy tree among a group of trees, but not always well hidden; groups of 3-4 roosting together include young of that year. This owl is by no means shy, and is at home around rural houses in Australia. It is the least nocturnal of Australian owls; sometimes calls during daytime, and on duller winter days may begin hunting before sunset. In middle Sepik region of New Guinea, it hunts in gardens and grassland and is usually found in pairs.

FOOD Mammals and birds, large insects and other invertebrates. In S Australia, it feeds particularly on rabbits. Also kills young hares, rats, mice, occasionally small bats and some marsupials, including possums. Takes birds up to the size of Australian Magpie *Gymnorhina tibicen* and Tawny Frogmouth *Podargus strigoides*. Any prey too big to be swallowed whole is torn up and eaten piece by piece; rear parts of victims are sometimes found beneath roost trees. It is also reported to clutch remains of prey while at roost. Stomach of a New Guinea specimen (from middle Sepik region) was filled with large black beetles.

BREEDING Breeding season July to September. Nests in tree hollows, usually from a few metres to 10m or more above ground; sometimes uses rock crevices or rabbit burrows. Male excavates a shallow depression in rotten wood or debris at the bottom of the cavity. The 2-3 dull white and roundish eggs (43-50 x 36-41mm) are laid at intervals of 2-3 days; female incubates alone for approximately 36 days. Young fledge early, by about 35 days, when still with much down, and are cared for by both parents for several months after fledging.

STATUS AND CONSERVATION In Australia nowhere common, except perhaps in parts of Queensland, and in Kimberleys of Western Australia. In Moluccas and New Guinea, it is generally thinly distributed, but locally sometimes not uncommon.

REMARKS This species' biology is in need of study.

REFERENCES Boyer & Hume (1991), Burton (1992), Diamond & LeCroy (1979), Gilliard & LeCroy (1966), Mees (1964), Hollands (1991).

185 SUMBA BOOBOOK
Ninox rudolfi   Plate 57

French: Chouette de Sumba
German: Sumbakauz

IDENTIFICATION A very distinctive, medium-sized owl (30-36cm) without ear-tufts, differing from all races of Southern Boobook [187] in its prominently white-spotted crown and mantle, heavily barred scapulars and wing coverts, and broadly rufous-banded rather than streaked or mottled underparts . **Similar species** No other *Ninox* species is currently known from Sumba.

VOCALISATIONS A long series of somewhat monotonous, short, hurried, cough-like notes may be the song. The notes are uttered at a rate of two per second (A. Lewis recording).

DISTRIBUTION Sumba, in Lesser Sundas.

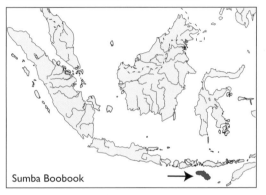

Sumba Boobook

MOVEMENTS Resident.

HABITAT Open forest and farmland in lowlands, to at least 500m.

DESCRIPTION Adult Head blackish, profusely spotted white, auriculars blackish; throat plain white, well defined; upperparts dark brown, covered with short white bars, these becoming longer and more prominent on scapulars and wing coverts; underparts white, heavily and broadly barred (not streaked) with rufescent-brown. Tarsi heavily feathered, extending onto tops of toes. **Juvenile** Undescribed. **Bare parts** Iris brown. Bill yellowish-brown. Toes pale yellow.

MEASUREMENTS AND WEIGHT Total length 30-36cm, males somewhat larger than females. Wing 227-243mm; tail 145mm. Weight: no data.

GEOGRAPHICAL VARIATION Monotypic: *Ninox rudolfi* Meyer, 1882.

HABITS Probably not much different from those of Southern Boobook. Occurs singly, in pairs or in small groups; occasionally seen during daytime.

FOOD Presumably much as for Southern Boobook, i.e. mainly insects.

BREEDING Unknown.

STATUS AND CONSERVATION Listed as Vulnerable by BirdLife International. Rare or uncommon. Surveys in

Sumba in 1989 and 1992 recorded small numbers in five localities, in monsoon forest and rain forest, both primary and secondary. Its population density has presumably suffered greatly from the extensive reduction in closed-canopy forest, which now covers less than 11% of the island. This habitat destruction for agricultural purposes is continuing steadily.

REMARKS Although this owl is sometimes regarded as a race of Southern Boobook, we take the view that it is specifically distinct. It is probably allopatric to *N. boobook* and, unlike the latter, it has brown eyes.

REFERENCES Coates & Bishop (1997), Collar *et al.* (1994), Eck & Busse (1973), Jones *et al.* (1996), Mees (1964; 1980 review by Schodde & Mason), White & Bruce (1986).

186 MOREPORK
Ninox novaeseelandiae   Plate 57

French: Chouette coucou de Nouvelle Seelandie
German: Neuseeland-Kuckuckskauz

IDENTIFICATION The only small (25-30cm), earless owl native to New Zealand. Very similar in appearance to Southern Boobook [187] of the Australian mainland, separation from which is based on a slight difference in wing shape, a darker facial disc and underwing-coverts, and bright golden-yellow eyes. **Similar species** Southern Boobook has pale yellowish-green eyes and is allopatric. In New Zealand, the introduced Little Owl [176] can be distinguished by its much less brown general coloration, its smaller size, comparatively short tail and the less rounded outline of the head. Without doubt, however, the most distinctive feature of Morepork is its peculiar song.

VOCALISATIONS The characteristic call is an individually variable *more-pork*, also rendered, probably more accurately, as *quor-quo* (somewhat similar to the well-known disyllabic, but clearer *boo-book* or *cu-coo* of Southern Boobook). A common variation is a repetitive and often prolonged *more-pork-pork-pork....* Also a scream and a vibrating *cree-cree*, heard mainly in the breeding season.

Morepork

DISTRIBUTION New Zealand: North Island and surrounding islands (Little and Greater Barrier, Three Kings, and Kapiti), South Island and Stewart Island, and the far-offshore Norfolk Island and Lord Howe Island. (Note that Schodde & Mason place the Norfolk and Lord Howe populations with Southern Boobook of the Australian continent.)

MOVEMENTS Resident.

HABITAT Forest and farmland; also urban areas and plantations.

DESCRIPTION *N. n. novaeseelandiae* **Adult** Plumage very variable, with many colour morphs. Facial disc dark brown, with narrow whitish eyebrows; rim around disc light buff. Upperparts dark-coloured, with ochraceous-buff spotting on head, neck and mantle. Tail dark brown with rather narrow ochraceous or buffy bars. Underparts brownish-white to light buff with dark chocolate-brown flecks and streaks. Tarsi feathered, yellowish-brown to reddish-buff; toes bare or with short bristles. **Juvenile** Chick has white down on hatching, this gradually replaced (from 10th days) by second down, which is dark smoky-brown. On leaving nest (at about 5 weeks old), much of second down remains and remnants of first down form a white 'halo' on crown and nape; distinct black 'spectacle-like' patches behind eyes. **Bare parts** Iris bright golden-yellow. Bill varies from dark brown with white culmen ridge, to white or yellow with dark brown cutting edges on both mandibles. Toes yellow to brownish-yellow. Claws dusky brown to blackish.

MEASUREMENTS AND WEIGHT Total length 25-30cm. Wing 186-222mm; tail 135-146mm. Weight 170-340g. Females normally somewhat larger and heavier.

GEOGRAPHICAL VARIATION We recognise three subspecies, one of them apparently extinct.
> *N. n. novaeseelandiae* (Gmelin, 1788). New Zealand. See Description. Wing 186-202mm.
> *N. n. albaria* Ramsay, 1888. Lord Howe Island: seemingly extinct. Light brown above, with light brown markings below. Wing 209-222mm.
> *N. n. undulata* (Latham, 1801). Norfolk Island. A little darker than preceding race. Wing 196-208mm.

HABITS Very similar to those of Southern Boobook. Commonly seen at dusk, when it begins to hawk for insects from a prominent perch. Frequently mobbed by small birds in daytime.

FOOD Very similar to that of Southern Boobook. Largely insects, especially wetas (Stenopelmatidae: large, wingless, long-horned insects), moths and beetles; also spiders. Pellets collected in urban area of Masterton revealed, in nearly every month of year, a high proportion of moths, with spiders and beetles of lesser importance, and a few remains of other invertebrates. Pellet ejection observed to occur generally in mid or late afternoon. Other dietary items are lizards, small birds, especially House Sparrow *Passer domesticus*, rats and mice. On outlying islands diet includes smaller petrels, as well as *Rattus exulans* and Short-tailed Bat. Aerial insects, such as moths and large beetles, are caught with the talons before being transferred to the bill.

BREEDING Laying begins in early October, with peak in November. Nesting sites are in hollow trees, tree holes, or dense clumps of vegetation (especially *Astelia*); sometimes in an exposed position in a tree fork, or even in a depression on the top of an old sparrow nest; once in a nestbox. The 2 (occasionally 3) roundish white eggs (38.0 x 32.7mm) are laid at a 2-day interval, and incubated for 30-31 days by the female alone, the male bringing food to his incubating mate. Later, both parents feed the chicks, which leave the nest by 34 days and are cared for by both parents for some time afterwards.

STATUS AND CONSERVATION Not uncommon in New Zealand, where it occupies all parts. Early records indicate that it was one of the native forest birds that adapted to modified and exotic vegetation in the earliest stages of human colonisation. It is common in farmland, urban areas, parks and streets, and is also present in larger exotic timber plantations (such as *Pinus radiata*). Commonly present in the Christchurch urban area until some time in the 1930s, but reported to have begun to decline there at about the time of a marked increase in numbers of Little Owls in that area.

The subspecies *albaria* from Lord Howe Island disappeared from the forest early in the 20th century, following the introduction of numerous owls, including Southern Boobook, to combat a plague of introduced black rats *Rattus rattus*. There were never many Moreporks on Lord Howe; the last *Ninox* were heard calling in 1950s, but the species could not be determined. Extinction was probably caused by competition with other introduced owls, which persisted since their introduction. Rats themselves, introduced in 1918, may cause breeding failure by predation of eggs and young.

The Norfolk Island subspecies *undulata* is endangered. A survey in October 1986 located a surviving female in an area where many calls were heard. For some years this female lived alone in a plantation of exotic trees with a few shrubs beneath the canopy, but later moved to native forest around Mt Pitt; she appears to avoid weed-infested native forest with a dense understorey. A co-operative agreement between the Norfolk Island Government, the Australian National Parks and Wildlife Service and the New Zealand Department of Conservation resulted in the importation of two males of the nominate race from New Zealand into the female's range in September 1987; nestboxes were erected and, after one unsuccessful year, two chicks were raised in 1989 and two more in 1990. Agriculture which leads to alteration of the native-forest structure through the development of a weedy understorey, the introduction of predatory rats (*Rattus exulans* and *R. rattus*), feral cats, competitors such as the Australian Kestrel *Falco cenchroides*, and other hole-nesters such as Crimson Rosella *Platycercus elegans* and Common Starling *Sturnus vulgaris* may all have contributed to the rarity of the owl, besides the activities of man. Most serious is the shortage of old growth to provide suitable nesting hollows, since most of the large trees have been felled. It is intended that owls should eventually be introduced to nearby Philip Island. Hybrid offspring from Norfolk Island could be selected for their phenotype and genotype resemblance to the female, and then back-crossed, to maximise the conservation of the Norfolk Island Morepork.

REMARKS The taxonomy of the 'boobook group' requires further study. Until very recently the Morepork has been treated as a subspecies of Southern Boobook, but the two are clearly allopatric species.

REFERENCES Boyer & Hume (1991), Burton (1992), Falla (1966), Garnett (1993), Mees (1964), Moon (1992), Norman *et al.* (1998b), Robertson (1974, 1985), Schodde & Mason (1980).

187 SOUTHERN BOOBOOK
Ninox boobook   Plate 57

French: Chouette coucou d'Australie
German: Kuckuckskauz

IDENTIFICATION A small (30-36cm), brown owl without ear-tufts. White spots on wings and back; underparts cream to buff with broad pale to dark brown streaks and mottling; indistinct facial disc much paler than general colour, with large dark patch behind each eye giving impression of large pale-rimmed goggles. Eyes pale greenish-yellow. An elusive species, however, its presence revealed chiefly by its characteristic song. **Similar species** No other owl on the Australian mainland has same size and colour pattern. Barking Owl [184] is larger (38-43cm) and greyer, has brilliant yellow eyes, and has grey to rufous streaks on whitish breast.

VOCALISATIONS The well-known two-syllable song, *boobook* or *mo-poke*, repeated at intervals, is unmistakable. The second syllable is slightly lower in pitch than the first. At a distance, this song resembes the call of the European Cuckoo *Cuculus canorus*. Also has a rarely heard yelping *yow*. A drawn-out rising cat-like *brrwow* and a monotonously repeated low *mor-mor-mor* are given, too. Young and female at the nest utter low trills.

DISTRIBUTION Timor to S New Guinea, and all parts (including drier areas) of Australia.

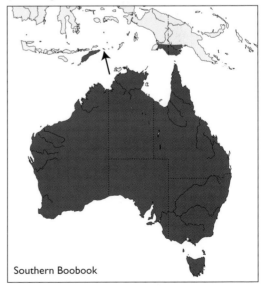

Southern Boobook

MOVEMENTS Resident, although sometimes makes nomadic movements to cereal-growing areas during mouse plagues.

HABITAT Very broad and varied. Common in all types of

country from forest to desert, and is found in towns suburbs with abundant trees. Habitats range from tropical rain forest to mallee and mulga scrub, and to margins of almost treeless plains, woodland, lightly timbered farming country, and cultivated land; also pine forest, orchards, parks, gardens and streets. Sometimes even roosts in caves in regions where trees are not plentiful. The NE Queensland race *lurida* (Red Boobook) lives in dense rain forest.

DESCRIPTION *N. b. boobook* **Adult** Sexes alike, but female sometimes slightly larger and darker. Considerable colour variation; in general, desert forms are paler and forest forms darker. Inconspicuous facial disc lighter-coloured or whitish, with large dark (nearly blackish) patches behind each eye. Upperparts pale to dark brown (depending on locality or individual; various morphs), with irregular pale or white spots on wings and back. Underparts reddish-brown with thick brown and white streaks or heavy irregular white mottling. Legs closely feathered; toes nearly bare, with bristles on upperside. **Juvenile** First down whitish or light buff; in later stage very dark, nearly black 'spectacles' develop around eyes, forming very striking pattern. **Bare parts** Eyes pale greenish-yellow; brown in juvenile. Bill blue-grey. Feet pale blue-grey.

MEASUREMENTS AND WEIGHT Total length 30-36cm, females sometimes larger. Wing 198-261mm (wide racial variation: see Geographical Variation); tail 127-162mm. Weight of males 170-298g, of females 194-360g.

GEOGRAPHICAL VARIATION We recognise nine sub-species, one of which may be a separate species.

N. b. boobook (Latham, 1801). S Queensland, New South Wales, Victoria and across S Australia. See Description. Wing 215-261mm. (We include the forms *rufigaster* from SW Australia, *marmorata* from S and SW Australia and *halmaturina* from Kangaroo Island as synonyms.)

N. b. rotiensis Johnstone & Darnell, 1997. Roti Island, in Lesser Sundas. A recently described subspecies (not examined.)

N. b. fusca (Vieillot, 1817). Timor, Roma and Leti in E Lesser Sundas, and Moa Island in Torres Strait: lowland forest and woodland up to 2,500m. A somewhat smaller, dark, cold grey-brown race, without any trace of warm brown or rufous; scapulars, secondaries, inner wing-coverts and (less marked) nape spotted with white; ventral streaking cold grey-brown. Wing 214-223mm. (We include *moae* from Moa, Leti and Romang as a synonym.)

N. b. plesseni Stresemann, 1929. W Alor (Tanglapoi, 1,000m) in E Lesser Sundas. Known only from holotype. General coloration similar to *fusca*, but entire upperparts marked with white and pale brown spots which show faint pattern of cross-barring, giving whole dorsal surface a mottled appearance; breast with longitudinal stripes, much as *fusca*, but tending to become ocellations on lower underparts; tail more strongly barred than in *fusca*. Wing 212mm.

N. b. cinnamomina Hartert, 1906. Tepa, Babar Islands, in E Lesser Sundas (7°55'S, 129°45'E). Very distinctive race. Deep cinnamon dorsally, browner on crown, and with deep cinnamon streaking below. Wing 210-215mm.

N. b. pusilla Mayr & Rand, 1935. Lowlands of S New Guinea (Oriomo and Wassi Kusa Rivers, west of Fly River), opposite Cape York. Overall plumage as *ocellata*, but distinctly smaller. Total length about 25cm; wing 193-200mm.

N. b. ocellata (Bonaparte, 1850). Tropical N Australia in Queensland and Northern Territory, also Sawu Island (between Timor and Sumba); Western Australia; South Australia (west of a line from Everard Ranges to Port Augusta, and in northern part of state perhaps farther east). Very variable, both in size and colour, but generally paler to much paler than other Australian races; odd individuals, however, can be very dark. Wing 205-240mm. (We include *melvillensis* from Melville Island, Northern Territory, and *remigialis* from Kai Islands as synonyms.)

N. b. leucopsis (Gould, 1826). Tasmania, perhaps straggling to S Australia. Eyes yellow. White dots on upperparts; underparts strongly ocellated rufous-orange. Smallest race. Wing 198-222mm.

N. (b.) lurida De Vis, 1899. Red Boobook. Restricted to forest of NE Queensland (Peterson's Pocket, Kirrima Range, Murray River, Bellenden-Ker Range). Very dark, the darkest race of Australian mainland. Upperparts without white spots; underparts dark, very cold brown, ocellated with white. Less vocal than nominate, and song harsher. Total length about 360mm; wing 207-221mm. (May be a separate species. The taxon *yorki*, wing 244mm, is probably a synonym of *lurida*.)

HABITS Roosts by day in thick foliage, singly, in pairs, or in family parties; lives in pairs, but usually only single birds seen at roost. Each bird or pair has a number of roosts. When disturbed, slips out silently. Southern Boobooks are mobbed incessantly by small passerines that discover them it their roost; the owl's position is often betrayed by the persistent mobbing calls of birds such as White-plumed Honeyeater *Lichenostomus penicillatus*. At dusk, sits watchfully on exposed perch; does not usually fly off when people walk past; at the approach of danger it sits bolt upright, feathers pressed tight against body, and turns side-on to the source of threat, appearing very long and slender. Looks dark and deceptively large in flight.

FOOD Feeds on birds up to the size of House Sparrow *Passer domesticus*, and small mammals, especially House Mouse *Mus musculus*. Takes more invertebrates than any other Australian owl; night-flying beetles and moths, especially, are important in its diet. Hunts from a perch, such as exposed branch, fence or telephone pole, from time to time flying up to capture aerial insects; has been seen catching large moths around street lights.

BREEDING Breeding season from August to October. Pair-members perch close together, the male giving long series of *por* notes. Female or both partners may roost in the nesting cavity for quite a long time before laying. A large variety of tree holes, 1-20m above ground, serves for nesting; male cleans hollow before female lays, and no nesting material is added; occasionally uses abandoned nests of corvids or babblers. The 2-5 (usually 3) dull white, rounded oval eggs (42 x 35mm) are laid at intervals of 1-2 days, and the female alone incubates for 31-35 days. Young leave the nest by about 5 weeks, sometimes earlier; they are fed and cared for by both parents for a further 2-3 months.

STATUS AND CONSERVATION This is the smallest and the most abundant of all Australian owls. Common throughout Australia wherever there are trees for nesting and roosting.

REMARKS The taxonomy of the whole 'boobook group' needs study. The form *lurida* ('Red Boobook') from NE Queensland may prove to be specifically distinct. Comparative bioacoustic studies are needed.

REFERENCES Boyer & Hume (1991), Burton (1992), Eck & Busse (1973), Hollands (1991), Johnstone & Darnell (1997), Mees (1964), Sayers (1976), White & Bruce (1986).

---

188 BROWN HAWK OWL
Ninox scutulata   Plate 58

French: Chouette hirsute
German: Falkenkauz

IDENTIFICATION A very hawk-like owl (about 32cm). Dark grey-brown above, with whitish forehead and irregular white patches around shoulders; throat and foreneck fulvous, streaked with brown, rest of underparts white with large drops of reddish-brown forming broken bars. Tail barred with black, tipped with white. Eyes golden-yellow. **Similar species** No other owl with such hawk-like appearance, except the other hawk owls in SE Asian region. Andaman Hawk Owl [189] is confined to the Andaman and Nicobar islands. Philippine Hawk Owl [191] has more white spots on scapulars and wings. Speckled Hawk Owl [196] from Sulawesi is smaller, much more speckled, and with white spots (not stripes) on breast; Ochre-bellied Hawk Owl [192] from the same island has an ochraceous-rufous breast and belly with faint darker spots. Jungle Hawk Owl [195] and Papuan Hawk Owl [202] are confined to New Guinea, Russet Hawk Owl [197] to the Bismarck Archipelago, and Solomon Hawk Owl [194] to the Solomon Islands.

VOCALISATIONS Very distinctive and diagnostic. Not particularly loud, but far-carrying, pleasant and almost musical song, *oo..uk, oo..uk, oo..uk* etc, in runs of 6-20 notes (mostly 9-13) at rate of about one per second, with a pause of a few seconds between each run. The female's song is slightly higher-pitched. The songs of the races in Japan, Nepal and Java are remarkably identical, although their ecology is somewhat different. Apart from the song, a number of other sounds, best described for the Japanese race (Oba 1996): this vocal repertoire consists of a low *hooh* (produced by both males and females) with hollow quality, not audible over more than 100m; a low powerful grunt, *guf*; a sharp, nasal, shrill *heeoo*; a quiet rolling, protracted *kerrrr* like purring of a cat; and a cat-like *mew* or *meew*, sometimes powerful, giving the bird the Japanese names Neko-dori ('cat-bird') or Miyah-tsuku ('miaow-owl').

DISTRIBUTION Indian subcontinent to E Siberia and Japan, south to the Andamans, Malay Peninsula, Great and Lesser Sundas, Sulawesi, Moluccas, Taiwan and Philippines; one record from Australia.

MOVEMENTS Movements poorly known. Migratory in the north, reaching Sundas, Taiwan, Philippines and NW Australia; resident in southern part of range. In SE Asia during the northern winter, two (or more) populations occur side by side (Java, Sumatra, etc), but the migratory race is non-vocal. In the Philippines, two migrant races (*japonica* and *totogo*) may occur at the same time. There is one record of *japonica* in Australia, from Ashmore Reef,

Brown Hawk Owl

about 300km northwest of NW Australia, between Timor and the Australian continent.

HABITAT In northern regions inhabits forest and woodland at low and high elevations (in mountains up to 1,300m). In Japan, occurs particularly in broadleaved deciduous and broadleaved evergreen woodland mixed with conifer plantations, and tends to frequent forest edges; also associates with human habitations and even breeds in urban areas, e.g. at Shinto shrines, Buddhist temples, in parks and gardens, provided these contain well-wooded areas with tall trees for daytime retreat, hunting and nesting. In India, from the outer Himalayas in W Pakistan eastwards to Assam south of the Brahmaputra River and south to C India, occurs in forest, well-wooded country and groves of trees, particularly in the neighbourhood of water and bordering forest streams or watercourses, often close to habitations. In SE Asia, resident races (e.g. *javensis*) occur exclusively in wet primary lowland rain forest, particularly far from human habitations.

DESCRIPTION *N. s. lugubris* **Adult** Lores and forehead white; bristles black or black-tipped. Crown, sides of head and neck pale grey-brown, palest next to forehead and grading into pure brown of back, rump, uppertail-coverts and wing-coverts; edge of shoulder of wing white. Tail banded dark brown and light brown (dark bars generally five), with whitish tip. Chin white; throat and foreneck fulvous, streaked with brown; rest of underparts white with large drops of light reddish-brown. Tarsi feathered, toes sparsely bristled or bare. **Juvenile** Overall the same colour, but with whitish neoptile down on feather tips of head; underparts more fluffy, less striated, with streaks dark brown. **Bare parts** Iris bright yellow. Cere dull green or greenish-brown. Bill horny-slate or bluish-black, paler at tip. Toes dull yellow of yellowish-green.

MEASUREMENTS AND WEIGHT Total length about 28-32cm, varying among subspecies; males tend to be larger than females. Wing 176-245mm (depending on race: see Geographical Variation); tail 98-142mm (also varying racially). Weight 172-227g.

GEOGRAPHICAL VARIATION Eleven subspecies are

recognised. The northern subspecies tend to be paler, larger and longer-winged than sedentary southern races.

N. s. japonica (Temminck & Schlegel, 1844). Ussuriland, SE Manchuria, N (and S?) Korea and Japan; migrates to Philippines (Calayan, Fuga, Camiguin Norte, Luzon, Mindoro, Masbate, Cuyo, Guimaras, Negros, Cebu, Mindanao, Basilan, Palawan, Sanga Sanga, Tawitawi, Bongao), Borneo and Sulawesi, probably also to Sumatra and Java (and one record from Ashmore Reef, between Timor and Australia). Large, pale race. Wing 222-245mm; tail 115-130mm. (We treat the taxa *macroptera* from Mindoro, *florensis* from Flores and some Philippine islands, and *ussuriensis* from Ussuriland and N Korea as synonyms.)

N. s. totogo Momiyama, 1931. Ryukyu Islands. Wing 206-216mm.

N. s. burmanica Hume, 1876. Assam to S Yunnan, south to Malay Peninsula, Thailand, Cambodia, Laos and Vietnam; migrates to Sumatra (?) and Java (?) (as probably does *japonica*). Differs from *lugubris* in being darker both above and below; head as dark as or darker than back, and much less grey. Wing 206-222mm.

N. s. scutulata (Raffles, 1822). Sumatra, Riau and Lingga Archipelagos, and Bangka. Dark resident race. Wings short and rounded. Wing 212-227mm. (We regard *malaccensis* from Malacca as a synonym.)

N. s. lugubris (Tickell, 1833). N India (Himalayas and submontane tracts) and C India (Bengal, Orissa, N Andhra Pradesh); southern limit rather ill-defined (Bombay region?). See Description. Wing 205-232mm.

N. s. hirsuta (Temminck, 1824). S India (south of about latitude of Bombay, about 19°N) and Sri Lanka. Very like *burmanica*, but still darker. Head always darker than back and more slaty-brown, less redbrown; very richly coloured below. Wing 190-212mm.

N. s. obscura Hume, 1873. Andaman and Nicobar Islands. Differs from other races in overall dark chocolate-brown colour, somewhat paler and rufous on abdomen; forehead mixed black and white; head and primary coverts generally darker and blacker than rest of upperparts. Wing 197-220mm.

N. s. javensis Stresemann, 1928. Java, perhaps also Bali; habitat primary lowland rain forest and hill forest. Small, round-winged, very dark and richly coloured race. Wing 178-183mm.

N. s. borneensis Bonaparte, 1850. Lowland rain forest of Borneo. Wing 176-197mm. (We regard *Ninox labuanensis* Sharpe, 1875 as a synonym.)

N. s. randi Deignan, 1951. Philippines: Luzon, Marinduque, Mindoro, Negros, Cebu, Siquijor, Mindanao, Basilan). Wing 218-242mm.

N. s. palawanensis Ripley & Rabor, 1962. Palawan. Wing 195mm.

HABITS Crepuscular and nocturnal. Occurs singly or in pairs, partners spending the daytime huddled together in the seclusion of a shady branch, often thickly smothered with creepers. When disturbed, will readily fly to another tree through dappled sunshine with no apparent unease. Normally not active before dusk, but sometimes on move during daytime in cloudy weather. Songpost often a bare branch high up in the top of a tree, usually used night after night. Flight with rapid wingbeats and glides; alights like a hawk, sweeping upwards to settle on a branch.

FOOD Mainly large insects such as beetles and grasshoppers, but also frogs, lizards, small birds, mice, and occasionally small insectivorous bats. Hunts at dusk from a perch on a tree stump or post, keeping lookout for prey. From time to time it springs upwards, sometimes almost vertically a metre or more, to take a passing insect in its claws, and dives back to its perch. Has also been observed hawking beetles and other insects in the air like a nightjar (Caprimulgidae).

BREEDING Very vocal during the breeding season, singing more or less continuously for hours, especially during moonlit nights. Male and female will join in irregular duets, or several distant birds will answer one another from all directions; sometimes choruses with birds in neighbouring territories. The male (sometimes the pair) has a particularly noisy round of calling in the twilight period of dawn, before retiring for the day. Occasionally calls also in daytime in cloudy weather.

Breeds at 5-20m above the ground in large irregular holes or hollow trees, the hole usually about 30-80cm deep, with diameter of 20-30cm. In Japan, often uses old *Zelkova serrata* and *Castanea crenata* trees, and the same nest hole is often used in successive years (over 20 years recorded for several pairs); also reported sometimes to nest on ground between garden rocks and piled timber, and in nestboxes. Courtship feeding outside the nest is recorded.

Season (eggs/incubation) end of May to late June in Japan, June-July in N India (Dehra Dun), and March-April in Sumatra. Eggs are laid on a layer of dead leaves and wood chips at the bottom of the hole. Northern races lay 2-5 eggs within 5-7 days; southern races usually 2 eggs. Eggs are white, roundish, measuring about 36 x 31mm. Female alone incubates through day and night, fed by the male, but she sometimes leaves the nest for short periods. Incubation, lasting about 24 days, usually starts with the third egg (Japan), suggesting synchronous hatching within 2 days; despite this, there are conspicuous size differences among the brood. Fledglings leave the nest hole 24-27 days after hatching. Both parents are involved in feeding of the young.

STATUS AND CONSERVATION Northern populations fairly common. Southern races more at risk from destruction of primary lowland rainforest, especially in Sumatra, Java and Borneo.

REMARKS The species' movements and biology are in need of more study. Taxonomy of several described forms unclear.

REFERENCES Boyer & Hume (1991), Burton (1992), Dickinson *et al.* (1991), Eck & Busse (1973), Mees (1970), Oba (1996), Rozendaal & Dekker (1989), Schodde & van Tets (1981), Voous (1988).

---

189 ANDAMAN HAWK OWL
Ninox affinis   Plate 58

French: Chouette des Andamanes
German: Andamanen-Falkenkauz

IDENTIFICATION Very similar to Brown Hawk Owl [187], especially of the Nicobar race obscura, but smaller (25-28cm) and browner, with distinct bright rufous streaking on underparts. Eyes yellow. **Similar species** No other owl in Andamans is of this size and with bright rufous spotting of underparts.

VOCALISATIONS The song is described as a loud *craw* repeated at intervals, and quite different from that of Brown Hawk Owl in Sri Lanka, which is a soft fluty double syllable.

DISTRIBUTION Andaman and Nicobar Islands.

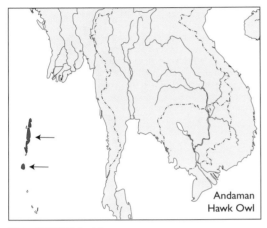

Andaman Hawk Owl

MOVEMENTS Resident.

HABITAT Presumably mainly lowland forest; in Nicobars, observed hawking moths in low secondary forest. Nothing further specifically recorded.

DESCRIPTION *N. a. affinis* **Adult** Facial disc greyish. Crown and mantle rather plain brown, outer webs of scapulars with some larger pale buffy areas. Flight and tail feathers barred brown and buff. Underparts pale buffy, usually streaked bright rufous-brown; underwing-coverts and axillaries almost unspotted orange-rufous, but wing-coverts more or less barred. Tarsi feathered to base of toes; latter bare or sparsely bristled. **Juvenile** Not described. **Bare parts** Iris yellow. Cere dull green. Bill greenish-horn, paler on culmen and tip. Toes yellowish. Claws blackish-horn.

MEASUREMENTS AND WEIGHT Total length about 25-28 cm. Wing 167-205mm; tail 102-130mm. Weight: no data.

GEOGRAPHICAL VARIATION Two subspecies.
N. a. affinis Beavan, 1867. Andaman Islands. See Description. Wing 167-169mm.
N. a. isolata Baker, 1926. Nicobar Islands. Distinctly larger than nominate, and browner, less ashy, on upperparts. Wing 185-205mm.

HABITS Very little known; presumably not much different from those of Brown Hawk Owl.

FOOD Probably mainly insectivorous. Davidson observed and shot a specimen hawking moths.

BREEDING Unknown.

STATUS AND CONSERVATION Listed as Near-threatened by BirdLife International. Probably endangered.

REMARKS This owl's biology and taxonomy require study.

REFERENCES Baker (1926, 1927), Boyer & Hume (1991), Burton (1992), Collar *et al.* (1994), Voous (1988).

190 MADAGASCAR HAWK OWL
Ninox superciliaris   Plate 58

French: Ninox à sourcils
German: Madagaskarkauz

IDENTIFICATION A medium-sized (23-30cm), plump owl with rounded head without ear-tufts. Upperparts brown, crown and sometimes mantle with small whitish spots, with prominent whitish eyebrows meeting at base of bill; underparts tan-white, boldly barred brown, abdomen plain whitish. Wings rather long, with pointed tips. Eyes brown. **Similar species** Madagascar Red Owl [4] has a heart-shaped facial disc, and orange-ochre plumage without any barring on underside. Madagascar Scops Owl [31] is smaller, with yellow eyes, and has a row of whitish dots across shoulder and small, erectile ear-tufts. Both also differ vocally.

VOCALISATIONS Poorly known. The song is probably a howling *wuhuoh* uttered at intervals; the notes at the beginning are often somewhat hoarse, *chruwuoh*. A series of about 15 powerful, barking *kuang* or *kuatt* notes, rising in volume and pitch at the beginning, may express aggression.

DISTRIBUTION NE and SW Madagascar.

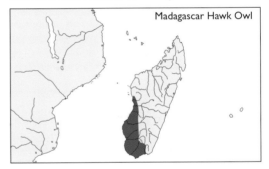

Madagascar Hawk Owl

MOVEMENTS Endemic resident.

HABITAT Rather varied: evergreen rain forest, gallery forest, forest clearings, dry deciduous forest, rather open landscape with subarid thorny shrubs and few trees, even in the vicinity of villages. From sea-level up to about 800m.

DESCRIPTION **Adult** Lighter and darker morphs occur, being similar in plumage pattern. Facial disc tan-grey; prominent white eyebrows meet on forehead at base of bill. Upperparts brown, crown sprinkled with whitish spots, back and mantle either uniform brown or mantle with some whitish dots; upperwing-coverts sparsely spotted white. Flight feathers diffusely barred light and dusky; tail brown with indistinct lighter narrow bars. Chin and throat brownish-white; underparts tan-white, boldly barred brown, the bars becoming diffuse in middle, especially on belly; undertail-coverts and underwing-coverts pure white. Tarsi feathered tan, toes bare. **Juvenile** Undescribed. **Bare parts** Eyes brown. Cere pale yellowish-brown (nostrils at front of cere). Bill whitish-horn. Toes yellowish-white. Claws horn.

MEASUREMENTS AND WEIGHT Total length 23-30cm. Wing 180-193mm; tail 88-102mm (once 119mm?). Weight about 236g.

GEOGRAPHICAL VARIATION Monotypic: *Ninox superciliaris* (Vieillot, 1817).

HABITS Strictly nocturnal. Activity begins at dusk and lasts to dawn. Very vocal, and located mainly by its song or other calls. Several individuals can quite frequently be heard calling to each other.

FOOD Chiefly insects, but probably also small vertebrates. Often perches on a branch overlooking open area, watching for prey; victim is generally caught by swooping down on to it.

BREEDING Territorial. Males claim territory by singing. Nesting has been observed from October to December. A shallow depression on the ground is used as nest; lays 3-5 shiny white eggs. Breeding biology poorly known.

STATUS AND CONSERVATION Endemic to Madagascar, where it is locally fairly common. The variety of habitats occupied shows that the species is less dependent on forest than are many other owls. Nevertheless, it may be threatened by the use of pesticides and by human persecution, as many villagers regard all owls as birds of ill omen.

REMARKS Although this handsome owl is still locally common, little is known of its biology, ecology and behaviour. In many publications, the colour of the iris figures as yellow or pale yellow; most recent observations, however, reveal that the eyes are brown, but whether there are exceptions to this (very old birds?) requires confirmation. Studies on Madagascar Hawk Owl are urgently needed, including with respect to its conservation.

REFERENCES Boyer & Hume (1991), Burton (1992), Eck & Busse (1973), Langrand (1990), R. Thorstrom (pers. comm. 1998).

---

191 PHILIPPINE HAWK OWL
Ninox philippensis   Plate 59

French: Chouette des Philippines
German: Philippinenkauz

IDENTIFICATION A small owl (15-20cm), extremely variable in appearance, but warm brown above, with white spots or bars on scapulars and upperwing-coverts; has dark tail with light bars. **Similar species** Brown Hawk Owl [188] differs in being larger, with longer tail (150 mm, as against 90 mm), plain brown (not rufous) above and without obvious white spots on scapulars and wing-coverts, more coarsely patterned below, and has a dark-barred tail. Mindoro Hawk Owl [192] is coarsely vermiculated and barred below, and differs vocally.

VOCALISATIONS According to tape recordings (by P. Morris), the song of the male is a long series of short, downward-inflected notes given at intervals of about 2 seconds, often increasing gradually in volume, becoming disyllabic and building up to a climax of three-note or four-note calls: *weuw weuw weuw…weuw-weuw weuw-weuw…weuw-kwe-weuw weuw-kwe-weuw….* Entire series can last about 2-3 minutes, especially when male and female duet. The highly excited song of the male is preceded by a melancholic *oohp*, followed by a higher trisyllabic sequence of notes: *oohp woiw-kwe-woik.* A loud shriek is occasionally given in response to playback.

Philippine Hawk Owl

DISTRIBUTION Endemic to Philippines, occurring on most islands except Mindoro (where replaced by Mindoro Hawk Owl). For details, see Geographical Variation.

MOVEMENTS Resident.

HABITAT Primary and secondary forest, including remnant patches of gallery forest.

DESCRIPTION *N. p. philippensis* **Adult** Facial disc ochraceous, with feathers whitish at base; narrow whitish eyebrows; sides of face brown, as crown, ear-coverts more dusky. Upperparts dark brown, washed rufous, head slightly darker (more chocolate-brown) and rather unmarked; scapulars with large white oval marks on outer webs, some of inner ones barred with ochraceous; wing-coverts dark brown, slightly washed with ochraceous, all distinctly spotted with white or ochraceous-white. Primaries brown, margined narrowly with ochraceous, and barred paler brown. Tail sepia-brown with 6-7 narrow bands of pale ochraceous. Chin whitish, throat marked with a few black streaks; underparts whitish, with ochraceous centres of feathers producing broadly streaked appearance. Tarsi feathered nearly to base of toes, latter rather densely bristled. **Juvenile** Natal down white. Fledged juveniles have upperparts almost entirely uniform rufous-chocolate but for a few buffy-white bars on outer scapulars; wing-coverts only a little darker than back, greaters distinctly spotted ochraceous and white on outer webs; white below, with broad fawn-coloured feather centres giving broadly streaked appearance. **Bare parts** Iris yellow. Bill greenish with yellow tip. Toes light yellow.

MEASUREMENTS AND WEIGHT Total length 15-20cm. Wing 158-194mm; tail 70-101mm. Weight of 1 male 125g.

GEOGRAPHICAL VARIATION We recognise seven subspecies, one or two of which may be separate species.
  N. p. philippensis Bonaparte, 1855. Luzon, Marinduque, Polillo, Buad, Catanduanes, Samar, Leyte. See Description. Wing 158-169mm; tail 75-88mm.
  N. p. proxima Mayr, 1945. Masbate. Differs from nominate in having upperparts darker brown, white spots on wings smaller, streaks below darker. Wing about 175mm; tail 79-82mm.

N. p. ticaoensis duPont, 1972. Sitio Calpi, Danao, San Jacinto, Ticao. Resembles previous race. (Taxonomic status doubtful; probably better treated as a synonym of *proxima*.)

N. p. centralis Mayr, 1945. Boracay, Carabao, Semirara, Panay, Guimaras, Negros, Bohol, Siquijor. Differs from *proxima* in having duller brown upperparts; also larger. Wing 181-191mm; tail 89-93mm.

N. (p.) spilocephala Tweeddale, 1879. Dinagat, Siargao, Mindanao, Basilan. Differs from nominate in having rufous spots or barring on head and neck; white spots on scapulars slightly larger; underparts streaked, with tendency to barring. Wing 163-190mm; tail 70-89mm.

N. p. reyi Oustalet, 1880. Sulu Archipelago, on Sulu, Siasi, Tawitawi, Bongao, Sanga Sanga, Sibutu. Differs from *spilocephala* in more prominent rufous barring on head and back; streaks below lacking on belly. Larger. Wing about 194mm. (We include *Ninox everetti* as a synonym.)

N. (p.) spilonota Bourns & Worcester, 1894. Tablas, Sibuyan, Cebu, Camiguin Sur. Differs from other species in having white underparts coarsely spotted and barred; also larger. Wing 188-194mm; tail 96-101mm. (Probably specifically distinct.)

HABITS Nocturnal.

FOOD Insects.

BREEDING Nestling in white down on Mindanao in March, another on Leyte in May. Normally uses a hollow in a tree for nesting.

STATUS AND CONSERVATION Locally common.

REMARKS The forms *spilonota* and *spilocephala* are sometimes regarded as separate species. Races sometimes also arranged in three relationship groups: *philippensis* + *proxima* + *ticaoensis* + *centralis*; *spilocephala* + *reyi*; and *spilonota*. Needs study on taxonomy and biology.

REFERENCES Boyer & Hume (1991), Burton (1992), Collar and Rasmussen (1998), Dickinson *et al.* (1991), Delacour & Mayr (1946), Dunning (1993), DuPont (1971), Mayr (1945), McGregor (1909).

---

192 MINDORO HAWK OWL
Ninox mindorensis   Plate 59

Syn: *Ninox plateni*

French: Chouette de Mindoro
German: Mindorokauz

IDENTIFICATION A small owl (about 20cm) without ear-tufts and with rather long, pointed wings. Dull brown above, with barred head, neck and mantle, scapulars with a few whitish spots; orange-rufous below, darker on upper breast, barred from neck to belly. Tarsi feathered nearly to toes, the latter bare with some bristles. Eyes yellow. **Similar species** Philippine Hawk Owl [191] is slightly smaller (normally less than 20cm), and is paler below with somewhat diffuse brownish shaft-streaks (not barred); also differs vocally.

VOCALISATIONS According to tape recordings (made by P. Morris), the song of the male is a series of very high-pitched growling whistles given at intervals of 1-2 seconds: *cheehrr cheehrr cheehrr...*, sometimes with an 'appendix', *cheehrr-ke cheehrr-ke....* (Since this is totally different from the song of Philippine Hawk Owl, and because the two have very different plumage patterns on the underparts, we treat them as separate species.)

DISTRIBUTION Endemic to Mindoro in the Philippines.

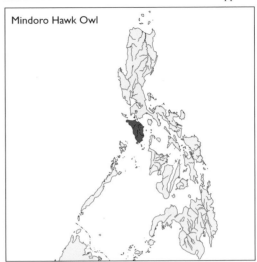
Mindoro Hawk Owl

MOVEMENTS Resident.

HABITAT Forest and wooded areas.

DESCRIPTION Adult Facial disc rufescent-brown without distinct rim; eyebrows between base of bill and eyes whitish, not very prominent; lores whitish. Narrow forehead whitish-buff; crown and nape rufescent-brown with fine buffy and dusky barring. Mantle rather uniform warm brown, back with whitish spots; outer webs of scapulars with large white spots; upperwing-coverts warm brown with pale buffy spots. Flight feathers brown with rows of lighter spots; tail warm brown with narrow buffy bars (number of bars fewer than in Philippine Hawk Owl). Throat whitish, with few dusky spots and streaks on upper foreneck; chest orange-brown, fading into whitish-buff on abdomen; entire underparts coarsely barred and vermiculated (not broadly streaked as Philippine Hawk Owl). Tarsi incompletely feathered orange-buff, leaving lower third bare; toes bristled. **Juvenile** Not described. **Bare parts** Eyes yellow. Cere and bill pale bluish-grey. Toes and bare parts of tarsi yellowish-grey. Claws dusky horn.

MEASUREMENTS AND WEIGHT Total length about 20cm. Wing 162-175mm; tail 77-89mm. Weight: no data.

GEOGRAPHICAL VARIATION Monotypic: *Ninox mindorensis* Ogilvie-Grant, 1896.

HABITS Nocturnal; activity begins at dusk.

FOOD Probably similar to that of other hawk owls of same size.

BREEDING Probably nests in holes in trees. Reproduction unknown.

STATUS AND CONSERVATION Uncertain.

REMARKS The Mindoro Hawk Owl has until now been considered a race of Philippine Hawk Owl. As demonstrated by recordings made recently by P. Morris, however, the two have totally different vocalisations, a fact which has convinced us that *mindorensis* should be treated as a full species and not as a subspecies of *N. philippensis*.

REFERENCES Collar & Rasmussen (pers. comm. 1999), Dickinson *et al.* (1991), P. Morris (pers. comm. 1999).

193 OCHRE-BELLIED HAWK OWL
Ninox ochracea   Plate 59

French: Chouette à ventre ocre
German: Ockerbauchkauz

IDENTIFICATION A medium-sized owl (25-26cm) without ear-tufts and with a relatively long tail (about 127mm). Brown-tinged dark chestnut above, crown more dusky, rather unmarked, with white spots on outer scapulars and white-spotted wing-coverts; remiges barred pale. Tail narrowly barred with whitish-buff. Throat white, upper breast cinnamon-tawny with few lighter bars, rest of underside tawny-ochre with indistinct darker markings on lower breast. Eyes yellow. **Similar species** No other owl of this size and colour pattern occurs in Sulawesi. Speckled Hawk Owl [196] has upperside reddish-brown with numerous small white spots, including on secondaries, wing-coverts and crown, a broad whitish stripe from forehead over eye to above ear-coverts, reddish-brown underparts barred white (bars more spot-like on abdomen), and brown eyes.

VOCALISATIONS A series of hoarse, guttural notes which develop into a series of double-note calls, *krurr-krurr* (duration of a single double note about 1.8 seconds) represents the territorial song of the male (according to recordings made by D. Bishop).

DISTRIBUTION Sulawesi and Butung Island, Indonesia.

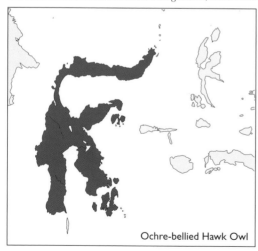

Ochre-bellied Hawk Owl

MOVEMENTS Resident.

HABITAT Primary forest at up to 1,780m.

DESCRIPTION Adult Facial disc brown, becoming lighter

towards eyes; narrow whitish eyebrows; chin whitish. Upperparts dark chestnut, tinged with brown, more dusky on crown; white scapular spots, white dots on wing-coverts. Buffy barring on flight feathers and relatively long tail. Prominent white throat (obvious when calling); rest of underparts tawny, with some indistinct lighter barring on upper breast, from lower breast towards belly shading gradually into ochraceous-tawny with some diffuse darker dots. Tarsi feathered to base of toes, latter bristled. **Juvenile** Undescribed. **Bare parts** Iris yellow. Cere and bill yellowish-horn. Toes yellowish-grey. Claws dark horn.

MEASUREMENTS AND WEIGHT Total length 25-26cm, females usually smaller than males. Wing 177-200mm; tail about 127mm. Weight: no data.

GEOGRAPHICAL VARIATION Monotypic: *Ninox ochracea* (Schlegel, 1856). (*Ninox perversa* Stresemann, 1938 is a synonym of *Ninox ochracea*.)

HABITS A rather elusive and little-known forest bird.

FOOD Probably insects.

BREEDING Unknown.

STATUS AND CONSERVATION Rather rare. No details known. Probably threatened by habitat destruction.

REMARKS Stresemann gave this species the name *Ninox perversa*, but the original description is of the same taxon and has priority.

REFERENCES Blasius (1897), Boyer & Hume (1991), Burton (1992), Coates & Bishop (1997), Holmes & Phillipps (1996), Mees (1964), Stresemann (1938).

194 SOLOMON HAWK OWL
Ninox jacquinoti   Plate 59

French: Chouette de Jacquinot
German: Jacquinotkauz

IDENTIFICATION A medium-sized owl (25-30cm), dark rufous-brown above, with or without white spots or bars, and whitish below with brownish bars or spots. Facial disc brownish, with white at base of bill and around eyes and narrow white eyebrows. Bill yellowish-horn; eyes yellow or brown. **Similar species** Fearful Owl [205] has much lighter yellowish-rufous upperparts which are densely mottled, with relatively large dark brown spots on forehead, hindneck and neck sides, and scapulars and wing-coverts yellowish-rufous with dark brown centres, remiges with distinct broad bars; also short tail, and powerful feet and bill, latter blackish.

VOCALISATIONS A series of somewhat throaty and unmusical double-notes with about 0.6 sec intervals between the two notes is probably the song of the male: *kwu, kwu, kwu, kwu* (based on tape-recordings by D. Bishop). In addition, single, hoarse calls are repeated at prolonged intervals. A single drawn-out whistle-like hoot with rising inflection at the end, and a lowish tremulous note often repeated, are vocalisations of uncertain function. Duetting between two birds commonly occurs, the calls rising in pitch and becoming more excited. Calls throughout the year.

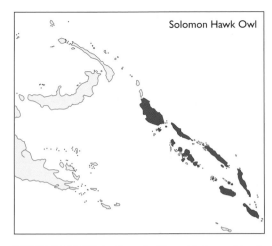

Solomon Hawk Owl

DISTRIBUTION Buka, Bougainville and Solomon Islands.

MOVEMENTS Resident.

HABITAT Frequents primary and tall secondary forest, from lowlands up to 1,500m. Also in forest patches and nearby gardens. Widespread.

DESCRIPTION *N. j. jacquinoti* **Adult** Facial disc brownish with some lighter concentric lines, and whitish zone around eyes and at base of bill; narrow white eyebrows. Upperparts dark rufous to blackish-brown, with numerous whitish flecks and pale edges to feathers of crown, neck and mantle; wing-coverts spotted whitish. Flight feathers dark brown with rows of whitish spots. Tail dark brown with 5-7 narrow whitish bars, central feathers sometimes unbarred. Throat whitish, upper breast brown with indistinct lighter barring; rest of underparts whitish with narrow brownish shaft-streaks. Tarsi feathered to base of toes, latter bristled. **Juvenile** Not specifically described. **Bare parts** Iris yellow to orange-yellow. Bill pale yellowish-horn or pale olive. Toes yellow or yellowish-cream. Claws dark horn.

MEASUREMENTS AND WEIGHT Total length 25-30cm. Wing 185-223mm; tail about 112mm. Weight: no data.

GEOGRAPHICAL VARIATION Numerous races have been described from the various islands, differing in spotting and barring of upperside and in size; the taxonomic status of some may be doubtful. We recognise seven subspecies, which can be divided more or less into two colour groups, with or without spotting and barring.

Group I
N. j. jacquinoti (Bonaparte, 1850). Santa Isabel. See Description. Wing 195-208mm.
N. j. eichhorni Hartert, 1927. Bougainville and Choiseul. Differs from nominate in smaller size and coarser barring above. Wing 185-197mm.
N. j. mono Mayr, 1935. Mono (or Treasure) Island. Differs from *eichhorni* in reduction of whitish bars on wings. Wing 190-196mm.
N. j. floridae Mayr, 1935. Florida Island. Differs from nominate only in larger size. Wing 218-223mm.

Group II
N. j. granti Sharpe, 1888. Guadalcanal. Lacks spotting and barring on head, back and scapulars, reduced spots and bars on wings and tail; underparts white

with heavy rufous-brown bars, more dense on breast and flanks. Eyes yellow. Wing 178-183mm.
N. j. malaitae Mayr, 1931. Malaita. Rather small. Wing 164-165mm.
N. j. roseoaxillaris (Hartert, 1929). Bauro and San Cristóbal. Upperside more rufous-cinnamon with some round ochraceous-buff nape spots; throat white, darker breast, cinnamon belly with creamy bars and spots, abdomen, undertail-coverts and thighs pale; axillaries pale pink. Eyes brown (sometimes yellow?). Small. Wing about 157mm.

HABITS Occurs singly or in pairs. Roosting sites include main forks of trees in the forest canopy and hollows beneath overhanging branches of large trees, usually 15m above ground.

FOOD Insects.

BREEDING Undescribed. Once seen to appear at the entrance of a hollow branch when two Cardinal Lories *Chalcopsitta cardinalis* tried to enter it.

STATUS AND CONSERVATION Widespread, and not uncommon. Rarer on San Cristobal and Malaita.

REMARKS The taxonomy and biology of this species need study.

REFERENCES Boyer & Hume (1991), Burton (1992), Coates (1985), Diamond (1975), Hadden (1981), Schodde (1977).

195 JUNGLE HAWK OWL
Ninox theomacha Plate 60

French: Chouette brune
German: Einfarbkauz

IDENTIFICATION A small to medium-sized owl (20-28cm) with uniform dark chocolate- or blackish-brown crown and upperparts. Face grey-brown to blackish-brown, with some white on forehead and at base of dark bill; uniform chestnut-brown below (one race more or less coarsely streaked). Iris yellow or golden-yellow. **Similar species** Southern Boobook [187], found only in S New Guinea (west of Fly River), has white underparts heavily streaked and mottled with red-brown on breast and streaked abdomen. Papuan Hawk Owl [202] is somewhat larger, and brown with dark brown to black bands on upperparts and wings, and buffy below with bold brown streaking. Rufous Owl [182] is much larger (41-51cm), with whitish to pale buffy underside with numerous rufous-brown bars. Barking Owl [184] is a robust medium-sized owl, with creamy-buff to whitish underparts boldly streaked brown to chestnut-brown.

VOCALISATIONS The territorial song consists of a series of double-notes of a hoarse, throaty quality with a marked downward inflection: *kreo-kreo, kreo-kreo*, somewhat resembling the song of Southern Boobook; it is repeated many times at intervals of a few seconds. Male and female duet during courtship, the voice of the female being higher in pitch.

DISTRIBUTION New Guinea and some western and eastern islands.

MOVEMENTS Resident.

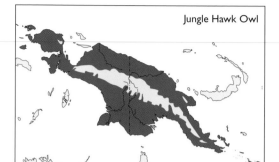

HABITAT Rain forest up to submontane and montane forest; frequents forest, forest edges and groves of trees in open country. Usually in lowlands up to 770m and 1,250m, but sometimes up to 2,000m.

DESCRIPTION *N. t. theomacha* **Adult** Facial disc blackish-brown, shading into pale greyish around bill. Sides of head blackish-brown to dark grey-brownish. Upperparts dark chocolate-brown, with or without few white spots on wing-coverts. Wings and tail (from above) unbarred, or with hint of faint bars. Throat pale chestnut to buff with some darker streaks; upper breast dark to medium chestnut-brown, nearly uniform; rest of underparts bright chestnut; under-wing with a few pale or whitish bars, undertail uniform fuscous. Tarsi feathered chestnut to base of toes, latter bristled. **Juvenile** Natal down grey. Mesoptile entirely fluffy dull brown. **Bare parts** Eyes yellow. Cere grey. Bill blackish with white or yellow tip. Feet yellowish. Claws black.

MEASUREMENTS AND WEIGHT Total length 20-28cm. Wing 175-227mm; tail about 100mm. Weight: no data.

GEOGRAPHICAL VARIATION Four subspecies.

N. t. theomacha (Bonaparte, 1855). All of New Guinea below 2500m. See Description. Wing 176-186mm.

N. t. hoedtii (Schlegel, 1871). Waigeo and Misool. Like nominate but duller, and sides of head brown (not sooty). Wing about 178mm.

N. t. goldii Gurney, 1883. D'Entrecasteaux Archipelago: Goodenough, Fergusson and Normanby Islands. Like nominate but larger, underparts lighter, lower breast and abdomen with bold streaks and spots. Wing 215-227mm.

N. t. rosseliana Tristram, 1889. Louisiade Archipelago: Tagula (or Sudest) and Rossel Islands. Like *goldii*, but white markings of underparts larger. Wing of 1 specimen 206mm, tail 127mm.

HABITS Little information.

FOOD Insects.

BREEDING Recorded in E Papua (Boneno, near Mt Simpson). Eggs were found in December in Central Province (Deva Deva and Mafulu); fledglings with much to little down were observed in October.

STATUS AND CONSERVATION Widely distributed. Locally common.

REMARKS This species' biology and taxonomy, as well as its vocalisations, require study.

REFERENCES Boyer & Hume (1991), Burton (1992), Coates (1985), Harrison & Frith (1970), Mayr & Rand (1937), Rand & Gilliard (1965).

196 SPECKLED HAWK OWL
Ninox punctulata
Plate 60

French: Chouette mouchetée
German: Pünktchenkauz

IDENTIFICATION A small owl (20-26 cm), dull reddish-brown above with profuse small white spots, including on wings and crown. Dark facial disc bordered below by conspicuous large white throat band; eyebrows white from base of bill to beyond eyes. Upper breast with brown band, bordered below by oval white patch; rest of underside whitish, obscurely barred or spotted reddish-brown. Eyes brown. **Similar species** Ochre-bellied Hawk Owl [193] has dark chestnut upperparts tinged with brown and crown more dusky, all without white spots, with breast cinnamon-tawny and belly tawny ochre; also relatively long tail, and yellow eyes.

VOCALISATIONS A long series of loud, clear whistles with rather sibilant quality, slightly rising in pitch and accelerating, is the song of the male: *toy-toy-toytoytoytoytoytoytoy*. Other descriptions transcribe it as *koi-kai-kai-keet*, sometimes *kai-koi-keet*, or just *koi-keet*; mostly trisyllabic, with first two notes short and the last longer, more screeching and emphasised. Variations occur within a series, also sometimes *hak-kai-tseek*. A low mumble, *kï-kï-kï* or *kohok-kohok*, often precedes the song. The native names 'totosik', 'cococik' or 'tatoke' (Minahassa, N Sulawesi) are good onomatopoeic imitations of the call.

DISTRIBUTION Sulawesi.

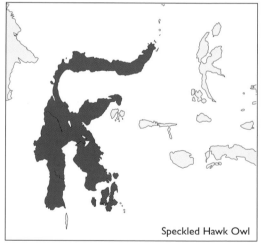

Speckled Hawk Owl

MOVEMENTS Resident.

HABITAT Forest, especially near narrow streams within primary forest; not confined to forest, however, and often occurs in cultivated areas and near habitations. Lowlands to 1,100m; once found in forest at 2,300m.

DESCRIPTION Adult Face blackish-brown, bordered above by whitish stripe from base of bill and forehead over eye to above ear-coverts. Upperparts dull reddish-brown, heavily spotted with white on crown, neck and mantle; secondaries and wing-coverts also with white spots, which more or less form short bars. Flight feathers dark brown with rows of whitish spots; tail brown with narrow pale bars. Large whitish throat patch or half-collar below dusky facial disc; rest of underparts rather variable, often with narrow white-spotted brown band across upper breast, with a whitish oval area below, bordered by another white-spotted brown band (sometimes underside reddish-brown, barred with white, and with whitish centre of lower breast and belly). Tarsi feathered, toes bristled. **Juvenile** Downy chick dark brown. Mesoptile dark brown above, with few small pale spots only on hindneck and mantle, underside mostly with dark brown down covering the abdomen; supercilium mixed dark brown and white; wing and tail feathers as adult. **Bare parts** Iris brown or coffee-brown. Cere and bill greyish-green. Toes greyish-white or grey.

MEASUREMENTS AND WEIGHT Total length 20-26cm. Wing 157-177mm; tail about 76mm. Weight about 200g.

GEOGRAPHICAL VARIATION Monotypic: *Ninox punctulata* (Quoi & Gaimard, 1830).

HABITS Very vocal, calling during the night throughout the year. Often duets, or calls in concert with birds of neighbouring territories.

FOOD Presumably mainly insects.

BREEDING Nestlings found in September.

STATUS AND CONSERVATION Widespread and common within restricted range.

REMARKS The biology of this species needs study.

REFERENCES Boyer & Hume (1991), Bruce (1986), Burton (1992), Coates & Bishop (1997), Coomans de Ruiter (1950), Holmes & Phillips (1996), Stresemann (1940), White & Bruce (1986).

---

197 RUSSET HAWK OWL
Ninox odiosa   Plate 60

Other name: New Britain Hawk Owl

French: Chouette de Nouvelle-Bretagne
German: Neubritannien-Kauz

IDENTIFICATION A small owl (20-23cm), rufous-brown above with pale-speckled head and neck, and with broad chocolate-brown band across upper breast spangled with buffy-white bar-like markings. Wing-coverts dark chocolate-brown with sparse white spots of varying size, wings with some white bars. Facial disc brown, with some white on eyebrows. Large area of white extending from throat to side of neck; lower breast and belly white, heavily spotted with brown or rufous-brown. Eyes golden-yellow to orange. **Similar species** Bismarck Hawk Owl [201], is somewhat larger, with forehead and hindneck unspotted, and with uniformly wide reddish-brown bars from breast to belly (no broad upper-breast band).

VOCALISATIONS Reported to have a long continuous song, a rapidly repeated monosyllable, sometimes lasting three minutes.

DISTRIBUTION Endemic to New Britain, in Bismarck Archipelago.

MOVEMENTS Resident.

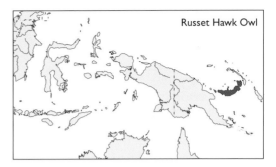

Russet Hawk Owl

HABITAT Occurs in lowland and hill forest, up to at least 1,200m.

DESCRIPTION Adult Facial disc brown, with some white on eyebrows; throat with large white area extending to sides of neck. Upperparts rufous-brown, forehead, crown, hindneck and neck sides with distinct small white or buffy-white spots, mantle and back more or less unspotted; wing-coverts dark chocolate-brown with variably sized sparse whitish spots. Flight feathers with some white bars; tail dark brown with a few white bars. Wide band across upper breast of chocolate-brown mixed with small buffy-white bar-like spots; lower breast and abdomen whitish, heavily spotted with pale rufous-brown, especially on flanks, with sharply defined brown or dark chocolate-brown shaft-streaks. Tarsi feathered, toes bristled. **Juvenile** Greyer, mottled; no clear eyebrows or throat stripe. **Bare parts** Eyes golden-yellow to orange. Cere and bill slaty or greenish-slate, bill with greenish-yellow tip. Toes yellowish-brown. Claws dusky horn with blackish tips.

MEASUREMENTS AND WEIGHT Total length 20-23cm. Wing 170-187mm. Weight of 1 female (Whiteman Mountains) 209g.

GEOGRAPHICAL VARIATION Monotypic: *Ninox odiosa* Sclater, 1877.

HABITS Occurs singly or in pairs. Nocturnal. Frequents the upper middle tier of primary lowland forest. Its presence is usually revealed by its vocalisations at night and by the mobbing of small birds which locate it during the day. Two observations involved a solitary owl and two birds together; in each case, small birds, including fly-catchers, drew attention to the owl by their mobbing activity.

FOOD Mainly insects, and probably occasional small vertebrates. The stomach of one specimen contained remains of long-legged insects. According to local folklore, it also preys on small bats.

BREEDING Unrecorded.

STATUS AND CONSERVATION Widely distributed and not rare. Apparently common in the lowlands.

REMARKS The biology of this species needs study.

REFERENCES Boyer & Hume (1991), Burton (1992), Coates (1985), Dunning (1993), Gilliard & LeCroy (1967), Hartert (1926).

198 MOLUCCAN HAWK OWL
Ninox squamipila   Plate 61

French: Chouette des Moluques
German: Molukkenkauz

IDENTIFICATION A medium-sized owl (25-36cm) without ear-tufts and with tail of 'normal' length. Dark reddish-brown above, with crown darker brown, scapulars with white bars, wings and tail with light rusty barring; breast rufous with dusky brown barring. **Similar species** Ochre-bellied and Speckled Hawk Owls [193, 196] can be excluded, as they occur only on Sulawesi. Barking Owl [184] is far less rufous, being dark brownish-grey above, and white below streaked (not barred) dark brownish-grey. Brown Hawk Owl [188] has a more hawk-like appearance with smaller head, its wings lack Moluccan's white and rusty bars, and its underparts have prominent reddish-brown droplet-like streaks (not bars).

VOCALISATIONS The song of the male is a sequence of croaking double-notes: *kwaor-kwaor, kwaor-kwaor*. The female's song is slightly higer in pitch. A loud *ko-ka-käkäkä* produced in a very aggressive way is described from observations on race *hantu*. The native name is 'kokakä' (onomatopoeic) in Buru. Further calls have been described, some of which may perhaps also be songs. This would suggest that *N. squamipila* possibly involves more than one species.

DISTRIBUTION Endemic to Moluccas and Tanimbar Islands.

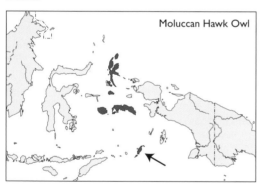

Moluccan Hawk Owl

MOVEMENTS Resident.

HABITAT Forest, groves and thickets. Encountered at sea-level (beach and coast zone), as well as in tropical lowland rain forest and mountain forest at up to 1,400m.

DESCRIPTION *N. s. squamipila* **Adult** Facial disc rufous-brown, becoming paler (rather whitish) towards eyes and base of bill; narrow whitish eyebrows. Upperside dark reddish-brown, darker on head; bar-like white scapular spots. Remiges and tail with light rusty barring. Throat white; breast rufous with dusky barring; abdomen white with rufous/rusty to blackish barring. Tarsi feathered, toes bristled. **Juvenile** Not described. **Bare parts** Iris dark brown (yellow in other races). Cere yellow. Bill light grey with white tip. Toes yellow or golden-yellow. Claws pale horn with darker tips.

MEASUREMENTS AND WEIGHT Total length 25-36cm, males often larger than females. Wing 190-241mm; tail 135-157mm. Weight of 1 nominate specimen 210g.

GEOGRAPHICAL VARIATION We recognise four sub-species.

N. s. hypogramma (G. R. Gray, 1860). Halmahera, Ternate and Bacan. Upperside dull rusty-brown, with cold dusky grey crown; breast reddish-brown with darker barring and some white barring, abdomen barred dark reddish and white. Eyes yellow. Wing 220-241mm.
N. s. hantu (Wallace, 1863). Buru. Upperside as *forbesi*, rather pale, wings less barred; light rusty-ochraceous below with only trace of barring or none. Wing 211-231mm.
N. s. squamipila (Bonaparte, 1850). Seram. See Description. Eyes brown. Wing 190-212mm.
N. s. forbesi Slater, 1883. Tanimbar Islands. All reddish-brown areas of plumage much lighter; crown also pale, not contrastingly darker. Wing 190-212mm.

HABITS Frequently heard in evening and at night, but in daytime very elusive and seldom seen. It seems to hide away by day in dense thickets or densely foliaged trees, in middle canopy. Occurs singly or in pairs.

FOOD Insects: grasshoppers recorded.

BREEDING Unknown.

STATUS AND CONSERVATION Locally rather common, at least formerly (e.g. Stresemann 1914). Said to be present everywhere on Buru.

REMARKS A rather complex species (group), having affinities with *N. theomacha* (New Guinea), *N. variegata* (Bismarck Archipelago) and *N. meeki* (Admiralty Islands). The geographically isolated *N. natalis* is regarded as more closely related to *N. boobook*: it differs from the other forms in some morphological features (plumage, eye colour) and particularly in its fundamentally different voice; it also has a somewhat different diet, and furthermore, its very isolated occurrence, 2,400km from the Moluccas (Buru) and 375km from W Java, makes a direct relationship unlikely.

REFERENCES Boyer & Hume (1991), Burton (1992), Coates & Bishop (1997), Siebers (1930), Stresemann (1914), White & Bruce (1986).

199 CHRISTMAS ISLAND HAWK OWL
Ninox natalis   Plate 61

French: Chouette de l'Ile de Noël
German: Christmaskauz

IDENTIFICATION A medium-sized owl (26-29cm), similar in coloration to race *hantu* of Moluccan Hawk Owl [198], but tarsi feathered to the base of the toes and differs vocally. Tawny-brown or cinnamon-rufous above, nearly unspotted, with tawny-brown face and a line of pale tawny or whitish feathers extending from above eye to base of bill and to some extent to side of bill; below, regular bars of same colour alternating with white, the spaces between about equal in breadth. Tail dark brown, barred rufous. Eyes lemon-yellow. **Similar species** No other owl species occur on Christmas Island. More rufous and paler than Moluccan Hawk Owl.

VOCALISATIONS Has a completely different song compared with that of Moluccan Hawk Owl and related species. Over a century ago, Lister (1888) described it as a low *ow-ow-ow* like the distant barking of a dog. The song of the male is a double note repeated at intervals of several seconds, a clear, somewhat clucking *glu-goog glu-goog...* . During the evening and the first half of the night the birds often call to each other, producing a peculiar sound somewhat resembling the barking of a dog but with a hollow, muffled quality (as though the animal were shut away in a thick-walled room): they usually begin with a low, scarcely audible *chuk-chuk*, which continues at intervals with gathering intensity, finally developing into a full, short bark; this is repeated a number of times, and mutual calling may go on for a considerable period, eventually fading gently as though the whole chorus were moving away, but occasionally the birds stop suddenly. The chinese workers on the island refer to this owl as 'the dog which no man feeds'.

Generally silent by day, even when disturbed, though it may emit a soft, throaty whine if extremely uneasy.

DISTRIBUTION Endemic to Christmas Island, 375km south of W Java.

Christmas Island Hawk Owl

MOVEMENTS Resident.

HABITAT Fairly evenly distributed over the whole island, frequenting dense rain forest and its fringes on both the plateau and the shore terrace; occasionally comes into the open at dusk, and at such times may stray on to verandas of houses or bungalows. Has also been seen hunting over clearings around Flying Fish Cove. Has also been recorded roosting for extended periods above well-used walkways.

DESCRIPTION Adult Forehead and lores with sparsely barbed white feathers with black shafts, except for line of pale tawny or whitish eyebrow feathers from above eye to base of bill; ear-coverts duller brown than nape, with white feather bases; chin feathers pale tawny with white shafts. Upperparts from crown to uppertail-coverts, and lesser upperwing-coverts, uniform reddish-tawny, with few sparse obscure paler spots on lateral nape and tail-coverts; concealed bars of feathers slaty-grey; greater coverts same colour as back, barred chiefly on outer webs with white, bordered by darker brown. Primaries dark brown, barred lighter brown and with paler outer edges. Tail dark brown with ten rufous bands, the contrast between bands and spaces between them becoming more conspicuous on outer feathers. Throat pale rufous; breast, belly and flanks white, somewhat obscurely barred with tawny-brown (bars and intervening spaces about equal in width), and with narrow brown shaft-streaks (individual variation in colour

not connected with sex or age: some birds rather whiter on underparts owing to rufous bars being paler or dark bars narrower, such birds also being faintly spotted on mantle, but there seems no reason for supposing them to be immatures). Tarsi feathered to the base of the toes; toes bristled. **Juvenile** Available material does not suggest a distinct juvenile plumage, including in bare-part colours. **Bare parts** Iris lemon-yellow; eyelids light bluish-grey, edged with black. Cere and bill yellowish-grey to bluish-grey. Toes pale yellow to straw-yellow. Claws horn.

MEASUREMENTS AND WEIGHT Total length 26-29cm, females slightly larger than males. Wing 178-199mm; tail 117-124mm. Weight 130-190g.

GEOGRAPHICAL VARIATION Monotypic: *Ninox natalis* Lister, 1888.

HABITS Rather secretive and shy. Mostly seen perched motionless on trees in jungle or thickets, usually about 3-4.5m from the ground.

FOOD The stomach of the bird collected by Lister (1888) contained feathers and bones. Stomachs examined later (seven) showed that the bird feeds chiefly on large insects, and to a lesser extent on lizards and white-eyes (*Zosterops citrinella natalis*). Insect remains included the elytra of several beetles, and recognisable fragments of a number of Orthoptera, including the large cricket *Gryllacris rufovaria*, the mantid *Hierodula dispar*, *Locusta migratoides* and a *Euconocephalus* species; reptiles were a gecko (*Gymnodactylus marmoratus*) and a skink (*Lygosoma atrocostatum*). Bird remains were found in only two of the seven stomachs examined.

BREEDING Little known. The majority of birds collected appeared to have undergone a full moult between May and August. The breeding season appears to be protracted with records in all quarters of the year. Only three nests recorded, all in hollows of large *Syzygium nervosum*. No nest material used. No details of eggs or clutch size. Incubation apparently by female only. Fledging period 68-77 days (n=2). Young dependent on parents for at least 2¹/₂ months after fledging.

STATUS AND CONSERVATION Estimates have indicated that clearance of primary rainforest after settlement probably reduced the population by about one quarter (Stokes 1988), but in 1933-40 the species was still considered quite common on the plateau and shore terraces. Between 1965 and 1974 the population was estimated at 10-100 pairs, but recent observations suggest that a higher figure is more accurate. Clearance of habitat such as rain forest is the main threat; a number of owls are also killed by cars, but such casualties are unlikely to affect the status of the population. Although the population is small, most of its habitat is now included in the National Park; the species is therefore not under immediate threat.

REMARKS Formerly treated as conspecific with Moluccan Hawk Owl, but distinct song and geographical isolation warrant separation. This opinion has recently been confirmed by DNA analysis.

REFERENCES Andrews (1900), Chasen (1933), Dunning (1993), Gibson-Hill (1947), Higgins (1999), Hill & Lill (1998a,b,c), Lister (1888), Norman *et al.* (1998a), Olsen & Stokes (1989), Phillips *et al.* (1991), Stokes (1988), van Tets (1975).

200 MANUS HAWK OWL
Ninox meeki   Plate 61

French: Chouette de Manus
German: Manuskauz

IDENTIFICATION A small owl (25-31cm) with rufous-brown upperparts, with or without some indistinct paler mottling. Nape distinctly barred; flight feathers and tail with white and dark brown bars. Throat pale tawny-ochraceous or whitish; underparts whitish-buff with rusty-brown streaks. Eyes pale yellow. **Similar species** No other owl of this size and colour pattern occurs on Manus Island.

VOCALISATIONS Gruff, slowly accelerating series of about 10 notes (G. Dutson *in litt.*).

DISTRIBUTION Endemic to Manus Island, in Admiralty Islands.

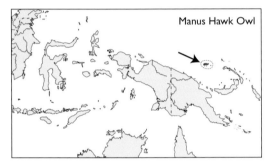

MOVEMENTS Resident.

HABITAT Forest.

DESCRIPTION Adult Crown uniform rufous-brown (female sometimes with some barring); ear-coverts dark brown. Upperparts similar, with distinct ochraceous tinge; distinctly barred nape, scapulars, wing-coverts, rump and tail. Throat pale tawny or whitish; breast whitish-buff with broad tawny or rusty streaks, rest of underparts white with rufous-brown streaks. Tarsi partly feathered and bristled, toes bristled. **Juvenile** Throat almost white, plain brown breast, white bars on wing-coverts heavier, rump mostly barred white, tail-bars wider and paler. **Bare parts** Iris pale yellow. Bill pale slaty-blue, tip pale horn. Toes creamy-yellow. Claws horn with darker tips.

MEASUREMENTS AND WEIGHT Total length 25-31cm. Wing 230-240mm; tail 120-130mm. Weight: no data.

GEOGRAPHICAL VARIATION Monotypic: *Ninox meeki* Rothschild & Hartert, 1914.

HABITS Undescribed.

FOOD Insects.

BREEDING Undescribed.

STATUS AND CONSERVATION Common locally.

REMARKS Very little is known about this owl; research required on all aspects.

REFERENCES Boyer & Hume (1991), Burton (1992), Coates (1985), Hartert (1914).

201 BISMARCK HAWK OWL
Ninox variegata   Plate 61

French: Chouette de Nouvelle Irlande
German: Neu-Irlandkauz

IDENTIFICATION A medium-sized (25-30cm), rather dark owl. Generally dark brown or rufous-brown above, with head often more greyish-brown, scapulars and wing-coverts with white bars or spots. Flight feathers and tail with lighter brown bars. Below, whitish with dark brown or orange-rufous bars. Eyes yellow, sometimes brown. **Similar species** The only other owl species of this size and colour in the E Bismarck Archipelago is Russet Hawk Owl [197], confined to New Britain: that is also chocolate-brown, but has distinct buffy-white spots and speckles on forehead, crown, hindneck and neck sides, a broad chocolate-brown band spangled with buff and white on upper breast, and fewer tail-bars.

VOCALISATIONS A frog-like double croak *kra-kra....kra-kra*; occasional single notes; duets (G. Dutson *in litt.*).

DISTRIBUTION: Endemic to New Hanover and New Ireland, in E Bismarck Archipelago.

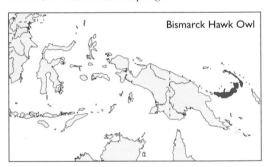

MOVEMENTS Resident.

HABITAT Forest; occurs in the lowland, hills and lower mountains up to 1,000m.

DESCRIPTION *N. v. variegata* **Adult** Facial disc brown. Head usually more greyish-brown than mantle; ear-coverts greyish-brown or brown. Upperparts dark sepia-brown or rufous-brown (two morphs), sometimes more or less faintly spotted with light and dark rufous; scapulars and wing-coverts with white bars and spots. Remiges and rectrices with dark brown and lighter brown bars. Underparts whitish with distinct barring of dark brown (dark morph) or orange-rufous (light morph), breast and sides of breast more uniform brown. Tarsi feathered, toes bristled. **Juvenile** Undescribed. **Bare parts** Iris yellow, sometimes brown. Bill pale yellowish-horn with lighter tip. Toes dull yellow. Claws dusky horn.

MEASUREMENTS AND WEIGHT Total length 25-30cm. Wing 192-224mm; tail about 117mm. Weight: no data.

GEOGRAPHICAL VARIATION Two subspecies.
  N. v. variegata (Quoy & Gaimard, 1830). New Ireland. See Description. Wing 192-210mm.
  N. v. superior Hartert, 1925. New Hanover. Paler brown above, forehead slightly spotted, face paler; distinctly spotted and barred on mantle, back and wings; large

pale throat patch, distinctly barred breast band, light-coloured underparts with fine brown barring on abdomen. Slightly larger race. Wing 211-224mm.

HABITS Little known. Nocturnal.

FOOD Presumably insects.

BREEDING Undescribed.

STATUS AND CONSERVATION Widespread. Fairly common in forest and forest edge.

REMARKS Sometimes also called *Ninox solomonis* (Sharpe, 1876), but this name is superseded by *variegata* (Quoy & Gaimard, 1830) according to rules of taxonomic precedence.

REFERENCES Boyer & Hume (1991), Burton (1992), Coates (1985).

Papuan Hawk Owl, Genus *Uroglaux* Mayr, 1937

Medium-sized owls with a rounded, relatively small head without ear-tufts. Tail relatively long and densely barred. Wings rather short in comparison with long tail, tips less pointed than in *Ninox*. Base of crown feathers whitish. One species on New Guinea and Yapen Island.

202 PAPUAN HAWK OWL
Uroglaux dimorpha   Plate 62

French: Chouette de Nouvelle Guinée
German: Rundflügelkauz

IDENTIFICATION A rather slim, medium-sized owl (30-34 cm), very similar to *Ninox* species, but head relatively smaller and tail longer. Crown and hindneck dark brown with brown to buffy-brown streaks; remainder of upperparts, including wings and tail, densely and evenly barred with blackish-brown and pale brown or rusty-brown. Face whitish, finely streaked black; inner eyebrows to forehead mainly white. Buffy to ochraceous-white below, with bold black streaking from throat to abdomen. Iris yellow. **Similar species** *Ninox* hawk owls are more chunky, distinctly shorter-tailed, and lack heavy barring above. Rufous Owl [182] has profuse but fine barring above and below.

VOCALISATIONS According to a recording by D. Bishop (April 1998), the song is a drawn-out whistle, repeated at intervals of several seconds. The whistle first rises in pitch, then keeps at the same level before finally dropping: *poweeeeho*, with emphasis on the *eeee*.

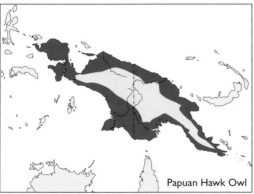

Papuan Hawk Owl

DISTRIBUTION New Guinea and Yapen Island. Probably occurs throughout New Guinea, but so far known only from the northwest (Vogelkop, Geelvink Bay, Weyland Mountains and Yapen Island) and southeast (Collingwood Bay, Milne Bay, Brown River, Port Moresby region and Mount Victoria). Endemic.

MOVEMENTS Resident

HABITAT Frequents rain forest, forest edges and gallery forest in savanna, occurring from near sea-level up to at least 1,500m.

DESCRIPTION Adult Facial disc whitish, finely streaked; eyebrows and forehead mainly white. Crown and hindneck dark brown, streaked with brown to buffy-brown. Upperparts, wings and tail profusely and evenly barred with dark brown and rusty-brown or rufous-brown. Underparts buffy to ochraceous-white, boldly streaked with black from throat to abdomen. Tarsus feathered to toe joint. **Juvenile** Downy fledglings are whitish. **Bare parts** Iris golden-yellow. Bill pale greyish-blue with dark tip. Toes pale yellow. Claws horn.

MEASUREMENTS AND WEIGHT Total length 30-34cm. Wing 200-225mm; tail 145-157mm. Weight: no data.

GEOGRAPHICAL VARIATION Monotypic: *Uroglaux dimorpha* (Salvadori, 1874).

HABITS Little known. Seldom observed.

FOOD Insects, rodents, and birds up to the size of Wompoo Fruit-dove *Ptilinopus magnificus*, about four-fifths of the body weight of the owl.

BREEDING Undescribed.

STATUS AND CONSERVATION Apparently very scarce to rare. Probably threatened by forest destruction.

REMARKS The biology and ecology of this species need study.

REFERENCES Beehler *et al.* (1986), Boyer & Hume (1991), Burton (1992), Coates (1985), Rand & Gilliard (1967).

Laughing Owl, Genus *Sceloglaux* Kaup, 1848

A medium-sized owl with a rounded head without ear-tufts. Wings long, broad and rather rounded. Tail relatively short. General coloration yellowish-brown, streaked dark brown below and above. Tarsi feathered yellowish to rufous-buff, toes bristled. One species, endemic to New Zealand, now probably extinct.

203 LAUGHING OWL
Sceloglaux albifacies   Plate 62

French: Chouette à joue blanche
German: Lachkauz

IDENTIFICATION A medium-sized (35.5-40cm), round-headed owl with yellowish-brown plumage striped with dark brown. White stripes on scapulars, sometimes also hindneck and mantle feathers edged with white rather than yellowish-brown. Facial disc white behind and below eye, greyish towards centre, with brown shaft-lines. Wings and tail with brownish-white bars. Tarsus with yellowish to reddish-buff feathers. Eyes dark orange. **Similar species** Morepork [186] is smaller and darker, with comparatively short tail. Little Owl [176] (introduced in New Zealand) is spotted light and greyish-brown and has sulphur-yellow eyes.

VOCALISATIONS The song has been variously described, and several vocalisations have obviously been mixed together. Species' vernacular name is derived from a loud cry consisting of a series of dismal shrieks, frequently repeated; 'a peculiar barking noise...just like the barking of a young dog'; a melancholy hooting note; also various whistling, chuckling and mewing notes (Buller, from observations of captive birds). Maori name 'Whekau' is onomatopoeic. According to early accounts, vocalisations were heard mainly on dark nights accompanied by rain or drizzle, or before rain.

DISTRIBUTION Was endemic to New Zealand, now extinct (no records since 1930s).

North Island: According to Maori tradition occurred in Urewera, but only two specimens have been collected, both in forest districts (Mt Egmont, about 1856; Wairarapa, about 1868); the second specimen formed the basis of Buller's description of the North Island subspecies. Sight records from Porirua and Te Karaka.

South Island: From early accounts and localities of collected specimens, inhabited mainly the low-rainfall districts of South Island (Nelson, Canterbury and Otago),

but penetrated deeply into the mountains of the central chain, also probably into Fiordland. Specimens obtained from Stewart Island about 1880.

MOVEMENTS Resident.

HABITAT Low-rainfall areas; most of the (early) specimens were obtained from fissures in rock areas. Possibly also in forest districts (North Island).

DESCRIPTION *S. a. albifacies* **Adult** Facial disc with white below and behind eye, becoming more grey with thin, dark brown shaft-lines towards centre; white eyebrows. Rest of plumage yellowish-brown, streaked with brown; white bars on scapulars; sometimes also white-edged rather than yellowish-brown on hindneck and mantle. Wings and tail brown with brownish-white bars Tarsus feathered yellowish to reddish-buff, toes bristled. **Juvenile** Newly hatched chick covered with coarse yellowish-white down. **Bare parts** Iris dark orange. Bill horn-coloured, black at base. Toes flesh-brown or pale yellow. Claws dark brown.

MEASUREMENTS AND WEIGHT Total length 35.5-40cm. Wing about 264mm; tail about 165mm. Weight: no data.

GEOGRAPHICAL VARIATION Two subspecies.
  S. a. albifacies (G. R. Gray, 1844). South Island and Stewart Island. See Description. Wing about 264mm; tail 165mm.
  S. a. rufifacies Buller, 1904. North Island. Plumage about the same as nominate, but face more rufous-washed, yellowish-brown upperparts (back and wings) more dark rufous-brown and underparts with more rufous tinge.

HABITS From observations of captive birds, this species fed much on the ground.

FOOD Pellets indicate that diet included beetles, rats and mice; captives also fed on these items, and readily took raw meat and lizards.

BREEDING Bred September-October. Nest a cavity among rocks, in rock fissure, lined with dry grass. Laid 2 roundish white eggs (44-51 x 38-43mm). Bred readily in captivity, with observations indicating that incubation was carried out solely by the female; incubation 25 days, male feeding female on nest.

STATUS AND CONSERVATION Extinct. When the first European settlers arrived in New Zealand in 1840, and during the early decades of colonisation, this owl was plentiful. By 1880, however, it had became extremely rare; there is no fully substantiated record since July 1914 (one individual found at Blue Cliffs, south Canterbury), but occasionally claimed, localities including south Canterbury (Hakataramea and adjacent districts), Wanaka and Te Anau. Egg fragments were found in Canterbury in 1960. Extinction appears to have coincided with European settlement (persecution, land-use changes) and the introduction of predators (cats, dogs, etc).

REMARKS The biology of this extinct species is poorly known.

REFERENCES Buller (1882, 1888), Burton (1992), Falla *et al.* (1966, 1993), Robertson (1985).

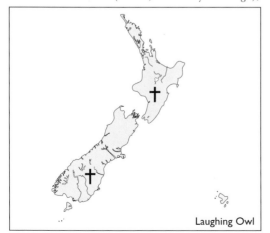

Laughing Owl

Northern Hawk Owl, Genus *Surnia* Duméril, 1806

A medium-sized dark greyish, white-spotted owl with a very long, graduated tail. Wings long and pointed, in flight similar to Common Kestrel *Falco tinnunculus*. Head rounded, without ear-tufts. Facial disc whitish, distinctly rimmed black; underparts whitish, densely barred dark grey-brown. Eyes yellow; tarsi and toes feathered. Largely diurnal. One species, distributed in northern Holarctic.

204 NORTHERN HAWK OWL
Surnia ulula   Plate 62

French: Chouette épervière
German: Sperbereule

IDENTIFICATION A medium-sized owl (36-41cm) lacking ear-tufts, with white-spotted dark grey upperparts. Facial disc whitish, broadly rimmed black; nape with indistinct occipital face. Tail long and graduated, wings long and pointed. Whitish below, rather densely barred dusky. Tarsi and toes feathered. Eyes light yellow. Largely diurnal. Flight kestrel-like, often hovers; perches in exposed sites. **Similar species** Tengmalm's Owl [178] is smaller, with relatively short tail, underparts not boldly barred but blotched and mottled, and is strictly nocturnal. Northern Saw-whet Owl [179] is much smaller and short-tailed, with, facial disc lacking broad black rim, and underparts diffusely streaked brown.

VOCALISATIONS The song of the male is a rapid, melodious, purring trill of 3-4 seconds' duration, resembling song of some American screech owls but lower in pitch: *kuhurrrrrrrrrrrr...*, about 15 notes per second. It begins softly, rises slightly in pitch and increases to a vibrating trill, breaking off abruptly. Such phrases are repeated at intervals of several seconds. The female utters a similar but higher-pitched, less clear song. Both sexes give a piercing *kiiiiirrl* and a kestrel-like *kwikikikikkik* when excited; screeching calls are also uttered. A soft *uhg* or *uih* is given as contact between partners. Young beg with a drawn-out *chchchiep*.

DISTRIBUTION Boreal zones of Eurasia, from Norway, Sweden and Finland east through Siberia to Kamchatka, Sakhalin and N China, in C Asia south to Tien Shan; boreal North America, from Alaska east to Labrador.

MOVEMENTS Moves widely within its area of distribution, breeding where food is abundant. In some autumns, invasions occur in areas south of normal range, with several records from W and C Europe. Largest distance covered by a ringed bird was 1,800km, from Finland to C Russia.

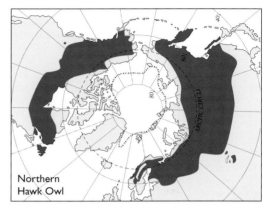

Northern Hawk Owl

HABITAT Rather open boreal coniferous forest with clearings and moors in lowlands or mountains. Hunts in semi-open country with scattered trees or groups of trees.

DESCRIPTION *S. u. ulula* Adult Facial disc whitish, broadly rimmed blackish at sides; eyebrows white. Upperparts dark grey to dusky greyish-brown, crown densely spotted whitish, nape with indistinct occipital face; mantle and back dusky grey with some whitish dots; scapulars mainly white, forming rather broad white band across shoulder. Flight feathers dark grey-brown with rows of white spots. Tail long and graduated, dark greyish-brown with several narrow whitish bars. Underparts whitish, barred with greyish-brown. Tarsi and toes feathered. **Juvenile** Downy chick whitish. Mesoptile with blackish facial disc with whitish lower part; crown and underparts pale grey, mottled darker; back similar to adult. When fledged, facial disc becomes whitish and dark barring of underparts begins to appear. **Bare parts** Eyes pale yellow; in juvenile, golden-yellow. Cere greyish-brown. Bill pale yellowish-green. Soles of toes dirty yellow. Claws dark brown with blackish tips.

MEASUREMENTS AND WEIGHT Total length 36-41cm. Wing 220-252mm; tail 164-203mm. Weight of males 273-326g (median 299g), of females 306-392g (median 345g).

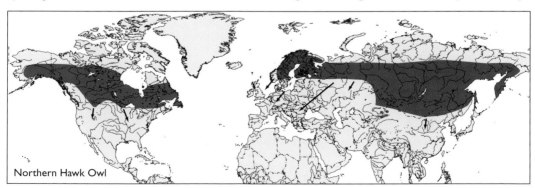

Northern Hawk Owl

GEOGRAPHICAL VARIATION Three subspecies.

S. u. ulula (Linnaeus, 1758). From Scandinavia through Siberia to Kamchatka, Sakhalin and N China. See Description. Wing of males 220-244mm, of females 225-250mm.

S. u. tianschanica Smallbones, 1906. Tien Shan. Dark areas more blackish, white purer than in nominate. Wing 235-252mm.

S. u. caparoch (Müller, 1776). Alaska to Labrador. Darker than nominate; scapulars less pronouncedly whitish; underparts more boldly and densely barred, sometimes with buffy tint on belly; tail with narrower whitish bars, mostly fewer in number than in nominate. Wing 226-246mm.

HABITS Not social; seen mostly singly or in pairs. Not shy. Active by day and night. Often perches in exposed sites, such as top of a dead vertical branch or treetop, on post, etc; flicks tail when excited. Flies in straight line with rapid wingbeats and open-winged glides; hovers over open places.

FOOD Small mammals (above all lemmings and other voles) make up the major part of its diet; also takes small birds, frogs and even fish. Weight of prey normally below 70g.

BREEDING Territorial. Monogamous during breeding season. Male advertises potential nest sites, female selects one. Cavities on top of broken trunks, natural tree holes, abandoned holes of large woodpeckers (e.g. Black Woodpecker *Dryocopus martius* in Europe) are used for breeding; also accepts nestboxes, and occasionally uses stick nests of larger birds; no nesting material is added. Laying occurs normally in April and first half of May. The 5-13 pure white eggs (36-44 x 29-34.4mm) are laid at intervals of about 2 days. Female incubates alone for 25-30 days, while fed by her mate, and broods chicks for 13-18 days. Young leave the nest at 23-30 days, not yet capable of flight; they are fed by both parents and at 5-6 weeks (about mid June) they fly well, becoming independent towards the end of August. Sexual maturity is reached towards the end of the first year.

STATUS AND CONSERVATION Uncertain. Species depends very much on the abundance of rodents. May be affected by the use of pesticides. Locally, the population may be increased by provision of nestboxes.

REMARKS Although a rather well-known owl, much of its biology merits further study.

REFERENCES Bezzel (1985), Boyer & Hume (1991), Burton (1992), Dementiev & Gladkov (1951), Dunning (1993), Eck & Busse (1973), Glutz & Bauer (1980), Hardy *et al.* (1989), Voous (1988).

Fearful Owl, Genus *Nesasio* Peters, 1937

Medium-sized owls with rounded head without ear-tufts. Bill and talons very powerful. General coloration ochraceous-brown, boldly streaked dusky. Wings and rather short tail barred ochraceous and dusky. Facial disc with blackish area around eyes; white eyebrows prominent. Eyes yellow. Endemic to Solomon Islands in the S Pacific. One species.

205 FEARFUL OWL
Nesasio solomonensis　　　　Plate 63

French: Chouette des Solomones
German: Salomonenkauz

IDENTIFICATION A medium-sized owl (30-38 cm) with very powerful bill, feet and claws. Face rufous, with white eyebrows, lores, chin and throat; upperparts densely mottled with rufous and dark brown; underparts deep ochre with narrow blackish shaft-streaks. Eyes yellow. **Similar species** Solomon Hawk Owl [193] is smaller (25-30cm), and much more slender and hawk-like, also rufous-brown above with numerous spots and bars, dark-spotted wings, and far less striped or barred below.

VOCALISATIONS Local inhabitants report that it utters a single drawn-out note with a ghostly, mournful, human quality, rising in pitch at the end.

DISTRIBUTION Bougainville and Solomon Islands (Choiseul and Santa Isabel).

MOVEMENTS Resident.

HABITAT Frequents primary and tall secondary lowland forest and hill forest. Found in forest over a range of altitudes, mostly in lowlands and hills to about 800m, on Santa Isabel, where large numbers of prey occurred.

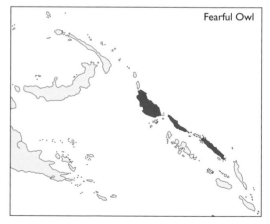

Fearful Owl

DESCRIPTION Adult Facial disc dusky around eyes, becoming rufous towards rim; rim around disc rather prominent; eyebrows, lores, chin and throat white. Upperparts and crown densely mottled and streaked rufous and dark brown. Flight and tail feathers barred light and dark. Underparts deep ochre with narrow dark brown to blackish shaft-streaks. Tarsi feathered tawny, toes bristled. **Juvenile** Undescribed. **Bare parts** Iris yellow. Cere dark grey. Bill blackish, very powerful. Toes ashy-grey. Claws horn with darker tips (very powerful).

MEASUREMENTS AND WEIGHT Total length 30-38cm. Wing about 300mm; tail about 170mm. Weight: no data.

GEOGRAPHICAL VARIATION Monotypic: *Nesasio solomonensis* (Hartert, 1901).

HABITS Little known.

FOOD According to local people, it feeds mainly on phalangers (*Phalanger orientalis*) or possums, later confirmed by research.

BREEDING Nests found high up in a huge tree on the edge of gardens, either in a hole in the trunk or in a crack

or hole in a limb; sometimes on epiphytes on large fig trees.

STATUS AND CONSERVATION Apparently rare and local. May be threatened by forest destruction.

REMARKS Remarkably, this species and Laughing Owl [203] are very similar in general appearance of plumage, in strong feet and bill and to some extent also in voice. Both are S Pacific island species. Whether the similarities are due to close relationship or convergence is uncertain.

REFERENCES Boyer & Hume (1991), Burton (1992), Coates (1985), Webb (1992).

Eared Owls and Allies, Genus *Asio* Brisson, 1760

Medium-sized owls with long wings, well-developed facial disc and mostly prominent, erectile ear-tufts. In two species, the ear-tufts are short (sometimes difficult to see) and placed near centre of forehead. Plumage boldly streaked below, often with cross-bars. Tarsi feathered; toes more or less feathered with short plumes. Seven species (one worldwide, one Holarctic, two Neotropical, three African).

206 STYGIAN OWL
Asio stygius   Plate 63

French: Hibou obscur
German: Styx-Eule
Spanish: Buho-cornudo oscuro, Lechuzón negruzco
Portuguese: Mocho-diabo

IDENTIFICATION A medium-sized (38-46cm), dusky owl with prominent, erectile ear-tufts. Dusky sooty-brown above, more or less spotted light on back and mantle, with short whitish eyebrows. Densely spotted dusky brown on upper chest; rest of underparts streaked dark, with distinct cross-bars. Wings very long, tail relatively short. Eyes yellow. Flies with rather slow wingbeats and glides. **Similar species** Great Horned Owl [94] is larger, with much more powerful talons, and is barred below. Striped Owl [210] is boldly streaked below and has dark brown eyes. Short-eared Owl [211] is smaller, streaked below, and has tiny ear-tufts and a blackish area around yellow eyes.

VOCALISATIONS The song of the male is a deep *whuof* with a downward inflection, repeated at intervals of several seconds. Female sometimes utters a higher-pitched song, often gives a cat-like *miah* in response to the male's song. Both sexes utter scratchy a *whag-whag-whag* when excited. A high-pitched, screaming *cheet* is uttered by female and fledged young when begging for food.

DISTRIBUTION From NW Mexico to Central America and the Caribbean, and South America patchily from Colombia and Ecuador to N and NE Argentina (Misiones) and SE Brazil.

MOVEMENTS Resident.

HABITAT Humid to semi-arid forest in montane areas, from about 700m up to 3,000m above sea-level, locally perhaps even higher if trees are present; also semi-open landscapes with groups of trees and bushes. Normally absent from lowlands, but locally at lower elevations. We found these owls in montane cloud forest of N Argentina (Salta) at about 1,500m above sea-level, living sympatrically

with Barn Owl, Montane Forest Screech Owl, Yungas Pygmy Owl and Buff-fronted Owl [1, 71, 157, 181]; otherwise, we heard several singing males in the Sierra de Misiones (NE Argentina) in semi-open secondary forest at about 700m, in the same area as Tropical and Long-tufted Screech Owls [68, 79], Rusty-barred Owl [139], Ferruginous Pygmy Owl [160] and, again, Buff-fronted Owl.

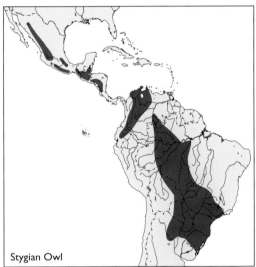

Stygian Owl

DESCRIPTION *A. s. stygius* **Adult** Facial disc brown, with finely speckled lateral rim; eyebrows short, whitish; ear-tufts long and prominent. Upperparts dark sooty-brown, forehead and crown mottled light, forehead appearing rather pale, contrasting with brown face; mantle and back nearly plain, feathers indistinctly edged light; outer webs of scapulars with faint light spots. Primaries nearly plain dark brown with rows of indistinct lighter spots, secondaries barred light and dark. Tail dark sooty-brown with narrow, indistinct lighter bars. Underparts pale buffy, heavily marked dusky on upper breast, rest with dark shaft-

423

streaks and cross-bars (herringbone pattern). Tarsi feathered, toes partly feathered with short plumes. **Juvenile** Downy chick whitish. Mesoptile pale buff, diffusely barred greyish; facial disc and wings sooty-black. **Bare parts** Eyes yellow to orange-yellow. Cere greyish-brown. Bill blackish. Toes brownish-flesh. Claws dark horn with blackish tips.

MEASUREMENTS AND WEIGHT Total length 38-46 cm. Wing 292-349mm; tail about 190mm. Weight about 675g, females heavier than males.

GEOGRAPHICAL VARIATION We recognise three subspecies, regarding three other taxa as synonyms.

A. s. stygius (Wagler, 1832). From Colombia, Venezuela and Ecuador through Peru, Bolivia and C Brazil to N Argentina and SE Brazil. See Description. (We regard *barberoi* as a synonym.)

A. s. robustus Kelso, 1934. Mexico, and locally in Central America to Nicaragua and Belize. Similar in size to nominate. Lighter, greyer above, scapulars and wing-coverts more distinctly spotted whitish; tail with 3-4 more distinct pale bars; underparts paler than nominate. (We include the form *lambi* as a synonym.)

A. s. siguapa (D'Orbigny, 1839). Cuba, Isle of Pines, Gonave, Hispaniola. Paler above and below (more whitish ground coloration) than nominate. Wing 295-305mm; tail about 157mm. (We regard *noctipetens* as a synonym.)

HABITS Strictly nocturnal. Roosts during daytime in dense foliage or on a branch covered with epiphytes, often close to the trunk. When alarmed, becomes very slim in erect posture, with ear-tufts erected vertically; when relaxed, ear-tufts are held flat and therefore nearly invisible. Territorial; male claims territory by singing from tree canopy. Flies with rather slow, rowing wingbeats, sometimes glides over some distance.

FOOD Small mammals (including bats), and birds up to the size of doves; other small vertebrates and insects. The prey is normally caught from a perch; bats are hawked on the wing.

BREEDING Poorly known. During courtship, male and female duet near nesting site; we tape-recorded a duetting pair in early September in montane forest near Salta (N Argentina). Male claps wings together below body in display flight. Uses abandoned stick nests of larger birds in trees; sometimes nests on the ground in a shallow depression. Normally lays 2 white eggs; female incubates alone, and young are fed by both parents.

STATUS AND CONSERVATION Uncertain. Probably threatened by forest destruction in some areas. Locally, perhaps less rare than it appears, as the owl is difficult to spot at night and its vocal activity is more frequent only in early breeding season.

REMARKS This species' biology, distribution and geographical variation are poorly known and need study.

REFERENCES Belton (1984), Boyer & Hume (1991), Burton (1992), Eck & Busse (1973), Fjeldså & Krabbe (1990), Hardy *et al.* (1989), Hilty & Brown (1986), Howell & Webb (1995), König (unpublished), Sick (1985).

207 LONG-EARED OWL
Asio otus   Plate 63

Other name: Common Long-eared Owl

French: Hibou moyen-duc
German: Waldohreule
Spanish: Buho chico

IDENTIFICATION A medium-sized (35-40cm), rather slim, long-winged owl with prominent erectile ear-tufts. Facial disc well developed, rimmed dusky. General coloration ochraceous-tawny with greyish wash, streaked and spotted blackish, with whitish on scapulars; pale ochraceous-tawny below, with dusky streaks on upper breast, below which heavily marked with herringbone-like pattern (dusky shaft-streaks with cross-bars). Bill blackish; eyes yellowish-orange to orange-red; tarsi and toes feathered. **Similar species** Stygian Owl [206] is darker and more boldly patterned below, with toes partly bare. Striped Owl [210] is streaked below and has dark brown eyes. Tawny Owl [130] has a broad, rounded head lacking ear-tufts, eyes blackish-brown, wings shorter and more rounded. Short-eared Owl [211] has very short ear-tufts and is boldly streaked below, with yellow eyes surrounded by blackish. Eurasian Eagle Owl [96] is much larger, with very powerful talons, and has crown and back largely blackish. Asian fish owls [110-113] have 'tousled' ear-tufts, are generally larger and have bare tarsi and toes (except the very large Blakiston's Fish Owl [112], which has feathered tarsi). Great Horned Owl [94] is larger and heavier, with yellow eyes and barred underparts. Scops and screech owls (genus *Otus*) are much smaller and have rather short ear-tufts. Marsh Owl [212] is generally brown, with fine mottling or barring below, and has brown eyes and tiny ear-tufts.

VOCALISATIONS The song of the male is a deep *whoop*, repeated at intervals of several seconds; normally starts with some hoots at slightly lower pitch before reaching full volume and quality. On calm nights, this song may be heard over a distance of 1-2km. Female gives a weak, much higher-pitched and less clear song with a 'nasal' character, resembling the sound produced with a toy trumpet, audible only at rather close range (less than 100m); it is uttered in duet with the male during courtship, also from the nest once selected and around the beginning of incubation (probably to call its mate to bring food). Both sexes utter cat-like, somewhat hoarse *jaiow* notes. When disturbed near nest with chicks or near fledged young, male and female give series of 'tinny' notes, *watt-watt-watt-watt*. During the period of courtship male flies around and flaps its wings below body, producing a clapping sound. As with many owls, both sexes and young utter hissing sounds and bill-snapping. Fledged young call with high-pitched, drawn-out *feeh* notes.

DISTRIBUTION Eurasia from Iberian Peninsula and the British Isles south to the Azores, Canary Islands and North Africa (Morocco to Tunisia), and east from Scandinavia to Siberia, Japan and Korea, and from Mediterranean islands to Asia Minor, the Middle East, Kashmir and C China. Widely distributed in North America, south to N Mexico.

MOVEMENTS Northern populations largely migratory, wandering south in autumn. Some birds (normally young) from C Europe may migrate southwest up to more than

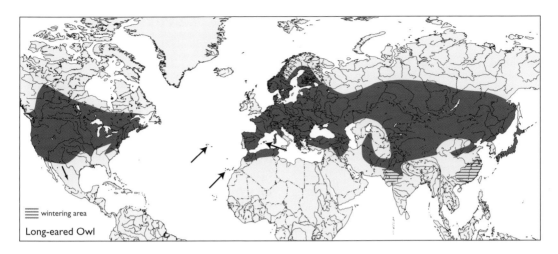

≡ wintering area

Long-eared Owl

2,000km southwest; C European adults are less migratory, merely wandering, often in small groups, roosting together during daytime. Birds from C Asia winter south to Egypt (Nile valley), Pakistan, N India and S China. In North America, migrates to Florida (infrequently), Georgia and N and S Mexico.

HABITAT Rather open landscapes with groups of trees, hedges or small woods, pastureland with rows of trees and bushes, forest (deciduous, mixed or coniferous) with clearings, forest edges, semi-open taiga forest, swampy areas with willows, alders and poplars, extensively managed orchards with old fruit trees, parks, cemeteries with trees and bushes, even gardens and timbered areas in villages and towns. From sea-level to near timberline.

DESCRIPTION *A. o. otus* **Adult** Facial disc pale ochraceous-tawny, rimmed blackish; short eyebrows whitish; erectile ear-tufts prominent, mainly blackish-brown with tawny edges. Upperparts ochraceous-tawny, finely peppered with dusky spots and blackish streaks on greyish 'veil'; crown finely mottled dusky, nape and hindeck with dusky shaft-streaks; outer webs of scapulars whitish, forming row across shoulder. Primaries basally uniform ochraceous-tawny, distally barred light and dark; secondaries barred ochraceous and dusky. Tail ochraceous-tawny with greyish wash, with 6-8 very narrow dark bars. Underparts pale ochraceous, foreneck and upper breast with blackish-brown streaks, rest becoming paler towards belly and marked with dusky shaft-streaks and narrow cross-bars (herringbone-like pattern); underwing with distinct barring, and with dark comma-like mark at wrist (Short-eared Owl has no barring on undersecondaries). Tarsi and toes feathered. **Juvenile** Downy chick whitish with pink skin. Mesoptile fluffy, greyish- to brownish-white, diffusely barred dusky; flight and tail feathers similar to adult, but ear-tufts not fully developed. **Bare parts** Eyes orange to yellowish-orange, occasionally chrome-yellow. Cere brownish-flesh. Bill grey. Toes feathered. Claws blackish-grey.

MEASUREMENTS AND WEIGHT Total length 35-40cm. Wing 257-320mm; tail 132-165mm. Weight 178-370g, females heavier than males.

GEOGRAPHICAL VARIATION Shows some individual variation in coloration, with some darker and others paler,

especially on underparts. We distinguish three subspecies.

A. o. otus (Linnaeus, 1758). Azores, NW Africa, Iberian Peninsula and British Isles east through C Asia to Sakhalin, Japan and N China; some populations winter Egypt, Pakistan, N India and S China. See Description. Wing 265-313mm.

A. o. canariensis Madarasz, 1901. Canary Islands. Smaller and darker than nominate. Eyes mostly reddish-orange. Wing 257-284mm.

A. o. wilsonianus (Lesson, 1830). North America from British Columbia south to California and east to Newfoundland and North Carolina; winters partly in Georgia (less frequently Florida), Texas and Mexico. Facial disc rufous, eyes yellow; markings on underparts more prominent, with more distinct cross-bars than nominate. Wing 284-305mm. (We include *tuftsi* from W North America as a synonym.)

HABITS Nocturnal. Activity normally begins at dusk. During daytime roosts in an upright position on a branch, often close to the trunk, sometimes within dense foliage, in winter often several quite close together in same tree or in a group of trees (e.g. in parks, large gardens or cemeteries). When approached, it 'freezes' with body stiffly upright, eyes closed to a narrow slit and ear-tufts erect; if approached closer, alternately opens and closes eyes, finally lowering ear-tufts, fluffing body plumage and flying to another roost. Often fair numbers of pellets and droppings present beneath well-used day roosts. When flying by day, it is often mobbed by diurnal birds, such as corvids and other birds of prey. Singing normally starts at dusk on calm evenings, continuing throughout the night; clear, windless moonlit nights are preferred. The song is normally delivered from a perch, mostly at medium height in trees or from the upper half near canopy, sometimes on the wing. May be stimulated or attracted by playback or imitation of song. Can be aggressive near nest with young; in defence, ruffles up the plumage and partly spreads the half-opened wings, trampling from one foot to the other, hissing and bill-snapping, and in this posture looks rather large. The flight is erratic, with slow, rowing wingbeats; sometimes glides on open wings.

FOOD Mostly small mammals (e.g. rodents, especially voles); also takes birds up to the size of Moorhen *Gallinula chloropus*, other small vertebrates and insects. Normally

425

hunts along hedges, forest edges or over open country by flying low, dashing suddenly on to prey on the ground or among foliage; sometimes hunts from a perch.

BREEDING Monogamous during breeding season. Territorial, but several pairs may nest rather close together (minimum distances between nests 50m and 150m). When food is abundant, about 10-12 pairs may nest within area of 100km². Male claims territory by singing and by display flights with wing-clapping. Female inspects potential nesting sites and duets with its mate; perched on a chosen nest, she sings to contact male; later, vocal activity is confined to weak calls heard only at short range. Normally breeds in stick nests of larger birds (crows *Corvus*, magpies *Pica*, raptors, herons *Ardea*, etc), occasionally in a rather open hollow in a rotten stump; artificial nesting platforms made of twigs are accepted. The nest is normally about 5-30m above ground, and can sometimes be so small that the bird's tail and head may be visible from below. Locally, a shallow depression on the ground at the base of a tree or under a bush is used for breeding.

Laying normally occurs in March/April. Generally lays 4-5 (sometimes more if food very abundant) pure white eggs (median 40.1 x 32.8mm, weight about 23g), at 2-day intervals, directly on to the bottom of the nest; no material is added. Incubation starts with the first egg and takes about 27-28 days per egg; female alone incubates, being fed by her mate, who brings food to the nest. The young hatch at 2-day intervals, their eyes opening at 5-7 days old. They are brooded by the female for about 2 weeks, the male roosting by day near the nest, watching it; female alone feeds chicks. Young leave the nest when about 20-25 days old, flightless, and climb around in the nest tree, although quite often they fall to the ground (if found, they should left alone or, if in the open, placed in a dense bush); they show a remarkable ability to climb up into trees or bushes, using their claws and bill and beating rapidly with their wings. At dusk they indicate their position with high-pitched calls. At about 35 days they are fully able to fly and follow their parents, which feed them for about 2 months after fledging; each night the young may be heard calling within the territory, their parents occasionally uttering the *watt-watt-...* series. Normally one clutch per year; occasionally double-brooded in years of vole abundance. In the wild, may reach 27-28 years of age.

STATUS AND CONSERVATION Rather common and widespread in many regions; density of populations depends on availability of food. Local threats include pesticides and persecution (e.g. shooting into stick nests occupied by owls in order to kill supposed breeding crows or magpies). Many are killed by road traffic. Breeding can be promoted by providing artificial platforms of twigs in bushes or trees. In severe winters, the owls' food supply can be augmented by setting up special feeding stations near day roosts, by offering live mice in a large trough with some straw, or by placing dead mice or 1-day-old domestic chicks on a feeding table.

REMARKS Although it is one of the commonest owls in C Europe and rather well studied, the taxonomy of this widely distributed species is not yet clear. In particular, geographical variation and the relationship of the Old and New World taxa require study.

REFERENCES Ali & Ripley (1969), Armstrong (1958), Bezzel (1985), Boyer & Hume (1991), Burton (1992),

Cramp (1985), Dementiev & Gladkov (1951), Eck & Busse (1973), Glutz & Bauer (1980), Hardy *et al.* (1989), Howell & Webb (1995), König (1967 and unpublished), Mikkola (1983), Saurola (1997), Voous (1988), Wendland (1957, 1958).

208 ABYSSINIAN LONG-EARED OWL
Asio abyssinicus   Plate 63

French: Moyen-duc d'Abyssinie
German: Äethiopien-Waldohreule

IDENTIFICATION A medium-sized (42-44cm), long-winged owl with prominent dark ear-tufts placed near centre of forehead, and rich tawny-brown facial disc. Dark brown above, mottled and spotted light and dark, without distinct stripe across shoulder; upper breast mottled tawny and dark brown, rest of underparts with irregular whitish and brown barring and brown shaft-streaks. Eyes orange-yellow; tarsi and toes feathered. **Similar species** Long-eared Owl [207] is smaller, lighter and slimmer, has lighter facial disc and is less boldly marked below, tail is more narrowly barred, and scapulars have whitish on outer webs; also differs vocally. Pharaoh and Cape Eagle Owls [97, 99] are larger, with much more powerful talons, and ear-tufts set more widely apart. Vermiculated Eagle Owl [102] is larger, densely vermiculated below, and has brown eyes. Spotted Eagle Owl [101] is also larger, with yellow eyes, and has dense barring below.

VOCALISATIONS Little known. The song of the male is a drawn-out, disyllabic *ooh-woomm*, rising slightly in pitch; it is repeated at intervals of several seconds.

DISTRIBUTION Ethiopian Highlands, Mt Kenya, Ruwenzori Mountains, south to E Zaïre (Mt Kabobo).

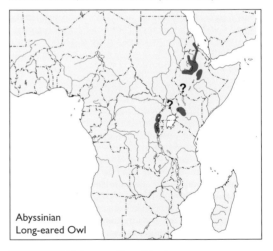

Abyssinian Long-eared Owl

MOVEMENTS Apparently resident.

HABITAT Giant heath, forested areas in highlands, humid forested valleys and gorges in high mountains up to about 2,800m and 3,900m above sea-level.

DESCRIPTION *A. a. abyssinicus* Adult Facial disc tawny-brown, rimmed dusky; ear-tufts (shorter than on Long-eared Owl) dark, set rather close to centre of forehead. Upperparts more dark golden-brown than Long-eared, mottled tawny, whitish parts of scapulars less prominent. Flight feathers distinctly barred light and dark. Tail greyish-brown, with dark bars broader than on Long-eared. Underparts mottled and streaked tawny and dark brown on upper breast; remainder tawny with distinct shaft-streaks and cross-bars, dividing incomplete, relatively broad whitish bars into blocks, giving 'chequered' effect. Tarsi and toes feathered. **Juvenile** Undescribed, but probably similar to Long-eared Owl. **Bare parts** Eyes orange-yellow. Cere greyish-brown. Bill blackish. Claws blackish-horn.

MEASUREMENTS AND WEIGHT Total length 42-44cm. Wing 347-360mm; tail 182-185mm. Weight unknown, but probably heavier than Long-eared Owl.

GEOGRAPHICAL VARIATION We distinguish two subspecies.
>   *A. a. abyssinicus* (Guérin-Méneville, 1843). Highlands of Ethiopia. See Description.
>   *A. a. graueri* Sassi, 1912. Mt Kenya, Ruwenzoris, south to E Zaire (Mt Kabobo). Smaller and greyer than nominate; markings more blackish. Wing 309-342mm.

HABITS Nocturnal. Roosts during daytime mostly on a branch close to the trunk; locally, in groves of giant heath, sometimes several birds together.

FOOD Largely small mammals, but also other small vertebrates and insects. Hunts much from the wing; sometimes hovers or hunts from a perch.

BREEDING Territorial. Male claims territory by singing. Normally breeds in stick nests of larger birds. Breeding biology probably similar to that of Long-eared Owl.

STATUS AND CONSERVATION Uncertain. Probably rare and locally endangered by habitat destruction or by the use of pesticides.

REMARKS Has been considered a race of Long-eared Owl, but has allopatric distribution and differs vocally, as well as biometrically. We consider it a full species.

REFERENCES Boyer & Hume (1991), Burton (1992), Dementiev & Gladkov (1951), Eck & Busse (1973), Fry *et al.* (1988), Voous (1988), Zimmerman *et al.* (1996).

---

209 MADAGASCAR LONG-EARED OWL
Asio madagascariensis Plate 63

French: Hibou de Madagascar
German: Madagaskar-Waldohreule

IDENTIFICATION A medium-sized owl (40-50cm) owl with prominent, long and thick ear-tufts set more widely apart than on other 'long-eared owls'. Female distinctly larger than male. Talons and blackish bill powerful. Mottled and spotted dark and yellowish-brown above; below, tan with heavy dusky streaking on upper breast, rest of underparts with prominent dark shaft-streaks and some cross-bars. Tarsi and toes feathered; eyes orange. **Similar species** In Madagascar, this is the only medium-sized owl with prominent ear-tufts and orange eyes.

VOCALISATIONS Poorly known. A loud, lilting *uluh*, uttered at intervals, seems to be the male's song. A sequence of barking, somewhat nasal calls, *wangwan-gwangwang...*, may express aggression. Fledged young utter upward-inflected, screeching calls, similar to begging-calls of young Long-eared Owls [207] but with hoarse quality: *chrreeh.*

DISTRIBUTION Endemic to Madagascar, where it occurs in the eastern parts.

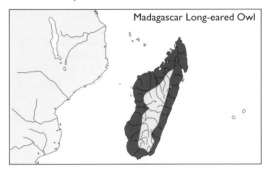

Madagascar Long-eared Owl

MOVEMENTS Resident.

HABITAT Evergreen rain forest, gallery forest and dry deciduous forest, from sea-level to about 1,800m.

DESCRIPTION Adult Facial disc yellowish-brown, shading into dark brown to blackish-brown around eyes; rim around disc dusky. Eyebrows short, slightly lighter than surrounding plumage; ear-tufts large and graduated (appearing rather thick or bushy), set wider apart than on other long-eared owls. Forehead and crown dark brown, flecked with tan. Upperparts dark brown with orange-buff and yellowish-brown markings, mantle and back with dusky shaft-streaks; scapulars with dark shaft-streaks, few cross-bars and a pale edge on outer webs. Flight feathers distinctly barred light and dusky; tail light brown with relatively broad dusky bars. Underparts yellowish-brown with whitish throat (visible only when calling); foreneck and upper breast broadly streaked dark brown, rest of underparts sparsely marked with prominent dusky shaft-streaks and some cross-bars; undertail-coverts plain tan. Tarsi feathered yellowish-brown, toes nearly totally covered with short tan plumes. **Juvenile** Downy chick white. Mesoptile whitish, with dark brown, almost blackish facial disc. **Bare parts** Eyes orange. Cere greyish-brown. Bill sooty-blackish with lighter tip. Bare parts of toes yellowish-brown. Claws dusky horn.

MEASUREMENTS AND WEIGHT Total length of males around 40cm, of females around 50cm. Wing of males 260-310mm, of females 274-340mm; tail 122-195mm. Weight unknown.

GEOGRAPHICAL VARIATION Monotypic: *Asio madagascariensis* (Smith, 1834).

HABITS Poorly known. Strictly nocturnal. Roosts during daytime in dense foliage. Secretive forest species.

FOOD Unknown. Probably small vertebrates (powerful bill and talons suggest perhaps larger prey than taken by other long-eared owls), and insects.

BREEDING Virtually unknown. Nesting has been observed between August and October.

STATUS AND CONSERVATION Apparently rare. Probably threatened by forest destruction and human persecution; as all owls, is regarded by villagers as a bird of ill omen.

REMARKS Doubtless a separate species, and not a race of Long-eared Owl. Its ecology and biology are rather unknown and need study, above all with regard to its conservation; its relationship to other taxa of the genus *Asio* also requires clarification.

REFERENCES Boyer & Hume (1991), Burton (1992), Eck & Busse (1973), Langrand (1990), Moreau (1966).

210 STRIPED OWL
Asio clamator   Plate 64

French: Hibou strié
German: Streifen-Ohreule
Spanish: Buho cornudo cariblanco, Lechuzón orejudo
Portuguese: Coruja-orelhuda

Striped Owl

IDENTIFICATION A medium-sized owl (30.5-38cm) with prominent ear-tufts and a pale, blackish-rimmed facial disc. Eyes dark brown. Scapulars with partly whitish outer webs. Below, pale ochraceous to creamy-white with dusky shaft-streaks. Tarsi and toes feathered. Wings shorter and with more rounded tips than on other 'long-eared owls'. **Similar species** Long-eared Owl [207] has a browner facial disc and orange or yellow eyes, and herringbone-like pattern below. Stygian Owl [206] is much darker, with rather dark brown facial disc and yellow eyes. Great Horned Owl [94] is larger, with more powerful talons, and below is spotted and distinctly barred dusky; eyes yellow. Short-eared Owl [211] is generally pale yellowish-brown below with bold streaking; eyes yellow, surrounded by blackish, and ear-tufts tiny and set near centre of forehead.

VOCALISATIONS The song of the male is a series of well-spaced hoots (intervals several seconds), higher in pitch than song of male Long-eared Owl. Also single, somewhat nasal hoots of about 1 second's duration are given, beginning softly, rising in pitch and volume, and declining at end: *nuuong*. Female gives a similar but higher-pitched song. A plaintive, screeching *chreeah* is uttered by the female when contacting mate. Single explosive barking notes, *wow*, are given by the male when disturbed. Both sexes utter series of barking calls, often duetting: *how-how-how-howhowowo*. Fledged young give high-pitched, drawn screams, *weehe*, with downward inflection.

DISTRIBUTION From S Mexico through Central America locally to Colombia, Venezuela, the Guyanas, E Peru, Bolivia, Brazil, Paraguay, N Argentina and Uruguay; also Caribbean islands.

MOVEMENTS Resident.

HABITAT Lives in open or semi-open grassland with scattered trees, small groves and bushes, and edges of open or semi-open woodland, also open marshland with bushes, pastures, agricultural country, even airstrips and rice fields; locally, large clearings near forest edges. Absent from heavy forest, and in general avoiding the Amazon basin. From sea-level up to about 1,600m.

DESCRIPTION *A. c. clamator* **Adult** Facial disc brownish-white, distinctly rimmed blackish; short eyebrows whitish; ear-tufts long and prominent, mostly blackish. Upperparts tawny-buff, heavily streaked dusky on forehead, crown and nape; mantle and back mottled and streaked dark; scapulars with whitish areas on outer webs. Flight feathers and tail barred light and dark brown; blackish patch at wrist, very obvious in flight (above and below). Throat white. Underparts pale tawny to buffy-whitish, prominently striped dark brown or blackish. Tarsi and toes feathered creamy. **Juvenile** Downy chick whitish. Mesoptile whitish-buff, diffusely barred greyish-brown above; pale cinnamon facial disc, rimmed dusky. **Bare parts** Eyes brown to cinnamon. Cere greyish. Bill and claws blackish.

MEASUREMENTS AND WEIGHT Total length 30.5-38cm. Wing 228-294mm; tail 130-165mm. Weight of males 335-347g, of females 400-502g.

GEOGRAPHICAL VARIATION Four subspecies are described, but we treat only three, as the form *oberi* from Tobago is known only from the type specimen and the species varies individually in coloration and plumage pattern.

A. c. clamator (Vieillot, 1807). Colombia, Venezuela, Peru and N and C Brazil outside Amazon forest. See Description. Darkest subspecies. Wing 236-277mm.
A. c. forbesi (Lowery & Dalquest, 1951). S Mexico to Costa Rica and Panama, and Caribbean Islands. Smaller and paler than nominate. Wing 228-239mm; tail 130mm.
A. c. midas (Schlegel, 1817). Bolivia, Paraguay, N and C Argentina to Uruguay and SE Brazil. Largest and palest subspecies. Wing 267-294mm.

HABITS Nocturnal; becomes active at dusk, sometimes at sunset. During daytime roosts in bushes or dense foliage of trees, sometimes within cover on the ground. Outside breeding season several may gather in flocks, roosting rather close togeather by day. Flies with rather shallow and rapid wingbeats over open areas.

FOOD Mostly small mammals and other small vertebrates, as well as insects. With its rather powerful talons with long claws, is able to catch larger prey than does Long-eared Owl (about equal in size, but with much lower body weight). Swoops down on prey spotted from rather low flight; often perches on fence posts watching for prey.

BREEDING Male claims territory by singing from perches; during courtship, male and female duet. Generally nests in a shallow depression on the ground or in flattened vegetation on it; sometimes uses low, rather open cavities in rotten stumps or dead leaf bases at trunks of palms (up to 3m above ground). The female lays 2-4 white eggs and incubates alone; incubation lasts about 4 weeks and starts with the first egg. Often only one chick is raised.

STATUS AND CONSERVATION Uncertain; locally, probably expanding its range because of logging of forested areas. May be affected by the use of pesticides.

REMARKS Striped Owl is often placed in a genus of its own, *Rhinoptynx*, but it is doubtless related to the long-eared owls of the genus *Asio*. Its distribution, biology, vocalisations and behaviour need more study.

REFERENCES Belton (1984), Boyer & Hume (1991), Burton (1992), Eck & Busse (1973), Hardy *et al.* (1989), Hilty & Brown (1986), Howell & Webb (1995), Kelso (1936), Ridgely (1976), Sick (1985), Stiles & Skutch (1989), Voous (1988).

---

211 SHORT-EARED OWL
Asio flammeus   Plate 64

French: Hibou brachyote
German: Sumpfohreule
Spanish: Lechuza campestre

IDENTIFICATION A medium-sized (33-41cm), long-winged owl with tiny ear-tufts set near centre of forehead but often concealed. General coloration lighter or darker yellowish-brown, heavily streaked dusky. Eyes relatively small and yellow, surrounded by blackish; rim around facial disc not prominent. In flight, dark area at wrist very distinct above and below, similar to Long-eared Owl [207], but secondaries from below more or less unbarred and tail less densely barred. Primaries from above with basal half rather plain ochraceous-buff, contrasting with blackish mark at wrist. **Similar species** Striped Owl [210] has prominent ear-tufts and brown eyes, and rim around facial disc blackish and very distinct. Long-eared Owl has prominent ear-tufts and orange or yellow eyes. Barn owls (*Tyto*) have heart-shaped facial disc and dark brown eyes. Tawny Owl [130] has a large head, prominent whitish scapular stripe and large dark brown eyes. Great Horned and Magellan Horned Owls [94, 95] are larger, barred below, and have prominent ear-tufts.

VOCALISATIONS The song of the male is a rather rapid series of deep hoots, first rising slightly and finally falling in pitch: *bubububububububog*. Such phrases are repeated at variable intervals, from a perch or in flight. Both sexes give hoarse *cheeaw* calls when disturbed in their nesting territory, and utter barking sounds such as *wow* and *jeff*. A low *gook* apparently has a contact function and is uttered by both sexes, the female's calls slightly higher in pitch. A screeching, drawn-out *cheearp* is given by the female when begging for food. Fledged young utter similar calls.

DISTRIBUTION Widely distributed. North America from Alaska and the Bering Strait east to Labrador, south to California and North Carolina; Hispaniola and some other Caribbean islands; Galápagos Islands, Juan Fernández Islands and Hawaii; Falkland Islands; locally South America, mainly the southern half; Greenland, British Isles and Atlantic coast of SW France and NW Spain, very locally in Iberian Peninsula, and from there and Norway eastwards through C Europe and C Asia to NE Siberia, Kamchatka, Sakhalin and N China; also some islands in the Bering Sea.

MOVEMENTS Northern populations are largely migratory. Those of N and C Europe winter in the Mediterranean and N Africa to Sahel zone; C Asian populations winter south to the Middle East, N India, Burma, S China and Taiwan; North American owls winter south of a line from British Columbia to the Great Lakes, reaching Mexico and Central America, as well as Cuba and other Caribbean islands. Birds breeding in tropical areas are mostly resident. Birds from the Falklands and Patagonia are partly migratory. In general, younger birds show a marked tendency to wander about. Concentrations of Short-eared Owls may be observed when voles are abundant, while the species is absent or very rare in the same areas when food is scarce. Distances of up to about 3,400km between breeding and wintering grounds have been recorded.

HABITAT Open areas with bushes or scattered trees, pastureland, moors, tundra, swampy areas, humid grassland, downland with patches of vegetation, dry, stony landscapes with areas of shrubs, large clearings near forest edges, páramo and puna above timberline in the Andes, and open, extensively cultivated landscapes. During migration and in winter occurs in varied open habitats, even potato fields. From sea-level up to about 4,000m (in the Andes).

DESCRIPTION *A. f. flammeus* **Adult** Facial disc ochraceous, shading into blackish around eyes; loral bristles and eyebrows whitish, contrasting with blackish mask around eyes. Ear-tufts tiny, set rather close together near centre of forehead, often barely if at all visible, erected only when excited. Crown and nape distinctly streaked dark on yellowish-tawny. Upperparts yellowish-tawny to pale ochraceous-buff with faint greyish cast, heavily streaked and spotted dusky; scapulars with dark centres and pale edges. Basal half of primaries above rather plain ochraceous, contrasting with narrow area of blackish feathers at wrist (distinctly visible in flight); rest of flight feathers barred light and dark. Tail slightly wedge-shaped, yellowish-tawny with faint greyish cast and 4-5 visible dark bars (Long-eared Owl has 6-8 much narrower bars). Underparts pale yellowish-tawny to ochre-whitish, distinctly streaked brown; undersides of secondaries nearly unbarred or plain. Tarsi and toes feathered pale tawny to whitish-cream. **Juvenile** Downy chick covered with pale ochraceous down. Mesoptile pale ochraceous-buff with dusky barring above and below; facial disc largely blackish, contrasting with yellow eyes and white eyebrows. **Bare parts** Eyes relatively small, light yellow to sulphur-yellow, sometimes brighter yellow (eyes contrast with dark mask). Cere greyish-brown. Bill blackish-horn. Claws greyish-horn with darker tips.

MEASUREMENTS AND WEIGHT Total length 33-41cm.

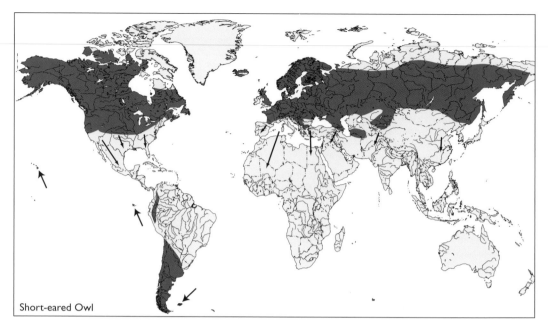

Short-eared Owl

Wing 281-335mm; tail 140-165mm. Weight of males 206-450g, of females 284-505g.

GEOGRAPHICAL VARIATION Like most owls, varies individually in coloration and plumage pattern. We recognise eight subspecies, regarding other taxa as synonyms as there is no clear evidence for subspecific recognition.

A. f. flammeus (Pontoppidan, 1763). North America, Europe, Asia, and NW Africa from Morocco to Tunisia. See Description. Wing 279-335mm.

A. f. bogotensis Chapman, 1915. N South America from Colombia and Venezuela to Surinam and from Ecuador south to Peru. Smaller and darker than nominate, with more rusty wash. (We include *pallidicaudus* as a synonym.)

A. f. suinda (Vieillot, 1817). From S Peru, C Chile, Bolivia and Brazil south to Tierra del Fuego. Similar to nominate in coloration, but somewhat darker; streaking on breast Y-shaped and reddish-brown. Wing 310-330mm.

A. f. sanfordi Bangs, 1919. Falkland Islands. Smaller and lighter than *suinda*.

A. f. sandwichensis (Bloxham, 1826). Hawaii. General coloration more yellowish-grey. Wing 285-304mm; tail 152-157mm.

A. f. ponapensis Mayr, 1933. Ponapé, in Caroline Islands in S Pacific. Shorter-winged than nominate.

A. f. domingensis (Müller, 1776). Hispaniola and Puerto Rico; recorded on Cuba. Smaller than nominate by about 12%. (We include *portoricensis* as a synonym.)

A. (f.) galapagoensis (Gould, 1837). Galápagos Islands. Differs greatly from all other races: very dark tawny with distinct blackish mask; underparts with indication of cross-bars; tarsal feathering barred and spotted dark. Wing 283-288mm; tail 136-143mm. (This taxon may well be specifically distinct.)

HABITS Largely diurnal, but most active at dusk and also at night; normally less active around noon and midnight. Often seen by day flying with deep, rather slow, rowing wingbeats and gliding on stretched wings over open landscapes. Often perches on fence posts, tops of bushes or other exposed sites. Roosts among bushes or in shelter of ground vegetation. Can be very aggressive near nest, and makes diving attacks even on human intruders. Outside breeding season may gather in flocks, roosting normally on the ground and hunting in groups at dusk over open landscapes.

FOOD Mostly small mammals (e.g. voles), but also other small vertebrates and insects; takes birds up to the size of a pigeon, and mammals to the size of brown rat *Rattus norvegicus* or young rabbit. When food is abundant, deposits surplus near the nest. Hunts from the wing by flying low over ground and swooping down on to prey; quite often hovers; also watches for prey from perches.

BREEDING Territorial during breeding season. Male claims territory by display flights with wing-clapping, and soars and makes sudden dives; also sings from perches or on the wing. Nest is a shallow depression on the ground, lined to some extent by the female, who gathers few dry grass stems, twigs or leaves from the area around the nest (this is one of the few owl species that shows a tendency to build a nest). Copulation normally occurs on the ground, sometimes on a fence post.

In Europe, laying normally occurs between late March and June. Generally lays 7-10 white eggs (40.4 x 31.3mm, fresh weight 20-23g) at intervals of about 2 days. Incubation, by the female alone, starts with the first egg, the male feeding female at the nest. Young hatch after an incubation of 24-28 days per egg. Breeding biology similar to that of Long-eared Owl. Young leave the nest flightless when about 2 weeks old and hide among vegetation; they are accompanied and fed by both parents for some weeks more, and in the following year reach sexual maturity. Normally one brood per year, but two broods have been recorded in years when food was very abundant. May reach an age of 12-13 years in the wild.

430

STATUS AND CONSERVATION Uncertain. Locally, threatened by habitat destruction and the use of pesticides; disappears from areas where intensive agriculture practised. Is very dependent on the abundance of food. In some areas, artificial feeding has proved successful in severe winters, as described for Long-eared Owl.

REMARKS This species' taxonomy requires study, especially with regard to the status of the Galápagos taxon. Some patterns suggest that latter may be a separate species, endemic to Galápagos Archipelago; bioacoustical and molecular-biological studies would be a great help.

REFERENCES Abs *et al.* (1965), Ali & Ripley (1969), Bezzel (1985), Clark (1975), Cramp (1985), Dementiev & Gladkov (1951), Dunning (1993), Eck & Busse (1973), Fjeldså & Krabbe (1990), Glue (1977), Glutz & Bauer (1980), Hardy *et al.* (1989), Hölzinger (1985), König (1967), Mikkola (1983), Saurola (1997), Voous (1988).

---

212 MARSH OWL
Asio capensis   Plate 64

French: Hibou des marais
German: Kap-Ohreule

IDENTIFICATION A medium-sized (31-38cm), generally earth-brown owl with rounded head and distinct pale facial disc. Upperparts sometimes with very fine speckles. Facial disc distinctly rimmed; blackish-brown area around dark brown eyes; erectile ear-tufts very tiny and mostly invisible, set near centre of forehead. Wings and tail barred tawny and dark brown. In flight, shows prominent dark patch at wrist (visible from above and below), upper primaries with rather plain tawny bases. Below, diffusely vermiculated dusky on lighter brown, appearing rather plain (birds from Madagascar more finely barred below). Tarsi feathered; toes partly covered with short plumes, outermost tips rather bare. **Similar species** Short-eared Owl [211] is generally pale yellowish-brown with distinct dusky streaking, especially on underparts; eyes pale yellow. Long-eared, Abyssinian Long-eared and Madagascar Long-eared Owls [207-209] have prominent ear-tufts, yellow to orange eyes and boldly patterned underparts. Tawny Owl [130] is more boldly patterned, has a broad, rounded head and large blackish-brown eyes (not surrounded by blackish) and has whitish outer webs to scapulars. African Wood Owl [135] has barred underparts and a whitish scapular stripe. Eagle owls (*Bubo*) are larger, with prominent ear-tufts. African fishing owls (*Scotopelia*) have bare tarsi and toes. African Grass Owl [8] is larger, dark brown above and light below, and has heart-shaped facial disc with relatively small, blackish eyes and relatively long legs with bristled toes.

VOCALISATIONS Little studied. Very different from all other members of this genus. Most common is a hoarse, grating call, uttered when perched or when circling overhead and clapping wings in display, sounding like the noise produced by breaking a dry branch by bending it slowly, *krrrrrr*; this is repeated at variable intervals. Also gives sequences of croaking, raven-like calls on the wing: *quarrk-quarrk-quarrk....* Female utters similar but higher-pitched and softer calls. These vocalisations might have the function of a territorial song, while the grating notes

perhaps express aggression against intruders. Female and fledged young utter far-carrying, wailing hisses with ventriloquial character: *shooeeh.* If disturbed at the nest, both sexes may fly around with croaking calls and high mewing screams.

DISTRIBUTION Africa and Madagascar. A rather isolated population in extreme NW Africa (Morocco, W Algeria); patchily distributed south of the Sahara from Senegambia and Ethiopia to the Cape.

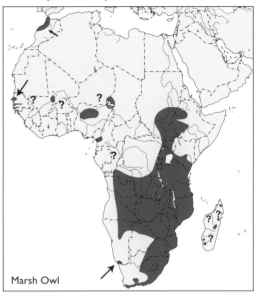

Marsh Owl

MOVEMENTS In general resident, but partly nomadic within sub-Saharan Africa and and intra-African migrant. Stragglers have been observed in S Iberian Peninsula and Canary Islands. Displacements are generally caused by food abundance (e.g. rodent plagues) or shortage, or the result of bush fires, floods, etc.

HABITAT Open country from coastal marshes to savanna, with or without scattered trees and bushes, also inland marshes, moors and montane grassland, from sea-level up to about 3,000m. Avoids extensive long grass, but favours landscapes with short vegetation and some patches of long grass or weeds; locally in rice fields and drainage strips in wooded savanna ('dambos'), sometimes open areas near or even in human settlements. Absent from forested areas, rocky landscapes and deserts.

DESCRIPTION *A. c. capensis* **Adult** Sexes alike, but males generally lighter in coloration than females; individually variable in tone. Facial disc pale buff, with dark brown area around eyes; distinct facial rim dark brown with buff speckles. Ear-tufts earth-brown, very tiny and rarely visible, set near centre of forehead. Upperparts plain earth-brown, crown and nape finely vermiculated buff; uppertail-coverts barred buff. Primaries with rather plain pale tawny-buff bases, contrasting with dusky patch at wrist; rest of flight feathers barred dark brown and tawny-buff. Tail dark brown, barred pale buff, with whitish tip. Underparts brown, finely vermiculated buff, becoming more uniform pale buff on thighs, belly and undertail-coverts; underwing-coverts buff with dark brown patch at wrist, very conspicuous in flight. Tarsi feathered pale tawny-buff;

toes covered with pale buffy plumes, leaving tips bare. **Juvenile** Downy chick covered with buff down; pink skin, blackish bill and pink toes. Mesoptile buff, barred brown above; facial disc darker than adult, with marked blackish rim. After moult (at age of about 10 weeks), distinguishable from adult by buff tips to scapulars and lower back feathers. **Bare parts** Eyes dark brown. Cere grey-brown. Bill blackish-horn. Bare parts of toes dark brown. Claws blackish.

MEASUREMENTS AND WEIGHT Total length 31-38cm. Wing 274-380mm; tail 147-180mm. Weight 227-376g.

GEOGRAPHICAL VARIATION We distinguish three subspecies.

> *A. c. capensis* (A. Smith, 1834). Africa south of Sahara. See Description. Wing 274-305mm; tail 150-170mm.
> *A. c. tingitanus* (Loche, 1867). Morocco and Algeria, occasionally straggling to S Iberia and Canary Islands. Darker than nominate, with rufous wash and some small whitish markings, especially below. Wing 280-318mm; tail 135-165mm.
> *A. c. hova* Stresemann, 1922. Madagascar. Largest subspecies. Underparts more barred and spotted; light parts of primaries paler. Bill and talons more powerful than in other races. Wing 322-380mm; tail 176-186mm.

HABITS Occurs singly or in pairs, sometimes in larger numbers (especially outside breeding season). Mostly crepuscular and nocturnal, but sometimes also active during cloudy days. By day, normally roosts on the ground in a hollow among grass or other vegetation. At dusk or by night, often perches on fence posts, stumps or tops of bushes watching for prey. May be aggressive near the nest or feign injury in order to distract potential enemies. Flight very similar to that of a harrier *Circus*.

FOOD Depends largely on availability. Normally small rodents form the major part of its diet, but sometimes small birds may be predominant; also takes other small vertebrates and insects. Prey includes mice, voles, rats, shrews, young hares, bats, birds up to the size of small ducks and doves, frogs, lizards, scorpions, beetles, grasshoppers, termite alates, etc. Most prey is captured by flying close to the ground with slow but powerful wing-beats, interspersed with fast swerves and hovering, before dropping on to victim; sometimes hawks flying insects, even those attracted by street lamps in urban areas.

BREEDING Monogamous and territorial. Sometimes nests in loose colonies. Territories normally 0.8-2km² in size, sometimes smaller when the population is denser; in South Africa, nests have been found about 75m apart. Hunting areas of neighbouring pairs may overlap. Male claims territory by circling over it, clapping wings and croaking; during courtship, pair-members often fly in wide circles at dusk and on moonlit nights, with wing-clapping and croaking calls (song?). Copulation normally occurs on ground. A hollow within a patch of tall grass or weeds, often beside a bush and with an 'entrance tunnel' from one side, is used for nesting, vegetation often being pulled over by the female to form a canopy. The depression itself is lined with some dry leaves to form a pad (this is probably done by the female, but needs confirmation). In Morocco, a nest was found about 4m above ground in an old corvid nest in a bush, the only case of a nest not being on the ground. Locally, nests in close vicinity to African Grass Owl, with one instance of nests only 20m apart.

Nesting normally occurs towards the end of the wet season. The female lays 2-6 (normally 3) white eggs (40 x 34.1mm), at intervals of about 2 days, and incubates alone, starting with the first egg. During incubation she is fed by her mate, who brings food to the nest in its talons, calls at his approach; he lands at the nest, walks in through the tunnel and delivers food mostly from bill to bill, but the female sometimes snatches it from his talons. If food is abundant, items may be cached at the nest by the female, or in deposits outside by the male. Incubation lasts 27-28 days for each egg. Chicks' eyes open at 7 days, and by 10 days the facial disc is well developed (showing characteristic blackish mask and black rim); up to this age they are regularly brooded by the female. At 18 days, when young still appear downy, they begin to leave the nest (sometimes as early as 10-14 days) and scatter in the surrounding vegetation; adults carry food directly to them, the young indicating their position by calls and a little 'tap-dance'. When 30 days old, young have acquired most contour feathers; by 70 days they are fully feathered, but are able to fly earlier, by 29-35 days. Both parents care for them for some time before they become independent.

STATUS AND CONSERVATION Uncertain. Rather scarce in NW Africa; south of the Sahara, locally common in years with abundant food. Is affected by bush fires, floods, overgrazing by cattle, and the use of pesticides. Several are killed by road traffic, or by entanglement in barbed wire. Some nests are destroyed by predators.

REMARKS This species, being the ecological counterpart in Africa of Short-eared Owl, has been supposed to be a close relative of the latter, but we believe the similarities in ecology and external appearance to be due to convergence and not to relationship. The totally different vocalisations support this view. In any case, it would not be wise to consider the two as representatives of a super-species, and certainly not as members of the same species. Marsh Owl's vocalisations, behaviour and reproductive biology are in need of further study, as is its taxonomy, including molecular biology.

REFERENCES Boyer & Hume (1991), Burton (1992), Cramp (1985), Dean (1978), de Naurois (1961), Dunning (1993), Eck & Busse (1973), Fry *et al.* (1988), König & Ertel (1979), Langrand (1990), Langrand & Meyburg (1984), Mikkola (1983), Smith & Killick-Kendrick (1964), Steyn (1982, 1983, 1984), Voous (1988), Zimmerman *et al.* (1996).

BIBLIOGRAPHY

ABDULALI, H. 1967. The birds of the Nicobar Islands, with notes on the Andaman birds. *J. Bombay Nat. Hist. Soc.* 64: 139-190.

ABDULALI, H. 1972. A catalogue of the birds in the collection of the Bombay Natural History Society, 11. Strigidae and Caprimulgidae. *J. Bombay Nat. Hist. Soc.* 69: 102-129.

ABDULALI, H. 1978. The birds of Great and Car Nicobars with some notes on wildlife conservation in the islands. *J. Bombay Nat. Hist. Soc.* 75: 744-772.

ABS, M., CURIO, E., KRAMER, P. & NIETHAMMER, J. 1965. Zur Ernährungsweise der Eulen auf Galapagos. *J. Orn.* 106: 49-57.

ALI, S. & RIPLEY, S. D. 1981. *Handbook of the birds of India and Pakistan*, 3. 2nd edition. Bombay: Oxford University Press.

ALI, S. 1949. *Indian hill birds*. Delhi: Oxford University Press.

ALI, S. 1964. *The book of Indian birds*. 7th edition. Bombay: Bombay Natural History Society.

ALI, S. 1977. *Field guide to the birds of the eastern Himalayas.* Delhi: Oxford University Press.

ALLEN, D. & BALLANTYNE, D. 1980. Wood Owl breeding in raptor nest. *Witwatersrand Bird Club News* 109: 17.

ALLEN, G. M. & GREENWAY, J. C. 1935. A specimen of *Tyto* (*Heliodilus*) *soumagnei*. *Auk* 52: 414-417.

AMADON, D. & BULL, J. 1988. Hawks and owls of the world. *Proc. Western Found. Vert. Zool.* 3: 295-347.

AMADON, D. & JEWETT, S. G. 1946. Notes on Philippine birds. *Auk* 63: 551-558.

AMADON, D. 1953. Avian systematics and evolution in the Gulf of Guinea. *Bull. Amer. Mus. Nat. Hist.* 100: 393-451.

ANGELL, T. 1974. *Owls.* Madison, Wisconsin: University of Wisconsin Press.

ARAYA M, B. & MILLIE H., G. 1986. *Guía de campo de las aves de Chile.* Santiago de Chile: Editorial Universitaria.

ARMSTRONG, W. H. 1958. Nesting and food habits of the Long-eared Owl in Michigan. *Michigan State University Biol. Ser.* 1: 69-96.

ARONSON, L. 1980. Hume's Tawny Owl *Strix butleri* in Israel. *Dutch Birding* 1: 18-19.

ATKINSON, P. E., KOROMA, A. P., RAUFF, R., ROWE, S. G. & WILKINSON, R. 1994. The status, identification and vocalization of African fishing-owls with particular reference to the Rufous Fishing-Owl *Scotopelia ussheri*. *Bull. African Bird Club* 1: 67-72.

ATMÜLLER, R. 1976. Schachtelbrut eines Schleiereulen-Weibchens (*Tyto alba*). *Vogelk. Ber. Nieders.* 8: 9-10.

AURIVILLIUS, M. & AURIVILLIUS, H. 1995. The Peregrine Fund – banbrytande fältornitologi på Madagascar. *Var Fågelvärld* 3: 21-23.

AUSTIN, O. L. 1948. The birds of Korea. *Bull. Mus. Comp. Zool.* 101: 1-301.

AUSTIN, O. L. & KURODA, N. 1953. The birds of Japan, their status and distribution. *Bull. Mus. Comp. Zool.* 109: 277-637.

AUSTING, G. R. 1957. The Saw-whet Owl. *Nat. Hist.* 66: 154-158.

AUSTING, G. R. & HOLT, J. B. 1966. *The world of the Great Horned Owl.* Philadelphia.

AVERY, G., ROBERTSON, A. S. PALMER, N. G. & PRINS, A. J. 1985. Prey of Giant Eagle Owls in the Lee Hoop Nature Reserve, Cape Province. *Ostrich* 56: 117-122.

BAKER, E. C. S. 1927. Remarks on Oriental owls with description of four new races. *Bull. Brit. Orn. Club* 47: 58-61.

BAKER, E. C. S. 1927. *The fauna of British India. Birds* IV. London: Taylor and Francis.

BAKER, J. K. 1962. The manner and efficiency of raptor depredations on bats. *Condor* 64: 500-504.

BAKER, R. H. 1951. The avifauna of Micronesia, its origin, evolution and distribution. *Publ. Univ. Kansas Mus. Nat. Hist.* 3: 1-159.

BALDWIN, P. H. & KOPLIN, J. R. 1966. The Boreal Owl as a Pleistocene relict in Colorado. *Condor* 68: 299-300.

van BALEN, S. 1991. Faunistic notes from Bali. *Kukila* 5: 125-132.

BANGS, O. & NOBLE, G. K. 1918. Birds of Peru. *Auk* 35: 448-449.

BANGS, O. & PENARD, T. E. 1921. Description of six new subspecies of American birds. *Proc. Biol. Soc. Washington.* 34: 89-92.

BANGS, O. 1899. A new barred owl from Corpus Christi, Texas. *Proc. New England Zool. Club* 1: 31-32.

BANNERMAN, D. A. 1953. *The birds of West and Equatorial Africa*, 2. Edinburgh & London: Oliver & Boyd.

BANNERMAN, D. A. 1968. *Birds of the Atlantic Islands*, 4. Edinburgh & London: Oliver & Boyd.

BARLOW, C., WACHER, T. & DISLEY, T. 1997. *A field guide to birds of the Gambia and Senegal.* Robertsbridge, U.K.: Pica Press.

BARROWS, C. W. 1981. Roost selection by Spotted Owls: an adaptation to heat and stress. *Condor* 83: 302-309.

BARROWS, C. W. & BARROWS, K. 1978. Roost characteristics and behavioural thermoregulation in the Spotted Owl. *Western Birds* 9: 1-8.

BARROWS, C. W. 1986. Cool spots in hot debate. *Living Bird Q.* Winter: 12-16.

BATES, G. L. 1937. Description of two new races of Arabian birds. *Bull. Brit. Orn. Club* 57: 150-151.

BAUDVIN, H., DESSOLIN, J.-H. & RIOLS, C. 1985. L'utilisation par la martre (*Martes martes*) des nichoirs à chouettes dans quelques forêts bourguignonnes. *Ciconia* 9: 61-104.

BAUER, H. G. & BERTHOLD, P. 1997. *Die Brutvögel Mitteleuropas, Bestand und Gefährung.* Wiesbaden.

BAUMGART, W. 1980. Wodurch ist der Steinkauz bedroht? *Falke* 27: 228-229.

BAUMGART, W. 1991. Gegenwärtiger Status und Gefährdungsgrad von Greifvögeln und Eulen in Syrien. *Birds of Prey Bull.* 4: 129-131.

BAVOUX, C. & BURNELEAU, G. 1985. Premières données sur la biologie de reproduction d'une population de Hiboux petits-ducs *Otus scops* (L). *Alauda* 53: 223-225.

BECKER, P. & RITTER, H. 1969. Habichtskauz (*Strix uralensis*) im Harz nachgewiesen. *Vogelk. Ber. Nieders.* 1: 55-56.

BECKING, J. H. 1994. On the biology and voice of the Javan Scops Owl *Otus angelinae*. *Bull. Brit. Orn. Club* 114: 211-224.

BEEHLER, B. M., PRATT, T. K. & ZIMMERMAN, D. K. 1986. *Birds of New Guinea*. Princeton: Princeton University Press.

BELCHER, C. & SMOOKER, G. D. 1936. Birds of the Colony of Trinidad and Tobago. III. *Ibis* (13)6. 1-35.

BELL, R. E. 1964. A sound-triangulation method for counting Barred Owls. *Wilson Bull.* 76: 292-294.

BELTON, W. 1984. Birds of Rio Grande do Sul, Brazil. Part 1. *Bull. Amer. Mus. Nat. Hist.* 178(4).

BENSON, C. W. 1960. Birds of the Comoro Islands. *Ibis* 103B: 5-106.

BENSON, C. W. 1962. The food of the Spotted Eagle-Owl *Bubo africanus*. Ostrich 33(4): 35.

BENSON, C. W. 1981. Ecological difference between the Grass Owl *Tyto capensis* and the Marsh Owl *Asio capensis*. *Bull. Brit. Orn. Club* 101: 372-376.

BENSON, C. W., BROOKE, R. K. DOWSETT, R. J. & IRWIN, M. P. S. 1971. *The birds of Zambia*. London: Collins.

BENSON, C. W. & IRWIN, M. P. S. 1967. The distribution and systematics of *Bubo capensis* Smith (Aves). *Arnoldia (Rhod.)* 3(19). 1-19.

BENT, A. C. 1938. *Life histories of North American birds of prey, II. Owls*. New York: Dover.

BERGIER, P. & BADAN, O. 1991. Evaluation of some breeding parameters in a population of Eagle Owls *Bubo bubo* in Provence (south-eastern France). *Birds of Prey Bull.* 4: 57-61.

BERGMANN, H.-H. & GANSO, M. 1965. Zur Biologie des Sperlingskauzes. *J. Orn.* 106: 255-284.

BERGMANN, H.-H. & HELB, H. W. 1982. *Stimmen der Vögel Europas*. München-Wien-Zürich.

von BERLEPSCH, H. & TACZANOWSKI, L. 1884. Deuxième liste des oiseaux recueillis dans l'Ecuadeur occidental par MM. Stolzmann et Siemiradski. *Proc. Zool. Soc. London*: 281-313.

von BERLEPSCH, H. & STOLZMANN, J. 1892. Résultats des recherches ornithologiques faites au Pérou par M. Jean Kalinowski. *Proc. Zool. Soc. London*: 371-411.

von BERLEPSCH, H. & STOLZMANN, J. 1902. On the ornithological researches of M. Jean Kalinowski in central Peru. *Proc. Zool. Soc. London*: 18-60.

BERTONI, E. 1910. *Glaucidium ferox rufus* – Kavuré-í puihta: descripción, costumbres, leyendas guaraní. *An. Cient. Paraguayos* 1: 179-185.

BEZZEL, E. 1985. *Kompendium der Vögel Mitteleuropas, Nonpasseriformes*. Wiesbaden: AULA-Verlag.

BEZZEL, E. & RANFTL, H. 1974. *Vogelwelt und Landschaftsplanung: eine Studie aus dem Werdenfelser Land (Oberbayern)*. Barmstedt.

BIGGS, H. C., KEMP, A. C., MENDELSOHN, H. P. & MENDELSOHN, J. M. 1979. Weights of southern African raptors and owls. *Durban Mus. Novit.* 12: 73-81.

BISHOP, K. D. 1989. Little known *Tyto* owls of Wallacea. *Kukila* 4: 37-43.

BISWAS, B. 1961. The birds of Nepal, 3. *J. Bombay Nat. Hist. Soc.* 58: 63-134.

BLAKE, E. R. 1963. *Birds of Mexico*. Chicago: University Chicago Press.

BLAKERS, M., DAVIES, S. J. J. F. & REILLY, P. N. 1984. *The atlas of Australian birds*. Melbourne: Melbourne University Press.

BLONDEL, J. & BADAN, O. 1976. La biologie du Hibou Grand-duc en Provence. *Nos Oiseaux* 33: 189-219.

BLÜTHGEN, J. 1964. *Allgemeine Klimageographie*. Berlin.

von BOETTICHER, H. 1927. Kurze Übersicht über die Raubvögel und Eulen Bulgariens. *Verh. Orn. Ges. Bayerns* 17: 535-549.

von BOETTICHER, H. 1929. Eine neue Rasse der Kanincheneule *Speotyto cunicularia* (Mol.). *Senckenbergiana* 11: 386-392.

BOND, J. 1942. Notes on the Devil Owl. *Auk* 59: 308-309.

BOND, J. 1975. Origin of the Puerto Rican Screech Owl *Otus nudipes*. *Ibis* 117: 244.

BOND, J. 1982. Comments on Hispaniolan Birds. *Publ. Parque Zool. Nac. Santo Domingo* 1: 1-4.

BOND, J. 1986. *Birds of the West Indies*. 5th Edition. London: Collins.

BOND, J. & MEYER de SCHAUENSEE, R. 1941. Description of new birds from Bolivia, IV. *Notulae Naturae* 93.

BONNEY, R. E. 1983. More than just a pretty face. *Living Bird Q.* Winter: 10-13.

BOUCHNER, M. & BARTA, D. 1979. *Greifvögel und Eulen*. Hanau (Dausien).

BOWDEN, C. G. R. & ANDREW, M. 1994. Mount Kupe and its birds. *Bull. African Bird Club* 1: 13-18.

BOWMAKER, J. K. & MARTIN, G. R. 1978. Visual pigments and colour vision in a nocturnal bird, *Strix aluco* (Tawny Owl). *Vision Res.* 18: 1125-1130.

BOYER, T. & HUME, R. 1991. *Owls of the world*. Limpsfield, U.K.: Dragon's World.

BRAHMACHARY, R. L., BASU, T. K. & SENGUPTA, A. 1972. On the daily screeching time of a colony of Spotted Owls *Athene brama* (Temminck). *J. Bombay Nat. Hist. Soc.* 69: 649-651.

BRANDT, T. & SEEBASS, C. 1994. *Die Schleiereule – Sammlung Vogelkunde*. Wiesbaden: Aula.

BRAZIL, M. A. 1991. *The Birds of Japan*. Christopher Helm, London.

BRAZIL, M. A. & YAMAMOTO, S. 1983. Nest boxes as a practical means of conservation of Blakiston's Fish Owl (*Ketupa blakistoni*) in Japan and notes on breeding behaviour. *Proc. 2nd East Asian Bird Protection Conference*: 80-86.

BRAZIL, M. A. & YAMAMOTO, S. 1989. The status and distribution of owls of Japan. Pp.389-401 in B.-U.

Meyburg & R. D. Chancellor, eds. *Raptors in the modern world*. London: World Working Group on Birds of Prey.

BRAZIL, M. A. & YAMAMOTO, S. 1989. The behavioural biology of Blakiston's Fish Owl *Ketupa blakistoni* in Japan: calling behaviour. Pp.403-410 in B.-U. Meyburg & R. D. Chancellor, eds. *Raptors in the modern world*. London: World Working Group on Birds of Prey.

BRETAGNOLLE, V. & ATTIÉ, C. 1995. Comments on a possible new species of Scops Owl *Otus* sp. on Réunion. *Bull. African Bird Club* 3: 36.

BRIFFETT, C. & SUFARI, S. B. 1993. *The birds of Singapore*. Oxford: Oxford University Press.

BRIGGS, M. A. 1954. Apparent neoteny in the Saw-whet Owl of Mexico and Central America. *Proc. Biol. Soc. Washington* 67: 179-182.

BRITTON, P. L., ed. 1980. *Birds of East Africa, their habitat, status and distribution*. Nairobi: East African Natural History Society.

BRODKORB, P. 1938. Further additions to the avifauna of Paraguay. *Occas. Pap. Mus. Zool. Univ. Michigan* 394.

BROOKE, R. K. 1973. Notes on the distribution and food of the Cape Eagle Owl in Rhodesia. *Ostrich* 44: 137-139.

BROWN, L. H. 1976. Observations on Pel's Fishing Owl *Scotopelia peli*. *Bull. Brit. Orn. Club* 96: 49-53.

BROWN, L. H. 1970. *African birds of prey*. London: Collins.

BROWNING, M. R. 1989. The type specimens of Hekstra's owls. *Proc. Biol. Soc. Washington* 102: 515-519.

BROWNING, M. R. 1990. Erroneous emendation to names proposed by Hekstra (Strigidae: *Otus*). *Proc. Biol. Soc. Washington* 103: 452.

BRÜLL, H. 1977. *Das Leben europäischer Greifvögel*. Third edition. Stuttgart.

BRÜLL, H. 1984. *Greifvögel und Eulen Mitteleuropas*. Minden (Philler).

BUCHANAN, O. M. 1971. The Mottled Owl *Ciccaba virgata* in Trinidad. *Ibis* 103: 105-106.

BÜHLER, P. 1981. Das Fütterungsverhalten der Schleiereule *Tyto alba*. *Ökol. Vögel* 3: 183-202.

BÜHLER, P. 1988. Anpassung des Kopf-Hals-Gefieders der Schleiereule (*Tyto alba*) an die akustische Ortung. *Proc. Int. 100. DO-G Meeting, Curr. Topics Avian Biol.* 49-55.

BÜHLER, P. & EPPLE, W. 1980. Die Lautäusserungen der Schleiereule (*Tyto alba*). *J. Orn.* 121; 36-70.

BULLER, W. L. 1888. *Birds of New Zealand*, Suppl, Vol. 2.

BULLER, W. L. 1892. *History of the Birds of New Zealand* 1. Second edition.

BULLER, W. L. 1904. On a new species of owl from New Zealand. *Ibis* (8)4: 639.

BUNN, D. S., WARBURTON, A. B. & WILSON, R. S. S. 1982. *The Barn Owl*. Calton, U.K.: T. & A. D. Poyser.

BURTON, J. A., ed. 1992. *Owls of the World: their Evolution, Structure and Ecology*. Peter Lowe/Eurobook.

BUTCHART, S. H. M., BROOKS, T. M., DAVIES, C. W. M., DHARMAPUTRA, G., DUTSON, G. C. L., LOWEN, J. C. & SAHU, A. 1996. The conservation status of forest birds on Flores and Sumbawa, Indonesia. *Bird Conserv. Internatn.* 6: 335-370.

BUTYNSKI, J. M., AGENONGA, U., NDERA, B. & HART, J. F. 1997. Rediscovery of the Congo Bay (Itombwe) Owl, *Phodilus prigoginei*. *Bull. African Bird Club* 4: 32-35.

BYERS, C. 1992. Scops Owl (*Otus scops*) and Striated Owl (*Otus brucei*). *Birding World* 5: 107-110.

CABANIS, J. 1855. Dr. Gundlachs Beiträge zur Ornithologie Cubas. *J. Orn.* 3: 465-467.

CABANIS, J. 1869. Übersicht der im Berliner Museum befindlichen Vögel von Costa Rica. *J. Orn.* 17: 204-213.

CARRILLO, J., NOGALES, M., DELGADO, G. & MARRERO, M. 1989. Preliminary data for a comparative study of the feeding habit of *Asio otus canariensis* on El Hierro and Gran Canaria, Canary Islands. Pp.451-457 in B.-U. Meyburg & R. D. Chancellor, eds. *Raptors in the modern world*. London: World Working Group on Birds of Prey.

CASSIN, J. 1862. *Birds of California and Texas*. Philadelphia: Lippincolt.

CASTRO, I. & PHILLIPS, A. 1996. *A guide to the birds of the Galápagos Islands*. London: Christopher Helm.

CAYLEY, N. W. 1959. *What bird is that?* 3rd Edition. Sydney: Angus & Robertson.

CHAPIN, J. B. 1930. Geographic variation on the African Scops Owl. *Amer. Mus. Novit.* 412.

CHAPMAN, F. M. 1922. Descriptions of apparently new birds from Colombia, Ecuador and Argentina. *Amer. Mus. Novit.* 31.

CHAPMAN, F. M. 1926. The distribution of bird-Life in Ecuador. *Bull. Amer. Mus. Nat. Hist.* 55.

CHAPMAN, F. M. 1929. New birds from Mt. Duida, Venezuela. *Amer. Mus. Novit.* 380.

CHAPPUIS, C. 1978. *Les oiseaux de l'ouest africain*. Sound supplement to ˙Alauda˝; Disc 9: Ala 17 & 18. Soc. d'études ornith., Paris.

CINQUINA, J. C. 1995. Split personality: experiencing the Jekyll and Hyde lifestyle of the Eastern Screech-Owl (*Otus asio*). *Birder's World* 9(5): 50-53.

CLAFFEY, P. M. 1997. The status of Pel's Fishing Owl *Scotopelia peli* in the Togo-Benin Gap. *Bull. African Bird Club* 4: 135-136.

CLARK, R. J. & SMITH, D. G. *Working bibliography of owls of the world* (2nd ed.) (in preparation).

CLARK, R. J. 1975. A field study of the Short-eared Owl *Asio flammeus* Pontoppidan in North America. *Wildlife Monogr.* 47: 1-67.

CLARK, R. J., SMITH, D. G. & KELSO, L. 1978. *Working bibliography of owls of the world*. Washington, D.C.: Raptor Information Center, National Wildlife Federation (Techn. Series 1).

CLARK, R. J. & MIKKOLA, H. 1989. A preliminary revision of threatened and near-threatened nocturnal birds of prey in the world. Pp.371-388 in B.-U. Meyburg & R. D. Chancellor, eds. *Raptors in the modern world*. London: World Working Group on Birds of Prey.

CLARK, R. J. 1997. A review of the taxonomy and distribution of the Burrowing Owl (*Speotyto cunicularia*). *Raptor Res. Report* 9: 14-23.

COATES, B. J. & BISHOP, K. D. 1997. *A guide to the birds of Wallacea: Sulawesi, the Moluccas and Lesser Sunda Islands, Indonesia.* Alderley, Queensland: Dove Publications.

COLLAR, N. J. & STUART, S. N. (1985) *Threatened birds of Africa and related islands: the ICBP/IUCN Red Data Book.* Cambridge, U.K.: International Council for Bird Preservation, and International Union for Conservation of Nature and Natural Resources.

COLLAR, N. J., CROSBY, M. J. & STATTERSFIELD, A. J. 1994. *Birds to watch 2: the world list of threatened birds.* Cambridge, U.K.: BirdLife International (BirdLife Conservation Series no.4).

COLLINS, C. T. 1963. Notes on the feeding behaviour, metabolism and weight of the Saw-whet Owl. *Condor* 65: 528-530.

CONNOR, J. 1988. Update Spotted Owl. *Living Bird Q.* Autumn: 32-34.

COOMANS de RUITER, L. & MAURENBRECHER, L. L. A. 1948. Stadsvogels van Makassar (zuid-Celebes). *Ardea* 36: 163-198.

CRAIGHEAD, J. J. & CRAIGHEAD, F. C. 1969. *Hawks, owls and wildlife.* New York: Dover.

CRAMP, S. ed. 1985. *The birds of the western Palearctic,* 4. Oxford: Oxford University Press.

CURIO, E., AUGST, H. J., BÖCKING, H. W., MILINSKI, M. & OHGUCHI, O. 1978. Wie Singvögel auf Feindrufe hassen lernen. *J. Orn.* 119: 231-233.

DANCE, S. P. 1991. *Die schönsten Naturgrafiken: Raubvögel.* Zug, Switzerland.

DASKAM, T. 1977. *Aves de Chile.* Lord Cochrane SA.

DAVIDSON, P. J., STONES, A. J., LUCKING, R. S., BEAN, N. J., VAN BALEN, B., RAHARJANINGTRAH, W. & BANJARANSARI, H. 1994. University of East Anglia Taliabu Expedition: preliminary report. Unpublished.

DAVIS, L. J. 1972. *A field guide to the birds of Mexico and Central America.* Austin, Texas.

DAVIS, T. J. 1986. Distribution and natural history of some birds from the departments of San Martín and Amazonas, northern Perú. *Condor* 88: 50-56.

DAWSON, W. L. 1923. *The birds of California.*

DEIGNAN, H. C. 1945. The birds of northern Thailand. *Bull. U. S. Natn. Mus.* 186.

DEIGNAN, H. C. 1950. The races of the Collared Scops Owl *Otus bakkamoena* Pennant. *Auk* 67: 189-201.

DELACOUR, J. 1941. On the species of *Otus scops. Zoologica* 26: 133-142.

DELACOUR, J. 1947. *Birds of Malaysia.* New York: Macmillan.

DELACOUR, J. & JABOUILLE, P. 1931. *Les oiseaux de l'Indochine Française.* Paris: Exposition Coloniale Internationale.

DELACOUR, J. & MAYR, E. 1945. Notes on the taxonomy of Philippine birds. *Zoologica* 30: 105-117.

DELACOUR, J. & MAYR, E. 1946. *Birds of the Philippines.* New York: Macmillan.

DEMENTIEV, G. P. 1933. Sur la position systématique de *Bubo doerriesi* Seebohm. *Alauda* 5: 383-388.

DEMENTIEV, G. P. & GLADKOV, N. A. 1951. [Birds of the Soviet Union], 1. Moscow.

DICKEY, D. R. & van ROSSEM, A. J. 1938. The birds of El Salvador. *Publ. Field Mus. Nat. Hist.* Zool. Ser. 23.

DICKINSON, E. C., KENNEDY, R. S. & PARKES, K. C. 1991. *The birds of the Philippines: an annotated check-list.* Tring, U.K.: British Ornithologists' Union (Check-list no. 12).

DIESENER, G. 1971. Pflege und Zucht des brasilianischen Sperlingskauzes (*Glaucidium brasilianum*). *Gefied. Welt* 95: 101-104.

DOWNER, A. & SUTTON, R. *Birds of Jamaica.* Cambridge, U.K.: Cambridge University Press.

DOWSETT, R. J. & DOWSETT-LEMAIRE, F. 1993. A contribution to the distribution and taxonomy of Afrotropical and Malagasy birds. *Tauraco Res. Rep.* 5. leige.

DOWSETT-LEMAIRE, F. 1996. A comment on the voice and status of Vermiculated Fishing Owl *Scotopelia bouvieri* and a correction to Dowsett-Lemaire (1992) on the Maned Owl *Jubula lettii. Bull. African Bird Club* 3: 134-135.

DRESSER, H. E. 1879-1896. *A history of the birds of Europe.*

DUCKETT, J. E. 1991. Management of the Barn Owl (*Tyto alba javanica*) as a predator of rats in oil palm (*Elaeis guineensis*) plantations in Malaysia. *Birds of Prey Bull.* 4: 11-23.

DUDGEON, G. C. 1900. The Large Barred Owlet (*Glaucidium cuculoides* Vigors) capturing Quail on the wing. *J. Bombay Nat. Hist. Soc.* 13: 530-531.

DUNNING, J. B. 1993. *CRC handbook of avian body masses.* Boca Raton, Florida.

DUNNING, J. S. 1982. *South American land birds.* Newtown Square, Pennsylvania: Harrowood Books.

DUPONT, J. E. 1971. *Philippine birds.* Greenville, Delaware: Delaware Museum of Natural History.

EARHART, C. M. & JOHNSON, N. K. 1970. Size dimorphism and food habits of North American owls. *Condor* 72: 251-264.

EATES, K. R. 1938. A note on the resident owls of Sind. *J. Bombay Nat. Hist. Soc.* 40: 750-755.

ECK, S. 1968. Der Zeichnungsparallelismus der *Strix varia. Zool. Abh. Staatl. Mus. Tierk.* Dresden 29: 283-288.

ECK, S. 1971. Katalog der Eulen des Staatlichen Museums für Tierkunde Dresden. *Zool. Abh. Staatl. Mus. Tierk.* Dresden 30: 173-218.

ECK, S. 1973. Katalog der ornithologischen Sammlung des Zoologischen Instituts der Karl-Marx-Universität Leipzig übernommen vom Staatl. Mus. für Tierkunde Dresden. *Zool. Abh. Staatl. Mus. Tierk.* Dresden 32: 156-169.

ECK, S. & BUSSE, H. 1973. *Eulen: die rezenten und fossilen Formen.* Wittenberg-Lutherstadt: Ziemsen.

EDWARDS, E. P. 1972. *A field guide to the birds of Mexico.* Sweet Briar, Virginia: E. P. Edwards.

ENGELMANN, F. 1928. *Die Raubvögel Europas,* I. Striges.

ENRIQUEZ-ROCHA, P., RANGEL-SALAZAR, J. L. & HOLT, D. W. 1994. The distribution of Mexican owls. Pp.567-574 in B.-U. Meyburg and R. D. Chancellor, eds. *Raptor conservation today.* London and Robertsbridge, U.K.: World Working Group on Birds of Prey, and Pica Press.

EPPLE, W. 1985. Ethologische Anpassungen im Fortpflanzungssystem der Schleiereulen (*T. alba* Scop. 1769). *Ökol. Vögel* 7: 1-95.

EPPLE, W. & ROGL, M. 1989 *Die Schleiereule.* Luzern.

ERARD, C. & ROUX, F. 1983. La Chevechette du Cap *Glaucidium capense* dans l'ouest africain. Description d'une race géographique nouvelle. *Oiseau et R.F.O.* 53: 97-104.

von ERLANGER, C. 1904. Beiträge zur Vogelkunde Nordostafrika. *J. Orn.* 45: 231-234.

ETCHÉCOPAR, R. D. & HÜE, F. 1967. *The birds of North Africa from the Canary Islands to the Red Sea.* Edinburgh & London: Oliver & Boyd.

ETCHÉCOPAR, R. D. & HÜE, F. 1978. *Les oiseaux de Chine de Mongolie et de Corée, non passereaux.* Tahiti: Editions de Pacifique.

EVANS, T. D., DUTSON, G. C. L. & BROOKS, T. M. 1993. *Cambridge Philippines Rainforest Project 1991 final report.* Cambridge, U.K.: BirdLife International (Study Report 54).

EVANS, T. D., WATSON, L. G., HIPKISS, A. J., KIURE, J., TIMMINS, R. J. & PERKIN, A. W. 1994. New records of Sokoke Scops Owl *Otus ireneae,* Usambara Eagle Owl *Bubo vosseleri* and East Coast Akalat *Sheppardia gunningi* from Tanzania. *Scopus* 18: 40-47.

EVERETT, M. 1977. *A natural history of owls.* London: Hamlyn.

EXO, K. M. 1984. Die akustische Unterscheidung von Steinkauzmännchen und -weibchen (*Athene noctua*). *J. Orn.* 125: 94-97.

FALLA, R. A., SIBSON, R. B. & TURBOTT, E. G. 1966. *A field guide to the birds of New Zealand and outlaying islands.* London: Collins.

FALLA, R. A., SIBSON, R. B. & TURBOTT, E. G. 1993. *Collins field guide to the birds of New Zealand.* Auckland: HarperCollins.

FARMER, R. 1984. Ear-tufts in a *Glaucidium* owl. *Malimbus* 6: 67-69.

FERGUSON-LEES, J. & FAULL, E. 1992. *Endangered birds.* London: George Philip.

FFRENCH, R. 1973. *A guide to the birds of Trinidad and Tobago.* Wynnewood, Pennsylvania: Livingston Publishing Company.

FINSCH, O. 1899. Über *Scops magicus* (S. Müller) und die verwandten Arten. *Notes Leyden Mus.* 20: 163-184.

FINSCH, O. 1906. On a new owl from Java. *Ibis* 8(6): 401-407.

FINSCH, O. 1912. Über eine neue Art Zwergohreule von Java. *Orn. Monatsb.* 20: 156-159.

FISHER, J. 1990. *Thornburn's birds.* London: Mermaid Books.

FITZPATRICK, J. W. & O'NEILL, J. P. 1986. *Otus petersoni,* a new screech-owl from the Eastern Andes, with systematic notes on *O. colombianus* and *O. ingens. Wilson Bull.* 98: 1-14.

FJELDSÅ, J. & KRABBE, N. 1989. An unpublished major collection of birds from the Bolivian highlands. *Zoologica Scripta* 18: 321-329.

FJELDSÅ, J. & KRABBE, N. 1990. *Birds of the high Andes.* Copenhagen: Zoological Museum (University of Copenhagen), and Svendborg: Apollo Books.

FLEAY, D. 1940. The Barking Owl mystery. *Victorian Naturalist* 57: 71-95.

FLEAY, D. 1944. Watching the Powerful Owl. *Emu* 44: 97-112.

FLEAY, D. 1949. The Tasmanian Masked Owl. *Emu* 55: 203-210.

FLEMING, J. H. 1916. The Saw-whet Owl of the Queen Charlotte Islands. *Auk* 33: 420-423.

FLEMING, R. L. & TRAYLOR, M. A. 1961. Notes on Nepal birds. *Fieldiana Zool.* 35: 441-487.

FLEMING, R. L. & TRAYLOR, M. A. 1968. Distributional notes on Nepal birds. *Fieldiana Zool.* 53: 145-203.

FLETCHER, B. S. 1998. A breeding record for Minahassa Owl *Tyto inexpectata* from Dumoga-Bone National Park, Sulawesi, Indonesia. *Forktail* 14: 80-81.

FLINT, V. E., BOEHME, R. L., KOSTIN, Y. V. & KUZNETSOV, A. A. 1984. *A field guide to birds of the USSR.* Princeton: Princeton University Press.

FORBUSH, E. H. & MAY, J. B. 1939. *A natural history of American birds of eastern and central North America.* New York: Bramhall.

von FRANTZIUS, A. 1869. Über die geographische Verbreitung der Vögel Costaricas und deren Lebensweise. *J. Orn.* 17: 195-204.

FREETHY, R. 1992. *Owls: a guide for ornithologists.* Hildenborough, U.K.: Bishopsgate Press.

FREMLIN, B. 1986. *A wildlife heritage of Western Australia.* Perth: St George Books.

FRIEDMANN, H. & DEIGNAN, H. G. 1939. Notes on some Asiatic owls of the genus *Otus,* with description of a new form. *J. Washington Acad.* Sci. 29: 287-291.

FRIEDMANN, H. 1949. The birds of North and Middle America, XI. *U.S. Natn. Mus. Bull.* 50.

FRIEDMANN, H. A new heron and a new owl from Venezuela. Smithsonian Coll., III(9): 2-3, Washington.

FRISCH, J. D. 1981. *Aves brasileiras* I. Sao Paulo: Dalgas Ecoltec Ecologia Técnica.

FRITH, C. & FRITH, D. 1985. *Australian tropical birds.* National Library of Australia.

FRY, C. H., KEITH, S. & URBAN, E. K. 1988. *The birds of Africa,* 3. London: Academic Press.

FUERTES, L. A. 1920. American birds of prey. *Natn. Geogr. Soc.* 38: 460-467.

GALEOTTI, P. & GARIBALDI, A. 1994. Territorial behaviour and habitat selection by the Scops Owl *Otus scops* in a karstic valley (N Italy). Pp.501-505 in B.-U. Meyburg and R. D. Chancellor, eds. *Raptor conservation today.* London and Robertsbridge, U.K.: World Working Group on Birds of Prey, and Pica Press.

GALLAGHER, M. D. & ROGER, T. D. 1980. On some birds of Dhofar and other parts of Oman. *Muscat Oman Stud. Spec. Report* 2: 369-371 (Strigidae).

GALLAGHER, M. D. & WOODCOCK, M. W. 1980. *The birds of Oman.* London: Quartet Books.

GALLAGHER, T. 1998. Lost and found. *Living Bird* 17: 24-28.

GEHLBACH, F. R. 1994. Recruitment in an Eastern Screech Owl *Otus asio* population: on components of fitness and inheritance. Pp.507-509 in B.-U. Meyburg and R. D. Chancellor, eds. *Raptor conservation today*. London and Robertsbridge, U.K.: World Working Group on Birds of Prey, and Pica Press.

GÉNOT, J.-C. 1994. Breeding biology of the Little Owl in France. Pp.511-520 in B.-U. Meyburg and R. D. Chancellor, eds. *Raptor conservation today*. London and Robertsbridge, U.K.: World Working Group on Birds of Prey, and Pica Press.

GERBER, R. 1960. *Die Sumpfohreule*. Wittenberg-Lutherstadt: Ziemsen.

GÉROUDET, P. 1979. *Les rapaces diurnes et nocturnes d'Europe*. Neuchatel: Delachaux & Niestlé.

GILL, L. E. 1964. *A first guide to South African birds*. Cape Town: Miller.

GILMAN, M. F. 1909. Some owls along the Gila River in Arizona. *Condor* 11: 145-150.

GINN, P. S., McILLERON, W. G. & MILSTEIN, P. le S. 1989. *The complete book of southern African birds*. Cape Town: Struik Winchester.

GLUE, D. E. 1972. Bird prey taken by British owls. *Bird Study* 19: 91-95.

GLUE, D. E. 1977. Breeding biology of Long-eared Owls. *Brit. Birds* 70: 318-331.

GLUTZ von BLOTZHEIM, U. N. & BAUER, K. M. 1980. *Handbuch der Vögel Mitteleuropas*, 9. Wiesbaden: Akademische Verlagsgesellschaft.

GLUTZ von BLOTZHEIM, U. N., ed. 1962. *Die Brutvögel der Schweiz*. Aargauer Tagblatt.

GOODMAN, S. M. & SABRY, H. 1984. A specimen record of Hume's Tawny Owl *Strix butleri* from Egypt. *Bull. Brit. Orn. Club* 104: 79-84.

GOSLER, A., ed. 1991. *Die Vögel der Welt*. Stuttgart: Franckh-Kosmos.

GOULD, G. I. 1977. Distribution of the Spotted Owl in California. *Western Birds* 8: 131-146.

GRASSÉ, P. P., ed. *Traité de Zoologie. Oiseaux*, XV. Paris: Masson.

GREENWAY, J. C. 1958. *Extinct and vanishing birds of the world*. New York: American Committee for International Wildlife Protection (Spec. Publ. 13).

GRIMMETT, R., INSKIPP. C. & INSKIPP, T. 1998. *Birds of the Indian Subcontinent*. Christoper Helm, London.

GRINNELL, J. 1913. Two new races of the Pygmy Owl from the Pacific coast. *Auk* 30: 222-224.

GRISCOM, L. 1931. Notes on rare and little-known neotropical pygmy-owls. *Proc. New England Zool. Club* 12: 37-43.

GRISCOM, L. 1932. The distribution of bird-life in Guatemala. *Bull. Amer. Mus. Nat. Hist.* 64.

de GROOT, R. S. 1983. Origin, status and ecology of the owls of Galápagos. *Ardea* 71: 167-182.

GROSSMANN, M. L. & HAMLET, J. 1964. *Birds of prey of the world*. London: Cassell.

GROSVENOR, G. & WETMORE, A., ed. 1937. *The book of birds*, 2. Washington, D.C.: National Geographic Society.

GURNEY, J. H. 1889. On an apparently undescribed species of owl from the Liu Kiu Islands. *Ibis*: 302.

HACHISUKA, M. 1934. *The Birds of the Philippine Islands* London: H. F. & G. Witherby.

HAFFER, J. 1987. Über Superspezies bei Vögeln. *Ann. Naturhist. Mus. Wien* 88/89 (B) 147-166.

HAFFER, J. 1991. Artbegriff und Artbegrenzung im Werk des Ornithologen Erwin Stresemann (1889-1972). *Mitt. Zool. Mus. Berlin* 67, Suppl.: *Ann. Orn.* 15: 77-91.

HAILS, C. & JARVIS, F. 1987. *Birds of Singapore*. Singapore: Times Editions.

HALL, B. P. 1957. Taxonomic notes on the Spotted Owl *Athene brama* and the Striated Weaver *Ploceus manyar* in Siam, including a new race of the latter. *Bull. Brit. Orn. Club* 77: 44-46.

HALLER, H. 1978. Zur Populationsökologie des Uhus *Bubo bubo* im Hochgebirge: Bestand, Bestandsentwicklung und Lebensraum in den Rät-Alpen. *Orn. Beob.* 75: 237-265.

HALLER, W. 1951. Zur Kièwitt-Frage (Steinkauz oder Waldkauz?). *Orn. Mitt.* 3: 199-301.

HANNECART, F. & LETOCART, Y. *Oiseaux de Nouvelle Calédonie et des Loyautés*, 2. Nouméa: Cardinalis.

HARDY, J. W., COFFEY, B. B. & REYNARD, G. B. 1989. *Voices of the New World owls*. Gainesville, Fl: Ara Records.

HARRIS, A., TUCKER, L. & VINICOMBE, K. 1991. *Vogelbestimmung für Fortgeschrittene*. Stuttgart: Franck-Kosmos.

HARRISON, C. 1975. *Jungvögel, Eier und Nester*. Hamburg & Berlin: Paul Parey.

HARRISON, J. M. 1957. Exhibition of a new race of the Little Owl from the Iberian Peninsula. *Bull. Brit. Orn. Club* 77: 2-3.

HARTERT, E. 1893. A new Scops Owl. (*P. solokensis* sp. nov.). *Bull. Brit. Orn. Club* 6: 5.

HARTERT, E. 1897. Striges (*Pisorhina silvicola alfredi*). *Novit. Zool.* 4: 527-528.

HARTERT, E. 1898. *Pisorhina sulaensis* sp. nov. *Novit. Zool.* 5: 126.

HARTERT, E. 1903. *Pisorhina manadensis kalidupae* ssp. nov. *Novit. Zool.* 10: 21-22.

HARTERT, E. 1904. *Pisorhina manadensis tempestatis* ssp. nov. and *Ninox ocellata* ssp. nov. *Novit. Zool.* 11: 190-191.

HARTERT, E. 1906. *Ninox boobook cinnamomina* ssp. nov. *Novit. Zool.* 13: 293.

HARTERT, E. 1910. Strigidae. *Novit. Zool.* 17: 204-206.

HARTERT, E. 1912-1921. *Die Vögel der Paläarktischen Fauna*, Berlin.

HARTERT, E. 1914. *Ninox meeki*. *Novit Zool.* 21: 289.

HARTERT, E. 1914. *Ninox squamipila* & *Otus m. magicus*. *Novit. Zool.* 21.

HARTERT, E. 1918. *Ninox goldii*. *Novit. Zool.* 25: 325.

HARTERT, E. 1925. *Ninox variegata*. *Novit. Zool.* 32: 289.

HARTERT, E. 1929. On various forms of the genus *Tyto*. *Novit. Zool.* 35: 93-104.

HARTERT, E. & STEINBACHER, F. 1932-1938. *Die Vögel der paläarktischen Fauna*. Supplement. Berlin.

HARTLAUB, G. & FINSCH, O. 1872. On birds from the Pelew and Mackenzie Islands. *Proc. Zool. Soc. London*: 90-91.

HARTLAUB, G. 1877. *Die Vögel Madagascars und der benachbarten Inseln*. Halle.

HAUG, E. A., MILLSAP, B. A. & MARTELL, M. S. 1993. Burrowing Owl *Speotyto cunicularia*. *The Birds of North America* No. 61: 1-19.

HAVERSCHMIDT, F. 1968. *Birds of Surinam*. Edinburgh & London: Oliver and Boyd.

HAVERSCHMIDT, F. 1970. Barn Owls hunting by daylight in Surinam. *Wilson Bull.* 82: 101.

HAYMAN, P. & BURTON, P. 1988. *Das goldene Kosmos-Vogelbuch*. Stuttgart: Franck-Kosmos.

HEIDRICH, H. P., KÖNIG, C. & WINK, B. M. 1995. Bioakustik, Taxonomie und molekulare Systematik amerikanischer Sperlingskäuze (Strigidae: *Glaucidium* spp.). *Stuttgarter Beitr. Naturk.* Ser. A, 534.

HEIDRICH, P., KÖNIG, C. & WINK, M. 1995. Molecular phylogeny of South American screech owls of the *Otus atricapillus* complex (Aves: Strigidae) inferred from nucleotide sequences of the mitochondrial Cytochrome-b gene. *Z-Naturforsch.* 50C: 294-302.

HEINTZELMANN, D. S. 1984. *Guide to owl watching in North America*. Piscataway, N.Y.:

HEKSTRA, G. P. 1982. Description of twenty-four new subspecies of American *Otus* (Aves, Strigidae). *Bull. Zool. Mus. Amsterdam* 9: 49-63.

HELLER, K.-G. & ARLETTAZ, R. 1994. Is there a sex ratio bias in the bushcricket prey of the Scops Owl due to predation of calling males? *J. Orthoptera Res.* 2: 41-42.

HENNICKE, C. R. 1905. *Naturgeschichte der Vögel Mitteleuropas*, 5. Berlin: Neuer Naumann.

HENRY, G. M. 1971. *A guide to the birds of Ceylon*. London: Oxford University Press.

HERKLOTS, G. A. C. 1964. *The birds of Trinidad and Tobago*. London: Collins.

HERREMANS, M., LOUETTE, M. & STEVENS, J. 1991. Conservation status and vocal and morphological description of the Grand Comoro Scops Owl *Otus pauliani* Benson 1960. *Bird Conserv. Internatn.* 1: 123-133.

von HEUGLIN, T. 1863. Beiträge zur Ornithologie N. O.-Afrikas. *J. Orn.* 1863: 12-13.

HIGGINS, P. J. (Ed.) 1999. *Handbook of Australian, New Zealand and Antarctic Birds. Volume 4: Parrots to Dollarbird*. Oxford University Press, Melbourne.

HIGUCHI, H. & MOMOSE, H. 1980. On the calls of the Collared Scops Owl *Otus bakkamoena* in Japan. *Tori* 29: 91-94.

HILL, F. A. R. & LILL, A. 1998a. Density and total population estimates for threatened Christmas Island Hawk-Owl *Ninox natalis*. *Emu* 98: 209-220.

HILL, F. A. R. & LILL, A. 1998b. Vocalisations of the Christmas Island Hawk-Owl *Ninox natalis*: Individual variation in advertisement calls. *Emu* 98: 221-226.

HILL, F. A. R. & LILL, A. 1998c. Diet and roost site characteristics of the Christmas Island Hawk-Owl *Ninox natalis*. *Emu* 98: 227-233.

HILTY, S. L. & BROWN, W. L. 1986. *A guide to the birds of Colombia*. Princeton: Princeton University Press.

HINKELMANN, C. 1987. *Otus petersoni* – eine neu entdeckte Eule aus Peru. *Trochilus* 8: 70-71.

HINKELMANN, C. 1990. Informationen über die Bergwald-Kreischeule *Otus hoyi* n. sp. und Anmerkungen zur Artzugehörigkeit südamerikanischer Zwergohreulen. *Trochilus* 11: 133-135.

HINKELMANN, C. 1992. Kanincheneulen (*Athene cunicularia*) – langbeinige Steinkäuze der amerikanischen Grassteppen. *Trop. Vögel* 13: 71-79.

HOESCH, W. & NIETHAMMER, G. 1940. Die Vogelwelt Deutsch-Südwest-afrikas. *J. Orn.* (spec. no.) 88: 1-404.

HÖGLUND, N. H. & LANSGREN, E. 1968. The Great Grey Owl and its prey in Sweden. *Viltrevy* 5: 363-421.

HÖLZINGER, J. 1987. *Die Vögel Baden-Württembergs: Gefährdung und Schutz*, 2. Stuttgart.

HOLLANDS, D. 1991. *Birds of the night*. Sydney: Reed Books.

HOLLANDS, D. 1995. Silent hunters of the night. *Nature Australia* Spring: 39-45.

HOLMES, D. & PHILLIPPS, K. 1996. *The birds of Sulawesi*. Oxford: Oxford University Press.

HOLMES, D. & NASH, S. 1989. *The birds of Java and Bali*. Oxford: Oxford University Press.

HOPPE, R. 1967. Kichernder Kauz aus Ecuadors Urwäldern. *Vogelkosmos* 67: 310-311.

HOSE, C. 1898. On the avifauna of Mount Dulit and the Baram District in the Territory of Sarawak. *Ibis* (6)5: 381-424.

HOSKING, E. & FLEGG, J. 1982. *Eric Hosking's owls*. London: Pelham.

HOUSSE, E. 1948. *Les oiseaux du Chili*. Paris: Masson.

HOWELL, S. N. G. & ROBBINS, M. B. 1995. Species limits of the Least and Pygmy-Owl (*Glaucidium minutissimum*) complex. *Wilson Bull.* 107: 7-25.

HOWELL, S. N. G. & WEBB, S. 1995. *A guide to the birds of Mexico and northern Central America*. Oxford: Oxford University Press.

HOWIE, R. R. & RITCHEY, R. 1987. Distribution, habitat selection and densities of Flammulated Owl in British Columbia. In Nero et al. 1987: 249-254.

HUBBARD, J. P. & CROSSIN, R. S. 1974. Notes on Northern Mexican birds. *Nemouria* 14.

HÜE, F. & ETCHÉCOPAR, R. D. 1970. *Les oiseaux du Proche et du Moyen Orient*. Paris.

HUEY, L. 1926. Birds of NW California. *Auk* 43: 360-362.

HUME, A. 1875. Novelties. *Stray Feathers* 3: 389-391.

HUMPHREY, P. S., BRIDGE, D., REYNOLDS, P. W. & PETERSON, R. T. 1970. *Birds of Isla Grande (Tierra del Fuego)*. Lawrence, Kansas: University of Kansas Museum of Natural History, for the Smithsonian Institution, Washington, D.C.

HUSSAIN, S. A. & KHAN, M. A. R. 1978. A new subspecies of Bay Owl (*Phodilus badius* Horsfield) from peninsular India. *J. Bombay Nat. Hist. Soc.* 74: 334-336.

INGLIS, C. M. 1945. The Northern Bay Owl. *J. Bengal Nat. Hist. Soc.* 19: 93-96.

IREDALE, T. 1956. *Birds of New Guinea*, I. Melbourne: Georgian House.

IRWIN, M. P. S. 1981. *The birds of Zimbabwe*. Salisbury, Zimbabwe: Quest Publishing.

ISHTIAQ, F. 1998. *Status survey of the Forest Spotted Owlet Athene blewitti in India*. Bombay Nat. Hist. Soc., Mumbai. 27pp.

JAKSIC, F. M., SEIB, R. L. & HERRERA, C. M. 1982. Predation by Barn Owl (*Tyto alba*) in Mediterranean habitats of Chile, Spain and California: a comparative approach. *Amer. Midland Nat.* 107: 151-162.

JANY, E. 1955. Neue Vogel-Formen von den Molukken. *J. Orn.* 96: 106.

JELLICOE, M. 1954. The Akun Eagle Owl. *Sierra Leone Studies* 154-167.

JIMÉNEZ, J. E. & JAKSIC, F. M. 1989. Biology of the Austral Pygmy Owl. *Wilson Bull.* 101: 377-389.

JOHANSEN, H. 1978. Nest site selection by the Ural Owl. *Fauna och Flora* 73: 207-210.

JOHNSGARD, P. A. 1988. *North American owls: biology and natural history*. Washington, D.C.

JOHNSGARD, P. A. 1991. Photo essay: Burrowing Owls. *Birders World* 6: 30-34.

JOHNSON, A. W. 1967. *The birds of Chile*, 2. Buenos Aires: Platt Establicimientos Gráficos.

JOHNSON, N. K. & JONES, R. E. 1990. Geographic differentation and distribution of the Peruvian Screech Owl. *Wilson Bull.* 102: 199-212.

JOHNSON, N. K. 1963. The supposed migratory status of the Flammulated Owl. *Wilson Bull.* 75: 174-178.

JOHNSON, W. D. 1975. Notes to the metabolism of the Cuckoo Owlet and Hawk Owl. *Bull. South Cal. Acad. Sci.* 74: 44-45.

JOHNSTON, R. F. 1956. Predation by Short-eared Owls on a *Salicornia* salt marsh. *Wilson Bull.* 68: 91-102.

JOHNSTONE, R.E. & DARNELL, J. C. 1997. Description of a new subspecies of Boobook Owl *Ninox novaeseelandiae* (Gmelin) from Roti Island, Indonesia. *W. Aust. Nat.* 21(3): 161-173.

JONSSON, L. 1992. *Die Vögel Europas und des Mittelmeerraumes*. Stuttgart: Franck-Kosmos.

KABAYA, T. & HIGUCHI, H. 1977. Songs and calls of the Scops Owl *Otus scops* in the Ryukyu Islands. *Tori* 26: 93-94.

KANAN, R. 1996. Another Bay Owl rediscovery. Rare bird found in Zaire. *W.C.S. News Section, Media Newsletter*, Sept. 1996, no. 4.

KAUP, J. J. 1862. Monograph of the Strigidae. *Trans. Zool. Soc. London* 1862: 201-260.

KELSO, E. H. 1936. A new striped owl from Tobago. *Auk* 53: 82.

KELSO, E. H. 1937. A new wood owl from Siam. *Auk* 54: 305.

KELSO, L. 1932. Synopsis of the American wood owls of the genus *Ciccaba*. Lancaster, Pa.

KELSO, L. 1934a. A key to the owls of the genus *Pulsatrix* Kaup. *Auk* 51: 234-236.

KELSO, L. 1934b. A new Stygian Owl. *Auk* 51: 522-523.

KELSO, L. 1937. A Costa Rican race of Jardine's Pygmy Owl. *Auk* 54: 304.

KELSO, L. 1940. Variation of the external ear-opening in the Strigidae. *Wilson Bull.* 52: 24-29.

KELSO, L. 1946. A study of the Spectacled Owls, genus *Pulsatrix*. *Biol. Leaflet* 33: 1-13.

KELSO, L. & KELSO, E. H. 1934. *A key to species of American owls and a list of the owls of America*. Washington, D.C.

KELSO, L. & KELSO, E. H. 1936a. The relation of feathering of feet of American owls to humidity of environment and to life zones. *Auk* 53: 51-56.

KELSO, L. & KELSO, E. H. 1936b. A new screech owl from Colombia. *Auk* 53: 448.

KEMP, A. & CALBURN, S. 1987. *The owls of southern Africa*. Cape Town.

KEMP, A. C. 1991. Estimation of biological indices for little-known African owls. Pp.441-449 in B.-U. Meyburg & R. D. Chancellor, eds. *Raptors in the modern world*. London: World Working Group on Birds of Prey.

KING, B. 1978. April bird observations in Saudi Arabia. *J. Saudi Arab. Nat. Hist. Soc.* 21: 1-23.

KING, B. 1997. *Checklist of the birds of Eurasia*. Vista, California: Ibis Publishing.

KING, B., DICKINSON, E. C. & WOODCOCK, M. 1975. *Field guide to the birds of South-East Asia*. London: Collins.

KING, B. & RASMUSSEN, P. C. 1998. The rediscovery of the Forest Owlet *Athene* (*Heteroglaux*) *blewitti*. *Forktail* 14: 51-53.

KIPP, F. 1959. Der Handflügel-Index als flugbiologisches Maß. *Vogelwarte* 20: 77-86.

KLAUS, S., VOGEL, F. & WIESNER, J. 1965. Ein Beitrag zur Biologie des Sperlingskauzes. Beobachtungen an einem Brutplatz von *Glaucidium passerinum* (L.) im Elbsandsteingebirge. *Zool. Abh. Mus. Tierk. Dresden* 28: 165-204.

KLAUS, S., KUCERA, L. & WIESNER, J. 1976. Zum Verhalten unverpaarter Männchen des Sperlingskauzes *Glaucidium passerinum*. *Orn. Mitt.* 28: 95-100.

KLAUS, S., BRÄSECKE, M. & BRÄSECKE, R. 1982. Beobachtungen an einem Brutplatz des Sperlingskauzes in der Belaer Tatra (Belanske Tatry, CSSR). *Falke* 29: 330-336.

KLEINSCHMIDT, O. 1906. *Strix flammea*. *Berajah*: 1-20. Leipzig.

KLEINSCHMIDT, O. 1907. *Strix athene. Berajah. Zoographia Infinita*: 1-6 (I-III), Leipzig (Nägele).

KLEINSCHMIDT, O. 1926. *Die Formenkreislehre und das Weltwerden des Lebens*. Halle: Gebauer-Schwetschke.

KLEINSCHMIDT, O. 1958. Raubvögel und Eulen der Heimat. Wittenberg-Lutherstadt: Ziemsen.

KNYSAUSTAS, A. J. V. & SIBNEV, J. B. 1987. *Die Vogelwelt Ussuriens*. Hamburg – Berlin.

KOBAYASHI, K. 1965. *Birds of Japan*. Osaka/Japan.

KOELZ, W. 1939. New birds from Asia, chiefly from India. *Proc. Biol. Soc. Washington* 52: 61-82.

KOELZ, W. 1950. New subspecies of birds from southwestern India. *Amer. Mus. Novit.* 1452.

KOENIG, A. 1936. *Die Vögel am Nil*, 2. Die Raubvögel. Bonn.

KOENIG, L. 1973. Das Aktionssystem der Zwergohreule *Otus scops scops*. *J. Comp. Ethol.* (Suppl.) 13: 1-124.

KOEPCKE, M. 1957. Aspectos de la distribución de las aves en el Perú. *Scientia*, U.N.M.S.M. Lima 4: 33-42.

KOEPCKE, M. (manuscript) Eine neue Eule von den Hochanden Perus. Ein Beitrag zur Kenntnis von *Otus roboratus*. Unpublished manuscript (courtesy of H. W. Koepcke).

KOEPCKE, M. 1964. *Las aves del departamento de Lima*. Lima.

KOEPCKE, H. W. & KOEPCKE, M. 1958. Los restos de bosques en las vertientes occidentales de los Andes. *Bol. Com. Nac. Protec. Nat.* 16: 22-30.

KOHL, S. 1977. Über die taxonomische Stellung der südosteuropäischen Habichtkäuze *Strix uralensis macroura* Wolf. *Studii si Communicarie Muzeum Brukenthal* 21: 309-344.

KOLLIBAY, P. 1910. On the ornithology of the Philippines. *Orn. Monatsb.* 18: 148-149.

KÖNIG, C. 1961. Schleiereule, *Tyto a. alba* Scop., 'schlägt fliegende Fledermäuse. *Beitr. Vogelk.* 7: 229-233.

KÖNIG, C. 1967 & 1970. *Europäische Vögel*, 2 & 3. Stuttgart: Belser.

KÖNIG, C. 1967. Der Sperlingskauz (*Glaucidium passerinum*) stirbt in Baden-Württemberg aus! *Veröff. Landesst. Natursch. & Landschaftspfl.* Baden-Württemburg 35: 39-44.

KÖNIG, C. 1968a. Lautäußerungen von Rauhfußkauz (*Aegolius funereus*) und Sperlingskauz (*Glaucidium passerinum*). *Vogelwelt* (suppl. 1): 115-138.

KÖNIG, C. 1968b. Zur Unterscheidung ähnlicher Rufe von Zwergohreule (*Otus scops*), Sperlingskauz (*Glaucidium passerinum*) und Geburtshelferkröte (*Alytes obstetricans*). *Orn. Mitt.* 20: p. 35.

KÖNIG, C. 1969. Sechsjährige Untersuchungen an einer Population des Rauhfußkauzes *Aegolius funereus*. *J. Orn.* 110: 133-147.

KÖNIG, C. 1969. Ordnung Eulen. Pp.377-406 in *Grzimeks Tierleben*. München: Kindler.

KÖNIG, C. 1972. Mobbing of small passerine birds in response to the song of the Pygmy Owl (*Glaucidium passerinum*). *Proc. XV Internatn. Orn. Congr.*: 661-662.

KÖNIG, C. 1975. Zur Situation von Uhu, Sperlings- und Rauhfußkauz. *Beih. Veröff. Landesst. Natursch. & Landschaftspfl.* Baden-Württemburg 7: 68-77.

KÖNIG, C. 1977. Der Sperlingskauz (*Glaucidium passerinum*) in Südwestdeutschland. *Ber. Deutsch. Sekt. Internatn. Rat Vogelsch.* 17: 77-80.

KÖNIG, C. 1981. Die Wiedereinbürgerung des Sperlingskauzes (*Glaucidium passerinum*) im Schwarzwald. *Forschber. Natn. Park Berchtesgaden* 3: 17-20.

KÖNIG, C. 1987. Zur Kenntnis des Patagonien-Sperlingskauzes *Glaucidium nanum* (King 1827). *Cour. Forsch.-Inst. Senckenberg* 97: 127-139.

KÖNIG, C. 1991a. Taxonomische und ökologische Untersuchungen an Kreischeulen (*Otus* sp.) des südlichen Südamerikas. *J. Orn.* 132: 209-214.

KÖNIG, C. 1991b. Zur Taxonomie und Ökologie der Sperlingskäuze (*Glaucidium* spp.) des Andenraumes. *Ökol. Vögel* 13: 15-76.

KÖNIG, C. 1993. Pygmy Owl in the Black Forest, SW Germany. *Re-introduction News* 7: 8-10.

KÖNIG, C. 1994a. Biological patterns in owl taxonomy, with emphasis on bioacoustical studies on Neotropical pygmy (*Glaucidium*) and screech owls (*Otus*). Pp.1-19 in B.-U. Meyburg and R. D. Chancellor, eds. *Raptor conservation today*. London and Robertsbridge, U.K.: World Working Group on Birds of Prey, and Pica Press.

KÖNIG, C. 1994b. Lautäußerungen als interspezifische Isolationsmechanismen bei Eulen der Gattung *Otus* (Aves: Strigidae) aus dem südlichen Südamerika. *Stuttgart. Beitr. Naturk.* Ser. A, 511.

KÖNIG, C. 1998. Lautäußerungen als interspezifische Differenzierungsmerkmale bei Eulen und ihre Bedeutung für die Taxonomie (Aves: Strigidae). *Zool. Abh. Staatl. Mus. Tierkde. Dresden* 50 (Suppl.): 51-62.

KÖNIG, C. 1999. Zur Ökologie und zum Lautinventar des Blaßstirnkauzes (*Aegolius harrisii*) in Nordargentinien. *Orn. Mitt.* 51: 127-138.

KÖNIG, C. & ERTEL, R. 1979. *Vögel Afrikas*, I. Stuttgart & Zürich: Belser.

KÖNIG, C. & KAISER, H. 1985. Der Sperlingskauz (*Glaucidium passerinum*) im Schwarzwald. *J. Orn.* 126: 443.

KÖNIG, C. & STRANECK, R. 1989. Eine neue Eule (Aves: Strigidae) aus Nordargentinien. *Stuttgart. Beitr. Naturk.* Ser. A, 428.

KÖNIG, C. & WINK, M. 1995. Eine neue Unterart des Brasil-Sperlingskauzes aus Zentralargentinien: *Glaucidium brasilianum stranecki* n. ssp. *J. Orn.* 136: 461-465.

KÖNIG, C., KAISER, H. & MÖRIKE, D. 1995. Zur Ökologie und Bestandsentwicklung des Sperlingskauzes (*Glaucidium passerinum*) im Schwarzwald. *Jh. Ges. Naturkde. Württemburg* 151: 457-500.

KÖNIG, C., HEIDRICH, P. & WINK, M. 1996. Zur Taxonomie der Uhus (*Bubo* ssp.) im südlichen Südamerika. *Stuttgart. Beitr. Naturk.* Ser. A, 540.

KRAHE, R. G. 1997. Überlebenstechniken nordischer Eulenarten. *S.C.R.O. Magazin* 1: 34-42.

KRATTER, A. W., SILLETT, T. S., CHESSER, R. T., O'NEILL, J. P., PARKER, T. A. & COSTELLO, A. 1993. Avifauna of a chaco locality in Bolivia. *Wilson Bull.* 105: 114-141.

KUHK, R. 1953. Lautäußerungen und jahreszeitliche Gesangstätigkeit des Rauhfußkauzes (*Aegolius funereus*). *J. Orn.* 94: 83-93.

KUHK, R. 1966. Aus der Sinneswelt des Rauhfußkauzes (*Aegolius funereus*). *Anz. Orn. Ges. Bayern* (spec. no.) 7: 714-716.

KULLBERG, C. 1995. Strategy of the Pygmy Owl while hunting avian and mammalian prey. *Ornis Fennica* 72: 72-78.

KURODA, N. 1931. A new subspecies of *Bubo blakistoni* from Sakhalin. *Tori* 31(7): 41-42.

KURODA, N. 1936. *Birds of the Island of Java*, 2. Tokyo: privately published.

LAFONTAINE, R. M. & MOULAERT, N. 1999. Une nouvelle espèce de petit-duc (*Otus*, Aves) aux Comores: taxonomie et statut de conservation. *Bull. African Bird Club* 6: 61-65.

LAMBERT, F. R. & RASMUSSEN, P. C. 1998. A new Scops Owl from Sangihe Island, Indonesia. *Bull. Brit. Orn. Club* 118: 204-217.

LAND, H. C. 1970. *Birds of Guatemala*. Wynnewood, Pennsylvania: Livingston Publishing Company.

LANGRAND, O. 1990. *Guide to the birds of Madagascar*. New Haven: Yale University Press.

LA TOUCHE, J. D. D. 1921. New races of *Bubo*. *Bull. Brit. Orn. Club* 42: 12-18, 29-32.

LAUDAR, E., LOPEZ, J., DIAZ, C. & COLMENARES, M. 1991. Population biology of the Barn Owl (*Tyto alba*) in Guarico State, Venezuela. *Birds of Prey Bull.* 4: 167-173.

LAWRENCE, G. N. 1878. On the members of *Gymnoglaux*. *Ibis* 20: 184-187.

LEGGE, W. V. 1880. *A history of the birds of Ceylon*, I. Republished 1983 by Tisara Prakasakayo, Dehiwala, Sri Lanka.

von LEHMANN, F. C. 1946. Two new birds from the Andes of Colombia. *Auk* 63: 218-221.

LEKAGUL, B. & ROUND, P. D. 1991. *A guide to the birds of Thailand*. Bangkok: Saha Karn Bhaet.

LESHEM, Y. 1979. Humes Waldkauz (*Strix butleri*) – die Lilith der Wüste. *Natur und Museum* 109: 375-377.

LESHEM, Y. 1981. Israel's raptors – the Negev and Iudean Desert. *Ann. Rep. Hawk Trust* 11: 30-35.

LESHEM, Y. 1981. The occurrence of Hume's Tawny Owl in Israel and Sinai. *Sandgrouse* 2: 100-102.

LEWINGTON, I., ALSTRÖM, P. & COLSTON, P. 1992. *Rare birds of Britain and Europe*. London: Collins.

LEWIS, A. 1995. In search of Badenga. *Bull. African Bird Club.* 3: 131-133.

LEWIS, A. 1998. Mayotte Scops Owl *Otus rutilus mayottensis*. *Bull. African Bird Club* 5: 33-34.

LIGON, J. D. 1968. The biology of the Elf Owl, *Micrathene whitneyi*. *Misc. Publ. Mus. Zool. Univ. Michigan* 136.

LISTER, J. J. 1888. On the natural history of Christmas Island. *Proc. Zool. Soc. London*: 512-531.

LIVERSIDGE, T. N. 1980. A study of Pel's Fishing Owl *Scotopelia peli* Bonaparte 1850 in the 'Pan Handle' region of the Okavango Delta, Botswana. *Proc. Pan-Afr. Orn. Congr.*: 291-299.

LLOYD, G. D. 1971. *Greifvögel und Eulen*. Stuttgart & Zürich.

LÖHRL, H. 1980. Alarmlaute der Tannenmeise. *J. Orn.* 121: 408-409.

LOUETTE, M. 1988. *Les oiseaux de Comores*. Tervuren.

LOUETTE, M., STEVENS, J., HERREMANS, M. & VANGELUWE, D. 1990. Red data bird: Grand Comoro Scops Owl. *World Birdwatch* 12(1-2): 13.

LOUETTE, M. & STEVENS, J. 1992. Conserving the endemic birds on the Comoro Islands, I: general considerations on survival prospects. *Bird Conserv. Internatn.* 2: 61-80.

LOWERY, G. H. & DALQUEST, W. W. 1951. Birds from the state of Veracruz, Mexico. *Univ. Kansas Publ. Mus. Hist. Nat.* 3: 533-649.

LOWERY, G. H. & NEWMAN, R. J. 1949. New birds from state of San Luis Potosí and the Tuxla Mountains of Veracruz, Mexico. *Occas. Pap. Mus. Zool. Louisiana State Univ.* 22: 1-4.

MACKAY, B. K. 1994. A celebration of owls. *Birds of the World* 3: 16-26.

MACKENZIE, J. P. S. 1986. *Birds of prey*. London: Harrap.

MACKINNON, J. 1990. *Birds of Java and Bali*. Yogyakarta, Java: Gadja Mada University Press.

MACKINNON, J. & PHILLIPPS, K. 1993. *A field guide to the birds of Borneo, Sumatra, Java and Bali*. Oxford: Oxford University Press.

MACKWORTH-PRAED, C. W. & GRANT, C. H. B. 1957. *Birds of eastern and north eastern Africa*, I. London: Longmans, Green & Co.

MACKWORTH-PRAED, C. W. & GRANT, C. H. B. 1962. *Birds of the southern third of Africa*, I. London: Longmans, Green & Co.

MACKWORTH-PRAED, C. W. & GRANT, C. H. B. 1970. *Birds of the west central and western Africa*, I. London: Longmans, Green & Co.

MACLEAN, G. L. 1985. *Roberts' birds of the southern Africa*. Fifth edition. Cape Town: Trustees of the John Voelker Bird Book Fund.

MAKATSCH, W. 1989. *Wir bestimmen die Vögel Europas*. Leipzig & Radebeul: Neumann.

MAGNIN, G. 1991. A record of Brown Fish-Owl *Ketupa zeylonensis* from Turkey. *Sandgrouse* 13: 42.

MANNEL, C. B. & GILLIARD, E. T. 1952. Undescribed and newly recorded Philippine birds. *Amer. Mus. Novit.* 1545.

MARCHANT, S. 1948. The West African Wood Owl. *Nigerian Field* 13: 16-20.

MARÍN A., M., KIFF, L. F. & PENA G., L. 1989. Notes on Chilean birds, with descriptions of two new subspecies. *Bull. Brit. Orn. Club* 109: 66-82.

van MARLE, J. G. 1940. Aanteekeningen omtrent de vogels van Minahassa (N. O. Celebes). *Limosa* 13: 65-70, 119-124.

MARPLES, B. J. 1942. A study of the Little Owl (*Athene noctua*) in New Zealand. *Trans. Proc. Roy. Soc. New Zealand* 72: 237-252.

MARSHALL, J. T. 1942. Food and habitat of Spotted Owl. *Condor* 44: 66-67.

MARSHALL, J. T. 1939. Territorial behaviour of the Flammulated Screech Owl. *Condor* 41: 71-78.

MARSHALL, J. T. 1949. The endemic avifauna of Saipan, Tinian, Guam and Palau. *Condor* 51: 200-221.

MARSHALL, J. T. 1957. Birds of pine-oak woodland in southern Arizona and adjacent Mexico. *Pacific Coast Avifauna* 32.

MARSHALL, J. T. 1966. Relationship of certain owls around the Pacific. *Nat. Hist. Bull. Siam Soc.* 21: 235-242.

MARSHALL, J. T. 1967. Parallel variation in North and Middle American screech owls. *Proc. Western Found. Vert. Zool.* 1-72.

MARSHALL, J. T. 1978. *Systematics of smaller Asian night birds based on voice*. Orn. Monogr. 25 (with disc).

MARSHALL, J. T. & KING, B. 1988. Genus *Otus*. Pp.331-336 in D. Amadon & J. Bull, Hawks and owls of the world: a distributional and taxonomic list. *Proc. Western Found. Vert. Zool*. 3: 295-357.

MARSHALL, J. T. 1991. Variable Screech Owl (*Otus atricapillus*) and its relatives. *Wilson Bull*. 103: 314-315.

MARSHALL, J. T., BEHRSTOCK, R. & KÖNIG, C. 1991. Review of the cassettes: Voices of the New World nightjars and their allies (Caprimulgiformes), Voices of the New World owls (Strigiformes). *Wilson Bull*. 103: 311-314.

MÄRZ, R. 1968. *Der Rauhfußkauz*. Wittenberg–Lutherstadt: Ziemsen.

MASON, I. J. 1983. A new subspecies of Masked Owl *Tyto novaehollandiae* from southern New Guinea. *Bull. Brit. Orn. Club* 103: 122-128.

MATHEWS, G. M. 1916. *The birds of Australia*, 5 (1). London: Witherby.

MAYR, E. 1929. Birds collected during the Whitney South Sea Expedition. *Amer. Mus. Novit*. 6-7.

MAYR, E. 1931. Birds of the Whitney Expedition XVII. *Amer. Mus. Novit*. 14-15.

MAYR, E. 1935. Whitney South Sea Expedition XXX. *Amer. Mus. Novit*. 820.

MAYR, E. 1943. *Ninox novaeseelandiae*: revision of Australasian races. *Emu* 43: 12-16.

MAYR, E. 1944. The birds of Timor and Sumba. *Bull. Amer. Mus. Nat. Hist*. 83: 123-194.

MAYR, E. 1945. The races of *Ninox philippinensis*. *Zoologica* 30: 46.

MAYR, E. & GILLIARD, E. T. 1954. Birds of central New Guinea. *Bull. Amer. Mus. Nat. Hist*. 103: 311-374.

MAYR, E. & MEYER de SCHAUENSEE, R. 1939. Birds of the island of Biak. *Proc. Acad. Nat. Sci. Philadelphia* 91: 1-37.

MAYR, E. & SHORT, L. L. 1970. Species taxa of North American birds. *Publ. Nuttall Orn. Club* 9.

McGREGOR, R. C. 1905. Birds from the islands of Romblon, Sibuyan and Cresta de Gallo. *Bur. Govern. Labor*. 25: 5-23.

McGREGOR, R. C. 1927. New or noteworthy Philippine birds, V. *Philippine J. Sci*. 32: 513-527.

McKITRICK, M. C. & ZINK, R. M. 1988. Species concepts in ornithology. *Condor* 90: 1-12.

MEBS, T. 1987. *Eulen und Käuze*. Stuttgart: Franck-Kosmos.

MEDWAY, Lord & WELLS, D. R. 1976. *The birds of the Malay Peninsula*, 5. London: H. F. & G. Witherby in association with Penerbit Universiti Malaya.

MEES, G. F. 1964a. Geographical variation in *Bubo sumatranus* (Raffles) (Aves, Strigidae). *Zool. Meded*. 40(13).

MEES, G. F. 1964b. A revision of the Australian owls. *Zool. Verhand*. 65: 1-62.

MEES, G. F. 1967. Zur Nomenklatur einiger Raubvögel und Eulen. *Zool. Meded*. 42(14): 143-146.

MEES, G. F. 1970. Birds from Formosa. *Zool. Meded*. 44: 285-297.

MEES, G. F. 1971. Birds from Borneo and Java. *Zool. Meded*. 45: 231-232.

MEES, G. F. 1982. Review of *Nocturnal birds of Australia* by R. Schodde & I. J. Mason. *Emu* 82: 182-184.

MEINERTZHAGEN, R. 1930. *Nicoll's Birds of Egypt*, 2. London: Hugh Rees for the Egyptian Government.

MEINERTZHAGEN, R. 1948. On the *Otus scops* (L.) group, and allied groups, with special reference to *Otus brucei* (Hume). *Bull. Brit. Orn. Club* 69: 8-11.

MEINERTZHAGEN, R. 1951. On the genera *Athene* Boie 1822 and *Speotyto* Gloger 1842. *Bull. Brit. Orn. Club* 70: 8-9.

MEINERTZHAGEN, R. 1954. *Birds of Arabia*. Edinburgh & London: Oliver and Boyd.

MEINERTZHAGEN, R. 1959. *Pirates and predators*. Edinburgh & London: Oliver and Boyd.

MEISE, W. 1933. Zur Systematik der Fischeulen. *Orn. Monatsb*. 41: 169-173.

MELDE, M. 1984. *Der Waldkauz*. Wittenberg-Lutherstadt: Ziemsen.

MERRIAM, G. H. 1893. The hawks and owls of the United States. *U.S. Dept. Agricult. Bull*. 3.

MEYER, A. B. 1882. On *Ninox rudolfi*, a new species of hawk owl in the Malay Archipelago. *Ibis* VI: 232.

MEYER de SCHAUENSEE, R. 1964. *The birds of Colombia*. Narberth, Pennsylvania: Livingston Publishing Company.

MEYER de SCHAUENSEE, R. 1966. *The species of birds of South America*. Narberth, Pennsylvania: Livingston Publishing Company.

MEYER de SCHAUENSEE, R. 1970. *A guide to the birds of South America*. Wynnewood, Pennsylvania: Livingston Publishing Company for the Academy of Natural Sciences of Philadelphia.

MEYER de SCHAUENSEE, R. 1984. *The birds of China*. Oxford: Oxford University Press.

MEYER DE SCHAUENSEE, R. & PHELPS, W. H. 1978. *A guide to the birds of Venezuela*. Princeton: Princeton University Press.

MIENIS, H. K. 1994. A case of 'pseudopredation' on landsnails by the Long-eared Owl *Asio otus*. *Orn. Soc. Middle East Bull*. 32: 20-21.

MIKKOLA, H. 1970. Zur Ernährung des Sperlingskauzes (*Glaucidium passerinum*) zur Brutzeit. *Orn. Mitt*. 22: 73-75.

MIKKOLA, H. 1973. Zur Ernährung der Sperbereule (*Surnia ulula*) zur Brutzeit. *Angew. Orn*. 3: 133-141.

MIKKOLA, H. 1981. *Der Bartkauz*. Wittenberg-Lutherstadt: Ziemsen.

MIKKOLA, H. 1983. *Owls of Europe*. Calton, U.K.: T. & A. D. Poyser.

MIKKOLA, H. 1986. Barn Owl *Tyto alba* in Bali. *Kukila* 2: 95.

MILLER, A. H. 1955. The avifauna of the Sierra del Carmen of Coahuila, Mexico. *Condor* 57: 154-178.

MILLER, A. H. 1963. Seasonal activity and ecology of the avifauna of an American equatorial cloud forest. *Univ. Calif. Publ. Zool.* 66: 1-78.

MILLER, A. H. 1965. The syringal structure of the Asiatic owl *Phodilus*. *Condor* 67: 536-538.

MILLER, A. H. & MILLER, L. 1951. Geographic variation of the screech owls of the desert of western North America. *Condor* 53: 161-177.

MISHIMA, T. 1956. Notes on *Ninox scutulata*. *Japan Wildlife Bull.* 15: 25-26.

MÖCKEL, R. 1980. Der Schutz von Spechthöhlen – eine notwendige Maßnahme zum Schutz bedrohter Vogelarten. *Naturschutzarb. Naturk. Heimatforsch. Sachsen* 22: 6-9.

MÖCKEL, R. & MÖCKEL, W. 1980. Zur Siedlungsdichte des Sperlingskauzes (*Glaucidium passerinum*) im Westerzgebirge. *Arch. Natursch. Landschaftsforsch.* 20: 155-165.

MOMIYAMA, T. T. 1928. New and known forms of the Ural Owl (*Strix uralensis*) from southeastern Siberia, Manchuria, Korea, Sakkalin and Japan. *Auk* 45: 177-185.

MONES, A., XIMÉNEZ, A. & CUELLA, J. 1973. Analisis del contenido de bolos de regurgitación de *Tyto alba tuidara* (J. E. Gray) con el hallazgo de un nuevo mamífero para el Uruguay. *Trab. V. Congr. Latinoamer. Zool.* 1: 166-167.

MONK, K. A., de FRETES, Y. & REKSODIHARJO-LILLEY, G. 1997. *The ecology of Nusa Tenggara and Maluku*. Hong Kong: Periplus (Ecology of Indonesia 5).

MONROE, B. L. 1968. A distributional survey of the birds of Honduras. *Orn. Monogr.* 7.

MONROE, B. L. & SIBLEY, C. 1993. *A world checklist of birds*. New Haven: Yale University Press.

MOON, G. 1992. *A field guide to New Zealand birds*. Singapore: Reed.

MOORE, R. T. 1941. Three new races in the genus *Otus* from central Mexico. *Proc. Biol. Soc. Washington* 54: 151-160.

MOORE, R. T. & MARSHALL, J. T. 1959. A new race of screech owl from Oaxaca: *Otus asio lambi*. *Condor* 61: 224-225.

MOORE, R. T. & PETERS, J. L. 1936. The genus *Otus* of Mexico and central America. *Auk* 56: 38-56.

MOREAU, R. E. 1964. The rediscovery of an African Owl, *Bubo vosseleri*. *Bull. Brit. Orn. Club* 84: 47-52.

MORRISON, A. 1948. Notes on the birds of the Pampas river valley, south Peru. *Ibis* 90: 119-126.

MOSHER, J. A. & HENRY, C. J. 1976. Thermal adaptiveness of plumage color in screech owls. *Auk* 93: 614-619.

MOUNTFORT, G. & ARLOTT, N. 1988. *Rare birds of the world*. London: Collins.

von MÜLLER, J. W. 1853-1854. *Beiträge zur Ornithologie Afrikas*.

MULSOW, D. 1964. Die Uhu-Pyramide. *Vogelkosmos* 11: 246-248.

MURPHY, R. & AMADON, D. 1953. *Land birds of America*. New York: McGraw-Hill.

MURRAY, G. A. 1976. Geographic variation in the clutch sizes of seven owl species. *Auk* 93: 602-613.

MYSTERUD, I. & DUNKER, H. 1979. Mammal ear mimicry: a hypothesis on the behavioural function of owl 'horns'. *Anim. Behaviour* 27: 315-316.

NAKAMURA, K. 1975. A record of a Brown Hawk Owl in the northern Pacific. *Tori* 23: 37-38.

NAROSKY, T. & YZURIETA, D. 1987. *Guía para la identificación de las aves de Argentina y Uruguay*. Buenos Aires: Asociación Ornitológica del Plata.

NATIONAL GEOGRAPHIC SOCIETY 1983. *Field guide to the birds of North America*. Washington, D.C.: National Geographic Society.

de NAUROIS, R. 1961. Recherches sur l'avifaune de la cote atlantique du Maroc, de détroit du Gibraltar aux iles de Mogador. *Alauda* 29: 241-259.

de NAUROIS, R. 1975. Le 'Scops' de l'Ile Sao Tomé *Otus hartlaubi* (Giebel). *Bonn. Zool. Beitr.* 26: 319-355.

de NAUROIS, R. 1982. Le statut de l'effraie de l'archipel du Cap Vert, *Tyto alba detorta*. *Riv. Ital. Orn.* 52: 154-166.

NELSON, A. W. 1901a. Description of a new genus and eleven new species and subspecies of birds from Mexico. *Proc. Biol. Soc. Washington* 14: 169-170.

NELSON, E. W. 1901b. Descriptions of five new birds from Mexico. *Auk* 18: 46.

NERO, R. W. 1988. Denizen of the northern forests: one researcher's account of the Great Gray Owl (*Strix nebulosa*). *Birder's World* 2(5): 20-25.

NERO, R. W., CLARK, R. J., KNAPTON, R. J. & HAMRE, R. H., eds. 1987. *Symposium proceedings on the biology and conservation of northern forest owls*. General Techn. USDA Forest Service RM – 142.

NEUMANN, O. 1911. *Glaucidium capense scheffleri* n. subsp. *Orn. Monatsb.* 19: 184.

NEUMANN, O. 1939. A new species and eight new races from Peleng and Taliaboe (*Tyto nigrobrunnea*). *Bull. Brit. Orn. Club* 59: 89-90.

NICOLAI, B., ed. 1993. *Atlas der Brutvögel Ostdeutschlands*. Stuttgart: Fischer.

NIETHAMMER, G. 1957. Ein weiterer Beitrag zur Vogelwelt des Ennedi-Gebirges. *Bonn. Zool. Beitr.* 8: 275-284.

NORBERG, R. A. 1978. Skull asymmetry, ear structure and function, and auditory localization in Tengmalm's Owl *Aegolius funereus*. *Phil. Trans. Roy. Soc. London* Biol. Ser. 282: 325-410.

NORMAN, J. A., CHRISTIDIS, L., WESTERMAN, M. & HILL, F. A. R. 1998a. Molecular data confirms the species status of the Christmas Isalnd Hawk-Owl *Ninox natalis*. *Emu* 98: 197-208.

NORMAN, J. *et al.* 1998b. Molecular genetics confirms taxonomic affinities of the endangered Norfolk Island Boobook *Ninox novaeseelandiae undulata*. *Biol. Conserv.* 86: 33-36.

NORTHERN, J. R. 1965. Notes on the owls of the Tres Marias Islands, Nayarit, Mexico. *Condor* 67: 358.

OATES, E. W. (Blanford, W. T. ed.) 1889-1898. *Fauna of British India: Birds*.

OBA, T. 1996. Vocal repertoire of the Japanese Brown

Hawk Owl *Ninox scutulata japonica* with notes on its natural history. *Nat. Hist. Res.* Spec. Issue 2: 1-64.

OBERHOLSER, H. C. 1908. A new Great Horned Owl from Venezuela with notes on the names of the American forms. *Mus. Brooklyn Inst. Arts & Sci. Bull.* 1(14): 371-374.

OBERHOLSER, H. C. 1915. Critical notes on the subspecies of the Spotted Owl *Strix occidentalis* (Xantus). *Proc. U.S. Natn. Mus.* 49: 251-257.

OBERHOLSER, H. C. 1922. A revision on the American Great Horned Owls. *Proc. U.S. Natn. Mus.*: 177-192.

OLNEY, P. J. 1984. The rare Nduk Eagle-Owl *Bubo poensis vosseleri* or *B. vosseleri* at the London Zoo. *Avicult. Mag.* 90: 129-134.

OLROG, C. C. 1974. Notas ornitológicas X. Sobre la colección del Instituto Miguel Lillo. *Acta zool. Lilloana* 31(8): 71-73.

OLROG, C. C. 1979. Notas ornitológicas XI. Sobre la colección del Instituto Miguel Lillo. *Acta zool. Lilloana* 33(2): 5-6.

OLROG, C. C. 1979. Nueva lista de la avifauna Argentina. *Opera Lilloana* 27.

OLSEN, P. D. & STOKES, T. 1989. State of knowledge of the Christmas Island Hawk-Owl *Ninox squamipila natalis*. Pp.411-414 in B.-U. Meyburg & R. D. Chancellor, eds. *Raptors in the modern world*. London: World Working Group on Birds of Prey.

OLSEN, P. D., MOONEY, N. J. & OLSEN, J. 1989. Status and conservation of the Norfolk Island Boobook *Ninox novaeseelandiae undulata*. Pp.415-422 in B.-U. Meyburg & R. D. Chancellor, eds. *Raptors in the modern world*. London: World Working Group on Birds of Prey.

OLSEN, P. D., HICKS, J., MOONEY, N. & GREENWOOD, D. 1994. Progress of the Norfolk Island Boobook Owl *Ninox novaeseelandiae undulata* re-establishment programme. Pp.575-578 in B.-U. Meyburg and R. D. Chancellor, eds. *Raptor conservation today*. London and Robertsbridge, U.K.: World Working Group on Birds of Prey, and Pica Press.

O'NEILL, J. P. & GRAVES, G. R. 1977. A new genus and species of owl (Aves: Strigidae) from Peru. *Auk* 94: 409-416.

OSCHE, G. 1966. Grundzüge der allgemeinen Phylogenetik. In F. Gessner, ed. *Handbuch der Biologie*. Vol 3/2. Frankfurt a. M.

OWEN, D. F. 1963a. Polymorphism in the Screech Owl in Eastern North America. *Wilson Bull.* 75: 183-190.

OWEN, D. F. 1963b. Variation in North American screech owls and the subspecies concept. *Syst. Zool.* 12: 8-14.

PACKLAND, R. L. 1954. Great Horned Owl attacking squirrel nests. *Wilson Bull.* 66: 272.

PAGE, W. T. 1920. The Bengal Eagle Owl. *Bird Notes* 3: 40-41.

PAKENHAM, R. H. W. 1937. *Otus pembaensis* sp. nov. *Bull. Brit. Orn. Club* 57: 112-114.

PALMER, D. A. 1986. Habitat selection, movements and activity of Boreal and Saw-whet Owls. Ph.D. thesis. Colorado State University, Fort Collins.

PANOV, E. N. 1973. [*The birds of south Ussuriland*]. Novosibirsk.

PARKER, T. A., PARKER, S. A. & PLENGE, M. A. 1982. *An annotated checklist of Peruvian birds*. Vermillion, South Dakota: Buteo Books.

PARKES, K. C. & PHILLIPS, A. R. 1978. Two new Caribbean Subspecies of Barn Owl (*Tyto alba*) with remarks on variation on other populations. *Ann. Carnegie Mus.* 47: 479-492.

PARMELEE, D. F. 1972. Canada's incredible arctic owls. *Beaver* 303: 30-41.

PARMELEE, D. F. & MACDONALD, S. D. 1960. The birds of west-central Ellsmere Island and adjacent areas. *Bull. Nat. Mus. Canada* Biol. Ser. 169: 1-103.

PARROT, 1908. *Athene cuculoides brügeli* nov. subsp. *Verh. Orn. Ges. Bayern* 8: 104-107.

PARTRIDGE, W. H. 1956. Variaciones geográficas en la Lechuza negra *Ciccaba huhula*. *Hornero* 10: 143-146.

PENARD, F. P. & PENARD, A. P. 1908. *De vogels van Guyana*. The Hague.

PENNY, M. 1974. *The birds of Seychelles and the outlying islands*. London: Collins.

PERRINS, C. M. 1992. *Die grosse Enzyklopädie der Vögel*. München: Mosaik.

PETERS, J. L. 1938. Systematic position of the genus *Ciccaba* Wagler. *Auk* 55: 179-186.

PETERS, J. L. 1940. *Check-list of the birds of the world*, 4. Cambridge, Mass.: Harvard University Press.

PETERSON, R. T. 1949. *How to know the birds*. New York: Mentor Book.

PETERSON, R. T. 1963. *A field guide to the birds of Texas*. Boston: Houghton Mifflin.

PETERSON, R. T. 1980. *A field guide to the birds east of the Rockies*. Boston: Houghton Mifflin.

PETERSON, R. T. 1990. *A field guide to western birds*. Boston: Houghton Mifflin.

PETERSON, R. T. & CHALIF, E. L. 1973. *A field guide to Mexican birds and adjacent Central America*. Boston: Houghton Mifflin.

PETERSON, R. T., MOUNTFORT, G. & HOLLOM, P. A. D. 1976. *Die Vögel Europas*. Hamburg & Berlin: Parey.

PETTERSSON, G. 1984. *Ugglor in Europa*. Göteborg: Wiken.

PETTY, S. J. 1994. Moult in Tawny Owls *Strix aluco* in relation to food supply and reproduction success. Pp.521-530 in B.-U. Meyburg and R. D. Chancellor, eds. *Raptor conservation today*. London and Robertsbridge, U.K.: World Working Group on Birds of Prey, and Pica Press.

PFISTER, O. 1999. Owls in Ladakh. *Bull. Oriental Bird Club* 29: 22-28.

PHELPS, W. H. & PHELPS, W. H. 1958. Lista de las aves de Venezuela con su distribución, I: no passeriformes. *Bol. Soc. Venezolana Cienc. Nat.* 19.

PHILIPPI, R. A. 1940. Notas ornitologicas. *Rev. Chil. Hist. Nat.* 4: 147-152.

PHILLIPS, A. R. 1942. Notes on the migration of the Elf and Flammulated Screech Owls. *Wilson Bull.* 54: 132-137.

PHILLIPS, A. R., MARSHALL, J. T. & MONSON, G. 1964. *The birds of Arizona*. Tucson.

PIECHOCKI, R. & MÄRZ, R. 1985. *Der Uhu*. Wittenberg-Lutherstadt: Ziemsen.

PINEAU, J. & GIRAUD-AUDINE, M. 1977. Notes sur les oiseaux nicheurs de l'extreme nord-ouest du Maroc: reproduction et mouvements. *Alauda* 45: 75-103.

PITMAN, C. R. S. & ADAMSON, J. 1978. Notes on the ecology and ethology of the Giant Eagle Owl *Bubo lacteus* (Temminck). *Honeyguide* 95: 3-23; 96: 26-43.

PIZZEY, G. 1981. *A field guide to the birds of Australia*. Sydney.

PLESNÍK, J. & DUSÍK, M. 1994. Reproductive output of the Tawny Owl *Strix aluco* in relation to small mammal dynamics in intensively cultivated farmland. Pp.531-535 in B.-U. Meyburg and R. D. Chancellor, eds. *Raptor conservation today*. London and Robertsbridge, U.K.: World Working Group on Birds of Prey, and Pica Press.

PLÓTNICK, R. 1956. Original comportamiento de un caburé. *Hornero* 10: 171-172.

POLIVANOV, V. M., SHEBAJEV, J. V. & LABSHUK, V. S. 1971. On the ecology of *Otus bakkamoena ussuriensis* But. Pp.85-91 in *Ecology and fauna of birds in the south of the Far East*. Vladivostok: Trudy Acad. Sci. USSR, 2.

PORTENKO, L. A. 1972. *Die Schneeeule*. Wittenberg–Lutherstadt: Ziemsen.

PRATT, H. D., BRUNER, P. L. & BERRETT, D. G. 1987. *The birds of Hawaii and the tropical Pacific*. Princeton: Princeton University Press.

PRIEST, C. D. 1939. The Southern White-faced Scops Owl. *Ostrich* 10: 51-53.

PRIGOGINE, A. 1973. Le statut de *Phodilus prigoginei* Schouteden. *Gerfaut* 63: 177-185.

PRIGOGINE, A. 1984. Un nouveau *Glaucidium* de l'Afrique Centrale. *Revue Zool. Afr.* 97: 886-895.

PUGET, A. & HÜE, F. 1970. La Chevéchette *Glaucidium brodiei* en Afghanistan. *Oiseau et R.F.O.* 40: 86-87.

PUKINSKI, J. 1975. *In der Ussuri-Taiga: Suche nach dem Riesenfischuhu*. Leipzig: Brockhaus.

PUKINSKY, Y. B. 1973. [On the ecology of the Eagle Owl (*Ketupa blakistoni doerriesi*) in the basin of the river Bikin.] *Byull. MOTP Otd. Biol.* 78: 40-47.

PYKAL, J. & KLOUBEC, B. 1994. Feeding ecology of Tengmalm's Owl *Aegolius funereus* in the Sumava National Park, Czechoslowakia. Pp.537-541 in B.-U. Meyburg and R. D. Chancellor, eds. *Raptor conservation today*. London and Robertsbridge, U.K.: World Working Group on Birds of Prey, and Pica Press.

PYLE, P. (1997). *Identification Guide to North American Birds*. Slate Creek Press, California.

RABOUR, D. S. 1997. *Philippine Birds and Mammals*. Manila: Univ. Philippines Press.

RAFFAELE, H. A. 1989. *A guide to the birds of Puerto Rico and the Virgin Islands*. Princeton: Princeton University Press.

RAND, A. L. 1950. A new race of owl, *Otus bakkamoena*, from Negros, Philippine Islands. *Nat. Hist. Misc. (Chicago)* 72.

RAND, A. L. 1951. Geographical variation on the Pearl-spotted Owlet. *Nat. Hist. Misc. (Chicago)* 86.

RAND, A. L. & FLEMING, R. L. 1957. Birds of Nepal. *Fieldiana Zool.* 41: 1-218.

RAND, A. L. & GILLIARD, E. T. 1967. *Handbook of New Guinea birds*. London: Weidenfeld & Nicolson.

RASMUSSEN, P. C. 1998a. The tracking of the Forest Spotted Owlet. *Hornbill* 1: 4-9.

RASMUSSEN, P. C. 1998b. A new Scops-owl from Great Nicobar Island. *Bull. Brit. Orn. Club* 118: 141-152.

RASMUSSEN, P. C. & COLLAR, N. J. 1998. Identification, distribution and status of the Forest Owlet *Athene* (*Heteroglaux*) *blewitti*. *Forktail* 14: 41-49.

RASMUSSEN, P. C. & COLLAR, N. J. 1999. Major specimen fraud in the Forest Owlet *Heteroglaux* (*Athene* auct.) *blewitti*: *Ibis* 141: 11-21.

RASMUSSEN. P. C. & ISHTIAQ, F. 1999. First notes on the behaviour and vocalisations of the Forest Owlet *Athene* (*Heteroglaux*) *blewitti*. *Forktail*.

REICHENOW, A. 1893. Diagnosen neuer Vogelarten aus Central-Africa. *Orn. Monatsber.* 1: 60-62.

REISER, O. 1927. Zoologische Ergebnisse der Walter Stötznerschen Expeditionen nach Szetschwan, Osttibet und Tschili, 4(1): Vogeleier. *Abh. Ber. Mus. Tierk. Völkerk. Dresden* 17: 1-6.

RENMAN, A. 1994. A possible new species of Scops Owl *Otus* sp. on Réunion?. *Bull. African Bird Club* 2: 54-55.

RICHMOND, C. W. 1903. Birds collected by Dr W. L. Abbott on the coast and islands of northwest Sumatra. *Proc. U.S. Natn. Mus.* 26: 485-524.

RIDGELY, R. S. & GWYNNE, J. A. 1989. *A guide to the birds of Panama, with Costa Rica, Nicaragua and Honduras*. Second edition. Princeton: Princeton University Press.

RIDGWAY, R. 1873. Genus *Glaucidium* Boie. *Proc. Boston Soc. Nat. Hist.* 16: 91-106.

RIDGWAY, R. 1895. On the correct subspecific names of the Texas and Mexican Screech-Owls. *Auk* 12: 389-390.

RIDGWAY, R. 1912. *Colour standards and colour nomenclature*. Washington.

RIDGWAY, R. 1914. Birds of North and Middle America. *U.S. Natn. Mus. Bull.* 50: 594-825.

RILEY, J. 1997. The birds of Sangihe and Talaud, north Sulawesi. *Kukila* 9: 3-36.

RIPLEY, S. D. 1964. Systematic and ecological study of New Guinea birds. *Peabody Mus. Bull.* 19: 1-87.

RIPLEY, S. D. 1966. A notable owlet from Kenya. *Ibis* 108: 136-137.

RIPLEY, S. D. 1976. Reconsideration of *Athene blewitti* (Hume). *J. Bombay Nat. Hist. Soc.* 73: 1-4.

RIPLEY, S. D. 1977. A revison of the subspecies of *Strix leptogrammica* Temm. 1831. *Proc. Biol. Soc. Washington* 90: 993-1001.

RIPLEY, S. D. & RABOR, D. S. 1958. Notes on collection of birds from Mindoro Island, Philippines. *Peabody Mus. Bull.* 13: 1-83.

RIPLEY, S. D. & BOND, G. M. 1966. The birds of Socotra and Abd-El-Kuri. *Smith. Misc. Coll.* 151(7).

RIPLEY, S. D. & RABOR, D. S. 1968. Two new subspecies of birds from the Philippines and comments on the validity of two others. *Proc. Biol. Soc. Washington* 81: 31-36.

RISDON, D. H. S. 1951. The rearing of a hybrid Virginian x European Eagle-Owl at Budley Zoo. *Avicult Mag.* 57: 199-201.

ROBBINS, M. B. & HOWELL, S. N. G. 1995. A new species of pygmy-owl (Strigidae: *Glaucidium*) from the eastern Andes. *Wilson Bull.* 107: 1-6.

ROBBINS, M. & STILES, F. G. 1999. A new species of pygmy owl (Strigidae, *Glaucidium*) from the Pacific slope of the northern Andes. *Auk* 116: 305-315.

ROBERTS, T. J. & KING, B. 1986. Vocalizations of the owls of the genus *Otus* in Pakistan. *Ornis Scand.* 17: 299-305.

ROBERTSON, W. R. 1959. Barred Owl nesting on the ground. *Auk* 76: 227-230.

ROBERTSON, C. J. R., ed. 1985. *Reader's Digest Complete Book of New Zealand Birds.* Sydney.

ROBINSON, H. C. 1927a. Exhibition and description of a new owl (*Athenoptera spilocephala stresemanni*) from Sumatra. *Bull. Brit. Orn. Club* 47: 126-127.

ROBINSON, H. C. 1927b. Note on *Phodilus* Less. with proposed new name *Phodilus badius saturatus*, for the birds from Sikkim. *Bull. Brit. Orn. Club* 47: 121-122.

ROBINSON, H. C. & CHASEN, F. N. 1939. *The birds of the Malay Peninsula*, 4. London: H. F. & G. Witherby.

van ROSSEM, A. J. 1932. A southern race of the Spotted Screech Owl. *Trans. San Diego Soc. Nat. Hist.* 7(17): 183-186.

van ROSSEM, A. J. 1937. The Ferruginous Pygmy-Owl of northwestern Mexico. *Proc. Biol. Soc. Washington* 50: 27-28.

ROTHSCHILD, W. & HARTERT, E. 1911. On some Australian forms of *Tyto*. *Novit. Zool.* 280-284.

ROZENDAAL, F. G. & DEKKER, R. W. R. J. 1989. Annotated checklist of the birds of the Dumogo-Bone National Park, North Sulawesi. *Kukila* 4: 85-109.

SAFFORD, R. J. 1993. Rediscovery, taxonomy and conservation of the Anjouan Scops Owl *Otus capnodes*. *Bird Conserv. Internatn.* 3: 57-74.

SALOMONSEN, F. 1951. *The birds of Greenland.* Copenhagen.

SALVADORI, T. A. 1882. On birds collected in New Britain. *Ibis*.

SARKER, S. U. 1985. Owls of Bangladesh and their conservation. *Bulletin* 2: 103-106.

SAUROLA, T. P. 1995. *Suomen pöllöt.* Helsinki.

SAYERS. B. 1976a. Blakiston's Fish Owl. *Avicult. Mag.* 82: 61-62.

SAYERS, B. C. 1976b. The Boobook Owl. *Avicult. Mag.* 82: 128-136.

SCHAAF, R. 1994. Die Wiederentdeckung der Anjouaneule (*Otus capnodes*). *Kauzbrief* 5: 10-13.

SCHERZINGER, W. 1965. Er lebt nicht im Urwald und heißt trotzdem Dschungelkauz. *Vogelkosmos* 5: 204-206.

SCHERZINGER, W. 1968. Mäuse – ein besonderer Imbiss. *Vogelkosmos* 68 (8).

SCHERZINGER, W. 1969. Eulen – Grimassenschneider unter den Vögeln. *Vogelkosmos* 7: 226-229.

SCHERZINGER, W. 1970. Zum Aktionssystem des Sperlingskauzes (*Glaucidium passerinum*). *Zoologica* 41: 1-120.

SCHERZINGER, W. 1974. Zur Ökologie des Sperlingskauzes *Glaucidium passerinum* im Bayerischen Wald. *Anz. Orn. Ges. Bayern* 13: 121-156.

SCHERZINGER, W. 1978. Vergleich der Stimmeninventare von fünf Arten der Gattung *Glaucidium. J. Orn.* 119: 475.

SCHERZINGER, W. 1981. Zum Nestbau der Kanincheneule *Speotyto cunicularia*. *Ökol. Vögel* 3: 213-222.

SCHERZINGER, W. 1983. Beobachtungen an Waldkauz-Habichtskauz-Hybriden (*Strix aluco* x *Strix uralensis*). *Zool. Garten* (NF) 53: 133-148.

SCHERZINGER, W. 1986. Kontrastzeichnungen im Kopfgefieder der Eulen als visuelle Kommunikationsmittel. *Ann. Naturhist. Mus. Wien* 88/89B: 37-56.

SCHERZINGER, W. 1990. Vergleichende Betrachtungen der Lautrepertoires innerhalb der Gattung *Athene* (Strigiformes). *Curr. Topics in Avian Biol. Proc. Int.* 100. *DO-G-Meeting* Bonn 1988: 89-96.

SCHLEGEL, H. 1878. On *Strix inexspectata* and *tenebricosa arfaki*. *Notes Leyden Mus.* 18: 50-52, 101.

SCHMITHÜSEN, J. 1961. *Allgemeine Vegetationsgeographie.* Berlin.

SCHNEIDER, W. & ECK, S. 1995. *Schleiereulen,* 3: Auflage. Heidelberg: Westarpp.

SCHODDE, R. & MASON, I. J. 1980. *Nocturnal birds of Australia.* Melbourne.

SCHÖNN, S. 1978. *Der Sperlingskauz.* Wittenberg-Lutherstadt: Ziemsen.

SCHÖNN, R. & SCHÖNN, S. 1987. *Auf leisen Schwingen.* Leipzig: Arnold.

SCHÖNN, S., SCHERZINGER, W. EXO, K.-M. & ILLE, R. 1991. *Der Steinkauz.* Wittenberg-Lutherstadt: Ziemsen.

SCHOUTEDEN, H. 1952. Un strigidé nouveau d'Afrique noire: *Phodilus prigoginei* nov. sp. *Rev. Zool. Bot. Afr.* 46(34): 423-428.

SCHOUTEDEN, H. 1954. Fauna du Congo Belge et du Ruanda-Urundi: III Oiseaux non passereaux. *Ann. Koninkl. Mus. Belgisch Kongo* 29: 1-437.

SCHOUTEDEN, H. 1966. Notes sur *Bubo shelleyi*. *Rev. Zool. Bot. Afr.* 73: 401-407.

SCHÜZ, E. 1957. Das Occipital-Gesicht bei Sperlingskäuzen (*Glaucidium*). *Vogelwarte* 19: 138-140.

SCHWERDTFEGER, O. 1994. The dispersion dynamics of Tengmalm's Owl *Aegolius funereus* in Central Europe. Pp.543-550 in B.-U. Meyburg and R. D. Chancellor, eds. *Raptor conservation today.* London and Robertsbridge, U.K.: World Working Group on Birds of Prey, and Pica Press.

SCLATER, P. L. 1859a. Decription of a new owl species of the genus *Ciccaba*. *Trans. Zool. Soc. London* 4.

SCLATER, P. L. 1859b. On some new or little-known species of Accipitres in the collection of the Norwich Museum. *Trans. Zool. Soc. London* 4.

SCLATER, P. L. 1877. Birds from New Britain. *Proc. Zool. Soc. London*: 108.

SCLATER, P. L. 1879. Remarks on the nomenclature of the British owls, on the arrangement of the order Striges. *Ibis* 3(4): 346-352.

SCLATER, P. L. & SALVIN, O. 1858. On new birds. *Proc. Zool. Soc. London*: 58-59.

SCLATER, P. L. & SALVIN, O. 1868. On new American birds. *Proc. Zool. Soc. London*: 327-329.

SCULLY, J. 1881. Ornithology of Gilgit. *Ibis* 423-425.

SERLE, W. 1949. New races of a warbler, a flycatcher and an owl, all from British Cameroons. *Bull. Brit. Orn. Club* 69: 74-76.

SEVERINGHAUS, L. L. 1986. The biology of Lanyu Scops Owl (*Otus elegans botelensis*). In: Sympos. Wildlife Cons. 1: 143-196, Nat. Ecol. Conserv. Soc, Taipei.

SEVERINGHAUS, L. L. 1989. The status and conservation of Lanyu Scops Owl (*Otus elegans botelensis*). Pp.423-431 in B.-U. Meyburg & R. D. Chancellor, eds. *Raptors in the modern world*. London: World Working Group on Birds of Prey.

SHALTER, M. D. 1978. Localization of passerine seeet and mobbing calls by Goshawks and Pygmy Owls. *Z. Tierpsych.* 46: 260-267.

SHARPE, R. 1875. *Catalogue of the Striges or nocturnal birds of prey in the collection of the British Museum*, 2. London: Trustees of the British Museum.

SHARPE, R. 1876. On new species of owl. *Proc. Zool. Soc. London*: 673.

SHARPE, R. 1888. Birds from Guadalcanal. *Proc. Zool. Soc. London*: 183-184.

SHARPE, R. 1888. Suborder Striges, *Heteroscops luciae*. *Ibis*: 77-79.

SHARPE, R. B. 1875. Contributions to a history of the Accipitres: the genus *Glaucidium*. *Ibis* : 35-59.

SHARPE, R. B. 1888. On a collection of birds from the island of Paláwan. *Ibis* (5)6: 193-204.

SHARPE, R. B. 1899. On a species of owl (*Gisella iheringi*) from Sao Paulo, Brazil. *Bull. Brit. Orn. Club* 12: 2-4.

SHAW, F. 1989. *Birds of America*. New York: Arch Cape Press.

SHELFORD, V. E. 1945. The relation of Snowy Owl migration to the abundance of the collared lemming. *Auk* 62: 592-596.

SHIELDS, J. & KING, G. 1990. Spotted Owls and forestry in the American northwest: a conflict of interest. *Birds Internat.* 2(1): 34-45.

SHIRIHAI, H. 1969. *The birds of Israel*. London: Academic Press.

SHORT, L. L. 1975. A zoogeographic analysis of the South American chaco avifauna. *Bull. Amer. Mus. Nat. Hist.* 154: 163-352.

SIBLEY, C. G. & MONROE, B. L. 1990. *Distribution and taxonomy of birds of the world*. New Haven: Yale University Press.

SIBNEV, B. K. 1963. Observations of the Brown Fish Owl (*Ketupa zeylonensis*) in Ussuri Krai. *Ornitologiya* 6: 486.

SICK, H. 1985. *Ornitologia Brasileira: uma introducao*. Brasília: Editora Universidade de Brasília.

SIEBERS, H. C. 1930. Fauna Buruana: Aves. *Treubia* 7 (suppl.): 165-303.

SIEBOLD, P. F. 1844. *Fauna Japonica. I. Description des Oiseaux.*

SILSBY, S. B. 1980. *Inland birds of Saudi Arabia*. London.

SIMMONS, K. 1976. Breeding of the Bengal Eagle Owl. *Avicult. Mag.* 82: 135-138.

SIMPSON, K. & DAY, N. 1989: *Field guide to the birds of Australia*. Australia: Viking O'Neill.

SINGER, D. 1992. *Greifvögel und Eulen*. Stuttgart: Franck-Kosmos.

SKEMP, J. R. 1955. Size and colour discrepancy in Tasmanian Masked Owls. *Emu* 55: 210-211.

SLATER, P. et al. 1970. *A field guide to Australian birds, non-passeres*. Perth & Edinburgh: Scottish Acad. Press.

SLATER, P., SLATER, P. & SLATER, R. 1989. *The Slater field guide to Australian birds*. Sydney: Weldon.

SMALLEY, M. E. 1983. Marsh Owl *Asio capensis*: a wet season migrant to the Gambia. *Malimbus* 5: 31-33.

SMITH, V. W. 1971. The breeding of the Algerian Marsh Owl (*Asio capensis tingitanus*) near Vom, northern Nigeria. *Nigerian Field* 36: 41-44.

SMITH-SVENSEN, T. 1969. Eulen die auf Hügeln brüten. *Vogelkosmos* 2: 54-57.

SMITHE, F. B. 1975. *Naturalist's Color Guide*. New York: American Museum of Natural History.

SMYTHIES, B. E. 1960. *The birds of Borneo*. Edinburgh & London: Oliver & Boyd.

SMYTHIES, B. E. 1986. *The Birds of Burma*. 3rd edition. Liss, Hants: Nimrod Press.

SOUTHERN, H. N. 1954. Tawny Owls and their prey. *Ibis* 96: 384-480.

SONOBE, K. 1982. *A field guide to the birds of Japan*. Tokyo: Wild Bird Society of Japan.

SPARKS, J. & SOPER, T. 1979. *Owls, their natural and unnatural history*. Newton Abbot: David & Charles.

STEINBACH, G. 1980. *Die Welt der Eulen*. Hamburg.

STEINBACH, G. 1981. *Vögel unserer Heimat*. Darmstadt: Habel.

STEINBACHER, J. 1962. Beiträge zur Kenntnis der Vögel von Paraguay. *Abh. Senckenberg Naturf. Ges.* 502: 1-106.

STEINBERG, R. 1997a. Die Queen Charlotte-Eule (*Aegolius acadicus brooksi*). *S. C. R. O. Magazin* 1: 24-30.

STEINBERG, R. 1997b. Der Philippinen-Uhu oder Streifenuhu (*Bubo philippensis*). *S. C. R. O. Magazin* 1: 31-32.

STEYN, P. 1979. Observations on the Pearl-spotted and Barred Owls. *Bokmakierie* 31(3): 50-60.

STEYN, P. 1982. *Birds of prey of southern Africa*. Beckenham, U.K.: Croom Helm.

STEYN, P. 1984. *A delight of owls: African owls observed*. Cape Town.

STILES, F. G. & SKUTCH, A. F. 1989. *A guide to the birds of Costa Rica*. London: Christopher Helm.

STONE, A. 1922. A new burrowing owl from Colombia. *Auk* 39: 84.

STONE, W. 1896. A revision of the North American Horned Owls with description of a new subspecies. *Auk* 13: 153-156.

STONE, W. 1899. On a collection of birds from the vicinity of Bogota with a review of South American species of *Speotyto* and *Trolodytes*. *Proc. Acad. Nat. Sci. Philadelphia*: 302-313.

STONES, A. J., DAVIDSON, P. J. A. & RAHARJANINGTRAH, W. 1997. Notes on the observation of a Taliabu Masked Owl *Tyto nigrobrunnea* on Taliabu Island, Indonesia. *Kukila* 9: 58-59.

STORER, R. W. 1972. The juvenile plumage and relationships of *Lophostrix cristata*. *Auk* 89: 452-455.

STORER, R. W. 1994. Avian exotica: the fishing owls. *Birder's World* 8(3): 66-67.

STRANECK, R., RIDGELY, R. & MATA, J. R. 1987. Dos nuevas lechuzas parta la Argentina: Caburé Andino *Glaucidium jardinii* y Lechuza Vermiculada *Otus guatemalae* (Aves, Strigidae). *Com. Mus. Arg. Cienc. Nat. 'Bernardino Rivadavia" (Zoología)* 4(18): 137-139.

STRANECK, R. & VIDOZ, F. 1995. Sobre el estado taxonómico de *Strix rufipes* (King) y de *Strix chacoensis* (Cherrie & Reichenberger). *Notulas Faunísticas* 74: 1-5.

STRESEMANN, E. 1923. Die Ergebnisse der Walter Stötznerschen Expeditionen nach Szetschwan, Osttibet und Tschili, 1(12): Striges-Ralli. *Abh. Ber. Mus. Tierk. Völkerk. Dresden* 16: 58-70.

STRESEMANN, E. 1924. Die Gattung *Strix* im Malayischen Archipel. *Orn. Monatsb.* 32: 110-111.

STRESEMANN, E. 1925. Beiträge zur Ornithologie der indo-australischen Region. *Mitt. Zool. Mus. Berlin* 12: 179-195.

STRESEMANN, E., ed. 1927-1934. Sauropoda: Aves. In W. Kükenthal, *Handbuch der Zoologie*. Berlin & Leipzig: de Gruyter.

STRESEMANN, E. 1939. Die Vögel von Celebes I, II. *J. Orn.* 87: 299-425.

STRESEMANN, E. 1941. Die Vögel von Celebes, III. Systematik u. Biologie. *J. Orn.* 89: 1-102.

STRESEMANN, E. & STRESEMANN, V. 1966. Die Mauser der Vögel. *J. Orn.*, Sonderheft 107: 357-375.

STUBBE, M. 1987. *Populationsökologie von Greifvögel- und Eulenarten*. Halle-Wittenberg: Martin-Luther-Universität.

SUBAH, A. 1984. Nesting by Hume's Tawny Owl in Nakhal Sekher. *Torgos* 3 (2) 7, 21-32, 105.

SUDHAUS, W. 1984. Artbegriff und Artbildung in zoologischer Sicht. *Z. Zool. Syst. Evol.-forschung* 22: 183-211.

SURESH KUMAR, T. 1985. The life history of the Spotted Owlet (*Athene brama brama* Temminck) in Andhra Pradesh. Monograph publ. No. 4. Raptor Research Centre, Hyderabad, India.

SUTTER, E. & BARRUEL, P. 1958. *Die Brutvögel Europas*, 2. Zürich: Silva.

SUTTON, G. M. & BURLEIGH, T. D. 1939. A new screech owl from Nuevo Leon. *Auk* 56: 174-175.

SWARTH, H. S. 1910. Two new owls from Arizona. *Univ. Calif. Publ. Zool.* 7(1): 1-8.

SWINHOE, R. 1879. On Chinese zoology. *Proc. Zool. Soc. London*: 447-448.

TAVERNER, P. A. 1942. Canadian races of the Great Horned Owl. *Auk* 59: 234-245.

TAVERNER, P. A. 1943. *Birds of Canada*.

TAYLOR, P. S. 1973. Behaviour of the Snowy Owl. *Living Bird*: 137-154.

TERBORGH, J. 1971. Distribution and environmental gradients: theory and preliminary interpretation of distributional patterns in the avifauna of the Cordillera de Vilcabamba, Perú. *Ecology* 52: 23-40.

THORSTROM, R., HART, J. & WATSON, R. T. 1997. New record, ranging, behaviour, vocalization and food of the Madagascar Red Owl *Tyto soumagnei*. *Ibis* 139: 477-481.

TICEHURST, C. B. 1922. Description of new races of Indian birds. *Bull. Brit. Orn. Club* 42: 57 & 122-123.

TODD, W. E. C. Two new owls from Bolivia. *Proc. Biol. Soc. Washington* 60: 90-96.

TRAYLOR, M. A. 1952. A new race of *Otus ingens* (Salvin) from Colombia. *Nat. Hist. Misc. (Chicago)* 99.

TRAYLOR, M. A. 1958. Variation in South American Great Horned Owls. *Auk* 75: 143-149.

TRISTRAM, C. 1889. On a small collection of birds from the Louisiade and d'Entrecasteaux Islands. *Ibis* 6(1): 557-558.

TRUSLOW, F. K. 1966. Ground-nesting Great Horned Owl: a photograpic study. *Living Bird*: 177-186.

TWEEDDALE, Marquis of 1878. Contributions to the ornithology of the Philippines. No. XI. On a collection made by Mr A. H. Everett at Zamboanga, in the island of Mindanao. *Proc. Zool. Soc. London*: 936-954.

ULLMAN, M. 1992. The Marsh Owl (*Asio capensis*) in Morocco. *Birding World* 5: 480-481.

VAURIE, C. 1960a. Systematic notes on Palaearctic birds, 41. Strigidae: the genus *Bubo*. *Amer. Mus. Novit.* 2000.

VAURIE, C. 1960b. Systematic notes on Palaearctic birds, 42. Strigidae: the genus *Athene*. *Amer. Mus. Novit.* 2015.

VAURIE, C. 1960c. Systematic notes on Palaearctic birds, Strigidae: the genera *Otus, Aegolius, Ninox* and *Tyto*. *Amer. Mus. Novit.* 2021.

VAURIE, C. 1965. *The birds of the Palaearctic fauna, non-passeres*. London: H. F. & G. Witherby.

van VEEN, J. C. & ten BROEKE, E. M. 1994. A silent method to record nesting events in hole-breeding owls. Pp.551-556 in B.-U. Meyburg and R. D. Chancellor, eds. *Raptor conservation today*. London and Robertsbridge, U.K.: World Working Group on Birds of Prey, and Pica Press.

VERNON, C. J. 1980. Prey of six species of owl at the Zimbabwe ruins. *Honeyguide* 101: 26-28.

VIELLIARD, J. 1989. Uma nova espécie de *Glaucidium* (Aves, Strigidae) da Amazônia. *Revta. Bras. Zoologia* 6: 685-693.

VIRANI, M. 1995. Sokoke Scops Owl in Tanzania. *Swara* 18(3): 34.

VOOUS, K. H. 1950. On the distribution and genetic origin of the intermediate populations of the Barn Owl (*Tyto alba*) in Europe. In *Syllegomena Biologica*. Wittenberg-Lutherstadt: Ziemsen.

VOOUS, K. H. 1960. *Atlas of European birds*. Edinburgh & London.

VOOUS, K. H. 1964. Wood owls of the genera *Strix* and *Ciccaba*. *Zool. Meded.* 39: 471-478.

VOOUS, K. H. 1966. The distribution of owls in Africa in relation to general zoogeographical problems. *Ostrich* (Suppl.) 6: 499-506.

VOOUS, K. H. 1983. *Birds of the Netherlands Antilles*. De Walberg Pers.

VOOUS, K. H. 1988. *Owls of the Northern Hemisphere*. London: Collins.

VOOUS, K. H. 1990. Species boundaries in non-tropical Northern Hemisphere owls. *Bijdragen Dierkunde* 60(3/4): 163-170.

VORDERMAN, A. G. 1895. Lampong-Vogels II. Natuurk. Tijdschr. Ned. Indië. *Batavia* 55: 137-156.

WALLACE, A. R. 1863. List of birds collected in the island of Bouru (one of the Moluccas), with descriptions of the new species. *Proc. Zool. Soc. London*: 18-32.

WALTER, H. 1962. *Die Vegetation der Erde in ökologischer Betrachtung*. Jena.

WATLING, D. 1983. Ornithological notes from Sulawesi. *Emu* 83: 247-261.

WATSON, J. 1980. A case of the vanishing owl. *Wildlife* 22: 38-39.

WEBSTER, J. D. & ORR, R. T. 1958. Variation in Great Horned Owls of Middle America. *Auk* 75: 134-142.

WEICK, F. 1994. An annotated checklist of the Strigiformes. Unpublished.

WELLS, D. R. 1986. Further parallels between the Asian Bay Owl *Phodilus badius* and *Tyto* species. *Bull. Brit. Orn. Club* 106: 12-15.

WELLS, D. R. 1999. *The Birds of the Thai-Malay Peninsula: Non-passerines*. London: Academic Press.

WESKE, J. S. & TERBORGH, J. W. 1981. *Otus marshalli*, a new species of screech-owl from Peru. *Auk* 98: 1-7.

WETMORE, A. 1922. New forms of Neotropical birds. *J. Washington Acad. Sci.* 12(14): 323-325.

WETMORE, A. 1926. Observations on the birds of Argentina, Paraguay and Chile. *U.S. Natn. Mus. Bull.* 133.

WETMORE, A. 1935. The type specimen of Newton's Owl. *Auk* 52: 186-187.

WETMORE, A. 1968. The birds of the republic of Panama, 2. *Smithsonian Misc. Coll.* 150(2).

WETMORE, A. & SWALES, B. H. 1931. The birds of Haiti and the Dominican Republic. *U.S. Natn. Mus. Bull.* 155.

van der WEYDEN, W. J. 1974. Vocal affinities of the Puerto Rican and Vermiculated Screech Owls (*Otus nudipes* and *Otus guatemalae*). *Ibis* 116: 369-372.

van der WEYDEN, W. J. 1975. Scops and screech owls: vocal evidence for a basic subdivision in the genus *Otus*. *Ardea* 63: 65-77.

WHEELER, L. 1938. A new wood-owl from Chile. *Field Mus. Nat. Hist., Publ. Zool. Ser.* 20: 471-482.

WHISTLER, H. 1949. *Popular handbook of Indian birds*. Fourth edition. Edinburgh & London: Oliver & Boyd.

WHITE, C. M. N. & BRUCE, M. D. 1986. *The birds of Wallacea*. London: British Ornithologists' Union (Check-list 7).

WHITE, G. B. 1974. Rarest Eagle-Owl in trouble. *Oryx* 12: 484-486.

WHITEHEAD, J. 1899. Field-notes on birds collected in the Philippine Islands in 1893-6. *Ibis* (7)5: 81-111.

WIDODO, W., COX, J. H. & RASMUSSEN, P. C. 1999. Rediscovery of the Flores Scops Owl *Otus alfredi* on Flores, Lesser Sunda Islands, Indonesia, and reaffirmation of its specific status. *Forktail* 15 (in press).

WIESNER, J. & RUDAT, V. 1983. Aktionsgebiet und Verhalten von Sperlingskauzfamilien (*Glaucidium passerinum*) in der Führungszeit. *Zool. Jb. Syst.* 110: 455-471.

WILEY, J. W. 1986. Status and conservation of raptors in the West Indies. *Birds of Prey Bull.* 3: 57-70.

WILLIAMS, J. G. 1963. *A field guide to the birds of East and Central Africa*. London: Collins.

WILLIAMS, J. G. 1971. *Säugetiere und seltene Vögel in den Nationalparks Ostafrikas*. Berlin & Hamburg: Paul Parey.

WILLIAMS, R. S. & TOBIAS, J. A. 1996. West Peruvian Screech Owl. *Cotinga* 6: 76-77.

WINDE, H. 1997. Osteologische Untersuchungen an einigen deutschen Eulenarten. *S.C.R.O. Magazin* 1: 42-51.

WITHERBY, H. F., JOURDAIN, F. C. R., TICEHURST, N. F. & TUCKER, B. W. 1938. *The handbook of British birds*, 2. London: H. F. & G. Witherby.

WITT, H.-H. 1984. Der 'kit-kit... Flugruf der Schleiereule (*Tyto alba*). *Vogelwelt* 105: 72-73.

WOLF, L. L. 1976. Avifauna of the Cerro de la Muerte region, Costa Rica. *Amer. Mus. Novit.* 2606.

WOLLE, J. 1994. Hilfe für die Schleiereule. *Mitt. Sächs. Orn.* 7. Beilage 1: 1-16.

WOLTERS, H. E. 1975-1982. *Die Vogelarten der Erde*. Hamburg & Berlin.

WOODS, R. W. 1975. *The birds of the Falkland Islands*. Oswestry: Anthony Nelson.

WÜST, W. 1986. *Avifauna Bavariae*, 2. München.

XIANJI, W. & LAN, Y. 1994. The distribution and conservation of Strigiformes in Yunnan Province, China. Pp.579-586 in B.-U. Meyburg and R. D. Chancellor, eds. *Raptor conservation today*. London and Robertsbridge, U.K.: World Working Group on Birds of Prey, and Pica Press.

XIAO-TI, Y. & DE-HAO, L. 1991. Past and future status of birds of prey and owls in China. *Birds of Prey Bull.* 4: 159-165.

YALDEN, D. W. 1973. Prey of the Abyssinian Long-eared Owl *Asio abyssinicus*. *Ibis* 115: 605-606.

YAMAMOTO, S. 1994. Mating behaviour of Blakiston's Fish Owl *Ketupa blakistoni*. Pp.587-590 in B.-U. Meyburg and R. D. Chancellor, eds. *Raptor conservation today*. London and Robertsbridge, U.K.: World Working Group on Birds of Prey, and Pica Press.

YEALLAND, J. J. 1968. Breeding of the Javan Fish-Owl at the London Zoo (*Ketupa ketupa*). *Avicult. Mag.* 74: 17-18.

YEALLAND, J. J. 1969. Breeding of the Magellan Eagle-Owl (*Bubo virginianus nacurutu*) at London Zoo. *Avicult. Mag.* 75: 53-54.

YEALLAND, J. J. 1969. Breeding of the West African Wood-Owl (*Ciccaba woodfordi nuchalis*) at London Zoo. *Avicult. Mag.* 75: 53.

ZEDLITZ, O. 1908. Kurze Notizen zur Ornis von Nordost-Afrika. *Orn. Monatsb.* 16: 172-174.

ZHENG, Z. *et al.* 1980. New records of China Birds from Xizang, Tibet. *Acta Zool. Sinica* 26: 286-287.

ZIMMERMAN, D. 1972. Avifauna of Kakamega Forest. *Bull. Amer. Mus. Nat. Hist.* 149: 291-292.

ZIMMERMAN, D., TURNER, D. A. & PEARSON, D. J. 1996. *Birds of Kenya and northern Tanzania*. London: Christopher Helm/A. & C. Black.

ZINK, R. M. & REMSEN, J. V. 1986. Evolutionary processes and patterns of geographic variation in birds. *Current Ornithology* 4: 1-69.

INDEX

Species are listed by their vernacular name (e.g. Barn Owl) and by their scientific name. Specific scientific names are followed by the generic name as used in the book (e.g. *alba, Tyto*) and subspecific names are followed by both the specific and generic names (e.g. *guttata, Tyto alba*). Numbers in *italic* refer to the first page of the relevant systematic entry. Numbers in **bold** type refer to the colour plate numbers.